A Comprehensive
HANDBOOK of the
UNITED
NATIONS

A Comprehensive HANDBOOK of the UNITED NATIONS

A Documentary Presentation in Two Volumes

VOLUME 2

Compiled and Edited by
DR. MIN-CHUAN KU
Professor of Political Science
Pembroke State University
The University of North Carolina

MONARCH PRESS

To all those who have dedicated themselves
to the principles of reason, justice and the
rule of law.

Published by
MONARCH PRESS
A Simon & Schuster division of
Gulf & Western Corporation
Simon & Schuster Building
1230 Avenue of the Americas
New York, N.Y. 10020

Manufactured in the United States of America

ISBN: 0-671-18787-2

Library of Congress Catalog Card Number: 77-71588

TABLE OF CONTENTS

[1] South West Africa was the only territory under mandate which had not been placed under the trusteeship system, and therefore, did not have a trusteeship agreement for it.

[2] Somoliland, the territory which was detached from an enemy state as a result of the Second World War, was placed under the administration of Italy by a resolution of the General Assembly on December 2, 1950 based on the Peace Treaty with Italy of 1946.

[3] Ryukyu Islands, another territory which was detached from an enemy state, was placed under the administration of the United States of America under the Peace Treaty with Japan, signed September 8, 1951, effective April 28, 1952. There was no trusteeship agreement for the Ryukyu Islands. Subsequent to the Peace Treaty of 1951, the United States undertook the administration of the Islands, and the responsibility for administering them was conferred on the Secretary of Defense by virtue of the Executive Orders No. 10713 of June 5, 1957 and No. 11010 of March 19, 1962.

PREFACE

A COMPREHENSIVE HANDBOOK OF THE UNITED NATIONS consists of basic laws, rules and regulations dealing with both substantive and procedural matters of all important organs of the United Nations and its affiliated agencies. It is designed to meet the needs of students, scholars, and publicists of international politics in general, and diplomats, policy makers of the Member States, and staff members of the United Nations and its affiliated agencies, especially those with policy-making authority, in particular. It is comprehensive in scope, complete in text, and dispassionate in presentation so as to reflect the skill, wisdom, vision, and far-sightedness, or, in certain cases the lack of them, on the part of the framers, and to serve the purpose of objective evaluation and historical review of the United Nations for many years to come.

The Handbook, in two volumes, comprises eight parts and a bibliography. Part I covers the background material which evolved and led to the adoption of the Charter of the United Nations. Part II lists basic laws, agreements, and statutes on which the United Nations has been formulated, and through which it has been operating. It also includes, *inter alia,* charts, diagrams and tables such as the comprehensive data of the Member States of the United Nations, members of different specialized agencies, structure of the Secretariat of the United Nations and structure and functions of the International Trusteeship System and the composition of the principal organs of the United Nations. Part III contains the rules of procedure of the principal organs of the United Nations and of the subordinate organs of the Economic and Social Council. Volume 2 begins with Part IV which includes a sketch and summary of the intergovernmental organizations, primarily the specialized agencies, their basic laws and their agreements with the United Nations. Part V enumerates all nongovernmental organizations which have relations with the United Nations, classified into three categories according to their relations with the United Nations. Part VI embraces all trusteeship agreements and describes the status of each trust territory primarily for historical review. Part VII covers important regional arrangements and/or basic laws of the regional agencies. Part VIII embraces important resolutions adopted by the General Assembly, classified into five fields. The bibliography consists mainly of plans, projects, and frameworks for an ideal international organization which are primarily the result of study and research done at different universities in the United States and in other countries.

Generally speaking, there are four approaches in the United Nations system designed to deal with international disputes or situations, namely: (1) *political,* exercised by the Security Council and the General Assembly in accommodating vicissitudes in international situations; (2) *legal,* typified by the judicial settlement of international disputes, of which the role of the International Court of Justice is of primary importance; (3) *regional,* designed to supplement or supplant the United Nations in case both the Security Council and the General Assembly fail to solve an international dispute, or when a regional solution to a dispute is more desirable; and (4) *functional,* performed by the Economic and Social Council, the Trusteeship Council, the intergovernmental and nongovernmental organizations, of which the fourteen specialized agencies are of special importance. These four approaches do not compete with each other but supplement or complement one another. Therefore, in order to master the machinery and mechanics of the United Nations, to see which approach is better suited to a particular case, one has to master the basic laws of the United Nations as well as of its principal and subsidiary organs. However, prior to the publication of this work, no previous attempt had been made to bring them together in a single set, readily available for execution, review and improvement.

Although more than a quarter of a century has elapsed since its inception, the United Nations is still not fully understood or appreciated by most people. This is so partly because of the complexity and diversity of its basic laws, and the dynamics of their growth and evolution, which are not easily understandable; and partly because of the fact that the organic and operative laws of the different organs are scattered throughout different documents, which are not readily accessible for reference, comparison, and cross-examination. This Handbook has been prepared to remedy this situation.

Min-chuan Ku
Pembroke State University
Pembroke, North Carolina

ACKNOWLEDGMENT

A.W. Sijthoff International Publishing Company and Kraus Reprint for permission to reprint the Statute of the Permanent Court of International Justice and related notes from the documents of the Court, entitled *Statute and Rules of Court,* Fourth Edition, 1940.

The World Peace Foundation for permission to quote the Declaration of London and the Declaration of Teheran from *Documents on American Foreign Relations,* Vol. III, 1941, p. 444 and Vol. VI, 1943, p. 235, respectively.

Acknowledgment is also due to the following organs and individuals of the United Nations and of the University of North Carolina Library for supplying or helping locate documents in their respective areas:

> The Office for Inter-Agency Affairs and Co-ordination,
> Mr. Patrizio Civili of the former Office for Inter-Agency Affairs,
> Mr. W. Martin Hill, Permanent Representative of the World Intellectual
>   Property Organization to the United Nations,
> Mrs. I. Baldina, Chief, Stack and Loan Section,
> Mrs. Madeleine Mitchell, Chief, Public Inquiries Unit,
> Mr. Michael Galatola of the Dag Hammarkjold Library,
> Miss Lillian Hope, secretary to the Committee on Contributions,
> Mrs. Jane Hu of the Statistic Office, and
> Mrs. Louise J. Hawkins, Chief, the Business Administration and Social
>   Science Division of the Library of The University of North
>   Carolina at Chapel Hill.

IV. INTER-GOVERNMENTAL AGENCIES

A. SKETCH OF THE AGENCIES
(Specialized Agencies, IAEA and GATT)

1. Specialized Agencies

NAME	LOCATION OF HQ.	DATE OF CREATION
International Labour Organization (ILO)	Geneva	1919
Food and Agriculture Organization of the United Nations (FAO)	Rome	1919
United Nations Educational, Scientific and Cultural Organization (UNESCO)	Paris	1945
World Health Organization (WHO)	Geneva	1946
International Bank for Reconstruction and Development (World Bank or IBRD)	Washington, D.C.	1914
International Finance Corporation (IFC)	Washington, D.C.	1956
International Development Association (IDA)	Washington, D.C.	1960
International Monetary Fund (Fund or IMF)	Washington, D.C.	1914
International Civil Aviation Organization (ICAO)	Montreal	1947
Universal Postal Union (UPU)	Berne	1875
International Telecommunications Union (ITU)	Geneva	1865
World Meteorological Organization (WMO)	Geneva	1950
Inter-Governmental Maritime Consultative Organization (IMCO)	London	1958
World Intellectual Property Organization (WIPO)	Geneva	1967

2. Other Agencies and Instruments

NAME	LOCATION OF HQ.	DATE OF CREATION
International Atomic Energy Agency (IAEA)[1]	Vienna	1957
General Agreement on Tariff and Trade (GATT)[2]		

---

[1] The International Atomic Energy Agency (IAEA) has a working relationship with the United Nations, but is not formally designated a specialized agency.

[2] An International Trade Organization (ITO) was planned as a specialized agency. The Charter of it has been signed but failed of required ratifications. The General Agreement serves as a standard of conduct for international trade.

1

B. SUMMARY OF THE AGENCIES HAVING WORKING RELATIONS WITH THE UNITED NATIONS

1. ABBREVIATIONS OF THE NAMES OF THE AGENCIES

Working in partnership with the United Nations in economic, social, scientific and technical fields is a group of intergovernmental organizations related to the United Nations by special agreements. They have their own legislative and executive bodies, their own secretariats and their own budgets.

The agencies are:

ILO	International Labour Organisation
FAO	Food and Agriculture Organization of the United Nations
UNESCO	United Nations Educational, Scientific and Cultural Organization
WHO	World Health Organization
IBRD	International Bank for Reconstruction and Development
IFC	International Finance Corporation
IDA	International Development Association
IMF	International Monetary Fund
ICAO	International Civil Aviation Organization
UPU	Universal Postal Union
ITU	International Telecommunication Union
WMO	World Meteorological Organization
IMCO	Inter-Governmental Maritime Consultative Organization
WIPO	World Intellectual Property Organization
IAEA	International Atomic Energy Agency
GATT	General Agreement on Tariffs and Trade

IAEA is an agency established "under the aegis of the United Nations"; it reports annually to the United Nations General Assembly and, as appropriate, to the Security Council and the Economic and Social Council.

The first 14 organizations are specialized agencies, a term used in Chapter IX of the United Nations Charter, which provides for international action to promote economic and social progress; they report annually to the Economic and Social Council under Article 64 of the Charter.

The United Nations and GATT co-operate at the secretariat and inter-governmental levels. The GATT secretariat was originally set up to serve as the secretariat for the Interim Commission for the International Trade Organization. (ITO has not been established).

These organizations of the United Nations family work together in common endeavours such as assistance to developing countries and in specific fields such as atomic energy and the environment. Their activities are inter-linked by the Administrative Committee on Co-ordination, a body under the chairmanship of the United Nations Secretary-General and in which the executive heads of the special programmes and organs of the United Nations also participate.

---

[1]U.N. Press Release SA/213/Rev. 14, March 19, 1976

2. SUMMARY OF THE AGENCIES

1. Specialized Agencies

Agency and Members[2]	Functions	Gross Budget[3] and Headquarters	Chief Officer and Number of Staff	Constitution and Agreement with United Nations
ILO 126	Brings together Government, labour and management to solve pressing international labour problems. Provides technical co-operation. Conducts World Employment Programme, which helps countries combat unemployment. Develops world labour standards for considerations by Governments. Run research and publications programmes centred on basic social and labour problems.	For 1976: $90,603,000 4, Route des Morillons CH-1211 Geneva 22 Switzerland	Director-General: Francis Blanchard (France) Staff: about 3,000, including about 900 experts in the field	Original Constitution came into force: 11 April 1919. Revised Constitution came into force 20 April 1948. Relationship with United Nations approved by General Assembly 14 December 1946.

[1] U.N. Press Release SA/213/Rev. 14, March 19, 1976.
[2] Number of members, as of 1 January 1976.
[3] Amounts are in United States dollars, except where otherwise indicated. The figures for agency budgets are from the latest annual report of the Advisory Committee on Administrative and Budgetary Questions on administrative and budgetary co-ordination with the specialized agencies (document A/10360) and are adjusted for comparability between budgets.

Agency and Members	Functions	Gross Budget and Headquarters	Chief Officer and Number of Staff	Constitution and Agreement with United Nations
FAO 131	Helps countries, through expert assistance, to increase production from farms, forests and fisheries, and to improve distribution, marketing and nutrition. Co-ordinates the Freedom-from-Hunger Campaign Action for Development. In collaboration with the United Nations, administers the World Food Programme, which provides food for economic development and relief.	For 1976: $87,174,000 Viale delle Terme di Caracalla Rome, Italy	Director-General: Edouard Saouma (Lebanon) Staff: over 5,000, including experts in the field	Constitution came into force: 16 October 1945. Relationship with United Nations approved by General Assembly 14 December 1946.
UNESCO 136 plus 3 associate members	Seeks to broaden the base of education in the world, bring benefits of science to all countries, and encourage cultural exchange and appreciation. 1975–1976 programme includes: Assistance for educational planning and development; Functional literacy projects combining literacy with economic advancement; Promoting research and co-operation in basic sciences, including hydrology and life sciences; special studies on preservation of the environment; improvement of science teaching; Peace studies; interdisciplinary studies on human rights; Protection of cultural heritage.	For 1976: $104,144,000 7 Place de Fontenoy 75700 Paris France	Director-General: Amadou-Mahtar M'Bow (Senegal) Staff: 3,504, including experts in the field	Constitution came into force: 4 November 1946. Relationship with United Nations approved by General Assembly 14 December 1946.

Agency and Members	Functions	Gross Budget and Headquarters	Chief Officer and Number of Staff	Constitution and Agreement with United Nations
WHO 146 plus 3 associate	Serves as directing and co-ordinating authority on international health work. Helps Governments, at their request, in carrying out public health programmes. Sets standards for drugs and vaccines, establishes guidelines and criteria in environmental health, and provides other technical services in international health. Promotes medical research.	For 1976: $153,436,000 20 Avenue Appia 1211 Geneva 27 Switzerland	Director-General: Dr. Halfdan Mahler (Denmark) Staff: over 4,300, including regional offices and field staff	Constitution came into force: 7 April 1948. Succeeded Interim Commission for WHO 1 September 1948. Relationship with United Nations approved by General Assembly 15 November 1947.
IBRD 125	Furthers economic development of members by loans for productive projects and by furnishing technical advice. All loans are made to or guaranteed by Governments. Loans totalling $29,748 million made by end of 1975.	$157,539,000 administrative budget for 1975 fiscal year (1 July 1974– 30 June 1975) for IBRD and IDA to be met from income 1818 H Street N.W. Washington, D.C. 20433	President: Robert S. McNamara (United States) Staff: about 4,000	Articles of Agreement came into force: 27 December 1945. Began operation 25 June 1946. Relationship with United Nations approved by General Assembly 15 November 1947.

Agency and Members	Functions	Gross Budget and Headquarters	Chief Officer and Number of Staff	Constitution and Agreement with United Nations
IFC 100	Seeks to assist less developed member countries by helping promote growth of private sector of their economies. Provides risk capital without government guarantee for productive private enterprises, assists development of local capital markets and stimulates the international flow of private capital. Gross commitments at 30 June 1975 totalled $1,262 million.	$10,446,809 administrative expenses for 1975 fiscal year (1 July 1974–30 June 1975) met from income 1818 H Street N.W. Washington, D.C. 20433	President: Robert S. McNamara (United States) Staff: 207 (IFC is an affiliate of IBRD.)	Charter came into force: 20 July 1956. Relationship with United Nations approved by General Assembly 20 February 1957.
IDA 113	Furthers economic development of members by providing finance on terms bearing less heavily on balance of payments of members than those of conventional loans. (Its credits have been for terms of 50 years, interest free.) Development credits totalled $9,150 million by end-1975.	(See IBRD.) 1818 H Street N.W. Washington, D.C. 20433	Same officers and staff as IBRD. (IDA is an affiliate of IBRD.)	Articles of Agreement came into force: 24 September 1960. Began operation 8 November 1960. Relationship with United Nations approved by General Assembly 27 March 1961.

Agency and Members	Functions	Gross Budget and Headquarters	Chief Officer and Number of Staff	Constitution and Agreement with United Nations
IMF 128	Promotes monetary co-operation and currency stabilization, facilitates trade expansion. Sells currency to help members meet temporary foreign payments difficulties. Aids Governments by consultation on financial problems. Supplements reserve assets of participants in Special Drawing Account. Members' drawing totalled 34,188.6 million Special Drawing Rights and repayments by repurchase totalled SDR 17,743 million at end of December 1975.	$60,976,755* administrative budget for 1976 fiscal year (1 July 1975– 30 June 1976) met from earnings 700 19th Street N.W. Washington, D.C. 20431	Managing Director: H. Johannes Witteveen (Netherlands) Staff: 1,447	Articles of Agreement came into force: 27 December 1945. Began operation 1 March 1947. Relationship with United Nations approved by General Assembly 15 November 1947.
ICAO 128	Promotes safety of international civil aviation by standardizing technical equipment, services and training, and by encouraging the use of safety measures; specifies location of air navigation services. Provides economic and statistical information. Works to reduce the red tape of customs, immigration and public health formalities. Extends technical assistance. Codifies international air law. Arranges joint financing of air navigation facilities and services.	For 1976: $18,101,000 International Aviation Bldg. 1080 University Street Montreal 101, P.Q. Canada	Secretary-General: Assad Kotaite (Lebanon) President of Council: Walter Binaghi (Argentina) Staff: 1,005, including regional office and technical assistance personnel.	Constitution came into force: 4 April 1947. Relationship with United Nations approved by General Assembly 14 December 1946.

*Budget in Special Drawing Rights; converted at the rate SDR 1= $1.17.

Agency and Members	Functions	Gross Budget and Headquarters	Chief Officer and Number of Staff	Constitution and Agreement with United Nations
UPU 153	Unites countries for reciprocal exchange of correspondence. Organizes and improves postal services and promotes international collaboration in this sphere. Every member agrees to transmit, as well as to admit in transit, mail of all other members by the best means used for its own mail.	For 1976: $5,287,000* Case Postale 3000 Berne 15 Switzerland	Director-General International Bureau of UPU: Mohamed J. Sobhi (Egypt) Staff: 121	Established in 1874. Constitution came into force: 1 January 1966. Additional Protocol on 1 January 1976. Relationship with United Nations approved by General Assembly 15 November 1947.
ITU 146	Regulates, standardizes, plans and co-ordinates international telecommunications (radio, telegraph, telephone and space radiocommunications). Promotes the development of technical facilities and their efficient operation. Is instrumental in allocating radio frequencies.	For 1976: $23,695,000* Place des Nations 1211 Geneva 20 Switzerland	Secretary-General: Mohamed Mili (Tunisia) Staff: 621	Originated as International Telegraph Union in 1865. Present title adopted under Convention of 1932. Relationship with United Nations approved by General Assembly 15 November 1947.

8

*Budget in Swiss francs; converted at the rate Sw. fr. 2.68 = $US 1.

Agency and Members	Functions	Gross Budget and Headquarters	Chief Officer and Number of Staff	Constitution and Agreement with United Nations
WMO 139	Promotes international co-operation in meteorology and operational hydrology, especially in establishment of world-wide network of meteorological stations and rapid exchange of weather data. Promotes standardization of observations and publication of observations and statistics. Furthers the application of meteorology to the activities of mankind, and encourages research and training in meteorology.	For 1976: $11,304,000 41 Avenue Giuseppe Motta 1211 Geneva 20 Switzerland	Secretary-General: David A. Davis (United Kingdom) Staff: 341, including field staff in technical assistance projects	Preceded by International Meteorological Organization, a non-governmental organization founded in 1873. Convention came into force: 23 March 1950. Began operation 4 April 1951. Relationship with United Nations approved by General Assembly 20 December 1951.
IMCO 92 plus 1 associate member	Promotes intergovernmental co-operation on technical matters affecting international shipping. Recommends and encourages adoption of highest practicable standards of maritime safety and navigation. Fosters international action, notably through technical and legal studies, to prevent marine pollution caused by ships and other craft. Drafts and concludes conventions, agreements and recommendations. Advises other international bodies on shipping matters.	For 1976: $4,648,000 101-104 Picadilly London, W1V OAE England	Secretary-General: C.P. Srivastava (India) Staff: 164	United Nations Maritime Conference in 1948 drew up IMCO Convention which came into force: 17 March 1958. Formally established 13 January 1959. Relationship with United Nations approved by General Assembly 18 November 1948.

Agency and Members	Functions	Gross Budget and Headquarters	Chief Officer and Number of Staff	Constitution and Agreement with United Nations
WIPO 74	Promotes protection of intellectual property, encourages conclusion of new international treaties and harmonization of national laws. Ensures administrative co-operation among intergovernmental "unions" by centralizing and supervising their administration. Assembles and disseminates information, carries out technical and legal studies, and maintains services for international registration or other administrative co-operation. Extends legal technical assistance to developing countries.	For 1976: $7,591,000 32 Chemin des Colombettes CH-1211 Geneva 20 Switzerland	Director-General: Arpad Bogsch (United States) Staff: 186, including experts in the field	Originated as International Bureau of Paris Union (1883) and of Berne Union (1886), and is successor to United International Bureau for the Protection of Intellectual Property (BIRPI). Convention came into force: 26 April 1970. Relationship with United Nations approved by General Assembly 17 December 1974.

2. Other Agencies and Instruments

Agency and Members	Functions	Gross Budget and Headquarters	Chief Officer and Number of Staff	Constitution and Agreement with United Nations
IAEA 104	Promotes uses of atomic energy for peaceful purposes; assists in atomic research and applications. Promotes information exchange, gives technical aid, and arranges supply of materials, equipment and facilities. Applies safeguards against diversion of materials to military use, and implements controls under the Treaty on Non-Proliferation of Nuclear Weapons. Sets safety standards, sends safety missions, and helps draft laws and conventions.	For 1976: $37,002,000 Karntner Ring 11-13 A-1010 Vienna Austria	Director-General: Sigvard Eklund (Sweden) Staff: about 1,000 at headquarters	IAEA Statute entered into force: 29 July 1957. Relationship with United Nations approved by General Assembly 14 Nomvember 1957.
GATT 83 Contracting parties, 22 additional countries participating under special arrangements	Establishes and administers code for orderly conduct of international trade. Helps Governments reduce customs tariffs and abolish other trade barriers, and provides forum for other trade negotiations. With United Nations Conference on Trade and Development, operates International Trade Centre, which provides export promotion assistance for developing countries. GATT rules govern some 80 per cent of international trade.	For 1976: $12,480,072* Villa Le Bocage Palais des Nations CH-1211 Geneva 10 Switzerland	Director-General: Olivier Long (Switzerland) Staff: 198, excluding about 200 staff and experts in International Trade Centre (a joint United Nations/GATT operation)	Charter of International Trade Organization drawn up at United Nations Conference in Havana in 1947-1949, but never ratified. GATT drawn up in 1947, came into force: 1 January 1948.

*Budget in Swiss francs; converted at the rate Sw.fr. 2.74 = $US 1.

C. MEMBERS OF THE AGENCIES AND CONTRACTING PARTIES TO THE GATT[1] (AS AT 1 JANUARY 1976)

ABBREVIATIONS

United Nations

UN   — United Nations

Specialized Agencies

ILO   — International Labor Organization

FAO   — Food and Agriculture Organization of the United Nations

UNESCO   — United Nations Educational, Scientific and Cultural Organization

WHO   — World Health Organization

IBRD   — International Bank for Reconstruction and Development

IDA   — International Development Association

IFC   — International Finance Corporation

IMF   — International Monetary Fund

ICAO   — International Civil Aviation Organization

UPU   — Universal Postal Union

ITU   — International Telecommunication Union

WMO   — World Meteorological Organization

IMCO   — Inter-Governmental Maritime Consultative Organization

WIPO   — World Intellectual Property Organization

Other Organizations

IAEA   — International Atomic Energy Agency

GATT   — General Agreement on Tariffs and Trade

[1] Information supplied by the Office for Inter-Agency Affairs and Coordination, United Nations, New York.

COUNTRY	UN	ILO	FAO	UNESCO	WHO	IBRD	IFC	IDA	IMF	ICAO	UPU	ITU	WMO	IMCO	IAEA	GATT	WIPO
Afghanistan	X	X	X	X	X	X	X	X	X	X	X	X	X	−	X	−	−
Albania	X	−	X	X	X	−	−	−	−	−	X	X	X	−	X	X	X
Algeria	X	X	X	X	X	X	−	X	X	X	X	X	X	X	X	−	X
Argentina	X	X	X	X	X	X	X	X	X	X	X	X	X	X	X	X	X
Australia	X	X	X	X	X	X	X	X	X	X	X	X	X	X	X	X	X
Austria	X	X	X	X	X	X	X	X	X	X	X	X	X	X	X	X	X
Bahamas	X	−	X	−	X	X	−	−	X	X	X	X	X	−	−	−	−
Bahrain	X	−	X	X	X	X	−	−	X	X	X	X	−	−	−	−	−
Bangladesh	X	X	X	X	X	X	−	X	X	X	X	X	X	−	X	X	−
Barbados	X	X	X	X	X	X	−	−	X	X	X	X	X	X	−	X	−
Belgium	X	X	X	X	X	X	X	X	X	X	X	X	X	X	X	X	X
Benin	X	X	X	X	X	X	−	X	X	X	X	X	X	−	−	X	X
Bhutan	X	−	−	−	−	−	−	−	−	−	X	−	−	−	−	−	−
Bolivia	X	X	X	X	X	X	X	X	X	X	X	X	X	−	X	−	−
Botswana	X	−	X	X	−	X	−	X	X	−	X	X	X	−	−	−	−
Brazil	X	X	X	X	X	X	X	X	X	X	X	X	X	X	X	X	X
Bulgaria	X	X	X	X	X	−	−	−	−	X	X	X	X	X	X	−	X
Burma	X	X	X	X	X	X	X	X	X	X	X	X	X	X	X	X	−
Burundi	X	X	X	X	X	X	−	X	X	X	X	X	X	−	−	X	−
Byelorussian SSR	X	X	−	X	X	−	−	−	−	−	X	X	X	−	X	−	X
Cambodia	X	X	X	X	X	X	−	X	X	X	X	X	X	X	X	−	−
Canada	X	X	X	X	X	X	X	X	X	X	X	X	X	X	X	X	X
Cape Verde	X	−	X	−	X	−	−	−	−	−	−	−	X	−	−	−	−
Central African Republic	X	X	X	X	X	X	−	X	X	X	X	X	X	−	−	X	−
Chad	X	X	X	X	X	X	−	X	X	X	X	X	X	−	−	X	X
Chile	X	X	X	X	X	X	X	X	X	X	X	X	X	X	X	X	X
China	X	−	X	X	X	−	−	−	−	X	X	X	X	X	−	−	−
Colombia	X	X	X	X	X	X	X	X	X	X	X	X	X	X	X	−	−
Comoros	X	−	−	−	X	−	−	−	−	−	X	−	−	−	−	−	−
Congo, People's Rep. of	X	X	X	X	X	X	−	X	X	X	X	X	X	X	−	X	X
Costa Rica	X	X	X	X	X	X	X	X	X	X	X	X	X	−	X	−	−
Cuba	X	X	X	X	X	−	−	−	−	X	X	X	X	X	X	X	X

COUNTRY	UN	ILO	FAO	UNESCO	WHO	IBRD	IFC	IDA	IMF	ICAO	UPU	ITU	WMO	IMCO	IAEA	GATT	WIPO
Cyprus	X	X	X	X	X	X	X	X	X	X	X	X	X	X	X	X	X
Czechoslovakia	X	X	X	X	X	—	—	—	—	X	X	X	X	X	X	X	X
Democratic People's Rep. of Korea, The	—	—	—	X	X	—	—	—	—	—	X	X	X	—	X	—	X
Democratic Republic of Vietnam	—	—	—	—	X	—	—	—	—	—	—	—	X	—	—	—	—
Democratic Yemen	X	X	X	X	X	X	—	X	X	X	X	X	X	—	—	—	—
Denmark	X	X	X	X	X	X	X	X	X	X	X	X	X	X	X	X	X
Dominican Republic	X	X	X	X	X	X	X	X	X	X	X	X	X	X	X	X	—
Ecuador	X	X	X	X	X	X	X	X	X	X	X	X	X	X	X	—	—
Egypt	X	X	X	X	X	X	X	X	X	X	X	X	X	X	X	X	X
El Salvador	X	X	X	X	X	X	X	X	X	X	X	X	X	—	X	—	—
Equatorial Guinea	X	—	—	—	—	X	—	X	X	X	X	X	—	X	—	—	—
Ethiopia	X	X	X	X	X	X	X	X	X	X	X	X	X	X	X	—	—
Fiji	X	X	X	—	X	X	—	X	X	X	X	X	—	—	—	—	X
Finland	X	X	X	X	X	X	X	X	X	X	X	X	X	X	X	X	X
France	X	X	X	X	X	X	X	X	X	X	X	X	X	X	X	X	X
Gabon	X	X	X	X	X	X	X	X	X	X	X	X	X	—	X	X	X
Gambia	X	—	X	X	X	X	—	X	X	—	X	X	—	—	—	X	—
German Democratic Rep.	X	X	—	X	X	—	—	—	—	X	X	X	X	X	—	—	X
Germany, Federal Rep. of	X	X	X	X	X	X	X	X	X	X	X	X	X	X	X	X	X
Ghana	X	X	X	X	X	X	X	X	X	X	X	X	X	X	X	X	—
Greece	X	X	X	X	X	X	X	X	X	X	X	X	X	X	X	X	X
Grenada	X	—	X	X	X	X	X	X	X	—	—	—	—	—	—	—	—
Guatemala	X	X	X	X	X	X	X	X	X	X	X	X	X	—	X	—	—
Guinea	X	X	X	X	X	X	—	X	X	X	X	X	X	X	—	—	—
Guinea-Bissau	X	—	X	X	X	—	—	—	—	—	X	X	—	—	—	—	—
Guyana	X	X	X	X	X	X	X	X	X	X	X	X	X	—	—	X	—
Haiti	X	X	X	X	X	X	X	X	X	X	X	X	X	X	X	X	—
Holy See	—	—	—	—	—	—	—	—	—	—	X	X	—	—	X	—	X
Honduras	X	X	X	X	X	X	X	X	X	X	X	X	X	X	—	—	—
Hungary	X	X	X	X	X	—	—	—	—	X	X	X	X	X	X	X	X
Iceland	X	X	X	X	X	X	X	X	X	X	X	X	X	X	X	X	—
India	X	X	X	X	X	X	X	X	X	X	X	X	X	X	X	X	X

COUNTRY	UN	ILO	FAO	UNESCO	WHO	IBRD	IFC	IDA	IMF	ICAO	UPU	ITU	WMO	IMCO	IAEA	GATT	WIPO
Indonesia	X	X	X	X	X	X	X	X	X	X	X	X	X	X	X	X	X
Iran	X	X	X	X	X	X	X	X	X	X	X	X	X	X	X	–	X
Iraq	X	X	X	X	X	X	X	X	X	X	X	X	X	X	X	–	–
Ireland	X	X	X	X	X	X	X	X	X	X	X	X	X	X	X	X	X
Israel	X	X	X	X	X	X	X	X	X	X	X	X	X	X	X	X	X
Italy	X	X	X	X	X	X	X	X	X	X	X	X	X	X	X	X	X
Ivory Coast	X	X	X	X	X	X	X	X	X	X	X	X	X	X	X	X	X
Jamaica	X	X	X	X	X	X	X	–	X	X	X	X	X	–	X	X	–
Japan	X	X	X	X	X	X	X	X	X	X	X	X	X	X	X	X	X
Jordan	X	X	X	X	X	X	X	X	X	X	X	X	X	X	X	–	X
Kenya	X	X	X	X	X	X	X	X	X	X	X	X	X	X	X	X	X
Kuwait	X	X	X	X	X	X	X	X	X	X	X	X	X	X	X	X	–
Lao People's Democratic Republic	X	X	X	X	X	X	–	X	X	X	X	X	X	–	–	–	–
Lebanon	X	X	X	X	X	X	X	X	X	X	X	X	X	X	X	–	–
Lesotho	X	–	X	X	X	X	X	X	X	X	X	X	–	–	–	–	–
Liberia	X	X	X	X	X	X	X	X	X	X	X	X	X	X	X	–	–
Libyan Arab Republic	X	X	X	X	X	X	X	X	X	X	X	X	X	X	X	–	–
Liechtenstein	–	–	–	–	–	–	–	–	–	–	X	X	–	–	X	–	X
Luxembourg	X	X	X	X	X	X	X	X	X	X	X	X	X	X	–	X	X
Madagascar	X	X	X	X	X	X	X	X	X	X	X	X	X	X	X	X	X
Malawi	X	X	X	X	X	X	X	X	X	X	X	X	X	–	–	X	X
Malaysia	X	X	X	X	X	X	X	X	X	X	X	X	X	X	X	X	–
Maldives	X	–	X	–	X	–	–	–	–	X	X	X	–	X	–	–	–
Mali	X	X	X	X	X	X	–	X	X	X	X	X	X	–	X	–	–
Malta	X	X	X	X	X	–	–	–	X	X	X	X	–	X	–	X	X
Mauritania	X	X	X	X	X	X	X	X	X	X	X	X	X	X	–	X	X
Mauritius	X	X	X	X	X	X	X	X	X	X	X	X	X	–	X	X	–
Mexico	X	X	X	X	X	X	X	X	X	X	X	X	X	X	X	–	X
Monaco	–	–	–	X	X	–	–	–	–	–	X	X	–	–	X	–	X
Mongolia	X	X	X	X	X	–	–	–	–	–	X	X	X	–	X	–	–
Morocco	X	X	X	X	X	X	X	X	X	X	X	X	X	X	X	–	X
Mozambique	X	–	–	–	X	–	–	–	–	–	–	X	–	–	–	–	–
Nauru	–	–	–	–	–	–	–	–	–	X	X	X	–	–	–	–	–

COUNTRY	UN	ILO	FAO	UNESCO	WHO	IBRD	IFC	IDA	IMF	ICAO	UPU	ITU	WMO	IMCO	IAEA	GATT	WIPO
Nepal	X	X	X	X	X	X	X	X	X	X	X	X	X	–	–	–	–
Netherlands	X	X	X	X	X	X	X	X	X	X	X	X	X	X	X	X	X
New Zealand	X	X	X	X	X	X	X	X	X	X	X	X	X	X	X	X	–
Nicaragua	X	X	X	X	X	X	X	X	X	X	X	X	X	–	–	X	–
Niger	X	X	X	X	X	X	–	X	X	X	X	X	X	–	X	X	X
Nigeria	X	X	X	X	X	X	X	X	X	X	X	X	X	X	X	X	–
Norway	X	X	X	X	X	X	X	X	X	X	X	X	X	X	X	X	X
Oman	X	–	X	X	X	X	X	X	X	X	X	X	X	–	–	–	–
Pakistan	X	X	X	X	X	X	X	X	X	X	X	X	X	X	X	X	–
Panama	X	X	X	X	X	X	X	X	X	X	X	X	X	X	X	–	–
Papua - New Guinea	X	–	X	–	–	X	X	X	X	–	–	X	X	–	–	–	–
Paraguay	X	X	X	X	X	X	X	X	X	X	X	X	X	–	X	–	–
Peru	X	X	X	X	X	X	X	X	X	X	X	X	X	X	X	X	–
Philippines	X	X	X	X	X	X	X	X	X	X	X	X	X	X	X	–	–
Poland	X	X	X	X	X	–	–	–	–	X	X	X	X	X	X	X	X
Portugal	X	X	X	X	X	X	X	–	X	X	X	X	X	–	X	X	X
Qatar	X	X	X	X	X	X	–	–	X	X	X	X	X	–	X	–	–
Republic of Korea	–	–	X	X	X	X	X	X	X	X	X	X	X	X	X	X	–
Republic of South Vietnam	–	X	X	X	X	X	X	X	X	X	X	X	X	–	X	–	X
Romania	X	X	X	X	X	X	–	–	X	X	X	X	X	X	X	X	X
Rwanda	X	X	X	X	X	X	X	X	X	X	X	X	X	–	–	X	–
San Marino	–	–	–	X	–	–	–	–	–	–	X	–	–	–	–	–	–
Sao Tome and Principe	X	–	–	–	–	–	–	–	–	–	–	–	–	–	–	–	–
Saudi Arabia	X	X	X	X	X	X	X	X	X	X	X	X	X	X	X	–	–
Senegal	X	X	X	X	X	X	X	X	X	X	X	X	X	X	X	X	X
Sierra Leone	X	X	X	X	X	X	X	X	X	X	X	X	X	X	X	X	–
Singapore	X	X	–	X	X	X	X	–	X	X	X	X	X	X	X	X	–
Somalia	X	X	X	X	X	X	X	X	X	X	X	X	X	–	–	–	–
South Africa	X	–	–	–	X	X	X	X	X	X	X	X	X	–	X	X	X
Spain	X	X	X	X	X	X	X	X	X	X	X	X	X	X	X	X	X
Sri Lanka	X	X	X	X	X	X	X	X	X	X	X	X	X	X	X	X	–
Sudan	X	X	X	X	X	X	X	X	X	X	X	X	X	X	X	–	X
Surinam	X	–	X	–	–	–	–	–	–	–	–	–	–	–	–	–	–

COUNTRY	UN	ILO	FAO	UNESCO	WHO	IBRD	IFC	IDA	IMF	ICAO	UPU	ITU	WMO	IMCO	IAEA	GATT	WIPO
Swaziland	X	X	X	—	X	X	X	X	X	X	X	X	—	—	—	—	—
Sweden	X	X	X	X	X	X	X	X	X	X	X	X	X	X	X	X	X
Switzerland	—	X	X	X	X	—	—	—	—	X	X	X	X	X	X	X	X
Syrian Arab Republic	X	X	X	X	X	X	X	X	X	X	X	X	X	X	X	—	X
Thailand	X	X	X	X	X	X	X	X	X	X	X	X	X	X	X	—	X
Togo	X	X	X	X	X	X	X	X	X	X	X	X	X	—	—	X	X
Tonga	—	—	—	—	X	—	—	—	—	—	X	X	—	—	—	—	—
Trinidad and Tobago	X	X	X	X	X	X	X	X	X	X	X	X	X	X	—	X	—
Tunisia	X	X	X	X	X	X	X	X	X	X	X	X	X	X	X	—	X
Turkey	X	X	X	X	X	X	X	X	X	X	X	X	X	X	X	X	X
Uganda	X	X	X	X	X	X	X	X	X	X	X	X	X	—	X	X	X
Ukrainian SSR	X	X	—	X	X	—	—	—	—	—	X	X	X	—	X	—	X
USSR	X	X	—	X	X	—	—	—	—	X	X	X	X	X	X	—	X
United Arab Emirates	X	X	X	X	X	X	—	—	X	X	X	X	—	—	X	—	X
United Kingdom	X	X	X	X	X	X	X	X	X	X	X	X	X	X	X	X	X
United Rep. of Cameroon	X	X	X	X	X	X	X	X	X	X	X	X	X	X	X	X	X
United Rep. of Tanzania	X	X	X	X	X	X	X	X	X	X	X	X	X	X	X	X	—
USA	X	X	X	X	X	X	X	X	X	X	X	X	X	X	X	X	X
Upper Volta	X	X	X	X	X	X	X	X	X	X	X	X	X	—	—	X	X
Uruguay	X	X	X	X	X	X	X	—	X	X	X	X	X	X	X	X	—
Venezuela	X	X	X	X	X	X	X	—	X	X	X	X	X	X	X	—	—
Western Samoa	—	—	—	—	X	X	X	X	X	—	—	—	—	—	—	—	—
Yemen Arab Republic	X	X	X	X	X	X	X	X	X	X	X	X	X	—	—	—	—
Yugoslavia	X	X	X	X	X	X	X	X	X	X	X	X	X	X	X	X	X
Zaire	X	X	X	X	X	X	X	X	X	X	X	X	X	X	X	X	X
Zambia	X	X	X	X	X	X	X	X	X	X	X	X	X	—	X	—	—
TOTALS	145	1) 127	136	2) 136	3) 146	4) 126	5) 104	6) 115	7) 127	8) 132	9) 153	146	10) 145	11) 92	106	12) 83	13) 74

---

[1] In information supplied by the ILO, China, although not represented, is included in the list of members of the Organization.

[2] UNESCO has three *associate members:* the British Eastern Caribbean Group, Namibia and Papua-New Guinea.

[3] WHO has three *associate members:* Southern Rhodesia, Namibia and Papua-New Guinea.

[4] In information supplied by the World Bank, China is included in the list of members of the Bank. However, with respect to China's representation, the Bank has not implemented General Assembly resolution 2758 (XXVI).

[5] In information supplied by the IFC, China is included in the list of members of the Corporation. However, with respect to China's representation, the IFC has not implemented General Assembly resolution 2758 (XXVI).

[6] In information supplied by the IDA, China is included in the list of members of the Association. However, with respect to China's representation, the IDA has not implemented General Assembly resolution 2758 (XXVI).

[7] In information supplied by the IMF, China is included in the list of members of the Fund. However, with respect to China's representation, the Fund has not implemented General Assembly resolution 2758 (XXVI).

[8] In ICAO, USSR membership includes the Byelorussian and Ukrainian SSR's.

[9] The 153 *members* of UPU include the following not listed in the table: Netherlands Antilles, Overseas Territories for the international relations of which the Government of the United Kingdom of Great Britain and Northern Ireland is responsible. Portuguese Provinces in East Africa, Asia and Oceania, Portuguese Provinces in West Africa, Spanish Territory in Africa, whole of the Territories of the United States of America, including the Trust Territory of the Pacific Islands, whole of the Territories represented by the French Office of Overseas Posts and Telecommunications.

[10] The 145 *members* of WMO include the 127 Member States listed in the table and the following 12 members not listed in the table which maintain their own meteorological service: British Caribbean Territories, Comoro Islands, French Polynesia, French Territory of the Afars and Issas, Hong Kong, Netherlands Antilles, New Caledonia, Portuguese East Africa, Portuguese West Africa, St. Pierre and Miquelon, Southern Rhodesia, Surinam.

[11] The 92 *members* of IMCO include one *associate member:* Hong Kong.

[12] The 83 contracting parties to GATT also include Rhodesia. In addition, there are three countries (Colombia, Philippines and Tunisia) which have provisionally acceded to the Agreement, and 18 countries (Algeria, Bahamas, Bahrain, Botswana, Equatorial Guinea, Fiji, Grenada, the Khmer Republic, Lesotho, Maldives, Mali, Papua-New Guinea, Qatar, Democratic Yemen, Swaziland, Tonga, United Arab Emirates and Zambia) to whose territories GATT has been applied before independence and which now as independent States maintain a *de facto* application of the GATT pending final decisions as to their future commercial policy.

[13] Includes States exercising membership right by virtue of article 21 of the WIPO Convention.

D. BASIC LAWS AND AGREEMENTS OF THE SPECIALIZED AGENCIES

1. INTERNATIONAL LABOUR ORGANIZATION

a. CONSTITUTION OF THE INTERNATIONAL LABOUR ORGANIZATION, EFFECTIVE MAY 22, 1963

TABLE OF CONTENTS

Text of the Constitution[1]

PREAMBLE

Whereas universal and lasting peace can be established only if it is based upon social justice;

And whereas conditions of labour exist involving such injustice, harship and privation to large numbers of people as to produce unrest so great that the peace and harmony of the world are imperilled; and an improvement of those conditions is urgently required: as, for example, by the regulation of the hours of work, including the establishment of a maximum working day and week, the regulation of the labour supply, the prevention of unemployment, the provision of an adequate living wage, the protection of the worker against sickness, disease and injury arising out of his employment, the protection of children, young persons and women, provision for old age and injury, protection of the interests of workers when employed in countries other than their own, recognition of the principle of equal remuneration for work of equal value, recognition of the principle of freedom of association, the organisation of vocational and technical education and other measures;

---

[1] The original text of the Constitution, established in 1919, has been modified by the amendment of 1922 which entered into force on 4 June 1934; the Instrument of Amendment of 1945 which entered into force on 26 September 1946; the Instrument of Amendment of 1946 which entered into force on 20 April 1948; the Instrument of Amendment of 1953 which entered into force on 20 May 1954; and the Instrument of Amendment of 1962 which entered into force on 22 May 1963.

Whereas also the failure of any nation to adopt humane conditions of labour is an obstacle in the way of other nations which desire to improve the conditions in their own countries;

The High Contracting Parties, moved by sentiments of justice and humanity as well as by the desire to secure the permanent peace of the world, and with a view to attaining the objectives set forth in this Preamble, agree to the following Constitution of the International Labour Organisation:

CHAPTER I — ORGANISATION

Article 1

Establishment
1. A permanent organisation is hereby established for the promotion of the objects set forth in the Preamble to this Constitution and in the Declaration concerning the aims and purposes of the International Labour Organisation adopted at Philadelphia on 10 May 1944 the text of which is annexed to this Constitution.

Membership
2. The Members of the International Labour Organisation shall be the States which were Members of the Organisation on 1 November 1945, and such other States as may become Members in pursuance of the provisions of paragraphs 3 and 4 of this article.

3. Any original Member of the United Nations and any State admitted to membership of the United Nations by a decision of the General Assembly in accordance with the provisions of the Charter may become a Member of the International Labour Organisation by communicating to the Director-General of the International Labour Office its formal acceptance of the obligations of the Constitution of the International Labour Organisation.

4. The General Conference of the International Labour Organisation may also admit Members to the Organisation by a vote concurred in by two-thirds of the delegates attending the session, including two-thirds of the Government delegates present and voting. Such admission shall take effect on the communication to the Director-General of the International Labour Office by the government of the new Member of its formal acceptance of the obligations of the Constitution of the Organisation.

Withdrawal
5. No Member of the International Labour Organisation may withdraw from the Organisation without giving notice of its intention so to do to the Director-General of the International Labour Office. Such notice shall take effect two years after the date of its reception by the Director-General, subject to the Member having at that time fulfilled all financial obligations arising out of its membership. When a Member has ratified any international labour Convention, such withdrawal shall not affect the continued validity for the period provided for in the Convention of all obligations arising thereunder or relating thereto.

Readmission
6. In the event of any State having ceased to be a Member of the Organisation, its readmission to membership shall be governed by the provisions of paragrah 3 or paragraph 4 of this article as the case may be.

Article 2

The permanent organisation shall consist of—

(a) a General Conference of representatives of the Members;

(b) a Governing Body composed as described in article 7; and

(c) an International Labour Office controlled by the Governing Body.

Conference

Article 3

Meetings and delegates

1. The meetings of the General Conference of representatives of the Members shall be held from time to time as occasion may require, and at least once in every year. It shall be composed of four representatives of each of the Members, of whom two shall be Government delegates and the two others shall be delegates representing respectively the employers and the workpeople of each of the Members.

Advisers

2. Each delegate may be accompanied by advisers, who shall not exceed two in number for each item on the agenda of the meeting. When questions specially affecting women are to be considered by the Conference, one at least of the advisers should be a woman.

Advisers from non-metropolitan territories

3. Each Member which is responsible for the international relations of non-metropolitan territories may appoint as additional advisers to each of its delegates—

(a) persons nominated by it as representatives of any such territory in regard to matters within the self-governing powers of that territory; and

(b) persons nominated by it to advise its delegates in regard to matters concerning non-self-governing territories.

4. In the case of a territory under the joint authority of two or more Members, persons may be nominated to advise the delegates of such Members.

Nomination of non-governmental representatives

5. The Members undertake to nominate non-Government delegates and advisers chosen in agreement with the industrial organisations, if such organisations exist, which are most representative of employers or workpeople, as the case may be, in their respective countries.

Status of advisers

6. Advisers shall not speak except on a request made by the delegate whom they accompany and by the special authorisation of the President of the Conference, and may not vote.

7. A delegate may by notice in writing addressed to the President appoint one of his advisers to act as his deputy, and the adviser, while so acting, shall be allowed to speak and vote.

Credentials

8. The names of the delegates and their advisers will be communicated to the International Labour Office by the government of each of the Members.

9. The credentials of delegates and their advisers shall be subject to scrutiny by the Conference, which may, by two-thirds of the votes cast by the delegates present, refuse to admit any delegate or adviser whom it deems not to have been nominated in accordance with this acticle.

Article 4

1. Every delegate shall be entitled to vote individually on all matters which are taken into consideration by the Conference.

2. If one of the Members fails to nominate one of the non-Government delegates whom it is entitled to nominate, the other non-Government delegate shall be allowed to sit and speak at the Conference, but not to vote.

3. If in accordance with article 3 the Conference refuses admission to a delegate of one of the Members, the provisions of the present article shall apply as if that delegate had not been nominated.

Place of meetings of the Conference

Article 5

The meetings of the Conference shall, subject to any decisions which may have been taken by the Conference itself at a previous meeting, be held at such place as may be decided by the Governing Body.

Seat of the International Labour Office

Article 6

Any change in the seat of the International Labour Office shall be decided by the Conference by a two-thirds majority of the votes cast by the delegates present.

Governing Body Composition

Article 7

1. The Governing Body shall consist of forty-eight persons—

Twenty-four representing governments,
Twelve representing the employers, and
Twelve representing the workers.

Government representatives

2. Of the twenty-four persons representing governments, ten shall be appointed by the Members of chief industrial importance, and fourteen shall be appointed by the Members selected for that purpose by the Government delegates to the Conference, excluding the delegates of the ten Members mentioned above.

States of chief industrial importance

3. The Governing Body shall as occasion requires determine which are the Members of the Organisation of chief industrial importance and shall make rules to ensure that all questions relating to the selection of the Members of chief industrial importance are considered by an impartial committee before being decided by the Governing Body. Any appeal made by a Member from the declaration of the Governing Body as to which are the Members of chief industrial importance shall be decided by the Conference, but an appeal to the Conference shall not suspend the application of the declaration until such time as the Conference decides the appeal.

Employers' and Workers' representatives

4. The persons representing the employers and the persons representing the workers shall be elected respectively by the Employers' delegates and the Workers' delegates to the Conference.

Term of office

5. The period of office of the Governing Body shall be three years. If for any reason the Governing Body elections do not take place on the expiry of this period, the Governing Body shall remain in office until such elections are held.

6. The method of filling vacancies and of appointing substitutes and other similar questions may be decided by the Governing Body subject to the approval of the Conference.

7. The Governing Body shall, from time to time, elect from its number a chairman and two vice-chairmen, of whom one shall be a person representing a government, one a person representing the employers, and one a person representing the workers.

8. The Governing Body shall regulate its own procedure and shall fix its own times of meeting. A special meeting shall be held if a written request to that effect is made by at least sixteen of the representatives on the Governing Body.

Article 8

1. There shall be a Director-General of the International Labour Office, who shall be appointed by the Governing Body, and, subject to the instructions of the Governing Body, shall be responsible for the efficient conduct of the International Labour Office and for such other duties as may be assigned to him.

2. The Director-General or his deputy shall attend all meetings of the Governing Body.

Article 9

1. The staff of the International Labour Office shall be appointed by the Director-General under regulations approved by the Governing Body.

2. So far as is possible with due regard to the efficiency of the work of the Office, the Director-General shall select persons of different nationalities.

3. A certain number of these persons shall be women.

4. The responsibilities of the Director-General and the staff shall be exclusively international in character. In the performance of their duties, the Director-General and the staff shall not seek or receive instructions from any government or from any other authority external to the Organisation. They shall refrain from any action which might reflect on their position as international officials responsible only to the Organization.

5. Each Member of the Organisation undertakes to respect the exclusively international character of the responsibilities of the Director-General and the staff and not to seek to influence them in the discharge of their responsibilities.

Article 10

1. The functions of the International Labour Office shall include the collection and distribution of information on all subjects relating to the international adjustment of conditions of industrial life and labour, and particularly the examination of subjects which it is proposed to bring before the Conference with a view to the conclusion of international Conventions, and the conduct of such special investigations as may be ordered by the Conference or by the Governing Body.

2. Subject to such directions as the Governing Body may give, the Office shall—

(a) prepare the documents on the various items of the agenda for the meetings of the Conference;

(b) accord to governments at their request all appropriate assistance within its power in connection with the framing of laws and regulations on the basis of the decisions of the Conference and the improvement of administrative practices and systems of inspection;

(c) carry out the duties required of it by the provisions of this Constitution in connection with the effective observance of Conventions;

(d) edit and issue, in such languages as the Governing Body may think desirable, publications dealing with problems of industry and employment of international interest.

3. Generally, it shall have such other powers and duties as may be assigned to it by the Conference or by the Governing Body.

Article 11

Relations with governments

The government departments of any of the Members which deal with questions of industry and employment may communicate directly with the Director-General through the representative of their government on the Governing Body of the International Labour Office or, failing any such representative, through such other qualified official as the government may nominate for the purpose.

Article 12

Relations with International organisations

1. The International Labour Organisation shall cooperate within the terms of this Constitution with any general international organisation entrusted with the coordination of the activities of public international organisations having specialised responsibilities and with public international organisations having specialised responsibilities in related fields.

2. The International Labour Organisation may make appropriate arrangements for the representatives of public international organisations to participate without vote in its deliberations.

3. The International Labour Organisation may make suitable arrangements for such consultation as it may think desirable with recognised non-governmental international organisations, including international organisations of employers, workers, agriculturists and co-operators.

Article 13

Financial and budgetary arrangements

1. The International Labour Organisation may make such financial and budgetary arrangements with the United Nations as may appear appropriate.

2. Pending the conclusion of such arrangements or if at any time no such arrangements are in force—

(a) each of the Members will pay the travelling and subsistence expenses of its delegates and their advisers and of its representatives attending the meetings of the Conference or the Governing Body, as the case may be;

(b) all other expenses of the International Labour Office and of the meetings of the Conference or Governing Body shall be paid by the Director-General of the International Labour Office out of the general funds of the International Labour Organisation;

(c) the arrangements for the approval, allocation and collection of the budget of the International Labour Organisation shall be determined by the Conference by a two-thirds majority of the votes cast by the delegates present, and shall provide for the approval of the budget and of the arrangements for the allocation of expenses among the Members of the Organisation by a committe of Government representatives.

3. The expenses of the International Labour Organisation shall be borne by the Members in accordance with the arrangements in force in virtue of paragraph 1 or paragraph 2 *(c)* of this article.

Arrears in payment of contributions

4. A Member of the Organisation which is in arrears in the payment of its financial contribution to the Organisation shall have no vote in the Conference, in the Governing Body, in any committee, or in the elections of members of the Governing Body, if the amount of its arrears equals or exceeds the amount of the contributions due from it for the preceding two full years: Provided that the Conference may by a two-thirds majority of the votes cast by the delegates present permit such a Member to vote if it is satisfied that the failure to pay is due to conditions beyond the control of the Member.

Financial responsibility of Director-General

5. The Director-General of the International Labour Office shall be responsible to the Governing Body for the proper expenditure of the funds of the International Labour Organisation.

CHAPTER II — PROCEDURE

Article 14

Agenda for Conference

1. The agenda for all meetings of the Conference will be settled by the Governing Body, which shall consider any suggestion as to the agenda that may be made by the government of any of the Members or by any representative organisation recognised for the purpose of article 3, or by any public international organisation.

Preparation for Conference

2. The Governing Body shall make rules to ensure through technical preparation and adequate consultation of the Members primarily concerned, by means of a preparatory conference or otherwise, prior to the adoption of a Convention or Recommendation by the Conference.

Transmission of agenda and reports for Conference

Article 15

1. The Director-General shall act as the Secretary-General of the Conference, and shall transmit the agenda so as to reach the Members four months before the meeting of the Conference, and, through them, the non-Government delegates when appointed.

2. The reports on each item of the agenda shall be despatched so as to reach the Members in time to permit adequate consideration before the meeting of the Conference. The Governing Body shall make rules for the application of this provision.

Article 16

Objections to agenda

1. Any of the government of the Members may formally object to the inclusion of any item or items in the agenda. The grounds for such objection shall be set forth in a statement addressed to the Director-General who shall circulate it to all the Members of the Organisation.

2. Items to which such objection has been made shall not, however, be excluded from the agenda, if at the Conference a majority of two-thirds of the votes cast by the delegates present is in favour of considering them.

Inclusion of new items by Conference

3. If the Conference decides (otherwise than under the preceding paragraph) by two-thirds of the votes cast by the delegates present that any subject shall be considered by the Conference, that subject shall be included in the agenda for the following meeting.

Article 17

Officers of Conference, procedure and committees

1. The Conference shall elect a president and three vice-presidents. One of the vice-presidents shall be a Government delegate, one an Employers' delegate and one a Workers' delegate. The Conference shall regulate its own procedure and may appoint committees to consider and report on any matter.

Voting

2. Except as otherwise expressly provided in this Constitution or by the terms of any Convention or other instrument conferring powers on the Conference or of the financial and budgetary arrangements adopted in virtue of article 13, all matters shall be decided by a simple majority of the votes cast by the delegates present.

Quorum

3. The voting is void unless the total number of votes cast is equal to half the number of the delegates attending the Conference.

Article 18

Technical experts

The Conference may add to any committees which it appoints technical experts without power to vote.

Article 19

Conventions and Recommendations

Decisions of the Conference

1. When the Conference has decided on the adoption of proposals with regard to an item on the agenda, it will rest with the Conference to determine whether these proposals should take the form: *(a)* of an international Convention, or *(b)* of a Recommendation to meet circumstances where the subject, or aspect of it, dealt with is not considered suitable or appropriate at tha time for a Convention.

Vote required

2. In either case a majority of two-thirds of the votes cast by the delegates present shall be necessary on the final vote for the adoption of the Convention or Recommendation, as the case may be, by the Conference.

Modifications for special local conditions

3. In framing any Convention or Recommendation of general application the Conference shall have due regard to those countries in which climatic conditions, the imperfect development of industrial organisation, or other special circumstances make the industrial conditions substantially different and shall suggest the modifications, if any, which it considers may be required to meet the case of such countries.

4. Two copies of the Convention or Recommendation shall be authenticated by the signatures of the President of the Conference and of the Director-General. Of these copies one shall be deposited in the archives of the International Labour Office and the other with the Secretary-General of the United Nations. The Director-General will communicate a certified copy of the Convention or Recommendation to each of the Members.

5. In the case of a Convention—

(a) the Convention will be communicated to all Members for ratification;

(b) each of the Members undertakes that it will, within the period of one year at most from the closing of the session of the Conference, or if it is impossible owing to exceptional circumstances to do so within the period of one year, then at the earliest practicable moment and in no case later than 18 months from the closing of the session of the Conference, bring the Convention before the authority or authorities within whose competence the matter lies, for the enactment of legislation or other action;

(c) Members shall inform the Director-General of the International Labour Office of the measures taken in accordance with this article to bring the Convention before the said competent authority or authorities, with particulars of the authority or authorities regarded as competent, and of the action taken by them;

(d) if the Member obtains the consent of the authority or authorities within whose competence the matter lies, it will communicate the formal ratification of the Convention to the Director-General and will take such action as may be necessary to make effective the provisions of such Convention;

(e) if the Member does not obtain the consent of the authority or authorities within whose competence the matter lies, no further obligation shall rest upon the Member except that it shall report to the Director-General of the International Labour Office, at appropriate intervals as requested by the Governing Body, the position of its law and practice in regard to the matters dealt with in the Convention, showing the extent to which effect has been given, or is proposed to be given, to any of the provisions of the Convention by legislation, administrative action, collective agreement or otherwise and stating the difficulties which prevent or delay the ratification of such Convention.

6. In the case of a Recommendation—

(a) the Recommendation will be communicated to all Members for their consideration with a view to effect being given to it by national legislation or otherwise;

(b) each of the Members undertakes that it will, within a period of one year at most from the closing of the session of the Conference, or if it is impossible owing to exceptional circumstances to do so within the period of one year, then at the earliest practicable moment and in no case later than 18 months after the closing of the Conference, bring the Recommendation before the authority or authorities within whose competence the matter lies for the enactment of legislation or other action;

(c) the Members shall inform the Director-General of the International Labour Office of the measures taken in accordance with this article to bring the Recommendation before the said competent

authority or authorities with particulars of the authority or authorities regarded as competent, and of the action taken by them;

(d) apart from bringing the Recommendation before the said competent authority or authorities, no further obligation shall rest upon the Members, except that they shall report to the Director-General of the International Labour Office, at appropriate intervals as requested by the Governing Body, the position of the law and practice in their country in regard to the matters dealt with in the Recommendation, showing the extent to which effect has been given, or is proposed to be given, to the provisions of the Recommendation and such modifications of these provisions as it has been found or may be found necessary to make in adopting or applying them.

Obligations of federal States

7. In the case of a federal State, the following provisions, shall apply:

(a) in respect of Conventions and Recommendations which the federal government regards as appropriate under its constitutional system for federal action, the obligations of the federal State shall be the same as those of Members which are not federal States;

(b) in respect of Conventions and Recommendations which the federal government regards as appropriate under its constitutional system, in whole or in part, for action by the constituent states, provinces, or cantons rather than for federal action, the federal government shall—

(i) make, in accordance with its Constitution and the Constitutions of the states, provinces or cantons concerned, effective arrangements for the reference of such Conventions and Recommendations not later than 18 months from the closing of the session of the Conference to the appropriate federal, state, provincial or cantonal authorities for the enactment of legislation or other action;

(ii) arrange, subject to the concurrence of the state, provincial or cantonal governments concerned, for periodical consultations between the federal and the state, provincial or cantonal authorities with a view to promoting within the federal State co-ordinated action to give effect to the provisions of such Conventions and Recommendations;

(iii) inform the Director-General of the International Labour Office of the measures taken in accordance with this article to bring such Conventions and Recommendations before the appropriate federal, state, provincial or cantonal authorities with particulars of the authorities regarded as appropriate and of the action taken by then;

(iv) in respect of each such Convention which it has not ratified, report to the Director-General of the International Labour Office, at appropriate intervals as requested by the Governing Body, the position of the law and practice of the federation and its constituent states, provinces or cantons in regard to the Convention, showing the extent to which effect has been given, or is proposed to be given, to any of the provisions of the Convention by legislation, administrative action, collective agreement, or otherwise;

(v) in respect of each such Recommendation, report to the Director-General of the International Labour Office, at appropriate intervals as requested by the Governing Body, the position of the law and practice of the federation and its constituent states, provinces or cantons in regard to the Recommendation, showing the extent to which effect has been given, or is proposed to be given, to the provisions of the Recommendation and such modifications of these provisions as have been found or may be found necessary in adopting or applying them.

Effect of Conventions and Recommendations on more favourable existing provisions

8. In no case shall the adoption of any Convention or Recommendation by the Conference, or the ratification of any Convention by any Member, be deemed to affect any law, award, custom or agreement which ensures more favourable conditions to the workers concerned than those provided for in the Convention or Recommendation.

Registration with the United Nations

Article 20

Any Convention so ratified shall be communicated by the Director-General of the International Labour Office to the Secretary-General of the United Nations for registration in accordance with the provisions of article 102 of the Charter of the United Nations but shall only be binding upon the Members which ratify it.

Conventions not adopted by the Conference

Article 21

1. If any Convention coming before the Conference for final consideration fails to secure the support of two-thirds of the votes cast by the delegates present, it shall nevertheless be within the right of any of the Members of the Organisation to agree to such Convention among themselves.

2. Any Convention so agreed to shall be communicated by the governments concerned to the Director-General of the International Labour Office and to the Secretary-General of the United Nations for registration in accordance with the provisions of article 102 of the Charter of the United Nations.

Annual reports on ratified Conventions

Article 22

Each of the Members agrees to make an annual report to the International Labour Office on the measures which it has taken to give to the provisions of Conventions to which it is a party. These reports shall be made in such form and shall contain such particulars as the Governing Body may request.

Examination and communication of reports

Article 23

1. The Director-General shall lay before the next meeting of the Conference a summary of the information and reports communicated to him by Members in pursuance of articles 19 and 22.

2. Each Member shall communicate to the representative organisations recognised for the purpose of article 3 copies of the information and reports communicated to the Director-General in pursuance of articles 19 and 22.

Article 24

In the event of any representation being made to the International Labour Office by an industrial association of employers or of workers that any of the Members has failed to secure in any respect the effective observance within its jurisdiction of any Convention to which it is a party, the Governing Body may communicate this representation to the government against which it is made, and may invite that government to make such statement on the subject as it may think fit.

Article 25

If no statement is received within a reasonable time from the government in question, or if the statement when received is not deemed to be satisfactory by the Governing Body, the latter shall have the right to publish the representation and the statement, if any, made in reply to it.

Article 26

1. Any of the Members shall have the right to file a complaint with the International Labour Office if it is not satisfied that any other Member is securing the effective observance of any Convention which both have ratified in accordance with the foregoing articles.

2. The Governing Body may, if it thinks fit, before referring such a complaint to a Commission of Inquiry, as hereinafter provided for, communicate with the government in question in the manner described in article 24.

3. If the Governing Body does not think it necessary to communicate the complaint to the government in question, or if, when it has made such communication, no statement in reply has been received within a reasonable time which the Governing Body considers to be satisfactory, the Governing Body may appoint a Commission of Inquiry to consider the complaint and to report thereon.

4. The Governing Body may adopt the same procedure either of its own motion or on receipt of a complaint from a delegate to the Conference.

5. When any matter arising out of article 25 or 26 is being considered by the Governing Body, the government in question shall, if not already represented thereon, be entitled to send a representative to take part in the proceedings of the Governing Body while the matter is under consideration. Adequate notice of the date on which the matter will be considered shall be given to the government in question.

Article 27

The Members agree that, in the event of the reference of a complaint to a Commission of Inquiry under article 26, they will each, whether directly concerned in the complaint or not, place at the disposal of the Commission all the information in their possession which bears upon the subject-matter of the complaint.

Report of Commission of Inquiry

Article 28

When the Commission of Inquiry has fully considered the complaint, it shall prepare a report embodying its findings on all questions of fact relevant to determining the issue between the parties and containing such recommendations as it may think proper as to the steps which should be taken to meet the complaint and the time within which they should be taken.

Action on report of Commission of Inquiry

Article 29

1. The Director-General of the International Labour Office shall communicate the report of the Commission of Inquiry to the Governing Body and to each of the governments concerned in the complaint, and shall cause it to be published.

2. Each of these governments shall within three months inform the Director-General of the International Labour Office whether or not it accepts the recommendations contained in the report of the Commission; and if not, whether it proposes to refer the complaint to the International Court of Justice.

Failure to submit Conventions or Recommendations to competent authorities

Article 30

In the event of any Member failing to take the action required by paragraphs 5 *(b)*, 6 *(b)* or 7 *(b)* (i) of article 19 with regard to a Convention or Recommendation, any other Member shall be entitled to refer the matter to the Governing Body. In the event of the Governing Body finding that there has been such a failure, it shall report the matter to the Conference.

Decisions of International Court of Justice

Article 31

The decision of the International Court of Justice in regard to a complaint or matter which has been referred to it in pursuance of article 29 shall be final.

Article 32

The International Court of Justice may affirm, vary or reverse any of the findings or recommendations of the Commission of Inquiry, if any.

Failure to carry out recommendations of Commission of Inquiry or ICJ

Article 33

In the event of any Member failing to carry out within the time specified the recommendations, if any, contained in the report of the Commission of Inquiry, or in the decision of the International Court of Justice, as the case may be, the Governing Body may recommend to the Conference such action as it may deem wise and expedient to secure compliance therewith.

Compilance
with recom-
mendations of
Commission of
Inquiry or
ICJ

Article 34

The defaulting government may at any time inform the Governing Body that it has taken the steps necessary to comply with the recommendations of the Commission of Inquiry or with those in the decision of the International Court of Justice, as the case may be, and may request it to constitute a Commission of Inquiry to verify its contention. In this case the provisions of articles 27, 28, 29, 31 and 32 shall apply, and if the report of the Commission of Inquiry or the decision of the International Court of Justice is in favour of the defaulting government, the Governing Body shall forthwith recommend the discontinuance of any action taken in pursuance of article 33.

CHAPTER III — GENERAL

Article 35

1. The Members undertake that Conventions which they have ratified in accordance with the provisions of this Constitution shall be applied to the non-metropolitan territories for whose international relations they are responsible, including any trust territories for which they are the administering authority, except where the subject-matter of the Convention is within the self-governing powers of the territory or the Convention is inapplicable owing to the local conditions or subject to such modifications as may be necessary to adapt the Convention to local conditions.

2. Each Member which ratifies a Convention shall as soon as possible after ratification communicate to the Director-General of the International Labour Office a declaration stating in respect of the territories other than those referred to in paragraphs 4 and 5 below the extent to which it undertakes that the provisions of the Convention shall be applied and giving such particulars as may be prescribed by the Convention.

3. Each Member which has communicated a declaration in virtue of the preceding paragraph may from time to time, in accordance with the terms of the Convention, communicate a further declaration modifying the terms of any former declaration and stating the present position in respect of such territories.

4. Where the subject-matter of the Convention is within the self-governing powers of any non-metropolitan territory the Member responsible for the international relations of that territory shall bring the Convention to the notice of the government of the territory as soon as possible with a view to the enactment of legislation or other action by such government. Thereafter the Member, in agreement with the government of the territory, may communicate to the Director-General of the International Labour Office a declaration accepting the obligations of the Convention on behalf of such territory.

5. A declaration accepting the obligations of any Convention may be communicated to the Director-General of the International Labour Office—

(a) by two or more Members of the Organisation in respect of any territory which is under their joint authority; or

(b) by any international authority responsible for the administration of any territory, in virtue of the Charter of the United Nations or otherwise, in respect of any such territory.

6. Acceptance of the obligations of a Convention in virtue of paragraph 4 or paragraph 5 shall involve the acceptance on behalf of the territory concerned of the obligations stipulated by the terms of the Convention and the obligations under the Constitution of the Organisation which apply to ratified Conventions. A declaration of acceptance may specify such modification of the provisions of the Conventions as may be necessary to adapt the Convention to local conditions.

7. Each Member or international authority which has communicated a declaration in virtue of paragraph 4 or paragraph 5 of this article may from time to time, in accordance with the terms of the Convention, communicate a further declaration modifying the terms of any former declaration or terminating the acceptance of the obligations of the Convention on behalf of the territory concerned.

8. If the obligations of a Convention are not accepted on behalf of a territory to which paragraph 4 or paragraph 5 of this article relates, the Member or Members or international authority concerned shall report to the Director-General of the International Labour Office the position of the law and practice of that territory in regard to the matters dealt with in the Convention and the report shall show the extent to which effect has been given, or is proposed to be given, to any of the provisions of the Convention by legislation, administrative action, collective agreement or otherwise and shall state the difficulties which prevent or delay the acceptance of such Convention.

Amendments to Constitution

Article 36

Amendments to this Constitution which are adopted by the Conference by a majority of two-thirds of the votes cast by the delegates present shall take effect when ratified or accepted by two-thirds of the Members of the Organisation including five of the ten Members which are represented on the Governing Body as Members of chief industrial importance in accordance with the provisions of paragraph 3 of article 7 of this Constitution.

Interpretation of Constitution and Conventions

Article 37

1. Any question or dispute relating to the interpretation of this Constitution or of any subsequent Convention concluded by the Members in pursuance of the provisions of this Constitution shall be referred for decision to the International Court of Justice.

2. Notwithstanding the provisions of paragraph 1 of this article the Governing Body may make and submit to the Conference for approval rules providing for the appointment of a tribunal for the expeditious determination of any dispute or question relating to the interpretation of a Convention which may be referred thereto by the Governing Body or in accordance with the terms of the Convention. Any applicable judgment or advisory opinion of the International Court of Justice shall be binding upon any tribunal established in virtue of this paragraph. Any award made by such a tribunal shall be circulated to the Members of the Organisation and any observations which they may make thereon shall be brought before the Conference.

Regional
Conferences

Article 38

1. The International Labour Organisation may convene such regional conferences and establish such regional agencies as may be desirable to promote the aims purposes of the Organisation.

2. The powers, functions and procedure of regional conferences shall be governed by rules drawn up by the Governing Body and submitted to the General Conference for confirmation.

CHAPTER IV — MISCELLANEOUS PROVISIONS

Legal status
of Organisation

Article 39

The International Labour Organisation shall possess full juridical personality and in particular the capacity—

(a) to contract;
(b) to acquire and dispose of immovable and movable property;
(c) to institute legal proceedings.

Privileges and
immunities

Article 40

1. The International Labour Organisation shall enjoy in the territory of each of its Members such privileges and immunities as are necessary for the fulfilment of its purposes.

2. Delegates to the Conference, members of the Governing Body and the Director-General and officials of the Office shall likewise enjoy such privileges and immunities as are necessary for the independent exercise of their functions in connection with the Organisation.

3. Such privileges and immunities shall be defined in a separate agreement to be prepared by the Organisation with a view to its acceptance by the States Members.

ANNEX

Declaration concerning the Aims and Purposes of the International Labour Organisation

The General Conference of the International Labour Organisation, meeting in its Twenty-sixth Session in Philadelphia, hereby adopts, this tenth day of May in the year nineteen hundred and forty-four, the present Declaration of the aims and purposes of the International Labour Organisation and of the principles which should inspire the policy of its Members.

I

The Conference reaffirms the fundamental principles on which the Organisation is based and, in particular, that—

(a) labour is not a commodity;
(b) freedom of expression and of association are essential to sustained progress;
(c) poverty anywhere constitutes a danger to prosperity everywhere;
(d) the war against want requires to be carried on with unrelenting vigour within each nation, and by continuous and concerted international effort in which the representatives or workers and employers, enjoying equal status with those of governments, join with them in free discussion and democratic decision with a view to the promotion of the common welfare.

II

Believing that experience has fully demonstrated the truth of the statement in the Constitution of the International Labour Organisation that lasting peace can be established only if it is based on social justice, the Conference affirms that—

(a) all human beings, irrespective of race, creed or sex, have the right to pursue both their material well-being and their spiritual development in conditions of freedom and dignity, of economic security and equal opportunity;

(b) the attainment of the conditions in which this shall be possible must constitute the central aim of national and international policy;

(c) all national and international policies and measures, in particular those of an economic and financial character, should be judged in this light and accepted only in so far as they may be held to promote and not to hinder the achievement of this fundamental objective;

(d) it is a responsibility of the International Labour Organisation to examine and consider all international economic and financial policies and measures in the light of this fundamental objective;

(e) in discharging the tasks entrusted to it the International Labour Organisation, having considered all relevant economic and financial factors, may include in its decisions and recommendations any provisions which it considers appropriate.

III

The Conference recognises the solemn obligation of the International Labour Organization to further among the nations of the world programmes which will achieve:

(a) full employment and the raising of standards of living;

(b) the employment of workers in the occupations in which they can have the satisfaction of giving the fullest measure of their skill and attainments and make their greatest contribution to the common well-being;

(c) the provision, as a means to the attainment of this end and under adequate guarantees for all concerned, of facilities for training and the transfer of labour, including migration for employment and settlement;

(d) policies in regard to wages and earnings, hours and other conditions or work calculated to ensure a just share of the fruits of progress to all, and a minimum living wage to all employed and in need of such protection;

(e) the effective recognition of the right of collective bargaining, the co-operation of management and labour in the continuous improvement of productive efficiency, and the collaboration of workers and employers in the preparation and application of social and economic measures;

(f) the extension of social security measures to provide a basic income to all in need of such protection and comprehensive medical care;

(g) adequate protection for the life and health of workers in all occupations;

(h) provision for child welfare and maternity protection;

(i) the provisions of adequate nutrition, housing and facilities for recreation and culture;

(j) the assurance of equality of educational and vocational opportunity.

IV

Confident that the fuller and broader utilisation of the world's productive resources necessary for the achievement of the objectives set forth in this Declaration can be secured by effective international and national action, including measures to expand production and consumption, to avoid severe economic fluctuations, to promote the economic and social advancement of the less developed regions of the world, to assure greater stability in world prices of primary products, and to promote a high and steady volume of international trade, the Conference pledges the full co-operation of the International Labour Organisation with such international bodies as may be entrusted with a share of the responsibility for this great task and for the promotion of the health, education and well-being of all peoples.

V

The Conference affirms that the principles set forth in this Declaration are fully application to all peoples everywhere and that, while the manner of their application must be determined with due regard to the stage of social and economic development reached by each people, their progressive application to peoples who are still dependent, as well as to those who have already achieved self-government, is a matter of concern to the whole civilised world.

b. STANDING ORDERS OF THE INTERNATIONAL LABOUR CONFERENCE, AMENDED UP TO AND DURING ITS FIFTY-SIXTH SESSION

TABLE OF CONTENTS

Part I

GENERAL STANDING ORDERS

Part II

STANDING ORDERS CONCERNING SPECIAL SUBJECTS

SECTION A. — ORDER OF BUSINESS AT THE OPENING OF EACH SESSION

SECTION D. — DISQUALIFICATION FROM VOTING OF MEMBERS WHICH ARE IN ARREARS IN THE PAYMENT OF THEIR CONTRIBUTIONS TO THE ORGANISATION

SECTION E. — CONVENTION AND RECOMMENDATION PROCEDURE

SECTION F. — PROCEDURE FOR THE CONSIDERATION BY THE CONFERENCE OF PROPOSED AMENDMENTS TO THE CONSTITUTION OF THE ORGANISATION

Text of the Standing Orders [1,2]

PART I

General Standing Orders

ARTICLE 1

Composition of the Conference

1. The Conference consists of all the delegates duly appointed by the Members of the International Labour Organisation.

Const. 3, 2-7 2. Each delegate may be accompanied by advisers who shall not exceed two in number for each item on the agenda of the meeting.

3. (1) In accordance with article 3 of the Constitution of the Organisation a delegate may by notice in writing addressed to the President appoint one of his advisers to act as his substitute.

(2) Such notice must be addressed to the President before the sitting, unless a new question comes up for discussion in the course of the sitting.

(3) The notice shall specify the sitting or sittings at which the substitute will act.

(4) Substitutes may take part in the debates and may vote under the same conditions as delegates.

ARTICLE 2

Right of Admission to Sittings of the Conference

1. The sittings of the Conference shall be public except in cases in which it has been expressly decided to the contrary.

2. Seats in the Conference hall shall be assigned to the delegates and their advisers by the Secretary-General.

3. Apart from delegates and advisers the only persons permitted to enter the body of the hall shall be—

(a) ministers whose departments deal with the questions discussed by the Conference and who are not delegates or advisers;

(b) representatives of official international organisations which have been invited by the Conference or the Governing Body to be represented at the Conference;

(c) members of the Governing Body who are not delegates or advisers;

(d) representatives of a State or province of a federal State who have been appointed to accompany a delegation by the Government of a Member of the Organisation;

(e) persons appointed as observers by a State invited to attend the Conference;

---

[1] Adopted on 21 November 1919 at the First Session of the Conference Revised and consolidated at the 27th Session. The present text includes all amendments adopted up to the 56th (1971) Session.

[2] The figures in the margin refer to the relevant provisions of the Constitution of the International Labour Organisation. *Articles* are indicated in bold type, *paragraphs* in light type.

(f) the Director-General of the International Labour Office and the officials of the Secretariat of the Conference;

(g) one secretary or interpreter for each delegation;

(h) the secretaries of the Employers' and Workers' groups;

(i) persons appointed by Members of the Organisation to occupy advisers' posts which may fall vacant in their delegations;

(j) representatives of non-governmental international organisations with which it has been decided to establish consultative relationships and with which standing arrangements for such representation have been made and representatives of other non-governmental international organisations which have been invited by the Conference or the Governing Body to be represented at the Conference.

4. Arrangements shall be made by the Secretary-General for the accommodation at public sittings of distinguished strangers and the press.

ARTICLE 3

Officers of the Conference

Const. 17, 1 1. The Conference shall elect as Officers a President and three Vice-Presidents, who shall all be of different nationalities and any of whom may be women.

2. The Government, Employers' and Workers' groups shall each nominate one of their number for election by the Conference as Vice-President.

ARTICLE 4

Selection Committee

1. The Conference shall appoint a Selection Committee consisting of twenty-four members nominated by the Government group, twelve members nominated by the Employers' group and twelve members nominated by the Workers' group. In none of these categories shall a country have more than one member.

2. It shall be the duty of the Selection Committee to arrange the programme of the Conference, to fix the time and agenda for the plenary sittings, to make proposals relating to the setting up and composition of other committees, and to report to the Conference on any other questions requiring a decision for the proper conduct of its business.

ARTICLE 5

Credentials Committee

1. The Conference shall, on the nomination of the Selection Committee, appoint a Credentials Committee consisting of one Government delegate, one Employers' delegate and one Workers' delegate.

2. The Credentials Committee shall examine the credentials of delegates and their advisers, and any objection relating thereto, in accordance with the provisions of Section B of Part II.

ARTICLE 6

Conference Drafting Committee

1. The Conference shall appoint on the nomination of the Selection Committee a Conference Drafting Committee consisting of at least three persons who need not be either delegates or advisers.

2. The Committee Drafting Committee appointed by each committee under article 59 (1) of these Standing Orders shall form part of the Conference Drafting Committee when any proposed Convention or Recommendation is submitted to the Conference by the committee concerned.

3. The Conference Drafting Committee shall have the functions entrusted to it by the rules concerning Convention and Recommendation procedure (Section E) and the rules concerning the procedure for the amendment of the Constitution of the Organisation (Section F) and shall, in general, be responsible for expressing in the form of Conventions and Recommendations the decisions adopted by the Conference and for ensuring agreement between the English and French versions of the texts of all formal instruments submitted to the Conference for adoption.

ARTICLE 7

Committee on the Application of Conventions and Recommendations

1. The Conference shall, as soon as possible, appoint a Committee to consider—

(a) the measures taken by Members to give effect to the provisions of Conventions to which they are parties and the information furnished by Members concerning the results of inspections;

(b) the information and reports concerning Conventions and Recommendations communicated by Members in accordance with article 19 of the Constitution;

(c) the measures taken by Members in accordance with article 35 of the Constitution.

2. The Committee shall submit a report to the Conference.

ARTICLE 7bis

Finance Committee of Government Representatives

1. The Conference shall, as soon as possible, appoint a Finance Committee consisting of one Government delegate from each Member of the Organisation represented at the Conference.

2. The Finance Committee shall consider—

(a) the arrangements for the approval, allocation and collective of the budget of the Organisation, including—

(i) the budget estimates;

(ii) the arrangements for the allocation of expenses among Members of the Organisation;

(b) the audited accounts of the Organisation, together with the Auditor's report thereon;

(c) any request or proposal that the Conference should permit a Member which is in arrears in the payment of its contribution to vote in accordance with article 13, paragraph 4, of the Constitution;

42

(d) any other matter referred to it by the Conference.

3. The Committee shall elect a Chairman and a Vice-Chairman.

4. The Director-General, accompanied by a tripartite delegation from the Governing Body, shall be entitled to attend the meetings of the Committee.

5. The decisions of the Committee shall be taken by a two-thirds majority of the votes cast by the members of the Committee present at the meeting.

6. The Committee shall submit a report, or reports, to the Conference.

ARTICLE 8

Other Committees

Const. The Conference may appoint a committee to consider and report on any
17, 1 matter.

ARTICLE 9

Procedure for the Appointment of Committees

The following rules shall apply to all committees appointed by the Conference with the exception of the Selection Committee, the Credentials Committee, the Finance Committee of Government Representatives and the Drafting Committee:

(a) when it has been decided to appoint a committee to which these rules apply, the Selection Committee shall fix the size of such committee and shall ask each group to furnish a list setting out in order of preference a larger number of names than there are places allocated to the group on the committee;

(b) the Selection Committee shall examine the lists furnished by the three groups and, if it appears desirable that any adjustment should be made in the composition of the committee so as to secure representation more adequate for the subject with which the committee will deal or more satisfactory as regards the allocation of seats to the various nationalities, shall endeavour to secure such adjustment, subject to the approval of the representatives of the groups who are present;

(c) the lists agreed upon by the Selection Committee shall be reported to the Conference for its approval;

(d) if a delegate has not been nominated by his group to sit on any committee, he may bring the matter to the notice of the Selection Committee which shall have power to place him on one or more committees, enlarging the number of members of such committee or committees accordingly. Any such request shall be made to the Chairman of the Selection Committee at latest at the sitting following that at which it fixed the composition of the committee or committees in question;

(e) in accordance with article 18 of the Constitution of the Organisation, the Conference may add to any committee to which these rules apply technical experts who shall have the right to take part in the discussions but not to vote.

ARTICLE 10

General Provisions concerning Committees

The work of the committees of the Conference, with the exception of the Credentials Committee and the Drafting Committee, shall be governed by the Standing Orders for the committees of the Conference set forth in Section H of Part II.

ARTICLE 11

Procedure for the Consideration of Proposed Conventions, Recommendations and Amendments to the Constitution

1. The procedure for the consideration of proposed Conventions and Recommendations shall be governed by the rules concerning Convention and Recommendation procedure set forth in Section E of Part II.

2. The procedure for the consideration of proposed amendments to the Constitution of the Organisation shall be governed by the rules concerning the procedure for the amendment of the Constitution of the Organisation set forth in Section F of Part II.

ARTICLE 12

Director-General's Report

1. During the session and at the times fixed by the Selection Committee the Conference shall discuss the report submitted by the Director-General of the International Labour Office on the steps taken to give effect to the decisions of previous sessions and the results achieved.

2. One delegate representing the Government, one delegate representing the Employers and one representing the Workers may participate in the discussion in respect of each member State, provided that a visiting minister may speak in addition to the Government delegate. No speaker may intervene in the discussion more than once.

ARTICLE 13

Duties of the President

1. The President shall declare the opening and close of the sittings. Before proceeding to the agenda, he shall bring before the Conference any communication which may concern it.

2. He shall direct the debates, maintain order, ensure the observance of the Standing Orders by such means as circumstances may demand, accord or withdraw the right to address the Conference, put questions to the vote and announce the result of the vote.

3. The President shall not take part in the debates and shall not vote. If he is himself a delegate he may appoint a substitute in accordance with the provisions of article 1, paragraph 3.

4. In the absence of the President during a sitting or any part thereof one of the Vice-Presidents, taken in rotation, shall preside.

5. A Vice-President acting as President shall have the same rights and duties as the President.

ARTICLE 14

Right to Address the Conference

1. No delegate shall address the Conference without having asked and obtained permission of the President.

2. Speakers shall be called upon in the order in which they have signified their desire to speak.

3. No delegate shall speak more than once upon the same motion, resolution or amendment, without the special permission of the Conference, provided that the mover of a motion, resolution or amendment shall have the right to speak twice unless the closure has been adopted in accordance with article 16.

4. The President may require a speaker to resume his seat if his remarks are not relevant to the subject under discussion.

5. A delegate may at any time rise to a point of order, which shall be decided forthwith by the President.

6. Except with the special consent of the Conference no speech, whether by a delegate, a visiting minister, an observer or a representative of an international organisation, shall exceed 15 minutes exclusive of the time for translation.

7. Interruptions and audible conversations are not permitted.

8. Ministers whose departments deal with the questions discussed by the Conference and who are not delegates or advisers, members of the Governing Body who are not delegates or advisers at the Conference, and the Director-General of the International Labour Office or his representative may address the Conference if invited to do so by the President.

9. Representatives of official international organisations which have been invited to be represented at the Conference may participate, without vote, in the discussions.

10. The President may, in agreement with the Vice-Presidents, permit representatives of non-governmental international organisations with which the International Labour Organisation has established consultative relationships and with which standing arrangements for representation at the Conference have been made, and representatives of other non-governmental international organisations which have been invited to be represented at the Conference, to make or circulate statements for the information of the Conference on questions which are being considered by the Conference other than administrative and financial questions. If agreement cannot be reached the matter shall be referred to the meeting for decision without discussion.

11. Persons appointed as observers by a State invited to attend the Conference may, with the permission of the President, address the Conference during the general discussions.

ARTICLE 15

Motions, Resolutions and Amendments

1. No motion, resolution or amendment shall be discussed unless it has been seconded.

2. (1) Motions as to procedure may be moved verbally and without previous notice. They may be moved at any time except after the President has called upon a speaker and before the speaker has terminated his speech.

(2) Motions as to procedure include the following:

(a) a motion to refer the matter back;
(b) a motion to postpone consideration of the question;
(c) a motion to adjourn the sitting;
(d) a motion to adjourn the debate on a particular question;
(e) a motion that the Conference proceed with the next item on the agenda for the sitting;
(f) a motion to ask for the opinion of the President, the Secretary-General or the Legal Adviser of the Conference;
(g) a motion for the closure of the discussion.

3. All resolutions and amendments other than motions as to procedure must be submitted in writing in one of the official languages or in Spanish.

4. (1) No resolution relating to an item on the agenda shall, unless it be a motions as to procedure, be moved at any sitting of the Conference unless a copy has been handed in to the Secretariat of the Conference at least two days previously.

(2) Any resolution thus handed in shall be translated and circulated by the Secretariat not later than the day following that on which it was received.

5. Resolutions relating to matters not included in the agenda of the Conference shall be subject, in addition to the applicable provisions of this article, to the special rules set forth in article 17.

6. Amendments to a resolution may be moved without previous notice if a copy of the text of the amendment is handed in to the Secretariat of the Conference before the amendment is moved.

7. (1) Amendments shall be voted on before the resolution to which they refer.

(2) If there are several amendments to a motion or resolution the President shall determine the order in which they shall be discussed and put to the vote, subject to the following provisions:

(a) every motion, resolution or amendment shall be put to the vote;
(b) amendments may be voted on either individually or against other amendments according as the President may decide, but if amendments are voted on against other amendments, the motion or resolution shall be deemed to be amended only after the amendment receiving the largest number of affirmative votes has been voted on individually and adopted;
(c) if a motion or resolution is amended as the result of a vote, that motion or resolution as amended shall be put to the meeting for a final vote.

8. (1) Any amendment may be withdrawn by the person who moved it unless an amendment to it is under discussion or has been adopted.

(2) Any amendment so withdrawn may be moved without previous notice by any other member of the Conference.

9. Any member may at any time draw attention to the fact that the Standing Orders are not being observed, and the President shall give an immediate ruling on any question so raised.

ARTICLE 16

Closure

1. Any delegate may move the closure of the discussion either on a particular resolution or amendment or on the general question.

2. The President shall put a motion for the closure of the discussion if it is supported by at least 30 delegates. Before putting it to the vote, however, he shall call out the names of those delegates who had signified their wish to speak before the closure had been moved.

3. If application is made for permission to speak against the closure, it shall be accorded subject to the condition that no speaker shall be allowed to speak for more than five minutes.

4. The President shall permit each group which makes a request to that effect through its Chairman to be heard on the question under discussion through one speaker appointed by the group, whether there has been a previous speaker or not representing the group.

5. Subject to the foregoing paragraphs no one shall be allowed to speak on a question after the closure has been voted.

ARTICLE 17

Resolutions relating to Matters Not Included in an Item on the Agenda

1. (1) No resolution relating to a matter not included in an item on the agenda of the Conference shall be moved at any sitting of the Conference unless a copy of the resolution has been deposited with the Director-General of the International Labour Office at least 15 days before the opening of the session of the Conference, by a delegate to the Conference.

(2) Copies of all resolutions shall be available to delegates at the International Labour Office not more than 48 hours after the expiry of the time limit laid down in the preceding subparagraph: Provided that the Director-General may decide to withhold circulation of the text of a particular resolution pending consultation of the Officers of the Governing Body.

(3) When circulation of a particular resolution has been withheld pending consultation of the Officers of the Governing Body, that resolution shall, unless the Officers decide unanimously to the contrary, be available to delegates not later than the date fixed for the opening of the session of the Conference.

2. The President may, with the approval of the three Vice-Presidents, permit a resolution relating to a matter not included in an item on the agenda of the Conference to be moved although it has not been deposited as required by paragraph 1 (1) if it relates either to urgent matters or to matters of an entirely formal nature.

3. All resolutions relating to matters not included in an item on the agenda shall be referred by the Conference for report to a Resolutions Committee.

4. The Resolutions Committee shall consider in respect of each resolution whether its satisfies the conditions of receivability set forth in paragraph 1.

5. The Resolutions Committee shall determine the order in which resolutions which have been declared receivable shall be examined, as follows:

(a) After having given the author, or one of the authors, of each resolution the possibility of moving it in a speech which shall not exceed tne minutes, the Committee shall, without discussion, determine by ballot the first five resolutions to be considered, in the following manner:

(i) each member of the Committee shall receive a ballot paper on which the titles of all the resolutions to be considered appear, and shall indicate thereon the five resolutions which he wishes to be discussed first, his first preference being marked "1," his second "2," and so forth; a ballot paper which does not indicate preferences for five resolutions shall be void;

(ii) whenever a resolution is indicated as a first preference, it shall be allotted five points, whenever it is indicated as a second preference, four points, and so forth; resolutions for which no preference has been indicated will receive no points;

(iii) where the Government, Employers' or Workers' members of the Committee are entitled to cast more than one vote, to take account of the unequal representation of the group on the Committee, the total number of points secured by each resolution shall be calculated separately for each group and multiplied by the multiplier applicable to the votes of members of the group;

(iv) the resolution obtaining the largest number of points, as determined in accordance with clauses (ii) and (iii), shall be discussed first, the resolution obtaining the second largest number of points shall be discussed second, and so forth for five resolutions; if the voting results in an equal number of points for each of two or more of the first five resolutions, priority shall be decided by lot in one or more castings, as appropriate.

(b) The Committee shall, at the beginning of its proceedings, set up a Working Party composed of three Government members, three Employers' members and three Workers' members to make recommendations as to the order in which the resolutions which were not included in the first five as a result of the procedure set forth in subparagraph (a) should be examined.

6. The Resolutions Committee shall begin its work as soon as possible after the opening of the session of the Conference, in order to enable it to complete its agenda, and shall terminate its work not later than the Saturday preceding the closing of the session. If, nevertheless, any resolution has not been considered by the Committee by the date on which it terminates its work, the Conference shall not discuss or act upon that resolution.

7. (1) If members of the Resolutions Committee having not less than one-quarter of the voting power of the Committee move that the Committee should take the view that a resolution is not within the competence of the Conference, or that its adoption is inexpedient, this preliminary question shall be determined by the Committee after hearing the author, or, where there are several, one of the authors of the resolution, not more than one speaker for and against the motion from each group, and the reply of the author or one of the authors.

(2) A recommendation by the Resolutions Committee that a resolution is not within the competence of the Conference, or that its adoption is inexpedient, shall be accompanied by a report of the discussion in the Committee and shall be put to the vote in the Conference without debate.

8. The Resolutions Committee may, after hearing the author or authors of a resolution, amend it in form or substance in such manner as it may consider desirable.

9. It shall be the special duty of the Resolutions Committee to distinguish, by appropriate drafting, resolutions the adoption of which by the Conference would involve exact legal consequences from resolutions intended for consideration by the Governing Body, governments or any other body, but not creating any legal obligation.

10. The Resolution Committee shall submit a report to the Conference.

ARTICLE 17*bis*

Prior Consultation in Respect of Proposals for New Activities relating to Matters of Direct Concern to the United Nations or Other Specialised Agencies

1. Where a proposal submitted to the Conference involves new activities to be undertaken by the International Labour Organisation relating to matters which are of direct concern to the United Nations or one or more specialised agencies other than the International Labour Organisation, the Director-General shall enter into consultation with the organisations concerned and report to the Conference on the means of achieving co-ordinated use of the resources of the respective organisations. Where a proposal put forward in the course of a meeting for new activities to be undertaken by the International Labour Organisation relates to matters which are of direct concern to the United Nations or one or more specialised agencies other than the International Labour Organisation, the Director-General shall, after such consultation with the representatives of the other organisation or organisations concerned attending the meeting as may be possible, draw the attention of the meeting to these implications of the proposal.

2. Before deciding on proposals referred to in the preceding paragraph, the Conference shall satisfy itself that adequate consultations have taken place with the organisations concerned.

ARTICLE 17*ter*

Time Limit for the Submission of Proposals for New Activities

1. Except as provided in paragraph 2 of the present article, no proposals for new activities to be undertaken by the International Labour Organisation shall be placed before a session of the Conference unless such proposal has been deposited with the Director-General of the International Labour Office at least six weeks before the opening of the Conference.

2. The requirements of paragraph 1 do not apply to—

(a) any proposal that a matter should be referred to the Governing Body or the Joint Maritime Commission for examination with a view to deciding whether action by the International Labour Organisation in regard to the matter is desirable, or

(b) matters or urgency in regard to which paragraph 2 of article 17 applies.

ARTICLE 18

Proposals Involving Expenditure

1. Any motion or resolution involving expenditure shall in the first instance, or in the case of resolutions referred to the Resolutions Committee as soon as that Committee is satisfied that the resolution is receivable and within the competence of the Conference, be referred to the Governing Body which, after consultation of its Financial and Administrative Committee, shall communicate its opinion to the Conference.

2. The opinion of the Governing Body shall be circulated to the delegates at least 24 hours before the motion or resolution is discussed by the Conference.

ARTICLE 19

Methods of Voting

1. The Conference shall vote by a show of hands or by a record vote.

2. Voting shall be by a show of hands except as hereinafter provided.

3. Votes by a show of hands shall be counted by the Secretariat and the result announced by the President.

4. In case of doubt as to the result, the President may cause a record vote to be taken.

5. A record vote shall be taken in all cases in which a majority of two-thirds of the votes is required by the Constitution of the Organisation, except when the Conference is voting on the inclusion in the agenda of the following session of an item already on the agenda of the session at which the decision is taken.

6. A record vote shall be taken on any question if the request is made by show of hands of not less than 50 delegates present at the sitting, or by the Chairman of a group, or by his representative duly appointed by notice in writing addressed to the President, whether such a request be made before or immediately after the vote by show of hands.

7. Record votes shall be taken by calling upon each delegate, each delegate voting in turn in the French alphabetical order of the names of the Members of the International Labour Organisation.

8. The vote shall be recorded by the Secretariat and announced by the President.

9. The names of the delegates voting in a record vote shall be inserted in the verbatim report of the sitting.

ARTICLE 20

Quorum

Const.
17, 3 1. (1) In accordance with article 17 of the Constitution of the Organisation a vote is not valid if the number of votes cast for and against is less than the number of delegates attending the Conference and entitled to vote.

(2) This number shall be provisionally fixed after the presentation of the brief report referred to in paragraph 2 of the rules of procedure concerning credentials set forth in article 26. It shall then be determined by the Credentials Committee.

(3) Any delegate who finally leaves the Conference before its termination and who gives formal notice of his departure to the Secretariat without authorising an adviser to act in his place shall be regarded as no longer attending the Conference for the purpose of calculating the quorum.

(4) If any delegate is not finally admitted the number constituting the quorum shall be modified accordingly for the subsequent sittings.

2. (1) Where a quorum has not been obtained in a vote by a show of hands the President may immediately take a record vote.

(2) He shall do so if a record vote is called for by 20 members present.

3. (1) Where a quorum has not been obtained in a vote by a show of hands or in a record vote, the President may take a record vote on the same question at one of the two next following sittings.

(2) The preceding subparagraph does not apply to a final vote for the adoption of a Convention or Recommendation.

ARTICLE 21

Majority

Const.
17, 2;
19, 1, 2
In order to determine the majorities by record vote all votes cast, for and against, shall be counted, so that, in order to be adopted, it is necessary that the proposal submitted to the Conference shall obtain more than one-half or two-thirds of the votes cast in accordance with the requirements of the Constitution, or of the Convention or other instrument conferring the powers which the Conference is exercising, or of the financial and budgetary arrangements adopted in virtue of article 13 of the Constitution.

ARTICLE 22

Secretariat of the Conference

1. The Director-General of the International Labour Office shall be the Secretary-General of the Conference and shall be responsible for the appointment and control of the Secretariat.

Const.
10, 3
2. The Secretariat of the Conference shall be responsible for--

(a) the receiving, printing, circulating and translation of documents, reports and resolutions;
(b) the interpretation of speeches at the sittings;
(c) the taking of shorthand notes;
(d) the printing and distribution of the reports of the proceedings;
(e) the custody of the records of the Conference;
(f) the publication of the final records of the session; and
(g) generally, for all other work which the Conference may think fit to entrust to it.

ARTICLE 23

Verbatim Reports

1. A verbatim report shall be printed at the conclusion of each sitting by the Secretariat. There shall be included in the report any texts adopted and the results of any votes taken.

2. Before the report is printed in its final form, any delegate may demand the right to revise any part of the report containing a speech which he has made. Speeches or parts of speeches that have not been delivered during the sitting shall not be published in the report.

3. In order that any proposed corrections may be inserted, they should be handed in to the Secretariat within seven days from the distribution of the number of the *Provisional Record* containing the report of the speech in question.

4. The verbatim reports shall be signed by the President of the Conference and the Secretary-General.

ARTICLE 24

Languages

1. The French and English languages shall be the official languages of the Conference.

2. Speeches made in French shall be summarised in English, and vice versa, by an interpreter belonging to the Secretariat of the Conference.

3. Speeches made in Spanish shall be summarised by the official interpreters, who shall also give a summary in Spanish of speeches made in English or French.

4. A delegate may speak in another non-official language, but his delegation must provide for a summarised translation of his speech into one of the two official languages by an interpreter attached to the delegation, unless an interpreter of the Conference for the official languages can be placed at its disposal by the Secretariat of the Conference. This summarised translation shall then be rendered in the other official language by an interpreter belonging to the Secretariat.

5. The translation and circulation of documents shall be in the hands of the Secretariat and all such documents shall appear in English, French and Spanish.

PART II

Standing Orders concerning Special Subjects

SECTION A

Order of Business at the Opening of Each Session

ARTICLE 25

1. The Conference shall be opened by the Chairman of the Governing Body of the International Labour Office, assisted by the other Officers of the Governing Body. These provisional Officers shall continue to act until the President of the Conference has assumed office.

2. The first business of the Conference shall be the election of the President.

3. The Government, Employers' and Workers' groups shall then meet separately to elect their own Officers and to decide on their nominations for the three Vice-Presidents of the Conference and for the members of the Selection Committee.

4. (1) In order to facilitate the choice of Officers of the Conference who are all of different nationalities as required by article 3, paragraph 1, of the Standing Orders, the three groups share priority of nomination for the designation of Vice-Presidents of the Conference in the rotation indicated in the following table:

Session	1st priority group	2nd priority group
56th	Employers'	Workers'
57th	Workers'	Government
58th	Government	Employers'
59th	Employers'	Workers'
60th	Workers'	Government
61st	Government	Employers'
62nd	Employers'	Workers'

and so forth.

(2) If a group nominates a Vice-President of the same nationality as the Vice-President nominated by a group possessing priority of nomination, such nomination shall be void.

5. In accordance with article 4, paragraph 1, of the Standing Orders, the Government group shall nominate twenty-four members for the Selection Committee and the Employers' and Workers' groups shall each nominate twelve members. In none of these groups shall any Member of the Organisation have more than one member.

6. The Conference shall then meet again in plenary sitting to receive the nominations made by the groups and shall proceed to elect the three Vice-Presidents and to appoint the Selection Committee.

7. The Selection Committee shall then meet and, after electing its Officers, shall proceed to frame proposals for the number of committees to be appointed by the Conference and their composition.

8. The proposals made by the Committee shall be submitteu to the Conference for approval.

9. The Government, Employers' and Workers' groups shall then meet to make their nominations for the membership of committees in accordance with the provisions of article 9.

SECTION B

Verification of Credentials

ARTICLE 26

Const.
3, 8, 9

1. The credentials of delegates and their advisers shall be deposited with the International Labour Office at least 15 days before the date fixed for the opening of the session of the Conference.

2. A brief report upon these credentials, drawn up by the Chairman of the Governing Body, shall, with the credentials, be open to inspection by the delegates on the day before the opening of the session of the Conference and shall be published as an appendix to the record of the first sitting.

3. The Credentials Committee appointed by the Conference in pursuance of article 5 of the Standing Orders of the Conference shall consider any objection concerning the nomination of any delegate or adviser which may have been lodged with the Secretary-General.

4. An objection shall not be receivable in the following cases:

(a) if the objection is not lodged with the Secretary-General within 72 hours from 10 o'clock a.m. of the date of the publication in the *Provisional Record* of the name and function of the person to whose nomination objection is taken: Provided that the above time limit may be extended by the Credentials Committee in the case of objections in the nomination of a delegate or adviser from a distant country;

(b) if the authors of the objection remain anonymous;

(c) if the author of the objection is serving as adviser to the delegate to whose nomination objection is taken;

(d) if the objection is based upon facts or allegations which the Conference, by a debate and a decision referring to identical facts or allegations, has already discussed and recognised to be irrelevant or devoid of substance.

5. The procedure for the determination of whether an objection is receivable shall be as follows:

(a) the Credentials Committee shall consider in respect of each objection whether on any of the grounds set forth in paragraph 4 the objection is irreceivable;

(b) if the Committee reaches a unanimous conclusion concerning the receivability of the objection, its decision shall be final;

(c) if the Credentials Committee does not reach a unanimous conclusion concerning the receivability of the objection, it shall refer the matter to the Conference which shall, on being furnished with a record of the Committee's discussions and with a report setting forth the opinion of the majority and minority of its members, decide without further discussion whether the objection is receivable.

6. In every case in which the objection is not declared irreceivable, the Credentials Committee shall consider whether the objection is well founded and shall as a matter of urgency submit a report thereon to the Conference.

7. If the Credentials Committee or any member thereof submits a report advising that the Conference should refuse to admit any delegate or adviser, the President shall submit this proposal to the Conference for decision, and the Conference, if it deems that the delegate or adviser has not been nominated in conformity with the requirements of the Constitution, may, in accordance with paragraph 9 of article 3 thereof, refuse by two-thirds of the votes cast by the delegates present to admit the delegate or adviser. Delegates who are in favour of refusing to admit the delegate or adviser shall vote "Yes;" delegates who are opposed to refusing to admit the delegate or adviser shall vote "No."

8. Pending final decision of the question of his admission, any delegate or adviser to whose nomination objection has been taken shall have the same rights as other delegates and advisers.

SECTION C

Admission of New Members

ARTICLE 27

Const.
1, 3   1. The acceptance of membership of the International Labour Organisation in pursuance of paragraph 3 of article 1 of the Constitution of the Organisation by a Member of the United Nations shall take effect on receipt by the Director-General of the International Labour Office of a formal and unconditional acceptance of the obligations of the Constitution of the Organisation.

2. The Director-General shall inform the Members of the Organisation and the International Labour Conference of the acceptance of membership of the International Labour Organisation by a Member of the United Nations.

ARTICLE 28

Const.
1, 4   1. The admission of new Members to the International Labour Organisation by the General Conference, in accordance with article 1 (4) of the Constitution of the Organisation, shall be governed by the provisions of the present article.

2. Each application for admission made to the Conference shall be referred in the first instance to the Selection Committee.

3. Unless the Selection Committee is of the opinion that no immediate action should be taken on the application, it shall refer the application to a subcommittee for examination.

4. Before submitting its report to the Selection Committee the subcommittee may consult any representative accredited to the Conference by the applicant.

5. The Selection Committee, after considering the report of the subcommittee, shall report on the question to the Conference.

6. In accordance with article 1 (4) of the Constitution of the Organisation—

(a) a vote concurred in by two-thirds of the delegates attending the session, including two-thirds of the Government delegates present and voting, shall be necessary for the admission of a new Member by the Conference;

(b) the admission shall take effect on the communication to the Director-General of the International Labour Office by the Government of the new Member of its formal acceptance of the obligations of the Constitution of the Organisation.

7. The readmission of former Members by the General Conference of the International Labour Organisation shall be governed by the provisions of the preceding paragraphs of the present article. When the subcommittee provided for by paragraph 3 above has before it an application for readmission by a former Member which had ratified international labour Conventions before its withdrawal from the Organisation, the subcommittee shall state in its report whether the applicant recognises that the obligations resulting from those Conventions continue to be binding.

SECTION D

Disqualification from Voting of Members Which Are in Arrears in the Payment of Their Contributions to the Organisation

ARTICLE 29

Notification to Member in Arrears

1. If the Director-General finds that the amount of the arrears due from a Member of the Organisation which is in arrears in the payment of its contribution to the Organisation will, in the event of no payment being received from the Member during the succeeding three months, increase so as to equal or exceed the amount of the contribution due from that Member for the two full years preceding the expiration of the said period of three months, he shall send to the Member in question a communication calling its attention to the terms of article 13, paragraph 4, of the Constitution.

2. When the amount of the arrears due to the International Labour Organisation from a Member which is in arrears in the payment of its contribution to the Organisation equals or exceeds the contribution due from that Member for the preceding two full years, the Director-General shall notify the Member in question of this fact and call its attention to the terms of article 13, paragraph 4, of the Constitution.

3. Contributions are due on 1 January of the year to which they relate, but the year in respect of which they are due shall be regarded as a period of grace and a contribution shall be regarded as being in arrears for the purpose of this article only if it has not been paid by 31 December of the year in respect of which it is due.

ARTICLE 30

Notification to Conference and Governing Body
that Member Is in Arrears

The notification provided for in paragraph 2 of article 29 shall be brought by the Director-General to the attention of the next sessions of the International Labour Conference, the Governing Body, and any other committee of the International Labour Organisation in which the question of the right to vote of the Member concerned may arise, and to the attention of the electoral colleges provided for in articles 49 and 50 of the Standing Orders of the Conference.

ARTICLE 31

Procedure Where Proposal is Made to Permit Member in Arrears to Vote

1. Any request or proposal that the Conference should nevertheless permit a Member which is in arrears in the payment of its contributions to vote in accordance with article 13, paragraph 4, of the Constitution shall be referred in the first instance to the Finance Committee of the Conference, which shall report thereon as a matter of urgency.

2. Pending a decision on the request or proposal by the Conference, the Member shall not be entitled to vote.

3. The Finance Committee shall submit to the Conference a report giving its opinion on the request or proposal.

4. If the Finance Committee, having found that the failure to pay is due to conditions beyond the control of the Member, thinks fit to propose to the Conference that the Member should nevertheless be permitted to vote in accordance with article 13, paragraph 4, of the Constitution, it shall in its report—

(a) explain the nature of the conditions beyond the Member's control;
(b) give an analysis of the financial relations between the Member and the Organisation during the preceding ten years; and
(c) indicate the measures which should be taken in order to settle the arrears.

5. Any decision which may be taken by the Conference to permit a Member which is in arrears in the payment of its contribution to vote notwithstanding such arrears may be made conditional upon the Member complying with any recommendations for settling the arrears which may be made by the Conference.

ARTICLE 32

Period of Validity of a Decision to Permit Member in Arrears to Vote

Any decision by the Conference permitting a Member which is in arrears in the payment of its contributions to vote shall be valid for the session of the Conference at which the decision is taken. Any such decision shall be operative in regard to the Governing Body and committees until the opening of the general session of the Conference next following that at which it was taken.

ARTICLE 33

Cessation of Disqualification from Voting

When, as a result of the receipt by the Director-General of the International Labour Office of payments made by a Member, article 13, paragraph 4, of the Constitution ceases to be applicable to that Member—

(a) The Director-General shall notify the Member that its right to vote is no longer suspended;

(b) if the International Labour Conference, the Governing Body, the electoral colleges provided for in articles 49 and 50 of the Standing Orders of the Conference, or any committee concerned, has received the notification provided for in article 30 of the present section, the Director-General shall inform it that the right to vote of the Member is no longer suspended.

SECTION E

Convention and Recommendation Procedure

ARTICLE 34[1]

General Provisions

1. When a proposal to place an item on the agenda of the Conference is discussed for the first time by the Governing Body, the Governing Body cannot, without the unanimous consent of the members present, take a decision until the following session.

2. When it is proposed to place on the agenda of the International Labour Conference an item which implies a knowledge of the laws in force in the various countries, the Office shall place before the Governing Body a concise statement of the existing laws and practice in the various countries relative to that item. This statement shall be submitted to the Governing Body before it takes its decision.

3. When considering the desirability of placing a question on the agenda of the International Labour Conference, the Governing Body may, if there are special circumstances which make this desirable, decide to refer the question to a preparatory technical conference with a view to such a conference making a report to the Governing Body before the question is placed on the agenda. The Governing Body may, in similar circumstances, decide to convene a preparatory technical conference when placing a question on the agenda of the Conference.

4. Unless the Governing Body has otherwise decided, a question placed on the agenda of the Conference shall be regarded as having been referred to the Conference with a view to a double discussion.

5. In cases of special urgency or where other special circumstances exist, the Governing Body may, by a majority of three-fifths of the votes cast, decide to refer a question to the Conference with a view to a single discussion.

ARTICLE 35

Method of Voting for Placing Items on the Agenda

1. The Governing Body shall decide by a first vote whether it will place on the agenda of the Conference all the items proposed, or whether it will eliminate some of them. If it decides to insert all the items proposed, the agenda of the Conference is considered as fixed by this first vote. If, on the other hand, it decides to eliminate some of them, the procedure shall be as follows.

---

[1] This article and the two following articles consist of provisions of the Standing Orders of the Governing Body which are included here for convenience of reference but are not part of the Standing Orders of the Conference.

2. Each member of the Governing Body receives a voting paper on which a list of all the questions proposed is given and each member voting is asked to cross out one question. Any voting paper on which no question is crossed out or on which more than one question is crossed out shall be regarded as invalid.

3. The question crossed out on the largest number of voting papers shall be regarded as having been eliminated. If there is an equal number of votes for the elimination of two questions, a vote is taken as between the two. If the voting is still equal, it shall be decided by lot which of the two questions should be eliminated. If there is an equal number of votes for the elimination of more than two questions, one of them shall be eliminated by applying to these questions alone the procedure of paragraph 2; if the voting continues to be equal the decision shall be taken by lot.

4. A fresh vote shall be taken by the same procedure until such time as only one question remains.

5. The remaining question shall be put to a vote, members being asked to vote for or against it. If it obtains the majority of the votes cast, it shall be regarded as having been placed on the agenda. If it does not obtain such a majority, the questions previously eliminated shall be put to a vote in the order of preference, the one eliminated last being taken first, until such time as one question obtains the majority and is thus placed on the agenda.

6. The Governing Body then decides whether it wishes to place another question on the agenda. If there is a majority in favour of placing another question on the agenda, it proceeds to take a vote for or against the other questions on which a vote has not been taken, taking them in the order of preference.

7. The procedure of paragraph 6 shall be repeated after the placing of each item on the agenda.

ARTICLE 36

Preparatory Conferences

1. When the Governing Body decides that a question shall be referred to a preparatory technical conference it shall determine the date, composition and terms of reference of the said preparatory conference.

2. The Governing Body shall be represented at such technical conferences which, as a general rule, be of a tripartite character.

3. Each delegate to such conferences may be accompanied by one or more advisers.

4. For each preparatory conference convened by the Governing Body, the Office shall prepare a report adequate to facilitate an exchange of views on all the issues referred to it and, in particular, setting out the law and practice in the different countries.

ARTICLE 37

Objections to Items on the Agenda

Const.
16, 2
If an objection has been lodged against any item on the agenda by the government of any of the Members, the Conference, after hearing any report upon the subject which the Governing Body may have presented, shall, in accordance with article 16 of the Constitution of the Organisation, decide whether such item is to be retained on the agenda or not.

Preparatory Stages of Single-Discussion Procedure

1. When a question is governed by the single-discussion procedure the International Labour Office shall communicate to the governments, so as to reach them not less than 12 months before the opening of the session of the Conference at which the question is to be discussed, a summary report upon the question containing a statement of the law and practice in the different countries and accompanied by a questionnaire drawn up with a view to the preparation of Conventions or Recommendations. This questionnaire shall request governments to give reasons for their replies. Such replies should reach the Office as soon as possible and not less than eight months before the opening of the session of the Conference at which the question is to be discussed. In the case of federal countries and countries where it is necessary to translate questionnaires into the national language the period of four months allowed for the preparation of replies shall be extended to five months if the government concerned so requests.

2. On the basis of the replies from the governments the Office shall draw up a final report which may contain one or more Conventions or Recommendations. This report shall be communicated by the Office to the governments as soon as possible and every effort shall be made to secure that the report shall reach them not less than four months before the opening of the session of the Conference at which the question is to be discussed.

3. These arrangements shall apply only in cases in which the question has been included in the agenda of the Conference not less than 18 months before the opening of the session of the Conference at which it is to be discussed. If the question has been included in the agenda less than 18 months before the opening of the session of the Conference at which it is to be discussed, a programme of reduced intervals shall be approved by the Governing Body; if the Officers of the Governing Body do not consider it practicable for the Governing Body to approve a detailed programme it shall be in their discretion to agree on a programme of reduced intervals with the Director-General.

4. If a question on the agenda has been considered at a preparatory technical conference the Office, according to the decision taken by the Governing Body in this connection, may either—

(a) communicate to the governments a summary report and a questionnaire as provided for in paragraph 1 above; or

(b) itself draw up on the basis of the work of the preparatory technical conference the final report provided for in paragraph 2 above.

ARTICLE 39

Preparatory Stages of Double-Discussion Procedure

1. When a question is governed by the double-discussion procedure, the International Labour Office shall prepare as soon as possible a preliminary report setting out the law and practice in the different countries and any other useful information, together with a questionnaire. The report and the questionnaire requesting the governments to give reasons for their replies shall be communicated by the Office to the governments so as to reach them not less than 12 months before the opening of the session of the Conference at which the question is to be discussed.

2. The replies of the governments should reach the Office as soon as possible and not less than eight months before the opening of the session of the Conference at which the question is to be discussed. In the case of federal countries and countries where it is necessary to translate questionnaires into the national language the period of four months allowed for the preparation of replies shall be extended to five months if the government concerned so requests.

3. The Office shall prepare a further report on the basis of the replies from governments indicating the principal questions which require consideration by the Conference. This report shall be communicated by the Office to the governments as soon as possible and every effort shall be made to secure that the report shall reach them not less than four months before the opening of the session of the Conference at which the question is to discussed.

4. These reports shall be submitted to a discussion by the Conference either in full sitting or in committee, and if the Conference decides that the matter is suitable to form the subject of Conventions or Recommendations it shall adopt such conclusions as it sees fit and may either—

(a) decide that the question shall be included in the agenda of the following session in accordance with article 16, paragraph 3, of the Constitution; or
(b) ask the Governing Body to include the question in the agenda of a later session.

5. The arrangements referred to in paragraphs 1 to 4 shall apply only in cases in which the question has been included in the agenda of the Conference not less than 18 months before the opening of the session of the Conference at which the first discussion is to take place. If the question has been included in the agenda less than 18 months before the opening of the session of the Conference at which the first discussion is to take place, a programme of reduced intervals shall be approved by the Governing Body; if the Officers of the Governing Body do not consider it practicable for the Governing Body to approve a detailed programme it shall be in their discretion to agree on a programme of reduced intervals with the Director-General.

6. On the basis of the replies from the governments to the questionnaire referred to in paragraph 1 and on the basis of the first disucssion by the Conference, the Office may prepare one or more Conventions or Recommendations and communicate them to the governments so as to reach them not later than two months from the closing of the session of the Conference, asking them to state within three months whether they have any amendments to suggest or comments to make.

7. On the basis of the replies from the governments the Office shall draw up a final report containing the text of Conventions or Recommendations with any necessary amendments. This report shall be communicated by the Office to the governments so as to reach them not less than three months before the opening of the session of the Conference at which the question is to be discussed.

8. The arrangements referred to in paragraphs 6 and 7 shall apply only in cases in which there exists a period of 11 months between the closing of the session of the Conference at which the first discussion took place and the opening of the next session of the Conference. If the period between the two sessions of the Conference is less than 11 months, a programme of reduced intervals shall be approved by the Governing Body; if the Officers of the Governing Body do not consider it practicable for the Governing Body to approve a detailed programme it shall be in their discretion to agree on a programme of reduced intervals with the Director-General.

ARTICLE 39*bis*

Consultation of the United Nations and Other Specialised Agencies

Where items are placed on the agenda of the Conference with a view to the adoption of a Convention or a Recommendation, the International Labour Office shall, at the same time as it is requesting governments for their comments on the proposed Convention or Recommendation, consult the United Nations and other specialised agencies in respect of any provision of the proposed Convention or Recommendation which affects the activities of such organisation or organisations, and the comments of such organisation or organisations shall be brought before the Conference, together with the comments received from governments.

ARTICLE 40

Procedure for the Consideration of Texts

1. The Conference shall decide whether it will take as the basis of discussion the Conventions or Recommendations prepared by the International Labour Office, and shall decide whether such Conventions or Recommendations shall be considered in full Conference or referred to a committee for report. These decisions may be preceded by a debate in full Conference on the general principles of the suggested Convention or Recommendation.

2. If the Convention or Recommendation is considered in full Conference each clause shall be placed before the Conference for adoption. During the debate and until all the clauses have been disposed of, no motion other than a motion to amend a clause of such Convention or Recommendation or a motion as to procedure shall be considered by the Conference.

3. If the Convention or Recommendation be referred to a committee, the Conference shall, after receiving the report of the committee, proceed to discuss the Convention or Recommendation in accordance with the rules laid down in paragraph 2. The discussions shall not take place before the day following that on which copies of the report have been circulated to the delegates.

4. During the discussion of the articles of a Convention or Recommendation, the Conference may refer one or more articles to a committee.

5. If a Convention contained in the report of a committee is rejected by the Conference, any delegate may ask the Conference to decide forthwith whether the Convention shall be referred back to the committee to consider the transformation of the Convention into a Recommendation. If the Conference decides to refer the matter back, the report of the committee shall be submitted to the approval of the Conference before the end of the session.

6. The provisions of a Convention or Recommendation as adopted by the Conference shall be referred to the Drafting Committee for the preparation of a final text. This text shall be circulated to the delegates.

7. No amendment shall be allowed to this text, but notwithstanding this provision the President, after consultation with the three Vice-Presidents, may submit to the Conference amendments which have been handed to the Secretariat the day after the circulation of the text as revised by the Drafting Committee.

Const.
19
8. On receipt of the text prepared by the Drafting Committee and after discussion of amendments, if any, submitted in accordance with the preceding paragraph, the Conference shall proceed to take a final vote on the adoption of the Convention or Recommendation in accordance with article 19 of the Constitution of the Organisation.

ARTICLE 41

Procedure If a Convention Fails to Obtain
a Two-Thirds Majority

If a Convention on a final vote fails to obtain the necessary two-thirds majority, but obtains a simple majority, the Conference shall decide forthwith whether the Convention shall be referred to the Drafting Committee to be drafted in the form of a Recommendation. If the Conference approves the reference to the Drafting Committee, the proposals contained in the Convention shall be submitted for the approval of the Conference in the form of a Recommendation before the end of the session.

ARTICLE 42

Official Translations

After the adoption of the French and English authentic texts, official translations of the Conventions and Recommendations may, at the request of interested governments, be drawn up by the Director-General of the International Labour Office. It will be open to the governments concerned to consider such translations as authoritative in their respective countries for the application of the Conventions and Recommendations.

ARTICLE 43[1]

Procedure for Placing on the Agenda of the Conference
the Question of Revising a Convention in Whole or in Part

1. When the Governing Body, in accordance with the provisions of a Convention, considers it necessary to present to the Conference a report on the working of the said Convention and to examine if it is desirable to place the question of its revision in whole or in part on the agenda of the Conference, the Office shall submit to the Governing Body all the information which it possesses, particularly on the legislation and practice relating to the said Convention in those countries which have ratified it and on the legislation relating to the subject of the Convention and its application in those which have not ratified it. The draft report of the Office shall be communicated for their observations to all Members of the Organisation.

2. After a lapse of six months from the date of circulation to members of the Governing Body and to governments of the draft report of the Office referred to in paragraph 1, the Governing Body shall fix the terms of the report and shall consider the question of placing the revision in whole or in part of the Convention on the agenda of the Conference.

3. If the Governing Body takes the view that it is not desirable to place the revision in whole or in part of the Convention on the agenda, the Office shall communicate the above-mentioned report to the Conference.

4. If the Governing Body takes the view that it is desirable that the question of placing the revision in whole or in part of the Convention on the agenda of the Conference should be further pursued, the Office shall send the report to the governments of the Members and shall ask them for their observations, drawing attention to the points which the Governing Body has considered specially worthy of attention.

---

[1] This article consists of provisions of the Standing Orders of the Governing Body which are included here for convenience of reference, but are not part of the Standing Orders of the Conference.

5. *The Governing Body shall, on the expiry of four months from the date of the despatch of the report to the governments, taking into account the replies of the governments, adopt the final report and define exactly the question or questions which it places on the agenda of the Conference.*

6. *If at any time other than a time at which the Governing Body, in accordance with the provisions of a Convention, considers it necessary to present to the Conference a report on the working of the said Convention, the Governing Body sould decide that it is desirable to consider placing upon the agenda of the Conference the revision in whole or in part of any Convention, the Office shall notify this decision to the governments of the Members and shall ask them for their observations, drawing attention to the points which the Governing body has considered specially worthy of attention.*

7. *The Governing Body shall, on the expiry of four months from the date of the despatch of this notification to the governments, taking into account the replies of the governments, define exactly the question or questions which it places on the agenda of the Conference.*

ARTICLE 44

Procedure in Case of Revision of a Convention

1. When the revision in whole or in part of a Convention which has been previously adopted by the Conference is included in the agenda, the Conference shall proceed in accordance with the following provisions:

2. The International Labour Office shall submit to the Conference draft amendments drawn up in accordance with the conclusions of the report of the Governing Body recommending the revision in whole or in part of the Convention previously adopted and corresponding to the question or questions in respect of which a proposal for revision has been placed on the agenda.

3. The Conference shall decide whether it will take as the basis of discussion the draft amendments prepared by the International Labour Office, and shall decide whether they shall be considered in full Conference or referred to a committee for report. These decisions may be preceded by a debate in full Conference on the general principles of the proposed revision in whole or in part within the limits permitted by the agenda.

4. If the draft amendments are considered in full Conference, each of them be placed successively before the Conference for adoption. During the debate, and until all the draft amendments have been disposed of, no motion other than a motion to amend the text of one of them or a motion as to procedure shall be considered by the Conference.

5. If the draft amendments be referred to a committee, the Conference shall, after receiving the report of the committee, proceed to discuss the text of each draft amendment in succession, in accordance with the rules laid down in the last preceding paragraph. The discussion shall not take place before the day following that on which copies of the report have been circulated to the delegates.

6. During the discussion of the draft amendments the Conference may refer one or more of them to a committee.

7. The amendments together with consequential amendments of the unamended provisions of the Convention under revision, as adopted by the Conference, shall be referred to the Conference Drafting Committee, which shall combine with them the unamended provisions of the Convention under revision, so as to establish the final text of the Convention in the revised form. This text shall be circulated to the delegates.

8. No amendment shall be allowed to this text but, notwithstanding this provision, the President, after consultation with the three Vice-Presidents, may submit to the Conference amendments which have been handed to the Secretariat the day after the circulation of the text as revised by the Drafting Committee.

9. On receipt of the text prepared by the Drafting Committee and after discussion of the amendments, if any, submitted in accordance with the preceding paragraph, the Conference shall proceed to take a final vote on the adoption of the Convention in accordance with article 19 of the Constitution of the Organisation.

10. In accordance with article 14 of the Constitution of the Organisation and subject in the provisions of article 16, paragraph 3, of the said Constitution, the Conference shall not at any stage of the procedure of revision revise in whole or in part a Convention which has previously been adopted by it, save in respect of a question or questions placed by the Governing Body on the agenda of the session.

ARTICLE 45

Procedure in Case of Revision of a Recommendation

Const.
14, 16,
3

1. When the revision in whole or in part of a Recommendation which has been previously adopted by the Conference is included in the agenda, the International Labour Office shall submit to the Conference draft amendments corresponding to the question or questions in respect of which a proposal for revision has been placed on the agenda.

2. The Conference shall decide whether it will take as the basis of discussion the draft amendments prepared by the International Labour Office, and shall decide whether they shall be considered in full Conference or referred to a committee for report. These decisions may be preceded by a debate in full Conference on the general principles of the proposed revision in whole or in part within the limits permitted by the agenda.

3. If the draft amendments are considered in full Conference, each of them shall be placed successively before the Conference for adoption. During the debate, and until all the draft amendments have been disposed of, no motion other than a motion to amend the text of one of them or a motion as to procedure shall be considered by the Conference.

4. If the draft amendments be referred to a committee, the Conference shall, after receiving the report of the committee, proceed to discuss the text of each draft amendment in succession, in accordance with the rules laid down in the last preceding paragraph. The discussion shall not take place before the day following that on which copies of the report have been circulated to the delegates.

5. During the discussion of the draft amendments the Conference may refer one or more of them to a committee.

6. The amendments, together with the consequential amendments of the unamended provisions of the Recommendation under revision, as adopted by the Conference, shall be referred to the Conference Drafting Committee, which shall combine with them the unamended provisions of the Recommendation under revision so as to establish the final text of the Recommendation in the revised form. This text shall be circulated to the delegates.

7. No amendment shall be allowed to this text but, notwithstanding this provision, the President, after consultation with the three Vice-Presidents, may

submit to the Conference amendments which have been handed to the Secretariat the day after the circulation of the text as revised by the Drafting Committee.

8. On receipt of the text prepared by the Drafting Committee and after discussion of the amendments, if any, submitted in accordance with the preceding paragraph, the Conference shall proceed to take a final vote on the adoption of the Recommendation in accordance with article 19 of the Constitution of the Organisation.

9. In accordance with article 14 of the Constitution of the Organisation, and subject to the provisions of article 16, paragraph 3, of the said Constitution, the Conference shall not revise in whole or in part a Recommendation which has previously been adopted by it, save in respect of a question or questions placed by the Governing Body on the agenda of the session.

SECTION F

Procedure for the Consideration by the Conference of Proposed Amendments to the Constitution of the Organisation[1]

ARTICLE 46

Inclusion of Proposals for the Amendment of the Constitution in the Agenda

1. Any proposal for the amendment of the Constitution of the Organisation shall only be considered by the Conference if it has been included in the agenda of the Conference by the Governing Body at least four months before the opening of the session at which it is to be considered in accordance with article 14 of the Constitution, or has been included in the agenda of the Conference by the preceding session of the Conference in accordance with paragraph 3 of article 16 of the Constitution.

2. When including any proposal for the amendment of the Constitution in the agenda the Governing Body or the Conference, as the case may be, shall define exactly the question or questions which it includes in the agenda of the Conference.

ARTICLE 47

Procedure for the Consideration of Proposed Amendments to the Constitution by the Conference

1. The International Labour Office shall submit to the Conference draft amendments corresponding to the question or questions in respect of which a proposal for amendment has been included in the agenda.

2. The Conference shall decide whether it will take as the basis of discussion the draft amendments prepared by the International Labour Office and shall decide whether they shall be considered in full Conference or referred to a committee for report. These decisions may be preceded by a general debate in full Conference on the question or questions in respect of which a proposal for amendment has been included in the agenda.

---

[1] The entry into force of amendments is governed by article 38 of the Constitution.

3. If the draft amendments are considered in full Conference, each of them shall be placed successively before the Conference for preliminary adoption by a two-thirds majority of the delegates present. During the debate, and until the draft amendments have been disposed of, no motion other than a motion to amend the text of one of them or a motion as to procedure shall be considered by the Conference.

4. If the draft amendments be referred to a committee, the Conference shall, after receiving the report of the committee, proceed to discuss the text of each draft amendment in succession, in accordance with the rules laid down in the last preceding paragraph. The discussion shall not take place before the day following that on which copies of the report have been circulated to the delegates.

5. During the discussion of the draft amendments the Conference may refer one or more of them to a committee.

6. The amendments as adopted by the Conference shall be referred to the Conference Drafting Committee which shall embody them, together with any necessary consequential amendments of the unamended provisions of the Constitution, in a draft instrument of amendment the text of which shall be circulated to the delegates.

7. No amendment shall be allowed to this text, but notwithstanding this provision the President, after consultation with the three Vice-Presidents, may submit to the Conference amendments which have been handed in to the Secretariat the day after the circulation of the text as revised by the Drafting Committee.

8. On receipt of the text prepared by the Drafting Committee and after discussion of the amendments, if any, submitted in accordance with the preceding paragraph, the Conference shall proceed to take a final vote on the adoption of the draft instrument of amendment in accordance with article 36 of the Constitution of the Organisation.

SECTION G

Governing Body Elections

ARTICLE 48

Periodicity of Elections

In accordance with article 7 of the Constitution of the Organisation the period of office of the members of the Governing Body shall be three years and meetings of the electoral colleges for the selection of fourteen States for representation on the Governing Body and for the election of the Employer and Worker members of the Governing Body shall be held every third year in the course of the Conference.

ARTICLE 49

Government Electoral College

1. Subject to the provisions of article 13, paragraph 4, of the Constitution and of Section D of the Standing Orders of the Conference, the Government electoral college shall consist of the government delegates of all Members of the Organisation excepting those of the ten Members of chief industrial importance.

2. Each member of the electoral college shall be entitled to cast one vote.

66

3. The Government electoral college shall select fourteen Members of the Organisation, the governments of which shall be entitled to appoint Government members of the Governing Body.

4. The Government electoral college shall also select fourteen other Members of the Organisation, the governments of which shall be entitled to appoint deputy Government members of the Governing Body.

ARTICLE 50

Employers' and Workers' Electoral Colleges

1. The Employers' and Workers' electoral colleges shall consist of the Employers' and Workers' delegates to the Conference respectively, excluding the Employers' and Workers' delegates of States disqualified from voting in pursuance of the provisions of article 13, paragraph 4, of the Constitution and of Section D of the Standing Orders of the Conference.

2. The Employers' and Workers' electoral colleges shall each elect by name twelve persons as regular members of the Governing Body and twelve persons as deputy members of the Governing Body.

ARTICLE 51

Notice of Elections

At least 24 hours' notice shall be given of meetings for election of members of the Governing Body.

ARTICLE 52

Procedure of Voting

1. Each electoral college shall vote by secret ballot.

2. The Chairman of each electoral college shall ask the representative of the President of the Conference to read the list of delegates who have the right to vote. Each delegate shall come forward as his name is called and place his voting paper in the ballot box.

3. The counting of the votes shall be carried out under the direction of the representative of the President of the Conference assisted by two returning officers appointed by the electoral college from among its members.

4. No State or person shall be considered to be elected unless it or he has obtained more than half of the votes cast by the members of the electoral college present at the meeting. If after the first vote one or more setas remain to be filled, one or more further votes shall be taken as may be necessary, each member of the electoral college being entitled to vote for a number of candidates equal to the number of seats which still remain to be filled.

5. On the conclusion of the voting the Chairman of the electoral college shall announce the result of the meeting and a report shall be drawn up for communication to the Conference and deposited in the archives of the International Labour Office. This report shall be signed by the Chairman of the electoral college and countersigned by the representative of the President of the Conference.

ARTICLE 53

[Deleted]

ARTICLE 54

Vacancies

1. If a State ceases, at a time when the Conference is meeting in ordinary session, to occupy one of the seats on the Governing Body reserved for the fourteen States selected by the Government electoral college, the Government electoral college shall meet during the course of the session to appoint, in accordance with the procedure laid down in this section, another State to take its place.

2. If a State ceases, during an interval between sessions of the Conference, to occupy one of the seats on the Governing Body reserved for the fourteen States selected by the Government electoral college, the Government group of the Governing Body shall proceed to replace it. The appointment thus made must be confirmed by the Government electoral college and communicated by it to the Conference. If such an appointment is not confirmed by the electoral college in question, a new election shall immediately be held in accordance with the relevant provisions of this section.

3. If a vacancy occurs, at any time whatsoever, owing to the decease or resignation of a Government representative, but the State concerned retains its seat on the Governing Body, the seat in question shall be occupied by the person whom the Government appoints to replace him.

4. If a vacancy occurs among the Employer or Worker members of the Governing Body at a time when the Conference is meeting in ordinary session, the electoral college concerned shall assemble during the course of the session to fill the vacancy, in accordance with the procedure laid down in this section.

5. If a vacancy occurs among the Employer or Worker members of the Governing Body during an interval between sessions of the Conference, the Governing Body group concerned shall proceed freely to fill the vacancy, without being required to appoint the new member from among the deputy members of the Governing Body. The appointment thus made must be confirmed by the electoral college concerned at the next session of the Conference and communicated by it to the Conference. If such an appointment is not confirmed by the electoral college in question, a new election shall immediately be held in accordance with the provisions of this section.

SECTION H

Committees of the Conference

ARTICLE 55

Scope

1. These Standing Orders apply to all committees appointed by the Conference except the Credentials Committee and the Drafting Committee.

2. The following provisions do not apply to the Selection Committee:
(a) article 56, paragraphs 6, 8 and 9;
(b) the words "in agreement with the Selection Committee" in article 60;
(c) article 63;
(d) paragraphs 3 and 4 of article 65;
(e) article 69.

3. These Standing Orders apply to the Finance Committee of Government Representatives, except in so far as they are inapplicable because that Committee is not tripartite in character and consists solely of Government representatives. In addition, the following provisions do not apply to the Finance Committee:

(a) article 56, paragraph 6;

(b) article 57, paragraph 2;

(c) the words "from each group" in the first sentence of article 64, paragraph 3; and the second sentence in that paragraph;

(d) article 65, paragraph 1;

(e) article 69.

4. These Standing Orders apply to the Resolutions Committee subject to the special provisions contained to articles 62, paragraph 4, and 64, paragraph 4.

ARTICLE 56

Composition of Committees and Right to Participate in Their Work

1. The Conference shall designate the governments to be represented on each committee by Government members and shall appoint the delegates or advisers to be Employers' and Workers' members of the said committee.

2. Each government designated in accordance with the preceding paragraph shall communicate to the secretariat of the committee the name of its regular representative and that of any substitute appointed.

3. The Employers' group and the Workers' group shall decide whether, and if so on what conditions, those of their members appointed to committees may be replaced by personal substitutes; the said groups shall inform the secretariat of the committee of their decisions.

4. When the need to mantain a balance between the groups represented on a committee does not permit the Conference to meet all requests for membership of the said committee, the Conference may designate governments who will be represented on the committee by Government deputy members nominated by them and may appoint Employers' and Workers' delegates or advisers to be Employers' and Workers' deputy members of the committee.

5. These deputy members shall have the same rights as the members of the committee except that they may vote only on the following conditions.

(a) Government deputy members may vote when they are so authorised by a written notification to the secretariat of the committee from a Government regular member of the committee who is not voting and has not been replaced by a substitute;

(b) Employers' and Workers' deputy members may vote in place of a regular Employers' or Workers' member on the conditions defined by their respective groups; the groups shall inform the secretariat of the committee of all decisions taken in this connection.

6. In addition to the members of the committee, any delegate or any adviser who has received a written authorisation for the purpose from the delegate to whom he is attached shall be entitled to be present at the meetings and shall have the full rights of the members of the committee except the right to vote.

7. Representatives of official international organisations which have been invited to be represented at the Conference shall be entitled to be present at the meetings of the committee and may participate, without vote, in the discussions.

8. The following persons shall be entitled to be present at the meetings of the committee and may participate in the discussions with the permission of the Chairman:

(a) persons appointed as observers by a State invited to attend the Conference;

(b) technical experts appointed to the committee by the Conference as assessors in accordance with article 18 of the Constitution of the Organisation.

9. Representatives of non-governmental international organisations with which the International Labour Organisation has established consultative relationships and with which standing arrangements for representation at the Conference have been made, and representatives of other non-governmental international organisations which the Conference has invited to be represented at the committee, may be present at the meetings of the committee. The Chairman may, in agreement with the Vice-Chairmen, permit such representatives to make or circulate statements for the information of the committee upon matters included in its agenda. If agreement cannot be reached the matter shall be referred to the meeting for decision without discussion. This paragraph does not apply to meetings dealing with administrative or financial matters.

ARTICLE 57

Officers of Committees

1. The first sitting of each committee shall be opened by an official of the Secretariat of the Conference appointed for the purpose by the Secretary-General. This official shall conduct the business until the Chairman has been elected.

2. Each committee shall elect a Chairman and two Vice-Chairmen, chosen one from each of the three groups.

3. Each committee shall then elect from among its members one or more Reporters to present the result of its deliberations to the Conference on its behalf. Before presenting a report to the committee for its approval, the Reporter or Reporters shall submit it to the Officers of the committee.

4. The Chairman, Vice-Chairmen and Reporters may be either delegates or advisers.

ARTICLE 58

Languages of Committees

1. The French and English languages shall be the official languages of the committees.

2. Speeches in French shall be summarised in English and vice versa by an interpreter belonging to the Secretariat of the Conference.

3. Speeches made in Spanish shall be summarised by the official interpreters, who shall also give a summary in Spanish of speeches made in English and French.

4. A delegate may speak in another non-official language, but his delegation must provide for a summarised translation of his speech into one of the two official languages by an interpreter attached to the delegation, unless an interpreter of the Conference for the official languages can be placed at its disposal by the Secretariat of the Conference. This summarised translation shall then be rendered in the other official language by an interpreter of the Secretariat.

5. In cases where at least one-fifth of the members of a committee taking an actual part in its work either as regular members or as substitutes declare individually and in writing that it is difficult for them to take part in the proceedings of the committee in either of the official languages or in Spanish and ask for an additional interpretation into another language with which they are conversant, the committee shall accede to that request provided that the Secretariat of the Conference is able to supply the necessary interpreters.

6. In cases where the number of members of a committee who ask for an additional interpretation into a non-official language in the conditions laid down in the above paragraph is less than one-fifth of the number of members, the committee shall decide whether it shall accede to the request as an exceptional measure and provided that the Secretariat of the Conference is able to furnish the necessary interpreters.

ARTICLE 59

Committee Drafting Committees; Subcommittees

1. Each committee to which the Conference, in accordance with article 40 of the rules of procedure for Conventions and Recommendations, refers as a basis of discussion texts of proposed Conventions or Recommendations shall set up at an early sitting a committee drafting committee consisting of one Government delegate, one Employers' delegate and one Workers' delegate together with the Reporter or Reporters of the committee and the Legal Adviser of the Conference. In so far as may be possible the committee drafting committee shall comprise members conversant with both official languages. The committee drafting committee may be assisted by the officials of the Secretariat of the Conference attached to each committee as experts on the particular item of the agenda concerned. The committee drafting committee shall form part of the Conference Drafting Committee when any Convention or Recommendation is submitted to the Conference by the committee concerned.

2. Each committee shall have power to set up subcommittees after due notice has been given to the three groups in the committee.

3. The Chairman of a committee shall be entitled to attend the meetings of the committee drafting committee and of the subcommittees set up by the committee.

ARTICLE 60

Sittings

The Chairman of the committee shall fix the date and time of the sittings after consulting the Vice-Chairmen and in agreement with the Selection Committee.

ARTICLE 61

Duties of the Chairman

1. The Chairman shall declare the opening and close of the sittings. Before proceeding to the agenda, he shall bring before the committee any communications which may concern it.

2. The Chairman shall direct the debates, maintain order, ensure the observance of the Standing Orders, accord or withdraw the right to address the committee in accordance with the provisions of the Standing Orders, put questions to the vote and announce the result of the vote.

3. The Chairman shall have the right to take part in the discussion and to vote except when replaced on the committee by a substitute, but he shall not have a casting vote.

4. In the absence of the Chairman during a sitting or any part thereof, the Vice-Chairmen shall preside alternately.

5. A Vice-Chairman acting as Chairman shall have the same rights and duties as the Chairman.

ARTICLE 62

Right to Address the Committee

1. No one shall be entitled to address a committee unless he has asked and obtained permission of the Chairman, who shall call upon speakers in the order in which they have signified their desire to speak.

2. The Chairman may withdraw the right to speak from any speaker whose remarks are not relevant to the subject under discussion.

3. Except with the special consent of the committee, no speech may exceed ten minutes, exclusive of the time for the translation.

4. In the case of the Resolutions Committee the Chairman may, after consultation with the two Vice-Chairmen, submit to the Committee for decision without debate a proposal to reduce the time limit for speeches on a specific topic to five minutes.

ARTICLE 63

Motions, Resolutions and Amendments

1. No motion, resolution or amendment shall be discussed unless it has been seconded.

2. (1) Motions as to procedure may be moved verbally and without previous notice. They may be moved at any time except after the Chairman has called upon a speaker and before the speaker has terminated his speech.

(2) Motions as to procedure include the following:
(a)   a motion to refer the matter back;
(b)   a motion to postpone consideration of the question;
(c)   a motion to adjourn the sitting;
(d)   a motion to adjourn the debate on a particular question;
(e)   a motion that the committee proceed with the next item on the agenda for the sitting;
(f)   a motion to ask for the opinion of the Chairman, the Secretariat or the Legal Adviser of the Conference;
(g)   a motion for the closure of the discussion.

3. All resolutions and amendments other than motions as to procedure must be submitted in writing in one of the official languages or in Spanish.

4. Resolutions and amendments must be handed in to the secretariat of the committee before 5 p.m. to enable the resolution or amendment to be discussed at a meeting to be held on the following morning or before 11 a.m. to enable the resolution or amendment to be discussed at a meeting to be held in the afternoon of the same day.

5. The texts of resolutions and amendments shall be translated and distributed before the discussion to all members of the committee present at the sitting.

6. Only amendments to amendments already submitted under the conditions referred to above may be submitted during a sitting of a committee for discussion at that sitting. Such amendments shall be submitted in writing in one of the official languages or in Spanish.

7. (1) Amendments shall be voted on before the resolution to which they refer.

(2) If therer are several amendments to a motion or resolution the Chairman shall determine the order in which they shall be discussed and put to the vote, subject to the following provisions:

(a) every motion, resolution or amendment shall be put to the vote;

(b) amendments may be voted on either individually or against other amendments according as the Chairman may decide, but if amendments are voted on against other amendments, the motion or resolution shall be deemed to be amended only after the amendment receiving the largest number of affirmative votes has been voted on individually and adopted;

(c) if a motion or resolution is amended as the result of a vote, that motion or resolution as amended shall be put to the meeting for a final vote.

8. (1) Any amendment may be withdrawn by the person who moved it unless an amendment to it is under discussion or has been adopted.

(2) Any amendment so withdrawn may be moved without previous notice by any other person entitled to take part in the discussions of the committee.

9. Any member may at any time draw attention to the fact that the Standing Orders are not being observed, and the Chairman shall give an immediate ruling on any question so raised.

ARTICLE 64

Closure

1. Any member of a committee may move the closure either on a particular amendment or on the general question.

2. The Chairman shall put a motion for the closure if it is supported by at least one-fifth of the members of the committee present at the sitting. Before putting it to the vote, however, he shall read out the names of those persons who have already signified their wish to speak and they shall still have the right to speak the closure has been voted.

3. If application is made for permission to speak against the closure, it shall be accorded to one speaker from each group. If the closure is voted, one member from each group, no member of which has already signified his wish to speak under the conditions provided for in the preceding paragraph, may speak on the question under discussion.

4. In the case of the Resolutions Committee only the sponsor of the motion, resolution or amendment under discussion, or one of the sponsors if there were several, shall have the right to speak on the question under discussion after the closure has been voted.

ARTICLE 65

Method of Voting

1. Decisions shall be taken by a simple majority of the votes cast by the members of the committee present at the sitting.

2. Each member of the committee shall, except in the cases provided for in paragraph 3 and 4 of this article, be entitled to cast one vote.

3. If the Conference has appointed to a committee twice as many Government members as Employers' or Workers' members,[1] each Government member shall be entitled to cast one vote and each Employers' or Workers' member shall be entitled to cast two votes.

4. If the Conference has appointed to a committee one-and-a-half times as many Government members as Employers' or Workers' members, each Government member shall be entitled to cast two votes and each Employers' or Workers' member shall be entitled to cast three votes.

5. Committees shall vote by a show of hands or by a record vote.

6. If the result of a vote by a show of hands is challenged, the Chairman shall cause a record vote to be taken.

7. A record vote shall also be taken if requested by show of hands by at least one-fifth of the members present at the sitting, whether such request be made before or immediately after the vote by show of hands.

8. The vote shall be recorded by the secretariat and announced by the Chairman.

9. No resolution, amendment or motion shall be adopted if an equal number of votes are cast for and against.

ARTICLE 66

Quorum

1. A vote is not valid if the number of votes cast for and against is less than two-fifths of the total voting power.

2. Where a quorum has not been obtained in a vote by show of hands, the Chairman may immediately take a record vote. He shall be obliged to do so if a record vote is called for by not less than one-fifth of the members of the committee present at the sitting.

ARTICLE 67

Amendments to Text Submitted by Committee Drafting Committee

Amendments to a text submitted to a committee by its drafting committee may be admitted by the Chairman after consultation with the Vice-Chairmen.

---

[1] In committees dealing with items on the agenda, it is the practice of the Conference to give equal representation to the three groups in the Conference—Governments, Employers and Workers. As it not infrequently happens that governments desire representation on a committee in numbers which it is impossible for one or both of the other groups to equal, the principle of equality between the three groups on the committee can be maintained only by the adoption of special systems of voting. Two systems are employed.

Under the first of these systems, the committee is constituted in the same proportions as the Conference, with twice as many Government members as there are Employers' or Workers' members, but each Government member casts one vote and each member of the other two groups casts two votes.

Under the second system, the Government members are one-and-a-half times as numerous as the Employers' or Workers's members, but each Government member casts two votes and each member of the other two groups casts three votes.

The composition of each committee is the subject of a proposal to the Conference by the Selection Committee, and the normal system of voting or one of two special systems is applied as the case may require.

ARTICLE 68

Secretariat

1. The Secretary-General of the Conference or his representatives may, with the permission of the Chairman, address committees, subcommittees or committee drafting committees.

2. The Secretary-General shall appoint an official of the Secretariat of the Conference to act as Secretary to each committee. This official will be required to undertake such additional duties as may be decided upon by the committee or the Chairman.

ARTICLE 69

Minutes

1. No verbatim record will made, but as soon as possible after each sitting of a committee the secretariat will draw up minutes which will be roneographed and circulated to the members. These minutes will only be a summarised record of the proceedings, their primary object being to record the decisions of a committee.

2. Any corrections to the minutes should be communicated within 24 hours to the secretariat of the committee, which will arrange for their distribution as early as possible to members of the committee. A copy of the minutes in which these corrections have been inserted will be kept in the archives of the International Labour Office.

SECTION I

Conference Groups

ARTICLE 70

Autonomy of Groups

Subject to the Standing Orders each group shall control its own procedure.

ARTICLE 71

Officers of Groups

1. At its first meeting each group shall elect a Chairman, at least one Vice-Chairman and a Secretary.

2. The Chairman and the Vice-Chairman or Vice-Chairmen shall be selected from among the delegates and advisers constituting the group; the Secretary may be elected from among persons outside the group.

ARTICLE 72

Official Meetings

1. Each group shall hold official meetings for the transaction of the following business:

(a) the nomination of a Vice-President of the Conference;
(b) the nomination of members of the Selection Committee;
(c) the nomination of members for other committees;
(d) elections for the Governing Body;

(e) any other matters referred to groups by the Selection Committee or by the Conference.

2. At the first official meeting of each group, which shall be held as soon as possible after the Conference meets, a representative of the Secretariat shall be present, if the group so desires, to inform the group as to procedure.

3. At official meetings only delegates shall vote, provided always that a delegate may, by notice in writing to the President, appoint one of his advisers to act as his substitute, if he himself is unable to be present, in accordance with the provisions concerning the meetings of the Conference contained in article 1 (3) of these Standing Orders.

4. The Secretary of each group shall report forthwith to the Officers of the Conference the results of all official meetings.

ARTICLE 73

Procedure of Voting at Elections

The President of the Conference or a person nominated by him shall direct the actual procedure of voting in elections required for the appointment or Vice-Presidents of the Conference, members of committees, and members of the Governing Body; he shall convoke in due the delegates who have a right to vote, shall see that the votes are regularly counted and shall communicate to the Conference the results of the election.

ARTICLE 74

Non-Official Meetings

Groups may at any time hold non-official meetings for discussion or the transaction of non-official business.

ARTICLE 75

Procedure for the Nomination of Members of Committees by the Government Group

1. In making nomination for committees, the Government group shall proceed as follows:

2. As soon as the Selection Committee has come to a decision as to the number of committees to be set up, the delegates of each government shall inform the Secretary of the group, in writing, upon which committees their government desires representation and in what order of preference.

3. The Secretary shall thereupon prepare for each committee a list showing what governments desire representation thereon and the order of their preference. These lists shall be communicated to the members of the group.

4. The group shall first make its nominations for that committee for which there are the largest number of candidates. After the members of the first committee have been nominated the same principle shall be followed in respect of the remaining committees.

2. FOOD AND AGRICULTURE ORGANIZATION

a. CONSTITUTION OF THE FOOD AND AGRICULTURE ORGANIZATION, AMENDED BY THE CONFERENCE OF THE ORGANIZATION UP TO 1969 AND ALL THE AMENDMENTS INCORPORATED IN THE 1972 EDITION[1]

Preamble

The Nations accepting this Constitution, being determined to promote the common welfare by furthering separate and collective action on their part for the purpose of:

raising levels of nutrition and standards of living of the peoples under their respective jurisdictions;

securing improvements in the efficiency of the production and distribution of all food and agricultural products;

bettering the condition of rural populations;

and thus contributing toward an expanding world economy and ensuring humanity's freedom from hunger;

hereby establish the Food and Agriculture Organization of the United Nations, hereinafter referred to as the "Organization," through which the Member will report to one another on the measures taken and the progress achieved in the field of action set forth above.

Article I

Functions of the Organization

1. The Organization shall collect, analyse, interpret and disseminate information relating to nutrition, food and agriculture. In this Constitution, the term "agriculture" and its derivatives include fisheries, marine products, forestry and primary forestry products.

2. The Organization shall promote and, where appropriate, shall recommend national and international action with respect to:

(a) scientific, technological, social and economic research relating to nutrition, food and agriculture;

(b) the improvement of education and administration relating to nutrition, food and agriculture, and the spread of public knowledge of nutritional and agricultural science and practice;

(c) the conservation of natural resources and the adoption of improved methods of agricultural production;

(d) the improvement of the processing, marketing and distribution of food and agricultural products;

(e) the adoption of policies for the provisions of adequate agricultural credit, national and international;

(f) the adoption of international policies with respect to agricultural commodity arrangements.

3. It shall also be the functions of the Organization:

(a) to furnish such technical assistance as governments may request;

(b) to organize, in cooperation with the governments concerned, such missions as

---

[1] As published by the Organization. This 1972 edition includes the amendments adopted by the tenth, eleventh, twelfth, thirteenth, fourteenth and fifteenth sessions of the Conference (Rome, 1959, 1961, 1963, 1965, 1967 and 1969). The Arabic, English, French and Spanish texts are equally authoritative. Prior to the seventh edition (June 1952) only the English editions were authentic; prior to the 1970 edition there was no authentic Arabic version.

may be needed to assist them to fulfil the obligation arising from their acceptance of the recommendations of the United Nations Conference on Food and Agriculture and of this Constitution; and

(c) generally to take all necessary and appropriate action to implement the purposes of the Organization as set forth in the Preamble.

Article II

Membership and Associate Membership

1. The original Member Nations of the Organization shall be such of the nations specified in Annex I as accept this Constitution, in accordance with the provisions of Article XXI.

2. The Conference may by a two-thirds majority of the votes cast, provided that a majority of the Member Nations of the Organization is present, decide to admit as an additional Member of the Organization any nation which has submitted an application for membership and a declaration made in a formal instrument that it will accept the obligations of the Constitution as in force at the time of admission.

3. The Conference may, under the same conditions regarding the required majority and quorum as prescribed in paragraph 2 above, decide to admit as an Associate Member of the Organization any territory or group of territories which is not responsible for the conduct of its international relations upon application made in its behalf by the Member Nation or authority having responsibility for its international relations, provided that such Member Nation of authority has submitted a declaration made in a formal instrument that it will accept on behalf of the proposed Associate Member the obligations of the Constitution as in force at the time of admission, and that it will assume responsibility for ensuring the observance of the provisions of paragraph 4 of Article VIII, paragraph 1 and 2 of Article XVI, and paragraphs 2 and 3 of Article XVIII of this Constitution with regard to the Associate Member.

4. The nature and extent of the rights and obligations of Associate Members are defined in the relevant provisions of this Constitution and the Rules and Regulations of the Organization.

5. Membership and Associate Membership shall become effective on the date on which the Conference approves the application.

Article III

The Conference

1. There shall be a Conference of the Organization in which each Member Nations and Associate Member shall be represented by one delegate. Associate Members shall have the right to participate in the deliberations of the Conference but shall not hold office nor have the right to vote.

2. Each Member Nation and Associate Member may appoint alternates, associates and advisers to its delegate. The Conference may determine the conditions for the participation of alternates, associates and advisers in its proceedings, but any such participation shall be without the right to vote, except in the case of an alternate, associate, of adviser participating in the place of a delegate.

3. No delegate may represent more than one Member Nation or Associate Member.

4. Each Member Nation shall have only one vote. A Member Nation which is in arrears in the payment of its financial contributions to the Organization shall have no vote in the Conference if the amount of its arrears equals or exceeds the amount of the contributions due from it for the two preceding calendar years. The Conference may, nevertheless, permit such a Member Nation to vote if it is satisfied that the failure to pay is

due to conditions beyond the control of the Member Nation.

5.   The Conference may invite any international organization which has responsibilities related to those of the Organization to be represented at its meetings on the conditions prescribed by the Conference.   No representative of such an organization shall have the right to vote.

6.   The Conference shall meet once in every two years in regular session.   It may meet in special session:

(a)   if at any regular session the Conference decides, by a majority of the votes cast, to meet in the following year;

(b)   if the Council so instructs the Director-General, of if at least one third of the Member Nations so request.

7.   The Conference shall elect its own officers.

8.   Except as otherwise expressly provided in this Constitution or by rules made by the Conference, all decisions of the Conference shall be taken by a majority of the votes cast.

Article IV

Functions of the Conference

1.   The Conference shall determine the policy and approve the budget of the Organization and shall exercise the other powers conferred upon it by this Constitution.

2.   The Conference shall adopt Rules of Procedure and Financial Regulations for the Organization.

3.   The Conference may, by a two-thirds majority of the votes cast, make recommendations to Member Nations and Associate Members concerning questions relating to food and agriculture, for consideration by them with a view to implementation by national action.

4.   The Conference may make recommendations to any international organization regarding any matter pertaining to the purposes of the Organization.

5.   The Conference may review any decision taken by the Council or by any commission or committee oftthe Conference or Council, or by any subsidiary body of such commissions or committees.

Article V

Council of the Organization

1.   A Council of the Organization consisting of forty-two Member Nations shall be elected by the Conference.   Each Member Nation on the Council shall have one representative and shall have only one vote.   Each Member of the Council may appoint alternates, associates and advisers to its representative.   The Council may determine the conditions for the participation of alternates, associates and advisers in its proceedings, but any such participation shall be without the right to vote, except in the case of an alternate, associate or adviser participating in the place of a representative.   No representative may represent more than one Member of the Council.   The tenure and other conditions of office of the Members of the Council shall be subject to rules made by the Conference.

2.   The Conference shall, in addition, appoint an independent Chairman of the Council.

3.   The Council shall have such powers as the Conference may delegate to it, but the Conference shall not delegate the powers set forth in paragraphs 2 and 3 of Article II, Article IV, paragraph I of Article VII, Article XII, paragraph 4 of Article XIII, paragraphs 1 and 6 of Article XIV and Article XX of this Constitution.

4. The Council shall appoint its officers other than the Chairman and, subject to any decisions of the Conference, shall adopt its own Rules of Procedure.

5. Except as otherwise expressly provided in this Constitution or by rules made by the Conference or Council, all decisions of the Council shall be taken by a majority of the votes cast.

6. To assist the Council in performing its functions, the Council shall appoint a Programme Committee, a Finance Committee, a Committee on Commodity Problems, a Committee on Fisheries and a Committee on Constitutional and Legal Matters. These committees shall report to the Council and their composition and terms of reference shall be governed by rules adopted by the Conference.

Article VI

Commissions, committees, conferences, working parties and consultations

1. The Conference or Council may establish commissions, the membership of which shall be open to all Member Nations and Associate Members, or regional commissions open to all Member Nations and Associate Members whose territories are situated wholly or in part in one or more regions, to advise on the formulation and implementation of policy and to coordinate the emplementation of policy. The Conference or Council may also establish, in conjunction with other intergovernmental organizations, joint commissions open to all Member Nations and Associate Members of the Organization and of the other organizations concerned, or joint regional commissions open to Member Nations and Associate Members of the Organization and of the other organizations concerned, whose territories are situated wholly or in part in the region.

2. The Conference, the Council, or the Director-General on the authority of the Conference or Council may establish committees and working parties to study and report on matters pertaining to the purpose of the Organization and consisting either of selected Member Nations and Associate Members, or of individuals appointed in their personal capacity because of their special competence in technical matters. The Conference, the Council, or the Director-General on the authority of the Conference or Council may, in conjunction with other intergovernmental organizations, also establish joint committees and working parties, consisting either of selected Member Nations and Associate Members of the Organization and of the other organizations concerned, or of individuals appointed in their personal capacity. The selected Member Nations and Associate Members shall, as regards the Organization, be designated either by the Conference or the Council, or by the Director-General if so decided by the Conference or Council. The individuals appointed in their personal capacity shall, as regards the Organization, be designated either by the Conference, the Council, selected Member Nations or Associate Members, or by the Director-General, as decided by the Conference or Council.

3. The Conference, the Council, or the Director-General on the authority of the Conference or Council, shall determine the terms of reference and reporting procedures, as appropriate of commissions, committees and working parties established by the Conference, the Council, or the Director-General as the case may be. Such commissions and committees may adopt their own rules of procedure and amendments thereto, which shall come into force upon approval by the Director-General subject to confirmation by the Conference or Council, as appropriate. The terms of reference and reporting procedures of joint commissions, committees and working parties established in conjunction with other intergovernmental organizations shall be determined in consultation with the other organizations concerned.

4. The Director-General may establish, in consultation with Member Nations, Associate Members and National FAO Committees, panels of experts, with a view to developing consultation with leading technicians in the various fields of activity of the Orga-

nization. The Director-General may convene meetings of some or all of these experts for consultation on specific subjects.

5.   The Conference, the Council, or the Director-General on the authority of the Conference or Council may convene general, regional, technical or other conferences, or working parties or consultations of Member Nations and Associate Members, laying down their terms of reference and reporting procedures, and may provide for participation in such conferences, working parties and consultations, in such manner as they may determine, of national and international bodies concerned with nutrition, food and agriculture.

6.   When the Director-General is satisfied that urgent action is required, he may establish the committees and working parties and convene the conferences, working parties and consultations provided for in paragraphs 2 and 5 above. Such action shall be notified by the Director-General to Member Nations and Associate Members and reported to the following session of the Council.

7.   Associate Members included in the membership of the commissions, committees or working parties, or attending the conferences, working parties or consultations referred to in paragraphs 1, 2 and 5 above, shall have the right to participate in the deliberations of such commissions, committees, conferences, working parties and consultations, but shall not hold office nor have the right to vote.

Article VII

The Director-General

1.   There shall be a Director-General of the Organization who shall be appointed by the Conference for a term of six years, after which he shall not be eligible for reappointment.

2.   The appointment of the Director-General under this Article shall be made by such procedures and on such terms as the Conference may determine.

3.   Should the office of Director-General become vacant during the above-mentioned term of office, the Conference shall, either at the next regular session or at a special session convened in accordance with Article III, paragraph 6 of this Constitution, appoint a Director-General in accordance with the provisions of paragraphs 1 and 2 of this Article. However, the duration of the term of office of a Director-General appointed at a special session shall expire at the end of the year of the third regular session of the Conference following the date of his appointment.

4.   Subject to the general supervision of the Conference and the Council, the Director-General shall have full power and authority to direct the work of the Organization.

5.   The Director-General or a representative designated by him shall participate, without the right to vote, in all meetings of the Conference and of the Council and shall formulate for consideration by the Conference and the Council proposals for appropriate action in regard to matters coming before them.

Article VIII

Staff

1.   The staff of the Organization shall be appointed by the Director-General in accordance with such procedure as may be determined by rules made by the Conference.

2.   The staff of the Organization shall be responsible to the Director-General. Their responsibilities shall be exclusively international in character and they shall not seek or receive instructions in regard to the discharge thereof from any authority external to the Organization. The Member Nations and Associate Members undertake fully to re-

spect the international character of the responsibilities of the staff and not to seek to influence any of their nationals in the discharge of such responsibilities.

3.   In appointing the staff, the Director-General shall, subject to the paramount importance of securing the highest standards of efficiency and of technical competence, pay due regard to the importance of selecting personnel recruited on as wide a geographical basis as is possible.

4.   Each Member Nation and Associate Member undertakes, insofar as it may be possible under its constitutional procedure, to accord to the Director-General and senior staff diplomatic privileges and immunities and to accord to other members of the staff all facilities and immunities accorded to nondiplomatic personnel attached to diplomatic missions, or alternatively, to accord to such other members of the staff the immunities and facilities which may hereafter be accorded to equivalent members of the staffs of other public international organizations.

Article IX

Seat

The seat of the Organization shall be determined by the Conference.

Article X

Regional and liaison offices

1.   There shall be such regional offices and subregional offices as the Director-General, with the approval of the Conference, may decide.

2.   The Director-General may appoint officials for liaison with particular countries or areas, subject to the agreement of the government concerned.

Article XI

Reports by Member Nations and Associate Members

1.   Each Member Nation and Associate Member shall communicate periodically to the Organization reports on the progress made toward achieving the purpose of the Organization set forth in the Preamble and on the action taken on the basis of recommendations made and conventions submitted by the Conference.

2.   These reports shall be made at such times and in such forms and shall contain such particulars as the Conference may request.

3.   The Director-General shall submit these reports, together with analyses thereof, to the Conference and shall publish such reports and analyses as may be approved for publication by the Conference, together with any reports relating thereto adopted by the Conference.

4.   The Director-General may request any Member Nation or Associate Member to submit information relating to the purpose of the Organization.

5.   Each Member Nation and Associate Member shall, on request, communicate to the Organization, on publication, all laws and regulations and official reports and statistics concerning nutrition, food and agriculture.

Article XII

Relations with the United Nations

1.   The Organization shall maintain relations with the United Nations as a specialized agency within the meaning of Article 57 of the Charter of the United Nations.[1]

2. Agreements defining the relations between the Organization and the United Nations shall be subject to the approval of the Conference.

Article XIII

Cooperation with organizations and persons

1. In order to provide for close cooperation between the Organization and other international organizations with related responsibilities, the Conference may enter into agreements with the competent authorities of such organizations, defining the distribution of responsibilities and methods of cooperation.

2. The Director-General may, subject to any decision of the Conference, enter into agreements with other intergovernmental organizations for the maintenance of common services, for common arrangements in regard to recruitment, training, conditions of service and other related matters, and for interchanges of staff.

3. The Conference may approve arrangements placing other international organizations dealing with questions relating to food and agriculture under the general authority of the Organization on such terms as may be agreed with the competent authorities of the organization concerned.

4. The Conference shall make rules laying down the procedure to be followed to secure proper consultation with governments in regard to relations between the Organization and national institutions or private persons.

Article XIV

Conventions and agreements

1. The Conference may, by a two-thirds majority of the votes cast and in conformity with rules adopted by the Conference, approve and submit to Member Nations conventions and agreements concerning questions relating to food and agriculture.

2. The Council, under rules to be adopted by the Conference, may, by a vote concurred in by at least two thirds of the membership of the Council, approve and submit to Member Nations:

(a) agreements concerning questions relating to food and agriculture which are of particular interest to Member Nations of geographical areas specified in such agreements and are designed to apply only to such areas;

(b) supplementary conventions of agreements designed to implement any convention or agreement which has come into force under paragraphs 1 or 2 *(a).*

3. Conventions, agreements, and supplementary conventions and agreements shall:

(a) be submitted to the Conference or Council through the Director-General on behalf of a technical meeting or conference comprising Member Nations, which has assisted in drafting the convention or agreement and has suggested that it be submitted to Member Nations concerned for acceptance;

---

[1] Article 57 reads as follows: "1. The various specialized agencies, established by intergovernmental agreement and having wide international responsibilities, as defined, in their basic instruments, in economic, social, cultural, educational, health and related fields, shall be brought into relationship with the United Nations in accordance with the provisions of Article 63.

"2. Such agencies thus brought into relationship with the United Nations are hereinafter referred to as specialized agencies."

Article 63 reads as follows: "1. The Economic and Social Council may enter into agreements with any of the agencies referred to in Article 57, defining the terms on which the agency concerned shall be brought into relationship with the United Nations. Such agreements shall be subject to approval by the General Assembly.

"2. It may coordinate the activities of the specialized agencies through consultation with and recommendations to such agencies and through recommendations to the General Assembly and to the members of the United Nations."

(b) contain provisions concerning the Member Nations of the Organization, and such nonmember nations as are members of the United Nations, which may become parties thereto and the number of acceptances by Member Nations necessary to bring such convention, agreement, supplementary convention or agreement into force, and thus ensure that it will constitute a real contribution to the achievement of its objectives. In the case of conventions, agreements, supplementary conventions and agreements establishing commissions or committees, participation by nonmember nations of the Organization that are members of the United Nations shall in addition be subject to prior approval by at least two thirds of the membership of such commissions or committees;

(c) not entail any financial obligations for Member Nations not parties to it other than their contributions to the Organization provided for in Article XVIII, paragraph 2 of this Constitution.

4. Any convention, agreement, supplementary convention or agreement approved by the Conference or Council for submission to Member Nations shall come into force for each contracting party as the convention, agreement, supplementary convention or agreement may prescribe.

5. As regards an Associate Member, conventions, agreements, supplementary conventions and agreements shall be submitted to the authority having responsibility for the international relations of the Associate Member.

6. The Conference shall make rules laying down the procedure to be followed to secure proper consultation with governments and adequate technical preparations prior to consideration by the Conference or the Council of proposed conventions, agreements, supplementary conventions and agreements.

7. Two copies in the authentic language or languages of any convention, agreement, supplementary convention or agreement approved by the Conference or the Council shall be certified by the Chairman of the Conference or of the Council respectively and by the Director-General. One of these copies shall be deposited in the archives of the Organization. The other copy shall be transmitted to the Secretary-General of the United Nations for registration once the convention, agreement, supplementary convention or agreement has come into force as a result of action taken under this Article. In addition, the Director-General shall certify copies of those conventions, agreements, supplementary conventions or agreements and transmit one copy to each Member Nation of the Organization and to such nonmember nations as may become parties to the conventions, agreements, supplementary conventions or agreements.

Article XV

Agreements between the Organization and Member Nations

1. The Conference may authorize the Director-General to enter into agreements with Member Nations for the establishment of international institutions dealing with questions relating to food and agriculture.

2. In pursuance of a policy decision taken by the Conference by a two-thirds majority of the votes cast, the Director-General may negotiate and enter into such agreements with Member Nations, subject to the provisions of paragraph 3 below.

3. The signature of such agreements by the Director-General shall be subject to the prior approval of the Conference by a two-thirds majority of the votes cast. The Conference may, in a particular case or cases, delegate the authority of approval to the Council, requiring a vote concurred in by at least two thirds of the membership of the Council.

Article XVI

Legal status

1. The Organization shall have the capacity of a legal person to perform any legal act appropriate to its purpose which is not beyond the powers granted to it by this Constitution.

2. Each Member Nation and Associate Member undertakes, insofar as it may be possible under its constitutional procedure, to accord to the Organization all the immunities and facilities which it accords to diplomatic missions, including inviolability of premises and archives, immunity from suit and exemptions from taxation.

3. The Conference shall make provision for the determination by an administrative tribunal of disputes relating to the conditions and terms of appointment of members of the staff.

Article XVII

Interpretation of the Constitution and settlement of legal questions

1. Any question or dispute concerning the interpretation of this Constitution, if not settled by the Conference, shall be referred to the International Court of Justice in conformity with the Statute of the Court or to such other body as the Conference may determine.

2. Any request by the Organization to the International Court of Justice for an advisory opinion on legal questions arising within the scope of its activities shall be in accordance with any agreement between the Organization and the United Nations.

3. The reference of any question or dispute under this Article, or any request for an advisory opinion, shall be subject to procedures to be prescribed by the Conference.

Article XVIII

Budget and contributions

1. The Director-General shall submit to each regular session of the Conference the budget of the Organization for approval.

2. Each Member Nation and Associate Member undertakes to contribute annually to the Organization its share of the budget, as apportioned by the Conference. When determining the contributions to be paid by Member Nation and Associate Members, the Conference shall take into account the difference in status between Member Nations and Associate Members.

3. Each Member Nation and Associate Member shall, upon approval of its application, pay as its first contribution a proportion, to be determined by the Conference, of the budget for the current financial period.

4. The financial period of the Organization shall be the two calendar years following the normal date for the regular session of the Conference, unless the Conference should otherwise determine.

5. Decisions on the level of the budget shall be taken by a two-thirds majority of the votes cast.

Article XIX

Withdrawal

Any Member Nation may give notice of withdrawal from the Organization at any time after the expiration of four years from the date of its acceptance of this Constitution. The notice of withdrawal of an Associate Member shall be given by the Member Nation or authority having responsibility for its international relations. Such notice shall take effect one year after the date of its communication to the Director-General. The financial obligation to the Organization of a Member Nation which has given notice of withdrawal, or of an Associate Member on whose behalf notice of withdrawal has been given, shall include the entire calendar year in which the notice takes effect.

Article XX

Amendment of Constitution

1. The Conference may amend this Constitution by a two-thirds majority of the votes cast, provided that such majority is more than one half of the Member Nations of the Organization.

2. An amendment not involving new obligations for Member Nations or Associate Members shall take effect forthwith, unless the resolution by which it is adopted provides otherwise. Amendments involving new obligations shall take effect for each Member Nation and Associate Member accepting the amendment or acceptance by two thirds of the Member Nations of the Organization and thereafter for each remaining Member Nation or Associate Member on acceptance by it. As regards an Associate Member, the acceptance of amendments involving new obligations shall be given on its behalf by the Member Nation or authority having responsibility for the international relations of the Associate Member.

3. Proposals for the amendment of the Constitution may be made either by the Council or by a Member Nation in a communication addressed to the Director-General. The Director-General shall immediately inform all Member Nations and Associate Members of all proposals for amendments.

4. No proposal for the amendment of the Constitution shall be included in the agenda of any session of the Conference unless notice thereof has been dispatched by the Director-General to Member Nations and Associate Members at least 120 days before the opening of the session.

Article XXI

Entry into force of Constitution

1. This Constitution shall be open to acceptance by the nations specified in Annex I.

2. The instruments of acceptance shall be transmitted by each governments to the United Nations Interim Commission on Food and Agriculture, which shall notify their receipt to the governments of the nations specified in Annex I. Acceptance may be notified to the Interim Commission through a diplomatic representative, in which case the instrument of acceptance must be transmitted to the Commission as soon as possible thereafter.

3. Upon the receipt by the Interim Commission of 20 notifications of acceptance, the Interim Commission shall arrange for this Constitution to be signed in a single copy by the diplomatic representatives duly authorized thereto of the nations who shall have notified their acceptance, and upon being so signed on behalf of not less than 20 of the nations specffied in Annex I, this Constitution shall come into force immediately.

4. Acceptances, the notification of which is received after the entry into force of this Constitution, shall become effective upon receipt by the Interim Commission or the Organization.

Article XXII

Authentic texts of Constitution

The Arabic, English, French and Spanish texts of this Constitution shall be equally authoritative.

Annex I

Nations eligible for original membership

Australia	India
Belgium	Iran
Bolivia	Iraq
Brazil	Liberia
Canada	Luxembourg
Chile	Mexico
China	Netherlands
Colombia	New Zealand
Costa Rica	Nicaragua
Cuba	Norway
Czechoslovakia	Panama
Denmark	Paraguay
Dominican Republic	Peru
Ecuador	Philippine Commonwealth
Egypt	Poland
El Salvador	Union of South Africa
Ethiopia	Union of Soviet Socialist Republics
France	United Kingdom
Greece	United States of America
Guatemala	Uruguay
Haiti	Venezuela
Honduras	Yugoslavia
Iceland	

3. UNITED NATIONS EDUCATIONAL, SCIENTIFIC AND CULTURAL ORGANIZATION

a. CONSTITUTION OF THE UNITED NATIONS EDUCATIONAL, SCIENTIFIC AND CULTURAL ORGANIZATION, AMENDED BY THE GENERAL CONFERENCE OF THE ORGANIZATION UP TO THE FIFTEENTH SESSION, DONE AT LONDON, NOVEMBER 16, 1945[1]

PREAMBLE

The Governments of the States Parties to this Constitution on behalf of their peoples declare:

That since wars begin in the minds of men, it is in the minds of men that the defences of peace must be constructed;

That ignorance of each other's ways and lives has been a common cause, throughout the history of mankind, of that suspicion and mistrust between the peoples of the world through which their differences have all too often broken into war;

That the great and terrible war which has now ended was a war made possible by the denial of the democratic principles of the dignity, equality and mutual respect of men, and by the propagation, in their place, through ignorance and prejudice, of the doctrine of the inequality of men and races;

That the wide diffusion of culture, and the education of humanity for justice and liberty and peace are indispensable to the dignity of man and constitute a sacred duty which all the nations must fulfil in a spirit of mutual assistance and concern;

That a peace based exclusively upon the political and economic arrangements of governments would not be a peace which could secure the unanimous, lasting and sincere support of the peoples of the world, and that the peace must therefore be founded, if it is not to fail, upon the intellectual and moral solidarity of mankind.

For these reasons, the States Parties to this Constitution, believing in full and equal opportunities for education for all, in the unrestricted pursuit of objective truth, and in the free exchange of ideas and knowledge, are agreed and determined to develop and to increase the means of communication between their peoples and to employ these means for the purposes of mutual understanding and a truer and more perfect knowledge of each other's lives;

In consequence whereof they do hereby create the United Nations Educational, Scientific and Cultural Organization for the purpose of advancing, through the educational and scientific and cultural relations of the peoples of the world, the objectives of international peace and of the common welfare of mankind for which the United Nations Organization was established and which its Charter proclaims.

ARTICLE I. — PURPOSES AND FUNCTIONS

1. The purpose of the Organization is to contribute to peace and security by promoting collaboration among the nations through education, science and culture in order to further universal respect for justice, for the rule of law and for the human rights and fundamental freedoms which are affirmed for the peoples of the world, without distinction of race, language or religion by the Charter of the United Nations.

---

[1] As published by the UNESCO.

Adopted in London on 16 November 1945 and amended by the General Conference at its 2nd, 3rd, 4th, 5th, 6th, 7th, 8th, 9th, 10th, 12th and 15th sessions.

2. To realize this purpose the Organization will:

   (a) Collaborate in the work of advancing the mutual knowledge and understanding of peoples, through all means of mass communication and to that end recommend such international agreements as may be necessary to promote the free flow of ideas by word and image;

   (b) Give fresh impulse to popular education and to the spread of culture;
   by collaborating with Members, at their request, in the development of educational activities;
   by instituting collaboration among the nations to advance the ideal of equality of educational opportunity without regard to race, sex or any distinctions, economic or social;
   by suggesting educational methods best suited to prepare the children of the world for the responsibilities of freedom;

   (c) Maintain, increase and diffuse knowledge;
   by assuring the conservation and protection of the world's inheritance of books, works of art and monuments of history and science, and recommending to the nations concerned the necessary international conventions;
   by encouraging co-operation among the nations in all branches of intellectual activity, including the international exchange of persons active in the fields of education, science and culture and the exchange of publications, objects of artistic and scientific interest and other materials of information;
   by initiating methods of international co-operation calculated to give the people of all countries access to the printed and published materials produced by any of them.

3. With a view to preserving the independence, integrity and fruitful diversity of the cultures and educational systems of the States members of this Organization, the Organization is prohibited from intervening in matters which are essentially within their domestic jurisdiction.

ARTICLE II. — MEMBERSHIP

1. Membership of the United Nations Organization shall carry with it the right to membership of the United Nations Educational, Scientific and Cultural Organization.

2. Subject to the conditions of the Agreement between this Organization and the United Nations Organization, approved pursuant to Article X of this Constitution, States not members of the United Nations Organization may be admitted to membership of the Organization, upon recommendation of the Executive Board, by a two-thirds majority vote of the General Conference.

3. Territories or groups of territories which are not responsible for the conduct of their international relations may be admitted as Associate Members by the General Conference by a two-thirds majority of Members present and voting, upon application made on behalf of such territory or group of territories by the Member or other authority having responsibility for their international relations. The nature and extent of the rights and obligations of Associate Members shall be determined by the General Conference.

4. Members of the Organization which are suspended from the exercise of the rights and privileges of membership of the United Nations Organization shall, upon the request of the latter, be suspended from the rights and privileges of this Organization.

5. Members of the Organization which are expelled from the United Nations Organization shall automatically cease to be members of this Organization.

6. Any Member State or Associate Member of the Organization may withdraw from the Organization by notice addressed to the Director-General. Such notice shall take effect on 31 December of the year following that during which the notice was given. No such withdrawal shall affect the financial obligations owed to the Organization on the date the withdrawal takes effect. Notice of withdrawal by an Associate Member shall be given on its behalf by the Member State or other authority having responsibility for its international relations.

ARTICLE III. — ORGANS

The Organization shall include a General Conference, and Executive Board and a Secretariat.

ARTICLE IV. — THE GENERAL CONFERENCE

A. Composition

1. The General Conference shall consist of the representatives of the States members of the Organization. The Government of each Member State shall appoint not more than five delegates, who shall be selected after consultation with the National Commission, if established, or with educational, scientific and cultural bodies.

B. Functions

2. The General Conference shall determine the policies and the main lines of work of the Organization. It shall take decisions on programmes submitted to it by the Executive Board.

3. The General Conference shall, when it deems desirable and in accordance with the regulations to be made by it, summon international conferences of States on education, the sciences and humanities or the dissemination of knowledge; non-governmental conferences on the same subjects may be summoned by the General Conference or by the Executive Board in accordance with such regulations.

4. The General Conference shall, in adopting proposals for submission to the Member States, distinguish between recommendations and international conventions submitted for their approval. In the former case a majority vote shall suffice; in the latter case a two-thirds majority shall be required. Each of the Member States shall submit recommendations or conventions to its competent authorities within a period of one year from the close of the session of the General Conference at which they were adopted.

5. Subject to the provisions of Article V, paragraph 5(c), the General Conference shall advise the United Nations Organization on the educational, scientific and cultural aspects of matters of concern to the letter; in accordance with the terms and procedure agreed upon between the appropriate authorities of the two Organizations.

6. The General Conference shall receive and consider the reports submitted periodically by Member States as provided by Article VIII.

7. The General Conference shall elect the members of the Executive Board and, on the recommendation of the Board, shall appoint the Director-General.

C. Voting

8. (a) Each Member State shall have one vote in the General Conference. Decisions shall be made by a simple majority except in cases in which a two-thirds majority is required by the provisions of this Constitution, or of the Rules of Procedure of the General Conference. A majority shall be a majority of the Member present and voting.

(b)   A Member State shall have no vote in the General Conference if the total amount of contributions due from it exceeds the total amount of contributions payable by it for the current year and the immediately preceding calendar year.

(c)   The General Conference may nevertheless permit such a Member State to vote, if it is satisfied that failure to pay is due to conditions beyond the control of the Member Nation.

D.   Procedure

9. (a)   The General Conference shall meet in ordinary session every two years. It may meet in extraordinary session if it decides to do so itself or if summoned by the Executive Board, or on the demand of at least one-third of the Member States.

(b)   At each Session the location of its next ordinary session shall be designated by the General Conference. The location of an extraordinary session shall be decided by the General Conference if the session is summoned by it, or otherwise by the Executive Board.

10. The General Conference shall adopt its own rules of procedure. It shall at each session elect a President and other officers.

11. The General Conference shall set up special and technical committees and such other subordinate bodies as may be necessary for its purposes.

12. The General Conference shall cause arrangements to be made for public access to meetings, subject to such regulations as it shall prescribe.

E.   Observers

13. The General Conference, on the recommendation of the Executive Board and by a two-thirds majority may, subject to its rules or procedure, invite as observers at specified sessions of the Conference or of its Commissions representatives of international organizations, such as those referred to in Article XI, paragraph 4.

14. When Consultative arrangements have been approved by the Executive Board for such international non-governmental or semi-governmental organizations in the manner provided in Article XI, paragraph 4, those organizations shall be invited to send observers to sessions of the General Conference and its Commissions.

ARTICLE V. — EXECUTIVE BOARD

A.   Composition

1. The Executive Board shall be elected by the General Conference from among the delegates appointed by the Member States and shall consist of thirty-four members each of whom shall represent the Government of the State of which he is a national. The President of the General Conference shall sit ex officio in an advisory capacity on the Executive Board.

2. In electing the members of the Executive Board the General Conference shall endeavour to include persons competent in the arts, the humanities, the sciences, education and the diffusion of ideas and qualified by their experience and capacity to fulfil the administrative and executive duties of the Board. It shall also have regard to the diversity of cultures and a balanced geographical distribution. Not more than one national of any Member State shall serve on the Board at any one time, the President of the Conference excepted.

3. Members of the Board shall serve from the close of the session of the General Conference which elected them until the close of the third ordinary session of the General Conference following that election. They shall not be immediately

eligible for a second term. The General Conference shall, at each of its ordinary sessions, elect the number of members required to fill the vacancies occuring at the end of the session.

4. In the event of the death or resignation of a member of the Executive Board, his replacement for the remainder of his term shall be appointed by the Executive Board on the nomination of the Government of the State the former member represented. The Government making the nomination and the Executive Board shall have regard to the factors set forth in paragraph 2 of this Article.

B. Functions

5. (a) The Executive Board shall prepare the agenda for the General Conference. It shall examine the programme of work for the Organization and corresponding budget estimates submitted to it by the Director-General in accordance with paragraph 3 of Article VI and shall submit them with such recommendations as it considers desirable to the General Conference.

(b) The Executive Board, acting under the authority of the General Conference, shall be responsible for the execution of the programme adopted by the Conference. In accordance with the decisions of the General Conference and having regard to circumstances arising between two ordinary sessions, the Executive Board shall take all necessary measures to ensure the effective and rational execution of the programme by the Director-General.

(c) Between ordinary sessions of the General Conference, the Board may discharge the functions of adviser to the United Nations, set forth in Article IV, paragraph 5, whenever the problem upon which advice is sought has already been dealt with in principle by the Conference, or when the solution is implicit in decisions of the Conference.

6. The Executive Board shall recommend to the General Conference the admission of new Member to the Organization.

7. Subject to decisions of the General Conference, the Executive Board shall adopt its own rules of procedure. It shall elect its officers from among its members.

8. The Executive Board shall meet in regular session at least twice a year and may meet in special session if convoked by the Chairman on his own initiative or upon the request of six members of the Board.

9. The Chairman of the Executive Board shall present, on behalf of the Board, to each ordinary session of the General Conference, with or without comments, the reports on the activities of the Organization which the Director-General is required to prepare in accordance with the provisions of Article VI.3(b).

10. The Executive Board shall make all necessary arrangements to consult the representatives of international organizations or qualified persons concerned with questions within its competence.

11. Between sessions of the General Conference, the Executive Board may request advisory opinions from the International Court of Justice on legal questions arising within the field of the Organization's activities.

12. Although the members of the Executive Board are representative of their respective Governments they shall exercise the powers delegated to them by the General Conference on behalf of the Conference as a whole.

C. Transitional Provisions

13. Notwithstanding the provisions of paragraph 3 of this Article, members of the Executive Board elected at the thirteenth and fourteenth sessions of the General Conference for a first term and members appointed by the Board in accordance

with the provisions of paragraph 4 of this Article to replace members with a four-year term shall be eligible for a second term of four years.

14. At the fifteenth session of the General Conference, nineteen members shall be elected to the Executive Board pursuant to the provisions of this Article. Thereafter, at each of its ordinary sessions, the General Conference shall elect the number of members required to fill the Vacancies occurring at the end of the session.

ARTICLE VI. — SECRETARIAT

1. The Secretariat shall consist of a Director-General and such staff as may be required.

2. The Director-General shall be nominated by the Executive Board and appointed by the General Conference for a period of six years, under such conditions as the Conference may approve, and shall be eligible for reappointment. He shall be the chief administrative officer of the Organization.

3. (a) The Director-General, or a deputy designated by him, shall participate, without the right to vote, in all meetings of the General Conference, of the Executive Board and of the Committees of the Organization. He shall formulate proposals for appropriate action by the Conference and the Board, and shall prepare for submission to the Board a draft programme of work for the Organization with corresponding budget estimates.

   (b) The Director-General shall prepare and communicate to Member States and to the Executive Board periodical reports on the activities of the Organization. The General Conference shall determine the periods to be covered by these reports.

4. The Director-General shall appoint the staff of the Secretariat in accordance with staff regulations to be approved by the General Conference. Subject to the paramount consideration of securing the highest standards of integrity, efficiency and technical competence, appointment to the staff shall be on as wide a geographical basis as possible.

5. The responsibilities of the Director-General and of the staff shall be exclusively international in character. In the discharge of their duties they shall not seek or receive instructions from any Government or from any authority external to the Organization. They shall refrain from any action which might prejudice their position as international officials. Each State member of the Organization undertakes to respect the international character of the responsibilities of the Director-General and the staff, and not to seek to influence them in the discharge of their duties.

6. Nothing in this Article shall preclude the Organization from entering into special arrangements within the United Nations Organization for common services and staff and for the interchange of personnel.

ARTICLE VII. — NATIONAL CO-OPERATING BODIES

1. Each Member State shall make such arrangements as suit its particular conditions for the purpose of associating its principal bodies interested in educational, scientific and cultural matters with the work of the Organization, preferably by the formation of a National Commission broadly representative of the Government and such bodies.

2. National Commissions or National Co-operating Bodies, where they exist, shall act in an advisory capacity to their respective delegations to the General Conference and to their Governments in matters relating to the Organization and shall function as agencies of liaison in all matters of interest to it.

3. The Organization may, on the request of a Member State, delegate, either temporarily or permanently, a member of its Secretariat to serve on the National Commission of that State, in order to assist in the development of its work.

ARTICLE VIII. — REPORTS BY MEMBER STATES

Each Member State shall report periodically to the Organization, in a manner to be determined by the General Conference, on its laws, regulations and statistics relating to educational, scientific and cultural life and institutions, and on the action taken upon the recommendations and conventions referred to in Article IV, paragraph 4.

ARTICLE IX. — BUDGET

1. The Budget shall be administered by the Organization.
2. The General Conference shall approve and give final effect to the budget and to the apportionment of financial responsibility among the States members of the Organization subject to such arrangement with the United Nations as may be provided in the agreement to be entered into pursuant to Article X.
3. The Director-General, with the approval of the Executive Board may receive gifts, bequests, and subventions directly from Governments, public and private institutions, associations and private persons.

ARTICLE X. — RELATIONS WITH THE UNITED NATIONS ORGANIZATIONS

This Organization shall be brought into relation with the United Nations Organization, as soon as practicable, as one of the Specialized Agencies referred to in Article 57 of the Charter of the United Nations. This relationship shall be effected through an agreement with the United Nations Organization under Article 63 of the Charter, which agreement shall be subject to the approval of the General Conference of this Organization. The agreement shall provide for effective cooperation between the two Organizations in the pursuit of their common purposes, and at the same time shall recognize the autonomy of this Organization, within the fields of its competence as defined in this Constitution. Such agreement may, among other matters, provide for the approval and financing of the budget of the Organization by the General Assembly of the United Nations.

ARTICLE XI. — RELATIONS WITH OTHER SPECIALIZED INTERNATIONAL
ORGANIZATIONS AND AGENCIES

1. This Organization may co-operate with other specialized inter-governmental organizations and agencies whose interests and activities are related to its purposes. To this end the Director-General, acting under the general authority of the Executive Board, may establish effective working relationships with such organizations and agencies and establish such joint committees as may be necessary to assure effective co-operation. Any formal arrangements entered into with such organizations or agencies shall be subject to the approval of the Executive Board.
2. Whenever the General Conference of this Organization and the competent authorities of any other specialized intergovernmental organizations or agencies whose purpose and functions lie within the competence of this Organization, deem it desirable to effect a transfer of their resources and activities to this Organization, the Director-General, subject to the approval of the Conference, may enter into mutually acceptable arrangements for this purpose.
3. This Organization may make appropriate arrangements with other intergovernmental organizations for reciprocal representation at meetings.
4. The United Nations Educational, Scientific and Cultural Organization may make suitable arrangements for consultation and co-operation with non-governmental

international organizations concerned with matters within its competence, and may invite them to undertake specific tasks. Such cooperation may also include appropriate participation by representatives of such organizations on advisory committees set up by the General Conference.

ARTICLE XII. — LEGAL STATUS OF THE ORGANIZATION

The provisions of Articles 104 and 105 of the Charter of the United Nations Organization concerning the legal status of that Organization, its privileges and immunities, shall apply in the same way to this Organization.

ARTICLE XIII. — AMENDMENTS

1. Proposals for amendments to this Constitution shall become effective upon receiving the approval of the General Conference by a two-thirds majority; provided, however, that those amendments which involve fundamental alterations in the aims of the Organization or new obligations for the Member States shall require subsequent acceptance on the part of two-thirds of the Member States before they come into force. The draft texts of proposed amendments shall be communicated by the Director-General to the Member States at least six months in advance of their consideration by the General Conference.

2. The General Conference shall have power to adopt by a two-thirds majority rules of procedure for carrying out the provisions of this Article.

ARTICLE XIV. — INTERPRETATION

1. The English and French texts of this Constitution shall be regarded as equally authoritative.

2. Any question or dispute concerning the interpretation of this Constitution shall be referred for determination to the International Court of Justice or to an arbitral tribunal, as the General Conference may determine under its rules of procedure.

ARTICLE XV. — ENTRY INTO FORCE

1. This Constitution shall be subject to acceptance. The instrument of acceptance shall be deposited with the Government of the United Kingdom.

2. This Constitution shall remain open for signature in the archives of the Government of the United Kingdom. Signature may take place either before of after the deposit of the instrument of acceptance. No acceptance shall be valid unless preceded or followed by signature.

3. This Constitution shall come into force when it has been accepted by twenty of its signatories. Subsequent acceptances shall take effect immediately.

4. The Government of the United Kingdom will inform all Members of the United Nations of the receipt of all instruments of acceptance and of the date on which the Constitution comes into force in accordance with the preceding paragraph.

In faith whereof, the undersigned, duly authorized to that effect, have signed this Constitution in English and French languages, both texts being equally authentic.

Done in London the sixteenth day of November, one thousand nine hundred and forty-five, in a single copy, in the English and French languages, of which certified copies will be communicated by the Government of the United Kingdom to the Governments of all the Members of the United Nations.

4. WORLD HEALTH ORGANIZATION

a. CONSTITUTION OF THE WORLD HEALTH ORGANIZATION, AMENDED AND BECAME EFFECTIVE OCTOBER 25, 1960[1]

THE STATES Parties to this Constitution declare, in conformity with the Charter of the United Nations, that the following principles are basic to the happiness, harmonious relations and security of all peoples:

Health is a state of complete physical, mental, and social well-being and not merely the absence of disease or infirmity.

The enjoyment of the highest attainable standard of health is one of the fundamental rights of every human being without distinction of race, religion, political belief, economic or social condition.

The health of all peoples is fundamental to the attainment of peace and security and is dependent upon the fullest co-operation of individuals and States.

The achievement of any State in the promotion and protection of health is of value to all.

Unequal development in different countries in the promotion of health and control of disease, especially communicable disease, is a common danger.

Healthy development of the child is of basic importance; the ability to live harmoniously in a changing total environment is essential to such development.

The extension to all peoples of the benefits of medical, psychological and related knowledge is essential to the fullest attainment of health.

Informed opinion and active co-operation on the part of the public are of the utmost importance in the improvement of the health of the people.

Governments have a responsibility for the health of their peoples which can be fulfilled only by the provision of adequate health and social measures.

ACCEPTING THESE PRINCIPLES, and for the purpose of cooperation among themselves and with others to promote and protect the health of all peoples, the Contracting Parties agree to the present Constitution and hereby establish the World Health Organization as a specialized agency within the terms of Article 57 of the Charter of the United Nations.

CHAPTER I — OBJECTIVE

Article 1

The objective of the World Health Organization (hereinafter called the Organization) shall be the attainment by all peoples of the highest possible level of health.

CHAPTER II — FUNCTIONS

Article 2

In order to achieve its objective, the functions of the Organization shall be:

(a) to act as the directing and co-ordinating authority on international health work;

(b) to establish and maintain effective collaboration with the United Nations, specialized agencies, governmental health administrations, professional groups and such other organizations as may be deemed appropriate;

---

[1] As published by the W.H.O.

(c) to assist Governments, upon request, in strengthening health services;

(d) to furnish appropriate technical assistance and, in emergencies, necessary aid upon the request or acceptance of Governments;

(e) to provide or assist in providing, upon the request of the United Nations, health services and facilities to special groups, such as the peoples of trust territories;

(f) to establish and maintain such administrative and technical services as may be required, including epidemiological and statistical services;

(g) to stimulate and advance work to eradicate epidemic, endemic and other diseases;

(h) to promote, in co-operation with other specialized agencies where necessary, the prevention of accidental injuries;

(i) to promote, in co-operation with other specialized agencies where necessary, the improvement of nutrition, housing, sanitation, recreation, economic or working conditions and other aspects of environmental hygiene;

(j) to promote co-operation among scientific and professional groups which contribute to the advancement of health;

(k) to propose conventions, agreements and regulations, and make recommendations with respect to international health matters and to perform such duties as may be assigned thereby to the Organization and are consistent with its objective;

(l) to promote maternal and child health and welfare and to foster the ability to live harmoniously in a changing total environment;

(m) to foster activities in the field of mental health, especially those affecting the harmony of human relations;

(n) to promote and conduct research in the field of health;

(o) to promote improved standards of teaching and training in the health, medical and related professions;

(p) to study and report on, in co-operation with other specialized agencies where necessary, administrative and social techniques affecting public health and medical care from preventive and curative points of view, including hospital services and social security;

(q) to provide information, counsel and assistance in the field of health;

(r) to assist in developing an informed public opinion among all peoples on matters of health;

(s) to establish and revise as necessary international nomenclatures of diseases, of causes of death and of public health practices;

(t) to standardize diagnostic procedures as necessary;

(u) to develop, establish and promote international standards with respect to food, biological, pharmaceutical and similar products;

(v) generally to take all necessary action to attain the objective of the Organization.

CHAPTER III — MEMBERSHIP AND ASSOCIATE MEMBERSHIP

Article 3

Membership in the Organization shall be open to all States.

Article 4

Members of the United Nations may become Members of the Organization by signing or otherwise accepting this Constitution in accordance with the provisions of Chapter XIX and in accordance with their constitutional processes.

Article 5

The States whose Governments have been invited to send observers to the International Health Conference held in New York, 1946, may become Members by signing or otherwise accepting this Constitution in accordance with the provisions of Chapter XIX and in accordance with their constitutional processes provided that such signature or acceptance shall be completed before the first session of the Health Assembly.

Article 6

Subject to the conditions of any agreement between the United Nations and the Organization, approved pursuant to Chapter XVI, States which do not become Members in accordance with Articles 4 and 5 may apply to become Members and shall be admitted as Members when their application has been approved by a simple majority vote of the Health Assembly.

Article 7

If a Member fails to meet its financial obligations to the Organization or in other exceptional circumstances, the Health Assembly may, on such conditions as it thinks proper, suspend the voting privileges and services to which a Member is entitled. The Health Assembly shall have the authority to restore such voting privileges and services.

Article 8

Territories or groups of territories which are not responsible for the conduct of their international relations may be admitted as Associate Members by the Health Assembly upon application made on behalf of such territory or group of territories by the Member or other authority having responsibility for their international relations. Representatives of Associate Members to the Health Assembly should be qualified by their technical competence in the field of health and should be chosen from the native population. The nature and extent of the rights and obligations of Associate Members shall be determined by the Health Assembly.

CHAPTER IV — ORGANS

Article 9

The work of the Organization shall be carried out by:
(a) The World Health Assembly (herein called the Health Assembly);
(b) The Executive Board (hereinafter called the Board);
(c) The Secretariat.

CHAPTER V — THE WORLD HEALTH ASSEMBLY

Article 10

The Health Assembly shall be composed of delegates representing Members.

Article 11

Each Member shall be represented by not more than three delegates, one of whom shall be designated by the Member as chief delegate. These delegates should be chosen from among persons most qualified by their technical competence in the field of health, preferably representing the national health administration of the Member.

Article 12

Alternates and advisers may accompany delegates.

Article 13

The Health Assembly shall meet in regular annual session and in such special sessions as may be necessary. Special sessions shall be convened at the request of the Board or of a majority of the Members.

Article 14

The Health Assembly, at each annual session, shall select the country or region in which the next annual session shall be held, the Board subsequently fixing the place. The Board shall determine the place where a special session shall be held.

Article 15

The Board, after consultation with the Secretary-General of the United Nations, shall determine the date of each annual and special session.

Article 16

The Health Assembly shall elect its President and other officers at the beginning of each annual session. They shall hold office until their successors are elected.

Article 17

The Health Assembly shall adopt its own rules of procedure.

Article 18

The functions of the Health Assembly shall be:

(a) to determine the policies of the Organization;
(b) to name the Members entitled to designate a person to serve on the Board;
(c) to appoint the Director-General;
(d) to review and approve reports and activities of the Board and of the Director-General and to instruct the Board in regard to matters upon which action, study, investigation or report may be considered desirable;
(e) to establish such committees as may be considered necessary for the work of the Organization;
(f) to supervise the financial policies of the Organization and to review and approve the budget;
(g) to instruct the Board and the Director-General to bring to the attention of Members and of international organizations, governmental or non-governmental, any matter with regard to health which the Health Assembly may consider appropriate;
(h) to invite any organization, international or national, governmental or non-governmental, which has responsibilities related to those of the Organization, to appoint representatives to participate, without right of vote, in its meetings or in those of the committees and conferences convened under its authority, on conditions prescribed by the Health Assembly; but in the case of national organizations, invitations shall be issued only with the consent of the Government concerned;
(i) to consider recommendations hearing on health made by the General Assembly, the Economic and Social Council, the Security Council or Trusteeship Council of the United Nations, and to report to them on the steps taken by the Organization to give effect to such recommendations;

(j) to report to the Economic and Social Council in accordance with any agreement between the Organization and the United Nations;

(k) to promote and conduct research in the field of health by the personnel of the Organization, by the establishment of its own institutions or by co-operation with official or non-official institutions of any Member with the consent of its Goverment;

(l) to establish such other institutions as it may consider desirable;

(m) to take any other appropriate action to further the objective of the Organization.

Article 19

The Health Assembly shall have authority to adopt conventions or agreements with respect to any matter within the competence of the Organization. A two-thirds vote of the Health Assembly shall be required for the adoption of such conventions or agreements, which shall come into force for each Member when accepted by it in accordance with its constitutional processes.

Article 20

Each Member undertakes that it will, within eighteen months after the adoption by the Health Assembly of a convention or agreement, take action relative to the acceptance of such convention or agreement. Each Member shall notify the Director-General of the action taken, and if it does not accept such convention or agreement within the time limit, it will furnish a statement of the reasons for non-acceptance. In case of acceptance, each Member agrees to make an annual report to the Director-General in accordance with Chapter XIV.

Article 21

The Health Assembly shall have authority to adopt regulations concerning:

(a) sanitary and quarantine requirements and other procedures designed to prevent the international spread of disease;

(b) nomenclatures with respect to diseases, causes of death and public health practices;

(c) standards with respect to diagnostic procedures for international use;

(d) standards with respect to the safety, purity and potency of biological, pharmaceutical and similar products moving in international commerce;

(e) advertising and labelling of biological, pharmaceutical and similar products moving in international commerce.

Article 22

Regulations adopted pursuant to Article 21 shall come into force for all Members after due notice has been given of their adoption by the Health Assembly except for such Members as may notify the Director-General of rejection or reservations within the period stated in the notice.

Article 23

The Health Assembly shall have authority to make recommendations to Members with respect to any matter within the competence of the Organization.

CHAPTER VI — THE EXECUTIVE BOARD

Article 24

The Board shall consist of twenty-four persons designated by as many Members. The Health Assembly, taking into account an equitable geographical distribution, shall elect the Members entitled to designate a person to serve on the Board. Each of these Members should appoint to the Board a person technically qualified in the field of health, who may be accompanied by alternates and advisers.

Article 25

These Members shall be elected for three years and may be re-elected, provided that of the twelve Members elected at the first session of the Health Assembly held after the coming into force of the amendment to this Constitution increasing the membership of the Board from eighteen to twenty-four the terms of two Members shall be for one year and the terms of two Members shall be for two years, as determined by lot.

Article 26

The Board shall meet at least twice a year and shall determine the place of each meeting.

Article 27

The Board shall elect its Chairman from among its members and shall adopt its own rules of procedure.

Article 28

The functions of the Board shall be:
(a) to give effect to the decisions and policies of the Health Assembly;
(b) to act as the executive organ of the Health Assembly;
(c) to perform any other functions entrusted to it by the Health Assembly;
(d) to advise the Health Assembly on questions referred to it by that body and on matters assigned to the Organization by conventions, agreements and regulations;
(e) to submit advice or proposals to the Health Assembly on its own initiative;
(f) to prepare the agenda of meetings of the Health Assembly;
(g) to submit to the Health Assembly for consideration and approval a general programme of work covering a specific period;
(h) to study all questions within its competence;
(i) to take emergency measures within the functions and financial resources of the Organization to deal with events requiring immediate action. In particular it may authorize the Director-General to take the necessary steps to combat epidemics, to participate in the organization of health relief to victims of a calamity and to undertake studies and research the urgency of which has been drawn to the attention of the Board by any Member or by the Director-General.

Article 29

The Board shall exercise on behalf of the whole Health Assembly the powers delegated to it by that body.

CHAPTER VII — THE SECRETARIAT

Article 30

The Secretariat shall comprise the Director-General and such technical and administrative staff as the Organization may require.

Article 31

The Director-General shall be appointed by the Health Assembly on the nomination of the Board on such terms as the Health Assembly determine. The Director-General, subject to the authority of the Board, shall be the chief technical and administrative officer of the Organization.

Article 32

The Director-General shall be *ex-officio* Secretary of the Health Assembly, of the Board, of all commissions and committees of the Organization and of conferences convened by it. He may delegate these functions.

Article 33

The Director-General or his representative may establish a procedure by agreement with Members, permitting him, for the purpose of discharging his duties, to have direct access to their various departments, especially to their health administrations and to national health organizations, governmental or non-governmental. He may also establish direct relations with international organizations whose activities come within the competence of the Organization. He shall keep regional offices informed on all matters involving their respective areas.

Article 34

The Director-General shall prepare and submit annually to the Board the financial statements and budget estimates of the Organization.

Article 35

The Director-General shall appoint the staff of the Secretariat in accordance with staff regulations established by the Health Assembly. The paramount consideration in the employment of the staff shall be to assure that the efficiency, integrity and internationally representative character of the Secretariat shall be maintained at the highest level. Due regard shall be paid also to the importance of recruiting the staff on as wide a geographical basis as possible.

Article 36

The conditions of service of the staff of the Organization shall conform as far as possible with those of other United Nations organizations.

Article 37

In the performance of their duties the Director-General and the staff shall not seek or receive instructions from any government or from any authority external to the Organization. They shall refrain from any action which might reflect on their position as international officers. Each Member of the Organization on its part undertakes to respect the exclusively international character of the Director-General and the staff and not to seek to influence them.

CHAPTER VIII — COMMITTEES

Article 38

The Board shall establish such committees as the Health Assembly may direct and, on its own initiative or on the proposal of the Director-General, may establish any other committees considered desirable to serve any purpose within the competence of the Organization.

Article 39

The Board, from time to time in any event annually, shall review the necessity for continuing each committee.

Article 40

The Board may provide for the creation of or the participation by the Organization in joint or mixed committees with other organizations and for the representation of the Organization in committees established by such other organizations.

CHAPTER IX — CONFERENCES

Article 41

The Health Assembly or the Board may convene local, general, technical or other special conferences to consider any matter within the competence of the Organization and may provide for the representation at such conferences of international organizations and, with the consent of the Government concerned, of national organizations, governmental or non-governmental. The manner of such representation shall be determined by the Health Assembly or the Board.

Article 42

The Board may provide for representation of the Organization at conferences in which the Board considers that the Organization has an interest.

CHAPTER X — HEADQUARTERS

Article 43

The location of the headquarters of the Organization shall be determined by the Health Assembly after consultation with the United Nations.

CHAPTER XI — REGIONAL ARRANGEMENTS

Article 44

(a) The Health Assembly shall from time to time define the geographical areas in which it is desirable to establish a regional organization.

(b) The Health Assembly may, with the consent of a majority of the Members situated within each area so defined, establish a regional organization to meet the special needs of such area. There shall not be more than one regional organization in each area.

Article 45

Each regional organization shall be an integral part of the Organization in accordance with this Constitution.

Article 46

Each regional organization shall consist of a regional committee and a regional office.

Article 47

Regional committees shall be composed of representatives of the Member States and Associate Members in the region concerned. Territories or groups of territories within the region, which are not responsible for the conduct of their international relations and which are not Associate Members, shall have the right to be represented and to participate in regional committees. The nature and extent of the rights and obligations of those territories or groups of territories in regional committees shall be determined by the Health Assembly in consultation with the Member or other authority having responsibility for the international relations of these territories and with the Member States in the region.

Article 48

Regional committees shall meet as often as necessary and shall determine the place of each meeting.

Article 49

Regional committees shall adopt their own rules of procedure.

Article 50

The functions of the regional committee shall be:

(a) to formulate policies governing matters of an exclusively regional character;
(b) to supervise the activities of the regional office;
(c) to suggest to the regional office the calling of technical conferences and such additional work or investigation in health matters as in the opinion of the regional committee would promote the objective of the Organization within the region;
(d) to co-operate with the respective regional committees of the United Nations and with those of other specialized agencies and with other regional international organizations having interests in common with the Organization;
(e) to tender advice, through the Director-General, to the Organization on international health matters which have wider than regional significance;
(f) to recommend additional regional appropriations by the Governments of the respective regions if the proportion of the central budget of the Organization allotted to that region is insufficient for the carrying-out of the regional functions;
(g) such other functions as may be delegated to the regional committee by the Health Assembly, the Board or the Director-General.

Article 51

Subject to the general authority of the Director-General of the Organization, the regional office shall be the administrative organ of the regional committee. It shall, in addition, carry out within the region the decisions of the Health Assembly and of the Board.

Article 52

The head of the regional office shall be the Regional Director appointed by the Board in agreement with the regional committee.

Article 53

The staff of the regional office shall be appointed in a manner to be determined by agreement between the Director-General and the Regional Director.

Article 54

The Pan American Sanitary Organization represented by the Pan American Sanitary Bureau and the Pan American Sanitary Conferences, and all other inter-governmental regional health organizations in existence prior to the date of signature of this Constitution, shall in due course be integrated with the Organization. This integration shall be effected as soon as practicable through common action based on mutual consent of the competent authorities expressed through the organizations concerned.

CHAPTER XII — BUDGET AND EXPENSES

Article 55

The Director-General shall prepare and submit to the Board the annual budget estimates of the Organization. The Board shall consider and submit to the Health Assembly such budget estimates, together with any recommendations the Board may deem advisable.

Article 56

Subject to any agreement between the Organization and the United Nations, the Health Assembly shall review and approve the budget estimates and shall apportion the expenses among the Members in accordance with a scale to be fixed by the Health Assembly.

Article 57

The Health Assembly or the Board acting on behalf of the Health Assembly may accept and administer gifts and bequests made to the Organization provided that the conditions attached to such gifts or bequests are acceptable to the Health Assembly or the Board and are consistent with the objective and policies of the Organization.

Article 58

A special fund to be used at the discretion of the Board shall be established to meet emergencies and unforessen contingencies.

CHAPTER XIII — VOTING

Article 59

Each Member shall have one vote in the Health Assembly.

Article 60

(a) Decisions of the Health Assembly on important questions shall be made by a two-thirds majority of the Members present and voting. These questions shall include: the adoption of conventions or agreements; the approval of agreements bringing the Organization into relation with the United Nations and inter-governmental organizations and agencies in accordance with Articles 69, 70 and 72; amendments to this Constitution.

(b) Decisions on other questions, including the determination of additional categories of questions to be decided by a two-thirds majority, shall be made by a majority of the Members present and voting.

(c) Voting on analogous matters in the Board and in committees of the Organization shall be made in accordance with paragraphs *(a)* and *(b)* of this Article.

CHAPTER XIV — REPORTS SUBMITTED BY STATES

Article 61

Each Member shall report annually to the Organization on the action taken and progress achieved in improving the health of its people.

Article 62

Each Member shall report annually on the action taken with respect to recommendations made to it by the Organization and with respect to conventions, agreements and regulations.

Article 63

Each Member shall communicate promptly to the Organization important laws, regulations, official reports and statistics pertaining to health which have been published in the State concerned.

Article 64

Each Member shall provide statistical and epidemiological reports in a manner to be determined by the Health Assembly.

Article 65

Each Member shall transmit upon the request of the Board such additional information pertaining to health as may be practicable.

CHAPTER XV — LEGAL CAPACITY, PRIVILEGES AND IMMUNITIES

Article 66

The Organization shall enjoy in the territory of each Member such legal capacity as may be necessary for the fulfilment of its objective and for the exercise of its functions.

Article 67

(a) The Organization shall enjoy in the territory of each Member such privileges and immunities as may be necessary for the fulfilment of its objective and for the exercise of its functions.

(b) Representatives of Members, persons designated to serve on the Board and technical and administrative personnel of the Organization shall similarly enjoy such privileges and immunities as are necessary for the independent exercise of their functions in connexion with the Organization.

Article 68

Such legal capacity, privileges and immunities shall be defined in a separate agreement to be prepared by the Organization in consultation with the Secretary-General of the United Nations and concluded between the Members.

CHAPTER XVI — RELATIONS WITH OTHER ORGANIZATIONS

Article 69

The Organization shall be brought into relation with the United Nations as one of the specialized agencies referred to in Article 57 of the Charter of the United Nations. The agreement or agreements bringing the Organization into relation with the United Nations shall be subject to approval by a two-thirds vote of the Health Assembly.

Article 70

The Organization shall establish effective relations and cooperate closely with such other inter-governmental organizations as may be desirable. Any formal agreement entered into with such organizations shall be subject to approval by a two-thirds vote of the Health Assembly.

Article 71

The Organization may, on matters within its competence, make suitable arrangements for consultation and co-operation with non-governmental international organizations and, with the consent of the Government concerned, with national organizations, governmental or non-governmental.

Article 72

Subject to the approval by a two-thirds vote of the Health Assembly, the Organization may take over from any other international organization or agency whose purpose and activities lie within the field of competence of the Organization such functions, resources and obligations as may be conferred upon the Organization by international agreement or by mutually acceptable arrangements entered into between the competent authorities of the respective organizations.

CHAPTER XVII — AMENDMENTS

Article 73

Texts of proposed amendments to this Constitution shall be communicated by the Director-General to Members at least six months in advance of their consideration by the Health Assembly. Amendments shall come into force for all Members when adopted by a two-thirds vote of the Health Assembly and accepted by two-thirds of the Members in accordance with their respective constitutional processes.

CHAPTER XVIII — INTERPRETATION

Article 74

The Chinese, English, French, Russian and Spanish texts of this Constitution shall be regarded as equally authentic.

Article 75

Any question or dispute concerning the interpretation or application of this Constitution which is not settled by negotiation or by the Health Assembly shall be referred to the International Court of Justice in conformity with the Statute of the Court, unless the parties concerned agree on another mode of settlement.

107

Article 76

Upon authorization by the General Assembly of the United Nations or upon authorization in accordance with any agreement between the Organization and the United Nations, the Organization may request the International Court of Justice for an advisory opinion on any legal question arising within the competence of the Organization.

Article 77

The Director-General may appear before the Court on behalf of the Organization in connexion with any proceedings arising out of any such request for an advisory opinion. He shall make arrangements for the presentation of the case before the Court, including arrangements for the argument of different views on the question.

CHAPTER XIX — ENTRY-INTO-FORCE

Article 78

Subject to the provisions of Chapter III, this Constitution shall remain open to all States for signature or acceptance.

Article 79

(a) States may become parties to this Constitution by
   (i) signature without reservation as to approval;
   (ii) signature subject to approval followed by acceptance; or
   (iii) acceptance.

(b) Acceptance shall be effected by the deposit of a formal instrument with the Secretary-General of the United Nations.

Article 80

This Constitution shall come into force when twenty-six Members of the United Nations have become parties to it in accordance with the provisions of Article 79.

Article 81

In accordance with Article 102 of the Charter of the United Nations, the Secretary-General of the United Nations will register this Constitution when it has been signed without reservation as to approval on behalf of one State or upon deposit of the first instrument of acceptance.

Article 82

The Secretary-General of the United Nations will inform States parties to this Constitution of the date when it has come into force. He will also inform them of the dates when other States have become parties to this Constitution.

IN FAITH WHEREOF the undersigned representatives, having been duly authorized for that purpose, sign this Constitution.

DONE in the City of New York this twenty-second day of July 1946, in a single copy in the Chinese, English, French, Russian and Spanish languages, each text being equally authentic. The original texts shall be deposited in the archives of the United Nations. The Secretary-General of the United Nations will send certified copies to each of the Governments represented at the Conference.

5. INTERNATIONAL BANK FOR RECONSTRUCTION
AND DEVELOPMENT

a. ARTICLES OF AGREEMENT OF THE INTERNATIONAL
BANK FOR RECONSTRUCTION AND DEVELOPMENT,
AMENDED AND BECAME EFFECTIVE
DECEMBER 17, 1965

LIST OF ARTICLES AND SECTIONS

ARTICLES OF AGREEMENT OF THE INTERNATIONAL BANK FOR RECONSTRUCTION AND DEVELOPMENT

(As amended effective December 17, 1965)

The Government on whose behalf the present Agreement is signed agree as follows:

INTRODUCTORY ARTICLE

The International Bank for Reconstruction and Development is established and shall operate in accordance with the following provisions:

ARTICLE I

PURPOSES

The purposes of the Bank are:

  (i) To assist in the reconstruction and development of territories of members by facilitating the investment of capital for productive purposes, including the restoration of economies destroyed or disrupted by war, the reconversion of productive facilities to peacetime needs and the encouragement of the development of productive facilities and resources in less developed countries.

 (ii) To promote private foreign investment by means of guarantees or participations in loans and other investments made by private investors; and when private capital is not available on reasonable terms, to supplement private investment by providing, on suitable conditions, finance for productive purposes out of its own capital, funds raised by it and its other resources.

(iii) To promote the long-range balanced growth of international trade and the maintenance of equilibrium in balances of payments by encouraging international investment for the development of the productive resources of members, thereby assisting in raising productivity, the standard of living and conditions of labor in their territories.

 (iv) To arrange the loans made or guaranteed by it in relation to international loans through other channels so that the more useful and urgent projects, large and small alike, will be dealt with first.

 (v) To conduct its operations with due regard to the effect of international investment on business conditions in the territories of members and, in the immediate postwar years, to assist in bringing about a smooth transition from a wartime to a peacetime economy.

The Bank shall be guided in all its decisions by the purposes set forth above.

ARTICLE II

MEMBERSHIP IN AND CAPITAL OF THE BANK

Section 1. *Membership*

(a) The original members of the Bank shall be those members of the International Monetary Fund which accept membership in the Bank before the date specified in Article XI, Section 2(e).

(b) Membership shall be open to other members of the Fund, at such times and in accordance with such terms as may prescribed by the Bank.

Section 2. *Authorized capital*

(a) The authorized capital of the Bank shall be $10,000,000,000,* in terms of United States dollars of the weight and fineness in effect on July 1, 1944. The capital stock shall be divided into 100,000 shares having a par value of $100,000 each, which shall be available for subscription only by members.

(b) The capital stock may be increased when the Bank deems it advisable by a three-fourths majority of the total voting power.

Section 3. *Subscription of shares*

(a) Each member shall subscribe shares of the capital stock of the Bank. The minimum number of shares to be subscribed by the original members shall be those set forth in Schedule A. The minimum number of shares to be subscribed by other members shall be determined by the Bank, which shall reserve a sufficient portion of its capital stocks for subscription by such members.

(b) The Bank shall prescribe rules laying down the conditions under which members may subscribe shares of the authorized capital stock of the Bank in addition to their minimum subscriptions.

(c) If the authorized capital stock of the Bank in increased, each member shall have a reasonable opportunity to subscribe, under such conditions as the Bank shall decide, a proportion of the increase of stock equivalent to the proportion which its stock theretofore subscribed bears to the total capital stock of the Bank, but no member shall be obligated to subscribe any part of the increased capital.

Section 4. *Issue price of shares*

Shares included in the minimum subscriptions of original members shall be issued at par. Other shares shall be issued at par unless the Bank by a majority of the total voting power decides in special circumstances to issue them on other terms.

Section 5. *Division and calls of subscribed capital*

The subscription of each member shall be divided into two parts as follows:
(i) twenty percent shall be paid or subject to call under Section 7 (i) of this Article as needed by the Bank for its operations;
(ii) the remaining eighty percent shall be subject to call by the Bank only when required to meet obligations of the Bank created under Article IV, Sections 1 (a) (ii) and (iii).
Calls on unpaid subscriptions shall be uniform on all shares.

Section 6. *Limitation on liability*

Liability or shares shall be limited to the unpaid portion of the issue price of the shares.

Section 7. *Method of payment of subscriptions for shares*

Payment of subscriptions for shares shall be made in gold or United States dollars and in the currencies of the members as follows:
(i) under Section 5 (i) if this Article, two percent of the price of each share shall be payable in gold or United States dollars, and, when calls are made, the remaining eighteen percent shall be paid in the currency of the member;
(ii) when a call is made under Section 5 (ii) of this Article, payment may be made at the option of the member either in gold, in United States dollars or in the currency required to discharge the obligations of the Bank for the purpose for which the call is made;

---

*As of December 31, 1970, the authorized capital stock of the Bank had been increased to $27,000,000,000, divided into 270,000 shares having a par value of $100,000 each.

(iii) when a member makes payments in any currency under (i) and (ii) above, such payments shall be made in amounts equal in value to the member's liability under the call. This liability shall be a proportionate part of the subscribed capital stock of the Bank as authorized and defined in Section 2 of this Article.

Section 8. *Time of payment of subscriptions*

(a) The two percent payable on each share in gold or United States dollars under Section 7 (i) of this Article, shall be paid within sixty days of the date on which the Bank begins operations, provided that

(i) any original member of the Bank whose metropolitan territory has suffered from enemy occupation or hostilities during the present war shall be granted the right to postpone payment of one-half percent until five years after that date;

(ii) an original member who cannot make such a payment because it has not recovered possession of its gold reserves which are still seized or immobilized as a result of the war may postpone all payment until such date as the Bank shall decide.

(b) The remainder of the price of each share payable under Section 7 (i) of this Article shall be paid as and when called by the Bank, provided that

(i) the Bank shall, within one year of its beginning operations, call not less than eight percent of the price of the share in addition to the payment of two percent referred to in (a) above;

(ii) not more than five percent of the price of the share shall be called in any period of three months.

Section 9. *Maintenance of value of certain currency holdings of the Bank*

(a) Whenever (i) the par value of a member's currency is reduced, or (ii) the foreign exchange value of a member's currency has, in the opinion of the Bank, depreciated to a significant extent within that member's territories, the member shall pay to the Bank within a reasonable time an additional amount of its own currency sufficient to maintain the value, as of the time of initial subscription, of the amount of the currency of such member which is held by the Bank and derived from currency originally paid in to the Bank by the member under Article II, Section 7 (i), from currency referred to in Article IV, Section 2 (b), or from any additional currency furnished under the provisions of the present paragraph, and which has not been repurchased by the member for gold or for the currency of any member which is acceptable to the Bank.

(b) Whenever the par value of a member's currency in increased, the Bank shall return to such member within a reasonable time an amount of that member's currency equal to the increase in the value of the amount of such currency described in (a) above.

(c) The provisions of the preceding paragraphs may be waived by the Bank when a uniform proportionate change in the par values of the currencies of all its members is made by the International Monetary Fund.

Section 10. *Restriction on disposal of shares*

Shares shall not be pledged on encumbered in any manner whatever and they shall be transferable only to the Bank.

ARTICLE III

GENERAL PROVISIONS RELATING TO LOANS AND GUARANTEES

Section 1. *Use of resources*

(a) The resources and the facilities of the Bank shall be used exclusively for the benefit of members with equitable consideration to projects for development and projects for reconstruction alike.

(b) For the purpose of facilitating the restoration and reconstruction of the economy of members whose metropolitan territories have suffered great devastation from enemy occupation or hostilities, the Bank, in determining the conditions and terms of loans made to such members, shall pay special regard to lightening the financial burden and expediting the completion of such restoration and reconstruction.

Section 2. *Dealings between members and the Bank*

Each member shall deal with the Bank only through its Treasury, central bank, stabilization fund or other similar fiscal agency, and the Bank shall deal with members only by or through the same agencies.

Section 3. *Limitations on guarantees and borrowings of the Bank*

The total amount oustanding of guarantees, participations in loans and direct loans made by the Bank shall not be increased at any time, if by such increase the total would exceed one hundred percent of the unimpaired subscribed capital, reserves and surplus of the Bank.

Section 4. *Conditions on which the Bank may guarantee or make loans*

The Bank may guarantee, participate in, or make loans to any member or any political sub-division thereof and any business, industrial, and agricultural enterprise in the territories of a member, subject to the following conditions:

(i) When the member in whose territories the project is located is not itself the borrower, the member or the central bank or some comparable agency of the member which is acceptable to the Bank, fully guarantees the repayment of the principal and the payment of interest and other charges on the loan.

(ii) The Bank is satisfied than in the prevailing marked conditions the borrower would be unable otherwise to obtain the loan under conditions which in the opinion of the Bank are reasonable for the borrower.

(iii) A competent committee, as provided for in Article V, Section 7, has submitted a written report recommending the project after a careful study of the merits of the proposal.

(iv) In the opinion of the Bank the rate of interest and other charges are reasonable and such rate, charges and the schedule for repayment of principal are appropriate to the project.

(v) In making or guaranteeing a loan, the Bank shall pay due regard to the prospects that the borrower, and, if the borrower is not a member, that the guarantor, will be in position to meet its obligations under the loan; and the Bank shall act prudently in the interests both of the particular member in whose territories the project is located and of the members as a whole.

(vi) In guaranteeing a loan made by other investors, the Bank receives suitable compensation for its risk.

(vii) Loans made or guaranteed by the Bank shall, except in special circumstances, be for the purpose of specific projects of reconstruction or development.

Section 5. *Use of loans guaranteed, participated in or made by the Bank*

(a) The Bank shall impose no conditions that the proceeds of a loan shall be spent in the territories of any particular member or members.

(b) The Bank shall make arrangements to ensure that the proceeds of any loan are used only for the purposes for which the loan was granted, with due attention to considerations of economy and efficiency and without regard to political or other non-economic influences or considerations.

(c) In the case of loans made by the Bank, it shall open an account in the name of the borrower and the amount of the loan shall be credited to this account in the currency or currencies in which the loan is made. The borrower shall be permitted by the Bank to draw on this account only to meet expenses in connection with the project as they are actually incurred.

Section 6. *Loans to the International Finance Corporation**

(a) The Bank may make, participate in, or guarantee loans to the International Finance Corporation, an affiliate of the Bank, for use in its lending operations. The total amount outstanding of such loans, participations and guarantees shall not be increased if, at the time or as a result thereof, the aggregate amount of debt (including the guarantee of any debt) incurred by the said Corporation from any source and then outstanding shall exceed an amount equal to four times its unimpaired subscribed capital and surplus.

(b) The provisions of Article III, Sections 4 and 5 (c) and of Article IV, Section 3 shall not apply to loans, participations and guarantees authorized by this Section.

ARTICLE IV

OPERATIONS

Section 1. *Methods of making or facilitating loans*

(a) The Bank may make or facilitate loans which satisfy the general conditions of Article III in any of the following ways:
  (i) By making or participating in direct loans out of its own funds corresponding to its unimpaired paid-up capital and surplus and, subject to Section 6 of this Article, to its reserves.
 (ii) By making or participating in direct loans out of funds raised in the market of a member, or otherwise borrowed by the Bank.
(iii) By guaranteeing in whole or in part loans made by private investors through the usual investment channels.

(b) The Bank may borrow funds under (a) (ii) above or guarantee loans under (a) (iii) above only with the approval of the member in whose markets the funds are raised and the member in whose currency the loan is denominated, and only if those members agree that the proceeds may be exchanged for the currency of any other member without restriction.

Section 2. *Availability and transferability of currencies*

(a) Currencies paid into the Bank under Article II, Section 7 (i), shall be loaned only with the approval in each case of the member whose currency is involved; provided, however, that if necessary, after the Bank's subscribed capital has been entirely called, such currencies shall, without restriction by the members whose currencies are offered, be used or exchanged for the currencies required to meet contractual payments of interest, other charges or amortization on the Bank's own borrowings, or to meet the Bank's liabilities with respect to such contractual payments on loans guaranteed by the Bank.

---

*Section added by amendment effective December 17, 1965.

115

(b) Currencies received by the Bank from borrowers or guarantors in payment on account of principal of direct loans made with currencies referred to in (a) above shall be exchanged for the currencies of other members or reloaned only with the approval in each case of the members whose currencies are involved; provided, however, that if necessary, after the Bank's subscribed capital has been entirely called, such currencies shall, without restriction by the members whose currencies are offered, be used or exchanged for the currencies required to meet contractual payments of interest, other charges or amortization on the Bank's own borrowings, or to meet the Bank's liabilities with respect to such contractual payments on loans guaranteed by the Bank.

(c) Currencies received by the Bank from borrowers or guarantors in payment on account of principal of direct loans made by the Bank under Section 1 (a) (ii) of this Article, shall be held and used, without restriction by the members, to make amortization payments, or to anticipate payment of or repurchase part or all of the Bank's own obligations.

(d) All other currencies available to the Bank, including those raised in the market or otherwise borrowed under Section 1 (a) (ii) of this Article, those obtained by the sale of gold, those received as payments of interest and other charges for direct loans made under Sections 1 (a) (i) and (ii), and those received as payments of commissions and other charges under Section 1 (a) (iii), shall be used or exchanged for other currencies or gold required in the operations of the Bank without restriction by the members whose currencies are offered.

(e) Currencies raised in the markets of members by borrowers on loans guaranteed by the Bank under Section 1 (a) (iii) of this Article, shall also be used or exchanged for other currencies without restriction by such members.

Section 3. *Provision of currencies for direct loans*

The following provisions shall apply to direct loans under Sections 1 (a) (i) and (ii) of this Article:

(a) The Bank shall furnish the borrower with such currencies of members, other than the member in whose territories the project is located, as are needed by the borrower for expenditures to be made in the territories of such other members to carry out the purpose of the loan.

(b) The Bank may, in exceptional circumstances when local currency required for the purposes of the loan cannot be raised by the borrower on reasonable terms, provide the borrower as part of the loan with an appropriate amount of that currency.

(c) The Bank, if the project gives rise indirectly to an increased need for foreign exchange by the member in whose territories the project is located, may in exceptional circumstances provide the borrower as part of the loan with an appropriate amount of gold or foreign exchange not in excess of the borrower's local expenditure in connection with the purposes of the loan.

(d) The Bank may, in exceptional circumstances, at the request of a member in whose territories a portion of the loan is spent, repurchase with gold or foreign exchange a part of that member's currency thus spent but in no case shall the part so repurchased exceed the amount by which the expenditure of the loan in those territories gives rise to an increased need for foreign exchange.

Section 4. *Payment provisions for direct loans*

Loan contracts under Section 1 (a) (i) or (ii) of this Article shall be made in accordance with the following payment provisions:

(a) The terms and conditions of interest and amortization payments, maturity and dates of payment of each loan shall be determined by the Bank. The Bank shall also determine the rate and any other terms and conditions of commission to be charged in connection with such loan.

In the case of loans made under Section 1 (a) (ii) of this Article during the first ten years of the Bank's operations, this rate of commission shall be not less than one percent per annum and not greater than one and one-half percent per annum, and shall be charged on the outstanding portion of any such loan. At the end of this period of ten years, the rate of commission may be reduced by the Bank with respect both to the outstanding portions of loans already made and to future loans, if the reserves accumulated by the Bank under Section 6 of this Article and out of other earnings are considered by it sufficient to justify a reduction. In the case of future loans the Bank shall also have discretion to increase the rate of commission beyond the above limit, if experience indicates that an increase in advisable.

(b) All loan contracts shall stipulate the currency or currencies in which payments under the contract shall be made to the Bank. At the option of the borrower, however, such payments may be made in gold, or subject to the agreement of the Bank, in the currency of a member other than that prescribed in the contract.

(i) In the case of loans made under Section 1 (a) (i) of this Article, the loan contracts shall provide that payments to the Bank of interest, other charges and amortization shall be made in the currency loaned, unless the member whose currency is loaned agrees that such payments shall be made in some other specified currency or currencies. These payments, subject to the provisions of Article II, Section 9 (c), shall be equivalent to the value of such contractual payments at the time the loans were made, in terms of a currency specified for the purpose by the Bank by a three-fourths majority of the total voting power.

(ii) In the case of loans made under Section 1 (a) (ii) of this Article, the total amount outstanding and payable to the Bank in any one currency shall at no time exceed the total amount of the outstanding borrowings made by the Bank under Section 1 (a) (ii) and payable in the same currency.

(c) If a member suffers from an acute exchange stringency, so that the service of any loan contracted by that member or guaranteed by it or by one of its agencies cannot be provided in the stipulated manner, the member concerned may apply to the Bank for a relaxation of the conditions of payment. If the Bank is satisfied that some relaxation is in the interests of the particular member and of the operations of the Bank and of its members as a whole, it may take action under either, or both, of the following paragraphs with respect to the whole, or part, of the annual service:

(i) The Bank may, in its discretion, make arrangements with the member concerned to accept service payments on the loan in the member's currency for periods not to exceed three years upon appropriate terms regarding the use of such currency and the maintenance of its foreign exchange value; and for the repurchase of such currency on appropriate terms.

(ii) The Bank may modify the terms of amortization or extend the life of the loan, or both.

Section 5. *Guarantees*

(a) In guaranteeing a loan placed through the usual investment channels, the Bank shall charge a guarantee commission payable periodically on the amount of the loan outstanding at a rate determined by the Bank. During the first ten years of the Bank's operations, this rate shall be not less than one percent per annum and not greater than one and one-half percent annum. At the end of this period of ten years, the rate of commission may be reduced by the Bank with respect both to the outstanding portions of loans already guaranteed and to future loans if the reserves accumulated by the Bank under Section 6 of this Article and out of other earnings are considered by it sufficient to justify a reduction. In the case of future loans the Bank shall also have discretion to increase the rate of commission beyond the above limit, if experience indicates that an increase is advisable.

(b) Guarantee commissions shall be paid directly to the Bank by the borrower.

(c) Guarantees by the Bank shall provide that the Bank may terminate its liability with respect to interest if, upon default by the borrower and by the guarantor, if any, the Bank offers to purchase, at par and interest accrued to a date designated in the offer, the bonds or other obligations guaranteed.

(d) The Bank shall have power to determine any other terms and conditions of the guarantee.

Section 6. *Special reserve*

The amount of commissions received by the Bank under Sections 4 and 5 of this Article shall be set aside as a special reserve, which shall be kept available for meeting liabilities of the Bank in accordance with Section 7 of this Article. The special reserve shall be held in such liquid form, permitted under this Agreement, as the Executive Directors may decide.

Section 7. *Methods of meeting liabilities of the Bank in case of defaults*

In cases of default on loans made, participated in, or guaranteed by the Bank:

(a) The Bank shall make such arrangements as may be feasible to adjust the obligations under the loans, including arrangements under or analogous to those provided in Section 4 (c) of this Article.

(b) The payments in discharge of the Bank's liabilities on borrowings or guarantees under Section 1 (a) (ii) and (iii) of this Article shall be charged:
  (i)   first, against the special reserve provided in Section 6 of this Article.
  (ii) then, to the extent necessary and at the discretion of the Bank, against the other reserves, surplus and capital available to the Bank.

(c) Whenever necessary to meet contractual payments of interest, other charges or amortization on the Bank's own borrowings, or to meet the Bank's liabilities with respect to similar payments on loans guaranteed by it, the Bank may call an appropriate amount of the unpaid subscriptions of members in accordance with Article II. Sections 5 and 7. Moreover, if it believes that a default may be of long duration, the Bank may call an additional amount of such unpaid subscriptions not to exceed in any one year one percent of the total subscriptions of the members for the following purposes:
  (i)   To redeem prior to maturity, or otherwise discharge its liability on, all or part of the outstanding principal of any loan guaranteed by it in respect of which the debtor is in default.
  (ii) To repurchase, or otherwise discharge its liability on, all or part of its own outstanding borrowings.

Section 8. *Miscellaneous operations*

In addition to the operations specified elsewhere in this Agreement, the Bank shall have the power:
  (i)   To buy and sell securities it has issued and to buy and sell securities which it has guaranteed or in which it has invested, provided that the Bank shall obtain the approval of the member in whose territories the securities are to be bought or sold.
  (ii) To guarantee securities in which it has invested for the purpose of facilitating their sale.
  (iii) To borrow the currency of any member with the approval of that member.
  (iv) To buy and sell such other securities as the Directors by a three-fourths majority of the total voting power may deem proper for the investment of all or part of the special reserve under Section 6 of this Article.

In exercising the powers conferred by this Section, the Bank may deal with any person, partnership, association, corporation or other legal entity in the territories of any member.

Section 9. *Warning to be placed on securities*

Every security guaranteed or issued by the Bank shall bear on its face a conspicuous statement to the effect that it is not an obligation of any government unless expressly stated on the security.

Section 10. *Political activity prohibited*

The Bank and its officers shall not interfere in the political affairs of any member; nor shall they be influenced in their decisions by the political character of the member or members concerned. Only economic considerations shall be relevant to their decisions, and these considerations shall be weighed impartially in order to achieve the purposes stated in Article I.

ARTICLE V

ORGANIZATION AND MANAGEMENT

Section 1. *Structure of the Bank*

The Bank shall have a Board of Governors, Executive Directors, a President and such other officers and staff to perform such duties as the Bank may determine.

Section 2. *Board of Governors*

(a) All the powers of the Bank shall be vested in the Board of Governors consisting of one governor and one alternate appointed by each member in such manner as it may determine. Each governor and each alternate shall serve for five years, subject to the pleasure of the member appointing him, and may be reappointed. No alternate may vote except in the absence of his principal. The Board shall select one of the governors as Chairman.

(b) The Board of Governors may delegate to the Executive Directors authority to exercise any powers of the Board, except the power to:
   (i) Admit new members and determine the conditions of their admission;
   (ii) Increase or decrease the capital stock;
   (iii) Suspend a member;
   (iv) Decide appeals from interpretations of this Agreement given by the Executive Directors;
   (v) Make arrangements to cooperate with other international organizations (other than informal arrangements of a temporary and administrative character);
   (vi) Decide to suspend permanently the operations of the Bank and to distribute its assets;
   (vii) Determine the distribution of the net income of the Bank.

(c) The Board of Governors shall hold an annual meeting and such other meetings as may be provided for by the Board or called by the Executive Directors. Meetings of the Board shall be called by the Directors whenever requested by five members or by members having one-quarter of the total voting power.

(d) A quorum for any meeting of the Board of Governors shall be a majority of the Governors, exercising not less than two-thirds of the total voting power.

(e) The Board of Governors may by regulation establish a procedure whereby the Executive Directors, when they deem such action to be in the best interests of the Bank, may obtain a vote of the Governors on a specific question without calling a meeting of the Board.

(f) The Board of Governors, and the Executive Directors to the extent authorized, may adopt such rules and regulations as may be necessary or appropriate to conduct the business of the Bank.

(g) Governors and alternates shall serve as such without compensation from the Bank, but the Bank shall pay them reasonable expenses incurred in attending meetings.

(h) The Board of Governors shall determine the remuneration to be paid to the Executive Directors and the salary and terms of the contract of service of the President.

Section 3. *Voting*

(a) Each member shall have two hundred fifty votes plus one additional vote for each share of stock held.

(b) Except as otherwise specifically provided, all matters before the Bank shall be decided by a majority of the votes cast.

Section 4. *Executive Directors*

(a) The Executive Directors shall be responsible for the conduct of the general operations of the Bank, and for this purpose, shall exercise all the powers delegated to them by the Board of Governors.

(b) There shall be twelve Executive Directors, who need not be governors, and of whom:

(i) five shall be appointed, one by each of the five members having the largest number of shares;

(ii) seven shall be elected according to Schedule B by all the Governors other than those appointed by the five members referred to in (i) above.

For the purpose of this paragraph, "members" means governments of countries whose names are set forth in Schedule A, whether they are original members or become members in accordance with Article II, Section 1 (b). When governments of other countries become members, the Board of Governors may, by a four-fifths majority of the total voting power, increase the total number of directors by increasing the number of directors to be elected.

Executive directors shall be appointed or elected every two years.

(c) Each executive director shall appoint an alternate with full power to act for him when he is not present. When the executive directors appointing them are present, alternates may participate in meetings but shall not vote.

(d) Directors shall continue in office until their successors are appointed or elected. If the office of an elected director becomes vacant more than ninety days before the end of his term, another directors shall be elected for the remainder of the term by the governors who elected the former director. A majority of the votes cast be required for election. While the office remains vacant, the alternate of the former director shall exercise his powers, except that of appointing an alternate.

(e) The Executive Directors shall function in continuous session at the principal office of the Bank and shall meet as often as the business of the Bank may require.

(f) A quorum for any meeting of the Executive Directors shall be a majority of the Directors, exercising not less than one-half of the total voting power.

(g) Each appointed director shall be entitled to cast the number of votes allotted under Section 3 of this Article to the member appointing him. Each elected director shall be entitled to cast the number of votes which counted toward his election. All the votes which a director is entitled to cast shall be cast as a unit.

(h) The Board of Governors shall adopt regulations under which a member not entitled to appoint a director under (b) above may send a representative to attend any meeting of the Executive Directors when a request made by, or a matter particularly affecting, that member is under consideration.

(i) The Executive Directors may appoint such committees as they deem advisable. Membership of such committees need not be limited to governors or directors or their alternates.

Section 5. *President and staff*

(a) The Executive Directors shall select a President who shall not be a governor or an executive director or an alternate for either. The President shall be Chairman of the Executive Directors, but shall have no vote except a deciding vote in case of an equal division. He may participate in meetings of the Board of Governors, but shall not vote at such meetings. The President shall cease to hold office when the Executive Directors so decide.

(b) The President shall be chief of the operating staff of the Bank and shall conduct, under the direction of the Executive Directors, the ordinary business of the Bank. Subject to the general control of the Executive Directors, he shall be responsible for the organization, appointment and dismissal of the officers and staff.

(c) The President, officers and staff of the Bank, in the discharge of their offices, owe their duty entirely to the Bank and to no other authority. Each member of the Bank shall respect the international character of this duty and shall refrain from all attempts to influence any of them in the discharge of their duties.

(d) In appointing the officers and staff the President shall, subject to the paramount importance of securing the highest standards of efficiency and of technical competence, pay due regard to the importance of recruiting personnel on as wide a geographical basis as possible.

Section 6. *Advisory Council*

(a) There shall be an Advisory Council of not less than seven persons selected by the Board of Governors including representatives of banking, commercial, industrial, labor, and agricultural interests, and with as wide a national representation as possible. In those fields where specialized international organizations exist, the members of the Council representative of those fields shall be selected in agreement with such organizations. The Council shall advise the Bank on matters of general policy. The Council shall meet annually and on such other occassions as the Bank may request.

(b) Councillors shall serve for two years and may be reappointed. They shall be paid their reasonable expenses incurred on behalf of the Bank.

Section 7. *Loan committees*

The committees required to report on loans under Article III, Section 4, shall be appointed by the Bank. Each such committee shall include an expert selected by the governor representing the member in whose territories the project is located and one or more members of the technical staff of the Bank.

Section 8. *Relationship to other international organizations*

(a) The Bank, within the terms of this Agreement, shall cooperate with any general international organization and with public international organizations having specialized responsibilities in related fields. Any arrangements for such cooperation which would involve a modification of any provision of this Agreement may be effected only after amendment to this Agreement under Article VIII.

(b) In making decisions on applications for loans or guarantees relating to matters directly within the competence of any international organization of the types specified in the preceding paragraph and participated in primarily by members of the Bank, the Bank shall give consideration to the views and recommendations of such organization.

Section 9. *Location of offices*

(a) The principal office of the Bank shall be located in the territory of the member holding the greatest number of shares.

(b) The Bank may establish agencies or branch offices in the territories of any member of the Bank.

Section 10. *Regional offices and councils*

(a) The Bank may establish regional offices and determine the location of, and the areas to be covered by, each regional office.

(b) Each regional office shall be advised by a regional council representative of the entire area and selected in such manner as the Bank may decide.

Section 11. *Depositories*

(a) Each member shall designate its central bank as a depository for all the Bank's holdings of its currency or, if it has no central bank, it shall designate such other institution as may be acceptable to the Bank.

(b) The Bank may hold other assets, including gold, in depositories designated by the five members having the largest number of shares and in such other designated depositories as the Bank may select. Initially, at least one-half of the gold holdings of the Bank shall be held in the depository designated by the member in whose territory the Bank has its principal office, and at least forty percent shall be held in the depositories designated by the remaining four members referred to above, each of such depositories to hold, initially, not less than the amount of gold paid on the shares of the member designating it. However, all transfers of gold by the Bank shall be made with due regard to the costs of transport and anticipated requirements of the Bank. In an emergency the Executive Directors may transfer all or any part of the Bank's gold holdings to any place where they can be adequately protected.

Section 12. *Form of holdings of currency*

The Bank shall accept from any member, in place of any part of the member's currency, paid in to the Bank under Article II, Section 7 (i), or to meet amortization payments on loans made with such currency, and not needed by the Bank in its operations, notes or similar obligations issued by the Governor of the member or the depository designated by such member, which shall be non-negotiable, non-interest-bearing and payable at their par value on demand by credit to the account of the Bank in the designated depository.

Section 13. *Publication of reports and provision of information*

(a) The Bank shall publish an annual report containing an audited statement of its accounts and shall circulate to members at intervals of three months or less a summary statement of its financial position and a frofit and loss statement showing the results of its operations.

(b) The Bank may publish such other reports as it deems desirable to carry out its purposes.

(c) Copies of all reports, statements and publications made under this section shall be distributed to members.

Section 14. *Allocation of net income*

(a) The Board of Governors shall determine annually what part of the Bank's net income, after making provision for reserves, shall be allocated to surplus and what part, if any, shall be distributed.

(b) If any part is distributed, up to two percent non-cumulative shall be paid, as a first charge against the distribution for any year, to each member on the basis of the average amount of the loans outstanding during the year made under Article IV, Section 1 (a) (i), out of currency corresponding to its subscription. If two percent is paid as a first charge, any balance remaining to be distributed shall be paid to all members in proportion to their shares. Payments to each member shall be made in its own currency, or if that currency is not available in other currency acceptable to the member. If such payments are made in currencies other than the member's own currency, the transfer of the currency and its use by the receiving member after payment shall be without restriction by the members.

ARTICLE VI

WITHDRAWAL AND SUSPENSION OF MEMBERSHIP; SUSPENSION OF OPERATIONS

Section 1. *Right of members to withdraw*

Any member may withdraw from the Bank at any time by transmitting a notice in writing to the Bank at its principal office. Withdrawal shall become effective on the date such notice is received.

Section 2. *Suspension of membership*

If a member fails to fulfill any of its obligations to the Bank, the Bank may suspend its membership by decision of majority of the Governors, exercising a majority of the total voting power. The member so suspended shall automatically cease to be a member one year from the date of its suspension unless a decision is taken by the same majority to restore the member to good standing.

While under suspension, a member shall not be entitled to exercise any rights under this Agreement, except the right of withdrawal, but shall remain subject to all obligations.

Section 3. *Cessation of membership in International Monetary Fund*

Any member which ceases to be a member of the International Monetary Fund shall automatically cease after three months to be a member of the Bank unless the Bank by three-fourths of the total voting power has agreed to allow it to remain a member.

Section 4. *Settlement of accounts with governments ceasing to be members*

(a) When a government ceases to be a member, it shall remain liable for its direct obligations to the Bank and for its contingent liabilities to the Bank so long as any part of the loans or guarantees contracted before it ceased to be a member are outstanding; but it shall cease to incur liabilities with respect to loans and guarantees entered into thereafter by the Bank and to share either in the income or the expenses of the Bank.

(b) At the time a government ceases to be a member, the Bank shall arrange for the repurchase of its shares as a part of the settlement of accounts with such government in accordance with the provisions of (c) and (d) below. For this purpose the repurchase price of the shares shall be the value shown by the books of the Bank on the day the government ceases to be a member.

(c) The payment for shares repurchased by the Bank under this section shall be governed by the following conditions:

  (i) Any amount due to the government for its shares shall be withheld so long as the government, its central bank or any of its agencies remains liable, as borrower or guarantor, to the Bank and such amount may, at the option of the Bank, be applied on any such liability as it matures. No amount shall be withheld on account of the liability of the government resulting from its subscription for shares under Article II, Section 5 (ii). In any event, no amount due to a member for its shares shall be paid until six months after the date upon which the government ceases to be a member.

 (ii) Payments for shares may be made from time to time, upon their surrender by the government, to the extent by which the amount due as the repurchase price in (b) above exceeds the aggregate of liabilities on loans and guarantees in (c) (i) above until the former member has received the full repurchase price.

(iii) Payments shall be made in the currency of the country receiving payment or at the option of the Bank in gold.

(iv) If losses are sustained by the Bank on any guarantees, participations in loans, or loans which were outstanding on the date when the government ceased to be a member, and the amount of such losses exceeds the amount of the reserve provided against losses on the date when the government ceased to be a member, such government shall be obligated to repay upon demand the amount by which the repurchase price of its shares would have been reduced, if the losses had been taken into account when the repurchase price was determined. In addition, the former member government shall remain liable on any call for unpaid subscriptions under Article II, Section 5 (ii), to the extent that it would have been required to respond if the impairment of capital had occurred and the call had been made at the time the repurchase price of its shares was determined.

(d) If the Bank suspends permanently its operations under Section 5 (b) of this Article, within six months of the date upon which any government ceases to be a member, all rights of such government shall be determined by the provisions of Section 5 of this Article.

Section 5. *Suspension of operations and settlement of obligations*

(a) In an emergency the Executive Directors may suspend temporarily operations in respect of new loans and guarantees pending an opportunity for further consideration and action by the Board of Governors.

(b) The Bank may suspend permanently its operations in respect of new loans and guarantees by vote of a majority of the Governors, exercising a majority of the total voting power. After such suspension of operations the Bank shall forthwith cease all activities, except those incident to the orderly realization, conservation, and preservation of its assets and settlement of its obligations.

(c) The liability of all members for uncalled subscriptions to the capital stock of the Bank and in respect of the depreciation of their own currencies shall continue until all claims of creditors, including all contingent claims, shall have been discharged.

(d) All creditors holding direct claims shall be paid out of the assets of the Bank, and then out of payments to the Bank on calls on unpaid subscriptions. Before making any payments to creditors holding direct claims, the Executive Directors shall make such arrangements as are necessary, in their judgment, to insure a distribution to holders of contingent claims ratably with creditors holding direct claims.

(e) No distribution shall be made to members on account of their subscriptions to the capital stock of the Bank until:
   (i)   all liabilities to creditors have been discharged or provided for, and
   (ii) a majority of the Governors, exercising a majority of the total voting power, have decided to make a distribution.

(f) After a decision to make a distribution has been taken under (e) above, the Executive Directors may by a two-thirds majority vote make successive distributions of the assets of the Bank to members until all of the assets have been distributed. This distribution shall be subject to the prior settlement of all outstanding claims of the Bank against each member.

(g) Before any distribution of assets is made, the Executive Directors shall fix the proportionate share of each member according to the ratio of its shareholding to the total outstanding shares of the Bank.

(h) The Executive Directors shall value the assets to be distributed as at the date of distribution and then proceed to distribute in the following manner:
   (i)   There shall be paid to each member in its own obligations or those of its official agencies or legal entities within its territories, insofar as they are available for distribution, an amount equivalent in value to its proportionate share of the total amount to be distributed.

(ii) Any balance due to a member after payment has been made under (i) above shall be paid, in its own currency, insofar as it is held by the Bank, up to an amount equivalent in value to such balance.

(iii) Any balance due to a member after payment has been made under (i) and (ii) above shall be paid in gold or currency acceptable to the member, insofar as they are held by the Bank, up to an amount equivalent in value to such balance.

(iv) Any remaining assets held by the Bank after payments have been made to members under (i), (ii), and (iii) above shall be distributed *pro rata* among the members.

(i) Any member receiving assets distributed by the Bank in accordance with (h) above, shall enjoy the same rights with respect to such assets as the Bank enjoyed prior to their distribution.

ARTICLE VII

STATUS, IMMUNITIES AND PRIVILEGES

Section 1. *Purposes of Article*

To enable the Bank to fulfill the functions with which it is entrusted, the status, immunities and privileges set forth in this Article shall be accorded to the Bank in the territories of each member.

Section 2. *Status of the Bank*

The Bank shall possess full juridical personality, and, in particular, the capacity:
  (i) to contract;
  (ii) to acquire and dispose of immovable and movable property;
  (iii) to institute legal proceedings.

Section 3. *Position of the Bank with regard to judicial process*

Actions may be brought against the Bank only in a court of competent jurisdiction in the territories of a member in which the Bank has an office, has appointed an agent for the purpose of accepting service or notice of process, or has issued or guaranteed securities. No actions shall, however, be brought by members or persons acting for or deriving claims from members. The property and assets of the Bank shall, wheresoever located and by whomsoever held, be immune from all forms of seizure, attachment or execution before the delivery of final judgment against the Bank.

Section 4. *Immunity of assets from seizure*

Property and assets of the Bank, wherever located and by whomsoever held, shall be immune from search, requisition, confiscation, expropriation or any other form of seizure by executive or legislative action.

Section 5. *Immunity of archives*

The archives of the Bank shall be inviolable.

Section 6. *Freedom of assets from restrictions*

To the extent necessary to carry out the operations provided for in this Agreement and subject to the provisions of this Agreement, all property and assets of the Bank shall be free from restrictions, regulations, controls and moratoria of any nature.

Section 7. *Privilege for communications*

The official communications of the Bank shall be accorded by each member the same treatment that it accords to the official communications of other members.

Section 8. *Immunities and privileges of officers and employees*

All governors, executive directors, alternates, officers and employees of the Bank

   (i) shall be immune from legal process with respect to acts performed by them in their official capacity except when the Bank waives this immunity;

  (ii) not being local nationals, shall be accorded the same immunities from immigration restrictions, alien registration requirements and national service obligations and the same facilities as regards exchange restrictions as are accorded by members to the representatives, officials, and employees of comparable rank of other members;

 (iii) shall be granted the same treatment in respect of travelling facilities as is accorded by members to representatives, officials and employers of comparable rank of other members.

Section 9. *Immunities from taxation*

(a) The Bank, its assets, property, income and its operations and transactions authorized by this Agreement, shall be immune from all taxation and from all customs duties. The Bank shall also be immune from liability for the collection or payment of any tax or duty.

(b) No tax shall be levied on or in respect of salaries and emoluments paid by the Bank to executive directors, alternates, officials or employees of the Bank who are not local citizens, local subjects, or other local nationals.

(c) No taxation of any kind shall be levied on any obligation or security issued by the Bank (including any dividend or interest thereon) by whomsoever held--

   (i) which discriminates against such obligation or security solely because it is issued by the Bank; or

  (ii) if the sole jurisdictional basis for such taxation is the place or currency in which it is issued, made payable or paid, or the location of any office or place of business maintained by the Bank.

(d) No taxation of any kind shall be levied on any obligation or security guaranteed by the Bank (including any dividend or interest thereon) by whomsoever held—

   (i) which discriminates against such obligation or security solely because it is guaranteed by the Bank; or

  (ii) if the sole jurisdictional basis for such taxation is the location of any office or place of business maintained by the Bank.

Section 10. *Application of Article*

Each member shall take such action as is necessary in its own territories for the purpose of making effective in terms of its own law the principles set forth in this Article and shall inform the Bank of the detailed action which it has taken.

ARTICLE VIII

AMENDMENTS

(a) Any proposal to introduce modifications in this Agreement, whether emanating from a member, a governor or the Executive Directors, shall be communicated to the Chairman of the Board of Governors who shall bring the proposal before the Board. If the proposed amendment is approved by the Board the Bank shall, by circular letter or telegram, ask all members whether they accept the proposed amendment. When three-fifths of the members, having four-fifths of the total voting power, have accepted the proposed amendments, the Bank shall certify the fact by formal communication addressed to all members.

(b) Notwithstanding (a) above, acceptance by all members is required in the case of any amendment modifying.

(i) the right to withdraw from the Bank provided in Article VI, Section 1;

(ii) the right secured by Article II, Section 3 (c);

(iii) the limitation on liability provided in Article II, Section 6.

(c) Amendments shall enter into force for all members three months after the date of the formal communication unless a shorter period is specified in the circular letter or telegram.

ARTICLE IX

INTERPRETATION

(a) Any question of interpretation of the provisions of this Agreement arising between any member and the Bank or between any members of the Bank shall be submitted to the Executive Directors for their decision. If the question particularly affects any member not entitled to appoint an executive director, it shall be entitled to representation in accordance with Article V, Section 4 (h).

(b) In any case where the Executive Directors have given a decision under (a) above, any member may require that the question be referred to the Board of Governors, whose decision shall be final. Pending the result of the reference to the Board, the Bank may, so far as it deems necessary, act on the basis of the decision of the Executive Directors.

(c) Whenever a disagreement arises between the Bank and a country which has ceased to be a member, or between the Bank and any member during the permanent suspension of the Bank, such disagreement shall be submitted to arbitration by a tribunal of three arbitrators, one appointed by the Bank, another by the country involved and an umpire who, unless the parties otherwise agree, shall be appointed by the President of the Permanent Court of International Justice or such other authority as may have been prescribed by regulation adopted by the Bank. The umpire shall have full power to settle all questions of procedure in any case where the parties are in disagreement with respect thereto.

ARTICLE X

APPROVAL DEEMED GIVEN

Whenever the approval of any member is required before any act may be done by the Bank, except in Article VIII, approval shall be deemed to have been given unless the member presents an objection within such reasonable period as the Bank may fix in notifying the member of the proposed act.

ARTICLE XI

FINAL PROVISIONS

Section 1. *Entry into force*

This Agreement shall enter into force when it has been signed on behalf of governments whose minimum subscriptions comprise not less than sixty-five percent of the total subscriptions set forth in Schedule A and when the instruments referred to in Section 2 (a) of this Article have been deposited on their behalf, but in no event shall this Agreement enter into force before May 1, 1945.

Section 2. *Signature*

(a) Each government on whose behalf this Agreement is signed shall deposit with the Government of the United States or America an instrument setting forth that it has accepted this Agreement in accordance with its law and has taken all steps necessary to enable it to carry out all of its obligations under this Agreement.

(b) Each government shall become a member of the Bank as from the date of the deposit on its behalf of the instrument referred to in (a) above, except that no government shall become a member before this Agreement enters into force under Section 1 of this Article.

(c) The Government of the United States of America shall inform the governments of all countries whose names are set forth in Schedule A, and all governments whose membership is approved in accordance with Article II, Section 1 (b), of all signatures of this Agreement and of the deposit of all instruments referred to in (a) above.

(d) At the time this Agreement is signed on its behalf, each government shall transmit to the Government of the United States of America one one-hundredth of one percent of the price of each share in gold or United States dollars for the purpose of meeting administrative expenses of the Bank. This payment shall be credited on account of the payment to be made in accordance with Article II, Section 8 (a). The Government of the United States of America shall hold such funds in a special deposit account and shall transmit them to the Board of Governors of the Bank when the initial meeting has been called under Section 3 of this Article. If this Agreement has not come into force by December 31, 1945, the Government of the United States of America shall return such funds to the governments that transmitted them.

(e) This Agreement shall remain open for signature at Washington on behalf of the governments of the countries whose names are set forth in Schedule A until December 31, 1945.

(f) After December 31, 1945, this Agreement shall be open for signature on behalf of the government of any country whose membership has been approved in accordance with Article II, Section 1 (b).

(g) By their signature of this Agreement, all governments accept it both on their own behalf and in respect of all their colonies, overseas territories, all territories under their protection, suzerainty, or authority and all territories in respect of which they exercise a mandate.

(h) In the case of governments whose metropolitan territories have been under enemy occupation, the deposit of the instrument referred to in (a) above may be delayed until one hundred and eighty days after the date on which these territories have been liberated. If, however, it is not deposited by any such government before the expiration of this period, the signature affixed on behalf of that government shall become void and the portion of its subscription paid under (d) above shall be returned to it.

(i) Paragraphs (d) and (h) shall come into force with regard to each signatory government as from the date of its signature.

Section 3. *Inauguration of the Bank*

(a) As soon as this Agreement enters into force under Section 1 of this Article, each member shall appoint a governor and the member to whom the largest number of shares is allocated in Schedule A shall call the first meeting of the Board of Governors.

(b) At the first meeting of the Board of Governors, arrangements shall be made for the selection of provisional executive directors. The governments of the five countries, to which the largest number of shares are allocated in Schedule A, shall appoint provisional executive directors. If one or more of such governments have not become members, the executive directorships which they would be entitled to fill shall remain vacant until they become members, or until January 1, 1946, whichever is the earlier. Seven provisional executive directors shall be elected in accordance with the provisions of Schedule B and shall remain in office until the date of the first regular election of executive directors which shall be held as soon as practicable after January 1, 1946.

(c) The Board of Governors may delegate to the provisional executive directors any powers except those which may not be delegated to the Executive Directors.

(d) The Bank shall notify members when it is ready to commence operations.

DONE at Washington, in a single copy which shall remain deposited in the archives of the Government of the United States of America, which shall transmit certified copies to all governments whose names are set forth in Schedule A and to all governments whose membership is approved in accordance with Article II, Section 1 (b).

SCHEDULE A

SUBSCRIPTIONS

(millions of dollars)		*(millions of dollars)*		*(millions of dollars)*	
Australia	200	Ethiopia	3	Norway	50
Belgium	225	France	450	Panama	.2
Bolivia	7	Greece	25	Paraguay	.8
Brazil	105	Guatemala	2	Peru	17.5
Canada	325	Haiti	2	Philippine Commonwealth	15
Chile	35	Honduras	1	Poland	125
China	600	Iceland	1	Union of South Africa	100
Colombia	35	India	400	Union of Soviet Socialist	
Costa Rica	2	Iran	24	Republics	1200
Cuba	35	Iraq	6	United Kingdom	1300
Czechoslovakia	125	Liberia	.5	United States	3175
*Denmark		Luxembourg	10	Uruguay	10.5
Dominican Republic	2	Mexico	65	Venezuela	10.5
Ecuador	3.2	Netherlands	275	Yugoslavia	40
Egypt	40	New Zealand	50	Total	9100
El Salvador	1	Nicaragua	.8		

SCHEDULE B

ELECTION OF EXECUTIVE DIRECTORS

1. The election of the elective executive directors shall be by ballot of the Governors eligible to vote under Article V, Section 4 (b).

2. In balloting for the elective executive directors, each governor eligible to vote shall cast for one person all of the votes to which the member appointing him is entitled under Section 3 of Article V. The seven persons receiving the greatest number of votes shall be executive directors, except that person who receives less than fourteen percent of the total of the votes which can be cast (eligible vote) shall be considered elected.

3. When seven persons are not elected on the first ballot, a second ballot shall be held in which the person who received the lowest number of votes shall be ineligible for election and in which there shall vote only (a) those governors who voted in the first ballot for a person not elected and (b) those governors whose votes for a person elected are deemed under 4 below to have raised the votes cast for that person above fifteen percent of the eligible votes.

4. In determining whether the votes cast by a governor are to be deemed to have raised the total of any person above fifteen percent of the eligible votes, the fifteen percent shall be deemed to include, first, the votes of the governor casting the largest number of votes for such person, then the votes of the governor casting the next largest number, and so on until fifteen percent is reached.

5. Any governor, part of whose votes must be counted in order to raise the total of any person above fourteen percent shall be considered as casting all of his votes for such person even if the total votes for such person thereby exceed fifteen percent.

6. If, after the second ballot, seven persons have not been elected, further ballots shall be held on the same principles until seven persons have been elected, provided that after six persons are elected, the seventh may be elected by a simple majority of the remaining votes and shall be deemed to have been elected by all such votes.

---

*The quota of Denmark shall be determined by the Bank after Denmark accepts membership in accordance with these Articles of Agreement.

b. BY-LAWS OF THE INTERNATIONAL BANK FOR
RECONSTRUCTION AND DEVELOPMENT, AMENDED
THROUGH AUGUST 21, 1969

These By-Laws are adopted under the authority of, and are intended to be complementary to, the Articles of Agreement of the International Bank for Reconstruction and Development; and they shall be construed accordingly. In the even of a conflict between anything in these By-Laws and any provision of requirement of the Articles of Agreement, the Articles of Agreement shall prevail.

SECTION 1. *Places of Business*

The principal office of the Bank shall be located within the metropolitan area of Washington, D.C., United States of America.

The Executive Directors may establish and maintain agencies or branch offices and regional offices at any place in the territories of any member, whenever it is necessary to do so in order to facilitate the efficient conduct of the business of the Bank.

SECTION 2. *Fund Represented*

The Executive Directors are authorized to invite the International Monetary Fund to send a representative of the Fund to meetings of the Board of Governors and Executive Directors who may participate in such meetings, but shall have no vote. The Executive Directors are authorized to accept invitations from the Fund to send a representative of the Bank to participate in meetings of the Board of Governors of Executive Directors of the Fund.

SECTION 3. *Meeting of the Board of Governors*

(a) The Annual Meeting of the Board of Governors shall be held at such time and place as the Board of Governors shall determine; provided, however, that, if the Executive Directors shall, because of special circumstances, deem it necessary to do so, the Executive Directors may change the time and place of such Annual Meeting.

(b) Special meetings of the Board of Governors may be called at any time by the Board of Governors of the Executive Directors and shall be called upon the request of five members of the Bank or of members of the Bank having in the aggregate one-fourth of the total voting power. Whenever any member of the Bank shall request the Executive Directors to call a special meeting of the Board of Governors, the President shall notify all members of the Bank of such request and of the reasons which shall have been given therefor.

(c) A quorum for any meeting of the Board of Governors shall be a majority of the Governors, exercising not less than two-thirds of the total voting power. Any meeting of the Board of Governors at which a quorum shall not be present may be adjourned from time to time by a majority of the Governors present and notice of the adjourned meeting need not be given.

SECTION 4. *Notice of Meetings of the Board of Governors*

The President shall cause notice of the time and place of each meeting of the Board of Governors to be given to each member of the Bank by telegram or cable which shall be dispatched not less than 42 days prior to the date set for such meeting, except that in urgent cases such notice shall be sufficient if dispatched by telegram of cable not less than 10 days prior to the date set for such meeting.

SECTION 5. *Attendance of Executive Directors and Observers at Meetings of the Board of Governors*

(a) The Executive Directors and their Alternates may attend all meetings of the Board of Governors and may participate in such meetings, but an Executive Director or his Alternate shall not be entitled to vote at any such meeting unless he shall be entitled to vote as a Governor or an Alternate or a temporary Alternate of a Governor.

(b) The Chairman of the Board of Governors, in consultation with the Executive Directors, may invite observers to attend any meeting of the Board of Governors.

SECTION 6. *Agenda of Meetings of the Board of Governors*

(a) Under the direction of the Executive Directors, the President shall prepare a brief agenda for each meeting of the Board of Governors and shall cause such agenda to be transmitted to each member of the Bank with the notice of such meeting.

(b) Additional subjects may be placed on the agenda for any meeting of Governors by any Governor provided that he shall give notice thereof to the President not less than seven days prior to the date set for such meeting. In special circumstances the President by direction of the Executive Directors may at any time place additional subjects on the agenda for any meeting of the Board of Governors. The President shall cause notice of the addition of any subjects to the agenda for any meeting of the Board of Governors to be given as promptly as possible to each member of the Bank.

(c) The Board of Governors may at any time authorize any subject to be placed on the agenda for any meeting of such Board even though the notice required by this section shall not have been given.

(d) Except as otherwise specifically directed by the Board of Governors, the Chairman of the Board of Governors jointly with the President shall have charge of all arrangements for the holding of meetings of the Board of Governors.

SECTION 7. *Election of Chairman and Vice Chairmen*

At each annual meeting the Board of Governors shall select a Governor to act as Chairman and at least two other Governors to act as Vice Chairmen until the next annual meeting.

In the absence of the Chairman the Vice-Chairman designated by the Chairman shall act in his place.

SECTION 8. *Secretary*

The Secretary of the Bank shall serve as Secretary of the Board of Governors.

SECTION 9. *Minutes*

The Board shall keep a summary record of its proceedings which shall be available to all members and which shall be filed with the Executive Directors for their guidance.

SECTION 10. *Report of Executive Directors*

The Executive Directors shall have prepared for presentation at the annual meeting of the Board of Governors an annual report in which shall be discussed the operations and policies of the Bank and which shall make recommendations to the Board of Governors on the problems confronting the Bank.

SECTION 11. *Voting*

Except as otherwise specifically provided in the Articles of Agreement, all decisions of the Board shall be made by a majority of the votes cast. At any meeting the Chairman may ascertain the sense of the meeting in lieu of a formal vote but he shall require a formal vote upon the request of any Governor. Whenever a formal vote is required the written text of the motion shall be distributed to the voting members.

SECTION 12. *Proxies*

No Governor or Alternate may vote at any meeting by proxy or by any other method than in person, but a member may make provision for the designation of a temporary Alternate to vote for the Governor at any Board Session at which the regularly designated Alternate is unable to be present.

SECTION 13. *Voting without Meeting*

Whenever, in the judgment of the Executive Directors, any action by the Bank must be taken by the Board of Governors which should not be postponed until the next regular meeting of the Board and does not warrant the calling of a special meeting of the Board, the Executive Directors shall present to each member by any rapid means of communication a motion embodying the proposed action with a request for a vote by its Governor. Votes shall be cast during such period as the Executive Directors may prescribe, provided that no Governor shall vote on any such motion until 7 days after despatch of the motion unless he is notified that the Executive Directors have waived this requirement. At the expiration of the period prescribed for voting, the Executive Directors shall record the results and the President shall notify all members. If the replies received do not include a majority of the Governors exercising two-thirds of the total voting power which are usually required for a quorum of the Board of Governors, the motion shall be considered lost.

SECTION 14. *Terms of Service*

(a) Governors and Alternates shall receive their actual transport expenses to and from the place of meeting in attending meetings and $75 for each night which attendance at such meeting requires them to spend away from their normal place of residence, this amount being reduced to $15 for each night when accommodation is included in the price of transporation.

(b) Pending the necessary action being taken by members to exempt from national taxation salaries and allowances paid out of the budget of the Bank, the Governors and the Executive Directors, and their Alternates, the President, and the staff members shall be reimbursed by the Bank for the taxes which they are required to pay on such salaries and allowances.

In computing the amount of tax adjustment to be made with respect to any individual, it shall be presumed for the purposes of the computation that the income received from the Bank is his total income. All salary scales and expense allowances prescribed by this Section are stated as net on the above basis.

(c) The salary of the President shall be $50,000 per annum. The Bank shall also pay any reasonable expenses incurred by the President in the interest of the Bank (including travel and transportation expenses for himself, and expenses for his family, and his personal effects in moving once to the seat of the Bank during or immediately before his term of office and in moving once from the seat during or immediately after his term of office). The initial contract of the President shall be for a term of five years. Any renewal of the contract may be for the same or for a shorter term.

(d) It shall be the duty of an Executive Director and his Alternate to devote all the time and attention to the business of the Bank that its interests require, and between them to be continuously available at the seat of the Bank. The periods of service of an Executive Director and his Alternate (other than service at meetings, when is absent on business of the Bank, or in similar appropriate circumstances provided for in regulations made by the Executive Directors) shall be mutually exclusive; provided, however, that this provision shall not apply to the extent that, where special circumstances exist, the Executive Director concerned, after consultation with the President, has advised the Bank that the performance of his duties so requires. An Executive Director who is unable to attend any meeting of the Executive Directors or a committee thereof may designate a temporary Alternate Executive Director to attend and act for him at such meeting. The terms Alternate and Alternate Executive Director whenever used in these By-Laws shall, unless the context shall otherwise require, include any such temporary Alternate Executive Director.

(e) Executive Directors and their Alternates shall be entitled to remuneration (as salary or expense allowance) for time spent by them in the service of the Bank at the rate of $35,000 per year for an Executive Director and $27,000 per year for an Alternate Executive Director. Such remuneration shall be prorated, in accordance with such rules and regulations as the Executive Directors shall from time to time approve, according to the time spent by the Executive Director or Alternate Executive Director in the service of the Bank. Such remuneration shall be in lieu of all other salary and expense allowances, including allowances for housing, entertainment and other expenses, except allowances provided pursuant to Sub-section (f) of this Section.

A Joint Committee on the Remuneration of Executive Directors and their Alternates, appointed by the Chairmen of the Boards of Governors of the Bank and Fund and consisting of one of the Chairmen and two former Governors or Alternate Governors of the Bank or Fund chosen by the Chairmen in consultation with the President of the Bank and the Managing Director of the Fund, shall be constituted in January of each year in which a regular election of Executive Directors is scheduled, starting with the year 1972, to consider the adequacy of the remuneration of Executive Directors of the Bank and the Fund, and their Alternates, and to prepare a report, which shall be submitted to the Board of Governors of the Bank by July 1 of that year, containing such recommendations for any changes in such remuneration or for any other action by the Board of Governors relating thereto as the Joint Committee shall deem appropriate.

(f) The Executive Directors may by regulation make appropriate provision whereby (i) each Executive Director or Alternate Executive Director who does not reside at or near the seat of the Bank shall be entitled to a reasonable allowance for expenses incurred by him in attending meetings of the Executive Directors or committees thereof; (ii) each Executive Director and Alternate Executive Director who shall at the request of the President perform designated service for the Bank shall be entitled to a reasonable allowance for expenses incurred by him in the performance thereof, and (iii) each Executive Director and Alternate Executive Director, but not a temporary Alternate Executive Director, shall be entitled to reasonable leave and resettlement allowances with due regard to the time spent by him in the service of the Bank. The allowances provided pursuant to this Sub-section shall be in addition to remuneration under Sub-section (e) of this Section.

(g) For any period in which an Executive Director or Alternate Executive Director shall also be an Executive Director or Alternate Executive Director of the International Monetary Fund, the aggregate of the remuneration and leave and resettlement allowances received by him from the Fund and the Bank shall not exceed the maximum to which he would be entitled if he served either the Bank or the Fund on a full-time basis.

(h) An individual claiming reimbursement or allowance for any expenses incurred by him shall include in his claim a representation that he has not received and will not claim reimbursement or allowance in respect to those expenses from any other source.

(i) Secretarial, staff services, office space, and other services incidental to the performance of the duties of the Executive Directors and Alternates shall be provided by the Bank.

SECTION 15. *Delegation of Authority*

The Executive Directors are authorized by the Board of Governors to exercise all the powers of the Bank except those reserved to the Board by Article V, Section 2 (b) and other provisions of the Articles of Agreement. The Executive Directors shall not take any action pursuant to powers delegated by the Board of Governors which is inconsistent with any action taken by the Board.

SECTION 16. *Rules and Regulations*

The Executive Directors are authorized by the Board of Governors to adopt such rules and regulations, including financial regulations, as may be necessary or appropriate to conduct the business of the Bank. Any rules and regulations so adopted, and any amendments thereof, shall be subject to review by the Board of Governors at their next annual meeting.

SECTION 17. *Vacant Directorships*

Whenever a new Director must be elected because of a vacancy requiring an election, the President shall notify the members who elected the former Director of the existence of the vacancy. He may convene a meeting of the Governors of such countries exclusively for the purpose of electing a new Director; or he may request nominations by mail or telegraph and conduct ballots by mail or telegraph. Successive ballots shall be cast until one candidate has a majority; and after each ballot, the candidate with the smallest number of votes shall be dropped from the next ballot.

When a new elective Director is named, the office of Alternate shall be deemed to be vacant and an Alternate shall be named by the newly-elected Director.

SECTION 18. *Representation of Members Not Entitled to Appoint a Director*

Whenever the Executive Directors are to consider a request made by, or a matter particularly affecting a member not entitled to appoint a Director, the member shall be promptly informed in writing of the date set for its consideration. No final action shall be taken by the Executive Directors, nor any question affecting the member submitted to the Board of Governors, until the member has been offered a reasonable opportunity to present its views and to be heard at a meeting of the Executive Directors of which the member has had reasonable notice. Any member, so electing, may waive this provision.

SECTION 19. *Budget and Audits*

The Executive Directors shall have an audit of the accounts of the Bank made at least once each year and on the basis of this audit shall submit a statement of its accounts, including a balance sheet and a statement of profit and loss, to the Board of Governors to be considered by them at their annual meeting.

The Executive Directors shall instruct the President to prepare an annual administrative budget to be presented to them for approval. The budget as approved shall be incorporated in the annual report to be presented to the Board of Governors at their annual meeting.

SECTION 20. *Application for Membership*

Subject to any special provisions that may be made for countries listed in Schedule A of the Articles of Agreement, any member of the International Monetary Fund may apply for membership in the Bank by filing with the Bank an application setting forth all relevant facts.

When submitting an application to the Board of Governors, the Executive Directors after consultation with the applicant country, shall recommend to the Board the number of shares of capital stock to be subscribed and such other conditions as, in the opinion of the Executive Directors, the Board of Governors may wish to prescribe.

SECTION 21. *Suspension of Membership*

Before any member is suspended from membership in the Bank, the matter shall be considered by the Executive Directors who shall inform the member in reasonable time of the complaint against it and allow the member an adequate opportunity for stating its case both orally and in writing. The Executive Directors shall recommend to the Board of Governors the action they deem appropriate. The member shall be informed of the recommendation and the date on which its case will be considered by the Board and shall be given a reasonable time within which to present its case to the Board both orally and in writing. Any member so electing may waive this provision.

SECTION 22. *Settlement of Disagreements*

The President of the International Court of Justice is prescribed as the authority to appoint an umpire whenever there arises a disagreement of the type referred to in Article IX (c) of the Articles of Agreement.

SECTION 23. *Amendment to By-Laws*

These By-Laws may be amended by the Board of Governors at any meeting thereof or by vote without a meeting as provided in Section 13.

6. INTERNATIONAL FINANCE CORPORATION

a. ARTICLES OF AGREEMENT OF THE INTERNATIONAL FINANCE CORPORATION, DONE AT WASHINGTON, D.C. JULY 20, 1956, AMENDED BY RESOLUTIONS AND BECAME EFFECTIVE SEPTEMBER 21, 1961 AND SEPTEMBER 1, 1965

The Governments on whose behalf this Agreement is signed agree as follows:

INTRODUCTORY ARTICLE

THE INTERNATIONAL FINANCE CORPORATION (hereinafter called the Corporation) is established and shall operate in accordance with the following provisions:

ARTICLE I

Purpose

The purpose of the Corporation is to further economic development by encouraging the growth of productive private enterprise in member countries, particularly in the less developed areas, thus supplementing the activities of the International Bank for Reconstruction and Development (hereinafter called the Bank). In carrying out this purpose, the Corporation shall:

(i) in association with private investors, assist in financing the establishment, improvement and expansion of productive private enterprises which would contribute to the development of its member countries by making investments, without guarantee of repayment by the member government concerned, in cases where sufficient private capital is not available on reasonable terms;

(ii) seek to bring together investment opportunities, domestic and foreign private capital, and experienced management; and

(iii) seek to stimulate, and to help create conditions conducive to, the flow of private capital, domestic and foreign, into productive investment in member countries.

The Corporation shall be guided in all its decisions by the provisions of this Article.

ARTICLE II

Membership and Capital

SECTION 1. *Membership*

(a) The original members of the Corporation shall be those members of the Bank listed in Schedule A hereto which shall, on or before the date specified in Article IX, Section 2(c), accept membership in the Corporation.

(b) Membership shall be open to other members of the Bank at such times and in accordance with such terms as may be prescribed by the Corporation.

SECTION 2. *Capital Stock*

(a) The authorized capital stock of the Corporation shall be $100,000,000, in terms of United States dollars.

(b) The authorized capital stock shall be divided into 100,000 shares having a par value of one thousand United States dollars each. Any such shares not initially subscribed by original members shall be available for subsequent subscription in accordance with Section 3 (d) of this Article.

(c) The amount of capital stock at any time authorized may be increased by the Board of Governors as follows:

  (i) by a majority of the votes cast, in case such increase is necessary for the purpose of issuing shares of capital stock on initial subscription by members other than original members, provided that the aggregate of any increases authorized pursuant to this subparagraph shall not exceed 10,000 shares;

  (ii) in any other case, by a three-fourths majority of the total voting power.

(d) In case of an increase authorized pursuant to paragraph (c) (ii) above, each member shall have a reasonable opportunity to subscribe, under such conditions as the Corporation shall decide, to a proportion of the increase of stock equivalent to the proportion which its stock theretofore subscribed bears to the total capital stock of the Corporation, but no member shall be obligated to subscribe to any part of the increased capital.

(e) Issuance of shares of stock, other than those subscribed either on initial subscription or pursuant to paragraph (d) above, shall require a three-fourths majority of the total voting power.

(f) Shares of stock of the Corporation shall be available for subscription only by, and shall be issued only to, members.

SECTION 3. *Subscriptions*

(a) Each original member shall subscribe to the number of shares of stock set forth opposite its name in Schedule A. The number of shares of stock to be subscribed by other members shall be determined by the Corporation.

(b) Shares of stock initially subscribed by original members shall be issued at par.

(c) The initial subscription of each original member shall be payable in full within 30 days after either the date on which the Corporation shall begin operations pursuant to Article IX, Section 3 (b), or the date on which such original member becomes a member, whichever shall be later, or at such date thereafter as the Corporation shall determine. Payment shall be made in gold or United States dollars in response to a call by the Corporation which shall specify the place or places of payment.

(d) The price and other terms of subscription of shares of stock to be subscribed, otherwise than on initial subscription by original members, shall be determined by the Corporation.

SECTION 4. *Limitation on Liability*

No member shall be liable, by reason of its membership, for obligations of the Corporation.

SECTION 5. *Restriction on Transfers and Pledges of Shares*

Shares of stock shall not be pledged or encumbered in any manner whatverver, and shall be transferable only to the Corporation.

ARTICLE III

Operations

SECTION 1. *Financing Operations*

The Corporation may make investments of its funds in productive private enterprises in the territories of its members. The existence of a government or other public interest in such an enterprise shall not necessarily preclude the Corporation from making an investment therein.

SECTION 2. *Forms of Financing*[*1] *Amended September 21, 1961*

The Corporation may make investments of its funds in such form or forms as it may deem appropriate in the circumstances.

SECTION 3. *Operational Principles*

The operations of the Corporation shall be conducted in accordance with the following principles:

(i) the Corporation shall not undertake any financing for which in its opinion sufficient private capital could be obtained on reasonable terms;

(ii) the Corporation shall not finance an enterprise in the territories of any member if the member objects to such financing;

(iii) The Corporation shall impose no conditions that the proceeds of any financing by it shall be spent in the territories of any particular country;

(iv) the Corporation shall not assume responsibility for managing any enterprise in which it has invested and shall not exercise voting rights for such purpose or for any other purpose which, in its opinion, properly is within the scope of managerial control;[2]
Amended September 21, 1961

(v) the Corporation shall undertake its financing on terms and conditions which it considers appropriate, taking into account the requirements of the enterprise, the risks being undertaken by the Corporation and the terms and conditions normally obtained by private investors for similar financing;

(vi) the Corporation shall seek to revolve its funds by selling its investments to private investors whenever it can appropriately do so on satisfactory terms;

(vii) the Corporation shall seek to maintain a reasonable diversification in its investments.

SECTION 4. *Protection of Interests*

Nothing in this Agreement shall prevent the Corporation, in the event of actual or threatened default on any of its investments, actual or threatened insolvency of the enterprise in which such investment shall have been made, or other situations which, in the opinion of the Corporation, threaten to jeopardize such investment, from taking such action and exercising such rights as it may deem necessary for the protection of its interests.

SECTION 5. *Applicability of Certain Foreign Exchange Restrictions*

Funds received by or payable to the Corporation in respect of an investment of the Corporation made in any member's territories pursuant to Section 1 of this Article shall not be free, solely by reason of any provision of this Agreement, from generally applicable foreign exchange restrictions, regulations and controls in force in the territories of that member.

---

[1] *Original Text:*

   (a) The Corporation's financing shall not take the form of investments in capital stock. Subject to the foregoing, the Corporation may make investments of its funds in such form or forms as it may deem appropriate in the circumstances, including (but without limitation) investments according to the holder thereof the right to participate in earnings and the right to subscribe to, or to convert the investment into, capital stock.

   (b) The Corporation shall not itself exercise any right to subscribe to, or to convert any investment into, capital stock.

[2] *Original Text:*

   (iv) The Corporation shall not assume responsibility for managing any enterprise in which it has invested;

138

SECTION 6. *Miscellaneous Operations*

In addition to the operations specified elsewhere in this Agreement, the Corporation shall have the power to:

(i) borrow funds, and in that connection to furnish such collateral or other security therefor as it shall determine; provided, however, that before making a public sale of its obligations in the markets of a member, the Corporation shall have obtained the approval of that member and of the member in whose currency the obligations are to be denominated; if and so long as the Corporation shall be indebted on loans from or guaranteed by the Bank, the total amount outstanding of borrowings incurred or guarantees given by the Corporation shall not be increased if, at the time or as a result thereof, the aggregate amount of debt (including the guarantee of any debt) incurred by the Corporation from any source and then outstanding shall exceed an amount equal to four times its unimpaired subscribed capital and surplus;*

(ii) invest funds not needed in its financing operations in such obligations as it may determine and invest funds held by it for pension or similar purposes in any marketable securities, all without being subject to the restrictions imposed by other sections of this Article;

(iii) guarantee securities in which it has invested in order to facilitate their sale;

(iv) buy and sell securities it has issued or guaranteed or in which it has invested;

(v) exercise such other powers incidental to its business as shall be necessary or desirable in furtherance of its purposes.

SECTION 7. *Valuation of Currencies*

Whenever it shall become necessary under this Agreement to value any currency in terms of the value of another currency, such valuation shall be as reasonably determined by the Corporation after consultation with the International Monetary Fund.

SECTION 8. *Warning To Be Placed on Securities*

Every security issued or guaranteed by the Corporation shall bear on its face a conspicuous statement to the effect that it is not an obligation of the Bank or, unless expressly stated on the security, of any government.

SECTION 9. *Political Activity Prohibited*

The Corporation and its officers shall not interfere in the political affairs of any member; nor shall they be influenced in their decisions by the political character of the member or members concerned. Only economic considerations shall be relevant to their decisions, and these considerations shall be weighed impartially in order to achieve the purposes stated in this Agreement.

ARTICLE IV

Organization and Management

SECTION 1. *Structure of the Corporation*

The Corporation shall have a Board of Governors, a Board of Directors, a Chairman of the Board of Directors, a President and such other officers and staff to perform such duties as the Corporation may determine.

Last clause added by amendment effective September 1, 1965

SECTION 2. *Board of Governors*

(a) All the powers of the Corporation shall be vested in the Board of Governors.

(b) Each Governor and Alternate Governor of the Bank appointed by a member of the Bank which is also a member of the Corporation shall *ex officio* be a Governor or Alternate Governor, respectively, of the Corporation. No Alternate Governor may vote except in the absence of his principal. The Board of Governors shall select one of the Governors as Chairman of the Board of Governors. Any Governor or Alternate Governor shall cease to hold office if the member by which he was appointed shall cease to be a member of the Corporation.

(c) The Board of Governors may delegate to the Board of Directors authority to exercise any its powers, except the power to:

  (i)   admit new members and determine the conditions of their admission;
  (ii)   increase or decrease the capital stock;
  (iii) suspend a member;
  (iv)   decide appeals from interpretations of this Agreement given by the Board of Directors;
  (v)   make arrangements to cooperate with other international organizations (other than informal arrangements of a temporary and administrative character);
  (vi)   decide to suspend permanently the operations of the Corporation and to distribute its assets;
  (vii) declare dividends;
  (viii) amend this Agreement.

(d) The Board of Governors shall hold an annual meeting and such other meetings as may be provided for by the Board of Governors or called by the Board of Directors.

(e) The annual meeting of the Board of Governors shall be held in conjunction with the annual meeting of the Board of Governors of the Bank.

(f) A quorum for any meeting of the Board of Governors shall be a majority of the Governors, exercising not less than two-thirds of the total voting power.

(g) The Corporation may by regulation establish a procedure whereby the Board of Directors may obtain a vote of the Governors on a specific question without calling a meeting of the Board of Governors.

(h) The Board of Governors, and the Board of Directors to the extent authorized, may adopt such rules and regulations as may be necessary or appropriate to conduct the business of the Corporation.

(i) Governors and Alternate Governors shall serve as such without compensation from the Corporation.

SECTION 3. *Voting*

(a) Each member shall have two hundred fifty votes plus one additional vote for each share of stock held.

(b) Except as otherwise expressly provided, all matters before the Corporation shall be decided by a majority of the votes cast.

SECTION 4. *Board of Directors*

(a) The Board of Directors shall be responsible for the conduct of the general operations of the Corporation, and for this purpose shall exercise all the powers given to it by this Agreement or delegated to it by the Board of Governors.

(b) The Board of Directors of the Corporation shall be composed *ex officio* of each Executive Director of the Bank who shall have been either (i) appointed by a member of the Bank which is also a member of the Corporation, or (ii) elected in an election in which the votes of at least one member of the Bank which is also a member of the

Corporation shall have counted toward his election. The Alternate to each such Executive Director of the Bank shall *ex officio* be an Alternate Director of the Corporation. Any Director shall cease to hold office if the member by which he was appointed, or if all the members whose votes counted toward his election, shall cease to be members of the Corporation.

(c) Each Director who is an appointed Executive Director of the Bank shall be entitled to cast the number of votes which the member by which he was so appointed is entitled to cast in the Corporation. Each Director who is an elected Executive Director of the Bank shall be entitled to cast the number of votes which the member or members of the Corporation whose votes counted toward his election in the Bank are entitled to cast in the Corporation. All the votes which a Director is entitled to cast shall be cast as a unit.

(d) An Alternate Director shall have full power to act in the absence of the Director who shall have appointed him. When a Director is present, his Alternate may participate in meetings but shall not vote.

(e) A quorum for any meeting of the Board of Directors shall be a majority of the Directors exercising not less than one-half of the total voting power.

(f) The Board of Directors shall meet as often as the business of the Corporation may require.

(g) The Board of Governors shall adopt regulations under which a member of the Corporation not entitled to appoint an Executive Director of the Bank may send a representative to attend any meeting of the Board of Directors of the Corporation when a request made by, or a matter particularly affecting, that member is under consideration.

SECTION 5. *Chairman, President and Staff*

(a) The President of the Bank shall be *ex officio* Chairman of the Board of Directors of the Corporation, but shall have no vote except a deciding vote in case of an equal division. He may participate in meetings of the Board of Governors but shall not vote at such meetings.

(b) The President of the Corporation shall be appointed by the Board of Directors on the recommendation of the Chairman. The President shall be chief of the operating staff of the Corporation. Under the direction of the Board of Directors and the general supervision of the Chairman, he shall conduct the ordinary business of the Corporation and under their general control shall be responsible for the organization, appointment and dismissal of the officers and staff. The President may participate in meetings of the Board of Directors but shall not vote at such meetings. The President shall cease to hold office by decision of the Board of Directors in which the Chairman concurs.

(c) The President, officers and staff of the Corporation, in the discharge of their offices, owe their duty entirely to the Corporation and to no other authority. Each member of the Corporation shall respect the international character of this duty and shall refrain from all attempts to influence any of them in the discharge of their duties.

(d) Subject to the paramount importance of securing the highest standards of efficiency and of technical competence, due regard shall be paid, in appointing the officers and staff of the Corporation, to the importance of recruiting personnel on as wide a geographical basis as possible.

SECTION 6. *Relationship to the Bank*

(a) The Corporation shall be an entity separate and distinct from the Bank and the funds of the Corporation shall be kept separate and apart from those of the Bank.* *Amended September 1, 1965.* The provisions of this Section shall not prevent the Corporation from making arrangements with the Bank regarding facilities, personnel and services and arrangements for reimbursement of administrative expenses paid in the first instance by either organization on behalf of the other.

(b) Nothing in this Agreement shall make the Corporation liable for the acts or obligations of the Bank, or the Bank liable for the acts or obligations of the Corporation.

SECTION 7. *Relations With Other International Organizations*

The Corporation, acting through the Bank, shall enter into formal arrangements with the United Nations and may enter into such arrangements with other public international organizations having specialized responsibilities in related fields.

SECTION 8. *Location of Offices*

The principal office of the Corporation shall be in the same locality as the principal office of the Bank. The Corporation may establish other offices in the territories of any member.

SECTION 9. *Depositories*

Each member shall designate its central bank as a depository in which the Corporation may keep holdings of such member's currency or other assets of the Corporation or, if it has no central bank, it shall designate for such purpose such other institution as may be acceptable to the Corporation.

SECTION 10. *Channel of Communication*

Each member shall designate an appropriate authority with which the Corporation may communicate in connection with any matter arising under this Agreement.

SECTION 11. *Publication of Reports and Provision of Information*

(a) The Corporation shall publish an annual report containing an audited statement of its accounts and shall circulate to members at appropriate intervals a summary statement of its financial position and a profit and loss statement showing the results of its operations.

(b) The Corporation may publish such other reports as it deems desirable to carry out its purposes.

(c) Copies of all reports, statements and publications made under this Section shall be distributed to members.

SECTION 12. *Dividends*

(a) The Board of Governors may determine from time to time what part of the Corporation's net income and surplus, after making appropriate provision for reserves, shall be distributed as dividends.

(b) Dividends shall be distributed *pro rata* in proportion to capital stock held by members.

(c) Dividends shall be paid in such manner and in such currency or currencies as the Corporation shall determine.

Original Text included the following:
"The Corporation shall not lend to or borrow from the Bank."

ARTICLE V

Withdrawal; Suspension of Membership; Suspension of Operations

SECTION 1. *Withdrawal by Members*

Any member may withdraw from membership in the Corporation at any time by transmitting a notice in writing to the Corporation at its principal office. Withdrawal shall become effective upon the date such notice is received.

SECTION 2. *Suspension of Membership*

(a) If a member fails to fulfill any of its obligations to the Corporation, the Corporation may suspend its membership by decision of a majority of the Governors, exercising a majority of the total voting power. The member so suspended shall automatically cease to be a member one year from the date of its suspension unless a decision is taken by the same majority to restore the member to good standing.

(b) While under suspension, a member shall not be entitled to exercise any rights under this Agreement except the right of withdrawal, but shall remain subject to all obligations.

SECTION 3. *Suspension or Cessation of Membership in the Bank*

Any member which is suspended from membership in, or ceases to be a member of, the Bank shall automatically be suspended from membership in, or cease to be a member of, the Corporation, as the case may be.

SECTION 4. *Rights and Duties of Governments Ceasing To Be Members*

(a) When a government ceases to be a member it shall remain liable for all amounts due from it to the Corporation. The Corporation shall arrange for the repurchase of such government's capital stock as a part of the settlement of accounts with it in accordance with the provisions of this Section, but the government shall have no other rights under this Agreement except as provided in this Section and in Article VIII (c).

(b) The Corporation and the government may agree on the repurchase of the capital stock of the government on such terms as may be appropriate under the circumstances, without regard to the provisions of paragraph (c) below. Such agreement may provide, among other things, for a final settlement of all obligations of the government to the Corporation.

(c) If such agreement shall not have been made within six months after the government ceases to be a member or such other time as the Corporation and such government may agree, the repurchase price of the government's capital stock shall be the value thereof shown by the book of the Corporation on the day when the government ceases to be a member. The repurchase of the capital stock shall be subject to the following conditions:

(i) payments for shares of stock may be made from time to time, upon their surrender by the government, in such instalments, at such times and in such available currency or currencies as the Corporation reasonably determines, taking into account the financial position of the Corporation;

(ii) any amount due to the government for its capital stock shall be withheld so long as the gonvernment or any of its agencies remains liable to the Corporation for payment of any amount and such amount may, at the option of the Corporation, be set off, as it becomes payable, against the amount due from the Corporation;

(iii) if the Corporation sustains a net loss on the investments made pursuant to Article III, Section 1, and held by it on the date when the government ceases to be a member, and the amount of such loss exceeds the amount of the reserves provided therefor on such date, such government shall repay on demand the amount by which the repurchase price of its shares of stock would have been reduced if such loss had been taken into account when the repurchase price was determined.

(d) In no event shall any amount due to a government for its capital stock under this Section be paid until six months after the date upon which the government ceases to be a member. If within six months of the date upon which any government ceases to be a member the Corporation suspends operations under Section 5 of this Article, all rights of such government shall be determined by the provisions of such Section 5 and such government shall be considered still a member of the Corporation for purposes of such Section 5, except that it shall have no voting rights.

SECTION 5. *Suspension of Operations and Settlement of Obligations*

(a) The Corporation may permanently suspend its operations by vote of a majority of the Governors exercising a majority of the total voting power. After such suspension of operations the Corporation shall forthwith cease all activities, except those incident to the orderly realization, conservation and preservation of its assets and settlement of its obligations. Until final settlement of such obligations and distribution of such assets, the Corporation shall remain in existence and all mutual rights and obligations of the Corporation and its members under this Agreement shall continue unimpaired, except that no member be suspended or withdraw and that no distribution shall be made to members except as in this Section provided.

(b) No distribution shall be made to members on account of their subscriptions to the capital stock of the Corporation until all liabilities to creditors shall have been discharged or provided for and until the Board of Governors, by vote of a majority of the Governors exercising a majority of the total voting power, shall have decided to make such distribution.

(c) Subject to the foregoing, the Corporation shall distribute the assets of the Corporation to members *pro rata* in proportion to capital stock held by them, subject, in the case of any member, to prior settlement of all outstanding claims by the Corporation against such member. Such distribution shall be made at such times, in such currencies, and in cash or other assets as the Corporation shall deem fair and equitable. The shares distributed to the several members need not necessarily be uniform in respect of the type of assets distributed or of the currencies in which they are expressed.

(d) Any member receiving assets distributed by the Corporation pursuant to this Section shall enjoy the same rights with respect to such assets as the Corporation enjoyed prior to their distribution.

ARTICLE VI

Status, Immunities and Privileges

SECTION 1. *Purposes of Article*

To enable the Corporation to fulfill the functions with which it is entrusted, the status, immunities and privileges set forth in this Article shall be accorded to the Corporation in the territories of each member.

SECTION 2. *Status of the Corporation*

The Corporation shall possess full juridical personality and, in particular, the capacity:

(i) to contract;
(ii) to acquire and dispose of immovable and movable property;
(iii) to institute legal proceedings.

144

SECTION 3. *Position of the Corporation with Regard to Judicial Process*

Actions may be brought against the Corporation only in a court of competent jurisdiction in the territories of a member in which the Corporation has an office, has appointed an agent for the purpose of accepting service or notice of process, or has issued or guaranteed securities. No actions shall, however, be brought by member or persons acting for or deriving claims from members. The property and assets of the Corporation shall, wheresoever located and by whomsoever held, be immune from all forms of seizure, attachment or execution before the delivery of final judgment against the Corporation.

SECTION 4. *Immunity of Assets from Seizure*

Property and assets of the Corporation, wherever located and by whomsoever held, shall be immune from search, requisition, confiscation, expropriation or any other form of seizure by executive or legislative action.

SECTION 5. *Immunity of Archives*

The archives of the Corporation shall be inviolable.

SECTION 6. *Freedom of Assets from Restrictions*

To the extent necessary to carry out the operations provided for in this Agreement and subject to the provisions of Article III, Section 5, and the other provisions of this Agreement, all property and assets of the Corporation shall be free from restrictions, regulations, controls and moratoria of any nature.

SECTION 7. *Privilege for Communications*

The official communications of the Corporation shall be accorded by each member the same treatment that it accords to the official communications of other members.

SECTION 8. *Immunities and Privileges of Officers and Employees*

All Governors, Directors, Alternates, officers and employees of the Corporation:
  (i) shall be immune from legal process with respect to acts performed by them in their official capacity;
 (ii) not being local nationals, shall be accorded the same immunities from immigration restrictions, alien registration requirements and national service obligations and the same facilities as regards exchange restrictions as are accorded by members to the representatives, officials, and employees of comparable rank of other members;
(iii) shall be granted the same treatment in respect of travelling facilities as is accorded by members to representatives, officials and employees of comparable rank of other members.

SECTION 9. *Immunities from Taxation*

(a) The Corporation, its assets, property, income and its operations and transactions authorized by this Agreement, shall be immune from all taxation and from all customs duties. The Corporation shall also be immune from liability for the collection or payment of any tax or duty.

(b) No tax shall be levied on or in respect of salaries and emoluments paid by the Corporation to Directors, Alternates, officials or employees of the Corporation who are not local citizens, local subjects, or other local nationals.

(c) No taxation of any kind shall be levied on any obligation or security issued by the Corporation (including any dividend or interest thereon) by whomsoever held:

(i) which discriminates against such obligation or security solely because it is issued by the Corporation; or

(ii) if the sole jurisdictional basis for such taxation is the place or currency in which it is issued, made payable or paid, or the location of any office or place of business maintained by the Corporation.

(d) No taxation of any kind shall be levied on any obligation or security guaranteed by the Corporation (including any dividend or interest thereon) by whomsoever held:

(i) which discriminates against such obligation or security solely because it is guaranteed by the Corporation; or

(ii) if the sole jurisdictional basis for such taxation is the location of any office or place of business maintained by the Corporation.

SECTION 10. *Application of Article*

Each member shall take such action as is necessary in its own territories for the purpose of making effective in terms of its own law the principles set forth in this Article and shall inform the Corporation of the detailed action which it has taken.

SECTION 11. *Waiver*

The Corporation in its discretion may waive any of the privileges and immunities conferred under this Article to such extent and upon such conditions as it may determine.

ARTICLE VII

Amendments

(a) This Agreement may be amended by vote of three-fifths of the Governors exercising four-fifths of the total voting power.

(b) Notwithstanding paragraph (a) above, the affirmative vote of all Governors is required in the case of any amendment modifying:

(i) the right to withdraw from the Corporation provided in Article V, Section 1;

(ii) the pre-emptive right secured by Article II, Section 2(d);

(iii) the limitation on liability provided in Article II, Section 4.

(c) Any proposal to amend this Agreement, whether emanating from a member, a Governor or the Board of Directors, shall be communicated to the Chairman of the Board of Governors who shall bring the proposal before the Board of Governors. When an amendment has been duly adopted, the Corporation shall so certify by formal communication addressed to all members. Amendments shall enter into force for all members three months after the date of the formal communication unless the Board of Governors shall specify a shorter period.

ARTICLE VIII

Interpretation and Arbitration

(a) Any question of interpretation of the provisions of this Agreement arising between any member and the Corporation or between any members of the Corporation shall be submitted to the Board of Directors for its decision. If the question particularly affects any member of the Corporation not entitled to appoint an Executive Director of the Bank, it shall be entitled to representation in accordance with Article IV, Section 4(g).

(b) In any case where the Board of Directors has given a decision under (a) above, any member may require that the question be referred to the Board of Governors, whose decision shall be final. Pending the result of the reference to the Board of Governors, the Corporation may, so far as it deems necessary, act on the basis of the decision of the Board of Directors.

(c) Whenever a disagreement arises between the Corporation and a country which has ceased to be a member, or between the Corporation and any member during the permanent suspension of the Corporation, such disagreement shall be submitted to arbitration by a tribunal of three arbitrators, one appointed by the Corporation, another by the country involved and an umpire who, unless the parties otherwise agree, shall be appointed by the President of the International Court of Justice or such other authority as may have been prescribed by regulation adopted by the Corporation. The umpire shall have full power to settle all questions of procedure in any case where the parties are in disagreement with respect thereto.

ARTICLE IX

Final Provisions

SECTION 1. *Entry into Force*

This Agreement shall enter into force when it has been signed on behalf of not less than 30 governments whose subscriptions comprise not less than 75 percent of the total subscriptions set forth in Schedule A and the instruments referred to in Section 2 (a) of this Article have been deposited on their behalf, but in no event shall this Agreement enter into force before October 1, 1955.

SECTION 2. *Signature*

(a) Each government on whose behalf this Agreement is signed shall deposit with the Bank an instrument setting forth that it has accepted this Agreement without reservation in accordance with its law and has taken all steps necessary to enable it to carry out all of its obligations under this Agreement.

(b) Each government shall become a member of the Corporation as from the date of the deposit on its behalf of the instrument referred to in paragraph (a) above except that no government shall become a member before this Agreement enters into force under Section 1 of this Article.

(c) This Agreement shall remain open for signature until the close of business on December 31, 1956, at the principal office of the Bank on behalf of the governments of the countries whose names are set forth in Schedule A.

(d) After this Agreement shall have entered into force, it shall be open for signature on behalf of the government of any country whose membership has been approved pursuant to Article II, Section 1 (b).

SECTION 3. *Inauguration of the Corporation*

(a) As soon as this Agreement enters into force under Section 1 of this Article the Chairman of the Board of Directors shall call a meeting of the Board of Directors.

(b) The Corporation shall begin operations on the date when such meeting is held.

(c) Pending the first meeting of the Board of Governors, the Board of Directors may exercise all the powers of the Board of Governors except those reserved to the Board of Governors under this Agreement.

DONE at Washington, in a single copy which shall remain deposited in the archives of the International Bank for Reconstruction and Development, which has indicated by its signature below its agreement to act as depository of this Agreement and to notify all governments whose names are set forth in Schedule A of the date when this Agreement shall enter into force under Article IX, Section 1 hereof.

SCHEDULE A

Subscription to Capital Stock of the International Finance Corporation

Country	Number of Shares	Amount (in United States dollars)
Australia	2,215	2,215,000
Austria	554	554,000
Belgium	2,492	2,492,000
Bolivia	78	78,000
Brazil	1,163	1,163,000
Burma	166	166,000
Canada	3,600	3,600,000
Ceylon	166	166,000
Chile	388	388,000
China	6,646	6,646,000
Colombia	388	388,000
Costa Rica	22	22,000
Cuba	388	388,000
Denmark	753	753,000
Dominican Republic	22	22,000
Ecuador	35	35,000
Egypt	590	590,000
El Salvador	11	11,000
Ethiopia	33	33,000
Finland	451	421,000
France	5,815	5,815,000
Germany	3,655	3,655,000
Greece	277	277,000
Guatemala	22	22,000
Haiti	22	22,000
Honduras	11	11,000
Iceland	11	11,000
India	4,431	4,431,000
Indonesia	1,218	1,218,000
Iran	372	372,000
Iraq	67	67,000
Israel	50	50,000
Italy	1,994	1,994,000
Japan	2,769	2,769,000
Jordan	33	33,000
Lebanon	50	50,000
Luxembourg	111	111,000
Mexico	720	720,000
Netherlands	3,046	3,046,000
Nicaragua	9	9,000
Norway	554	554,000
Pakistan	1,108	1,108,000
Panama	2	2,000
Paraguay	16	16,000
Peru	194	194,000
Philippines	166	166,000
Sweden	1,108	1,108,000
Syria	72	72,000
Thailand	139	139,000
Turkey	476	476,000
Union of South Africa	1,108	1,108,000
United Kingdom	14,400	14,400,000
United States	35,168	35,168,000
Uruguay	116	116,000
Venezuela	116	116,000
Yugoslavia	443	443,000
Total:	100,000	$100,000,000

b. BY-LAWS OF THE INTERNATIONAL FINANCE CORPORATION, DONE AT WASHINGTON, D.C., OCTOBER 1, 1956[1]

These By-Laws are adopted under the authority of, and are intended to be complementary to, the Articles of Agreement of the International Finance Corporation (hereinafter called the Corporation), and they shall be construed accordingly. In the event of a conflict between anything in these By-Laws and any provision or requirement of the Articles of Agreement, the Articles of Agreement shall prevail.

SECTION 1. *Meetings of the Board of Governors*

(a) Special meetings of the Board of Governors may be called at any time by the Board of Governors or the Board of Directors.

(b) Any meeting of the Board of Governors at which a quorum shall not be present may be adjourned from time to time by a majority of the Governors present and notice of the adjourned meeting need not be given.

SECTION 2. *Notice of Meetings of the Board of Governors*

The Chairman of the Board of Directors shall cause notice of the time and place of each of the Board of Governors to be given to each member of the Corporation by any rapid means of communication which shall be dispatched not less than 42 days prior to the date set for such meeting, except that in urgent cases such notice shall be sufficient if dispatched by telegram or cable not less than 10 days prior to the date set for such meeting.

SECTION 3. *Attendance of Directors and Observers at Meetings of the Board of Governors*

(a) The Directors and their Alternates may attend all meetings of the Board of Governors and may participate in such meetings, but a Director or his Alternate shall not be entitled to vote at any such meeting unless he shall be entitled to vote as a Governor or an Alternate or a temporary Alternate of a Governor.

(b) The Chairman of the Board of Governors, in consultation with the Board of Directors, may invite observers to attend any meeting of the Board of Governors.

SECTION 4. *Agenda of Meetings of the Board of Governors*

(a) Under the direction of the Board of Directors, the Chairman of the Board of Directors shall prepare a brief agenda for each meeting of the Board of Governors and shall cause such agenda to be transmitted to each member of the Corporation with the notice of such meeting.

(b) Additional subjects may be placed on the agenda for any meeting of the Board of Governors by any Governor provided that he shall give notice thereof to the Chairman of the Board of Directors not less than seven days prior to the date set for such meeting. In special circumstances the Chairman of the Board of Directors by direction of the Board of Directors may at any time place additional subjects on the agenda for any meeting of the Board of Governors. The Chairman of the Board of Directors shall cause notice of the addition of any subjects to the agenda for any meeting of the Board of Governors to be given as promptly as possible to each member of the Corporation.

---

[1] As published by the Corporation.

(c) The Board of Governors may at any time authorize any subject to be placed on the agenda for any meeting of such Board even though the notice required by this section shall not have been given.

(d) Except as otherwise specifically directed by the Board of Governors, the Chairman of the Board of Governors jointly with the Chairman of the Board of Directors shall have charge of all arrangements for the holding of meetings of the Board of Governors.

SECTION 5. *Chairman and Vice Chairmen*

The Chairman and Vice Chairmen of the Board of Governors of the International Bank for Reconstruction and Development (hereinafter called the Bank) shall be, provided that they are Governors of the Corporation, the Chairman and Vice Chairmen, respectively, of the Board of Governors of the Corporation. If, however, the Chairman of the Board of Governors of the Bank shall not be a Governor of the Corporation, the Board of Governors of the Corporation at its annual meeting shall select a Governor to act as Chairman. As used in this Section, the term "Chairman of the Board of Governors of the Bank" shall include any Vice Chairman acting in his place.

SECTION 6. *Secretary*

The Secretary of the Corporation shall serve as Secretary of the Board of Governors.

SECTION 7. *Minutes*

The Board of Governors shall keep a summary record of its proceedings which shall be available to all members and which shall be filed with the Board of Directors for its guidance.

SECTION 8. *Annual Report*

The Board of Directors shall have prepared for presentation at the annual meeting of the Board of Governors one or more reports in which shall be discussed the operations and policies of the Corporation and which shall make recommendations to the Board of Governors on the problems confronting the Corporation.

SECTION 9. *Voting*

Except as otherwise specifically provided in the Articles of Agreement, all decisions of the Board of Governors shall be made by a majority of the votes cast. At any meeting the Chairman may ascertain the sense of the meeting in lieu of a formal vote but he shall require a formal vote upon the request of any Governor. Whenever a formal vote is required the written text of the motion shall be distributed to the voting members.

SECTION 10. *Proxies*

No Governor or Alternate may vote at any meeting by proxy or by any other method than in person, but a member may make provision for the designation of a temporary Alternate to vote for the Governor at any Board session at which the regularly designated Alternate is unable to be present.

SECTION 11. *Voting without Meeting*

Whenever, in the judgment of the Board of Directors, any action by the Corporation must be taken by the Board of Governors which should not be postponed until the next regular meeting of the Board and does not warrant the calling of a special meeting of the Board, the Board of directors shall present to each member by any rapid means of communication a motion embodying the proposed action with a request for a vote by the Board of Governors. Votes shall be cast during such period as the Board of Directors may prescribe, provided that no Governor shall vote on any such motion until 7 days after dispatch of the motion unless he is notified that the Board of Directors has waived this requirement. At the expiration of the period prescribed for voting, the Board of Directors shall record the results and the Chairman of the Board of Directors shall notify all members. If the replies received do not include a majority of the Governors exercising two-thirds of the total voting power, the motion shall be considered lost.

SECTION 12. *Terms of Service*

(a) Governors and Alternates shall be reimbursed for their expenses in attending meetings on behalf of the Corporation on the same basis as they are reimbursed for expenses in attending meetings on behalf of the Bank; provided, however, that with respect to any meeting held on behalf of the Corporation at or about the same time as a meeting held on behalf of the Bank, they shall be reimbursed only for additional expenses incurred in attending the meeting on behalf of the Corporation.

(b) The Corporation shall reimburse Governors and Directors and their Alternates, the Chairman of the Board of Directors, the President and staff members for taxes they are required to pay on their salaries and allowances on the same basis that tax reimbursement is made by the Bank on corresponding salaries and allowances.

(c) The Chairman of the Board of Directors shall serve without compensation. The Corporation shall pay any reasonable expenses incurred by him in the interest of the Corporation.

(d) They salary of the President and the term of his contract shall be as determined by the Board of Directors. The Corporation shall also pay any reasonable expenses incurred by the President in the interest of the Corporation (including travel and transportation expenses for himself, and expenses for his family and his personal effects in moving once to the seat of the Corporation during or immediately before his term of office and in moving once from the seat during or immediately after his term of office).

(e) It shall be the duty of a Director and his Alternate to devote all the time and attention to the buisness of the Corporation that its interests require, and between them to be continuously available at the seat of the Corporation. A Director who is unable to attend any meeting of the Board of Directors or a committee thereof may designate a temporary Alternate Director to attend and act for him at such meeting. The terms Alternate and Alternate Director whenever used in these By-Laws shall, unless the context shall otherwise require, include any such temporary Alternate Director.

(f) A Director or Alternate Director receiving compensation on a full-time basis for services as Executive Director or Alternate Executive Director, respectively, of the Bank, or of the Bank and the International Monetary Fund (hereinafter called the Fund), shall not receive any additional compensation for services as a Director or Alternate Director of the Corporation. A Director or Alternate Director receiving compensation on a part-time basis for services to the Bank, or to the Bank and Fund, shall receive compensation for such additional time as he may spend in the service of the Corporation at the same rate applicable to his services to the Bank. The aggregate of the remuneration and leave and resettlement allowances received for such services by a Director or Alternate Director from the Corporation and the Bank (or from the Corporation, the Bank and the Fund) shall not exceed the maximum to which he would be entitled if he served either the Bank or the Fund, as the case may be, on a full-time basis.

(g) Compensation received by a Director or an Alternate Director pursuant to paragraph (f) above shall be in lieu of all other salary and expense allowances, including allowances for housing, entertainment and other expenses, except as provided hereinafter. Each Director or Alternate Director who does not reside at or near the seat of the Corporation shall be entitled to a reasonable allowance for expenses incurred by him in attending of the Board of Directors or committees thereof, but only over and above those which would have been incurred in any event in attending meetings of the Executive Directors of the Bank. Each Director and Alternate Director who shall at the request of the President perform designated service for the Corporation shall be entitled to a reasonable allowance for expenses incurred by him in the performance thereof. Nothing herein shall preclude the Corporation from entering into appropriate arrangements with the Bank for sharing remuneration, allowances and other expenses paid to the Director and Alternates by either institution.

(h) An individual claiming reimbursement or allowance for any expenses incurred by him shall include in his claim a representation that he has not received and will not claim reimbursement or allowance in respect to those expenses from any other source.

(i) Administration of this Section shall be governed, to the extent applicable, by the established practices of the Bank.

SECTION 13. *Delegation of Authority*

The Board of Directors may exercise all the powers of the Corporation except those reserved to the Board of Governors by Article IV, Section 2 (c) and other provisions of the Articles of Agreement. The Board of Directors shall not take any action pursuant to powers delegated by the Board of Governors which is inconsistent with any action taken by the Board of Governors.

SECTION 14. *Rules and Regulations*

The Board of Directors may adopt such rules and regulations, including financial regulations, as may be necessary or appropriate to conduct the business of the Corporation. Any rules and regulations so adopted, and any amendments thereof, shall be subject to review by the Board of Governors at its next annual meeting.

SECTION 15. *Representation of Members Not Entitled to Appoint a Director*

Whenever the Board of Directors is to consider a request made by, or a matter particularly affecting a member not entitled to appoint an Executive Director of the Bank, the member shall be promptly informed in writing of the date set for its consideration. No final action shall be taken by the Board of Directors, nor any question affecting the member submitted to the Board of Governors, until the member has been offered a reasonable opportunity to present its views and to be heard at a meeting of the Board of Directors of which the member has had reasonable notice. Any member so electing may waive this provision.

SECTION 16. *Budget and Audits*

The Board of Directors shall have an audit of the accounts of the Corporation made at least once each year and on the basis of this audit shall submit a statement of its accounts, including a balance sheet and a statement of profit and loss, to the Board of Governors to be considered by it at its annual meeting.

The Board of Directors shall instruct the President to prepare an annual administrative budget for the Board's approval. The budget as approved shall be presented to the Board of Governors at its annual meeting.

SECTION 17. *Application for Membership*

Subject to any special provisions that may be made for countries listed in Schedule A of the Articles of Agreement, any member of the Bank may apply for membership in the Corporation by filing with the Corporation an application setting forth all relevant facts.

When submitting an application to the Board of Governors, the Board of Directors, after consultation with the applicant country, shall make recommendations to the Board of Governors as to the number of shares of capital stock to be subscribed and such other conditions as, in the opinion of the Board of Directors, should be prescribed by the Board of Governors.

SECTION 18. *Suspension of Membership*

Before any member is suspended from membership in the Corporation (other than under Section 3 of Article V of the Articles of Agreement), the matter shall be considered by the Board of Directors which shall inform the member in reasonable time of the complaint against it and allow the member an adequate opportunity for stating its case both orally and in writing. The Board of Directors shall recommend to the Board of Governors the action it deems appropriate. The member shall be informed of the recommendation and the date on which its case will be considered by the Board of Governors and shall be given a reasonable time within which to present its case to the Board of Governors both orally and in writing. Any member so electing may waive this provision.

SECTION 19. *Amendment to By-Laws*

These By-Laws may be amended by the Board of Governors at any meeting thereof or by vote without a meeting as provided in Section 11.

7. INTERNATIONAL DEVELOPMENT ASSOCIATION

a. ARTICLES OF AGREEMENT OF THE INTERNATIONAL DEVELOPMENT ASSOCIATION, EFFECTIVE SEPTEMBER 24, 1960

LIST OF ARTICLES AND SECTIONS

ARTICLES OF AGREEMENT OF THE
INTERNATIONAL DEVELOPMENT ASSOCIATION

The Governments on whose behalf this Agreement is signed,

Considering:

That mutual cooperation for constructive economic purposes, healthy development of the world economy and balanced growth of international trade foster international relationships conductive to the maintenance of peace and world prosperity;

That an acceleration of economic development which will promote higher standards of living and economic and social progress in the less-developed countries is desirable not only in the interests of those countries but also in the interests of the international community as a whole;

That achievement of these objectives would be facilitated by an increase in the international flow of capital, public and private, to assist in the development of the resources of the less-developed countries, do hereby agree as follows:

INTRODUCTORY ARTICLE

The INTERNATIONAL DEVELOPMENT ASSOCIATION (hereinafter called "the Association)" is established and shall operate in accordance with the following provisions:

ARTICLE I

PURPOSES

The purposes of the Association are to promote economic development, increase productivity and thus raise standards of living in the less-developed areas of the world included within the Association's membership, in particular by providing finance to meet their important developmental requirements on terms which are more flexible

155

and bear less heavily on the balance of payments than those of conventional loans, thereby furthering the developmental objectives of the International Bank for Reconstruction and Development (hereinafter called "the Bank)" and supplementing its activities.

The Association shall be guided in all its decisions by the provisions of this Article.

ARTICLE II

MEMBERSHIP; INITIAL SUBSCRIPTIONS

SECTION 1. *Membership*

(a) The original members of the Association shall be those members of the Bank listed in Schedule A hereto which, on or before the date specified in Article XI, Section 2 (c), accept membership in the Association.

(b) Membership shall be open to other members of the Bank at such times and in accordance with such terms as the Association may determine.

SECTION 2. *Initial Subscriptions*

(a) Upon accepting membership, each member shall subscribe funds in the amount assigned to it. Such subscriptions are herein referred to as initial subscriptions.

(b) The initial subscription assigned to each original member shall be in the amount set forth opposite its name in Schedule A, expressed in terms of United States dollars of the weight and fineness in effect on January 1, 1960.

(c) Ten percent of the initial subscription of each original member shall be payable in gold or freely convertible currency as follows: fifty percent within thirty days after the date on which the Association shall begin operations pursuant to Article XI, Section 4, or on the date on which the original member becomes a member, whichever shall be later; twelve and one-half percent one year after the beginning of operations of the Association; and twelve and one-half percent each year thereafter at annual intervals until the ten percent portion of the initial subscription shall have been paid in full.

(d) The remaining ninety percent of the initial subscription of each original member shall be payable in gold or freely convertible currency in the case of members listed in Part I of Schedule A, and in the currency of the subscribing member in the case of members listed in Part II of Schedule A. This ninety percent portion of initial subscriptions of original members shall be payable in five equal annual instalments as follows: the first such instalment within thirty days after the date on which the Association shall begin operations pursuant to Article XI, Section 4, or on the date on which the original member becomes a member, whichever shall be later; the second instalment one year after the beginning of operations of the Association, and succeeding instalments each year thereafter at annual intervals until the ninety percent portion of the initial subscription shall have been paid in full.

(e) The Association shall accept from any member, in place of any part of the member's currency paid in or payable by the member under the preceding subsection (d) or under Section 2 of Article IV and not needed by the Association in its operations, notes or similar obligations issued by the government of the member or the depository designated by such member, which shall be non-negotiable, non-interest-bearing and payable at their par value on demand to the account of the Association in the designated depository.

(f) For the purposes of this Agreement the Association shall regard as "freely convertible currency:"

(i) currency of a member which the Association determines, after consultation with the International Monetary Fund, is adequately convertible into the currencies of other members for the purposes of the Association's operations; or

156

(ii) currency of a member which such member agrees, on terms satisfactory to the Association, to exchange for the currencies of other members for the purposes of the Association's operations.

(g) Except as the Association may otherwise agree, each member listed in Part I of Schedule A shall maintain, in respect of its currency paid in by it as freely convertible currency pursuant to subsection (d) of this Section, the same convertibility as existed at the time of payment.

(h) The conditions on which the initial subscriptions of members other than original members may be made, and the amounts and the terms of payment thereof, shall be determined by the Association pursuant to Section 1 (b) of this Article.

SECTION 3. *Limitation on Liability*

No member shall be liable, by reason of its membership, for obligations of the Association.

ARTICLE III

ADDITIONS TO RESOURCES

SECTION 1. *Additional Subscriptions*

(a) The Association shall at such time as it deems appropriate in the light of the schedule for completion of payments on initial subscriptions of original members, and at intervals of approximately five years thereafter, review the adequacy of its resources and, if it deems desirable, shall authorize a general increase in subscriptions. Notwithstanding the foregoing, general or individual increases in subscriptions may be authorized at any time, provided that an individual increase shall be considered only at the request of the member involved. Subscriptions pursuant to this Section are herein referred to as additional subscriptions.

(b) Subject to the provisions of paragraph (c) below, when additional subscriptions are authorized, the amounts authorized for subscription and the terms and conditions relating thereto shall be as determined by the Association.

(c) When any additional subscription is authorized, each member shall be given an opportunity to subscribe, under such conditions as shall be reasonably determined by the Association, an amount which will enable it to maintain its relative voting power, but no member shall be obligated to subscribe.

(d) All decisions under this Section shall be made by a two-thirds majority of the total voting power.

SECTION 2. *Supplementary Resources Provided by a Member in the Currency of Another Member*

(a) The Association may enter into arrangements, on such terms and conditions consistent with the provisions of this Agreement as may be agreed upon, to receive from any member, in addition to the amounts payable by such member on account of its initial or any additional subscription, supplementary resources in the currency of another member, provided that the Association shall not enter into any such arrangement unless the Association is satisfied that the member whose currency is involved agrees to the use of such currency as supplementary resources and to the terms and conditions governing such use. The arrangements under which any such resources are received may include provisions regarding the disposition of earnings on the resources and regarding the disposition of the resources in the event that the member providing them ceases to be a member or the Association permanently suspends its operations.

(b) The Association shall deliver to the contributing member a Special Development Certificate setting forth the amount and currency of the resources so contributed and the terms and conditions of the arrangement relating to such resources. A special Development Certificate shall not carry any voting rights and shall be transferable only to the Association.

(c) Nothing in this Section shall preclude the Association from accepting resources from a member in its own currency on such terms as may be agreed upon.

ARTICLE IV

CURRENCIES

SECTION 1. *Use of Currencies*

(a) Currency of any member listed in Part II of Schedule A, whether or not freely convertible, received by the Association pursuant to Article II, Section 2 (d), in payment of the ninety percent portion payable thereunder in the currency of such member, and currency of such member derived therefrom as principal, interest or other charges, may be used by the Association for administrative expenses incurred by the Association in the territories of such member and, insofar as consistent with sound monetary policies, in payment for goods and services produced in the territories of such member and required for projects financed by the Association and located in such territories; and in addition when and to the extent justified by the economic and financial situation of the member concerned as determined by agreement between the member and the Association, such currency shall be freely convertible or otherwise usable for projects financed by the Association and located outside the territories of the member.

(b) The usability of currencies received by the Association in payment of subscriptions other than initial subscriptions of original members, and currencies derived therefrom as principal, interest or other charges, shall be governed by the terms and conditions on which such subscriptions are authorized.

(c) The usability of currencies received by the Association as supplementary resources other than subcriptions, and currencies derived therefrom as principal, interest or other charges, shall be governed by the terms of the arrangements pursuant to which such currencies are received.

(d) All other currencies received by the Association may be freely used and exchanged by the Association and shall not be subject to any restriction by the member whose currency is used or exchanged; provided that the foregoing shall not preclude the Association from entering into any arrangements with the member in whose territories any project financed by the Association is located restricting the use by the Association of such member's currency received as principal, interest or other charges in connection with such financing.

(e) The Association shall take appropriate steps to ensure that, over reasonable intervals of time, the portions of the subscriptions paid under Article II, Section 2 (d) by members listed in Part I of Schedule A shall be used by the Association on an approximately *pro rata* basis, provided, however, that such portions of such subscriptions as are paid in gold or in a currency other than that of the subscribing member may be used more rapidly.

SECTION 2. *Maintenance of Value of Currency Holdings*

(a) Whenever the par value of a member's currency is reduced or the foreign exchange value of a member's currency has, in the opinion of the Association, depreciated to a significant extent within that member's territories, the member shall pay to the Association within a reasonable time an additional amount of its own currency sufficient to maintain the value, as of the time of subscription, of the amount of the currency of such member paid in to the Association by the member under Article II,

Section 2 (d), and currency furnished under the provisions of the present paragraph, whether or not such currency is held in the form of notes accepted pursuant to Article II, Section 2 (e), provided, however, that the foregoing shall apply only so long as and to the extent that such currency shall not have been initially disbursed or exchanged for the currency of another member.

(b) Whenever the par value of a member's currency is increased, or the foreign exchange value of a member's currency has, in the opinion of the Association, appreciated to a significant extent within that member's territories, the Association shall return to such member within a reasonable time an amount of that member's currency equal to the increase in the value of the amount of such currency to which the provisions of paragraph (a) of this Section are applicable.

(c) The provisions of the preceding paragraphs may be waived by the Association when a uniform proportionate change in the par value of the currencies of all its members is made by the International Monetary Fund.

(d) Amounts furnished under the provisions of paragraph (a) of this Section to maintain the value of any currency shall be convertible and usable to the same extent as such currency.

ARTICLE V

OPERATIONS

SECTION 1. *Use of Resources and Conditions of Financing*

(a) The Association shall provide financing to further development in the less-developed areas of the world included within the Association's membership.

(b) Financing provided by the Association shall be for purposes which in the opinion of the Association are of high developmental priority in the light of the needs of the area or areas concerned and, except in special circumstances, shall be for specific projects.

(c) The Association shall not provide financing if in its opinion such financing is available from private sources on terms which are reasonable for the recipient or could be provided by a loan of the type made by the Bank.

(d) The Association shall not provide financing except upon the recommendation of a competent committee, made after a careful study of the merits of the proposal. Each such committee shall be appointed by the Association and shall include a nominee of the Governor or Governors representing the member or members in whose territories the project under consideration is located and one or more members of the technical staff of the Association. The requirement that the committee include the nominee of a Governor or Governors shall not apply in the case of financing provided to a public international or regional organization.

(e) The Association shall not provide financing for any project if the member in whose territories the project is located objects to such financing, except that it shall not be necessary for the Association to assure itself that individual members do not object in the case of financing provided to a public international or regional organization.

(f) The Association shall impose no conditions that the proceeds of its financing shall be spent in the territories of any particular member or members. The foregoing shall not preclude the Association from complying with any restrictions on the use of funds imposed in accordance with the provisions of these Articles, including restrictions attached to supplementary resources pursuant to agreement between the Association and the contributor.

(g) The Association shall make arrangements to ensure that the proceeds of any financing are used only for the purposes for which the financing was provided, with due attention to considerations of economy, efficiency and competitive international trade and without regard to political or other non-economic influences or considerations.

(h) Funds to be provided under any financing operation shall be made available to the recipient only to meet expenses in connection with the project as they are actually incurred.

SECTION 2. *Form and Terms of Financing*

(a) Financing by the Association shall take the form of loans. The Association may, however, provide other financing, either

    (i) out of funds subscribed pursuant to Article III, Section 1, and funds derived therefrom as principal, interest or other charges, if the authorization for such subscriptions expressly provides for such financing; or

    (ii) in special circumstances, out of supplementary resources furnished to the Association, and funds derived therefrom as principal, interest or other charges, if the arrangements under which such resources are furnished expressly authorize such financing.

(b) Subject to the foregoing paragraph, the Association may provide financing in such forms and on such terms as it may deem appropriate, having regard to the economic position and prospects of the area or areas concerned and to the nature and requirements of the project.

(c) The Association may provide financing to a member, the government of a territory included within the Association's membership, a political subdivision of any of the foregoing, a public or private entity in the territories of a member or members, or to a public international or regional organization.

(d) In the case of a loan to an entity other than a member, the Association may, in its discretion, require a suitable governmental or other guarantee or guarantees.

(e) The Association, in special cases, may make foreign exchange available for local expenditures.

SECTION 3. *Modifications of Terms of Financing*

The Association may, when and to the extent it deems appropriate in the light of all relevant circumstances, including the financial and economic situation and prospects of the member concerned, and on such conditions as it may determine, agree to a relaxation or other modification of the terms on which any of its financing shall have been provided.

SECTION 4. *Cooperation with Other International Organizations and Members Providing Development Assistance*

The Association shall cooperate with those public international organizations and members which provide financial and technical assistance to the less-developed areas of the world.

SECTION 5. *Miscellaneous Operations*

In addition to the operations specified elsewhere in this Agreement, the Association may:

    (i) Borrow funds with the approval of the member in whose currency the loan is denominated;

    (ii) guarantee securities in which it has invested in order to facilitate their sale;

    (iii) buy and sell securities it has issued or guaranteed or in which it has invested;

(iv) in special cases, guarantee loans from other sources for purposes not inconsistent with the provisions of these Articles;

(v) provide technical assistance and advisory services at the request of a member; and

(vi) exercise such other powers incidental to its operations as shall be necessary or desirable in furtherance of its purposes.

SECTION 6. *Political Activity Prohibited*

The Association and its officers shall not interfere in the political affairs of any member; nor shall they be influenced in their decisions by the political character of the member or members concerned. Only economic considerations shall be relevant to their decisions, and these considerations shall be weighed impartially in order to achieve the purposes stated in this Agreement.

ARTICLE VI

ORGANIZATION AND MANAGEMENT

SECTION 1. *Structure of the Association*

The Association shall have a Board of Governors, Executive Directors, a President and such other officers and staff to perform such duties as the Association as the Association may determine.

SECTION 2. *Board of Governors*

(a) All the powers of the Association shall be vested in the Board of Governors.

(b) Each Governor and Alternate Governor of the Bank appointed by a member of the Bank which is also a member of the Association shall *ex officio* be a Governor and Alternate Governor, respectively, of the Association. No Alternate Governor may vote except in the absence of his principal. The Chairman of the Board of Governors of the Bank shall *ex officio* be Chairman of the Board of Governors of the Association except that if the Chairman of the Board of Governors of the Bank shall represent a state which is not a member of the Association, then the Board of Governors shall select one of the Governors as Chairman of the Board of Governors. Any Governor or Alternate Governor shall cease to hold office if the member by which he was appointed shall cease to be a member of the Association.

(c) The Board of Governors may delegate to the Executive Directors authority to exercise any of its powers, except the power to:

(i) admit new members and determine the conditions of their admission;

(ii) authorize additional subscriptions and determine the terms and conditions relating thereto;

(iii) suspend a member;

(iv) decide appeals from interpretations of this Agreement given by the Executive Directors;

(v) make arrangements pursuant to Section 7 of this Article to cooperate with other international organizations (other than informal arrangements of a temporary and administrative character);

(vi) decide to suspend permanently the operations of the Association and to distribute its assets;

(vii) determine the distribution of the Association's net income pursuant to Section 12 of this Article; and

(viii) approve proposed amendments to this Agreement.

(d) The Board of Governors shall hold an annual meeting and such other meetings as may be provided for by the Board of Governors or called by the Executive Directors.

(e) The annual meeting of the Board of Governors shall be held in conjunction with the annual meeting of the Board of Governors of the Bank.

(f) A quorum for any meeting of the Board of Governors shall be a majority of the Governors, exercising not less than two-thirds of the total voting power.

(g) The Association may by regulation establish a procedure whereby the Executive Directors may obtain a vote of the Governors on a specific question without calling a meeting of the Board of Governors.

(h) The Board of Governors, and the Executive Directors to the extent authorized, may adopt such rules and regulations as may be necessary or appropriate to conduct the business of the Association.

(i) Governors and Alternate Governors shall serve as such without compensation from the Association.

SECTION 3. *Voting*

(a) Each original member shall, in respect of its initial subscription, have 500 votes plus one additional vote for each $5,000 of its initial subscription. Subscriptions other than initial subscriptions of original members shall carry such voting rights as the Board of Governors shall determine pursuant to the provisions of Article II, Section 1 (b) or Article III, Section 1 (b) and (c), as the case may be. Additions to resources other than subscriptions under Article II, Section 1 (b) and additional subscriptions under Article III, Section 1, shall not carry voting rights.

(b) Except as otherwise specifically provided, all matters before the Association shall be decided by a majority of the votes cast.

SECTION 4. *Executive Directors*

(a) The Executive Directors shall be responsible for the conduct of the general operations of the Association, and for this purpose shall exercise all the powers given to them by this Agreement or delegated to them by the Board of Governors.

(b) The Executive Directors of the Association shall be composed *ex officio* of each Executive Director of the Bank who shall have been (i) appointed by a member of the Bank which is also a member of the Association, or (ii) elected in an election in which the votes of at least one member of the Bank which is also a member of the Association shall have counted toward his election. The Alternate to each such Executive Director of the Bank shall *ex officio* be an Alternate Director of the Association. Any Director shall cease to hold office if the member by which he was appointed, or if all the members whose votes counted toward his election, shall cease to be members of the Association.

(c) Each Director who is an appointed Executive Director of the Bank shall be entitled to cast the number of votes which the member by which he was appointed is entitled to cast in the Association. Each Director who is an elected Executive Director of the Bank shall be entitled to cast the number of votes which the member or members of the Association whose votes counted toward his election in the Bank are entitled to cast in the Association. All the votes which a Director is entitled to cast shall be cast as a unit.

(d) An Alternate Director shall have full power to act in the absence of the Director who shall have appointed him. When a Director is present, his Alternate may participate in meetings but shall not vote.

(e) A quorum for any meeting of the Executive Directors shall be a majority of the Directors exercising not less than one-half of the total voting power.

(f) The Executive Directors shall meet as often as the business of the Association may require.

(g) The Board of Governors shall adopt regulations under which a member of the Association not entitled to appoint an Executive Director of the Bank may send a representative to attend any meeting of the Executive Directors of the Association when a request made by, or a matter particularly affecting, that member is under consideration.

SECTION 5. *President and Staff*

(a) The President of the Bank shall be *ex officio* President of the Association. The President shall be Chairman of the Executive Directors of the Association but shall have no vote except a deciding vote in case of an equal division. He may participate in meetings of the Board of Governors but shall not vote at such meetings.

(b) The President shall be chief of the operating staff of the Association. Under the direction of the Executive Directors he shall conduct the ordinary business of the Association and under their general control shall be responsible for the organization, appointment and dismissal of the officers and staff. To the extent practicable, officers and staff of the Bank shall be appointed to serve concurrently as officers and staff of the Association.

(c) The President, officers and staff of the Association, in the discharge of their offices, owe their duty entirely to the Association and to no other authority. Each member of the Association shall respect the international character of this duty and shall refrain from all attempts to influence any of them in the discharge of their duties.

(d) In appointing officers and staff the President shall, subject to the paramount importance of securing the highest standards of efficiency and of technical competence, pay due regard to the importance of recruiting personnel on as wide a geographical basis as possible.

SECTION 6. *Relationship to the Bank*

(a) The Association shall be an entity separate and distinct from the Bank and the funds of the Association shall be kept separate and apart from those of the Bank. The Association shall not borrow from or lend to the Bank, except that this shall not preclude the Association from investment funds not needed in its financing operations in obligations of the Bank.

(b) The Association may make arrangements with the Bank regarding facilities, personnel and services and arrangements for reimbursement of administrative expenses paid in the first instance by either organization on behalf of the other.

(c) Nothing in this Agreement shall make the Association liable for the acts or obligations of the Bank, or the Bank liable for the acts or obligations of the Association.

SECTION 7. *Relations with Other International Organizations*

The Association shall enter into formal arrangments with the United Nations and may enter into such arrangements with other public international organizations having specialized responsibilities in related fields.

SECTION 8. *Location of Offices*

The principal office of the Association shall be the principal office of the Bank. The Association may establish other offices in the territories of any member.

SECTION 9. *Depositories*

Each member shall designate its central bank as a depository in which the Association may keep holdings of such member's currency or other assets of the Association, or, if it has no central bank, it shall designate for such purpose such other institution as may be acceptable to the Association. In the absence of any different designation, the depository designated for the Bank shall be the depository for the Association.

SECTION 10. *Channel of Communication*

Each member shall designate an appropriate authority with which the Association may communicate in connection with any matter arising under this Agreement. In the absence of any different designation, the channel of communication designated for the Bank shall be the channel for the Association.

SECTION 11. *Publication of Reports and Provision of Information*

(a) The Association shall publish an annual report containing an audited statement of its accounts and shall circulate to members at appropriate intervals a summary statement of its financial position and of the results of its operations.

(b) The Association may publish such other reports as it deems desirable to carry out its purposes.

(c) Copies of all reports, statements and publications made under this Section shall be distributed to members.

SECTION 12. *Disposition of Net Income*

The Board of Governors shall determine from time to time the disposition of the Association's net income, having due regard to provision for reserves and contingencies.

ARTICLE VII

WITHDRAWAL; SUSPENSION OF MEMBERSHIP;
SUSPENSION OF OPERATIONS

SECTION 1. *Withdrawal by Members*

Any member may withdraw from membership in the Association at any time by transmitting a notice in writing to the Association at its principal office. Withdrawal shall become effective upon the date such notice is received.

SECTION 2. *Suspension of Membership*

(a) If a member fails to fulfill any of its obligations to the Association, the Association may suspend its membership by decision of a majority of the Governors, exercising a majority of the total voting power. The member so suspended shall automatically cease to be a member one year from the date of its suspension unless a decision is taken by the majority to restore the member to good standing.

(b) While under suspension, a member shall not be entitled to exercise any rights under this Agreement except the right of withdrawal, but shall remain subject to all obligations.

SECTION 3. *Suspension or Cessation of Membership in the Bank*

Any member which is suspended from membership in, or ceases to be a member of, the Bank shall automatically be suspended from membership in, or cease to be a member of, the Association, as the case may be.

SECTION 4. *Rights and Duties of Governments Ceasing to be Members*

(a) When a government ceases to be a member, it shall have no rights under this Agreement except as provided in this Section and in Article X (c), but it shall, except as in this Section otherwise provided, remain liable for all financial obligations under-taken by it to the Association, whether as a member, borrower, guarantor or other-wise.

(b) When a government ceases to be a member, the Association and the government shall proceed to a settlement of accounts. As part of such settlement of accounts, the Association and the government may agree on the amounts to be paid to the govern-ment on account of its subscription and on the time and currencies of payment. The term "subscription" when used in relation to any member government shall for the purposes of this Article be deemed to include both the initial subscription and any ad-ditional subscription of such member government.

(c) If no such agreement is reached within six months from the date when the gov-ernment ceased to be a member, or such other time as may be agreed upon by the As-sociation and the government, the following provisions shall apply:

(i) The government shall be relieved of any further liability to the Association on account if its subscription, except that the government shall pay to the Asso-ciation forthwith amounts due and unpaid on the date when the government ceased to be a member and which in the opinion of the Association are needed by it to meet its commitments as of that date under its financing operations.

(ii) The Association shall return to the government funds paid in by the govern-ment on account of its subscription or derived therefrom as principal repay-ments and held by the Association on the date when the government ceased to be a member, except to the extent that in the opinion of the Association such funds will be needed by it meet its commitments as of that date under its fi-nancing operations.

(iii) The Association shall pay over to the government a *pro rata* share of all princi-pal repayments received by the Association after the date on which the govern-ment ceases to be a member on loans contracted prior thereto, except those made out of supplementary resources provided to the Association under ar-rangements specifying special liquidation rights. Such share shall be such pro-portion of the total principal amount of such loans as the total amount paid by the government on account of its subscription and not returned to it pur-suant to clause (ii) above shall bear to the total amount paid by all members on account of their subscriptions which shall have been used or in the opin-ion of the Association will be needed by it to meet its commitments under its financing operations as of the date on which the government ceases to be a member. Such payment by the Association shall be made in instalments when and as such principal repayments are received by the Association, but not more frequently than annually. Such instalments shall be paid in the cur-rencies received by the Association except that the Association may in its dis-cretion make payment in the currency of the government concerned.

(iv) Any amount due to the government on account of its subscription may be withheld so long as that government, or the government of any territory in-cluded within its membership, or any political subdivision or any agency of any of the foregoing remains liable, as borrower or guarantor, to the Associa-tion, and such amount may, at the option of the Association, be applied against any such liability as it matures.

(v) In no event shall the government receive under this paragraph (c) an amount exceeding, in the aggregate, the lesser of the two following: (a) the amount paid by the government on account of its subscription, or (b) such propor-tion of the net assets of the Association, as shown on the books of the Asso-ciation as of the date on which the government ceased to be a member, as the amount of its subscription shall bear to the aggregate amount of the subscrip-tions of all members.

(vi) All calculations required hereunder shall be made on such basis as shall be rea-sonably determined by the Association.

(d) In no event shall any amount due to a government under this Section be paid until six months after the date upon which the government ceases to be a member. If within six months of the date upon which any government ceases to be a member the Association suspends operations under Section 5 of this Article, all rights of such government shall be determined by the provisions of such Section 5 and such government shall be considered a member of the Association for purposes of such Section 5, except that it shall have no voting rights.

SECTION 5. *Suspension of Operations and Settlement of Obligations*

(a) The Association may permanently suspend its operations by vote of a majority of the Governors exercising a majority of the total voting power. After such suspension of operations the Association shall forthwith cease all activities, except those incident to the orderly realization, conservation and preservation of its assets and settlement of its obligations. Until final settlement of such obligations and distribution of such assets, the Association shall remain in existence and all mutual rights and obligations of the Association and its members under this Agreement shall continue unimpaired, except that no member shall be suspended or shall withdraw and that no distribution shall be made to members except as in this Section provided.

(b) No distribution shall be made to members on account of their subscriptions until all liabilities to creditors shall have been discharged or provided for and until the Board of Governors, by vote of a majority of the Governors exercising a majority of the total voting power, shall have decided to make such distribution.

(c) Subject to the foregoing, and to any special arrangements for the disposition of supplementary resources agreed upon in connection with the provision of such resources to the Association, the Association shall distribute its assets to members *pro rata* in proportion to amounts paid in by them on account of their subscriptions. Any distribution pursuant to the foregoing provision of this paragraph (c) shall be subject, in the case of any member, to prior settlement of all outstanding claims by the Association against such member. Such distribution shall be made at such times, in such currencies, and in cash or other assets as the Association shall deem fair and equitable. Distribution to the several members need not be uniform in respect of the type of assets distributed or of the currencies in which they are expressed.

(d) Any member receiving assets distributed by the Association pursuant to this Section or Section 4 shall enjoy the same rights with respect to such assets as the Association enjoyed prior to their distribution.

ARTICLE VIII

STATUS, IMMUNITIES AND PRIVILEGES

SECTION 1. *Purposes of Article*

To enable the Association to fulfill the functions with which it is entrusted, the status, immunities and privileges provided in this Article shall be accorded to the Association in the territories of each member.

SECTION 2. *Status of the Association*

The Association shall possess full juridical personality and, in particular, the capacity:
  (i) to contract;
  (ii) to acquire and dispose of immovable and movable property;
  (iii) to institute legal proceedings.

166

SECTION 3. *Position of the Association with Regard to Judicial Process*

Actions may be brought against the Association only in a court of competent jurisdiction in the territories of a member in which the Association has an office, has appointed an agent for the purpose of accepting service or notice of process, or has issued or guaranteed securities. No actions shall, however, be brought by members or persons acting for or deriving claims from members. The property and assets of the Association shall, wheresoever located and by whomsoever held, be immune from all forms of seizure, attachment or execution before the delivery of final judgment against the Association.

SECTION 4. *Immunity of Assets from Seizure*

Property and assets of the Association, wherever located and by whomsoever held, shall be immune from search, requisition, confiscation, expropriation or any other form of seizure by executive or legislative action.

SECTION 5. *Immunity of Archives*

The archives of the Association shall be inviolable.

SECTION 6. *Freedom of Assets from Restrictions*

To the extent necessary to carry out the operations provided for in this Agreement and subject to the provisions of this Agreement, all property and assets of the Association shall be free from restrictions, regulations, controls and moratoria of any nature.

SECTION 7. *Privilege for Communications*

The official communications of the Association shall be accorded by each member the same treatment that it accords to the official communications of other members.

SECTION 8. *Immunities and Privileges of Officers and Employees*

All Governors, Executive Directors, Alternates, officers and employees of the Association

(i) shall be immune from legal process with respect to acts performed by them in their official capacity except when the Association waives this immunity;

(ii) not being local nationals, shall be accorded the same immunities from immigration restrictions, alien registration requirements and national service obligations and the same facilities as regards exchange restrictions as are accorded by members to the representatives, officials, and employees of comparable rank of other members;

(iii) shall be granted the same treatment in respect of travelling facilities as is accorded by members to representatives, officials and employees of comparable rank of other members.

SECTION 9. *Immunities from Taxation*

(a) The Association, its assets, property, income and its operations and transactions authorized by this Agreement, shall be immune from all taxation and from all customs duties. The Association shall also be immune from liability for the collection or payment of any tax or duty.

(b) No tax shall be levied on or in respect of salaries and emoluments paid by the Association to Executive Directors, Alternates, officials or employees of the Association who are not local citizens, local subjects, or other local nationals.

(c) No taxation of any kind shall be levied on any obligation or security issued by the Association (including any dividend or interest thereon) by whomsoever held

    (i) which discriminates against such obligation or security solely because it is is-
sued by the Association; or

   (ii) if the sole jurisdictional basis for such taxation is the place or currency in which
it is issued, made payable or paid, or the location of any office or place of business maintained by the Association.

  (d) No taxation of any kind shall be levied on any obligation or security guaranteed
by the Association (including any dividend or interest thereon) by whomsoever held

    (i) which discriminates against such obligation or security solely because it is guar-
anteed by the Association; or

   (ii) if the sole jurisdictional basis for such taxation is the location of any office or
place of business maintained by the Association.

SECTION 10. *Application of Article*

Each member shall take such action as is necessary in its own territories for the purpose of making effective in terms of its own law the principles set forth in this Article
and shall inform the Association of the detailed action which it has taken.

ARTICLE IX

AMENDMENTS

(a) Any proposal to introduce modifications in this Agreement, whether emanating
from a member, a Governor or the Executive Directors, shall be communicated to the
Chairman of the Board of Governors who shall bring the proposal before the Board.
If the proposed amendments approved by the Board, the Association shall, by circular
letter or telegram, ask all members whether they accept the proposed amendment.
When three-fifths of the members, having four-fifths of the total voting power, have
accepted the proposed amendments, the Association shall certify the fact by formal
communication addressed to all members.

(b) Notwithstanding (a) above, acceptance by all members is required in the case of
any amendment modifying

   (i) the right to withdraw from the Association provided in Article VII, Section 1;

  (ii) the right secured by Article III, Section 1 (c);

 (iii) the limitation on liability provided in Article II, Section 3.

(c) Amendments shall enter into force for all members three months after the date
of the formal communication unless a shorter period is specified in the circular letter
or telegram.

ARTICLE X

INTERPRETATION AND ARBITRATION

(a) Any question of interpretation of the provisions of this Agreement arising between any member and the Association or between any members of the Association
shall be submitted to the Executive Directors for their decision. If the question particularly affects any member of the Association not entitled to appoint an Executive
Director of the Bank, it shall be entitled to representation in accordance with Article
VI, Section 4 (g).

(b) In any case where the Executive Directors have given a decision under (a)
above, any member may require that the question be referred to the Board of Governors, whose decision shall be final. Pending the result of the reference to the Board
of Governors, the Association may, so far as it deems necessary, act on the basis of the
decision of the Executive Directors.

(c) Whenever a disagreement arises between the Association and a country which
has ceased to be a member, or between the Association and any member during the

permanent suspension of the Association, such disagreement shall be submitted to arbitration by a tribunal of three arbitrators, one appointed by the Association, another by the country involved and an umpire who, unless the parties otherwise agree, shall be appointed by the President of the International Court of Justice or such other authority as may have been prescribed by regulation adopted by the Association. The umpire shall have full power to settle all questions of procedure in any case where the parties are in disagreement with respect thereto.

ARTICLE XI

FINAL PROVISIONS

SECTION 1. *Entry into Force*

This Agreement shall enter into force when it has been signed on behalf of governments whose subscriptions comprise not less than sixty-five percent of the total subscriptions set forth in Schedule A and when the instruments referred to in Section 2 (a) of this Article have been deposited on their behalf, but in no event shall this Agreement enter into force before September 15, 1960.

SECTION 2. *Signature*

(a) Each government on whose behalf this Agreement is signed shall deposit with the Bank an instrument setting forth that it has accepted this Agreement in accordance with its law and has taken all steps necessary to enable it to carry out all of its obligations under this Agreement.

(b) Each government shall become a member of the Association as from the date of the deposit on its behalf of the instrument referred to in paragraph (a) above except that no government shall become a member before this Agreement enters into force under Section 1 of this Article.

(c) This Agreement shall remain open for signature until the close of business on December 31, 1960, at the principal office of the Bank, on behalf of the governments of the states whose names are set forth in Schedule A, provided that, if this Agreement shall not have entered into force by that date, the Executive Directors of the Bank may extend the period during which this Agreement shall remain open for signature by not more than six months.

(d) After this Agreement shall have entered into force, it shall be open for signature on behalf of the government of any state whose membership shall have been approved pursuant to Article II, Section 1 (b).

SECTION 3. *Territorial Application*

By its signature of this Agreement, each government accepts it both on its own behalf and in respect of all territories for whose international relations such government is responsible except those which are excluded by such government by written notice to the Association.

SECTION 4. *Inauguration of the Association*

(a) As soon as this Agreement enters into force under Section 1 of this Article the President shall call a meeting of the Executive Directors.

(b) The Association shall begin operations on the date when such meeting is held.

(c) Pending the first meeting of the Board of Governors, the Executive Directors may exercise all the powers of the Board of Governors except those reserved to the Board of Governors under this Agreement.

SECTION 5. *Registration*

The Bank is authorized to register this Agreement with the Secretariat of the United Nations in accordance with Article 102 of the Charter of the United Nations and the Regulations thereunder adopted by the General Assembly.

DONE at Washington, in a single copy which shall remain deposited in the archives of the International Bank for Reconstruction and Development, which has indicated by its signature below its agreement to act as depository of this Agreement, to register this Agreement with the Secretariat of the United Nations and to notify all governments whose names are set forth in Schedule A of the date when this Agreement shall have entered into force under Article XI, Section 1 hereof.

SCHEDULE A--INITIAL SUBSCRIPTIONS
(US $ Millions)*

PART I

Australia	20.18	France	52.96	Norway	6.72
Austria	5.04	Germany	52.96	Sweden	10.09
Belgium	22.70	Italy	18.16	Union of South	
Canada	37.83	Japan	33.59	Africa	10.09
Denmark	8.74	Luxembourg	1.01	United Kingdom	131.14
Finland	3.83	Netherlands	27.74	United States	320.29

763.07

PART II

Afghanistan	1.01	Haiti	0.76	Panama	0.02
Argentina	18.83	Honduras	0.30	Paraguay	0.30
Bolivia	1.06	Iceland	0.10	Peru	1.77
Brazil	18.83	India	40.35	Philippines	5.04
Burma	2.02	Indonesia	11.10	Saudi Arabia	3.70
Ceylon	3.03	Iran	4.54	Spain	10.09
Chile	3.53	Iraq	0.76	Sudan	1.01
China	30.26	Ireland	3.03	Thailand	3.03
Colombia	3.53	Israel	1.68	Tunisia	1.51
Costa Rica	0.20	Jordan	0.30	Turkey	5.80
Cuba	4.71	Korea	1.26	United Arab	
Dominican Republic	0.40	Lebanon	0.45	Republic	6.03
Ecuador	0.65	Libya	1.01	Uruguay	1.06
El Salvador	0.30	Malaya	2.52	Venezuela	7.06
Ethiopia	0.50	Mexico	8.74	Viet-Nam	1.51
Ghana	2.36	Morocco	3.53	Yugoslavia	4.04
Greece	2.52	Nicaragua	0.30		
Guatemala	0.40	Pakistan	10.09		

236.93

TOTAL   1000.00

*In terms of United States dollars of the weight and fineness in effect on January 1, 1960.

b. REPORT OF THE EXECUTIVE DIRECTORS OF THE INTERNATIONAL BANK FOR RECONSTRUCTION AND DEVELOPMENT ON THE ARTICLES OF AGREEMENT OF THE INTERNATIONAL DEVELOPMENT ASSOCIATION, APPROVED JANUARY 26, 1960[1]

1. Resolution No. 136, adopted by the Board of Governors of the International Bank for Reconstruction and Development (herein called "the Bank") on October 1, 1959, provides as follows:

> "RESOLVED: That with respect to the question of creating an International Development Association as an affiliate of the Bank, the Executive Directors, having regard to the views expressed by Governors and considering the broad principles on which such an Association should be established and all other aspects of the matter, are requested to formulate articles of agreement of such an Association for submission to the member Governments of the Bank."

2. The Executive Directors of the Bank, acting pursuant to the foregoing Resolution, have formulated Articles of Agreement for an International Development Association (herein called "the Association") and, on January 26, 1960, approved the text of such Articles, as attached hereto, for submission to member governments of the Bank. The Executive Directors' approval of the Agreement for submission to governments does not, of course, imply that governments are committed to take action on the Agreement.

3. The Executive Directors invite attention to the provisions of Article XI, Section 1, pursuant to which the attached Agreement will enter into force at any time on or after September 15, 1960, when it has been signed on behalf of governments whose subscriptions aggregate at least $650 million, and to the provisions of Article XI, Section 2(c), pursuant to which, unless an extension of time is granted, the Agreement will remain open for signature by original members only until the close of business on December 31, 1960.

4. While the provisions of the attached text are for the most part self-explanatory, the Executive Directors believe that brief comment on a few principal features may be useful to member governments in their consideration of the Agreement.

Initial Subscriptions

5. The Articles provide for initial subscriptions which will aggregate $1 billion if all present members of the Bank become original members of the Association. The initial subscription to be made by each original member, as listed in Schedule A to the Articles of Agreement, is designed to be proportionate to that member's subscription to the capital stock of the Bank. For purposes of calculating proportionality, the Bank's capitalization and each member's subscription in the Bank have been taken as if the recently authorized capital increases had already become effective as follows: (a) all members of the Bank had doubled their capital subscriptions pursuant to Resolution No. 128 of the Board of Governors, except China which has reserved its position; (b) the individual special increases in subscriptions authorized by Resolutions No. 130 and No. 132 of the Board of Governors had been effected; and (c) the "small quota" increases in subscriptions authorized by Resolution No. 130 of the Board of Governors had been effected only by Bolivia, Burma, Ethiopia, Guatemala, Iraq, Libya, Tunisia and Viet-Nam, the only members which at December 31, 1959, had indicated their intention to effect such increases.

---

[1] As published by the Association.

6. Article II, Section 2, divides the initial subscription of original members into a 10% component, which must be paid by all members in gold or freely convertible currency (as defined by Article II, Section 2 (f)), and a 90% component. The 90% component is payable in gold or freely convertible currency by members listed in Part I of Schedule A, and in national currency by members listed in Part II. Pursuant to Article IV, Section 1, the national currency paid in by a member listed in Part II of Schedule A may be converted by the Association, or used by it to finance exports from the member's territories, only with the member's consent. Part I lists only those members whose economic and financial situation is such, in the opinion of the Executive Directors, as to justify making the entire amount of their subscriptions available on a freely convertible basis. While the members listed in Part II have no legal obligation to make more than 10% of their initial subscription available to the Association on a freely convertible basis, it is hoped that the more developed of these countries, upon accepting membership in the Association or reasonably soon thereafter, will be in a position to release at least some part of the 90% portion of their subscriptions.

7. Article II, Section 2, also provides that the 90% component of the initial subscriptions of original members shall be payable in five equal annual instalments amounting to 18% each and that, in connection with each such payment, members may substitute non-negotiable, non-interest-bearing demand notes for their own currency until the funds are needed by the Association. The remaining 10% component of the initial subscription of original members, which, as already noted, must be paid in gold or freely convertible currency, is also payable in five annual instalments: 5% the first year and 1¼% each year thereafter. Thus the first instalment of each member's initial subscription amounts to 23% of the total (18% plus 5%) and each of the other four instalments amounts to 19¼% (18% plus 1¼%).

8. Two other features concerning initial subscriptions to the Association deserve mention. The first relates to the maintenance of value obligation imposed upon each member by Article IV, Section 2 (a), with respect to its own currency paid in by it as the 90% component of its initial subscription; unlike the situation under the Bank's Articles, this maintenance of value obligation extends only until the member's currency has been initially disbursed or exchanged by the Association for the currency of another member. The second feature is the provisions of Article IV, Section 1 (e), that the 90% component of the initial subscriptions of all members listed in Part I of Schedule A shall be used by the Association, over reasonable intervals of time, on an approximately *pro rata* basis.

Voting Rights

9. The voting rights of original members in respect of their initial subscriptions, prescribed by Article VI, Section 3, are in general based on the Bank pattern of voting rights. Assuming that all members of the Bank become original members of the Association, members will have approximately the same relative voting power in the Association as in the Bank following completion of the recent capital increases, but adjusted to restore the voting power of the smaller Bank members which was somewhat diluted by those capital increases.

10. Voting rights on subscriptions other than initial subscriptions of original members are left to be determined by the Association.

Additions to Resources

11. Article III, 1 (a), provides for a periodic review by the Association of the adequacy of its resources and for the authorization, if, when to the extent deemed desirable, of general increases in subscriptions. In formulating these provisions, the Executive Directors considered that, as in the case of the initial subscriptions, any general increases in subscriptions should normally be designed to provide the Association with

funds for a five-year period. Section 1 (c) of Article III requires the Association, when authorizing any general or individual increase in subscriptions, to give each member an opportunity to subscribe an amount enabling it to maintain its relative voting power. This provision permits the Association either to give each member an option to subscribe to all or part of the amount authorized for it, or to require each member to choose between subscribing the entire amount authorized for it or nothing at all.

12. Article III, Section 2, expressly authorizes the Association to enter into arrangements, upon such terms and conditions as may be agreed, to accept from any member supplementary resources in the currency of another member, provided that the member whose currency is involved agrees to the use of such currency as supplementary resources and to the terms and conditions governing such use. The inclusion of this express authorization to accept supplementary resources of a particular type is not intended to preclude the Association from accepting other types of contributions for purposes and on terms consistent with the provisions of the Agreement.

Operations

13. Article V, Section 1 (a) states that the Association shall provide financing to further development in the less-developed areas of the world included within the Association's membership. Under this provision, the Association's financing is to be for less-developed member countries and less-developed dependent and associated territories included within the membership of member countries.

14. The other provisions of Article V have been drafted in very general terms, in order to give the Association wide latitude to shape its financing to meet the needs of actual cases as they arise. For example, the Association is authroized to finance any project which is of high developmental priority, that is, which will make an important contribution to the development of the area or areas concerned, whether or not the project is revenue-producing or directly productive. Thus projects such as water supply, sanitation, pilot housing and the like are eligible for financing, although it is expected that a major part of the Association's financing is likely to be for projects of the type financed by the Bank.

15. Section 1 (b) of Article V specifies that the Association's financing shall normally be in support of specific projects. The words "specific projects" are intended to include, as in the Bank's practice, such proposals as a railway program, an agricultural credit program, or a group of related projects forming part of a development program. Section 1 (b) permits the Association to provide financing for other than specific projects in special circumstances.

16. The only directives contained in the Agreement with respect to the terms and forms of the Association's financing are the provisions of Article I that the terms shall be "more flexible and bear less heavily on the balance of payments than those of conventional loans," and the provisions of Article V, Section 2 (a), the effect of which is to require that financing out of initial subscriptions take the form of loans. The broad language of Article V is designed to permit the Association to carry out the directive of Article I, in the case of loans made from its freely convertible resources, in any of a number of ways: for example, by providing for lenient terms of repayment (such as loans repayable in foreign exchange with long maturities or long periods of grace or both, or loans repayable wholly or partly in local currency), by lending free of interest or at a low rate of interest, or by some combination of the foregoing.

17. Section 2 (c) of Article V provides that the Association may provide financing not only to governments but to public or private entities in the territories of a member or members and, in addition, to public international or regional organizations. Section 2 (d) provides that, in the case of a loan to an entity other than a member, the Association may require a suitable governmental or other guarantee; unlike the situation under the Bank's Articles, a governmental guarantee of such a loan is discretionary, not mandatory.

18. Section 1 (g) of Article V provides that the Association, in making arrangements with respect to the use of the proceeds of any financing, including currencies accepted as supplementary resources, shall give due regard to considerations of competitive international trade. It is expected that the Association, like the Bank, will require that the choice of equipment and services to be purchased with funds supplied by the Association shall normally be determined on the basis of international competition.

19. One of the powers conferred upon the Association by Article V, Section 5, is the power to provide technical assistance and advisory services at the request of a member. Such assistance may, in the discretion of the Association, be provided with or without reimbursement.

Organization and Management

20. Under Article VI of the Agreement, the Association is to be organized as an affiliate of the Bank, as required by Resolution No. 136 of the Board of Governors. As in the case of the International Finance Corporation, each member of the Association is to be represented on the Assocation's Board of Governors by the same Governor and Alternate Governor who represent it on the Board of Governors of the Bank, and each Executive Director and Alternate Director of the Bank is to serve *ex officio* in a corresponding capacity for the Association, provided that he represents at least one country which is a member of the Association. Unlike the International Finance Corporation, however, the Association will not have a separate President; the President of the Bank, who is also Chairman of the Bank's Executive Directors, is to serve as both President and Chairman of the Executive Directors of the Association.

21. Section 5 (b) of Article VI provides that, to the extent practicable, officers and staff of the Bank are to be appointed to serve concurrently as officers and staff of the Association, and it is contemplated that, at least initially, the Association will have no separate officers or staff. It is further expected that, as and when the aggregate volume of work of the Bank and Association requires, officers and staff serving both institutions concurrently will be augmented, with responsibilities assigned as seems appropriate from time to time. However, should a different course at any time appear desirable, Article VI is sufficiently flexible to permit the appointment of officers (other than the President) and staff who would be concerned solely with the affairs of the Association.

Status, Immunities and Privileges

22. Article VIII, dealing with status, immunities and privileges, follows exactly the corresponding provisions of the Bank's Articles of Agreement.

c. BY-LAWS OF THE INTERNATIONAL DEVELOPMENT
ASSOCIATION, NOVEMBER 30, 1962[1]

These By-Laws are adopted under the authority of, and are intended to be complementary to, the Articles of Agreement of the International Development Association (hereinafter called the Association), and they shall be construed accordingly. In the event of a conflict between anything in these By-Laws and any provision or requirement of the Articles of Agreement, the Articles of Agreement shall prevail.

SECTION 1. *Meetings of the Board of Governors*

(a) The provisions of Sections 4, 5, 6 and 9 of the By-Laws of the International Bank for Reconstruction and Development (hereinafter called the Bank) as amended from time to time (hereinafter called the By-Laws of the Bank) shall apply *mutatis mutandis.*

(b) Any meeting of the Board of Governors at which a quorum shall not be present may be adjourned from time to time by a majority of the Governors present and notice of the adjourned meeting need not be given.

(e) The Secretary of the Association shall serve as Secretary of the Board of Governors.

SECTION 2. *Annual Report*

The provisions of Section 10 of the By-Laws of the Bank shall apply *mutatis mutandis.*

SECTION 3. *Voting by Governors*

The provisions of Sections 11, 12 and 13 of the By-Laws of the Bank shall apply *mutatis mutandis.*

SECTION 4. *Terms of Service*

(a) Governors and Alternates shall be reimbursed for their expenses in attending meetings on behalf of the Association on the same basis as they are reimbursed for expenses in attending meetings on behalf of the Bank; provided, however, that with respect to any meeting held on behalf of the Association at or about the same time as a meeting held on behalf of the Bank or the International Finance Corporation, they shall be reimbursed only for additional expenses incurred in attending the meeting on behalf of the Association.

(b) In the event that the Association shall make any direct payment on account of salaries or allowances to Governors or Executive Directors or their Alternates, the President, officers or staff, the Association shall reimburse such persons for taxes they are required to pay on such salaries and allowances on the same basis as that on which tax reimbursement is made by the Bank on corresponding salaries and allowances paid by the Bank.

(c) The Executive Directors, Alternate Executive Directors, the President and the officers and staff of the Bank whom the President shall appoint to serve concurrently as officers and staff of the Association shall serve without compensation from the As-

---

[1] As published by the Association.

sociation. Nothing herein shall preclude the Association from entering into appropriate arrangements with the Bank for sharing remuneration, allowances and other expenses paid by either institution.

(d) Each Executive Director or Alternate Executive Director who does not reside at or near the Seat of the Association shall be entitled to a reasonable allowance for expenses incurred by him in attending meetings of the Executive Directors or committees thereof, but only over and above those which would have been incurred in any event in attending meetings of the Executive Directors of the Bank or of the Board of Directors of the International Finance Corporation. Each Executive Directors and Alternate Executive Director who shall at the request of the President perform designated service for the Association shall be entitled to a reasonable allowance for expenses incurred by him in the performance thereof.

SECTION 5. *Delegation of Authority*

The Executive Directors may exercise all the powers of the Association except those reserved to the Board of Governors by Article VI, Section 2 (c) and other provisions of the Articles of Agreement. The Executive Directors shall not take any action pursuant to powers delegated by the Board of Governors which is inconsistent with any action taken by the Board of Governors.

SECTION 6. *Rules and Regulations*

The provisions of Section 16 of the By-Laws of the Bank shall apply *mutatis mutandis.*

SECTION 7. *Representation of Members Not Represented by an Appointed Executive Director*

The provisions of Section 18 of the By-Laws of the Bank shall apply *mutatis mutandis.*

SECTION 8. *Budget and Audits*

The provisions of Section 19 of the By-Laws of the Bank shall apply *mutatis mutandis.*

SECTION 9. *Application for Membership*

Subject to any special provisions that may be made for countries listed in Schedule A of the Articles of Agreement, any member of the Bank may apply for membership in the Association by filing with the Association an application setting forth all relevant facts.

When submitting an application to the Board of Governors, the Executive Directors, after consultation with the applicant country, shall make recommendations to the Board of Governors as to the initial subscription and such other conditions as, in the opinion of the Executive Directors, should be prescribed by the Board of Governors.

SECTION 10. *Suspension of Membership*

Except in connection with a suspension of membership under Section 3 of Article VII of the Articles of Agreement, the provisions of Section 21 of the By-Laws of the Bank shall apply *mutatis mutandis* to the Association.

SECTION 11. *Amendment to By-Laws*

These By-Laws may be amended by the Board of Governors at any meeting thereof or by vote without a meeting as provided in Section 3.

8. INTERNATIONAL MONETARY FUND

a. ARTICLES OF AGREEMENT OF THE INTERNATIONAL MONETARY FUND, ADOPTED JULY 22, 1944, AMENDED AND BECAME EFFECTIVE JULY 28, 1969

Adopted at the United Nations Monetary and Financial Conference, Bretton Woods, New Hampshire, July 22, 1944. Entered into force December 27, 1945. Amended effective July 28, 1969, by the modifications approved by the Board of Governors in Resolution No. 23-5, adopted May 31, 1968.

TABLE OF CONTENTS

————

ARTICLES OF AGREEMENT

OF THE

INTERNATIONAL MONETARY FUND

The Governments on whose behalf the present Agreement is signed agree as follows:

Introductory Article

(i) The International Monetary Fund is established and shall operate in accordance with the provisions of this Agreement as originally adopted, and as subsequently amended in order to institute a facility based on special drawing rights and to effect certain other changes.

(ii) To enable the Fund to conduct its operations and transactions, the Fund shall maintain a General Account and a Special Drawing Account. Membership in the Fund shall give the right to participation in the Special Drawing Account.

(iii) Operations and transactions authorized by this Agreement shall be conducted through the General Account except that operations and transactions involving special drawing rights shall be conducted through the Special Drawing Account.

Article I

Purposes

The purposes of the International Monetary Fund are:

(i) To promote international monetary cooperation through a permanent institution which provides the machinery for consultation and collaboration on international monetary problems.

(ii) To facilitate the expansion and balanced growth of international trade, and to contribute thereby to the promotion and maintenance of high levels of employment and real income and to the development of the productive resources of all members as primary objectives of economic policy.

(iii) To promote exchange stability, to maintain orderly exchange arrangements among members, and to avoid competitive exchange depreciation.

(iv) To assist in the establishment of a multilateral system of payments in respect of current transactions between members and in the elimination of foreign exchange restrictions which hamper the growth of world trade.

(v) To give confidence to members by making the Fund's resources temporarily available to them under adequate safeguards, thus providing them with opportunity to correct maladjustments in their balance of payments without resorting to measures destructive of national or international prosperity.

(vi) In accordance with the above, to shorten the duration and lessen the degree of disequilibrium in the international balances of payments of members.

The Fund shall be guided in all its policies and decisions by the purposes set forth in this Article.

Article II

Membership

Section 1. *Original members*

The original members of the Fund shall be those of the countries represented at the United Nations Monetary and Financial Conference whose governments accept membership before the date specified in Article XX, Section 2 *(e)*.

Section 2. *Other members*

Membership shall be open to the governments of other countries at such times and in accordance with such terms as may be prescribed by the Fund.

Article III

Quotas and Subscriptions

Section 1. *Quotas*

Each member shall be assigned a quota. The quotas of the members represented at the United Nations Monetary and Financial Conference which accept membership before the date specified in Article XX, Section 2 *(e)*, shall be those set forth in Schedule A. The quotas of other members shall be determined by the Fund.

Section 2. *Adjustment of quotas*

The Fund shall at intervals of not more than five years conduct a general review, and if it deems it appropriate propose an adjustment, of the quotas of the members. It may also, if it thinks fit, consider at any other time the adjustment of any particular quota at the request of the member concerned. An eighty-five percent majority of the total voting power shall be required for any change in quotas proposed as the result of a general review and a four-fifths majority of the total voting power shall be required for any other change in quotas. No quota shall be changed without the consent of the member concerned.

Section 3. *Subscriptions: time, place, and form of payment*

(a) The subscription of each member shall be equal to its quota and shall be paid in full to the Fund at the appropriate depository on or before the date when the member becomes eligible under Article XX, Section 4 *(c)* or *(d)*, to buy currencies from the Fund.

(b) Each member shall pay in gold, as a minimum, the smaller of

   (i) twenty-five percent of its quota; or

  (ii) ten percent of its net official holdings of gold and United States dollars as at the date when the Fund notifies members under Article XX, Section 4 *(a)* that it will shortly be in a position to begin exchange transactions.

Each member shall furnish to the Fund the data necessary to determine its net official holdings of gold and United States dollars.

(c) Each member shall pay the balance of its quota in its own currency.

(d) If the net official holdings of gold and United States dollars of any member as at the date referred to in *(b)* (ii) above are not ascertainable because its territories have been occupied by the enemy, the Fund shall fix an appropriate alternative date for determining such holdings. If such date is later than that on which the country becomes eligible under Article XX, Section 4 *(c)* or *(d)*, to buy currencies from the Fund, the Fund and the member shall agree on a provisional gold payment to be made under *(b)* above, and the balance of the member's subscription shall be paid in the member's currency, subject to appropriate adjustment between the member and the Fund when the net official holdings have been ascertained.

Section 4. *Payments when quotas are changed*

(a) Each member which consents to an increase in its quota shall, within thirty days after the date of its consent, pay to the Fund twenty-five percent of the increase in gold and the balance in its own currency. If, however, on the date when the member consents to an increase, its monetary reserves are less than its new quota, the Fund may reduce the proportion of the increase to be paid in gold.

(b) If a member consents to a reduction in its quota, the Fund shall, within thirty days after the date of the consent, pay to the member an amount equal to the reduction. The payment shall be made in the member's currency and in such amount of gold as may be necessary to prevent reducing the Fund's holdings of the currency below seventy-five percent of the new quota.

(c) A majority of eighty-five percent of the total voting power shall be required for any decisions dealing with the payment, or made with the sole purpose of mitigating the effects of the payment, of increases in quotas proposed as the result of a general review of quotas.

Section 5. *Substitution of securities for currency*

The Fund shall accept from any member in place of any part of the member's currency which in the judgment of the Fund is not needed for its operations, notes or similar obligations issued by the member or the depository designated by the member under Article XIII, Section 2, which shall be non-negotiable, non-interest bearing and payable at their par value on demand by crediting the account of the Fund in the designated depository. This Section shall apply not only to currency subscribed by members but also to any currency otherwise due to, or acquired by, the Fund.

Article IV

Par Values of Currencies

Section 1. *Expression of par values*

(a) The par value of the currency of each member shall be expressed in terms of gold as a common denominator or in terms of the United States dollar of the weight and fineness in effect on July 1, 1944.

(b) All computations relating to currencies of members for the purpose of applying the provisions of this Agreement shall be on the basis of their par values.

Section 2. *Gold purchases based on par values*

The Fund shall prescribe a margin above and below par value for transactions in gold by members, and no member shall buy gold at a price above par value plus the prescribed margin, or sell gold at a price below par value minus the prescribed margin.

Section 3. *Foreign exchange dealings based on parity*

The maximum and the minimum rates for exchange transactions between the currencies of members taking place within their territories shall not differ from parity

(i)   in the case of spot exchange transactions, by more than one percent. and

(ii) in the case of other exchange transactions, by a margin which exceeds the margin for spot exchange transactions by more than the Fund considers reasonable.

Section 4. *Obligations regarding exchange stability*

(a) Each member undertakes to collaborate with the Fund to promote exchange stability, to maintain orderly exchange arrangements with other members, and to avoid competitive exchange alterations.

(b) Each member undertakes, through appropriate measures consistent with this Agreement, to permit within its territories exchange transactions between its currency and the currencies of other members only within the limits prescribed under Section 3 of this Article. A member whose monetary authorities, for the settlement of international transactions, in fact freely buy and sell gold within the limits prescribed by the Fund under Section 2 of this Article shall be deemed to be fulfilling this undertaking.

Section 5. *Changes in par values*

(a) A member shall not propose a change in the par value of its currency except to correct a fundamental disequilibrium.

(b) A change in the par value of a member's currency may be made only on the proposal of the member and only after consultation with the Fund.

(c) When a change is proposed, the Fund shall first take into account the changes, if any, which have already taken place in the initial par value of the member's currency as determined under Article XX, Section 4. If the proposed change, together with all previous changes, whether increases or decreases,

(i)   does not exceed ten percent of the initial par value, the Fund shall raise no objection,

(ii) does not exceed a further ten percent of the initial par value, the Fund may either concur or object, but shall declare its attitute within seventy-two hours if the member so requests,

(iii) is not within (i) or (ii) above, the Fund may either concur or object, but shall be entitled to a longer period in which to declare its attitude.

(d) Uniform changes in par values made under Section 7 of this Article shall not be taken into account in determining whether a proposed change falls within (i), (ii), or (iii) of *(c)* above.

(e) A member may change the par value of its currency without the concurrence of the Fund if the change does not affect the international transactions of members of the Fund.

(f) The Fund shall concur in a proposed change which is within the terms of *(c)* (ii) or *(c)* (iii) above if it is satisfied that the change is necessary to correct a fundamental disequilibrium. In particular, provided it is so satisfied, it shall not object to a proposed change because of the domestic social or political policies of the member proposing the change.

Section 6. *Effect of unauthorized changes*

If a member changes the par value of its currency despite the objection of the Fund, in cases where the Fund is entitled to object, the member shall be ineligible to use the resources of the Fund unless the Fund otherwise determines; and if, after the expiration of a reasonable period, the difference between the member and the Fund continues, the matter shall be subject to the provisions of Article XV, Section 2 *(b)*.

Section 7. *Uniform changes in par values*

Notwithstanding the provisions of Section 5 *(b)* of this Article, the Fund by an eighty-five percent majority of the total voting power may make uniform proportionate changes in the par values of the currencies of all members. The par value of a member's currency shall, however, not be changed under this provision if, within seventy-two hours of the Fund's action, the member informs the Fund that it does not wish the par value of its currency to be changed by such action.

Section 8. *Maintenance of gold value of the Fund's assets*

(a) The gold value of the Fund's assets shall be maintained notwithstanding changes in the par or foreign exchange value of the currency of any member.

(b) Whenever (i) the par value of a member's currency is reduced, or (ii) the foreign exchange value of a member's currency has, in the opinion of the Fund, depreciated to a significant extent within that member's territories, the member shall pay to the Fund within a reasonable time an amount of its own currency equal to the reduction in the gold value of its currency held by the Fund.

(c) Whenever the par value of a member's currency is increased, the Fund shall return to such member within a reasonable time an amount in its currency equal to the increase in the gold value of its currency held by the Fund.

(d) The provisions of this Section shall apply to a uniform proportionate change in the par values of the currencies of all members, unless at the time when such a change is made the Fund decides otherwise by an eighty-five percent majority of the total voting power.

Section 9. *Separate currencies within a member's territories*

A member proposing a change in the par value of its currency shall be deemed, unless it declares otherwise, to be proposing a corresponding change in the par value of the separate currencies of all territories in respect of which it has accepted this Agreement under Article XX, Section 2 *(g)*. It shall, however, be open to a member to declare that its proposal relates either to the metropolitan currency alone, or only to one or more specified separate currencies, or to the metropolitan currency and one or more specified separate currencies.

Article V

Transactions with the Fund

Section 1. *Agencies dealing with the Fund*

Each member shall deal with the Fund only through its Treasury, central bank, stabilization fund or other similar fiscal agency and the Fund shall deal only with or through the same agencies.

Section 2. *Limitation on the Fund's operations*

Except as otherwise provided in this Agreement, operations on the account of the Fund shall be limited to transactions for the purpose of supplying a member, on the initiative of such member, with the currency of another member in exchange for gold or for the currency of the member desiring to make the purchase.

Section 3. *Conditions governing use of the Fund's resources*

(a) A member shall be entitled to buy the currency of another member from the Fund in exchange for its own currency subject to the following conditions:

   (i) The member desiring to purchase the currency represents that it is presently needed for making in that currency payments which are consistent with the provisions of this Agreement;

  (ii) The Fund has not given notice under Article VII, Section 3, that its holdings of the currency desired have become scarce;

 (iii) The proposed purchase would be a gold tranche purchase, or would not cause the Fund's holdings of the purchasing member's currency to increase by more than twenty-five percent of its quota during the period of twelve-months ending on the date of the purchase or to exceed two hundred percent of its quota;

 (iv) The Fund has not previously declared under Section 5 of this Article, Article IV, Section 6, Article VI, Section 1, or Article XV, Section 2 *(a)*, that the member desiring to purchase is ineligible to use the resources of the Fund.

(b) A member shall not be entitled without the permission of the Fund to use the Fund's resources to acquire currency to hold against forward exchange transactions.

(c) A member's use of the resources of the Fund shall be in accordance with the purposes of the Fund. The Fund shall adopt policies on the use of its resources that will assist members to solve their balance of payments problems in a manner consistent with the purposes of the Fund and that will establish adequate safeguards for the temporary use of its resources.

(d) A representation by a member under *(a)* above shall be examined by the Fund to determine whether the proposed purchase would be consistent with the provisions of this Agreement and with the policies adopted under them, with the exception that proposed gold tranche purchases shall not be subject to challenge.

Section 4. *Waiver of conditions*

The Fund may in its discretion, and on terms which safeguard its interests, waive any of the conditions prescribed in Section 3 *(a)* of this Article, especially in the case of members with a record of avoiding large or continuous use of the Fund's resources. In making a waiver it shall take into consideration periodic or exceptional requirements of the member requesting the waiver. The Fund shall also take into consideration a member's willingness to pledge as collateral security gold, silver, securities, or other acceptable assets having a value sufficient in the opinion of the Fund to protect its interests and may require as a condition of waiver the pledge of such collateral security.

Section 5. *Ineligibility to use the Fund's resources*

Whenever the Fund is of the opinion that any member is using the resources of the Fund in a manner contrary to the purposes of the Fund, it shall present to the member a report setting forth the views of the Fund and prescribing a suitable time for reply. After presenting such a report to a member, the Fund may limit the use of its resources by the member. If no reply to the report is received from the member within the prescribed time, or if the reply received is unsatisfactory, the Fund may continue to limit the member's use of the Fund's resources or may, after giving reasonable notice to the member, declare it ineligible to use the resources of the Fund.

Section 6. *Purchases of currencies from the Fund for gold*

(a) Any member desiring to obtain, directly or indirectly, the currency of another member for gold shall, provided that it can do so with equal advantage, acquire it by the sale of gold to the Fund.

(b) Nothing in this Section shall be deemed to preclude any member from selling in any market gold newly produced from mines located within its territories.

Section 7. *Repurchase by a member of its currency held by the Fund*

(a) A member may repurchase from the Fund and the Fund shall sell for gold any part of the Fund's holdings of its currency in excess of its quota.

(b) At the end of each financial year of the Fund, a member shall repurchase from the Fund with each type of monetary reserve, as determined in accordance with Schedule B, part of the Fund's holdings of its currency under the following conditions:

    (i) Each member shall use in repurchases of its own currency from the Fund and amount of its monetary reserves equal in value to the following changes that have occurred during the year: one-half of any increase in the Fund's holdings of the member's currency, plus one-half of any increase, or minus one-half of any decrease, in the member's monetary reserves, or, if the Fund's holdings of the member's currency have decreased, one-half of any increase in the member's monetary reserves minus one-half of the decrease in the Fund's holdings of the member's currency. This rule shall not apply when a member's monetary reserves have decreased during the year by more than the Fund's holdings of its currency have increased.

   (ii) If after the repurchase described in (i) above (if required) has been made, a member's holdings of another member's currency (or of gold acquired from that member) are found to have increased by reason of transactions in terms of that currency with other members or persons in their territories, the member whose holdings of such currency (or gold) have thus increased shall use the increase to repurchase its own currency from the Fund.

(c) None of the adjustments described in *(b)* above shall be carried to a point at which

    (i) the member's monetary reserves are below one hundred fifty percent of its quota, or

   (ii) the Fund's holdings of its currency are below seventy-five percent of its quota, or

 (iii) the Fund's holdings of any currency required to be used are above seventy-five percent of the quota of the member concerned, or

 (iv) the amount repurchased exceeds twenty-five percent of the quota of the member concerned.

(d) The Fund by an eighty-five percent majority of the total voting power may revise the percentages in *(c)* (i) and (iv) above and revise and supplement the rules in paragraph 1 *(c)*, *(d)*, and *(e)* and *(e)* and paragraph 2 *(b)* of Schedule B.

186

Section 8. *Charges*

(a) Any member buying the currency of another member from the Fund in exchange for its own currency shall pay, in addition to the parity price, a service charge uniform for all members of not less than one-half percent and not more than one percent, as determined by the Fund, provided that the Fund in its discretion may levy a service charge of less than one-half percent on gold tranche purchases.

(b) The Fund may levy a reasonable handling charge on any member buying gold from the Fund or selling gold to the Fund.

(c) The Fund shall levy charges uniform for all members which shall be payable by any member on the average daily balances of its currency held by the Fund in excess of its quota. These charges shall be at the following rates:

  (i) *On amounts not more than twenty-five percent in excess of the quota:* no charge for the first three months; one-half percent per annum for the next nine months; and thereafter an increase in the charge of one-half percent for each subsequent year.

  (ii) *On amounts more than twenty-five percent and not more than fifty percent in excess of the quota:* an additional one-half percent for the first year; and an additional one-half percent for each subsequent year.

  (iii) *On each additional bracket of twenty-five per-percent in excess of the quota:* an additional one-half percent for the first year; and an additional one-half percent for each subsequent year.

(d) Whenever the Fund's holdings of a member's currency are such that the charge applicable to any bracket for any period has reached the rate of four percent per annum, the Fund and the member shall consider means by which the Fund's holdings of the currency can be reduced. Thereafter; the charges shall rise in accordance with the provisions of *(c)* above until they reach five percent and failing agreement, the Fund may then impose such charges as it deems appropriate.

(e) The rates referred to in *(c)* and *(d)* above may be changed by a three-fourths majority of the total voting power.

(f) All charges shall be paid in gold. If, however, the member's monetary reserves are less than one-half of its quota, it shall pay in gold only that proportion of the charges due which such reserves bear to one-half of its quota, and shall pay the balance in its own currency.

Section 9. *Remuneration*

(a) The Fund shall pay remuneration, at a rate uniform for all members, on the amount by which seventy-five percent of a member's quota exceeded the average of the Fund's holdings of the member's currency, provided that no account shall be taken of holdings in excess of seventy-five percent of quota. The rate shall be one and one-half percent per annum, but the Fund in its discretion may increase or reduce this rate, provided that a three-fourths majority of the total voting power shall be required for any increase above two percent per annum or reduction below one percent per annum.

(b) Remuneration shall be paid in gold or a member's own currency as determined by the Fund.

Article VI

Capital Transfers

Section 1. *Use of the Fund's resources for capital transfers*

(a) A member may not use the Fund's resources to meet a large or sustained outflow of capital except as provided in Section 2 of this Article, and the Fund may

request a member to exercise controls to prevent such use of the resources of the Fund. If, after receiving such a request, a member fails to exercise appropriate controls, the Fund may declare the member ineligible to use the resources of the Fund.

(b) Nothing in this Section shall be deemed

(i) to prevent the use of the resources of the Fund for capital transactions of reasonable amount required for the expansion of exports or in the ordinary course of trade, banking or other business, or

(ii) to affect capital movements which are met out of a member's own resources of gold and foreign exchange, but members undertake that such capital movements will be in accordance with the purposes of the Fund.

Section 2. *Special provisions for capital transfers*

A member shall be entitled to make gold tranche purchases to meet capital transfers.

Section 3. *Controls of capital transfers*

Members may exercise such controls as are necessary to regulate international capital movements, but no member may exercise these controls in a manner which will restrict payments for current transactions or which will unduly delay transfers of funds in settlement of commitments, except as provided in Article VII, Section 3 *(b)*, and in Article XIV, Section 2.

Article VII

Scarce Currencies

Section 1. *General scarcity of currency*

If the Fund finds that a general scarcity of a particular currency is developing, the Fund may so inform members and may issue a report setting forth the causes of the scarcity and containing recommendations designed to bring it to an end. A representative of the member whose currency is involved shall participate in the preparation of the report.

Section 2. *Measures to replenish the Fund's holdings of scarce currencies*

The Fund may, if it deems such action appropriate to replenish its holdings of any member's currency, take either or both of the following steps:

(i) Propose to the member that, on terms and conditions agreed between the Fund and the member, the latter lend its currency to the Fund or that, with the approval of the member, the Fund borrow such currency from some other source either within or outside the territories of the member, but no member shall be under any obligation to make such loans to the Fund or to approve the borrowing of its currency by the Fund from any other source.

(ii) Require the member to sell its currency to the Fund for gold.

Section 3. *Scarcity of the Fund's holdings*

(a) If it becomes evident to the Fund that the demand for a member's currency seriously threatens the Fund's ability to supply that currency, the Fund, whether or not it has issued a report under Section 1 of this Article, shall formally declare such currency scarce and shall thenceforth apportion its existing and accruing supply of the scarce currency with due regard to the relative needs of members, the general international economic situation and any other pertinent considerations. The Fund shall also issue a report concerning its action.

(b) A formal declaration under *(a)* above shall operate as an authorization to any member, after consultation with the Fund, temporarily to impose limitations on the freedom of exchange operations in the scarce currency. Subject to the provisions of

Article IV, Sections 3 and 4, the member shall have complete jurisdiction in determining the nature of such limitations, but they shall be no more restrictive than is necessary to limit the demand for the scarce currency to the supply held by, or accruing to, the member in question; and they shall be relaxed and removed as rapidly as conditions permit.

(c) The authorization under *(b)* above shall expire whenever the Fund formally declares the currency in question to be no longer scarce.

Section 4. *Administration of restrictions*

Any member imposing restrictions in respect of the currency of any other member pursuant to the provisions of Section 3 *(b)* of this Article shall give sympathetic consideration to any representations by the other member regarding the administration of such restrictions.

Section 5. *Effect of other international agreements on restrictions*

Members agree not to invoke the obligations of any engagements entered into with other members prior to this Agreement in such a manner as will prevent the operation of the provisions of this Article.

Article VIII

General Obligations of Members

Section 1. *Introduction*

In addition to the obligations assumed under other articles of this Agreement, each member undertakes the obligations set out in this Article.

Section 2. *Avoidance of restrictions on current payments*

(a) Subject to the provisions of Article VII, Section 3 *(b)*, and Article XIV, Section 2, no member shall, without the approval of the Fund, impose restrictions on the making of payments and transfers for current international transactions.

(b) Exchange contracts which involve the currency of any member and which are contrary to the exchange control regulations of that member maintained or imposed consistently with this Agreement shall be unenforceable in the territories of any member. In addition, members may, by mutual accord, cooperate in measures for the purpose of making the exchange control regulations of either member more effective, provided that such measures and regulations are consistent with this Agreement.

Section 3. *Avoidance of discriminatory currency practices*

No member shall engage in, or permit any of its fiscal agencies referred to in Article V, Section 1, to engage in, any discriminatory currency arrangements or multiple currency practices except as authorized under this Agreement or approved by the Fund. If such arrangements and practices are engaged in at the date when this Agreement enters into force the member concerned shall consult with the Fund as to their progressive removal unless they are maintained or imposed under Article XIV, Section 2, in which case the provisions of Section 4 of that Article shall apply.

Section 4. *Convertibility of foreign held balances*

(a) Each member shall buy balances of its currency held by another member if the latter, in requesting the purchase, represents

(i) that the balances to be bought have been recently acquired as a result of current transactions; or

(ii) that their conversion is needed for making payments for current transactions.

The buying member shall have the option to pay either in the currency of the member making the request or in gold.

(b) The obligation in (a) above shall not apply

(i) when the convertibility of the balances has been restricted consistently with Section 2 of this Article, or Article VI, Section 3; or

(ii) when the balances have accumulated as a result of transactions effected before the removal by a member of restrictions maintained or imposed under Article XIV, Section 2; or

(iii) when the balances have been acquired contrary to the exchange regulations of the member which is asked to buy them; or

(iv) when the currency of the member requesting the purchase has been declared scarce under Article VII, Section 3 (a); or

(v) when the member requested to make the purchase is for any reason not entitled to buy currencies of other members from the Fund for its own currency.

Section 5. *Furnishing of information*

(a) The Fund may require members to furnish it with such information as it deems necessary for its operations, including, as the minimum necessary for the effective discharge of the Fund's duties, national data on the following matters:

(i) Official holdings at home and abroad, of (1) gold, (2) foreign exchange.

(ii) Holdings at home and abroad by banking and financial agencies, other than official agencies, of (1) gold, (2) foreign exchange.

(iii) Production of gold.

(iv) Gold exports and imports according to countries of destination and origin.

(v) Total exports and imports of merchandise, in terms of local currency values, according to countries of destination and origin.

(vi) International balance of payments, including (1) trade in goods and services, (2) gold transactions, (3) known capital transactions, and (4) other items.

(vii) International investment position, *i.e.*, investments within the territories of the member owned abroad and investments abroad owned by persons in its territories so far as it is possible to furnish this information.

(viii) National income.

(ix) Price indices, *i.e.*, indices of commodity prices in wholesale and retail markets and of export and import prices.

(x) Buying and selling rates for foreign currencies.

(xi) Exchange controls, *i.e.*, a comprehensive statement of exchange controls in effect at the time of assuming membership in the Fund and details of subsequent changes as they occur.

(xii) Where official clearing arrangements exist, details of amounts awaiting clearance in respect of commercial and financial transactions, and of the length of time during which such arrears have been outstanding.

(b) In requesting information the Fund shall take into consideration the varying ability of members to furnish the data requested. Members shall be under no obligation to furnish information in such detail that the affairs of individuals or corporations are disclosed. Members undertake, however, to furnish the desired information in as detailed and accurate a manner as is practicable, and, so far as possible, to avoid mere estimates.

(c) The Fund may arrange to obtain further information by agreement with members. It shall act as a centre for the collection and exchange of information on monetary and financial problems, thus facilitating the preparation of studies designed to assist members in developing policies which further the purposes of the Fund.

Section 6. *Consultation between members regarding existing international agreements*

Where under this Agreement a member is authorized in the special or temporary circumstances specified in the Agreement to maintain or establish restrictions on exchange transactions, and there are other engagements between members entered into prior to this Agreement which conflict with the application of such restrictions, the parties to such engagements will consult with one another with a view to making such mutually acceptable adjustments as may be necessary. The provisions of this Article shall be without prejudice to the operation of Article VII, Section 5.

Article IX

Status, Immunities and Privileges

Section 1. *Purposes of Article*

To enable the Fund to fulfill the functions with which it is entrusted, the status, immunities and privileges set forth in this Article shall be accorded to the Fund in the territories of each member.

Section 2. *Status of the Fund*

The Fund shall possess full juridical personality, and, in particular, the capacity:
- (i) to contract;
- (ii) to acquire and dispose of immovable and movable property;
- (iii) to institute legal proceedings.

Section 3. *Immunity from judicial process*

The Fund, its property and its assets, wherever located and by whomsoever held, shall enjoy immunity from every form of judicial process except to the extent that it expressly waives its immunity for the purpose of any proceedings or by the terms of any contract.

Section 4. *Immunity from other action*

Property and assets of the Fund, wherever located and by whomsoever held, shall be immune from search, requisition, confiscation, expropriation or any other form of seizure by executive or legislative action.

Section 5. *Immunity of archives*

The archives of the Fund shall be inviolable.

Section 6. *Freedom of assets from restrictions*

To the extent necessary to carry out the operations provided for in this Agreement, all property and assets of the Fund shall be free from restrictions, regulations, controls and moratoria of any nature.

Section 7. *Privilege for communications*

The official communications of the Fund shall be accorded by members the same treatment as the official communications of other members.

Section 8. *Immunities and privileges of officers and employees*

All governors, executive directors, alternates, officers and employees of the Fund.
- (i) shall be immune from legal process with respect to acts performed by them in their official capacity except when the Fund waives this immunity.
- (ii) not being local nationals, shall be granted the same immunities from immigration restrictions, alien registration requirements and national service obli-

gations and the same facilities as regards exchange restrictions as are accorded by members to the representatives, officials, and employees of comparable rank of other members.

(iii) shall be granted the same treatment in respect of traveling facilities as is accorded by members to representatives, officials and employees of comparable rank of other members.

Section 9. *Immunities from taxation*

(a) The Fund, its assets, property, income and its operations and transactions authorized by this Agreement, shall be immune from all taxation and from all customs duties. The Fund shall also be immune from liability for the collection or payment of any tax or duty.

(b) No tax shall be levied on or in respect of salaries and emoluments paid by the Fund to executive directors, alternates, officers or employees of the Fund who are not local citizens, local subjects, or other local nationals.

(c) No taxation of any kind shall be levied on any obligation or security issued by the Fund, including any dividend or interest thereon, by whomsoever held,

(i) which discriminates against such obligation or security solely because of its origin; or

(ii) if the sole jurisdictional basis for such taxation is the place or currency in which it is issued, made payable or paid, or the location of any office or place of business maintained by the Fund.

Section 10. *Application of Article*

Each member shall take such action as is necessary in its own territories for the purpose of making effective in terms of its own law the principles set forth in this Article and shall inform the Fund of the detailed action which it has taken.

Article X

Relations with Other International Organizations

The Fund shall cooperate within the terms of this Agreement with any general international organization and with public international organizations having specialized responsibilities in related fields. Any arrangements for such cooperation which would involve a modification of any provision of this Agreement may be effected only after amendment to this Agreement under Article XVII.

Article XI

Relations with Non-Member Countries

Section 1. *Undertakings regarding relations with non-member countries*

Each member undertakes:

(i) Not to engage in, nor to permit any of its fiscal agencies referred to in Article V, Section 1 to engage in, any transactions with a non-member or with persons in a non-member's territories which would be contrary to the provisions of this Agreement or the purposes of the Fund;

(ii) Not to cooperate with a non-member or with persons in a non-member's territories in practices which would be contrary to the provisions of this Agreement or the purposes of the Fund; and

(iii) To cooperate with the Fund with a view to the application in its territories of appropriate measures to prevent transactions with non-members or with persons in their territories which would be contrary to the provisions of this Agreement or the purposes of the Fund.

Section 2. *Restrictions on transactions with non-member countries*

Nothing in this Agreement shall affect the right of any member to impose restrictions on exchange transactions with non-members or with persons in their territories unless the Fund finds that such restrictions prejudice the interests of members and are contrary to the purposes of the Fund.

Article XII

Organization and Management

Section 1. *Structure of the Fund*

The Fund shall have a Board of Governors, Executive Directors, a Managing Director and a staff.

Section 2. *Board of Governors*

(a) All powers of the Fund shall be vested in the Board of Governors, consisting of one governor and one alternate appointed by each member in such manner as it may determine. Each governor and each alternate shall serve for five years, subject to the pleasure of the member appointing him, and may be reappointed. No alternate may vote except in the absence of his principal. The Board shall select one of the governors as chairman.

(b) The Board of Governors may delegate to the Executive Directors authority to exercise any powers of the Board, except the power to:

(i) Admit new members and determine the conditions of their admission.
(ii) Approve a revision of quotas, or to decide on the payment, or on the mitigation of the effects of payment, of increases in quotas proposed as the result of a general review of quotas.
(iii) Approve a uniform change in the par values of the currencies of all members, or to decide when such a change is made that the provisions relating to the maintenance of gold value of the Fund's assets shall not apply.
(iv) Make arrangements to cooperate with other international organizations (other than informal arrangements of a temporary or administrative character).
(v) Determine the distribution of the net income of the Fund.
(vi) Require a member to withdraw.
(vii) Decide to liquidate the Fund.
(viii) Decide appeals from interpretations of this Agreement given by the Executive Directors.
(ix) Revise the provisions on repurchase or to revise and supplement the rules for the distribution of repurchases among types of reserves.
(x) Make transfers to general reserve from any special reserve.

(c) The Board of Governors shall hold an annual meeting and such other meetings as may be provided for by the Board or called by the Executive Directors. Meetings of the Board shall be called by the Directors whenever requested by five members or by members having one quarter of the total voting power.

(d) A quorum for any meeting of the Board of Governors shall be a majority of the governors exercising not less than two-thirds of the total voting power.

(e) Each governor shall be entitled to cast the number of votes allotted under Section 5 of this Article to the member appointing him.

(f) The Board of Governors may by regulation establish a procedure whereby the Executive Directors, when they deem such action to be in the best interests of the Fund, may obtain a vote of the governors on a specific question without calling a meeting of the Board.

(g) The Board of Governors, and the Executive Directors to the extent authorized, may adopt such rules and regulations as may be necessary or appropriate to conduct the business of the Fund.

(h) Governors and alternates shall serve as such without compensation from the Fund, but the Fund shall pay them reasonable expenses incurred in attending meetings.

(i) The Board of Governors shall determine the remuneration to be paid to the Executive Directors and the salary and terms of the contract of service of the Managing Director.

Section 3. *Executive Directors*

(a) The Executive Directors shall be responsible for the conduct of the general operations of the Fund, and for this purpose shall exercise all the powers delegated to them by the Board of Governors.

(b) There shall be not less than twelve directors who need not be governors, and of whom

   (i) Five shall be appointed by the five members having the largest quotas;
   (ii) Not more than two shall be appointed when the provisions of *(c)* below apply;
   (iii) Five shall be elected by the members not entitled to appoint directors, other than the American Republics; and
   (iv) Two shall be elected by the American Republics not entitled to appoint directors.

For the purposes of this paragraph, members means governments of countries whose names are set forth in Schedule A, whether they become members in accordance with Article XX or in accordance with Article II, Section 2. When governments of other countries become members, the Board of Governors may, by a four-fifths majority of the total voting power, increase the number of directors to be elected.

(c) If, at the second regular election of directors and thereafter, the members entitled to appoint directors under *(b)* (i) above do not include the two members, the holdings of whose currencies by the Fund have been, on the average over the preceding two years, reduced below their quotas by the largest absolute amounts in terms of gold as a common denominator, either one or both of such members, as the case may be, shall be entitled to appoint a director.

(d) Subject to Article XX, Section 3 *(b)* elections of elective directors shall be conducted at intervals of two years in accordance with the provisions of Schedule C, supplemented by such regulations as the Fund deems appropriate. Whenever the Board of Governors increases the number of directors to be elected under *(b)* above, it shall issue regulations making appropriate changes in the proportion of votes required to elect directors under the provisions of Schedule C.

(e) Each director shall appoint an alternate with full power to act for him when he is not present. When the directors appointing them are present, alternates may participate in meetings but may not vote.

(f) Directors shall continue in office until their successors are appointed or elected. If the office of an elected director becomes vacant more than ninety days before the end of his term, another director shall be elected for the remainder of the term by the members who elected the former director. A majority of the votes cast shall be re-

quired for election. While the office remains vacant, the alternate of the former director shall exercise his powers, except that of appointing an alternate.

(g) The Executive Directors shall function in continuous session at the principal office of the Fund and shall meet as often as the business of the Fund may require.

(h) A quorum for any meeting of the Executive Directors shall be a majority of the directors representing not less than one-half of the voting power.

(i) Each appointed director shall be entitled to cast the number of votes allotted under Section 5 of this Article to the member appointing him. Each elected director shall be entitled to cast the number of votes which counted towards his election. When the provisions of Section 5 *(b)* of this Article are applicable, the votes which a director would otherwise be entitled to cast shall be increased or decreased correspondingly. All the votes which a director is entitled to cast shall be cast as a unit.

(j) The Board of Governors shall adopt regulations under which a member not entitled to appoint a director under *(b)* above may send a representative to attend any meeting of the Executive Directors when a request made by, or a matter particularly affecting, that member is under consideration.

(k) The Executive Directors may appoint such committees as they deem advisable. Membership of committees need not be limited to governors or directors or their alternates.

Section 4. *Managing Director and staff*

(a) The Executive Directors shall select a Managing Director who shall not be a governor or an executive director. The Managing Director shall be chairman of the Executive Directors, but shall have no vote except a deciding vote in case of an equal division. He may participate in meetings of the Board of Governors, but shall not vote at such meetings. The Managing Director shall cease to hold office when the Executive Directors so decide.

(b) The Managing Director shall be chief of the operating staff of the Fund and shall conduct, under the direction of the Executive Directors, the ordinary business of the Fund. Subject to the general control of the Executive Directors, he shall be responsible for the organization, appointment and dismissal of the staff of the Fund.

(c) The Managing Director and the staff of the Fund, in the discharge of their functions, shall owe their duty entirely to the Fund and to no other authority. Each member of the Fund shall respect the international character of this duty and shall refrain from all attempts to influence any of the staff in the discharge of his functions.

(d) In appointing the staff the Managing Director shall, subject to the paramount importance of securing the highest standards of efficiency and of technical competence, pay due regard to the importance of recruiting personnel on as wide a geographical basis as possible.

Section 5. *Voting*

(a) Each member shall have two hundred fifty votes plus one additional vote for each part of its quota equivalent to one hundred thousand United States dollars.

(b) Whenever voting is required under Article V, Section 4 or 5, each member shall have the number of votes to which it is entitled under *(a)* above, adjusted:

  (i) by the addition of one vote for the equivalent of each four hundred thousand United States dollars of net sales of its currency up to the date when the vote is taken, or
  (ii) by the subtraction of one vote for the equivalent of each four hundred thousand United States dollars of its net purchases of the currencies of other members up to the date when the vote is taken

provided, that neither net purchases nor net sales shall be deemed at any time to exceed an amount equal to the quota of the member involved.

(c) For the purpose of all computations under this Section, United States dollars shall be deemed to be of the weight and fineness in effect on July 1, 1944, adjusted for any uniform change under Article IV, Section 7, if a waiver is made under Section 8*(d)* of that Article.

(d) Except as otherwise specifically provided, all decisions of the Fund shall be made by a majority of the votes cast.

Section 6. *Reserves and distribution of net income*

(a) The Board of Governors shall determine annually what part of the Fund's net income shall be placed to reserve and what part, if any, shall be distributed.

(b) If any distribution is made of the net income of any year, there shall first be distributed to members eligible to receive remuneration under Article V, Section 9, for that year an amount by which two percent per annum exceeded any remuneration that has been paid for that year. Any distribution of the net income of that year beyond that amount shall be made to all members in proportion to their quotas. Payments to each member shall be made in its own currency.

(c) The Fund may make transfer to general reserve from any special reserve.

Section 7. *Publication of reports*

(a) The Fund shall publish an annual report containing an audited statement of its accounts, and shall issue, at intervals of three months or less, a summary statement of its transactions and its holdings of gold and currencies of members.

(b) The Fund may publish such other reports as it deems desirable for carrying out its purposes.

Section 8. *Communication of views to members*

The Fund shall at all times have the right to communicate its views informally to any member on any matter arising under this Agreement. The Fund may, by a two-thirds majority of the total voting power, decide to publish a report made to a member regarding its monetary or economic conditions and developments which directly tend to produce a serious disequilibrium in the international balance of payments of members. If the member is not entitled to appoint an executive director, it shall be entitled to representation in accordance with Section 3 *(j)* of this Article. The Fund shall not publish a report involving changes in the fundamental structure of the economic organization of members.

Article XIII

Offices and Depositories

Section 1. *Location of offices*

The principal office of the Fund shall be located in the territory of the member having the largest quota, and agencies or branch offices may be established in the territories of other members.

Section 2. *Depositories*

(a) Each member country shall designate its central bank as a depository for all the Fund's holdings of its currency, or if it has no central bank it shall designate such other institution as may be acceptable to the Fund.

(b) The Fund may hold other assets, including gold, in the depositories designated by the five members having the largest quotas and in such other designated depositories as the Fund may select. Initially, at least one-half of the holdings of the Fund shall be held in the depository designated by the member in whose territories the Fund has its principal office and at least forty percent shall be held in the depositories

designated by the remaining four members referred to above. However, all transfers of gold by the Fund shall be made with due regard to the costs of transport and anticipated requirements of the Fund. In an emergency the Executive Directors may transfer all or any part of the Fund's gold holdings to any place where they can be adequately protected.

Section 3. *Guarantee of the Fund's assets*

Each member guarantees all assets of the Fund against loss resulting from failure or default on the part of the depository designated by it.

Article XIV

Transitional Period

Section 1. *Introduction*

The Fund is not intended to provide facilities for relief or reconstruction or to deal with international indebtedness arising out of the war.

Section 2. *Exchange restrictions*

In the post-war transitional period members may, notwithstanding the provisions of any other articles of this Agreement, maintain and adapt to changing circumstances (and, in the case of members whose territories have been occupied by the enemy, introduce where necessary) restrictions on payments and transfers for current international transactions. Members shall, however, have continuous regard in their foreign exchange policies to the purposes of the Fund; and, as soon as conditions permit, they shall take all possible measures to develop such commercial and financial arrangements with other members as will facilitate international payments and the maintenance of exchange stability. In particular, members shall withdraw restrictions maintained or imposed under this Section as soon as they are satisfied that they will be able, in the absence of such restrictions, to settle their balance of payments in a manner which will not unduly encumber their access to the resources of the Fund.

Section 3. *Notification to the Fund*

Each member shall notify the Fund before it becomes eligible under Article XX, Section 4 *(c)* or *(d)*, to buy currency from the Fund, whether it intends to avail itself of the transitional arrangements in Section 2 of this Article, or whether it is prepared to accept the obligations of Article VIII, Sections 2, 3, and 4. A member availing itself of the transitional arrangements shall notify the Fund as soon thereafter as it is prepared to accept the above-mentioned obligations.

Section 4. *Action of the Fund relating to restrictions*

Not later than three years after the date on which the Fund begins operations and in each year thereafter, the Fund shall report on the restrictions still in force under Section 2 of this Article. Five years after the date on which the Fund begins operations, and in each year thereafter, any member still retaining any restrictions inconsistent with Article VIII, Sections 2, 3, or 4, shall consult the Fund as to their further retention. The Fund may, if it deems such action necessary in exceptional circumstances, make representations to any member that conditions are favorable for the withdrawal of any particular restriction, or for the general abandonment of restrictions, inconsistent with the provisions of any other articles of this Agreement. The member shall be given a suitable time to reply to such representations. If the Fund finds that the members persists in maintaining restrictions which are inconsistent with the purposes of the Fund, the member shall be subject to Article XV, Section 2 *(a)*.

Section 5. *Nature of transitional period*

In its relations with members, the Fund shall recognize that the post-war transitional period will be one of change and adjustment and in making decisions on requests occasioned thereby which are presented by any member it shall give the member the benefit of any reasonable doubt.

Article XV

Withdrawal from Membership

Section 1. *Right of members to withdraw*

Any member may withdraw from the Fund at any time by transmitting a notice in writing to the Fund at its principal office. Withdrawal shall become effective on the date such notice is received.

Section 2. *Compulsory withdrawal*

(a) If a member fails to fulfill any of its obligations under this Agreement, the Fund may declare the member ineligible to use the resources of the Fund. Nothing in this Section shall be deemed to limit the provisions of Article IV, Section 6, Article V, Section 5, or Article VI, Section 1.

(b) If, after the expiration of a reasonable period the member persists in its failure to fulfill any of its obligations under this Agreement, or a difference between a member and the Fund under Article IV, Section 6, continues, that member may be required to withdraw from membership in the Fund by a decision of the Board of Governors carried by a majority of the governors representing a majority of the total voting power.

(c) Regulations shall be adopted to ensure that before action is taken against any member under *(a)* or *(b)* above, the member shall be informed in reasonable time of the complaint against it and given an adequate opportunity for stating its case, both orally and in writing.

Section 3. *Settlement of accounts with members withdrawing*

When a member withdraws from the Fund, normal transactions of the Fund in its currency shall cease and settlement of all accounts between it and the Fund shall be made with reasonable despatch by agreement between it and the Fund. If agreement is not reached promptly, the provisions of Schedule D shall apply to the settlement of accounts.

Article XVI

Emergency Provisions

Section 1. *Temporary suspension*

(a) In the event of an emergency or the development of unforeseen circumstances threatening the operations of the Fund, the Executive Directors by unanimous vote may suspend for a period of not more than one hundred twenty days the operation of any of the following provisions:

(i) Article IV, Sections 3 and 4 *(b)*
(ii) Article V, Sections 2, 3, 7, 8 *(a)* and *(f)*
(iii) Article VI, Section 2
(iv) Article XI, Section 1

(b) Simultaneously with any decision to suspend the operation of any of the foregoing provisions, the Executive Directors shall call a meeting of the Board of Governors for the earliest practicable date.

(c) The Executive Directors may not extend any suspension beyond one hundred twenty days. Such suspension may be extended, however, for an additional period of not more than two hundred forty days, if the Board of Governors by a four-fifths majority of the total voting power so decides, but it may not be further extended except by amendment of this Agreement pursuant to Article XVII.

(d) The Executive Directors may, by a majority of the total voting power, terminate such suspension at any time.

Section 2. *Liquidation of the Fund*

(a) The Fund may not be liquidated except by decision of the Board of Governors. In an emergency, if the Executive Directors decide that liquidation of the Fund may be necessary, they may temporarily suspend all transactions, pending decision by the Board.

(b) If the Board of Governors decides to liquidate the Fund, the Fund shall forthwith cease to engage in any activities except those incidental to the orderly collection and liquidation of its assets and the settlement of its liabilities, and all obligations of members under this Agreement shall cease except those set out in this Article, in Article XVIII, paragraph *(c)*, in Schedule D, paragraph 7, and in Schedule E.

(c) Liquidation shall be administered in accordance with the provisions of Schedule E.

Article XVII

Amendments

(a) Any proposal to introduce modifications in this Agreement, whether emanating from a member, a governor or the Executive Directors, shall be communicated to the chairman of the Board of Governors who shall bring the proposal before the Board. If the proposed amendment is approved by the Board the Fund shall, by circular letter or telegram, ask all members whether they accept the proposed amendment. When three-fifths of the members, having four-fifths of the total voting power, have accepted the proposed amendment, the Fund shall certify the fact by a formal communication addressed to all members.

(b) Notwithstanding *(a)* above, acceptance by all members is required in the case of any amendment modifying

   (i) the right to withdraw from the Fund (Article XV, Section 1);
  (ii) the provision that no change in a member's quota shall be made without its consent (Article III, Section 2);
 (iii) the provision that no change may be made in the par value of a member's currency except on the proposal of that member (Article IV, Section 5 *(b)*).

(c) Amendments shall enter into force for all members three months after the date of the formal communication unless a shorter period is specified in the circular letter or telegram.

Article XVIII

Interpretation

(a) Any question of interpretation of the provisions of this Agreement arising between any member and the Fund or between any members of the Fund shall be submitted to the Executive Directors for their decision. If the question particularly affects any member not entitled to appoint an executive director it shall be entitled to representation in accordance with Article XII, Section 3 *(j)*.

(b) In any case where the Executive Directors have given a decision under *(a)* above, any member may require, within three months from the date of the decision,

199

that the question be referred to the Board of Governors, whose decision shall be final. Any question referred to the Board of Governors shall be considered by a Committee on Interpretation of the Board of Governors. Each Committee member shall have one vote. The Board of Governors shall establish the membership, procedures, and voting majorities of the Committee. A decision of the Committee shall be the decision of the Board of Governors unless the Board by an eighty-five percent majority of the total voting power decides otherwise. Pending the result of the reference to the Board the Fund may, so far as it deems necessary, act on the basis of the decision of the Executive Directors.

(c) Whenever a disagreement arises between the Fund and a member which has withdrawn, or between the Fund and any member during liquidation of the Fund, such disagreement shall be submitted to arbitration by a tribunal of three arbitrators, one appointed by the Fund, another by the member or withdrawing member and an umpire who, unless the parties otherwise agree, shall be appointed by the President of the Permanent Court of International Justice or such other authority as may have been prescribed by regulation adopted by the Fund. The umpire shall have full power to settle all questions of procedure in any case where the parties are in disagreement with respect thereto.

Article XIX

Explanation of Terms

In interpreting the provisions of this Agreement the Fund and its members shall be guided by the following:

(a) A member's monetary reserves means its official holdings of gold, of convertible currencies of other members, and of the currencies of such non-members as the Fund may specify.

(b) The official holdings of a member means central holdings (that is, the holdings of its Treasury, central bank, stabilization fund, or similar fiscal agency).

(c) The holdings of other official institutions or other banks within its territories may, in any particular case, be deemed by the Fund, after consultation with the member, to be official holdings to the extent that they are substantially in excess of working balances; provided that for the purpose of determining whether, in a particular case, holdings are in excess of working balances, there shall be deducted from such holdings amounts of currency due to official institutions and banks in the territories of members or non-members specified under *(d)* below.

(d) A member's holdings of convertible currencies means its holdings of the currencies of other members which are not availing themselves of the transitional arrangements under Article XIV, Section 2, together with its holdings of the currencies of such non-members as the Fund may from time to time specify. The term currency for this purpose includes without limitation coins, paper money, bank balances, bank acceptances, and government obligations issued with a maturity not exceeding twelve months.

(e) The sums deemed to be official holdings of other official institutions and other banks under *(c)* above shall be included in the member's monetary reserves.

(f) The Fund's holdings of the currency of a member shall include any securities accepted by the Fund under Article III, Section 5.

(g) The Fund, after consultation with a member which is availing itself of the transitional arrangements under Article XIV, Section 2, may deem holdings of the currency of that member which carry specified rights of conversion into another currency or into gold to be holdings of convertible currency for the purpose of the calculation of monetary reserves.

(h) For the purpose of calculating gold subscriptions under Article III, Section 3, a member's net official holdings of gold and United States dollars shall consist of its

official holdings of gold and United States currency after deducting central holdings of its currency by other countries and holdings of its currency by other official institutions and other banks if these holdings carry specified rights of conversion into gold or United States currency.

(i) Payments for current transactions means payments which are not for the purpose of transferring capital, and includes, without limitation:

(1) All payments due in connection with foreign trade, other current business, including services, and normal short-term banking and credit facilities;
(2) Payments due as interest on loans and as net income from other investments;
(3) Payments of moderate amount for amortization of loans or for depreciation of direct investments;
(4) Moderate remittances for family living expenses.

The Fund may, after consultation with the members concerned, determine whether certain specific transactions are to be considered current transactions or capital transactions.

(j) Gold tranche purchase means a purchase by a member of the currency of another member in exchange for its own currency which does not cause the Fund's holdings of the member's currency to exceed one hundred percent of its quota, provided that for the purposes of this definition the Fund may exclude purchases and holdings under policies on the use of its resources for compensatory financing of export fluctuations.

Article XX

Inaugural Provisions

Section 1. *Entry into force*

This Agreement shall enter into force when it has been signed on behalf of governments having sixty-five percent of the total of the quotas set forth in Schedule A and when the instruments referred to in Section 2 *(a)* of this Article have been deposited on their behalf, but in no event shall this Agreement enter into force before May 1, 1945.

Section 2. *Signature*

(a) Each government on whose behalf this Agreement is signed shall deposit with the Government of the United States of America an instrument setting forth that is has accepted this Agreement in accordance with its law and has taken all steps necessary to enable it to carry out all of its obligations under this Agreement.

(b) Each government shall become a member of the Fund as from the date of the deposit on its behalf of the instrument referred to in *(a)* above, except that no government shall become a member before this Agreement enters into force under Section 1 of this Article.

(c) The Government of the United States of America shall inform the governments of all countries whose names are set forth in Schedule A, and all governments whose membership is approved in accordance with Article II, Section 2, of all signatures of this Agreement and of the deposit of all instruments referred to in *(a)* above.

(d) At the time this Agreement is signed on its behalf, each government shall transmit to the Government of the United States of America one one-hundredth of one percent of its total subscription in gold or United States dollars for the purpose of meeting administrative expenses of the Fund. The Government of the United States of America shall hold such funds in a special deposit account and shall transmit them to the Board of Governors of the Fund when the initial meeting has been called under Section 3 of this Article. If this Agreement has not come into force by December

31, 1945, the Government of the United States of America shall return such funds to the governments that transmitted them.

(e) This Agreement shall remain open for signature at Washington on behalf of the governments of the countries whose names are set forth in Schedule A until December 31, 1945.

(f) After December 31, 1945, this Agreement shall be open for signature on behalf of the government of any country whose membership has been approved in accordance with Article II, Section 2.

(g) By their signature of this Agreement, all governments accept it both on their own behalf and in respect of all their colonies, overseas territories, all territories under their protection, suzerainty, or authority and all territories in respect of which they exercise a mandate.

(h) In the case of governments whose metropolitan territories have been under enemy occupation, the deposit of the instrument referred to in *(a)* above may be delayed until one hundred eighty days after the date on which these territories have been liberated. If, however, it is not deposited by any such government before the expiration of this period the signature affixed on behalf of that government shall become void and the portion of its subscription paid under *(d)* above shall be returned to it.

(i) Paragraphs *(d)* and *(h)* shall come into force with regard to each signatory goverment as from the date of its signature.

Section 3. *Inauguration of the Fund*

(a) As soon as this Agreement enters into force under Section 1 of this Article, each member shall appoint a governor and the member having the largest quota shall call the first meeting of the Board of Governors.

(b) At the first meeting of the Board of Governors, arrangements shall be made for the selection of provisional executive directors. The governments of the five countries for which the largest quotas are set forth in Schedule A shall appoint provisional executive directors. If one or more of such governments have not become members, the executive directorships they would be entitled to fill shall remain vacant until they become members, or until January 1, 1946, whichever is the earlier. Seven provisional executive directors shall be elected in accordance with the provisions of Schedule C and shall remain in office until the date of the first regular election of executive directors which shall be held as soon as practicable after January 1, 1946.

(c) The Board of Governors may delegate to the provisonal executive directors any powers except those which may not be delegated to the Executive Directors.

Section 4. *Initial determination of par values*

(a) When the Fund is of the opinion that it will shortly be in a position to begin exchange transactions, it shall so notify the members and shall request each member to communicate within thirty days the par value of its currency based on the rates of exchange prevailing on the sixtieth day before the entry into force of this Agreement. No member whose metropolitan territory has been occupied by the enemy shall be required to make such a communication while that territory is a theater of major hostilities or for such period thereafter as the Fund may determine. When such a member communicates the par value of its currency the provisions of *(d)* below shall apply.

(b) The par value communicated by a member whose metropolitan territory has not been occupied by the enemy shall be the par value of that member's currency for the purposes of this Agreement unless, within ninety days after the request referred to in *(a)* above has been received, (i) the member notifies the Fund that it regards the par value as unsatisfactory, or (ii) the Fund notifies the member that in its opinion the par value cannot be maintained without causing recourse to the Fund on the part of that member or others on a scale prejudicial to the Fund and to members. When notification is given under (i) or (ii) above, the Fund and the member shall, within a period determined by the Fund in the light of all relevant circumstances, agree upon a

suitable par value for that currency. If the Fund and the member do not agree within the period so determined, the member shall be deemed to have withdrawn from the Fund on the date when the period expires.

(c) When the par value of a member's currency has been established under *(b)* above, either by the expiration of ninety days without notification, or by agreement after notification, the member shall be eligible to buy from the Fund the currencies of other members to the full extent permitted in this Agreement, provided that the Fund has begun exchange transactions.

(d) In the case of a member whose metropolitan territory has been occupied by the enemy, the provisions of *(b)* above shall apply, subject to the following modifications:

  (i) The period of ninety days shall be extended so as to end on a date to be fixed by agreement between the Fund and the member.

  (ii) Within the extended period the member may, if the Fund has begun exchange transactions, buy from the Fund with its currency the currencies of other members, but only under such conditions and in such amounts as may be prescribed by the Fund.

  (iii) At any time before the date fixed under (i) above, changes may be made by agreement with the Fund in the par value communicated under *(a)* above.

(e) If a member whose metropolitan territory has been occupied by the enemy adopts a new monetary unit before the date to be fixed under *(d)* (i) above, the par value fixed by that member for the new unit shall be communicated to the Fund and the provisions of *(d)* above shall apply.

(f) Changes in par values agreed with the Fund under this Section shall not be taken into account in determining whether a proposed change falls within (i), (ii), or (iii) of Article IV, Section 5 *(c)*.

(g) A member communicating to the Fund a par value for the currency of its metropolitan territory shall simultaneously communicate a value, in terms of that currency, for each separate currency, where such exists, in the territories in respect of which it has accepted this Agreement under Section 2 *(g)* of this Article, but no member shall be required to make a communication for the separate currency of a territory which has been occupied by the enemy while that territory is a theater of major hostilities of for such period thereafter as the Fund may determine. On the basis of the par values so communicated, the Fund shall compute the par value of each separate currency. A communication or notification to the Fund under *(a)*, *(b)* or *(d)* above regarding the par value of a currency, shall also be deemed, unless the contrary is stated, to be a communication or notification regarding the par value of all the separate currencies referred to above. Any member may, however, make a communication or notification relating to the metropolitan or any of the separate currencies alone. If the member does so, the provisions of the preceding paragraphs (including *(d)* above, if a territory where a separate currency exists has been occupied by the enemy) shall apply to each of these currencies separately.

(h) The Fund shall begin exchange transactions at such date as it may determine after members having sixty-five percent of the total of the quotas set forth in Schedule A have become eligible, in accordance with the preceding paragraphs of this Section, to purchase the currencies of other members, but in no event until after major hostilities in Europe have ceased.

(i) The Fund may postpone exchange transactions with any member if its circumstances are such that, in the opinion of the Fund, they would lead to use of the resources of the Fund in a manner contrary to the purposes of this Agreement or prejudicial to the Fund or the members.

(j) The par values of the currencies of governments which indicate their desire to become members after December 31, 1945, shall be determined in accordance with the provisions of Article II, Section 2.

Article XXI

Special Drawing Rights

Section 1. *Authority to allocate special drawing rights*

To meet the need, as and when it arises, for a supplement to existing reserve assets, the Fund is authorized to allocate special drawing rights to members that are participants in the Special Drawing Account.

Section 2. *Unit of value*

The unit of value of special drawing rights shall be equivalent to 0.888 671 gram of fine gold.

Article XXII

General Account and Special Drawing Account

Section 1. *Separation of operations and transactions*

All operations and transactions involving special drawing rights shall be conducted through the Special Drawing Account. All other operations and transactions of the Fund authorized by or under this Agreement shall be conducted through the General Account. Operations and transactions pursuant to Article XXIII, Section 2, shall be conducted through the General Account as well as the Special Drawing Account.

Section 2. *Separation of assets and property*

All assets and property of the Fund shall be held in the General Account, except that assets and property acquired under Article XXVI, Section 2, and Articles XXX and XXXI and Schedules H and I shall be held in the Special Drawing Account. Any assets or property held in one Account shall not be available to discharge or meet the liabilities, obligations, or losses of the Fund incurred in the conduct of the operations and transactions of the other Account, except that the expenses of conducting the business of the Special Drawing Account shall be paid by the Fund from the General Account which shall be reimbursed from time to time by assessments under Article XXVI, Section 4, made on the basis of a reasonable estimate of such expenses.

Section 3. *Recording and information*

All changes in holdings of special drawing rights shall take effect only when recorded by the Fund in the Special Drawing Account. Participants shall notify the Fund of the provisions of this Agreement under which special drawing rights are used. The Fund may require participants to furnish it with such other information as it deems necessary for its functions.

Article XXIII

Participants and Other Holders of Special Drawing Rights

Section 1. *Participants*

Each member of the Fund that deposits with the Fund an instrument setting forth that it undertakes all the obligations of a participant in the Special Drawing Account in accordance with its law and that it has taken all steps necessary to enable it to carry out all of these obligations shall become a participant in the Special Drawing Account as of the date the instrument is deposited, except that no member shall become a participant before Articles XXI through XXXII and Schedules F through I have entered into force and instruments have been deposited under this Section by members that have at least seventy-five percent of the total of quotas.

Section 2. *General Account as a holder*

The Fund may accept and hold special drawing rights in the General Account and use them, in accordance with the provisions of this Agreement.

Section 3. *Other holders*

The Fund by an eighty-five percent majority of the total voting power may prescribe:

(i) as holders, non-members, members that are non-participants, and institutions that perform functions of a central bank for more than one member;

(ii) the terms and conditions on which these holders may be permitted to accept, hold, and use special drawing rights, in operations and transactions with participants; and

(iii) the terms and conditions on which participants may enter into operations and transactions with these holders.

The terms and conditions prescribed by the Fund for the use of special drawing rights by prescribed holders and by participants in operations and transactions with them shall be consistent with the provisions of this Agreement.

Article XXIV

Allocation and Cancellation of Special Drawing Rights

Section 1. *Principles and considerations governing allocation and cancellation*

(a) In all its decisions with respect to the allocation and cancellation of special drawing rights the Fund shall seek to meet the long-term global need, as and when it arises, to supplement existing reserve assets in such manner as will promote the attainment of its purposes and will avoid economic stagnation and deflation as well as excess demand and inflation in the world.

(b) The first decision to allocate special drawing rights shall take into account, as special considerations, a collective judgment that there is a global need to supplement reserves, and the attainment of a better balance of payments equilibrium, as well as the likelihood of a better working of the adjustment process in the future.

Section 2. *Allocation and cancellation*

(a) Decisions of the Fund to allocate or cancel special drawing rights shall be made for basic periods which shall run consecutively and shall be five years in duration. The first basic period shall begin on the date of the first decision to allocate special drawing rights or such later date as may be specified in that decision. Any allocations or cancellations shall take place at yearly intervals.

(b) The rates at which allocations are to be made shall be expressed as percentages of quotas on the date of each decision to allocate. The rates at which special drawing rights are to be cancelled shall be expressed as percentages of net cumulative allocations of special drawing rights on the date of each decision to cancel. The percentages shall be the same for all participants.

(c) In its decision for any basic period the Fund may provide, notwithstanding *(a)* and *(b)* above, that:

(i) the duration of the basic period shall be other than five years; or

(ii) the allocations or cancellations shall take place at other than yearly intervals; or

(iii) the basis for allocations or cancellations shall be the quotas or net cumulative allocations on dates other than the dates of decisions to allocate or cancel.

(d) A member that becomes a participant after a basic period starts shall receive allocations beginning with the next basic period in which allocations are made after it

becomes a participant unless the Fund decides that the new participant shall start to receive allocations beginning with the next allocation after it becomes a participant. If the Fund decides that a member that becomes a participant during a basic period shall receive allocations during the remainder of that basic period and the participant was not a member on the dates established under *(b)* or *(c)* above, the Fund shall determine the basis on which these allocations to the participant shall be made.

(e) A participant shall receive allocations of special drawing rights made pursuant to any decision to allocate unless:

 (i) the governor for the participant did not vote in favor of the decision; and
 (ii) the participant has notified the Fund in writing prior to the first allocation of special drawing rights under that decision that it does not wish special drawing rights to be allocated to it under the decision. On the request of a participant, the Fund may decide to terminate the effect of the notice with respect to allocations of special drawing rights subsequent to the termination.

(f) If on the effective date of any cancellation the amount of special drawing rights held by a participant is less than its share of the special drawing rights that are to be cancelled, the participant shall eliminate its negative balance as promptly as its gross reserve position permits and shall remain in consultation with the Fund for this purpose. Special drawing rights acquired by the participant after the effective date of the cancellation shall be applied against its negative balance and cancelled.

Section 3. *Unexpected major developments*

The Fund may change the rates or intervals of allocation or cancellation during the rest of a basic period or change the length of a basic period or start a new basic period, if at any time the Fund finds it desirable to do so because of unexpected major developments.

Section 4. *Decisions on allocations and cancellations*

(a) Decisions under Section 2*(a)*, *(b)*, and *(c)* or Section 3 of this Article shall be made by the Board of Governors on the basis of proposals of the Managing Director concurred in by the Executive Directors

(b) Before making any proposal, the Managing Director, after having satisfied himself that it will be consistent with the provisions of Section 1 *(a)* of this Article, shall conduct such consultations as will enable him to ascertain that there is broad support among participants for the proposal. In addition, before making a proposal for the first allocation, the Managing Director shall satisfy himself that the provisions of Section 1 *(b)* of this Article have been met and that there is broad support among participants to begin allocations; he shall make a proposal for the first allocation as soon after establishment of the Special Drawing Account as he is so satisfied.

(c) The Managing Director shall make proposals:

 (i) not later than six months before the end of each basic period;
 (ii) if no decision has been taken with respect to allocation or cancellation for a basic period, whenever he is satisfied that the provisions of *(b)* above have been met;
 (iii) when, in accordance with Section 3 of this Article, he considers that it would be desirable to change the rate or intervals of allocation or cancellation or change the length of a basic period or start a new basic period; or
 (iv) within six months of a request by the Board of Governors or the Executive Directors;

provided that, if under (i), (iii), or (iv) above the Managing Director ascertains that there is no proposal which he considers to be consistent with the provisions of Section 1 of this Article that has broad support among participants in accordance with *(b)* above, he shall report to the Board of Governors and to the Executive Directors.

(d) A majority of eighty-five percent of the total voting power shall be required for decisions under Section 2 *(a)*, *(b)*, and *(c)* or Section 3 of this Article except for decisions under Section 3 with respect to a decrease in the rates of allocation.

Article XXV

Operations and Transactions in Special Drawing Rights

Section 1. *Use of special drawing rights*

Special drawing rights may be used in the operations and transactions authorized by or under this Agreement.

Section 2. *Transactions between participants*

(a) A participant shall be entitled to use its special drawing rights to obtain an equivalent amount of currency from a participant designated under Section 5 of this Article.

(b) A participant, in agreement with another participant, may use its special drawing rights:

    (i) to obtain an equivalent amount of its own currency held by the other participant; or

    (ii) to obtain an equivalent amount of currency from the other participant in any transactions, prescribed by the Fund, that would promote reconstitution by the other participant under Section 6 *(a)* of this Article; prevent or reduce a negative balance of the other participant; offset the effect of a failure by the other participant to fulfill the expectation in Section 3 *(a)* of this Article, or bring the holdings of special drawing rights by both participants closer to their net cumulative allocations. The Fund by an eighty-five percent majority of the total voting power may prescribe additional transactions or categories of transactions under this provision. Any transactions or categories of transactions prescribed by the Fund under this subsection *(b)* (ii) shall be consistent with the other provisions of this Agreement and with the proper use of special drawing rights in accordance with this Agreement.

(c) A participant that provides currency to a participant using special drawing rights shall receive an equivalent amount of special drawing rights.

Section 3. *Requirement of need*

(a) In transactions under Section 2 of this Article, except as otherwise provided in *(c)* below, a participant will be expected to use its special drawing rights only to meet balance of payments needs or in the light of developments in its official holdings of gold, foreign exchange, and special drawing rights, and its reserve position in the Fund, and not for the sole purpose of changing the composition of the foregoing as between special drawing rights and the total of gold, foreign exchange, and reserve position in the Fund.

(b) The use of special drawing rights shall not be subject to challenge on the basis of the expectation in *(a)* above, but the Fund may make representations to a participant that fails to fulfill this expectation. A participant that persists in failing to fulfill this expectation shall be subject to Article XXIX, Section 2 *(b)*.

(c) Participants may use special drawing rights without fulfilling the expectation in *(a)* above to obtain an equivalent amount of currency from another participant in any transactions, prescribed by the Fund, that would promote reconstitution by the other participant under Section 6 *(a)* of this Article; prevent or reduce a negative balance of the other participant; offset the effect of a failure by the other participant to fulfill the expectation in *(a)* above; or bring the holdings of special drawing rights by both participants closer to their net cumulative allocations.

Section 4. *Obligation to provide currency*

A participant designated by the Fund under Section 5 of this Article shall provide on demand currency convertible in fact to a participant using special drawing rights under Section 2 *(a)* of this Article. A participant's obligation to provide currency shall not extend beyond the point at which its holdings of special drawing rights in excess of its net cumulative allocation are equal to twice its net cumulative allocation or such higher limit as may be agreed between a participant and the Fund. A participant may provide currency in excess of the obligatory limit or any agreed higher limit.

Section 5. *Designation of participants to provide currency*

(a) The Fund shall ensure that a participant will be able to use its special drawing rights by designating participants to provide currency for specified amounts of special drawing rights for the purposes of Sections 2 *(a)* and 4 of this Article. Designations shall be made in accordance with the following general principles supplemented by such other principles as the Fund may adopt from time to time:

   (i) A participant shall be subject to designation if its balance of payments and gross reserve position is sufficiently strong, but this will not preclude the possibility that a participant with a strong reserve position will be designated even though it has a moderate balance of payments deficit. Participants shall be designated in such manner as will promote over time a balanced distribution of holdings of special drawing rights among them.

  (ii) Participants shall be subject to designation in order to promote reconstitution under Section 6 *(a)* of this Article; to reduce negative balances in holdings of special drawing rights; or to offset the effect of failures to fulfill the expectation in Section 3 *(a)* of this Article.

 (iii) In designating participants the Fund normally shall give priority to those that need to acquire special drawing rights to meet the objectives of designation under (ii) above.

(b) In order to promote over time a balanced distribution of holdings of special drawing rights under *(a)* (i) above, the Fund shall apply the rules for designation in Schedule F or such rules as may be adopted under *(c)* below.

(c) The rules for designation shall be reviewed before the end of the first and each subsequent basic period and the Fund may adopt new rules as the result of a review. Unless new rules are adopted, the rules in force at the time of the review shall continue to apply.

Section 6. *Reconstitution*

(a) Participants that use their special drawing rights shall reconstitute their holdings of them in accordance with the rules for reconstitution in Schedule G or such rules as may be adopted under *(b)* below.

(b) The rules for reconstitution shall be reviewed before the end of the first and each subsequent basic period and new rules shall be adopted if necessary. Unless new rules are adopted or a decision is made to abrogate rules for reconstitution, the rules in force at the time of the review shall continue to apply. An eighty-five percent majority of the total voting power shall be required for decisions to adopt, modify, or abrogate the rules for reconstitution.

Section 7. *Operations and transactions through the General Account*

(a) Special drawing rights shall be included in a member's monetary reserves under Article XIX for the purposes of Article III, Section 4 *(a)*, Article V, Section 7 *(b)* and *(c)*, Article V, Section 8 *(f)*, and Schedule B, paragraph 1. The Fund may decide that in calculating monetary reserves and the increase in monetary reserves during any year for the purpose of Article V, Section 7 *(b)* and *(c)*, no account shall be taken of any

increase or decrease in those monetary reserves which is due to allocations or cancellations of special drawing rights during the year.

(b) The Fund shall accept special drawing rights:

(i) in repurchases accruing in special drawing rights under Article V, Section 7 *(b)*; and

(ii) in reimbursement pursuant to Article XXVI, Section 4.

(c) The Fund may accept special drawing rights to the extent it may decide:

(i) in payment of charges; and

(ii) in repurchases other than those under Article V, Section 7 *(b)*, in proportions which, as far as feasible, shall be the same for all members.

(d) The Fund, if it deems such action appropriate to replenish its holdings of a participant's currency and after consultation with that participant on alternative ways of replenishment under Article VII, Section 2, may require that participant to provide its currency for special drawing rights held in the General Account subject to Section 4 of this Article. In replenishing with special drawing rights, the Fund shall pay due regard to the principles of designation under Section 5 of this Article.

(e) To the extent that a participant may receive special drawing rights in a transaction prescribed by the Fund to promote reconstitution by it under Section 6 *(a)* of this Article, prevent or reduce a negative balance, or offset the effect of a failure by it to fulfill the expectation in Section 3 *(a)* of this Article, the Fund may provide the participant with special drawing rights held in the General Account for gold or currency acceptable to the Fund.

(f) In any of the other operations and transactions of the Fund with a participant conducted trought the General Account the Fund may use special drawing rights by agreement with the participant.

(g) The Fund may levy reasonable charges uniform for all participants in connection with operations and transactions under this Section.

Section 8. *Exchange rates*

(a) The exchange rates for operations or transactions between participants shall be such that a participant using special drawing rights shall receive the same value whatever currencies might be provided and whichever participants provide those currencies, and the Fund shall adopt regulations to give effect to this principle.

(b) The Fund shall consult a participant on the procedure for determining rates of exchange for its currency.

(c) For the purpose of this provision the term participant includes a terminating participant.

Article XXVI

Special Drawing Account Interest and Charges

Section 1. *Interest*

Interest at the same rate for all holders shall be paid by the Fund to each holder on the amount of its holdings of special drawing rights. The Fund shall pay the amount due to each holder whether or not sufficient charges are received to meet the payment of interest.

Section 2. *Charges*

Charges at the same rate for all participants shall be paid to the Fund by each participant on the amount of its net cumulative allocation of special drawing rights plus any negative balance of the participant or unpaid charges.

Section 3. *Rate of interest and charges*

The rate of interest shall be equal to the rate of charges and shall be one and one-half percent per annum. The Fund in its discretion may increase or reduce this rate, but the rate shall not be greater than two percent or the rate of remuneration decided under Article V, Section 9, whichever is higher, or smaller than one percent or the rate of remuneration decided under Article V, Section 9, whichever is lower.

Section 4. *Assessments*

When it is decided under Article XXII, Section 2, that reimbursement shall be made, the Fund shall levy assessments for this purpose at the same rate for all participants on their net cumulative allocations.

Section 5. *Payment of interest, charges, and assessments*

Interest, charges, and assessments shall be paid in special drawing rights. A participant that needs special drawing rights to pay any charge or assessment shall be obligated and entitled to obtain them, at its option for gold or currency acceptable to the Fund, in a transaction with the Fund conducted through the General Account. If sufficient special drawing rights cannot be obtained in this way, the participant shall be obligated and entitled to obtain them with currency convertible in fact from a participant which the Fund shall specify. Special drawing rights acquired by a participant after the date for payment shall be applied against its unpaid charges and cancelled.

Article XXVII

Administration of the General Account and the Special Drawing Account

(a) The General Account and the Special Drawing Account shall be administered in accordance with the provisions of Article XII, subject to the following:

  (i) The Board of Governors may delegate to the Executive Directors authority to exercise any powers of the Board with respect to special drawing rights except those under Article XXIII, Section 3, Article XXIV, Section 2 *(a)*, *(b)*, and *(c)*, and Section 3, the penultimate sentence of Article XXV, Section 2 *(b)*, Article XXV, Section 6 *(b)*, and Article XXXI *(a)*.

 (ii) For meetings of or decisions by the Board of Governors on matters pertaining exclusively to the Special Drawing Account only requests by or the presence and the notes of governors appointed by members that are participants shall be counted for the purpose of calling meetings and determining whether a quorum exists or whether a decision is made by the required majority.

(iii) For decisions by the Executive Directors on matters pertaining exclusively to the Special Drawing Account only directors appointed or elected by at least one member that is a participant shall be entitled to vote. Each of these directors shall be entitled to cast the number of votes allotted to the member which is a participant that appointed him or to the members that are participants whose votes counted towards his election. Only the presence of directors appointed or elected by members that are participants and the votes allotted to members that are participants shall be counted for the purpose of determining whether a quorum exists or whether a decision is made by the required majority.

 (iv) Questions of the general administration of the Fund, including reimbursement under Article XXII, Section 2, and any question whether a matter pertains to both Accounts or exclusively to the Special Drawing Account shall be decided as if they pertained exclusively to the General Account. Decisions with respect to the acceptance and holding of special drawing rights in the General Account and the use of them, and other decisions affecting the operations and transsactions conducted through both the General Account and the Special Drawing Account shall be made by the majorities required for decisions on matters pertaining exclusively to each Account. A decision on a matter pertaining to the Special Drawing Account shall so indicate.

(b) In addition to the privileges and immunities that are accorded under Article IX of this Agreement, no tax of any kind shall be levied on special drawing rights or on operations or transactions in special drawing rights.

(c) A question of interpretation of the provisions of this Agreement on matters pertaining exclusively to the Special Drawing Account shall be submitted to the Executive Directors pursuant to Article XVIII *(a)* only on the request of a participant. In any case where the Executive Directors have given a decision on a question of interpretation pertaining exclusively to the Special Drawing Account only a participant may require that the question be referred to the Board of Governors under Article XVIII *(b)*. The Board of Governors shall decide whether a governor appointed by a member that is not a participant shall be entitled to vote in the Committee on Interpretation on questions pertaining exclusively to the Special Drawing Account.

(d) Whenever a disagreement arises between the Fund and a participant that has terminated its participation in the Special Drawing Account or between the Fund and any participant during the liquidation of the Special Drawing Account with respect to any matter arising exclusively from participation in the Special Drawing Account, the disagreement shall be submitted to arbitration in accordance with the procedures in Article XVIII *(c)*.

Article XXVIII

General Obligations of Participants

In addition to the obligations assumed with respect to special drawing rights under other Articles of this Agreement, each participant undertakes to collaborate with the Fund and with other participants in order to facilitate the effective functioning of the Special Drawing Account and the proper use of special drawing rights in accordance with this Agreement.

Article XXIX

Suspension of Transactions in Special Drawing Rights

Section 1. *Emergency provisions*

In the event of an emergency or the development of unforeseen circumstances threatening the operations of the Fund with respect to the Special Drawing Account, the Executive Directors by unanimous vote may suspend for a period of not more than one hundred twenty days the operation of any of the provisions relating to special drawing rights, and the provisions of Article XVI, Section 1 *(b)*, *(c)*, and *(d)*, shall then apply.

Section 2. *Failure to fulfill obligations*

(a) If the Fund finds that a participant has failed to fulfill its obligations under Article XXV, Section 4, the right of the participant to use its special drawing rights shall be suspended unless the Fund otherwise determines.

(b) If the Fund finds that a participant has failed to fulfill any other obligation with respect to special drawing rights, the Fund may suspend the right of the participant to use special drawing rights it acquires after the suspension.

(c) Regulations shall be adopted to ensure that before action is taken against any participant under *(a)* or *(b)* above, the participant shall be informed immediately of the complaint against it and given an adequate opportunity for stating its case, both

orally and in writing. Whenever the participant is thus informed of a complaint relating to *(a)* above, it shall not use special drawing rights pending the disposition of the complaint.

(d) Suspension under *(a)* or *(b)* above or limitation under *(c)* above shall not affect a participant's obligation to provide currency in accordance with Article XXV, Section 4.

(e) The Fund may at any time terminate a suspension under *(a)* or *(b)* above, provided that a suspension imposed on a participant under *(b)* above for failure to fulfill the obligation under Article XXV, Section 6 *(a)*, shall not be terminated until one hundred eighty days after the end of the first calendar quarter during which the participant complies with the rules for reconstitution.

(f) The right of a participant to use its special drawing rights shall not be suspended because it has become ineligible to use the Fund's resources under Article IV, Section 6, Article V, Section 5, Article VI, Section 1, or Article XV, Section 2 *(a)*. Article XV, Section 2, shall not apply because a participant has failed to fulfill any obligations with respect to special drawing rights.

Article XXX

Termination of Participation

Section 1. *Right to terminate participation*

(a) Any participant may terminate its participation in the Special Drawing Account at any time by transmitting a notice in writing to the Fund at its principal office. Termination shall become effective on the date the notice is received.

(b) A participant that withdraws from membership in the Fund shall be deemed to have simultaneously terminated its participation in the Special Drawing Account.

Section 2. *Settlement on termination*

(a) When a participant terminates its participation in the Special Drawing Account, all operations and transactions by the terminating participant in special drawing rights shall cease except as otherwise permitted under an agreement made pursuant to *(c)* below in order to facilitate a settlement or as provided in Sections 3, 5, and 6 of this Article or in Schedule H. Interest and charges that accrued to the date of termination and assessments levied before that date but not paid shall be paid in special drawing rights.

(b) The Fund shall be obligated to redeem all special drawing rights held by the terminating participant, and the terminating participant shall be obligated to pay to the Fund an amount equal to its net cumulative allocation and any other amounts that may be due and payable because of its participation in the Special Drawing Account. These obligations shall be set off against each other and the amount of special drawing rights held by the terminating participant that is used in the setoff to extinguish its obligation to the Fund shall be cancelled.

(c) A settlement shall be made with reasonable dispatch by agreement between the terminating participant and the Fund with respect to any obligation of the terminating participant or the Fund after the setoff in *(b)* above. If agreement on a settlement is not reached promptly the provisions of Schedule H shall apply.

Section 3. *Interest and charges*

After the date of termination the Fund shall pay interest on any outstanding balance of special drawing rights held by a terminating participant and the terminating participant shall pay charges on any outstanding obligation owed to the Fund at the times and rates prescribed under Article XXVI. Payment shall be made in special drawing rights. A terminating participant shall be entitled to obtain special drawing rights with currency convertible in fact to pay charges or assessments in a transaction with a participant specified by the Fund or by agreement from any other holder, or to dispose of special drawing rights received as interest in a transaction with any participant designated under Article XXV, Section 5, or by agreement with any other holder.

Section 4. *Settlement of obligation to the Fund*

Gold or currency received by the Fund from a terminating participant shall be used by the Fund to redeem special drawing rights held by participants in proportion to the amount by which each participant's holdings of special drawing rights exceed its net cumulative allocation at the time the gold or currency is received by the Fund. Special drawing rights so redeemed and special drawing rights obtained by a terminating participant under the provisions of this Agreement to meet any installment due under an agreement on settlement or under Schedule H and set off against that installment shall be cancelled.

Section 5. *Settlement of obligation to a terminating participant*

Whenever the Fund is required to redeem special drawing rights held by a terminating participant, redemption shall be made with currency or gold provided by participants specified by the Fund. These participants shall be specified in accordance with the principles in Article XXV, Section 5. Each specified participant shall provide at its option the currency of the terminating participant or currency convertible in fact or gold to the Fund and shall receive an equivalent amount of special drawing rights. However, a terminating participant may use its special drawing rights to obtain its own currency, currency convertible in fact, or gold from any holder, if the Fund so permits.

Section 6. *General Account transactions*

In order to facilitate settlement with a terminating participant the Fund may decide that a terminating participant shall:

(i) use any special drawing rights held by it after the setoff in Section 2 *(b)* of this Article, when they are to be redeemed, in a transaction with the Fund conducted through the General Account to obtain its own currency or currency convertible in fact at the option of the Fund; or

(ii) obtain special drawing rights in a transaction with the Fund conducted through the General Account for a currency acceptable to the Fund or gold to meet any charges or installment due under an agreement or the provisions of Schedule H.

Article XXXI

Liquidation of the Special Drawing Account

(a) The Special Drawing Account may not be liquidated except by decision of the Board of Governors. In an emergency, if the Executive Directors decide that liquidation of the Special Drawing Account may be necessary, they may temporarily suspend allocations or cancellations and all transactions in special drawing rights pending decision by the Board. A decision by the Board of Governors to liquidate the Fund shall be a decision to liquidate both the General Account and the Special Drawing Account.

(b) If the Board of Governors decides to liquidate the Special Drawing Account, all allocations or cancellations and all operations and transactions in special drawing rights and the activities of the Fund with respect to the Special Drawing Account shall cease except those incidental to the orderly discharge of the obligations of participants and of the Fund with respect to special drawing rights, and all obligations of the Fund and of participants under this Agreement with respect to special drawing rights shall cease except those set out in this Article, Article XVIII *(c)*, Article XXVI, Article XXVII *(d)*, Article XXX and Schedule H, or any agreement reached under Article XXX subject to paragraph 4 of Schedule H, Article XXXII, and Schedule I.

(c) Upon liquidation of the Special Drawing Account, interest and charges that accrued to the date of liquidation and assessments levied before that date but not paid shall be paid in special drawing rights. The Fund shall be obligated to redeem all special drawing rights held by holders and each participant shall be obligated to pay the Fund an amount equal to its net cumulative allocation of special drawing rights and such other amounts as may be due and payable because of its participation in the Special Drawing Account.

(d) Liquidation of the Special Drawing Account shall be administered in accordance with the provisions of Schedule I.

Article XXXII

Explanation of Terms with Respect to Special Drawing Rights

In interpreting the provisions of this Agreement with respect to special drawing rights the Fund and its members shall be guided by the following:

(a) Net cumulative allocation of Special drawing rights means the total amount of special drawing rights allocated to a participant less its share of special drawing rights that have been cancelled under Article XXIV, Section 2 *(a)*.

(b) Currency convertible in fact means.

(1) a participant's currency for which a procedure exists for the conversion of balances of the currency obtained in transactions involving special drawing rights into each other currency for which such procedure exists, at rates of exchange prescribed under Article XXV, Section 8, and which is the currency of a participant that

    (i) has accepted the obligations of Article VIII, Sections 2, 3, and 4, or

    (ii) for the settlement of international transactions in fact freely buys and sells gold within the limits prescribed by the Fund under Section 2 of Article IV, or

(2) currency convertible into a currency described in paragraph (1) above at rates of exchange prescribed under Article XXV, Section 8.

(c) A participant's reserve position in the Fund means the sum of the gold tranche purchases it could make and the amount of any indebtedness of the Fund which is readily repayable to the participant under a loan agreement.

[The signature and depository clause reproduced below followed the text of Article XX in the original Articles of Agreement]

Done at Washington, in a single copy which shall remain deposited in the archives of the Government of the United States of America, which shall transmit certified copies to all governments whose names are set forth in Schedule A and to all governments whose membership is approved in accordance with Article II, Section 2.

Quotas

(In millions of United States dollars)

Australia	200	India	400
Belgium	225	Iran	25
Bolivia	10	Iraq	8
Brazil	150	Liberia	.5
Canada	300	Luxembourg	10
Chile	50	Mexico	90
China	550	Netherlands	275
Colombia	50	New Zealand	50
Costa Rica	5	Nicaragua	2
Cuba	50	Norway	50
Czechoslovakia	125	Panama	.5
Denmark*	*	Paraguay	2
Dominican Republic	5	Peru	25
Ecuador	5	Philippine Commonwealth	15
Egypt	45	Poland	125
El Salvador	2.5	Union of South Africa	100
Ethiopia	6	Union of Soviet Socialist	
France	450	Republics	1200
Greece	40	United Kingdom	1300
Guatemala	5	United States	2750
Haiti	5	Uruguay	15
Honduras	2.5	Venezuela	15
Iceland	1	Yugoslavia	60

*The quota of Denmark shall be determined by the Fund after the Danish Government has declared its readiness to sign this Agreement but before signature takes place.

Schedule B

Provisions with Respect to Repurchase by a Member of Its Currency Held by the Fund

1. In determining the extent to which repurchase of a member's currency from the Fund under Article V, Section 7 *(b)*, shall be made with each convertible currency and each of the other types of monetary reserve, the following rule, subject to 2 below, shall apply:

   (a) If the member's monetary reserves have not increased during the year, the amount payable to the Fund shall be distributed among all types of reserves in proportion to the member's holdings thereof at the end of the year.

   (b) If the member's monetary reserves have increased during the year, a part of the amount payable to the Fund equal to one-half of the increase, minus one-half of any decrease in the Fund's holdings of the member's currency that has occurred during the year, shall be distributed among those types of reserves which have increased in proportion to the amount by which each of them has increased. The remainder of the sum payable to the Fund shall be distributed among all types of reserves in proportion to the member's remaining holdings thereof.

(c) If after the repurchases required under Article V, Section 7 *(b)*, had been made, the result would exceed either of the limits specified in Article V, Section 7*(c)* (i) or (ii), the Fund shall require such repurchases to be made by the member proportionately in such manner that these limits will not be exceeded.

(d) If after all the repurchases required under Article V, Section 7 *(b)*, had been made, the result would exceed the limit specified in Article V, Section 7 *(c)* (iii), the amount by which the limit would be exceeded shall be discharged in convertible currencies as determined by the Fund without exceeding that limit.

(e) If a repurchase required under Article V, Section 7 *(b)*, would exceed the limit specified in Article V, Section 7 *(c)* (iv), the amount by which the limit would be exceeded shall be repurchased at the end of the subsequent financial year or years in such a way that total repurchases under Article V, Section 7 *(b)*, in any year would not exceed the limit specified in Article V, Section 7 *(c)* (iv).

2. *(a)* The Fund shall not acquire the currency of any non-member under Article V, Section 7 *(b)* and *(c)*.

(b) Any amount payable in the currency of a non-member under 1 *(a)* or 1 *(b)* above shall be paid in the convertible currencies of members as determined by the Fund.

3. In calculating monetary reserves and the increase in monetary reserves during any year for the purpose of Article V, Section 7 *(b)* and *(c)*, no account shall be taken, unless deductions have otherwise been made by the member for such holdings, of any increase in those monetary reserves which is due to currency previously inconvertible having become convertible during the year; or to holdings which are the proceeds of a long-term or medium-term loan contracted during the year; or to holdings which have been transferred or set aside for repayment of a loan during the subsequent year.

4. In the case of members whose metropolitan territories have been occupied by the enemy, gold newly produced during the five years after the entry into force of this Agreement from mines located within their metropolitan territories shall not be included in computations of their monetary reserves or of increases in their monetary reserves.

5. In calculating monetary reserves and the increase in monetary reserves during any year for the purpose of Article V, Section 7 *(b)* and *(c)*, the Fund may decide in its discretion, on the request of a member, that deductions shall be made for obligations outstanding as the result of transactions between members under a reciprocal facility by which a member agrees to exchange on demand its currency for the currency of the other member up to a maximum amount and on terms requiring that each such transaction be reversed within a specified period not in excess of nine months.

6. In calculating monetary reserves and the increase in monetary reserves for the purpose of Article V. Section 7 *(b)* and *(c)*, Article XIX *(e)* shall apply except that the following provision shall apply at the end of a financial year if it was in effect at the beginning of that year:

"A member's monetary reserves shall be calculated by deducting from its central holdings the currency liabilities to the Treasuries, central banks, stabilization funds or similar fiscal agencies of other members or non-members specified under *(d)* above, together with similar liabilities to other official institutions and other banks in the territories of members, or non-members specified under *(d)* above. To these net holdings shall be added the sums deemed to be official holdings of other official institutions and other banks under *(c)* above."

216

Schedule C

Election of Executive Directors

1. The election of the elective executive directors shall be by ballot of the governors eligible to vote under Article XII, Section 3 *(b)* (iii) and (iv).

2. In balloting for the five directors to be elected under Article XII, Section 3 *(b)* (iii), each of the governors eligible to vote shall cast for one person all of the votes to which he is entitled under Article XII, Section 5 *(a)*. The five persons receiving the greatest number of votes shall be directors, provided that no person who received less than nineteen percent of the total number of votes that can be cast (eligible votes) shall be considered elected.

3. When five persons are not elected in the first ballot, a second ballot shall be held in which the person who received the lowest number of votes shall be ineligible for election and in which there shall vote only *(a)* those governors who voted in the first ballot for a person not elected, and *(b)* those governors whose votes for a person elected are deemed under 4 below to have raised the votes cast for that person above twenty percent of the eligible votes.

4. In determining whether the votes cast by a governor are to be deemed to have raised the total of any person above twenty percent of the eligible votes the twenty percent shall be deemed to include, first, the votes of the governor casting the largest number of votes for such person, then the votes of the governor casting the next largest number, and so on until twenty percent is reached.

5. Any governor part of whose votes must be counted in order to raise the total of any person above nineteen percent shall be considered a casting all of his votes for such person even if the total votes for such person thereby exceed twenty percent.

6. If, after the second ballot, five persons have not been elected, further ballots shall be held on the same principles until five persons have been elected, provided that after four persons are elected, the fifth may be elected by a simple majority of the remaining votes and shall be deemed to have been elected by all such votes.

7. The directors to be elected by the American Republics under Article XII, Section 3 *(b)* (iv) shall be elected as follows:

   (a) Each of the directors shall be elected separately.

   (b) In the election of the first director, each governor representing an American Republic eligible to participate in the election shall cast for one person all the votes to which he is entitled. The person receiving the largest number of votes shall be elected provided that he has received not less than forty-five percent of the total votes.

   (c) If no person is elected on the first ballot, further ballots shall be held, in each of which the person receiving the lowest number of votes shall be eliminated, until one person received a number of votes sufficient for election under *(b)* above.

   (d) Governors whose votes contributed to the election of the first director shall take no part in the election of the second director.

   (e) Persons who did not succeed in the first election shall not be ineligible for election as the second director.

   (f) A majority of the votes which can be cast shall be required for election of the second director. If at the first ballot no person receives a majority, further ballots shall be held in each of which the person receiving the lowest number of votes shall be eliminated, until some person obtains a majority.

   (g) The second director shall be deemed to have been elected by all the votes which could have been cast in the ballot securing his election.

Schedule D

Settlement of Accounts with Members Withdrawing

1. The Fund shall be obligated to pay to a member withdrawing an amount equal to its quota, plus any other amounts due to it from the Fund, less any amounts due to the Fund, including charges accruing after the date of its withdrawal; but no payment shall be made until six months after the date of withdrawal. Payments shall be made in the currency of the withdrawing member.

2. If the Fund's holdings of the currency of the withdrawing member are not sufficient to pay the net amount due from the Fund, the balance shall be paid in gold, or in such other manners as may be agreed. If the Fund and the withdrawing member do not reach agreement within six months of the date of withdrawal, the currency in question held by the Fund shall be paid forthwith to the withdrawing member. Any balance due shall be paid in ten half-yearly installments during the ensuing five years. Each such installment shall be paid, at the option of the Fund, either in the currency of the withdrawing member acquired after its withdrawal or by the delivery of gold.

3. If the Fund fails to meet any installment which is due in accordance with the preceding paragraphs, the withdrawing member shall be entitled to require the Fund to pay the installment in any currency held by the Fund with the exception of any currency which has been declared scarce under Article VII, Section 3.

4. If the Fund's holdings of the currency of a withdrawing member exceed the amount due to it, and if agreement on the method of settling accounts is not reached within six months of the date of withdrawal, the former member shall be obligated to redeem such excess currency in gold or, at its option, in the currencies of members which at the time of redemption are convertible. Redemption shall be made at the parity existing at the time of withdrawal from the Fund. The withdrawing member shall complete redemption within five years of the date of withdrawal, or within such longer period as may be fixed by the Fund, but shall not be required to redeem in any half-yearly period more than one-tenth of the Fund's excess holdings of its currency at the date of withdrawal plus further acquisitions of the currency during such half-yearly period. If the withdrawing member does not fulfill this obligation, the Fund may in an orderly manner liquidate in any market the amount of currency which should have been redeemed.

5. Any member desiring to obtain the currency of a member which has withdrawn shall acquire it by purchase from the Fund, to the extent that such member has access to the resources of the Fund and that such currency is available under 4 above.

6. The withdrawing member guarantees the unrestricted use at all times of the currency disposed of under 4 and 5 above for the purchase of goods or for payment of sums due to it or to persons within its territories. It shall compensate the Fund for any loss resulting from the difference between the par value of its currency on the date of withdrawal and the value realized by the Fund on disposal under 4 and 5 above.

7. In the event of the Fund going into liquidation under Article XVI, Section 2, within six months of the date on which the member withdraws, the account between the Fund and that government shall be settled in accordance with Article XVI, Section 2, and Schedule E.

Schedule E

Administration of Liquidation

1. In the event of liquidation the liabilities of the Fund other than the repayment of subscriptions shall have priority in the distribution of the assets of the Fund. In meeting each such liability the Fund shall use its assets in the following order:

(a) the currency in which the liability is payable;

(b) gold;

(c) all other currencies in proportion, so far as may be practicable, to the quotas of the members.

2. After the discharge of the Fund's liabilities in accordance with 1 above, the balance of the Fund's assets shall be distributed and apportioned as follows:

(a) The Fund shall distribute its holdings of gold among the members whose currencies are held by the Fund in amounts less than their quotas. These members shall share the gold so distributed in the proportions of the amounts by which their quotas exceed the Fund's holdings of their currencies.

(b) The Fund shall distribute to each member one-half the Fund's holdings of its currency but such distribution shall not exceed fifty percent of its quota.

(c) The Fund shall apportion the remainder of its holdings of each currency among all the members in proportion to the amounts due to each member after the distributions under *(a)* and *(b)* above.

3. Each member shall redeem the holdings of its currency apportioned to other members under 2 *(c)* above, and shall agree with the Fund within three months after a decision to liquidate upon an orderly procedure for such redemption.

4. If a member has not reached agreement with the Fund within the three-month period referred to in 3 above, the Fund shall use the currencies of other members apportioned to that member under 2 *(c)* above to redeem the currency of that member apportioned to other members. Each currency apportioned to a member which has not reached agreement shall be used, so far as possible, to redeem its currency apportioned to the members which have made agreements with the Fund under 3 above.

5. If a member has reached agreement with the Fund in accordance with 3 above, the Fund shall use the currencies of other members apportioned to that member under 2 *(c)* above to redeem the currency of that member apportioned to other members which have made agreements with the Fund under 3 above. Each amount so redeemed shall be redeemed in the currency of the member to which it was apportioned.

6. After carrying out the preceding paragraphs, the Fund shall pay to each member the remaining currencies held for its account.

7. Each member whose currency has been distributed to other members under 6 above shall redeem such currency in gold or, at its option, in the currency of the member requesting redemption, or in such other manner as may be agreed between them. If the members involved do not otherwise agree, the member obligated to redeem shall complete redemption within five years of the date of distribution, but shall not be required to redeem in any half-yearly period more than one-tenth of the amount distributed to each other member. If the member does not fulfill this obligation, the amount of currency which should have been redeemed may be liquidated in an orderly manner in any market.

8. Each member whose currency has been distributed to other members under 6 above guarantees the unrestricted use of such currency at all times for the purchase of goods or for payment of sums due to it or to persons in its territories. Each member so obligated agrees to compensate other members for any loss resulting from the difference between the par value of its currency on the date of the decision to liquidate the Fund and the value realized by such members on disposal of its currency.

Schedule F

Designation

During the first basic period the rules for designation shall be as follows:

(a) Participants subject to designation under Article XXV, Section 5 *(a)* (i), shall be designated for such amounts as will promote over time equality in

the ratios of the participants' holdings of special drawing rights in excess of their net cumulative allocations to their official holdings of gold and foreign exchange.

(b) The formula to give effect to (a) above shall be such that participants subject to designation shall be designated:

(i) in proportion to their official holdings of gold and foreign exchange when the ratios described in (a) above equal; and

(ii) in such manner as gradually to reduce the difference between the ratios described in (a) above that are low and the ratios that are high.

Schedule G

Reconstitution

1. During the first basic period the rules for reconstitution shall be as follows:

(a) (i) A participant shall so use and reconstitute its holdings of special drawing rights that, five years after the first allocation and at the end of each calendar quarter thereafter, the average of its total daily holdings of special drawing rights over the most recent five-year period will be not less than thirty percent of the average of its daily net cumulative allocation of special drawing rights over the same period.

(ii) Two years after the first allocation and at the end of each calendar month thereafter the Fund shall make calculations for each participant so as to ascertain whether and to what extent the participant would need to acquire special drawing rights between the date of the calculation and the end of any five-year period in order to comply with the requirement in (a) (i) above. The Fund shall adopt regulations with respect to the bases on which these calculations shall be made and with respect to the timing of the designation of participants under Article XXV, Section 5 (a) (ii), in order to assist them to comply with the requirement in (a) (i) above.

(iii) The Fund shall give special notice to a participant when the calculations under (a) (ii) above indicate that it is unlikely that the participant will be able to comply with the requirement in (a) (i) above unless it ceases to use special drawing rights for the rest of the period for which the calculation was made under (a) (ii) above.

(iv) A participant that needs to acquire special drawing rights to fulfill this obligation shall be obligated and entitled to obtain them, at its option for gold or currency acceptable to the Fund, in a transaction with the Fund conducted through the General Account. If sufficient special drawing rights to fulfill this obligation cannot be obtained in this way, the participant shall be obligated and entitled to obtain them with currency convertible in fact from a participant which the Fund shall specify.

(b) Participants shall also pay due regard to the desirability of pursuing over time a balanced relationship between their holdings of special drawing rights and their holdings of gold and foreign exchange and their reserve positions in the Fund.

2. If a participant fails to comply with the rules for reconstitution, the Fund shall determine whether or not the circumstances justify suspension under Article XXIX, Section 2 (b).

Schedule H

Termination of Participation

1. If the obligation remaining after the setoff under Article XXX, Section 2 *(b)*, is to the terminating participant and agreement on settlement between the Fund and the terminating participant is not reached within six months of the date of termination, the Fund shall redeem this balance of special drawing rights in equal half-yearly installments within a maximum of five years of the date of termination. The Fund shall redeem this balance as it may determine, either *(a)* by the payment to the terminating participant of the amounts provided by the remaining participants to the Fund in accordance with Article XXX, Section 5, or *(b)* by permitting the terminating participant to use its special drawing rights to obtain its own currency or currency convertible in fact from a participant specified by the Fund, the General Account, or any other holder.

2. If the obligation remaining after the setoff under Article XXX, Section 2 *(b)*, is to the Fund and agreement on settlement is not reached within six months of the date of termination, the terminating participant shall discharge this obligation in equal half-yearly installments within three years of the date of termination or within such longer period as may be fixed by the Fund. The terminating participant shall discharge this obligation, as the Fund may determine, either *(a)* by the payment to the Fund of currency convertible in fact or gold at the option of the terminating participant, or *(b)* by obtaining special drawing rights, in accordance with Article XXX, Section 6, from the General Account or in agreement with a participant specified by the Fund or from any other holder, and the setoff of these special drawing rights against the installment due.

3. Installments under either 1 or 2 above shall fall due six months after the date of termination and at intervals of six months thereafter.

4. In the event of the Special Drawing Account going into liquidation under Article XXXI within six months of the date a participant terminates its participation, the settlement between the Fund and that government shall be made in accordance with Article XXXI and Schedule I.

Schedule I

Administration of Liquidation of the Special Drawing Account

1. In the event of liquidation of the Special Drawing Account, participants shall discharge their obligations to the Fund in ten half-yearly installments, or in such longer period as the Fund may decide is needed, in currency convertible in fact and the currencies of participants holdings special drawing rights to be redeemed in any installment to the extent of such redemption, as determined by the Fund. The first half-yearly payment shall be made six months after the decision to liquidate the Special Drawing Account.

2. If it is decided to liquidate the Fund within six months of the date of the decision to liquidate the Special Drawing Account, the liquidation of the Special Drawing Account shall not proceed until special drawing rights held in the General Account have been distributed in accordance with the following rule:

> After the distribution made under 2 *(a)* of Schedule E, the Fund shall apportion its special drawing rights held in the General Account among all members that are participants in proportion to the amounts due to each participant after the distribution under 2 *(a)*. To determine the amount due to each member for the purpose of apportioning the remainder of its holdings of each currency under 2 *(c)* of Schedule E, the Fund shall deduct the distribution of special drawing rights made under this rule.

3. With the amounts received under 1 above, the Fund shall redeem special drawing rights held by holders in the following manner and order:

(a) Special drawing rights held by governments that have terminated their participation more than six months before the date the Board of Governors decides to liquidate the Special Drawing Account shall be redeemed in accordance with the terms of any agreement under Article XXX or Schedule H.

(b) Special drawing rights held by holders that are not participants shall be redeemed before those held by participants, and shall be redeemed in proportion to the amount held by each holder.

(c) The Fund shall determine the proportion of special drawing rights held by each participant in relation to its net cumulative allocation. The Fund shall first redeem special drawing rights from the participants with the highest proportion until this proportion is reduced to that of the second highest proportion; the Fund shall then redeem the special drawing rights held by these participants in accordance with their net cumulative allocations until the proportions are reduced to that of the third highest proportion; and this process shall be continued until the amount available for redemption is exhausted.

4. Any amount that a participant will be entitled to receive in redemption under 3 above shall be set off against any amount to be paid under 1 above.

5. During liquidation the Fund shall pay interest on the amount of special drawing rights held by holders, and each participant shall pay charges on the net cumulative allocation of special drawing rights to it less the amount of any payments made in accordance with 1 above. The rates of interest and charges and the time of payment shall be determined by the Fund. Payments of interest and charges shall be made in special drawing rights to the extent possible. A participant that does not hold sufficient special drawing rights to meet any charges shall make the payment with gold or a currency specified by the Fund. Special drawing rights received as charges in amounts needed for administrative expenses shall not be used for the payment of interest, but shall be transferred to the Fund and shall be redeemed first and with the currencies used by the Fund to meet its expenses.

6. While participant is in default with respect to any payment required by 1 or 5 above, no amounts shall be paid to it in accordance with 2 or 5 above.

7. If after the final payments have been made to participants each participant not in default does not hold special drawing rights in the same proportion to its net cumulative allocation, those participants holding a lower proportion shall purchase from those holding a higher proportion such amounts in accordance with arrangements made by the Fund as will make the proportion of their holdings of special drawing rights the same. Each participant in default shall pay to the Fund its own currency in an amount equal to its default. The Fund shall apportion this currency and any residual claims among participants in proportion to the amount of special drawing rights held by each and these special drawing rights shall be cancelled. The Fund shall then close the books of the Special Drawing Account and all of the Fund's liabilities arising from the allocations of special drawing rights and the administration of the Special Drawing Account shall cease.

8. Each participant whose currency is distributed to other participants under this Schedule guarantees the unrestricted use of such currency at all times for the purchase of goods or for payments of sums due to it or to persons in its territories. Each participant so obligated agrees to compensate other participants for any loss resulting from the difference between the value at which the Fund distributed its currency under this Schedule and the value realized by such participants on disposal of its currency.

b. BY-LAWS, RULES AND REGULATIONS OF THE INTERNATIONAL MONETARY FUND, TWENTY-NINTH ISSUE, NOVEMBER 30, 1970 AND ITS SUPPLEMENT

CONTENTS

I. BY-LAWS OF THE INTERNATIONAL MONETARY FUND

II. RULES AND REGULATIONS OF THE INTERNATIONAL MONETARY FUND

CERTIFICATE

I hereby certify that this is a full and true copy of the By-Laws and of the Rules and Regulations of the International Monetary Fund, as amended to November 30, 1970.

W. Lawrence Hebbard
Secretary

Washington, D.C.
November 30, 1970

BY-LAWS OF THE INTERNATIONAL MONETARY FUND

These By-Laws are adopted under the authority of, and are intended to be complementary to, the Articles of Agreement of the International Monetary Fund; and they shall be construed accordingly. In the event of a conflict between anything in these By-Laws and any provision or requirement of the Articles of Agreement, the Articles of Agreement shall prevail.

SEC. 1. PLACES OF BUSINESS

The principal office of the Fund shall be located within the metropolitan area of Washington, D.C., United States of America.

The Executive Directors may establish and maintain agencies or branch offices at any place in the territories of other members, whenever it is necessary to do so in order to facilitate the efficient conduct of the business of the Fund.

Adopted March 16, 1946

SEC. 2. GENERAL ACCOUNT AND SPECIAL DRAWING ACCOUNT

In matters pertaining exclusively to the Special Drawing Account the references in these By-Laws, other than in Section 4, 5, and 13 (b), to members of the Fund or to Governors and Executive Directors shall be understood to refer only to members that are participants or to Governors appointed by members that are participants and Executive Directors appointed or elected by at least one member that is a participant.

Adopted October 2, 1969

SEC. 3. MEETINGS OF THE BOARD OF GOVERNORS

(a) The annual meeting of the Board of Governors shall be held at such time and place as the Board of Governors shall determine; provided, however, that, if the Executive Directors shall, because of special circumstances, deem it necessary to do so, the Executive Directors may change the time and place of such annual meeting.

(b) Special meetings of the Board of Governors may be called at any time by the Board of Governors or the Executive Directors and shall be called upon the request of five members of the Fund or of members of the Fund having in the aggregate one-fourth of the total voting power. Whenever any member of the Fund shall request the Executive Directors to call a special meeting of the Board of Governors, the Managing Director shall notify all members of the Fund of such request and of the reasons which shall have been given therefor.

(c) A quorum for any meeting of the Board of Governors shall be a majority of the Governors, exercising not less than two-thirds of the total voting power.

Adopted March 16, 1946, amended October 2, 1946

SEC. 4. NOTICE OF MEETINGS OF THE BOARD OF GOVERNORS

The Managing Director shall cause notice of the time and place of each meeting of the Board of Governors to be given to each member of the Fund by telegram or cable which shall be dispatched not less than 42 days prior to the date set for such meeting, except that in urgent cases such notice shall be sufficient if dispatched by telegram or cable not less than ten days prior to the date set for such meeting.

Adopted March 16, 1946, amended October 2, 1946

SEC. 5. ATTENDANCE AT MEETINGS

(a) The Executive Directors and their Alternates may attend all meetings of the Board of Governors and may participate in such meetings, but an Executive Director or his Alternate shall not be entitled to vote at any such meeting unless he shall be entitled to vote as a Governor or an Alternate or temporary Alternate of a Governor.

(b) The Chairman of the Board of Governors in consultation with the Executive Directors, may invite observers to attend any meeting of the Board of Governors.

(c) The Executive Directors are authorized to invite the International Bank for Reconstruction and Development to send a representative of the Bank to meetings of the Board of Governors and Executive Directors who may participate in such meetings, but shall have no vote.

(d) The Executive Directors are authorized to accept invitations from the Bank to send a representative of the Fund to participate in meetings of the Board of Governors or Executive Directors of the Bank.

Adopted March 16, 1946, amended October 2, 1946; paragraphs (c) and (d) were adopted as Sec. 2 on March 16, 1946

SEC. 6. AGENDA OF MEETINGS OF THE BOARD OF GOVERNORS

(a) Under the direction of the Executive Directors, the Managing Director shall prepare a brief agenda for each meeting of the Board of Governors and shall cause such agenda to be transmitted to each member of the Fund with the notice of such meeting.

(b) Additional subjects may be placed on the agenda for any meeting of the Board of Governors by any Governor provided that he shall give notice thereof to the Managing Director not less than seven days prior to the date set for such meeting. In special circumstances the Managing Director, by direction of the Executive Directors, may at any time place additional subjects on the agenda for any meeting of the Board of Governors. The Managing Director shall cause notice of the addition of any subjects to the agenda for any meeting of the Board of Governors to be given as promptly as possible to each member of the Fund.

(c) The Board of Governors may at any time authorize any subject to be placed on the agenda for any meeting of such Board even though the notice required by this section shall not have been given.

(d) Except as otherwise specifically directed by the Board of Governors, the Chairman of the Board of Governors jointly with the Managing Director, shall have charge of all arrangements for the holding of meetings of the Board of Governors.

Adopted March 16, 1946, amended October 2, 1946

SEC 7. ELECTION OF CHAIRMAN AND VICE-CHAIRMEN

At each annual meeting the Board of Governors shall select a Governor to act as Chairman and at least two other Governors to act as Vice-Chairmen until the next annual meeting.

In the absence of the Chairman, the Vice-Chairman designated by the Chairman shall act in his place.

Adopted March 16, 1946

SEC. 8. SECRETARY

The Secretary of the Fund shall serve as Secretary of the Board of Governors.

Adopted March 16, 1946

SEC. 9. MINUTES

The Board shall keep a summary record of its proceedings which shall be available to all members and which shall be filed with the Executive Directors for their guidance.

Adopted March 16, 1946

SEC. 10. REPORT OF EXECUTIVE DIRECTORS

The Executive Directors shall have prepared for presentation at the annual meeting of the Board of Governors an annual report in which shall be discussed the operations and policies of the Fund and which shall make recommendations to the Board of Governors on the problems confronting the Fund. The Executive Directors shall review, as part of the annual report, both the operation of the Special Drawing Account and the adequacy of global reserves.

Adopted March 16, 1946, amended October 2, 1969

SEC. 11. VOTING

Except as otherwise specifically provided in the Articles of Agreement, all decisions of the Board shall be made by a majority of the votes cast. At any meeting the Chairman may ascertain the sense of the meeting in lieu of a formal vote but he shall require a formal vote upon the request of any Governor. Whenever a formal vote is required the written text of the motion shall be distributed to the voting members.

Adopted March 16, 1946

SEC. 12. PROXIES

No Governor or Alternate may vote at any meeting by proxy or by any other method than in person, but a member may make provision for the designation of a temporary Alternate to vote for the Governor at any Board session at which the regularly designated Alternate is unable to be present.

Adopted March 16, 1946

SEC. 13. VOTING WITHOUT MEETING

(a) Whenever, in the judgment of the Executive Directors, any action by the Fund must be taken by the Board of Governors which should not be postponed until the next regular meeting of the Board and does not warrant the calling of a special meeting of the Board, the Executive Directors shall request Governors to vote without meeting.

(b) The Executive Directors shall present to each member by any rapid means of communication a motion embodying the proposed action.

(c) Votes shall be cast during such period as the Executive Directors may prescribe, provided that no Governor shall vote on any such motion until 7 days after dispatch of the motion, unless he is notified that the Executive Directors have waived this requirement. At the expiration of the period prescribed for voting, the Executive Directors shall record the results and the Managing Director shall notify all members. If the replies received do not include a majority of the Governors exercising two-thirds of the total voting power, which is required for a quorum of the Board of Governors, the motion shall be considered lost.

Adopted March 16, 1946, amended October 2, 1969

SEC. 14. TERMS OF SERVICE

(a) Governors and Alternates shalll receive their actual transport expenses to and from the place of meeting in attending meetings, and $75 for each night which attendance at such meetings requires them to spend away from their normal place of residence, this amount being reduced to $15 for each night when accommodation is included in the price of transportation.

(b) Pending the necessary action being taken by members to exempt from national taxation salaries and allowances paid out of the budget of the Fund, the Governors and the Executive Directors, and their Alternates, the Managing Director and the staff members shall be reimbursed by the Fund for the taxes which they are required to pay on such salaries and allowances.

In computing the amount of tax adjustment to be made with respect to any individual, it shall be presumed for the purposes of the computation that the income received from the Fund is his total income. All salary scales and expense allowances prescribed by this section are stated as net on the above basis.

(c) The salary of the Managing Director shall be $50,000 per annum. The Fund shall also pay any reasonable expenses incurred by the Managing Director in the interest of the Fund (including travel and transportation expenses for himself, and expenses for his family, and his personal effects in moving once to the seat of the Fund during or immediately before his term of office and in moving once from the seat during or immediately after his term of office). The contract of the Managing Director shall be for a term of five years and may be renewed for the same term or for a shorter term at the discretion of the Executive Directors, provided that no person shall be initially appointed to the post of Managing Director after he had reached his sixty-fifth birthday and that no Managing Director shall hold such post beyond his seventieth birthday.

(d) It shall be the duty of an Executive Director and his Alternate to devote all the time and attention to the business of the Fund that its interests require, and, between them, to be continuously available at the principal office of the Fund; however, in the event that both an Executive Director and his Alternate are unable to be available at the principal office of the Fund for reasons of health, absence while on business of the Fund, or similar reasons, the Executive Director may designate a temporary Alternate to act for him for periods of time which shall not in the aggregate exceed fifteen business days in the course of any financial year. A temporary Alternate shall receive no salary or expense allowance.

(e) The maximum salary and expense allowance including housing, entertainment and all other expenses [except those specified in subsection (f)] shall be $35,000 per year for Executive Directors and $27,000 per year for Alternates. If will be the duty of each Executive Director and each Alternate to state how much of these amounts he intends to draw whether as salary or as expense allowance.

A Joint Committee on the Remuneration of Executive Directors and their Alternates, appointed by the Chairmen of the Boards of Governors of the Fund and Bank and consisting of one of the Chairmen and two former Governors or Alternate Governors of the Fund or Bank chosen by the Chairmen in consultation with the Managing Director of the Fund and the President of the Bank, shall be constituted in January of each year in which a regular election of Executive Directors is scheduled, starting with the year 1972, to consider the adequacy of the remuneration of Executive Directors of the Fund and the Bank, and their Alternates, and to prepare a report, which shall be submitted to the Board of Governors of the Fund by July 1 of that year, containing such recommendations for any changes in such remuneration of for any other action by the Board of Governors relating thereto as the Joint Committee shall deem appropriate.

(f) The Executive Directors and their Alternates are to be reimbursed, in addition, for all reasonable expenses incurred during absence from the seat of the Fund while on official Fund business, and for reasonable expenses actually incurred by them in Washington or in the place of the annual meeting of the Board of Governors in connection with official Fund business to entertain senior officials coming from the countries that appointed, elected, or designated them. They shall also be reimbursed for travel and transportation expenses for themselves, their families, and their personal effects in moving once to the seat of the Fund during or immediately before their periods of service, and in moving once from the seat during or within a reasonable period after their periods of service.

In addition, any Executive Director or Alternate shall in the third year of continuous full-time service in either capacity and in every second year of such service thereafter be entitled to reimbursement for the cost of transportation expenses for his family in traveling once to and from the country of which he or his wife is a national, provided that in cases where the wife is a national of another country the reimbursement for transportation expenses to and from her country does not exceed that to and from the country of which he is a national. For home leave travel more frequent than every third year, reimbursement shall be made on the basis of cabin- or economy-class accommodations.

(g) Where not specified, it is assumed that the Director and Alternate will be a full-time Director and Alternate. Where it is intended that he shall not devote his full time, it shall be so indicated. Where an Executive Director or Alternate indicates that he intends to devote only part of his time to the Fund, his remuneration shall be pro-rated on the basis of a representation by him of the proportion of his time he has devoted to the interests of the Fund. He may make such representation each month.

(h) Where an individual is serving both Fund and Bank, the aggregate of salary received from both shall not exceed the full annual single salary indicated above.

In all cases of salaries or expenses involving dual offices in the Fund or Bank, or both, the individual affected is entitled to take his choice as to which salary or expense he elects, but he shall not be entitled to both.

(i) An individual putting forward a claim for reimbursement for any expenses incurred by him shall include therewith a representation that he has not received and will not claim reimbursement in respect to those expenses from any other source.

(j) Secretarial, staff services, office space, and other services incidental to the performance of the duties of the Executive Directors and Alternates shall be provided by the Fund.

Adopted March 16, 1946; paragraph (a) amended March 18, 1946 and June 6, 1966; paragraph (c) amended July 27, 1951; December 14, 1960, effective December 1, 1960; and February 13, 1969, effective November 1, 1968; paragraph (d) amended September 17, 1947; paragraph (e) amended January 5, 1951, effective January 1, 1951; December 2, 1957, effective November 1, 1957; December 28, 1959, effective November 1, 1959; November 7, 1962, effective September 1, 1962; August 8, 1966, effective November 1, 1965; February 13, 1969, effective November 1, 1968; and July 30, 1969, effective August 1, 1969; paragraph (f) amended September 17, 1947, September 30, 1948, August 18, 1961, September 10, 1964, and February 13, 1969.

SEC. 15. DELEGATION OF AUTHORITY

The Executive Directors are authorized by the Board of Governors to exercise all the powers of the Fund except those reserved to the Board by Article XII, Section 2 *(b)*, Article XXVII *(a)* (i), and other provisions of the Articles of Agreement. The Executive Directors shall not take any action pursuant to powers delegated by the Board of Governors which is inconsistent with any action taken by the Board.

Adopted March 16, 1946, amended October 2, 1969

SEC. 16. RULES AND REGULATIONS

The Executive Directors are authorized by the Board of Governors to adopt such Rules and Regulations, including financial regulations, as may be necessary or appropriate to conduct the business of the Fund. Any Rules and Regulations so adopted, and any amendments thereof, shall be subject to review by the Board of Governors at their next annual meeting.

Adopted March 16, 1946

SEC. 17. VACANT DIRECTORSHIPS

Whenever a new Director must be elected because of a vacancy requiring an election, the Managing Director shall notify the members who elected the former Director of the existence of the vacancy. He may convene a meeting of the Governors of such countries exclusively for the purpose of electing a new Director; or he may request nominations by mail or telegraph and conduct ballots by mail or telegraph. Successive ballots shall be cast until one candidate has a majority; and after each ballot, the candidate with the smallest number of votes shall be dropped from the next ballot.

When a new elective Director is named, the office of Alternate shall be deemed to be vacant and an Alternate shall be named by the newly-elected Director.

Adopted March 16, 1946

SEC. 18. ADDITIONAL DIRECTORS

At least one month before the second and subsequent regular elections of Directors, the Managing Director shall notify all members of the two members whose currencies held by the Fund have been, on the average over the preceding two years, reduced below their quotas by the largest absolute amounts. He shall state whether either or both are entitled to appoint a Director in accordance with Article XII, Section 3 *(c)* of the Articles of Agreement.

When a member becomes entitled to appoint a Director in accordance with Article XII, Section 3 *(b)* (i) and 3 *(c)* of the Articles of Agreement, it shall not participate in the election of any Director.

Adopted March 16, 1946

SEC. 19. REPRESENTATION OF MEMBERS NOT ENTITLED TO APPOINT A DIRECTOR

(a) Each member not entitled to appoint a Director may, in accordance with the regulations provided in this section, send a representative to attend any meeting of the Executive Directors when a request made by, or a matter particularly affecting, that member is under consideration. A member, so electing, may waive its rights under this provision. The Executive Directors shall determine whether a matter under consideration particularly affects a member not entitled to appoint a Director, which determination shall be final.

(b) Whenever a member nor entitled to appoint a Director desires to present its views at the meeting of the Executive Directors at which a request the member has made is to be considered, it shall so notify the Fund when it makes the request and shall designate a representative for this purpose who shall be available at the seat of the Fund. Failure to give such notice or to designate an available representative shall constitute a waiver of the member's right to present its views at the meeting.

(c) Whenever the Executive Directors are to consider a matter which has been determined particularly to affect a member not entitled to appoint a Director, the member shall be promptly informed by rapid means of communication of the date set for its consideration. No final action shall be taken by the Executive Directors with respect to such matter, nor any question particularly affecting such member submitted to the Board of Governors, until the member has either waived its rights under paragraph (a) of this section or has been given an opportunity to present its views through an appropriately authorized representative at a meeting of the Executive Directors, of which the member has had reasonable notice.

Adopted March 16, 1946, amended September 17, 1947

SEC. 20. BUDGET AND AUDITS

(a) The Executive Directors shall instruct the Managing Director to prepare an annual administrative budget to be presented to them for approval. The budget so approved shall be incorporated in the annual report to be presented to the Board of Governors at their annual meeting.

(b) An external audit of the financial records and transactions of the Fund shall be made annually and such audit shall relate to the period representing the fiscal year of the Fund. The Executive Directors shall submit the Fund's audited balance sheet and audited statement of income and expense to the Board of Governors to be considered by them at their annual meeting.

The annual audit shall be made by an audit committee consisting of either three or five persons each of whom shall be nominated by a different member of the Fund and confirmed by the Executive Directors. At least one person serving on each audit committee shall be nominated by one of the six members of the Fund having the largest quotas, and at least one person shall be nominated by a member that is also a participant. The Executive Directors shall determine, in the case of each audit, whether the audit committee shall consist of three or five persons and which members of the Fund shall be requested to nominate persons to serve on the committee. The service of the members of each audit committee shall terminate upon completion of the annual audit and submission of the report on audit.

Each audit committee shall elect one of its members as chairman, shall determine its own procedure, and shall otherwise be independent of the Management of the Fund in conducting the annual audit according to generally accepted auditing standards.

The annual audit shall be comprehensive with respect to examination of the financial records of the Fund; shall extend, insofar as practicable, to the ascertainment that operations and transactions conducted through the General Account or the Special Drawing Account during the period under review are supported by the necessary authority; and shall determine that there is adequate and faithful accounting for the assets and liabilities of the Fund and for special drawing rights. It shall thereby establish an appropriate basis for conclusion concerning the financial position of the Fund at the close of the fiscal year and the results of its operations and transactions during that year. For this purpose, the audit committee shall have access to the accounting records of the Fund and other supporting evidence of its operations and transactions, and shall be furnished by the Management of the Fund with such information and representations as may be required in connection with the audit. The members of the audit committee shall respect the confidential nature of their service and the information made available for purposes of the audit.

All accounts of the General Account shall be summarized in United States dollars; and for this purpose gold shall be valued in terms of United States dollars at the par value of the United States dollar, and all members' currencies shall be converted at their par values or in accordance with a decision of the Fund pursuant to Article IV, Section 8 of the Articles of Agreement. The accounts of the Special Drawing Account shall be summarized in units of value of special drawing rights.

The Executive Directors shall decide all questions of policy raised by requests of the audit committee for particular information or the inspection of particular records or documents. The refusal of any such requests for reasons of policy shall be explained in the comments of the Executive Directors forwarded to the Board of Governors with the report on audit.

Any question the audit committee may have concerning interpretation of the Articles of Agreement, the By-Laws, or the Rules and Regulations shall be discussed with the Managing Director, or officials designated by him, and if the reply is not completely satisfactory to the audit committee, shall be referred to the Executive Directors through the Managing Director.

The audit committee shall submit its report on audit to the Board of Governors for consideration by them at their annual meeting. Such submission shall be made through the Managing Director and the Executive Directors who shall forward with the report on audit their comments thereon. The audit committee shall afford the Managing Director an opportunity for explanation to them before deciding that any matter seems to require criticism in the report on audit.

The audit committee may formally furnish the Managing Director and Executive Directors their views and suggestions concerning the system of accounting, internal financial control, and documentary or other procedure which may technically strengthen or improve the administration of the Fund's financial affairs. Such matters need not be dealt with in the report on audit unless the audit committee believes they are of such moment as to warrant inclusion.

The Managing Director shall determine what expenses are necessary and reasonable in connection with each annual audit and the Fund shall bear such expenses.

Adopted March 16, 1946, amended September 17, 1947 and October 2, 1969

SEC. 21. APPLICATIONS FOR MEMBERSHIP

Subject to any special provisions that may be made for countries listed in Schedule A of the Articles of Agreement, any country may apply for membership in the Fund by filing with the Fund an application setting forth all relevant facts.

When submitting an application to the Board of Governors, the Executive Directors after consultation with the applicant country shall recommend to the Board the amount of the quota, the form of payment, the parity of the currency, conditions regarding exchange restrictions, and such other conditions as, in the opinion of the Executive Directors, the Board of Governors may wish to prescribe.

Adopted March 16, 1946

SEC. 22. COMPULSORY WITHDRAWAL

Before any member is required to withdraw from membership in the Fund, the matter shall be considered by the Executive Directors who shall inform the member in reasonable time of the complaint against it and allow the member an adequate opportunity for stating its case both orally and in writing. The Executive Directors shall recommend to the Board of Governors the action they deem appropriate. The member shall be informed of the recommendation and the date on which its case will be considered by the Board and shall be given a reasonable time within which to present its case to the Board both orally and in writing. Any member so electing may waive this provision.

Adopted March 16, 1946

SEC. 23. COMMITTEE ON INTERPRETATION
[to be adopted]

SEC. 24. SETTLEMENT OF DISAGREEMENTS

The President of the International Court of Justice is prescribed as the authority to appoint an umpire whenever there arises a disagreement of the type referred to in Article XVIII *(c)* or Article XXVII *(d)* of the Articles of Agreement.

Adopted as Sec. 23 March 16, 1946, amended October 2, 1969

SEC. 25. OTHER HOLDERS

Applications to be permitted to accept, hold, and use special drawing rights under Article XXIII, Section 3, shall be filed with the Fund with all relevant facts. When submitting an application to the Board of Governors, the Executive Directors after consultation with the applicant shall recommend to the Board such terms and conditions as, in the opinion of the Executive Directors, the Board of Governors may wish to prescribe.

Adopted October 2, 1969

SEC. 26. AMENDMENT OF BY-LAWS

These By-Laws may be amended by the Board of Governors at any meeting thereof or by vote without a meeting as provided in Section 13.

Adopted as Sec. 24 October 2, 1946

RULES AND REGULATIONS OF THE
INTERNATIONAL MONETARY FUND

A—SCOPE OF RULES AND REGULATIONS

A-1. These Rules and Regulations supplement the Fund Agreement and the By-Laws adopted by the Board of Governors. They are not intended to replace any provision of either the Agreement or the By-Laws. The Rules and Regulations attempt to provide such operating rules, procedures, regulations, and interpretation as are necessary and desirable to carry out the purposes and powers contained in the Agreement, as supplemented by the By-Laws. If any provision in the Rules and Regulations is found to be in conflict with any provision in the Agreement or in the By-Laws, the Agreement and By-Laws shall prevail and an appropriate amendment should be made to these Rules and Regulations.

Adopted September 25, 1946

A-2 Additions to, and changes of, the Rules and Regulations will be made as experience brings to light new problems or suggests modifications in procedures already adopted.

Adopted September 25, 1946

B—TERMS, DEFINITIONS, AND SYMBOLS EMPLOYED IN THIS DOCUMENT

B-1. Executive Director, except where otherwise specified, shall include the Alternate or the temporary Alternate, as the case may be. In matters pertaining exclusively to the Special Drawing Account references in these Rules and Regulations to Executive Director, other than in Rules C-1, C-5 (a), C-15, and C-16, shall apply to an Executive Director appointed or elected by at least one member that is a participant.

Adopted September 25, 1946, amended August 14, 1947, effective September 17, 1947, and September 18, 1969

B-2. Executive Board refers to the Executive Directors presided over by the Chairman.

Adopted September 25, 1946

B-3. Chairman, except where otherwise specified, shall refer to the Chairman or Acting Chairman of the Executive Board.

Adopted September 25, 1946

B-4. Agenda ordinarily refers to both the list of items to be considered at a meeting and the supplementary documents pertinent thereto.

Adopted September 25, 1946

B-5. Fund Agreement refers to the Articles of Agreement of the International Monetary Fund and, where the context is clear, Agreement shall also refer to the Articles of Agreement.

Adopted September 25, 1946

B-6. FA refers to the Fund Agreement.

BL refers to the By-Laws of the International Monetary Fund as adopted by the Board of Governors.

RR refers to these Rules and Regulations.

Adopted September 25, 1946

B-7. Executive Session refers to a Meeting of the Executive Directors in which no person is present except the Executive Directors, Managing Director, and, with the approval of the Board granted separately for each Executive Session, the Secretary of the Board.

Adopted September 25, 1946

B-8. Business day[1] refers to the normal working hours of the Fund, 9:00 a.m. to 5:30 p.m. at the official time for the District of Columbia, on Monday through Friday of each week with the following exceptions (which will include the preceding Friday whenever one of the dates below falls on a Saturday and the following Monday whenever one falls on a Sunday):

New Year's Day, January 1
Washington's Birthday, the third Monday in February
Memorial Day, the last Monday in May
Independence Day, July 4
Labor Day, the first Monday in September
Columbus Day, the second Monday in October
Veterans Day, the fourth Monday in October
Thanksgiving Day, the fourth Thursday in November
Christmas Day, December 25

Adopted May 28, 1947, amended March 8, 1948, October 27, 1961, and November 24, 1970

C—MEETINGS OF THE EXECUTIVE BOARD

Meetings

C-1. Meetings of the Executive Directors shall be called by the Chairman as the business of the Fund may require. Except in special circumstances the Chairman shall notify all Executive Directors of meetings at least two business days in advance.

Adopted September 25, 1946, amended May 28, 1947

C-2. The Chairman shall call a meeting at the request of any Executive Director.

Adopted September 25, 1946

C-3. Meetings of the Executive Board shall be open to attendance by the Secretary and such members of the staff as the Chairman indicates. At the request of the Chairman or any Executive Director meetings may be held in Executive Session, or the Executive Board may determine which particular members of the staff may attend any session.

Adopted September 25, 1946, amended January 15, 1948

C-4. The Executive Directors shall meet at the principal office of the Fund unless it is decided that a particular meeting shall be held elsewhere.

Adopted September 25, 1946

C-5. (a)   Any Executive Director may participate in any meeting of the Executive Board or committees of the Executive Board.

---

[1] The definition of "business day" does not affect in any way the arrangements which have been made for the receipt of messages at all times and for prompt action upon them as required by circumstances and the Fund Agreement, By-Laws and Rules and Regulations.

(b) In the absence of the Managing Director, the Deputy Managing Director shall act as Chairman and shall have a deciding vote in case of an equal division. In the absence of both the Managing Director and the Deputy Managing Director, the Executive Director selected by the Executive Board shall act as Chairman. An Executive Director shall retain his right to vote when serving as Acting Chairman.

Adopted September 25, 1946, amended November 12, 1948 and September 18, 1969

Agenda

C-6. The agenda for each meeting shall be prepared by the Chairman. The agenda shall include any item requested by an Executive Director.

Adopted September 25, 1946

C-7. Except in special circumstances the Chairman shall notify Executive Directors of new items on the agenda at least two full business days before their consideration in meetings. Additional advance notice shall be given at the discretion of the Chairman before the consideration of new items of especial importance which may require consultation with members of the return to the seat of the Fund of Executive Directors who are absent.

Adopted September 25, 1946, amended May 28, 1947

C-8. Matters not on the agenda for a meeting may be considered at that meeting only by unanimous consent of the Executive Directors present.

Adopted September 25, 1946

C-9. Any item of the agenda for a meeting, consideration of which has not been completed at that meeting, shall, unless the Executive Directors decide otherwise, be automatically included in the agenda of the next meeting.

Adopted September 25, 1946

Voting

C-10. The Chairman will ordinarily ascertain the sense of the meeting in lieu of a formal vote. Any Executive Director may require a formal vote to be taken with votes cast as prescribed in Article XII, Section 3 *(i)*, or Article XXVII *(a)* (iii).

Adopted September 25, 1946, amended September 18, 1969

C-11. There shall be no formal voting in committees and subcommittees. The Chairman of the committee or subcommittee shall determine the sense of the meeting (including alternative points of view) which shall be reported.

Adopted September 25, 1946

C-12. No Executive Director may vote at any meeting by proxy or by any other method than in person.

Adopted September 25, 1946

Language

C-13. The working language of the Fund will be English. The discussion, documents, and reports of meetings will ordinarily be in English. Speeches or papers presented in other languages shall be translated into English.

Adopted September 25, 1946

Minutes

C-14. Under the direction of the Managing Director, the Secretary shall be responsible for the preparation of a summary record of the proceedings of the Executive Board.

Adopted September 25, 1946

C-15. Verbatim records will be taken only if the Chairman, the Executive Board or an Executive Director so requests. In such case, the Secretariat shall be given advance notice of the desire for verbatim recording.

Adopted September 25, 1946

C-16. Draft minutes will be circulated to all Executive Directors as quickly as possible after meetings. They will normally be submitted for approval at the next meeting of the Executive Board following the day they are circulated, and in any case will be submitted for approval not later than the third succeding meeting.

Adopted September 25, 1946, amended May 28, 1947 and August 14, 1947

D—APPLICATION FOR MEMBERSHIP, CHANGES IN QUOTAS, AND APPLICATION TO BE AN OTHER HOLDER OF SPECIAL DRAWING RIGHTS

Application for Membership

D-1. When a country applies for membership in the Fund, and the application is placed before the Executive Board, the Chairman shall announce a reasonable time to be allowed for discussion and preliminary investigation by the Executive Board before a decision is reached to proceed with the formal investigation. If this decision is in the affirmative the Fund may proceed to obtain all relevant information and discuss with the applicant any matters relating to its application. Any Executive Director may request such information to be added to the list requested of the applicant as in his opinion is relevant to the decision to be made. The Executive Board shall then decide whether to submit an application for membership with its views to the Board of Governors for a telegraphic vote or hold the application until the next meeting of the Board of Governors.

Adopted September 25, 1946

Quotas

D-2. When a member requests an adjustment of its quota, the Executive Board, after consulting the member, shall submit a written report on the request to the Board of Governors at its next meeting. If the Board of Governors approves an increase in the quota of a member, and on the date the member consents to the increase its monetary reserves are less than its new quota, the Executive Board may reduce the proportion of the increase to be paid in gold. The member shall, if it desires such a reduction, transmit to the Fund by rapid means of communication within ten days after its consent, the data necessary to determine its monetary reserves as at the date of the consent. The decision of the Executive Board shall be made within ten days after receipt of such data.

Adopted September 25, 1946, amended May 28, 1947

D-3. At last one year prior to the time when a review of quotas must be undertaken by the Fund, the Executive Board shall appoint a committee to study the problem and to prepare a written report.

Adopted September 25, 1946

Other Holders

D-4. When an application to be permitted to accept, hold, and use special drawing rights under Article XXIII, Section 3, is received by the Fund and it is placed before the Executive Board, the Chairman shall announce a reasonable time to be allowed for discussion and preliminary investigation by the Executive Board before a decision is reached to proceed with the formal investigation. If this decision is in the affirmative the Fund may proceed to obtain all relevant information and discuss with the applicant any matters relating to its application. Any Executive Director may request such information to be added to the list requested of the applicant as in his opinion is relevant to the decision to be made. The Executive Board shall then decide whether to submit an application with its views to the Board of Governors for a telegraphic vote of hold the application until the next meeting of the Board of Governors.

Adopted September 18, 1969

E--SUBSCRIPTIONS

E-1. Gold depositories of the Fund shall be established in the United States, United Kingdom, France, and India. The gold of the Fund shall be held with the depositories designated by the members in whose territories they are located at places agreed with the Fund. A member may pay its gold subscription to the Fund at one or more of the specified gold depositories within the terms of Article XIII, Section 2.

Adopted September 25, 1946, amended November 29, 1956

E-2. A member shall pay its currency subscription to the Fund at the designated depository. Each member is authorized to substitute in accordance with Article III, Section 5, non-negotiable, non-interest hearing notes payable to the Fund on demand for that part of the currency holdings of the Fund which exceed 1 per cent of the member's quota, and the depository shall gold such notes for the account of the Fund. Such notes shall not be accepted until the Fund is satisfied that they are in proper form and that their issue has been authorized. The balances held in the administrative accounts of the Fund shall not be considered as part of the currency holdings of the Fund for the application of this Rule.

Adopted September 25, 1946, amended February 20, 1950

E-3. The Executive Board may agree to alter the 1 per cent requirement in the case of any member should circumstances in the opinion of the Executive Board warrant a different percentage.

Adopted September 25, 1946, amended February 20, 1950

E-4. The member is allowed 24 hours in which to deposit the currency necessary to maintain the amount required under E-2 and E-3.

Adopted September 25, 1946

E-5. For purposes of Article III, Section 3, initial gold payments in excess of the minimum shall be accepted on the same basis as the minimum payment.

Adopted September 25, 1946

F—PAR VALUES

F-1. The Fund shall arrange through the fiscal agencies of members that frequent and regular information as to the market rates of members' currencies bought and sold in their territories is made available to the Fund.

Adopted September 25, 1946

F-2. Members shall notify the Fund whether for the settlement of international transactions they, in fact, freely buy and sell gold within the prescribed limits of price and shall notify the Fund of any changes in such policy.

Adopted September 25, 1946

F-3. A member desiring to change the par value of its currency shall give the Fund as much notice as the circumstances allow, and shall submit a full and reasoned statement why, in its opinion, such a change is necessary to correct a fundamental disequilibrium.

Adopted September 25, 1946

F-4. For transactions in gold by a member the margin above and below par value shall be, at the option of the member, either:

    1. One quarter of one per cent plus the following charges:

        (a) The actual or computed cost of converting the gold transferred into good delivery bars at the normal center for dealing in gold of either the buying member whose currency is exchanged for the gold;

        (b) The actual or computed cost of transporting the gold transferred to the normal center for dealing in gold of either the buying member or the member whose currency is exchanged for the gold;

        (c) Any charges made by the custodian of the gold transferred for effecting the transfer; or

    2. One per cent, which one per cent shall be taken to include all of the charges set forth in 1 above.

Adopted June 10, 1947, amended October 15, 1954 and extended November 5, 1954

G—OPERATIONS AND TRANSACTIONS

G-1. Each member shall designate a fiscal agency in accordance with Article V, Section 1, and may change the agency after notifying the Fund.

Adopted September 25, 1946, amended September 18, 1969

Foreign Exchange

G-2. Each request from a member to purchase currency from the Fund shall be made by the fiscal agency designated in accordance which Article V, Section 1, such request to be authenticated in the manner agreed upon by the Fund and the agency. In its operations on behalf of the Fund a depository will act only on instructions authenticated in such manner as may be agreed upon by the Fund and the depository.

Adopted September 25, 1946, amended February 20, 1947

G-3. When a duly authenticated request for the purchase of foreign exchange in accordance with Article V, Section 3, is received, the Fund shall, on the third business day following the day of receipt of the request, instruct the appropriate depository to make the transfer, except in cases which the Executive Board may indicate. The first business day after receipt of the request shall be regarded as the first of the three days.

Adopted September 25, 1946, amended February 7, 1947

G-4. When a member expects to purchase from the Fund, in a single transaction or a series of transactions, an unusually large sum of any other member's currency (unusually large relative to the quota of that other member), the member shall give the Fund as much notice of the proposed transaction or transactions as can reasonably be effected.

Adopted September 25, 1946

G-5. When the request of a member, if consummated, would increase to more than 5 per cent of its quota the aggregate purchases by the member pursuant or Article V, Section 3, during the thirty-day period preceding the date of action specified in G-3, the Managing Director shall notify each Executive Director (or his Alternate if the Executive Director is not available) on the first business day after receipt of the request. If neither the Executive Director nor the Alternate is in Washington or its environs, the notification will be assumed to have been duly delivered if appropriate notice is delivered to his office.

At the request of any Executive Director or on the initiative of the Managing Director, a special meeting shall be called by the Managing Director to discuss the request as soon as feasible, but not later than the morning of the second business day.

Adopted February 7, 1947

Gold

G-6. Gold due to the Fund may be delivered at any gold depository of the Fund. Whenever the Fund accepts gold situated elsewhere than at a gold depository of the Fund, the member delivering such gold may be required to assume the actual or estimated costs, as the case may be, of moving the gold to the Fund's nearest gold depository. Where the member is required to reimburse the Fund for such actual or estimated costs, the Fund shall advise the member in what form reimbursement shall be made.

Adopted July 30, 1948

G-7. When any member sells gold to the Fund pursuant to Article V, Section 6 *(a)*, the member may be required to assume the estimated costs that would be incurred by the Fund if it used the gold so acquired to purchase the currency it has sold. The Fund shall advise the member in what form such payment shall be made.

Adopted July 30, 1948

H— EXCHANGE CONTROLS, CURRENCY PRACTICES, AND AGREEMENTS

H-1. The Fund shall keep all exchange controls under review and shall consult with members with a view to the progressive removal of exchange restrictions in accordance with the Fund Agreement.

Adopted September 25, 1946

H-2. If a member complains to the Executive Board that another member is not complying with its obligations concerning exchange controls, discriminatory currency arrangements, or multiple currency practices, the complaint shall give all facts pertinent to an examination.

Adopted September 25, 1946

H-3. Upon receipt of a complaint from a member, the Executive Board shall make arrangements promptly for consultation with the members directly involved.

Adopted September 25, 1946

H-4. All requests by a member under Article VIII, Sections 2 and 3, that the Fund approve the imposition of restrictions on the making of payments and transfers for current international transactions, or the use of discriminatory currency arrangements or multiple currency practices, shall be submitted to the Executive Board in writing, with a statement of the reasons for making the request.

Adopted September 25, 1946

H-5. The Executive Board shall decide each request for approval expeditiously.

Adopted September 25, 1946

I— REPURCHASES AND CHARGES IN RESPECT OF
GENERAL ACCOUNT TRANSACTIONS

I-1. The first time that a member has to make a gold payment to the Fund it shall deliver gold of designated weight and fineness at least sufficient in value to meet the payment. Any surplus balance of gold shall be held by the Fund under earmark at the disposal of the member and may be used to meet other payments incurred in the future.

Adopted September 25, 1946

I-2. The service charge payable by a member buying the currency of another member in exchange for its own currency shall be paid at the time the transaction is consummated. The service charge payable for such transactions taking place after November 30, 1951, shall be ½ of 1 per cent, except that beginning July 28, 1969, no service charge shall be payable in respect of any purchase to the extent that it is a gold tranche purchase. The service charge shall be reviewed in connection with any review of charges under Rule I-4.

Adopted September 25, 1946, amended November 19, 1951, November 14, 1952, June 26, 1953, October 14, 1953, December 23, 1953, December 15, 1954, December 27, 1955, May 23, 1956, December 21, 1956, December 9, 1957, December 12, 1958, March 20, 1959, April 20, 1959, April 19, 1960, April 17, 1961, April 25, 1962, April 24, 1963, April 13, 1964, April 28, 1965, April 22, 1966, and September 18, 1969

I-3. Rule I-3, adopted September 25, 1946, was eliminated on July 30, 1948, and the substance of the Rule was incorporated into Rule G-6 on that date.

I-4. (a) As soon as possible after July 31, October 31, January 31 and April 30, the Fund shall notify each member by cable of the charges it owes to the Fund pursuant to Article V, Section 8 *(c)* or *(d)*, for the three calendar months ending on each such date. These charges shall be payable within thirty days after the sending of such notice.

Adopted September 25, 1946, amended July 30, 1948 and February 24, 1954

(b) Such charges payable by each member shall be computed on the basis of the "average of the holdings" which, as used in this section, means the average daily balances of its currency held by the Fund in excess of its quota calculated as follows:

(i) At the end of each calendar month there shall be averaged for each member the daily amounts by which the Fund's holdings of its currency on the Fund's books at the close of each day during that month have exceeded its quota on each such day;

(ii) The Fund's holdings of each member's currency shall consist of all of its currency except amounts, not in excess of $1/10$ of 1 per cent of the member's quota, in a special account to meet administrative expenses and amounts in sundry cash accounts.

Adopted July 30, 1948, amended November 1, 1968

(c) The period of time during which the Fund's holdings of a member's currency have been at a particular level shall be the continuous period of time during which the average of the holdings has not fallen below that level, and, in determining periods of time for the application of the charges, changes in the average of the holdings shall affect the calculation of time periods in the following way:

(i) Each increase in the average of the holdings shall create a new segment of the holdings which will be equal to the amount of the increase and the period of time during which each segment is held shall be measured from the beginning of the month in which the increase in the average of the holdings occurs.

(ii) Each decrease in the average of the holdings shall terminate the period of time during which the holdings have been in excess of the new average and the period of time shall terminate at the end of the month preceding that in which the decrease in the average of the holdings occurs.

Adopted July 30, 1948

[Rule I-4 (d) and (e) have been omitted because the charges provided thereunder are no longer applicable to any segment of the Fund's holdings. For the text, see the 22nd issue of the By-Laws and Rules and Regulations.]

(f) (1) With respect to each segment of the holdings of a member's currency to the extent that it represents the acquisition of that currency by the Fund from January 1, 1954 through April 30, 1963:

    (i) The charge to be levied on each segment to the extent that it is within the first bracket of 50 per cent in excess of the quota shall be nil for the first three months, 2 per cent per annum for the next fifteen months, and an additional ½ per cent per annum for each subsequent six months.

    (ii) The charge to be levied on each segment to the extent that it is within the second bracket of more than 50 per cent and not more than 75 per cent in excess of the quota shall be nil for the first three months, 2 per cent per annum for the next nine months, and an additional ½ per cent per annum for each subsequent six months.

    (iii) The charge to be levied on each segment to the extent that it is within the third bracket of more than 75 per cent and not more than 100 per cent in excess of the quota shall be nil for the first three months, 2 per cent per annum for the next three months, and an additional ½ per cent per annum for each subsequent six months.

Adopted as I-4 (f) December 23, 1953, amended December 15, 1954, December 27, 1955, May 23, 1956, December 21, 1956, December 9, 1957, December 12, 1958, March 20, 1959, April 20, 1959, April 19, 1960, April 17, 1961, April 25, 1962, and April 24, 1963

(2) With respect to each segment of the holdings of a member's currency to the extent that it represents the acquisition of that currency by the Fund after April 30, 1963:

    (i) The charge to be levied on each segment to the extent that it is within the first bracket of 50 per cent in excess of the quota shall be nil for the first three months, 2 per cent per annum for the next fifteen months, and an additional ½ per cent per annum for each subsequent six months.

    (ii) The charge to be levied on each segment to the extent that it is within the second bracket of more than 50 per cent and not more than 100 per cent in excess of the quota shall be nil for the first three months, 2 per cent per annum for the next nine months, and an additional ½ per cent per annum for each subsequent six months.

    (iii) The charge to be levied on each segment to the extent that it is within the third bracket of more than 100 per cent in excess of the quota shall be nil for the first three months, 2 per cent per annum for the next three months, and an additional ½ per cent per annum for each subsequent six months.

Adopted April 24, 1963, amended April 13, 1964, April 28, 1965, and April 22, 1966

(g) The Fund and the member shall consider means by which the Fund's holdings of the currency can be reduced whenever the Fund's holdings of a member's currency are such that the charge under *(f)* above applicable to any segment for any period has reached the rate of 4 per cent per annum. Thereafter, the charges shall rise in accordance with (f) above, provided that the rate shall not increase beyond 5 per cent per annum when agreement is reached under this Rule for repurchase within three to five years after a drawing in accordance with Executive Board Decision No. 102-(52/11). In the case of agreements on means to reduce the Fund's holdings beyond five years, the Fund may adopt higher maximum rates. In the absence of agreement on means to reduce the Fund's holdings, the Fund may impose such charges as it deems appropriate after the rate of 5 per cent is reached. When an agreement for repurchase within three to five years after a drawing is not reached or observed, the charges to be imposed shall rise in accordance with (f) above, provided that when the charges payable on any segment have reached 6 per cent the Fund will review the charges to be imposed thereafter. In the case of non-observance, if 5 per cent is payable on any segment at the date of non-observance, it shall continue to be payable only for that part of a period of six months for which it has not yet been payable; and when the repurchases for which the non-observance relates are made or a new agreement for repurchase not later than five years after the drawing is made all charges in excess of 5 per cent shall be reduced to 5 per cent.

Adopted as I-4 (f) November 19, 1951, amended December 23, 1953, April 27, 1959, February 25, 1963, and April 24, 1963

I-5. (a) If, in accordance with Article V, Section 8 *(f)*, a member wishes to pay in its own currency part of any charge due to the Fund pursuant to I-4, the proportion to be paid in such currency shall be calculated on the basis of its monetary reserves at the end of the quarter of the financial year of the Fund to which such charges apply.

Adopted September 25, 1946, amended May 28, 1947 and July 30, 1948

(b) If, in accordance with Article V, Section 8 *(f)*, a member wishes to pay in its own currency part of any charge due to the Fund pursuant to I-2 or I-8, the proportion to be paid in such currency shall be calculated on the basis of its monetary reserves on the day before the day on which the charge is due; provided, however, that if the member would encounter undue difficulties in providing for that day the data required by the Fund in the monetary reserve report forms sent to members, the proportion to be paid in the member's currency shall be calculated on the basis of its monetary reserves at the end of the quarter of the financial year of the Fund in which the charge becomes due. The member, when making a provisional payment in accordance with (c) below, shall advise the Fund whether the member will provide monetary reserve data for the day before the day on which the charge becomes due or for the end of the quarter in which the charge becomes due.

Adopted July 30, 1948, amended March 24, 1950

(c) Whenever a charge is due under I-2, I-4, or I-8, and the member wishes to pay part thereof in its own currency, the member shall make a provisional payment in gold and currency on the basis of its own estimate of its monetary reserves for the appropriate day or end of quarter of the financial year of the Fund as specified in (a) or (b) above. The member shall provide the

Fund with the data, for such appropriate day or end of quarter, required by the Fund in the monetary reserve report forms sent to members, and such data shall be provided to the Fund not later than six months from the aforesaid appropriate day or end of quarter. On the basis of such data, the Fund shall make a final determination of the proportions of the charge to be paid in gold and in currency, and final adjustment of the provisional payment shall be made on the date specified by the Fund. If the member fails to provide its monetary reserve data within the period prescribed herein, the whole of the charge shall be finally payable in gold.

Adopted July 30, 1948

I-6. (a) Within six months after the end of each financial year of the Fund, each member shall furnish the data necessary for the calculation of its monetary reserves and its repurchase obligation, if any. Such data shall be supplied to the Fund in the monetary reserve report forms sent to members by the Fund.

(b) Each member's monetary reserves and repurchase obligation, if any, shall be computed on the basis of the aforesaid data.

(c) When a repurchase obligation has thus been computed for a member, the Managing Director, after consultation with the Executive Director appointed or elected by the member, shall notify the member by letter containing all the necessary details of the computation, including the distribution of the amount payable among the types of reserves and any amount to be postponed.

(d) If the member is in agreement with the aforesaid computation, the member shall so advise the Fund within thirty days from the day on which the member receives notice thereof. The Managing Director shall then send to the member a formal request for payment, and shall at the same time notify the Board of such request. The member shall discharge the amount due within thirty days from the day on which the member receives the formal request for payment.

(e) If the member disagrees with the computation notified to it under (c) above, it shall so advise the Fund within thirty days from the day on which the member receives notice thereof, and shall at the same time or within the said thirty days inform the Fund of its reasoned objections. If agreement with the member is not reached within a period regarded by the Managing Director as reasonable in the circumstances of the case, the Managing Director, after consultation with the Executive Director appointed or elected by the member, shall refer the matter to the Executive Board.

(f) After agreement with the member if reached under (e) above, or after a decision by the Executive Board determining the member's repurchase obligation, the Managing Director shall send to the member a formal request for payment, and shall at the same time notify the Board of such request. The member shall discharge the amount due within thirty days from the day on which the member receives the formal request for payment or within such other period as may be decided by the Executive Board.

(g) The Managing Director shall report to the Executive Board any case in which it appears the above procedure has not been followed.

Adopted September 25, 1946, amended July 28, 1950; paragraphs (c), (d), and (f) amended May 20, 1970

I-7. For the purposes of Article V, Section 7, the term "financial year" shall be defined as beginning on May 1 and ending on the succeeding April 30; provided, however, that the first financial year shall begin on March 1, 1947 and end on April 30, 1948.

For purposes of the Fund's accounts and reports, its fiscal year shall begin on May 1 and end on the succeeding April 30; provided, however, that the fiscal year 1946/47 shall begin on July 1, 1946 and end on June 30, 1947, and the fiscal year 1947/48 shall begin on July 1, 1947 and end on April 30, 1948.

Adopted February 7, 1947, amended May 28, 1947, effective September 17, 1947

I-8. When any member sells gold to the Fund pursuant to Article V, Section 6 *(a)*, or buys gold from the Fund, the Fund may levy a handling charge which shall be paid in accordance with Article V, Section 8 *(f)*.

Adopted February 7, 1947, amended July 30, 1948

I-9. (a) Remuneration shall accrue daily and shall be paid as of the end of each financial year of the Fund. Remuneration shall be paid in gold to the extent that receipts of gold, during the financial year, in payment of charges under Article V, Section 8 *(f)*, exceed payments during that year of gold as transfer charges and interest on borrowings. If the amount of gold thus available is less than the total remuneration to be paid, the gold shall be paid to each member in proportion to the remuneration to which it is entitled.

(b) Payments in gold pursuant to (a) above shall be made only to the extent that these can be effected in bars.

(c) Any remuneration due to each member and not payable in gold shall be paid in that member's currency.

(d) The Executive Board shall review from time to time the rate of remuneration and the extent to which remuneration shall be paid in gold.

Adopted September 18, 1969

J—ACCOUNTING AND REPORTING

Accounts

J-1. (a) The accounts of the General Account shall be kept in terms of the currencies held in the General Account and United States dollars on the basis of the established parities.

(b) The accounts of the Special Drawing Account shall be kept in terms of the unit of value of special drawing rights.

Adopted September 25, 1946, amended September 18, 1969

J-2. The accounts of the General Account and the Special Drawing Account shall be kept in a manner that will show clearly the nature and amount of each operation and transaction, the position of the General Account and the Special Drawing Account, the position of each participant and each other holder, and the nature and amount of all operations and transactions in special drawing rights.

Adopted September 25, 1946, amended September 18, 1969

J-3. (a) A summary statement of the operations nad transactions conducted through the General Account and the holdings in the General Account of gold, special drawing rights, and currencies of members shall be issued at intervals of three months or less, and a monthly statement of balances shall be sent to all members.

(b) A summary statement of all operations and transactions in special drawing rights, and the position of each participant and each other holder shall be issued at intervals of three months or less, and a monthly statement of balances of special drawing rights shall be sent to participants and other holders.

(c) A monthly summary statement of all transactions under Article XXV, Section 2 *(a)*, *(b)* (i), and *(b)* (ii), shall be sent to all participants.

Adopted September 25, 1946, amended September 18, 1969

Annual Budget

J-4. The Managing Director shall prepare an annual administrative budget, which shall include a projection of the expense of conducting the business of the Special Drawing Account, for presentation to the Executive Board for approval not later than April 1 of each year.

Adopted September 25, 1946, amended February 20, 1948 and September 18, 1969

Annual Report

J-5. Not later than June 30 of each year, the Managing Director shall present to the Executive Board a summary of the matters which in his opinion should be included in the annual report to the Board of Governors. At least one month before the annual meeting of the Board of Governors, the Managing Director shall submit to the Executive Board for its consideration, a draft of the annual report.

Adopted September 25, 1946

Audit

J-6. At least one month before the annual meeting of the Board of Governors, the audited accounts of the Fund shall be submitted to the Executive Board for its consideration.

Adopted September 25, 1946

K—LIMITATION AND INELIGIBILITY

K-1. The Managing Director shall report to the Executive Board any case in which it appears to him that a member is not fulfilling obligations under the Fund Agreement that could lead to the application of the provisions of Article XV, Section 2.

Adopted September 25, 1946, amended September 18, 1969

K-2. Whenever the Executive Board would be authorized to declare a member ineligible to use the resources of the Fund it may refrain from making the declaration and indicate the circumstances under which, and/or the extent to which, the member may make use of the resources.

Adopted September 25, 1946

K-3. When a member has changed the par value of its currency despite the objection of the Fund, in cases where the Fund is entitled to object, the Executive Board may determine the circumstances under which, and the extent to which, a member may use the resources of the Fund.

Adopted September 25, 1946

K-4. Before any member is declared, pursuant to Article XV, Section 2 *(a)*, ineligible to use the resources of the Fund, the matter shall be considered by the Executive Board, who shall inform the member in reasonable time of the complaint against it and allow the member an adequate opportunity for stating its case both orally and in writing.

Adopted September 25, 1946

K-5. When any member that is ineligible to use the resources of the Fund, or whose use of the resources has been limited, according to K-2 or K-3 above, requests the Executive Board to permit the resumption of exchange transactions with or without special limitations and the Executive Board decides not to permit such resumption, a written report shall be made to the member starting what further action is required before such resumption will be permitted.

Adopted September 25, 1946, corrected October 18, 1950

L—CAPITAL TRANSFERS

L-1. If there is taking place a large or sustained outflow of capital from a member country:

> (a) that member or any other member may notify the Fund, presenting such information as it deems necessary; and may request the Fund's views with respect to such capital movement; and
> (b) the Fund may present to the member or members concerned a report setting forth its views, and may request the member or members to report on the situation within a suitable time.

Adopted September 25, 1946

L-2. Whenever the Fund has requested a member to exercise controls to prevent use of the resources of the Fund to meet a large or sustained outflow of capital, the Fund shall request the member to notify it promptly and in detail of the measures taken.

Adopted September 25, 1946

L-3. Each member shall inform the Fund in detail of the measures it is taking to regulate international capital movements and of changes made in such measures.

Adopted September 25, 1946

L-4. If the Fund is of the opinion that the controls exercised by a member to regulate international capital movements are restrictive of payments for current transactions, or unduly delay transfers of funds in settlement of commitments, the Fund shall, subject to the provisions of Article VII, Section 3 *(b)* and Article XIV, Section 2, consult with the member on the manner in which the controls are exercised. If, after consultation, the Fund is not satisfied that the controls are exercised in a manner consistent with the Fund Agreement, it shall so inform the member in a written report and request it to modify the controls.

Adopted September 25, 1946

M—RELATIONS WITH NON-MEMBERS

M-1. The Fund may request the cooperation of any member with a view to the application of appropriate measures to prevent transactions with non-members or with persons in their territories, contrary to the provisions of the Agreement or the purposes of the Fund.

Adopted September 25, 1946

M-2. When the Fund finds that a member or any of its fiscal agencies referred to in Article V, Section 1, engages in any transaction with or cooperates in practices with a non-member or with persons in a non-member's territory, contrary to the provisions of the Agreement or the purposes of the Fund, it shall present to the member a report setting forth its views and may request the cessation or modification of the transactions or practices.

Adopted September 25, 1946

M-3. A member shall inform the Fund promptly and in detail of any restrictions which it imposes on exchange transactions with non-members or with persons in their territories.

Adopted September 25, 1946

M-4. Any member may notify the Fund of restrictions imposed by a member on exchange transactions with non-members or with persons in their territories which are deemed to prejudice the interests of members and to be contrary to the purposes of the Fund.

Adopted September 25, 1946

M-5. When the Fund finds that the restrictions imposed by a member on exchange transactions with non-members or with persons in their territories are prejudicial to the interests of members and contrary to the purposes of the Fund, it shall present to the member a report setting forth its views and may request the abolition or modification of the restrictions.

Adopted September 25, 1946

M-6. The Fund deems that it would be prejudicial to the interests of members and contrary to the purposes of the Fund for a member to impose restrictions on exchange transactions with those non-members having entered into special exchange agreements under the General Agreement on Tariffs and Trade, or with persons in their territories, which the member would not in similar circumstances be authorized to impose on exchange transactions with other members or persons in their territories. Therefore, pursuant to Article XI, Section 2, members should not institute restrictions on exchange transactions with such non-members, or persons in their territories, unless the restrictions (a) if instituted on transactions with other members, or persons in their territories, would be authorized under the Fund Agreement, or (b) have been approved in advance by the Fund. Requests for prior approval shall be submitted in writing with a statement of reasons.

Adopted June 7, 1950

N—STAFF REGULATIONS

Personnel

N-1. The employment, classification, promotion, and assignment of personnel in the Fund shall be made without discriminating against any person because of sex, race or creed.

Adopted September 25, 1946

N-2. Persons on the staff of the Fund shall be nationals of members of the Fund unless the Executive Board authorizes exceptions in particular cases.

Adopted September 25, 1946

N-3. In the discharge of their functions, the persons on the staff owe their duty entirely to the Fund and to no other authority.

Adopted September 25, 1946

N-4. All persons on the staff must avoid any action, and in particular any kind of pronouncement, which may reflect unfavorably upon their position as employees of an international organization, either in their own country or elsewhere. They should always bear in mind the reserve and tact incumbent upon them by reason of their international functions, and they are required to exercise the utmost discretion in regard to matters of official business. At no time should they in any way use to private advantage information known to them by reason of their official position.

Adopted September 25, 1946

N-5. Except in the course of his official duties or by express authorization of the Managing Director, no person on the staff may, during the term of his appointment of service, publish, cause to be published, or assist in the publication of any book, pamphlet, article, letter, or other document relative to the policies or activities of the Fund or to any national political questions; deliver any speech, lecture, or radio broadcast, or grant any press interview on such policies, activities, or questions; or communicate to any person any unpublished information known to him by reason of his official position. After termination of his period of service with the Fund, a person formerly on the staff may not, without the express authorization of the Managing Director, disclose any confidential information he has received during his service with the Fund by reason of his official position.

Adopted September 25, 1946

N-6. No person on the staff shall hold other public or private employment or engage in any occupation or profession which in the Fund's opinion is incompatible with the proper performance of his official duties.

Adopted September 25, 1946

N-7. A person on the staff may retain re-employment rights or pension rights acquired in the service of a public or private organization.

Adopted September 25, 1946

N-8. Any person on the staff who accepts a public office of a political character shall immediately resign from the Fund.

Adopted September 25, 1946

N-9. No person on the staff may accept any honor, decoration, favor, gift, or bonus from any government, or from any other authority or person external to the Fund, for services rendered during the period of his appointment or service with the Fund.

Adopted September 25, 1946

N-10. Upon appointment, each person on the staff will subscribe in writing to the following affirmation:

I solemnly affirm:

That, to the best of my ability, I will carry out my responsibilities in a manner that will further the purposes of the International Monetary Fund;

That I will refrain from communicating confidential information to persons outside the Fund;

That I will not use to private advantage information known to me by reason of my official position; and

That I will accept no instruction in regard to the performance of my duties from any government or authority external to the Fund.

Adopted September 25, 1946

N-11. All persons appointed to permanent positions on the staff shall be classified by grades or positions according to the nature of their duties and responsibilities. Salary increases within each grade will be progressively available upon the successful completion of successive periods of work or upon the recommendation of supervisors.

Adopted September 25, 1946

N-12. The salary scale for permanent employees of the Fund shall, so far as practicable, conform to the salary scale of the United Nations.

Adopted September 25, 1946

N-13. The Managing Director shall inform the Executive Board at least two weeks in advance of any action to appoint or initiate the dismissal of any person at or above the rank of division chief within a department or office or receiving a salary equal to or more than that of a division chief within a department. All other appointments to the staff shall be made by the Managing Director or his designated representative.

Adopted September 25, 1946, amended July 1, 1959

N-14. The Managing Director is authorized to issue General Orders, with the approval of the Executive Board, concerning the general personnel policies which shall apply to the operating staff of the Fund.

Adopted September 25, 1946

Travel

N-15. (a) Official travel will be undertaken by staff members only with the approval of the Managing Director or officials designated by him. In the case of travel outside the continental United States, however, the specific approval of the Managing Director is required.

Adopted September 25, 1946, amended February 11, 1948

(b) The Managing Director will inform the Executive Board of all such travel at least once a month.

Adopted February 11, 1948

(c) Staff participation in activities of national agencies and staff travel to a member's territory require consultation in advance with the Executive Director appointed or elected by the member.

Adopted February 11, 1948

(d) Staff participation in deliberations or activities of international agencies or conferences as well as staff travel to a member's territory, undertaken in response to a formal invitation, require the advance approval of the Executive Board.

Adopted February 11, 1948

O—TRANSACTIONS INVOLVING SPECIAL DRAWING RIGHTS

Currency Convertible in Fact

O-1. In deciding whether currency is convertible in fact under Article XXXII *(b)*, the Fund will consult participants with respect to

(i) procedures for the convertibility of currencies in accordance with Article XXXII *(b)* (1), and
(ii) arrangements for the conversion of balances of currency into a currency convertible in accordance with Article XXXII *(b)* (1).

The Fund shall inform all participants of the procedures or arrangements for conversion. Participants shall consult the Fund with respect to any changes they propose to make in their procedures or arrangements.

Adopted September 18, 1969

O-2. (a) Currency shall cease to be convertible in fact if

(i) the issuer of that currency notifies the Fund that the currency will no longer be convertible in fact; or
(ii) the Fund decides after consultation with the issuer of the currency that the currency is no longer convertible in fact.

(b) If a participant receives currency in a transaction under Article XXV, Section 2 *(a)*, which cannot be converted into the currency desired in accordance with Rule O-6 it shall inform the Managing Director and may return the currency to the designated participant which shall substitute other currency convertible in fact.

Adopted September 18, 1969

Exchange Rates

O-3. The exchange rate in terms of special drawing rights for a currency provided in a transaction between participants or involved in a conversion associated with such a transaction, shall be

    (i) for the United States dollar: its par value;

    (ii) for the currency of a participant having an exchange market in which the Fund finds that a representative rate for spot delivery for the United States dollar can be readily ascertained: that representative rate;

    (iii) for the currency of a participant having an exchange market in which the Fund finds that a representative rate for spot delivery for the United States dollar cannot be readily ascertained but in which a representative rate can be readily ascertained for spot delivery for a currency as described in (ii): the rate calculated by reference to the representative rate for spot delivery for that currency and the rate ascertained pursuant to (ii) above for the United States dollar in terms of that currency;

    (iv) for any other currency; a rate determined by the Fund.

Adopted September 18, 1969

O-4. The exchange rate for each currency for the purposes of Rule O-3 shall be determined as of:

    (i) the date of dispatch of the Fund's designation instruction in a transaction under Article XXV, Section 2 *(a)*, or

    (ii) the date of dispatch of the notification under Rule O-10 by the participant using special drawing rights in any other transaction.

Adopted September 18, 1969

O-5. Exchange rates shall be determined under Rules O-3 and O-4 by procedures established in consultation between the Fund and the participants.

Adopted September 18, 1969

Provision and Conversion of Currency

O-6. A participant shall inform the Fund of its intention to use special drawing rights in a transaction under Article XXV, Section 2 *(a)*. If it desires a particular currency convertible in fact pursuant to Rule O-1 (i), the participant shall indicate this in its communication.

Adopted September 18, 1969

O-7. In a transaction under Article XXV, Section 2 *(a)*, the instructions for any conversion of currency provided pursuant to Rule O-1 (i) or Rule O-1 (ii) shall be given by the Fund in accordance with the indication under Rule O-6. In any other transaction, a participant using special drawing rights may ask the Fund in its notification under Rule O-10 to give instructions for any conversion of currency.

Adopted September 18, 1969

O-8. Currency convertible in fact shall be provided at, or converted through, an official agency of the participant issuing the currency and in accordance with the procedures or arrangements under Article XXXII *(b)* and Rule O-1. Instructions for the provision or conversion of any currency shall be carried out promptly.

Adopted September 18, 1969

O-9. No participant shall levy any charge in respect of the provision or conversion of currency in connection with the use of special drawing rights.

Adopted September 18, 1969

Notification

O-10. Both parties to a transaction, except for participants designated under Article XXV, Section 5, or the General Account, shall notify the Fund under which provision of the Articles, or prescription under Article XXV, Section 2 *(b)* (ii), that transaction is undertaken.

Adopted September 18, 1969

O-11. A participant using special drawing rights under Article XXV, Section 2, shall declare in its notification under Rule O-10 that the use is in accordance with Article XXV, Section 3 *(a)*, or a specific prescription under Article XXV, Section 3 *(c)*.

Adopted September 18, 1969

Recording

O-12. A participant using special drawing rights shall inform the Fund immediately of the receipt of currency in accordance with the Articles of Agreement and these Rules and Regulations.

Adopted September 18, 1969

O-13. The Fund shall record a transaction in the Special Drawing Account when it is satisfied that the transaction is in conformity with the obligations of participants under the Articles of Agreement and with the Rules and Regulations and any applicable decisions of the Fund. A transaction shall be recorded as of the date on which currency is provided.

Adopted September 18, 1969

Designation of Participants to Provide Currency

O-14. At quarterly intervals the Executive Board shall decide, in accordance with Article XXV, Section 5, and Schedule F, on the plan, including the amounts, by which designations will be made until the next decision takes effect.

On the request of any participant, an Executive Director, or the Managing Director, the Executive Board shall review, and if necessary amend, any plan adopted pursuant to this Rule.

Adopted September 18, 1969

O-15. The Executive Board may prescribe transactions or categories of transactions under Article XXV, Section 2 *(b)* (ii), without designation under Article XXV, Section 5, in which a participant in agreement with any other participant may use its special drawing rights. The Managing Director shall inform participants from time to time of the participants and the amounts of special drawing rights each may receive under any prescription made under this Rule.

Adopted September 18, 1969

Transactions Without the Requirement of Need

O-16. The Executive Board may prescribe transactions or categories of transactions under Article XXV, Section 3 *(c)*, in which a participant may use its special drawing rights without regard to the requirement of need in Article XXV, Section 3 *(a)*. The Managing Director shall inform participants from time to time of the participants and the amounts each may use under any prescription made under this Rule.

Adopted September 18, 1969

P— RECONSTITUTION

P-1. Any period of five years ending five years after the first allocation or at the end of any calendar quarter thereafter shall be a reconstitution period under Schedule G, paragraph 1.

Adopted September 18, 1969

P-2. The calculations for each participant under Schedule G, paragraph 1 *(a)* (ii), shall be based on the assumptions that the Executive Board makes from time to time with respect to allocations or cancellations during the remainder of any reconstitution period and on the assumptions that a participant will

   (i) make no use of special drawing rights during the remainder of the reconstitution period for which the calculation is made; and

   (ii) obtain any net additional amount of special drawing rights which it needs to hold, in addition to allocations assumed pursuant to this Rule, in order to comply with the requirement in Schedule G, paragraph 1 *(a)* (i), in equal quarterly amounts on the fifteenth day of each calendar quarter during the remainder of the reconstitution period for which the calculation is made.

Adopted September 18, 1969

P-3. When these calculations indicate that a participant would need to obtain special drawing rights in order to comply with the requirement in Schedule G, paragraph 1 *(a)* (i), the Managing Director shall inform the participant of the amount it would have to obtain quarterly and hold during the remainder of the reconstitution period in order to comply with this requirement.

Adopted September 18, 1969

P-4. When these calculations indicate that a participant would need to obtain special drawing rights for any reconstitution period in an amount per quarter that equals or exceeds ten per cent of the participant's net cumulative allocation at the end of the reconstitution period, the participant shall be subject to designation under Article

XXV, Section 5 *(a)* (ii), as of the beginning of the calendar quarter following the calculation, for an amount of special drawing rights equal to the largest amount per quarter calculated for any reconstitution period.

Adopted September 18, 1969

P-5. The Managing Director shall give the special notice required under Schedule G, paragraph 1 *(a)* (iii), when these calculations indicate that the quarterly amount of special drawing rights which the participant needs to obtain in order to comply with the reconstitution requirement in Schedule G, paragraph 1 *(a)* (i), for any reconstitution period equals or exceeds 50 per cent of its net cumulative allocation at the end of the reconstitution period.

Adopted September 18, 1969

P-6. To the extent that a participant may receive special drawing rights in a transaction under any prescription to promote reconstitution by it, the Fund shall provide special drawing rights held in the General Account to the participant at its request for gold or currency acceptable to the Fund. A participant shall consult the Managing Director before making a request under this Rule.

Adopted September 18, 1969

P-7. The Fund shall specify the participant and the amount of special drawing rights it shall provide when is required by Schedule G, paragraph 1 *(a)* (iv); XXVI, Section 5; and Article XXX, Section 3.

Adopted September 18, 1969

Q—INTEREST, CHARGES, AND ASSESSMENTS IN RESPECT OF SPECIAL DRAWING RIGHTS

Q-1. Interest and charges in respect of special drawing rights shall accrue daily and shall be paid promptly as of the end of each financial year of the Fund. The accounts of participants shall be credited with the excess of interest due over charges or debited with the excess of charges over the interest due. The accounts of holders that are not participants shall be credited with the interest due.

Adopted September 18, 1969

Q-2. Assessments shall be levied promptly, as of the end of each financial year of the Fund, on the basis of a reasonable estimate of the expenses of conducting the business of the Special Drawing Account for the financial year, and the accounts of participants shall be debited with the amounts of the assessments.

Adopted September 18, 1969

R—SUSPENSION OF USE OF SPECIAL DRAWING RIGHTS

R-1. The Managing Director shall report to the Executive Board any facts on the basis of which it appears to him that a participant is not fulfilling obligations under the Fund Agreement that could lead to suspension under Article XXIX, Section 2, and may include a complaint in his report.

Adopted September 18, 1969

R-2. A participant may complain that another participant is not fulfilling obligations under the Fund Agreement that could lead to suspension under Article XXIX, Section 2, and the Managing Director shall transmit the complaint to the Executive Board with his comments. Any complaint shall be made in writing or by any rapid means of communication, and it shall be accompanied by a statement of the facts on which the participant bases its complaint.

Adopted September 18, 1969

R-3. The Managing Director shall immediately inform a participant of any complaint against it and the statement of the facts on which the complaint is based.

Adopted September 18, 1969

R-4. If the complaint is that the participant has failed to fulfill its obligations under Article XXV, Section 4, the participant shall not use special drawing rights and this limitation shall continue pending the disposition of the complaint.

Adopted September 18, 1969

R-5. A participant against which a complaint has been made under Rule R-1 or Rule R-2, the Managing Director, or an Executive Director may request the Executive Board to dismiss the complaint. The Executive Board shall consider the request forthwith.

Adopted September 18, 1969

R-6. If the right of a participant to use special drawing rights has been limited under Rule R-4, and a request under Rule R-5 has been made by a participant, the complaint shall be deemed to have been dismissed at the end of ten business days after the request, or at the end of such longer period as the participant states in the request, unless within this time the Executive Board has taken a decision disposing of the complaint.

Adopted September 18, 1969

R-7. If the right of a participant to use its special drawing rights under Article XXIX, Section 2, has been suspended, the participant may request the Executive Board to terminate the suspension. If the Executive Board decides not to terminate the suspension, a written report shall be made to the participant stating the circumstances under which the suspension would be terminated.

Adopted September 18, 1969

R-8. All procedures under Rules R-1 through R-7 shall be conducted as expeditiously as possible, and shall allow the participant and adequate opportunity to state its case both orally and in writing.

Adopted September 18, 1969

SUPPLEMENT

To Twenty-Ninth Issue
November 30, 1970

RULES AND REGULATIONS

I-2. The service charge payable by a member buying, in exchange for its own currency, the currency of another member or special drawing rights shall be 1/2 of 1 per cent, except that no service charge shall be payable in respect of any purchase to the extent that it is a gold tranche purchase. The service charge shall be paid at the time the transaction is consummated. The service charge shall be reviewed in connection with any review of charges under Rule I-4.

Adopted September 25, 1946, amended November 19, 1951, November 14, 1952, June 26, 1953, October 14, 1953, December 23, 1953, December 15, 1954, December 27, 1955, May 23, 1956, December 21, 1956, December 9, 1957, December 12, 1958, March 20, 1959, April 20, 1959, April 19, 1960, April 17, 1961, April 25, 1962, April 24, 1963, April 13, 1964, April 28, 1965, April 22, 1966, September 18, 1969, and September 10, 1971.

I-6. (a) Each member shall furnish the data necessary for the calculation of its monetary reserves and its repurchase obligation, if any, within two months after the end of each financial year of the Fund, subject to (h) below. All data shall be supplied to the Fund in the monetary reserve report forms sent to members by the Fund.

(h) Notwithstanding (a) above, a member which is unable to report within two months after the end of a financial year of the Fund the necessary data with respect to holdings of its other official institutions and the other banks within its territories and the amounts of currency due to official institutions and banks in the territories of members or nonmembers specified by the Fund shall furnish these data not later than six months after the end of the financial year of the Fund. On the basis of these data and Article XIX *(c)* the Fund may decide to recalculate the member's monetary reserves and repurchase obligation calculated in accordance with (b) above. Paragraphs (c) through (g) above shall apply to the recalculated repurchase obligation.

Rule I-6 adopted September 25, 1946, amended July 28, 1950, May 20, 1970, and April 21, 1971.

9. INTERNATIONAL CIVIL AVIATION ORGANIZATION

a. CONVENTION ON INTERNATIONAL CIVIL AVIATION, SIGNED AT CHICAGO, DECEMBER 7, 1944, AMENDED BY THE ICAO ASSEMBLY APRIL 1, 1969[1]

FOREWORD

1.   This document contains, except for the six Articles mentioned in paragraph 2 *(a)* and *(b)* below:

— the text of the Convention on International Civil Aviation in the English language, as signed at Chicago on 7 December 1944, and

— the text of the said Convention in the French and Spanish languages annexed to the Protocol on the Authentic Trilingual Text of the Convention on International Civil Aviation (Chicago, 1944) which was signed at Buenos Aires on 24 September 1968 and which came into force, as among the States which had signed it without reservation as to acceptance, on 24 October 1968 (the Protocol being hereinafter referred to as the "Buenos Aires Protocol").

In addition, this document contains the text of the above-mentioned Buenos Aires Protocol.

Note. — Under Article I of the Buenos Aires Protocol the text of the Convention in the French and Spanish languages annexed to the Protocol, together with the text of the Convention in the English language, constitutes the text equally authentic in the three languages as specifically referred to in the last paragraph of the Convention.

2.   In the body of the above-mentioned texts of the Convention, in English, French and Spanish, as presented in this document, are incorporated all the amendments' made to the Convention which are in force at this date, 1 April 1969, namely in respect of the Articles specified in *(a)* and *(b)* below:

(a) Articles 45, 48 *(a)*, 49 *(e)*, 50 *(a)* and 61 of the Convention were partly amended by the Assembly at its Eighth and Thirteenth Sessions and the wording of the amended parts of these Articles is of equal authenticity in English, French and Spanish. In this document, the English text of these Articles is the text signed at Chicago, as so amended; and the French and Spanish texts of these Articles are the texts thereof as annexed to the Buenos Aires Protocol but after including therein the amendments in question. Attention is invited to the footnotes to these Articles.

(b) Article 93 *bis* was adopted by the Assembly at its First Session in English, French and Spanish, each text being of equal authenticity. The Article is incorporated in this document.

3.   The Assembly, at its Fourteenth Session, adopted another amendment to Article 48 *(a)* of the Convention but that amendment is not incorporated in the text of Article 48 *(a)* presented in this document because the amendment has not yet entered into force.

4.   Following the signature of the Buenos Aires Protocol, the Assembly, at its Sixteenth Session, adopted Resolution A16-16 with a view to bringing into use as soon as possible the text of the Convention in the French and Spanish languages annexed to that Protocol. That Resolution reads as follows:

---

[1] As published by the International Civil Aviation Organization in Doc. 7300/4.

RESOLUTION A16-16

French and Spanish Texts of the Convention

WHEREAS Resolution A3-2 invited the Council to take action with a view to providing the Organization with texts in French and Spanish of the Convention on International Civil Aviation, such texts to be used only for internal purposes of the Organization;

WHEREAS the Council, pursuant to that Resolution, and for the said purposes, adopted the French and Spanish texts of the Convention which are found in Doc 7300/3;

WHEREAS the International Conference on the Authentic Trilingual Text of the Convention on International Civil Aviation (Chicago, 1944) adopted, on 20 September 1968, at Buenos Aires, and opened for signature, on 24 September 1968, a Protocol (hereinafter referred to as the "Buenos Aires Protocol)" to which is annexed a text of the said Convention in the French and Spanish languages; and

WHEREAS it is desirable that the text of the Convention in the French and Spanish languages attached to the Buenos Aires Protocol come into use as soon as possible;

THE ASSEMBLY:

(1) URGES all Contracting States to accept the Buenos Aires Protocol as soon as possible;

(2) RESOLVES that the text of the Convention in the French and Spanish languages attached to the Buenos Aires Protocol be used henceforth by the Organization;

(3) RECOMMENDS to Contracting States that, for reference purposes in their relations with the Organization or with other Contracting States, they use, in their communications in the French or Spanish language, only the text of the Convention in those languages which is attached to the Buenos Aires Protocol; and

(4) RESCINDS Resolution A3-2.

TABLE OF CONTENTS

CONVENTION[1]

ON INTERNATIONAL CIVIL AVIATION

Signed at Chicago, on 7 December 1944

PREAMBLE

WHEREAS the future development of international civil aviation can greatly help to create and preserve friendship and understanding among the nations and peoples of the world, yet its abuse can become a threat to the general security; and

WHEREAS it is desirable to avoid friction and to promote that cooperation between nations and peoples upon which the peace of the world depends;

THEREFORE, the undersigned governments having agreed on certain principles and arrangements in order that international civil aviation may be developed in a safe and orderly manner and that international air transport services may be established on the basis of equality of opportunity and operated soundly and economically;

Have accordingly concluded this Convention to that end.

PART I

AIR NAVIGATION

CHAPTER I

GENERAL PRINCIPLES AND APPLICATION OF THE CONVENTION

Article 1

Sovereignty

The contracting States recognize that every State has complete and exclusive sovereignty over the airspace above its territory.

---

[1] Came into force on 4 April 1947, the thirtieth day after deposit with the Government of the United States of America of the twenty-sixth instrument of ratification thereof of notification of adherence thereto, in accordance with Article 91 *(b)*.

261

Article 2

Territory

For the purposes of this Convention the territory of a State shall be deemed to be the land areas and territorial waters adjacent thereto under the sovereignty, suzerainty, protection or mandate of such State.

Article 3

Civil and state aircraft

(a) This Convention shall be applicable only to civil aircraft, and shall not be applicable to state aircraft.

(b) Aircraft used in military, customs and police services shall be deemed to be state aircraft.

(c) No state aircraft of a contracting State shall fly over the territory of another State or land thereon without authorization by special agreement or otherwise, and in accordance with the terms thereof.

(d) The contracting States undertake, when issuing regulations for their state aircraft, that they will have due regard for the safety of navigation of civil aircraft.

Article 4

Misuse of civil aviation

Each contracting State agrees not to use civil aviation for any purpose inconsistent with the aims of this Convention.

CHAPTER II

FLIGHT OVER TERRITORY OF CONTRACTING STATES

Article 5

Right of non-scheduled flight

Each contracting State agrees that all aircraft of the other contracting States, being aircraft not engaged in scheduled international air services shall have the right, subject to the observance of the terms of this Convention, to make flights into or in transit non-stop across its territory and to make stops for non-traffic purposes without the necessity of obtaining prior permission, and subject to the right of the State flown over to require landing. Each contracting State nevertheless reserves the right, for reasons of safety of flight, to require aircraft desiring to proceed over regions which are inaccessible or without adequate air navigation facilities to follow prescribed routes, or to obtain special permission for such flights.

Such aircraft, if engaged in the carriage of passengers, cargo, or mail for remuneration or hire on other than scheduled international air services, shall also, subject to the provisions of Article 7, have the privilege of taking on or discharging passengers, cargo, or mail, subject to the right of any State where such embarkation or discharge takes place to impose such regulations, conditions or limitations as it may consider desirable.

Article 6

Scheduled air services

No scheduled international air service may be operated over or into the territory of a contracting State, except with the special permission or other authorization of that State, and in accordance with the terms of such permission or authorization.

Article 7

Cabotage

Each contracting State shall have the right to refuse permission to the aircraft of other contracting States to take on in its territory passengers, mail and cargo carried for remuneration or hire and destined for another point within its territory. Each contracting State undertakes not to enter into any arrangements which specifically grant any such privilege on an exclusive basis to any other State or an airline of any other State, and not to obtain any such exclusive privilege from any other State.

Article 8

Pilotless aircraft

No aircraft capable of being flown without a pilot shall be flown without a pilot over the territory of a contracting State without special authorization by that State and in accordance with the terms of such authorization. Each contracting State undertakes to insure that the flight of such aircraft without a pilot in regions open to civil aircraft shall be so controlled as to obviate danger to civil aircraft.

Article 9

Prohibited areas

(a) Each contracting State may, for reasons of military necessity or public safety, restrict or prohibit uniformly the aircraft of other States from flying over certain areas of its territory, provided that no distinction in this respect is made between the aircraft of the State whose territory is involved, engaged in international scheduled airline services, and the aircraft of the other contracting States likewise engaged. Such prohibited areas shall be of reasonable extent and location so as not to interfere unnecessarily with air navigation. Descriptions of such prohibited areas in the territory of a contracting State, as well as any subsequent alterations therein, shall be communicated as soon as possible to the other contracting States and to the International Civil Aviation Organization.

(b) Each contracting State reserves also the right, in exceptional circumstances or during a period of emergency, or in the interest of public safety, and with immediate effect, temporarily to restrict or prohibit flying over the whole or any part of its territory, on condition that such restriction or prohibition shall be applicable without distinction of nationality to aircraft of all other States.

(c) Each contracting State, under such regulations as it may prescribe, may require any aircraft entering the areas contemplated in subparagraphs *(a)* or *(b)* above to effect a landing as soon as practicable thereafter at some designated airport within its territory.

Article 10

Landing at customs airport

Except in a case where, under the terms of this Convention or a special authorization, aircraft are permitted to cross the territory of a contracting State without landing, every aircraft which enters the territory of a contracting State shall, if the regulations of that State so require, land at an airport designated by that State for the purpose of customs and other examination. On departure from the territory of a contracting State, such aircraft shall depart from a similarly designated customs airport. Particulars of all designated customs airports shall be published by the State and transmitted to the International Civil Aviation Organization established under Part II of this Convention for communication to all other contracting States.

Article 11

Applicability of air regulations

Subject to the provisions of this Convention, the laws and regulations of a contracting State relating to the admission to or departure from its territory of aircraft engaged in international air navigation, or to the operation and navigation of such aircraft while within its territory, shall be applied to the aircraft of all contracting States without distinction as to nationality, and shall be complied with by such aircraft upon entering or departing from or while within the territory of that State.

Article 12

Rules of the air

Each contracting State undertakes to adopt measures to insure that every aircraft flying over or maneuvering within its territory and that every aircraft carrying its nationality mark, wherever such aircraft may be, shall comply with the rules and regulations relating to the flight and maneuver of aircraft there in force. Each contracting State undertakes to keep its own regulations in these respects uniform, to the greatest possible extent, with those established from time to time under this Convention. Over the high seas, the rules in force shall be those established under this Convention. Each contracting State undertakes to insure the prosecution of all persons violating the regulations applicable.

Article 13

Entry and clearance regulations

The laws and regulations of a contracting State as to the admission to or departure from its territory of passengers, crew or cargo of aircraft, such as regulations relating to entry, clearance, immigration, passports, customs, and quarantime shall be complied with by or on behalf of such passengers, crew or cargo upon entrance into or departure from, or while within the territory of that State.

Article 14

Prevention of spread of disease

Each contracting State agrees to take effective measures to prevent the spread by means of air navigation of cholera, typhus (epidemic), smallpox, yellow fever, plague, and such other communicable diseases as the contracting States shall from time to time decide to designate, and to that end contracting States will keep in close consultation with the agencies concerned with international regulations relating to sanitary measures applicable to aircraft. Such consultation shall be without prejudice to the application of any existing international convention on this subject to which the contracting States may be parties.

Article 15

Airport and similar charges

Every airport in a contracting State which is open to public use by its national aircraft shall likewise, subject to the provisions of Article 68, be open under uniform conditions to the aircraft of all the other contracting States. The like uniform conditions shall apply to the use, by aircraft of every contracting State, of all air navigation facilities, including radio and meteorological services, which may be provided for public use for the safety and expedition of air navigation.

Any charges that may be imposed or permitted to be imposed by a contracting State for the use of such airports and air navigation facilities by the aircraft of any other contracting State shall not be higher,

(a) As to aircraft not engaged in scheduled international air services, than those that would be paid by its national aircraft of the same class engaged in similar operations, and

(b) As to aircraft engaged in scheduled international air services, than those that would be paid by its national aircraft engaged in similar international air services.

All such charges shall be published and communicated to the International Civil Aviation Organization: provided that, upon representation by an interested contracting State, the charges imposed for the use of airports and other facilities shall be subject to review by the Council, which shall report and make recommendations thereon for the consideration of the State or States concerned. No fees, dues or other charges shall be imposed by any contracting State in respect solely of the right of transit over or entry into or exit from its territory of any aircraft of a contracting State or persons or property thereon.

Article 16

Search of aircraft

The appropriate authorities of each of the contracting States shall have the right, without unreasonable delay, to search aircraft of the other contracting States on landing or departure, and to inspect the certificates and other documents prescribed by this Convention.

CHAPTER III

NATIONALITY OF AIRCRAFT

Article 17

Nationality of aircraft

Aircraft have the nationality of the State in which they are registered.

Article 18

Dual registration

An aircraft cannot be validly registered in more than one State, but its registration may be changed from one State to another.

Article 19

National laws governing registration

The registration or transfer of registration of aircraft in any contracting State shall be made in accordance with its laws and regulations.

Article 20

Display of marks

Every aircraft engaged in international air navigation shall bear its appropriate nationality and registration marks.

Article 21

Reports of registrations

Each contracting State undertakes to supply to any other contracting State or to the International Civil Aviation Organization, on demand, information concerning the registration and ownership of any particular aircraft registered in that State. In addition, each contracting State shall furnish reports to the International Civil Aviation Organization, under such regulations as the latter may prescribe, giving such pertinent data as can be made available concerning the ownership and control of aircraft registered in that State and habitually engaged in international air navigation. The data thus obtained by the International Civil Aviation Organization shall be made available by it on request to the other contracting States.

CHAPTER IV

MEASURES TO FACILITATE AIR NAVIGATION

Article 22

Facilitation of formalities

Each contracting State agrees to adopt all practicable measures, through the issuance of special regulations or otherwise, to facilitate and expedite navigation by aircraft between the territories of contracting States, and to prevent unnecessary delays to aircraft, crews, passengers and cargo, especially in the administration of the laws relating to immigration, quarantine, customs and clearance.

Article 23

Customs and immigration procedures

Each contracting State undertakes, so far as it may find practicable, to establish customs and immigration procedures affecting international air navigation in accordance with the practices which may be established or recommended from time to time, pursuant to this Convention. Nothing in this Convention shall be construed as preventing the establishment of customs-free airports.

Article 24

Customs duty

(a) Aircraft on a flight to, from, or across the territory of another contracting State shall be admitted temporarily free of duty, subject to the customs regulations of the State. Fuel, lubricating oils, spare parts, regular equipment and aircraft stores on board an aircraft of a contracting State, on arrival in the territory of another contracting State and retained on board on leaving the territory of that State shall be exempt from customs duty, inspection fees or similar national or local duties and charges. This exemption shall not apply to any quantities or articles unloaded, except in accordance with the customs regulations of the State, which may require that they shall be kept under customs supervision.

(b) Spare parts and equipment imported into the territory of a contracting State for incorporation in or use on an aircraft of another contracting State engaged in international air navigation shall be admitted free of customs duty, subject to compliance with the regulations of the State concerned, which may provide that the articles shall be kept under customs supervision and control.

Article 25

Aircraft in distress

Each contracting State undertakes to provide such measures of assistance to aircraft in distress in its territory as it may find practicable, and to permit, subject to control by its own authorities, the owners of the aircraft or authorities of the State in which the aircraft is registered to provide such measures of assistance as may be necessitated by the circumstances. Each contracting State, when undertaking search for missing aircraft will collaborate in coordinated measures which may be recommended from time to time pursuant to this Convention.

Article 26

Investigation of accidents

In the event of an accident to an aircraft of a contracting State occurring in the territory of another contracting State, and involving death or serious injury, or indicating serious technical defect in the aircraft or air navigation facilities, the State in which the accident occurs will institute an inquiry into the circumstances of the accident, in accordance, so far as its laws permit, with the procedure which may be recommended by the International Civil Aviation Organization. The State in which the aircraft is registered shall be given the opportunity to appoint observers to be present at the inquiry and the State holding the inquiry shall communicate the report and findings in the matter to that State.

Article 27

Exemption from seizure on patent claims

(a) While engaged in international air navigation, any authorized entry of aircraft of a contracting State into the territory of another contracting State or authorized transit across the territory of such State with or without landings shall not entail any seizure or detention of the aircraft or any claim against the owner or operator thereof or any other interference therewith by or on behalf of such State or any person therein, on the ground that the construction, mechanism, parts accessories or operation of the aircraft is an infringement of any patent, design, or model duly granted or registered in the State whose territory is entered by the aircraft, it being agreed that no deposit of security in connection with the foregoing exemption from seizure or detention of the aircraft shall in any case be required in the State entered by such aircraft.

(b) The provisions of paragraph *(a)* of this Article shall also be applicable to the storage of spare parts and spare equipment for the aircraft and the right to use and install the same in the repair of an aircraft of a contracting State in the territory of any other contracting State, provided that any patented part or equipment so stored shall not be sold or distributed internally in or exported commercially from the contracting State entered by the aircraft.

(c) The benefits of this Article shall apply only to such States, parties to this Convention, as either (1) are parties to the International Convention for the Protection of Industrial Property and to any amendments thereof; or (2) have enacted patent laws which recognize and give adequate protection to inventions made by the nationals of the other States parties to this Convention.

Article 28

Air navigation facilities and standard systems

Each contracting State undertakes, so far as it may find practicable, to:

(a) Provide, in its territory, airports, radio services, meteorological services and

other air navigation facilities to facilitate international air navigation, in accordance with the standards and practices recommended or established from time to time, pursuant to this Convention;

(b) Adopt and put into operation the appropriate standard systems of communications procedure, codes, markings, signals, lighting and other operational practices and rules which may be recommended or established from time to time, pursuant to this Convention;

(c) Collaborate in international measures to secure the publication of aeronautical maps and charts in accordance with standards which may be recommended or established from time to time, pursuant to this Convention.

CHAPTER V

CONDITIONS TO BE FULFILLED WITH RESPECT TO AIRCRAFT

Article 29

Documents carried in aircraft

Every aircraft of a contracting State, engaged international navigation, shall carry the following documents in conformity with the conditions prescribed in this Convention:

(a) Its certificate of registration;

(b) Its certificate or airworthiness;

(c) The appropriate licenses for each member of the crew;

(d) Its journey log book;

(e) If it is equipped with radio apparatus, the aircraft radio station license;

(f) If it carries passengers, a list of their names and places of embarkation and destination;

(g) If it carries cargo, a manifest and detailed declarations of the cargo.

Article 30

Aircraft radio equipment

(a) Aircraft of each contracting State may, in or over the territory of other contracting States, carry radio transmitting apparatus only if a license to install and operate such apparatus has been issued by the appropriate authorities of the State in which the aircraft is registered. The use of radio transmitting apparatus in the territory of the contracting State whose territory if flown over shall be in accordance with the regulations prescribed by that State.

(b) Radio transmitting apparatus may be used only by members of the flight crew who are provided with a special license for the purpose, issued by the appropriate authorities of the State in which the aircraft is registered.

Article 31

Certificates of airworthiness

Every aircraft engaged in international navigation shall be provided with a certificate of airworthiness issued or rendered valid by the State in which it is registered.

Article 32

Licenses of personnel

(a) The pilot of every aircraft and the other members of the operating crew of every aircraft engaged in international navigation shall be provided with certificates of com-

petency and licenses issued or rendered valid by the State in which the aircraft is registered.

(b) Each contracting State reserves the right to refuse to recognize, for the purpose of flight above its own territory, certificates of competency and licenses granted to any of its nationals by another contracting State.

Article 33

Recognition of certificates and licenses

Certificates of airworthiness and certificates of competency and licenses issued or rendered valid by the contracting State in which the aircraft is registered, shall be recognized as valid by the other contracting States, provided that the requirements under which such certificates or licenses were issued or rendered valid are equal to or above the minimum standards which may be established from time to time pursuant to this Convention.

Article 34

Journey log books

There shall be maintained in respect of every aircraft engaged in international navigation a journey log book in which shall be entered particulars of the aircraft, its crew and of each journey, in such form as may be prescribed from time to time pursuant to this Convention.

Article 35

Cargo restrictions

(a) No munitions of war or implements of war may be carried in or above the territory of a State in aircraft engaged in international navigation, except by permission of such State. Each State shall determine by regulations what constitutes munitions of war or implements of war for the purposes of this Article, giving due consideration, for the purposes of uniformity, to such recommendations as the International Civil Aviation Organization may from time to time make.

(b) Each contracting State reserves the right, for reasons of public order and safety, to regulate or prohibit the carriage in or above its territory of articles other than those enumerated in paragraph *(a)*: provided that no distinction is made in this respect between its national aircraft engaged in international navigation and the aircraft of the other States so engaged; and provided further that no restriction shall be imposed which may interfere with the carriage and use on aircraft of apparatus necessary for the operation or navigation of the aircraft or the safety of the personnel or passengers.

Article 36

Photographic apparatus

Each contracting State may prohibit or regulate the use of photographic apparatus in aircraft over its territory.

CHAPTER VI

INTERNATIONAL STANDARDS AND RECOMMENDED PRACTICES

Article 37

Adoption of international standards and procedures

Each contracting State undertakes to collaborate in securing the highest practicable degree of uniformity in regulations, standards, procedures, and organization in relation to aircraft, personnel, airways and auxiliary services in all matters in which such uniformity will facilitate and improve air navigation.

To this end the International Civil Aviation Organization shall adopt and amend from time to time, as may be necessary, international standards and recommended practices and procedures dealing with:

   (a) Communications systems and air navigation aids, including ground marking;
   (b) Characteristics of airports and landing areas;
   (c) Rules of the air and air traffic control practices;
   (d) Licensing of operating and mechanical personnel;
   (e) Airworthiness of aircraft;
   (f) Registration and identification of aircraft;
   (g) Collection and exchange of meteorological information;
   (h) Log books;
   (i) Aeronautical maps and charts;
   (j) Customs and immigration procedures;
   (k) Aircraft in distress and investigation of accidents;

and such other matters concerned with the safety, regularity, and efficiency of air navigation as may from time to time appear appropriate.

Article 38

Departures from international standards and procedures

Any State which finds it impracticable to comply in all respects with any such international standard or procedure, or to bring its own regulations or practices into full accord with any international standard or procedure after amendment of the latter, or which deems it necessary to adopt regulations or practices differing in any particular respect from those established by an international standard, shall give immediate notification to the International Civil Aviation Organization of the differences between its own practice and that established by the international standard. In the case of amendments to international standards, any State which does not make the appropriate amendments to its own regulations or practices shall give notice to the Council within sixty days of the adoption of the amendment to the international standard, or indicate the action which it proposes to take. In any such case, the Council shall make immediate notification to all other states of the difference which exists between one or more features of an international standard and the corresponding national practice of that State.

Article 39

Endorsement of certificates and licenses

   (a) Any aircraft or part thereof with respect to which there exists an international standard of airworthiness or performance, and which failed in any respect to satisfy that standard at the time of its certification, shall have endorsed on or attached to its airworthiness certificate a complete enumeration of the details in respect of which it so failed.

(b) Any person holding a license who does not satisfy in full the conditions laid down in the international standard relating to the class of license or certificate which he holds shall have endorsed on or attached to his license a complete enumeration of the particulars in which he does not satisfy such conditions.

Article 40

Validity of endorsed certificates and licenses

No aircraft or personnel having certificates or licenses so endorsed shall participate in international navigation, except with the permission of the State or States whose territory is entered. The registration or use of any such aircraft, or of any certificated aircraft part, in any State other than that in which it was originally certificated shall be at the discretion of the State into which the aircraft or part is imported.

Article 41

Recognition of existing standards of airworthiness

The provisions of this Chapter shall not apply to aircraft and aircraft equipment of types of which the prototype is submitted to the appropriate national authorities for certification prior to a date three years after the date of adoption of an international standard of airworthiness for such equipment.

Article 42

Recognition of existing standards of competency of personnel

The provisions of this Chapter shall not apply to personnel whose licenses are originally issued prior to a date one year after initial adoption of an international standard of qualification for such personnel; but they shall in any case apply to all personnel whose licenses remain valid five years after the date of adoption of such standard.

PART II

THE INTERNATIONAL CIVIL AVIATION ORGANIZATION

CHAPTER VII

THE ORGANIZATION

Article 43

Name and composition

An organization to be named the International Civil Aviation Organization is formed by the Convention. It is made up of an Assembly, a Council, and such other bodies as may be necessary.

Article 44

Objectives

The aims and objectives of the Organization are to develop the principles and techniques of international air navigation and to foster the planning and development of international air transport so as to:

(a) Insure the safe and orderly growth of international civil aviation throughout the world;

271

(b) Encourage the arts of aircraft design and operation for peaceful purposes;

(c) Encourage the development of airways, airports, and air navigation facilities for international civil aviation;

(d) Meet the needs of the peoples of the world for safe, regular, efficient and economical air transport;

(e) Prevent economic waste caused by unreasonable competition;

(f) Insure that the rights of contracting States are fully respected and that every contracting State has a fair opportunity to operate international airlines;

(g) Avoid discrimination between contracting States;

(h) Promote safety of flight in international air navigation;

(i) Promote generally the development of all aspects of international civil aeronautics.

Article 45*

Permanent seat

The permanent seat of the Organization shall be at such place as shall be determined at the final meeting of the Interim Assembly of the Provisional International Civil Aviation Organization set up by the Interim Agreement on International Civil Aviation signed at Chicago on December 7, 1944. The seat may be temporarily transferred elsewhere by decision of the Council, and otherwise than temporarily by decision of the Assembly, such decision to be taken by the number of votes specified by the Assembly. The number of votes so specified will not be less than three-fifths of the total number of contracting States.

Article 46

First meeting of Assembly

The first meeting of the Assembly shall be summoned by the Interim Council of the above-mentioned Provisional Organization as soon as the Convention has come into force, to meet at a time and place to be decided by the Interim Council.

Article 47

Legal capacity

The Organization shall enjoy in the territory of each contracting State such legal capacity as may be necessary for the performance of its functions. Full juridical personality shall be granted wherever compatible with the constitution and laws of the State concerned.

This is the text of the Article as amended by the Eighth Session of the Assembly on 14 June 1954; it entered into force on 16 May 1958. Under Article 94(a)* of the Convention, the amended text is in force in respect of those States which have ratified the amendment. In respect of the States which have not ratified the amendment, the original text is still in force and, therefore, that text is reproduced below:

"The permanent seat of the Organization shall be at such place as shall be determined at the final meeting of the Interim Assembly of the Provisional International Civil Aviation Organization set up by the Interim Agreement on International Civil Aviation signed at Chicago on December 7, 1944. The seat may be temporarily transferred elsewhere by decision of the Council."

CHAPTER VIII

THE ASSEMBLY

Article 48

Meetings of Assembly and voting

(a) The Assembly shall meet not less than once in three years and shall be convened by the Council at a suitable time and place. Extraordinary meetings of the Assembly may be held at any time upon the call of the Council or at the request of any ten contracting States addressed to the Secretary General.*

(b) All contracting States shall have an equal right to be represented at the meetings of the Assembly and each contracting State shall be entitled to one vote. Delegates representing contracting States may be assisted by technical advisers who may participate in the meetings but shall have no vote.

(c) A majority of the contracting States is required to constitute a quorum for the meetings of the Assembly. Unless otherwise provided in this Convention, decisions of the Assembly shall be taken by a majority of the votes cast.

Article 49

Powers and duties of Assembly

The powers and duties of the Assembly shall be to:

(a) Elect at each meeting its President and other officers;

(b) Elect the contracting States to be represented on the Council, in accordance with the provisions of Chapter IX;

(c) Examine and take appropriate action on the reports of the Council and decide on any matter referred to it by the Council;

(d) Determine its own rules of procedure and establish such subsidiary commissions as it may consider to be necessary or desirable;

(e) Vote annual budgets and determine the financial arrangements of the Organization, in accordance with the provisions of Chapter XII;*

(f) Review expenditures and approve the accounts of the Organization;

(g) Refer, at its discretion, to the Council, to subsidiary commissions, or to any other body any matter within its sphere of action;

(h) Delegate to the Council the powers and authority necessary or desirable for the discharge of the duties of the Organization and revoke or modify the delegations of authority at any time;

---

*This is the text of the Article as amended by the Eighth Session of the Assembly on 14 June 1954; it entered into force on 12 December 1956. Under Article 94 *(a)* of the Convention, the amended text is in force in respect of those States which have ratified the amendment. In respect of the States which have not ratified the amendment, the original text is still in force and, therefore, that text is reproduced below:

"*(a)* The Assembly shall meet annually and shall be convened by the Council at a suitable time and place. Extraordinary meetings of the Assembly may be held at any time upon the call of the Council or at the request of any ten contracting States addressed to the Secretary General."

---

*This is the text of the Article as amended by the Eighth Session of the Assembly on 14 June 1954; it entered into force on 12 December 1956. Under Article 94 *(a)* of the Convention, the amended text is in force in respect of those States which have ratified the amendment. In respect of the States which have not ratified the amendment, the original text is still force and, therefore, that text is reproduced below:

"*(e)* Vote an annual budget and determine the financial arrangements of the Organization, in accordance with the provisions of Chapter XII;",

(i) Carry out the appropriate provisions of Chapter XIII;

(j) Consider proposals for the modification or amendment of the provisions of this Convention and, if it approves of the proposals, recommend them to the contracting States in accordance with the provisions of Chapter XXI;

(k) Deal with any matter within the sphere of action of the Organization not specifically assigned to the Council.

CHAPTER IX

THE COUNCIL

Article 50

Composition and election of Council

(a) The Council shall be a permanent body responsible to the Assembly. It shall be composed of twenty-seven contracting States elected by the Assembly. An election shall be held at the first meeting of the Assembly and thereafter every three years, and the members of the Council so elected shall hold office until the next following election.*

(b) In electing the members of the Council, the Assembly shall give adequate representation to (1) the States of chief importance in air transport; (2) the States not otherwise included which make the largest contribution to the provision of facilities for international civil air navigation; and (3) the States not otherwise included whose designation will insure that all the major geographic areas of the world are represented on the Council. Any vacancy on the Council shall be filled by the Assembly as soon as possible; any contracting State so elected to the Council shall hold office for the unexpired portion of its predecessor's term of office.

(c) No representative of a contracting State on the Council shall be actively associated with the operation of an international air service or financially interested in such a service.

Article 51

President of Council

The Council shall elect its President for a term of three years. He may be reelected. He shall have no vote. The Council shall elect from among its members one or more Vice-Presidents who shall retain their right to vote when serving as acting President. The President need not be selected from among the representatives of the members of the Council but, if a representative is elected, his seat shall be deemed vacant and it shall be filled by the State which he represented. The duties of the President shall be to:

(a) Convene meetings of the Council, the Air Transport Committee, and the Air Navigation Commission;

(b) Serve as representative of the Council; and

(c) Carry out on behalf of the Council the functions which the Council assigns to him.

*This is the text of the Article as amended by the Thirteenth (Extraordinary) Session of the Assembly on 19 June 1961; it entered into force on 17 July 1962. Under Article 94 *(a)* of the Convention, the amended text is in force in respect of those States which have ratified the amendment. In respect of the States which have not ratified the amendment, the original text is still in force and, therefore, that text is reproduced below:

"*(a)* The Council shall be a permanent body responsible to the Assembly. It shall be composed of twenty-one contracting States elected by the Assembly. An election shall be held at the first meeting of the Assembly and thereafter every three years, and the members of the Council so elected shall hold office until the next following election."

Article 52

Voting in Council

Decisions by the Council shall require approval by a majority of its members. The Council may delegate authority with respect to any particular matter to a committee of its members. Decisions of any committee of the Council may be appealed to the Council by any interested contracting State.

Article 53

Participation without a vote

Any contracting State may participate, without a vote, in the consideration by the Council and by its committees and commissions of any question which especially affects its interests. No member of the Council shall vote in the consideration by the Council of a dispute to which it is a party.

Article 54

Mandatory functions of Council

The Council shall:

(a) Submit annual reports to the Assembly;

(b) Carry out the directions of the Assembly and discharge the duties and obligations which are laid on it by this Convention;

(c) Determine its organization and rules of procedure;

(d) Appoint and define the duties of an Air Transport Committee, which shall be chosen from among the representatives of the members of the Council, and which shall be responsible to it;

(e) Establish an Air Navigation Commission, in accordance with the provisions of Chapter X;

(f) Administer the finances of the Organization in accordance with the provisions of Chapters XII and XV;

(g) Determine the emoluments of the President of the Council;

(h) Appoint a chief executive officer who shall be called the Secretary General, and make provision for the appointment of such other personnel as may be necessary, in accordance with the provisions of Chapter XI;

(i) Request, collect, examine and publish information relating to the advancement of air navigation and the operation of international air services, including information about the costs of operation and particulars of subsidies paid to airlines from public funds;

(j) Report to contracting States any infraction of this Convention, as well as any failure to carry out recommendations or determinations of the Council;

(k) Report to the Assembly any infraction of this Convention where a contracting State has failed to take appropraite action within a reasonable time after notice of the infraction;

(l) Adopt, in accordance with the provisions of Chapter VI of this Convention, international standards and recommended practices; for convenience, designate them as Annexes to this Convention; and notify all contracting States of the action taken;

(m) Consider recommendations of the Air Navigation Commission for amendment of the annexes and take action in accordance with the provisions of Chapter XX;

(n) Consider any matter relating to the Convention which any contracting State refers to it.

Article 55

Permissive functions of Council

The Council may:

(a) Where appropriate and as experience may show to be desirable, create subordinate air transport commissions on a regional or other basis and define groups of states or airlines with or through which it may deal to facilitate the carrying out of the aims of this Convention;

(b) Delegate to the Air Navigation Commission duties additional to those set forth in the Convention and revoke or modify such delegations of authority at any time;

(c) Conduct research into all aspects of air transport and air navigation which are of international importance, communicate the results of its research to the contracting States, and facilitate the exchange of information between contracting States on air transport and navigation matters;

(d) Study any matters affecting the organization and operation of international air transport, including the international ownership and operation of international air services on trunk routes, and submit to the Assembly plans in relation thereto;

(e) Investigate, at the request of any contracting State, any situation which may appear to present avoidable obstacles to the development of international air navigation; and, after such investigation, issue such reports as may appear to it desirable.

CHAPTER X

THE AIR NAVIGATION COMMISSION

Article 56

Nomination and appointment of Commission

The Air Navigation Commission shall be composed of twelve members appointed by the Council from among persons nominated by contracting States. These persons shall have suitable qualifications and experience in the science and practice of aeronautics. The Council shall request all contracting States to submit nominations. The President of the Air Navigation Commission shall be appointed by the Council.

Article 57

Duties of Commission

The Air Navigation Commission shall:

(a) Consider, and recommend to the Council for adoption, modifications of the Annexes to this Convention;

(b) Establish technical subcommissions on which any contracting State may be represented, if it so desires;

(c) Advice the Council concerning the collection and communication to the contracting States of all information which it considers necessary and useful for the advancement of air navigation.

CHAPTER XI

PERSONNEL

Article 58

Appointment of personnel

Subject to any rules laid down by the Assembly and to the provisions of this Convention, the Council shall determine the method of appointment and of termination of appointment, the training, and the salaries, allowances, and conditions of service of the Secretary General and other personnel of the Organization, and may employ or make use of the services of nationals of any contracting State.

Article 59

International character of personnel

The President of the Council, the Secretary General, and other personnel shall not seek or receive instructions in regard to the discharge of their responsibilities from any authority external to the Organization. Each contracting State undertakes fully to respect the international character of the responsibilities of the personnel and not to seek to influence any of its nationals in the discharge of their responsibilities.

Article 60

Immunities and privileges of personnel

Each contracting State undertakes, so far as possible under its constitutional procedure, to accord to the President of the Council, the Secretary General, and the other personnel of the Organization, the immunities and privileges which are accorded to corresponding personnel of other public international organizations. If a general international agreement on the immunities and privileges of international civil servants is arrived at, the immunities and privileges accorded to the President, the Secretary General, and the other personnel of the Organization shall be the immunities and privileges accorded under that general international agreement.

CHAPTER XII

FINANCE

Article 61*

Budget and apportionment of expenses

The Council shall submit to the Assembly annual budgets, annual statements of accounts and estimates of all receipts and expenditures. The Assembly shall vote budgets with whatever modification it sees fit to prescribe, and, with the exception of assessments under Chapter XV to States consenting thereto, shall apportion the expenses of the Organization among the contracting States on the basis which it shall from time to time determine.

*This is the text of the Article as amended by the Eighth Session of the Assembly on 14 June 1954; it entered into force on 12 December 1956. Under Article 94(a) of the Convention, the amended text is in force in respect of those States which have ratified the amendment. In respect of the States which have not ratified the amendment, the original text is still in force and, therefore, that text is reproduced below:

"The Council shall submit to the Assembly an annual budget, annual statements of accounts, and estimates of all receipts and expenditures. The Assembly shall vote the budget with whatever modification it sees fit to prescribe, and, with the exception of assessments under Chapter XV to States consenting thereto, shall apportion the expenses of the Organization among the contracting States on the basis which it shall from time to time determine."

Article 62

Suspension of voting power

The Assembly may suspend the voting power in the Assembly and in the Council of any contracting State that fails to discharge within a reasonable period its financial obligations to the Organization,

Article 63

Expenses of delegations and other representatives

Each contracting State shall bear the expenses of its own delegation to the Assembly and the remuneration, travel, and other expenses of any person whom it appoints to serve on the Council, and of its nominees or representatives on any subsidiary committees or commissions of the Organization.

CHAPTER XIII

OTHER INTERNATIONAL ARRANGEMENTS

Article 64

Security arrangements

The Organization may, with respect to air matters within its competence directly affecting world security, by vote of the Assembly enter into appropriate arrangements with any general organization set up by the nations of the world to preserve peace.

Article 65

Arrangements with other international bodies

The Council, on behalf of the Organization, may enter into agreements with other international bodies for the maintenance of common services and for common arrangements concerning personnel and, with the approval of the Assembly, may enter into such other arrangements as may facilitate the work of the Organization.

Article 66

Functions relating to other agreements

(a) The Organization shall also carry out the functions placed upon it by the International Air Services Transit Agreement and by the International Air Transport Agreement drawn up at Chicago on December 7, 1944, in accordance with the terms and conditions therein set forth.

(b) Members of the Assembly and the Council who have not accepted the International Air Services Transit Agreement of the International Air Transport Agreement drawn up at Chicago on December 7, 1944 shall not have the right to vote on any questions referred to the Assembly or Council under the provisions of the relevant Agreement.

PART III

INTERNATIONAL AIR TRANSPORT

CHAPTER XIV

INFORMATION AND REPORTS

Article 67

File reports with Council

Each contracting State undertakes that its international airliness shall, in accordance with requirements laid down by the Council, file with the Council traffic reports, cost statistics and financial statements showing among other things all receipts and the sources thereof.

CHAPTER XV

AIRPORTS AND OTHER AIR NAVIGATION FACILITIES

Article 68

Designation of routes and airports

Each contracting State may, subject to the provisions of this Convention, designate the route to be followed within its territory by any international air service and the airports which any such service may use.

Article 69

Improvement of air navigation facilities

If the Council is of the opinion that the airports or other air navigation facilities, including radio and meteorological services, of a contracting State are not reasonably adequate for the safe, regular, efficient, and economical operation of international air services, present or contemplated, the Council shall consult with the State directly concerned, and other States affected, with a view to finding means by which the situation may be remedied, and may make recommendations for that purpose. No contracting State shall be guilty on an infraction of this Convention if it fails to carry out these recommendations.

Article 70

Financing of air navigation facilities

A contracting State, in the circumstances arising under the provisions of Article 69, may conclude an arrangement with the Council for giving effect to such recommendations. The State may elect to bear all of the costs involved in any such arrangement. If the State does not so elect, the Council may agree, at the request of the State, to provide for all or a portion of the costs.

Article 71

Provision and maintenance of facilities by Council

If a contracting State so requests, the Council may agree to provide, man, maintain, and administer any or all of the airports and other air navigation facilities including radio and meteorological services, required in its territory for the safe, regular, efficient and economical operation of the international air services of the other contracting States, and may specify just and reasonable charges for the use of the facilities provided.

Article 72

Acquisition or use of land

Where land is needed for facilities financed in whole or in part by the Council at the request of a contracting State, that State shall either provide the land itself, retaining title if it wishes, or facilitate the use of the land by the Council on just and reasonable terms and in accordance with the laws of the State concerned.

Article 73

Expenditure and assessment of funds

Within the limit of the funds which may be made available to it by the Assembly under Chapter XII, the Council may make current expenditures for the purposes of this Chapter from the general funds of the Organization. The Council shall assess the capital funds required for the purposes of this Chapter is previously agreed proportions over a reasonable period of time to the contracting States consenting thereto whose airlines use the facilities. The Council may also assess to States that consent any working funds that are required.

Article 74

Technical assistance and utilization of revenues

When the Council, at the request of a contracting State, advances funds or provides airports or other facilities in whole or in part, the arrangement may provide, with the consent of that State, for technical assistance in the supervision and operation of the airports and other facilities, and for the payment, from the revenues derived from the operation of the airports and other facilities, of the operating expenses of the airports and the other facilities, and of interest and amortization charges.

Article 75

Taking over of facilities from Council

A contracting State may at any time discharge any obligation into which it has entered under Article 70, and take over airports and other facilities which the Council has provided in its territory pursuant to the provisions of Articles 71 and 72, by paying to the Council an amount which in the opinion of the Council is reasonable in the circumstances. If the State considers that the amount fixed by the Council is unreasonable it may appeal to the Assembly against the decision of the Council and the Assembly may confirm or amend the decision of the Council.

Article 76

Return of funds

Funds obtained by the Council through reimbursement under Article 75 and from receipts of interest and amortization payments under Article 74 shall, in the case of advances originally financed by States under Article 73, be returned to the States which were orginally assessed in the proportion of their assessments, as determined by the Council.

CHAPTER XVI

JOINT OPERATING ORGANIZATIONS AND POOLED SERVICES

Article 77

Joint operating organizations permitted

Nothing in this Convention shall prevent two or more contracting States from constituting joint air transport operating organizations or international operating agencies and from pooling their air services on any routes or in any regions, but such organizations or agencies and such pooled services shall be subject to all the provisions of this Convention, including those relating to the registration of agreements with the Council. The Council shall determine in what manner the provisions of this Convention relating to nationality of aircraft shall apply to aircraft operated by international operating agencies.

Article 78

Function of Council

The Council may suggest to contracting States concerned that they form joint organizations to operate air services on any routes or in any regions.

Article 79

Participation in operating organizations

A State may participate in joint operating organizations or in pooling arrangements, either through its government or through an airline company or companies designated by its government. The companies may, at the sole discretion of the State concerned, be state-owned or partly state-owned or privately owned.

PART IV

FINAL PROVISIONS

CHAPTER XVII

OTHER AERONAUTICAL AGREEMENTS AND ARRANGEMENTS

Article 80

Paris and Habana Conventions

Each contracting State undertakes, immediately upon the coming into force of this Convention, to give notice of denunciation of the Convention relating to the Regulation of Aerial Navigation signed at Paris on October 13, 1919 or the Convention on Commercial Aviation signed at Habana on February 20, 1928, if it is a party to either.

As between contracting States, this Convention supersedes the Conventions of Paris and Habana previously referred to.

Article 81

Registration of existing agreements

All aeronautical agreements which are in existence on the coming into force of this Convention, and which are between a contracting State and any other State or between an airline of a contracting State and any other State or the airline of any other State, shall be forthwith registered with the Council.

Article 82

Abrogation of inconsistent arrangements

The contracting States accept this Convention as abrogating all obligations and understandings between them which are inconsistent with its terms, and undertake not to enter into any such obligations and understandings. A contracting State which, before becoming a member of the Organization has undertaken any obligations toward a non-contracting State or a national of a contracting State or of a non-contracting State inconsistent with the terms of this Convention, shall take immediate steps to procure its release from the obligations. If an airline of any contracting State has entered into any such inconsistent obligations, the State of which it is a national shall use its best efforts to secure their termination forthwith and shall in any event cause them to be terminated as soon as such action can lawfully be taken after the coming into force of this Convention.

Article 83

Registration of new arrangements

Subject to the provisions of the preceding Article, any contracting State may make arrangements not inconsistent with the provisions of this Convention. Any such arrangement shall be forthwith registered with the Council, which shall make it public as soon as possible.

CHAPTER XVIII

DISPUTES AND DEFAULT

Article 84

Settlement of disputes

If any disagreement between two or more contracting States relating to the interpretation or application of this Convention and its Annexes cannot be settled by negotiation, it shall, on the application of any State concerned in the disagreement, be decided by the Council. No member of the Council shall vote in the consideration by the Council of any dispute to which it is a party. Any contracting State may, subject to Article 85, appeal from the decision of the Council to an *ad hoc* arbitral tribunal agreed upon with the other parties to the dispute or to the Permanent Court of International Justice. Any such appeal shall be notified to the Council within sixty days of receipt of notification of the decision of the Council.

Article 85

Arbitration procedure

If any contracting State party to a dispute in which the decision of the Council is under appeal has not accepted the Statute of the Permanent Court of International Justice and the contracting States parties to the dispute cannot agree on the choice of the arbitral tribunal, each of the contracting States parties to the dispute shall name a single arbitrator who shall name an umpire. If either contracting State party to the dispute fails to name an arbitrator within a period of three months from the date of the appeal, an arbitrator shall be named on behalf of that State by the President of the Council from a list of qualified and available persons maintained by the Council. If, within thirty days, the arbitrators cannot agree on an umpire, the President of the Council shall designate an umpire from the list previously referred to. The arbitrators and the umpire shall then jointly constitute an arbitral tribunal. Any arbitral tribunal established under this or the preceding Article shall settle its own procedure and give its decisions by majority vote, provided that the Council may determine procedural questions in the event of any delay which in the opinion of the Council is excessive.

Article 86

Appeals

Unless the Council decides otherwise any decision by the Council on whether an international airline is operating in conformity with the provisions of this Convention shall remain in effect unless reversed on appeal. On any other matter, decisions of the Council shall, if appealed from, be suspended until the appeal is decided. The decisions of the Permanent Court of International Justice and of an arbitral tribunal shall be final and binding.

Article 87

Penalty for non-conformity of airline

Each contracting State undertakes not to allow the operation of an airline of a contracting State through the airspace above its territory if the Council has decided that the airline concerned is not conforming to a final decision rendered in accordance with the previous Article.

Article 88

Penalty for non-conformity by State

The Assembly shall suspend the voting power in the Assembly and in the Council of any contracting State that is found in default under the provisions of this Chapter.

CHAPTER XIX

WAR

Article 89

War and emergency conditions

In case of war, the provisions of this Convention shall not affect the freedom of action of any of the contracting States affected, whether as belligerents or as neutrals.

The same principle shall apply in the case of any contracting State which declares a state of national emergency and notifies the fact to the Council.

CHAPTER XX

ANNEXES

Article 90

Adoption and amendment of Annexes

(a) The adoption by the Council of the Annexes described in Article 54, subparagraph (l), shall require the vote of two-thirds of the Council at a meeting called for that purpose and shall then be submitted by the Council to each contracting State. Any such Annex or any amendment of an Annex shall become effective within three months after its submission to the contracting States or at the end of such longer period of time as the Council may prescribe, unless in the meantime a majority of the contracting States register their disapproval with the Council.

(b) The Council shall immediately notify all contracting States of the coming into force of any Annex or amendment thereto.

CHAPTER XXI

RATIFICATIONS, ADHERENCES, AMENDMENTS, AND DENUNCIATIONS

Article 91

Ratification of Convention

(a) This Convention shall be subject to ratification by the signatory States. The instruments of ratification shall be deposited in the archives of the Government of the United States of America, which shall give notice of the date of the deposit to each of the signatory and adhering States.

(b) As soon as this Convention has been ratified or adhered to by twenty-six States it shall come into force between them on the thirtieth day after deposit of the twenty-sixth instrument. It shall come into force for each State ratifying thereafter on the thirtieth day after the deposit of its instrument of ratification.

(c) It shall be the duty of the Government of the United States of America to notify the government of each of the signatory and adhering States of the date on which this Convention comes into force.

Article 92

Adherence to Convention

(a) This Convention shall be open for adherence by members of the United Nations and States associated with them, and States which remained neutral during the present world conflict.

(b) Adherence shall be effected by a notification addressed to the Government of the United States of America and shall take effect as from the thirtieth day from the receipt of the notification by the Government of the United States of America, which shall notify all the contracting States.

Article 93

Admission of other States

States other than those provided for in Articles 91 and 92 *(a)* may, subject to approval by any general international organization set up by the nations of the world to preserve peace, be admitted to participation in this Convention by means of a four-fifths vote of the Assembly and on such conditions as the Assembly may prescribe: provided that in each case the assent of any State invaded or attacked during the present war by the State seeking admission shall be necessary.

Article 93 bis*

(a) Notwithstanding the provisions of Articles 91, 92 and 93 above:

(1) A State whose government the General Assembly of the United Nations has recommended be debarred from membership in international agencies established by or brought into relationship with the United Nations shall automatically cease to be a member of the International Civil Aviation Organization;

(2) A State which has been expelled from membership in the United Nations shall automatically cease to be a member of the International Civil Aviation Organization unless the General Assembly of the United Nations attaches to its act of expulsion a recommendation to the contrary.

(b) A State which ceases to be a member of the International Civil Aviation Organization as a result of the provisions of paragraph *(a)* above may, after approval by the General Assembly of the United Nations, be readmitted to the International Civil Aviation Organization upon application and upon approval by a majority of the Council.

(c) Members of the Organization which are suspended from the exercise of the rights and privileges of membership in the United Nations shall, upon the request of the latter, be suspended from the rights and privileges of membership in this Organization.

Article 94

Amendment of Convention

(a) Any proposed amendment to this Convention must be approved by a two-thirds vote of the Assembly and shall then come into force in respect of States which have ratified such amendment when ratified by the number of contracting States specified by the Assembly. The number so specified shall not be less than two-thirds of the total number of contracting States.

(b) If in its opinion the amendment is of such a nature as to justify this course, the Assembly in its resolution recommending adoption may provide that any State which has not ratified within a specified period after the amendment has come into force shall thereupon cease to be a member of the Organization and a party to the Convention.

Article 95

Denunciation of Convention

(a) Any contracting State may give notice of denunciation of this Convention three years after its coming into effect by notification addressed to the Government of the United States of America, which shall at once inform each of the contracting States.

(b) Denunciation shall take effect one year from the date of the receipt of the notification and shall operate only as regards the State effecting the denunciation.

*On 27 May 1947 the Assembly decided to amend the Chicago Convention by introducing Article 93 *bis*. Under Article 94 *(a)* of the Convention the amendment came into force on 20 March 1961 in respect of States which ratified it.

CHAPTER XXII

DEFINITIONS

Article 96

For the purpose of this Convention the expression:

(a) "Air service" means any scheduled air service performed by aircraft for the public transport of passengers, mail or cargo.

(b) "International air service" means an air service which passes through the air space over the territory of more than one State.

(c) "Airline" means any air transport enterprise offering or operating an international air service.

(d) "Stop for non-traffic purposes" means a landing for any purpose other than taking on or discharging passengers, cargo or mail.

SIGNATURE OF CONVENTION

IN WITNESS WHEREOF, the undersigned plenipotentiaries, having been duly authorized, sign this Convention on behalf of their respective governments on the dates appearing opposite their signatures.

DONE at Chicago the seventh day of December 1944, in the English language. A text drawn up in the English, French and Spanish languages, each of which shall be of equal authenticity, shall be open for signature at Washington, D.C. Both texts shall be deposited in the archives of the Government of the United States of America, and certified copies shall be transmitted by that Government to the governments of all the States which may sign or adhere to this Convention.

PROTOCOL[1]

ON THE AUTHENTIC TRILINGUAL TEXT OF THE CONVENTION
ON INTERNATIONAL CIVIL AVIATION

(CHICAGO, 1944)

Signed at Buenos Aires, on 24 September 1968

THE UNDERSIGNED GOVERNMENTS

CONSIDERING that the last paragraph of the Convention on International Civil Aviation, hereinafter called "the Convention," provides that a text of the Convention, drawn up in the English, French and Spanish languages, each of which shall be of equal authenticity, shall be open for signature;

CONSIDERING that the Convention was opened for signature, at Chicago, on the seventh day of December, 1944, in a text in the English language;

CONSIDERING, accordingly, that it is appropriate to make the necessary provision for the text to exist in three languages as contemplated in the Convention;

CONSIDERING that in making such provision, it should be taken into account that there exist amendments to the Convention in the English, French and Spanish languages, and that the text of the Convention in the French and Spanish languages should not incorporate those amendments because, in accordance with Article 94*(a)* of the Convention, each such amendment can come into force only in respect of any State which has ratified it;

HAVE AGREED as follows:

---

[1] Came into force on 24 October 1968.

Article I

The text of the Convention in the French and Spanish languages annexed to this Protocol, together with the text of the Convention in the English language, constitutes the text equally authentic in the three languages as specifically referred to in the last paragraph of the Convention.

Article II

If a State party to this Protocol has ratified or in the future ratifies any amendment made to the Convention in accordance with Article 94 *(a)* thereof, then the text of such amendment in the English, French and Spansih languages shall be deemed to refer to the text, equally authentic in the three languages, which results from this Protocol.

Article III

1) The States members of the International Civil Aviation Organization may become parties to this Protocol either by:

(a) signature without reservation as to acceptance, or

(b) signature with reservation as to acceptance followed by acceptance, or

(c) acceptance.

2) This Protocol shall remain open for signature at Buenos Aires until the twenty-seventh day of September 1968 and thereafter at Washington, D.C.

3) Acceptance shall be effected by the deposit of an instrument of acceptance with the Government of the United States of America.

4) Adherence to or ratification or approval of this Protocol shall be deemed to be acceptance thereof.

Article IV

1) This Protocol shall come into force on the thirtieth day after twelve States shall, in accordance with the provisions of Article III, have signed it without reservation as to acceptance or accepted it.

2) As regards any State which shall subsequently become a party to this Protocol, in accordance with Article III, the Protocol shall come into force on the date of its signature without reservation as to acceptance or of its acceptance.

Article V

Any future adherence of a State to the Convention shall be deemed to be acceptance of this Protocol.

Article VI

As soon as this Protocol comes into force, it shall be registered with the United Nations and with the International Civil Aviation Organization by the Government of the United States of America.

Article VII

1) This Protocol shall remain in force so long as the Convention is in force.

2) This Protocol shall cease to be in force for a State only when that State ceases to be a party to the Convention.

Article VIII

The Government of the United States of America shall give notice to all States members of the International Civil Aviation Organization and to the Organization itself:

(a) of any signature of this Protocol and the date thereof, with an indication whether the signature is with or without reservation as to acceptance;

(b) of the deposit of any instrument of acceptance and the date thereof;

(c) of the date on which this Protocol comes into force in accordance with the provisions of Article IV, paragraph 1.

Article IX

This Protocol, drawn up in the English, French and Spanish languages, each text being equally authentic, shall be deposited in the archives of the Government of the United States of America, which shall transmit duly certified copies thereof to the Government of the States members of the International Civil Aviation Organization.

IN WITNESS WHEREOF, the undersigned Plenipotentiaries, duly authorized, have signed this Protocol.

DONE at Buenos Aires this twenty-fourth day of September, one thousand nine hundred and sixty-eight.

10. UNIVERSAL POSTAL UNION

a. CONSTITUTION OF THE UNIVERSAL POSTAL UNION, SIGNED AT VIENNA, JULY 10, 1964[1]

TABLE OF CONTENTS

---

[1]The Universal Postal Union Constitution and the Final Protocol thereto, signed at Vienna on 10 July 1964, as published by the Universal Postal Union, documents of the 1969 Tokyo Congress, Vol. III.

FINAL PROTOCOL TO THE CONSTITUTION OF THE UNIVERSAL POSTAL UNION

1. Accession to the Constitution.

CONSTITUTION
OF THE UNIVERSAL POSTAL UNION

PREAMBLE

With a view to developing communications between peoples by the efficient operation of the postal services, and to contributing to the attainment of the noble aims of international collaboration in the cultural, social and economic fields.

the plenipotentiaries of the Governments of the Contracting Countries have, subject to ratification adopted this Constitution.

SECTION I

ORGANIC PROVISIONS

CHAPTER I

GENERAL

Article 1

Scope and objectives of the Union

1. The Countries adopting this Constitution comprise, under the title of the Universal Postal Union, a single postal territory for the reciprocal exchange of letter post items. Freedom of transit is guaranteed throughout the entire territory of the Union.

2. The aim of the Union is to secure the organisation and improvement of the postal services and to promote in this sphere the development of international collaboration.

3. The Union takes part, as far as possible, in postal technical assistance sought by its Member Countries.

Article 2

Members of the Union

Member Countries of the Union are:
(a) Countries which have membership status at the date on which this constitution comes into force.
(b) Countries admitted to membership in accordance with Article 11.

Article 3

Jurisdiction of the Union

The Union has within its jurisdiction:
(a) the territories of Member Countries;
(b) post offices set up by Member Countries in territories not included in the Union.
(c) territories which, without being members of the Union, are included in it because from the postal point of view they are dependent on Member Countries.

Article 4

Exceptional relations

Postal Administrations which provide a service with territories not included in the Union are bound to act as intermediaries for other Administrations. The provisions of the Convention and its Detailed Regulations are applicable to such exceptional relations.

Article 5

Seat of the Union

The seat of the Union and of its permanent organs shall be at Berne.

Article 6

Official language of the Union

The official language of the Union is French.

Article 7

Monetary standard

The franc adopted as the monetary unit in the Acts of the Union is the gold franc of 100 centimes weighing 10/31 of a gramme and of a fineness of 0.900.

Article 8

Restricted Unions. Special Agreements

1. Member countries, or their Postal Administrations if the legislation of those countries so permits, may establish Restricted Unions and make Special Agreements concerning the international postal service, provided always that they do not introduce provisions less favourable to the public than those provided for by the Acts to which the member countries concerned are parties.

2. Restricted Unions may send observers to Congresses, Conferences and meetings of the Union, to the Executive Council and to the Consultative Committee for Postal Studies.

3. The Union may send observers to Congresses, Conferences and meetings of Restricted Unions.

Article 9

Relations with the United Nations

The relations between the Union and the United Nations are governed by the Agreements whose texts are annexed to this Constitution.

Article 10

Relations with international organisations

In order to secure close co-operation in the international postal sphere, the Union may collaborate with international organisations having related interests and activities.

CHAPTER II

ACCESSION OR ADMISSION TO THE UNION
WITHDRAWAL FROM THE UNION

Article 11

Accession or admission to the Union. Procedure

1. Any member of the United Nations may accede to the Union.

2. Any sovereign Country which is not a member of the United Nations may apply for admission as a member country of the Union.

3. Accession or application for admission to the Union entails a formal declaration of accession to the Constitution and to the obligatory Acts of the Union. It shall be addressed through diplomatic channels to the Government of the Swiss Confederation and by that Government to member countries.

4. A country which is not a member of the United Nations will be deemed to be admitted as a member country if its application is approved by at least two thirds of the member countries of the Union. Member countries which have not replied within a period of four months are considered as having abstained.

5. Accession or admission to membership shall be notified by the Government of the Swiss Confederation to the Governments of member countries. It shall take effect from the date of such notification.

Article 12

Withdrawal from the Union. Procedure

1. Each member country may withdraw from the Union by notice of denunciation of the Constitution given through diplomatic channels to the Government of the Swiss Confederation and by that Government to the Governments of member countries.

2. Withdrawal from the Union becomes effective one year after the day on which the notice of denunciation provided for in paragraph 1 is received by the Government of the Swiss Confederation.

CHAPTER III

ORGANISATION OF THE UNION

Article 13

Organs of the Union

1. The organs of the Union are Congress, Administrative Conferences, the Executive Council, the Consultative Committee for Postal Studies, Special Committees and the International Bureau.

2. The permanent organs of the Union are the Executive Council, the Consultative Committee for Postal Studies and the International Bureau.

Article 14

Congress

1. Congress is the supreme organ of the Union.

2. Congress consists of the representatives of member countries.

Article 15

Extraordinary Congresses

An Extraordinary Congress may be convened at the request or with the consent of at least two thirds of the Member Countries of the Union.

Article 16

Administrative Conferences

Conferences entrusted with the examination of questions of an administrative nature may be convened at the request or with the consent of at least two thirds of the Postal Administrations of Member Countries.

Article 17

Executive Council

1. Between Congresses the Executive Council (EC) ensures the continuity of the work of the Union in accordance with the provisions of the Acts of the Union.

2. Members of the Executive Council carry out their functions in the name and in the interests of the Union.

Article 18

Consultative Committee for Postal Studies

The Consultative Committee for Postal Studies (CCPS) is entrusted with carrying out studies and giving opinions on technical, operational and economic questions concerning the postal service.

Article 19

Special Committees

Special Committees may be entrusted by a Congress or by an Administrative Conference with the study of one or more specific questions.

Article 20

International Bureau

A central office operating at the seat of the Union under the title of the International Bureau of the Universal Postal Union, directed by a Director General and placed under the general supervision of the Government of the Swiss Confederation, serves as an organ of liaison, information and consultation for Postal Administrations.

CHAPTER IV

FINANCES OF THE UNION

Article 21

Expenditure of the Union. Contributions of Member Countries

1. Each Congress shall fix the maximum amount which the ordinary expenditure of the Union may reach annually.

2. The maximum amount for ordinary expenditure referred to in paragraph 1 may be exceeded if circumstances so require, provided that the relevant provisions of the General Regulations are observed.

3. The extraordinary expenses of the Union are those occasioned by the convening of a Congress, an Administrative Conference or a Special Committee as well as special tasks entrusted to the international Bureau.

4. The ordinary expenses of the Union, including applicable the expenditure envisaged in paragraph 2, together with the extraordinary expenses of the Union, shall be borne in common by Member Countries, which shall be divided by Congress for this purpose into a specific number of contribution classes.

5. In the case of accession or admission to the Union under Article 11, the Government of the Swiss Confederation shall fix, by agreement with the Government of the Country concerned, the contribution class into which the latter Country is to be placed for the purpose of apportioning the expenses of the Union.

SECTION II

ACTS OF THE UNION

CHAPTER I

GENERAL

Article 22

Acts of the Union

1. The Constitution is the basic Act of the Union. It contains the organic rules of the Union.

2. The General Regulations embody those provisions which ensure the application of the Constitution and the working of the Union. They shall be binding on all Member Countries.

3. The Universal Postal Convention and its Detailed Regulations embody the rules applicable throughout the international postal service and the provisions concerning the letter post services. These Acts shall be binding on all Member Countries.

4. The Agreements of the Union, and their Detailed Regulations, regulate the services other than those of the letter post between those Member Countries which are parties to them. They shall be binding on those Countries only.

5. The Detailed Regulations, which contain the rules of application necessary for the implementation of the Convention and of the Agreements, shall be drawn up by the Postal Administrations of the Member Countries concerned.

6. The Final Protocols annexed to the Acts of the Union referred to in paragraphs 3, 4 and 5 contain the reservations to those Acts.

Article 23

Application of the Acts of the Union to Territories for whose international relations a Member Country is responsible.

1. Any Country may declare at any time that its acceptance of the Acts of the Union includes all the Territories for whose international relations it is responsible, or certain of them only.

2. The declaration provided for in paragraph 1 must be addressed to the Government:
   (a) of the Country where Congress is held, if made at the time of signature of the Act or Acts in question:
   (b) of the Swiss Confederation in all other cases.

3. Any Member Country may at any time address to the Government of the Swiss Confederation a notification of its intention to denounce the application of these Acts of the Union in respect of which it has made the declaration provided for in paragraph 1. Such notification shall take effect one year after the date of its receipt by the Government of the Swiss Confederation.

4. The declaration and notifications provided for in paragraphs 1 and 3 shall be communicated to Member Countries by the Government of the Country which has received them.

5. Paragraphs 1 to 4 shall not apply to Territories having the status of a member of the Union and for whose international relations a Member Country is responsible.

Article 24

National legislation

The provisions of the Acts of the Union do not derogate from the legislation of any Member Country in respect of anything which is not expressly provided for by those Acts.

CHAPTER II

ACCEPTANCE AND DENUNCIATION OF THE ACTS OF THE UNION

Article 25

Signature, ratification and other forms of approval of the Acts on the Union

1. Signature of the Acts of the Union by Plenipotentiaries shall take place at the end of Congress.

2. The Constitution shall be ratified as soon as possible by the signatory Countries.

3. Approval of the Acts of the Union other than the Constitution is governed by the constitutional regulations of each signatory Country.

4. When a Country does not ratify the Constitution or does not approve the other Acts which it has signed, the Constitution and other Acts shall be no less valid for the other Countries that have ratified or approved them.

Article 26

Notification of ratifications and other forms of approval of the Acts of the Union

The instruments of ratification of the Constitution and, where appropriate, of approval of the other Acts of the Union shall be addressed as soon as possible to the Government of the Swiss Confederation and by that Government to the Governments of Member Countries.

Article 27

Accession to the Agreements

1. Member Countries may, at any time, accede to one or more of the Agreements provided for in Article 22, paragraph 4.

2. Accession of Member Countries to the Agreements is notified in accordance with Article 11, paragraph 3.

Article 28

Denunciation of an Agreement

Each Member Country may cease being a party to one or more of the Agreements, under the conditions laid down in Article 12.

CHAPTER III

AMENDMENT OF THE ACTS OF THE UNION

Article 29

Presentation of proposals

1. The Postal Administration of a Member Country has the right to present, either to Congress or between Congresses, proposals concerning the Acts of the Union to which its Country is a party.

2. However, proposals concerning the Constitution and the General Regulations may be submitted only to Congress.

Article 30

Amendment of the Constitution

1. To be adopted, proposals submitted to congress and relating to this Constitution must be approved by at least two thirds of the Member Countries of the Union.

2. Amendments adopted by a Congress shall form the subject of an additional protocol and, unless that Congress decides otherwise, shall enter into force at the same time as the Acts renewed in the course of the same Congress. They shall be ratified as soon as possible by Member Countries and the instruments of such ratification shall be dealt with in accordance with the procedure laid down in Article 26.

Article 31

Amendment of the Convention, the General Regulations and
the Agreements

1. The Convention, the General Regulations and the Agreements define the conditions to be fulfilled for the approval of proposals which concern them.

2. The Acts referred to in paragraph 1 shall enter into force simultaneously and shall have the same duration. As from the day fixed by Congress for the entry into force of these Acts the corresponding Acts of the preceding Congress shall be abrogated.

CHAPTER IV

SETTLEMENT OF DISPUTES

Article 32

Arbitration

In the event of a dispute between two or more Postal Administrations of Member Countries concerning the interpretation of the Acts of the Union or the responsibility imposed on a Postal Administration by the application of those Acts, the question at issue shall be settled by arbitration.

SECTION III

FINAL PROVISIONS

Article 33

Coming into operation and Duration of the Constitution

This Constitution shall come into operation on 1st January, 1966 and shall remain in force for an indefinite period.

In witness whereof, the Plenipotentiaries of the Governments of the Contracting Countries have signed this Constitution in a single original which shall be deposited in the Archives of the Government of the Country in which the seat of the Union is situated. A copy thereof shall be delivered to each Party by the Government of the Country in which Congress is held.

Done at Vienna, the 10th of July, 1964.

b. FINAL PROTOCOL TO THE CONSTITUTION OF THE UNIVERSAL POSTAL UNION, SIGNED AT VIENNA, JULY 10, 1964

At the moment of proceeding to signature of the Constitution of the Universal Postal Union concluded this day, the undersigned Plenipotentiaries have agreed the following:

SOLE ARTICLE

Accession to the Constitution

Member Countries of the Union which have not signed the Constitution may accede to it at any time. Instruments of accession shall be addressed through diplomatic channels to the Government of the Country in which the seat of the Union is situated and by that Government to the Governments of the Member Countries of the Union.

In witness whereof, the undermentioned Plenipotentiaries have drawn up this Protocol, which shall have the same force and the same validity as if its provisions were inserted in the text of the Constitution itself, and they have signed it in a single original which shall be deposited in the Archives of the Government of the Country in which the seat of the Union is situated. A copy thereof shall be delivered to each Party by the Government of the Country in which Congress is held.

Done at Vienna, the 10th of July, 1964.

ADDITIONAL PROTOCOL
TO THE
CONSTITUTION OF THE UNIVERSAL POSTAL UNION

CONTENTS

Art.

ADDITIONAL PROTOCOL TO THE
CONSTITUTION OF THE UNIVERSAL POSTAL UNION

The Plenipotentiaries of the Governments of the Member Countries of the Universal Postal Union, met in Congress at Tokyo, in view of Article 30, § 2, of the Constitution of the Universal Postal Union concluded at Vienna on 10 July 1964 have adopted, subject to ratification, the following amendments to that Constitution.

299

Article I

(Article 8 amended)

Restricted Unions. Special Agreements

1. Member Countries or their postal administrations, if the legislation of those countries so permits, may establish Restricted Unions and make Special Agreements concerning the international postal service, provided always that they do not introduce provisions less favourable to the public than those provided for by the Acts to which the Member Countries concerned are parties.

2. Restricted Union may send observers to Congresses, Conferences and meetings of the Union, to the Executive Council and to the Consultative Council for Postal Studies.

3. The Union may send observers to Congresses, Conferences and meetings of restricted Unions.

Article II

(Article 11 amended)

Accession or admission to the Union. Procedure

1. Any member of the United Nations may accede to the Union.

2. Any sovereign country which is not a member of the United Nations may apply for admission as a member country of the Union.

3. Accession or application for admission to the Union shall entail a formal declaration of accession to the Constitution and to the compulsory Acts of the Union. It shall be addressed through diplomatic channels to the Government of the Swiss Confederation, which shall notify the accession or consult the member countries on the application for admission, as the case may be.

4. A country which is not a member of the United Nations shall be deemed to be admitted as a Member Country if its application is approved by at least two-thirds of the Member Countries of the Union. Member Countries which have not replied within a period of four months shall be considered to have abstained.

5. Accession or admission to membership shall be notified by the Government of the Swiss Confederation to the Governments of Member Countries. It shall take effect from the date of such notification.

Article III

(Article 13 amended)

The Union's bodies

1. The Union's bodies shall be Congress. Administrative Conferences, the Executive Council, the Consultative Council for Postal Studies, Special Committees and the International Bureau.

2. The Union's permanent bodies shall be the Executive Council, the Consultative Council for Postal Studies and the International Bureau.

Article IV

(Article 18 amended)

Consultative Council for Postal Studies

The Consultative Council for Postal Studies (CCPS) shall carry out studies and give opinions on technical, operational and economic questions concerning the postal service.

Article V

(Article 21 amended)

Expenditure of the Union. Contributions of Member Countries

1. Each Congress shall fix the maximum amount which:
(a) the expenditure of the Union may reach annually;
(b) the expenditure relating to the organization of the next Congress may reach.

2. The maximum amount for expenditure referred to in § 1 may be exceeded if circumstances so require, provided that the relevant provisions of the General Regulations are observed.

3. The expenses of the Union, including where applicable the expenditure envisaged in § 2, shall be jointly borne by the Member Countries of the Union. For this purpose, each Member Country shall be classed by Congress in one of the contribution classes, the number of which shall be determined by the General Regulations.

4. In the case of accession or admission to the Union under Article 11, the Government of the Swiss Confederation shall fix, by agreement with the Government of the country concerned, the contribution class into which the latter country is be placed for the purpose of apportioning the expenses of the Union.

Article VI

(Article 26 amended)

Notification of ratifications and other forms of approval of the Acts of the Union

The instruments of ratification of the Constitution and, where appropriate, of approval of the other Acts of the Union shall be deposited as soon as possible with the Government of the Swiss Confederation which shall notify the Member Countries of these deposits.

Article VII

Accession to the Additional Protocol and to the other Acts of the Union

1. Member Countries which have not signed the present Protocol may accede to it at any time.

2. Member Countries which are party to the Acts renewed by Congress but which have not signed them, shall accede thereto as soon as possible.

3. Instruments of accession relative to the cases set forth in § 1 and 2 shall be sent through diplomatic channels to the Government of the country in which the seat of the Union is situated, which shall notify the Member Countries of these deposits.

Article VIII

Entry into force of the Additional Protocol
to the Constitution of the Universal Postal Union

This Additional Protocol shall come into force on 1 July 1971, with the exception of Article V which shall come into force on 1 January 1971, and shall remain in force for an indefinite period.

In witness whereof the Plenipotentiaries of the Governments of the Member Countries have drawn up this Additional Protocol, which shall have the same force and the same validity as if its provisions were inserted in the text of the Constitution itself and they have signed it in a single original which shall be deposited in the Archives of the Government of the country in which the seat of the Union is situated. A copy thereof shall be delivered to each party by the Government of the country in which Congress is held.

Done at Tokyo, 14 November 1969.

c. UNIVERSAL POSTAL CONVENTION, DONE AT TOKYO, NOVEMBER 14, 1969

CONTENTS

CHAPTER II

REGISTERED ITEMS

CHAPTER III

LIABILITY

CHAPTER IV

ALLOCATION OF CHARGES. TRANSIT CHARGES

UNIVERSAL POSTAL CONVENTION

The undersigned, Plenipotentiaries of the Governments of the member countries of the Union, having regard to Article 22, § 3, of the Constitution of the Universal Postal Union concluded at Vienna on 10 July 1964, have by common consent and subject to Article 25, § 3, of the Constitution drawn up in this Convention the rules applicable in common throughout the international postal service and the provisions concerning the letter-post services.

PART I

RULES APPLICABLE IN COMMON THROUGHOUT THE INTERNATIONAL POSTAL SERVICE

CHAPTER I

GENERAL PROVISIONS

Article 1

Freedom of transit

1. Freedom of transit, the principle of which is set forth in Article 1 of the Constitution, shall carry with it the obligation for each postal administration to forward always by the quickest routes which it uses for its own items, closed mails and *a decouvert* letter-post items which are passed to it by another administration. This obligation shall also apply to air-mail correspondence, whether or not the intermediate postal administrations take part in reforwarding it.

2. Member countries which do not participate in the exchange of letters containing perishable biological substances or radioactive substances shall have the option of not admitting these items in transit *a decouvert* through their territory. The same shall apply to the items referred to in Article 29, § 5.

3. Member countries not providing the insured letters and boxes service or not accepting liability for insured items carried by their sea or air services may not, however, refuse transit of such items in closed mails through their territory or conveyance of them by their sea or air services; but those countries' liability shall be limited to that laid down for registered items.

4. Freedom of transit for postal parcels to be forwarded by land and sea routes shall be limited to the territory of the countries taking part in this service.

5. Freedom of transit for air parcels shall be guaranteed throughout the territory of the Union. Nevertheless, member countries which are not parties to the Postal Parcels Agreement shall not be required to forward air parcels by surface.

6. Member countries which are parties to the Postal Parcels Agreement but which do not provide an insured parcels service or which do not accept liability for insured items carried by their sea or air services, may not, however, refuse transit of such parcels in closed mails through their territory or conveyance of them by their sea or air services; but those countries' liability shall be limited to that laid down for uninsured parcels of the same weight.

Article 2

Failure to give freedom of transit

When a member country fails to observe the provisions of Article 1 of the Constitution and of Article of the Convention regarding freedom of transit, postal administrations of other member countries may discontinue their postal service with that country. They shall give prior notice of this step to the administrations concerned by telegram, and inform the international Bureau of the fact.

Article 3

Temporary suspension of services

When, owing exceptional circumstances, a postal administration is obliged to suspend temporarily its services wholly or in part, it shall announce the fact immediately, if need be by telegram, to the administration on administrations concerned.

Article 4

Ownership of postal items

A postal item shall remain the property of the sender until it is delivered to the rightful owner, except when the item has been seized in pursuance of the legislation of the country of destination.

Article 5

Charges

1. The charges for the various international postal services shall be laid down in the Convention and the Agreements.

2. No postal charge of any kind may be collected other than those provided for in the Convention and Agreements.

Article 6

Equivalents

In each member country, the charges shall be fixed on the basis of the closest possible equivalent of the value of the gold franc in the currency of that country.

Article 7

Postage stamps

Postage stamps for denoting payment of postage shall be issued by postal administrations only.

Article 8

Forms

1. Forms for the use of administrations in their relations with one another shall be drawn up in French with or without interlinear translation unless the administrations concerned arrange otherwise by direct agreement.

2. Forms for the use of the public shall bear an interlinear translation in French when they are not printed in that language.

3. The texts, colours and dimensions of the forms mentioned in 8 § 1 and 2 shall be prescribed in the Detailed Regulations of the Convention and of the Agreements.

Article 9

Postal identity cards

1. Each postal administration may issue to persons who apply for them postal identity cards valid as proof of identity for postal transactions effected in member countries which have not announced their refusal to recognize them.

2. The administration which issues a card shall be authorized to collect, on this account, a charge which may not exceed 2 francs.

3. Administrations shall be relieved of all liability when it is established that the delivery of a postal item or the payment of a monetary article was effected on presentation of a genuine card. Moreover, they shall not be liable for consequences arising from the loss, theft or fraudulent use of a genuine card.

4. A card shall be valid for a period of five years from the date of issue. Nevertheless, it shall cease to be valid when the appearance of the holder is altered to such an extent that it no longer corresponds to the photograph or to the description.

Article 10

Settlement of accounts

Settlements between postal administrations of international accounts arising from postal traffic may be regarded as current transactions and effected in accordance with the current international obligations of the member countries concerned, when there are agreements to this effect. In the absence of such agreements, accounts shall be settled in accordance with the provisions of the Detailed Regulations.

Article 11

Undertakings regarding penal measures

The Governments of member countries shall undertake to adopt, or to propose to the legislatures of their countries, the necessary measures:

(a) for punishing the counterfeiting of postage stamps, even if withdrawn from circulation, of international reply coupons and of postal identity cards;
(b) for punishing the use or uttering:
    (i) of counterfeit postage stamps (even if withdrawn from circulation) or used postage stamps, as well as of counterfeit or used impressions of franking machines or printing presses;
    (ii) of counterfeit international reply coupons;
    (iii) of counterfeit postal identity cards;
(c) for punishing the fraudulent use of genuine postal identity cards;
(d) for prohibiting and suppressing all fraudulent operations of manufacturing and uttering adhesive stamps and stamped impressions in use in the postal service, counterfeited or imitated in such a manner that they could be mistaken for the

adhesive stamps and stamped impressions issued by the postal administration of a member country;

(e) for preventing and, if necessary, for punishing the insertion in postal items of opium, morphine, cocaine or other narcotics as well as explosive or easily inflammable substances, where their insertion has not been expressly authorized by the Convention and the Agreements.

CHAPTER II

EXEMPTION FROM POSTAL CHARGES

Article 12

Exemption from postal charges

Cases of exemption from postal charges are expressly laid down by the Convention and the Agreements.

Article 13

Exemption from postal charges on letter-post items relating to the postal service

Subject to the provisions of Article 56, § 4, letter-post items relating to the postal service shall be exempted from all postal charges if sent by postal administrations or exchanged between the following:

(a) postal administrations and bodies of the Universal Postal Union;
(b) postal administrations and Restricted Unions;
(c) bodies of the Universal Postal Union and Restricted Unions;
(d) bodies of the Universal Postal Union;
(e) Restricted Unions;
(f) post offices of member countries;
(g) post offices and postal administrations.

Article 14

Exemption from postal charges of items which concern prisoners of war and civilian internees

1. Subject to the provisions of Article 56, § 2, letter-post items, insured letters and boxes, postal parcels and monetary articles addressed to or sent by prisoners of war, either direct or though the Information Bureaux and the Central Prisoner-of-War Information Agency provided for in Articles 122 and 123 respectively of the Geneva Convention of 12 August 1949 relative to the treatment of prisoners of war, shall be exempted from all charges. Belligerents apprehended and internal in a neutral country shall be classed with prisoners of war proper so far as the application of the foregoing provisions is concerned.

2. § 1 shall also apply to letter-post items, insured letters and boxes, postal parcels and monetary articles originating in other countries and addressed to or sent by civilian internees as defined by the Geneva Convention of 12 August 1949 relative to the protection of civilian persons in time of war, either direct or through the information Bureaux and the Central Information Agency prescribed in Articles 136 and 140 respectively of that Convention.

3. The national Information Bureaux and the Central Information Agencies mentioned above shall also enjoy exemption from postal charges in respect of letter-post items, insured letters and boxes, postal parcels and monetary articles which concern the persons referred to in § 1 and 2, which they send or receive, either direct or as intermediaries, under the conditions laid down in those paragraphs.

4. Parcels shall be admitted fee of postage up to a weight of 5 kg. The weight limit shall be increased to 10 kg in the case of parcels the contents of which cannot be split up and of parcels addressed to a camp or the prisoners' representatives there (*"hommes de confiance"*) for distribution to the prisoners.

Article 15

Exemption of literature for the blind from postal charges

Subject to the provisions of Article 56, § 2, literature for the blind shall be exempted from postage as well as the special charges for registration, advice or delivery, express, inquiry and cash-on-delivery.

PART II

PROVISIONS CONCERNING THE LETTER POST

CHAPTER I

GENERAL PROVISIONS

Article 16

Letter-post items

Letter-post items shall include letters, postcards, printed papers, literature for the blind and small packets.

Article 17

Charges and general conditions

1. The postage rates for the conveyance of letter-post items throughout the entire extent of the Union, and also the limits of weight and size, shall be fixed in accordance with the table below. Except in the cases provided for in Article 19, § 3, these charges shall cover delivery of the items to the place of address provided that there is a delivery service in the country of destination:

Category	Weight Step	Charge	Limits of Weight	Limits of Size
1	2	3	4	5
Letters	up to 20 g	30		Maxima: length, width and depth combined: 900 mm but the greatest dimension may not exceed 600 mm. In roll form: length plus twice the diameter, 1040 mm but the greatest dimension may not exceed 900 mm.
	Above 20 g up to 50 g ⎤ optional Above 50 g up to 100 g ⎦ weight steps	55 70		Minima: to have a surface measuring not less than 90 x 140 mm, with a tolerance of 2 mm. In roll form: length plus twice the diameter: 170 mm, but the greatest dimension may not be less than 100 mm.
	or		2 kg	
	Above 20 g up to 100 g Above 100 g up to 250 g Above 250 g up to 500 g Above 500 g up to 1000 g Above 1000 g up to 2000 g	70 160 300 500 800		Items of smaller dimensions than the minima set out above shall nevertheless be admitted if they bear a rectangular address label of card or strong paper, the dimensions of which are not less than 70 x 100 mm.
Postcards		20		Maxima: 105 x 148 mm, with a tolerance of 2 mm. Minima: as for letters.

(continued on next page)

Category	Weight Step	Charge	Limits of Weight	Limits of Size
1	2	3	4	5
Printed Papers	up to 20 g	15	2 kg	
	Above 20 g up to 50 g ⎤ optional	⎡ 20	(for books	
	Above 50 g up to 100 g ⎦ weight steps	⎣ 25	5 kg; this limit of weight may be raised to 10 kg after agreement between the admin-istrations concerned)	⎤
	or			
	Above 20 g up to 100 g	25		
	Above 100 g up to 250 g	40		├ As for letters
	Above 250 g up to 500 g	70		
	Above 500 g up to 1000 g	120		
	Above 1000 g up to 2000 g	200		
	Per additional step of 1000 g	100		
Literature for the blind	See Article 15		7 kg	
Small Packets	up to 100 g	30	1 kg	
	Above 100 g up to 250 g	60		
	Above 250 g up to 500 g	100		
	Above 500 g up to 1000 g	180		⎦

2. In connection with the provisions of § 1 and subject to Article 122 of the De-tailed Regulations of the Convention, rectangular items shall be considered standard-ized if their length is not less than their width multiplied by § 2 (approximate value: 1.4) and if they satisfy the following conditions:

(a)   for items in envelopes:
minimum dimensions: as provided in § 1;
maximum dimensions: 120 x 235 mm with a tolerance of 2 mm;
maximum weight: 20g;
maximum thickness: 5 mm;
in addition, the address shall be written on the envelope on the plain side which is not provided with the closing flap;

(b)   for items in card form:
dimensions and consistency of postcards:

(c)   for all items:
on the address side, a rectangular area 40 mm (–2 mm) in depth from the upper edge and 74 mm in width from the right-hand edge shall be reserved for affixing the postage stamp or stamps and the cancellation impression. Inside this area the postage stamps or franking impression shall be applied in the top right-hand corner.

The following items shall not be considered standardized:
items which do not comply with the above conditions, even if they are pro-vided with an address label meeting the requirements set out in § 1 column 5 of the table, third subparagraph; folded cards.

3. The administration of origin may apply to non-standardized letters and printed papers in envelopes of the first weight step and to letters in the form of cards which do not meet the conditions laid down in § 2 first paragraph and, (b), a charge which may not be higher than the charge relating to items of the second weight step.

4. The limits of weight and size laid down in § 1 shall no apply to letter-post items sent on postal service, as mentioned in Article 13. Printed papers for the same addressee at the same address, when enclosed in one or more special bags, shall cease to be subject to the limits of weight fixed in § 1 for this category of item.

5. The charge applicable to printed papers for the same addressee at the same ad-dress enclosed in a special bag shall be calculated by weight steps of 1 kilogramme up

to the total weight of the bag. Each administration may allow a reduction in the charge of up to 10% for pointed papers sent by special bags.

6. Perishable biological substances made up and packed in accordance with the provisions of the Detailed Regulations shall be subject to the tariff for letters and shall be forwarded by the quickest route, normally by air, subject to payment of the corresponding air surcharges. They may be exchanged only between officially recognized qualified laboratories. This exchange shall, moreover, be restricted to those member countries whose postal administrations have declared their willingness to admit such items, whether reciprocally or in one direction only.

7. Radioactive materials made up and packed in accordance with the provisions of the Detailed Regulations shall be subject to the tariff for letters and shall be forwarded by the quickest route, normally by air, subject to payment of the corresponding air surcharges. They may be posted only by duly authorized senders. This exchange shall, moreover, be restricted to those member countries whose postal administrations have declared their willingness to admit such items, whether reciprocally or in one direction only.

8. Each postal administration may allow a reduction of not more than 50% of the tariff for printed papers, for newspapers and periodicals published in its country, while reserving the right to restrict this reduction to newspapers and periodicals which fulfil the conditions required by internal regulations for transmission at the tariff for newspapers. This reduction shall not extend to commercial printed papers such as catalogues, prospectuses, price-lists etc., no matter how regularly they are issued; the same shall apply to advertisements printed on sheets annexed to newspapers and periodicals.

9. Administrations may likewise concede the same reduction for books and pamphlets, for musical scores and for maps, provided they contain no publicity matter or advertisement other than that appearing on the cover or the fly leaves.

10. Items other than registered letters in a closed envelope may not contain coin, bank notes, currency notes or securities of any kind payable to bearer, platinum, gold or silver, manufactured or not, precious stones, jewels and other valuable articles.

11. Administrations of countries of origin and of destination may deal, according to their legislation, with letters containing documents having the character of current and personal correspondence exchanged between persons other the sender and the addressee or persons living with them.

12. Apart from the exceptions provided for in the Detailed Regulations, printed papers, literature for the blind and small packets:
(a) shall be made up in such a manner that they may be easily examined;
(b) shall not bear any inscription or contain any document having the character of current and personal correspondence;
(c) shall not contain any postage stamp or form of prepayment, whether cancelled or not, or any paper representing a monetary value.

13. The combining in one item of articles on which different charges are payable shall be authorized. The charge applicable to the total weight of the item in this case shall be that of the category with the highest rate.

14. Apart from the exceptions provided for in the Convention and its Detailed Regulations, items not fulfilling the conditions laid down in this article and the Detailed Regulations shall not be forwarded. Items which have been wrongly admitted shall be returned to the administration of origin. Nevertheless, the administration of destination shall be authorized to deliver them to the addressees. In that event it shall collect on them, as necessary the charges prescribed for the category of the letter post to which they belong by reason of their contents, weight or size items of which the weight exceeds the maximum limits laid down in § 1 may be charged according to their actual weight.

Article 18

Special charges

The charges prescribed in the Convention which are collected in addition to the postage charges mentioned in Article 17 shall be known as "special charges" Their amount shall be fixed in accordance with the indications in the table below:

Description of Charge 1	Amount 2	Observations 3
(a) Additional charge for items handed over after the latest time of posting (Article 19, §1)	Charge collected at the rate laid down by internal legislation	
(b) *Poste restante* charge (Article 19, §2)	Same charge as in internal service	
(c) Charge for delivery to the addressee of a small packet exceeding 500 g. (Article 19, §3)	60 centimes at most	This charge may be increased by 30 centimes at most when the item is delivered to the place of address
(d) Storage charge (Article 20)	Charge collected at the rate laid down by internal legislation for printed papers and small packets exceeding 500 g.	
(e) Charge on unpaid or underpaid correspondence (Article 24, §1)	Charge fixed at double the amount of the deficient postage, multiplied by the ratio between the charge adopted for letters at the first weight step by the country of delivery and the same charge adopted by the country of origin.	Not less than 10 centimes. This charge shall be fixed at the single amount of the deficient postage in the cases provided for in Articles 37, §5 and §138, §3, §4 and §5, of the Detailed Regulations
(f) Express charge (Article 26, §2, §3 and §6)	Charge which may not be less than the amount of postage pre-payable on an unregistered single-rate letter and not more than 1.60 francs or the amount of the charge applied in the internal service of the country of origin if this is higher.	For each bag containing the items mentioned in Article 17, §4, second sentence, administrations shall collect, instead of the charge per item, a bulk charge not exceeding five times the charge per item. When express delivery involves special demands an additional charge may be levied in accordance with the provisions governing items of the same kind in the internal service. If the addressee asks for express delivery, the charge of the internal service may be collected.
(g) Charge for a request for withdrawal from the post or alteration of address (Article 27, §2)	2 francs at most	
(h) Charge for request for redirection (Article 28, §3)	Same charge as in internal service.	
(i) Customs clearance charge (Article 32)	1.50 francs at most	For each bag containing the items mentioned in Article 17, §4, second sentence, administrations shall collect, instead of the charge per item, a bulk charge not exceeding 3 francs.

(continued on next page)

Description of Charge 1	Amount 2	Observations 3
(j) Charge collected for delivery of an item free of charges and fees (Article 34, §1 and §3)	(i) Commission charge not exceeding 1 franc; (ii) Charge not exceeding 2 francs per request made after posting	
(k) Charge for inquiry or request for information (Article 36, §4)	90 centimes at most	
(l) Registration charge (Article 37, §2(b))	60 centimes at most	For each bag containing the items mentioned in Article 17, §4, second sentence, administrations shall collect, instead of the charge per item, a bulk charge not exceeding five times the amount of the charge per item.
(m) Charge for cover against risks due to "force majeure" (Article 37, §4)	40 centimes at most for each registered item.	
(n) Advice of delivery charge (Article 38, §1 and §2)	(i) At the time of posting 60 centimes at most; (ii) After posting 1.20 francs at most.	
(o) Charge for delivery of a registered item to the addressee in person (Article 39, §1)	20 centimes or the fee charged in the country of origin	

Article 19

Charge on items posted after the latest time of posting
Poste restante charge. Charge for delivery of small packets

1. Administrations shall be authorized to collect from the sender an additional charge, according to the provisions of their legislation, on items handed over for dispatch after the latest time of posting.

2. Administrations of countries of destination may collect on items addressed *poste restante* the special charge, if any, prescribed by their legislation for items of the same kind in their internal service.

3. Administrations of countries of destination shall be authorized to collect on each small packet exceeding the weight of 500 grammes delivered to the addressee, the special charge laid down in Article 18, (c).

Article 20

Storage charge

The administration of destination shall be authorized to collect, according to the provisions of its legislation, a storage charge for printed papers and small packets weighing more than 500 grammes of which the addressee has not taken delivery within the period during which they are held at his disposal free of charge.

Article 21

Payment of postage

1. As a general rule, items mentioned in Article 16, with the exception of those which are dealt with in Article 13 to 15 shall be fully prepaid by the sender.

2. Unpaid or underpaid items other than letters and postcards shall not be forwarded.

3. When unpaid or underpaid letters or postcards are posted in bulk, the administration of the country of origin may return them to the sender.

Article 22

Methods of denoting prepayment

1. Prepayment shall be denoted either by means of postage stamps, valid in the country of origin, printed on or affixed to the items, or by means of impressions of officially approved franking machines operating under the direct supervision of the postal administration, or by means of impressions made by a printing press or other printing or stamping procees when such a system is authorized by the regulations of the administration of origin.

2. Prepayment of printed papers for the same addressee at the address which are enclosed in a special bag shall be denoted by one of the methods referred to in § 1 and the total amount shown on the label outside the bag.

3. The following shall be considered as duly prepaid: items properly paid for their first transmission and on which the supplementary charge has been paid before their redirection, and also newspapers or packets of newspapers and periodicals which bear on the address side the indication *"Abonnement-poste"* or *"Abonnement direct"* and which are sent under the Subscription to Newspapers and Periodicals Agreement. The inscription *"Abonnement-poste"* or *"Abonnement direct"* shall be followed by the endorsement *"Tax percue" (T.P.)* or *"Port paye" (P.P.)*.

Article 23

Prepayment of letter-post items on board ship

1. Items posted on board ship at the two terminal points of the voyage or at any intermediate port of call shall be prepaid by means of postage stamps and according to the rates of the country in whose waters the ship is lying.

2. If the items are posted on board on the high seas, they may be prepaid, in the absence of special agreement between the administrations concerned, by means of the postage stamps and according to the rates of the country to which the ship appertains or is under contract.

Article 24

Charge on unpaid or underpaid correspondence

1. Apart from the exceptions laid down in Article 37, § 5, for registered items and in Article 138, § 3, 4 and 5, of the Detailed Regulations for certain classes of redirected items, unpaid or underpaid letters and postcards shall be liable to the special charge, payable by the addressee or, in the case of the undeliverable items by the sender, laid down in Article 18 (e).

2. The same treatment may be applied in similar circumstances to other letter-post items which have been incorrectly forwarded to the country of destination.

Article 25

International reply coupons

1. International reply coupons shall be placed on sale in member countries.

2. Their selling price shall be fixed by the administrations concerned, but it may not be less than 60 centimes.

3. Reply coupons shall be exchangeable in any member country for one or more postage stamps representing the postage prepayable on an unregistered letter of the first weight-step sent abroad by surface mail. If the regulations of the administration of the country of exchange permit, reply coupons shall also be exchangeable for postal stationery. When a sufficient number of reply coupons are presented, administrations shall be required to supply the postage stamps necessary for prepaying an unregistered letter weighing not more than 20 grammes for dispatch by air as a surcharged item.

4. The administration of a member country may, in addition, reserve the right to require the reply coupons and the items to be prepaid in exchange for those reply coupons to be presented at the same time.

Article 26

Express items

1. At the senders' request, letter post items shall be delivered at the place of address by special messenger immediately after arrival, in countries where the administration agrees to perform the service.

2. These items, styled "express," shall be subject, in addition to the ordinary postage, to the special charge laid down in Article 18 (f). This charge shall be fully paid in advance.

3. When express delivery involves special demands on the administration of destination as regards either the situation of the addressee's address or the day or time of arrival at the office of destination, the delivery of the item and the possible collection of an additional charge shall be governed by the provisions relating to items of the same kind in the internal service.

4. Express items on which the total amount of the charges payable in advance has not been completely paid shall be delivered as ordinary mail unless they have been treated as express by the office of origin. In the latter event a charge shall be collected on them in accordance with Article 24.

5. Administrations may confine themselves to making only one attempt at express delivery. It that attempt fails, the item may be treated as an ordinary item.

6. If the regulations of the administration of destination permit, addressees may ask the delivery office to deliver to them by express immediately on arrival any registered or other item arriving for them. In that case the administration of destination shall be authorized to collect, on delivery, the charge that applies in its internal service.

Article 27

Withdrawal from the post. Alteration or correction of address

1. The sender of a letter-post item may have it withdrawn from the post, or have address altered, so long as the item:

(a) has not been delivered to the addressee;

(b) has not been confiscated or destroyed by the competent authorities because of infringement of Article 29;

(c)   has not been seized by virtue of the legislation of the country of destination.

2. The request to be made to this effect shall be forwarded by post or by telegraph at the expense of the sender who shall pay, for each request, the special charge laid down in Article 18 (g). If the request to be forwarded by air or by telegraph the sender shall pay in addition the appropriate air surcharge or telegraph charge.

3. If its legislation permits, each administration shall be bound to accept requests for withdrawal from the post or alteration of the address in respect of any letter-post item posted in the service of other administrations.

4. If the sender wishes to be informed by air or by telegraph of the action taken by the office of destination on his request for withdrawal from the post or alteration of the address, he shall pay for this purpose the relative air surcharge or telegraph charge.

5. The charges or surcharges prescribed in § 2 shall be levied only once for each request for withdrawal from the post or alteration of address involving several items posted at the same time, at the same office, by the same sender to the same addressee.

6. A request for simple correction of address (without alteration of the name or status of the addressee) may be made direct to the office of destination by the sender, that is to say, without compliance with the formalities and without payment of the charges prescribed in § 2.

7. An item shall be returned to origin or redirected to the new destination by air following a request for withdrawal from the post or alteration of address when the sender undertakes to pay the corresponding air surcharge.

Article 28

Redirection. Undeliverable items

1. If an addressee changes his address, letter post items shall be reforwarded to him forthwith, under the conditions prescribed in the internal service, unless the sender has forbidden redirection by means of a note on the address side in a language known in the country of destination. Nevertheless, reforwarding from one country to another shall be effected only if the items satisfy the conditions for the further conveyance. In the case of redirection or return to origin by air, Articles 63, § 2 to 4 of the Convention and 178 of the Detailed Regulations shall be applied.

2. Each administration may lay down a redirection period in accordance with that in force in its internal service.

3. Administrations which collect a charge for requests for redirection in their internal services shall be authorized to collect this same charge in the international service.

4. Undeliverable items shall be returned forthwith to the country of origin.

5. The period of retention for items held at the disposal of the addressees *poste restante* shall be fixed by the regulations of the administration of destination. As a general rule, however, this period may not exceed one month, except in particular cases when the administration of destination considers it necessary to extend it to a maximum of two months. Return to the country of origin shall be effected within a shorter period if the sender has requested it by a note on the address side in a language known in the country of destination.

6. Postcards which do not bear the address of the sender shall not be returned. Moreover the return to origin of undeliverable printed papers shall not be compulsory, unless the sender has asked for their return by means of a note on the item in a language known in the country of destination. Books and registered printed papers shall always be returned.

7. Apart from the exceptions provided for in the Detailed Regulations, no additional charge may be collected for the redirection of letter post items from country to country or their return to the country of origin.

8. Letter-post items which are redirected or returned to origin as underliverable items shall be delivered to the addressees or senders on payment of the charges incurred on departure, on arrival, or in course of transmission due to redirection after the first transmission, without prejudice to the payment of customs duty or other special charges which the country of destination does not cancel.

9. In the event of redirection to another country or of non-delivery, the *poste restante* charge, the customs clearance charge, the storage charge, the commission charge, the additional express charge and the charge for delivery of small packets to the addressees shall be cancelled.

Article 29

Prohibitions

1. The insertion in letter-post items of the following articles shall be prohibited:
- (a) articles which, by their nature or their packing, may expose officials to danger, or soil or damage letter-post items or postal equipment. Metal fasteners used for closing items shall not have sharp edges, nor shall they hamper the performance of postal operations;
- (b) articles subject to customs duty (apart from the exceptions mentioned in Article 30);
- (c) opium, morphine, cocaine and other narcotics;
- (d) live animals, except:
  - (i) bees, leeches and silkworms;
  - (ii) parasites and destroyers of noxious insects intended for the control of those insects and exchanged between officially recognized institutions;
- (e) explosive, flammable or other dangerous substances; nevertheless, the perishable biological substances and radioactive substances mentioned in Article 17, § 6 and 7, shall not come within this prohibition;
- (f) obscene or immoral articles;
- (g) articles of which the importation and circulation is prohibited in the country of destination.

2. Items containing articles mentioned in § 1 which have been wrongly admitted to the post shall be dealt with according to the legislation of the country of the administration establishing their presence.

3. Nevertheless, items containing articles mentioned in § 1 (c), (e) and (f) shall in no circumstances be forwarded to their destination, delivered to the addressees or returned to origin. The administration of destination may deliver to the addressee the part of the contents which is not subject to a prohibition.

4. When items wrongly admitted to the post are neither returned to origin nor delivered to the addressee, the administration of origin shall be told exactly how they have been dealt with.

5. Moreover, the right of every member country shall be reserved to deny conveyance in transit *a decouvert* over its territory to letter-post items, other than letters and postcards, which do not satisfy the legal requirements governing the conditions of their publication or circulation in that country. Such items shall be returned to the administration of origin.

Article 30

Articles subject to customs duty

1. Printed papers and small packets subject to customs duty shall be admitted.

2. The same shall apply to letters containing articles subject to customs duty, where the country of destination has given its consent. Nevertheless, each postal administration may restrict to the registered letter service letters containing articles subject to customs duty.

3. Consignments of serums and vaccines and also of medicines urgently required and difficult to obtain shall be admitted in every case.

Article 31

Customs control

The postal administrations of the countries of origin and destination shall be authorized to submit to customs control, according to their legislation, the items mentioned in Article 30 and, if necessary, to open them officially.

Article 32

Customs clearance charge

Items submitted to customs control in the country of origin or of destination, as the case may be, may be subject either for submission to customs and customs clearance or for submission to customs only, as a postal charge, to the special charge laid down in in Article 18, (i).

Article 33

Customs duty and other fees

Postal administrations shall be authorized to collect from the senders or addressees of items, as the case may be, the customs duty and all other fees which may be due.

Article 34

Items for delivery free of charges and fees

1. In the service between those member countries whose postal administrations have notified their agreement to that effect senders may, by means of a previous declaration at the office of origin, undertake to pay the whole of the charges and fees to which the items are subject on delivery. So long as an item has not been delivered to the addressee, the sender may ask after posting, on payment of the special charge laid down in Article 18, (j), (ii), that the item be delivered free of charges and fees. It the request is to be forwarded by air or by telegraph, the sender shall pay in addition the appropriate air surcharge or telegraph charge.

2. In the cases prvided for in § 1, senders shall undertake to pay the amounts which may be claimed by the office of destination and, if necessary, pay a sufficient deposit.

3. The administration of destination shall be authorized to collect on each item the commission charge laid down in Article 18, (j), (i). This charge shall be independent of that prescribed in Article 32.

4. Every administration may restrict to registered items the service of delivery free of charges and fees.

Article 35

Cancellation of customs duty and other fees

Postal administrations shall undertake to seek from the appropriate services in their country cancellation of customs duty and other fees on items returned to origin, destroyed because of total damage to the contents or redirected to a third country.

Article 36

Inquiries and requests for information

1. Inquiries shall be entertained within a period of a year from the day after that on which the item was posted.

2. Inquiries initiated by an administration shall be in order and shall be dealt with, provided only that they reach the administration concerned within 15 months from the day after the date of posting of the items under inquiry. Each administration shall be bound to deal with requests for information as early as possible.

3. Each administration shall be bound to accept inquiries and requests for information relating to any item posted in the service of another administration.

4. Unless the sender has already paid the charge for an advice of delivery, the special charge laid down in Article 18 (k) may be collected on each inquiry or request for information. If a request is made for transmission by telegraph, the cost of the telegram and, where applicable, of the reply shall be collected in addition to the inquiry charge.

5. If the inquiry or request for information relates to several items posted at the same time at the same office by the same sender and addressed to the same addressee, only one charge shall be collected. However, in the case of registered items which had, at the sender's request, to be forwarded by different routes, a separate charge shall be collected for each of the routes used.

6. If the inquiry or request for information has been occasioned by a service error, the charge collected for it shall be refunded.

CHAPTER II

REGISTERED ITEMS

Article 37

Charges

1. The letter-post items specified in Article 16 may be sent as registered items.

2. The charge on registered items shall be paid in advance. It shall be made up of:
(a)   the ordinary postage, according to the category of item;
(b)   the fixed registration charge laid down in Article 18 (i)

3. A receipt shall be handed over free of charge to the sender of a registered item at the time of posting.

4. Postal administrations prepared to cover risks of *"force majeure"* shall be authorized to collect the special charge laid down in Article 18 (m).

5. Unpaid or underpaid registered items which have been incorrectly forwarded to the country of destination shall be liable to the charge, payable by the addressee or, in the case of undeliverable items, by the sender, laid down in Articles 18 (e) and 24, § 1, but calculated on the basis of the single amount of the deficient postage.

Article 38

Advice on delivery

1. The sender of a registered item may apply for an advice of delivery on payment at the time of posting of the fixed charge laid down in Article 18, (n), (i). This advice shall be sent to him by air if he pays, in addition to the fixed charge mentioned, an additional charge not exceeding the air surcharge corresponding to the weight of the form.

2. The advice of delivery may be applied for after the posting of an item, against payment of the fixed charge laid down in Article 18, (n), (ii), and under the conditions laid down in Article 36. Nevertheless, the corresponding air surcharge may be collected when the sender has asked for the request to be sent and the advice of delivery returned by air.

3. When the sender inquiries about an advice of delivery which he has not received within a normal period, neither a second advice or delivery charge nor the charge prescribed in Article 36 for inquiries and requests for information shall be collected.

Article 39

Delivery to the addressee in person

1. In the service between those administrations which have given their consent, registered items shall, at the sender's request, be delivered to the addressee in person. Administrations may agree to allow this option only for registered items accompanied by an advice of delivery. In both cases, the sender shall pay the special charge laid down in Article 18, (o).

2. Administrations shall make two attempts to deliver such items.

CHAPTER III

LIABILITY

Article 40

Principle and extent of liability of postal administrations

1. Postal administrations shall be liable only for the loss of registered items. Their liability shall be as binding for items conveyed *a decouvert* as for those forwarded in closed mails.

2. The sender shall be entitled on this account to an indemnity the amount of which shall be fixed at 40 francs per item; this amount may be raised to 200 francs for each special bag of printed papers such as is mentioned in Article 17, § 4, second sentence.

3. The sender may waive this right in favour of the addressee.

Article 41

Non-liability of postal administrations

1. Postal administrations shall cease to be liable for registered items which they have delivered according either to the conditions laid down in their regulations for items of the same kind or to those set out in Article 9, § 3.

2. They shall not be liable:

(i) for the loss of registered items:
    (a) in cases of *"force majeure."* The administration in whose service the loss occurred shall decide, according to the laws of its country, whether the loss is due to circumstances amounting to a case of *"force majeure."* these circumstances shall be communicated to the administration of the country of origin if the latter administration so requests. Nevertheless, the administration of the dispatching country shall still be liable if it has undertaken to cover risks of *"force majeure"* (Article 37, § 4);
    (b) when they cannot account for items owing to the destruction of official records by *"force majeure,"* provided that proof of their liability has not been otherwise produced;
    (c) in the case of items whose contents fall within the prohibitions specified in Articles 17, § 10 and 12 (c), and 20, § 1, in so far as these items have been confiscated or destroyed by the competent authority because of their contents;
    (d) when the sender has made no inquiry within the period of one year prescribed in Article 36;
(ii) for registered items seized under the legislation of the country of destination.
3. Postal administrations shall not be liable on account of customs declarations in whatever form these are made nor for decisions taken by the customs on examination of letter-post items submitted to customs control.

Article 42

Sender's liability

1. The sender of a letter-post item shall be liable, within the same limits as administrations themselves, for any damage caused to other postal items as a result of the dispatch of articles not acceptable for conveyance or by the non-observance of the conditions of acceptance, provided there has been no fault or negligence on the part of administrations or carriers.

2. The acceptance by the office of posting of such an item shall not relieve the sender of his liability.

3. Where appropriate, it shall be for the administration of origin to take action against the sender.

Article 43

Determination of liability between postal administrations

1. Until the contrary is provided, liability for the loss of a registered item shall rest with the postal administration which, having received it without comment and being furnished with all the prescribed means of inquiry, cannot prove either delivery to the addressee or, where appropriate, correct transfer to another administration.

2. Until the contrary is proved, and subject to § 3, an intermediate administration or administration of destination shall be relieved of all liability:
(a) when it has observed the provisions of Article 3 of the Convention and Articles 151, § 5 and 152, § 4 of the Detailed Regulations.
(b) when it can prove that it was not informed of the inquiry until after the destruction of the official records relating to the item in question, the period of retention prescribed in Article 108 of the Detailed Regulations having expired: this reservation shall not prejudice the rights of the applicant.
(c) when, in the case of individual entry of registered items, correct delivery of the lost item cannot be proved because the administration of origin did not observe Article 147, § 2, concerning the detailed entry of registered items on the C 12 letter bill or on the C 13 special lists.

3. If, however, the loss occurs in course of conveyance without it being possible to establish in which country's territory or service it happened, the administrations concerned shall bear the loss equally.

4. When a registered item has been lost due to *"force majeure,"* the administration in whose territory or service the loss occurred shall not be liable to the dispatching administration unless the two countries undertake to cover risks of *"force majeure."*

5. Customs duty and other fees of which it has not been possible to secure cancellation shall be borne by the administrations liable for the loss.

6. An administration which has paid the indemnity shall take over the rights, up to the amount of the indemnity, of the person who has received it in any action which may be taken against the addressee, the sender or third parties.

Article 44

Payment of indemnity

1. Subject to the right of recourse against the administration which is liable, the obligation to pay the indemnity shall rest either with the administration of origin or, in the case mentioned in Article 40, § 3, of the administration of destination.

2. This payment shall be made as soon as possible and, at the latest, within a period of six months from the day following the day of inquiry.

3. When the administration responsible for the payment does not undertake to cover risks of *"force majeure"* and when, at the end of the period prescribed in § 2, the question of whether the loss is due to such causes has not been decided, it may, exceptionally, postpone payment of the indemnity beyond that period.

4. The administration of origin or destination, as the case may be, shall be authorized to indemnify the rightful claimant on behalf of any of the other administrations sharing in the conveyance, which, although duly informed, has allowed five months to pass without settling the matter or without informing the administration of origin or destination, as the case may be, that the loss appeared to be due to *"force majeure."*

Article 45

Reimbursing the administration which paid the indemnity

1. The administration which is liable or on behalf of which payment is made in accordance with Article 44 shall be bound to reimburse the administration which paid the indemnity, and which is called the paying administration, the amount of indemnity actually paid to the rightful claimant: this payment shall be made within four months of dispatch of the notice of payment.

2. If the indemnity is due to be borne by several administrations in accordance with Article 43, the whole of the indemnity shall be paid to the paying administration, within the period mentioned in § 1, by the first administration which, having duly received the item claimed for, is unable to prove its correct transfer to the next service. It shall rest with this administration to recover from the other administrations which are liable, each one's share of the indemnity paid to the rightful claimant.

3. Reimbursement of the creditor administration shall be made in accordance with the rules for payment laid down in Article 10.

4. When liability has been admitted, as well as in the case provided for in Article 44, § 4, the amount of the indemnity may also be automatically recovered from the administration which is liable through any liquidation account, either direct or through the intermediary of an administration which regularly draws up liquidation accounts with the administration which is liable.

5. The paying administration may only claim reimbursement from the administration which is liable within a period of one year from the date of dispatch of notice that payment has been made to the rightful claimant.

6. The administration whose liability is duly established and which has at first declined to pay the indemnity shall assume all additional costs resulting from the unwarranted delay in payment.

7. Administrations may agree to settle periodically for the indemnities which they have paid to the rightful claimants and which they have accepted as justified.

Article 46

Possible recovery of the indemnity from the sender or the addressee

1. If, after payment of the indemnity, a registered item or part of such an item previously considered as lost is found, the addressee and the sender shall be informed of the fact; the latter or, where Article 40, § 3, applies, the addressee shall be further advised that he may take delivery of it within a period of three months on repayment of the amount of the indemnity received. If the sender or the addressee, as the case may be, does not claim the item within this period, the same approach shall be made to the addressee or the sender as the case may be.

2. If the sender or the addressee takes delivery of the item against repayment of the amount of the indemnity, that sum shall be refunded to the administration or, where appropriate, administrations which bore the loss.

3. If the sender and the addressee refuse to take delivery of the item, it shall become the property of the administration or, where appropriate, administrations which bore the loss.

4. When proof of delivery is supplied after the period of five months laid down in Article 44, § 4, the indemnity paid shall continue to be borne by the intermediate administration or administration of destination if the sum paid cannot, for any reason, be recovered from the sender.

CHAPTER IV

ALLOCATION OF CHARGES. TRANSIT CHARGES

Article 47

Allocation of charges

Except where otherwise provided by the Convention and the Agreement each postal administration shall retain the charges which it has collected.

Article 48

Transit charges

1. Subject to Article 50, closed mails exchanged between two administrations or between two offices of the same country by means of the services of one or more other administrations (third party services) shall be subject to the transit charges indicated in the table below, payable to each of the countries which are crossed or whose services take part in the conveyance. These charges shall be payable by the administration of the country of origin of the mail. Nevertheless, costs of conveyance between two offices of the country of destination shall be borne by that country.

Distances Traversed 1		Charge per kg gross 2
(i) Distances traversed by land expressed in kilometres		fr.
Up to 300 km		0.11
Above 300 up to 600		0.18
600 1000		0.26
1000 1500		0.35
1500 2000		0.45
2000 2500		0.55
2500 3000		0.64
3000 3800		0.77
3800 4600		0.91
4600 5500		1.06
5500 6500		1.23
6500 7500		1.40
7500 for each additional 1000		0.17
(ii) Distances traversed by sea		
(a) Expressed in nautical miles	(b) Expressed in kilometres after conversion on the basis of 1 nautical mile for 1.852 km.	
Up to 300 nautical miles	Up to 556 km	0.21
Above 300 up to 600	Above 556 up to 1111	0.28
600 1000	1111 1852	0.33
1000 1500	1852 2778	0.37
1500 2000	2778 3704	0.41
2000 2500	3704 4630	0.44
2500 3000	4630 5556	0.47
3000 3500	5556 6482	0.50
3500 4000	6482 7408	0.52
4000 5000	7408 9260	0.55
5000 6000	9260 11112	0.58
6000 7000	11112 12964	0.61
7000 8000	12964 14816	0.64
8000	14816	0.67

2. In the absence of special agreement direct sea conveyance between two countries by the ships of one of them shall be regarded as a third party service.

3. The distances used to determine the transit charges according to the table in § 1 shall be taken from the "List of kilometric distances relating to land sectors of mails in transit" provided for in Article 111, § 2 (c) of the Detailed Regulations, as regards distances traversed by land, and from the "List of shipping lines" provided for in Article 111, § 2 (d) of the Detailed Regulations, as regards distances traversed by sea.

4. Sea transit shall begin when the mails are deposited on the quay serving the ship in the port of departure and shall end when they are delivered on the quay of the port of destination.

5. For the payment of transit charges, mis-sent mails shall be considered to have followed their normal route, consequently, administrations concerned in the conveyance of such mails shall not be entitled on that account to demand a payment from the dispatching administrations, but the latter shall remain liable for the appropriate transit charges to the countries whose services they normally use.

Article 49

Payment for internal costs caused by inward international mail

1. Each administration, which, in its exchanges with another administration, receives a larger quantity of letter-mail items than it sends shall have the right to collect from the dispatching administration, as compensation, a payment for the costs incurred by the conveyance, sorting and delivery of the excess international mail received.

2. The payment provided for in § 1 shall be 50 centimes per kilogramme of mail received in excess.

3. The dispatching administration shall be exempt from any payment if the relevant annual account does not exceed 2000 francs.

4. Any administration may waive wholly or in part the payment provided for in § 1.

Article 50

Exemption from transit charges

Items exempted from postal charges under Articles 13 to 15, as well as dispatches of empty mail bags, shall be exempted from all land and sea transit charges.

Article 51

Extraordinary services

The transit charges specified in Article 48 shall not be applicable to conveyance by extraordinary services specially established or maintained by a postal administration at the request of one or more other administrations. The conditions of this class of conveyance shall be regulated by mutual consent between the administrations concerned.

Article 52

Accounting for transit charges

1. General accounting for transit charges shall take place annually on the basis of statistical returns taken once every three years, over a period of fourteen days. This period shall be extended to twenty-eight days for mails handled less than five times a week by the services of one and the same intermediary country. The Detailed Regulations shall fix the incidence of the statistics and the duration of their application.

2. When the annual balance between two administrations does not exceed 25 francs, the debtor administration shall be exempted from any payment.

3. Every administration shall be authorized to submit for the consideration of a committee of arbitrator the results of statistics which in its opinion differ too much from reality. The arbitration shall be arranged as laid down in Article 125 of the General Regulations.

4. The arbitrators shall be empowered to fix in a fair and reasonable manner the transit charges to be paid.

Article 53

Exchange of closed mails with military units placed at the disposal of the United Nations and with warships or military aircraft

1. Closed mails may be exchanged between the post offices of any member country and the commanding officers of military units placed at the disposal of the United Nations, and between the commanding officer of one of those military units and the commanding officer of another military unit placed at the disposal of the United Nations, through the intermediary of the land, sea or air services of other countries.

2. Closed mails may also be exchanged between the post offices of any member country and the commanding officers of naval or air units or warships or military aircraft of the same country stationed abroad, or between the commanding officer of one of those naval or air units or of any of those warships or military aircraft and the commanding officer of another unit or of another warship or military aircraft of the same country, through the intermediary of the land, sea or air services of other countries.

3. Letter-post items in the mails referred to in § 1 and 2 shall be confined to items addressed to or sent by members of military units or the officers and crews of the ships or aircraft to or from which the mails are forwarded. The rates and conditions of dispatch applicable to them shall be fixed, according to its regulations, by the postal administration of the country which has made the military unit available or to which the ships or aircraft belong.

4. In the absence of special agreement, the administration of the country which has made the military unit available or to which the warships or military aircraft belong shall be liable to the intermediate administrations for the transit charges for the mails, calculated in accordance with Article 48, and for air conveyance dues, calculated in accordance with Article 65.

PART III

AIR CONVEYANCE OF LETTER-POST ITEMS

CHAPTER I

GENERAL PROVISIONS

Article 54

Air-mail correspondence

Letter-post items conveyed by air shall be called "air-mail correspondence"

Article 55

Aerogrammes

1. Each administration may admit aerogrammes, which are air-mail correspondence.

2. An aerogramme shall consist of a sheet of paper suitably folded and gummed preferably on all sides, the dimensions of which, in that form, shall be the following:
   (a) minimum dimensions: identical to those prescribed for letters;
   (b) maximum dimensions: 110 x 220 mm;
and such that the length is equal to or greater than the width multipled by § 2 (approximate value: 1.4). The front of the sheet when folded in this way shall be re-

served for the address: it shall bear the printed indication *"Aerogramme"* and may also bear an equivalent indication in the language of the country of origin. An aerogramme shall not contain any enclosure. It may be registered if the regulations of the country of origin so permit.

3. Each administration shall fix, within the limits defined in § 2, the conditions of issue, manufacture and sale of aerogrammes.

4. Items of air-mail correspondence posted as aerogrammes, but not fulfilling the conditions fixed above shall be treated in accordance with Article 59. Administrations may, however, forward them in all cases by surface.

Article 56

Surcharged and unsurcharged air-mail correspondence

1. Air-mail correspondence shall be divided, as regards charges, into surcharged air-mail correspondence and unsurcharged air-mail correspondence.

2. In principle, air-mail correspondence shall be subject, in addition to the charges authorized by the Convention and various Agreements, to surchages for air conveyance; the postal items mentioned in Articles 14 and 15 shall be liable to the same surcharges. All such correspondence shall be described as surcharged air-mail correspondence.

3. Administrations shall be permitted not to collect a surcharge for air conveyance, provided that they inform the administrations of the countries of destination of the fact: items accepted under these conditions shall be described as unsurcharged air-mail correspondence.

4. With the exception of those originating from the bodies of the Universla Postal Union and from the Restricted Unions, items on postal service mentioned in Article 13 shall be exempt from air surcharge.

5. Aerogrammes, as described in Article 55, shall be subject to a charge at least equal to that applicable in the country of origin to an unsurcharged letter of the first weight step.

Article 57

Air surcharges or combined charges

1. Administrations shall fix the air-surcharges to be collected for forwarding. They may adopt, for fixing of surcharges, smaller weight steps than those laid down in Article 17.

2. Administrations may fix combined charges for the prepayment of surcharged air-mail correspondence.

3. The surcharges shall be closely related to conveyance costs and, as a general rule, the sum thereof shall not in total exceed the costs payable for such conveyance.

4. Surcharges shall be uniform for the whole of the territory of a country of destination whatever the route used.

5. Air surcharges shall be paid before dispatch.

6. In calculating the air surcharge for an air-mail item, each administration shall be authorized to take into account the weight of any forms used by the public which may be attached to the item.

Article 58

Methods of denoting prepayment

Apart from the methods laid down in Article 22, the prepayment of surcharged air-mail correspondence may be represented by a manuscript indication, in figures, of the sum collected, expressed in the currency of the country of origin, for example in the form: *"Taxe percue:* . . . dollars . . . cents" (Amount collected: . . . dollars . . . cents). This indication may appear either in a special stamp impression or on a special stamp or label, or simply be marked by any method on the address side of the item. In every case the indication shall be authenticated by a date-stamp impression of the office of origin.

Article 59

Unpaid or underpaid surcharged air-mail correspondence

1. Unpaid or underpaid surcharged air-mail correspondence which it is not possible to have regularized by the senders shall be treated as follows:

(a) in the event of complete absence of prepayment, surcharged air-mail correspondence shall be treated in accordance with Articles 21 and 24; items on which the payment of postage is not obligatory before dispatch shall be forwarded by the means of transport normally used;

(b) in the event of underpayment, surcharged air-mail correspondence shall be forwarded by air if the charges paid represent at least the amount of the air surcharge, nevertheless, the administration of origin shall be permitted to send these items by air when the charges paid represent at least 75% of the surcharge. Below this limit, items shall be treated as laid down to Article 21. In the preceding cases, Article 24 shall be applicable.

2. If the amount of the charge to be collected has not been indicated by the administration of origin, the administration of destination shall be permitted to deliver, without collecting a charge, underpaid surcharged air-mail correspondence on which the charges paid by the sender represent at least the postage for an unsurcharged item of the same weight and category.

Article 60

Routeing

1. Administrations shall be bound to forward by the air communications they use for the conveyance of their own air-mail correspondence the items of this type which reach them from other administrations.

2. Administrations of countries without an air service shall forward air-mail correspondence by the most rapid means used for mails; the same shall apply if for any reason routeing by surface means is more advantageous than the use of airlines.

3. Closed air mails shall forwarded by the route requested by the administration of the country of origin, provided that it is used by the administration of the country of transit for the transmission of its own mails. If that is not possible or if there is insufficient time for the transhipment the administration of the country of origin shall be so informed.

Article 61

Operations at airports

Administrations shall take the necessary steps to ensure the best conditions for the receipt and onward transmission of air mails at airports in their country.

Article 62

Customs control of air-mail correspondence

Administrations shall take all necessary steps to speed up the operations relating to the customs control of air-mail correspondence addressed to their countries.

Article 63

Redirection or return to origin of air-mail correspondence

1. In principle, all air-mail correspondence addressed to an addressee who has changed his address shall be redirected to its new destination by the means of transport normally used for unsurcharged correspondence. For this purpose, Article 28, § 1 to 3, shall be applicable by analogy. The same means of transport shall be used for the return to origin of undeliverable air-mail correspondence.

2. At the express request of the addressee (in the case of redirection) or of the sender (in the case of return to origin) and if the person concerned undertakes to pay the air surcharges on the new air route, or indeed if these surcharges are paid at the redirecting office by a third person, the items in question may be reforwarded by air: in the first two cases the air surcharge shall be collected, in principle, at the time of delivery of the item and retained by the delivering administration.

3. Correspondence sent by surface on its first transmission may be reforwarded abroad or returned to origin by air, under the conditions laid down in § 2. Redirection by air of such articles within the country of destination shall be governed by the internal regulations of that country.

4. The special C 6 envelopes and bags, used for collective redirection and made up in accordance with Article 139 of the Detailed Regulations, shall be forwarded to the new destination by the means of transport normally used for unsurcharged correspondence, unless the surcharges are paid in advance to the redirecting office, or the addressee or the sender, as the case may be, undertakes to pay the air surcharges on the new air route in accordance with § 2.

CHAPTER II

AIR CONVEYANCE DUES

Article 64

General principles

1. The air conveyance dues for the whole distance flown shall be borne:
(a) in the case of closed mails, by the administration of the country of origin of the mails.
(b) in the case of air-mail correspondence in transit *a decouvert*, including missent items, by the administration which forwards this correspondence to another administration.

2. These same regulations shall be applicable to air mails and air-mail correspondence in transit *a decouvert* exempt from transit charges.

3. Conveyance dues shall, for a particular sector, be uniform for all administrations which use the sector without sharing in the running costs of the air service or services operating over it.

4. Unless agreement has been reached that no charge should be made, air conveyance dues within the country of destination shall be uniform for all air-mails originating abroad whether or not this mail is reforwarded by air.

5. In the absence of special agreement between the administrations concerned. Article 48 shall apply to air-mail correspondence for any transit by land or by sea: nevertheless, no transit charges shall be payable for:

(a) the transhipment of air mails between two airports serving the same town;

(b) the conveyance of such mails from an airport serving a town to a depot situated in the same town and the return of the same mails for reforwarding.

Article 65

Basic rates and calculation of air conveyance dues relating to closed mails

1. The basic rates applicable to the settlement of accounts between administrations in respect of air conveyance shall be fixed per kilogramme of gross weight and per kilometre. These rates, detailed below, shall apply proportionally to fractions of a kilogramme:

(a) for LC items (letters, aerogrammes, postcards, postal money orders, COD money orders, bills for collection, insured letters and boxes, advices of payment, entry and delivery): 3 thousandths of a franc at most;

(b) for AO items (items other than LC): 1 thousandth of a franc at most.

2. Air conveyance dues shall be calculated according to, on the one hand, the actual basic rates (fixed within the limits of the basic rates specified in   1) and the kilometric distances given in the "List of air-mail distances" referred to in Article 201, § 1, (b), of the Detailed Regulations, and, on the other, the gross weight of the mails; no account shall be taken of the weight of *sacs collecteurs*.

3. Where dues are payable for air conveyance in the interior of the country of destination, they shall be fixed in the form of a single rate for each of the two categories, LC and AO. These dues shall be calculated on the basis of the rates prescribed in § 1, and according to the weighted average distances of the sectors flown by international mail on the internal network. The weighted average distance shall be determined in terms of the gross weight of all the air mails arriving at the country of destination, including the mail which is not reforwarded by air in the interior of that country.

4. The sum of the dues referred to in § 3 may not exceed in total the amounts which actually have to be paid for conveyance.

5. The rates for internal and international air conveyance (obtained by multiplying the effective basic rate by the distance), which are used in calculating the dues mentioned in § 2 and 3, shall be rounded up or down to the nearest 10 gold centimes according to whether or not the number made up by the figure of hundredths and that of thousandths exceeds 50.

Article 66

Calculation of and accounting for air conveyance dues for air-mail correspondence in transit *a decouvert*

1. Air conveyance dues for air-mail correspondence in transit *a decouvert* shall be calculated, in principle, as indicated in Article 65, § 2, but according to the net weight of such correspondence. Nevertheless, when the territory of the country of destination is served by one or more lines with several stops in that territory the conveyance dues shall be calculated on the basis of a weighted average rate taking into account the weight of the mail offloaded at each stop. The total amount of these dues shall be increased by 5%.

2. The intermediate administration shall, however, be entitled to calculate conveyance dues for *a decouvert* correspondence on the basis of not more than twenty average

rates, each relating to a group of countries of destination and fixed according to the weight of mail offloaded at different destinations within the group. The sum of these dues may not exceed in total the amounts which have to be paid for conveyance.

3. Accounting for air conveyance dues for air-mail correspondence in transit *a decouvert* shall take place, in principle, on the basis of the data of statistical returns compiled once a year over a period of fourteen days.

4. Accounting shall take place on the basis of actual weight in the case of misrouted correspondence or correspondence posted on board ship or sent at irregular intervals or in too varying amounts. However, this accounting shall be done only if the intermediate administration asks to be paid for the conveyance of this correspondence.

Article 67

Payment of air conveyance dues

1. Air conveyance dues shall be payable, apart from the exceptions provided for in § 2 to the administration of the country which controls the air service used.

2. Notwithstanding § 1:
(a) the conveyance dues may be paid to the administration of the country in which the airport is situated at which the air-mails taken over by the air carrier, subject to an agreement between this administration and that of the country which controls the air service concerned;
(b) the administration which hands over air mails to an air carrier may settle direct with that carrier, for the conveyance dues for all or part of the distance flown, subject to the agreement of the administration of the countries which control the air service used.

3. Conveyance dues for air-mail correspondence in transit *a decouvert* shall be paid to the administration which reforwards it.

Article 68

Air conveyance dues for diverted mails

1. The administration of origin of a mail which has gone off its route in course of conveyance shall pay the conveyance dues for the mail as far as the airport of offloading initially provided for on the AV 7 delivery bill.

2. It shall also settle the reforwarding dues relating to the sectors actually covered subsequently by the mail in order to reach its place of destination.

3. The supplementary dues relating to the sectors subsequently covered by the diverted mail shall be reimbursed as follows:
(a) by the administration whose services have committed the error in the case of misrouteing;
(b) by the administration which has collected the conveyance dues paid to the airline when the latter has offloaded in a place other than that shown on the AV 7 delivery bill.

Article 69

Air conveyance dues for mail lost or destroyed

In case of loss or destruction of mail as the result of an accident occurring to the aircraft or through any other cause involving the liability of the air carrier, the administration of origin shall be exempt from any payment in respect of the air conveyance of the mail lost or destroyed, for any part of the flight of the route used.

PART IV

FINAL PROVISIONS

Article 70

Conditions of approval of proposals concerning the Convention
and its Detailed Regulations

1. To become effective, proposals submitted to Congress relating to this Convention and its Detailed Regulations must be approved by a majority of the member countries present and voting. Half of the member countries represented at Congress shall be present at the time of voting.

2. To become effective, proposals introduced between two Congresses relating to this Convention and its Detailed Regulations must obtain:

(a) unanimity of votes if they involve amendments to Articles 1 to 15 (Part 1), 16, 17, 18, (e), (l), (m) and (n), 21, 24, 37, 38, 40 to 53 (Part II), 70 and 71 (Part IV) of the Convention, to any of the Articles of its Final Protocol or to Articles 102 to 104, 105, § 1, 125, 155, 159, 170, 171 and 202 of its Detailed Regulations;

(b) two-thirds of the votes if they involve amendments of substance to provisions other than those mentioned under (a);

(c) a majority of the votes if they involve;

(i) drafting amendments to the provisions of the Convention and its Detailed Regulations other than those mentioned under (a);

(ii) interpretation of the provisions of the Convention, its Final Protocol and its Detailed Regulations, except in case of a dispute to be submitted to arbitration as provided for in Article 32 of the Constitution.

Article 71

Entry into force and duration of the Convention

This Convention shall come into force on 1 July 1971 and shall remain in operation until the entry into force of the Acts of the next Congress.

In witness whereof the Plenipotentiaries of the Governments of the member countries have signed this Convention in a single original which shall be deposited in the Archives of the Government of the country in which the seat of the Union is situated. A copy thereof shall be delivered to each party by the Government of the country in which Congress is held.

Done at Tokyo, 14 November 1969.

d. FINAL PROTOCOL TO THE UNIVERSAL POSTAL CONVENTION, DONE AT TOKYO NOVEMBER 14, 1969

At the moment of proceeding to signature of the Universal Postal Convention concluded this day, the undersigned Plenipotentiaries have agreed the following:

Article I

Ownership of postal items

1. Article 4 shall not apply to the Republic of South Africa, the Commonwealth of Australia, Barbados, Bhutan, the Republic of Botswana, Canada, the Republic of Cyprus, Ghana, the United Kingdom of Great Britain and Northern Ireland, the Overseas Territories for whose international relations the Government of the United Kingdom of Great Britain and Northern Ireland is responsible, Guyana, Ireland, Jamaica, Kenya, Kuwait, Malaysia, Malawi, Malta, Mauritius, the Republic of Nauru, the Federal Republic of Nigeria, New Zealand, Uganda, Qatar, the United Arab Republic, Sierra Leone, Singapore, the Kingdom of Swaziland, the United Republic of Tanzania, Trinidad and Tobago, the Arab Republic of Yemen, the People's Republic of Southern Yemen, and the Republic of Zambia.

2. Nor shall that article apply to Denmark, whose internal legislation does not allow withdrawal from the post or alteration of the address of correspondence, at the request of the sender, from the time when the addressee has been informed of the arrival of an item addressed to him.

Article II

Exception to the exemption of literature for the blind from postal charges

Notwithstanding Article 15, those member countries which do not concede exemption from postal charges to literature for the blind in their internal service may collect the postage and special charges mentioned in Article 15 which may not, however, exceed those in their internal service.

Article III

Equivalents. Maximum and minimum limits

1. Each member country may increase by 60% or reduce by 30%, at most, the charges prescribed in Article 17, § 1, in accordance with the following table:

Category	Weight Step		Charges	
			Upper limit	Lower limit
1	2		3	4
			c	c
Letters	Up to	20 g	48	21
	⌈ Above 20 g up to 50 g ⌉ (optional		⌈ 88	38.5
	⌊ 50 g 100 g ⌋ weight steps)		⌊ 112	49
	Above 20 g up to 100 g		112	49
	100 g 250 g		256	112
	250 g 500 g		480	210
	500 g 1000 g		800	350
	1000 g 2000 g		1280	560

(continued on next page)

		Charges	
Category	Weight Step	Upper limit	Lower limit
1	2	3	4
Postcards		32	14
Printed Papers	Up to 20 g	24	10.5
	⌈ Above 20 g up to 50 g ⌉ (optional	⌈ 32	14
	⌊ 50 g 100 g ⌋ weight steps)	⌊ 40	17.5
	Above 20 g up to 100 g	40	17.5
	100 g 250 g	64	28
	250 g 500 g	112	49
	500 g 1000 g	192	84
	1000 g 2000 g	320	140
	Per additional step of 1000 g	160	70
Literature for the Blind	–	–	–
Small Packets	Up to 100 g	48	21
	Above 100 g up to 250 g	96	42
	250 g 500 g	160	70
	500 g 1000 g	288	126

2. The charges adopted shall, as far as possible, bear the same proportions to one another as the basic charges, each postal administration being free to round its charges up or down, whichever is best adapted to its monetary system.

3. Exceptionally and notwithstanding the provisions of § 1 and 2, member countries shall be authorized to raise the margin of increase from 60% to 100% at most for letters up to 100 g, for postcards, for printed papers up to 100g, and for smallpackets up to 100 g, and, in consequence, to apply the following upper limits in those cases:

Category	Weight Step	Upper Limit
1	2	3
		c
Letters	Up to 20 g	60
	⌈ Above 20 g up to 50 g ⌉ (optional	⌈ 110
	⌊ 50 g 100 g ⌋ weight steps)	⌊ 140
	Above 20 g up to 110 g	140
Postcards		40
Printed Papers	Up to 20 g	30
	⌈ Above 20 g up to 50 g ⌉ (optional	⌈ 40
	⌊ 50 g 100 g ⌋ weight steps)	⌊ 50
	Above 20 g up to 100 g	50
Small Packets	Up to 100 g	60

4. Notwithstanding § 2, member countries shall be authorized, provisionally and until 1 October 1972 at the latest, to apply to the first weight step and, if appropriate, to the optional 50 gramme step of the printed papers category, a charge reduction different from that applied to other letter-post items. Under no circumstances may the charge for the first weight step of the printed papers category be less than 9 centimes, nor may that for the optional 60 gramme step be less than 12 centimes.

Article IV

Additional charges

Notwithstanding Article 17, member countries shall exceptionally have the right to apply uniformly to items other than letters and postcards additional charges which enable them to compensate for the expenses incurred by the payment of the internal costs for inward international surface mail prescribed in Article 49 within the maximum limits given in § 1 and 3 of Article III in the Final Protocol.

Article V

Exception to the application of the tariff for printed papers

Exceptionally, member countries shall be authorized to raise the charge for printed papers up to those prescribed by their legislation for items of the same nature in their internal service.

Article VI

Ounce and pound avoirdupois

Notwithstanding the table in Article 17, § 1, member countries which by reason of their internal system are unable to adopt the metric-decimal system of weight may substitute for the weight steps specified in Article 17, § 1, the following equivalents:

Up to	20 g	1 oz
Up to	50 g	2 oz
Up to	100 g	4 oz
Up to	250 g	8 oz
Up to	500 g	1 lb
Up to	1000 g	2 lb
Per additional	1000 g	2 lb

Article VII

Dimensions of items in envelopes

Notwithstanding Article 17, § 1, items in envelopes with minimum dimensions of 70 x 100 mm shall be admitted until 1 October 1973.

Article VIII

Standardized items

Article 17, § 2, concerning standardized items shall take effect from 1 October 1973.

Article IX

Exception concerning the dimensions of items in envelopes

The administrations of Canada, Kenya, Tanzania, Uganda, and the United States of America shall not be obliged to discourage the use of envelopes whose formal exceeds the recommended dimensions when those envelopes are widely used in their countries.

Article X

Minimum dimensions of aerogrammes

Notwithstanding Article 17, § 1 (table) and Article 55, the postal administrations of Barbados, Bhutan, Guyana, India, Nigeria and Pakistan shall be authorized to adopt, for aerogrammes, minimum dimensions not less than 70 x 100 mm until 1 October 1973.

Article XI

Small packets

The obligation to participate in the exchange of small packets exceeding 500 g in weight shall not apply to member countries which find it impossible to operate such an exchange.

Article XII

Exception to the provisions concerning printed papers

Notwithstanding Article 17, § 1, postal administrations shall be authorized to apply a first weight step of 50 g to printed papers.

Article XIII

Exception to the inclusion of articles of value in registered letters

1. Notwithstanding Article 17, § 10, the postal administrations of the following countries shall be authorized not to admit in registered letters the articles of value mentioned in the said § 10, the Argentine Republic, Bhutan, the Federative Republic of Brazil, Chile, El Salvador, Iran, Mexico, Nepal, Pakistan, Peru, Saudi Arabia, the United Arab Republic and the Republic of Venezuela.

2. Notwithstanding Article 17, § 10, the postal administration of India shall be authorized not to admit the articles of value mentioned in the said § 10 in ordinary or registered letters.

Article XIV

Posting abroad of letter post items

A member country shall not be bound to forward or deliver to the addressees letter-post items which senders resident in its territory post or cause to be posted in a foreign country with the object of profiting by the lower charges in force there: the same shall apply to such items posted in large quantities whether or not such postings are made with a view to benefiting from lower charges. The rule shall be applied without distinction both to correspondence made up in the country where the sender resides and then carried across the frontier and to correspondence made up in a foreign country. The administration concerned may either return the items in question to origin or charge postage on them at its internal rates. The method by which the charges are collected shall be left to its discretion.

Article XV

International reply coupons

Notwithstanding Article 25, § 1, postal administrations shall be permitted not to undertake the sale of international reply coupons, or to limit their sale.

Article XVI

Withdrawal from the post. Alteration or correction of address

Article 27 shall not apply to the Republic of South Africa, the Commonwealth of Australia, Barbados, Bhutan, Burma, the Republic of Botswana, Canada, the Republic of Cyprus, the United Kingdom of Great Britain and Northern Ireland, to those of the Overseas Territories for whose international relations the Government of the United Kingdom of Great Britain and Northern Ireland is responsible, Guyana, Ireland, Jamaica, Kenya, Kuwait, the Kingdom of Lesotho, Malaysia, Malawi, Malta, Mauritius, the Republic of Nauru, the Federal Republic of Nigeria, New Zealand, Uganda, Qatar, Sierra Leone, Singapore, the Kingdom of Swaziland, the United Republic of Tanzania, Trinidad and Tobago, the People's Republic of Southern Yemen, and the Republic of Zambia, whose legislation does not permit withdrawal from the post or alteration of address of letter-post items at the sender's request. The Argentine Republic shall not, for its part, give effect to requests for withdrawal from the post or alteration of the address originating from countries which have made reservations regarding Article 27.

Article XVII

Special charges other than postage

1. Member countries whose internal service special charges, other than the postage rates laid down in Article 17, are higher than those which are fixed in Article 18 shall be authorized to apply them also in the international service.

2. Notwithstanding Article 18, (l) column 3, the postal administrations of the Argentine Republic, the Republic of Cuba, Peru and the Philippines shall be authorized not to accept printed papers dispatched in special registered bags. Consequently the special indemnity laid down for these items in Article 40, § 2, cannot be claimed from those administrations.

Article XVIII

Special transit charges for conveyance in transit by the Trans-Siberian and Trans-Andine and via Lake Nasser

1. The postal administration of the Union of Soviet Socialist Republics shall be authorized to collect a supplement of 1 franc 50 centimes in addition to the transit charges indicated in Article 48, § 1, (i) (distances traversed by land) for each kilogramme of letter-post items conveyed in transit over the Trans-Siberian route.

2. The postal administration of the Argentine Republic shall be authorized to collect a supplement of 30 centimes over and above the transit charges indicated in Article 48, § 1, (i) (distances traversed by land) for each kilogramme of letter-post items conveyed in transit over the Argentine section of the "Ferrocarril Trasandino."

3. The postal administrations of the United Arab Republic and the Democratic Republic of the Sudan shall be authorized to collect a supplement of 50 centimes in addition to the transit charges indicated in Article 48, § 1, for each bag of letter-post in transit via Lake Nasser between Shallal (UAR) and Wadi Halfa (Sudan).

Article XIX

Special transit conditions for Afghanistan

Notwithstanding Article 48, § 1, the postal administration of Afghanistan shall be authorized provisionally, because of its special difficulties as regards means of conveyance and communication, to effect the transit of closed mails and *a decouvert* correspondence across its territory on terms specially agreed with the postal administrations concerned.

Article XX

Special storage charges at Aden

Exceptionally, the postal administration of the People's Republic of Southern Yemen shall be authorized to collect a charge of 40 centimes per bag for all mails stored at Aden, provided that that administration does not receive any payment in respect of land or sea transit for those mails.

Article XXI

Exceptional air surcharge

By reason of the special geographical situation of the U.S.S.R., the postal administration of that country shall reserve the right to apply a uniform air surcharge throughout the whole territory of the U.S.S.R., for all the countries of the world. This surcharge shall not exceed the actual costs occasioned by the conveyance of letter-post items by air.

Article XXII

Compulsory routeing indicated by the country of origin

1. The Federal Socialist Republic of Yugoslavia will recognize only the costs of the conveyance effected in accordance with the provision concerning the line shown on the bag labels (AV 8) of air-mail dispatches.

2. The postal administrations of the Byelorussian Soviet Socialist Republic, the Romanian Socialist Republic, the Ukrainian Soviet Socialist Republic and the Union of Soviet Socialist Republics will recognise only the costs of the conveyance effected in accordance with the provision concerning the line shown on the bag labels (AV 8) of air-mail dispatches and on the AV 7 delivery bills.

In witness whereof, the Plenipotentiaries below have drawn up this Protocol, which shall have the same force and the same validity as if its provisions were inserted in the text of the Convention itself, and they have signed it in a single original which shall be deposited in the Archives of the Government of the country in which the seat of the Union is situated. A copy thereof shall be delivered to each party by the Government of the country in which Congress is held.

Done at Tokyo, 14 November 1969.

11. INTERNATIONAL TELECOMMUNICATION UNION

a. INTERNATIONAL TELECOMMUNICATION CONVENTION, DONE AT MONTREUX, NOVEMBER 12, 1965, AND BECAME EFFECTIVE JANUARY 1, 1967[1]

TABLE OF CONTENTS

---

[1] As published by the General Secretariat of the International Telecommunication Union

CHAPTER III

Relations with the United Nations and with International Organizations

CHAPTER IV

General Provisions relating to Telecommunications

CHAPTER V

Special Provisions for Radio

CHAPTER VI

Definitions

INTERNATIONAL TELECOMMUNICATION CONVENTION

PREAMBLE

1   While fully recognizing the sovereign right of each country to regulate its telecommunication, the plenipotentiaries of the Contracting Governments, with the object of facilitating relations and co-operation between the peoples by means of efficient telecommunication services, have agreed to conclude the following Convention.

2   The countries and groups of territories which become parties to the present Convention constitute the International Telecommunication Union.

CHAPTER I

Composition, Purposes and Structure of the Union

ARTICLE 1

Composition of the Union

3   1. The International Telecommunication Union shall comprise Members and Associate Members.

4   2. A Member of the Union shall be:

a) any country or group of territories listed in Annex 1 upon signature and ratification of, or accession to, this Convention by it or on its behalf;

5   *b)* any country, not listed in Annex 1, which becomes a Member of the United Nations and which accedes to this Convention in accordance with Article 19;

6   *c)* any sovereign country, not listed in Annex 1 and not a Member of the United Nations, which applies for Membership of the Union and which, after having secured approval of such application by two-thirds of the Members of the Union, accedes to this Convention in accordance with Article 19.

7   3. An Associate Member of the Union shall be:

a) any country which has not become a Member of the Union in accordance with 4 to 6, by acceding to this Convention in accordance with Article 19, after its application for Associate Membership has received approval by a majority of the Members of the Union;

8   *b)* any territory or group of territories not fully responsible for the conduct of its international relations, in behalf of which a Member of the Union has signed and ratified or has acceded to this Convention in accordance with Article 19 or 20, provided that its application for Associate Membership is sponsored by such a Member, after the application has received approval by a majority of the Members of the Union;

9   *c)* any trust territory on behalf of which the United Nations has acceded to this Convention in accordance with Article 21, and the application of which for Associate Membership has been sponsored by the United Nations.

10   4. If any territory or group of territories, forming part of a group of territories constituting a Member of the Union, becomes or has become an Associate Member of the Union in accordance with 8, its rights and obligations under this Convention shall be those of an Associate Member only.

342

11   5. For the purpose of 6, 7 and 8, if an application for Membership or Associate Membership is made, by diplomatic channel and through the intermediary of the country of the seat of the Union, during the interval between two Plenipotentiary Conferences, the Secretary-General shall consult the Members of the Union; a Member shall be deemed to have abstained if it has not replied within four months after its opinion has been requested.

ARTICLE 2

Rights and Obligations of Members and Associate Members

12   1. (1) All Members shall be entitled to participate in conferences of the Union and shall be eligible for election to any of its organs.

13   (2) Each Member shall have one vote at all conferences of the Union, at meetings of the International Consultative Committees in which it participates and, if it is a Member of the Administrative Council, at all sessions of that Council.

14   (3) Each Member shall also have one vote in all consultations carried out by correspondence.

15   2. Associate Members shall have the same rights and obligations as Members of the Union, except that they shall not have the right to vote in any conference or other organ of the Union or to nominate candidates for membership of the International Frequency Registration Board. They shall not be eligible for election to the Administrative Council.

ARTICLE 3

Seat of the Union

16   The seat of the Union shall be at Geneva.

ARTICLE 4

Purposes of the Union

17   1. The purposes of the Union are:

    a) to maintain and extend international cooperation for the improvement and rational use of telecommunications of all kinds;

18   *b)* to promote the development of technical facilities and their most efficient operation with a view to improving the efficiency of telecommunication services, increasing their usefulness and making them, so far as possible, generally available to the public;

19   *c)* to harmonize the actions of nations in the attainment of those common ends.

20   2. To this end, the Union shall in particular:

    a) effect allocation of the radio frequency spectrum and registration of radio frequency assignments in order to avoid harmful interference between radio stations of different countries;

21   *b)* coordinate efforts to eliminate harmful interference between radio stations of different countries and to improve the use made of the radio frequency spectrum;

22   *c)* foster collaboration among its Members and Associate Members with a view to the establishment of rates at levels as low as possible consistent with an efficient service and taking into account the necessity for maintaining independent financial administration of telecommunication on a sound basis;

23   *d)* foster the creation, development and improvement of telecommunication equipment and networks in new or developing countries by every means at its disposal, especially its participation in the appropriate programmes of the United Nations;

24   *e)* promote the adoption of measures for ensuring the safety of life through the cooperation of telecommunication services;

25   *f)* undertake studies, make regulations, adopt resolutions, formulate recommendations and opinions, and collect and publish information concerning telecommunication matters for the benefit of all Members and Associate Members.

ARTICLE 5

Structure of the Union

26   The organization of the Union shall be as follows:

    1. the Plenipotentiary Conference, which is the supreme organ of the Union;

27   2. Administrative Conferences;

28   3. the Administrative Council;

29   4. the permanent organs of the Union, which are:

    a) the General Secretariat;

30   *b)* the International Frequency Registration Board (I.F.R.B.);

31   *c)* the International Radio Consultative Committee (C.C.I.R.);

32   *d)* the International Telegraph and Telephone Consultative Committee (C.C.I.T.T.).

ARTICLE 6

Plenipotentiary Conference

33   1. The Plenipotentiary Conference, supreme organ of the Union, shall be composed of delegations representing Members and Associate Members.

34   2. The Plenipotentiary Conference shall:

    a) determine the general policies for fulfilling the purposes of the Union prescribed in Article 4 of this Convention;

35   *b)* consider the report by the Administrative Council on its activities and those of the Union since the previous Plenipotentiary Conference;

36   *c)* establish the basis for the budget of the Union and determine a fiscal limit for the expenditure of the Union until the next Plenipotentiary Conference;

37   *d)* fix the basic salaries, the salary scales and the system of allowances and pensions for all the officials of the Union;

38   *e)* finally approve the accounts of the Union;

39   *f)* elect the Members of the Union which are to serve on the Administrative Council;

40   *g)* elect the Secretary-General and the Deputy Secretary-General and fix the dates of their taking office;

41   *h)* revise the Convention if it considers this necessary;

42   *i)* conclude or revise, if necessary, agreements between the Union and other international organizations, examine any provisional agreements with such organizations concluded, on behalf of the Union, by the Administrative Council, and take such measures in connection therewith as it deems appropriate;

43   *j)* deal with such other telecommunication questions as may be necessary.

44   3. The Plenipotentiary Conferences shall normally meet at a date and place decided on by the preceding Plenipotentiary Conference.

45   4. (1) The date and place of the next Plenipotentiary Conference, or either one of these, may be changed:

46   *a)* when at least one-quarter of the Members and Associate Members of the Union have individually proposed a change to the Secretary-General, or,

47   *b)* on a proposal of the Administrative Council.

48   (2) In either case a new date or place or both shall be determined with the concurrence of a majority of the Members of the Union.

ARTICLE 7

Administrative Conferences

49   1. Administrative conferences of the Union shall comprise:
     a) world administrative conferences;

50   *b)* regional administrative conferences.

51   2. Administrative conferences shall normally be convened to consider specific telecommunication matters. Only items included in their agenda may be discussed by such conferences. The decisions of such conferences must in all circumstances be in conformity with the provisions of the Convention.

52   3. (1) The agenda of a world administrative conference may include:
     a) the partial revision of the Administrative Regulations listed in **203**;

53   *b)* exceptionally, the complete revision of one or more of those Regulations;

54   *c)* any other question of a worldwide character within the competence of the conference.

55   (2) The agenda of a regional administrative conference may provide only for specific telecommunication questions of a regional nature, including instructions to the International Frequency Registration Board regarding its activities in respect of the region concerned, provided such instructions do not conflict with the interests of other regions. Furthermore, the decisions of such a conference must in all circumstances be in conformity with the provisions of the Administrative Regulations.

56   4. (1) The agenda of an administrative conference shall be determined by the Administrative Council with the concurrence of a majority of the Members of the Union in the case of a world administrative conference, or of a majority of the Members belonging to the region concerned in the case of a regional administrative conference, subject to the provisions of **76**.

57   (2) This agenda shall include any question which a Plenipotentiary Conference has directed to be placed on the agenda.

58   (3) The following items may also be included in the agenda of a world administrative conference dealing with radiocommunication:
     a) the election of the members of the international Frequency Registration Board in accordance with **172** to **174**;

59   *b)* instructions to the Board regarding its activities and a review of those activities.

60   5. (1) A world administrative conference shall be convened:
     a) by a decision of a Plenipotentiary Conference which may fix the date and place of its meeting;

61   *b)* on the recommendation of a previous world administrative conference;

62   *c)* at the request of at least one-quarter of the Members and Associate Members of the Union, who shall individually address their requests to the Secretary-General; or

63   *d)* on a proposal of the Administrative Council.

64   (2) In the cases specified in **61, 62** and **63** and, if necessary, in the case specified in **60**, the date and place of meeting shall be determined by the Administrative Council with the concurrence of a majority of the Members of the Union, subject to the provisions of **76**.

65   6. (1) A regional administrative conference shall be convened:

        a) by a decision of a Plenipotentiary Conference;

66   *b)* on the recommendation of a previous world or regional administrative conference;

67   *c)* at the request of at least one-quarter of the Members and Associate Members belonging to the region concerned, who shall individually address their requests to the Secretary-General; or

68   *d)* on a proposal of the Administrative Council.

69   (2) In the cases specified in **66, 67** and **68** and, if necessary, in the case specified in **65**, the date and place of meeting shall be determined by the Administrative Council with the concurrence of a majority of the Members of the Union belonging to the region concerned, subject to the provisions of **76**.

70   7. (1) The agenda, or date or place of an administrative conference may be changed:

        a) at the request of at least one-quarter of the Members and Associate Members of the Union, in the case of a world administrative conference, or of at least one-quarter of the Members and Associate Members of the Union belonging to the region concerned in the case of a regional administrative conference. Their requests shall be addressed individually to the Secretary-General, who shall transmit them to the Administrative Council for approval; or

71   *b)* on a proposal of the Administrative Council.

72   (2) In cases specified in **70** and **71**, the changes proposed shall not be finally adopted until accepted by a majority of the Members of the Union, in the case of a world administrative conference, or of a majority of the Members of the Union belonging to the region concerned, in the case of a regional administrative conference, subject to the provisions of **76**.

73   8. (1) The Administrative Council may deem it advisable for the main session of an administrative conference to be preceded by a preparatory meeting to draw up proposals for the technical bases of the work of the conference.

74   (2) The convening of such a preparatory meeting and its agenda must be approved by a majority of the Members of the Union in the case of a world administrative conference, or by a majority of the Members of the Union belonging to the region concerned in the case of a regional administrative conference, subject to the provisions of **76**.

75   (3) Unless the Plenary Meeting of a preparatory session of an administrative conference decides otherwise the texts finally approved by it will be assembled in a report which will also be approved by a Plenary Meeting and signed by the Chairman.

76   9. In the consultations referred to in **56, 64, 69, 72** and **74**, Members of the Union who have not replied within the time limits specified by the Administrative Council shall be regarded as not participating in the consultaitons, and in consequence shall not be taken into account in computing the majority. If the number of replies does not exceed one-half of the Members consulted, a further consultation shall take place.

ARTICLE 8

Rules of Procedure of Conferences and Assemblies

77   For the organization of their work and the conduct of their discussions, confer-

ences and assemblies shall apply the Rules of Procedure in the General Regulations annexed to the Convention. However, each conference or assembly may adopt such rules of procedure, in amplification of those in Chapter 9 of the General Regulations, which it considers to be indispensable, provided that such additional rules of procedure are compatible with the Convention and the General Regulations.

ARTICLE 9

Administrative Council

A. *Organization and working arrangements*

78 1. (1) The Administrative Council shall be composed of twenty-nine Members of the Union elected by the Plenipotentiary Conference with due regard to the need for equitable representation of all parts of the world. The Members of the Union elected to the Council shall hold office until the date on which a new Council is elected by the Plenipotentiary Conference. They shall be eligible for re-election.

79 (2) If between two Plenipotentiary Conferences a seat becomes vacant on the Administrative Council, it shall pass by right to the Member of the Union from the same region as the Member whose seat is vacated, which had obtained at the previous election the largest number of votes among those not elected.

80 (3) A seat on the Administrative Council shall be considered vacant:

a) when a Council Member does not have a representative in attendance at two consecutive annual sessions of the Administrative Council:

81 b) when a Member of the Union resigns its membership on the Council.

82 2. Each of the Members of the Administrative Council shall appoint to serve on the Council a person who shall, so far as possible, be an official serving in, or directly responsible to, or for, their telecommunications administration and qualified in the field of telecommunication services.

83 3. Each Member of the Administrative Council shall have one vote.

84 4. The Administrative Council shall adopt its own Rules of Procedure.

85 5. The Administrative Council shall elect its own Chairman and Vice-Chairman at the beginning of each annual session. They shall serve until the opening of the next annual session and shall be eligible for re-election. The Vice-Chairman shall serve as Chairman in the absence of the latter.

86 6. (1) The Administrative Council shall hold an annual session at the seat of the Union.

87 (2) During this session it may decide to hold, exceptionally, an additional session.

88 (3) Between ordinary sessions, it may be convened, as a general rule at the seat of the Union, by its Chairman at the request of a majority of its Members.

89 7. The Secretary-General and the Deputy Secretary-General, the Chairman and the Vice-Chairman of the International Frequency Registration Board and the Directors of the International Consultative Committees may participate as of right in the deliberations of the Administrative Council, but without taking part in the voting. Nevertheless, the Council may hold meetings confined to its own members.

90 8. The Secretary-General shall act as Secretary of the Administrative Council.

91 9. (1) In the interval between Plenipotentiary Conferences, the Administrative Council shall act on behalf of the Plenipotentiary Conference within the limits of the powers delegated to it by the latter.

92 (2) The Council shall act only in formal session.

93 10. The representative of each Member of the Administrative Council shall have the right to attend, as an observer, all meetings of the permanent organs of the Union mentioned in **30, 31** and **32**.

94   11. Only the travelling and subsistence expenses incurred by the representative of each Member of the Administrative Council in this capacity at Council sessions shall be borne by the Union.

B. *Duties*

95   12. (1) The Administrative Council shall be responsible for taking all steps to facilitate the implementation by the Members and Associate Members of the provisions of the Convention, of the Regulations, of the decisions of the Plenipotentiary Conference, and, where appropriate, of the decisions of other conferences and meetings of the Union.

96   (2) It shall ensure the efficient coordination of the work of the Union.

97   13. In particular, the Administrative Council shall:

  a) perform any duties assigned to it by the Plenipotentiary Conference;

98   *b)* in the interval between Plenipotentiary Conferences, be responsible for effecting the coordination with all international organizations referred to in Articles **29** and **30,** and to this end, shall conclude, on behalf of the Union, provisional agreements with the international organizations referred to in Article **30,** and with the United Nations in application of the Agreement between the United Nations and the International Telecommunication Union; these provisional agreements shall be submitted to the next Plenipotentiary Conference in accordance with **42;**

99   *c)* decide on the numbers and grading of the staff of the General Secretariat and of the specialized secretariats of the permanent organs of the Union, taking into account the general directives given by the Plenipotentiary Conference;

100   *d)* draw up such regulations as it may consider necessary for the administrative and financial activities of the Union; and also the administrative regulations to take account of current practice of the United Nations and of the specialized agencies applying the Common System of pay, allowances and pensions;

101   *e)* supervise the administrative functions of the Union;

102   *f)* review and approve the annual budget of the Union, ensuring the strictest possible economy;

103   *g)* arrange for the annual of the accounts of the Union prepared by the Secretary-General and approve them for submission to the next Plenipotentiary Conference;

104   *h)* adjust as necessary;

  1. the basic salary scales for staff in the professional categories and above, excluding the salaries for posts filled by election, to accord with any changes in the basic salary scales adopted by the United Nations for the corresponding Common System categories;

105   2. the basic salary scales for staff in the general service categories to accord with changes in the rates applied by the United Nations organization and the specialized agencies at the seat of the Union;

106   3. the post adjustment for professional categories and above, including posts filled by election, in accordance with decisions of the United Nations for application at the seat of the Union;

107   4. the allowances for all staff of the Union, in accordance with any changes adopted in the United Nations Common System;

108   5. the contributions payable by the Union and the staff to the United Nations Joint Pension Fund, in accordance with the decisions of the United Nations Joint Staff Pension Board;

| 109 | | 6. the cost-of-living allowances granted to beneficiaries of the Union Staff Superannuation and Benevolent Funds on the basis of practice in the United Nations. |

110   *i)* arrange for the convening of plenipotentiary and administrative conferences of the Union in accordance with Articles **6** and **7**;

111   *j)* offer to the Plenipotentiary Conference of the Union any recommendations deemed useful;

112   *k)* coordinate the activities of the permanent organs of the Union, take such action as it deems appropriate on requests or recommendations made to it by such organs, and review their annual reports;

113   *l)* provide, if it considers it desirable, for the filling ad interim of a vacancy for Deputy Secretary-General;

114   *m)* provide for the filling ad interim of vacancies for Directors of the International Consultative Committees;

115   *n)* perform the other functions prescribed for it in this Convention and, within the framework of the Convention and the Regulations, any functions deemed necessary for the proper administration of the Union;

116   *o)* take the necessary steps, with the agreement of a majority of the Members of the Union, provisionally to resolve questions which are not covered by the Convention and its Annexes and cannot await the next competent conference for settlement;

117   *p)* submit a report on its activities and those of the Union for consideration by the Plenipotentiary Conference;

118   *q)* send to Members and Associate Members of the Union, as soon as possible after each of its sessions, summary reports on the activities of the Administrative Council and other documents deemed useful;

119   *r)* promote international cooperation for the provision of technical cooperation to the new or developing countries by every means at its disposal, especially through the participation of the Union in the appropriate programmes of the United Nations; and, in accordance with the purposes of the Union, to promote by all possible means, the development of telecommunication.

ARTICLE 10

General Secretariat

120 1.   (1) The General Secretariat shall be directed by a Secretary-General, assisted by one Deputy Secretary-General.

121   (2) The Secretary-General and the Deputy Secretary-General shall take up their duties on the dates determined at the time of their election. They shall normally remain in office until dates determined by the following Plenipotentiary Conference, and they be eligible for re-election.

122   (3) The Secretary-General shall be responsible to the Administrative Council for all the administrative and financial aspects of the Union's activities. The Deputy Secretary-General shall be responsible to the Secretary-General.

123   (4) If the post of Secretary-General falls vacant, the Deputy Secretary-General shall discharge the duties ad interim.

124 2.   The Secretary-General shall:

     a) coordinate the activities of the permanent organs of the Union with the assistance of the Coordination Committee referred to in Article 11;

125   *b)* organize the work of the General Secretariat and appoint the staff of that Secretariat in accordance with directives of the Plenipotentiary Conference and the rules established by the Administrative Council;

126 *c)* undertake administrative arrangements for the specialized secretariats of the permanent organs of the Union and appoint the staff of those secretariats in agreement with the Head of each permanent organ; the appointments shall be made on the basis of the latter's choice, but the final decision for appointment or dismissal shall rest with the Secretary-General;

127 *d)* report to the Administrative Council any decisions taken by the United Nations and the specialized agencies which affect Common System conditions of service, allowances and pensions;

128 *e)* ensure the application of the financial and administrative regulations approved by the Administrative Council;

129 *f)* supervise, for administrative purposes only, the staff of those specialized secretariats who shall work directly under the orders of the Heads of the permanent organs of the Union;

130 *g)* undertake secretarial work preparatory to, and following, conferences of the Union;

131 *h)* provide, where appropriate in cooperation with the inviting government, the secretariat of every conference of the Union and provide the facilities and services for meetings of the permanent organs of the Union in collaboration with their respective Heads. The Secretary-General may also, when so requested, provide the secretariat of other telecommunication meetings on a contractual basis;

132 *i)* keep up-to-date the official lists, compiled from data supplied for this purpose by the permanent organs of the Union or by Administrations, with the exception of the master register and such other essential records as may be related to the duties of the International Frequency Registration Board;

133 *j)* publish the recommendations and principal reports of the permanent organs of the Union;

134 *k)* publish international and regional telecommunication agreements communicated to him by the parties thereto, and keep up-to-date records of these agreements;

135 *l)* publish the technical standards of the International Frequency Registration Board, as well as such other data concerning the assignment and utilization of frequencies as are prepared by the Board in the discharge of its duties;

136 *m)* prepare, publish and keep up-to-date with the assistance, where appropriate, of the other permanent organs of the Union:

137   1. a record of the composition and structure of the Union;

138   2. the general statistics and the official service documents of the Union as prescribed by the Regulations annexed to the Convention;

139   3. such other documents as conferences or the Administrative Council may direct;

140 *n)* distribute the published documents;

141 *o)* collect and publish, in suitable form, data, both national and international, regarding telecommunication throughout the world;

142 *p)* assemble and publish, in cooperation with the other permanent organs of the Union, both technical and administrative information that might be specially useful to new or developing countries in order to help them to improve their telecommunication networks. Their attention shall also be drawn to the possibilities offered by the international programmes under the auspices of the United Nations;

143 *q)* collect and publish such information as would be of assistance to Members and Associate Members regarding the development of technical methods with a view to achieving the most efficient operation of telecommunication services and especially the best possible use of radio frequencies so as to diminish interference;

144 *r)* publish periodically, with the help of information put at his disposal or which he may collect, including that which he may obtain from other international organizations, a journal of general information and documentation concerning telecommunication;

145 *s)* prepare and submit to the Administrative Council annual budget estimates which, after approval by the Council, shall be transmitted for information to all Members and Associate Members;

146 *t)* prepare a financial operating report and accounts to be submitted annually to the Administrative Council and recapitulative accounts immediately preceding each Plenipotentiary Conference; these accounts, after audit and approval by the Administrative Council, shall be circulated to the Members and Associate Members and be submitted to the next Plenipotentiary Conference for examination and final approval;

147 *u)* prepare an annual report on the activities of the Union which, after approval by the Administrative Council, shall be transmitted to all Members and Associate Members;

148 *v)* perform all other secretarial functions of the Union;

149 *w)* act as the legal representative of the Union.

150 3. The Deputy Secretary-General shall assist the Secretary-General in the performance of his duties and undertake such specific tasks as may be entrusted to him by the Secretary-General. He shall perform the duties of the Secretary-General in the absence of the latter.

151 4. The Secretary-General or the Deputy Secretary-General may participate, in a consultative capacity, in Plenary Assemblies of the International Consultative Committees and in all conferences of the Union; the Secretary-General or his representative may participate in a consultative capacity in all other meetings of the Union; their participation in the meetings of the Administrative Council is governed by **89.**

ARTICLE 11
Coordination Committee

152 1. (1) The Secretary-General shall be assisted by a Coordination Committee which shall advise him on administrative, financial and technical cooperation matters affecting more than one permanent organ and on external relations and public information.

153 (2) The Committee shall also consider any important matters referred to it by the Administrative Council. After examining them, the Committee will report, through the Secretary-General, to the Council.

154 (3) The Committee shall, in particular, help the Secretary-General in the duties assigned to him under **144, 145, 146** and **147.**

155 (4) The Committee shall examine the progress of the work of the Union in technical cooperation and submit recommendations, through the Secretary-General, to the Administrative Council.

156 (5) The Committee shall be responsible for ensuring coordination with all the international organizations mentioned in Articles **29** and **30** as regards representation of the permanent organs of the Union at conferences of such organizations.

157 2. The Committee shall endeavour to reach conclusions unanimously. The Secretary-General may, however, take decisions even when he does not have the support of two or more other members of the Committee, provided that he judges the matters in question to be of an urgent nature. In such circumstances he shall, if requested by the Committee, report on such matters to the Administrative Council in terms approved by all the members of the Committee. If, in similar circumstances, the matters are not urgent but are important, they shall be referred for consideration to the next session of the Administrative Council.

158 3. The Committee shall be presided over by the Secretary-General and shall be composed of the Deputy Secretary-General, the Directors of the International Consultative Committees and the Chairman of the International Frequency Registration Board.

159 4. The Committee shall meet when convened by its Chairman and, in general, at least once a month.

ARTICLE 12

Elected Officials and Staff of the Union

160 1. The Secretary-General, the Deputy Secretary-General and the Directors of the International Consultative Committees shall all be nationals of different countries, Members of the Union. At their election, due consideration should be given to the principles embodied in 164 and to the appropriate geographical representation of the regions of the world.

161 2. (1) In the performance of their duties, neither the elected officials nor the staff of the Union shall seek or accept instructions from any government or from any other authority outside the Union. They shall refrain from acting in any way which is incompatible with their status as international officials.

162 (2) Each Member and Associate Member shall respect the exclusively international characters of the duties of the elected officials and of the staff of the Union, and refrain from trying to influence them in the performance of their work.

163 (3) No elected official or any member of the staff of the Union shall participate in any manner or have any financial interest whatsoever in any enterprise concerned with telecommunications, except as part of their duties. However, the term "financial interest" is not to be construed as applying to the continuation of retirement benefits accruing in respect of previous employment or service.

164 3. The paramount consideration in the recruitment of staff and in the determination of the conditions of service shall be the necessity of securing for the Union the highest standards of efficiency, competence and integrity. Due regard must be paid to the importance of recruiting the staff on as wide a geographical basis as possible.

ARTICLE 13

International Frequency Registration Board

165 1. The essential duties of the International Frequency Registration Board shall be:

   a) to effect an orderly recording of frequency assignments made by the different countries so as to establish, in accordance with the procedure provided for in the Radio Regulations and in accordance with any decisions which may be taken by competent conferences of the Union, the date, purpose and technical characteristics of each of these assignments, with a view to ensuring formal international recognition thereof;

166 b) to furnish advice to Members and Associate Members with a view to the operation of the maximum practicable number of radio channels in those portions of the spectrum where harmful interference may occur;

167 c) to perform any additional duties, concerned with the assignment and utilization of frequencies, prescribed by a competent conference of the Union, or by the Administrative Council with the consent of a majority of the Members of the Union, in preparation for or in pursuance of the decisions of such a conference;

168 d) to maintain such essential records as may be related to the performance of its duties.

169 2. (1) The International Frequency Registration Board shall consist of five independent members designated in accordance with **172** to **180**.

170 (2) The members of the Board shall be thoroughly qualified by technical training in the field of radio and shall possess practical experience in the assignment and utilization of frequencies.

171 (3) Moreover, for the more effective understanding of the problems coming before the Board under **166**, each member shall be familiar with geographic, economic and demographic conditions within a particular area of the world.

172 3. (1) The five members of the Board shall be elected at intervals of not less than five years by a world administrative conference dealing with general radiocommunication matters. These members shall be chosen from the candidates sponsored by countries, Members of the Union. Each Member of the Union may propose only one candidate who shall be a national of its country. Each candidate shall possess the qualifications described in **170** and **171**.

173 (2) The election procedure shall be established by the conference itself in such a way as to ensure equitable representation of the various parts of the world.

174 (3) At each election any serving member of the Board may be proposed again as a candidate by the country of which he is a national.

175 (4) The members of the Board shall take up their duties on the date determined by the world administrative conference which elected them. They shall normally remain in office until the date determined by the conference which elects their successors.

176 (5) If in the interval between two world administrative conferences which elect members of the Board, an elected member of the Board should resign or abandon his duties without good cause for a period exceeding thirty days or should die, the country, Member of the Union, of which he is a national shall be asked by the Chairman of the Board to provide a replacement as soon as possible, who shall also be a national of that country.

177 (6) If the country, Member of the Union, concerned does not provide a replacement within a period of three months from the date of this request, it shall lose its right to designate a person to serve on the Board for the unexpired period of its current term.

178 (7) If in the interval between two world administrative conferences which elect members of the Board, the replacement should resign or abandon his duties without good cause for a period exceeding thirty days or should die, the country, Member of the Union, of which he is a national shall not be entitled to designate a further replacement.

179 (8) In the circumstances described in **177** and **178**, the Chairman of the Board shall request the Secretary-General to invite the countries, Members of the Union, of the region concerned to propose candidates for the election of a replacement at the next annual session of the Administrative Council.

180 (9) In order to safeguard the efficient operation of the Board, any country, a national of which has been elected to the Board, shall refrain, as far as possible, from recalling that person between two world administrative conferences which elect members of the Board.

181 4. (1) The working arrangment of the Board are defined in the Radio Regulations.

182 (2) The members of the Board shall elect from their own numbers a Chairman and a Vice-Chairman, for a period of one year. Thereafter, the Vice-Chairman shall succeed the Chairman each year and a new Vice-Chairman shall be elected.

183 (3) The Board shall be assisted by a specialized secretariat.

184 5. (1) The members of the Board shall serve, not as representatives of their respective countries, or of a region, but as custodians of an international public trust.

185   (2) No member of the Board shall request or receive instructions relating to the exercise of his duties from any government or a member thereof, or from any public or private organization or person. Furthermore, each Member and Associate Member must respect the international character of the Board and of the duties of its members and shall refrain from any attempt to influence any of them in the exercise of their duties.

ARTICLE 14

International Consultative Committees

186 1. (1) The duties of the International Radio Consultative Committee (C.C.I.R.) shall be to study technical and operating questions relating specifically to radiocommunication and to issue recommendations on them.

187   (2) The duties of the International Telegraph and Telephone Consultative Committee (C.C.I.T.T.) shall be to study technical, operating and tariff questions relating to telegraphy and telephony and to issue recommendations on them.

188   (3) In the performance of its duties, each Consultative Committee shall pay due attention to the study of questions and to the formulation of recommendations directly connected with the establishment, development and improvement of telecommunication in new or developing countries in both the regional and international fields.

189   (4) At the request of the countries concerned, each Consultative Committee may also study and offer advice concerning their national telecommunication problems. The study of such problems should be in accordance with **190.**

190 2. (1) The questions studied by each International Consultative Committee, on which it shall issue recommendations, shall be those referred to it by the Plenipotentiary Conference, by an administrative conference, by the Administrative Council, by the other Consultative Committee, or by the International Frequency Registration Board, in addition to those decided upon by the Plenary Assembly of the Consultative Committee itself, or, in the interval between its Plenary Assemblies, when requested or approved by correspondence by at least twenty Members and Associate Members of the Union.

191   (2) The Plenary Assemblies of the International Consultative Committees are authorized to submit to administrative conferences proposals arising directly from their recommendations or from findings on questions under their study.

192 3. The International Consultative Committees shall have as members:

a) of right, the administrations of all Members and Associate Members of the Union;

193   b) any recognized private operating agency which, with the approval of the Member or Associate Member which has recognized it, expresses a desire to participate in the work of these Committees.

194 4. Each Consultative Committee shall work through the medium of:

a) the Plenary Assembly, normally meeting every three years. When a corresponding world administrative conference has been convened, the Plenary Assembly should meet, if possible, at least eight months before this conference;

195   b) study groups, which shall be set up by the Plenary Assembly to deal with questions to be examined;

196   c) a Director elected by the Plenary Assembly initially for a period equal to twice the interval between two consecutive Plenary Assemblies, i.e. normally for six years. He shall be eligible for re-election at each subsequent Plenary Assembly and if re-elected shall then remain in office until the date of the next Plenary Assembly, normally for three years. When the position becomes unexpectedly vacant, the following Plenary Assembly shall elect the new Director;

197   *d)* a specialized secretariat, which assists the Director;

198   *e)* laboratories of technical installations set up by the Union.

199   5. There shall be a World Plan Committee, and such Regional Plan Committees as may be jointly approved by the Plenary Assemblies of the International Consultative Committees. These Plan Committees shall develop a General Plan for the international telecommunication network to help in planning international telecommunication network to help in planning international telecommunication services. They shall refer to the International Consultative Committees questions the study of which is of particular interest to new or developing countries and which are within the terms of reference of those Consultative Committees.

200   6. The Plenary Assemblies and the study group meetings of the Consultative Committees shall observe the Rules of Procedure contained in the General Regulations, annexed to this Convention. They may also adopt additional rules of procedure in accordance with **77**. These additional rules of procedure shall be published in the form of a Resolution in the documents of the Plenary Assemblies.

201   7. The working arrangements of the Consultative Committees are defined in Part II of the General Regulations annexed to this Convention.

ARTICLE 15

Regulations

202   1. Subject to the provisions of Article 8, the General Regulations contained in Annex 4 to this Convention shall have the same force and duration as the Convention.

203   2. (1) The provisions of the Convention are completed by the following sets of Administrative Regulations:

Telegraph Regulations,
Telephone Regulations,
Radio Regulations,
Additional Radio Regulations.

204   (2) Ratification of this Convention in accordance with Article **18** or accession in accordance with Article **19** involves acceptance of the General and Administrative Regulations in force at the time of ratification or accession.

205   (3) Members and Associate Members shall inform the Secretary-General of their approval of any revision of these Regulations by competent administrative conferences. The Secretary-General shall inform Members and Associate Members promptly regarding receipt of such notifications of approval.

206   3. In case of inconsistency between a provision of the Convention and a provision of the Regulations, the Convention shall prevail.

ARTICLE 16

Finances of the Union

207   1. The expenses of the Union shall comprise the costs of:

a) the Administrative Council, the General Secretariat, the International Frequency Registration Board, the secretariats of the International Consultative Committees, and the Union's laboratories and technical equipment;

208   *b)* Plenipotentiary Conferences and world administrative conferences;

209   *c)* all meetings of the International Consultative Committees.

210   2. Expenses incurred by the regional administrative conferences referred to in **50** shall be borne in accordance with their unit classification by all the Members and Associate Members of the region concerned and, where appropriate, on the same basis by any Members and Associate Members of other regions which have participated in such conferences.

211 3. The Administrative Council shall review and approve the annual budget of the Union, taking account of the limits for expenditure set by the Plenipotentiary Conference.

212 4. The expenses of the Union shall be met from the contributions of the Members and Associate Members, each Member and Associate Member paying a sum proportional to the number of units in the class of contribution it has chosen from the following scale:

30 Unit class	8 Unit class
25 ” ”	5 ” ”
20 ” ”	4 ” ”
18 ” ”	3 ” ”
15 ” ”	2 ” ”
13 ” ”	1 ” ”
10 ” ”	½ ” ”

213 5. Members and Associate Members shall be free to choose their class of contribution for defraying Union expenses.

214 6. (1) At least six months before the Convention comes into force, each Member and Associate Member shall inform the Secretary-General of the class of contribution it has chosen.

215 (2) The Secretary-General shall communicate this decision to Members and Associate Members.

216 (3) Members and Associate Members who have failed to make known their decision before the date specified in 214 shall retain the class of contribution previously notified to the Secretary-General.

217 (4) Members and Associate Members may at any time choose a class of contribution higher than the one already adopted by them.

218 (5) No reduction in a unit classification established in accordance with 214 to 216 can take effect during the life of the Convention.

219 7. Members and Associate Members shall pay in advance their annual contributory shares, calculated on the basis of the budget approved by the Administrative Council.

220 8. (1) Every new Member or Associate Member shall, in respect of the year of its accession, pay a contribution calculated as from the first day of the month of accession.

221 (2) Should the Convention be denounced by a Member or Associate Member, its contribution shall be paid up to the last day of the month in which such denunciation takes effect.

222 9. The amounts due shall bear interest from the beginning of each financial year of the Union at 3% (three per cent) per annum during the first six months, and at 6% (six per cent) per annum from the beginning of the seventh month.

223 10. The following provisions shall apply to contributions by recognized private operating agencies, scientific or industrial organizations and international organizations:

224 a) Recognized private operating agencies and scientific or industrial organization shall share in defraying the expenses of the International Consultative Committees in the work of which they have agreed to participate. Recognized private operating agencies shall likewise share in defraying the expenses of the administrative conferences in which they have agreed to participate, or have participated, in accordance with 621 of the General Regulations;

225 b) International organizations shall also share in defraying the expenses of the conferences or meetings in which they have been allowed to participapate, unless exempted by the Administrative Council on condition of reciprocity;

226   *c)* Recognized private operating agencies, scientific or industrial organizations and international organizations which share in defraying the expenses of conferences or meetings in accordance with **224** and **225**, shall freely choose from the scale in **212** their class of contribution for defraying Union expenses, and inform the Secretary-General of the class chosen;

227   *d)* Recognized private operating agencies, scientific or industrial organizations and international organizations which share in defraying the expenses of conferences or meetings may at any time choose a class of contribution higher than the one already adopted by them;

228   *e)* No reduction in the number of contributory units shall take effect during the life of the Convention;

229   *f)* In the case of denunciation of participation in the work of an International Consultative Committee, the contribution shall be paid up to the last day of the month in which such denunciation takes effect;

230   *g)* The amount of the contribution per unit payable by recognized private operating agencies and scientific or industrial organizations or international organizations towards the expenses of the International Consultative Committees in the work of which they have agreed to participate shall be fixed annually by the Administrative Council. The contributions shall be considered as Union income. They shall bear interest in accordance with the provisions of **222**;

231   *h)* The amount of the contribution per unit payable towards the expenses of administrative conferences by recognized private operating agencies which participate in accordance with **621** of the General Regulations and by participating international organizations shall be fixed by dividing the total amount of the budget of the Conference in question by the total number of units contributed by Members and Associate Members as their share of Union expenses. The contributions shall be considered as Union income. They shall bear interest from the sixtieth day following the day on which accounts are sent out, at the rates fixed in **222**.

232 11. Expenses incurred by laboratories and technical installations of the Union in measurements, testing, or special research for individual Members or Associate Members, groups of Members or Associate Members, or regional organizations or others, shall be borne by those Members or Associate Members, groups, organizations or others.

233 12. The sale price of documents sold to administrations, recognized private operating agencies or individuals, shall be determined by the Secretary-General, in collaboration with the Administrative Council, bearing in mind that the cost of printing and distribution should, in general, be covered by the sale of the documents.

ARTICLE 17

Languages

234 1. (1) The official languages of the Union shall be Chinese, English, French, Russian and Spanish.

235   (2) The working languages of the Union shall be English, French and Spanish.

236   (3) In case of dispute, the French text shall be authentic.

237 2. (1) The final documents of the plenipotentiary and administrative conferences, their final acts, protocols, resolutions, recommendations and opinions shall be drawn up in the official languages of the Union, in versions equivalent in form and content.

238   (2) All other documents of these conferences shall be issued in the working languages of the Union.

239 3. (1) The official service documents of the Union as prescribed by the Administrative Regulations shall be published in the five official languages.

240   (2) All other documents for general distribution prepared by the Secretary-General in the course of his duties shall be drawn up in the three working languages.

241 4. Any of the documents referred to in **237** to **240** may be published in languages other than those there specified, provided that the Members or Associate Members requesting such publication undertake to defray the whole of the cost of translation and publication involved.

242 5. (1) At conferences of the Union and whenever it is necessary at meetings of its permanent organs and of the Administrative Council, the debates shall be conducted with the aid of an efficient system of reciprocal interpretation between the three working languages and Russian.

243   (2) When all participants in a meeting agree, the debates may be conducted in fewer than the four languages mentioned above.

244 6. (1) At conferences of the Union and at meetings of its permanent organs and of the Administrative Council, languages other than those mentioned in **235** and **242** may be used:

245   *a)* if an application is made to the Secretary-General or to the Head of the permanent organ concerned to provide for the use of an additional language or languages, oral or written, provided that the additional cost so incurred shall be borne by those Members and Associate Members which have made or supported the application;

246   *b)* if any delegation itself makes arrangements at its own expense for oral translation from its own language into any one of the languages referred to in **242**.

247   (2) In the case provided for in **245**, the Secretary-General or the Head of the permanent organ concerned shall comply to the extent practicable with the application, having first obtained from the Members or Associate Members concerned an undertaking that the cost incurred will be duly repaid by them to the Union.

248   (3) In the case provided for in **246**, the delegation concerned may, furthermore, if it wishes, arrange at its own expense for oral translation into its own language from one of the languages referred to in **242**.

CHAPTER II

Application of the Convention and Regulations

ARTICLE 18

Ratification of the Convention

249 1. This Convention shall be ratified by the signatory governments in accordance with the constitutional rules in force in their respective countries. The instruments of ratification shall be deposited, in as short a time as possible, with the Secretary-General by diplomatic channel through the intermediary of the government of the country of the seat of the Union. The Secretary-General shall notify the Members and Associate Members of each deposit of ratification.

250 2. (1) During a period of two years from the date of entry into force of this Convention, a signatory government, even though it may not have deposited an instrument of ratification in accordance with **249**, shall enjoy the rights conferred on Members of the Union in **12** to **14**.

251 (2) From the end of a period of two years from the date of entry into force of this Convention, a signatory government which has not deposited an instrument of ratification in accordance with **249** shall not be entitled to vote at any conference of the Union, or at any session of the Administrative Council, or at any meeting of any of the peemanent organs of the Union, or during consultation by correspondence conducted in accordance with the provisions of the Convention until it has so deposited such an instrument. Its rights, other than voting rights, shall not be affected.

252 3. After the entry into force of this Convention in accordance with Article 53, each instrument of ratification shall become effective on the date of its deposit with the Secretary-General.

253 4. If one or more of the signatory governments do not ratify the Convention, it shall not thereby be less valid for the governments which have ratified it.

ARTICLE 19

Accession to the Convention

254 1. The government of a country, not a signatory of this Convention, may accede thereto at any time subject to the provisions of Article 1.

255 2. The instrument of accession shall be deposited with the Secretary-General by diplomatic channel through the intermediary of the government of the country of the seat of the Union. Unless otherwise specified therein, it shall become effective upon the date of its deposit. The Secretary-General shall notify the Members and Associate Members of each accession when it is received and shall forward to each of them a certified copy of the act of accession.

ARTICLE 20

Application of the Convention to Countries or Territories for whose Foreign Relations Members of the Union are responsible

256 1. Members of the Union may declare at any time that their acceptance of this Convention applies to all or a group or a single one of the countries or territories for whose foreign relations they are responsible.

257 2. A declaration made in accordance with **256** shall be communicated to the Secretary-General, who shall notify the Members and Associate Members of each such declaration.

258 3. The provisions of **256** and **257** shall not be deemed to be obligatory in respect of any country, territory or group of territories listed in Annex 1 of this Convention.

ARTICLE 21

Application of the Convention to Trust Territories of the United Nations

259 The United Nations shall have the right to accede to this Convention on behalf of any territory or group of territories placed under its administration in accordance with a trusteeship agreement as provided for in Article 75 of the Charter of the United Nations.

ARTICLE 22

Execution of the Convention and Regulations

260 1. The Members and Associate Members are bound to abide by the provisions of this Convention and the Regulations annexed thereto in all telecommunication offices and stations established or operated by them which engage in international services or which are capable of causing harmful interference to radio services of other countries, except in regard to services exempted from there obligations in accordance with the provisions of Article 51 of this Convention.

261 2. They are also bound to take the necessary steps to impose the observance of the provisions of this Convention and of the Regulations annexed thereto upon private operating agencies authorized by them to establish and operate telecommunications and which engage in international services or which operate stations capable of causing harmful interference to the radio services of other countries.

ARTICLE 23

Denunciation of the Convention

262 1. Each Member and Associate Member which has ratified, or acceded to, this Convention shall have the right to denounce it by a notification addressed to the Secretary-General by diplomatic channel through the intermediary of the government of the country of the seat of the Union. The Secretary-General shall advise the other Members and Associate Members thereof.

263 2. This denunciation shall take effect at the expiration of a period of one year from the day of the receipt of notification of it by the Secretary-General.

ARTICLE 24

Denunciation of the Convention on behalf of Countries or Territories for whose Foreign Relations Members of the Union are responsible

264 1. The application of this Convention to a country, territory or group of territories in accordance with Article 20 may be terminated at any time, and such country, territory or group of territories, if it is an Associate Member, ceases upon termination to be such.

265 2. The declaration of denunciation contemplated in the above paragraph shall be notified in conformity with the conditions set out in 262; it shall take effect in accordance with the provisions of 263.

ARTICLE 25

Abrogation of the earlier Convention

266 This Convention shall abrogate and replace, in relations between the Contracting Governments, the International Telecommunication Convention (Geneva, 1959).

ARTICLE 26

Validity of Administrative Regulations in force

267 The Administrative Regulations referred to in 203 are those in force at the time of signature of this Convention. They shall be regarded as annexed to this Convention and shall remain valid, subject to such partial revisions as may be adopted in consequence of the provisions of 52 until the time of entry into force of new Regulations drawn up by the competent world administrative conferences to replace them as annexes to this Convention.

ARTICLE 27

Relations with Non-contracting States

268 1. Each Member and Associate Member reserves to itself and to the recognized private operating agencies the right to fix the conditions under which it admits telecommunications exchanged with a State which is not a party to this Convention.

269 2. If a telecommunication originating in the territory of such a non-contracting State is accepted by a Member or Associate Member, it must be transmitted and, in so far as it follows the telecommunication channels of a Member or Associate Member, the obligatory provisions of the Convention and Regulations and the usual charges shall apply to it.

ARTICLE 28

Settlement of Disputes

270 1. Members and Associate Members may settle their disputes on questions relating to the application of this Convention or of the Regulations contemplated in Article 15, through diplomatic channels, or according to procedures established by bilateral or multilateral treaties concluded between them for the settlement of international disputes, or by any other method mutually agreed upon.

271 2. If none of these methods of settlement is adopted, any Member or Associate Member party to a dispute may submit the dispute to arbitration in accordance with the procedure defined in Annex 3, or in the Optional Additional Protocol, as the case may be.

CHAPTER III

Relations with the United Nations and with International Organizations

ARTICLE 29

Relations with the United Nations

272 1. The relationship between the United Nations and the International Telecommunication Union is defined in the Agreement concluded between these two Organizations.

273 2. In accordance with the provision of Article XVI of the above-mentioned Agreement, the telecommunication operating services of the United Nations shall be entitled to the rights and bound by the obligations of this Convention and of the Administrative Regulations annexed thereto. Accordingly, they shall be entitled to attend all conferences of the Union, including meetings of the International Consultative Committees, in a consultative capacity.

ARTICLE 30

Relations with International Organizations

274 In furtherance of complete international coordination on matters affecting telecommunication, the Union shall cooperate with international organizations having related interests and activities.

CHAPTER IV

General Provisions relating to Telecommunications

ARTICLE 31

The Right of the Public to use the International Telecommunication Service

275 Members and Associate Members recognize the right of the public to correspond by means of the international service of public correspondence. The services, the charges and the safeguards shall be the same for all users in each category of correspondence without any priority or preference.

ARTICLE 32

Stoppage of Telecommunications

276 1. Members and Associate Members reserve the right to stop the transmission of any private telegram which may appear dangerous to the security of the State or contrary to their laws, to public order or to decency, provided that they immediately notify the office of origin of the stoppage of any such telegram or any part thereof, except when such notification may appear dangerous to the security of the State.

277 2. Members and Associate Members also reserve the right to cut off any other private telecommunications which may appear dangerous to the security of the State or contrary to their law, to public order or to decency.

ARTICLE 33

Suspension of Services

278 Each Member and Associate Member reserves the right to suspend the international telecommunication service for an indefinite time, either generally or only for certain relations and/or for certain kinds of correspondence, outgoing, incoming or in transit, provided that it immediately notifies such action to each of the other Members and Associate Members through the medium of the Secretary-General.

ARTICLE 34

Responsibility

279 Members and Associate Members accept no responsibility towards users of the international telecommunication services, particularly as regards claims for damages.

ARTICLE 35

Secrecy of Telecommunications

280 1. Members and Associate Members agree to take all possible measures, compatible with the system of telecommunication used, with a view to ensuring the secrecy of international correspondence.

281 2. Nevertheless, they reserve the right to communicate such correspondence to the competent authorities in order to ensure the application of their internal laws or the execution of international conventions to which they are parties.

ARTICLE 36

Establishment, Operation, and Protection of Telecommunication Installations and Channels

282 1. Members and Associate Members shall take such steps as may be necessary to ensure the establishment, under the best technical conditions, of the channels and installations necessary to carry on the rapid and uninterrupted exchange of international telecommunications.

283 2. So far as possible, these channels and installations must be operated by the methods and procedures which practical operating experience has shown to be the best. They must be maintained in proper operating condition and kept abreast of scientific and technical progress.

284 3. Members and Associate Members shall safeguard these channels and installations within their jurisdiction.

285 4. Unless other conditions are laid down by special arrangements, each Member and Associate Member shall take such steps as may be necessary to ensure maintenance of those sections of international telecommunication circuits within its control.

ARTICLE 37

Notification of Infringements

286 In order to facilitate the application of the provisions of Article **22** of this Convention, Members and Associate Members undertake to inform one another of infringements of the provisions of this Convention and of the Regulations annexed thereto.

ARTICLE 38

Charges and Free Services

287 The provisions regarding charges for telecommunications and the various cases in which free services are accorded are set forth in the Regulations annexed to this Convention.

ARTICLE 39

Priority of Telecommunications concerning Safety of Life

288 The international telecommunication services must give absolute priority to all telecommunications concerning safety of life at sea, on land, in the air or in outer space, as well as to epidemiological telecommunications of exceptional urgency of the World Health Organization.

ARTICLE 40

Priority of Government Telegrams and Telephone Calls

289 Subject to the provisions of Articles **39** and **49** of this Convention, government telegrams shall enjoy priority over other telegrams when priority is requested for them by the sender. Government telephone calls may also be given priority, upon specific request and to the extent practicable, over other telephone calls.

ARTICLE 41

Secret Language

290 1. Government telegrams and service telegrams may be expressed in secret language in all relations.

291 2. Private telegrams in secret language may be admitted between all countries with the exception of those which have previously notified, through the medium of the Secretary-General, that they do not admit this language for those categories of correspondence.

292 3. Members and Associate Members which do not admit private telegrams in secret language originating in or destined for their own territory must let them pass in transit, except in the case of suspension of service provided for in Article **33** of this Convention.

ARTICLE 42

Rendering and Settlement of Accounts

293 1. Administrations of Members and Associate Members and recognized private operating agencies which operate international telecommunication services, shall come to an agreement with regard to the amount of their credits and debits.

294 2. The statements of accounts in respect to debits and credits referred to in **293** shall be drawn up in accordance with the provisions of the Regulations annexed to this Convention, unless special arrangements have been concluded between the parties concerned.

295 3. The settlement of international accounts shall be regarded as current transactions and shall be effected in accordance with the current international obligations of the countries concerned, in those cases where their governments have concluded arrangements on this subject. Where no such arrangements have been concluded, and in the absence of special agreements made under Article 44 of this Convention, these settlements shall be effected in accordance with the Regulations.

ARTICLE 43

Monetary Unit

296 The monetary unit used in the composition of the tariffs of the international telecommunication services and in the establishment of the international accounts shall be the gold franc of 100 centimes, of a weight of 10/31 of a gramme and of a fineness of 0.900.

ARTICLE 44

Special Agreements

297 Members and Associate Members reserve for themselves, for the private operating agencies recognized by them and for other agencies duly authorized to do so, the right to make special agreements on telecommunication matters which do not concern Members and Associate Members in general. Such agreements, however, shall not be in conflict with the terms of this Convention or of the Regulations annexed thereto, so far as concerns the harmful interference which their operation might be likely to cause to the radio services of other countries.

ARTICLE 45

Regional Conferences, Agreements and Organizations

298 Members and Associate Members reserve the right to convene regional conferences, to conclude regional agreements and to form regional organizations, for the purpose of settling telecommunication questions which are susceptible of being treated on a regional basis. Such agreements shall not be in conflict with this Convention.

CHAPTER V

Special Provisions for Radio

ARTICLE 46

Rational Use of the Radio Frequency Spectrum

299 Members and Associate Members recognize that it is desirable to limit the number of frequencies and the spectrum space used to the minimum essential to provide in a satisfactory manner the necessary services. To that end it is desirable that the latest technical advances be applied as soon as possible.

ARTICLE 47

Intercommunication

300 1. Stations performing radiocommunication in the mobile service shall be bound, within the limits of their normal employment, to exchange radiocommunications reciprocally without distinction as to the radio system adopted by them.

301 2. Nevertheless, in order not to impede scientific progress, the provisions of 300 shall not prevent the use of a radio system incapable of communicating with other systems, provided that such incapacity is due to the specific nature of such system and is not the result of devices adopted solely with the object of preventing intercommunication.

302 3. Notwithstanding the provisions of 300, a station may be assigned to a restricted international service of telecommunication, determined by the purpose of such service, or by other circumstances independent of the system used.

ARTICLE 48

Harmful Interference

303 1. All stations, whatever their purpose, must be established and operated in such a manner as not to cause harmful interference to the radio services or communications of other Members or Associate Members or of recognized private operating agencies, or of other duly authorized operating agencies which carry on radio service, and which operate in accordance with the provisions of the Radio Regulations.

304 2. Each Member or Associate Member undertakes to require the private operating agencies which it recognizes and the other operating agencies duly authorized for this purpose, to observe the provisions of 303.

305 3. Further, the Members and Associate Members recognize the desirability of taking all practicable steps to prevent the operation of electrical apparatus and installations of all kinds from causing harmful interference to the radio services or communications mentioned in 303.

ARTICLE 49

Distress Calls and Messages

306 Radio stations shall be obliged to accept, with absolute priority, distress calls and messages regardless of their origin, to reply in the same manner to such messages, and immediately to take such action in regard thereto as may be required.

ARTICLE 50

False or Deceptive Distress, Urgency, Safety or Identification Signals

307 Members and Associate Members agree to take the steps required to prevent the transmission or circulation of false or deceptive distress, urgency, safety or identification signals, and to collaborate in locating and identifying stations transmitting such signals from their own country.

ARTICLE 51

Installations for National Defence Services

308 1. Members and Associate Members retain their entire freedom with regard to military radio installations of their army, naval and air forces.

309 2. Nevertheless, these installations must, so far as possible, observe statutory provisions relative to giving assistance in case of distress and to the measures to be taken to prevent harmful interference, and the provisions of the Regulations concerning the types of emission and the frequencies to be used, according to the nature of the service performed by such installations.

310 3. Moreover, when these installations take part in the service of public correspondence or other services governed by the Regulations annexed to this Convention, they must, in general, comply with the regulatory provisions for the conduct of such services.

CHAPTER VI

Definitions

ARTICLE 52

Definitions

311 In this Convention, unless the context otherwise requires,
    a) the terms which are defined in Annex 2 to this Convention shall have the meanings therein assigned to them;

312 *b)* other terms which are defined in the Regulations referred to in Article 15 shall have the meanings therein assigned to them.

CHAPTER VII

Final Provisions

ARTICLE 53

Effective Date of the Convention

313 The present Convention shall enter into force on January first nineteen hundred and sixty-seven between countries, territories or groups of territories, in respect of which instruments of ratification or accession have been deposited before that date.

IN WITNESS WHEREOF the respective plenipotentiaries have signed the Convention in each of the Chinese, English, French, Russian and Spanish languages, in a single copy in which, in case of dispute, the French text shall be authentic, and which shall remain deposited in the archives of the International Telecommunication Union, which shall forward a copy to each of the signatory countries.

Done at Montreaux, 12 November 1965.

12. WORLD METEOROLOGICAL ORGANIZATION

a. CONVENTION OF THE WORLD METEOROLOGICAL ORGANIZATION, DONE AT WASHINGTON, D.C., OCTOBER 11, 1947[1]

With a view to co-ordinating, standardizing and improving world meteorological activities, and to encouraging an efficient exchange of meteorological information between countries in the aid of human activities, the contracting States agree to the present Convention, as follows:

PART I

Establishment

ARTICLE 1

The World Meteorological Organization (hereinafter called "the Organization)" is hereby established.

PART II

ARTICLE 2

Purposes

The purposes of the Organization shall be:

(a) To facilitate world-wide co-operation in the establishment of networks of stations for the making of meteorological observations or other geophysical observations related to meteorology, and to promote the establishment and maintenance of meteorological centres charged with the provision of meteorological services;

(b) To promote the establishment and maintenance of systems for the rapid exchange of meteorological information;

(c) To promote standardization of meteorological observations and to ensure the uniform publication of observations and statistics;

(d) To further the application of meteorology to aviation, shipping, water problems, agriculture and other human activities; and

(e) To encourage research and training in meteorology and to assist in co-ordinating the international aspects of such research and training.

PART III

Membership

ARTICLE 3

Members

The following may become Members of the Organization by the procedure set forth in the present Convention:

---

[1]Material supplied by the United Nations.

(a) Any State represented at the Conference of Directors of the International Meteorological Organization convened at Washington, D.C., on 22 September 1947, as listed in Annex I attached hereto and which signs the present Convention and ratifies it in accordance with Article 32, or which accedes thereto, in accordance with Article 33;

(b) Any Member of the United Nations having a Meteorological Service by acceding to the present Convention in accordance with Article 33;

(c) Any State fully responsible for the conduct of its international relations and having a Meteorological Service, not listed in Annex I of the present Convention and not a Member of the United Nations, after submission of a request for membership to the Secretariat of the Organization and after its approval by two-thirds of the Members of the Organization as specified in paragraphs *(a)*, *(b)* and *(c)* of this Article, by acceding to the present Convention in accordance with Article 33;

(d) Any territory or group of territories maintaining its own Meteorological Service and listed in Annex II attached hereto, upon application of the present Convention on its behalf, in accordance with paragraph *(a)* of Article 34, by the State or States responsible for its international relations and represented at the Conference of Directors of the International Meteorological Organization convened at Washington, D.C., on 22 September 1947, as listed in Annex 1 of the present Convention;

(e) Any territory or group of territories not listed in Annex II of the present Convention, maintaining its own Meteorological Service but not responsible for the conduct of its international relations, on behalf of which the present Convention is applied in accordance with paragraph *(b)* of Article 34; provided that the request for membership is presented by the Member responsible for its international relations, and secures approval by two-thirds of the Members of the Organization as specified in paragraphs *(a)*, *(b)* and *(c)* of this Article;

(f) Any trust territory or group of trust territories maintaining its own Meteorological Service, and administered by the United Nations, to which the United Nations applies the present Convention in accordance with Article 34.

Any request for membership in the Organization shall state in accordance with which paragraph of this Article membership is sought.

PART IV

Organization

ARTICLE 4

(a) The Organization shall comprise:
   (1) The World Meteorological Congress (hereinafter called "Congress");
   (2) The Executive Committee;
   (3) Regional Meteorological Associations (hereinafter called "the Regional Associations");
   (4) Technical Commissions;
   (5) The Secretariat.

(b) There shall be a President and three Vice-Presidents of the Organization who shall also be President and Vice-Presidents of Congress and of the Executive Committee.

ARTICLE 5

The activities of the Organization and the conduct of its affairs shall be decided by the Members of the Organization.

(a) Such decisions shall normally be taken by Congress in session.

(b) However, except on matters reserved in the Convention for decisions by Con-

gress, decisions may also be taken by Members by correspondence, when urgent action is required between sessions of Congress. Such a vote shall be taken upon receipt by the Secretary-General of the request of a majority of the Members of the Organization, or when so decided by the Executive Committee.

Such votes shall be conducted in accordance with Articles 11 and 12 of the Convention and with the General Regulations (hereinafter referred to as "the Regulations").

PART V

Officers of the Organization and members of the Executive Committee

ARTICLE 6

(a) Eligibility for election to the offices of President and Vice-Presidents of the Organization, of President and Vice-President of the Regional Associations, and for membership, subject to the provisions of Article 13 *(c)* (ii) of the Convention, of the Executive Committee, shall be confined to persons who are designated as the Directors of their Meteorological Service by the Members of the Organization for the purpose of this Convention.

(b) In the performance of their duties, all officers of the Organization and members of the Executive Committee shall act as representatives of the Organization and not as representatives of particular Members thereof.

PART VI

The World Meteorological Congress

ARTICLE 7

Composition

(a) The Congress is the general assembly of delegates representing Members and as such is the supreme body of the Organization.

(b) Each Member shall designate one of its delegates, who should be the Director of its Meteorological Service, as its principal delegate at Congress.

(c) With a view to securing the widest possible technical representation, any Director of a Meteorological Service or any other individual may be invited by the President to be present at and to participate in the discussions of Congress in accordance with the provisions of the Regulations.

ARTICLE 8

Functions

In addition to the functions set out in other Articles of the Convention, the primary duties of Congress shall be:

(a) To determine general policies for the fulfilment of the purposes of the Organization as set forth in Article 2;

(b) To make recommendations to Members on matters within the purposes of the Organization;

(c) To refer to any body of the Organization any matter within the provisions of the Convention upon which such a body is empowered to act;

(d) To determine regulations prescribing the procedures of the various bodies of the Organization, in particular the General, Technical, Financial and Staff Regulations;

(e) To consider the reports and activities of the Executive Committee and to take appropriate action in regard thereto;

(f) To establish Regional Associations in accordance with the provisions of Article 18; to determine their geographical limits, co-ordinate their activities, and consider their recommendations;

(g) To establish Technical Commissions in accordance with the provisions of Article 19; to define their terms of reference, co-ordinate their activities, and consider their recommendations;

(h) To determine the location of the Secretariat of the Organization;

(i) To elect the President and Vice-Presidents of the Organization, and members of the Executive Committee other than the Presidents of the Regional Associations.

Congress may also take any other appropriate action on matters affecting the Organization.

ARTICLE 9

Execution of Congress decisions

(a) All Members shall do their utmost to implement the decisions of Congress.

(b) If, however, any Member finds it impracticable to give effect to some requirement in a technical resolution adopted by Congress, such Member shall inform the Secretary-General of the Organization whether its inability to give effect to it is provisional or final, and state its reasons therefor.

ARTICLE 10

Sessions

(a) Congress shall normally be convened at intervals as near as possible to four years, at a place and on a date to be decided by the Executive Committee.

(b) An extraordinary Congress may be convened by decision of the Executive Committee.

(c) On receipt of requests for an extraordinary Congress from one-third of the Members of the Organization the Secretary-General shall conduct a vote by correspondence, and if a simple majority of the Members are in favour an extraordinary Congress shall be convened.

ARTICLE 11

Voting

(a) In a vote in Congress each Member shall have one vote. However, only Members of the Organization which are States (hereinafter referred to as "Members which are States") shall be entitled to vote or to take a decision on the following subjects:

(1) Amendment or interpretation of the Convention or proposals for a new Convention;

(2) Requests for Membership of the Organization;

(3) Relations with the United Nations and other intergovernmental organizations;

(4) Election of the President and Vice-Presidents of the Organization and of the members of the Executive Committee other than the Presidents of the Regional Associations.

(b) Decisions shall be by a two-thirds majority of the votes cast for and against, except that elections of individuals to serve in any capacity in the Organization shall be by simple majority of the votes cast. The provisions of this paragraph, however, shall not apply to decisions taken in accordance with Articles 3, 10 *(c)*, 25, 26 and 28 of the Convention.

ARTICLE 12

Quorum

The presence of delegates of a majority of the Members shall be required to constitute a quorum for meetings of Congress. For those meetings of Congress at which decisions are taken on the subjects enumerated in paragraph *(a)* of Article 11, the presence of delegates of a majority of the Members which are States shall be required to constitute a quorum.

PART VII

The Executive Committee

ARTICLE 13

Composition

The Executive Committee shall consist of:

(a) The President and the Vice-Presidents of the Organization;

(b) The Presidents of Regional Associations who can be replaced at sessions by their alternates, as provided for in the Regulations;

(c) Fourteen Directors of Meteorological Services of Members of the Organization, who can be replaced at sessions by alternates, provided:

    (i) That these alternates shall be as provided for in the Regulations;

    (ii) That not more than seven and not less than two members of the Executive Committee, comrpising the President and Vice-Presidents of the Organization, the Presidents of Regional Associations and the fourteen elected Directors, shall come from one Region, this Region being determined in the case of each member in accordance with the Regulations.

ARTICLE 14

Functions

The Executive Committee is the executive body of the Organization and is responsible to Congress for the co-ordination of the programme of the Organization and for the utilization of its budgetary resources in accordance with the decisions of Congress.

In addition to functions set out in other Articles of the Convention, the primary functions of the Executive Committee shall be:

(a) To implement the decisions taken by the Members of the Organization either in Congress or by means of correspondence and to conduct the activities of the Organization in accordance with the intention of such decisions;

(b) To examine the programme and budget estimates for the following financial period prepared by the Secretary-General and to present its observations and its recommendations thereon to Congress;

(c) To consider and, where necessary, take action on behalf of the Organization on resolutions and recommendations of Regional Associations and Technical Commissions in accordance with the procedures laid down in the Regulations;

(d) To provide technical information, counsel and assistance in the field of meteorology;

(e) To study and make recommendations on any matter affecting international meteorology and the operation of Meteorological Services;

(f) To prepare the agenda for Congress and to give guidance to the Regional Associations and Technical Commissions in the preparation of their agenda;

(g) To report on its activities to each session of Congress;

(h) To administer the finances of the Organization in accordance with the provisions of Part XI of the Convention.

The Executive Committee may also perform such other functions as may be conferred on it by Congress or by Members collectively.

ARTICLE 15

Sessions

(a) The Executive Committee shall normally hold a session at least once a year, at a place and on a date to be determined by the President of the Organization after consultation with other members of the Committee.

(b) An extraordinary session of the Executive Committee shall be convened according to the procedures contained in the Regulations, after receipt by the Secretary-General of requests from a majority of the members of the Executive Committee. Such a session may also be convened by agreement between the President and the three Vice-Presidents of the Organization.

ARTICLE 16

Voting

(a) Decisions of the Executive Committee shall be by two-thirds majority of the votes for and against. Each member of the Executive Committee shall have only one vote, notwithstanding that he may be a member in more than one capacity.

(b) Between sessions the Executive Committee may vote by correspondence. Such votes shall be conducted in accordance with Articles 16 *(a)* and 17 of the Convention.

ARTICLE 17

Quorum

The presence of two-thirds of the members shall be required to constitute a quorum for meetings of the Executive Committee.

PART VIII

Regional Associations

ARTICLE 18

(a) Regional Associations shall be composed of the Members of the Organization, the networks of which lie in or extend into the Region.

(b) Members of the Organization shall be entitled to attend the meetings of Regional Associations to which they do not belong, to take part in the discussions and to present their views upon questions affecting their own Meteorological Service, but shall not have the right to vote.

(c) Regional Associations shall meet as often as necessary. The time and place of the meeting shall be determined by the Presidents of the Regional Associations in agreement with the President of the Organization.

(d) The functions of the Regional Associations shall be:

    (i) To promote the execution of the resolutions of Congress and the Executive Committee in their respective Regions;

    (ii) To consider matters brought to their attention by the Executive Committee;

(iii) To discuss matters of general meteorological interest and to co-ordinate meteorological and associated activities in their respective Regions;

(iv) To make recommendations to Congress and the Executive Committee on matters within the purposes of the Organization;

(v) To perform such other functions as may be conferred on them by Congress.

(e) Each Regional Association shall elect its President and Vice-President.

PART IX

Technical Commissions

ARTICLE 19

(a) Commissions consisting of technical experts may be established by Congress to study and make recommendations to Congress and the Executive Committee on any subject within the purpose of the Organization.

(b) Members of the Organization have the right to be represented on the Technical Commissions.

(c) Each Technical Commission shall elect its President and Vice-President.

(d) Presidents of Technical Commissions may participate without vote in the meetings of Congress and of the Executive Committee.

PART X

The Secretariat

ARTICLE 20

The permanent Secretariat of the Organization shall be composed of a Secretary-General and such technical and clerical staff as may be required for the work of the Organization.

ARTICLE 21

(a) The Secretary-General shall be appointed by Congress on such terms as Congress may approve.

(b) The staff of the Secretariat shall be appointed by the Secretary-General with the approval of the Executive Committee in accordance with regulations established by the Congress.

ARTICLE 22

(a) The Secretary-General is responsible to the President of the Organization for the technical and administrative work of the Secretariat.

(b) In the performance of their duties, the Secretary-General and the staff shall not seek or receive instructions from any authority external to the Organization. They shall refrain from any action which might reflect on their position as international officers. Each Member of the Organization on its part shall respect the exclusively international character of the responsibilities of the Secretary-General and the staff and not seek to influence them in the discharge of their responsibilities to the Organization.

PART XI

Finances

ARTICLE 23

(a) Congress shall determine the maximum expenditure which may be incurred by the Organization on the basis of the estimates submitted by the Secretary-General after prior examination by, and with the recommendations of, the Executive Committee.

(b) Congress shall delegate to the Executive Committee such authority as may be required to approve the annual expenditures of the Organization within the limitations determined by Congress.

ARTICLE 24

The expenditures of the Organization shall be apportioned among the Members of the Organization in the proportions determined by Congress.

PART XII

Relations with the United Nations

ARTICLE 25

The Organization shall be in relationship to the United Nations pursuant to Article 57 of the Charter of the United Nations. Any agreement concerning such relationship shall require approval by two-thirds of the Members which are States.

PART XIII

Relations with other organizations

ARTICLE 26

(a) The Organization shall establish effective relations and co-operate closely with such other intergovernmental organizations as may be desirable. Any formal agreement entered into with such organizations shall be made by the Executive Committee, subject to approval by two-thirds of the Members which are States, either in Congress or by correspondence.

(b) The Organization may on matters within its purposes make suitable arrangements for consultation and co-operation with non-governmental international organizations and, with the consent of the government concerned, with national organizations, governmental or non-governmental.

(c) Subject to approval by two-thirds of the Members which are States, the Organization may take over from any other international organization or agency, the purpose and activities of which lie within the purposes of the Organization, such functions, resources and obligations as may be transferred to the Organization by international agreement or by mutually acceptable arrangements entered into between competent authorities of the respective organizations.

374

PART XIV

Legal status, privileges and immunities

ARTICLE 27

(a) The Organization shall enjoy in the territory of each Member such legal capacity as may be necessary for the fulfilment of its purposes and for the exercise of its functions.

(b) (i) The Organization shall enjoy in the territory of each Member to which the present Convention applies such privileges and immunities as may be necessary for the fulfilment of its purposes and for the exercise of its functions.

(ii) Representatives of Members, officers and officials of the Organization, as well as members of the Executive Committee, shall similarly enjoy such privileges and immunities as are necessary for the independent exercise of their functions in connexion with the Organization.

(c) In the territory of any Member which is a State and which has acceded to the Convention on the Privileges and Immunities of the Specialized Agencies adopted by the General Assembly of the United Nations on 21 November 1947, such legal capacity, privileges and immunities shall be those defined in the said Convention.

PART XV

Amendments

ARTICLE 28

(a) The text of any proposed amendment to the present Convention shall be communicated by the Secretary-General to Members of the Organization at least six months in advance of its consideration by Congress.

(b) Amendments to the present Convention involving new obligations for Members shall require approval by Congress, in accordance with the provisions of Article 11 of the present Convention, by a two-thirds majority vote, and shall come into force on acceptance by two-thirds of the Members which are States for each such Member accepting the amendment, and thereafter for each remaining such Member on acceptance by it. Such amendments shall come into force for any Member not responsible for its own international relations upon the acceptance on behalf of such a Member by the Member responsible for the conduct of its international relations.

(c) Other amendments shall come into force upon approval by two-thirds of the Members which are States.

PART XVI

Interpretation and disputes

ARTICLE 29

Any question or dispute concerning the interpretation or application of the present Convention which is not settled by negotiation or by Congress shall be referred to an independent arbitrator appointed by the President of the International Court of Justice, unless the parties concerned agree on another mode of settlement.

PART XVII

Withdrawal

ARTICLE 30

(a) Any Member may withdraw from the Organization on twelve months' notice in writing given by it to the Secretary-General of the Organization, who shall at once inform all the Members of the Organization of such notice of withdrawal.

(b) Any Member of the Organization not responsible for its own international relations may be withdrawn from the Organization on twelve months' notice in writing given by the Member or other authority responsible for its international relations to the Secretary-General of the Organization, who shall at once inform all the Members of the Organization of such notice of withdrawal.

PART XVIII

Suspension

ARTICLE 31

If any Member fails to meet its financial obligations to the Organization or otherwise fails in its obligations under the present Convention, Congress may by resolution suspend it from exercising its rights and enjoying privileges as a Member of the Organization until it has met such financial or other obligations.

PART XIX

Ratification and accession

ARTICLE 32

The present Convention shall be ratified by the signatory States and the instruments of ratification shall be deposited with the Government of the United States of America, which will notify each signatory and acceding State of the date of deposit thereof.

ARTICLE 33

Subject to the provisions of Article 3 of the present Convention, accession shall be effected by the deposit of an instrument of accession with the Government of the United States of America, which shall notify each Member of the Organization thereof.

ARTICLE 34

Subject to the provisions of Article 3 of the present Convention:

(a) Any contracting State may declare that its ratification of, or accession to, the present Convention includes any territory or group of territories for the international relations of which it is responsible.

(b) The present Convention may at any time thereafter be applied to any such territory or group of territories upon a notification in writing to the Government of the United States of America and the present Convention shall apply to the territory or group of territories on the date of the receipt of the notification by the Government of the United States of America, which will notify each signatory and acceding State thereof.

(c) The United Nations may apply the present Convention to any trust territory or group of trust territories for which it is the administering authority. The Government of the United States of America will notify all signatory and acceding States of any such application.

PART XX

Entry into force

ARTICLE 35

The present Convention shall come into force on the thirtieth day after the date of the deposit of the thirtieth instrument of ratification or accession. The present Convention shall come into force for each State ratifying or acceding after that date on the thirtieth day after the deposit of its instrument of ratification or accession.

The present Convention shall bear the date on which it is opened for signature and shall remain open for signature for a period of one hundred and twenty days thereafter.

IN WITNESS WHEREOF the undersigned, being duly authorized by their respective governments, have signed the present Convention.

DONE at Washington this eleventh day of October 1947, in the English and French languages, each equally authentic, the original of which shall be deposited in the archives of the Government of the United States of America. The Government of the United States of America shall transmit certified copies thereof to all the signatory and acceding States.

The signatures of the delegates of the countries follow here.

SIGNATORY COUNTRIES

The Convention, which was opened for signature on 11 October 1947, at Washington and remained open for signature for a period of one hundred and twenty days thereafter, has been signed on behalf of the following countries:

ARGENTINA	INDIA
AUSTRALIA	IRELAND
BELGIUM	ITALY
(including the Belgian Congo)	MEXICO
BRAZIL	KINGDOM OF THE NETHERLANDS
BURMA	NEW ZEALAND
CANADA	NORWAY
CHILE	PAKISTAN
CHINA	PARAGUAY
COLOMBIA	POLAND
CUBA	PORTUGAL
CZECHOSLOVAKIA	REPUBLIC OF THE PHILIPPINES
DENMARK	SIAM
DOMINICAN REPUBLIC	SWEDEN
ECUADOR	SWITZERLAND
EGYPT	TURKEY
FINLAND	UNION OF SOUTH AFRICA
FRANCE	UNITED KINGDOM OF GREAT BRITAIN
GREECE	and NOTHERN IRELAND
GUATEMALA	UNITED STATES OF AMERICA
HUNGARY	URUGUAY
ICELAND	YUGOSLAVIA

ANNEX I

States represented at the Conference of Directors
of the International Meteorological Organization convened
at Washington, D.C., on 22 September 1947

ARGENTINA

AUSTRALIA

BELGIUM

BRAZIL

BURMA

CANADA

CHILE

CHINA

COLOMBIA

CUBA

CZECHOSLOVAKIA

DENMARK

DOMINICAN REPUBLIC

ECUADOR

EGYPT

FINLAND

FRANCE

GREECE

GUATEMALA

HUNGARY

ICELAND

INDIA

IRELAND

ITALY

MEXICO

NETHERLANDS

NEW ZEALAND

NORWAY

PAKISTAN

PARAGUAY

PHILIPPINES

POLAND

PORTUGAL

RUMANIA

SIAM

SWEDEN

SWITZERLAND

TURKEY

UNION OF SOUTH AFRICA

UNION OF SOVIET SOCIALIST
   REPUBLICS

UNITED KINGDOM OF GREAT BRITAIN
   AND NORTHERN IRELAND

UNITED STATES OF AMERICA

URUGUAY

VENEZUELA

YUGOSLAVIA

ANNEX II

Territories or groups of territories which maintain their own Meteorological Services
and of which the States responsible for their international relations are represented
at the Conference of Directors of the International Meteorological Organization
convened at Washington, D.C., on 22 September 1947

ANGLO EGYPTIAN SUDAN

BELGIAN CONGO

BERMUDA

BRITISH EAST AFRICA

BRITISH GUIANA

BRITISH WEST AFRICA

CAMEROONS

CAPE VERDE ISLANDS

CEYLON

CURACAO

FRENCH EQUATORIAL AFRICA

FRENCH OCEANIC COLONIES

FRENCH SOMALILAND

FRENCH TOGOLAND

FRENCH WEST AFRICA

HONG KONG

INDO-CHINA

JAMAICA

MADAGASCAR

MALAYA

MAURITIUS

MOROCCO
   (not including the Spanish Zone)

NETHERLANDS INDIES

NEW CALEDONIA

PALESTINE

PORTUGUESE EAST AFRICA

PORTUGUESE WEST AFRICA

RHODESIA

SURINAM

TUNISIA

13. INTER-GOVERNMENTAL MARITIME CONSULTATIVE ORGANIZATION

a. CONVENTION ON THE INTER-GOVERNMENTAL MARITIME CONSULTATIVE ORGANIZATION, DONE AT GENEVA, MARCH 6, 1948 AND AMENDED IN ACCORDANCE WITH ASSEMBLY RESOLUTIONS ADOPTED ON SEPTEMBER 15, 1964 AND SEPTEMBER 29, 1965[1]

PART I

Purposes of the Organization

Article 1

The purposes of the Organization are:

(a) To provide machinery for co-operation among Governments in the field of governmental regulation and practices relating to technical matters of all kinds affecting shipping engaged in international trade, and to encourage the general adoption of the highest practicable standards in matters concerning maritime safety and efficiency of navigation;

(b) To encourage the removal of discriminatory action and unnecessary restrictions by Governments affecting shipping engaged in international trade so as to promote the availability of shipping services to the commerce of the world without discrimination; assistance and encouragement given by a Government for the development of its national shipping and for purposes of security does not in itself constitute discrimination, provided that such assistance and encouragement is not based on measures designed to restrict the freedom of shipping of all flags to take part in international trade;

(c) To provide for the consideration by the Organization of matters concerning unfair restrictive practices by shipping concerns in accordance with Part II;

(d) To provide for the consideration by the Organization of any matters concerning shipping that may be referred to it by an organ or specialized agency of the United Nations;

(e) To provide for the exchange of information among Governments on matters under consideration by the Organization.

PART II

Functions

Article 2

The functions of the Organization shall be consultative and advisory.

Article 3

In order to achieve the purposes set out in Part I, the functions of the Organization shall be:

---

[1]Material supplied by the United Nations.

(a) Subject to the provisions of Article 4, to consider and make recommendations upon matters arising under Article 1 *(a)*, *(b)* and *(c)* that may be remitted to it by Members, by any organ or specialized agency of the United Nations or by any other inter-governmental organization or upon matters referred to it under Article 1 *(d)*;

(b) To provide for the drafting of conventions, agreements, or other suitable instruments, and to recommend these to Governments and to intergovernmental organizations, and to convene such conferences as may be necessary;

(c) To provide machinery for consultation among Members and the exchange of information among Governments.

Article 4

In those matters which appear to the Organization capable of settlement through the normal processes of international shipping business the Organization shall so recommend. When in the opinion of the Organization, any matter concerning unfair restrictive practices by shipping concerns is incapable of settlement through the normal processes of international shipping business, or has in fact so proved, and provided it shall first have been the subject of direct negotiations between the Members concerned, the Organization shall, at the request of one of those Members, consider the matter.

PART III

Membership

Article 5

Membership in the Organization shall be open to all States, subject to the provisions of Part III.

Article 6

Members of the United Nations may become Members of the Organization by becoming parties to the Convention in accordance with the provisons of Article 57.

Article 7

States not Members of the United Nations which have been invited to send representatives to the United Nations Maritime Conference convened in Geneva on 19 February 1948, may become Members by becoming parties to the Convention in accordance with the provisions of Article 57.

Article 8

Any State not entitled to become a Member under Article 6 or 7 may apply through the Secretary-General of the Organization to become a Member and shall be admitted as a Member upon its becoming a party to the Convention in accordance with the provisions of Article 57 provided that, upon the recommendation of the Council, its application has been approved by two-thirds of the Members other than Associate Members.

Article 9

Any Territory or group of Territories to which the Convention has been made applicable under Article 58, by the Member having responsibility for its international relations or by the United Nations, may become an Associate Member of the Organization by notification in writing given by such Member or by the United Nations, as the case may be, to the Secretary-General of the United Nations.

Article 10

An Associate Member shall have the rights and obligations of a Member under the Convention except that it shall not have the right to vote in the Assembly or be eligible for membership on the Council or in the Maritime Safety Committee and subject to this the word "Member" in the Convention shall be deemed to include Associate Member unless the context otherwise requires.

Article 11

No State or Territory may become or remain a Member of the Organization contrary to a resolution of the General Assembly of the United Nations.

PART IV

Organs

Article 12

The Organization shall consist of an Assembly, a Council, a Maritime Safety Committee, and such subsidiary organs as the Organization may at any time consider necessary; and a Secretariat.

PART V

The Assembly

Article 13

The Assembly shall consist of all the Members.

Article 14

Regular sessions of the Assembly shall take place once every two years. Extraordinary sessions shall be convened after a notice of sixty days whenever one-third of the Members give notice to the Secretary-General that they desire a session to be arranged, or at any time if deemend necessary by the Council, after a notice of sixty days.

Article 15

A majority of the Members other than Associate Members shall constitute a quorum for the meetings of the Assembly.

Article 16

The functions of the Assembly shall be:

(a) To elect at each regular session from among its Members, other than Associate Members, its President and two Vice-Presidents who shall hold office until the next regular session;

(b) To determine its own Rules of Procedure except as otherwise provided in the Convention;

(c) To establish any temporary or, upon recommendation of the Council, permanent subsidiary bodies it may consider to be necessary;

(d) To elect the Members to be represented on the Council, as provided in Article 17, and on the Maritime Safety Committee as provided in Article 28;

(e) To receive and consider the reports of the Council, and to decide upon any question referred to it by the Council;

(f) To vote the budget and determine the financial arrangements of the Organization, in accordance with Part IX;

(g) To review the expenditures and approve the accounts of the Organization;

(h) To perform the functions of the Organization, provided that in matters relating to Article 3 *(a)* and *(b)*, the Assembly shall refer such matters to the Council for formulation by it of any recommendations or instruments thereon; provided further that any recommendations or instruments submitted to the Assembly by the Council and not accepted by the Assembly shall be referred back to the Council for further consideration with such observations as the Assembly may make;

(i) To recommend to Members for adoption regulations concerning maritime safety, or amendments to such regulations, which have been referred to it by the Maritime Safety Committee thorugh the Council;

(j) To refer to the Council for consideration or decision any matters within the scope of the Organization, except that the function of making recommendations under paragraph *(i)* of this Article shall not be delegated.

PART VI

The Council

Article 17

The Council shall be composed of eighteen Members elected by the Assembly.

Article 18

In electing the Members of the Council, the Assembly shall observe the following principles:

(a) Six shall be Governments of States with the largest interest in providing international shipping services;

(b) Six shall be Governments of other States with the largest interest in international seaborne trade;

(c) Six shall be Government of States not elected under *(a)* or *(b)* above, which have special interests in maritime transport or navigation, and whose election to the Council will ensure the representation of all major geographic areas of the world.

Article 19

Members represented on the Council in accordance with Article 17 shall hold office until the end of the next regular session of the Assembly. Members shall be eligible for re-election.

Article 20

(a) The Council shall elect its Chairman and adopt its own Rules of Procedure except as otherwise provided in the Convention.

(b) Twelve Members of the Council shall constitute a quorum.

(c) The Council shall meet upon one month's notice as often as may be necessary for the efficient discharge of its duties upon the summons of its Chairman or upon request by not less than four of its Members. It shall meet at such places as may be convenient.

Article 21

The Council shall invite any Member to participate, without vote, in its deliberations on any matter of particular concern to that Member.

Article 22

(a) The Council shall receive the recommendations and reports of the Maritime Safety Committee and shall transmit them to the Assembly and, when the Assembly is not in session, to the Members for information, together with the comments and recommendations of the Council.

(b) Matters within the scope of Article 29 shall be considered by the Council only after obtaining the views of the Maritime Safety Committee thereon.

Article 23

The Council, with the approval of the Assembly, shall appoint the Secretary-General. The Council shall also make provision for the appointment of such other personnel as may be necessary, and determine the terms and conditions of service of the Secretary-General and other personnel, which terms and conditions shall conform as far as possible with those of the United Nations and its specialized agencies.

Article 24

The Council shall make a report to the Assembly at each regular session on the work of the Organization since the previous regular session of the Assembly.

Article 25

The Council shall submit to the Assembly the budget estimates and the financial statements of the Organization, together with its comments and recommendations.

Article 26

The Council may enter into agreements or arrangements covering the relationship of the Organization with other organizations, as provided for in Part XII. Such agreements or arrangements shall be subject to approval by the Assembly.

Article 27

Between sessions of the Assembly, the Council shall perform all the functions of the Organization, except the function of making recommendations under Article 16 *(i)*.

PART VII

Maritime Safety Committee

Article 28*

The Maritime Safety Committee shall consist of sixteen Members elected by the Assembly from Members, Governments of those States having an important interest in maritime safety of which:

---

*The amended text of Article 28 printed here was adopted by the Assembly of the Organization on 28 September 1965 and the date of its entry into force is 3 November 1968. The original text of the Article is as follows:

(a) Eight Members shall be elected from among the ten largest shipowning States;

(b) Four Members shall be elected in such manner as to ensure that, under this sub-paragraph, a State in each of the following areas is represented:

     I.   Africa
    II.   The Americas
   III.   Asia and Oceania
   IV.   Europe

(c) The remaining four Members shall be elected from among States not otherwise represented on the Committee.

For the purpose of this Article, States having an important interest in maritime safety shall include, for example, States interested in the supply of large numbers of crews or in the carriage of large numbers of berthed or unberthed passengers.

Members of the Maritime Safety Committee shall be elected for a term of four years and shall be eligible for re-election.

Article 29

(a) The Maritime Safety Committee shall have the duty of considering any matter within the scope of the Organization and concerned with aids to navigation, construction and equipment of vessels, manning from a safety standpoint, rules for the prevention of collisions, handling of dangerous cargoes, maritime safety procedures and requirements, hydrographic information, log-books and navigational records, marine casualty investigation, salvage and rescue, and any other matters directly affecting maritime safety.

(b) The Maritime Safety Committee shall provide machinery for performing any duties assigned to it by the Convention, or by the Assembly, or any duty within the scope of this Article which may be assigned to it by any other inter-governmental instrument.

(c) Having regard to the provisions of Part XII, the Maritime Safety Committee shall have the duty of maintaining such close relationship with other inter-governmental bodies concerned with transport and communications as may further the object of the Organization in promoting maritime safety and facilitate the co-ordination of activities in the fields of shipping, aviation, telecommunications and meteorology with respect to safety and rescue.

Article 30

The Maritime Safety Committee, through the Council, shall:

(a) Submit to the Assembly at its regular sessions proposals made by Members for safety regulations or for amendments to existing safety regulations, together with its comments or recommendations thereon;

(b) Report to the Assembly on the work of the Maritime Safety Committee since the previous regular session of the Assembly.

Article 28

(a) The Maritime Safety Committee shall consist of fourteen Members elected by the Assembly from the Members, Governments of those nations having an important interest in maritime safety, of which not less than eight shall be the largest shipowning nations, and the remainder shall be elected so as to ensure adequate representation of Members, Governments of other nations with an important interest in maritime safety, such as nations interested in the supply of large numbers of crews or in the carriage of large numbers of berthed and unberthed passengers, and of major geographical areas.

(b) Members shall be elected for a term of four years and shall be eligible for re-election.

Article 31

The Maritime Safety Committee shall meet once a year and at other times upon request of any five of its Members. It shall elect its officers once a year and shall adopt its own Rules of Procedure. A majority of its Members shall constitute a quorum.

Article 32

The Maritime Safety Committee shall invite any Member to participate, without vote, in its deliberations on any matter of particular concern to that Member.

PART VIII

The Secretariat

Article 33

The Secretariat shall comprise the Secretary-General, a Secretary of the Maritime Safety Committee and such staff as the Organizaiton may require. The Secretary-General shall be the chief administrative officer of the Organization, and shall, subject to the provisions of Article 23, appoint the above mentioned personnel.

Article 34

The Secretariat shall maintain all such records as may be necessary for the efficient discharge of the functions of the Organization and shall prepare, collect and circulate the papers, documents, agenda, minutes and information that may be required for the work of the Assembly, the Council, the Maritime Safety Committee, and such subsidiary organs as the Organization may establish.

Article 35

The Secretary-General shall prepare and submit to the Council the financial statements for each year and the budget estimates on a biennial basis, with the estimates for each year shown separately.

Article 36

The Secretary-General shall keep Members informed with respect to the activities of the Organization. Each Member may appoint one or more representatives for the purpose of communication with the Secretary-General.

Article 37

In the performance of their duties the Secretary-General and the staff shall not seek or receive instructions from any Government or from any authority external to the Organization. They shall refrain from any action which might reflect on their position as international officials. Each Member on its part undertakes to respect the exclusively international character of the responsibilities of the Secretary-General and the staff and not to seek to influence them in the discharge of their responsibilities.

Article 38

The Secretary-General shall perform such other tasks as may be assigned to him by the Convention, the Assembly, the Council and the Maritime Safety Committee.

PART IX

Finances

Article 39

Each Member shall bear the salary, travel and other expenses of its own delegation to the Assembly and of its representatives on the Council, the Maritime Safety Committee, other committees and subsidiary bodies.

Article 40

The Council shall consider the financial statements and budget estimates prepared by the Secretary-General and submit them to the Assembly with its comments and recommendations.

Article 41

(a) Subject to any agreement between the Organization and the United Nations, the Assembly shall review and approve the budget estimates.

(b) The Assembly shall apportion the expenses among the Members in accordance with a scale to be fixed by it after consideration of the proposals of the Council thereon.

Article 42

Any Member which fails to discharge its financial obligation to the Organization within one year from the date on which it is due, shall have no vote in the Assembly, the Council, or the Maritime Safety Committee unless the Assembly, at its discretion, waives this provision.

PART X

Voting

Article 43

The following provisions shall apply to voting in the Assembly, the Council and the Maritime Safety Committee:

(a) Each Member shall have one vote.

(b) Except as otherwise provided in the Convention or in any international agreement which confers functions on the Assembly, the Council, or the Maritime Safety Committee, decisions of these organs shall be by a majority vote of the Members, present and voting and, for decisions where a two-thirds majority vote is required, by a two-thirds majority vote of those present.

(c) For the purpose of the Convention, the phrase "Members present and voting" means "Members present and casting an affirmative or negative vote." Members which abstain from voting shall be considered as not voting.

PART XI

Headquarters of the Organization

Article 44

(a) The headquarters of the Organization shall be established in London.

(b) The Assembly may by a two-thirds majority vote change the site of the headquarters if necessary.

(c) The Assembly may hold sessions in any place other than the headquarters if the Council deems it necessary.

PART XII

Relationship with the United Nations and other Organizations

Article 45

The Organization shall be brought into relationship with the United Nations in accordance with Article 57 of the Charter of the United Nations as the specialized agency in the field of shipping. This relationship shall be effected through an agreement with the United Nations under Article 63 of the Charter of the United Nations, which agreement shall be concluded as provided in Article 26.

Article 46

The Organization shall co-operate with any specialized agency of the United Nations in matters which may be the common concern of the Organization and of such specialized agency, and shall consider such matters and act with respect to them in accord with such specialized agency.

Article 47

The Organization may, on matters within its scope, co-operate with other intergovernmental organizations which are not specialized agencies of the United Nations, but whose interests and activities are related to the purposes of the Organization.

Article 48

The Organization may, on matters within its scope, make suitable arrangements for consultation and co-operation with non-governmental international organizations.

Article 49

Subject to approval by a two-thirds majority vote of the Assembly, the Organization may take over from any other international organizations, governmental or nongovernmental, such functions, resources and obligations within the scope of the Organization as may be transferred to the Organization by international agreements or by mutually acceptable arrangements entered into between competent authorities of the respective organizations. Similarly, the Organization may take over any administrative functions which are within its scope and which have been entrusted to a Government under the terms of any international instrument.

PART XIII

Legal Capacity, Privileges and Immunities

Article 50

The legal capacity, privileges and immunities to be accorded to, or in connexion with, the Organization, shall be derived from and governed, by the General Convention on the Privileges and Immunities of the Specialized Agencies approved by the General Assembly of the United Nations on 21 November 1947, subject to such modifications as may be set forth in the final (or revised) text of the Annex approved by the Organization in accordance with Sections 36 and 38 of the said General Convention.

Article 51

Pending its accession to the said General Convention in respect of the Organization, each Member undertakes to apply the provisions of Appendix II to the present Convention.

PART XIV

Amendments

Article 52

Texts of proposed amendments to the Convention shall be communicated by the Secretary General to Members at least six months in advance of their consideration by the Assembly. Amendments shall be adopted by a two-thirds majority vote of the Assembly, including the concurring votes of a majority of the Members represented on the Council. Twelve months after its acceptance by two-thirds of the Members of the Organization, other than Associate Members, each amendment shall come into force for all Members except those which, before it comes into force, make a declaration that they do not accept the amendment. The Assembly may by a two-thirds majority vote determine at the time of its adoption that an amendment is of such a nature that any Member which has made such a declaration and which does not accept the amendment within a period of twelve months after the amendment comes into force shall, upon the expiration of this period, cease to be a party to the Convention.

Article 53

Any amendment adopted under Article 52 shall be deposited with the Secretary-General of the United Nations, who will immediately forward a copy of the amendment to all Members.

Article 54

A declaration or acceptance under Article 52 shall be made by the communication of an instrument to the Secretary-General for deposit with the Secretary-General of the United Nations. The Secretary-General will notify Members of the receipt of any such instrument and of the date when the amendment enters into force.

PART XV

Interpretation

Article 55

Any question or dispute concerning the interpretation or application of the Convention shall be referred for settlement to the Assembly, or shall be settled in such other manner as the parties to the dispute agree. Nothing in this Article shall preclude the Council or the Maritime Safety Committee from settling any such question or dispute that may arise during the exercise of their functions.

Section 2. (a) The Organization shall enjoy in the territory of each of its Members such privileges and immunities as are necessary for the fulfilment of its purposes and the exercise of its functions.

(b) Representatives of Members including alternates and advisers, and officials and employees of the Organization shall similarly enjoy such privileges and immunities as are necessary for the independent exercise of their functions in connexion with the Organization.

Section 3. In applying the provisions of Sections 1 and 2 of this Appendix, the Members shall take into account as far as possible the standard clauses of the General Convention on the Privileges and Immunities of the Specialized Agencies.

Article 56

Any legal question which cannot be settled as provided in Article 55 shall be referred by the Organization to the International Court of Justice for an advisory opinion in accordance with Article 96 of the Charter of the United Nations.

PART XVI

Miscellaneous Provisions

Article 57. Signature and Acceptance

Subject to the provisions of Part III the present Convention shall remain open for signature or acceptance and States may become parties to the Convention by:

(a) Signature without reservation as to acceptance;
(b) Signature subject to acceptance followed by acceptance; or
(c) Acceptance.

Acceptance shall be effected by the deposit of an instrument with the Secretary-General of the United Nations.

Article 58. Territories

(a) Members may make a declaration at any time that their participation in the Convention includes all or a group or a single one of the Territories for whose international relations they are responsible.

(b) The Convention does not apply to Territories for whose international relations Members are responsible unless a declaration to that effect has been made on their behalf under the provisions of paragraph *(a)* of this Article.

(c) A declaration made under paragraph *(a)* of this Article shall be communicated to the Secretary-General of the United Nations and a copy of it will be forwarded by him to all States invited to the United Nations Maritime Conference and to such other States as may become Members.

(d) In cases where under a Trusteeship Agreement the United Nations is the administering authority, the United Nations may accept the Convention on behalf of one, several, or all of the Trust Territories in accordance with the procedure set forth in Article 57.

Article 59. Withdrawal

(a) Any Member may withdraw from the Organization by written notification given to the Secretary-General of the United Nations, who will immediately inform the other Members and the Secretary-General of the Organization of such notification. Notification of withdrawal may be given at any time after the expiration of twelve months from the date on which the Convention has come into force. The withdrawal shall take effect upon the expiration of twelve months from the date on which such written notification is received by the Secretary-General of the United Nations.

(b) The application of the Convention to a Territory or group of Territories under Article 58 may at any time be terminated by written notification given to the Secretary-General of the United Nations by the Member responsible for its international relations or, in the case of a Trust Territory of which the United Nations is the administering authority, by the United Nations. The Secretary-General of the United Nations will immediately inform all Members and the Secretary-General of the Organization

of such notification. The notification shall take effect upon the expiration of twelve months from the date on which it is received by the Secretary-General of the United Nations.

PART XVII

Entry into Force

Article 60

The present Convention shall enter into force on the date when 21 States, of which seven shall each have a total tonnage of not less than 1,000,000 gross tons of shipping, have become parties to the Convention in accordance with Article 57.

Article 61

The Secretary-General of the United Nations will inform all States invited to the United Nations Maritime Conference and such other States as may have become Members, of the date when each State becomes party to the Convention, and also of the date on which the Convention enters into force.

Article 62

The present Convention, of which the English, French and Spanish texts are equally authentic, shall be deposited with the Secretary-General of the United Nations, who will transmit certified copies thereof to each of the States invited to the United Nations Maritime Conference and to such other States as may have become Members.

Article 63

The United Nations is authorized to effect registration of the Convention as soon as it comes into force.[1]

IN WITNESS WHEREOF the undersigned[2] being duly authorized by their respective Governments for that purpose have signed the present Convention.[3]

Done in Geneva on 6 March 1948.

APPENDIX I

(This Appendix, referred to in the text of Article 17 prior to its amendment on 17 October 1967, provided for the composition of the first Council of the Organization and has no relevance to the existing text of Article 17).

---

[1] Entered into force on 17 March 1958.
[2] Signatures omitted.
[3] The delegates at the Conference placed their signatures after the English text only although it was understood that all three texts were equally authentic.

APPENDIX II

(Referred to in Article 51)

Legal Capacity, Privileges and Immunities

The following provisions on legal capacity, privileges and immunities shall be applied by Members to, or in connexion with, the Organization pending their accession to the General Convention on Privileges and Immunities of Specialized Agencies in respect of the Organization.

Section 1. The Organization shall enjoy in the territory of each of its Members such legal capacity as is necessary for the fulfilment of its purposes and the exercise of its functions.

14. WORLD INTELLECTUAL PROPERTY ORGANIZATION

a. CONVENTION ESTABLISHING THE WORLD INTELLECTUAL PROPERTY ORGANIZATION, SIGNED AT STOCKHOLM, JULY 14, 1967 AND BECAME EFFECTIVE APRIL 26, 1970[1,2]

The Contracting Parties,

Desiring to contribute to better understanding and cooperation among States for their mutual benefit on the basis of respect for their sovereignty and equality,

Desiring, in order to encourage creative activity, to promote the protection of intellectual property throughout the world,

Desiring to modernize and render more efficient the administration of the Unions established in the fields of the protection of industrial property and the protection of literary and artistic works, while fully respecting the independence of each of the Unions,

Agree as follows:

Article 1

Establishment of the Organization

The World Intellectual Property Organization is hereby established.

Article 2

Definitions

For the purposes of this Convention:

(i) "Organization" shall mean the World Intellectual Property Organization (WIPO);

(ii) "International Bureau" shall mean the International Bureau of Intellectual Property;

(iii) "Paris Convention" shall mean the Convention for the Protection of Industrial Property signed on March 20, 1883, including any of its revisions;

(iv) "Berne Convention" shall mean the Convention for the Protection of Literary and Artistic Works signed on September 9, 1886, including any of its revisions;

(v) "Paris Union" shall mean the International Union established by the Paris Convention;

(vi) "Berne Union" shall mean the International Union established by the Berne Convention;

(vii) "Unions" shall mean the Paris Union, the Special Unions and Agreements established in relation with that Union, the Berne Union, and any other international agreement designed to promote the protection of intellectual property whose administration is assumed by the Organization according to Article 4 (iii);

---

[1] The Convention entered into force on April 26, 1970 (According to *General Information* published by World Intellectual Property Organization, Geneva, 1974, p. 35).

[2] The Convention was published by United International Bureaux for the Protection of International Property (BIRPI), Geneva, 1967 in its document 251 (E), and supplied by the Permanent Representative of the Organization to the United Nations.

(viii)   "intellectual property" shall include the rights relating to:
- -- literary, artistic and scientific works,
- — performances of performing artists, phonograms, and broadcasts,
- — inventions in all fields of human endeavor,
- — scientific discoveries,
- -- industrial designs,
- — trademarks, service marks, and commercial names and designations,
- — protection against unfair competition,

and all other rights resulting from intellectual activity in the industrial, scientific, literary or artistic fields.

Article 3

Objectives of the Organization

The objectives of the Organization are:

   (i)   to promote the protection of intellectual property throughout the world through cooperation among States and, where appropriate, in collaboration with any other international organization,

  (ii)   to ensure administrative cooperation among the Unions.

Article 4

Functions

In order to attain the objectives described in Article 3, the Organization, through its appropriate organs, and subject to the competence of each of the Unions:

    (i)   shall promote the development of measures designed to facilitate the efficient protection of intellectual property throughout the world and to harmonize national legislation in this field;

   (ii)   shall perform the administrative tasks of the Paris Union, the Special Unions established in relation with that Union, and the Berne Union;

  (iii)   may agree to assume, or participate in, the administration of any other international agreement designed to promote the protection of intellectual property;

  (iv)   shall encourage the conclusion of international agreements designed to promote the protection of intellectual property;

   (v)   shall offer its cooperation to States requesting legal-technical assistance in the field of intellectual property;

  (vi)   shall assemble and disseminate information concerning the protection of intellectual property, carry out and promote studies in this field, and publish the results of such studies;

 (vii)   shall maintain services facilitating the international protection of intellectual property and, where appropriate, provide for registration in this field and the publication of the data concerning the registrations;

(viii)   shall take all other appropriate action.

Article 5

Membership

1. Membership in the Organization shall be open to any State which is a member of any of the Unions as defined in Article 2 (vii).

2. Membership in the Organization shall be equally open to any State not a member of any of the Unions, provided that:

(i)   it is a member of the United Nations, any of the Specialized Agencies brought into relationship with the United Nations, or the International Atomic Energy Agency, or is a party to the Statute of the International Court of Justice, or

(ii)   it is invited by the General Assembly to become a party to this Convention.

Article 6

General Assembly

1. *(a)* There shall be a General Assembly consisting of the States party to this Convention which are members of any of the Unions.

(b) The Government of each State shall be represented by one delegate, who may be assisted by alternate delegates, advisors, and experts.

(c) The expenses of each delegation shall be borne by the Government which has appointed it.

2. The General Assembly shall:

(i)   appoint the Director General upon nomination by the Coordination Committee;

(ii)   review and approve reports of the Director General concerning the Organization and give him all necessary instructions;

(iii)   review and approve the reports and activities of the Coordination Committee and give instructions to such Committee;

(iv)   adopt the triennial budget of expenses common to the Unions;

(v)   approve the measures proposed by the Director General concerning the administration of the international agreements referred to in Article 4 (iii);

(vi)   adopt the financial regulations of the Organization;

(vii)   determine the working languages of the Secretariat, taking into consideration the practice of the United Nations;

(viii)   invite States referred to under Article 5 (2) (ii) to become party to this Convention;

(ix)   determine which States not Members of the Organization and which intergovernmental and international non-governmental organizations shall be admitted to its meetings as observers;

(x)   exercise such other functions as are appropriate under this Convention.

3. *(a)* Each State, whether member of one or more Unions, shall have one vote in the General Assembly.

(b) One-half of the States members of the General Assembly shall constitute a quorum.

(c) Notwithstanding the provisions of subparagraph *(b)*, if, in any session, the number of States represented is less than one-half but equal to or more than one-third of the States members of the General Assembly, the General Assembly may make decisions but, with the exception of decisions concerning its own procedure, all such decisions shall take effect only if the following conditions are fulfilled. The International Bureau shall communicate the said decisions to the States members of the General Assembly which were not represented and shall invite them to express in writing their vote or abstention within a period of three months from the date of the communication. If, at the expiration of this period, the number of States having thus expressed their vote or abstention attains the number of States which was lacking for attaining the quorum in the session itself, such decisions shall take effect provided that at the same time the required majority still obtains.

(d) Subject to the provisions of subparagraphs *(e)* and *(f)*, the General Assembly shall make its decisions by a majority of two-thirds of the votes cast.

(e) The approval of measures concerning the administration of international agreements referred to in Article 4 (iii) shall require a majority of three-fourths of the votes cast.

(f) The approval of an agreement with the United Nations under Articles 57 and 63 of the Charter of the United Nations shall require a majority of nine-tenths of the votes cast.

(g) For the appointment of the Director General (paragraph (2) (i), the approval of measures proposed by the Director General concerning the administration of international agreements (paragraph (2) (v)), and the transfer of headquarters (Article 10), the required majority must be attained not only in the General Assembly but also in the Assembly of the Paris Union and the Assembly of the Berne Union.

(h) Abstentions shall not be considered as votes.

(i) A delegate may represent, and vote in the name of, one State only.

4. *(a)* The General Assembly shall meet once in every third calendar year in ordinary session, upon convocation by the Director-General.

(b) The General Assembly shall meet in extraordinary session upon convocation by the Director General either at the request of the Coordination Committee or at the request of one-fourth of the States members of the General Assembly.

(c) Meetings shall be held at the headquarters of the Organization.

5. States party to this Convention which are not members of any of the Unions shall be admitted to the meetings of General Assembly as observers.

6. The General Assembly shall adopt its own rules procedure.

Article 7

Conference

1. *(a)* There shall be a Conference consisting of the States party to this Convention whether or not they are members of any of the Unions.

(b) The Government of each State shall be represented by one delegate, who may be assisted by alternate delegates, advisors, and experts.

(c) The expenses of each delegation shall be borne by the Government which has appointed it.

2. The Conference shall:
   (i) discuss matters of general interest in the field of intellectual property and may adopt recomendations relating to such matters, having regard for the competence and autonomy of the Unions;
   (ii) adopt the triennial budget of the Conference;
   (iii) within the limits of the budget of the Conference, establish the triennial program of legal-technical assistance;
   (iv) adopt amendments to this Convention as provided in Article 17;
   (v) determine which States not Members of the Organization and which intergovernmental and international nongovernmental organizations shall be admitted to its meetings as observers;
   (vi) exercise such other functions as are appropriate under this Convention.

3. *(a)* Each Member State shall have one vote in the Conference.

(b) One-third of the Member States shall constitute a quorum.

(c) Subject to the provisions of Article 17, the Conference shall make its decisions by a majority of two-thirds of the votes cast.

(d) The amounts of the contributions of States party to this Convention not members of any of the Unions shall be fixed by a vote in which only the delegates of such States shall have the right to vote.

(e) Abstentions shall not be considered as votes.

(f) A delegate may represent, and vote in the name of, one State only.

4. *(a)* The Conference shall meet in ordinary session, upon convocation by the Director General, during the same period and at the same as the General Assembly.

(b) The Conference shall meet in extraordinary session, upon convocation by the Director General, at the request of the majority of the Member States.

5. The Conference shall adopt its own rules of procedure.

Article 8

Coordination Committee

1. *(a)* There shall be a Coordination Committee consisting of the States party to this Convention which are members of the Executive Committee of the Paris Union, or the Executive Committee of the Berne Union, or both. However, if either of these Executive Committees is composed of more than one-fourth of the number of the countries members of the Assembly which elected it, then such Executive Committee shall designate from among its members the States which will be members of the Coordination Committee, in such a way that their number shall not exceed the one-fourth referred to above, it being understood that the country on the territory of which the Organization has its headquarters shall not be included in the computation of the said one-fourth.

(b) The Government of each State member of the Coordination Committee shall be represented by one delegate, who may be assisted by alternate delegates, advisors, and experts.

(c) Whenever the Coordination Committee considers either matters of direct interest to the program or budget of the Conference and its agenda, or proposals for the amendment of this Convention which would affect the rights or obligations of States party to this Convention not members of any of the Unions, one-fourth of such States shall participate in the meetings of the Cordination Committee with the same rights as members of that Committee. The Conference shall, at each of its ordinary sessions, designate these States.

(d) The expenses of each delegation shall be borne by the Government which has appointed it.

2. If the other Unions administered by the Organization wish to be represented as such in the Coordination Committee, their representatives must be appointed from among the States members of the Coordination Committee.

3. The Coordination Committee shall:

   (i) give advice to the organs of the Unions, the General Assembly, the Conference, and the Director General, on all administrative, financial and other matters of common interest either to two or more of the Unions, or to one or more of the Unions and the Organization, and in particular on the budget of expenses common to the Unions;

   (ii) prepare the draft agenda of the General Assembly;

   (iii) prepare the draft agenda and the draft program and budget of the Conference;

   (iv) on the basis of the triennial budget of expenses common to the Unions and the triennial budget of the Conference, as well as on the basis of the triennial program of legal-technical assistance, establish the corresponding annual budgets and programs;

   (v) when the term of office of the Director General is about to expire, or when there is a vacancy in the post of the Director General, nominate a candidate for appointment to such position by the General Assembly; if the General Assembly does not appoint its nominee, the Coordination Committee shall nominate another candidate; this procedure shall be repeated until the latest nominee is appointed by the General Assembly;

   (vi) if the post of the Director General becomes vacant between two sessions of the General Assembly, appoint an Acting Director General for the term preceding the assuming of office by the new Director General;

   (vii) perform such other functions as are allocated to it under this Convention.

4. *(a)* The Coordination Committee shall meet once every year in ordinary session, upon convocation by the Director General. It shall normally meet at the headquarters of the Organization.

(b) The Coordination Committee shall meet in extraordinary session, upon convo-

cation by the Director General, either on his own initiative, or at the request of its Chairman or one-fourth of its members.

5. *(a)* Each State, whether a member of one or both of the Executive Committees referred to in paragraph (1) *(a)*, shall have one vote in the Coordination Committee.

(b) One-half of the members of the Coordination Committee shall constitute a quorum.

(c) A delegate may represent, and vote in the name of, one State only.

6. *(a)* The Coordination Committee shall express its opinions and make its decisions by a simple majority of the votes cast. Abstentions shall not be considered as votes.

(b) Even if a simple majority is obtained, any member of the Coordination Committee may, immediately after the vote, request that the votes be the subject of a special recount in the following manner: two separate lists shall be prepared, one containing the names of the States members of the Executive Committee of the Paris Union and the other the names of the States members of the Executive Committee of the Berne Union; the vote of each State shall be inscribed opposite its name in each list in which it appears. Should this special recount indicate that a simple majority has not been obtained in each of those lists, the proposal shall not be considered as carried.

7. Any State Member of the Organization which is not a member of the Coordination Committee may be represented at the meetings of the Committee by observers having the right to take part in the debates but without the right to vote.

8. The Coordination Committee shall establish its own rules of procedure.

Article 9

International Bureau

1. The International Bureau shall be the Secretariat of the Organization.

2. The International Bureau shall be directed by the Director General, assisted by two or more Deputy Directors General.

3. The Director General shall be appointed for a fixed term, which shall be not less than six years. He shall be eligible for reappointment for fixed terms. The periods of the initial appointment and possible subsequent appointments, as well as all other conditions of the appointment, shall be fixed by the General Assembly.

4. *(a)* The Director General shall be the chief executive of the Organization.

(b) He shall represent the Organization.

(c) He shall report to, and conform to the instructions of, the General Assembly as to the internal and external affairs of the Organization.

5. The Director General shall prepare the draft programs and budgets and periodical reports on activities. He shall transmit them to the Governments of the interested States and to the competent organs of the Unions and the Organization.

6. The Director General and any staff member designated by him shall participate, without the right to vote, in all meetings of the General Assembly, the Conference, the Coordination Committee, and any other committee or working group. The Director General or a staff member designated by him shall be ex officio secretary of these bodies.

7. The Director General shall appoint the staff necessary for the efficient performance of the tasks of the International Bureau. He shall appoint the Deputy Directors General after approval by the Coordination Committee. The conditions of employment shall be fixed by the staff regulations to be approved by the Coordination Committee on the proposal of the Director General. The paramount consideration in the employment of the staff and in the determination of the conditions of service shall be the necessity of securing the highest standards of efficiency, competence, and integrity. Due regard shall be paid to the importance of recruiting the staff on as wide a geographical basis as possible.

8. The nature of the responsibilities of the Director General and of the staff shall be exclusively international. In the discharge of their duties they shall not seek or receive instructions from any Government or from any authority external to the Organization. They shall refrain from any action which might prejudice their position as international officials. Each Member State undertakes to respect the exclusively international character of the responsibilities of the Director General and the staff, and not to seek to influence them in the discharge of their duties.

Article 10

Headquarters

1. The headquarters of the Organization shall be at Geneva.
2. Its transfer may be decided as provided for in Article 6 (3) *(d)* and *(g)*.

Article 11

Finances

1. The Organization shall have two separate budgets: the budget of expenses common to the Unions, and the budget of the Conference.
2. *(a)* The budget of expenses common to the Unions shall include provision for expenses of interest to several Unions.
   (b) This budget shall be financed from the following sources:
   (i) contributions of the Unions, provided that the amount of the contribution of each Union shall be fixed by the Assembly of that Union, having regard to the interest the Union has in the common expenses;
   (ii) charges due for services performed by the International Bureau not in direct relation with any of the Unions or not received for services rendered by the International Bureau in the field of legal-technical assistance;
   (iii) sale of, or royalties on, the publications of the International Bureau not directly concerning any of the Unions;
   (iv) gifts, bequests, and subventions, given to the Organization, except those referred to in paragraph (3) *(b)* (iv);
   (v) rents, interests, and other miscellaneous income, of the Organization.
3. *(a)* The budget of the Conference shall include provision for the expenses of holding sessions of the Conference and for the cost of the legal-technical assistance program.
   (b) This budget shall be financed from the following sources:
   (i) contributions of States party to this Convention not members of any of the Unions;
   (ii) any sums made available to this budget by the Unions, provided that the amount of the sum made available by each Union shall be fixed by the Assembly of that Union and that each Union shall be free to abstain from contributing to the said budget;
   (iii) sums received for services rendered by the International Bureau in the field of legal-technical assistance;
   (iv) gifts, bequests, and subventions, given to the Organization for the purposes referred to in subparagraph *(a)*.
4. *(a)* For the purpose of establishing its contribution towards the budget of the Conference, each State party to this Convention not member of any of the Unions shall belong to a class, and shall pay its annual contributions on the basis of a number of units fixed as follows:

Class A 10

Class B   3

Class C   1

(b) Each such State shall, concurrently with taking action as provided in Article 14 (1), indicate the class to which it wishes to belong. Any such State may change class. If it chooses a lower class, the State must announce it to the Conference at one of its ordinary sessions. Any such change shall take effect at the beginning of the calendar year following the session.

(c) The annual contribution of each such State shall be an amount in the same proportion to the total sum to be contributed to the budget of the Conference by all such States as the number of its units is to the total of the units of all the said States.

(d) Contributions shall become due on the first of January of each year.

(e) If the budget is not adopted before the beginning of a new financial period, the budget shall be at the same level as the budget of the previous year, in accordance with the financial regulations.

5. Any State party to this Convention not member of any of the Unions which is in arrears in the payment of its financial contributions under the present Article, and any State party to this Convention member of any of the Unions which is in arrears in the payment of its contributions to any of the Unions, shall have no vote in any of the bodies of the Organization of which it is a member, if the amount of its arrears equals or exceeds the amount of the contributions due from it for the preceding two full years. However, any of these bodies may allow such a State to continue to exercise its vote in that body if, and as long as, it is satisfied that the delay in payment arises from exceptional and unavoidable circumstances.

6. The amount of the fees and charges due for services rendered by the International Bureau in the field of legal-technical assistance shall be established, and shall be reported to the Coordination Committee, by the Director General.

7. The Organization, with the approval of the Coordination Committee, may receive gifts, bequests, and subventions, directly from Governments, public or private institutions, associations or private persons.

8. *(a)* The Organization shall have a working capital fund which shall be constituted by a single payment made by the Unions and by each State party to this Convention not member of any Union. If the fund becomes insufficient, it shall be increased.

(b) The amount of the single payment of each Union and its possible participation in any increase shall be decided by its Assembly.

(c) The amount of the single payment of each State party to this Convention not member of any Union and its part in any increase shall be a proportion of the contribution of that State for the year in which the fund is established or the increase decided. The proportion and the terms of payment shall be fixed by the Conference on the proposal of the Director General and after it has heard the advice of the Coordination Committee.

9. *(a)* In the headquarters agreement concluded with the State on the territory of which the Organization has its headquarters, it shall be provided that, whenever the working capital fund is insufficient, such State shall grant advances. The amount of these advances and the conditions on which they are granted shall be the subject of separate agreements, in each case, between such State and the Organization. As long as it remains under the obligation to grant advances, such State shall have an ex officio seat on the Coordination Committee.

(b) The State referred to in subparagraph *(a)* and the Organization shall each have the right to denounce the obligation to grant advances, by written notification. Denunciation shall take effect three years after the end of the year in which it has been notified.

10. The auditing of the accounts shall be effected by one or more Member States,

or by external auditors, as provided in the financial regulations. They shall be designated, with their agreement, by the General Assembly.

Article 12

Legal Capacity; Privileges and Immunities

1. The Organization shall enjoy on the territory of each Member State, in conformity with the laws of that State, such legal capacity as may be necessary for the fulfilment of the Organization's objectives and for the exercise of its functions.

2. The Organization shall conclude a headquarters agreement with the Swiss Confederation and with any other State in which the headquarters may subsequently he located.

3. The Organization may conclude bilateral or multilateral agreements with the other Member States with a view to the enjoyment by the Organization, its officials, and representatives of all Member States, of such privileges and immunities as may be necessary for the fulfilment of its objectives and for the exercise of its functions.

4. The Director General may negotiate and, after approval by the Coordination Committee, shall conclude and sign on behalf of the Organization the agreements referred to in paragraphs (2) and (3).

Article 13

Relations with Other Organizations

1. The Organization shall, where appropriate, establish working relations and cooperate with other intergovernmental organizations. Any general agreement to such effect entered into with such organizations shall be concluded by the Director General after approval by the Coordination Committee.

2. The Organization may, on matters within its competence, make suitable arrangements for consultation and cooperation with international non-governmental organizations and, with the consent of the Governments concerned, with national organizations, governmental or non-governmental. Such arrangements shall be made by the Director General after approval by the Coordination Committee.

Article 14

Becoming Party to the Convention

1. States referred to in Article 5 may become party to this Convention and Member of the Organization by:
   (i) signature without reservation as to ratification, or
   (ii) signature subject to ratification followed by the deposit of an instrument of ratification, or
   (iii) deposit of an instrument of accession.

2. Notwithstanding any other provision of this Convention, a State party to the Paris Convention, the Berne Convention, or both Conventions, may become party to this Convention only if it concurrently ratifies or accedes to, or only after it has ratified or acceded to:
   (i) either the Stockholm Act of the Paris Convention in its entirety or with only the limitation set forth in Article 20 (1) *(b)* (i) thereof.
   (ii) or the Stockholm Act of the Berne Convention in its entirety or with only the limitation set forth in Article 28 (1) *(b)* (i) thereof.

3. Instruments of ratification or accession shall be deposited with the Director General.

Article 15

Entry into Force of the Convention

1. This Convention shall enter into force three months after ten States members of the Paris Union and seven States members of the Berne Union have taken action as provided in Article 14 (1), it being understood that, if a State is a member of both Unions, it will be counted in both groups. On that date, this Convention shall enter into force also in respect of States which, not being members of either of the two Unions, have taken action as provided in Article 14 (1) three months or more prior to that date.

2. In respect to any other State, this Convention shall enter into force three months after the date on which such State takes action as provided in Article 14 (1).

Article 16

Reservations

No reservations to this Convention are permitted.

Article 17

Amendments

1. Proposals for the amendment of this Convention may be initiated by any Member State, by the Coordination Committee, or by the Director General. Such proposals shall be communicated by the Director General to the Member States at least six months in advance of their consideration by the Conference.

2. Amendments shall be adopted by the Conference. Whenever amendments would affect the rights and obligations of States party to this Convention not members of any of the Unions, such States shall also vote. On all other amendments proposed, only States party to this Convention members of any Union shall vote. Amendments shall be adopted by a simple majority of the votes cast, provided that the Conference shall vote only on such proposals for amendments as have previously been adopted by the Assembly of the Paris Union and the Assembly of the Berne Union according to the rules applicable in each of them regarding the adoption of amendments to the administrative provisions of their respective Conventions.

3. Any amendment shall enter into force one month after written notifications of acceptance, effected in accordance with their respective constitutional processes, have been received by the Director General from three-fourths of the States Members of the Organization, entitled to vote on the proposal for amendment pursuant to paragraph (2), at the time the Conference adopted the amendment. Any amendments thus accepted shall bind all the States which are Members of the Organization at the time the amendment enters into force or which become Members at a subsequent date, provided that any amendment increasing the financial obligations of Member States shall bind only those States which have notified their acceptance of such amendment.

Article 18

Denunciation

1. Any Member State may denounce this Convention by notification addressed to the Director General.

2. Denunciation shall take effect six months after the day on which the Director General has received the notification.

Article 19

Notifications

The Director General shall notify the Governments of all Member States of:
  (i) the date of entry into force of the Convention,
  (ii) signatures and deposits of instruments of ratification or accession,
  (iii) acceptances of an amendment to this Convention, and the date upon which the amendment enters into force,
  (iv) denunciations of this Convention.

Article 20

Final Provisions

1. *(a)* This Convention shall be signed in a single copy in English, French, Russian and Spanish, all texts being equally authentic, and shall be deposited with the Government of Sweden.

(b) This Convention shall remain open for signature at Stockholm until January 13, 1968.

2. Official texts shall be established by the Director General, after consultation with the interested Governments, in German, Italian and Portuguese, and such other languages as the Conference may designate.

3. The Director General shall transmit two duly certified copies of this Convention and of each amendment adopted by the Conference to the Governments of the States members of the Paris or Berne Unions, to the Government of any other State when it accedes to this Convention, and, on request, to the Government of any other State. The copies of the signed text of the Convention transmitted to the Governments shall be certified by the Government of Sweden.

4. The Director General shall register this Convention with the Secretariat of the United Nations.

Article 21

Transitional Provisions

1. Until the first Director General assumes office, references in this Convention to the International Bureau or to the Director General shall be deemed to be references to the United International Bureaux for the Protection of Industrial, Literary and Artistic Property (also called the United International Bureaux for the Protection of Intellectual Property (BIRPI)), or its Director, respectively.

2. *(a)* States which are members of any of the Unions but which have not become party to this Convention may, for five years from the date of entry into force of this Convention, exercise, if they so desire, the same rights as if they had become party to this Convention. Any State desiring to exercise such rights shall give written notification to this effect to the Director General; this notification shall be effective on the date of its receipt. Such States shall be deemed to be members of the General Assembly and the Conference until the expiration of the said period.

(b) Upon expiration of this five-year period, such States shall have no right to vote in the General Assembly, the Conference, and the Coordination Committee.

(c) Upon becoming party to this Convention, such States shall regain such right to vote.

3. *(a)* As long as there are States members of the Paris or Berne Unions which have not become party to this Convention, the International Bureau and the Director General shall also function as the United International Bureaux for the Protection of Industrial, Literary and Artistic Property, and its Director, respectively.

(b) The staff in the employment of the said Bureaux on the date of entry into force of this Convention shall, during the transitional period referred to in subparagraph *(a)*, be considered as also employed by the International Bureau.

4. *(a)* Once all the States members of the Paris Union have become Members of the Organization, the rights, obligations, and property, of the Bureau of that Union shall devolve on the International Bureau of the Organization.

(b) Once all the States members of the Berne Union have become Members of the Organization, the rights, obligations, and property, of the Bureau of that Union shall devolve on the International Bureau of the Organization.

E. STATUTE OF THE INTERNATIONAL ATOMIC ENERGY AGENCY, AMENDED UP TO JANUARY 31, 1963[1]

CONTENTS

STATUTE OF THE INTERNATIONAL ATOMIC ENERGY AGENCY

ARTICLE I

Establishment of the Agency

The Parties hereto establish an International Atomic Energy Agency (hereinafter referred to as "the Agency") upon the terms and conditions hereinafter set forth.

---

[1] As published by the Agency. This Statute was approved on 23 October 1956 by the Conference on the Statute of the International Atomic Energy Agency, which was held at the Headquarters of the United Nations. It was opened for signature on 26 October 1956 and came into force on 29 July 1957.

On 4 October 1961 the General Conference of the Agency approved an amendment to the first sentence of Article VI.A.3, which came into force on 31 January 1963.

ARTICLE II

Objectives

The Agency shall seek to accelerate and enlarge the contribution of atomic energy to peace, health and prosperity throughout the world. It shall ensure, so far as it is able, that assistance provided by it or at its request or under its supervision or control is not used in such a way as to further any military purpose.

ARTICLE III

Functions

A. The Agency is authorized:

1. To encourage and assist research on, and development and practical application of, atomic energy for peaceful uses throughout the world; and, if requested to do so, to act as an intermediary for the purposes of securing the performance of services or the supplying of materials, equipment, or facilities by one member of the Agency for another; and to perform any operation or service useful in research on, or development or practical application of, atomic energy for peaceful purposes;

2. To make provision, in accordance with this Statute, for materials, services, equipment, and facilities to meet the needs of research on, and development and practical application of, atomic energy for peaceful purposes, including the production of electric power, with due consideration for the needs of the under-developed areas of the world;

3. To foster the exchange of scientific and technical information on peaceful uses of atomic energy;

4. To encourage the exchange and training of scientists and experts in the field of peaceful uses of atomic energy;

5. To establish and administer safeguards designed to ensure that special fissionable and other materials, services, equipment, facilities, and information made available by the Agency or at its request or under its supervision or control are not used in such a way as to further any military purpose; and to apply safeguards, at the request of the parties, to any bilateral or multilateral arrangement, or at the request of a State, to any of that State's activities in the field of atomic energy;

6. To establish or adopt, in consultation and, where appropriate, in collaboration with the competent organs of the United Nations and with the specialized agencies concerned, standards of safety for protection of health and minimization of danger to life and property (including such standards for labour conditions), and to provide for the application of these standards to its own operations as well as to the operations making use of materials, services, equipment, facilities, and information made available by the Agency or at its request or under its control or supervision; and to provide for the application of these standards, at the request of the parties, to operations under any bilateral or multilateral arrangement, or, at the request of a State, to any of that State's activities in the field of atomic energy;

7. To acquire or establish any facilities, plant and equipment useful in carrying out its authorized functions, whenever the facilities, plant, and equipment otherwise available to it in the area concerned are inadequate or available only on terms it deems unsatisfactory.

B. In carrying out its functions, the Agency shall:

1. Conduct its activities in accordance with the purposes and principles of the United Nations to promote peace and international co-operation, and in conformity with policies of the United Nations furthering the establishment of safeguarded worldwide disarmament and in conformity with any international agreements entered into pursuant to such policies;

2. Establish control over the use of special fissionable materials received by the Agency, in order to ensure that these materials are used only for peaceful purposes;

3. Allocate its resources in such a manner as to secure efficient utilization and the greatest possible general benefit in all areas of the world, bearing in mind the special needs of the under-developed areas of the world;

4. Submit reports on its activities annually to the General Assembly of the United Nations and, when appropriate, to the Security Council: if in connexion with the activities of the Agency there should arise questions that are within the competence of the Security Council, the Agency shall notify the Security Council; as the organ bearing the main responsibility for the maintenance of international peace and security, and may also take the measures open to it under this Statute, including those provided in paragraph C of article XII;

5. Submit reports to the Economic and Social Council and other organs of the United Nations on matters within the competence of these organs.

C. In carrying out its functions, the Agency shall not make assistance to members subject to any political, economic, military, or other conditions incompatible with the provisions of this Statute.

D. Subject to the provisions of this Statute and to the terms of agreements concluded between a State or a group of States and the Agency which shall be in accordance with the provisions of the Statute, the activities of the Agency shall be carried out with due observance of the sovereign rights of States.

ARTICLE IV

Membership

A. The initial members of the Agency shall be those States Members of the United Nations or of any of the specialized agencies which shall have signed this Statute within ninety days after it is opened for signature and shall have deposited an instrument of ratification.

B. Other members of the Agency shall be those States, whether or not Members of the United Nations or of any of the specialized agencies, which deposit an instrument of acceptance of this Statute after their membership has been approved by the General Conference upon the recommendation of the Board of Governors. In recommending and approving a State for membership, the Board of Governors and the General Conference shall determine that the State is able and willing to carry out the obligations of membership in the Agency, giving due consideration to its ability and willingness to act in accordance with the purposes and principles of the Charter of the United Nations.

C. The Agency is based on the principle of the sovereign equality of all its members, and all members, in order to ensure to all of them the rights and benefits resulting from membership, shall fulfil in good faith the obligations assumed by them in accordance with this Statute.

ARTICLE V

General Conference

A. A General Conference consisting of representatives of all members shall meet in regular annual session and in such special sessions as shall be convened by the Director General at the request of the Board of Governors or of a majority of members. The sessions shall take place at the headquarters of the Agency unless otherwise determined by the General Conference.

B. At such sessions, each member shall be represented by one delegate who may be accompanied by alternates and by advisers. The cost of attendance of any delegation shall be borne by the member concerned.

C. The General Conference shall elect a President and such other officers as may be required at the beginning of each session. They shall hold office for the duration of the session. The General Conference, subject to the provisions of this Statute, shall adopt its own rules of procedure. Each member shall have one vote. Decisions pursuant to paragraph H of article XIV, paragraph C of article XVIII and paragraph B of article XIX shall be made by a two-thirds majority of the members present and voting. Decisions on other questions, including the determination of additional questions or categories of questions to be decided by a two-thirds majority, shall be made by a majority of the members present and voting. A majority of members shall constitute a quorum.

D. The General Conference may discuss any questions or any matters within the scope of this Statute or relating to the powers and functions of any organs provided for in this Statute, and may make recommendations to the membership of the Agency or to the Board of Governors or to both on any such questions or matters.

E. The General Conference shall:

1. Elect members of the Board of Governors in accordance with article VI;

2. Approve States for membership in accordance with article IV;

3. Suspend a member from the privileges and rights of membership in accordance with article XIX;

4. Consider the annual report of the Board;

5. In accordance with article XIV, approve the budget of the Agency recommended by the Board or return it with recommendations as to its entirety or parts to the Board, for resubmission to the General Conference;

6. Approve reports to be submitted to the United Nations as required by the relationship agreement between the Agency and the United Nations, except reports referred to in paragraph C of article XII, or return them to the Board with its recommendations;

7. Approve any agreement or agreements between the Agency and the United Nations and other organizations as provided in article XVI or return such agreements with its recommendations to the Board, for resubmission to the General Conference;

8. Approve rules and limitations regarding the exercise of borrowing powers by the Board, in accordance with paragraph G of article XIV; approve rules regarding the acceptance of voluntary contributions to the Agency; and approve, in accordance with paragraph F of article XIV, the manner in which the general fund referred to in that paragraph may be used;

9. Approve amendments to this Statute in accordance with paragraph C of article XVIII;

10. Approve the appointment of the Director General in accordance with paragraph A of article VII.

F. The General Conference shall have the authority:

1. To take decisions on any matter specifically referred to the General Conference for this purpose by the Board;

2. To propose matters for consideration by the Board and request from the Board reports on any matter relating to the functions of the Agency.

ARTICLE VI

Board of Governors

A. The Board of Governors shall be composed as follows:

1. The outgoing Board of Governors (or in the case of the first Board, the Preparatory Commission referred to in Annex I) shall designate for membership on the Board the five members most advanced in the technology of atomic energy including the production of source materials and the member most advanced in the technology of atom-

ic energy including the production of source materials in each of the following areas not represented by the aforesaid five:

(1) North America
(2) Latin America
(3) Western Europe
(4) Eastern Europe
(5) Africa and the Middle East
(6) South Asia
(7) South East Asia and the Pacific
(8) Far East.

2. The outgoing Board of Governors (or in the case of the first Board, the Preparatory Commission referred to in Annex I) shall designate for membership on the Board two members from among the following other producers of source materials: Belgium, Czechoslovakia, Poland, and Portugal; and shall also designate for membership on the Board one other member as a supplier of technical assistance. No member in this category in any one year will be eligible for redesignation in the same category for the following year.

3. The General Conference shall elect twelve members to membership on the Board of Governors, with due regard to equitable representation on the Board as a whole of the members in the areas listed in sub-paragraph A-1 of this article, so that the Board shall at all times include in this category three representatives of the area of Latin America, three representatives of the area of Africa and the Middle East and a representative of each of the remaining areas except North America. Except for the five members chosen for a term of one year in accordance with paragraph D of this article, no member in this category in any one term of office will be eligible for re-election in the same category for the following term of office.

B. The designations provided for in subparagraphs A-1 and A-2 of this article shall take place not less than sixty days before each regular annual session of the General Conference. The elections provided for in sub-paragraph A-3 of this article shall take place at regular annual sessions of the General Conference.

C. Members represented on the Board of Governors in accordance with sub-paragraphs A-1 and A-2 of this article shall hold office from the end of the next regular annual session of the General Conference after their designation until the end of the following regular annual session of the General Conference.

D. Members represented on the Board of Governors in accordance with sub-paragraph A-3 of this article shall hold office from the end of the regular annual session of the General Conference at which they are elected until the end of the second regular annual session of the General Conference thereafter. In the election of these members for the first Board, however, five shall be chosen for a term of one year.

E. Each member of the Board of Governors shall have one vote. Decisions on the amount of the Agency's budget shall be made by a two-thirds majority of those present and voting, as provided in paragraph H of article XIV. Decisions on other questions, including determination of additional questions or categories of questions to be decided by a two-thirds majority, shall be made by a majority of those present and voting. Two-thirds of all members of the Board shall constitute a quorum.

F. The Board of Governors shall have authority to carry out the functions of the Agency in accordance with this Statute, subject to its responsibilities to the General Conference as provided in this Statute.

G. The Board of Governors shall meet at such times as it may determine. The meetings shall take place at the headquarters of the Agency unless otherwise determined by the Board.

H. The Board of Governors shall elect a Chairman and other officers from among its members and, subject to the provisions of this Statute, shall adopt its own rules of procedure.

I. The Board of Governors may establish such committees as it deems advisable. The Board may appoint persons to represent it in its relations with other organizations.

J. The Board of Governors shall prepare an annual report to the General Conference concerning the affairs of the Agency and any projects approved by the Agency. The Board shall also prepare for submission to the General Conference such reports as the Agency is or may be required to make to the United Nations or to any other organization the work of which is related to that of the Agency. These reports, along with the annual reports, shall be submitted to members of the Agency at least one month before the regular annual session of the General Conference.

ARTICLE VII

Staff

A. The staff of the Agency shall be headed by a Director General. The Director General shall be appointed by the Board of Governors with the approval of the General Conference for a term of four years. He shall be the chief administrative officer of the Agency.

B. The Director General shall be responsible for the appointment, organization, and functioning of the staff and shall be under the authority of and subject to the control of the Board of Governors. He shall perform his duties in accordance with regulations adopted by the Board.

C. The staff shall include such qualified scientific and technical and other personnel as may be required to fulfil the objectives and functions of the Agency. The Agency shall be guided by the principle that its permanent staff shall be kept to a minimum.

D. The paramount consideration in the recruitment and employment of the staff and in the determination of the conditions of service shall be to secure employees of the highest standards of efficiency, technical competence, and integrity. Subject to this consideration, due regard shall be paid to the contributions of members to the Agency and to the importance of recruiting the staff on as wide a geographical basis as possible.

E. The terms and conditions on which the staff shall be appointed, remunerated, and dismissed shall be in accordance with regulations made by the Board of Governors, subject to the provisions of this Statute and to general rules approved by the General Conference on the recommendation of the Board.

F. In the performance of their duties, the Director General and the staff shall not seek or receive instructions from any source external to the Agency. They shall refrain from any action which might reflect on their position as officials of the Agency; subject to their responsibilities to the Agency, they shall not disclose any industrial secret or other confidential information coming to their knowledge by reason of their official duties for the Agency. Each member undertakes to respect the international character of the responsibilities of the Director General and the staff and shall not seek to influence them in the discharge of their duties.

G. In this article the term "staff" includes guards.

ARTICLE VIII

Exchange of information

A. Each member should make available such information as would, in the judgement of the member, be helpful to the Agency.

B. Each member shall make available to the Agency all scientific information developed as a result of assistance extended by the Agency pursuant to article XI.

C. The Agency shall assemble and make available in an accessible form the information made available to it under paragraph A and B of this article. It shall take positive steps to encourage the exchange among its members of information relating to the nature and peaceful uses of atomic energy and shall serve as an intermediary among its members for this purpose.

ARTICLE IX

Supplying of materials

A. Members may make available to the Agency such quantities of special fissionable materials as they deem advisable and on such terms as shall be agreed with the Agency. The material made available to the Agency may, at the discretion of the member making them available, be stored either by the member concerned or, with the agreement of the Agency, in the Agency's depots.

B. Members may also make available to the Agency source materials as defined in article XX and other materials. The Board of Governors shall determine the quantities of such materials which the Agency will accept under agreements provided for in article XIII.

C. Each member shall notify the Agency of the quantities, form, and composition of special fissionable materials, source materials, and other materials which that member is prepared, in conformity with its laws, to make available immediately or during a period specified by the Board of Governors.

D. On request of the Agency a member shall, from the materials which it has made available, without delay deliver to another member or group of members such quantities of such materials as the Agency may specify, and shall without delay deliver to the Agency itself such quantities of such materials as are really necessary for operations and scientific research in the facilities of the Agency.

E. The quantities, form and composition of materials made available by any member may be changed at any time by the member with the approval of the Board of Governors.

F. An initial notification in accordance with paragraph C of this article shall be made within three months of the entry into force of this Statute with respect to the member concerned. In the absence of a contrary decision of the Board of Governors, the materials initially made available shall be for the period of the calendar year succeeding the year when this Statute takes effect with respect to the member concerned. Subsequent notifications shall likewise, in the absence of a contrary action by the Board, relate to the period of the calendar year following the notification and shall be made no later the first day of November of each year.

G. The Agency shall specify the place and method of delivery and, where appropriate, the form and composition, of materials which it has requested a member to deliver from the amounts which that member has notified the Agency it is prepared to make available. The Agency shall also verify the quantities of materials delivered and shall report those quantities periodically to the members.

H. The Agency shall be responsible for storing and protecting materials in its possesion. The Agency shall ensure that these materials shall be safeguarded against (1) hazards of the weather, (2) unauthorized removal or diversion, (3) damage or destruction, including sabotage, and (4) forcible seizure. In storing special fissionable materials in its possession, the Agency shall ensure the geographical distribution of these materials in such a way as not to allow concentration of large amounts of such materials in any country or region of the world.

I. The Agency shall as soon as practicable establish or acquire such of the following as may be necessary:

1. Plant, equipment, and facilities for the receipt, storage, and issue of materials;

2. Physical safeguards;

3. Adequate health and safety measures;

4. Control laboratories for the analysis and verification of materials received;

5. Housing and administrative facilities for any staff required for the foregoing.

J. The materials made available pursuant to this article shall be used as determined by the Board of Governors in accordance with the provisions of this Statute. No member shall have the right to require that the materials it makes available to the Agency be kept separately by the Agency or to designate the specific project in which they must be used.

ARTICLE X

Services, equipment, and facilities

Members may make available to the Agency services, equipment, and facilities which may be of assistance in fulfilling the Agency's objectives and functions.

ARTICLE XI

Agency projects

A. Any member or group of members of the Agency desiring to set up any project for research on, or development or practical application of, atomic energy for peaceful purposes may request the assistance of the Agency in securing special fissionable and other materials, services, equipment, and facilities necessary for this purpose. Any such request shall be accompanied by an explanation of the purpose and extent of the project and shall be considered by the Board Governors.

B. Upon request, the Agency may also assist any member or group of members to make arrangements to secure necessary financing from outside sources to carry out such projects. In extending this assistance, the Agency will not be required to provide any guarantees or to assume any financial responsibility for the project.

C. The Agency may arrange for the supplying of any materials, services, equipment, and facilities necessary for the project by one or more members or may itself undertake to provide any or all of these directly, taking into consideration the wishes of the member or members making the request.

D. For the purpose of considering the request, the Agency may send into the territory of the member or group of members making the request a person or persons qualified to examine the project. For this purpose the Agency may, with the approval of the member or group of members making the request, use members of its own staff or employ suitably qualified nationals of any member.

E. Before approving a project under this article, the Board of Governors shall give due consideration to:

1. The usefulness of the project, including its scientific and technical feasibility;

2. The adequacy of plans, funds, and technical personnel to assure the effective execution of the project;

3. The adequacy of proposed health and safety standards for handling and storing materials and for operating facilities;

4. The inability of the member of group of members making the request to secure the necessary finances, materials, facilities, equipment, and services;

5. The equitable distribution of materials and other resources available to the Agency;

6. The special needs of the under-developed areas of the world; and

7. Such other matters as may be relevant.

F. Upon approving a project, the Agency shall enter into an agreement with the member or group of members submitting the project, which agreement shall:

1. Provide for allocation to the project of any required special fissionable or other materials;

2. Provide for transfer of special fissionable materials from their then place of custody, whether the materials be in the custody of the Agency or of the member making them available for use in Agency projects, to the member or group of members submitting the project, under conditions which ensure the safety of any shipment required and meet applicable health and safety standards;

3. Set forth the terms and conditions, including charges, on which any materials, services, equipment, and facilities are to be provided by the Agency itself, and, if any such materials, services, equipment, and facilities are to be provided by a member, the terms and conditions as arranged for by the member or group of members submitting the project and the supplying member;

4. Include undertakings by the member or group of members submitting the project: *(a)* that the assistance provided shall not be used in such a way as to further any military purpose; and *(b)* that the project shall be subject to the safeguards provided for in article XII, the relevant safeguards being specified in the agreement;

5. Make appropriate provision regarding the rights and interests of the Agency and the member or members concerned in any inventions or discoveries, or any patents therein, arising from the project;

6. Make appropriate provision regarding settlement of disputes;

7. Include such other provisions as may be appropriate.

G. The provisions of this article shall also apply where appropriate to a request for materials, services, facilities, or equipment in connexion with an existing project.

ARTICLE XII

Agency safeguards

A. With respect to any Agency project, or other arrangement where the Agency is requested by the parties concerned to apply safeguards, the Agency shall have the following rights and responsibilities to the extent relevant to the project or arrangement:

1. To examine the design of specialized equipment and facilities, including nuclear reactors, and to approve it only from the view-point of assuring that it will not further any military purpose, that it complies with applicable health and safety standards, and that it will permit effective application of the safeguards provided for in this article;

2. To require the observance of any health and safety measures prescribed by the Agency;

3. To require the maintenance and production of operating records to assist in ensuring accountability for source and special fissionable materials used or produced in the project or arrangement;

4. To call for and receive progress reports;

5. To approve the means to be used for the chemical processing of irradiated materials solely to ensure that this chemical processing will not lend itself to diversion of materials for military purposes and will comply with applicable health and safety standards; to require that special fissionable materials recovered or produced as a by-product be used for peaceful purposes under continuing Agency safeguards for research or in reactors, existing or under construction, specified by the member or members concerned; and to require deposit with the Agency of any excess of any special fissionable materials recovered or produced as a by-product over what is needed for the above-stated uses in order to prevent stock-piling of these materials, provided that thereafter at the request of the member or members concerned special fissionable materials so deposited with the Agency shall be returned promptly to the member or members concerned for use under the same provisions as stated above;

6. To send into the territory of the recipient State or States inspectors, designated by the Agency after consultation with the State or States concerned, who shall have

access at all times to all places and data and to any person who by reason of his occupation deals with materials, equipment, or facilities which are required by this Statute to be safeguarded, as necessary to account for source and special fissionable materials supplied and fissionable products and to determine whether there is compliance with the undertaking against use in furtherance of any military purpose referred to in sub-paragraph F-4 of article XI, with the health and safety measures referred to in sub-paragraph A-2 of this article, and with any other conditions prescribed in the agreement between the Agency and the State or States concerned. Inspectors designated by the Agency shall be accompanied by representatives of the authorities of the State concerned, if that State so requests, provided that the inspectors shall not thereby be delayed or otherwise impeded in the exercise of their functions;

7. In the event of non-compliance and failure by the recipient State or States to take requested corrective steps within a reasonable time, to suspend or terminate assistance and withdraw any materials and equipment made available by the Agency or a member in furtherance of the project.

B. The Agency shall, as necessary, establish a staff of inspectors. The staff of inspectors shall have the responsibility of examining all operations conducted by the Agency itself to determine whether the Agency is complying with the health and safety measures prescribed by it for application to projects subject to its approval, supervision or control, and whether the Agency is taking adequate measures to prevent the source and special fissionable materials in its custody or used or produced in its own operations from being used in furtherance of any military purpose. The Agency shall take remedial action forthwith to correct any non-compliance or failure to take adequate measures.

C. The staff of inspectors shall also have the responsibility of obtaining and verifying the accounting referred to in sub-paragraph A-6 of this article and of determining whether there is compliance with the undertaking referred to in sub-paragraph F-4 of article XI, with the measures referred to in sub-paragraph A-2 of this article, and with all other conditions of the project prescribed in the agreement between the Agency and the State or States concerned. The inspectors shall report any non-compliance to the Director General who shall thereupon transmit the report to the Board of Governors. The Board shall call upon the recipient State or States to remedy forthwith any non-compliance which it finds to have occurred. The Board shall report the non-compliance to all members and to the Security Council and General Assembly of the United Nations. In the event of failure of the recipient State or States to take fully corrective action within a reasonable time, the Board may take one or both of the following measures: direct curtailment or suspension of assistance being provided by the Agency or by a member, and call for the return of materials and equipment made available to the recipient member or group of members. The Agency may also, in accordance with article XIX, suspend any noncomplying member from the exercise of the privileges and rights of membership.

ARTICLE XIII

Reimbursement of members

Unless otherwise agreed upon between the Board of Governors and the member furnishing to the Agency materials, services, equipment, or facilities, the Board shall enter into an agreement with such member providing for reimbursement for the items furnished.

ARTICLE XIV

Finance

A. The Board of Governors shall submit to the General Conference the annual budget estimates for the expenses of the Agency. To facilitate the work of the Board in this regard, the Director General shall initially prepare the budget estimates. If the General Conference does not approve the estimates, it shall return them together with its recommendations to the Board. The Board shall then submit further estimates to the General Conference for its approval.

B. Expenditures of the Agency shall be classified under the following categories:

1. Administrative expenses: these shall include:

(a) Costs of the staff of the Agency other than the staff employed in connexion with materials, services, equipment, and facilities referred to in sub-paragraph B-2 below; costs of meetings; and expenditures required for the preparation of Agency projects and for the distribution of information;

(b) Costs of implementing the safeguards referred to in article XII in relation to Agency projects or, under sub-paragraph A-5 of article III, in relation to any bilateral or multilateral arrangement, together with the costs of handling and storage of special fissionable material by the Agency other than the storage and handling charges referred to in paragraph E below;

2. Expenses, other than those included in sub-paragraph 1 of this paragraph, in connexion with any materials, facilities, plant, and equipment acquired or established by the Agency in carrying out its authorized functions, and the costs of materials, services, equipment, and facilities provided by it under agreements with one or more members.

C. In fixing the expenditures under subparagraph B-1 *(b)* above, the Board of Governors shall deduct such amounts as are recoverable under agreements regarding the application of safeguards between the Agency and parties to bilateral or multilateral arrangements.

D. The Board of Governors shall apportion the expenses referred to in sub-paragraph B-1 above, among members in accordance with a scale to be fixed by the General Conference. In fixing the scale the General Conference shall be guided by the principles adopted by the United Nations in assessing contributions of Member States to the regular budget of the United Nations.

E. The Board of Governors shall establish periodically a scale of charges, including reasonable uniform storage and handling charges, for materials, services, equipment, and facilities furnished to members by the Agency. The scale shall be designed to produce revenues for the Agency adequate to meet the expenses and costs referred to in sub-paragraph B-2 above, less any voluntary contributions which the Board of Governors may, in accordance with paragraph F, apply for this purpose. The proceeds of such charges shall be placed in a separate fund which shall be used to pay members for any materials, services, equipment, or facilities furnished by them and to meet other expenses referred to in sub-paragraph B-2 above which may be incurred by the Agency itself.

F. Any excess of revenues referred to in paragraph E over the expenses and costs there referred to, and any voluntary contributions to the Agency, shall be placed in a general fund which may be used as the Board of Governors, with the approval of the General Conference, may determine.

G. Subject to rules and limitations approved by the General Conference, the Board of Governors shall have the authority to exercise borrowing powers on behalf of the Agency without however, imposing on members of the Agency any liability in respect of loans entered into pursuant to this authority, and to accept voluntary contributions made to the Agency.

H. Decisions of the General Conference on financial questions and of the Board of

Governors on the amount of the Agency's budget shall require a two-thirds majority of those present and voting.

ARTICLE XV

Privileges and immunities

A. The Agency shall enjoy in the territory of each member such legal capacity and such privileges and immunities as are necessary for the exercise of its functions.

B. Delegates of members together with their alternates and advisers, Governors appointed to the Board together with their alternates and advisers, and the Director General and the staff of the Agency, shall enjoy such privileges and immunities as are necessary in the independent exercise of their functions in connexion with the Agency.

C. The legal capacity, privileges, and immunities referred to in this article shall be defined in a separate agreement or agreements between the Agency, represented for this purpose by the Director General acting under instructions of the Board of Governots, and the members.

ARTICLE XVI

Relationship with other organizations

A. The Board of Governors, with the approval of the General Conference, is authorized to enter into an agreement or agreements establishing an appropriate relationship between the Agency and the United Nations and any other organizations the work of which is related to that of the Agency.

B. The agreement or agreements establishing the relationship of the Agency and the United Nations shall provide for:

1. Submission by the Agency of reports as provided for in sub-paragraphs B-4 and B-5 of article III;

2. Consideration by the Agency of resolutions relating to it adopted by the General Assembly or any of the Councils of the United Nations and the submission of reports, when requested, to the appropriate organ of the United Nations on the action taken by the Agency or by its members in accordance with this Statute as a result of such consideration.

ARTICLE XVII

Settlement of disputes

A. Any questions or dispute concerning the interpretation or application of this Statute which is not settled by negotiation shall be referred to the International Court of Justice in conformity with the Statute of the Court, unless the parties concerned agree on another mode of settlement.

B. The General Conference and the Board of Governors are separately empowered, subject to authorization from the General Assembly of the United Nations, to request the International Court of Justice to give an advisory opinion on any legal question arising within the scope of the Agency's activities.

ARTICLE XVIII

Amendments and withdrawals

A. Amendments to this Statute may be proposed by any member. Certified copies of the text of any amendment proposed shall be prepared by the Director General and communicated by him to all members at least ninety days in advance of its consideration by the General Conference.

B. At the fifth annual session of the General Conference following the coming into force of this Statute, the question of a general review of the provisions of this Statute shall be placed on the agenda of that session. On approval by a majority of the members present and voting, the review will take place at the following General Conference. Thereafter, proposals on the question of a general review of this Statute may be submitted for decision by the General Conference under the same procedure.

C. Amendments shall come into force for all members when:

(i) Approved by the General Conference by a two-thirds majority of those present and voting after consideration of observations submitted by the Board of Governors on each proposed amendment, and

(ii) Accepted by two-thirds of all the members in accordance with their respective constitutional processes. Acceptance by a member shall be effected by the deposit of an instrument of acceptance with the depository Government referred to in paragraph C of article XXI.

D. At any time after five years from the date when this Statute shall take effect in accordance with paragraph E of article XXI or whenever a member is unwilling to accept an amendment to this Statute, it may withdraw from the Agency by notice in writing to that effect given to the depositary Government referred to in paragraph C of article XXI, which shall promptly inform the Board of Governors and all members.

E. Withdrawal by a member from the Agency shall not affect its contractual obligations entered into pursuant to article XI or its budgetary obligations for the year in which it withdraws.

ARTICLE XIX

Suspension of privileges

A. A member of the Agency which is in arrears in the payment of its financial contributions to the Agency shall have no vote in the Agency if the amount of its arrears equals or exceeds the amount of the contributions due from it for the preceding two years. The General Conference may, nevertheless, permit such a member to vote if it is satisfied that the failure to pay is due to conditions beyond the control of the member.

B. A member which has persistently violated the provisions of this Statute or of any agreement entered into by it pursuant to this Statute may be suspended from the exercise of the privileges and rights of membership by the General Conference acting by a two-thirds majority of the members present and voting upon recommendation by the Board of Governors.

ARTICLE XX

Definitions

As used in this Statute:

1. The term "special fissionable material" means plutonium-239; uranium-233; uranium enriched in the isotopes 235 or 233; any material containing one or more of the foregoing; and such other fissionable material as the Board of Governors shall from time to time determine; but the term "special fissionable material" does not include source material.

2. The term "uranium enriched in the isotopes 235 or 233" means uranium containing the isotopes 235 or 233 or both in an amount such that the abundance ratio of the sum of these isotopes to the isotope 238 is greater than the ratio of the isotope 235 to the isotope 238 occurring in nature.

3. The term "source material" means uranium containing the mixture of isotopes occurring in nature; uranium depleted in the isotope 235; thorium; any of the foregoing in the form of metal, alloy, chemical compound, or concentrate; any other material containing one or more of the foregoing of such concentration as the Board of Governors shall from time to time determine; and such other material as the Board of Governors shall from time to time determine.

ARTICLE XXI

Signature, acceptance, and entry into force

A. This Statute shall be open for signature on 26 October 1956 by all States Members of the United Nations or of any of the specialized agencies and shall remain open for signature by those States for a period of ninety days.

B. The signatory States shall become parties to this Statute by deposit of an instrument of ratification.

C. Instruments of ratification by signatory States and instruments of acceptance by States whose membership has been approved under paragraph B of article IV of this Statute shall be deposited with the Government of the United States of America, hereby designated as depositary Government.

D. Ratification or acceptance of this Statute shall be effected by States in accordance with their respective constitutional processes.

E. This Statute, apart from the Annex, shall come into force when eighteen States have deposited instruments of ratification in accordance with paragraph B of this article, provided that such eighteen States shall include at least three of the following States: Canada, France, the Union of Soviet Socialist Republics, the United Kingdom of Great Britain and Northern Ireland, and the United States of America. Instruments of ratification and instruments of acceptance deposited thereafter shall take effect on the date of their receipt.

F. The depositary Government shall promptly inform all States signatory to this Statute of the date of each deposit of ratification and the date of entry into force of the Statute. The depositary Government shall promptly inform all signatories and members of the dates on which States subsequently become parties thereto.

G. The Annex to this Statute shall come into force on the first day this Statute is open for signature.

ARTICLE XXII

Registration with the United Nations

A. This Statute shall be registered by the depositary Government pursuant to Article 102 of the Charter of the United Nations.

B. Agreements between the Agency and any member or members, agreements between the Agency and any other organization or organizations, and agreements between members subject to approval of the Agency, shall be registered with the Agency. Such agreements shall be registered by the Agency with the United Nations if registration is required under Article 102 of the Charter of the United Nations.

ARTICLE XXIII

Authentic texts and certified copies

This Statute, done in the Chinese, English, French, Russian and Spanish languages, each being equally authentic, shall be deposited in the archives of the depositary Government. Duly certified copies of this Statute shall be transmitted by the depositary Government to the Governments of the other signatory States and to the Governments of States admitted to membership under paragraph B of article IV.

417

In witness whereof the undersigned, duly authorized, have signed this Statute.

DONE at the Headquarters of the United Nations, this twenty-sixth day of October, one thousand nine hundred and fifty-six.

ANNEX I

Preparatory Commission

A. A Preparatory Commission shall come into existence on the first day this Statute is open for signature. It shall be composed of one representative each of Australia, Belgium, Brazil, Canada, Czechoslovakia, France, India, Portugal, Union of South Africa, Union of Soviet Socialist Republics, United Kingdom of Great Britain and Northern Ireland, and United States of America, and one representative each of six other States to be chosen by the International Conference on the Statute of the International Atomic Energy Agency. The Preparatory Commission shall remain in existence until this Statute comes into force and thereafter until the General Conference has convened and a Board of Governors has been selected in accordance with article VI.

B. The expenses of the Preparatory Commission may be met by a loan provided by the United Nations and for this purpose the Preparatory Commission shall make the necessary arrangements with the appropriate authorities of the United Nations, including arrangements for repayment of the loan by the Agency. Should these funds be insufficient, the Preparatory Commission may accept advances from Governments. Such advances may be set off against the contributions of the Governments concerned to the Agency.

C. The Preparatory Commission shall:

1. Elect its own officers, adopt its own rules of procedure, meet as often as necessary, determine its own place of meeting and establish such committees as it deems necessary;

2. Appoint an executive secretary and staff as shall be necessary, who shall exercise such powers and perform such duties as the Commission may determine;

3. Make arrangements for the first session of the General Conference, including the preparation of a provisional agenda and draft rules of procedure, such session to be held as soon as possible after the entry into force of this Statute;

4. Make designations for membership on the first Board of Governors in accordance with sub-paragraphs A-1 and A-2 and paragraph B of article VI;

5. Make studies, reports, and recommendations for the first session of the General Conference and for the first meeting of the Board of Governors on subjects of concern to the Agency requiring immediate attention, including *(a)* the financing of the Agency; *(b)* the programmes and budget for the first year of the Agency; *(c)* technical problems relevant to advance planning of Agency operations; *(d)* the establishment of a permanent Agency staff; and *(e)* the location of the permanent headquarters of the Agency;

6. Make recommendations for the first meeting of the Board of Governors concerning the provisions of a headquarters agreement defining the status of the Agency and the rights and obligations which will exist in the relationship between the Agency and the host Government;

7. *(a)* Enter into negotiations with the United Nations with a view to the preparation of a draft agreement in accordance with article XVI of this Statute, such draft agreement to be submitted to the first session of the General Conference and to the first meeting of the Board of Governors; and *(b)* make recommendations to the first session of the General Conference and to the first meeting of the Board of Governors concerning the relationship of the Agency to other international organizations as contemplated to article XVI of this Statute.

F. GENERAL AGREEMENT ON TARIFFS AND TRADE, SIGNED AT GENEVA, OCTOBER 30, 1947[1]

I. *(a)* *Final Act adopted at the conclusion of the second session of the Preparatory Committee of the United Nations Conference on Trade and Employment. Signed at Geneva, on 30 October 1947.*

   (b) *General Agreement on Tariffs and Trade. (The schedules of tariff concessions annexed to this Agreement are published in Volumes 56 to 61).*

   (c) *Protocol of Provisional Application of the General Agreement on Tariffs and Trade. Signed at Geneva, on 30 October 1947.*

I. *(a)* FINAL ACT ADOPTED AT THE CONCLUSION OF THE SECOND SESSION OF THE PREPARATORY COMMITTEE OF THE UNITED NATIONS CONFERENCE ON TRADE AND EMPLOYMENT. SIGNED AT GENEVA, ON 30 OCTOBER 1947.

In accordance with the Resolution adopted at the First Session of the Preparatory Committee of the United Nations Conference on Trade and Employment, established by the Economic and Social Council of the United Nations on February 18, 1946,[2]

The Governments of the COMMONWEALTH OF AUSTRALIA, the KINGDOM OF BELGIUM, the UNITED STATES OF BRAZIL, BURMA, CANADA, CEYLON, the REPUBLIC OF CHINA, the REPUBLIC OF CUBA, the CZECHOSLOVAK REPUBLIC, the FRENCH REPUBLIC, INDIA, LEBANON, the GRAND-DUCHY OF LUXEMBURG, the KINGDOM OF THE NETHERLANDS, NEW ZEALAND, the KINGDOM OF NORWAY, PAKISTAN, SOUTHERN RHODESIA, SYRIA, the UNION OF SOUTH AFRICA, the UNITED KINGDOM OF GREAT BRITAIN AND NORTHERN IRELAND, and the UNITED STATES OF AMERICA,

Initiated negotiations between their representatives, at Geneva on April 10, 1947, directed to the substantial reduction of tariffs and other trade barriers and to the elimination of preferences, on a reciprocal and mutually advantageous basis. These negotiations have terminated today and have resulted in the framing of a General Agreement on Tariffs and Trade and of a Protocol of Provisional Application, the texts of which are annexed hereto. These texts are hereby authenticated.

The signature of this Final Act, or of the Protocol of Provisional Application, by any of the above-mentioned Governments does not in any way prejudice their freedom of action at the United Nations Conference on Trade and Employment.

This Final Act, including the texts of the General Agreement on Tariffs and Trade and of the Protocol of Provisional Application, will be released by the Secretary-General of the United Nations for publication on November 18, 1947, provided that the Protocol of Provisional Application shall have been signed by November 15, 1947, on behalf of all the countries named therein.

In WITNESS WHEREOF the respective Representatives have signed the present Act.

DONE at Geneva, in a single copy, in the English and French languages, both texts authentic, this thirtieth day of October, one thousand nine hundred and forty-seven.

---

[1] United Nations document E/PC/T 33.

[2] Applied provisionally as from 1 January 1948 pursuant to the Protocol of Provisional Application.

States which have undertaken to apply provisionally the General Agreement:

(a) By signature of the Protocol of Provisional Application (territories other than metropolitan territories in respect of which notice of application was received by the Secretary-General of the United Nations, in accordance with paragraph 2 of the said Protocol, are listed under the respective States and the effective date of such notice is given):

State	As from	State	As from
Australia	1 January 1948	Mandated territory of	
Belgium	1 January 1948	Palestine***	19 April 1948
Belgian Congo	1 January 1948	All the territories for	
Canada	1 January 1948	the international rela-	
China*	21 May 1948	tions of which they	
France	1 January 1948	are responsible, with	
All the overseas territo-		the exception of	
ries of the French		Jamaica	28 July 1948
Union listed in an-		United States of America	1 January 1948
nex B of the Gene-		Brazil	30 July 1948
ral Agreement with		Burma	29 July 1948
the exception of Mo-		Ceylon	29 July 1948
rocco	12 June 1949	Cuba	1 January 1948
Luxembourg	1 January 1948	Czechoslovakia	20 April 1948
Netherlands	1 January 1948	India	8 July 1948
Overseas territories of		Lebanon	29 July 1948
the Kingdom of the		New Zealand	30 July 1948
Netherlands	12 March 1948	Norway	10 July 1948
United Kingdom of Great		Pakistan	30 July 1948
Britain and Northern		Southern Rhodesia	11 July 1948
Ireland	1 January 1948	Syria	30 July 1948
Newfoundland**	1 January 1948	Union of South Africa	18 June 1948

(b) Pursuant to the Protocol for the Accession of Signatories of the Final Act (see No. 814 III. a), Volume 62 of this Series):

Chile . . . . 16 March 1949

(c) Pursuant to the provisions of the Annecy Protocol of Terms of Accession (see No. 814 V, Volume 63 of this *Series*):

Denmark	28 May 1950	Greece	1 March 1950
Not including the ter-		Haiti	1 January 1950
ritory of the Faroe		Italy	30 May 1950
Islands.		Liberia****	20 May 1950
Dominican Republic	10 May 1950	Nicaragua	28 May 1950
Finland	25 May 1950	Sweden	30 April 1950

(d) Pursuant to the provisions of article XXVI (4) of the General Agreement on Tariffs and Trade:

Indonesia . . . . 24 February 1950

*China, having undertaken to apply provisionally the General Agreement on Tariffs and Trade as from 21 May 1948 by virtue of signature on 21 April 1948 of the Protocol of Provisional Application, notified the Secretary-General of the United Nations on 6 March 1950 of the withdrawal of such application. In accordance with paragrpah 5 of the Protocol of Provisional Application this notice of withdrawal became effective on 5 May 1950.

**The Government of the United Kingdom ceased to be responsible for Newfoundland on 31 March 1949 and Newfoundland became a part of the customs territory of Canada.

***The Government of the United Kingdom ceased to be responsible for the mandated territory of Palestine on 15 May 1948.

****Liberia also deposited with the Secretary-General on 17 May 1950 an instrument of acceptance to the General Agreement on Tariffs and Trade of 30 October 1947.

In accordance with the provisions of paragraph 8(a) of the Annecy Protocol of Terms of Accession, and subject to the conditions stipulated therein, this acceptance shall take effect on the day on which the General Agreement enters into force pursuant to article XXVI.

For the Commonwealth of Australia:	C. E. MORTON
For the Kingdom of Belgium:	P. A. FORTHOMME
For the United States of Brazil:	A. DE FERREIRA BRAGA
For Burma:	MAUNG NYUN
For Canada:	L. D. WILGRESS
For Ceylon:	J. COREA
For the Republic of Chile:	A. FAIVOVICH
For the Republic of China:	WUNSZ KING
For the Republic of Cuba:	SERGIO I. CLARK
For the Czechoslovak Republic:	Z. AUGENTHALER
For the French Republic:	PIERRE BARADUC
For India:	S. RANGANATHAN
For Lebanon:	J. MIKAOUI

I. *(b)* GENERAL AGREEMENT ON TARIFFS AND TRADE[1]

———————————

The Governments of the Commonwealth of Australia, the Kingdom of Belgium, the United States of Brazil, Burma, Canada, Ceylon, the Republic of Chile, the Republic of China, the Republic of Cuba, the Czechoslovak Republic, the French Republic, India, Lebanon, the Grand-Duchy of Luxemburg, the Kingdom of the Netherlands, New Zealand, the Kingdom of Norway, Pakistan, Southern Rhodesia, Syria, the Union of South Africa, the United Kingdom of Great Britain and Northern Ireland, and the United States of America:

Recognizing that their relations in the field of trade and economic endeavour should be conducted with a view to raising standards of living, ensuring full employment and a large and steadily growing volume of real income and effective demand, developing the full use of the resources of the world and expanding the production and exchange of goods;

Being desirous of contributing to these objectives by entering into reciprocal and mutually advantageous arrangements directed to the substantial reduction of tariffs and other barriers to trade and to the elimination of discriminatory treatment in international commerce;

Have through their Representatives agreed as follows:

PART I

Article I[1]

GENERAL MOST-FAVOURED-NATION TREATMENT

1. With respect to customs duties and charges of any kind imposed on or in connection with importation or exportation or imposed on the international transfer of payments for imports or exports, and with respect to the method of levying such duties and charges, and with respect to all rules and formalities in connection with importation and exportation, and with respect to all matters referred to in paragraphs 1 and 2

———————

[1]Paragraphs 1, 2 and 3 of Article I have been amended by the Protocol modifying part I and article XXIX of the General Agreement on Tariffs and Trade, signed at Geneva, on 14 September 1948, which, at the date of registration of the General Agreement on Tariffs and Trade, had not yet entered into force.

of Article III, any advantage, favour, privilege or immunity granted by any contracting party to any product originating in or destined for any other country shall be accorded immediately and unconditionally to the like product originating in or destined for the territories of all other contracting parties.

2.   The provisions of paragraph 1 of this Article shall not require the elimination of any preferences in respect of import duties or charges which do not exceed the levels provided for in paragraph 3 of this Article and which fall within the following descriptions:

(a)   preferences in force exclusively between two or more of the territories listed in Annex A, subject to the conditions set forth therein;

(b)   preferences in force exclusively between two or more territories which on July 1, 1939, were connected by common sovereignty or relations of protection or suzerainty and which are listed in Annexes B, C and D, subject to the conditions set forth therein;

(c)   preferences in force exclusively between the United States of America and the Republic of Cuba;

(d)   preferences in force exclusively between neighbouring countries listed in Annexes E and F.

3.   The margin of preference on any product in respect of which a preference is permitted under paragraph 2 of this Article but is not specifically set forth as a maximum margin of preference in the appropriate Schedule annexed to this Agreement shall not exceed:

(a)   in respect of duties or charges on any product described in such Schedule, the difference between the most-favoured-nation and preferential rates provided for therein; if no preferential rate is provided for, the preferential rate shall for the purposes of this paragraph be taken to be that in force on April 10, 1947, and, if no most-favoured-nation rate is provided for, the margin shall not exceed the difference between the most-favoured-nation and preferential rates existing on April 10, 1947:

(b)   in respect of duties or charges on any product not described in the appropriate Schedule, the difference between the most-favoured-nation and preferential rates existing on April 10, 1947.

In the case of the contracting parties named in Annex G, the date of April 10, 1947, referred to in subparagraphs (a) and (b) of this paragraph shall be replaced by the respective dates set forth in that Annex.

Article II

SCHEDULES OF CONCESSIONS[1]

1.   (a) Each contracting party shall accord to the commerce of the other contracting parties treatment no less favourable than that provided for in the appropriate Part of the appropriate Schedule annexed to this Agreement.

(b) The products described in Part I of the Schedule relating to any contracting party, which are the products of territories of other contracting parties, shall, on their importation into the territory to which the Schedule relates, and subject to the terms, conditions or qualifications set forth in that Schedule, be exempt from ordinary customs duties in excess of those set forth and provided for therein. Such products shall also be exempt from all other duties or charges of any kind imposed on or in connection with importation in excess of those imposed on the date of this Agreement or

---

[1]United Nations *Treaty Series*, Volumes 56 to 61.

those directly and mandatorily required to be imposed thereafter by legislation in force in the importing territory on that date.

(c) The products described in Part II of the Schedule relating to any contracting party, which are the products of territories entitled under Article I to receive preferential treatment upon importation into the territory to which the Schedule relates, shall, on their importation into such territory, and subject to the terms, conditions or qualifications set forth in that Schedule, be exempt from ordinary customs duties in excess of those set forth and provided for in Part II of that Schedule. Such products shall also be exempt from all other duties or charges of any kind imposed on or in connection with importation in excess of those imposed on the date of this Agreement or those directly and mandatory required to be imposed thereafter by legislation in force in the importing territory on that date. Nothing in this Article shall prevent any contracting party from maintaining its requirements existing on the date of this Agreement as to the eligibility of goods for entry at preferential rates of duty.

2.[1] Nothing in this Article shall prevent any contracting party from imposing at any time on the importation of any product.

(a) a charge equivalent to an internal tax imposed consistently with the provisions of paragraph I of Article III in respect of the like domestic product or in respect of an article from which the imported product has been manufactured or produced in whole or in party;

(b) any anti-dumping or countervailing duty applied consistently with the provisions of Article VI;

(c) fees or other charges commensurate with the cost of services rendered.

3. No contracting party shall alter its method of determining dutiable value or of converting currencies so as to impair the value of any of the concessions provided for in the appropriate Schedule annexed to this Agreement.

4. If any contracting party establishes, maintains or authorizes, formally or in effect, a monopoly of the importation of any product described in the appropriate Schedule annexed to this Agreement, such monopoly shall not, except as provided for in that Schedule or as otherwise agreed between the parties which initially negotiated the concession, operate so as to afford protection on the average in excess of the amount of protection provided for in that Schedule. The provisions of this paragraph shall not limit the use by contracting parties of any form of assistance to domestic producers permitted by other provisions of this Agreement.

5. If any contracting party considers that a product is not receiving from another contracting party the treatment which the first contracting party believes to have been contemplated by a concession provided for in the appropriate Schedule annexed to this Agreement, it shall bring the matter directly to the attention of the other contracting party. If the latter agrees that the treatment contemplated was that claimed by the first contracting party, but declares that such treatment cannot be accorded because a court or other proper authority has ruled to the effect that the product involved cannot be classified under the tariff laws of such contracting party so as to permit the treatment contemplated in this Agreement, the two contracting parties, together with any other contracting parties substantially interested, shall enter promptly into further negotiations with a view to a compensatory adjustment of the matter.

6. *(a)* The specific duties and charges included in the Schedules relating to contracting parties members of the International Monetary Fund, and margins of preference in specific duties and charges maintained by such contracting parties, are expressed in the appropriate currency at the par value accepted or provisionally recognized by the Fund at the date of this Agreement. Accordingly, in case this par value is reduced consis-

---

[1] Paragraph 2 *(a)* of article II has been amended by the Protocol modifying part I and article XXIX of the General Agreement on Tariffs and Trade, signed at Geneva, on 14 September 1948, which, at the date of registration of the General Agreement on Tariffs and Trade, had not yet entered into force.

tently with the Articles of Agreement of the International Monetary Fund by more than twenty per centum, such specific duties and charges and margins of preference may be adjusted to take account of such reduction; *Provided* that the CONTRACTING PARTIES (i.e. the contracting parties acting jointly as provided for in Article XXV) concur that such adjustments will not impair the value of the concessions provided for in the appropriate Schedule or elsewhere in this Agreement, due account being taken of all factors which may influence the need for, or urgency of, such adjustments.

(b) Similar provisions shall apply to any contracting party not a member of the Fund, as from the date on which such contracting party becomes a member of the Fund or enters into a special exchange agreement in pursuance of Article XV.

7. The Schedules[1] annexed to this Agreement are hereby made an integral part of Part I of this Agreement.

PART II

Article III[2]

NATIONAL TREATMENT ON INTERNAL TAXATION AND REGULATION

1. The products of the territory of any contracting party imported into the territory of any other contracting party shall be exempt from internal taxes and other internal charges of any kind in excess of those applied directly or indirectly to like products of national origin. Moreover, in cases in which there is no substantial domestic production of like products of national origin, no contracting party shall apply new or increased internal taxes on the products of the territories of other contracting parties for the purpose of affording protection to the production of directly competitive or substitutable products which are not similarly taxed; and existing internal taxes of this kind shall be subject to negotiation for their reduction or elimination.

2. The products of the territory of any contracting party imported into the territory of any other contracting party shall be accorded treatment no less favourable than that accorded to like products of national origin in respect of all laws, regulations and requirements affecting their internal sale, offering for sale, purchase, transportation, distribution, or use. The provisions of this paragraph shall not prevent the application of differential transportation charges which are based exclusively on the economic operation of the means of transport and not on the nationality of the product.

3. In applying the principles of paragraph 2 of this Article to internal quantitative regulations relating to the mixture, processing or use of products in specified amounts or proportions, the contracting parties shall observe the following provisions:

   (a) no regulations shall be made which, formally or in effect, require that any specified amount or proportion of the product in respect of which such regulations are applied must be supplied from domestic sources;

   (b) no contracting party shall, formally or in effect, restrict the mixing, processing or use of a product of which there is no substantial domestic production with a view to affording protection to the domestic production of a directly competitive or substitutable product.

4. The provisions of paragraph 3 of this Article shall not apply to:

   (a) any measure of internal quantitative control in force in the territory of any contracting party on July 1, 1939 or April 10, 1947, at the option of that contracting party: *Provided* that any such measure which would be in conflict with the provisions of paragraph 3 of this Article shall not be modified to the detriment of imports and shall be subject to negotiation for its limitation, liberalization or elimination;

---

[1] These schedules are published in Volumes 56, 57, 58, 59, 60 and 61 of this *Series*.
[2] Article III has been amended by the Protocol modifying part II and article XXVI, of the General Agreement on Tariffs and Trade, signed at Geneva, on 14 September 1948. See Volume 62.

(b) any internal quantitative regulation relating to exposed cinematograph films and meeting the requirements of Article IV.

5.   The provisions of this Article shall not apply to the procurement by governmental agencies of products purchased for governmental purposes and not for resale or use in the production of goods for sale, nor shall they prevent the payment to domestic producers only of subsidies provided for under Article XVI, including payments to domestic producers derived from the proceeds of internal taxes or charges and subsidies effected through governmental purchases of domestic products.

Article IV

SPECIAL PROVISIONS RELATING TO CINEMATOGRAPH FILMS

If any contracting party establishes or maintains internal quantitative regulations relating to exposed cinematograph films, such regulations shall take the form of screen quotas which shall conform to the following requirements:

(a) screen quotas may require the exhibition of cinematograph films of national origin during a specified minimum proportion of the total screen time actually utilized, over a specified period of not less than one year, in the commercial exhibition of all films of whatever origin, and shall be computed on the basis of screen time per theatre per year or the equivalent thereof;

(b) with the exception of screen time reserved for films of national origin under a screen quota, screen time including that released by administrative action from screen time reserved for films of national origin, shall not be allocated formally or in effect among sources of supply;

(c) notwithstanding the provisions of sub-paragraph *(b)* of this Article, any contracting party may maintain screen quotas conforming to the requirements of sub-paragraph *(a)* of this Article which reserve a minimum proportion of screen time for films of a specified origin other than that of the contracting party imposing such screen quotas; *Provided* that no such minimum proportion of screen time shall be increased above the level in effect on April 10, 1947;

(d) screen quotas shall be subject to negotiation for their limitation, liberalization or elimination.

Article V

FREEDOM OF TRANSIT

1.   Goods (including baggage), and also vessels and other means of transport shall be deemed to be in transit across the territory of a contracting party when the passage across such territory, with or without trans-shipment, warehousing, breaking bulk, or change in the mode of transport, is only a portion of a complete journey beginning and terminating beyond the frontier of the contracting party across whose territory the traffic passes. Traffic of this nature is termed in this Article "traffic in transit."

2.   There shall be freedom of transit through the territory of each contracting party, via the routes most convenient for international transit, for traffic in transit to or from the territory of other contracting parties. No distinction shall be made which is based on the flag of vessels, the place of origin, departure, entry, exit or destination, or on any circumstances relating to the ownership of goods, or vessels or of other means of transport.

3.   Any contracting party may require that traffic in transit through its territory be entered at the proper custom house, but, except in cases of failure to comply with applicable customs laws and regulations, such traffic coming from or going to the territory of other contracting parties shall not be subject to any unnecessary delays

or restrictions and shall be exempt from customs duties and from all transit duties or other charges imposed in respect of transit, except charges for transportation or those commensurate with administrative expenses entailed by transit or with the cost of services rendered.

4. All charges and regulations imposed by contracting parties on traffic in transit to or from the territories of other contracting parties shall be reasonable, having regard to the conditions of the traffic.

5. With respect to all charges, regulations and formalities in connection with transit, each contracting party shall accord to traffic in transit to or from the territory of any other contracting party treatment no less favourable than the treatment accorded to traffic in transit to or from any third country.

6. Each contracting party shall accord to products which have been in transit through the territory of any other contracting party treatment no less favourable than that which would have been accorded to such products had they been transported from their place of origin to their destination without going through the territory of such other contracting party. Any contracting party shall, however, be free to maintain its requirements of direct consignment existing on the date of this Agreement, in respect of any goods in regard to which such direct consignment is a requisite condition of eligibility for entry of the goods at preferential rates of duty or has relation to the contracting party's prescribed method of valuation for duty purposes.

7. The provisions of this Article shall not apply to the operation of aircraft in transit, but shall apply to air transit of goods (including baggage).

Article VI[1]

ANTI-DUMPING AND COUNTERVAILING DUTIES

1. No anti-dumping duty shall be levied on any product of the territory of any contracting party imported into the territory of any other contracting party in excess of an amount equal to the margin of dumping under which such product is being imported. For the purposes of this Article, the margin of dumping shall be understood to mean the amount by which the price of the product exported from one country to another.

   (a) is less than the comparable price, in the ordinary course of trade, for the like product when destined for consumption in the exporting country; or,

   (b) in the absence of such domestic price, is less than either

   (i) the highest comparable price for the like product for export to any third country in the ordinary course of trade, or

   (ii) the cost of production of the product in the country of origin plus a reasonable addition for selling cost and profit.

Due allowance shall be made in each case for differences in conditions and terms of sale, for differences in taxation, and for other differences affecting price comparability.

2. No countervailing duty shall be levied on any product of the territory of any contracting party imported into the territory of another contracting party in excess of an amount equal to the estimated bounty or subsidy determined to have been granted, directly or indirectly, on the manufacture, production or export of such product in the country of origin or exportation, including any special subsidy to the transportation of a particular product. The term "countervailing duty" shall be understood to mean a special duty levied for the purpose of offsetting any bounty or subsidy bestowed, directly or indirectly, upon the manufacture, production or exportation of any merchandise.

---

[1] Article VI has been amended by the Protocol modifying part II and article XXVI of the General Agreement on Tariffs and Trade, signed at Geneva, on 14 September 1948. See Volume 62.

3.   No product of the territory of any contracting party imported into the territory of any other contracting party shall be subject to anti-dumping or countervailing duty by reason of the exemption of such product from duties or taxes borne by the like product when destined for consumption in the country of origin or exportation, or by reason of the refund of such duties or taxes.

4.   No product of the territory of any contracting party imported into the territory of any other contracting party shall be subject to both anti-dumping and countervailing duties to compensate for the same situation of dumping or export subsidication.

5.   No contracting party shall levy any anti-dumping or countervaling duty on the importation of any product of the territory of another contracting party unless it determines that the effect of the dumping or subsidization, as the case may be, is such as to cause or threaten material injury to an established domestic industry, or is such as to prevent or materially retard the establishment of a domestic industry. The CON-TRACTING PARTIES may waive the requirements of this paragraph so as to permit a contracting party to levy an anti-dumping or countervailing duty on the importation of any product for the purpose of offsetting dumping or subsidization which causes or threatens material injury to an industry in the territory of another contracting party exporting the product concerned to the territory of the importing contracting party.

6.   A system for the stabilization of the domestic price or of the return to domestic producers of a primary commodity, independently of the movements of export prices, which results at times in the sale of the product for export at a price lower than the comparable price charged for the like product to buyers in the domestic market, shall be considered not to result in material injury within the meaning of paragraph 5 of this Article, if it is determined by consultation among the contracting parties substantially interested in the product concerned:

   (a)   that the system has also resulted in the sale of the product for export at a price higher than the comparable price charged for the like product to buyers in the domestic market, and

   (b)   that the system is so operated, either because of the effective regulation of production or otherwise, as not to stimulate exports unduly or otherwise seriously prejudice the interests of other contracting parties.

7.   No measures other than anti-dumping or countervailing duties shall be applied by any contracting party in respect of any product of the territory of any other contracting party for the purpose of offsetting dumping or subsidization.

Article VII

VALUATION FOR CUSTOMS PURPOSES

1.   The contracting parties recognize the validity of the general principles of valuation set forth in the following paragraphs of this Article, and they undertake to give effect to such principles, in respect of all products subject to duties or other charges or restrictions on importation and exportation based upon or regulated in any manner by value, at the earliest practicable date. Moreover, they shall, upon a request by another contracting party, review the operation of any of their laws or regulations relating to value for customs purposes in the light of these principles. The CONTRACTING PARTIES may request from contracting parties reports on steps taken by them in pursuance of the provisions of this Article.

2.   *(a)* The value for customs purposes of imported merchandise should be based on the actual value of the imported merchandise on which duty is assessed, or of like merchandise, and should not be based on the value of merchandise of national origin or on arbitrary or fictitious values.

   (b) "Actual value" should be the price at which, at a time and place determined by the legislation of the country of importation, and in the ordinary course of trade, such or like merchandise is sold or offered for sale under fully competitive conditions.

To the extent to which the price of such or like merchandise is governed by the quantity in a particular transaction, the price to be considered should uniformly be related to either (i) comparable quantities, or (ii) quantities not less favourable to importers than those in which the greater volume of the merchandise is sold in the trade between the countries of exportation and importation.

(c) When the actual value is not ascertainable in accordance with sub-paragraph *(b)* of this paragraph, the value for customs purposes should be based on the nearest ascertainable equivalent of such value.

3. The value for customs purposes of any imported product should not include the amount of any internal tax, applicable within the country of origin or export, from which the imported product has been exempted or has been or will be relieved by means of refund.

4. *(a)* Except as otherwise provided for in this paragraph, where it is necessary for the purposes of paragraph 2 of this Article for a contracting party to convert into its own currency a price expressed in the currency of another country, the conversion rate of exchange to be used shall be based on the par values of the currencies involved as established pursuant to the Articles of Agreement of the International Monetary Fund[1] or by special exchange agreements entered into pursuant to Article XV of this Agreement.

(b) Where no such par value has been established, the conversion rate reflect effectively the current value of such currency in commercial transactions.

(c) The CONTRACTING PARTIES, in agreement with the International Monetary Fund, shall formulate rules governing the conversion by contracting parties of any foreign currency in respect of which multiple rates of exchange are maintained consistently with the Articles of Agreement of the International Monetary Fund. Any contracting party may apply such rules in respect of such foreign currencies for the purposes of paragraph 2 of this Article as an alternative to the use of par values. Until such rules are adopted by the CONTRACTING PARTIES, any contracting party may employ, in respect of any such foreign currency, rules of conversion for the purposes of paragraph 2 of this Article which are designed to reflect effectively the value of such foreign currency in commercial transactions.

(d) Nothing in this paragraph shall be construed to require any contracting party to alter the method of converting currencies for customs purposes which is applicable in its territory on the date of this Agreement, if such alteration would have the effect of increasing generally the amounts of duty payable.

5. The bases and methods for determining the value of products subject to duties or other charges or restrictions based upon or regulated in any manner by value should be stable and should be given sufficient publicity to enable traders to estimate, with a reasonable degree of certainty, the value for customs purposes.

Article VIII

FORMALITIES CONNECTED WITH IMPORTATION AND EXPORTATION

1. The contracting parties recognise that fees and charges, other than duties, imposed by governmental authorities on or in connection with importation or exportation, should be limited in amount to the approximate cost of services rendered and should not represent an indirect protection to domestic products or a taxation of imports or exports for fiscal purposes. The contracting parties also recognize the need for reducing the number and diversity of such fees and charges, for minimizing the incidence and complexity of import and export formalities, and for decreasing and simplifying import and export documentation requirements.

---

[1] United Nations *Treaty Series,* Volume 2, page 39, and Volume 19, page 280.

2.   The contracting parties shall take action in accordance with the principles and objectives of paragraph 1 of this Article at the earliest practicable date. Moreover, they shall, upon request by another contracting party, review the operation of any of their laws and regulations in the light of these principles.

3.   No contracting party shall impose substantial penalties for minor breaches of customs regulations or procedural requirements. In particular, no penalty in respect of any omission or mistake in customs documentation which is easily rectifiable and obviously made without fraudulent intent or gross negligence shall greater than necessary to serve merely as a warning.

4.   The provisions of this Article shall extend to fees, charges, formalities and requirements imposed by governmental authorities in connection with importation and exportation, including those relating to:

> *(a)* consular transactions, such as consular invoices and certificates;
> *(b)* quantitative restrictions;
> *(c)* licensing;
> *(d)* exchange control;
> *(e)* statistical services;
> *(f)* documents, documentation and certification;
> *(g)* analysis and inspection; and
> *(h)* quarantine, sanitation and fumigation.

Article IX

MARKS OF ORIGIN

1.   Each contracting party shall accord to the products of the territories of other contracting parties treatment with regard to marking requirements no less favourable than the treatment accorded to like products of any third country.

2.   Whenever it is administratively practicable to do so, contracting parties should permit required marks of origin to be affixed at the time of importation.

3.   The laws and regulations of contracting parties relating to the marking of imported products shall be such as to permit compliance without seriously damaging the products, or materially reducing their value, or unreasonably increasing their cost.

4.   As a general rule no special duty or penalty should be imposed by any contracting party for failure to comply with marking requirements prior to importation unless corrective marking is unreasonably delayed or deceptive marks have been affixed or the required marking has been intentionally omitted.

5.   The contracting parties shall co-operate with each other with a view to preventing the use of trade names in such manner as to misrepresent the true origin of a product, to the detriment of such distinctive regional or geographical names of products of the territory of a contracting party as are protected by its legislation. Each contracting party shall accord full and sympathetic consideration to such requests or representations as may be made by any other contracting party regarding the application of the undertaking set forth in the preceding sentence to names of products which have been communicated to it by the other contracting party.

Article X

PUBLICATION AND ADMINISTRATION OF TRADE REGULATIONS

1.   Laws, regulations, judicial decisions and administrative rulings of general application, made effective by any contracting party, pertaining to the classification or the valuation of products for customs purposes, or to rates of duty, taxes or other charges, or to requirements, restrictions or prohibitions on imports or exports or on the transfer of payments therefor, or affecting their sale, distribution, transportation, insurance,

warehousing, inspection, exhibition, processing, mixing or other use, shall be published promptly in such a manner as to enable governments and traders to become acquainted with them. Agreements affecting international trade policy which are in force between the government or a governmental agency of any contracting party and the government or governmental agency of any other contracting party shall also be published. The provisions of this paragraph shall not require any contracting party to disclose confidential information which would impede law enforcement of otherwise be contrary to the public interest or would prejudice the legitimate commercial interests of particular enterprises, public or private.

2.   No measure of general application taken by any contracting party effecting an advance in a rate of duty or other charge on imports under an established and uniform practice, or imposing a new or more burdensome requirement, restriction or prohibition on imports, or on the transfer of payments therefor, shall be enforced before such measure has been officially published.

3.   *(a)* Each contracting party shall administer in a uniform, impartial and reasonable manner all its laws, regulations, decisions and rulings of the kind described in paragraph 1 of this Article.

   (b) Each contracting party shall maintain, or institute as soon as practicable, judicial, arbitral or administrative tribunals or procedures for the purpose, *inter alia*, of the prompt review and correction of administrative action relating to customs matters. Such tribunals or procedures shall be independent of the agencies entrusted with administrative enforcement and their decisions shall be implemented by, and shall govern the practice of, such agencies unless an appeal is lodged with a court or tribunal of superior jurisdiction within the time prescribed for appeals to be lodged by importers; *Provided* that the central administration of such agency may take steps to obtain a review of the matter in another proceeding if there is good cause to believe that the decision is inconsistent with established principles of law or the actual facts.

   (c) The provisions of sub-paragraph *(b)* of this paragraph shall not require the elimination or substitution of procedures in force in the territory of a contracting party on the date of this Agreement which in fact provide for an objective and impartial review of administrative action even though such procedures are not fully or formally independent of the agencies entrusted with administrative enforcement. Any contracting party employing such procedures shall, upon request, furnish the CONTRACTING PARTIES with full information thereon in order that they may determine whether such procedures conform to the requirements of this sub-paragraph.

Article XI

GENERAL ELIMINATION OF QUANTITATIVE RESTRICTIONS

1.   No prohibitions or restrictions other than duties, taxes or other charges, whether made effective through quotas, import or export licenses or other measures, shall be instituted or maintained by any contracting party on the importation of any product of the territory of any other contracting party or on the exportation or sale for export of any product destined for the territory of any other contracting party.

2.   The provisions of paragraph 1 of this Article shall not extend to the following:

   (a)   export prohibitions or restrictions temporarily applied to prevent or relieve critical shortages of foodstuffs or other products essential to the exporting contracting party;

   (b)   import and export prohibitions or restrictions necessary to the application of standards or regulations for the classification, grading or marketing of commodities in international trade;

   (c)   import restrictions on any agricultural or fisheries product, imported in any form, necessary to the enforcement of governmental measures which operate:

(i) to restrict the quantities of the like domestic product permitted to be marketed or produced, or, if there is no substantial domestic production of the like product, of a domestic product for which the imported product, can be directly substituted; or

(ii) to remove a temporary surplus of the like domestic product, or, if there is no substantial domestic production of the like product, of a domestic product for which the imported product can be directly substituted, by making the surplus available to certain groups of domestic consumers free of charge or at prices below the current market level; or

(iii) to restrict the quantities permitted to be produced of any animal product the production of which is directly dependent, wholly or mainly, on the imported commodity, if the domestic production of that commodity is relatively negligible.

Any contracting party applying restrictions on the importation of any product pursuant to sub-paragraph *(c)* of this paragraph shall give public notice of the total quantity or value of the product permitted to be imported during a specified future period and of any change in such quantity or value. Moreover, any restrictions applied under (i) above shall not be such as will reduce the total of imports relative to the total of domestic production, as compared with the proportion which might reasonably be expected to rule between the two in the absence of restrictions. In determining this proportion, the contracting party shall pay due regard to the proportion prevailing during a previous representative period and to any special factors which may have affected or may be affecting the trade in the product concerned.

3.   Throughout Articles XI, XII, XIII and XIV the terms "import restrictions" or "export restrictions" include restrictions made effective through state-trading operations.

Article XII

RESTRICTIONS TO SAFEGUARD THE BALANCE OF PAYMENTS

1.   Notwithstanding the provisions of paragraph 1 of Article XI, any contracting party, in order to safeguard its external financial position and balance of payments, may restrict the quantity or value of merchandise permitted to be imported, subject to the provisions of the following paragraphs of this Article.

2.   *(a)* No contracting party shall institute, maintain or intensify import restrictions under this Article except to the extent necessary.

(i) to forestall the imminent threat of, or to stop, a serious decline in its monetary reserves, or

(ii) in the case of a contracting party with very low monetary reserves, to achieve a reasonable rate of increase in its reserves.

Due regard shall be paid in either case to any special factors which may be affecting the contracting party's reserves or need for reserves, including, where special external credits or other resources are available to it, the need to provide for the appropriate use of such credits or resources.

(b) Contracting parties applying restrictions under sub-paragraph *(a)* of this paragraph shall progressively relax them as such conditions improve, maintaining them only to the extent that the conditions specified in that sub-paragraph still justify their application. They shall eliminate the restrictions when conditions would no longer justify their institution or maintenance under that sub-paragraph.

3.   *(a)* The contracting parties recognize that during the next few years all of them will be confronted in varying degrees with problems of economic adjustment resulting from the war. During this period the CONTRACTING PARTIES shall, when required to take decisions under this Article or under Article XIV, take full account of the difficulties of post-war adjustment and of the need which a contracting party may have to

use import restrictions as a step towards the restoration of equilibrium in its balance of payments on a sound and lasting basis.

(b) The contracting parties recognize that, as a result of domestic policies directed toward the achievement and maintenance of full and productive employment and large and steadily growing demand or toward the reconstruction or development of industrial and other economic resources and the raising of standards of productivity, such a contracting party may experience a high level of demand for imports. Accordingly,

(i) notwithstanding the provisions of paragraph 2 of this Article, no contracting party shall be required to withdraw or modify restrictions on the ground that a charge in the policies referred to above would render unnecessary the restrictions which it is applying under this Article;

(ii) any contracting party applying import restrictions under this Article may determine the incidence of the restrictions on imports of different products or classes of products in such a way as to give priority to the importation of those products which are more essential in the light of such policies.

(c) Contracting parties undertake, in carrying out their domestic policies:

(i) to pay due regard to the need for restoring equilibrium in their balance of payments on a sound and lasting basis and to the desirability of assuring an economic employment of productive resources;

(ii) not to apply restrictions so as to prevent unreasonably the importation of any description of goods in minimum commercial quantities, the exclusion of which would impair regular channels of trade, or restrictions which would prevent the importation of commercial samples, or prevent compliance with patent, trademark, copyright, or similar procedures; and

(iii) to apply restrictions under this Article in such a way as to avoid unnecessary damage to the commercial or economic interests of any other contracting party.

4. *(a)* Any contracting party which is not applying restrictions under this Article, but is considering the need to do so, shall, before instituting such restrictions (or, in circumstances in which prior consultation is impracticable, immediately after doing so), consult with the CONTRACTING PARTIES as to the nature of its balance-of-payments difficulties, alternative corrective measures which may be available, and the possible effect of such measures on the economies of other contracting parties. No contracting party shall be required in the course of consultations under this sub-paragraph to indicate in advance the choice or timing of any particular measures which it may ultimately determine to adopt.

(b) The CONTRACTING PARTIES may at any time invite any contracting party which is applying import restrictions under this Article to enter into such consultations with them, and shall invite any contracting party substantially intensifying such restrictions to consult within thirty days. A contracting party thus invited shall participate in such discussions. The CONTRACTING PARTIES may invite any other contracting party to take part in these discussions. Not later than January 1, 1951, the CONTRACTING PARTIES shall review all restrictions existing on that day and still applied under this Article at the time of the review.

(c) Any contracting party may consult with the CONTRACTING PARTIES with a view to obtaining their prior approval for restrictions which the contracting party proposes, under this Article, to maintain, intensify or institute, or for the maintenance, intensification or institution of restrictions under specified future conditions. As a result of such consultations, the CONTRACTING PARTIES may approve in advance the maintenance, intensification or institution of restrictions by the contracting party in question insofar as the general extent, degree of intensity and duration of the restrictions are concerned. To the extent to which such approval has been given, the requirements of sub-paragraph *(a)* of this paragraph shall be deemed to have been fulfilled, and the action of the contracting party applying the restrictions shall not be open to

challenge under sub-paragraph *(d)* of this paragraph on the ground that such action is inconsistent with the provisions of paragraph 2 of this Article.

(d) Any contracting party which considers that another contracting party is applying restrictions under this Article inconsistently with the provisions of paragraphs 2 or 3 of this Article or with those of Article XIII (subject to the provisions of Article XIV) may bring the matter for discussion to the CONTRACTING PARTIES; and the contracting party applying the restrictions shall participate in the discussion. The CONTRACTING PARTIES, if they are satisfied that there is a *prima facie* case that the trade of the contracting party initiating the procedure is adversely affected, shall submit their views to the parties with the aim of achieving a settlement of the matter in question which is satisfactory to the parties and to the CONTRACTING PARTIES. If no such settlement is reached and if the CONTRACTING PARTIES determine that the restrictions are being applied inconsistently with the provisions of paragraphs 2 or 3 of this Article or with those of Article XIII (subject to the provisions of Article XIV), they shall recommend the withdrawal or modification of the restrictions. If the restrictions are not withdrawn or modified in accordance with the recommendation of the CONTRACTING PARTIES within sixty days, they may release any contracting party from specified obligations under this Agreement towards the contracting party applying the restrictions.

(e) It is recognized that premature disclosure of the prospective application, withdrawal or modification of any restriction under this Article might stimulate speculative trade and financial movements which would tend to defeat the purposes of this Article. Accordingly, the CONTRACTING PARTIES shall make provision for the observance of the utmost secrecy in the conduct of any consultation.

5. If there is a persistent and widespread application of import restrictions under this Article, indicating the existence of a general disequilibrium which is restricting international trade, the CONTRACTING PARTIES shall initiate discussions to consider whether other measures might be taken, either by those contracting parties whose balances of payments are under pressure or by those whose balances of payments are tending to be exceptionally favourable, or by any appropriate inter-governmental organization, to remove the underlying causes of the disequilibrium. On the invitation of the CONTRACTING PARTIES, contracting parties shall participate in such discussions.

Article XIII

NON-DISCRIMINATORY ADMINISTRATION OF QUANTITATIVE RESTRICTIONS

1. No prohibition or restriction shall be applied by any contracting party on the importation of any product of the territory of any other contracting party or on the exportation of any product destined for the territory of any other contracting party, unless the importation of the like product of all third countries or the exportation of the like product to all third countries is similarly prohibited or restricted.

2. In applying restrictions to any product, contracting parties shall aim at a distribution of trade in such product approaching as closely as possible to the shares which the various contracting parties might be expected to obtain in the absence of such restrictions, and to this end shall observe the following provisions:

   (a) wherever practicable, quotas representing the total amount of permitted imports (whether allocated among supplying countries or not) shall be fixed, and notice given of their amount in accordance with paragraph 3 *(b)* of this Article;

   (b) in cases in which quotas are not practicable, the restrictions may be applied by means of import licences or permits without a quota;

(c) contracting parties shall not, except for purposes of operating quotas allocated in accordance with sub-paragraph *(d)* of this paragraph, require that import licences or permits be utilized for the importation of the product concerned from a particular country or source;

(d) in cases in which a quota is allocated among supplying countries, the contracting party applying the restrictions may seek agreement with respect to the allocation of shares in the quota with all other contracting parties having a substantial interest in supplying the product concerned. In cases in which this method is not reasonably practicable, the contracting party concerned shall allot to contracting parties having a substantial interest in supplying the product shares based upon the proportions, supplied by such contracting parties during a previous representative period, of the total quantity or value of imports of the product, due account being taken of any special factors which may have affected or may be affecting the trade in the product. No conditions or formalities shall be imposed which would prevent any contracting party from utilizing fully the share of any such total quantity or value which has been allotted to it, subject to importation being made within any prescribed period to which the quota may relate.

3. *(a)* In cases in which import licences are issued in connection with import restrictions, the contracting party applying the restrictions shall provide, upon the request of any contracting party having an interest in the trade in the product concerned, all relevant information concerning the administration of the restrictions, the import licences granted over a recent period and the distribution of such licences among supplying countries; *Provided* that there shall be no obligation to supply information as to the names of importing or supplying enterprises.

   (b) In the case of import restrictions involving the fixing of quotas, the contracting party applying the restrictions shall give public notice of the total quantity or value of the product or products which will be permitted to be imported during a specified future period and of any change in such quantity or value. Any supplies of the product in question which were en route at the time at which public notice was given shall not be excluded from entry; *Provided* that they may be counted so far as practicable, against the quantity permitted to be imported in the period in question, and also, where necessary, against the quantities permitted to be imported in the next following period or periods, and *Provided* further that if any contracting party customarily exempts from such restrictions products entered for consumption or withdrawn from warehouse for consumption during a period of thirty days after the day of such public notice, such practice shall be considered full compliance with this sub-paragraph.

   (c) In the case of quotas allocated among supplying countries, the contracting party applying the restrictions shall promptly inform all other contracting parties having an interest in supplying the product concerned of the shares in the quota currently allocated, by quantity or value, to the various supplying countries and shall give public notice thereof.

4. With regard to restrictions applied in accordance with paragraph 2 *(d)* of this Article or under paragraph 2 *(c)* of Article XI, the selection of a representative period for any product and the appraisal of any special factors affecting the trade in the product shall be made initially by the contracting party applying the restriction; *Provided* that such contracting party shall upon the request of any other contracting party having a substantial interest in supplying that product or upon the request of the CONTRACTING PARTIES, consult promptly with the other contracting party or the CONTRACTING PARTIES regarding the need for an adjustment of the proportion determined or of the base period selected, or for the reappraisal of the special factors involved, or for the elimination of conditions, formalities or any other provisions established unilaterally relating to the allocation of an adequate quota or its unrestricted utilization.

5.[1] The provisions of this Article shall apply to any tariff quota instituted or maintained by any contracting party, and, insofar as applicable, the principles of this Article shall also extend to export restrictions and to any internal regulation or requirement under paragraphs 3 and 4 of Article III.

Article XIV [2]

EXCEPTIONS TO THE RULE OF NON-DISCRIMINATION

1. *(a)* The contracting parties recognize that when a substantial and widespread disequilibrium prevails in international trade and payments a contracting party applying restrictions under Article XII may be able to increase its imports from certain sources without unduly depleting its monetary reserves, if permitted to depart from the provisions of Article XIII. The contracting parties also recognize the need for close limitation of such departures so as not to handicap achievement of multilateral international trade.

(b) Accordingly, when a substantial and widespread disequilibrium prevails in international trade and payments, a contracting party applying import restrictions under Article XII may relax such restrictions in a manner which departs from the provisions of Article XIII to the extent necessary to obtain additional imports above the maximum total of imports which it could afford in the light of the requirements of paragraph 2 of Article XII if its restrictions were fully consistent with the provisions of Article XIII, provided that

  (i) levels of delivered prices for products so imported are not established substantially higher than those ruling for comparable goods regularly available from other contracting parties, and that any excess of such price levels for products so imported is progressively reduced over a reasonable period;

  (ii) the contracting party taking such action does not do so as part of any arrangement by which the gold or convertible currency which the contracting party currently receives directly or indirectly from its exports to other contracting parties not party to the arrangement is appreciably reduced below the level it could otherwise have been reasonably expected to attain;

  (iii) such action does not cause unnecessary damage to the commercial or economic interests of any contracting party.

(c) Any contracting party taking action under this paragraph shall observe the principles of sub-paragraph *(b)* of this paragraph. A contracting party shall desist from transactions which prove to be inconsistent with that sub-paragraph, but the contracting party shall not be required to satisfy itself, when it is not practicable to do so, that the requirements of that sub-paragraph are fulfilled in respect of individual transactions.

(d) Contracting parties undertake, in framing and carrying out any programme for additional imports under this paragraph, to have due regard to the need to facilitate the termination of any exchange arrangements which deviate from the obligations of Sections 2, 3 and 4 of Article VIII of the Articles of Agreement of the International Monetary Fund and to the need to restore equilibrium in their balances of payments on a sound and lasting basis.

2. Any contracting party taking action under paragraph 1 of this Article shall keep the CONTRACTING PARTIES regularly informed regarding such action and shall provide such available relevant information as they may request.

---

[1] Paragraph 5 of article XIII has been amended by the Protocol modifying part II and article XXVI of the General Agreement on Tariffs and Trade, signed at Geneva on 14 September 1948. See Volume 62.

[2] Article XIV has been amended by the Special Protocol modifying article XIV of the General Agreement on Tariffs and Trade, signed at Havana, on 24 March 1948. See Volume 62.

3. *(a)* Not later than March 1, 1952 (five years after the date on which the International Monetary Fund began operations) and in each year thereafter, any contracting party maintaining or proposing to institute action under paragraph 1 of this Article shall seek the approval of the CONTRACTING PARTIES which shall thereupon determine whether the circumstances of the contracting party justify the maintenance or institution of action by it under paragraph 1 of this Article. After March 1, 1952, no contracting party shall maintain or institute such action without determination by the CONTRACTING PARTIES that the contracting party's circumstances justify the maintenance or institution of such action, as the case may be, and the subsequent maintenance or institution of such action by the contracting party shall be subject to any limitations which the CONTRACTING PARTIES may prescribe for the purpose of ensuring compliance with the provisions of paragraph 1 of this Article; *Provided* that the CONTRACTING PARTIES shall not require that prior approval be obtained for individual transactions.

(b) If at any time the CONTRACTING PARTIES find that import restrictions are being applied by a contracting party in a discriminatory manner inconsistent with the exceptions provided for under paragraph 1 of this Article, the contracting party shall, within sixty days, remove the discrimination or modify it as specified by the CONTRACTING PARTIES; *Provided* that any action under paragraph 1 of this Article, to the extent that it has been approved by the CONTRACTING PARTIES under sub-paragraph *(a)* of this paragraph or to the extent that it has been approved by them at the request of a contracting party under a procedure analogous to that of paragraph 4 *(c)* of Article XII, shall not be open to challenge under this sub-paragraph or under paragraph 4 *(d)* of Article XII on the ground that it is inconsistent with the provisions of Article XIII.

(c) Not later than March 1, 1950, and in each year thereafter so long as any contracting parties are taking action under paragraph 1 of this Article, the CONTRACTING PARTIES shall report on the action still taken by contracting parties under that paragraph. On or about March 1, 1952, and in each year thereafter so long as any contracting parties are taking action under paragraph 1 of this Article, and at such times thereafter as they may decide, the CONTRACTING PARTIES shall review the question whether there then exists such a substantial and widespread disequilibrium in international trade and payments as to justify resort to paragraph 1 of this Article by contracting parties. If it appears at any date prior to March, 1, 1952, that there has been a substantial and general improvement in international trade and payments, the CONTRACTING PARTIES may review the situation at that date. If, as a result of any such review, the CONTRACTING PARTIES determine that no such disequilibrium exists, the provisions of paragraph 1 of this Article shall be suspended, and all actions authorized thereunder shall cease six months after such determination.

4. The provisions of Article XIII shall not preclude restrictions in accordance with Article XII which either
  (a) are applied against imports from other countries, but not as among themselves, by a group of territories having a common quota in the International Monetary Fund, on condition that such restrictions are in all other respects consistent with the provisions of Article XIII, or
  (b) assist, in the period up to December 31, 1951, by measures not involving substantial departure from the provisions of Article XIII, another country whose economy has been disrupted by war.

5. The provisions of this Agreement shall not preclude:
  (a) restrictions with equivalent effect to exchange restrictions authorized under Section 3 *(b)* of Article VII of the Articles of Agreement of the International Monetary Fund; or
  (b) restrictions under the preferential arrangements provided for in Annex A of this Agreement, subject to the conditions set forth therein.

6. *(a)* The provisions of Article XIII shall not enter into force in respect of import restrictions applied by any contracting party pursuant to Article XII in order to safeguard its external financial position and balance of payments, and the provisions of paragraph 1 of Article XI and Article XIII shall not enter into force in respect of export restrictions applied by any contracting party for the same reason, until January 1, 1949; *Provided* that this period may with the concurrence of the CONTRACTING PARTIES, be extended for such further periods as they may specify in respect of any contracting party whose supply of convertible currencies is inadequate to enable it to apply the above-mentioned provisions.

(b) If a measure taken by a contracting party in the circumstances referred to in sub-paragraph *(a)* of this paragraph affects the commerce of another contracting party to such an extent as to cause the latter to consider the need of having recourse to the provisions of Article XII, the contracting party having taken that measure shall, if the affected contracting party so requests, enter into immediate consultation with a view to arrangements enabling the affected contracting party to avoid having such recourse, and, if special circumstances are put forward to justify such action, shall temporarily suspend application of the measure for a period of fifteen days.

Article XV

EXCHANGE ARRANGEMENTS

1. The CONTRACTING PARTIES shall seek co-operation with the International Monetary Fund to the end that the CONTRACTING PARTIES and the Fund may pursue a co-ordinated policy with regard to exchange questions within the jurisdiction of the Fund and questions of quantitative restrictions and other trade measures within the jurisdiction of the CONTRACTING PARTIES.

2. In all cases in which the CONTRACTING PARTIES are called upon to consider or deal with problems concerning monetary reserves, balances of payments or foreign exchange arrangements, they shall consult fully with the International Monetary Fund. In such consultation, the CONTRACTING PARTIES shall accept all findings of statistical and other facts presented by the Fund relating to foreign exchange, monetary reserves and balances of payments, and shall accept the determination of the Fund as to whether action by a contracting party in exchange matters is in accordance with the Articles of Agreement of the International Monetary Fund, or with the terms of a special exchange agreement between that contracting party and the CONTRACTING PARTIES. The CONTRACTING PARTIES, in reaching their final decision in cases involving the criteria set forth in paragraph 2 *(a)* of Article XII, shall accept the determination of the Fund as to what constitutes a serious decline in the contracting party's monetary reserves, a very low level of its monetary reserves or a reasonable rate of increase in its monetary reserves, and as to the financial aspects of other matters covered in consultation in such cases.

3. The CONTRACTING PARTIES shall seek agreement with the Fund regarding procedures for consultation under paragraph 2 of this Article.

4. Contracting parties shall not, by exchange action, frustrate the intent of the provisions of this Agreement, nor, by trade action, the intent of the provisions of the Articles of Agreement of the International Monetary Fund.

5. If the CONTRACTING PARTIES consider, at any time, that exchange restrictions on payments and transfers in connection with imports are being applied by a contracting party in a manner inconsistent with the exceptions provided for in this Agreement for quantitative restrictions, they shall report thereon to the Fund.

6. Any contracting party which is not a member of the Fund shall, within a time to be determined by the CONTRACTING PARTIES after consultation with the Fund, become a member of the Fund, or, failing that, into a special exchange agreement with the CONTRACTING PARTIES. A contracting party which ceases to be a member of the Fund shall

forthwith enter into a special exchange agreement with the CONTRACTING PARTIES. Any special exchange agreement entered into by a contracting party under this paragraph shall thereupon become part of its obligations under this Agreement.

7. *(a)* A special exchange agreement between a contracting party and the CONTRACT-ING PARTIES under paragraph 6 of this Article shall provide to the satisfaction of the CONTRACTING PARTIES that the objectives of this Agreement will not be frustrated as a result of action in exchange matters by the contracting party in question.

(b) The terms of any such agreement shall not impose obligations on the contract-ing party in exchange matters generally more restrictive than those imposed by the Arti-cles of Agreement of the International Monetary Fund on members of the Fund.

8. A contracting party which is not a member of the Fund shall furnish such informa-tion within the general scope of Section 5 of Article VIII of the Articles of Agreement of the International Monetary Fund as the CONTRACTING PARTIES may require in order to carry out their functions under this Agreement.

9.[1] Subject to the provisions of paragraph 4 of this Article, nothing in this Agreement shall preclude:

(a) the use by a contracting party of exchange controls or exchange restrictions in accordance with the Articles of Agreement of the International Monetary Fund or with that contracting party's special exchange agreement with the CONTRACT-ING PARTIES, or

(b) the use by a contracting party of restrictions or controls on imports or exports, the sole effect of which, additional to the effects permitted under Articles XI, XII, XIII and XIV, is to make effective such exchange controls or exchange restrictions.

Article XVI

SUBSIDIES

If any contracting party grants or maintains any subsidy, including any form of in-come or price support, which operates directly or indirectly to increase exports of any product from, or to reduce imports of any product into, its territory, it shall notify the CONTRACTING PARTIES in writing of the extent and nature of the subsidization, of the estimated effect of the subsidization on the quantity of the affected product or prod-uct imported into or exported from its territory and of the circumstances making the subsidization necessary. In any case in which it is determined that serious prejudice to the interests of any other contracting party is caused or threatened by any such subsidization, the contracting party granting the subsidy shall, upon request, discuss with the other contracting party or parties concerned, or with the CONTRACTING PAR-TIES, the possibility of limiting the subsidization.

Article XVII

NON-DISCRIMINATORY TREATMENT
ON THE PART OF STATE-TRADING ENTERPRISES

1. *(a)* Each contracting party undertakes that if it establishes or maintains a State enterprise, wherever located, or grants to any enterprise, formally or in effect, exclu-sive or special privileges, such enterprise shall, in its purchases or sales involving either imports or exports, act in a manner consistent with the general principles of non-dis-criminatory treatment prescribed in this Agreement for governmental measures affect-ing imports or exports by private traders.

(b) The provisions of sub-paragraph *(a)* of this paragraph shall be understood to require that such enterprises shall, having due regard to the other provisions of this Agreement, make any such purchases or sales solely in accordance with commercial considerations, including price, quality, availability, marketability, transportation and

other conditions of purchase or sale, and shall afford the enterprises of the other contracting parties adequate opportunity, in accordance with customary business practice, to compete for participation in such purchases or sales.

(c) No contracting party shall prevent any enterprise (whether or not an enterprise described in sub-paragraph *(a)* of this paragraph) under its jurisdiction from acting in accordance with the principles of sub-paragraphs *(a)* and *(b)* of this paragraph.

2.   The provisions of paragraph 1 of this Article shall not apply to imports of products for immediate or ultimate consumption in governmental use and not otherwise for resale or for use in the production of goods for sale. With respect to such imports, each contracting party shall accord to the trade of the other contracting parties fair and equitable treatment.

Article XVIII[1]

ADJUSTMENTS IN CONNECTION WITH ECONOMIC DEVELOPMENT

1.   The contracting parties recognize that special governmental assistance may be required to promote the establishment, development or reconstruction of particular industries or particular branches of agriculture, and that in appropriate circumstances the grant of such assistance in the form of protective measures is justified. At the same time they recognize that an unwise use of such measures would impose undue burdens on their own economies and unwarranted restrictions on international trade, and might increase unnecessarily the difficulties of adjustment for the economies of other countries.

2.   *(a)* If a contracting party, in the interest of its programme of economic development or reconstruction, considers it desirable to adopt any non-discriminatory measure which would conflict with any obligation which it has assumed under Article II, or with any other provision of this Agreement, such applicant contracting party shall so notify the CONTRACTING PARTIES and shall transmit to them a written statement of the considerations in support of the adoption of the proposed measures.

(b) The CONTRACTING PARTIES shall promptly transmit such statement to all other contracting parties, and any contracting party which considers that its trade would be substantially affected by the proposed measure shall transmit its views to the CONTRACTING PARTIES within such period as shall be prescribed by them.

(c) The CONTRACTING PARTIES shall then promptly examine the proposed measure to determine whether they concur in it, with or without modification, and shall in their examination have regard to the provisions of this Agreement, to the considerations presented by the applicant contracting party and its stage of economic development or reconstruction, to the views presented by contracting parties which may be substantially affected, and to the effect which the proposed measure, with or without modification, is likely to have on international trade.

3.   *(a)* If, as a result of their examination pursuant to paragraph 2 *(c)* of this Article, the CONTRACTING PARTIES concur in principle in any proposed measure, with or without modification, which would be inconsistent with any obligation that the applicant contracting party has assumed under Article II, or which would tend to nullify or impair the benefit to any other contracting party or parties of any such obligation, the CONTRACTING PARTIES shall sponsor and assist in negotiations between the applicant contracting party and the other contracting party or parties which would be substantially affected with a view to obtaining substantial agreement. The CONTRACTING PARTIES shall establish and communicate to the contracting parties concerned a time schedule for such negotiations.

---

[1] Article XVIII has been amended by the Protocol modifying part II and article XXVI of the General Agreement on Tariffs and Trade, signed at Geneva, on 14 September 1948. See Volume 62.

(b) Contracting parties shall commence the negotiations provided for in sub-paragraph *(a)* of this paragraph within such period as the CONTRACTING PARTIES may prescribe and shall thereafter, unless the CONTRACTING PARTIES decide otherwise, proceed continuously with such negotiations with a view to reaching substantial agreement in accordance with the time schedule laid down by the CONTRACTING PARTIES.

(c) Upon substantial agreement being reached, the CONTRACTING PARTIES may release the applicant contracting party from the obligation referred to in paragraph *(a)* of this paragraph or from any other elevant obligation under this Agreement, subject to such limitations as may have been agreed upon in the negotiations between the contracting parties concerned.

4. *(a)* If, as a result of their examination pursuant to paragraph 2 *(c)* of this Article, the CONTRACTING PARTIES concur in any proposed measure, with or without modification, other than a measure referred to in paragraph 3 *(a)* of this Article, which would be inconsistent with any provision of this Agreement, the CONTRACTING PARTIES may release the applicant contracting party from any obligation under such provisions, subject to such limitations as they may impose.

(b) If, having regard to the provisions of paragraph 2 *(c)* of this Article, it is established in the course of such examination that such measure is unlikely to be more restrictive of international trade than any other practicable and reasonable measure permitted under this Agreement which could be imposed without undue difficulty and that it is the one most suitable for the purpose having regard to the economies of the industry or the branch of agriculture concerned and to the current economic condition of the applicant contracting party, the CONTRACTING PARTIES shall concur in such measure and grant such release as may be required to enable such measure to be made effective.

(c) If in anticipation of the concurrence of the CONTRACTING PARTIES in the adoption of a measure concerning which notice has been given under paragraph 2 of this Article, other than a measure referred to in paragraph 3 *(a)* of this Article, there should be an increase or threatened increase in the importations of the product or products concerned, including products which can be directly substituted therefor, so substantial as to jeopardize the plans of the applicant contracting party for the establishment, development or reconstruction of the industry or industries or branches of agriculture concerned, and if no preventive measures consistant with this Agreement can be found which seem likely to prove effective, the applicant contracting party may, after informing, and when practicable consulting with, the CONTRACTING PARTIES, adopt such other measures as the situation may require pending a determination by the CONTRACTING PARTIES, provided that such measures do not reduce imports below the level obtaining in the most recent representative period preceding the date on which the contracting party's original notifications was made under paragraph 2 of this Article.

5. *(a)* In the case of measures referred to in paragraph 3 of this Article, the CONTRACTING PARTIES shall, at the earliest opportunity but ordinarily within fifteen days after receipt of the statement referred to in paragraph 2 *(a)* of this Article, advise the applicant contracting party of the date by which they will notify it whether or not they concur in principle in the proposed measure, with or without modification.

(b) In the case of measures referred to in paragraph 4 of this Article, the CONTRACTING PARTIES shall, as in sub-paragraph *(a)* of this paragraph, advise the applicant contracting party of the date by which they will notify it whether or not it is released from such obligation or obligations as may be relevant; *Provided* that, if the applicant contracting party does not receive a final reply by the date fixed by the CONTRACTING PARTIES, it may, after communicating with the CONTRACTING PARTIES, institute the proposed measure upon the expiration of a further thirty days from such date.

6. Any contracting party may maintain any non-discriminatory measure, in force on September 1, 1947, which has been imposed for the establishment, development or reconstruction of particular industries or particular branches of agriculture and which is not otherwise permitted by this Agreement; *Provided* that any such contracting party shall have notified the other contracting parties, not later than October 10, 1947, of each product on which any such existing measure is to be maintained and of the nature and purpose of such measure. Any contracting party maintaining any such measure shall, within sixty days of becoming a contracting party, notify the CONTRACTING PARTIES of the measure concerned, the considerations in support of its maintenance and the period for which it wishes to maintain the measure. The CONTRACTING PARTIES shall, as soon as possible but in any case within twelve months from the day on which such contracting party becomes a contracting party, examine and give a decision concerning the measure as if it had been submitted to the CONTRACTING PARTIES for their concurrence under the provisions of the preceding paragraphs of this Article. The CONTRACTING PARTIES, in making a decision under this paragraph specifying a date by which any modification in or withdrawal of the measure is to be made, shall have regard to the possible need of a contracting party for a suitable period of time in which to make such modification or withdrawal.

7. The provisions of paragraph 6 of this Article shall not apply, in respect of any contracting party, to any product described in the appropriate Schedule annexed to this Agreement.

Article XIX

EMERGENCY ACTION ON IMPORTS OF PARTICULAR PRODUCTS

1. *(a)* If, as a result of unforeseen developments and of the effect of the obligations incurred by a contracting party under this Agreement, including tariff concessions, any product is being imported into the territory of that contracting party in such increased quantities and under such conditions as to cause or threaten serious injury to domestic producers in that territory of like or directly competitive products, the contracting party shall be free, in respect of such product, and to the extent and for such time as may be necessary to prevent or remedy such injury, to suspend the obligation in whole or in part or to withdraw or modify the concession.

(b) If any product, which is the subject of a concession with respect to a preference, is being imported into the territory of a contracting party in the circumstances set forth in sub-paragraph *(a)* of this paragraph, so as to cause or threaten serious injury to domestic producers of like or directly competitive products in the territory of a contracting party which receives or received such preference, the importing contracting party shall be free, if that other contracting party so requests, to suspend the relevant obligation in whole or in part or to withdraw or modify the concession in respect of the product, to the extent and for such time as may be necessary to prevent or remedy such injury.

2. Before any contracting party shall take action pursuant to the provisions of paragraph 1 of this Article, it shall give notice in writing to the CONTRACTING PARTIES as far in advance as may be practicable and shall afford the CONTRACTING PARTIES and those contracting parties having a substantial interest as exporters of the product concerned an opportunity to consult with it in respect of the proposed action. When such notice is given in relation to a concession with respect to a preference, the notice shall name the contracting party which has requested the action. In critical circumstances, where delay would cause damage which it would be difficult to repair, action under paragraph 1 of this Article may be taken provisionally without prior consultation, on the condition that consultation shall be effected immediately after taking such action.

3.   *(a)* If agreement among the interested contracting parties with respect to the action is not reached, the contracting party which proposes to take or continue the action shall, nevertheless, be free to do so, and if such action is taken or continued, the affected contracting parties shall then be free, not later than ninety days after such action is taken, to suspend, upon the expiration of thirty days from the day on which written notice of such suspension is received by the CONTRACTING PARTIES, the application to the trade of the contracting party taking such action, or, in the case envisaged in paragraph 1 *(b)* of this Article, to the trade of the contracting party requesting such action, of such substantially equivalent obligations or concessions under this Agreement the suspension of which the CONTRACTING PARTIES do not disapprove.

   (b) Notwithstanding the provisions of sub-paragraph *(a)* of this paragraph, where action is taken under paragraph 2 of this Article without prior consultation and causes or threatens serious injury in the territory of a contracting party to the domestic producers of products affected by the action, that contracting party shall, where delay would cause damage difficult to repair, be free to suspend, upon the taking of the action and throughout the period of consultation, such obligations or concessions as may be necessary to prevent or remedy the injury.

Article XX[1]

GENERAL EXCEPTIONS

   Subject to the requirement that such measures are not applied in a manner which would constitute a means of arbitrary or unjustifiable discrimination between countries where the same conditions prevail, or a disguised restriction on international trade, nothing in this Agreement shall be construed to prevent the adoption or enforcement by any contracting party of measures:

I.   *(a)* necessary to protect public morals;
  (b) necessary to protect human, animal or plant life or health;
  (c) relating to the importation or exportation of gold or silver;
  (d) necessary to secure compliance with laws or regulations which are not inconsistent with the provisions of this Agreement, including those relating to customs enforcement, the enforcement of monopolies operated under paragraph 4 of Article II and Article XVII, the protection of patents, trade marks and copyrights, and the prevention of deceptive practices;
  (e) relating to the products of prison labour;
  (f) imposed for the protection of national treasures of artistic, historic or archaeological value;
  (g) relating to the conservation of exhaustible natural resources if such measures are made effective in conjunction with restrictions on domestic production or consumption;
  (h) undertaken in pursuance of obligations under intergovernmental commodity agreements, conforming to the principles approved by the Economic and Social Council of the United Nations in its Resolution of March 28, 1947, establishing an Interim Co-ordinating Committee for International Commodity Arrangements;[2] or

---

[1] Article XX has been amended by the Protocol of Rectifications, signed at Havana, on 24 March 1948. See Volume 62.

[2] United Nations document E/437.

(i) involving restrictions on exports of domestic materials necessary to assure essential quantities of such materials to a domestic processing industry during periods when the domestic price of such materials is held below the world price as part of a governmental stabilization plan; *Provided* that such restrictions shall not operate to increase the exports of or the protection afforded to such domestic industry, and shall not depart from the provisions of this Agreement relating to non-discrimination;

II. *(a)* essential to the acquisition or distribution of products in general or local short supply; *Provided* that any such measures shall be consistent with any multilateral arrangements directed to an equitable international distribution of such products or, in the absence of such arrangements, with the principle that all contracting parties are entitled to an equitable share of the international supply of such products;

   (b) essential to the control of prices by a contracting party undergoing shortages subsequent to the war; or

   (c) essential to the orderly liquidation of temporary surpluses of stocks owned or controlled by the government of any contracting party or of industries developed in the territory of any contracting party owing to the exigencies of the war which it would be uneconomic to maintain in normal conditions; *Provided* that such measures shall not be instituted by any contracting party except after consultation with other interested contracting parties with a view to appropriate international action.

Measures instituted or maintained under part II of this Article which are inconsistent with the other provisions of this Agreement shall be removed as soon as the conditions giving rise to them have ceased, and in any event not later than January 1, 1951; *Provided* that this period may, with the concurrence of the CONTRACTING PARTIES, be extended in respect of the application of any particular measure to any particular product by any particular contracting party for such further periods as the CONTRACTING PARTIES may specify.

Article XXI

SECURITY EXCEPTIONS

Nothing in this Agreement shall be construed

(a) to require any contracting party to furnish any information the disclosure of which it considers contrary to its essential security interests; or

(b) to prevent any contracting party from taking any action which it considers necessary for the protection of its essential security interests

   (i) relating to fissionable materials or the materials from which they are derived;

   (ii) relating to the traffic in arms, ammunition and implements of war and to such traffic in other goods and materials as is carried on directly of indirectly for the purpose of supplying a military establishment;

   (iii) taken in time of war or other emergency in international relations; or

(c) to prevent any contracting party from taking any action in pursuance of its obligations under the United Nations Charter for the maintenance of international peace and security.

Article XXII

CONSULTATION

Each contracting party shall accord sympathetic consideration to, and shall afford adequate opportunity for consultation regarding, such representations as may be made by any other contracting party with respect to the operation of customs regulations and formalities, anti-dumping and countervailing duties, quantitative and exchange regulations, subsidies, state-trading operations, sanitary laws and regulations for the protection of human, animal or plant life or health, and generally all matters affecting the operation of this Agreement.

Article XXIII

NULLIFICATION OR IMPAIRMENT

If any contracting party should consider that any benefit accruing to it directly of indirectly under this Agreement is being nullified or impaired or that the attainment of any objective of the Agreement is being impeded as the result of *(a)* the failure of another contracting party to carry out its obligations under this Agreement, or *(b)* the application by another contracting party of any measure, whether or not it conflicts with the provisions of this Agreement, or *(c)* the existence of any other situation, the contracting party may, with a view to the satisfactory adjustment of the matter, make written representations or proposals to the other contracting party or parties which it considers to be concerned. Any contracting party thus approached shall give sympathetic consideration to the representations or proposals made to it.

2. If no satisfactory adjustment is effected between the contracting parties concerned within a reasonable time, or if the difficulty is of the type described in paragraph 1 *(c)* of this Article, the matter may be referred to the CONTRACTING PARTIES. The CONTRACTING PARTIES shall promptly investigate any matter so referred to them and shall make appropriate recommendations to the contracting parties which they consider to be concerned, or give a ruling on the matter, as appropriate. The CONTRACTING PARTIES may consult with contracting parties, with the Economic and Social Council of the United Nations and with any appropriate inter-governmental organization in cases where they consider such consultation necessary. If the CONTRACTING PARTIES consider that the circumstances are serious enough to justify such action, they may authorize a contracting party or parties to suspend the application to any other contracting party or parties of such obligations or concessions under this Agreement as they determine to be appropriate in the circumstances. If the application to any contracting party of any obligation or concession is in fact suspended, that contracting party shall then be free, not later than sixty days after such action is taken, to advise the Secretary-General of the United Nations in writing of its intention to withdraw from this Agreement and such withdrawal shall take effect upon the expiration of sixty days from the day on which written notice of such withdrawal is received by him.

PART III

Article XXIV[1]

TERRITORIAL APPLICATION — FRONTIER TRAFFIC — CUSTOMS UNIONS

1. The rights and obligations arising under this Agreement shall be deemed to be in force between each and every territory which is a separate customs territory and in respect of which this Agreement has been accepted under Article XXVI or is being applied under the Protocol of Provisional Application.
2. The provisions of this Agreement shall not be construed to prevent:
   (a) advantages accorded by any contracting party to adjacent countries in order to facilitate frontier traffic;

---

[1] Article XXIV has been amended by the Special Protocol relating to article XXIV of the General Agreement on Tariffs and Trade, signed at Havana, on 24 March 1948. See Volume 62.

(b) the formation of a customs union or the adoption of an interim agreement necessary for the attainment of a customs union; *Provided* that the duties and other regulations of commerce imposed by, or any margin of preference maintained by, any such union or agreement in respect of trade with other contracting parties shall not on the whole be higher or more stringent than the average level of the duties and regulations of commerce or margins of preference applicable in the constituent territories prior to the formation of such union or the adoption of such agreement; and *Provided* further that any such interim agreement shall include a definite plan and schedule for the attainment of such a customs union within a reasonable length of time.

3.   *(a)* Any contracting party proposing to enter into a customs union shall consult with the CONTRACTING PARTIES and shall make available to them such information regarding the proposed union as will enable them to make such reports and recommendations to contracting parties as may be deemed appropriate.

   (b) No contracting party shall institute or maintain any interim agreement under the provisions of paragraph 2 *(b)* of this Article if, after a study of the plan and schedule proposed in such agreement, the CONTRACTING PARTIES find that such agreement is not likely to result in such a customs union within a reasonable length of time.

   (c) The plan or schedule shall not be substantially altered without consultation with the CONTRACTING PARTIES.

4.   For the purpose of this Article a customs territory shall be understood to mean any territory with respect to which separate tariffs or other regulations of commerce are maintained for a substantial part of the trade of such territory with other territories. A customs union shall be under stood to mean the substitution of a single customs territory for two or more customs territories, so that all tariffs and other restrictive regulations of commerce as between the territories of members of the union are substantially eliminated and substantially the same tariffs and other regulations of commerce are applied by each of the members of the union to the trade of territories not included in the union.

5.   Taking into account the exceptional circumstances arising out of the establishment of India and Pakistan as independent States and recognizing the fact that they have long constituted an economic unit, the contracting parties agree that the provisions of this Agreement shall not prevent the two countries from entering into special arrangements with respect to the trade between them, pending the establishment of their mutual trade relations on a definitive basis.

6.   Each contracting party shall take such reasonable measures as may be available to it to assure observance of the provisions of this Agreement by the regional and local governments and authorities within its territory.

Article XXV

JOINT ACTION BY THE CONTRACTING PARTIES

1.   Representatives of the contracting parties shall meet from time to time for the purpose of giving effect to those provisions of this Agreement which involve joint action and, generally, with a view to facilitating the operation and furthering the objectives of this Agreement. Wherever reference is made in this Agreement to the contracting parties acting jointly they are designated as the CONTRACTING PARTIES.

2.   The Secretary-General of the United Nations is requested to convene the first meeting of the CONTRACTING PARTIES which shall take place not later than March 1, 1948.

3.   Each contracting party shall be entitled to have one vote at all meetings of the CONTRACTING PARTIES.

4.   Except as otherwise provided for in this Agreement, decisions of the CONTRACTING PARTIES shall be taken by a majority of the votes cast.

5.[1] In exceptional circumstances not elsewhere provided for in this Agreement, the CONTRACTING PARTIES may waive and obligation imposed upon a contracting party by this Agreement: *Provided* that any such decision shall be approved by a two-thirds majority of the votes cast and that such majority shall comprise more than half of the contracting parties. The CONTRACTING PARTIES may also by such a vote

(a) define certain categories of exceptional circumstances to which other voting requirements shall apply for the waiver of obligations, and

(b) prescribe such criteria as may be necessary for the application of this paragraph.

Article XXVI[1]

ACCEPTANCE, ENTRY INTO FORCE AND REGISTRATION

1.   The present Agreement shall bear the date of the signature of the Final Act adopted at the conclusion of the Second Session of the Preparatory Committee of the United Nations Conference on Trade and Employment and shall be open to acceptance by any government signatory to the Final Act.

2.   This Agreement, done in a single English original and in a single French original, both texts authentic, shall be deposited with the Secretary-General of the United Nations, who shall furnish certified copies thereof to all interested governments.

3.   Each government accepting this Agreement shall deposit an instrument of acceptance with the Secretary-General of the United Nations, who will inform all interested governments of the date of deposit of each instrument of acceptance and of the day on which this Agreement enters into force under paragraph 5 of this Article.

4.[2]   Each government accepting this Agreement does so in respect of its metropolitan territory and of the other territories for which it has international responsibility; *Provided* that it may at the time of acceptance declare that any separate customs territory for which it has international responsibility possesses full autonomy in the conduct of its external commercial relations and of the other matters provided for in this Agreement, and that its acceptance does not relate to such territory; and *Provided* further that if any of the customs territories on behalf of which a contracting party has accepted this Agreement possesses or acquires full autonomy in the conduct of its external commercial relations and of the other matters provided for in this Agreement, such territory shall, upon sponsorship through a declaration by the responsible contracting party establishing the above-mentioned fact, be deemed to be a contracting party.

5.[3]   (a) This Agreement shall enter into force, as among the governments which have accepted it, on the thirtieth day following the day on which instruments of acceptance have been deposited with the Secretary-General of the United Nations on behalf of governments signatory to the Final Act the territories of which account for eighty-five per centum of the total external trade of the territories of the signatories to the Final Act adopted at the conclusion of the Second Session of the Preparatory Committee of the United Nations Conference on Trade and Employment. Such percentage shall be determined in accordance with the table set forth in Annex H. The instrument of acceptance of each other government signatory to the Final Act shall take effect on the thirtieth day following the day on which such instrument is deposited.

(b) Notwithstanding the provisions of sub-paragraph (a) of this paragraph, this Agreement shall not enter into force under this paragraph until any agreement necessary under the provisions of paragraph 2 (a) of Article XXIX has been reached.

---

[1] Paragraph 5 of article XXV has been amended by the Special Protocol relating to article XXIV of the General agreement on Tariffs and Trade, signed at Havana, on 24 March 1948. See Volume 62.

[2] Paragraph 4 of article XXVI has been amended by the Protocol modifying article XXVI of the General Agreement on Tariffs and Trade, signed at Annecy, on 13 August 1949. See Volume 62.

[3] Paragraph 5 of article XXVI has been amended by the Protocol modifying part II and article XXVI of the General Agreement on Tariffs and Trade, signed at Geneva, on 14 September 1948. See Volume 62.

6.   The United Nations is authorized to effect registration of this Agreement as soon as it enters into force.

Article XXVII

WITHHOLDING OR WITHDRAWAL OF CONCESSIONS

Any contracting party shall at any time be free to withhold or to withdraw in whole or in part any concession, provided for in the appropriate Schedule annexed to this Agreement, in respect of which such contracting party determines that it was initially negotiated with a government which has not become, or has ceased to be, a contracting party. The contracting party taking such action shall give notice to all other contracting parties and, upon request, consult with the contracting parties which have a substantial interest in the product concerned.

Article XXVIII

MODIFICATION OF SCHEDULES

1.   On or after January 1, 1951, any contracting party may, by negotiation and agreement with any other contracting party with which such treatment was initially negotiated, and subject to consultation with such other contracting parties as the CONTRACTING PARTIES determine to have a substantial interest in such treatment, modify, or cease to apply, the treatment which it has agreed to accord under Article II to any product described in the appropriate Schedule annexed to this Agreement. In such negotiations and agreement, which may include provision for compensatory adjustment with respect to other products, the contracting parties concerned shall endeavour to maintain a general level of reciprocal and mutually advantageous concessions not less favourable to trade than that provided for in the present Agreement.

2.   *(a)* If agreement between the contracting parties primarily concerned cannot be reached, the contracting party which proposes to modify or cease to apply such treatment shall, nevertheless, be free to do so, and if such action is taken the contracting party with which such treatment was initially negotiated, and the other contracting parties determined under paragraph 1 of this Article to have a substantial interest, shall then be free, not later than six months after such action is taken, to withdraw, upon the expiration of thirty days from the day on which written notice of such withdrawal is received by the CONTRACTING PARTIES, substantially equivalent concessions initially megotiated with the contracting party taking such action.

(b) If agreement between the contracting parties primarily concerned is reached but any other contracting party determined under paragraph 1 of this Article to have a substantial interest is not satisfied, such other contracting party shall be free, not later than six months after action under such agreement is taken, to withdraw, upon the expiration of thirty days from the day on which written notice of such withdrawal is received by the CONTRACTING PARTIES, substantially equivalent concessions initially negotiated with a contracting party taking action under such agreement.

Article XXIX

RELATION OF THIS AGREEMENT TO THE CHARTER FOR AN INTERNATIONAL TRADE ORGANIZATION

1.   The contracting parties, recognizing that the objectives set forth in the preamble of this Agreement can best be attained through the adoption by the United Nations Conference on Trade and Employment, of a Charter heading to the creation of an International Trade Organization, undertake, pending their acceptance of such a

Charter in accordance with their constitutional procedures, to observe to the fullest extent of their executive authority the general principles of the Draft Charter submitted to the Conference by the Preparatory Committee.[1]

2. *(a)* On the day on which the Charter[2] of the International Trade Organization enters into force, Article I and Part II of this Agreement shall be suspended and superseded by the corresponding provisions of the Charter; *Provided* that within sixty days of the closing of the United Nations Conference on Trade and Employment any contracting party may lodge with the other contracting parties an objection to any provision or provisions of this Agreement being so suspended and superseded;[3] in such case the contracting parties shall, within sixty days after the final date for the lodging of objections, confer to consider the objection in order to agree whether the provisions of the Charter to which objection has been lodged, or the corresponding provisions of this Agreement in its existing form or any amended form, shall apply.

(b) The contracting parties will also agree concerning the transfer to the International Trade Organization of their functions under Article XXV.

3. If any contracting party has not accepted the Charter when it has entered into force, the contracting parties shall confer to agree whether, and if so in what way, this Agreement, insofar as it affects relations between the contracting party which has not accepted the Charter and other contracting parties, shall be supplemented or amended.

4. During the month of January 1949, should the Charter not have entered into force, or at such earlier time as may be agreed if it is known that the Charter will not enter into force, or at such later time as may be agreed if the Charter ceases to be in force, the contracting parties shall meet to agree whether this Agreement shall be amended, supplemented or maintained.

5. The signatories of the Final Act which are not at the time contracting parties shall be informed of any objection lodged by a contracting party under the provisions of paragraph 2 of this Article and also of any agreement which may be reached between the contracting parties under paragraphs 2, 3 or 4 of this Article.

Article XXX

AMENDMENTS

1. Except where provision for modification is made elsewhere in this Agreement, amendments of the provisions of Part I of this Agreement or the provisions of Article XXIX or of this Article shall become effective upon acceptance by all the contracting parties, and other amendments to this Agreement shall become effective, in respect of those contracting parties which accept them, upon acceptance by two-thirds of the contracting parties and thereafter for each other contracting party upon acceptance by it.

2. Any contracting party accepting an amendment to this Agreement shall deposit an instrument of acceptance with the Secretary-General of the United Nations within such period as the CONTRACTING PARTIES may specify. The CONTRACTING PARTIES may decide that any amendment made effective under this Article is of such a nature that any contracting party which has not accepted it within a period specified by the CONTRACTING PARTIES shall be free to withdraw from this Agreement, or to remain a contracting party with the consent of the CONTRACTING PARTIES.

---

[1] Article XXIX has been amended by the Protocol modifying part I and article XXIX of the General Agreement on Tariffs and Trade, signed at Geneva, on 14 September 1948, which, at the date of registration of the General Agreement on Tariffs and Trade, had not yet entered into force.

[1] United Nations document E/PC/T/186.
[2] United Nations publication 1948.II.D.4.
[3] See Declaration, signed at Havana on 24 March 1948. (No. 814 II. *(b)*, Volume 62).

Article XXXI

WITHDRAWAL

Without prejudice to the provisions of Article XXIII or of paragraph 2 of Article XXX, any contracting party may, on or after January 1, 1951, withdraw from this Agreement, or may separately withdraw on behalf of any of the separate customs territories for which it has international responsibility and which at the time possesses full autonomy in the conduct of its external commercial relations and of the other matters provided for in this Agreement. The withdrawal shall take effect on or after January 1, 1951, upon the expiration of six months from the day on which written notice of withdrawal is received by the Secretary-General of the United Nations.

Article XXXII

CONTRACTING PARTIES

1.[1] The contracting parties to this Agreement shall be understood to mean those governments which are applying the provisions of this Agreement under Article XXVI or pursuant to the Protocol of Provisional Application.

2. At any time after the entry into force of this Agreement pursuant to paragraph 5 of Article XXVI, those contracting parties which have accepted this Agreement pursuant to paragraph 3 of Article XXVI may decide that any contracting party which has not so accepted it shall cease to be a contracting party.

Article XXXIII[2]

ACCESSION

A government not party to this Agreement or a government acting on behalf of a separate customs territory possessing full autonomy in the conduct of its external commercial relations and of the other matters provided for in this Agreement, may accede to this Agreement, on its own behalf or on behalf of that territory, on terms to be agreed between such government and the contracting parties.

Article XXXIV[3]

ANNEXES

The annexes to this Agreement are hereby made an integral part of this Agreement.

---

[1] Paragraph 1 of article XXXII has been amended by the Protocol modifying Certain Provisions of the General Agreement on Tariffs and Trade, signed at Havana, on 24 March 1948. See Volume 62.

[2] Article XXXIII has been amended by the Protocol modifying Certain Provisions of the General Agreement on Tariffs and Trade, signed at Havana, on 24 March 1948. See Volume 62.

[3] The Protocol modifying Certain Provisions of the General Agreement on Tariffs and Trade, signed at Havana, on 24 March 1948, provides for the insertion of a new Article XXXV. See Volume 62.

ANNEX A[1]

United Kingdom of Great Britain and Northern Ireland
Dependent territories of the United Kingdom of Great Britain and Northern Ireland
Canada
Commonwealth of Australia
Dependent territories of the Commonwealth of Australia
New Zealand
Dependent territories of New Zealand
Union of South Africa including South West Africa
Ireland
India (as on April 10, 1947)
Newfoundland
Southern Rhodesia
Burma
Ceylon

Certain of the territories listed above have two or more preferential rates in force for certain products. Any such territory may, by agreement with the other contracting parties which are principal suppliers of such products at the most-favoured-nation rate, substitute for such preferential rates a single preferential rate which shall not on the whole be less favourable to suppliers at the most-favoured-nation rate than the preferences in force prior to such substitution.

The imposition of an equivalent margin of tariff preference to replace a margin of preference in an internal tax existing on April 10, 1947, exclusively between two or more of the territories listed in this Annex or to replace the preferential quantitative arrangements described in the following paragraph, shall not be deemed to constitute an increase in a margin of tariff preference.

The preferential arrangements referred to in paragraph 5 *(b)* of Article XIV are those existing in the United Kingdom on April 10, 1947, under contractual agreements with the Governments of Canada, Australia and New Zealand, in respect of chilled and frozen beef and veal, frozen mutton and lamb, chilled and frozen pork, and bacon. It is the intention, without prejudice to any action taken under part I *(h)* of Article XX, that these arrangements shall be eliminated or replaced by tariff preferences, and that negotiations to this end shall take place as soon as practicable among the countries substantially concerned or involved.

The film hire tax in force in New Zealand on April 10, 1947, shall, for the purposes of this Agreement, be treated as a customs duty under Article I. The renters' film quota in force in New Zealand on April 10, 1947, shall, for the purposes of this Agreement, be treated as a screen quota under Article IV.

---

[1] A paragraph has been added to the annex A by the Protocol modifying part I and article XXIX of the General Agreement on Tariffs and Trade, signed at Geneva, on 14 September 1948, which, at the date of registration of the General Agreement on Tariffs and Trade, had not yet entered into force.

ANNEX B

LIST OF TERRITORIES OF THE FRENCH UNION REFERRED TO IN PARAGRAPH 2 *(b)* OF ARTICLE I

France
French Equatorial Africa (Treaty Basin of the Congo* and other territories)
French West Africa
Cameroons under French Mandate*
French Somali Coast and Dependencies
French Establishments in India*
French Establishments in Oceania
French Establishments in the Condominium of the New Hebrides*
Guadeloupe and Dependencies
French Guiana
Indo-China
Madagascar and Dependencies
Morocco (French zone)*
Martinique
New Caledonia and Dependencies
Reunion
Saint-Pierre and Miquelon
Togo under French Mandate*
Tunisia

*For imports into Metropolitan France[1]

ANNEX C[2]

LIST OF TERRITORIES OF THE CUSTOMS UNION OF BELGIUM, LUXEMBOURG AND THE NETHERLANDS REFERRED TO IN PARAGRAPH 2 *(b)* OF ARTICLE I

The Economic Union of Belgium and Luxembourg
Belgian Congo
Ruanda Urundi
Netherlands
Netherlands Indies[3]
Surinam
Curacao

For imports into the metropolitan territories constituting the Customs Union.

---

[1] This note has been amended by the Protocol of Rectification to the General Agreement on Tariffs and Trade, signed at Havana, on 24 March 1948.

[2] Annex C has been amended by the Third Protocol of Rectifications to the General Agreement on Tariffs and Trade, signed at Annecy, on 13 August 1949, and by the Fourth Protocol of Rectifications to the General Agreement signed at Geneva, on 3 April 1950, which, at the time of registration of the General Agreement on Tariffs and Trades had not yet entered into force.

[3] Following a declaration made by the Netherlands Government in virtue of article XXVI, paragraph 4, of the General Agreement on Tariffs and Trade, and the acceptance by the Republic of the United States of Indonesia of all the obligations arising out of the provisional application of the General Agreement, the Contracting Parties decided on 24 February 1950 that the United States of Indonesia become a Contracting Party in their own right by virtue of the above-mentioned article.

The schedules of tariff concessions (XXI) relating to the United States of Indonesia are set forth in the Fourth Protocol of Rectifications of the General Agreement, signed at Geneva on 3 April 1950, which was not yet in force at the date of registration of the General Agreement.

ANNEX D

United States of America (customs territory)
Dependent territories of the United States of America
Republic of the Philippines

The imposition of an equivalent margin of tariff preference to replace a margin of preference in an internal tax existing on April 10, 1947, exclusively between two or more of the territories listed in this Annex shall not be deemed to constitute an increase in a margin of tariff preference.

ANNEX E

LIST OF TERRITORIES COVERED BY PREFERENTIAL ARRANGEMENTS BETWEEN CHILE
AND NEIGHBOURING COUNTRIES REFERRED TO IN PARAGRAPH 2 *(d)* OF ARTICLE I

Preferences in force exclusively between Chile, on the one hand, and

1. Argentina
2. Bolivia
3. Peru

on the other hand.

ANNEX F

LIST OF TERRITORIES COVERED BY PREFERENTIAL ARRANGEMENTS BETWEEN
LEBANON AND SYRIA AND NEIGHBOURING COUNTRIES REFERRED TO IN PARAGRAPH 2 *(d)* OF ARTICLE I

Preferences in force exclusively between the Lebano-Syrian Customs Union, on the one hand, and

1. Palestine
2. Transjordan

on the other hand.

ANNEX G

DATES ESTABLISHING MAXIMUM MARGINS OF PREFERENCE
REFERRED TO IN PARAGRAPH 3 OF ARTICLE I

Australia	October	15, 1946
Canada	July	1, 1939
France	January	1, 1939
Lebano-Syrian Customs Union	November	30, 1939
Union of South Africa	July	1, 1938
Southern Rhodesia	May	1, 1941

ANNEX H

PERCENTAGE SHARES OF TOTAL EXTERNAL TRADE TO BE USED FOR THE PURPOSE OF MAKING THE DETERMINATION REFERRED TO IN ARTICLE XXVI

(Based on the average of 1938 and the latest twelve months for which figures are available)

	Percentage
Australia	3.2
Belgium-Luxembourg-Netherlands	10.9
Brazil	2.8
Burma	0.7
Canada	7.2
Ceylon	0.6
Chile	0.6
China	2.7
Cuba	0.9
Czechoslovakia	1.4
French Union	9.4
India	3.3*
Pakistan	
New Zealand	1.2
Norway	1.5
Southern Rhodesia	0.3
Lebano-Syrian Customs Union	0.1
Union of South Africa	2.3
United Kingdom of Great Britain and Northern Ireland	25.7
United States of America	25.2
	100.0

Note: These percentages have been determined taking into account the trade of all territories for which countries mentioned above have international responsibility and which are not self-governing in matters dealt with in the General Agreement on Tariffs and Trade.

*The allocation of this percentage will be made by agreement between the Governments of India and Pakistan and will be communicated as soon as possible to the Secretary-General of the United Nations.

ANNEX I

INTERPRETATIVE NOTES

ad Article I

Paragraph 1[1]

The obligations incorporated in paragraph 1 of Article I by reference to paragraphs 1 and 2 of Article III and those incorporated in paragraph 2 *(b)* of Article II by reference to Article VI shall be considered as falling within Part II for the purposes of the Protocol of Provisional Application.

---

[1] This paragraph has been amended and a second paragraph has been inserted by the Protocol modifying part I and article XXIX of the General Agreement on Tariffs and Trade, signed at Geneva on 14 September 1948, which, at the date of registration of the General Agreement on Tariffs and Trade, had not yet entered into force.

Paragraph 3[2]

The term "margin of preference" means the absolute difference between the most-favoured-nation rate of duty and the preferential rate of duty for the like product, and not the proportionate relation between those rates. As examples:

1) If the most-favoured-nation rate were 36 per cent, *ad valorem* and the preferential rate were 24 per cent, *ad valorem*, the margin of preference would be 12 per cent, *ad valorem*, and not one-third of the most-favoured-nation rate;

2) If the most-favoured-nation rate were 36 per cent, *ad valorem* and the preferential rate were expressed as two-thirds of the most-favoured-nation rate, the margin of preference would be 12 per cent, *ad valorem;*

3) If the most-favoured-nation rate were 2 francs per kilogram and the preferential rate were 1.50 francs per kilogram, the margin of preference would be 0.50 francs per kilogram.

The following kinds of customs action, taken in accordance with established uniform procedures, would not be contrary to a general binding of margins of preference:

(i) the re-application to an imported product of a tariff classification or rate of duty, properly applicable to such product, in cases in which the application of such classification or rate to such product was temporarily suspended or inoperative on April 10, 1947; and

(ii) the clasiffication of a particular product under a tariff item other than that under which importations of that product were classified on April 10, 1947, in cases in which the tariff law clearly contemplates that such product may be classified under more than one tariff item.

ad Article II [1]

Paragraph 2 (b)

See the note relating to paragraph 1 of Article I.

Paragraph 4[2]

Except where otherwise specifically agreed between the contracting parties which initially negotiated the concession, the provisions of this paragraph will be applied in the light of the provisions of Article 31 of the Draft Charter referred to in Article XXIX of this Agreement. [3]

ad Article V

Paragraph 5

With regard to transportation charges, the principle laid down in paragraph 5 refers to like products being transported on the same route under like conditions.

---

[2] The heading "paragraph 3" has been amended by the Protocol modifying part I and article XXIX of the General Agreement on Tariffs and Trade, signed at Geneva on 14 September 1948, which, at the date of registration of the General Agreeement on Tariffs and Trade, had not yet entered into force.

[1] A paragraph has been added immediately after this heading by the Protocol modifying part I and article XXIX of the General Agreement on Tariffs and Trade signed at Geneva on 14 September 1948, which, at the date of registration of the General Agreement on Tariffs and Trade, had not yet entered into force.

[2] This paragraph has been amended by the Protocol modifying part I and article XXIX of the General Agreement on Tariffs and Trade, signed at Geneva on 14 September 1948, which, at the date of registration of the General Agreement on Tariffs and Trade, had not yet entered into force.

[3] See the Protocol modifying part II and article XXVI of the General Agreement on Tariffs and Trade, signed at Geneva on 14 September 1948 (Volume 62), for insertion of the interpretative notes relating to article III.

ad Article VI[1]

Paragraph 1

Hidden dumping by associated houses (that is, a sale by an importer at a price below that corresponding to the price invoiced by an exporter with whom the importer is associated, and also below the price in the exporting country) constitutes a form of price dumping.

Paragraph 2

Multiple currency practices can in certain circumstances constitute a subsidy to exports which may be met by countervailing duties under paragraph 2 or can constitute a form of dumping by means of a partial depreciation of a country's currency which may be met by action under paragraph 1 of this Article. By "multiple currency practices" is meant practices by governments or sanctioned by governments.

Paragraph 7

The obligations set forth in paragraph 7, as in the case of other obligations under this Agreement, are subject to the provisions of Article XIX.

ad Article VII

Paragraph 1

Consideration was given to the desirability of replacing the words "at the earliest practicable date" by a definite date or, alternatively, by a provision for a specified limited period to be fixed later. It was appreciated that it would not be possible for all contracting parties to give effect to these principles by a fixed time, but it was nevertheless understood that a majority of the contracting parties would give effect to them at the time the Agreement enters into force.

Paragraph 2

It would be in conformity with Article VII to presume that "actual value" may be represented by the invoice price, plus any non-included charges for legitimate costs which are proper elements of "actual value" and plus any abnormal discount or other reduction from the ordinary competitive price.

It would be in conformity with Article VII, paragraph 2 *(b)*, for a contracting party to construe the phrase "in the ordinary course of trade," read in conjunction with "under fully competitive conditions," as excluding any transaction wherein the buyer and seller are not independent of each other and price is not the sole consideration.

The prescribed standard of "fully competitive conditions" permits contracting parties to exclude from consideration distributors' prices which involve special discounts limited to exclusive agents.

The wording of sub-paragraphs *(a)* and *(b)* permits a contracting party to assess duty uniformly either (1) on the basis of a particular exporter's prices of the imported merchandise, or (2) on the basis of the general price level of like merchandise.

---

[1] The interpretative notes concerning article VI have been amended by the Protocol modifying part II and article XXVI of the General Agreement on Tariffs and Trade, signed at Geneva on 14 September 1948. See Volume 62.

ad Article VIII

While Article VIII does not cover the use of multiple rates of exchange as such, paragraphs 1 and 4 condemn the use of exchange taxes or fees as a device for implementing multiple currency practices; if, however, a contracting party is using multiple currency exchange fees for balance-of-payments reasons with the approval of the International Monetary Fund, the provisions of paragraph 2 fully safeguard its position since that paragraph merely requires that the fees be eliminated at the earliest practicable date.

ad Article XI

Paragraph 2 (c)

The term "in any form" in this paragraph covers the same products when in any early stage of processing and still perishable, which compete directly with the fresh product and if freely imported would tend to make the restriction on the fresh product ineffective.

Paragraph 2, last sub-paragraph

The term "special factors" includes changes in relative productive efficiency as between domestic and foreign producers, or as between different foreign producers, but not changes artificially brought about by means not permitted under the Agreement.

ad Article XII

Paragraph 3 (b) (i)

The phrase "notwithstanding the provisions of paragraph 2 of this Article" has been included in the text to make it quite clear that a contracting party's import restrictions otherwise "necessary" within the meaning of paragraph 2 (a) shall not be considered unnecessary on the ground that a change in domestic policies as referred to in the text could improve a contracting party's monetary reserve position. The phrase is not intended to suggest that the provisions of paragraph 2 are affected in any other way.

Consideration was given to the special problems that might be created for contracting parties which, as a result of their programmes of full employment, maintenance of high and rising levels of demand and economic development, find themselves faced with a high level of demand for imports, and in consequence maintain quantitative regulation of their foreign trade. It was considered that the present text of Article XII together with the provision for export controls in certain parts of the Agreement, e.g. in Article XX, fully meet the position of these economies.

ad Article XIII

Paragraph 2 (d)

No mention was made of "commercial considerations" as a rule for the allocation of quotas because it was considered that its application by governmental authorities might not always be practicable. Moreover, in cases where it is practicable, a contracting party could apply these considerations in the process of seeking agreement, consistently with the general rule laid down in the opening sentence of paragraph 2.

Paragraph 4

See note relating to "special factors" in connection with the last subparagraph of paragraph 2 of Article XI.

ad Article XIV[1]

Paragraph 3

It was not considered necessary to make express reference in paragraph 3 to the need for the CONTRACTING PARTIES to consult with the International Monetary Fund, since such consultation in all appropriate cases was already required by virtue of the provisions of paragraph 2 of Article XV.

Paragraph 6 (b)

Suspension of any measure for a period of fifteen days would be for the purpose of making the consultation effective and among the special circumstances which would justify such suspension would be the immediate damage caused to producers of perishable commodities ready for shipment or to consumers of essential goods of which the importing country had no stocks.

ad Article XV

Paragraph 4

The word "frustrate" is intended to indicate, for example, that infringements of the letter of any Article of this Agreement by exchange action shall not be regarded as a violation of that Article if, in practices, there is no appreciable departure from the intent of the Article. Thus, a contracting party which, as part of its exchange control operated in accordance with the Articles of Agreement of the International Monetary Fund, requires payment to be received for its exports in its own currency or in the currency or in the currency of one or more members of the International Monetary Fund will not thereby be deemed to contravene Article XI or Article XIII. Another example would be that of a contracting party which specifies on an import licence the country from which the goods may be imported, for the purpose not of introducing any additional element of discrimination in its import licensing system but of enforcing permissible exchange controls.

ad Article XVII

Paragraph 1

The operations of Marketing Boards, which are established by contracting parties and are engaged in purchasing or selling, are subject to the provisions of sub-paragraphs *(a)* and *(b)*.

The activities of Marketing Boards which are established by contracting parties and which do not purchase or sell but lay down regulations covering private trade are governed by the relevant Articles of this Agreement.

The charging by a State enterprise of different prices for its sales of a product in different markets is not precluded by the provisions of this Article, provided that such different prices are charged for commercial reasons, to meet conditions of supply and demand in export markets.

---

[1] The interpretative notes concerning article XIV have been amended by the Special Protocol modifying article XIV of the General Agreement on Tariffs and Trade, signed at Havana, on 24 March 1948. See Volume 62.

Paragraph 1 (a)

Governmental measures imposed to ensure standards of quality and efficiency in the operation of external trade, or privileges granted for the exploitation of national natural resources but which do not empower the government to exercise control over the trading activities of the enterprise in question, do not constitute "exclusive or special privileges."

Paragraph 1 (b)

A country receiving a "tied loan" is free to take this loan into account as a "commercial consideration" when purchasing requirements abroad.

Paragraph 2

The term "goods" is limited to products as understood in commercial practice, and is not intended to include the purchase or sale of services.[1]

ad Article XXIV[2]

Paragraph 5

Measures adopted by India and Pakistan in order to carry out definitive trade arrangements between them, once they have been agreed upon, might depart from particular provisions of this Agreement, but these measures would in general be consistent with the objectives of the Agreement.

ad Article XXVI

Territories for which the contracting parties have international responsibility do not include areas under military occupation.[3,4]

Final note

The applicability of the General Agreement on Tariffs and Trade to the trade of contracting parties with the under military occupation has not been dealt with and is reserved for further study at an early date. Meanwhile, nothing in this Agreement shall be taken to prejudge the issues involved. This, of course, does not affect the applicability of the provisions of Articles XXII and XXIII to matters arising from such trade.

---

[1] See the Protocol modifying part II and article XXVI of the General Agreement on Tariffs and Trade, signed at Geneva, on 14 September 1948 (Volume 62), for insertion relating to article XVIII.

[2] The interpretative notes concerning article XXIV have been amended by the Special Protocol relating to article XXIV of the General Agreement on Tariffs and Trade, signed at Havana, on 24 March 1948. See Volume 62.

The first of the two interpretative notes concerning article XXIV, as amended by the Special Protocol relating to article XXIV, has been further amended by the Third Protocol of Rectifications to the General Agreement on Tariffs and Trade, signed at Annecy, on 13 August 1949, which, at the date of registration of the General Agreement on Tariffs and Trade, had not yet entered into force.

[3] Interpretative notes relating to article XXIX have been added by the Protocol modifying part I and article XXIX of the General Agreement on Tariffs and Trade, signed at Geneva on 14 September 1948, which, at the date of registration of the General Agreement on Tariffs and Trade, had not yet entered into force.

[4] See the Special Protocol modifying article XIV of the General Agreement on Tariffs and Trade, signed at Havana on 24 March 1948 (Volume 62), concerning the addition of annex J and interpretative note to annex J.

INDEX TO LIST OF SCHEDULES

These schedules are published in the following volumes of the *Treaty Series:*

I. (c) PROTOCOL OF PROVISIONAL APPLICATION OF THE GENERAL AGREEMENT ON TARIFFS AND TRADE. SIGNED AT GENEVA, ON 30 OCTOBER 1947.

—————

1. The Governments of the COMMONWEALTH OF AUSTRALIA, the KINGDOM OF BELGIUM (in respect of its metropolitan territory), CANADA, the FRENCH REPUBLIC (in respect of its metropolitan territory), the GRAND-DUCHY OF LUXEMBURG, the KINGDOM OF THE NETHERLANDS (in respect of its metropolitan territory), the UNITED KINGDOM OF GREAT BRITAIN AND NORTHERN IRELAND (in respect of its metropolitan territory), and the UNITED STATES OF AMERICA, undertake, provided that this Protocol shall have been signed on behalf of all the foregoing Governments not later than November 15, 1947, to apply provisionally on and after January 1, 1948:

   (a)   Parts I and III of the General Agreement on Tariffs and Trade, and
   (b)   Part II of that Agreement to the fullest extent not inconsistent with existing legislation.

2. The foregoing Governments shall make effective such provisional application of the General Agreement, in respect of any of their territories other than their metropolitan territories, on or after January 1, 1948, upon the expiration of thirty days from the day on which notice of such application is received by the Secretary-General of the United Nations.

3. Any other Government signatory to this Protocol shall make effective such provisional application of the General Agreement, on or after January 1, 1948, upon the expiration of thirty days from the day of signature of this Protocol on behalf of such Government.

4. This Protocol shall remain open for signature at the Headquarters of the United Nations, (a) until November 15, 1947, on behalf of any Government named in paragraph 1 of this Protocol which has not signed it on this day, and (b) until June 1948, on behalf of any other Government signatory to the Final Act[1] adopted at the conclusion of the Second Session of the Preparatory Committee of the United Nations Conference on Trade and Employment which has not signed it on this day.

5. Any Government applying this Protocol shall be free to withdraw such application, and such withdrawal shall take effect upon the expiration of sixty days from the day on which written notice of such withdrawal is received by the Secretary-General of the United Nations.

6. The original of this Protocol shall be deposited with the Secretary-General of the United Nations, who will furnish certified copies thereof to all interested Governments.

IN WITNESS WHEREOF the respective Representatives, after having communicated their full powers, found to be in good and due form, have signed this Protocol.

DONE at Geneva, in a single copy, in the English and French languages, both texts authentic, this thirtieth day of October, one thousand nine hundred and forty-seven.

—————

[1] See Protocol for the accession of signatories of the Final Act of 30 October 1947, signed at Geneva, on 14 September 1948 (United Nations *Treaty Series*, Volume 62, No. 814 III. *(a).)*

For the Kingdom of Belgium:	P.A. FORTHOMME
For Canada:	L.D. WILGRESS
For the Grand-Duchy of Luxemburg:	J. STURM
For the Kingdom of the Netherlands:	A.B. SPEEKENBRINK
For the United Kingdom of Great Britain and Northern Ireland:	T.M. SNOW
For the United States of America:	WINTHROP BROWN
For the Commonwealth of Australia:	HERBERT V. EVATT New York 13/11/47
For the French Republic:	ANDRE PHILIP New York, le 13 november 1947

(b) That upon the expiration of thirty days from the date of signature by me, the Government of India would give provisional effect to the agreed tariff concessions on most, but not all, of the items in schedule XII to the agreement, *vide* paragraph 3 of Protocol. The excepted items are indicated below:

(1) Ex 20 (1): certain fruit juices.
(2) Ex 20 (2): certain canned fruits.
(3) Ex 20 (2): pine-apples canned.
(4) 24 (3): tobacco, un-manufactured.
(5) Ex 28: certain chemicals, drugs and medicines.
(6) 75 (1): motor cars and parts and accessories thereof.[1]

P.P. PILLAI
8th June 1948

For the Kingdom of Norway:	FINN MOE New York, le 10 juin 1948
For Southern Rhodesia:	ALEXANDER CADOGAN New York, June 11, 1948

Note by the Secretariat:

The six tariff items listed in the second of India's reservations (paragraph *b*) were made applicable on 11 February 1949 and hence this reservation is no longer operative.

Note du Secretariat:

Les six positions du tarif mentionnees dans la reserve *b*) ci-dessus ont ete rendues applicable le 11 fevrier 1949. En consequence cette reserve n'a plus d'effect.

---

[1] *Traduction:*

a) Le Gouvernement de l'Inde se reserve, conformement a l'Article XXXV, d'accorder son consentement a l'application de l'Accord entre l'Inde et l'Union Sud-Africaine au cas ou l'Union Sud-Africaine deviendrait partie contractante;

b) A l'expiration d'un delai de trente jours a compter de la date a laquelle le Representant de l'Inde aura appose sa signature, le Gouvernement de l'Inde appliquera a trite provisoire les concessions tarifaires consenties a la plus grande partie, mais non a la totalite des produits figurant sur la liste XII annexee a l'Accord, conformement au paragraphe 3 du Protocole. Les produits pour lesquels les concessions ne seront pas appliquees sont:

1) Ex 20 (1): Certains jus de fruits.
2) Ex 20 (2): Certains fruits en boites de fer-blane.
3) Ex 20 (2): Ananas en boites de fer-blane.
4) 24 (3): Tabac non manufacture.
5) Ex 28: Certains produits chimiques, drogues et medicaments.
6) 75 (1): Automobiles ainsi que parties et accessoires de ces vehicles.

For Pakistan: Signed subject to the following reservation:

Under Article XXXV of the General Agreement, Pakistan will not extend most-favoured-nation treatment in applying the provisions of this Agreement to South Africa at present.

M.A.H. ISPAHANI
New York, June 30 1948

For Brazil: Joao Carlos Muniz
New York, June 30th 1948

G. AGREEMENTS BETWEEN THE UNITED NATIONS AND THE SPECIALIZED AGENCIES AND THE INTERNATIONAL ATOMIC ENERGY AGENCY[1]

PREFATORY NOTE

There have been assembled in this chapter the agreements and supplementary agreements between the United Nations, on the one hand, and the specialized agencies and the International Atomic Energy Agency, on the other, which have entered into force after approval by the General Assembly and the appropriate bodies of the respective agencies. Also included are the protocols concerning the entry into force of these agreements. Not included is the agreement between the United Nations and the International Refugee Organization,[2] the latter having gone into liquidation on 1 March 1952.

Subsidiary agreements or arrangements made between the Secretary-General and the executive heads of some of the agencies—for example, on public information—do not appear here.

April 1961

TABLE OF CONTENTS

---

[1] U.N. Doc. ST/SG/14.
[2] The text of this agreement may be found in the United Nations publication entitled "Agreements between the United Nations and the Specialized Agencies" (ST/SG/1), Sales No. : 51.X.1.

1. AGREEMENT BETWEEN THE UNITED NATIONS AND THE INTERNATIONAL LABOUR ORGANIZATION APPROVED BY THE GENERAL ASSEMBLY ON DECEMBER 14, 1946

PROTOCOL CONCERNING THE ENTRY INTO FORCE OF THE AGREEMENT
BETWEEN THE UNITED NATIONS AND THE INTERNATIONAL LABOUR
ORGANISATION

Article 57 of the Charter of the United Nations provides that specialized agencies established by intergovernmental agreement and having wide international responsibilities as defined in their basic instruments in economic, social, cultural, educational, health and related fields shall be brought into relationship with the United Nations. Article 63 of the Charter provides that the Economic and Social Council may enter into agreements with any of the agencies referred to in Article 57, defining the terms on which the agency concerned shall be brought into relationship with the United Nations, and specifies that such agreements shall be subject to approval by the General Assembly.

The International Labour Conference, meeting in its twenty-seventh session in Paris on 3 November 1945, adopted a resolution confirming the desire of the International Labour Organisation to enter into relationship with the United Nations on terms, to be determined by agreement, which will permit the International Labour Organisation, in which the representatives of workers and employers enjoy equal status with those of Governments, to co-operate fully for the attainment of the ends of the United Nations, while retaining the authority essential for the discharge of its responsibilities under the Constitution of the Organisation and the Declaration of Philadelphia, and authorizing the Governing Body of the International Labour Office to enter, subject to the approval of the Conference, into such agreements with the appropriate authorities of the United Nations as might be necessary or desirable for this purpose.

The Economic and Social Council, during its first session, in January-February 1946, adopted a resolution establishing a Committee of the Council on Negotiations with Specialized Agencies which was directed to enter into negotiations as early as possible with the International Labour Organisation.

Negotiations between the Committee on Negotiations with Specialized Agencies of the Economic and Social Council and the Negotiating Delegation of the International Labour Organisation took place in New York on 28 and 29 May 1946 and resulted in an Agreement. This Agreement was signed on 30 May 1946 by Sir A. Ramaswami Mudaliar, President of the Economic and Social Council and Chairman of the Committee on Negotiations with Specialized Agencies, and Mr. G. Myrddin Evans, Chairman of the Governing Body of the International Labour Office and of the Negotiating Delegation of the International Labour Organisation.

On 21 June 1946, the Economic and Social Council, during its second session, unanimously recommended the Agreement between the United Nations and the International Labour Organisation to the General Assembly for its approval.

Article XX of the Agreement provides that the Agreement shall come into force on its approval by the General Assembly of the United Nations and the General Conference of the International Labour Organisation.

The Agreement was approved by the General Assembly of the United Nations on 14 December 1946 and by the General Conference of the International Labour Organisation on 2 October 1946.

The Agreement accordingly came into force on 14 December 1946.

A copy of the authentic text of the Agreement is attached hereto.

IN FAITH WHEREOF we have appended our signatures this nineteenth day of December, one thousand nine hundred and forty-six, to two original copies of the present Protocol, the text of which consists of versions in the English and French languages which are equally authentic. One of the original copies will be filed and recorded with the Secretariat of the United Nations and the other will be deposited in the archives of the International Labour Office.

Trygve LIE
Secretary-General of the United Nations

Edward PHELAN
Director-General of the International Labour Office

AGREEMENT BETWEEN THE UNITED NATIONS AND THE INTERNATIONAL LABOUR ORGANISATION

Article 57 of the Charter of the United Nations provides that specialized agencies established by intergovernmental agreement and having wide international responsibilities as defined in their basic instruments in economic, social, cultural, educational, health and related fields shall be brought into relationship with the United Nations.

The International Labour Conference, meeting in its twenty-seventh session in Paris on 3 November 1945, adopted a resolution confirming the desire of the International Labour Organisation to enter into relationship with the United Nations on terms to be determined by agreement.

Therefore, the United Nations and the International Labour Organisation agree as follows:

Article I

The United Nations recognizes the International Labour Organisation as a specialized agency responsible for taking such action as may be appropriate under its basic instrument for the accomplishment of the purposes set forth therein.

Article II

RECIPROCAL REPRESENTATION

1. Representatives of the United Nations shall be invited to attend the meetings the International Labour Conference (hereinafter called the Conference) and its committees, the Governing Body and its committees, and such general, regional or other special meetings as the International Labour Organisation may convene, and to participate, without vote, in the deliberations of these bodies.

2. Representatives of the International Labour Organisation shall be invited to attend meetings of the Economic and Social Council of the United Nations (hereinafter called the Council) and of its commissions and committees and to participate, without vote, in the deliberations of these bodies with respect to items on their agenda in which the International Labour Organisation has indicated that it has an interest.

3. Representatives of the International Labour Organisation shall be invited to attend, in a consultative capacity, meetings of the General Assembly and shall be afforded full opportunity for presenting to the General Assembly the views of the International Labour Organisation on questions within the scope of its activities.

4. Representatives of the International Labour Organisation shall be invited to attend meetings of the main committees of the General Assembly in which the International Labour Organisation has an interest and to participate, without vote in the deliberations thereof.

5. Representatives of the International Labour Organisation shall be invited to attend the meetings of the Trusteeship Council and to participate, without vote, in the deliberations thereof with respect to items on the agenda in which the International Labour Organisation has indicated that it has an interest.

6. Written statements of the Organisation shall be distributed by the Secretariat of the United Nations to all Members of the General Assembly, the Council and its commissions and the Trusteeship Council as appropriate.

Article III

PROPOSAL OF AGENDA ITEMS

Subject to such preliminary consultation as may be necessary, the International Labour Organisation shall include on the agenda of the Governing Body items proposed to it by the United Nations. Similarly, the Council and its commissions and the Trusteeship Council shall include on their agenda items proposed by the International Labour Organisation.

Article IV

RECOMMENDATIONS OF THE GENERAL ASSEMBLY AND OF THE COUNCIL

1. The International Labour Organisation, having regard to the obligation of the United Nations to promote the objectives set forth in Article 55 of the Charter and the function and power of the Council, under Article 62 of the Charter, to make or initiate studies and reports with respect to international economic, social, cultural, educational, health and related matters and to make recommendations concerning these matters to the specialized agencies concerned, and having regard, also the responsibility of the United Nations, under Articles 58 and 63 of the Charter, to make recommendations for the co-ordination of the policies and activities of such specialized agencies, agrees to arrange for the submission, as soon as possible, to the Governing Body, the Conference or such other organ of the International Labour Organisation, as may be appropriate, of all formal recommendations which the General Assembly or the Council may make to it.

2. The International Labour Organisation agrees to enter into consultation with the United Nations upon request, with respect to such recommendations, and in due course to report to the Nations on the action taken, by the Organisation or by its members, to give effect to such recommendations, or on the other results of their consideration.

3. The International Labour Organisation affirms its intention of co-operating in whatever further measures may be necessary to make co-ordination of the activities of specialized agencies and those of the United Nations fully effective. In particular, it agrees to participate in, and to co-operate with, any body or bodies which the Council may establish for the purpose of facilitating such co-ordination, and to furnish such information as may be required for the carrying out of this purpose.

Article V

EXCHANGE OF INFORMATION AND DOCUMENTS

1. Subject to such arrangements as may be necessary for the safeguarding of confidential material, the fullest and promptest exchange of information and documents shall be made between the United Nations and the International Labour Organisation.

2. Without prejudice to the generality of the provisions of paragraph 1:

(a) The International Labour Organisation agrees to transmit to the United Nations regular reports on the activities of the International Labour Organisation;

(b) The International Labour Organisation agrees to comply to the fullest extent practicable with any request which the United Nations may make for the furnishing of special reports, studies or information, subject to the conditions set forth in article XV; and

(c) The Secretary-General shall, upon request, consult with the Director regarding the provision to the International Labour Organisation of such information as may be of special interest to the Organisation.

Article VI

ASSISTANCE TO THE SECURITY COUNCIL

The International Labour Organisation agrees to co-operate with the Economic and Social Council in furnishing such information and rendering such assistance to the Security Council as that Council may request including assistance in carrying out decisions of the Security Council for the maintenance or restoration of international peace and security.

Article VII

ASSISTANCE TO THE TRUSTEESHIP COUNCIL

The International Labour Organisation agrees to co-operate with the Trusteeship Council in the carrying out of its functions and in particular agrees that it will, to the greatest extent possible, render such assistance as the Trusteeship Council may request, in regard to matters with which the Organization is concerned.

Article VIII

NON-SELF-GOVERNING TERRITORIES

The International Labour Organisation agrees to co-operate with the United Nations in giving effect to the principles and obligations set forth in Chapter XI of the Charter with regard to matters affecting the well-being and development of the peoples of Non-Self-Governing Territories.

Article IX

RELATIONS WITH THE INTERNATIONAL COURT OF JUSTICE

1. The International Labour Organisation agrees to furnish any information which may be requested by the International Court of Justice in pursuance of Article 34 of the Statute of the Court.

2. The General Assembly authorizes the International Labour Organisation to request advisory opinions of the International Court of Justice on legal questions arising within the scope of its activities other than questions concerning the mutual relationships of the Organisation and the United Nations or other specialized agencies.

3. Such request may be addressed to the Court by the Conference, or by the Governing Body acting in pursuance of an authorization by the Conference.

4. When requesting the International Court of Justice to give an advisory opinion, the International Labour Organisation shall inform the Economic and Social Council of the request.

Article X

HEADQUARTERS AND REGIONAL OFFICES

1. The International Labour Organisation, having regard to the desirability of the headquarters of specialized agencies being situated at the permanent seat of the United Nations, and to the advantages that flow from such centralization, agrees to consult

the United Nations before making any decision concerning the location of its permanent headquarters.

2. Any regional or branch offices which the International Labour Organisation may establish shall, so far as practicable, be closely associated with such regional or branch offices as the United Nations may establish.

Article XI

PERSONNEL ARRANGEMENTS

1. The United Nations and the International Labour Organisation recognize that the eventual development of a single unified international civil service is desirable from the standpoint of effective administrative co-ordination, and with this end in view, agree to develop common personnel standards, methods and arrangements designed to avoid serious discrepancies in terms and conditions of employment, to avoid competition in recruitment of personnel, and to facilitate interchange of personnel in order to obtain the maximum benefit from their services.

2. The United Nations and the International Labour Organisation agree to co-operate to the fullest extent possible in achieving these ends and in particular they agree to:

(a) Consult together concerning the establishment of an International Civil Service Commission to advise on the means by which common standards of recruitment in the secretariats of the United Nations and of the specialized agencies may be ensured;

(b) Consult together concerning other matters relating to the employment of their officers and staff, including conditions of service, duration of appointments, classification, salary scales and allowances, retirement and pension rights and staff regulations and rules with a view to securing as much uniformity in these matters as shall be found practicable;

(c) Co-operate in the interchange of personnel, when desirable, on a temporary or permanent basis, making due provision for the retention of seniority and pension rights;

(d) Co-operate in the establishment and operation of suitable machinery for the settlement of disputes arising in connexion with the employment of personnel and related matters.

Article XII

STATISTICAL SERVICES

1. The United Nations and the International Labour Organisation agree to strive for maximum co-operation, the elimination of all undesirable duplication between them, and the most efficient use of their technical personnel in their respective collection, analysis, publication and dissemination of statistical information. They agree to combine their efforts to secure the greatest possible usefulness and utilization of statistical information and to minimize the burdens placed upon national governments and other organizations from which such information may be collected.

2. The International Labour Organisation recognizes the United Nations as the central agency for the collection, analysis, publication, standardization and improvement of statistics serving the general purposes of international organizations.

3. The United Nations recognizes the International Labour Organisation as the appropriate agency for the collection, analysis, publication, standardization and improvement of statistics within its special sphere, without prejudice to the right of the United Nations to concern itself with such statistics so far as they may be essential for its own purposes or for the improvement of statistics throughout the world.

4. The United Nations shall develop administrative instruments and procedures through which effective statistical co-operation may be secured between the United Nations and the agencies brought into relationship with it.

5. It is recognized as desirable that the collection of statistical information should not be duplicated by the United Nations or any of the specialized agencies whenever

it is practicable for any of them to utilize information or materials which another may have available.

6. In order to build up a central collection of statistical information for general use, it is agreed that data supplied to the International Labour Organisation for incorporation in its basic statistical series or special reports, should, so far as practicable, be made available to the United Nations.

Article XIII

ADMINISTRATIVE AND TECHNICAL SERVICES

1. The United Nations and the International Labour Organisation recognize the desirability, in the interest of administrative and technical uniformity and of the most efficient use of personnel and resources, of avoiding, whenever possible, the establishment and operation of competitive or overlapping facilities and services among the United Nations and the specialized agencies.

2. Accordingly, the United Nations and the International Labour Organisation agree to consult together concerning the establishment and use of common administrative and technical services and facilities in addition to those referred to in articles XI, XII and XIV, in so far as the establishment and use of such services may from time to time be found practicable and appropriate.

3. Arrangements shall be made between the United Nations and the International Labour Organisation in regard to the registration and deposit of official documents.

Article XIV

BUDGETARY AND FINANCIAL ARRANGEMENTS

1. The International Labour Organisation recognizes the desirability of establishing close budgetary and financial relationships with the United Nations in order that the administrative operations of the United Nations and of the specialized agencies shall be carried out in the most efficient and economical manner possible, and that the maximum measure of co-ordination and uniformity with respect to these operations shall be secured.

2. The United Nations and the International Labour Organisation agree to co-operate to the fullest extent possible in achieving these ends and, in particular, shall consult together concenring the desirability of making appropriate arrangements for the inclusion of the budget of the Organisation within a general budget of the United Nations. Any such arrangements which may be made shall be defined in a supplementary agreement between the two organizations.

3. In the preparation of the budget of the International Labour Organisation the Organisation shall consult with the United Nations.

4. The International Labour Organisation agrees to transmit its proposed budget to the United Nations annually at the same time as such budget is transmitted to its members. The General Assembly shall examine the budget or proposed budget of the Organisation and may make recommendations to it concerning any item or items contained therein.

5. Representatives of the International Labour Organisation shall be entitled to participate, without vote, in the deliberations of the General Assembly or any committee thereof at all times when the budget of the Organisation or general administrative or financial questions affecting the Organisation are under consideration.

6. The United Nations may undertake the collection of contributions from those members of the International Labour Organisation which are also Members of the United Nations in accordance with such arrangements as may be defined by a later agreement between the United Nations and the International Labour Organisation.

7. The United Nations shall, upon its own initiative or upon the request of the International Labour Organisation, arrange for studies to be undertaken concerning other financial and fiscal questions of interest to the Organisation and to other specialized agencies with a view to the provision of common services and the securing of uniformity in such matters.

8. The International Labour Organisation agrees to conform as far as may be practicable to standard practices and forms recommended by the United Nations.

Article XV

FINANCING OF SPECIAL SERVICES

1. In the event of the International Labour Organisation being faced with the necessity of incurring substantial extra expense as a result of any request which the United Nations may make for special reports, studies or assistance in accordance with articles V, VI, or VII or with other provisions of this agreement, consultation shall take place with a view to determining the most equitable manner in which such expense shall be borne.

2. Consultation between the United Nations and the International Labour Organisation shall similarly take place with a view to making such arrangements as may be found equitable for covering the costs of central administrative, technical or fiscal services or facilities or other special assistance provided by the United Nations.

Article XVI

INTER-AGENCY AGREEMENTS

The International Labour Organisation agrees to inform the Council of the nature and scope of any formal agreement between the International Labour Organisation and any other specialized agency or intergovernmental organization and in particular agrees to inform the Council before any such agreement is concluded.

Article XVII

LIAISON

1. The United Nations and the International Labour Organisation agree to the foregoing provisions in the belief that they will contribute to the maintenance of effective liaison between the two organizations. They affirm their intention of taking whatever further measures may be necessary to make this liaison fully effective.

2. The liaison arrangements provided for in the foregoing articles of this Agreement shall apply as far as appropriate to the relations between such branch or regional offices as may be established by the two organizations as well as between their central machinery.

Article XVIII

IMPLEMENTATION OF THE AGREEMENT

The Secretary-General and the Director may enter into such supplementary arrangements for the implementation of this Agreement as may be found desirable in the light of the operating experience of the two organizations.

Article XIX

REVISION

This Agreement shall be subject to revision by agreement between the United Nations and the International Labour Organisation.

Article XX

ENTRY INTO FORCE

This Agreement shall come into force on its approval by the General Assembly of the United Nations and the General Conference of the International Labour Organization.

2. AGREEMENT BETWEEN THE UNITED NATIONS AND THE FOOD AND AGRICULTURE ORGANIZATION OF THE UNITED NATIONS APPROVED BY THE GENERAL ASSEMBLY ON DECEMBER 14, 1946

PROTOCOL CONCERNING THE ENTRY INTO FORCE OF THE AGREEMENT BETWEEN THE UNITED NATIONS AND THE FOOD AND AGRICULTURE ORGANIZATION OF THE UNITED NATIONS

Article 57 of the Charter of the United Nations provides that specialized agencies established by intergovernmental agreement and having wide international responsibilities as defined in their basic instruments in economic, social, cultural, educational, health and related fields shall be brought into relationship with the United Nations. Article 63 of the Charter provides that the Economic and Social Council may enter into agreements with any of the agencies referred to in Article 57, defining the terms on which the agency concerned shall be brought into relationship with the United Nations, and specifies that such agreements shall be subject to approval by the General Assembly.

The Food and Agriculture Organization of the United Nations, meeting in its first session in Quebec, Canada, 16 October to 1 November 1945, adopted a resolution stating that, in pursuance of Article XIII of the Constitution of the Food and Agriculture Organization (which provides that the Organization shall constitute a part of any general international organization to which may be entrusted the co-ordination of the activities of international organization with specialized responsibilities), the Organization should, without prejudice to its purposes and limitations as set out in the Constitution, so order its procedure and practice as to achieve the closest relationship with the United Nations; and that in order to give effect to this provision the Director-General should, with the approval of the Executive Committee, negotiate agreements between the Organization and the United Nations.

The Economic and Social Council, during its first session, in January-February 1946, adopted a resolution establishing a Committee of the Council on Negotiations with Specialized Agencies which was directed to enter into negotiations as early as possible with the Food and Agriculture Organization of the United Nations.

The Director-General of the Food and Agriculture Organization of the United Nations, with the approval of the Executive Committee, in March 1946, appointed a negotiating committee to enter into negotiations with the United Nations.

Negotiations between the Committee on Negotiations with Specialized Agencies of the Economic and Social Council and the Negotiating Committee of the Food and Agriculture Organization of the United Nations took place in New York on 6 and 7 June 1946 and resulted in a draft agreement. In this draft agreement a decision regarding relations with the International Court of Justice was deferred pending further consideration thereof by the Economic and Social Council.

This draft agreement was initialled on 10 June 1946 by Sir A. Ramaswami Mudaliar, President of the Economic and Social Council and Chairman of the Committee on Negotiations with Specialized Agencies, and Professor Andre Mayer, Chairman of the Executive Committee and of the Negotiating Committee of the Food and Agriculture Organization of the United Nations.

On 21 June 1946, the Economic and Social Council, during its second session, unanimously recommended the Agreement between the United Nations and the Food and Agriculture Organization of the United Nations to the General Assembly for its approval.

The second session of the Conference of the Food and Agriculture Organization of the United Nations held in Copenhagen from 2 to 14 September 1946, adopted a resolution approving the Agreement and instructing the Director-General to sign on behalf of the Organization upon approval by the United Nations.

The Conference also approved the request of the Negotiating Committee of the Food and Agriculture Organization of the United Nations that Article IX provide that the Food and Agriculture Organization of the United Nations be authorized to request directly advisory opinions of the International Court of Justice on legal questions arising within the scope of its activities.

On 3 October 1946, the Economic and Social Council, during its third session, recommended to the General Assembly that it approve the insertion in the draft agreement of the authorization regarding relations with the International Court of Justice requested by the Food and Agriculture Organization of the United Nations.

The Agreement was approved by the General Assembly of the United Nations on 14 December 1946.

Article XX of the Agreement provides that the Agreement shall come into force on its approval by the General Assembly of the United Nations and by the Conference of the Food and Agriculture Organization of the United Nations.

The Agreement accordingly came into force on 14 December 1946.

A copy of the authentic text of the Agreement is attached hereto.

IN FAITH WHEREOF we have appended our signatures, this third day of February, one thousand nine hundred and forty-seven, to two original copies of the present Protocol, the text of which consists of versions in the English and French languages which are equally authentic. One of the original copies will be filed and recorded with the Secretariat of the United Nations and the other will be deposited in the archives of the Food and Agriculture Organization of the United Nations.

Trygve LIE
Secretary-General of the United Nations

John Boyd ORR
*Director-General of the Food and Agriculture Organization
of the United Nations*

AGREEMENT BETWEEN THE UNITED NATIONS AND THE FOOD AND AGRICULTURE ORGANIZATION OF THE UNITED NATIONS

Articles 57 of the Charter of the United Nations provides that specialized agencies, established by inter-governmental agreement and having wide international responsibilities as defined in their basic instruments in economic, social, cultural, educational, health and related fields shall be brought into relationship with the United Nations.

Article XIII of the Constitution of the Food and Agriculture Organization of the United Nations provides that the Organization shall constitute a part of any general international organization to which may be entrusted the co-ordination of the activities of international organizations with specialized responsibilities.

Therefore, the United Nations and the Organization agree as follows:

Article I

The United Nations recognizes the Food and Agriculture Organization of the United Nations as a specialized agency and as being responsible for taking such action as may be appropriate under its basic instrument for the accomplishment of the purposes set forth therein.

Article II

RECIPROCAL REPRESENTATION

1. Representatives of the United Nations shall be invited to attend the meetings of the Conference of the Food and Agriculture Organization of the United Nations and its committees, the Executive Committee, and such general, regional or other special meetings as the Organization may convene, and to participate, without vote, in the deliberations of these bodies.

2. Representatives of the Food and Agriculture Organization of the United Nations shall be invited to attend meetings of the Economic and Social Council of the United Nations (hereinafter called the Council) and of its commissions and committees and to participate, without vote, in the deliberations of these bodies with respect to items on their agenda relating to matters within the scope of its activities.

3. Representatives of the Food and Agriculture Organization of the United Nations shall be invited to attend meetings of the General Assembly for purposes of consultation on matters within the scope of its activities.

4. Representatives of the Food and Agriculture Organization of the United Nations shall be invited to attend meetings of the main committees of the General Assembly when matters within the scope of its activities are under discussion and to participate, without vote, in such discussions.

5. Representatives of the Food and Agriculture Organization of the United Nations shall be invited to attend the meetings of the Trusteeship Council and to participate, without vote, in the deliberations thereof with respect to items on the agenda relating to matters within the scope of its activities.

6. Written statements of the Food and Agriculture Organization of the United Nations shall be distributed by the Secretariat of the United Nations to all Members of the General Assembly, the Council and its commissions, and the Trusteeship Council as appropriate.

Article III

PROPOSAL OF AGENDA ITEMS

Subject to such preliminary consultation as may be necessary, the Food and Agriculture Organization of the United Nations shall include on the agenda of the Conference or Executive Committee items proposed to it by the United Nations. Similarly, the Council and its commissions and the Trusteeship Council shall include on their agenda items proposed by the Conference or Executive Committee of the Organization.

Article IV

RECOMMENDATIONS OF THE UNITED NATIONS

1. The Food and Agriculture Organization of the United Nations, having regard to the obligation of the United Nations to promote the objectives set forth in Article 55 of the Charter and the function and power of the Council, under Article 62 of the Charter, to make or initiate studies and reports with respect to international, economic, social, cultural, educational, health and related matters and to make recommendations concerning these matters to the specialized agencies concerned, and having regard also to the responsibility of the United Nations, under Articles 58 and 63 of the Charter, to make recommendations for the co-ordination of the policies and activities

of such specialized agencies, agrees to arrange for the submission, as soon as possible, to the appropriate organ of the Organization, of all formal recommendations which the United Nations may make to it.

2. The Food and Agriculture Organization of the United Nations agrees to enter into consultation with the United Nations upon request with respect to such recommendations, and in due course to report to the United Nations on the action taken by the Organization or by its members to give effect to such recommendations, or on the other results of their consideration.

3. The Food and Agriculture Organization of the United Nations affirms its intention of co-operating in whatever further measures may be necessary to make co-ordination of the activities of specialized agencies and those of the United Nations fully effective. In particular, it agrees to participate in and to co-operate with any body or bodies which the Council may establish for the purpose of facilitating such co-ordination and to furnish such information as may be required for the carrying out of this purpose.

Article V

EXCHANGE OF INFORMATION AND DOCUMENTS

1. Subject to such arrangements as may be necessary for the safeguarding of confidential material, the fullest and promptest exchange of information and documents shall be made between the United Nations and the Food and Agriculture Organization of the United Nations.

2. Without prejuduce to the generality of the provisions of paragraph 1:

(a) The Food and Agriculture Organization of the United Nations agrees to transmit to the United Nations regular reports on the activities of the Organization;

(b) The Food and Agriculture Organization of the United Nations agrees to comply to the fullest extent practicable with any request which the United Nations may make for the furnishing of special reports, studies, or information, subject to the conditions set forth in article XV;

(c) The Secretary-General shall, upon request, consult with the Director-General regarding the provision to the Food and Agriculture Organization of the United Nations of such information as may be of special interest to the Organization.

Article VI

ASSISTANCE TO THE SECURITY COUNCIL

The Food and Agriculture Organization of the United Nations agrees to cooperate with the Economic and Social Council in furnishing such information and rendering such assistance to the Security Council as that Council may request, including assistance in carrying out decisions of the Security Council for the maintenance or restoration of international peace and security.

Article VII

ASSISTANCE TO THE TRUSTEESHIP COUNCIL

The Food and Agriculture Organization of the United Nations agrees to co-operate with the Trusteeship Council in the carrying out of its functions and in particular agrees that it will, to the greatest extent possible, render such assistance as the Trusteeship Council may request in regard to matters with which the Organization is concerned.

Article VIII

NON-SELF-GOVERNING TERRITORIES

The Food and Agriculture Organization of the United Nations agrees to cooperate with the United Nations in giving effect to the principles and obligations set forth in Chapter XI of the Charter with regard to matters affecting the well-being and development of the peoples of Non-Self-Governing Territories.

Article IX

RELATIONS WITH THE INTERNATIONAL COURT OF JUSTICE

1. The Food and Agriculture Organization of the United Nations agrees to furnish any information which may be requested by the International Court of Justice in pursuance of Article 34 of the Statute of the Court.

2. The General Assembly authorizes the Food and Agriculture Organization of the United Nations to request advisory opinions of the International Court of Justice on legal questions arising within the scope of its activities other than questions concerning the mutual relationships of the Organization and the United Nations or other specialized agencies.

3. Such request may be addressed to the Court by the Conference or by the Executive Committee acting in pursuance of an authorization by the Conference.

4. When requesting the International Court of Justice to give an advisory opinion the Food and Agriculture Organization of the United Nations shall inform the Economic and Social Council of the request.

Article X

HEADQUARTERS AND REGIONAL OFFICES

1. The permanent headquarters of the Food and Agriculture Organization of the United Nations shall be situated at the permanent seat of the United Nations subject to:

(a) The permanent headquarters of the United Nations being situated at a place where the Food and Agriculture Organization of the United Nations can effectively and economically discharge its duties and maintain effective liaison with those specialized agencies with which it is particularly concerned;

(b) Satisfactory arrangements being made in a subsequent agreement between the Food and Agriculture Organization of the United Nations and the United Nations regarding the provision of a site and necessary facilities for the establishment of such headquarters.

The United Nations shall provide the Food and Agriculture Organization of the United Nations with appropriate assistance in the establishment of the permanent headquarters of the Organization at the permanent seat of the United Nations.

2. Any regional or branch offices which the Food and Agriculture Organization of the United Nations may establish shall, so far as practicable, be closely associated with such regional or branch offices as the United Nations may establish.

Article XI

PERSONNEL ARRANGEMENTS

1. The United Nations and the Food and Agriculture Organization of the United Nations recognize that the eventual development of a single unified international civil service is desirable from the standpoint of effective administrative co-ordination, and

with this end in view agree to develop common personnel standards, methods and arrangements designed to avoid serious discrepancies in terms and conditions of employment, to avoid competition in recruitment of personnel, and to facilitate interchange of personnel in order to obtain the maximum benefit from their services.

2. The United Nations and the Food and Agriculture Organization of the United Nations agree to co-operate to the fullest extent possible in achieving these ends and in particular they agree to:

(a) Consult together concerning the establishment of an International Civil Service Commission to advise on the means by which common standards of recruitment in the secretariats of the United Nations and of the specialized agencies may be ensured;

(b) Consult together concerning other matters relating to the employment of their officers and staff, including conditions of service, duration of appointments, classification, salary scales and allowances, retirement and pension rights and staff regulations and rules with a view to securing as much uniformity in these matters as shall be found practicable;

(c) Co-operate in the interchange of personnel when desirable on a temporary or permanent basis, making due provision for the retention of seniority and pension rights;

(d) Co-operate in the establishment and operation of suitable machinery for the settlement of disputes arising in connexion with the employment of personnel and related matters.

Article XII

STATISTICAL SERVICES

1. The United Nations and the Food and Agriculture Organization of the United Nations agree to strive for maximum co-operation, the elimination of all undesirable duplication between them, and the most efficient use of their technical personnel in their respective collection, analysis, publication and dissemination of statistical information. They agree to combine their efforts to secure the greatest possible usefulness and utilization of statistical information and to minimize the burdens placed upon national governments and other organizations from which such information may be collected.

2. The Food and Agriculture Organization of the United Nations recognizes the United Nations as the central agency for the collection, analysis, publication, standardization and improvement of statistics serving the general purposes of international organizations.

3. The United Nations recognizes the Food and Agriculture Organization of the United Nations as the appropriate agency for the collection, analysis, publication, standardization and improvement of statistics within its special sphere, without prejudice to the right of the United Nations to concern itself with such statistics so far as they may be essential for its own purposes or for the improvement of statistics throughout the world.

4. The United Nations shall in consultation with the specialized agencies develop administrative instruments and procedures through which effective statistical co-operation may be secured between the United Nations and the agencies brought into relationship with it.

5. It is recognized as desirable that the collection of statistical information should not be duplicated by the United Nations or any of the specialized agencies whenever it is practicable for any of them to utilize information or materials which another may have available.

6. In order to build up a central collection of statistical information for general use, it is agreed that data supplied to the Food and Agriculture Organization of the United Nations for incorporation in its basic statistical series or special report should, so far as practicable, be made available to the United Nations.

Article XIII

ADMINISTRATIVE AND TECHNICAL SERVICES

1. The United Nations and the Food and Agriculture Organization of the United Nations recognize the desirability, in the interest of administrative and technical uniformity and of the most efficient use of personnel and resources, of avoiding, whenever possible, the establishment and operation of competitive or overlapping facilities and services among the United Nations and the specialized agencies.

2. Accordingly, the United Nations and the Food and Agriculture Organization of the United Nations agree to consult together concerning the establishment and use of common administrative and technical services and facilities in addition to those referred to in articles XI, XII and XIV, in so far as the establishment and use of such services may from time to time be found practicable and appropriate.

3. Arrangements shall be made between the United Nations and the Food and Agriculture Organization of the United Nations in regard to the registration and deposit of official documents.

Article XIV

BUDGETARY AND FINANCIAL ARRANGEMENTS

1. The Food and Agriculture Organization of the United Nations recognizes the desirability of establishing close budgetary and financial relationships with the United Nations in order that the administrative operations of the United Nations and of the specialized agencies shall be carried out in the most efficient and economical manner possible, and that the maximum measure of co-ordination and uniformity with respect to these operations shall be secured.

2. The United Nations and the Food and Agriculture Organization of the United Nations agree to co-operate to the fullest extent possible in achieving these ends and, in particular, shall consult together concerning appropriate arrangements for the inclusion of the budget of the Organization within a general budget of the United Nations. Such arrangements shall be defined in a supplementary agreement between the two organizations.

3. Pending the conclusion of such agreement, the following arrangements shall govern budgetary and financial relationships between the Food and Agriculture Organization of the United Nations and the United Nations:

(a) The Secretary-General and the Director-General shall arrange for consultation in connexion with the preparation of the budget of the Food and Agriculture Organization of the United Nations;

(b) The Food and Agriculture Organization of the United Nations agrees to transmit its proposed budget to the United Nations annually at the same time as such budget is transmitted to its members. The General Assembly shall examine the budget or proposed budget of the Organization and may make such recommendations as it may consider necessary;

(c) Representatives of the Food and Agriculture Organization of the United Nations shall be entitled to participate, without vote, in the deliberations of the General Assembly or any committee thereof at all times when the budget of the Food and Agriculture Organization of the United Nations or general administrative or financial questions affecting the Organization are under consideration;

(d) The United Nations may undertake the collection of contributions from those members of the Food and Agriculture Organization of the United Nations which are also Members of the United Nations in accordance with such arrangements as may be defined by a later agreement between the United Nations and the Organization;

(e) The United Nations shall, upon its own initiative or upon the request of the Food and Agriculture Organization of the United Nations, arrange for studies to be undertaken concerning other financial and fiscal questions of interest to the Organization and to other specialized agencies with a view to the provision of common services and the securing of uniformity in such matters;

(f) The Food and Agriculture Organization of the United Nations agrees to conform, as far as may be practicable, to standard practices and forms recommended by the United Nations.

Article XV

FINANCING OF SPECIAL SERVICES

1. In the event of the Food and Agriculture Organization of the United Nations being faced with the necessity of incurring substantial extra expense as a result of any request which the United Nations may make for special reports, studies or assistance in accordance with articles V, VII, VII, or with other provisions of this agreement, consultation shall take place with a view to determining the most equitable manner in which such expense shall be borne.

2. Consultation between the United Nations and the Food and Agriculture Organization of the United Nations shall similarly take place with a view to making such arrangements as may be found equitable for covering the cost of central administrative, technical or fiscal services or facilities or other special assistance provided by the United Nations.

*Article XVI**

INTER-AGENCY AGREEMENTS

The Food and Agriculture Organization of the United Nations agrees to inform the Council of the nature and scope of any formal agreement between the Organization and any other specialized agency, inter-governmental organization or non-governmental organization and in particular agrees to inform the Council before any such agreement concluded.

*Article XVII**

LIAISON

1. The United Nations and the Food and Agriculture Organization of the United Nations agree to the foregoing provisions in the belief that they will contribute to the maintenance of effective liaison between the two organizations. They affirm their intention of taking whatever further measure may be necessary to make this liaison fully effective.

2. The liaison arrangements provided for in the foregoing articles of this agreement shall apply as far as appropriate to the relations between such branch or regional offices as may be established by the two organizations as well as between their central machinery.

*Article XVIII**

IMPLEMENTATION OF THE AGREEMENT

The Secretary-General and the Director-General may enter into such supplementary arrangements for the implementation of this Agreement as may be found desirable in the light of the operating experience of the two organizations.

---

*These articles should be re-numbered in accordance with Article 11 of the supplementary agreement.

Article XIX*

REVISION

This Agreement shall be subject to revision by agreement between the United Nations and the Food and Agriculture Organization of the United Nations.

Article XX*

ENTRY INTO FORCE

This Agreement shall come into force on its approval by the General Assembly of the United Nations and the Conference of the Food and Agriculture Organization of the United Nations.

SUPPLEMENTARY AGREEMENT TO THE AGREEMENT BETWEEN THE UNITED NATIONS AND THE FOOD AND AGRICULTURE ORGANIZATION OF THE UNITED NATIONS.

Whereas the Secretary-General of the United Nations has been requested by resolution 136 (VI) of the Economic and Social Council adopted on 25 February 1948 to conclude with any specialized agency which may so desire, a supplementary agreement to extend to the officials of that agency the provisions of article VII of the Convention on the Privileges and Immunities of the United Nations and to submit such supplementary agreement to the General Assembly for approval; and

Whereas the Food and Agriculture Organization of the United Nations is desirous of entering into such supplementary agreement to the agreement between the United Nations and the Food and Agriculture Organization of the United Nations entered into under Article 63 of the Charter;

It is hereby agreed as follows:

Article I

The following provision shall be added to the agreement between the United Nations and the Food and Agriculture Organization of the United Nations:

"The officials of the Food and Agriculture Organization of the United Nations shall have the right to use the *laissez-passer* of the United Nations in accordance with special arrangements to be negotiated between the Secretary-General of the United Nations and the Director-General of the Food and Agriculture Organization of the United Nations."

Article II

The above provision shall be inserted as article XVI of the agreement aforesaid, and articles XVI, XVII, XVIII, XIX and XX of that agreement shall be renumbered so as to become articles XVII, XVIII, XIX, XX and XXI respectively.

Article III

This agreement shall come into force on its approval by the General Assembly of the United Nations and the Conference of the Food and Agriculture Organization of the United Nations.

IN FAITH WHEREOF we have appended our signatures to two original copies of the present agreement, the text of which is done in duplicate in the English and French languages both equally authentic.

For the United Nations:

14 July 1948

(Signed) Trygve LIE
Secretary-General

For the Food and Agriculture Organization of the United Nations:

21 July 1948

(Signed) Norris E. DODD
Director-General

3. AGREEMENT BETWEEN THE UNITED NATIONS AND THE UNITED NATIONS EDUCATIONAL, SCIENTIFIC AND CULTURAL ORGANIZATION APPROVED BY THE GENERAL ASSEMBLY ON DECEMBER 14, 1946

PROTOCOL CONCERNING THE ENTRY INTO FORCE OF THE AGREEMENT BETWEEN THE UNITED NATIONS AND THE UNITED NATIONS EDUCATIONAL, SCIENTIFIC AND CULTURAL ORGANIZATION

Article 57 of the Charter of the United Nations provides that specialized agencies established by inter-governmental agreement and having wide international responsibilities as defined in their basic instruments in economic, social, cultural, educational, health and related fields shall be brought into relationship with the United Nations. Article 63 of the Charter provides that the Economic and Social Council may enter into agreements with any of the agencies referred to in Article 57, defining the terms on which the agency concerned shall be brought into relationship with the United Nations, and specifies that such agreements shall be subject to approval by the General Assembly.

Article X of the Constitution of the United Nations Educational, Scientific and Cultural Organization provides that the Organization shall be brought into relation with the United Nations. This relationship shall be effected through an agreement with the United Nations under Article 63 of the Charter.

The Economic and Social Council, during its first session in January-February 1946, adopted a resolution establishing a Committee of the Council on Negotiations with Specialized Agencies. This Committee was directed to enter into negotiations as early as possible with the United Nations Educational, Scientific and Cultural Organization.

The Executive Committee of the Preparatory-Commission of the United Nations Educatinal, Scientific and Cultural Organization agreed at its meeting on London on 19 March 1946 to appoint four representatives of the Executive Committee as a Delegation to negotiate an Agreement bringing the United Nations Educational, Scientific and Cultural Organization into relationship with the United Nations.

Negotiations between the Committee on Negotiations with Specialized Agencies of the Economic and Social Council and the Negotiating Delegation of the United Nations Educational, Scientific and Cultural Organization took place in New York on 3 June 1946 and resulted in an Agreement. This Agreement was signed on 4 June 1946 by Sir A. Ramaswami Mudaliar, President of the Economic and Social Council and Chairman of the Committee on Negotiations with Specialized Agencies, and Mr. Roger Seydoux, Member of the Executive Committee and Chairman of the Negotiating Delegation of the Preparatory Commission of the United Nations Educational, Scientific and Cultural Organization.

On 21 June 1946, the Economic and Social Council, during its second session, unanimously recommended the Agreement between the United Nations and the United Nations Educational, Scientific and Cultural Organization to the General Assembly for its approval. On 5 July 1946 the Preparatory Commission of the United Nations Educational, Scientific and Cultural Organization recommended the Agreement to the General

Conference of the United Nations Educational, Scientific and Cultural Organization for its approval.

On 3 October 1946, the Economic and Social Council, during its third session, recommended to the General Assembly that it authorize the Secretary-General to offer to the United Nations Educational, Scientific and Cultural Organization to replace Article XI of the Agreement with that Organization, which deals with relations with the International Court of Justice, by an article which will extend to the United Nations Educational, Scientific and Cultural Organization the same procedure in this respect as is specified in the Agreements with the other specialized agencies. This recommendation was accepted by both the General Assembly of the United Nations and the General Conference of the United Nations Educational, Scientific and Cultural Organization, and Article XI of the Agreement was revised accordingly.

Article XXII of the Agreement provides that it shall come into force on its approval by the General Assembly of the United Nations and the General Conference of the United Nations Educational, Scientific and Cultural Organization.

The Agreement as a whole was approved by the General Assembly of the United Nations on 14 December 1946 and by the General Conference of the United Nations Educational, Scientific and Cultural Organization on 6 December 1946.

The Agreement accordingly came into force on 14 December 1946.

A copy of the authentic text of the Agreement is attached hereto.

IN FAITH WHEREOF we have appended our signatures this third day of February, one thousand nine hundred and forty-seven, to two original copies of the present Protocol, the text of which consists of versions in the English and French languages which are equally authentic. One of the original copies will be filed and recorded with the Secretariat of the United Nations and the other will be deposited in the archives of the United Nations Educational, Scientific and Cultural Organization.

Trygve LIE
Secretary-General of the United Nations

Julian HUXLEY
Director-General of the United Nations Educational, Scientific and
Cultural Organization

AGREEMENT BETWEEN THE UNITED NATIONS AND THE UNITED NATIONS EDUCATIONAL, SCIENTIFIC AND CULTURAL ORGANIZATION

1. Article 57 of the Charter of the United Nations provides that specialized agencies, established by inter-governmental agreement and having wide international responsibilities as defined in their basic instruments in economic, social, cultural, educational, health, and related fields, shall be brought into relationship with the United Nations.

2. Articles X and IV, paragraph B, sub-paragraph 5, of the constitution establishing the United Nations Educational, Scientific and Cultural Organization provide that this Organization shall be brought into relation with the United Nations as soon as practicable, as one of the specialized agencies referred to in Article 57 of the Charter of the United Nations, with the function of advising the United Nations on the educational, scientific and cultural aspects of matters of concern to the latter.

Therefore the United Nations and the United Nations Educational, Scientific and Cultural Organization agree as follows:

Article I

The United Nations recognizes the United Nations Educational, Scientific and Cultural Organization (UNESCO) as a specialized agency responsible for taking such action as may be appropriate under its basic instrument for the accomplishment of the purposes set forth therein.

Article II

ADMISSION OF STATES NOT MEMBERS OF THE UNITED NATIONS

Applications submitted by States not members of the United Nations for admission to the United Nations Educational, Scientific and Cultural Organization shall be immediately transmitted by the secretariat of the Organization to the Economic and Social Council of the United Nations (hereinafter called the Council). The Council may recommend the rejection of such applications and any such recommendations shall be accepted by the Organization. If, within six months of the receipt of an application by the Council, no such recommendation has been made, the application shall be dealt with according to article II, paragraph 2, of the constitution of the Organization.

Article III

RECIPROCAL REPRESENTATION

1. Representatives of the United Nations shall be invited to attend the meetings of the General Conference of the United Nations Educational, Scientific and Cultural Organization and its committees, the Executive Board and its committees, and such general, regional or other special meetings as the Organization may convene, and to participate, without vote, in the deliberations of these bodies.

2. Representatives of the United Nations Educational, Scientific and Cultural Organization shall be invited to attend meetings of the Economic and Social Council and of its commissions and committees and to participate, without vote, in the deliberations of these bodies with respect to items on their agenda relating to educational scientific and cultural matters.

3. Representatives of the United Nations Educational, Scientific and Cultural Organization shall be invited to attend meetings of the General Assembly of the United Nations for the purposes of consultation on educational, scientific and cultural matters.

4. Representatives of the United Nations Educational, Scientific and Cultural Organization shall be invited to attend meetings of the main committees of the General Assembly when educational, scientific or cultural matters are under discussion, and to participate, without vote, in such discussions.

5. Representatives of the United Nations Educational, Scientific and Cultural Organization shall be invited to attend the meetings of the Trusteeship Council of the United Nations and to participate, without vote, in the deliberations thereof, with respect to items on the agenda relating to educational, scientific and cultural matters.

6. Written statements of the United Nations Educational, Scientific and Cultural Organization shall be distributed by the Secretariat of the United Nations to all Members of the General Assembly, the Council and its commissions, and the Trusteeship Council as appropriate.

Article IV

PROPOSAL OF AGENDA ITEMS

Subject to such preliminary consultation as may be necessary, the United Nations Educational, Scientific and Cultural Organization shall include on the agenda of the General Conference or Executive Board items proposed to it by the United Nations.

Similarly, the Council and its commissions and the Trusteeship Council shall include on their agenda items proposed by the General Conference or Executive Board of the Organization.

Article V

RECOMMENDATIONS OF THE UNITED NATIONS

1. The United Nations Educational, Scientific and Cultural Organization, having regard to the obligation of the United Nations to promote the objectives set forth in Article 55 of the Charter and the function and power of the Council, under Article 62 of the Charter, to make or initiate studies and reports with respect to international economic, social, cultural, educational, health and related matters and to make recommendations concerning these matters to the specialized agencies concerned, and having regard also to the responsibility of the United Nations, under Articles 58 and 63 of the Charter, to make recommendations for the co-ordination of the policies and activities of such specialized agencies, agrees to arrange for the submission, as soon as possible, to the appropriate organ of the Organization, of all formal recommendations which the United Nations may make to it.

2. The United Nations Educational, Scientific and Cultural Organization agrees to enter into consultation with the United Nations upon request with respect to such recommendations, and in due course to report to the United Nations on the action taken by the Organization or by its members to give effect to such recommendations, or on the other results of their consideration.

3. The United Nations Educational, Scientific and Cultural Organization affirms its intention of co-operating in whatever further measures may be necessary to make co-ordination of the activities of specialized agencies and those of the United Nations, fully effective. In particular, it agrees to participate in, and to co-operate with, any body or bodies which the Council may establish for the purpose of facilitating such co-ordination and to furnish such information as may be required for the carrying out of this purpose.

Article VI

EXCHANGE OF INFORMATION AND DOCUMENTS

1. Subject to such arrangements as may be necessary for the safeguarding of confidential material, the fullest and promptest exchange of information and documents shall be made between the United Nations and the United Nations Educational, Scientific and Cultural Organization.

2. Without prejudice to the generality of the provisions of paragraph 1:

(a) The United Nations Educational, Scientific and Cultural Organization agrees to transmit to the United Nations regular reports on the activities of the Organization;

(b) The United Nations Educational, Scientific and Cultural Organization agrees to comply to the fullest extent practicable with any request which the United Nations may make for the furnishing of special reports, studies or information, subject to the conditions set forth in article XVII;

(c) The Secretary-General shall, upon request, consult with the Director-General regarding the provision to the United Nations Educational, Scientific and Cultural Organization of such information as may be of special interest to the Organization.

Article VII

PUBLIC INFORMATION

Having regard to the functions of the United Nations Educational, Scientific and Cultural Organization, as defined in article I, paragraphs 2 *(a)* and *(c)*, of its constitution, to collaborate in the work of advancing the mutual knowledge and understanding of peoples through all means of mass communication, and with a view to co-ordinating the activities of the Organization in this field with the operations of the information services of the United Nations, a subsidiary agreement regarding these matters shall be concluded as soon as possible after the coming into force of the present agreement.

Article VIII

ASSISTANCE TO THE SECURITY COUNCIL

The United Nations Educational, Scientific and Cultural Organization agrees to co-operate with the Economic and Social Council in furnishing such information and rendering such assistance to the Security Council as that Council may request, including assistance in carrying out decisions of the Security Council for the maintenance or restoration of international peace and security.

Article IX

ASSISTANCE TO THE TRUSTEESHIP COUNCIL

The United Nations Educational, Scientific and Cultural Organization agrees to co-operate with the Trusteeship Council in the carrying out of its functions and in particular agrees that it will, to the greatest extent possible, render such assistance as the Trusteeship Council may request in regard to matters with which the Organization is concerned.

Article X

NON-SELF-GOVERNING TERRITORIES

The United Nations Educational, Scientific and Cultural Organization agrees to co-operate with the United Nations in giving effect to the principles and obligations set forth in Chapter XI of the Charter with regard to matters affecting the well-being and development of the peoples of Non-Self-Governing Territories.

Article XI

RELATIONS WITH THE INTERNATIONAL COURT OF JUSTICE

1. The United Nations Educational, Scientific and Cultural Organization agrees to furnish any information which may be requested by the International Court of Justice in pursuance of Article 34 of the Statute of the Court.
2. The General Assembly authorized the United Nations Educational, Scientific and Cultural Organization to request advisory opinions of the International Court of Justice on legal questions arising within the scope of its activities other than questions concerning the mutual relationships of the Organization and the United Nations or other specialized agencies.
3. Such request may be addressed to the Court by the General Conference or by the Executive Board acting in pursuance of an authorization by the Conference.
4. When requesting the International Court of Justice to give an advisory opinion the United Nations Educational, Scientific and Cultural Organization shall inform the Economic and Social Council of the request.

Article XII

REGIONAL OFFICES

Any regional or branch offices which the United Nations Educational, Scientific and Cultural Organization may establish shall, so far as practicable, be closely associated with such regional or branch offices as the United Nations may establish.

Article XIII

PERSONNEL ARRANGEMENTS

1. The United Nations and the United Nations Educational, Scientific and Cultural Organization recognize that the eventual development of a single unified international civil service is desirable from the standpoint of effective administrative co-ordination, and with this end in view agree to develop common personnel standards, methods and arrangements designed to avoid serious discrepancies in terms and conditions of employment, to avoid competition in recruitment of personnel, and to facilitate interchange of personnel in order to obtain the maximum benefit from their services.

2. The United Nations and the United Nations Educational, Scientific and Cultural Organization agree to co-operate to the fullest extent possible in achieving these ends and in particular they agree to:

(a) Consult together concerning the establishment of an international Civil Service Commission to advise on the means by which common standards of recruitment in the secretariats of the United Nations and of the specialized agencies may be ensured;

(b) Consult together concerning other matters relating to the employment of their officers and staff, including conditions of service, duration of appointments, classification, salary scales and allowances, retirement and pension rights and staff regulations and rules with a view to securing as much uniformity in these matters as shall be found practicable;

(c) Co-operate in the interchange of personnel when desirable on a temporary or permanent basis, making due provision for the retention of seniority and pension rights;

(d) Co-operate in the establishment and operation of suitable machinery for the settlement of disputes arising in connexion with the employment of personnel and related matters.

Article XIV*

STATISTICAL SERVICES

1. The United Nations and the United Nations Educational, Scientific and Cultural Organization agree to strive for maximum co-operation, the elimination of all undesirable duplication between them, and the most efficient use of their technical personnel in their respective collection, analysis, publication and dissemination of statistical information. They agree to combine their efforts to secure the greatest possible usefulness and utilization of statistical information and to minimize the burdens placed upon national governments and other organizations from which such information may be collected.

---

*These articles should be re-numbered in accordance with Article 11 of the supplementary agreement.

2. The United Nations Educational, Scientific and Cultural Organization recognizes the United Nations as the central agency for the collection, analysis, publication, standardization and improvement of statistics serving the general purposes of international organizations.

3. The United Nations recognizes the United Nations Educational, Scientific and Cultural Organization as the appropriate agency for the collection, analysis, publication, standardization and improvement of statistics within its special sphere, without prejudice to the right of the United Nations to concern itself with such statistics so far as they may be essential for its own purposes or for the improvement of statistics throughout the world.

4. The United Nations shall develop administrative instruments and procedures through which effective statistical co-operation may be secured between the United Nations and the agencies brought into relationship with it.

5. It is recognized as desirable that the collection of statistical information should not be duplicated by the United Nations or any of the specialized agencies whenever it is practicable for any of them to utilize information or materials which another may have available.

6. In order to build up a central collection of statistical information for general use, it is agreed that data supplied to the United Nations Educational, Scientific and Cultural Organization for incorporation in its basic statistical series or special reports should, so far as practicable, be made available to the United Nations.

Article XV*

ADMINISTRATIVE AND TECHNICAL SERVICES

1. The United Nations and the United Nations Educational, Scientific and Cultural Organization recognize the desirability, in the interest of administrative and technical uniformity and of the most efficient use of personnel and resources, of avoiding, whenever possible, the establishment and operation of competitive or overlapping facilities and services among the United Nations and the specialized agencies.

2. Accordingly, the United Nations and the United Nations Educational, Scientific and Cultural Organization agree to consult together concerning the establishment and use of common administrative and technical services and facilities in addition to those referred to in articles XIII, XIV and XVI, in so far as the establishment and use of such services may from time to time be found practicable and appropriate.

3. Arrangements shall be made between the United Nations Educational, Scientific and Cultural Organization in regard to the registration and deposit of official documents.

Article XVI*

BUDGETARY AND FINANCIAL ARRANGEMENTS

1. The United Nations Educational, Scientific and Cultural Organization recognizes the desirability of establishing close budgetary and financial relationships with the United Nations in order that the administrative operations of the United Nations and of the specialized agencies shall be carried out in the most efficient and economical manner possible, and that the maximum measure of co-ordination and uniformity with respect to these operations shall be secured.

2. The United Nations and the United Nations Educational, Scientific and Cultural Organization agree to co-operate to the fullest extent possible in achieving these ends and, in particular, shall consult together concerning appropriate arrangements for the inclusion of the budget of the Organization within a general budget of the United Na-

tions. Such arrangements shall be defined in a supplementary agreement between the two organizations.

3. Pending the conclusion of such agreement, the following arrangements shall govern budgetary and financial relationships between the United Nations and the United Nations Educaional, Scientific and Cultural Organization:

(a) In the preparation of the budget of the United Nations Educational, Scientific and Cultural Organization, the Organization shall consult with the United Nations;

(b) The United Nations Educational, Scientific and Cultural Organization agrees to transmit its proposed budget to the United Nations annually at the same time as such budget is transmitted to its members. The General Assembly shall examine the budget or proposed budget of the Organization and may make recommendations to it concerning any item or items contained therein;

(c) Representatives of the United Nations Educational, Scientific and Cultural Organization shall be entitled to participate, without vote, in the deliberations of the General Assembly or any committee thereof at all times when the budget of the Organization or general administrative financial questions affecting the Organization are under consideration;

(d) The United Nations may undertake the collection of contributions from those members of the United Nations Educational, Scientific and Cultural Organization which are also Members of the United Nations in accordance with such arrangements as may be defined by a later agreement between the United Nations and the Organization;

(e) The United Nations shall, upon its own initiative or upon the request of the United Nations Educational, Scientific and Cultural Organization, arrange for studies to be undertaken concerning other financial and fiscal questions of interest to the Organization and to other specialized agencies with a view to the provision of common services and the securing of uniformity in such matters;

(f) The United Nations Educational, Scientific and Cultural Organization agrees to conform, as far as may be practicable, to standard practices and forms recommended by the United Nations.

Article XVII*

FINANCING OF SPECIAL SERVICES

1. In the event of the United Nations Educational, Scientific and Cultural Organization being faced with the necessity of incurring substantial extra expense as a result of any request which the United Nations may make for special reports, studies or assistance in accordance with articles VII, VIII, or IX or with other provisions of this agreement, consultation shall take place with a view to determining the most equitable manner in which such expense shall be borne.

2. Consultation between the United Nations and the United Nations Educational, Scientific and Cultural Organization shall similarly take place with a view to making such arrangements as may be found equitable for covering the costs of central administrative, technical or fiscal services or facilities or other special assistance provided by the United Nations.

Article XVIII*

INTER-AGENCY AGREEMENTS

The United Nations Educational, Scientific and Cultural Organization agrees to inform the Council of the nature and scope of any formal agreement between the Organization and any other specialized agency, intergovernmental or non-governmental organization, and in particular agrees to inform the Council before any such agreement is concluded.

Article XIX*

LIAISON

1. The United Nations and the United Nations Educational, Scientific and Cultural Organization agree to the foregoing provisions to the belief that they will contribute to the maintenance of effective liaison between the two organizations. They affirm their intention of taking whatever further measures may be necessary to make this liaison fully effective.

2. The liaison arrangements provided for in the foregoing articles of this agreement shall apply as far as appropriate to the relations between such branch or regional offices as may be established by the two organizations as well as between their central machinery.

Article XX*

IMPLEMENTATION OF THE AGREEMENT

The Secretary-General and the Director-General may enter into such supplementary arrangements for the implementation of this Agreement as may be found desirable in the light of the operating experience of the two organizations.

Article XXI*

REVISION

This Agreement shall be subject to revision by agreement between the United Nations and the United Nations Educational, Scientific and Cultural Organization, and shall be reviewed not later than three years after the Agreement has come into force.

Article XXII*

ENTRY INTO FORCE

This Agreement shall come into force on its approval by the General Assembly of the United Nations and the General Conference of the United Nations Educational, Scientific and Cultural Organization.

SUPPLEMENTARY AGREEMENT TO THE AGREEMENT BETWEEN THE UNITED NATIONS AND THE UNITED NATIONS EDUCATIONAL, SCIENTIFIC AND CULTURAL ORGANIZATION.

Whereas, the Secretary-General of the United Nations has been requested by resolution 136 (VI) of the Economic and Social Council adopted on 25 February 1948 to conclude with any specialized agency which may so desire, a supplementary agreement to extend to the officials of that agency the provisions of article VII of the Convention on the Privileges and Immunities of the United Nations and to submit such supplementary agreement to the General Assembly for approval; and

Whereas the United Nations Educational, Scientific and Cultural Organization is desirous of entering into such supplementary agreement to the agreement between the United Nations and the United Nations Educational, Scientific and Cultural Organization entered into under Article 63 of the Charter;

It is hereby agreed as follows:

Article I

The following provision shall be added to the agreement between the United Nations and the United Nations Educational, Scientific and Cultural Organization:

"The officials of the United Nations Educational, Scientific and Cultural Organization shall have the right to use the *laissez-passer* of the United Nations in accordance with special arrangements to be negotiated between the Secretary-General of the United Nations and the competent authority of the United Nations Educational, Scientific and Cultural Organization."

Article II

The above provision shall be inserted as Article XIV of the agreement aforesaid, and articles XIV, XV, XVI, XVII, XVIII, XIX, XX, XXI and XXII of that agreement shall be renumbered so as to become articles XV, XVI, XVII, XVIII, XIX, XX, XXI, XXII, and XXIII respectively.

Article III

This agreement shall come into force on its approval by the General Assembly of the United Nations and the General Conference of the United Nations Educational, Scientific and Cultural Organization.

IN FAITH WHEREOF we have appended our signature to two original copies of the present agreement, the text of which is done in duplicate in the English and French languages both equally authentic.

For the United Nations:
24 June 1948

(Signed) Trygve LIE
Secretary-General

For the United Nations Educational, Scientific and Cultural Organization:
10 July 1948

(Signed) Julian HUXLEY
Director-General

4. AGREEMENT BETWEEN THE UNITED NATIONS AND THE INTERNATIONAL CIVIL AVIATION ORGANIZATION APPROVED BY THE GENERAL ASSEMBLY ON DECEMBER 14, 1946

PROTOCOL CONCERNING THE ENTRY INTO FORCE OF THE AGREEMENT BETWEEN THE UNITED NATIONS AND THE INTERNATIONAL CIVIL AVIATION ORGANIZATION

Article 57 of the Charter of the United Nations provides that specialized agencies established by inter-governmental agreement and having wide international responsibilities as defined in their basic instruments in economic, social, cultural, educational, health and related fields shall be brought into relationship with the United Nations. Article 63 of the Charter provides that the Economic and Social Council may enter into agreements with any of the agencies referred to in Article 57, defining the terms on which the agency concerned shall be brought into relationship with the United Nations, and specifies that such agreements shall be subject to approval by the General Assembly.

Article 64 of the Convention on International Civil Aviation provides that the International Civil Aviation Organization may, with respect to air matters within its competence directly affecting world security, enter into appropriate arrangements with any general organization set up by the nations of the world to preserve peace. Article 65 of the Convention provides that the Organization may enter into agreements with international bodies for the maintenance of common services, for common arrangements concerning personnel and for the facilitation of its work.

The Economic and Social Council on 21 June 1946 directed its Committee on Negotiations with Specialized Agencies to enter into negotiations with the Provisional International Civil Aviation Organization for the purpose of bringing it into relationship with the United Nations and to submit a report of the negotiations to the third session of the Council, including therein a draft preliminary agreement based on these negotiations.

The Interim Council of the Provisional International Civil Aviation Organization, having been informed of the decision of the Economic and Social Council aforementioned, appointed a committee to enter into negotiations with the Committee on Negotiations with Specialized Agencies to prepare a draft agreement.

Negotiations between the Committee on Negotiations with Specialized Agencies of the Economic and Social Council and the Negotiating Committee of the Interim Council took place at Lake Success on 27 and 28 September 1946 and resulted in a draft agreement between the United Nations and the International Civil Aviation Organization. In this draft agreement a decision regarding relations with the International Court of Justice was deferred pending consideration thereof by the Economic and Social Council.

This draft agreement was signed on 30 September 1946 by Mr. Roland Lebeau, Acting Chairman of the Committee of the Economic and Social Council on Negotiations with Specialized Agencies, and Sir James Cotton, Chairman of the Negotiations Delegation of the Provisional International Civil Aviation Organization. On 3 October 1946 the Economic and Social Council recommended that the Agreement between the

United Nations and the International Civil Aviation Organization be approved by the General Assembly with the insertion in the Agreement of the authorization regarding relations with the International Court of Justice.

The Interim Council of the Provisional International Civil Aviation Organization decided on 29 October 1946 to recommend to the Assembly of the International Civil Aviation Organization the approval of the draft agreement.

The General Assembly of the United Nations decided on 14 December 1946 to approve the Agreement with the International Civil Aviation Organization, provided "that Organization complies with any decision of the General Assembly regarding Franco Spain."

The General Assembly decided to recommend "that the Franco Government of Spain be debarred from membership in international agencies established by or brought into relationship with the United Nations, and from participation in conferences or other activities which may be arranged by the United Nations or by these agencies, until a new and acceptable government is formed in Spain."

On 13 May 1947 the Assembly of the International Civil Aviation Organization approved an agreement between it and the United Nations by a resolution, of which a certified copy is appended to this Protocol as Annex A. On the same date the Assembly of the International Civil Aviation Organization acted to comply with the recommendation contained in the aforesaid resolution of the General Assembly of the United Nations relating to debarment of the Franco Government of Spain from membership in international agencies, a certified copy of which is appended to this Protocol as Annex B.

Article XXII of the Agreement provides that the Agreement shall come into force on its approval by the General Assembly of the United Nations and by the Assembly of the International Civil Aviation Organization. The Agreement accordingly came into force on 13 May 1947. A copy of the authentic text of the Agreement is attached hereto.

IN FAITH WHEREOF we have appended our signatures this first day of October one thousand nine hundred and forty-seven to two original copies of the present Protocol, the text of which consists of versions in the English and French languages, which are equally authentic. One of the original copies will be filed and recorded with the Secretariat of the United Nations, and the other will be deposited in the archives of the International Civil Aviation Organization.

(Signed) Trygve LIE
Secretary-General of the United Nations

(Signed) Edward WARNER
President of the Council of the
International Civil Aviation Organization

ANNEXES TO THE PROTOCOL

Annex A

RESOLUTION ADOPTED BY THE FIRST ASSEMBLY
OF THE INTERNATIONAL CIVIL AVIATION ORGANIZATION

Whereas the Interim Council of PICAO has negotiated a draft agreement of relationship between ICAO and the United Nations in accordance with resolution XXI of the Interim Assembly of PICAO and has submitted this Agreement to the Assembly of ICAO for approval, and

Whereas it is the wish of the Assembly of ICAO to enter into an agreement with the United Nations in the terms submitted by the Interim Council of PICAO;

Now, therefore, the Assembly of ICAO hereby approves the Agreement of relationship with the United Nations and resolves:

(a) To authorize the Council to enter into such supplementary arrangements with the Secretary-General of the United Nations for the implementation of the Agreement, in accordance with article XIX thereof, as may be found desirable in the light of the operating experience of the two Organizations;

(b) To authorize the Council to enter into negotiations with the United Nations for the conclusion of further appropriate arrangements between ICAO and the United Nations with respect to air matters within the competence of ICAO, as provided for in article XX. Such arrangements, however, shall be subject to final approval by the Assembly;

(c) To authorize the President of the Council to sign with the appropriate official of the United Nations a protocol bringing the agreement of relationship between the United Nations and ICAO into force;

(d) To authorize the Council to enter into negotiations with the United Nations for revising the agreement of relationship, as provided for in article XXI thereof. Revisions negotiated by the Council shall be subject to the final approval of the Assembly.

Annex B

RESOLUTION ADOPTED BY THE FIRST ASSEMBLY OF THE
INTERNATIONAL CIVIL AVIATION ORGANIZATION

Whereas the General Assembly of the United Nations has recommended that the Franco Government of Spain be debarred from membership in specialized agencies established by or brought into relationship with the United Nations and from participation in conference or other activities which may be arranged by the United Nations or by these agencies until a new and acceptable government is formed in Spain; and

Whereas the General Assembly, in approving the draft agreement between the United Nations and ICAO, made it a condition of its approval that ICAO comply with any decision of the General Assembly regarding Franco Spain;

Now, therefore, the Assembly of ICAO, wishing to conform with the recommendation of the General Assembly and to comply with the condition of the General Assembly to its approval of the draft agreement between the United Nations and ICAO, hereby approves the following proposed amendment to the Convention on International Civil Aviation, in accordance with article 94 of the Convention:

Article 93 bis

"*(a)* Notwithstanding the provision of articles 91, 92 and 93 above.

"(1) A State whose government the General Assembly of the United Nations has recommended be debarred from membership in international agencies established by or brought into relationship with the United Nations shall automatically cease to be a member of the International Civil Aviation Organization.

"(2) A State which has been expelled from membership in the United Nations shall automatically cease to be a member of the International Civil Aviation Organization unless the General Assembly of the United Nations attaches to its act of expulsion a recommendation to the contrary.

"*(b)* A State which ceases to be a member of the International Civil Aviation Organization as a result of the provisions of paragraph *(a)* above may, after approval by the General Assembly of the United Nations, be readmitted to the International Civil Aviation Organization upon application and upon approval by a majority of the Council.

"*(c)* Members of the Organization which are suspended from the exercise of the rights and privileges of membership in the United Nations shall, upon request of the latter, be suspended from the rights and privileges of membership in this Organization."

AGREEMENT BETWEEN THE UNITED NATIONS AND THE INTERNATIONAL CIVIL AVIATION ORGANIZATION

PREAMBLE

Article 57 of the Charter of the United Nations makes provision for bringing the specialized agencies, established by inter-governmental agreement and having wide international responsibilities as defined in their basic instruments in economic, social, cultural, educational, health and related fields, into relationship with the United Nations.

Article 64 of the Convention on International Civil Aviation provides that the International Civil Aviation Organization may, with respect to air matters within its competence, directly affecting world security, enter into appropriate arrangements with any general organization set up by the nations of the world to preserve peace. Article 65 of the Convention provides that the Organization may enter into agreements with international bodies for the maintenance of common service, for common arrangements concerning personnel and for the facilitation of its work.

Therefore the United Nations and the International Civil Aviation Organization agree as follow:

Article I

The United Nations recognizes the International Civil Aviation Organization as the specialized agency responsible for taking such action as may be appropriate under its basic instrument for the accomplishment of the purposes set forth therein.

Article II

APPLICATIONS FOR MEMBERSHIP BY CERTAIN STATES

Any application submitted to the International Civil Aviation Organization by States other than those provided for in articles 91 and 92 *(a)* of the Convention on International Civil Aviation to become parties to the Convention, shall be immediately transmitted by the secretariat of the Organization to the General Assembly of the United Nations. The General Assembly may recommend the rejection of such application, and any such recommendation shall be accepted by the Organization. If no such recommendation is made by the General Assembly at the first session following receipt of the application, the application shall be decided upon by the Organization in accordance with the procedure established in article 93 of the Convention.

Article III

RECIPROCAL REPRESENTATION

1. Representatives of the United Nations shall be invited to attend the meetings of the Assembly of the International Civil Aviation Organization, the Council of the Organization and their commissions and committees and such general regional or other special meetings as the Organization may convene, and to participate, without vote, in the deliberations of these bodies.

2. Representatives of the International Civil Aviation Organization shall be invited to attend meetings of the Economic and Social Council and of its own commissions and committees and to participate, without vote, in the deliberations of these bodies with respect to items on their agenda relating to civil aviation matters.

3. Representatives of the International Civil Aviation Organization shall be invited to attend meetings of the General Assembly of the United Nations for the purposes of consultation on civil aviation matters.

4. Representatives of the International Civil Aviation Organization shall be invited to attend meetings of the main Committees of the General Assembly when civil aviation matters are under discussion, and to participate, without vote, in such discussions.

5. Representatives of the International Civil Aviation Organization shall be invited to attend meetings of the Trusteeship Council of the United Nations and to participate, without vote, in the deliberations thereof, with respect to items on its agenda relating to civil aviation matters.

6. Written statements submitted by the International Civil Aviation Organization on matters relating to civil aviation shall be distributed as soon as possible by the Secretariat of the United Nations to all members of the principal and subsidiary organs of the United Nations, and their commissions or committees as appropriate. Similarly, written statements of any of the principal or subsidiary organs of the United Nations and their commissions or committees shall be distributed as soon as possible by the secretariat of the Organization to all members of the Assembly or Council of the Organization as appropriate.

Article IV

PROPOSAL OF AGENDA ITEMS

After such preliminary consultation as may be necessary, the International Civil Aviation Organization shall include on the agenda of the Assembly or Council of the Organization items proposed to it by the United Nations. Reciprocally the Economic and Social Council and its commissions, and the Trusteeship Council, shall include on their agenda items proposed by the Assembly or Council of the Organization.

Article V

RECOMMENDATIONS OF THE UNITED NATIONS

1. The International Civil Aviation Organization, having regard to the obligation of the United Nations to promote the objectives set forth in Article 55 of the Charter

and the function and power of the Economic and Social Council, under Article 62 of the Charter, to make or initiate studies and reports with respect to international, economic, social, cultural, educational, health and related matters and to make recommendations concerning these matters to the specialized agencies concerned, and having regard also to the responsibility of the United Nations, under Articles 58 and 63 of the Charter, to make recommendations for the co-ordination of the policies and activities of such specialized agencies, agrees to arrange for the submission, as soon as possible, to its appropriate organ of all formal recommendations which the United Nations may make to it.

2. The International Civil Aviation Organization agrees to enter into consultation with the United Nations upon request, with respect to such recommendations, and in due course to report to the United Nations on the action taken by the Organization or by its members to give effect to such recommendations, or on the other results of their consideration.

3. The International Civil Aviation Organization affirms its intention of co-operating in whatever measures may be necessary to make co-ordination of the activities of specialized agencies and those of the United Nations fully effective. In particular, it agrees to participate in, and to co-operate with any body or bodies which the Economic and Social Council may establish for the purpose of facilitating such co-ordination, and to furnish such information as may be required for the carrying out of this purpose.

Article VI

EXCHANGE OF INFORMATION AND DOCUMENTS

1. Subject to such arrangements as may be necessary for the safeguarding of confidential material, the fullest and promptest exchange of information and documents shall be made between the United Nations and the International Civil Aviation Organization.

2. Without prejudice to the generality of the provisions of paragraph 1:

(a) The International Civil Aviation Organization agrees to transmit to the United Nations regular reports on its activities;

(b) The International Civil Aviation Organization agrees to comply to the fullest extent practicable with any request which the United Nations may make for the furnishing of special reports, studies or information, subject to the condition set forth in article XVI; and

(c) The Secretary-General of the United Nations shall, upon request, consult with the appropriate officer of the Organization with respect to the furnishing to the Organization of such information as may be of special interest to it.

Article VII

ASSISTANCE TO THE SECURITY COUNCIL

The International Civil Aviation Organization agrees to co-operate with the Economic and Social Council in furnishing such information and rendering such assistance to the Security Council as that Council may request, including assistance in carrying out decisions of the Security Council for the maintenance of restoration of international peace and security.

Article VIII

ASSISTANCE TO THE TRUSTEESHIP COUNCIL

The International Civil Aviation Organization agrees to co-operate with the Trusteeship Council in the carrying out of its functions, and in particular agrees that it will to the greatest extent possible render such assistance as the Trusteeship Council may request in regard to matters with which the Organization is concerned.

Article IX

NON-SELF-GOVERNING TERRITORIES

The International Civil Aviation Organization agrees to co-operate with the United Nations in giving effect to the principles and obligations set forth in Chapter XI of the Charter with regard to matters affecting the well-being development of the peoples of Non-Self-Governing Territories.

Article X

RELATIONS WITH THE INTERNATIONAL COURT OF JUSTICE

1. The International Civil Aviation Organization agrees to furnish any information which may be requested by the International Court of Justice in pursuance of Article 34 of the Statute of the Court.

2. The General Assembly of the United Nations authorizes the International Civil Aviation Organization to request advisory opinions of the International Court of Justice on legal questions arising within the scope of its activities other than questions concerning the mutual relationships of the International Civil Aviation Organization and the United Nations or other specialized agencies.

3. Such request may be addressed to the Court by the Assembly or the Council of the International Civil Aviation Organization.

4. When requesting the International Court of Justice to give an advisory opinion, the International Civil Aviation Organization shall inform the Economic and Social Council of the request.

Article XI

HEADQUARTERS AND REGIONAL OFFICES

1. The International Civil Aviation Organization, having regard to the desirability of the headquarters of specialized agencies being situated at the permanent seat of the United Nations and to the advantages that flow from such centralization, agrees to consult the United Nations before making any further decision concerning the location of its permanent headquarters.

2. Having due regard to the special needs of international civil aviation, any regional or branch offices which the International Civil Aviation Organization may establish shall, so far as is practicable, be closely associated with such regional or branch offices as the United Nations may establish.

Article XII

PERSONNEL ARRANGEMENTS

1. The United Nations and the International Civil Aviation Organization recognize that the eventual development of a single unified international civil service is desirable from the standpoint of effective administrative co-ordination, and with this end in view agree to develop common personnel standards, methods and arrangements designed to avoid unjustified differences in terms and conditions of employment, to avoid competition in recruitment of personnel, and to facilitate interchange of personnel in order to obtain the maximum benefit from their services.

2. The United Nations and the International Civil Aviation Organization agree to co-operate to the fullest extent possible in achieving these ends and in particular they agree:

(a) To consult together concerning the establishment of an International Civil Service Commission to advise on the means by which common standards of recruitment in the secretariats of the United Nations and of the specialized agencies may be ensured;

(b) To consult together concerning other matters relating to the employment of their officers and staff, including conditions of service, duration of appointments, classification, salary scales and allowances, retirement and pension rights and staff regulations and rules, with a view to securing as much uniformity in these matters as shall be found practicable;

(c) To co-operate in the interchange of personnel, when desirable, on a temporary or a permanent basis, making due provisions for the retention of seniority and pension rights;

(d) To co-operate in the establishment and operation of suitable machinery for the settlement of disputes arising in connexion with the employment of personnel and related matters.

Article XIII

STATISTICAL SERVICES

1. The United Nations and the International Civil Aviation Organization agree to strive for maximum co-operation, the elimination of all undesirable duplication between them, and the most efficient use of their technical personnel in their respective collection, analysis, publication, standardization, improvement and dissemination of statistical information. They agree to combine their efforts to secure the greatest possible usefulness and utilization of statistical information and to minimize the burdens placed upon national Governments and other organizations from which such information may be collected.

2. The International Civil Aviation Organization recognizes the United Nations as the central agency for the collection, analysis, publication, standardization, improvement and dissemination of statistics serving the general purposes of international organizations.

3. The United Nations recognizes the International Civil Aviation Organization as the central agency responsible for the collection, analysis, publication, standardization, improvement and dissemination of statistics within its special sphere, without prejudice to the rights of the United Nations to concern itself with such statistics so far as they may be essential for its own purposes or for the improvement of statistics throughout the world.

4. The United Nations shall, in consultation with the International Civil Aviation Organization and with the other specialized agencies where appropriate, develop administrative instruments and procedures through which effective statistical cooperation

may be secured between the United Nations and the agencies brought into relationship with it.

5. It is recognized as desirable that the collection of statistical information shall not be duplicated by the United Nations or any of its specialized agencies whenever it is practicable for any of them to utilize information or material which another may have available.

6. In order to build up a central collection of statistical information for general use, it is agreed that data supplied to the International Civil Aviation Organization for incorporation in its basic statistical series or special reports should, so far as practicable, be made available to the United Nations.

7. It is agreed that data supplied to the United Nations for incorporation in its basic statistical series or special reports should, so far as practicable and appropriate, be made available to the International Civil Aviation Organization.

Article XIV

ADMINISTRATIVE AND TECHNICAL SERVICES

1. The United Nations and the International Civil Aviation Organization recognize the desirability, in the interest of administrative and technical uniformity and of the most efficient use of personnel and resources, of avoiding whenever possible the establishment and operation of competitive or overlapping facilities and services among the United Nations and the specialized agencies.

2. Accordingly, the United Nations and the International Civil Aviation Organization agree to consult together concerning the establishment and use of common administrative and technical services and facilities in addition to those referred to in articles XII, XIII and XV, in so far as the establishment and use of such services may from time to time be found practicable and appropriate.

3. Arrangements shall be made between the United Nations and the International Civil Aviation Organization with regard to the registration and deposit of official documents.

Article XV

BUDGETARY AND FINANCIAL ARRANGEMENTS

1. The International Civil Aviation Organization recognizes the desirability of establishing close budgetary and financial relationships with the United Nations in order that the administrative operations of the United Nations and of the specialized agencies shall be carried out in the most efficient and economical manner possible, and that the maximum measure of co-ordination and uniformity with respect to these operations shall be secured.

2. The United Nations and the International Civil Aviation Organization agree to co-operate to the fullest extent possible in achieving these ends, and to consult together concerning the desirability of making appropriate arrangements for the inclusion of the budget of the Organization within a general budget of the United Nations. Any such arrangements which may be made shall be defined in a supplementary agreement between the two Organizations.

3. The Secretary-General of the United Nations and the appropriate officer of the

International Civil Aviation Organization shall arrange for consultation in connexion with the preparation of the budget.

4. The International Civil Aviation Organization agrees to transmit its proposed budget to the United Nations annually at the same time as such budget is transmitted to its members. The General Assembly shall examine the administrative budget or proposed budget of the Organization and may make such recommendations as it may consider necessary.

5. Representatives of the International Civil Aviation Organization shall be entitled to participate, without vote, in the deliberations of the General Assembly or any Committee thereof at all times when the budget of the Organization or general administrative or financial questions affecting the Organization are under consideration.

6. The United Nations may undertake the collection of contributions from those members of the International Civil Aviation Organization which are also Members of the United Nations, in accordance with such arrangements as may be defined by a later agreement between the United Nations and the Organization.

7. The United Nations shall, upon its own initiative or upon the request of the International Civil Aviation Organization, arrange for studies to be undertaken concerning other financial and fiscal questions of interest to the Organization and to other specialized agencies, with a view to the provision of common services and the securing of uniformity in such matters.

8. The International Civil Aviation Organization agrees to conform, as far as may be practicable, to standard practices and forms recommended by the United Nations.

Article XVI

FINANCING OF SPECIAL SERVICES

1. In the event of the International Civil Aviation Organization's being faced with the necessity of incurring substantial extra expense as a result of any request which the United Nations may make for special reports, studies or assistance in accordance with articles VI, VII, VIII, or with other provisions of this Agreement, consultation shall take place with a view to determining the most equitable manner in which such expense shall be borne.

2. Consultation between the United Nations and the International Civil Aviation Organization shall similarly take place with a view to making such arrangements as may be found equitable for covering the cost of central administrative, technical or fiscal services or facilities or other special assistance provided by the United Nations.

*Article XVII**

INTER-AGENCY AGREEMENTS

The International Civil Aviation Organization agrees to inform the Economic and Social Council of the nature and scope of any formal agreement between the Organization and any other specialized agency, inter-governmental or non-governmental organization, and to inform the Economic and Social Council before any such agreement is concluded.

---

*These articles should be re-numbered in accordance with Article II of the supplementary agreement.

Article XVIII*

LIAISON

1. The United Nations and the International Civil Aviation Organization agree to the foregoing provisions in the belief that they will contribute to the maintenance of effective liaison between the two Organizations. They affirm their intention of taking whatever further measure may be necessary to make this liaison fully effective.

2. The liaison arrangements provided for in the foregoing articles of this Agreement shall apply as far as appropriate to the relations between such branch or regional offices as may be established by the two Organizations, as well as between their headquarters.

Article XIX*

IMPLEMENTATION OF THE AGREEMENT

The Secretary-General of the United Nations and the appropriate officer of the International Civil Aviation Organization may enter into such supplementary arrangements for the implementation of this Agreement as may be found desirable, in the light of the operating experience of the two Organizations.

Article XX*

OTHER ARRANGEMENTS

The present Agreement shall not preclude the conclusion of further appropriate arrangements between the International Civil Aviation Organization and the United Nations with respect to air matters within the competence of the Organization directly affecting world security as contemplated in the Convention on International Civil Aviation.

Article XXI*

REVISION

This Agreement shall be subject to revision by agreement between the United Nations and the International Civil Aviation Organization.

Article XXII*

ENTRY INTO FORCE

This Agreement shall come into force on its approval by the General Assembly of the United Nations and the Assembly of the International Civil Aviation Organization.

SUPPLEMENTARY AGREEMENT TO THE AGREEMENT BETWEEN THE UNITED NATIONS AND THE INTERNATIONAL CIVIL AVIATION ORGANIZATION

Whereas the Secretary-General of the United Nations has been requested by resolution 136 (VI) of the Economic and Social Council adopted on 25 February 1948 to conclude with any specialized agency which may so desire, a supplementary agreement to extend to the officials of that agency the provisions of article VII of the Convention on the Privileges and Immunities of the United Nations and to submit such supplementary agreement to the General Assembly for approval; and

Whereas the International Civil Aviation Organization is desirous of entering into such supplementary agreement to the agreement between the United Nations and the International Civil Aviation Organization entered into under Article 63 of the Charter;

It is hereby agreed as follows:

Article I

The following provision shall be added to the agreement between the United Nations and the International Civil Aviation Organization:

"The officials of the International Civil Aviation Organization shall have the right to use the *laissez-passer* of the United Nations in accordance with special arrangements to be negotiated between the Secretary-General of the United Nations and the competent authority of the International Civil Aviation Organization."

Article II

The above provision shall be inserted as article XVII of the agreement aforesaid, and articles XVII, XVIII, XIX, XX, XXI and XXII of that agreement shall be renumbered so as to become articles XVIII, XIX, XX, XXI, XXII and XXIII respectively.

Article III

This agreement shall come into force on its approval by the General Assembly of the United Nations and the Assembly of the International Civil Aviation Organization.

IN FAITH WHEREOF, we have appended our signatures to two original copies of the present agreement, the text of which is done in duplicate in the English and French languages both equally authentic.

For the United Nations:
10 May 1948

(Signed) Trygve LIE
Secretary-General

For the International Civil Aviation Organization:
31 May 1948

(Signed) Edward WARNER
President of the Council

5. AGREEMENT BETWEEN THE UNITED NATIONS AND THE WORLD HEALTH ORGANIZATION APPROVED BY THE GENERAL ASSEMBLY ON NOVEMBER 15, 1947

PROTOCOL CONCERNING THE ENTRY INTO FORCE OF THE AGREEMENT BETWEEN THE UNITED NATIONS AND THE WORLD HEALTH ORGANIZATION

Article 57 of the Charter of the United Nations provides that specialized agencies established by inter-governmental agreement and having wide international responsibilities as defined in their basic instruments in economic, social, cultural, educational, health and related fields shall be brought into relationship with the United Nations. Article 63 of the Charter provides that the Economic and Social Council may enter into agreements with any of the agencies referred to in Article 57, defining the terms on which the agency concerned shall be brought into relationship with the United Nations, and specifies that such agreements shall be subject to approval by the General Assembly.

Article 69 of the Constitution of the World Health Organization provides that the Organization shall be brought into relation with the United Nations as one of the specialized agencies referred to in Article 57 of the Charter.

On 3 October 1946, the Economic and Social Council, during its third session, directed the Secretary-General to initiate as soon as possible conversations with the Interim Commission of the World Health Organization for the purpose of preparing an agreement to be negotiated at an early session of the Economic and Social Council.

The Interim Commission of the World Health Organization, having been informed of the aforementioned decision of the Economic and Social Council, appointed a Committee to enter into negotiations with the United Nations Committee on Negotiations with Specialized Agencies to prepare a draft agreement.

Negotiations between the Committee on Negotiations with Specialized Agencies of the Economic and Social Council and the Negotiating Delegation of the World Health Organization took place at Lake Success on 4 August 1947 and resulted in an Agreement. This draft agreement was signed on 8 August 1947 by Mr. Jan Papanek, Acting Chairman of the Committee of the Economic and Social Council on Negotiations with Specialized Agencies, and Dr. W.A. Timmerman, Chairman of the Negotiating Committee of the World Health Organization.

On 13 August 1947, the Economic and Social Council, during its fifth session, unanimously recommended the agreement between the United Nations and the World Health Organization ot the General Assembly for its approval.

The Interim Commission of the World Health Organization, at its fourth session held in Geneva, approved on 12 September 1947 the draft agreement between the United Nations and the World Health Organization.

On 20 October 1947, the Secretary-General of the United Nations, upon request of the Executive Secretary of the Interim Commission of the World Health Organization, proposed to the General Assembly and additional article on the use of the United Nations *laissez-passer*, to be inserted in the draft agreement.

The Agreement between the United Nations and the World Health Organization, with the insertion in the Agreement of the article on the use of the United Nations *laissez-passer*, was approved by the General Assembly during its second regular session on 15 November 1947 and by the First World Health Assembly on 10 July 1948.

Article XXII of the Agreement provides that this agreement shall come into force on its approval by the General Assembly of the United Nations and the World Health Assembly.

The Agreement accordingly came into force on 10 July 1948.

A copy of the authentic text of the Agreement is attached hereto.

IN FAITH WHEREOF we have appended our signatures this twelfth day of November, one thousand nine hundred and forty-eight, to two original copies of the present Protocol, the text of which consists of versions in the English and French languages which are equally authentic. One of the original copies will be deposited with the Secretariat of the United Nations and the other will be deposited with the Secretariat of the World Health Organization.

Trygve LIE
Secretary-General of the United Nations

Brock CHISHOLM
Director-General of the World Health Organization

PREAMBLE

Article 57 of the Charter of the United Nations provides that specialized agencies established by inter-governmental agreement and having wide international responsibilities as defined in their basic instruments in economic, social, cultural, educational, health and related fields shall be brought into relationship with the United Nations.

Article 69 of the Constitution of the World Health Organization provides that the Organization shall be brought into relation with the United Nations as one of the specialized agencies referred to in Article 57 of the Charter.

Therefore, the United Nations and the World Health Organization agree as follows:

Article I

The United Nations recognizes the World Health Organization as the specialized agency responsible for taking such action as may be appropriate under its Constitution for the accomplishment of the objectives set forth therein.

Article II

RECIPROCAL REPRESENTATION

1. Representatives of the United Nations shall be invited to attend the meetings of the World Health Assembly and its committees, the Executive Board, and such general, regional or other special meetings as the Organization may convene, and to participate, without vote, in the deliberations of these bodies.

2. Representatives of the World Health Organization shsll be invited to attend meetings of the Economic and Social Council of the United Nations (hereinafter called the Council) and of its commissions and committees, and to participate, without vote, in the deliberations of these bodies with respect to items on their agenda relating to health matters.

3. Representatives of the World Health Organization shall be invited to attend meetings of the General Assembly for purposes of consultation on matters within the scope of its competence.

4. Representatives of the World Health Organization shall be invited to attend meetings of the main committees of the General Assembly when matters within the scope of its competence are under discussion, and to participate, without vote, in such discussions.

5. Representatives of the World Health Organization shall be invited to attend the meetings of the Trusteeship Council, and to participate, without vote, in the deliberations thereof with respect to items on the agenda relating to matters within the competence of the World Health Organization.

6. Written statements of the World Health Organization shall be distributed by the Secretariat of the United Nations to all members of the General Assembly, the Council and its commissions, and the Trusteeship Council, as appropriate. Similarly, written statements presented by the United Nations shall be distributed by the World Health Organization to all members of the World Health Assembly or the Executive Board, as appropriate.

Article III

PROPOSAL OF AGENDA ITEMS

Subject to such preliminary consultation as may be necessary, the World Health Organization shall include in the agenda of the Health Assembly or Executive Board, as appropriate, items proposed to it by the United Nations. Similarly, the Council and its commissions and the Trusteeship Council shall include in their agenda items proposed by the World Health Organization.

Article IV

RECOMMENDATIONS OF THE UNITED NATIONS

1. The World Health Organization, having regard to the obligation of the United Nations to promote the objectives set forth in Article 55 of the Charter, and the function and power of the Council, under Article 62 of the Charter, to make or initiate studies and reports with respect to international economic, social, cultural, educational, health and related matters and to make recommendations concerning these matters to the specialized agencies concerned, and having regard also to the responsibility of the United Nations, under Articles 58 and 63 of the Charter, to make recommendations for the co-ordination of the policies and activities of such specialized agencies, agrees to arrange for the submission, as soon as possible, to the Health Assembly, the Executive Board or such other organ of the World Health Organization as may be appropriate, of all formal recommendations which the United Nations may make to it.

2. The World Health Organization agrees to enter into consultation with the United Nations upon request with respect to such recommendations, and in due course to report to the United Nations on the action taken by the Organization or by its members to give effect to such recommendations, or on the other results of their consideration.

3. The World Health Organization affirms its intention of co-operating in whatever further measures may be necessary to make co-ordination of the activities of specialized agencies and those of the United Nations fully effective. In particular, it agrees to participate in and to co-operate with any body or bodies which the Council may establish for the purpose of facilitating such co-ordination, and to furnish such information as may be required for the carrying out of this purpose.

Article V

EXCHANGE OF INFORMATION AND DOCUMENTS

1. Subject to such arrangements as may be necessary for the safeguarding of confidential material, the fullest and promptest exchange of information and documents shall be made between the United Nations and the World Health Organization.

2. Without prejudice to the generality of the provisions of paragraph 1:

(a) The World Health Organization agrees to transmit to the United Nations regular reports on the activities of the Organization;

(b) The World Health Organization agrees to comply to the fullest extent practicable with any request which the United Nations may make for the furnishing of special reports, studies or information, subject to the conditions set forth in article XVI;

(c) The Secretary-General shall, upon request, transmit to the Director-General of the World Health Organization such information, documents or other material as may from-time to time be agreed between them.

Article VI

PUBLIC INFORMATION

Having regard to the functions of the World Health Organization, as defined in article 2, paragraphs *(q)* and *(r)*, of its Constitution, to provide information in the field of health and to assist in developing an informed public opinion among all peoples on matters of health, and with a view to furthering co-operation and developing joint services in the field of public information between the Organization and the United Nations, a subsidiary agreement on such matters shall be concluded as soon as possible after the coming into force of the present agreement.

Article VII

ASSISTANCE TO THE SECURITY COUNCIL

The World Health Organization agrees to co-operate with the Council in furnishing such information and rendering such assistance for the maintenance or restoration of international peace and security as the Security Council may request.

Article VIII

ASSISTANCE TO THE TRUSTEESHIP COUNCIL

The World Health Organization agrees to co-operate with the Trusteeship Council in the carrying out of its functions and in particular agrees that it will, to the greatest extent possible, render such assistance as the Trusteeship Council may request in regard to matters with which the Organization is concerned.

Article IX

NON-SELF-GOVERNING TERRITORIES

The World Health Organization agrees to co-operate with the United Nations in giving effect to the principles and obligations set forth in Chapter XI of the Chapter with regard to matters affecting the well-being and development of the peoples of Non-Self-Governing Territories.

Article X

RELATIONS WITH THE INTERNATIONAL COURT OF JUSTICE

1. The World Health Organization agrees to furnish any information which may be requested by the International Court of Justice in pursuance of Article 34 of the Statute of the Court.
2. The General Assembly authorizes the World Health Organization to request advisory opinions of the International Court of Justice on legal questions arising within the scope of its competence other than questions concerning the mutual relationships of the Organization and the United Nations or other specialized agencies.

3. Such request may be addressed to the Court by the Health Assembly or by the Executive Board acting in pursuance of an authorization by the Health Assembly.

4. When requesting the International Court of Justice to give and Advisory opinion, the World Health Organization shall inform the Economic and Social Council of the request.

Article XI

HEADQUARTERS AND REGIONAL OFFICES

1. The World Health Organization agrees to consult with the United Nations before making any decision concerning the location of its permanent headquarters.

2. Any regional or branch offices which the World Health Organization may establish shall, so far as is practicable, be closely associated with such regional or branch offices as the United Nations may establish.

Article XII

PERSONNEL ARRANGEMENTS

1. The United Nations and the World Health Organization recognize that the eventual development of a single unified international civil service is desirable from the standpoint of effective administrative co-ordination, and with this end in view agree to develop, as far as is practicable, common personnel standards, methods and arrangements designed to avoid serious discrepancies in terms and conditions of employment, to avoid competition in recruitment of personnel, and to facilitate interchange of personnel in order to obtain the maximum benefit from their services.

2. The United Nations and the World Health Organization agree to co-operate to the fullest extent possible in achieving these ends and in particular they agree to:

(a) Consult together concerning the establishment of an international civil service commission to advise on the means by which common standards of recruitment in the secretariats of the United Nations and of the specialized agencies may be ensured;

(b) Consult together concerning other matters relating to the employment of their officers and staff, including conditions of service, duration of appointments, classification, salary scales and allowances, retirement and pension rights and staff regulations and rules with a view to securing as much uniformity in these matters as shall be found practicable;

(c) Co-operate in the interchange of personnel when desirable on a temporary or permanent basis, making due provision for the retention of seniority and pension rights;

(d) Co-operate in the establishment and operation of suitable machinery for the settlement of disputes arising in connexion with the employment of personnel and related matters.

Article XIII

STATISTICAL SERVICES

1. The United Nations and the World Health Organization agree to strive for maximum co-operation, the elimination of all undesirable duplication between them, and

the most efficient use of their technical personnel in their respective collection, analysis, publication and dissemination of statistical information. They agree to combine their efforts to secure the greatest possible usefulness and utilization of statistical information and to minimize the burdens placed upon national Governments and other organizations from which such information may be collected.

2. The World Health Organization recognizes the United Nations as the central agency for the collection, analysis, publication, standardization, dissemination and improvement of statistics serving the general purposes of international organizations.

3. The United Nations recognizes the World Health Organization as the appropriate agency for the collection, analysis, publication, standardization, dissemination and improvement of statistics within its special sphere, without prejudice to the right of the United Nations to concern itself with such statistics so far as they may be essential for its own purpose or for the improvement of statistics throughout the world.

4. The United Nations shall, in consultation with the specialized agencies, develop administrative instruments and procedures through which effective statistical co-operation may be secured between the United Nations and the agencies brought into relationship with it.

5. It is recognized as desirable that the collection of statistical information should not be duplicated by the United Nations or any of the specialized agencies whenever it is practicable for any of them to utilize information or materials which another may have available.

6. In order to build up a central collection of statistical information for general use, it is agreed that data supplied to the World Health Organization for incorporation in its basic statistical series or special reports should, so far as is practicable, be made available to the United Nations.

Article XIV

ADMINISTRATIVE AND TECHNICAL SERVICES

1. The United Nations and the World Health Organization recognize the desirability, in the interest of administrative and technical uniformity and of the most efficient use of personnel and resources, of avoiding, whenever possible, the establishment and operation of competitive or overlapping facilities and services among the United Nations and the specialized agencies.

2. Accordingly, the United Nations and the World Health Organization agree to consult together concerning the establishment and use of common administrative and technical services and facilities in addition to those referred to in articles XII, XIII and XV, in so far as the establishment and use of such services may from time to time be found practicable and appropriate.

3. Arrangements shall be made between the United Nations and the World Health Organization with regard to registration and deposit of official documents.

Article XV

BUDGETARY AND FINANCIAL ARRANGEMENTS

1. The World Health Organization recognizes the desirability of establishing close budgetary and financial relationships with the United Nations in order that the admin-

istrative operations of the United Nations and of the specialized agencies shall be carried out in the most efficient and economical manner possible, and that the maximum measure of co-ordination and uniformity with respect to these operations shall be secured.

2. The United Nations and the World Health Organization agree to co-operate to the fullest extent possible in achieving these ends and, in particular, shall consult together concerning the desirability of the inclusion of the budget of the Organization within a general budget of the United Nations. Any arrangements to this effect shall be defined in a supplementary agreement between the two organizations.

3. Pending the conclusion of any such agreement, the following arrangements shall govern budgetary and financial relationships between the World Health Organization and the United Nations:

(a) The Secretary-General and the Director-General shall arrange for consultation in connexion with the preparation of the budget of the World Health Organization.

(b) The World Health Organization agrees to transmit its proposed budget to the United Nations annually at the same time as such budget is transmitted to its members. The General Assembly shall examine the budget or proposed budget of the Organization and may make recommendations to it concerning any item or items contained therein.

(c) Representatives of the World Health Organization shall be entitled to participate, without vote, in the deliberations of the General Assembly or any committee thereof at all times when the budget of the World Health Organization or general administrative or financial questions affecting the Organization are under consideration.

(d) The United Nations may undertake the collection of contributions from those members of the World Health Organization which are also Members of the United Nations in accordance with such arrangements as may be defined by a later agreement between the United Nations and the Organization.

(e) The United Nations shall, upon its own initiative or upon the request of the World Health Organization, arrange for studies to be undertaken concerning other financial and fiscal questions of interest to the Organization and to other specialized agencies with a view to the provision of common services and the securing of uniformity in such matters.

(f) The World Health Organization agrees to conform, as far as may be practicable, to standard practices and forms recommended by the United Nations.

Article XVI

FINANCING OF SPECIAL SERVICES

1. In the event of the World Health Organization being faced with the necessity of incurring substantial extra expense as a result of any request which the United Nations may make for special reports, studies or assistance in accordance with articles V, VII, VIII, or with other provisions of this agreement, consultation shall take place with a view to determining the most equitable manner in which such expense shall be borne.

2. Consultation between the United Nations and the World Health Organization shall similarly take place with a view to making such arrangements as may be found equitable for covering the costs of central administrative, technical or fiscal services or facilities or other special assistance provided by the United Nations, in so far as they apply to the World Health Organization.

Article XVII

UNITED NATIONS "LAISSEZ-PASSER"

Officials of the World Health Organization shall have the right to use the *laissez-passer* of the United Nations in accordance with the special arrangements to be negotiated between the Secretary-General of the United Nations and the Director-General of the World Health Organization.

Article XVIII

INTER-AGENCY AGREEMENTS

The World Health Organization agrees to inform the Council of any formal agreement between the Organization and any other specialized agency, inter-governmental organization or non-governmental organization, and in particular agrees to inform the Council of the nature and scope of any such agreement before it is concluded.

Article XIX

LIAISON

1. The United Nations and the World Health Organization agree to the foregoing provisions in the belief that they will contribute to the maintenance of effective liaison between the two organizations. They affirm their intention of taking whatever further measures may be necessary to make this liaison fully effective.

2. The liaison arrangements provided for in the foregoing articles of this agreement shall apply, as far as is appropriate, to the relations between such branch or regional offices as may be established by the two organizations, as well as between their central headquarters.

Article XX

IMPLEMENTATION OF THE AGREEMENT

The Secretary-General and the Director-General may enter into such supplementary arrangements for the implementation of this agreement as may be found desirable in the light of the operating experience of the two organizations.

Article XXI

REVISION

This agreement shall be subject to revision by agreement between the United Nations and the World Health Organization.

Article XXII

ENTRY INTO FORCE

This agreement shall come into force on its approval by the General Assembly of the United Nations and the World Health Assembly.

6. AGREEMENT BETWEEN THE UNITED NATIONS AND THE INTERNATIONAL BANK FOR RECONSTRUCTION AND DEVELOPMENT APPROVED BY THE GENERAL ASSEMBLY ON NOVEMBER 15, 1947

PROTOCOL CONCERNING THE ENTRY INTO FORCE OF THE AGREEMENT BETWEEN THE UNITED NATIONS AND THE INTERNATIONAL BANK FOR RECONSTRUCTION AND DEVELOPMENT

Article 57 of the Charter of the United Nations provides that specialized agencies established by inter-governmental agreement and having wide international responsibilities as defined in their basic instruments in economic, social, cultural, educational, health and related fields shall be brought into relationship with the United Nations. Article 63 of the Charter provides that the Economic and Social Council may enter into agreements with any of the agencies referred to in Article 57, defining the terms on which the agency concerned shall be brought into relationship with the United Nations, and specifies that such agreements shall be subject to approval by the General Assembly.

Article V, section 8 *(a)* of the Articles of Agreement of the International Bank for Reconstruction and Development provides that the Bank, within the terms of the Articles of Agreement, shall co-operate with any general international organization and with public international organizations having specialized responsibilities in related fields.

The Economic and Social Council, during its first session, on 16 February 1946, adopted a resolution establishing a Committee of the Council on Negotiations with Specialized Agencies which was directed to enter into negotiations as early as possible with the International Bank for Reconstruction and Development.

The Economic and Social Council, during its third session, on 3 October 1946, adopted a resolution directing the Secretary-General to strengthen and extend working relationships between the United Nations and the International Bank for Reconstruction and Development, and to continue consultations with the representatives of that Organization with a view to initiating formal negotiations as soon as practicable.

Negotiations between the Committee on Negotiations with Specialized Agencies of the Economic and Social Council and the Negotiating Delegation of the International Bank for Reconstruction, and Development took place in New York on 15 August 1947 and resulted in an Agreement. These negotiations were conducted simultaneously with negotiations between the Committee on Negotiations with Specialized Agencies of the Economic and Social Council and the Negotiating Delegation of the International Monetary Fund.

On 16 August 1947, the Economic and Social Council, during its fifth session, recommended the Agreement between the United Nations and the International for Reconstruction and Development to the General Assembly for its approval.

Article XIII, paragraph 4, of the Agreement provides that the Agreement shall come into force when it shall have been approved by the General Assembly of the United Nations and the Board of Governors of the International Bank for Reconstruction and Development.

The Agreement was approved by the General Assembly of the United Nations on 15 November 1947 and by the Board of Governors of the International Bank for Reconstruction and Development on 16 September 1947.

The Agreement accordingly came into force on 15 November 1947.

A copy of the text of the Agreement in both English and French is attached hereto, the English text being the authentic text.

IN FAITH WHEREOF we have appended our signatures this fifteenth day of April, one thousand nine hundred and forty eight, to two original copies of the present Protocol, the text of which consists of versions in the English and French languages which are equally authentic. One of the original copies will be filed and recorded with the Secretariat of the United Nations and the other will be deposited in the archives of the International Bank for Reconstruction and Development.

Trygve LIE
Secretary-General of the United Nations

John J. MCCLOY
President of the International Bank for Reconstruction and Development

AGREEMENT BETWEEN THE UNITED NATIONS AND THE INTER-NATIONAL BANK FOR RECONSTRUCTION AND DEVELOPMENT

Article I

GENERAL

1. This agreement, which is entered into by the United Nations pursuant to the provisions of Article 63 of its Charter, and by the International Bank for Reconstruction and Development (hereinafter called the Bank) pursuant to the provisions of Section 8 *(a)* of article V of its Articles of Agreement, is intended to define the terms on which the United Nations and the Bank shall be brought into relationship.

2. The Bank is a specialized agency established by agreement among its member Governments and having wide international responsiblities, as defined in its Articles of Agreement, in economic and related fields within the meaning of Article 57 of the Charter of the United Nations. By reason of the nature of its international responsibilities and the terms of its Articles of Agreement, the Bank is, and is required to function as, an independent international organization.

3. The United Nations and the Bank are subject to certain necessary limitations for the safeguarding of confidential material furnished to them by their members or others, and nothing in this agreement shall be construed to require either of them to furnish any information the furnishing of which would, in its judgment, constitute a violation of the confidence of any of its members or anyone from whom it shall have received such information, or which would otherwise interfere with the orderly conduct of its operations.

Article II

RECIPROCAL REPRESENTATION

1. Representatives of the United Nations shall be entitled to attend, and to participate without vote in, meetings of the Board of Governors of the Bank. Representatives of the United Nations shall be invited to participate without vote in meetings especially called by the Bank for the particular purpose of considering the United Nations point of view in matters of concern to the United Nations.

2. Representatives of the Bank shall be entitled to attend meetings of the General Assembly of the United Nations for purposes of consultation.

3. Representatives of the Bank shall be entitled to attend, and to participate without vote in, meetings of the committees of the General Assembly, meetings of the Economic and Social Council, of the Trusteeship Council and of their respective subsidiary bodies dealing with matters in which the Bank has an interest.

4. Sufficient advance notice of these meetings and their agenda shall be given so that, in consultation, arrangements can be made for adequate representation.

Article III

PROPOSAL OF AGENDA ITEMS

In preparing the agenda for meetings of the Board of Governors, the Bank will give due consideration to the inclusion in the agenda of items proposed by the United Nations. Similarly, the Council and its commissions and the Trusteeship Council will give due consideration to the inclusion in their agenda of items proposed by the Bank.

Article IV

CONSULTATION AND RECOMMENDATIONS

1. The United Nations and the Bank shall consult together and exchange views on matters of mutual interest.

2. Neither organization, nor any of their subsidiary bodies, will present any formal recommendations to the other without reasonable prior consultation with regard thereto. Any formal recommendations made by either organization after such consultation will be considered as soon as possible by the appropriate organ of the other.

3. The United Nations recognizes that the action to be taken by the Bank on any loan is a matter to be determined by the independent exercise of the Bank's own judgment in accordance with the Bank's Articles of Agreement. The United Nations recognizes, therefore, that it would be sound policy to refrain from making recommendations to the Bank with respect to particular loans or with respect to terms or conditions of financing by the Bank. The Bank recognizes that the United Nations and its organs may appropriately make recommendations with respect to the technical aspects of reconstruction or development plants, programmes or projects.

Article V

EXCHANGE OF INFORMATION

The United Nations and the Bank will, to the fullest extent practicable and subject to paragraph 3 of article I, arrange for the current exchange of information and publications of mutual interest, and the furnishing of special reports and studies upon request.

Article VI

SECURITY COUNCIL

1. The Bank takes note of the obligation assumed, under paragraph 2 of Article 48 of the United Nations Charter, by such of its members as are also Members of the United Nations, to carry out the decisions of the Security Council through their action in the appropriate specialized agencies of which they are members, and will, in the conduct of its activities, have due regard for decisions of the Security Council under Articles 41 and 42 of the United Nations Charter.

2. The Bank agrees to assist the Security Council by furnishing to it information in accordance with the provisions of article V of this agreement.

Article VII

ASSISTANCE TO THE TRUSTEESHIP COUNCIL

The Bank agrees to co-operate with the Trusteeship Council in the carrying out of its functions by furnishing information and technical assistance upon request and in such other similar ways as may be consistent with the Articles of Agreement of the Bank.

Article VIII

INTERNATIONAL COURT OF JUSTICE

The General Assembly of the United Nations hereby authorizes the Bank to request advisory opinions of the International Court of Justice on any legal questions arising within the scope of the Bank's activities other than questions relating to the relationship between the Bank and the United Nations or any specialized agency. Whenever the Bank shall request the Court for an advisory opinion, the Bank will inform the Economic and Social Council of the request.

Article IX

STATISTICAL SERVICES

1. In the interests of efficiency and for the purpose of reducing the burden on national governments and other organizations, the United Nations and the Bank agree to co-operate in eliminating unnecessary duplication in the collection, analysis, publication and dissemination of statistical information.

2. The Bank recognizes the United Nations as the central agency for the collection, analysis, publication, standardization and improvement of statistics serving the general purposes of international organizations, without prejudice to the right of the Bank to concern itself with any statistics so far as they may be essential for its own purposes.

3. The United Nations recognizes the Bank as the appropriate agency for the collection, analysis, publication, standardization and improvement of statistics within its special sphere, without prejudice to the right of the United Nations to concern itself with any statistics so far as they may be essential for its own purposes.

4. *(a)* In its statistical activities the Bank agrees to give full consideration to the requirements of the United Nations and of the specialized agencies.

(b) In its statistical activities the United Nations agrees to give full consideration to the requirements of the Bank.

5. The United Nations and the Bank agree to furnish each other promptly with all their non-confidential statistical information.

Article X

ADMINISTRATIVE RELATIONSHIPS

1. The United Nations and the Bank will consult from time to time concerning personnel and other administrative matters of mutual interest, with a view to securing as much uniformity in these matters as they shall find practicable and to assuring the most efficient use of the services and facilities of the two organizations. These consultations shall include determination of the most equitable manner in which special services furnished by one organization to the other should be financed.

2. To the extent consistent with the provisions of this agreement, the Bank will participate in the work of the Co-ordination Committee and its subsidiary bodies.

3. The Bank will furnish to the United Nations copies of the annual report and the quarterly financial statements prepared by the Bank pursuant to section 13 *(a)* of article V of its Articles of Agreement. The United Nations agrees that, in the interpretation of paragraph 3 of Article 17 of the United Nations Charter it will take into consideration that the Bank does not rely for its annual budget upon contributions from its members, and that the appropriate authorities of the Bank enjoy full autonomy in deciding the form and content of such budget.

4. The officials of the Bank shall have the right to use the *laissez-passer* of the United Nations in accordance with special arrangements to be negotiated between the Secretary-General of the United Nations and the competent authorities of the Bank.

Article XI

AGREEMENTS WITH OTHER ORGANIZATIONS

The Bank will inform the Economic and Social Council of any formal agreement which the Bank shall enter into with any specialized agency, and in particular agrees to inform the Council of the nature and scope of any such agreement before it is concluded.

Article XII

LIAISON

1. The United Nations and the Bank agree to the foregoing provisions in the belief that they will contribute to the maintenance of effective co-operation between the two organizations. Each agrees that it will establish within its own organization such administrative machinery as may be necessary to make the liaison, as provided for in this agreement, fully effective.

2. The arrangements provided for in the foregoing articles of this agreement shall apply, as far as is appropriate, to relations between such branch or regional offices as may be established by the two organizations, as well as between their central machinery.

Article XIII

MISCELLANEOUS

1. The Secretary-General of the United Nations and the President of the Bank are authorized to make such supplementary arrangements as they shall deem necessary or proper to carry fully into effect the purposes of this agreement.

2. This agreement shall be subject to revision by agreement between the United Nations and the Bank from the date of its entry into force.

3. This agreement may be terminated by either party thereto on six months' written notice to the other party, and thereupon all rights and obligations of both parties hereunder shall cease.

4. This agreement shall come into force when it shall have been approved by the General Assembly of the United Nations and the Board of Governors of the Bank.

7. AGREEMENT BETWEEN THE UNITED NATIONS AND THE INTERNATIONAL MONETARY FUND APPROVED BY THE GENERAL ASSEMBLY ON NOVEMBER 15, 1947

PROTOCOL CONCERNING THE ENTRY INTO FORCE OF THE AGREEMENT BETWEEN THE UNITED NATIONS AND THE INTERNATIONAL MONETARY FUND

Articles 57 of the Charter of the United Nations provides that specialized agencies established by inter-governmental agreement and having wide international responsibilities, as defined in their basic instruments in economic, social, cultural, educational, health and related fields, shall be brought into relationship with the United Nations. Article 63 of the Charter provides that the Economic and Social Council may enter into agreements with any of the agencies referred to in Article 57, defining the terms on which the agency concerned shall be brought into relationship with the United Nations, and specifies that such agreements shall be subject to approval by the General Assembly.

Article X of the Articles of Agreement of the International Monetary Fund provides that the Fund shall co-operate, within the terms of the Articles of Agreement, with any general international organization and with public international organizations having specialized responsibilities in related fields.

The Economic and Social Council, during its first session, on 16 February 1946, adopted a resolution establishing a Committee of the Council on Negotiations with Specialized Agencies which was directed to enter into negotiations as early as possible with the International Monetary Fund.

The Economic and Social Council, during its third session, on 3 October 1946, adopted a resolution directing the Secretary-General to strengthen and extend working relationships between the United Nations and the International Monetary Fund, and to continue consultations with the representatives of that Organization with a view to initiating formal negotiations as soon as practicable.

Negotiations between the Committee on Negotiations with Specialized Agencies of the Economic and Social Council and the Negotiating Delegation of the International Monetary Fund took place in New York on 15 August 1947 and resulted in an Agreement. These negotiations were conducted simultaneously with negotiations between the Committee on Negotiations with Specialized Agencies of the Economic and Social Council and the Negotiating Delegation of the International Bank for Reconstruction and Development.

On 16 August 1947, the Economic and Social Council during its fifth session recommended the Agreement between the United Nations and the International Monetary Fund to the General Assembly for its approval.

Article XIII, paragraph 4, of the Agreement provides that the Agreement shall come into force when it shall have been approved by the General Assembly of the United Nations and the Board of Governors of the International Monetary Fund.

The Agreement was approved by the General Assembly of the United Nations on 15 November 1947 and by the Board of Governors of the International Monetary Fund on 17 September 1947.

The Agreement accordingly came into force on 15 November 1947.

A copy of the text of the Agreement in both English and French is attached hereto, the English text being the authentic text.

IN FAITH WHEREOF we have appended our signatures this fifteenth day of April, one thousand nine hundred and forty-eight, in two original copies of the present Protocol, the text of which consists of versions in the English and French languages which are equally authentic. One of the original copies will be filed and recorded with the Secretariat of the United Nations and the other will be deposited in the archives of the International Monetary Fund.

Trygve LIE
Secretary-General of the United Nations

GUTT
Managing Director of the International Monetary Fund

AGREEMENT BETWEEN THE UNITED NATIONS AND THE INTERNATIONAL MONETARY FUND

Article I

GENERAL

1. This agreement, which is entered into by the United Nations pursuant to the provisions of Article 63 of its Charter, and by the International Monetary Fund (hereinafter called the Fund), pursuant to the provisions of article X of its Articles of Agreement, is intended to define the terms on which the United Nations and the Fund shall be brought into relationship.

2. The Fund is a specialized agency established by agreement among its member governments and having wide international responsibilities, as defined in its Articles of Agreement, in economic and related fields within the meaning of Article 57 of the Charter of the United Nations. By reason of the nature of its international responsibilities and the terms of its Articles of Agreement, the Fund is, and is required to function as, an independent international organization.

3. The United Nations and the Fund are subject to certain necessary limitations for the safeguarding of confidential material furnished to them by their members or others, and nothing in this agreement shall be construed to require either of them to furnish any information the furnishing of which would, in its judgment, constitute a violation of the confidence of any of its members or anyone from whom it shall have received such information, or which would otherwise interfere with the orderly conduct of its operations.

Article II

RECIPROCAL REPRESENTATION

1. Representatives of the United Nations shall be entitled to attend, and to participate without vote in, meetings of the Board of Governors of the Fund. Representatives of the United Nations shall be invited to participate without vote in meetings especially called by the Fund for the particular purpose of considering the United Nations point of view in matters of concern to the United Nations.

2. Representatives of the Fund shall be entitled to attend meetings of the General Assembly of the United Nations for purposes of consultation.

3. Representatives of the Fund shall be entitled to attend, and to participate without vote in, meetings of the committees of the General Assembly, meetings of the Economic and Social Council, of the Trusteeship Council and of their respective subsidiary bodies, dealing with matters in which the Fund has an interest.

4. Sufficient advance notice of these meetings and their agenda shall be given so that, in consultation, arrangements can be made for adequate representation.

Article III

PROPOSAL OF AGENDA ITEMS

In preparing the agenda for meetings of the Board of Governors, the Fund will give due consideration to the inclusion in the agenda of items proposed by the United Nations. Similarly, the Council and its commissions and the Trusteeship Council will give due consideration to the inclusion in their agenda of items proposed by the Fund.

Article IV

CONSULTATION AND RECOMMENDATIONS

1. The United Nations and the Fund shall consult together and exchange views on matters of mutual interest.

2. Neither organization, nor any of their subsidiary bodies, will present any formal recommendations to the other without reasonable prior consultation with regard thereto. Any formal recommendations made by either organization after such consultation will be considered as soon as possible by the appropriate organ of the other.

Article V

EXCHANGE OF INFORMATION

The United Nations and the Fund will, to the fullest extent practicable and subject to paragraph 3 of article I, arrange for the current exchange of information and publications of mutual interest, and the furnishing of special reports and studies upon request.

Article VI

SECURITY COUNCIL

1. The Fund takes note of the obligation assumed, under paragraph 2 of Article 48 of the United Nations Charter, by such of its members as are also Members of the United Nations, to carry out the decisions of the Security Council through their action in the appropriate specialized agencies of which they are members, and will, in the conduct of its activities, have due regard for decisions of the Security Council under Articles 41 and 42 of the United Nations Charter.

2. The Fund agrees to assist the Security Council by furnishing to it information in accordance with the provisions of article V of this agreement.

Article VII

ASSISTANCE TO THE TRUSTEESHIP COUNCIL

The Fund agrees to co-operate with the Trusteeship Council in the carrying out of its functions by furnishing information and technical assistance upon request, and in such other similar ways as may be consistent with the Articles of Agreement of the Fund.

Article VIII

INTERNATIONAL COURT OF JUSTICE

The General Assembly of the United Nations hereby authorizes the Fund to request advisory opinions of the International Court of Justice on any legal questions arising within the scope of the Fund's activities other than questions relating to the relationship between the Fund and the United Nations or any specialized agency. Whenever the Fund shall request the Court for an advisory opinion, the Fund will inform the Economic and Social Council of the request.

Article IX

1. In the interests of efficiency and for the purpose of reducing the burden on national Governments and other organizations, the United Nations and the Fund agree to co-operate in eliminating unnecessary duplication in the collection, analysis, publication and dissemination of statistical information.

2. The Fund recognizes the United Nations as the central agency for the collection, analysis, publication, standardization and improvement of statistics serving the general purposes of international organizations, without prejudice to the right of the Fund to concern itself with any statistics so far as they may be essential for its own purposes.

3. The United Nations recognizes the Fund as the appropriate agency for the collection, analysis, publication, standardization and improvement of statistics within its special sphere, without prejudice to the right of the United Nations to concern itself with any statistics so far as they may be essential for its own purposes.

4. *(a)* In its statistical activities the Fund agrees to give full consideration to the requirements of the United Nations and of the specialized agencies.

(b) In its statistical activities the United Nations agrees to give full consideration to the requirements of the Fund.

5. The United Nations and the Fund agree to furnish each other promptly with all their non-confidential statistical information.

Article X

ADMINISTRATIVE RELATIONSHIPS

1. The United Nations and the Fund will consult from time to time concerning personnel and other administrative matters of mutual interest, with a view to securing as much uniformity in these matters as they shall find practicable and to assuring the most efficient use of the services and facilities of the two organizations. These consultations shall include determination of the most equitable manner in which special services furnished by one organization to the other should be financed.

2. To the extent consistent with the provisions of this agreement, the Fund will participate in the work of the Co-ordination Committee and its subsidiary bodies.

3. The Fund will furnish to the United Nations copies of the annual report and the quarterly financial statements prepared by the Fund pursuant to section 7 *(a)* of article V of its Articles of Agreement. The United Nations agrees that, in the interpretation of paragraph 3 of Article 17 of the United Nations Charter it will take into consideration that the Fund does not rely for its annual budget upon contributions from its members, and that the appropriate authorities of the Fund enjoy full autonomy in deciding the form and content of such budget.

4. The officials of the Fund shall have the right to use the *laissez-passer* of the United Nations in accordance with special arrangements to be negotiated between the Secretary-General of the United Nations and the competent authorities of the Fund.

Article XI

AGREEMENTS WITH OTHER ORGANIZATIONS

The Fund will inform the Economic and Social Council of any formal agreement which the Fund shall enter into with any specialized agency, and in particular agrees to inform the Council of the nature and scope of any such agreement before it is concluded.

Article XII

LIAISON

1. The United Nations and the Fund agree to the foregoing provisions in the belief that they will contribute to the maintenance of effective co-operation between the two organizations. Each agrees that it will establish within its own organizations such administrative machinery as may be necessary to make the liaison, as provided for in this agreement, fully effective.

2. The arrangements provided for in the foregoing articles of this agreement shall apply, as far as is appropriate, to relations between such branch or regional offices as may be established by the two organizations, as well as between their central machinery.

Article XIII

MISCELLANEOUS

1. The Secretary-General of the United Nations and the Managing Director of the Fund are authorized to make such supplementary arrangements as they shall deem necessary or proper to carry fully into effect the purposes of this agreement.

2. This agreement shall be subject to revisions by agreement between the United Nations and the Fund from the date of its entry into force.

3. This agreement may be terminated by either party thereto on six months' written notice to the other party, and thereupon all rights and obligations of both parties hereunder shall cease.

4. This agreement shall come into force when it shall have been approved by the General Assembly of the United Nations and the Board of Governors of the Fund.

8. AGREEMENT BETWEEN THE UNITED NATIONS AND AND THE UNIVERSAL POSTAL UNION APPROVED BY THE GENERAL ASSEMBLY ON NOVEMBER 15, 1947

PROTOCOL CONCERNING THE ENTRY INTO FORCE OF THE AGREEMENT BETWEEN THE UNITED NATIONS AND THE UNIVERSAL POSTAL UNION

Article 57 of the Charter of the United Nations provides that specialized agencies established by inter-governmental agreement and having wide international responsibilities as defined in their basic instruments in economic, social, cultural, educational, health and related fields shall be brought into relationship with the United Nations. Article 63 of the Charter provides that the Economic and Social Council may enter into agreement with any of the agencies referred to in Article 57, defining the terms on which the agency concerned shall be brought into relationship with the United Nations, and specifies that such agreements shall be subjected to approval by the General Assembly.

The Economic and Social Council, on 28 March 1947, directed its Committee on Negotiations with Specialized Agencies to enter into negotiations at the appropriate time with the Universal Postal Union for the purpose of bringing it into relationship with the United Nations and to submit a report on the negotiations to the Council including therein a draft preliminary agreement based upon these negotiations.

The Congress of the Universal Postal Union, which met in Paris in June 1947, having been informed of the aforementioned decision of the Economic and Social Council, appointed a Committee to enter into negotiations with the United Nations Committee on Negotiations with Specialized Agencies to prepare a draft agreement.

Negotiations between the Committee on Negotiations with Specialized Agencies of the Economic and Social Council and the Negotiating Committee of the Universal Postal Union took place in Paris on 17, 18 and 20 June 1947 and resulted in a draft agreement. This draft agreement, after certain subsequent adjustments made in accordance with the alternatives accepted in advance by both negotiating committees during the negotiating sessions, was initialled on 4 July 1948 by Mr. Jan Papanck, Acting Chairman of the Committee of the Economic and Social Council on Negotiations with Specialized Agencies, and Mr. J.J. Le Mouel, Chairman of the XIIth Congress of the Universal Postal Union.

On 4 July 1947 the Congress of the Universal Postal Union which met in Paris for the purpose of revising the Universal Postal Convention unanimously approved the draft agreement which subsequently was annexed to the revised Convention.

On 4 August 1947 the Economic and Social Council, during its fifth session, recommended the agreement between the United Nations and the Universal Postal Union to the General Assembly for its approval.

Article XV of the Agreement provides that this agreement being annexed to the Universal Postal Convention concluded in Paris in 1947 shall come into force after its approval by the General Assembly of the United Nations, and, at the earliest, at the same time as this Convention.

The Agreement between the United Nations and the Universal Postal Union was approved by the General Assembly during its second regular session on 15 November 1947. The Universal Postal Convention came into force on 1 July 1948. The Agreement accordingly came into force on 1 July 1948.

A copy of the authentic text of the Agreement is attached hereto.

IN FAITH WHEREOF we have appended our signatures this fifteenth day of November, one thousand nine hundred and forty-eight, to two original copies of the present Protocol, the text of which consists of versions in the English and French languages which are equally authentic. One of the original copies will be deposited with the Secretariat of the United Nations and the other will be deposited in the Bureau of the Universal Postal Union.

Trygve LIE
Secretary-General of the United Nations

MURI
Director of the International Bureau
of the Universal Postal Union

AGREEMENT BETWEEN THE UNITED NATIONS
AND THE UNIVERSAL POSTAL UNION

PREAMBLE

In consideration of the obligations placed upon the United Nations by Article 57 of the Charter of the United Nations, the United Nations and the Universal Postal Union agree as follows:

Article I

The United Nations recognizes the Universal Postal Union (hereinafter called the Union) as the specialized agency responsible for taking such action as may be appropriate under its basic instrument for the accomplishment of the purposes set forth therein.

Article II

RECIPROCAL REPRESENTATION

1. Representatives of the United Nations shall be invited to attend all the Union's congresses, administrative conferences and commissions, and to participate, without vote, in the deliberations of these meetings.

2. Representatives of the Union shall be invited to attend meetings of the Economic and Social Council of the United Nations (hereinafter called the Council), of its commissions and committees, and to participate, without vote, in the deliberations thereof with respect to items on the agenda in which the Union may be concerned.

3. Representatives of the Union shall be invited to attend the meetings of the General Assembly during which questions within the competence of the Union are under discussion, for purposes of consultation, and to participate without vote, in the deliberations of the main committees of the General Assembly with respect to items concerning the Union.

4. Written statements presented by the Union shall be distributed by the Secretariat of the United Nations to the Members of the General Assembly, the Council and its commissions, and the Trusteeship Council, as appropriate. Similarly, written statements presented by the United Nations shall be distributed by the Union to its members.

Article III

PROPOSAL OF AGENDA ITEMS

Subject to such preliminary consultation as may be necessary, the Union shall include in the agenda of its congresses, administrative conferences or commissions, or, as the case may be, shall submit to its members in accordance with the provisions of the Universal Postal Convention, items proposed to it by the United Nations. Similarly, the Council, its commissions and committees, and the Trusteeship Council shall include in their agenda items proposed by the Union.

Article IV

RECOMMENDATIONS OF THE UNITED NATIONS

1. The Union agrees to arrange for the submission as soon as possible, for appropriate action, to its congresses or its administrative conferences or commissions, or to its members, in conformity with the provisions of the Universal Postal Convention, of all formal recommendations which the United Nations may make to it. Such recommendations will be addressed to the Union and not directly to its members.

2. The Union agrees to enter into consultation with the United Nations, upon re-

529

quest, with respect to such recommendations, and in due course to report to the United Nations on the action taken by the Union or by its members to give effect to such recommendations, or on the other results of their consideration.

3. The Union will co-operate in whatever further measures may be necessary to make co-ordination of the activities of specialized agencies and those of the United Nations fully effective. In particular, it will co-operate with any body which the Council may establish for the purpose of facilitating such co-ordination and will furnish such information as may be requested for the carrying out of this purpose.

Article V

EXCHANGE OF INFORMATION AND DOCUMENTS

1. Subject to such arrangements as may be necessary for the safeguarding of confidential material, the fullest and promptest exchange of information and documents shall be made between the United Nations and the Union.

2. Without prejudice to the generality of the provisions of the preceding paragraph:

(a) The Union shall submit to the United Nations an annual report on its activities;

(b) The Union shall comply to the fullest extent practicable with any request which the United Nations may make for the furnishing of special reports, studies or information, subject to the conditions set forth in article XI;

(c) The Union shall furnish written advice on questions within its competence as may be requested by the Trusteeship Council;

(d) The Secretary-General of the United Nations shall, upon request, consult with the Director of the International Bureau of the Union regarding the provision to the Union of such information as may be of special interest to it.

Article VI

ASSISTANCE TO THE UNITED NATIONS

The Union agrees to co-operate with and to give assistance to the United Nations, its principal and subsidiary organs, so far as is consistent with the provisions of the Universal Postal Convention.

As regards the Members of the United Nations, the Union agrees that in accordance with Article 103 of the Charter no provision in the Universal Postal Convention or related agreements shall be construed as preventing or limiting any State in complying with its obligations to the United Nations.

Article VII

PERSONNEL ARRANGEMENTS

The United Nations and the Union agree to co-operate as necessary to ensure as much uniformity as possible in the conditions of employment of personnel, and to avoid competition in the recruitment of personnel.

Article VIII

STATISTICAL SERVICES

1. The United Nations and the Union agree to co-operate with a view to securing the greatest possible usefulness and utilization of statistical information and data.

2. The Union recognizes the United Nations as the central agency for the collection, analysis, publication, standardization and improvement of statistics serving the general purposes of international organizations.

3. The United Nations recognizes the Union as the appropriate agency for the collection, analysis, publication, standardization and improvement of statistics within

its special sphere, without prejudice to the right of the United Nations to concern itself with such statistics so far as it may be essential for its own purposes or for the improvement of statistics throughout the world.

Article IX

ADMINISTRATIVE AND TECHNICAL SERVICES

1. The United Nations and the Union recognize the desirability, in the interests of the most efficient use of personnel and resources, of avoiding the establishing of competitive or overlapping services.

2. Arrangements shall be made between the United Nations and the Union with regard to the registration and deposit of official documents.

Article X

BUDGETARY ARRANGEMENTS

The annual budget of the Union shall be transmitted to the United Nations, and the General Assembly may make recommendations thereon to the Congress of the Union.

Article XI

FINANCING OF SPECIAL SERVICES

In the event of the Union being faced with the necessity of incurring substantial extra expense as a result of any request which the United Nations may make for special reports, studies or information in accordance with article V or with any other provisions of this agreement, consultation shall take place with a view to determining the most equitable manner in which such expense shall be borne.

Article XII

INTER-AGENCY AGREEMENTS

The Union will inform the Council of the nature and scope of any agreement between the Union and any specialized agency or other inter-governmental organization, and further agrees to inform the Council of the preparation of any such agreements.

Article XIII

LIAISON

1. The United Nations and the Union agree to the foregoing provisions in the belief that they will contribute to the maintenance of effective liaison between the two organizations. They affirm their intention of taking in agreement whatever measures may be necessary to this end.

2. The liaison arrangements provided for in this agreement shall apply, as far as is appropriate, to the relations between the Union and the United Nations, including its branch and regional offices.

Article XIV

IMPLEMENTATION OF THE AGREEMENT

The Secretary-General of the United Nations and the President of the Executive and Liaison Commission of the Union may enter into such supplementary arrangements for the implementation of this agreement as may be found desirable in the light of operating experience of the two organizations.

531

Article XV

ENTRY INTO FORCE

This agreement is annexed to the Universal Postal Convention concluded in Paris in 1947. It will come into force after approval by the General Assembly of the United Nations, and, at the earliest, at the same time as this Convention.

Article XVI

REVISION

On six months' notice given on either part, the agreement shall be subject to revision by agreement between the United Nations and the Union.

SUPPLEMENTARY AGREEMENT TO THE AGREEMENT BETWEEN THE UNITED NATIONS AND THE UNIVERSAL POSTAL UNION

WHEREAS the Secretary-General of the United Nations has been requested by Resolution No. 136 (VI) of the Economic and Social Council, adopted on 25 February 1948, to conclude with any Specialized Agency which may so desire, a supplementary agreement to extend to the officials of that agency the provisions of article VII of the Convention on the Privileges and Immunities of the United Nations and to submit such supplementary agreement to the General Assembly for approval; and

WHEREAS the UNIVERSAL POSTAL UNION is desirous of entering into such supplementary agreement to the Agreement between the UNITED NATIONS and the UNIVERSAL POSTAL UNION entered into under Article 63 of the Charter;

IT IS HEREBY AGREED AS FOLLOWS:

Article I

The following provision shall be added as an additional article to the Agreement between the UNITED NATIONS and the UNIVERSAL POSTAL UNION:

"The officials of the Universal Postal Union shall have the right to use the *laissez-passer* of the United Nations in accordance with special arrangements to be negotiated under Article XIV."

Article II

This Agreement shall come into force on its approval by the General Assembly of the UNITED NATIONS and the UNIVERSAL POSTAL UNION.

For the United Nations:
Lake Success, New York 27 July 1949

> (*Signed*) Byron PRICE
> *Acting Secretary-General*

For the Universal Postal Union:
Paris, 13 July 1949

> (*Signed*) J.J. LE MOUEL
> *Chairman of the Executive and Liaison Commission*
> *of the Universal Postal Union*

9. AGREEMENT BETWEEN THE UNITED NATIONS AND THE INTERNATIONAL TELECOMMUNICATIONS UNION APPROVED BY THE GENERAL ASSEMBLY ON NOVEMBER 15, 1947

PROTOCOL CONCERNING THE ENTRY INTO FORCE OF THE AGREEMENT BETWEEN THE UNITED NATIONS AND THE INTERNATIONAL TELECOMMUNICATION UNION

Article 57 of the Charter of the United Nations provides that specialized agencies established by inter-governmental agreement and having wide international responsibilities as defined in their basic instruments in economic, social, cultural, educational, health and related fields shall be brought into relationship with the United Nations. Article 63 of the Charter provides that the Economic and Social Council may enter into agreements with any of the agencies referred to in Article 57, defining the terms on which the agency concerned shall be brought into relationship with the United Nations, and specifies that such agreements shall be subject to approval by the General Assembly.

On 28 March 1947, the Economic and Social Council, during its fourth session, directed its Committee on Negotiations with Inter-Governmental Agencies to enter into negotiations at the appropriate time with the International Telecommunication Union for the purpose of bringing it into relationship with the United Nations and to submit a report on the negotiations to the Council including therein a draft preliminary agreement based upon these negotiations.

The Plenipotentiary Conference of the International Telecommunication Union which met in Atlantic City from May to October 1947, having been informed of the aforementioned decision of the Economic and Social Council, appointed a Committee to enter into negotiations with the United Nations Committee on Negotiations with Inter-Governmental Agencies to prepare a draft agreement.

Negotiations between the Committee on Negotiations with Inter-Governmental Agencies of the Economic and Social Council and the Negotiating Committee of the International Telecommunication Union took place at Lake Success on 12, 13 and 14 August 1947 and resulted in a draft agreement, which was signed by Mr. Walter M. Kotschnig, Acting Chairman of the Committee of the Economic and Social Council on Negotiations with Inter-Governmental Agencies, and Sir Harold Shoobert, Chairman of the Negotiating Committee of the International Telecommunication Union.

On 16 August 1947 the Economic and Social Council, during its fifth session, recommended the agreement between the United Nations and the International Telecommunication Union to the General Assembly for its approval, with the reservation that approval of the agreement would be conditional on a decision by the Plenipotentiary Conference of the Union, having the effect of bringing the Union into full compliance with the resolution passed by the General Assembly on 12 December 1946 with regard to Franco Spain.

On 4 September 1947 the Plenipotentiary Conference of the International Telecommunication Union which met in Atlantic City for the purpose of revising the International Telecommunication Convention unanimously approved the draft agreement which subsequently was annexed to the revised Convention.

On 2 October 1947 the Plenipotentiary Conference of the International Telecommunication Union approved Article I of the revised Convention on the composition of the Union the provisions of which had the effect of bringing the Union into full compliance with the resolution passed by the General Assembly on 12 December 1946 with regard to Franco Spain.

On 11 October 1947 the Secretary-General of the United Nations, upon request of the Secretary-General of the International Telecommunication Conferences at Atlantic City, proposed to the General Assembly an additional article on the use of the United Nations *laissez-passer*, to be inserted in the draft agreement.

The Agreement between the United Nations and the International Telecommunication Union, with the insertion in the Agreement of the article on the use of the United Nations *laissez-passer*, was approved by the General Assembly during its second regular session on 15 November 1947.

Article XVIII of the Agreement provides that this Agreement shall come into force provisionally on its approval by the General Assembly of the United Nations and the Plenipotentiary Telecommunication Conference at Atlantic City in 1947. The Agreement accordingly came into force provisionally on 15 November 1947.

Article XVIII of the Agreement further provides that subject to the aforementioned approval, the Agreement shall formally enter into force at the same time as the International Telecommunication Convention concluded at Atlantic City in 1947. The International Telecommunication Convention entered into force on 1 January 1949.

The Agreement accordingly came into force on 1 January 1949.

IN FAITH WHEREOF we have appended our signatures this 26th day of April one thousand nine hundred and forty-nine, to two original copies of the present Protocol, the text of which consists of versions in the English and French languages which are equally authentic. One of the original copies will be deposited with the Secretariat of the United Nations and the other will be deposited with the Secretariat of the International Telecommunication Union.

Trygve LIE
Secretary-General of the United Nations

Pr. V. ERNST
*Secretary-General
of the International Telecommunication Union*

AGREEMENT BETWEEN THE UNITED NATIONS
AND THE INTERNATIONAL TELECOMMUNICATION UNION

PREAMBLE

In consideration of the provisions of Article 57 oftthe Charter of the United Nations and of article 26 of the Convention of the International Telecommunication Union of Atlantic City 1947, the United Nations and the International Telecommunication Union agree as follows:

Article I

The United Nations recognizes the International Telecommunication Union (thereinafter called Union) as the specialized agency responsible for taking such action as may be appropriate under its basic instrument for the accomplishment of the purposes set forth therein.

Article II

RECIPROCAL REPRESENTATION

1. The United Nations shall be invited to send representatives to participate, without vote, in the deliberations of all the plenipotentiary and administrative conferences of the Union. It shall also, after appropriate consultation, be invited to send representatives to attend international consultative committees or any other meetings convened by the Union, with the right to participate, without vote, in the discussion of items of interest to the United Nations.

2. The Union shall be invited to send representatives to attend meetings of the General Assembly of the United Nations for the purposes of consultation on telecommunication matters.

3. The Union shall be invited to send representatives to be present at the meetings of the Economic and Social Council of the United Nations and of the Trusteeship Council and of their commissions or committees, and to participate, without vote, in the deliberations thereof with respect to items on the agenda in which the Union may be concerned.

4. The Union shall be invited, to send representatives to attend meetings of the main committees of the General Assembly when matters within the competence of the Union are under discussion, and to participate, without vote, in such discussions.

5. Written statements presented by the Union shall be distributed by the Secretariat of the United Nations to the members of the General Assembly, the Economic and Social Council and its commissions, and the Trusteeship Council, as appropriate. Similarly, written statements presented by the United Nations shall be distributed by the Union to its members.

Article III

PROPOSAL OF AGENDA ITEMS

After such preliminary consultation as may be necessary, the Union shall include in the agenda of plenipotentiary or administrative conferences or meetings of other organs of the Union, items proposed to it by the United Nations. Similarly, the Economic and Social Council and its commissions and the Trusteeship Council shall include in their agenda items proposed by the conferences or other organs of the Union.

Article IV

RECOMMENDATIONS OF THE UNITED NATIONS

1. The Union, having regard to the obligation of the United Nations to promote the objectives set forth in Article 55 of the Charter, and the function and power of the Economic and Social Council under Article 62 of the Charter to make or initiate studies and reports with respect to international economic, social, cultural, educational, health and related matters and to make recommendations concerning these matters to the specialized agencies concerned, and having regard also to the responsibility of the United Nations, under Articles 58 and 63 of the Charter, to make recommendations for the co-ordination of the policies and activities of such specialized agencies, agrees to arrange for the submission as soon as possible to its appropriate organ, for such action as may seem proper, of all formal recommendations which the United Nations may make to it.

2. The Union agrees to enter into consultation with the United Nations upon request with respect to such recommendations, and in due course to report to the United Nations on the action taken by the Union or by its members to give effect to such recommendations, or on the other results of their consideration.

3. The Union will co-operate in whatever further measures may be necessary to make co-ordination of the activities of specialized agencies and those of the United Nations fully effective. In particular, it agrees to co-operate with any body or bodies which the Economic and Social Council may establish for the purpose of facilitating such co-ordination, and to furnish such information as may be required for the carrying out of this purpose.

Article V

EXCHANGE OF INFORMATION AND DOCUMENTS

1. Subject to such arrangements as may be necessary for the safeguarding of confidential material, the fullest and promptest exchange of appropriate information and documents shall be made between the United Nations and the Union to meet the requirements of each.

2. Without prejudice to the generality of the provisions of the preceding paragraph:

(a) The Union shall submit to the United Nations an annual report on its activities;

(b) The Union shall comply to the fullest extent practicable with any request which the United Nations may make for the furnishing of special reports, studies or information;

(c) The Secretary-General of the United Nations shall, upon request, consult with the appropriate authority of the Union with a view to providing to the Union such information as may be of special interest to it.

Article VI

ASSISTANCE TO THE UNITED NATIONS

The Union agrees to co-operate with and to render all possible assistance to the United Nations, its principal and subsidiary organs, in accordance with the United Nations Charter and the International Telecommunication Convention, taking fully into account the particular position of the individual members of the Union who are not members of the United Nations.

Article VII

RELATIONS WITH THE INTERNATIONAL COURT OF JUSTICE

1. The Union agrees to furnish any information which may be requested by the International Court of Justice in pursuance of Article 34 of the Statute of the Court.

2. The General Assembly authorizes the Union to request advisory opinions of the International Court of Justice on legal questions arising within the scope of its competence other than questions concerning the mutual relationships of the Union and the United Nations or other specialized agencies.

3. Such request may be addressed to the Court by the Plenipotentiary Conference or the Administrative Council acting in pursuance of an authorization by the Plenipotentiary Conference.

4. When requesting the International Court of Justice to give an advisory opinion the Union shall inform the Economic and Social Council of the request.

Article VIII

PERSONNEL ARRANGEMENTS

1. The United Nations and the Union agree to develop, as far as is practicable, common personnel standards, methods and arrangements designed to avoid serious discrepancies in terms and conditions of employment, to avoid competition in recruitment of personnel, and to facilitate any mutually desirable interchange of personnel in order to obtain the maximum benefit from their services.

2. The United Nations and the Union agree to co-operate to the fullest extent possible in achieving these ends.

Article IX

STATISTICAL SERVICES

1. The United Nations and the Union agree to strive for maximum co-operation, the elimination of all undesirable duplication between them, and the most efficient use of their technical personnel in their respective collection, analysis, publication, standardization, improvement and dissemination of statistical information. They agree to combine their efforts to secure the greatest possible usefulness and utilization of statistical information and to minimize the burdens placed upon national Government and other organizations from which such information may be collected.

2. The Union recognizes the United Nations as the central agency for the collection, analysis, publication, standardization, improvement and dissemination of statistics serving the general purposes of international organizations.

3. The United Nations recognizes the Union as the central agency responsible for the collection, analysis, publication, standardization, improvement and dissemination of statistics within its special sphere, without prejudice to the rights of the United Nations to concern itself with such statistics so far as that may be essential for its own purposes or for the improvement of statistics throughout the world. All decisions as to the form in which its service documents are complied rest with the Union.

4. In order to build up a central collection of statistical information for general use, it is agreed that data supplied to the Union for incorporation in its basic statistical series or special reports should, as far as is practicable, be made available to the United Nations upon request.

5. It is agreed that data supplied to the United Nations for incorporation in its basic statistical series or special reports should, so far as is practicable and appropriate, be made available to the Union upon request.

Article X

ADMINISTRATIVE AND TECHNICAL SERVICES

1. The United Nations and the Union recognize the desirability, in the interests of the most efficient use of personnel and resources, of avoiding, whenever possible, the establishment of competitive or overlapping services, and when necessary to consult thereon to achieve these ends.

2. Arrangements shall be made between the United Nations and the Union with regard to the registration and deposit of official documents.

Article XI

BUDGETARY AND FINANCIAL ARRANGEMENTS

1. The budget or the proposed budget of the Union shall be transmitted to the United Nations at the same time as such budget is transmitted to the members of the Union, and the General Assembly may make recommendations thereon to the Union.

2. The Union shall be entitled to send representatives to participate, without vote, in the deliberations of the General Assembly or any committee thereof at all times when the budget of the Union is under consideration.

Article XII

FINANCING OF SPECIAL SERVICES

1. In the event of the Union being faced with the necessity of incurring substantial extra expense as a result of any request which the United Nations may make for special reports, studies or assistance in accordance with article VI or with any other provisions of this agreement, consultation shall take place with a view to determining the most equitable manner in which such expense shall be borne.

2. Consultation between the United Nations and the Union shall similarly take place with a view to making such arrangements as may be found equitable for covering the costs of central administrative, technical or fiscal services or facilities or other special assistance requested by the Union and provided by the United Nations.

Article XIII

UNITED NATIONS LAISSEZ-PASSER

Officials of the Union shall have the right to use the *laissez-passer* of the United Nations in accordance with special arrangements to be negotiated between the Secretary-General of the United Nations and the competent authorities of the Union.

Article XIV

INTER-AGENCY AGREEMENTS

1. The Union agrees to inform the Economic and Social Council of the nature and scope of any formal agreement contemplated between the Union and any other specialized agency or other inter-governmental organization or international non-governmental organization, and further will inform the Economic and Social Council of the details of any such agreement, when concluded.

2. The United Nations agrees to inform the Union of the nature and scope of any formal agreement contemplated by any other specialized agencies on matters which might be of concern to the Union and further will inform the Union of the details of any such agreement, when concluded.

Article XV

LIAISON

1. The United Nations and the Union agree to the foregoing provisions in the belief that they will contribute to the maintenance of effective liaison between the two Organizations. They affirm their intention of taking whatever measures may be necessary to this end.

2. The liaison arrangements provided for in this agreement shall apply, as far as is appropriate, to the relations between the Union and the United Nations, including its branch and regional offices.

Article XVI

UNITED NATIONS TELECOMMUNICATION SERVICES

1. The Union recognizes that it is important the United Nations shall benefit by the same rights as the members of the Union for operating telecommunication services.

2. The United Nations undertakes to operate the telecommunication services under its control in accordance with the terms of the International Telecommunication Convention and the regulations annexed thereto.

3. The precise arrangements for implementing this article shall be dealt with separately.

Article XVII

IMPLEMENTATION OF AGREEMENT

The Secretary-General of the United Nations and the appropriate authority of the Union may enter into such supplementary arrangements for the implementation of this agreement as may be found desirable.

Article XVIII

REVISION

On six months' notice given on either side, this agreement shall be subject to revision by agreement between the United Nations and the Union.

Article XIX

ENTRY INTO FORCE

1. This agreement will come into force provisionally after approval by the General Assembly of the United Nations and the Plenipotentiary Telecommunication Conference at Atlantic City in 1947.

2. Subject to the aforementioned approval, the agreement will formally enter into force at the same time as the International Telecommunication Convention concluded at Atlantic City in 1947, or at some earlier date as may be arranged for by a decision of the Union.

10. AGREEMENT BETWEEN THE UNITED NATIONS AND THE WORLD METEOROLOGICAL ORGANIZATION APPROVED BY THE GENERAL ASSEMBLY ON ON DECEMBER 20, 1951

PROTOCOL CONCERNING THE ENTRY INTO FORCE OF THE AGREEMENT BETWEEN THE UNITED NATIONS AND THE WORLD METEOROLOGICAL ORGANIZATION

Article 57 of the Charter of the United Nations provides that specialized agencies established by inter-governmental agreement and having wide international responsibilities as defined in their basic instruments in economic, social, cultural, educational, health and related fields shall be brought into relationship with the United Nations. Article 63 of the Charter provides that the Economic and Social Council may enter into agreements with any of the agencies referred to in Article 57, defining the terms on which the agency concerned shall be brought into relationship with the United Nations, and specifies that such agreements shall be subject to approval by the General Assembly.

Article 25 of the Convention of the World Meteorological Organization provides that the Organization shall be brought into relationship with the United Nations subject to the approval of the terms of the agreement by two-thirds of the members which are States.

On 10 March 1948, the Economic and Social Council, during its sixth session, directed its Committee on Negotiations with Inter-Governmental Agencies to enter into negotiations at the appropriate time with the World Meteorological Organization for the purpose of bringing it into relationship with the United Nations and to submit a report on the negotiations to the Council including therein a draft preliminary agreement based on these negotiations.

During the twelfth session of the Council, the Committee on Negotiations with Inter-Governmental Agencies requested its Chairman forthwith to negotiate an agreement on its behalf with the World Meteorological Organization.

The Congress of the World Meteorological Organization, at its first session which was held in Paris in March and April 1951, appointed its President and two Vice-Presidents as negotiating officers to undertake negotiations with the Chairman of the United Nations Committee on Negotiations with Inter-Governmental Agencies to prepare a draft agreement.

Negotiations between the Chairman of the Committee on Negotiations with Inter-Governmental Agencies of the Economic and Social Council and authorized officers of the World Meteorological Organization took place on 5 April 1951 in Paris and resulted in a draft agreement. This draft agreement was signed on 5 April 1951 by Sir Ramaswami Mudaliar, Chairman of the Committee on Negotiations with Inter-Governmental Agencies, and Sir Nelson K. Johnson, Head of the negotiating officers of the World Meteorological Organization.

On 9 August 1951 the Economic and Social Council, during its thirteenth session, recommended the Agreement between the United Nations and the World Meteorological Organization to the General Assembly for its approval.

Article XVIII of the Agreement provides that this Agreement shall come into force on its approval by the General Assembly of the United Nations and by the World Meteorological Organization in accordance with Article 25 of the Convention of the World Meteorological Organization. The Agreement was approved by the Congress of the World Meteorological Organization during its first session on 10 April 1951 and by the General Assembly of the United Nations during its sixth regular session on 20 December 1951. The Agreement accordingly came into force on 20 December 1951.

A copy of the authentic text of this Agreement is attached hereto.

IN FAITH WHEREOF we have appended our signatures this 19th day of February, one thousand nine hundred and fifty two, to two original copies of the present Protocol, the text of which consists of versions in the English and French languages which are equally authentic. One of the original copies will be deposited with the Secretariat of the United Nations and the other will be deposited with the Secretariat of the World Meteorological Organization.

Trygve LIE
Secretary-General of the United Nations

G. SWOBODA
Secretary-General of the World Meteorological Organization

AGREEMENT BETWEEN THE UNITED NATIONS AND THE WORLD METEOROLOGICAL ORGANIZATION

PREAMBLE

In consideration of the provisions of Article 57 of the Charter of the United Nations and of Article 25 of the Convention of the World Meteorological Organization, the United Nations and the World Meteorological Organization agree as follows:

Article I

The United Nations recognizes the World Meteorological Organization (hereinafter called "the Organization") as the specialized agency responsible for taking such action as may be appropriate under its basic instrument for the accomplishment of the purposes set forth therein.

Article II

RECIPROCAL REPRESENTATION

1. The United Nations shall be invited to send representatives to participate, without vote, in the deliberations of all the Congresses and Meetings of the Executive Committee and Regional Associations. It shall also, after appropriate consultation, be invited to send representatives to attend meetings of the Technical Commissions or any other meetings convened by the Organization with the right to participate without vote in the discussion of items of interest to the United Nations.

2. The Organization shall be invited to send representatives to attend meetings of the Economic and Social Council of the United Nations (thereinafter called "the Council)," of its Commissions and Committees and to participate, without vote, in the deliberations thereof with respect to items on the agenda in which the Organization may be concerned.

3. The Organization shall be invited to send representatives to attend the meetings of the General Assembly during which questions within the competence of the Organization are under discussion for purposes of consultation, and to participate, without vote, in the deliberations of the main Committees of the General Assembly with respect to items concerning the Organization.

4. The Organization shall be invited to send representatives and to attend meetings of the Trusteeship Council of the United Nations and to participate, without vote, in the deliberations thereof, with respect to items on its agenda relating to meteorological matters.

5. Written statements presented by the Organization shall be distributed by the Secretariat of the United Nations to the members of the General Assembly, the Council and its Commissions, and the Trusteeship Council as appropriate. Similarly, written statements presented by the United Nations shall be distributed by the Organization to its Members.

Article III

PROPOSAL OF AGENDA ITEMS

Subject to such preliminary consultation as may be necessary, the Organization shall include on the agenda of its Congresses and Meetings of the Executive Committee, Regional Associations and Technical Commissions or, as the case may be, shall submit to its Members items proposed to it by the United Nations. Similarly, the Council, its Commissions and Committees and the Trusteeship Council shall include on their agenda items proposed by the Organization.

Article IV

RECOMMENDATIONS OF THE UNITED NATIONS

1. The Organization, having regard to the obligations of the United Nations to promote the objectives set forth in Article 55 of the Charter, and the functions and power of the Economic and Social Council under Article 62 of the Charter to make or initiate studies and reports with respect to international economic, social, cultural, educational, health and related matters and to make recommendations concerning these matters to the specialized agencies concerned, and having regard also to the responsibility of the United Nations, under Articles 58 and 63 of the Charter, to make recommendations for the co-ordination of the policies and activities of such specialized agencies, agree to arrange for the submission as soon as possible to its appropriate organ or to its Members for such action as may seem proper, of all formal recommendations which the United Nations may make to it.

2. The Organization agrees to enter into consultation with the United Nations upon request with respect to such recommendations and in due course to report to the United Nations on the action taken by the Organization or by its Members to give effect to such recommendations, or on the other results of their consideration.

3. The Organization agrees to co-operate in whatever further measures may be necessary to make co-ordination of the activities of specialized agencies and those of the United Nations fully effective. In particular, it agrees to co-operate with any body or bodies which the Council may establish for the purposes of facilitating such co-ordination and furnish such information as may be required for the carrying out of this purpose.

Article V

EXCHANGE OF INFORMATION AND DOCUMENTS

1. Subject to such arrangements as may be necessary for the safeguarding of confidential material, the fullest and promptest exchange of information and documents shall be made between the United Nations and the Organization to meet the requirements of each.

2. Without prejudice to the generality of the provisions of the preceding paragraph:

(a) The Organization shall submit to the United Nations an annual report on its activities.

(b) The Organization shall comply to the fullest extent practicable with any request which the United Nations may make for the furnishing of special reports, studies or information, subject to the conditions set forth in Article XIII.

(c) The Secretary-General of the United Nations shall, upon request, consult with the Secretary-General of the Organization regarding the provision to the Organization of such information as may be of special interest to it.

Article VI

ASSISTANCE TO THE UNITED NATIONS

The Organization agrees to co-operate with and to render all possible assistance to the United Nations, its principal and subsidiary organs, in accordance with the United Nations Charter and the World Meteorological Convention, taking fully into account the particular position of the individual Members of the Organization which are not members of the United Nations.

Article VII

RELATIONS WITH THE INTERNATIONAL COURT OF JUSTICE

1. The Organization agrees to furnish any information which may be requested by the International Court of Justice in pursuance of Article 34 of the Statute of the Court.

2. The General Assembly authorities the Organization to request advisory opinions of the International Court of Justice on legal questions arising within the scope of its competence other than questions concerning the mutual relationships of the Organization with the United Nations or with other specialized agencies.

3. Such requests may be addressed to the Court by the Congress or the Executive Committee acting in pursuance of an authorization by the Congress.

4. When requesting the International Court of Justice to give an advisory opinion, the Organization shall inform the Council of the request.

Article VIII

HEADQUARTERS AND REGIONAL OFFICES

1. The World Meteorological Organization agrees to consult with the United Nations before making any decision concerning the location of its permanent headquarters.

2. Having due regard to the special needs of world meteorology, any regional or branch office which the World Meteorological Organization may establish shall so far as is practicable be closely associated with such regional or branch offices as the United Nations or other specialized agencies may establish.

Article IX

PERSONNEL ARRANGEMENTS

1. The United Nations and the Organization agree to develop as far as practicable common personnel standards, methods, and arrangements designed to avoid serious discrepancies in terms and conditions of employment, to avoid competition in recruitment of personnel, and to facilitate any mutually desirable interchange of personnel in order to obtain the maximum benefit from their services.

2. The United Nations and the Organization agree to co-operate to the fullest extent possible in achieving these ends and to consult in regard to the participation of the Organization in the work of the International Civil Service Advisory Board and the United Nations Joint Staff Pension Fund.

3. The United Nations and the Organization agree further to consult as to the desirability of concluding a special agreement extending the competence of the United Nations Administrative Tribunal to the Organization.

Article X

STATISTICAL SERVICES

1. The United Nations and the Organization agree to strive for maximum co-operation; the elimination of all undesirable duplication between them, and the most efficient use of their technical personnel in their respective collection, analysis, publication, standardization, improvement and dissemination of statistical information. They agree to combine their efforts to secure the greatest possible usefulness and utilization of statistical information and to minimize the burdens placed upon national governments and other organizations from which such information may be collected.

2. The Organization recognizes the United Nations as the central agency for the collection, analysis, publication, standardization, improvement and dissemination of statistics serving the general purposes of international organizations.

3. In view of the fact that meteorological statistics of universal application to scientific research, aviation, shipping, agriculture, health and other human activities can best be derived from data collected and compiled by or through the Organization, the United Nations recognizes the Organization as the specialized agency responsible in conformity with Article 2 of its Convention for the collection, analysis, publication, standardization, improvement and dissemination of statistics in the field of meteorology and its applications, and for the supply of such statistics to other specialized agencies without prejudice to the right of the United Nations to concern itself with such statistics so far as it may be essential for its own purposes or for the improvement of statistics throughout world. All decisions as to the form in which its service documentation shall be compiled rest with the Organization.

4. The United Nations shall in consultation with the Organization, and with the other specialized agencies where appropriate, develop administrative instruments and procedures through which effective statistical co-operation may be secured between the United Nations and the specialized agencies and among the specialized agencies themselves.

5. It is recognized as important that the collection of meteorological statistical information shall not be duplicated by the United Nations or any of its other specialized agencies whenever it is practicable for any of them to utilize information or material which the Organization has or can make available.

6. In order to build up a central collection of statistical information for general use, it is agreed that data supplied to the Organization for incorporation in its basic statistical series or special reports should so far as practicable be made available to the United Nations upon request.

7. It is agreed that data supplied to the United Nations by other sources than that of the Organization for incorporation in its basic statistical series or special reports or for other purposes should so far as practicable and appropriate be made available to the latter upon request.

Article XI

ADMINISTRATIVE AND TECHNICAL SERVICES

1. The United Nations and the Organization recognize the desirability, in the interest of the most efficient use of personnel and resources, of avoiding, whenever possible, the establishment of competitive or overlapping services, and agree when necessary to consult thereon to achieve these ends.

2. Arrangements shall be made between the United Nations and the Organization in regard to the registration and deposit of official documents.

3. Officials of the Organization shall have the right to use the *laissez-passer* of the United Nations in accordance with special arrangements to be negotiated between the Secretary-General of the United Nations and the competent authorities of the Organization.

Article XII

BUDGETARY AND FINANCIAL ARRANGEMENTS

1. The Organization recognizes the desirability of establishing close budgetary and financial relationships with the United Nations in order that the administrative operations of the United Nations and of the specialized agencies shall be carried out in the most efficient and economical manner possible and that the maximum measure of co-ordination and uniformity with respect to these operations shall be secured.

2. The United Nations and the Organization agree to co-operate to the fullest extent possible in achieving these ends and, in particular, shall if it appears expedient to both Organizations consult together concerning the desirability of making appropriate arrangements for the inclusion of the budget of the Organization within a general bud-

get of the United Nations. Any such arrangements shall be defined in a supplementary agreement between the two Organizations.

3. Pending the conclusion of any such agreement, the following arrangement shall govern budgetary and financial relationships between the United Nations and the Organization:

(a) In the preparation of the budget of the Organization, the Secretariat of the Organization shall consult with the Secretary-General of the United Nations with a view to achieving, in so far as practicable, uniformity in presentation of the budgets of the United Nations and of the specialized agencies for the purpose of providing a basis for comparison of the several budgets.

(b) The Organization agrees to transmit its budget or budgetary estimates to the United Nations by 1 July of the preceding year or such other date as may be agreed upon by the United Nations and the Organization. The General Assembly shall examine the budget or budgetary estimates of the Organization and may make such recommendations as it may consider necessary.

(c) Representatives of the Organization shall be entitled to participate, without vote, in the deliberations of the General Assembly or any committee thereof or established by it, at all times when the budget of the Organization or general administrative or financial questions affecting the Organization are under consideration.

(d) The United Nations may undertake the collection of contributions from those members of the Organization which are also members of the United Nations in accordance with such arrangements as may be defined by a later agreement between the United Nations and the Organization.

(e) The United Nations shall, upon its own initiative or upon the request of the Organization, arrange for studies to be undertaken concerning other financial and fiscal questions of interest to the Organization and to other specialized agencies with a view to the provision of common services and the securing of uniformity in such matters.

(f) The Organization agrees to conform, as far as may be practicable, to standard practices and forms recommended by the United Nations.

Article XIII

FINANCING OF SPECIAL SERVICES

1. In the event of the Organization being faced with the necessity of incurring substantial extra expenses as a result of any request which the United Nations may make for special reports, studies or assistance in accordance with Article VI or with any other provisions of this agreement, the Organization shall consult with the United Nations prior to incurring such expense with a view to determining the most equitable manner in which such expense shall be borne.

2. Consultation between the United Nations and the Organization shall similarly take place with a view to making such arrangements as may be found equitable for covering the costs of central administrative, technical or fiscal services or facilities or other special assistance requested by the Organization and provided by the United Nations.

Article XIV

INTER-AGENCY AGREEMENTS

1. The Organization agrees to inform the Council of the nature and scope of any formal agreement contemplated between the Organization and any other specialized agency or other inter-governmental organization or international non-governmental organization, and further to inform the Council of the details of any such agreement when concluded.

2. The United Nations agrees to inform the Organization of the nature and scope of any formal agreement contemplated by any other specialized agencies on matters which might be of concern to the Organization and further will inform the Organization of the details of any such agreement, when concluded.

Article XV

LIAISON

1. The United Nations and the Organization agree to the foregoing provisions in the belief that they will contribute to the maintenance of effective liaison between the two organizations. They affirm their intention of taking whatever further measures may be necessary to this end.

2. The liaison arrangements provided for in this Agreement shall apply, as far as appropriate, to the relations between such branch and regional offices as may be established by the two organizations as well as between their central headquarters.

Article XVI

IMPLEMENTATION OF AGREEMENT

The Secretary-General of the United Nations and the appropriate authority of the Organization may enter into such supplementary arrangements for the implementation of this Agreement as may be found desirable.

Article XVII

REVISION

On six months' notice given on either part, this Agreement shall be subject to revision by agreement between the United Nations and the Organization.

Article XVIII

ENTRY INTO FORCE

This Agreement shall come into force on its approval by the General Assembly of the United Nations and by the Organization in accordance with Article 25 of the World Meteorological Convention.

11. AGREEMENT BETWEEN THE UNITED NATIONS AND THE INTERNATIONAL FINANCE CORPORATION APPROVED BY THE GENERAL ASSEMBLY ON FEBRUARY 20, 1957

PROTOCOL CONCERNING THE ENTRY INTO FORCE OF THE AGREEMENT BETWEEN THE UNITED NATIONS AND THE INTERNATIONAL BANK FOR RECONSTRUCTION AND DEVELOPMENT (ACTING FOR AND ON BEHALF OF THE INTERNATIONAL FINANCE CORPORATION) ON RELATIONSHIP BETWEEN THE UNITED NATIONS AND THE INTERNATIONAL FINANCE CORPORATION.

Article 57 of the Charter of the United Nations provides that specialized agencies established by inter-governmental agreement and having wide international responsibilities as defined in their basic instruments in economic, social, cultural, educational, health and related fields shall be brought into relationship with the United Nations. Article 63 of the Charter provides that the Economic and Social Council may enter into agreements with any of the agencies referred to in Article 57, defining the terms on which the agency concerned shall be brought into relationship with the United Nations, and specifies that such agreements shall be subject to approval by the General Assembly.

Section 7 of article IV of the Articles of Agreement of the International Finance Corporation provides that the Corporation, acting through the International Bank for Reconstruction and Development, shall enter into formal arrangements with the United Nations and may enter into such arrangements with other public international organizations having specialized responsibilities in related fields.

By a communication dated 14 November 1956 the President of the International Bank for Reconstruction and Development informed the Secretary-General of the United Nations that the Bank had been authorized and requested by the Board of Directors of the International Finance Corporation to negotiate an agreement with the United Nations on terms substantially corresponding to the terms of the Agreement between the United Nations and the Bank.

The Economic and Social Council, having been informed of the aforementioned communication from the President of the International Bank for Reconstruction and Development, adopted a resolution on 17 December 1956, during its resumed twenty-second session, requesting the President of the Council to negotiate with the appropriate authorities of the Bank an agreement for the purpose of bringing the International Finance Corporation into relationship with the United Nations.

Negotiations between the President of the Council and a Vice-President of the International Bank for Reconstruction and Development took place in New York on 17 December 1956 and resulted in an Agreement.

On 19 December 1956 the Economic and Social Council, during its resumed twenty-second session, recommended the Agreement between the United Nations and the International Bank for Reconstruction and Development, acting for and on behalf of the International Finance Corporation, on relationship between the United Nations and the International Finance Corporation to the General Assembly for its approval.

Paragraph 3 of the Agreement provides that the Agreement shall enter into force when it shall have been approved by the General Assembly of the United Nations, the Board of Governors of the International Bank for Reconstruction and Development and the Board of Governors of the International Finance Corporation.

The Agreement was approved by the General Assembly of the United Nations on 20 February 1957, and by the Board of Governors of the International Bank for Reconstruction and Development and the Board of Governors of the International Finance Corporation on 31 January 1957.

The Agreement accordingly came into force on 20 February 1957.

A copy of the text of the Agreement in both English and French is attached hereto, the English text being the authentic text.

IN FAITH WHEREOF we have appended our signatures to three original copies of the present Protocol, the text of which consists of versions in the English and French languages which are equally authentic. One of the original copies will be filed and recorded with the Secretariat of the United Nations, one will be deposited in the archives of the International Bank for Reconstruction and Development, and one will be deposited in the archives of the International Finance Corporation.

Dag HAMMARSKJOLD
Secretary-General of the United Nations
17 April 1957

Eugene R. BLACK
President of the International Bank for Reconstruction and Development,
acting for and on behalf of the International Finance Corporation
18 April 1957

AGREEMENT BETWEEN THE UNITED NATIONS AND THE INTERNATIONAL BANK FOR RECONSTRUCTION AND DEVELOPMENT (ACTING FOR AND ON BEHALF OF THE INTERNATIONAL FINANCE CORPORATION) ON RELATIONSHIP BETWEEN THE UNITED NATIONS AND THE INTERNATIONAL FINANCE CORPORATION

WHEREAS Article 63 of the Charter of the United Nations provides that the Economic and Social Council may enter into agreements with any of the specialized agencies, defining the terms on which the agency concerned shall be brought into relationship with the United Nations;

WHEREAS the International Bank for Reconstruction and Development (hereinafter called the Bank) entered into an agreement (hereinafter called the Bank Agreement) with the United Nations which defines the terms on which the United Nations and the Bank were brought into relationship and which was approved by the Board of Governors of the Bank on 16 September 1947, and by the General Assembly of the United Nations on 15 November 1947;

WHEREAS the Articles of Agreement of the International Finance Corporation (hereinafter called the Corporation) entered into force, in accordance with session 1 of article IX of the said Articles of Agreement, on 20 July 1956;

WHEREAS section 7 of article IV of the said Articles of Agreement provides that the Corporation, acting through the Bank, shall enter into formal arrangements with the United Nations;

WHEREAS the Corporation has authorized the Bank to act for and on behalf of the Corporation in entering into such arrangements with the United Nations on terms substantially corresponding to the terms of the Bank Agreement;

NOW THEREFORE the United Nations and the Bank, acting for and on behalf of the Corporation, hereby agree as follows:

1. The relationship between the United Nations and the Corporation shall be gov-

erned by the Bank Agreement, and to that end the term "Bank" in the Bank Agreement shall be deemed to refer to the Corporation for purposes of this Agreement; except that, for the purposes of this Agreement,

(a) Paragraph 1 of article 1 of the Bank Agreement shall be deemed to read:

"This agreement, which is entered into by the United Nations pursuant to the provisions of Article 63 of its Charter, and by the International Bank for Reconstruction and Development, acting for and on behalf of the International Finance Corporation, pursuant to the provisions of section 7 of article IV of the Corporation's Articles of Agreement, is intended to define the terms on which the United Nations and the Corporation shall be brought into relationship;"

"(b) The last sentence of paragraph 3 of article IV of the Bank Agreement shall be deemed to read:

"The Corporation recognizes that the United Nations and its organs may appropriately make recommendations with respect to the technical aspects of programmes or projects for the development of productive private enterprise;"

(c) The first sentence of paragraph 3 of article X of the Bank Agreement shall be deemed to read:

"Copies of the annual report and the financial statements prepared by the Corporation pursuant to section 11, paragraph *(a)*, of article IV of its Articles of Agreement will be furnished to the United Nations;"

(d) The reference in paragraph 1 of article XIII of the Bank Agreement to the President of the Bank shall be deemed to continue to refer to the President of the Bank;

(e) Paragraph 2 of article XIII of the Bank Agreement shall be deemed to read;

"This agreement shall be subject to revision by agreement between the United Nations and the Bank, acting for and on behalf of the Corporation, from the date of its entry into force;"

(f) Paragraph 4 of article XIII of the Bank Agreement shall be deemed to be deleted, and to be replaced by paragraph 3 of this Agreement;

2. The Corporation shall act to the fullest extent practicable through the Bank in fulfilling its obligations under this Agreement;

3. This Agreement shall come into force when it shall have been approved by the General Assembly of the United Nations, the Board of Governors of the Bank, and the Board of Governors of the Corporation.

12. AGREEMENT BETWEEN THE UNITED NATIONS AND THE INTERNATIONAL ATOMIC ENERGY AGENCY APPROVED BY THE GENERAL ASSEMBLY ON NOVEMBER 14, 1957

PROTOCOL CONCERNING THE ENTRY INTO FORCE OF THE AGREEMENT CONCERNING THE RELATIONSHIP BETWEEN THE UNITED NATIONS AND THE INTERNATIONAL ATOMIC ENERGY AGENCY

Article XVI of the Statute of the International Atomic Energy Agency authorizes the Agency to enter into an agreement establishing an appropriate relationship between the Agency and the United Nations, which agreement shall provide for the submission by the Agency of reports to the United Nations and the consideration by the Agency of resolutions relating to it adopted by the General Assembly or any of the Councils of the United Nations.

Annex I of the Statute adopted by the Conference on the Statute of the International Atomic Energy Agency directed the Preparatory Commission of the Agency to enter into negotiations with the United Nations with a view to the preparation of a draft agreement for submission to the General Conference and to the Board of Governors.

The General Assembly of the United Nations, during its eleventh session in 1956, adopted a resolution authorizing the Secretary-General's Advisory Committee on the Peaceful Uses of Atomic Energy to negotiate with the Preparatory Commission of the International Atomic Energy Agency a draft relationship agreement for submission to the General Assembly, based on the principles set forth in a study prepared by the Secretary-General in consultation with the Advisory Committee.

After some preliminary negotiations, a joint meeting was held on 24 June 1957 between the Advisory Committee on the Peaceful Uses of Atomic Energy and the Preparatory Commission of the International Atomic Energy Agency. At that time the text of the draft agreement was considered and approved, with the exception of the word "primarily" which had originally appeared in the phrase "The United Nations recognizes the International Atomic Energy Agency. . . as the agency under the aegis of the United Nations as specified in this Agreement primarily responsible for international activities concerned with the peaceful uses of atomic energy. . ." (Article I, par. 1). In an exchange of correspondence between Mr. Carlos A. Bernardes, President of the Preparatory Commission, and Mr. Dag Hammarskjold, Secretary-General of the United Nations and Chairman of the Advisory Committee, it was agreed that the following statement should be included in the record, as indicating the understanding of the parties concerning this provision of the agreement:

"With regard to paragraph 1 of Article 1 of the draft agreement, it is noted that the Agency, which is established for the specific purpose of dealing with the peaceful uses of atomic energy, will have the leading position in this field."

The Board of Governors of the International Atomic Energy Agency on 11 October 1957 recommended to the General Conference of the Agency the adoption of the Agreement. On 23 October 1957, the General Conference, during its first special session, approved the Agreement, taking note of the exchange of correspondence between the President of the Preparatory Commission and the Secretary-General of the United Nations.

The Advisory Committee on the Peaceful Uses of Atomic Energy recommended approval of the Agreement to the General Assembly of the United Nations. On 14 November 1957 the General Assembly, during its twelfth session, approved the Agreement, taking note of the exchange of correspondence between the President of the Preparatory Commission and the Secretary-General of the United Nations.

Article XXIV of the Agreement provides that it shall come into force on its approval by the General Assembly of the United Nations and the General Conference of the International Atomic Energy Agency.

The Agreement accordingly came into force on 14 November 1957.

A copy of the authentic text of the Agreement is attached hereto.

IN FAITH WHEREOF we have appended our signatures on the dates appearing beneath our respective names to two original copies of the present Protocol, the text of which consists of versions in the English and French languages which are equally authentic. One of the original copies will be filed and recorded with the Secretariat of the United Nations and the other will be deposited in the archives of the International Atomic Energy Agency.

This 10th day of August 1959.

Dag HAMMARSKJOLD
Secretary-General of the United Nations

This 19th day of June 1959

Sterling COLE
Director-General of the International Atomic Energy Agency

AGREEMENT CONCERNING THE RELATIONSHIP BETWEEN THE UNITED NATIONS AND
THE INTERNATIONAL ATOMIC ENERGY AGENCY

The United Nations and the International Atomic Energy Agency,

Desiring to make provision for an effective system of relationship whereby the discharge of their respective responsibilities may be facilitated,

Taking into account for this purpose the provisions of the Charter of the United Nations and the statute of the Agency,

Have agreed as follows:

Article I

PRINCIPLES

1. The United Nations recognizes the International Atomic Energy Agency (hereinafter referred to as the Agency) as the agency, under the aegis of the United Nations as specified in this Agreement, responsible for international activities concerned with the peaceful uses of atomic energy in accordance with its Statute, without prejudice to the rights and responsibilities of the United Nations in this field under the Charter.

2. The United Nations recognizes that the Agency, by virtue of its inter-governmental character and international responsibilities, will function under its statute as an autonomous international organization in the working relationship with the United Nations established by this Agreement.

3. The Agency recognizes the responsibilities of the United Nations, in accordance with the Charter in the fields of international peace and security and economic and social development.

4. The Agency undertakes to conduct its activities in accordance with the purposes and principles of the United Nations Charter to promote peace and international cooperation, and in conformity with policies of the United Nations furthering the establishment of safeguarded world-wide disarmament and in conformity with any international agreements entered into pursuant to such policies.

Article II

CONFIDENTIAL INFORMATION

The United Nations or the Agency may find it necessary to apply certain limitations for the safeguarding of confidential material furnished to them by their members or others, and, subject to the provisions of article IX, nothing in this Agreement shall be construed to require either of them to furnish any information the furnishing of which would, in its judgement, constitute a violation of the confidence of any of its members or anyone from whom it shall have received such information.

Article III

REPORTS OF THE AGENCY TO THE UNITED NATIONS

1. The Agency shall keep the United Nations informed of its activities. Accordingly it shall:

(a) Submit reports covering its activities to the General Assembly at each regular session;

(b) Submit reports, when appropriate, to the Security Council and notify the Council whenever, in connexion with the activities of the Agency, questions within the competence of the Council arise;

(c) Submit reports to the Economic and Social Council and to other organs of the United Nations on matters within their respective competences.

2. The Agency shall report to the Security Council and the General Assembly any case of non-compliance within the meaning of article XII, paragraph C, of its statute.

Article IV

REPORT OF THE SECRETARY-GENERAL OF THE UNITED NATIONS

1. The Secretary-General of the United Nations shall report to the United Nations, as appropriate, on the common activities of the United Nations and the Agency and on the development of relations between them.

2. Any written report circulated under paragraph 1 of this article shall be transmitted to the Agency by the Secretary-General.

Article V

RESOLUTIONS OF THE UNITED NATIONS

The Agency shall consider any resolution relating to the Agency adopted by the General Assembly or by a Council of the United Nations. Any such resolution shall be referred to the Agency together with the appropriate records. Upon request, the Agency shall submit report on any action taken in accordance with the statute of the Agency by it or by its members as a result of its consideration of any resolution referred to it under this article.

Article VI

EXCHANGE OF INFORMATION AND DOCUMENTS

1. There shall be the fullest and promptest exchange between the United Nations and the Agency of appropriate information and documents.

2. The Agency, in conformity with its statute and to the extent practicable, shall furnish special studies or information requested by the United Nations.

3. The United Nations shall likewise furnish the Agency, upon request, with special studies or information relating to matters within the competence of the Agency.

Article VII

RECIPROCAL REPRESENTATION

1. The Secretary-General of the United Nations shall be entitled to attend and participate without vote on matters of common interest in sessions of the General Conference and of the Board of Governors of the Agency. The Secretary-General shall also be invited as appropriate to attend and participate without vote in such other meetings as the Agency may convene at which matters of interest to the United Nations are under consideration. The Secretary-General may, for the purposes of this paragraph, designate any person as his representative.

2. The Director General of the Agency shall be entitled to attend plenary meetings of the General Assembly of the United Nations for the purposes of consultation. He shall be entitled to attend and participate without vote in meetings of the Committees of the General Assembly, and meetings of the Economic and Social Council, the Trusteeship Council and, as appropriate, their subsidiary bodies. At the invitation of the Security Council, the Director General may attend its meetings to supply it with information or give it other assistance with regard to matters within the competence of the Agency. The Director General may, for the purposes of this paragraph, designate any person as his representative.

3. Written statements presented by the United Nations to the Agency for distribution shall be distributed by the Agency to all members of the appropriate organ or organs of the Agency. Written statements presented by the Agency to the United Nations for distribution shall be distributed by the Secretariat of the United Nations to all members of the appropriate organ or organs of the United Nations.

Article VIII

AGENDA ITEMS

1. The United Nations may propose items for consideration by the Agency. In such cases, the United Nations shall notify the Director General of the Agency of the item or items concerned, and the Director General shall include any such item or items in the provisional agenda of the General Conference or Board of Governors or such other organ of the Agency as may be appropriate.

2. The Agency may propose items for consideration by the United Nations. In such cases, the Agency shall notify the Secretary-General of the United Nations of the item or items concerned and the Secretary-General, in accordance with his authority, shall bring such item or items to the attention of the General Assembly, the Security Council, the Economic and Social Council or the Trusteeship Council, as appropriate.

Article IX

CO-OPERATION WITH THE SECURITY COUNCIL

The Agency shall co-operate with the Security Council by furnishing to it at its request such information and assistance as may be required in the exercise of its responsibility for the maintenance or restoration of international peace and security.

Article X

INTERNATIONAL COURT OF JUSTICE

1. The United Nations will take the necessary action to enable the General Conference or the Board of Governors of the Agency to seek an advisory opinion of the International Court of Justice on any legal question arising within the scope of the activities of the Agency, other than a question concerning the mutual relationships of the Agency and the United Nations or the specialized agencies.

2. The Agency agrees, subject to such arrangements as it may make for the safeguarding of confidential information, to furnish any information which may be requested by the International Court of Justice in accordance with the Statute of that Court.

Article XI

CO-ORDINATION

The United Nations and the Agency recognize the desirability of achieving effective co-ordination of the activities of the Agency with those of the United Nations and the specialized agencies, and of avoiding the overlapping and duplication of activities. Accordingly, the Agency agrees to co-operate, in accordance with its statute, in measures recommended by the United Nations for this purpose. Furthermore, the Agency agrees to participate in the work of the Administrative Committee on Co-ordination and, as appropriate, of any other bodies which have been or may be established by the United Nations to facilitate such co-operation and co-ordination. The Agency may also consult with appropriate bodies established by the United Nations on matters within their competence and on which the Agency requires expert advice. The United Nations, on its part, agrees to take such action as may be necessary to facilitate such participation and consultation.

Article XII

CO-OPERATION BETWEEN SECRETARIATS

1. The Secretariat of the United Nations and the staff of the Agency shall maintain a close working relationship in accordance with such arrangements as may be agreed upon from time to time between the Secretary-General of the United Nations and the Director General of the Agency.

2. It is recognized that similar close working relationships between the secretariats of the specialized agencies and the staff of the Agency are desirable and should be established and maintained in accordance with such arrangements as may be made between the Agency and the specialized agency or agencies concerned.

Article XIII

ADMINISTRATIVE CO-OPERATION

1. The United Nations and the Agency recognize the desirability of co-operation in administrative matters of mutual interest.

2. Accordingly, the United Nations and the Agency undertake to consult together from time to time concerning these matters, particularly the most efficient use of facilities, staff and services and appropriate methods of avoiding the establishment and operation of competitive or overlapping facilities and services among the United Nations, the specialized agencies and the Agency, and with a view to securing, within the limits of the Charter of the United Nations and the statute of the Agency, as much uniformity in these matters as shall be found practicable.

3. The consultations referred to in this article shall be utilized to establish the most equitable manner in which any special services or assistance furnished by the Agency to the United Nations or by the United Nations to the Agency shall be financed.

Article XIV

STATISTICAL SERVICES

The United Nations and the Agency, recognizing the desirability of maximum co-operation in the statistical field and of minimizing the burdens placed on national Governments and other organizations from which information may be collected, undertake to avoid undesirable duplication between them with respect to the collection, compilation and publication of statistics, and agree to consult with each other on the most efficient use of resources and of technical personnel in the field of statistics.

Article XV

TECHNICAL ASSISTANCE

The United Nations and the Agency recognize the desirability of co-operation concerning the provision of technical assistance in the atomic energy field. They undertake to avoid undesirable duplication of activities and services relating to technical assistance and agree to take such action as may be necessary to achieve effective co-ordination of their technical assistance activities within the framework of existing co-ordination machinery in the field of technical assistance, and the Agency agrees to give consideration to the common use of available services as far as practicable. The United Nations will make available to the Agency its administrative services in this field for use as requested.

Article XVI

BUDGETARY AND FINANCIAL ARRANGEMENTS

1. The Agency recognizes the desirability of establishing close budgetary and financial relationships with the United Nations in order that the administrative operations of the United Nations, the Agency and the specialized agencies shall be carried out in the most efficient and economical manner possible, and that the maximum measure of co-ordination and uniformity with respect to these operations shall be secured.

2. The Agency agrees to conform, as far as may be practicable and appropriate, to standard practices and forms recommended by the United Nations.

3. The Agency agrees to transmit its annual budget to the United Nations for such recommendations as the General Assembly may wish to make on the administrative aspects thereof.

4. The United Nations may arrange for studies to be undertaken concerning financial and fiscal questions of interest to the Agency and to the specialized agencies with a view to the provision of common services and the securing of uniformity in such matters.

Article XVII

PUBLIC INFORMATION

The United Nations and the Agency shall co-operate in the field of public information with a view to avoiding overlapping or uneconomical services and, where necessary or appropriate, to establishing common or joint services in this field.

Article XVIII

PERSONNEL ARRANGEMENTS

1. The United Nations and the Agency agree to develop, in the interests of uniform standards of international employment and to the extent feasible, common personnel standards, methods and arrangements designed to avoid unjustified difference in terms and conditions of employment to avoid competition in recruitment of personnel, and to facilitate interchange of personnel in order to obtain the maximum benefit from their services.

2. The United Nations and the Agency agree:

(a) To consult together from time to time concerning matters of common interest relating to the terms and conditions of employment of the officers and staff with a view to securing as much uniformity in these matters as may be feasible;

(b) To co-operate in the interchange of personnel, when desirable, on a temporary or a permanent basis, making due provision for the retention of seniority and pension rights;

(c) To co-operate, on such terms and conditions as may be agreed, in the operation of a common pension fund;

(d) To co-operate in the establishment and operation of suitable machinery for the settlement of disputes arising in connexion with the employment of personnel and related matters.

3. The terms and conditions on which any facilities or services of the Agency or the United Nations in connexion with the matters referred to in this article are to be extended to the other shall, where necessary, be the subject of subsidiary agreements concluded for this purpose after the entry into force of this Agreement.

Article XIX

ADMINISTRATIVE RIGHTS AND FACILITIES

1. Members of the staff of the Agency shall be entitled, in accordance with such administrative arrangements as may be concluded between the Secretary-General of the United Nations and the Director General of the Agency, to use the United Nations and the Director General of the Agency, to use the United Nations *laissez-passer* as a valid travel document where such use is recognized by States parties to the Convention on the Privileges and Immunities of the United Nations.

2. Subject to the provisions of article XVIII, the Secretary-General of the United Nations and the Director General of the Agency shall consult together as soon as may be practicable after the entry into force of this Agreement regarding the extension to the Agency of such other administrative rights and facilities as may be enjoyed by organizations within the United Nations system.

3. The United Nations shall invite, and provide the necessary facilities to, any representative of a member of the Agency, representative of the Agency, or member of the staff of the Agency desiring to proceed to the United Nations Headquarters district on official business connected with the Agency, whether at the initiative of any organ of the United Nations, of the Agency or of the member thereof.

Article XX

INTER-AGENCY AND OTHER AGREEMENTS

The agency shall inform the United Nations before the conclusion of any formal agreement between the Agency and any specialized agency or intergovernmental organization or any non-government organization enjoying consultative status with the United Nations, of the nature and scope of any such agreement, and shall inform the United Nations of the conclusion of any such agreement.

Article XXI

REGISTRATION OF AGREEMENTS

The United Nations and the Agency shall consult together as may be necessary with regard to the registration with the United Nations of agreements within the meaning of article XXII B of the statute of the Agency.

Article XXII

IMPLEMENTATION OF THIS AGREEMENT

The Secretary-General of the United Nations and the Director General of the Agency may enter into such arrangements for the implementation of this Agreement as may be found desirable in the light of the operating experience of the two organizations.

Article XXIII

AMENDMENTS

This Agreement may be amended by agreement between the United Nations and the Agency. Any amendment so agreed upon shall enter into force on its approval by the General Conference of the Agency and the General Assembly of the United Nations.

Article XXIV

ENTRY INTO FORCE

This Agreement shall enter into force on its approval by the General Assembly of the United Nations and the General Conference of the Agency.

EXCHANGE OF LETTERS

I

LETTER DATED 3 JULY 1957 FROM THE PRESIDENT OF THE PREPARATORY COMMISSION OF THE INTERNATIONAL ATOMIC ENERGY AGENCY ADDRESSED TO THE SECRETARY-GENERAL

I have the honour to refer to our previous conversations regarding the wording of article I, paragraph 1, of the draft agreement between the United Nations and the International Atomic Energy Agency.

At the joint meeting of the Advisory Committee on the Peaceful Uses of Atomic Energy and the Preparatory Commission of the International Atomic Energy Agency, which was held on 24 June 1957, you, as Chairman of the Advisory Committee and on behalf of the majority of its members, favoured the deletion of the word "primarily" in the phrase "The United Nations recognizes the International Atomic Energy Agency. . . as the agency, under the aegis of the United Nations as specified in this Agreement, primarily responsible for international activities concerned with the peaceful uses of atomic energy in accordance with its Statute. ." . After that meeting you suggested that a statement might be included in the record to cover the preoccupations of the Preparatory Commission on this point to the following effect:

With regard to paragraph 1 of article I of the draft agreement, it is noted that the Agency, which is established for the specific purpose of dealing with the peaceful uses of atomic energy, will have the leading position in this field."

The Preparatory Commission has discussed this question again and is prepared to agree to the deletion of the word "primarily" in view of the objection to it expressed by you as Chairman of the Advisory Committee and in the light of the inclusion of the above-quoted statement in the record, although it still feels that the original wording would have helped to clarify the relationship of the future Agency with other international organizations which also have an interest in certain aspects of atomic energy. The main concern of the Commission in this matter is to avoid duplication of effort and to ensure proper co-ordination.

I would suggest that the above-quoted statement might be included in the record, as indicated in the attached copy of the provisional record, and would be grateful for your agreement to this addition. This insertion could then be regarded as the interpretation of paragraph 1, article I, of the draft agreement, agreed by both parties and might as such be communicated to the General Conference.

(Signed) Carlos A. BERNARDES
President

II

LETTER DATED 19 JULY 1957 FROM THE SECRETARY-GENERAL ADDRESSED TO THE PRESIDENT OF THE PREPARATORY COMMISSION OF THE INTERNATIONAL ATOMIC ENERGY AGENCY

I have the honour to refer to your letter of 3 July concerning the wording of article I, paragraph 1, of the draft agreement to be entered into between the United Nations and the International Atomic Energy Agency.

It is noted that the Preparatory Commission is prepared to agree that the word "primarily" not be included in article I, paragraph 1, if the statement quoted in paragraph 2 of your letter, which had been suggested by me, is inserted in the record of the joint meeting of the Advisory Committee and the Preparatory Commission held on 24 June 1957 (IAEA/PC/OR.42;ST/SG/AC.I/SR.32).

As Chairman of the Advisory Committee and on its behalf, I agree to the inclusion of this statement in the record as reflecting the understanding of the two parties with regard to the interpretation of paragraph 1 of article I of the draft of the agreement.

(Signed) Dag HAMMARSKJOLD
Secretary-General

13. AGREEMENT BETWEEN THE UNITED NATIONS AND THE INTER-GOVERNMENTAL MARITIME CONSULTATIVE ORGANIZATION APPROVED BY THE GENERAL ASSEMBLY ON NOVEMBER 18, 1948

PROTOCOL CONCERNING THE ENTRY INTO FORCE OF THE AGREEMENT BETWEEN THE UNITED NATIONS AND THE INTER-GOVERNMENTAL MARITIME CONSULTATIVE ORGANIZATION

Article 57 of the Charter of the United Nations provides that the various specialized agencies, established by intergovernmental agreement and having wide international responsibilities, as defined in their basic instruments, in economic, social, cultural, educational, health, and related fields, shall be brought into relationship with the United Nations. Article 63 of the Charter provides that the Economic and Social Council may enter into agreements with any of the agencies referred to in Article 57, defining the terms on which the agency concerned shall be brought into relationship with the United Nations, and specifies that such agreements shall be subject to approval by the General Assembly.

Article 45 of the Convention on the Inter-Governmental Maritime Consultative Organization provides that the Organization shall be brought into relationship with the United Nations subject to the approval of the terms of the agreement by the Assembly.

On 10 March 1948, the Economic and Social Council, during its sixth session, authorized its Committee on Negotiations with Inter-Governmental Agencies to enter into negotiations at the appropriate time with the Inter-Governmental Maritime Consultative Organization or its Preparatory Committee for the purpose of bringing the Organization into relationship with the United Nations.

Negotiations between the Chairman of the Committee on Negotiations with Inter-Governmental Agencies of the Economic and Social Council and authorized representatives of the Negotiating Committee of the Preparatory Committee of the Inter-Governmental Maritime Consultative Organization took place on 10 August 1948 in Geneva and resulted in a draft agreement. This draft agreement was signed on 12 August 1948 by Mr. Walter Kotschnig, Chairman of the Committee on Negotiations with Inter-Governmental Agencies, and Mr. J.J. Oyevaar, Chairman of the Negotiating Committee of the Preparatory Committee of the Inter-Governmental Maritime Consultative Organization.

Article XIX of the draft agreement provides that the Agreement shall come into force on its approval by the General Assembly of the United Nations and the Assembly of the Organization.

On 27 August 1948, the Economic and Social Council, during its seventh session, recommended the draft agreement between the United Nations and the Inter-Governmental Maritime Consultative Organization to the General Assembly for its approval.

The Agreement was approved by the General Assembly of the United Nations during its third regular session on 18 November 1948 and by the Assembly of the Intergovernmental Maritime Consultative Organization during its first regular session on

13 January 1959. The Agreement accordingly came into force on 13 January 1959.
A copy of the authentic text of the Agreement is attached hereto.

IN FAITH WHEREOF we have appended our signatures this 17th day of February one thousand nine hundred and fifty-nine to two original copies of the present Protocol, the text of which consists of versions in the English and French languages which are equally authentic. One of the original copies will be deposited with the Secretariat of the United Nations and the other will be deposited with the Secretariat of the Inter-Governmental Maritime Consultative Organization.

Dag HAMMARSKJOLD
Secretary-General of the United Nations

O. NIELSEN
*Secretary-General of the Inter-Governmental
Maritime Consultative Organization*

AGREEMENT BETWEEN THE UNITED NATIONS AND THE INTER-
GOVERNMENTAL MARITIME CONSULTATIVE ORGANIZATION

PREAMBLE

Article 57 of the Charter of the United Nations provides that specialized agencies established by inter-governmental agreement and having wide international responsibilities as defined in their basic instruments in economic, social, cultural, educational, health and related fields shall be brought into relationship with the United Nations.

Part XII of the Convention on the Inter-Governmental Maritime Consultative Organization provides that the Inter-Governmental Maritime Consultative Organization (hereinafter called the Organization) shall be brought into relationship with the United Nations as one of the specialized agencies referred to in Article 57 of the Charter of the United Nations.

Therefore the United Nations and the Organization agree as follows:

Article I

The United Nations recognized the Organization as the specialized agency responsible for taking such action as may be appropriate under its basic instrument for the accomplishment of the purposes set forth therein.

Article II

RECIPROCAL REPRESENTATION

1. The United Nations shall be invited to send representatives to attend the meetings of the Assembly of the Organization, the Council, the Maritime Safety Committee, any subsidiary organs and such conferences as the Organization may convene, and to participate, without vote, in the deliberations of these bodies.

2. The Organization shall be invited to send representatives to attend meetings of the Economic and Social Council of the United Nations and of its commissions and committees, and to participate, without vote, in the deliberations of these bodies with respect to items on their agenda relating to matters within the scope of the activities of the Organization.

3. The Organization shall be invited to send representatives to attend meetings of the General Assembly of the United Nations for purposes of consultation on matters within the scope of the activities of the Organization.

4. The Organization shall be invited to send representatives to attend meetings of the main committees of the General Assembly when matters within the scope of its activities are under discussions and to participate, without vote, in such discussions.

5. The Organization shall be invited to send representatives to attend the meetings of the Trusteeship Council and to participate, without vote, in the deliberations thereof with respect to items on the agenda relating to matters within the scope of its activities.

6. Written statements of the Organization shall be distributed by the Secretariat of the United Nations to the Members of the General Assembly, the Economic and Social Council and its commissions, and the Trusteeship Council, as appropriate. Similarly, written statements presented by the United Nations shall be distributed as soon as possible by the secretariat of the Organization to all members of the Organization.

Article III

PROPOSAL OF AGENDA ITEMS

Subject to such preliminary consultation as may be necessary, the Organization shall include in the agenda of the Assembly, Council and the Maritime Safety Committee items proposed to it by the United Nations. Similarly, the Economic and Social Council and its commissions and the Trusteeship Council shall include in their provisional agenda items proposed by the Assembly or Council.

Article IV

RECOMMENDATIONS OF THE UNITED NATIONS

1. The Organization, having regard to the obligation of the United Nations to promote the objectives set forth in Article 55 of the Charter and the functions and powers of the Economic and Social Council, under Article 62 of the Charter to make or initiate studies and reports with respect to international economic, social, cultural, educational, health and related matters and to make recommendations concerning these matters to the specialized agencies concerned, and having regard also to the responsibility of the United Nations, under Articles 58 and 63 of the Charter, to make recommendations for the co-ordination of the policies and activities of such specialized agencies, agrees to arrange for the submission, as soon as possible, to the Assembly or the Council, as appropriate, of all formal recommendations which the United Nations may make to it.

2. The Organization agrees to enter into consultation with the United Nations upon request with respect to such recommendations, and in due course to report to the United Nations on the action taken by the Organization or by its members to give effect to such recommendations, or on the other results of their consideration.

3. The Organization affirms its intention of co-operating in whatever further measures may be necessary to make co-ordination of the policy and activities of specialized agencies and those of the United Nations fully effective. In particular, it agrees to participate in and to co-operate with, any bodies which the Economic and Social Council has established or may establish for the purpose of facilitating such co-ordination, and to furnish such information as may be required for the carrying out of this purpose.

Article V

EXCHANGE OF INFORMATION AND DOCUMENTS

1. Subject to such arrangements as may be necessary for the safeguarding of confidential material, the fullest and promptest exchange of appropriate information and documents shall be made between the United Nations and the Organization.

2. Without prejudice to the generality of the provisions of paragraph 1:

(a) The Organization agrees to transmit to the United Nations regular reports on the activities of the Organization and programmes of operation for each ensuing year;

(b) The Organization agrees to comply to the fullest extent practicable with any request which the United Nations may make for the furnishing of special reports, studies or information, subject to the conditions set forth in article XIV; and

(c) The Secretary-General of the United Nations shall, upon request, consult with the Secretary-General of the Organization regarding the provision to the Organization of such information as may be of special interest to the Organization.

Article VI

ASSISTANCE TO THE SECURITY COUNCIL

The Organization agrees to co-operate with the Economic and Social Council in furnishing such information and rendering such assistance to the Security Council as that Council may request, including assistance in carrying out decisions of the Security Council for the maintenance or restoration of international peace and security.

Article VII

ASSISTANCE TO THE TRUSTEESHIP COUNCIL

The Organization agrees to co-operate with the Trusteeship Council in the carrying out of its functions and in particular agrees that it will, to the greatest extent possible, render such assistance as the Trusteeship Council may request in regard to matters with which the Organization is concerned.

Article VIII

NON-SELF-GOVERNING TERRITORIES

The Organization agrees to co-operate within the limits of its functions with the United Nations in giving effect to the principles and obligations set forth in Chapter XI of the Charter of the United Nations with regard to matters affecting the well-being and development of the peoples of non-self-governing territories.

Article IX

RELATIONS WITH THE INTERNATIONAL COURT OF JUSTICE

1. The Organization agrees to furnish any information which may be requested by the International Court of Justice in pursuance of article 34 of the Statute of the Court.

2. The General Assembly authorizes the Organization to request advisory opinions of the International Court of Justice on legal questions arising within the scope of its activities other than questions concerning the mutual relationships of the Organization and the United Nations or other specialized agencies.

3. Such request may be addressed to the Court by the Assembly or by the Council acting in pursuance of an authorization by the Assembly.

4. When requesting the International Court of Justice to give an advisory opinion, the Organization shall inform the Economic and Social Council of the request.

Article X

PERSONNEL ARRANGEMENTS

1. The United Nations and the Organization recognize that the eventual development of a single unified international civil service is desirable from the standpoint of effective administrative co-ordination, and-with this end in view agree to develop common personnel standards, methods and arrangements designed to avoid serious discrepancies in terms and conditions of employment, to avoid competition in recruitment of personnel and to facilitate interchange of personnel in order to obtain the maximum benefit from their services.

2. The United Nations and the Organization agree to co-operate to the fullest extent possible in achieving these ends and in particular they agree:

(a) To participate in the International Civil Service Advisory Board established for the purpose of contributing to the improvement of recruitment and related phases of personnel administration in all of the international organizations;

(b) To consult together concerning other matters relating to the employment of their officers and staff, including conditions of service, duration of appointments, classification, salary scales and allowances, retirement and pension rights and staff regulations and rules with a view to securing as much uniformity in these matters as shall be found practicable;

(c) To co-operate in the interchange of personnel, when desirable, on a temporary or permanent basis, making due provision of the retention of seniority and pension rights; and

(d) To co-operate in the establishment and operation of suitable machinery for the settlement of disputes arising in connexion with the employment of personnel and related matters.

Article XI

STATISTICAL SERVICES

1. The United Nations and the Organization agree to strive for maximum co-operation, the elimination of all undesirable duplication between them and the most efficient use of their technical personnel in their respective collection, analysis, publication and dissemination of statistical information. They agree to combine their efforts to secure the greatest possible usefulness and utilization of statistical information and to minimize the burdens placed upon national Governments and other organizations from which such information may be collected.

2. The Organization recognizes the United Nations as the central agency for the collection, analysis, publication, standardization and improvement of statistics serving the general purposes of international organizations.

3. The United Nations recognizes the Organization as the appropriate agency for the collection, analysis, publication, standardization and improvement of statistics within its special sphere, without prejudice to the right of the United Nations to concern itself with such statistics so far as they may be essential for its own purposes or for the improvement of statistics throughout the world.

4. The United Nations shall, in consultation with the Organization and other specialized agencies, develop administrative instruments and procedures through which effective statistical co-operation may be secured between the United Nations, the Organization and other agencies brought into relationship with it.

5. It is recognized as desirable that the collection of statistical information should not be duplicated by the United Nations or any of the specialized agencies whenever it is practicable for any of them to utilize information or materials which another may have available.

6. In order to build up a central collection of statistical information for general use, it is agreed that data supplied to the Organization for incorporation in its basic statistical series of special reports should, so far as practicable, be made available to the United Nations on request.

Article XII

ADMINISTRATIVE AND TECHNICAL SERVICES

1. The United Nations and the Organization recognize the desirability, in the interest of administrative and technical uniformity and of the most efficient use of personnel and rexources, of avoiding, whenever possible, the establishment and operation of competitive or overlapping facilities and services among the United Nations and the specialized agencies.

2. Accordingly, the United Nations and the Organization agree to consult together concerning the establishment and use of common administrative and technical services and facilities in addition to those referred to in articles X, XI and XIII, in so far as the establishing and use of such services may from time to time be found practicable and appropriate.

3. Arrangements shall be made between the United Nations and the Organization in regard to the registration and deposit of official documents.

4. Officials of the Organization shall have the right to use the *laissez-passer* of the United Nations in accordance with special arrangements to be negotiated between the Secretary-General of the United Nations and the competent authorities of the Organization.

Article XIII

BUDGETARY AND FINANCIAL ARRANGEMENTS

1. The Organization recognizes the desirability of establishing close budgetary and financial relationships with the United Nations in order that the administrative operations of the United Nations and of the specialized agencies shall be carried out in the most efficient and economical manner possible and that the maximum measure of coordination and uniformity with respect to these operations shall be secured.

2. The United Nations and the Organization agree to co-operate to the fullest extent possible in achieving these ends and, in particular, shall consult together concerning the desirability of making appropriate arrangements for the inclusion of the budget of the Organization within a general budget of the United Nations. Any such arrangements shall be defined in a supplementary agreement between the two Organizations.

3. Pending the conclusion of any such agreement, the following arrangements shall govern budgetary and financial relationships between the United Nations and the Organization:

(a) In the preparation of the budget of the Organization the Secretariat of the Organization shall consult with the Secretary-General of the United Nations with a view to achieving, in so far as practicable, uniformity in presentation of the budgets of the United Nations and of the specialized agencies for the purposes of providing a basis for comparison of the several budgets.

(b) The Organization agrees to transmit its budget or budgetary estimates to the United Nations by July of the preceding year of such other date as may be agreed upon by the United Nations and the Organization. The General Assembly shall examine the budgetary estimates of the Organization and may make such recommendations as it may consider necessary.

(c) Representatives of the Organization shall be entitled to participate, without vote, in the deliberations of the General Assembly or any committee thereof or established by it at all times when the budget of the Organization or general administrative or financial questions affecting the Organization are under consideration.

(d) The United Nations may undertake the collection of contributions from those members of the Organization which are also Members of the United Nations in accordance with such arrangements as may be defined by a later agreement between the United Nations and the Organization.

(e) The United Nations shall, upon its own initiative or upon the request of the Organization, arrange for studies to be undertaken concerning other financial and fiscal questions of interest to the Organization and to other specialized agencies with a view to the provision of common services and the securing of uniformity in such matters.

(f) The Organization agrees to conform, as far as may be practicable, to standard practices and forms recommended by the United Nations.

Article XIV

FINANCING OF SPECIAL SERVICES

1. In the event of the Organization being faced with the necessity of incurring substantial extra expenses as a result of any request which the United Nations may make for special reports, studies or assistance in accordance with articles V, VI, or VII, or with other provisions of this agreement, consultation shall take place with view to determining the most equitable manner in which such expense shall be borne.

2. Consultation between the United Nations and the Organization shall similarly take place with a view to making such arrangements as may be found equitable for covering the costs of central administrative, technical or fiscal services or facilities or other special assistance provided by the United Nations.

Article XV

INTER-AGENCY AGREEMENTS

The Organization agrees to inform the Economic and Social Council of the nature and scope of any formal agreement contemplated and to notify the Council of the conclusions of any formal agreement between the Organization and any other specialized agency, inter-governmental organization, or non-governmental organization.

Article XVI

LIAISON

1. The United Nations and the Organization agree to the foregoing provisions in the belief that they will contribute to the maintenance of effective liaison between the two organizations. They affirm their intention of taking whatever further measures may be necessary to make this liaison fully effective.

2. The liaison arrangements provided for in the foregoing articles of this agreement shall apply as far as appropriate to the relations between such branch or regional offices as may be established by the two Organizations as well as between their central machinery.

Article XVII

IMPLEMENTATION OF THE AGREEMENT

The Secretary-General of the United Nations and the appropriate authority of the Organization may enter into such supplementary arrangements for the implementation of this agreement as may be found desirable.

14. AGREEMENT BETWEEN THE UNITED NATIONS AND THE INTERNATIONAL DEVELOPMENT ASSOCIATION APPROVED BY THE GENERAL ASSEMBLY ON MARCH 27, 1961

PROTOCOL CONCERNING THE ENTRY INTO FORCE OF THE AGREEMENT BETWEEN THE UNITED NATIONS AND THE INTERNATIONAL DEVELOPMENT ASSOCIATION

Article 57 of the Charter of the United Nations provides that specialized agencies established by inter-governmental agreement and having wide international responsibilities as defined in their basic instruments in economic, social, cultural, educational, health and related fields, shall be brought into relationship with the United Nations. Article 63 of the Charter provides that the Economic and Social Council may enter into agreements with any of the agencies referred to in Article 57, defining the terms on which the agency concerned shall be brought into relationship with the United Nations, and specifies that such agreements shall be subject to approval by the General Assembly.

Section 7 of article of the Articles of Agreement of the International Development Association provides that the Association shall enter into formal arrangements with the United Nations and may enter into such arrangements with other public international organizations having specialized responsibilities in related fields.

By a communication dated 16 December 1960 the President of the International Development Association informed the Secretary-General of the United Nations that the management of the Association had been authorized by the Executive Directors of the Association to negotiate na agreement with the United Nations on terms substantially corresponding to the terms of the Agreement between the United Nations and the Bank, and that the Executive Directors of the Association had also authorized the inclusion within such an agreement of a provisions which would establish a liaison committee composed of the Secretary-General of the United Nations and the President of the Bank and of the Association, or their representatives, which the Managing Director of the United Nations Special Fund and the Executive Chairman of the United Nations Technical Assistance Board, or their representatives, would be invited to join as full participants. This proposed liaison committee would be designed to enable the participants to keep one another fully informed, and to consult with one another as required, on their current programmes and future plans in areas of common interest and concern, thereby assuring co-ordination of their technical assistance and other development activities.

The Economic and Social Council, having been informed of the aforementioned communication from the President of the International Development Association, adopted a resolution on 21 December 1960, during its resumed thirtieth session, requesting the President of the Council to negotiate with the appropriate authorities of the International Development Association an agreement for the purpose of bringing the Association into relationship with the United Nations.

Negotiations between the President of the Council and a Vice-President of the International Development Association took place in New York on 21 December 1960 and resulted in an Agreement.

On 22 December 1969 the Economic and Social Council, during its resumed thirtieth session, recommended the Agreement between the United Nations and the International Development Association on relationship between the United Nations and the International Development Association, to the General Assembly for its approval.

Article III of the Agreement provides that the Agreement shall enter into force when it shall have been approved by the General Assembly of the United Nations and the Board of Governors of the International Development Association.

The Agreement was approved by the General Assembly of the United Nations on 27 March 1961, and by the Board of Governors of the International Development Association on 24 February 1961.

The Agreement accordingly came into force on 27 March 1961.

A copy of the text of the Agreement in both English and French is attached hereto, the English text being the authentic text.

IN FAITH WHEREOF we have appended our signatures to two original copies of the present Protocol, the text of which consists of versions in the English and French languages which are equally authentic. One of the original copies will be filed and recorded with the Secretariat of the United Nations and one will be deposited in the archives of the International Development Association.

16 April 1961

Dag HAMMARSKJOLD
Secretary-General of the United Nations

10 April 1961

Eugene R. BLACK
President of the International Development Association

AGREEMENT BETWEEN THE UNITED NATIONS AND THE INTERNATIONAL DEVELOPMENT ASSOCIATION

Whereas Article 57 of the Charter of the United Nations provides that specialized agencies established by inter-governmental agreement and having wide international responsibilities as defined in their basic instruments in economic, social, cultural, educational, health and related fields, shall be brought into relationship with the United Nations, and Article 58 provides that the United Nations shall make recommendations for the co-ordination of the policies and activities of the specialized agencies.

Whereas the International Development Association (hereinafter called the Association) is an international agency established by agreement among its member Governments and having wide international responsibilities, as defined in its Articles of Agreement, in economic and related fields,

Whereas the Association has been organized as an affiliate of the International Bank for Reconstruction and Development (hereinafter called the Bank),

Whereas article VI, section 7 of the Articles of Agreement of the Association provides that the Association shall enter into formal arrangements with the United Nations,

Whereas it is desirable to establish on a formal basis arrangements for exchange of information and for consultation as required, among the United Nations, the Bank, and the Association, so as to ensure co-ordination of their technical assistance and other development activities,

Now therefore the United Nations and the Association hereby agree as follows:

Article I

The United Nations and the Association shall have the same rights and obligations toward each other as the United Nations and the Bank have under the Agreement approved by the General Assembly of the United Nations on 15 November 1947 and by the Board of Governors of the Bank on 16 September 1947, which Agreement shall *mutatis mutandis* govern the relationship between the United Nations and the Association.

Article II [1]

There is hereby created a Liaison Committee composed of the Secretary-General of the United Nations and the President of the Bank and of the Association, or their representatives, which the Executive Chairman of the United Nations Technical Assistance Board and the Managing Director of the United Nations Special Fund, or their representatives, shall be invited to join as full participants. Through this Liaison Committee, which shall meet periodically and not less often than four times a year, the participants shall keep each fully informed, and shall consult each other as required, on their current programmes and future plans in areas of common interest and concern, thereby assuring co-ordination of their technical assistance and other development activities.

Article III

This Agreement shall come into force when it shall have been approved by the General Assembly of the United Nations and the Board of Governors of the Association.

---

[1] The Bank has agreed to participate in the Liaison Committee created by article II of the Agreement.

15. AGREEMENT BETWEEN THE UNITED NATIONS AND THE WORLD INTELLECTUAL PROPERTY ORGANIZATION, ADOPTED BY THE GENERAL ASSEMBLY OF THE UNITED NATIONS, DECEMBER 17, 1974[1]

PREAMBLE

In consideration of the provisions of Article 57 of the Charter of the United Nations and of article 13, paragraph 1, of the Convention Establishing the World Intellectual Property Organization, the United Nations and the World Intellectual Property Organization agree as follows:

Article 1

RECOGNITION

The United Nations recognizes the World Intellectual Property Organization (hereinafter called the "Organization") as a specialized agency and as being responsible for taking appropriate action in accordance with its basic instrument, treaties and agreements administered by it, *inter alia,* for promoting creative intellectual activity and for facilitating the transfer of technology related to industrial property to the developing countries in order to accelerate economic, social and cultural development, subject to the competence and responsibilities of the United Nations and its organs, particularly the United Nations Conference on Trade and Development, the United Nations Development Programme and the United Nations Industrial Development Organization, as well as of the United Nations Educational, Scientific and Cultural Organization and of other agencies within the United Nations system.

Article 2

CO-ORDINATION AND CO-OPERATION

In its relations with the United Nations, its organs and the agencies within the United Nations system, the Organization recognized the responsibilities for co-ordination of the General Assembly and of the Economic and Social Council under the Charter of the United Nations. Accordingly, the Organization agrees to co-operate in whatever measures may be necessary to make co-ordination of the policies and activities of the United Nations and those of the organs and agencies within the United Nations system fully effective. The Organization agrees further to participate in the work of any United Nations bodies which have been established or may be established for the purpose of facilitating such co-operation and co-ordination, in particular through membership in the Administrative Committee on Co-ordination.

Article 3

RECIPROCAL REPRESENTATION

(a) Representatives of the United Nations shall be invited to attend the sessions of all the bodies of the Organization and all such other meetings convened by the

---

[1] The Agreement was adopted by the General Assembly of the United Nations on December 17, 1974 and annexed to its resolution 3346 (XXIX).

Organization, and to participate, without the right to vote, in the deliberations of such bodies and at such meetings. Written statements presented by the United Nations shall be distributed by the Organization to its members.

(b) Representatives of the Organization shall be invited to attend meetings and to participate, without the right to vote, in the deliberations of the Economic and Social Council, its commissions and committees, of the main committees and the organs of the General Assembly, and of other conferences and meetings of the United Nations, with respect to items on the agenda relating to intellectual property matters within the scope of the activities of the Organization and other matters of mutual interest. Written statements presented by the Organization shall be distributed by the Secretariat of the United Nations to the members of the above-mentioned bodies, in accordance with the rules of procedure.

(c) Representatives of the Organization shall be invited, for purposes of consultation, to attend meetings of the General Assembly of the United Nations when questions as defined in paragraph (b) above are under discussion.

Article 4

PROPOSAL OF AGENDA ITEMS

Subject to such preliminary consultation as may be necessary, the Organization shall arrange for the inclusion in the provisional agenda of its appropriate bodies of items proposed by the United Nations, and the Economic and Social Council, its commissions and committees shall arrange for the inclusion in their provisional agenda of items proposed by the Organization.

Article 5

RECOMMENDATIONS OF THE UNITED NATIONS

(a) The Organization, having regard to the obligation of the United Nations to promote the objectives set forth in Article 55 of the Charter of the United Nations and the function and power of the Economic and Social Council, under Article 62 of the Charter, to make or initiate studies and reports with respect to international economic, social, cultural, educational, health and related matters and to make recommendations concerning these matters to the specialized agencies concerned, and having regard also to the responsibility oftthe United Nations, under Articles 58 and 63 of the Charter, to make recommendations for the co-ordination of the policies and activities of such specialized agencies, agrees to arrange for the submission, as soon as possible, to the appropriate organ of the Organization, of all formal recommendations which the United Nations may make to it.

(b) The Organization agrees to enter into consultation with the United Nations upon request with respect to such recommendations, and in due course to report to the United Nations on the action taken by the Organization or by its members to give effect to such recommendations, or on the other results of their consideration.

Article 6

INFORMATION AND DOCUMENTS

(a) Subject to such arrangements as may be necessary for the safeguarding of confidential material, full and prompt exchange of appropriate information and documents shall be made between the United Nations and the Organization.

(b) The Organization shall submit to the United Nations an annual report on its activities.

Article 7

STATISTICAL SERVICES

(a) The United Nations and the Organization agree to strive for the maximum co-operation, the elimination of all undersirable duplication between them and the most efficient use of their technical personnel in their respective collection, analysis, publication and dissemination of statistical information. They agree to combine their efforts to secure the greatest possible usefulness and utilization of statistical information and to minimize the burden placed upon Governments and other organizations from which such information may be collected.

(b) The Organization recognizes the United Nations as the central agency for the collection, analysis, publication, standardization and improvement of statistics serving the general purposes of international organizations.

(c) The United Nations recognizes the Organization as an appropriate agency for the collection, analysis, publication, standardization and improvement of statistics within its special sphere, without prejudice to the right of the United Nations, its organs and other agencies within the United Nations system to concern themselves with such statistics in so far as they may be essential for their own purposes or for the improvement of statistics throughout the world.

(d) The United Nations shall, in consultation with the Organization and other agencies within the United Nations system, develop administrative instruments and procedures through which effective statistical co-operation may be secured between the United Nations, the Organization and other agencies within the United Nations system brought into relationship with it.

(e) It is recognized as desirable that the collection of statistical information should not be duplicated by the United Nations or any of the agencies within the United Nations system whenever it is practicable for any of them to utilize information or materials which another may have available.

(f) In order to collect statistical information for general use, it is agreed that data supplied to the Organization for incorporation in its basic statistical series or special reports should, so far as practicable, be made available to the United Nations on request.

(g) It is agreed that data supplied to the United Nations for incorporation in its basic statistical series or special reports should, so far as is practicable and appropriate, be made available to the Organization upon request.

Article 8

ASSISTANCE TO THE UNITED NATIONS

The Organization shall, in accordance with the Charter of the United Nations and the basic instrument of the Organization, treaties and agreements administered by the Organization, co-operate with the United Nations by furnishing to it such information, special reports and studies, and by rendering such assistance to it, as the United Nations may request.

Article 9

TECHNICAL ASSISTANCE

The United Nations and the Organization undertake to co-operate in the provision of technical assistance for development in the field of intellectual creation. They also undertake to avoid undersirable duplication of activities and services relating to such technical assistance and agree to take such action as may be necessary to achieve effective co-ordination of their technical assistance activities within the framework of existing co-ordination machinery in the field of technical assistance. To this end, the Organization agrees to give consideration to the common use of available services as far as practicable. The United Nations will make available to the Organization its administrative services in this field for use as requested.

Article 10

TRANSFER OF TECHNOLOGY

The Organization agrees to co-operate within the field of its competence with the United Nations and its organs, particularly the United Nations Conference on Trade and Development, the United Nations Development Programme and the United Nations Industrial Development Organization, as well as the agencies within the United Nations system, in promoting and facilitating the transfer of technology to developing countries in such a manner as to assist these countries in attaining their objectives in the fields of science and technology and trade and development.

Article 11

TRUST, NON-SELF-GOVERNING AND OTHER TERRITORIES

The Organization agrees to co-operate within the field of its competence with the United Nations in giving effect to the principles and obligations set forth in Chapters XI, XII and XIII of the Charter of the United Nations and in the Declaration on the Granting of Independence to Colonial Countries and Peoples, with regard to matters affecting the well-being and development of the peoples of the Trust, Non-Self-Governing and other Territories.

Article 12

INTERNATIONAL COURT OF JUSTICE

(a) The Organization agrees to furnish any information which may be requested by the International Court of Justice in pursuance of Article 34 of the Statute of the Court.

(b) The General Assembly of the United Nations authorizes the Organization to request advisory opinions of the International Court of Justice on legal questions arising within the scope of its competence other than questions concerning the mutual relationships of the Organization and the United Nations or other specialized agencies.

(c) Such requests may be addressed to the International Court of Justice by the General Assembly of the Organization, or by the Co-ordination Committee of the Organization acting in pursuance of an authorization by the General Assembly of the Organization.

(d) When requesting the International Court of Justice to give an advisory opinion, the Organization shall inform the Economic and Social Council of the request.

Article 13

RELATIONS WITH OTHER INTERNATIONAL ORGANIZATIONS

Before the conclusion of any formal agreement between the Organization and any other specialized agency, any intergovernmental organization other than a specialized agency or any non-governmental organization, the Organization shall inform the Economic and Social Council of the nature and scope of the proposed agreement; furthermore, the Organization shall inform the Economic and Social Council of any matter of interagency concern within its competence.

Article 14

ADMINISTRATIVE CO-OPERATION

(a) The United Nations and the Organization recognize the desirability of co-operation in administrative matters of natural interest.

(b) Accordingly, the United Nations and the Organization undertake to consult together from time to time concerning these matters, particularly the most efficient use of facilities, staff and services and the appropriate methods of avoiding the establishment and operation of competitive or overlapping facilities and services among the United Nations and the agencies within the United Nations system and the Organization and with a view to securing, within the limits of the Charter of the United Nations and the Convention Establishing the Organization, as much uniformity in these matters as shall be found practicable.

(c) The consultations referred to in this article shall be utilized to establish the most equitable manner in which any special services or assistance furnished, on request, by the Organization to the United Nations or by the United Nations to the Organization shall be financed.

Article 15

PERSONNEL ARRANGEMENTS

(a) The United Nations and the Organization agree to develop, in the interests of uniform standards of international employment and to the extent feasible, common personnel standards, methods and arrangements designed to avoid unjustified differences in terms and conditions of employment, to avoid competition in recruitment of personnel, and to facilitate any mutually desirable and beneficial interchange of personnel.

(b) The United Nations and the Organization agree:

(i) To consult together from time to time concerning matters of mutual interest relating to the terms and conditions of employment of the officers and staff, with a view to securing as much uniformity in these matters as may be feasible;

(ii) To co-operate in the interchange of personnel when desirable, on a temporary or a permanent basis, making due provision for the retention of seniority and pension rights;

(iii) To co-operate, on such terms and conditions as may be agreed, in the operation of a common pension fund;

(iv) To co-operate in the establishment and operation of suitable machinery for the settlement of disputes arising in connexion with the employment of personnel and related matters.

(c) The terms and conditions on which any facilities or services of the Organization or the United Nations in connexion with the matters referred to in this article are to be extended to the other shall, where necessary, be the subject of subsidiary agreements concluded for this purpose after the entry into force of this Agreement.

Article 16

BUDGETARY AND FINANCIAL MATTERS

(a) The Organization recognizes the desirability of establishing close budgetary and financial relationships with the United Nations in order that the administrative operations of the United Nations and the agencies within the United Nations system shall be carried out in the most efficient and economical manner possible, and that the maximum measure of co-ordination and uniformity with respect to these operations shall be secured.

(b) The Organization agrees to conform, as far as may be practicable and appropriate, to standard practices and forms recommended by the United Nations.

(c) In the preparation of the budget of the Organization, the Director-General of the Organization shall consult with the Secretary-General of the United Nations with a view to achieving, in so far as is practicable, uniformity in presentation of the budgets of the United Nations and of the agencies within the United Nations system for the purposes of providing a basis for comparison of the several budgets.

(d) The Organization agrees to transmit to the United Nations its draft triennial and annual budgets not later than when the said draft budgets are transmitted to its members so as to give the General Assembly sufficient time to examine the said draft budgets, or budgets, and make such recommendations as it deems desirable.

(e) The United Nations may arrange for studies to be undertaken concerning financial and fiscal questions of interest both to the Organization and to the other agencies within the United Nations system, with a view to the provision of common services and the securing of uniformity in such matters.

Article 17

UNITED NATIONS LAISSEZ-PASSER

Officials of the Organization shall be entitled, in accordance with such special arrangements as may be concluded between the Secretary-General of the United Nations and the Director-General of the Organization, to use the laissez-passer of the United Nations.

Article 18

IMPLEMENTATION OF THE AGREEMENT

The Secretary-General of the United Nations and the Director-General of the Organization may enter into such supplementary arrangements for the implementation of this Agreement as may be found desirable.

Article 19

AMENDMENT AND REVISION

This Agreement may be amended or revised by agreement between the United Nations and the Organization and any such amendment or revision shall come into force on approval by the General Assembly of the United Nations and the General Assembly of the Organization.

Article 20

ENTRY INTO FORCE

This Agreement shall enter into force on its approval by the General Assembly of the United Nations and the General Assembly of the Organization.

V. NON-GOVERNMENTAL ORGANIZATIONS
STATUS WITH THE ECONOMIC AND SOCIAL COUNCIL, THE
SPECIALIZED AGENCIES, OR OTHER UNITED NATIONS
BODIES IN 1977[1]

The non-governmental organizations in consultative status as of May 1977 as a result of action taken by the Council at its sixty second session, are listed below. Of these, 26 are in category I, 205 in category II, and 103 are on the Roster. Another 27 organizations are on the Roster by action of the Secretary-General. An additional 374 organizations are on the Roster by virtue of their status with the specialized agencies or other United Nations bodies.

A. CATEGORY I

International Alliance of Women – Equal Rights, Equal Responsibilities
International Association of French-Speaking Parliamentarians
International Chamber of Commerce
International Confederation of Free Trade Unions
International Co-operative Alliance
International Council of Voluntary Agencies (ICVA)
International Council of Women
International Council on Social Welfare
International Federation of Agricultural Producers
International Organization for Standardization (ISO)
International Organization of Consumers Unions (IOCU)
International Organization of Employers
International Planned Parenthood Federation
International Union of Local Authorities
International Youth and Student Movement for the United Nations
Inter-Parliamentary Union
League of Red Cross Societies
Organization of African Trade Union Unity (OATUU)
United Towns Organization
Women's International Democratic Federation
World Assembly of Youth (WAY)
World Confederation of Labour
World Federation of Democratic Youth (WFDY)
World Federation of Trade Unions (WFTU)
World Federation of United Nations Associations (WFUNA)
World Veterans Federation

B. CATEGORY II

Afro-Asian Organization for Economic Co-operation
Afro-Asian Peoples' Solidarity Organization
Agudas Israel World Organization
Airport Associations Coordinating Council (AACC)
All-India Women's Conference
All-Pakistan Women's Association
American Field Service, Inc.
Amnesty International

---

[1]U.N. Doc. E/INF/162, August 31, 1977.

Anti-*apartheid* Movement, The
Anti-Slavery Society, The
Arab Lawyers Union
Associated Country Women of the World
Association for Childhood Education International
Association for the Study of the World Refugee Problem
Baha'i International Community
Baptist World Alliance
Boy Scouts World Bureau
CARE (Cooperative for American Relief Everywhere, Inc.)
Caritas Internationalis (International Confederation of Catholic Charities)
Carnegie Endowment for International Peace
Catholic International Union for Social Service
Centre for Latin American Monetary Studies
Chamber of Commerce of the United States of America
Christian Democratic World Union
Christian Peace Conference
Church World Service, Inc.
Commission of the Churches on International Affairs, The
Commonwealth Human Ecology Council (CHEC)
Consultative Council of Jewish Organizations
Co-ordinating Board of Jewish Organizations (CBJO)
Co-ordinating Committee for International Voluntary Service
Eastern Regional Organization for Public Administration
European Association of National Productivity Centres
European Insurance Committee
European League for Economic Co-operation
Federation for the Respect of Man and Humanity
Federation of Arab Economists, The
Foundation for the Peoples of the South Pacific, Inc., The
Friends World Committee for Consultation
Howard League for Penal Reform
Ibero-American Institute of Aeronautic and Space Law and Commercial Aviation
Institute for Policy Studies – Transnational
Institute of Electrical and Electronic Engineers, Inc.
Inter-American Council of Commerce and Production
Inter-American Federation of Public Relations Association
Inter-American Federation of Touring and Automobile Clubs (FITAC)
Inter-American Planning Society
Inter-American Press Association
Inter-American Statistical Institute
International Abolitionist Federation
International Air Transport Association
International Association Against Painful Experiments on Animals
International Association for Religious Freedom (IARF)
International Association for Social Progress
International Association for the Promotion and Protection of Private
    Foreign Investments
International Association for the Protection of Industrial Property
International Association for Water Law (IAWL)
International Association of Democratic Lawyers
International Association of Educators for World Peace
International Association of Penal Law
International Association of Ports and Harbours (IAPH)
International Association of Schools of Social Work

International Association of Youth Magistrates
International Astronautical Federation
International Automobile Federation (FIA)
International Bar Association
International Cargo Handling Co-ordination Association
International Catholic Child Bureau
International Catholic Migration Commission
International Catholic Union of the Press
International Centre for Local Credit
International Chamber of Shipping
International Christian Union of Business Executives (UNIAPAC)
International Civil Airport Association
International College of Surgeons
International Commission of Jurists
International Commission on Irrigation and Drainage
International Committee of the Red Cross
International Co-operation for Socio-Economic Development (CIDSE)
International Council for Adult Education (ICAE)
International Council for Building Research, Studies and Documentation
International Council of Environmental Law
International Council of Jewish Women
International Council of Monuments and Sites (ICOMOS)
International Council of Scientific Unions
International Council of Social Democratic Women
International Council of Societies of Industrial Design (ICSID)
International Council of Alcohol and Addictions
International Council on Jewish Social and Welfare Services
International Defence and Aid Fund for Southern Africa
International Federation for Housing and Planning
International Federation for Human Rights
International Federation of Beekeepers' Associations
International Federation of Business and Professional Women
International Federation of Journalists
International Federation of Landscape Architects
International Federation of Resistance Movements
International Federation of Senior Police Officers
International Federation of Settlements and Neighbourhood Centres
International Federation of Social Workers
International Federation of University Women
International Federation of Women in Legal Careers
International Federation of Women Lawyers
International Hotel Association
International Indian Treaty Council
International Institute for Vital Registration and Statistics (IIVRS)
International Institute of Administrative Sciences
International Institute of Public Finance
International Islamic Federation of Student Organizations
International Law Association
International League for Human Rights
International League of Societies for the Mentally Handicapped
International Movement for Fraternal Union Among Races and Peoples (UFER)
International Organization – Justice and Development
International Organization of Journalists (IOJ)
International Organization of Supreme Audit Institutions (INTOSAI)
International Petroleum Industry Environmental Conservation Association (IPIECA)

580

International Prisoners Aid Association
International Road Federation
International Road Transport Union
International Rural Housing Association
International Savings Banks Institute
International Senior Citizens Association, Inc., The
International Social Service
International Society for Criminology
International Society of Social Defence
International Statistical Institute
International Touring Alliance
International Union for Child Welfare
International Union for Conservation of Nature and Natural Resources
International Union for Inland Navigation
International Union for the Scientific Study of Population
International Union of Architects
International Union of Building Societies and Savings Associations
International Union of Family Organizations
International Union of Lawyers
International Union of Producers and Distributors of Electrical Energy
International Union of Public Transport
International Union of Railways
International University Exchange Fund
International Young Christian Workers
Jaycees International
Latin American Association of Finance Development Institutions (ALIDE)
Latin American Iron and Steel Institute
Lions International – The International Association of Lions Clubs
Lutheran World Cooperation
Movement for Colonial Freedom
Muslim World League (MWL)
Mutual Assistance of the Latin American Government Oil Companies
    (ARPEL)
Organization for International Economic Relations (IER)
OXFAM
Panafrican Institute for Development
Pan African Women's Organization
Pan American Federation of Engineering Societies (UPADI)
Pan-Pacific and South-East Asia Women's Association
Pax Romana
    International Catholic Movement for Intellectual and Cultural Affairs
    International Movement of Catholic Students
Permanent International Association of Road Congresses (PIARC)
Rehabilitation International
Rotary International
Salvation Army, The
Save the Children Federation
Socialist International
Society for Comparative Legislation
Society for International Development (SID)
Société internationale de prophylaxie criminelle
Soroptimist International
St. Joan's International Alliance
Studies and Expansion Society – International Scientific Association (SEC)
Union of Arab Jurists

Union of International Associations
Union of International Fairs
United Kingdom Standing Conference on the Second United Nations
  Development Decade
Universal Federation of Travel Agents Associations
Vienna Institute for Development
War Resisters International
Women's International League for Peace and Freedom
Women's International Zionist Organization
World Alliance of Young Men's Christian Associations
World Association of Girl Guides and Girl Scouts
World Association of World Federalists
World Confederation of Organizations of the Teaching Profession
World Conference on Religion and Peace
World Council for the Welfare of the Blind
World Council of Credit Unions, Inc. (WOCCU)
World Council of Management
World Energy Conference
World Federation for Mental Health
World Federation for the Protection of Animals
World Federation of Catholic Youth
World Federation of the Deaf
World Jewish Congress
World Leisure and Recreation Association
World Movement of Mothers
World Muslim Congress
World Peace Through Law Centre
World Population Society
World Student Christian Federation
World Trade Centers Association
World Union Catholic Women's Organizations
World Union of Organizations for the Safeguard of Youth
World University Service
World Women's Christian Temperance Union
World Young Women's Christian Association
Zonta International

C. ROSTER ORGANIZATIONS-504 ORGANIZATIONS

1. ORGANIZATIONS (103) INCLUDED ON THE ROSTER
BY THE ECONOMIC AND SOCIAL COUNCIL

African Medical and Research Foundation International
American Foreign Insurance Association
Asian Development Center
Asian Youth Council
Battelle Memorial Institute
Center for Inter-American Relations
Commission to Study the Organization of Peace
Comité d'études économiques de l'industrie du gaz
Committee for Economic Development
Committee for European Construction Equipment
Confederation of Asian Chambers of Commerce
Congress of Racial Equality (CORE)
Council of European National Youth Committees (CENYC)
Engineers Joint Council
Environmental Coalition for North America (ENCONA)

European Alliance of Press Agencies
European Association of Refrigeration Enterprises (AEEF)
European Confederation of Woodworking Industries
European Container Manufacturers' Committee
European Mediterranean Commission Water Planning
Ex-Volunteers International
Federation of International Furniture Removers
Foundation for the Establishment of an International Criminal Court, The
Institute of International Container Lessors
International Association for Bridge and Structural Engineeering
International Association for Hydrogen Energy
International Association for Research Into Income and Wealth
International Association for the Exchange of Students for Technical
    Experience (IASTE)
International Association of Chiefs of Police
International Association of Gerontology
International Board of Co-operation for the Developing Countries (EMCO)
International Bureau for the Suppression of Traffic in Persons
International Bureau of Motor-Cycle Manufacturers
International Committee of Outer Space Onomastics (ICOSO)
International Center for Dynamics of Development
International Confederation of Associations of Experts and Consultants
International Container Bureau
International Federation for Documentation
International Federation of Chemical Energy and General Workers' Unions
International Federation of Cotton and Allied Textile Industries
International Federation of Forwarding Agents Associations
International Federation of Free Journalists
International Federation of Operational Research Societies
International Federation of Pedestrians
International Federation of Surveyors
International Federation of the Blind
International Federation on Ageing
International Fiscal Association
International Inner Wheel
International League of Surveillance Societies, The
International Movement Science and Service for a Just and Free World
International Olive Growers Federation
International Organization for Commerce
International Organization of Experts (ORDINEX)
International Peace Academy
International Peace Bureau
International Permanent Bureau of Automobile Manufacturers
International Playground Association
International Police Association
International Progress Organisation (IPO)
International Public Relations Association (IPRA)
International Real Estate Federation
International Schools Association
International Shipping Federation
International Society for Prosthetics and Orthotics
International Society for the Protection of Animals
International Solar Energy Society
International Union of Judges
International Union of Marine Insurance

International Union of Police Federations
International Union of Social Democratic Teachers
International Union of Tenants
International Voluntary Service
International Working Group for the Construction of Sports Premises
    (IAKS)
Latin American Confederation of Tourist Organizations (COTAL)
Latin American Official Workers' Confederation (CLATE)
Minority Rights Group
Movement Against Racism, Antisemitism and for Peace
National Indian Brotherhood
National Organization for Women (NOW)
National Parks and Conservation Association
OISCA – International (Organization for Industrial, Spiritual and Cultural
    Advancement – International)
Open Door International (for the Economic Emancipation of the Woman
    Worker)
Pan American Development Foundation
Pax Christi, International Catholic Peace Movement
Permanent International Association of Navigation Congresses
Pio Mansú International Research Centre for Environmental Structures, The
Planetary Citizens
Population Council, The
Prévention routière internationale, La (International Road Safety Association)
Quota International
SERVAS International
Society for Social Responsibility in Science
United Nations of Yoga (UNY)
United Way of America
World Alliance of Reformed Churches
World Association for Christian Communication
World Confederation for Physical Therapy
World Development Movement
World Federation of Christian Life Communities
World Union for Progressive Judaism
Young Lawyers International Association (AIJA)

2. ORGANIZATIONS (27) PLACED ON THE ROSTER BY
THE SECRETARY-GENERAL

American Association for the Advancement of Science
Asian Environmental Society
Association for the Advancement of Agricultural Sciences in Africa
Center of Concern
Committee for International Co-ordination of National Research in Demography
    (CICRED)
Fauna Preservation Society, The
Foresta Institute for Ocean and Mountain Studies
Friends of the Earth (F.O.E.)
Institut de la vie
International Advisory Committee on Population and Law
International Association Against Noise

584

International Association on Water Pollution Research (IAWPR)
International Educational Development, Inc.
International Institute for Environment and Development
International Ocean Institute
International Society for Community Development
International Studies Association
International Union of Anthropological and Ethnological Sciences
National Audubon Society
Natural Resources Defence Council, Inc.
Organisation Internationale pour le developpement rural
Population Crisis Committee
Population Institute
Sierra Club
Trilateral Commission, The
World Education Inc.
World Society of Ekistics

3. ORGANIZATIONS (374) PLACED ON THE ROSTER BY VIRTUE OF THEIR CONSULTATIVE STATUS WITH SPECIALIZED AGENCIES OR OTHER UNITED NATIONS BODIES

Aerospace Medical Association	ICAO
African Insurance Organization	UNCTAD
Afro-Asian Writers' Union	UNESCO
Agency for the Security of Aerial Navigation in Africa and Madagascar	WMO
Arab Federation of Chemical Fertilizer Producers	UNIDO
Asian Broadcasting Union	UNESCO, FAO
Associación Latinoamericana de Educación Radiofónica	UNESCO
Association des universités partiellement ou entierement de langue francaise	UNESCO
Association for the Promotion of the International Circulation of the Press	UNESCO
Association of African Universities	UNESCO
Association of Arab Universities	UNESCO
Association of Commonwealth Universities	UNESCO
Association of European Jute Industries	UNCTAD
Association of Official Analytical Chemists	FAO
Association of South East Asian Institutions of Higher Education	UNESCO
Baltic and International Maritime Conference, The	IMCO, UNCTAD
Biometric Society, The	WHO
B'nai B'rith International Council	UNESCO
Catholic International Education Office	UNESCO, UNICEF
Central Council for Health Education	WHO
Christian Medical Commission	WHO
Commonwealth Medical Association	WHO
Co-ordination Committee for the Textile Industries in the European Common Market	UNCTAD
Council for International Organizations of Medical Sciences (CIOMS)	WHO, UNESCO
Council of European and Japanese National Shipowners' Associations, The (CENSA)	UNCTAD
Engineering Committee on Oceanic Resources (ECOR)	IMCO
European Association for Animal Production	FAO

European Association for Personnel Management	ILO
European Association for the Trade in Jute Products	UNCTAD
European Association of Management Consultants Associations	UNIDO
European Association of Management Training Centres	UNIDO
European Association of Nitrogen Manufacturers	IMCO
European Atomic Forum	IAEA
European Broadcasting Union	UNESCO
European Centre for International Co-operation (CECI)	UNIDO
European Centre for Overseas Industrial Development	UNIDO
European Centre for the Perfection and Research for Artists taking in the Productions	UNESCO
European Committee of Sugar Manufacturers	UNCTAD
European Confederation of Agriculture	FAO, IAEA
European Council of Chemical Manufacturers Federations	IMCO, UNCTAD
European Federation of Associations of Engineers and Heads of Industrial Safety Services and Industrial Physicians	ILO
European Federation of National Associations of Engineers	UNESCO
European Federation of National Maintenance Societies	UNIDO
European Industrial Space Study Group – EUROSPACE	IMCO
European Mechanical Handling Confederation	ILO
European Nitrogen Producers' Association	IMCO
European Oceanic Association	UNIDO
European Society of Culture	UNESCO
European Tea Committee	FAO
European Training and Research Centre for Theatrical Performers	UNESCO
European Tugowners Association (ETA)	IMCO
European Union of Coachbuilders	UNIDO
European Union of Public Relations	UNIDO
Eurosat S.A.	IMCO
Experiment in International Living, The	UNESCO
Federation of Arab Teachers	UNESCO
Federation of Indian Chambers of Commerce and Industry	UNCTAD
Federation of Indian Export Organizations	UNCTAD
Federation of National Associations of Ship Brokers and Agents	UNCTAD
General Arab Insurance Federation	UNCTAD
Hemispheric Insurance Conference	UNCTAD
Ibero-American Television Organization	ITU
Institut du transport aerien	ICAO
Institute of International Law	ICAO
Institute on Man and Science	UNESCO
Inter-American Association of Broadcasters	UNESCO
Inter-American Association of Sanitary Engineering	WHO
Inter-American Council of Commerce and Production	UNCTAD
International Academy of Aviation and Space Medicine	ICAO
International Academy of Pathology	WHO
International Aeronautical Federation	ICAO
International Agency for the Prevention of Blindness (Vision International)	UNICEF, WHO
International Aircraft Brokers Association	ICAO
International Airline Navigators Council	ICAO, WHO
International Air Safety Association	ICAO

International Association for Accidents and Traffic Medicine	WHO
International Association for Cereal Chemistry (ICC)	UNIDO
International Association for Child Psychiatry and Allied Professions	WHO
International Association for Earthquake Engineering	UNESCO
International Association for Educational and Vocational Guidance	UNESCO, ILO UNICEF
International Association for Educational and Vocational Information	UNESCO, ILO
International Association for Mass Communication Research	UNESCO
International Association for Mutual Assistance	ILO
International Association for Prevention of Blindness	WHO
International Association for the Advancement of Educational Research	UNESCO
International Association for the Evaluation of Educational Achievement	UNESCO
International Association for the Physical Sciences of the Ocean	ICAO
International Association of Agricultural Economists	FAO
International Association of Agricultural Librarians and Documentalists	FAO
International Association of Agricultural Medicine	WHO, ILO
International Association of Art – Painting, Sculpture, Graphic Art	UNESCO
International Association of Art Critics	UNESCO
International Association of Classification Societies	IMCO
International Association of Conference Interpreters	ILO, UNESCO
International Association of Crafts and Small and Medium-Sized Enterprises	UNIDO
International Association of Drilling Contractors (IADC)	IMCO
International Association of Fish Meal Manufacturers	FAO
International Association of Horticultural Producers	FAO
International Association of Insurance and Reinsurance Intermediaries	UNCTAD
International Association of Institutes of Navigation (IAIN)	IMCO
International Association of Legal Science	UNESCO
International Association of Lighthouse Authorities	IMCO
International Association of Literary Critics	UNESCO
International Association of Logopedics and Phoniatrics	UNESCO, WHO UNICEF
International Association of Medical Laboratory Technologists	WHO
International Association of Microbiological Societies	WHO
International Association of Physical Oceanography (IAPO)	ICAO
International Association of Producers of Insurance and Reinsurance (BIPAR)	IMCO
International Association of Scientific Experts in Tourism	UNESCO
International Association of Students in Economics and Management	UNESCO, ILO
International Association of Theatre Critics	UNESCO
International Association of Universities	UNESCO
International Association of University Professors and Lecturers	UNESCO

International Association of Workers for Maladjusted Children	UNESCO
International Astronomical Union	WMO
International Baccalaureate Office	UNESCO
International Board on Books for Young People	UNESCO, UNICEF
International Brain Research Organization	UNESCO, WHO
International Bureau of Social Tourism	ILO, UNESCO
International Cell Research Organization	UNESCO
International Centre for Industry and Environment (ICIE)	UNIDO
International Centre for Wholesale Trade	UNCTAD
International Centre of Films for Children and Young People	UNESCO, UNICEF
International Centre of Insect Physiology and Ecology	UNESCO
International Centre of Research and Information on Collective Economy	ILO
International Cocoa Trade Federation	UNCTAD
International Commission Against Concentration Camp Practices	ILO
International Commission of Agricultural Engineering	FAO, UNESCO
International Commission on Illumination	IMCO, ICAO, ILO
International Commission on Radiation Units and Measurements	WHO, IAEA
International Commission on Radiological Protection	WHO, IAEA
International Committee for Plastics in Agriculture	UNIDO
International Committee for Social Science Information and Documentation	UNESCO
International Committee of Catholic Nurses and Medico-Social Workers	WHO, ILO
International Committee on Laboratory Animals	WHO
International Community of Booksellers Associations	UNESCO
International Confederation of European Beet Growers	UNCTAD
International Confederation of Midwives	WHO, ILO, UNICEF
International Confederation of Societies of Authors and Composers	UNESCO
International Congress of University Adult Education	UNESCO
International Coordinating Committee for the Presentation of Science and the Development of Out-of-School Scientific Activities	UNESCO
International Coordinating Council of Aerospace Industries Associations	ICAO
International Copyright Society	UNESCO
International Council for Philosophy and Humanistic Studies	UNESCO
International Council for Educational Films	ILO
International Council of Aircraft Owner and Pilot Associations	ICAO
International Council of Graphic Design Associations	UNESCO
International Council of Marine Industry Associations (ICOMIA)	IMCO
International Council of Museums	UNESCO
International Council of Nurses	WHO, ILO, UNESCO, UNICEF
International Council of Societies of Pathology	WHO
International Council of Sport and Physical Education	UNESCO
International Council on Archives	UNESCO

International Council on Correspondence Education	UNESCO
International Council on Education for Teaching	UNESCO
International Cystic Fibrosis (Mucoviscidosis) Association	WHO
International Dairy Federation	FAO, UNICEF
International Dance Council	UNESCO
International Dental Federation	WHO
International Diabetes Federation	WHO
International Economic Association	UNESCO
International Electrotechnical Commission	IMCO, WHO
International Spidemiological Association	WHO
International Ergonomics Association	ILO, WHO
International Falcon Movement	UNESCO
International Federation for Information Processing	UNESCO
International Federation for Medical and Biological Engineering	WHO
International Federation for Parent Education	UNESCO, UNICEF
International Federation of Actors	UNESCO
International Federation of Air Line Pilots Associations	ICAO, WMO
International Federation of Automatic Control	UNIDO, UNESCO
International Federation of Catholic Universities	UNESCO
International Federation of Children's Communities	UNESCO
International Federation of Clinical Chemistry	WHO
International Federation of Fertility Societies	WHO
International Federation of Free Teachers' Unions	UNESCO
International Federation of Gynecology and Obstetrics	WHO
International Federation of Home Economics	FAO, UNESCO
International Federation of Independent Air Transport	ICAO
International Federation of Industrial Producers of Electricity for own Consumption	IAEA
International Federation of Inventors' Associations (IFIA)	UNCTAD, UNIDO
International Federation of Library Associations	UNESCO
International Federation of Margarine Associations	FAO
International Federation of Medical Students' Associations	WHO
International Federation of Multiple Sclerosis Societies	WHO
International Federation of Musicians	UNESCO
International Federation of Newspaper Publishers	UNESCO
International Federation of Ophthalmological Societies	WHO
International Federation of Organizations of School Correspondence and Exchanges	UNESCO
International Federation of Patent Agents	UNCTAD
International Federation of Pharmaceutical Manufacturers Associations	WHO
International Federation of Physical Medicine and Rehabilitation	WHO
International Federation of Plantation, Agricultural and Allied Workers	FAO
International Federation of Popular Travel Organizations	UNESCO
International Federation of Purchasing and Materials Management (IFPMM)	UNCTAD
International Federation of Shipmasters' Associations (IFSMA)	IMCO
International Federation of Sports Medicine	WHO
International Federation of Surgical Colleges	WHO
International Federation of the Periodical Press	UNESCO
International Federation of the Phonographic Industry	UNESCO

International Federation of the Training Centres for the Promotion of Progressive Education	UNESCO
International Federation of Translators	UNESCO
International Federation of Workers' Educational Associations	UNESCO
International Fertility Association	WHO
International Film and Television Council	UNESCO
International Food Policy Research Institute	UNCTAD
International Geographical Union	ICAO
International Group of Scientific, Technical and Medical Publishers	UNESCO
International Hospital Federation	WHO
International Humanistic and Ethical Union	UNESCO
International Hydatidological Association	WHO
International Institute for Industrial Planning	UNIDO
International Institute of Music, Dance and Theatre in the Audio-Visual Media	UNESCO
International League Against Epilepsy	WHO
International League Against Rheumatism	WHO, UNICEF
International League for Child and Adult Education	UNESCO
International League of Dermatological Societies	WHO
International Leprosy Association	WHO
International Lifesaving Appliance Manufacturers' Association (ILAMA)	IMCO
International Literary and Artistic Association	UNESCO
International Maritime Committee	IMCO, UNCTAD
International Maritime Pilots' Association	IMCO
International Maritime Radio Association	ICAO, IMCO
International Measurement Confederation	UNIDO
International Medical Association for the Study of Living Conditions and Health	FAO
International Movement of Catholic Agricultural and Rural Youth	FAO, ILO, UNESCO
International Music Council	UNESCO
International Organization Against Trachoma	WHO
International Organization for Rural Development	UNICEF
International Paediatric Association	WHO, UNICEF
International Peace Research Association	UNESCO
International Peat Society	FAO
International PEN	UNESCO
International Pharmaceutical Federation	WHO
International Political Science Association	UNESCO
International Publishers Association	UNESCO
International Radiation Protection Association	WHO
International Radio and Television Organization	UNESCO
International Radio-Maritime Committee	IMCO, ICAO, WMO
International Reading Association	UNESCO
International Round Table for the Advancement of Counselling (IRTAC)	ILO, UNICEF
International Rayon and Synthetic Fibres Committee	UNCTAD
International Salvage Union (ISU)	IMCO
International Scientific Film Association	UNESCO
International Scientific Radio Union	WMO
International Secretariat of Catholic Technologists, Agriculturists and Economists	ILO

International Ship Owners Association	UNCTAD
International Social Science Council	UNESCO, ILO
International Society for Burn Injuries	WHO
International Society for Education through Art	UNESCO
International Society for Human and Animal Mycology	WHO
International Society for Labour Law and Social Legislation	ILO
International Society for Photogrammetry	UNESCO
International Society for Research on Moors	FAO
International Society of Biometeorology	WHO, WMO
International Society of Blood Transfusion	WHO
International Society of Cardiology	WHO
International Society of Chemotherapy	WHO
International Society of Citriculture	FAO
International Society of Endocrinology	WHO
International Society of Hematology	WHO
International Society of Orthopaedic Surgery and Traumatology	WHO
International Society of Radiographers and Radiological Technicians	WHO
International Society of Radiology	WHO
International Society of Soil Science	FAO, UNESCO, WMO
International Sociological Association	UNESCO
International Solid Wastes and Public Cleansing Association	WHO
International Superphosphate and Compound Manufacturers' Association Limited	UNIDO
International Theatre Institute	UNESCO
International Transport Workers' Federation	ICAO
International Travel Journalists and Writers Federation	UNESCO
International Union Against Cancer	WHO
International Union Against the Venereal Diseases and the Treponematoses	WHO, UNICEF
International Union Against Tuberculosis	WHO, ILO, UNICEF
International Union for Health Education	WHO, UNESCO UNICEF
International Union for the Liberty of Education	UNESCO
International Union of Aviation Insurers	ICAO
International Union of Biological Sciences	WHO
International Union of Food and Allied Workers Associations	FAO
International Union of Forestry Research Organizations	FAO
International Union of Geodesy and Geophysics	ICAO
International Union of Immunological Societies	WHO
International Union of Independent Laboratories	UNIDO
International Union of Leather Technologists and Chemists Societies	UNIDO, FAO
International Union of Nutritional Sciences	FAO, WHO, UNICEF
International Union of Pharmacology	WHO
International Union of Psychological Science	UNESCO
International Union of Pure and Applied Chemistry	WHO, FAO
International Union of School and University Health and Medicine	WHO, UNESCO
International Union of Socialist Youth	UNESCO, ILO, UNICEF
International Union of Students	UNESCO

International Water Supply Association	WHO
International Writers Guild	UNESCO
International Young Catholic Students	UNESCO
International Youth Federation for Environmental Studies and Conservation	UNESCO
International Youth Hostel Federation	UNESCO
Japan Atomic Industrial Forum, Inc.	IAEA
Joint Commission on International Aspects of Mental Retardation	WHO
Latin American and Caribbean Federation of Exporters' Associations	UNCTAD
Latin American Plastics Institute	UNIDO
Latin American Shipowners Association	UNCTAD, IMCO
Latin-American Social Science Council	UNESCO
Liaison Office of the Rubber Industries of the European Economic Community	UNCTAD
Medical Women's International Association	WHO, UNICEF
Miners' International Federation	UNCTAD
National Shippers' Councils of Europe	UNCTAD
Oil Companies' International Marine Forum	IMCO
Oil Industry International Exploration and Production Forum (E and P Forum)	IMCO
Organization for Flora Neotropica	UNESCO
Pacific Science Association	UNESCO, WMO
Pan-African Youth Movement	UNESCO
Pan-American Union of Association of Engineering	UNESCO
Permanent Commission and International Association on Occupational Health	WHO, ILO
Permanent International Committee on Canned Foods	FAO
Permanent Joint Technical Commission for Nile Waters	WMO
Society for Chemical Industry	UNIDO
Society for General Systems Research	UNESCO
Society of African Culture	UNESCO
Sri Aurobindo Society	UNESCO
Standing Conference of Chambers of Commerce and Industry of the European Economic Community	UNCTAD
Standing Conference of Rectors and Vice-Chancellors of the European Universities	UNESCO
Trade Unions International of Agricultural, Forestry and Plantation Workers	FAO
Trade Union International of Food, Tobacco, Hotel and Allied Industries' Workers	FAO
Transplantation Society	WHO
UNDA – Catholic International Association for Radio and Television	UNESCO
Union of Industries of the European Community	UNIDO, UNCTAD
Union of International Engineering Organizations	UNESCO, UNIDO
Union of Latin American Universities	UNESCO
Union of National Radio and Television Organizations of Africa	UNESCO, ILO
Union of Producers, Conveyors and Distributors of Electric Power in African Countries, Madagascar and Mauritius	UNIDO
United Schools International	UNESCO
United Seamen's Service	ILO
Universal Esperanto Association	UNESCO

World Association for Animal Production	FAO
World Association for Public Opinion Research	UNESCO
World Association for the School as an Instrument of Peace	UNESCO
World Association of Industrial and Technological Research Organizations	UNIDO
World Association of Societies of Pathology	WHO
World Confederation of Teachers	UNESCO
World Crafts Council	UNESCO, UNICEF
World Education Fellowship, The	UNESCO
World Federation for Medical Education	WHO
World Federation of Agricultural Workers	FAO
World Federation of Associations of Clinical Toxicology Centers and Poison Control Centers	WHO
World Federation of Engineering Organizations	UNESCO, UNIDO
World Federation of Foreign Language Teachers Associations	UNESCO
World Federation of Hemophilia	WHO
World Federation of Neurology	WHO
World Federation of Neurosurgical Societies	WHO
World Federation of Nuclear Medicine and Biology	WHO
World Federation of Occupational Therapists	WHO
World Federation of Parasitologists	WHO, FAO
World Federation of Proprietary Medicine Manufacturers (WFPMM)	WHO
World Federation of Public Health Associations	WHO
World Federation of Scientific Workers	UNESCO
World Federation of Societies of Anaesthesiologists	WHO
World Federation of Teachers' Unions	UNESCO
World Federation of Workers of Food, Tobacco and Hotel Industries	FAO
World Fellowship of Buddhists	UNESCO
World Future Studies Federation	UNESCO
World Medical Association	WHO, ILO
World Movement of Christian Workers	ILO
World Organization for Early Childhood Education	UNESCO, UNICEF
World ORT Union	ILO
World OSE Union (Worldwide Organisation for Child Care, Health and Hygiene Among Jews)	WHO, UNICEF
World Packaging Organization	UNIDO
World Peace Council	UNESCO, UNCTAD
World's Poultry Science Association	FAO
World Psychiatric Association	WHO
World Union of Catholic Teachers	UNESCO
World Veterinary Association	WHO, FAO
Young Christian Workers	UNESCO, ILO

VI. TRUSTEESHIP SYSTEM

A. TRUSTEESHIP AGREEMENTS AND OTHER MEANS BY WHICH TERRITORIES HAVE BEEN PLACED UNDER THE TRUSTEESHIP SYSTEM AND THE SITUATION OF SOUTH WEST AFRICA

1. TRUSTEESHIP AGREEMENT FOR THE TERRITORY OF WESTERN SAMOA, APPROVED BY THE GENERAL ASSEMBLY OF THE UNITED NATIONS ON 13 DECEMBER 1946[1]

Whereas the Territory of Western Samoa has been administered in accordance with Article 22 of the Covenant of the League of Nations and pursuant to a mandate conferred upon His Britannic Majesty to be exercised on his behalf by the Government of New Zealand;

Whereas Article 75[2] of the Charter of the United Nations signed at San Francisco on 26 June 1945, provides for the establishment of an International Trusteeship System for the administration and supervision of such territories as may be the subject of trusteeship agreements;

Whereas, under Article 77 of the said Charter, the International Trusteeship System may be applied to territories now held under mandate;

Whereas the Government of New Zealand have indicated their willingness that the said International Trusteeship System be applied to Western Samoa;

And whereas the said Charter provides further that the terms of trusteeships are to be approved by the United Nations,

Now, therefore, the General Assembly of the United Nations hereby resolves to approve the following terms of trusteeship for Western Samoa, in substitution for the terms of the aforesaid mandate:

Article 1

The Territory to which this Agreement applies is the territory known as Western Samoa comprising the islands of Upolu, Savai'i, Manono, and Apolima, together with all other islands and rocks adjacent thereto.

Article 2

The Government of New Zealand is hereby designated as the Administering Authority for Western Samoa.

Article 3

The Administering Authority shall have full powers of administration, legislation and jurisdiction over the Territory, subject to the provisions of this Agreement, and of the Charter of the United Nations, and may apply to the Territory, subject to any modifications which the Administering Authority may consider desirable, such of the laws of New Zealand as may seem appropriate to local conditions and requirements.

---

[1] United Nations *Treaty Series*, Vol. 8, 1947, pp. 72-80.
[2] Came into force on 13 December 1946, date of approval of the Agreement by the General Assembly of the United Nations (resolution 63 (I)).

Article 4

The Administering Authority undertakes to administer Western Samoa in such a manner as to achieve, in that Territory, the basic objectives of the International Trusteeship System, as expressed in Article 76 of the Charter of the United Nations, namely:

"a. to further international peace and security;

"b. to promote the political, economic, social and educational advancement of the inhabitants of the Trust Territories, and their progressive development towards self-government or independence as may be appropriate to the particular circumstances of each Territory and its peoples and the freely expressed wishes of the peoples concerned, and as may be provided by the terms of such Trusteeship Agreement;

"c. to encourage respect for human rights and for fundamental freedoms for all without distinction as to race, sex, language or religion, and to encourage recognition of the interdependence of the peoples of the world; and

"d. to ensure equal treatment in social, economic, and commercial matters for all Members of the United Nations and their nationals, and also equal treatment for the latter in the administration of justice, without prejudice to the attainment of the foregoing objectives and subject to the provisions of Article 80."

Article 5

The Administering Authority shall promote the development of free political institutions suited to Western Samoa. To this end and as may be appropriate to the particular circumstances of the Territory and its peoples, the Administering Authority shall assure, to the inhabitants of Western Samoa, a progressively increasing share in the administrative and other services of the Territory, shall develop the participation of the inhabitants of Western Samoa in advisory and legislative bodies and in the government of the Territory, and shall take all other appropriate measures with a view to the political advancement of the inhabitants of Western Samoa in accordance with Article 76 b of the Charter of the United Nations.

Article 6

In pursuance of its undertakings to promote the social advancement of the inhabitants of the Trust Territory, and without in any way limiting its obligations thereunder, the Administering Authority shall:

1. Prohibit all forms of slavery and slavetrading;

2. Prohibit all forms of forced or compulsory labour, except for essential public works and services as specifically authorized by the local administration and then only in times of public emergency, with adequate remuneration and adequate protection of the welfare of the workers;

3. Control the traffic in arms and ammunition;

4. Control, in the interest of the inhabitants, the manufacture, importation and distribution of intoxicating spirits and beverages; and

5. Control the production, importation, manufacture, and distribution of opium and narcotic drugs.

Article 7

The Administering Authority undertakes to apply, in Western Samoa, the provisions of any international conventions and recommendations as drawn up by the United Nations or its specialized agencies which are, in the opinion of the Administering Authority, appropriate to the needs and conditions of the Trust Territory, and conducive to the achievement of the basic objectives of the International Trusteeship System.

Article 8

In framing the laws to be applied in Western Samoa, the Administering Authority shall take into consideration Samoan customs and usages and shall respect the rights and safeguard the interests, both present and future, of the Samoan population.

In particular, the laws relating to the holding or transfer of land shall ensure that no native land may be transferred save with the prior consent of the competent public authority and that no right over native land in favour of any person not a Samoan may be created except with the same consent.

Article 9

The Administering Authority shall ensure, in the Territory, freedom of conscience and the free exercise of all forms of workship, and shall allow missionaries, nationals of any State Member of the United Nations, to enter into, travel and reside in the Territory for the purpose of prosecuting their calling. The provisions of this article shall not, however, affect the right and duty of the Administering Authority to exercise such control as it may consider necessary for the maintenance of peace, order and good government.

Article 10

The Administering Authority shall ensure that the Trust Territory of Western Samoa shall play its part, in accordance with the Charter of the United Nations, in the maintenance of international peace and security. To this end the administering Authority shall be entitled:

1. To establish naval, military and air bases and to erect fortifications in the Trust Territory;

2. To station and employ armed forces in the Territory;

3. To make use of volunteer forces, facilities and assistance from the Trust Territory in carrying out the obligations toward the Security Council undertaken in this regard by the Administering Authority, as well as for local defence and the maintenance of law and order within the Trust Territory;

4. To take all such other measures in accordance with the purposes and principles of the Charter of the United Nations as are, in the opinion of the Administering Authority, necessary for the maintenance of international peace and security and the defence of Western Samoa.

Article 11

The Administering Authority shall, as may be appropriate to the circumstance of the Trust Territory, continue and extend a general system of education, including post-primary education and professional training.

Article 12

Subject only to the requirements of public order, the Administering Authority shall guarantee to the inhabitants of the Trust Territory freedom of speech, of the press, of assembly and of petition.

Article 13

The Administering Authority may arrange for the co-operation of Western Samoa in any regional advisory commission, regional technical organization or other voluntary association of States, any specialized international bodies, public or private, or other forms of international activity not inconsistent with the Charter of the United Nations.

Article 14

The Administering Authority shall make, to the General Assembly of the United Nations, an annual report on the basis of a questionnaire drawn up by the Trusteeship Council in accordance with the Charter of the United Nations and shall otherwise collaborate fully with the Trusteeship Council in the discharge of all the Council's functions in accordance with Articles 87 and 88 of the Charter. The Administering Authority shall arrange to be represented at the sessions of the Trusteeship Council at which the reports of the Administering Authority with regard to Western Samoa are considered.

Article 15

The terms of this Agreement shall not be altered or amended except as provided in Article 79 of the Charter of the United Nations.

Article 16

If any dispute should arise between the Administering Authority and another Member of the United Nations, relating to the interpretation or application of the provisions of this Agreement, such dispute, if it cannot be settled by negotiation or similar means, shall be submitted to the International Court of Justice.

2. TRUSTEESHIP AGREEMENT FOR THE TERRITORY OF TANGANYIKA, APPROVED BY THE GENERAL ASSEMBLY OF THE UNITED NATIONS ON 13 DECEMBER 1946[1]

Whereas the Territory known as Tanganyika has been administered in accordance with Article 22 of the Covenant of the League of Nations under a mandate conferred on His Britannic Majesty; and

Whereas Article 75 of the United Nations Charter, signed at San Francisco on 26 June 1945, provides for the establishment of an International Trusteeship System for the administration and supervision by such territories as may be placed thereunder by subsequent individual agreements; and

Whereas under Article 77 of the said Charter the International Trusteeship System may be applied to territories now held under mandate, and

Whereas His Majesty has indicated his desire to place Tanganyika under the said International Trusteeship System; and

Whereas, in accordance with Articles 75 and 77 of said Charter, the placing of a territory under the International Trusteeship System is to be effected by means of a trusteeship agreement,

Now, therefore, the General Assembly of the United Nations hereby resolves to approve the following terms of Trusteeship for Tanganyika:

---

[1] United Nations *Treaty Series* Vol. 8, 1947, pp. 92-103. Came into force on 13 December 1946, date of approval of the Agreement by the General Assembly of the United Nations (resolution 63 (I)).

Article 1

The Territory to which this Agreement applies comprises that part of East Africa lying within the boundaries defined by article 1 of the British mandate for East Africa, and by the Anglo-Belgian Treaty of 22 November 1931[2] regarding the boundary between Tanganyika and Ruanda-Urundi.

Article 2

His Majesty is hereby designated as Administering Authority for Tanganyika, the responsibility for the administration of which will be undertaken by His Majesty's Government in the United Kingdom of Great Britain and Northern Ireland.

Article 3

The Administering Authority undertakes to administer Tanganyika in such a manner as to achieve the basic objectives of the International Trusteeship system laid down in Article 76 of the United Nations Charter. The Administering Authority further undertakes to collaborate fully with the General Assembly of the United Nations and the Trusteeship Council in the discharge of all their functions as defined in Article 87 of the United Nations Charter, and to facilitate any periodic visits to Tanganyika which they may deem necessary, at times to be agreed upon with the Administering Authority.

Article 4

The Administering Authority shall be responsible *(a)* for the peace, order, good government and defence of Tanganyika, and *(b)* for ensuring that it shall play its part in the maintenance of international peace and security.

Article 5

For the above-mentioned purposes and for all purposes of this Agreement, as may be necessary, the Administering Authority:

(a) Shall have full powers of legislation, administration, and jurisdiction in Tanganyika, subject to the provisions of the United Nations Charter and of this Agreement;

(b) Shall be entitled to constitute Tanganyika into a customs, fiscal or administrative union or federation with adjacent territories under his sovereignty or control, and to establish common services between such territories and Tanganyika where such measures are not inconsistent with the basic objectives of the International Trusteeship System and with the terms of this Agreement;

(c) And shall be entitled to establish naval, military and air bases, to erect fortifications, to station and employ his own forces in Tanganyika and to take all such other measures as are in his opinion necessary for the defence of Tanganyika and for ensuring that the territory plays its part in the maintenance of international peace and security. To this end the Administering Authority may make use of volunteer forces, facilities and assistance from Tanganyika in carrying out the obligations towards the Security Council undertaken in this regard by the Administering Authority, as well as for local defence and the maintenance of law and order within Tanganyika.

Article 6

The Administering Authority shall promote the development of free political institutions suited to Tanganyika. To this end, Administering Authority shall assure to the

[2]League of Nations, *Treaty Series*, Volume CXC, page 95.

inhabitants of Tanganyika a progressively increasing share in the administrative and other services of the Territory; shall develop the participation of the inhabitants of Tanganyika in advisory and legislative bodies and in the government of the Territory, both central and local, as may be appropriate to the particular circumstances of the Territory and its peoples; and shall take all other appropriate measures with a view to the political advancement of the inhabitants of Tanganyika in accordance with Article 76 b of the United Nations Charter.

Article 7

The Administering Authority undertakes to apply, in Tanganyika, the provisions of any international conventions and recommendations already existing or hereafter drawn up by the United Nations or by the specialized agencies referred to in Article 57 of the Charter, which may be appropriate to the particular circumstances of the Territory and which would conduce to the achievement of the basic objectives of the International Trusteeship System.

Article 8

In framing laws relating to the holding or transfer of land and natural resources, the Administering Authority shall take into consideration native laws and customs, and shall respect the rights and safeguard the interests, both present and future, of the native population. No native land or natural resources may be transferred, except between natives, save with the previous consent of the competent public authority. No real rights over native land or natural resources in favour of non-natives may be created except with the same consent.

Article 9

Subject to the provisions of article 10 of this Agreement, the Administering Authority shall take all necessary steps to ensure equal treatment in social, economic, industrial and commercial matters for all Members of the United Nations and their nationals and to this end:

(a) Shall ensure the same rights to all nationals of Members of the United Nations as to his own nationals in respect of entry into and residence in Tanganyika, freedom of transit and navigation, including freedom of transit and navigation by air, acquisition of property both movable and immovable, the protection of person and property, and the exercise of professions and trades;

(b) Shall not discriminate on grounds of nationality against nationals of any Member of the United Nations in matters relating to the grant of concessions for the development of the natural resources of Tanganyika and shall not grant concessions having the character of a general monopoly;

(c) Shall ensure equal treatment in the administration of justice to the nationals of all Members of the United Nations.

The rights conferred by this article on nationals of Members of the United Nations apply equally to companies and associations controlled by such nationals and organized in accordance with the law of any Member of the United Nations.

Article 10

Measures taken to give effect to article 9 of this Agreement shall be subject always to the overriding duty of the Administering Authority, in accordance with Article 76 of the United Nations Charter, to promote the political, economic, social and educational advancement of the inhabitants of Tanganyika, to carry out the other basic objectives of the International Trusteeship System, and to maintain peace, order and good government. The Administering Authority shall in particular be free:

(a) To organize essential public services and works on such terms and conditions as he thinks just;

(b) To create monopolies of a purely fiscal character in order to provide Tanganyika with the fiscal resources which seem best suited to local requirements, or otherwise to serve the interests of the inhabitants of Tanganyika;

(c) Where the interests of the economic advancement of the inhabitants of Tanganyika may require it, to establish, or permit to be established, for specific purposes, other monopolies or undertakings having in them an element of monopoly, under conditions or proper public control; provided that, in the selection of agencies to carry out the purposes of this paragraph, other than agencies controlled by the Government or those in which the Government participates, the Administering Authority shall not discriminate on grounds of nationality against Members of the United Nations or their nationals.

Article 11

Nothing in this Agreement shall entitle any Member of the United Nations to claim for itself or for its nationals, companies and associations the benefits of article 9 of this Agreement in any respect in which it does not give to the inhabitants, companies and associations of Tanganyika equality of treatment with the nationals, companies and associations of the State which it treats most favourably.

Article 12

The Administering Authority shall, as may be appropriate to the circumstances of Tanganyika, continue and extend a general system of elementary education designed to abolish illiteracy and to facilitate the vocational and cultural advancement of the population, child and adult, and shall similarly provide such facilities as may prove desirable and practicable, in the interests of the inhabitants, for qualified students to receive secondary and higher education, including professional training.

Article 13

The Administering Authority shall ensure, in Tanganyika, complete freedom of conscience and, so far as is consistent with the requirements of public order and morality, freedom of religious teaching and the free exercise of all forms of worship. Subject to the provisions of article 8 of this Agreement and the local law, missionaries who are nationals of Members of the United Nations shall be free to enter Tanganyika and to travel and reside therein, to acquire and possess property, to erect religious buildings and to open schools and hospitals in the Territory. The provisions of this article shall not, however, affect the right and duty of the Administering Authority to exercise such controls as he may consider necessary for the maintenance of peace, order and good government and for the educational advancement of the inhabitants of Tanganyika, and to take all measures required for such control.

Article 14

Subject only to the requirements of public order, the Administering Authority shall guarantee to the inhabitants of Tanganyika freedom of speech, of the press, of assembly and of petition.

Article 15

The Administering Authority may arrange for the co-operation of Tanganyika in any regional advisory commission, regional technical organization or other voluntary association of States, any specialized international bodies, public or private, or other forms of international activity not inconsistent with the United Nations Charter.

Article 16

The Administering Authority shall make, to the General Assembly of the United Nations, an annual report on the basis of a questionnaire drawn up by the Trusteeship Council in accordance with Article 88 of the United Nations Charter. Such reports shall include information concerning the measures taken to give effect to suggestions and recommendations of the General Assembly and the Trusteeship Council. The Administering Authority shall designate an accredited representative to be present at the sessions of the Trusteeship Council at which the reports of the Administering Authority with regard to Tanganyika are considered.

Article 17

Nothing in this Agreement shall affect the right of the Administering Authority to propose, at any future date, the amendment of this Agreement for the purpose of designating the whole or part of Tanganyika as a strategic area or for any other purpose not inconsistent with the basic objectives of the International Trusteeship System.

Article 18

The terms of this Agreement shall not be altered or amended except as provided in Article 79 and Article 83 or 85, as the case may be, of the United Nations Charter.

Article 19

If any dispute whatever should arise between the Administering Authority and another Member of the United Nations relating to the interpretation or application of the provisions of this Agreement, such dispute, if it cannot be settled by negotiation or other means, shall be submitted to the International Court of Justice, provided for in Chapter XIV of the United Nations Charter.

3. TRUSTEESHIP AGREEMENT FOR THE TERRITORY OF RUANDA-URUNDI, APPROVED BY THE GENERAL ASSEMBLY OF THE UNITED NATIONS ON 13 DECEMBER 1946[1]

———————————

Whereas the Territory known as Ruanda-Urundi has been administered in accordance with Article 22 of the Covenant of the League of Nations under mandate conferred upon Belgium;

Whereas Article 75 of the United Nations Charter, signed at San Francisco on 26 June 1945, provides for the establishment of an International Trusteeship System for the administration and supervision of such territories as may be placed thereunder by subsequent individual agreements;

———————————

[1] United Nations *Treaty Series*, Vol. 8, 1947, pp. 106-117. Came into force on 13 December 1946, date of approval of the Agreement by the General Assembly of the United Nations (resolution 63 (I)).

Whereas under Article 77 of the said Charter the International Trusteeship System may be applied to territories now held under mandate;

Whereas the Belgian Government has indicated its desire to place Ruanda-Urundi under the International Trusteeship System; and

Whereas, under Articles 75 and 77 of the Charter, the placing of a territory under the International Trusteeship System is to be effected by means of a trusteeship agreement;

Now, therefore, the General Assembly of the United Nations hereby resolves to approve the following terms of Trusteeship for Ruanda-Urundi:

Article 1

The present Trusteeship Agreement shall apply to the whole of the Territory of Ruanda-Urundi as at present administered by Belgium and as defined by article 1 of the Belgian mandate and by the Treaty concluded in London on 22 November 1934[2] by Belgium and the United Kingdom.

Article 2

By the present Agreement, the Belgian Government is designated as Administering Authority for Ruanda-Urundi in accordance with Article 75 of the Charter. The said Government shall assume responsibility for the administration of the said Territory.

Article 3

The Administering Authority undertakes to administer Ruanda-Urundi in such a manner as to achieve the basic objectives of the International Trusteeship System laid down in Article 76 of the United Nations Charter. The Administering Authority further undertakes to collaborate fully with the General Assembly of the United Nations and with the Trusteeship Council in the discharge of all their functions as defined in Article 87 of the United Nations Charter.

It likewise undertakes to facilitate such periodic visits to the Trust Territory as the General Assembly or the Trusteeship Council may decide to arrange, to decide, jointly with these organs, the dates on which such visits shall take place and also to agree jointly with them on all questions concerned with the organization and accomplishment of these visits.

Article 4

The Administering Authority shall ensure the maintenance of peace and order as well as the good government and defence of the Territory. The said Authority shall ensure that the Territory shall play its part in the maintenance of international peace and security.

Article 5

For the above-mentioned purposes, and in order to fulfill the obligations arising under the Charter and the present Agreement, the Administering Authority:

1. Shall have full powers of legislation, administration and jurisdiction in the Territory of Ruanda-Urundi and shall administer it in accordance with Belgian law as an integral part of Belgian territory, subject to the provisions of the Charter and of this Agreement;

[2]League of Nations, *Treaty Series,* Volume CXC, page 95.

2. Shall be entitled to constitute Ruanda-Urundi into a customs, fiscal or administrative union or federation with adjacent territories under its sovereignty and to establish common services between such territories and Ruanda-Urundi, provided that such measures are not inconsistent with the objectives of the International Trusteeship System and with the provisions of this Agreement;

3. May establish, on the Trust Territory, military bases, including air bases, erect fortifications, station its own armed forces and raise volunteer contingents therein.

The Administering Authority may likewise, within the limits laid down by the Charter, take all measures of organization and defence appropriate for ensuring:

(a) The participation of the Territory in the maintenance of international peace and security;

(b) The respect for obligations concerning the assistance and facilities to be given by the Administering Authority to the Security Council;

(c) The respect for internal law and order;

(d) The defence of the Territory within the framework of special agreements for the maintenance of international peace and security.

Article 6

The Administering Authority shall promote the development of free political institutions suited to Ruanda-Urundi. To this end the Administering Authority shall assure to the inhabitants of Ruanda-Urundi an increasing share in the administration and services, both central and local, of the Territory; it shall further such participation of the inhabitants in the representative organs of the population as may be appropriate to the particular conditions of the Territory.

In short, the Administering Authority shall take all measures conducive to the political advancement of the population of Ruanda-Urundi in accordance with Article 76 b of the Charter of the United Nations.

Article 7

The Administering Authority undertakes to apply to Ruanda-Urundi the provisions of all present or future international conventions and recommendations which may be appropriate to the particular conditions of the Territory and which would be conducive to the achievement of the basic objectives of the International Trusteeship System.

Article 8

In framing laws relating to the ownership of land and the rights over natural resources, and to their transfer, the Administering Authority shall take into consideration native laws and customs and shall respect the rights and safeguard the interests, both present and future, of the native population. No native land or native-owned natural resources may be transferred, except between natives, save with the previous consent of the competent public authority. No real rights over native land or native-owned resources of the sub-soil, in favour of non-natives, may be created except with the same consent.

Article 9

Subject to the provisions of the following article, the Administering Authority shall take all necessary steps to ensure equal treatment in social, economic, industrial and commercial matters for all States Members of the United Nations and their nationals and to this end:

1. Shall ensure to all nationals of Members of the United Nations the same rights

as are enjoyed by its own nationals in respect of entry into and residence in Ruanda-Urundi, freedom of transit and navigation, including freedom of transit and navigation by air, the acquisition of property, both movable and immovable, the protection of person and property, and the exercise of professions and trades;

2. Shall not discriminate on grounds of nationality against nationals of any Member of the United Nations in matters relating to the grant of concessions for the development of natural resources of the Territory and shall not grant concessions having the character of a general monopoly;

3. Shall ensure equal treatment in the administration of justice to the nationals of all Members of the United Nations.

The rights conferred by this article on the nationals of States Members of the United Nations apply equally to companies or associations controlled by such nationals and formed in accordance with the law of any Member of the United Nations.

Article 10

Measures taken to give effect to the provisions of the preceding article shall be subject always to the overriding duty of the United Nations and of the Administering Authority to promote the political, economic, social and cultural advancement of the inhabitants of the Territory, and to pursue the other objectives of the Trusteeship System as laid down in Article 76 of the Charter of the United Nations.

The Administering Authority shall, in particular, be free:

1. To organize essential public services and works on such terms and such conditions as it thinks just;

2. To create, in the interests of Ruanda-Urundi, monopolies of a purely fiscal character in order to provide the Territory with the resources which seem best suited to local requirements;

3. Where the interest or the economic advancement of the inhabitants of the Territory may require it, to establish or permit to be established, for specific purposes, other monopolies or undertakings having in them an element of monopoly, under conditions of proper public control, provided that, in the selection of agencies to carry out the purposes of this paragraph, other than agencies controlled by the Government or those in which the Government participates, the Administering Authority shall not discriminate on grounds of nationality against Members of the United Nations or their nationals.

Article 11

Nothing in this Agreement shall entitle any Member of the United Nations to claim for itself or for its nationals, companies or associations, the benefits of article 9 of this Agreement in any respect in which it does not give to the inhabitants, companies and associations of Ruanda-Urundi equality of treatment with the nationals, companies and associations of the State which it treats most favourably.

Article 12

The Administering Authority shall develop the system of elementary education in the Trust Territory in order to reduce the number of illiterates, to train the inhabitants in manual skill, and to improve the education of the population. The Administering Authority shall, so far as possible, provide the necessary facilities to enable qualified students to receive higher education, more especially professional education.

Article 13

The Administering Authority shall ensure, throughout the Trust Territory complete freedom of conscience, freedom or religious teaching and the free exercise of all forms of worship which are consistent with public order and morality; all missionaries who are nationals of any State Member of the United Nations shall be free to enter, travel and reside in the Trust Territory, to acquire and possess property, to erect religious buildings and to open schools and hospitals therein. The provisions of the present article shall not, however, affect the duty of the Administering Authority to exercise such control as may be necessary for the maintenance of public order and good government and also the quality and progress of education.

Article 14

Subject only to the requirements of public order, the Administering Authority shall guarantee to the inhabitants of the Trust Territory freedom of speech, of the press, or assembly and of petition.

Article 15

The Administering Authority may, on behalf of the Trust Territory, accept membership in any advisory regional commission (regional authority), technical organization, or other voluntary association of States. It may co-operate with specialized agencies, whether public or private, and participate in other forms of international co-operation not inconsistent with the Charter.

Article 16

The Administering Authority shall make, to the General Assembly of the United Nations, an annual report on the basis of the questionnaire drawn up by the Trusteeship Council in accordance with Article 88 of the Charter of the United Nations.

Such reports shall include information regarding the measures taken in order to give effect to the suggestions and recommendations of the General Assembly and of the Trusteeship Council.

The Administering Authority shall appoint an accredited representative to attend the meetings of the Trusteeship Council at which the reports of the Administering Authority for Ruanda-Urundi will be examined.

Article 17

Nothing in this Agreement shall affect the right of the Administering Authority to propose at any future date the designation of the whole or part of the Territory as a strategic area in accordance with Articles 82 and 83 of the Charter.

Article 18

The terms of the present Trusteeship Agreement may not be altered or amended except as provided in Articles 79, 83 or 85 of the Charter.

Article 19

If any dispute whatever should arise between the Administering Authority and another Member of the United Nations relating to the interpretation or the application of the provisions of the present Trusteeship Agreement, such dispute, if it cannot be settled by negotiation or other means, shall be submitted to the International Court of Justice, provided for by Chapter XIV of the Charter of the United Nations.

4. TRUSTEESHIP AGREEMENT FOR THE TERRITORY OF THE CAMEROONS UNDER BRITISH ADMINISTRATION, APPROVED BY THE GENERAL ASSEMBLY OF THE NATIONS ON 13 DECEMBER 1946[1]

Whereas the Territory known as the Cameroons under British Mandate[2] and hereinafter referred to as the Territory has been administered in accordance with Article 22 of the Covenant of the League of Nations under a mandate conferred on His Britannic Majesty; and

Whereas Article 75 of the United Nations Charter, signed at San Francisco on 26 June 1945, provides for the establishment of an International Trusteeship System for the administration and supervision of such territories as may be placed thereunder by subsequent individual agreements; and

Whereas, under Article 77 of the said Charter, the International Trusteeship System may be applied to territories now held under mandate; and

Whereas His Majesty has indicated his desire to place the Territory under the said International Trusteeship System; and

Whereas, in accordance with Articles 75 and 77 of the said Charter, the placing of a territory under the International Trusteeship System is to be effected by means of a trusteeship agreement,

Now, therefore, the General Assembly of the United Nations hereby resolves to approve the following terms of Trusteeship for the Territory:

Article 1

The Territory to which this Agreement applies comprises that part of the Cameroons lying to the west of the boundary defined by the Franco-British Declaration of 10 July 1919,[3] and more exactly defined in the Declaration made by the Governor of the Colony and Protectorate of Nigeria and the Governor of the Cameroons under French mandate which was confirmed by the exchange of Notes between His Majesty's Government in the United Kingdom and the French Government of 9 January 1931.[4] This line may, however, be slightly modified by mutual agreement between His Majesty's Government in the United Kingdom and the Government of the French Republic where an examination of the localities shows that it is desirable in the interests of the inhabitants.

Article 2

His Majesty is hereby designated as Administering Authority for the Territory, the responsibility of the administration of which will be undertaken by His Majesty's Government in the United Kingdom of Great Britain and Northern Ireland.

Article 3

The Administering Authority undertakes to administer the Territory in such a manner as to achieve the basic objectives of the International Trusteeship System laid down

---

[1] United Nations *Treaty Series*, Vol. 8, 1947, pp. 120-133. Came into force on 13 December 1946, date of approval of the Agreement by the General Assembly of the United Nations (resolution 63 (I)).

[2] League of Nations, *Official Journal*, Volume 2 (1922), pp. 869-871.

[3] *British and Foreign State Papers*, Volume 118, page 887.

[4] *British and Foreign State Papers*, Volume 134, page 238.

in Article 76 of the United Nations Charter. The Administering Authority further undertakes to collaborate fully with the General Assembly of the United Nations and the Trusteeship Council in the discharge of all their functions as defined in Article 87 of the United Nations Charter, and to facilitate any periodic visits to the Territory which they may deem necessary, at times to be agreed upon with the Administering Authority.

Article 4

The Administering Authority shall be responsible: *(a)* for the peace, order, good government and defence of the Territory and *(b)* for ensuring that it shall play its part in the maintenance of international peace and security.

Article 5

For the above-mentioned purposes and for all purposes of this Agreement, as may be necessary, the Administering Authority:

(a) Shall have full powers of legislation, administration and jurisdiction in the Territory and shall administer it in accordance with the authority's own laws as an integral part of its territory with such modification as may be required by local conditions and subject to the provisions of the United Nations Charter and of this Agreement;

(b) Shall be entitled to constitute the Territory into a customs, fiscal or administrative union or federation with adjacent territories under its sovereignty or control, and to establish common services between such territories and the Territory where such measures are not inconsistent with the basic objectives of the International Trusteeship System and with the terms of this Agreement;

(c) And shall be entitled to establish naval, military and air bases, to erect fortifications, to station and employ its own forces in the Territory and to take all such other measures as are in its opinion necessary for the defence of the Territory and for ensuring that it plays its part in the maintenance of international peace and security. To this end the Administering Authority may make use of volunteer forces, facilities and assistance from the Territory in carrying out the obligations towards the Security Council undertaken in this regard by the Administering Authority, as well as for local defence and the maintenance of law and order within the Territory.

Article 6

The Administering Authority shall promote the development of free political institutions suited to the Territory. To this end the Administering Authority shall assure to the inhabitants of the Territory a progressively increasing share in the administrative and other services of the Territory; shall develop the participation of the inhabitants of the Territory in advisory and legislative bodies and in the government of the Territory, both central and local, as may be appropriate to the particular circumstances of the Territory and its people; and shall take all other appropriate measures with a view to the political advancement of the inhabitants of the Territory in accordance with Article 76 b of the United Nations Charter. In considering the measures to be taken under this article the Administering Authority shall, in the interests of the inhabitants, have special regard to the provisions of article 5 *(a)* of this Agreement.

Article 7

The Administering Authority undertakes to apply in the Territory the provisions of any international conventions and recommendations already existing or hereafter drawn up by the United Nations or by the specialized agencies referred to in Article 57 of the Charter, which may be appropriate to the particular circumstances of the Territory and which would conduce to the achievement of the basic objectives of the International Trusteeship System.

Article 8

In framing laws relating to the holding or transfer of land and natural resources, the Administering Authority shall take into consideration native laws and customs, and shall respect the rights and safeguard the interests, both present and future, of the native population. No native land or natural resources may be transferred except between natives, save with the previous consent of the competent public authority. No real rights over native land or natural resources in favour of non-natives may be created except with the same consent.

Article 9

Subject to the provisions of article 10 of this Agreement, the Administering Authority shall take all necessary steps to ensure equal treatment in social, economic, industrial and commercial matters for all Members of the United Nations and their nationals and to this end:

(a) Shall ensure the same rights to all nationals of Members of the United Nations as to its own nationals in respect of entry into and residence in the Territory, freedom of transit and navigation, including freedom of transit and navigation by air, acquisition of property both movable and immovable, the protection of persons and property and the exercise of professions and trades;

(b) Shall not discriminate on grounds of nationality against nationals of any Member of the United Nations in matters relating to the grant of concessions for the development of the natural resources of the Territory, and shall not grant concessions having the character of a general monopoly;

(c) Shall ensure equal treatment in the administration of justice to the nationals of all Members of the United Nations.

The rights conferred by this article on nationals of Members of the United Nations apply equally to companies and associations controlled by such nationals and organized in accordance with the law of any Member of the United Nations.

Article 10

Measures taken to give effect to article 9 of this Agreement shall be subject always to the overriding duty of the Administering Authority in accordance with Article 76 of the United Nations Charter to promote the political, economic, social and educational advancement of the inhabitants of the Territory, to carry out the other basic objectives of the International Trusteeship System, and to maintain peace, order and good government. The Administering Authority shall in particular be free:

(a) To organize essential public services and works on such terms and conditions as it thinks just;

(b) To create monopolies of a purely fiscal character in order to provide the Territory with the fiscal resources which seem best suited to local requirements, or otherwise to serve the interests of the inhabitants of the Territory;

(c) Where the interests of the economic advancement of the inhabitants of the Territory may require it, to establish or permit to be established, for specific purposes, other monopolies or undertakings having in them an element of monopoly, under conditions of proper public control; provided that, in the selection of agencies to carry out the purposes of this paragraph, other than agencies controlled by the Government or those in which the Government participates, the Administering Authority

shall not discriminate on grounds of nationality against Members of the United Nations or their nationals.

Article 11

Nothing in this Agreement shall entitle any Member of the United Nations to claim for itself or for its nationals, companies and associations, the benefits of article 9 of this Agreement in any respect in which it does not give to the inhabitants, companies and associations of the Territory equality of treatment with the nationals, companies and associations of the State which it treats most favorably.

Article 12

The Administering Authority shall, as may be appropriate to the circumstances of the Territory, continue and extend a general system of elementary education designed to abolish illiteracy and to facilitate the vocational and cultural advancement of the population, child and adult, and shall similarly provide such facilities as may prove desirable and practicable in the interests of the inhabitants for qualified students to receive secondary and higher education, including professional training.

Article 13

The Administering Authority shall ensure, in the Territory, complete freedom of conscience and, so far as is consistent with the requirements of public order and morality, freedom of religious teaching and the free exercise of all forms of worship. Subject to the provisions of article 8 of this Agreement and the local law, missionaries who are nationals of Members of the United Nations shall be free to enter the Territory and to travel and reside therein, to acquire and possess property, to erect religious buildings and to open schools and hospitals in the Territory. The provisions of this article shall not, however, affect the right and duty of the Administering Authority to exercise such control as he may consider necessary for the maintenance of peace, order and good government and for the educational advancement of the inhabitants of the Territory, and to take all measures required for such control.

Article 14

Subject only to the requirements of public order, the Administering Authority shall guarantee to the inhabitants of the Territory freedom of speech, of the press, of assembly and of petition.

Article 15

The Administering Authority may arrange for the co-operation of the Territory in any regional advisory commission, regional technical organization, or other voluntary association of States, any specialized international bodies, public or private, or other forms of international activity not inconsistent with the United Nations Charter.

Article 16

The Administering Authority shall make to the General Assembly of the United Nations an annual report on the basis of a questionnaire drawn up by the Trusteeship Council in accordance with Article 88 of the United Nations Charter. Such reports shall include information concerning the measures taken to give effect to suggestions and recommendations of the General Assembly and the Trusteeship Council. The Administering Authority shall designate an accredited representative to be present at the sessions of the Trusteeship Council at which the reports of the Administering Authority with regard to the Territory are considered.

Article 17

Nothing in this Agreement shall affect the right of the Administering Authority to propose, at any future date, the amendment of this Agreement for the purpose of designating the whole or part of the Territory as a strategic area or for any other purpose not inconsistent with the basic objectives of the International Trusteeship System.

Article 18

The terms of this Agreement shall not be altered or amended except as provided in Article 79 and Article 83 or 85, as the case may be, of the United Nations Charter.

Article 19

If any dispute whatever should arise between the Administering Authority and another Member of the United Nations relating to the interpretation or application of the provisions of this Agreement, such dispute, if it cannot be settled by negotiation or other means, shall be submitted to the International Court of Justice, provided for in Chapter XIV of the United Nations Charter.

5. TRUSTEESHIP AGREEMENT FOR THE TERRITORY OF THE CAMEROONS UNDER FRENCH ADMINISTRATION, APPROVED BY THE GENERAL ASSEMBLY OF THE UNITED NATIONS ON 13 DECEMBER 1946[1]

Whereas the Territory known as the Cameroons lying to the east of the line agreed upon in the Declaration signed on 10 July 1919[2] has been under French administration in accordance with the mandate defined under the terms of the instrument of 20 July 1922,[3] and

Whereas, in accordance with article 9 of that instrument, this part of the Cameroons has since then been "administered in accordance with the laws of the Mandatory as an integral part of his territory and subject to the provisions" of the mandate, and it is of importance, in the interests of the population of the Cameroons, to pursue the administrative and political development of the territories in question, in such a way as to promote the political, economic and social advancement of the inhabitants in accordance with Article 76 of the Charter of the United Nations; and

Whereas France has indicated its desire to place under trusteeship in accordance with Articles 75 and 77 of the said Charter that part of the Cameroons which is at present administered by it; and

Whereas Article 85 of the said Charter provides that the terms of Trusteeship are to be submitted for approval by the General Assembly,

Now, therefore, the General Assembly of the United Nations approves the following terms of Trusteeship for the said Territory:

---

[1]United Nations *Treaty Series*, Vol. 8, 1947, pp. 136-149. Came into force on 13 December 1946, date of approval of the Agreement by the General Assembly of the United Nations (resolution 63 (I)).
[2]*British and Foreign State Papers*, Volume 118, page 887.
[3]League of Nations, *Official Journal*, Volume 2 (1922), pp. 874-877.

Article 1

The Territory to which the present Trusteeship Agreement applies comprises that part of the Cameroons lying to the east of the boundary defined by the Franco-British Declaration of 10 July 1919.

Article 2

The French Government, in its capacity of Administering Authority for this Territory under the terms of Article 81 of the Charter of the United Nations undertakes to exercise therein the duties of trusteeship as defined in the said Charter, to promote the basic objectives of the Trusteeship System laid down in Article 76 and to collaborate fully with the General Assembly and the Trusteeship Council in the discharge of their functions as defined in Articles 87 and 88.

Accordingly the French Government undertakes:

1. To make to the General Assembly of the United Nations the annual report provided for in Article 88 of the Charter, on the basis of the questionnaire drawn up by the Trusteeship Council in accordance with the said Article, and to attach to that report such memoranda as may be required by the General Assembly or the Trusteeship Council;

To include in that report information relating to the measures taken to give effect to the suggestions and recommendations of the General Assembly or of the Trusteeship Council;

To appoint a representative and, where necessary, qualified experts to attend the meetings of the Trusteeship Council or of the General Assembly at which the said reports and memoranda will be examined;

2. To appoint a representative and, where necessary, qualified experts to participate, in consultation with the General Assembly or the Trusteeship Council, in the examination of petitions received by those bodies;

3. To facilitate such periodic visits to the Territory as the General Assembly or the Trusteeship Council may decide to arrange; to decide jointly with these bodies the dates on which such visits shall take place, and also to agree jointly with them on all questions concerned with the organization and accomplishment of these visits;

4. To render general assistance to the General Assembly or the Trusteeship Council in the application of these arrangements, and of such other arrangement as these bodies may make in accordance with the terms of the present Agreement.

Article 3

The Administering Authority shall be responsible for the peace, order and good government of the Territory.

It shall also be responsible for the defence of the said Territory and ensure that it shall play its part in the maintenance of international peace and security.

Article 4

For the above-mentioned purposes and in order to fulfil its obligations under the Charter and the present Agreement, the Administering Authority:

A

1. Shall have full powers of legislation, administration and jurisdiction in the Territory and shall administer it in accordance with French law as an integral part of French territory, subject to the provisions of the Charter and of the Agreement;

2. Shall be entitled, in order to ensure better administration, with the consent of

the territorial representative assembly, to constitute this Territory into a customs, fiscal or administrative union or federation with adjacent territories under its sovereignty or control and to establish common services between such territories and the Trust Territory, provided that such measures shall promote the objectives of the International Trusteeship System;

B

1. May establish, on the Territory, military, naval or air bases, station national forces and raise volunteer contingents therein;

2. May within the limits laid down in the Charter, take all measures of organization and defence appropriate for ensuring:

The participation of the Territory in the maintenance of international peace and security,

The respect for obligations concerning the assistance and facilities to be given by the Administering Authority to the Security Council;

The respect for internal law and order;

The defence of the Territory within the framework of the special agreements for the maintenance of international peace and security.

Article 5

The Administering Authority shall take measures to ensure to the local inhabitants a share in the administration of the Territory by the development of representative democratic bodies, and, in due course, to arrange appropriate measures to enable the inhabitants freely to express an opinion in their political regime and ensure the attainment of the objectives prescribed in Article 76 b of the Charter.

Article 6

The Administering Authority undertakes to maintain the application to the Territory of the international agreements and conventions which are at present in force there, and to apply therein any conventions and recommendations made by the United Nations or the specialized agencies referred to in Article 57 of the Charter, the application of which would be in the interests of the population and consistent with the basic objectives of the Trusteeship System and the terms of the present Agreement.

Article 7

In framing laws relating to the holding or transfer of land, the Administering Authority shall, in order to promote the economic and social progress of the native population, take into consideration local laws and customs.

No land belonging to a native or to a group of natives may be transferred except between natives, save with the previous consent of the competent public authority, who shall respect the rights and safeguard the interests, both present and future, of the natives. No real rights over native land in favour of non-natives may be created except with the same consent.

Article 8

Subject to the provisions of the following article, the Administering Authority shall take all necessary steps to ensure equal treatment in social, economic, industrial and commercial matters for all States Members of the United Nations and their nationals and to this end:

1. Shall grant to all nationals of Members of the United Nations freedom of transit and navigation, including freedom of transit and navigation by air, and the

protection of person and property, subject to the requirements of public order and on condition of compliance with the local law;

2. Shall ensure the same rights to all nationals of Members of the United Nations as to his own nationals in respect of entry into and residence in the Territory, acquisition of property, both movable and immovable, and the exercise of professions and trades;

3. Shall not discriminate on grounds of nationality against nationals of any Member of the United Nations in matters relating to the grant of concessions for the development of the natural resources of the Territory, and shall not grant concessions having the character of a general monopoly;

4. Shall ensure equal treatment in the administration of justice to the nationals of all Members of the United Nations.

The rights conferred by this article on the nationals of Members of the United Nations apply equally to companies and associations controlled by such nationals and formed in accordance with the law of any Member of the United Nations.

Nevertheless, pursuant to Article 76 of the Charter, such equal treatment shall be without prejudice to the attainment of the trusteeship objectives as prescribed in the said Article 76 and particularly in paragraph b of that Article.

Should special advantages of any kind be granted by a Power enjoying the equality of treatment referred to above to another Power, or to a territory whether self-governing or not, the same, advantages shall automatically apply reciprocally to the Trust Territory and to its inhabitants, especially in the economic and commercial field.

Article 9

Measures taken to give effect to the preceding article of this Agreement shall be subject to the overriding duty of the Administering Authority, in accordance with Article 76 of the Charter, to promote the political, economic, social and educational advancement of the inhabitants of the Territory, to carry out the other basic objectives of the International Trusteeship System and to maintain peace, order and good government. The Administering Authority shall in particular be free, with the consent of the territorial representative Assembly:

1. To organize essential public services and works on such terms and such conditions as it thinks just;

2. To create monopolies of a purely fiscal character in the interest of the Territory and in order to provide the Territory with the fiscal resources which seem best suited to local requirements;

3. To establish or to permit to be established under conditions of proper public control, in conformity with Article 76, paragraph d of the Charter, such public enterprises or joint undertakings as appear to the Administering Authority to be in the interest of the economic advancement of the inhabitants of the Territory.

Article 10

The Administering Authority shall ensure, in the Territory, complete freedom of thought and the free exercise of all forms of worship and of religious teaching which are consistent with public order and morality. Missionaries who are nationals of States Members of the United Nations shall be free to enter the Territory and to reside therein, to acquire and possess property, to erect religious buildings and to open schools and hospitals throughout the Territory.

The provisions of this article shall not, however, affect the right and duty of the Administering Authority to exercise such control as may be necessary for the maintenance of public order and morality, and for the educational advancement of the inhabitants of the Territory.

The Administering Authority shall continue to develop elementary, secondary and technical education for the benefit of both children and adults. To the full extent compatible with the interests of the population it shall afford to qualified students the opportunity of receiving higher general or professional education.

The Administering Auhtority shall guarantee to the inhabitants of the Territory freedom of speech, of the press, of assembly and of petition, subject only to the requirements of public order.

Article 11

Nothing in this Agreement shall affect the right of the Administering Authority to propose at any future date the designation of the whole or part of the Territory thus placed under its trusteeship as a strategic area in accordace with Articles 82 and 83 of the Charter.

Article 12

The terms of the present Trusteeship Agreement shall not be altered or amended except as provided in Articles 79, 82, 83 and 85, as the case may be of the Charter.

Article 13

If any dispute whatever should arise between the Administering Authority and another Member of the United Nations, relating to the interpretation or the application of the provisions of the present Trusteeship Agreement, such dispute, if it cannot be settled by negotiation or other means, shall be submitted to the International Court of Justice, provided for by Chapter XIV of the Charter of the United Nations.

Article 14

The Administering Authority may enter, on behalf of the Territory, any consultative regional commission, technical organ or voluntary association of States which may be constituted. It may also collaborate, on behalf of the Territory, with international public or private institutions or participate in any form of international co-operation in accordance with the spirit of the Charter.

Article 15

The present Agreement shall enter into force as soon as it has received the approval of the General Assembly of the United Nations.

6. TRUSTEESHIP AGREEMENT FOR THE TERRITORY OF TOGOLAND UNDER BRITISH ADMINISTRATION, APPROVED BY THE GENERAL ASSEMBLY OF THE UNITED NATIONS ON 13 DECEMBER 1946[1]

———————

Whereas the Territory known as Togoland under British Mandate[2] and hereinafter referred to as the Territory has been administered in accordance with Article 22 of

---

[1] United Nations *Treaty Series*, Vol. 8, 1947, pp. 152-163. Came into force on 13 December 1946, date of approval of the Agreement by the General Assembly of the United Nations (resolution 63 (I)).

[2] League of Nations, *Official Journal*, Volume 2 (1922), pp. 869-871.

the Covenant of the League of Nations under a mandate conferred on His Britannic Majesty; and

Whereas Article 75 of the United Nations Charter, signed at San Francisco on 26 June 1945 provides for the establishment of an International Trusteeship System for the administration and supervision of such territories as may be placed thereunder by subsequent individual agreements; and

Whereas under Article 77 of the said Charter, the International Trusteeship System may be applied to territories now held under mandate; and

Whereas His Majesty has indicated his desire to place the Territory under the said International Trusteeship System; and

Whereas in accordance with Articles 75 and 77 of the said Charter, the placing of a territory under the International Trusteeship System is to be effected by means of a trusteeship agreement,

Now therefore the General Assembly of the United Nations hereby resolves to approve the following terms of trusteeship for the Territory:

Article 1

The Territory to which this Agreement applies comprises that part of Togoland lying to the west of the boundary defined by the Franco-British Declaration of 10 July 1919,[3] as delimited and modified by the Protocol of 21 October 1929,[4] executed by the Commissioners appointed in the execution of article 2 (1) of the said Declaration.

Article 2

His Majesty is hereby designated as Administering Authority for the Territory, the responsibility for the administration of which will be undertaken by His Majesty's Government in the United Kingdom of Great Britain and Northern Ireland.

Article 3

The Administering Authority undertakes to administer the Territory in such a manner as to achieve the basic objectives of the International Trusteeship System laid down in Article 76 of the United Nations Charter. The Administering Authority further undertakes to collaborate fully with the General Assembly of the United Nations and the Trusteeship Council in the discharge of all their functions as defined in Article 87 of the United Nations Charter, and to facilitate any periodic visits to the Territory which they may deem necessary, at times to be agreed upon with the Administering Authority.

Article 4

The Administering Authority shall be responsible: *(a)* for the peace, order, good government and defence of the Territory and *(b)* for ensuring that it shall play its part in the maintenance of international peace and security.

Article 5

For the above-mentioned purposes and for all purposes of this Agreement as may be necessary, the Administering Authority:

---

[3]*British and Foreign State Papers*, Volume 118, page 893.
[4]*British and Foreign State Papers*, Volume 132, page 248.

(a) Shall have full powers of legislation, administration and jurisdiction in the Territory, and shall administer it in accordance with its own laws as any integral part of its territory with such modifications as may be required by local conditions and subject to the provisions of the United Nations Charter and of this Agreement;

(b) Shall be entitled to constitute the Territory into a customs, fiscal or administrative union or federation with adjacent territories under his sovereignty or control, and to establish common services between such territories and the Territory where such measures are not inconsistent with the basic objectives of the International Trusteeship System and with the terms of this Agreement;

(c) And shall be entitled to establish naval, military and air bases, to erect fortifications, to station and employ his own forces in the Territory and to take all such other measures as are, in his opinion, necessary for the defence of the Territory and for ensuring that it plays its part in the maintenance of international peace and security. To this end the Administering Authority may make use of volunteer forces, facilities and assistance from the Territory in carrying out the obligations towards the Security Council undertaken in this regard by the Administering Authority, as well as for local defence and the maintenance of law and order within the Territory.

Article 6

The Administering Authority shall promote the development of free political institutions suited to the Territory. To this end, the Administering Authority shall assure, to the inhabitants of the Territory, a progressively increasing share in the administrative and other services of the Territory; shall develop the participation of the inhabitants of the Territory in advisory and legislative bodies and in the government of the Territory, both central and local, as may be appropriate to the particular circumstances of the Territory and its peoples; and shall take all other appropriate measures with a view to the political advancement of the inhabitants of the Territory in accordance with Article 76 b of the United Nations Charter. In considering the measures to be taken under this Article the Administering Authority shall, in the interests of the inhabitants, have special regard to the provisions of article 5 *(a)* of this Agreement.

Article 7

The Administering Authority undertakes to apply, in the Territory, the provisions of any international conventions and recommendations already existing or hereafter drawn up by the United Nations or by the specialized agencies referred to in Article 57 of the Charter, which may be appropriate to the particular circumstances of the Territory and which would conduce to the achievement of the basic objectives of the International Trusteeship System.

Article 8

In framing laws relating to the holding or transfer of land and natural resources, the Administering Authority shall take into consideration native laws and customs, and shall respect the rights and safeguard the interests, both present and future, of the native population. No native land or natural resources may be transferred, except between natives, save with the previous consent of the competent public authority. No real rights over native land or natural resources in favour of non-natives may be created, except with the same consent.

Article 9

Subject to the provisions of Article 10 of this Agreement, the Administering Authority shall take all necessary steps to ensure equal treatment in social, economic, industrial and commercial matters for all Members of the United Nations and their nationals and to this end:

(a) Shall ensure the same rights to all nationals of Members of the United Nations as to his own nationals in respect of entry into and residence in the Territory, freedom of transit and navigation, including freedom of transit and navigation by air, acquisition of property both movable and immovable, the protection of person and property, and the exercise of professions and trades;

(b) Shall not discriminate on grounds of nationality against nationals of any Member of the United Nations in matters relating to the grant of concessions for the development of the natural resources of the Territory, and shall not grant concessions having the character of a general monopoly;

(c) Shall ensure equal treatment in the administration of justice to the nationals of all Members of the United Nations.

The rights conferred by this article on nationals of Members of the United Nations apply equally to companies and associations controlled by such nationals and organized in accordance with the law of any Member of the United Nations.

Article 10

Measures taken to give effect to article 9 of this Agreement shall be subject always to the overriding duty of the Administering Authority, in accordance with Article 76 of the United Nations Charter, to promote the political, economic, social and educational advancement of the inhabitants of the Territory, to carry out the other basic objectives of the International Trusteeship System, and to maintain peace, order and good government. The Administering Authority shall in particular be free:

(a) To organize essential public services and works on such terms and conditions as he thinks just;

(b) To create monopolies of a purely fiscal character in order to provide the Territory with the fiscal resources which seem best suited to local requirements, or otherwise to serve the interests of the inhabitants of the Territory;

(c) Where the interests of the economic advancement of the inhabitants of the Territory may require it, to establish or permit to be established, for specific purposes, other monopolies or undertakings having in them an element of monopoly, under conditions of proper public control; provided that, in the selection of agencies to carry out the purposes of this paragraph, other than agencies controlled by the Government or those in which the Government participates, the Administering Authority shall not discriminate on grounds of nationality against Members of the United Nations or their nationals.

Article 11

Nothing in this Agreement shall entitle any Member of the United Nations to claim for itself or for its nationals, companies and associations the benefits of article 9 of this Agreement in any respect in which it does not give to the inhabitants, companies and associations of the Territory equality of treatment with the nationals, companies and associations of the State which it treats most favourably.

Article 12

The Administering Authority shall, as may be appropriate to the circumstances of the Territory, continue and extend a general system of elementary education designed to abolish illiteracy and to facilitate the vocational and cultural advancement of the population, child and adult, and shall similarly provide such facilities as may prove desirable and practicable, in the interests of the inhabitants, for qualified students to receive secondary and higher education, including professional training.

Article 13

The Administering Authority shall ensure in the Territory complete freedom of conscience and, so far as is consistent with the requirements of public order and morality, freedom of religious teaching and the free exercise of all forms of workship. Subject to the provisions of article 8 of this Agreement and the local law, missionaries who are nationals of Members of the United Nations shall be free to enter the Territory and to travel and reside therein, to acquire and possess property, to erect religious buildings and to open schools and hospitals in the Territory. The provisions of this article shall not, however, affect the right and duty of the Administering Authority to exercise such control as he may consider necessary for the maintenance of peace, order and good government and for the educational advancement of the inhabitants of the Territory and to take all measures required for such control.

Article 14

Subject only to the requirements of public order, the Administering Authority shall guarantee to the inhabitants of the Territory freedom of speech, of the press, of assembly and of petition.

Article 15

The Administering Authority may arrange for the co-operation of the Territory in any regional advisory commission, regional technical organization, or other voluntary association of States, any specialized international bodies, public or private, or other forms of international activity not inconsistent with the United Nations Charter.

Article 16

The Administering Authority shall make, to the General Assembly of the United Nations, an annual report on the basis of a questionnaire drawn up by the Trusteeship Council in accordance with Article 88 of the United Nations Charter. Such reports shall include information concerning the measures taken to give effect to suggestions and recommendations of the General Assembly and the Trusteeship Council. The Administering Authority shall designate an accredited representative to be present at the sessions of the Trusteeship Council at which the reports of the Administering Authority with regard to the Territory are considered.

Article 17

Nothing in this Agreement shall affect the right of the Administering Authority to propose, at any future date, the amendment of this Agreement for the purpose of designating the whole or part of the Territory as a strategic area or for any other purpose not inconsistent with the basic objectives of the International Trusteeship System.

Article 18

The terms of this Agreement shall not be altered or amended except as provided for in Article 79 and Articles 83 or 85, as the case may be, of the United Nations Charter.

Article 19

If any dispute whatever should arise between the Administering Authority and another Member of the United Nations relating to the interpretation or application of the provisions of this Agreement, such dispute, if it cannot be settled by negotiation or other means, shall be submitted to the International Court of Justice, provided for in Chapter XIV of the United Nations Charter.

7. TRUSTEESHIP AGREEMENT FOR THE TERRITORY OF TOGOLAND UNDER FRENCH ADMINISTRATION, APPROVED BY THE GENERAL ASSEMBLY OF THE UNITED NATIONS ON 13 DECEMBER 1946[1]

Whereas the Territory known as Togoland lying to the east of the line agreed upon in the Declaration, signed on 10 July 1919,[2] has been under French administration in accordance with the mandate defined under the terms of the instrument of 20 July 1922,[3] and

Whereas, in accordance with article 9 of that instrument this part of Togoland has since then been "administered in accordance with the laws of the mandatory as an integral part of his territory and subject to the provisions" of the mandate, and it is of importance, in the interests of the population of Togoland to pursue the administrative and political development of the Territories in question in such a way as to promote the political, economic and social advancement of the inhabitants in accordance with Article 76 of the Charter of the United Nations; and

Whereas France has indicated its desire to place under trusteeship in accordance with Articles 75 and 77 of the said Charter that part of Togoland which is at present administered by it; and

Whereas Article 85 of the said Charter provides that the terms of the trusteeship agreements are to be submitted for approval by the General Assembly,

Now, therefore, the General Assembly of the United Nations approves the following terms of trusteeship for the said Territory:

Article 1

The Territory to which the present Trusteeship Agreement applies comprises that part of Togoland lying to the east of the boundary defined by the Franco-British Declaration of 10 July 1919.

Article 2

The French Government, in its capacity of Administering Authority for this Territory under the terms of Article 81 of the Charter of the United Nations undertakes to exercise the duties of trusteeship as defined in the said Charter to promote the basic objectives of the Trusteeship System laid down in Article 76, and to collaborate fully with the General Assembly and the Trusteeship Council in the discharge of their functions as defined in Articles 87 and 88.

Accordingly, the French Government undertakes:

1. To make, to the General Assembly of the United Nations, the annual report provided for in Article 88 of the Charter, on the basis of the questionnaire drawn up by the Trusteeship Council in accordance with the said Article and to attach to that report such memoranda as may be required by the General Assembly or the Trusteeship Council;

To include in that report information relating to the measures taken to give effect to the suggestions and recommendations of the General Assembly or of the Trusteeship Council;

---

[1] United Nations *Treaty Series,* Vol. 8, 1947, pp. 166-179. Came into force on 13 December 1946, date of approval of the Agreement by the General Assembly of the United Nations (resolution 63 (I)).

[2] *British and Foreign State Papers,* Volume 118, page 893.

[3] League of Nations, *Official Journal,* Volume 2 (1922), pp. 886-889.

To appoint a representative and, where necessary, qualified experts to attend the meetings of the Trusteeship Council or of the General Assembly at which the said reports and memoranda will be examined;

2. To appoint a representative and, when necessary, qualified experts to participate, in consultation with the General Assembly or the Trusteeship Council, in the examination of petitions received by those bodies;

3. To facilitate such periodic visits to the Territory as the General Assembly or the Trusteeship Council may decide to arrange; to decide jointly with these bodies the dates on which such visits shall take place, and also to agree with them on all questions concerned with the organization and accomplishment of these visits;

4. To render general assistance to the General Assembly or to the Trusteeship Council in the application of these arrangements, and of such other arrangements as those bodies may make in accordance with the terms of the present Agreement.

Article 3

The Administering Authority shall be responsible for the peace, order and good government of the Territory,

It shall also be responsible for the defence of the said Territory and for ensuring that it shall play its part in the maintenance of international peace and security.

Article 4

For the above-mentioned purposes and in order to fulfil its obligations under the Charter and the present Agreement, the Administering Authority:

A

1. Shall have full powers of legislation, administration and jurisdiction in the Territory and shall administer it in accordance with French law as an integral part of French territory, subject to the provisions of the Charter and of this Agreement;

2. Shall be entitled, in order to ensure better administration, with the consent of the territorial representative assembly, to constitute this Territory into a customs, fiscal or administrative union or federation with adjacent territories under its sovereignty or control to establish common services between such territories and the Trust Territory, provided that such measures should promote the objectives of the International Trusteeship System;

B

1. May establish, on the Territory, military, naval or air bases, station national forces, and raise volunteer contingents therein;

2. May, within the limits laid down in the Charter, take all measures of organization and defence appropriate for ensuring:

(a) The participation of the Territory in the maintenance of international peace and security;

(b) The respect for obligations concerning the assistance and facilities to be given by the Administering Authority to the Security Council;

(c) The respect for internal law and order;

(d) The defence of the Territory within the framework of the special agreements for the maintenance of international peace and security.

Article 5

The Administering Authority shall take measures to ensure to the local inhabitants a share in the administration of the Territory by the development of representative democratic bodies, and in due course to arrange appropriate consultations to enable the inhabitants freely to express an opinion on their political regime and ensure the attainment of the objectives prescribed in Article 76 b of the Charter.

Article 6

The Administering Authority undertakes to maintain the application to the Territory of the international agreements and conventions which are at present in force there, and to apply therein any conventions and recommendations made by the United Nations or the specialized agencies referred to in Article 57 of the Charter, the application of which would be in the interests of the population and consistent with the basic objectives of the Trusteeship System and the terms of the present Agreement.

Article 7

In framing laws relating to the holding or transfer of land, the Administering Authority shall, in order to promote the economic and social progress of the native population, take into consideration local laws and customs.

No land belonging to a native or to a group of natives may be transferred except between natives, save with previous consent of the competent public authority, who shall respect the rights and safeguard the interests, both present and future, of the native population. No real rights over native land in favour of non-natives may be created except with the same consent.

Article 8

Subject to the provisions of the following article, the Administering Authority shall take all necessary steps to ensure equal treatment in social, economic, industrial and commercial matters for all Members of the United Nations and their nationals, and to this end:

1. Shall grant to all nationals of Members of the United Nations, freedom of transit and navigation, including freedom of transit and navigation by air, and the protection of person and property, subject to the requirements of public order, and on condition of compliance with the local law;

2. Shall ensure the same rights to all nationals of Member of the United Nations as to its own nationals in respect of entry into and residence in the Territory, acquisition of property, both movable and immovable, and the exercise of professions and trades;

3. Shall not discriminate on grounds of nationality against nationals of any Member of the United Nations in matters relating to the grant of concessions for the development of the natural resources of the Territory, and shall not grant concessions having the character of a general monopoly;

4. Shall ensure equal treatment in the administration of justice to the nationals of all Members of the United Nations.

The rights conferred by this article on nationals of Members of the United Nations apply equally to companies and associations controlled by such nationals and formed in accordance with the law of any Member of the United Nations.

Nevertheless, pursuant to Article 76 of the Charter, such equal treatment shall be without prejudice to the attainment of the trusteeship objectives as prescribed in the said Article 76 and particularly in paragraph b of that Article.

Should special advantages of any kind be granted by a Power enjoying the equality of treatment referred to above to another Power, or to a territory whether self-governing or not, the same advantages shall automatically apply reciprocally to the Trust Territory and to its inhabitants, especially in the economic and commercial field.

Article 9

Measures taken to give effect to the preceding article of this Agreement shall be subject always to the overriding duty of the Administering Authority in accordance with Article 76 of the Charter, to promote the political, economic, social and educational advancement of the inhabitants of the Territory, to carry out the other basic objectives of the International Trusteeship System and to maintain peace, order and good government. The Administering Authority shall in particular be free, with the consent of the territorial representative Assembly:

1. To organize essential public services and works on such terms and such conditions as it thinks just;

2. To create monopolies of a purely fiscal character in the interest of the Territory and in order to provide the Territory with the fiscal resources which seem best suited to local requirements;

3. To establish, or to permit to be established, under conditions of proper public control, in conformity with Article 76, paragraph d of the Charter, such public enterprises or joint undertakings as appear to the Administering Authority to be in the interest of the economic advancement of the inhabitants of the Territory.

Article 10

The Administering Authority shall ensure, in the Territory, complete freedom of thought and the free exercise of all forms of worship and of religious teaching which are consistent with public order and morality. Missionaries who are nationals of States Members of the United Nations shall be free to enter the Territory and to reside therein, to acquire and possess property, to erect religious buildings and to open schools and hospitals throughout the Territory.

The provisions of this article shall not, however, affect the right and duty of the Administering Authority to exercise such control as may be necessary for the maintenance of public order and morality and for the educational advancement of the inhabitants of the Territory.

The Administering Authority shall continue to develop elementary, secondary and technical education for the benefit of both children and adults. To the full extent compatible with the interests of the population, it shall afford to qualified students the opportunity of receiving higher general or professional education.

The Administering Authority shall guarantee to the inhabitants of the Territory freedom of speech, of the press, of assembly and of petition, subject only to the requirements of public order.

Article 11

Nothing in this Agreement shall affect the right of the Administering Authority to propose, at any future date, the designation of the whole or part of the Territory thus placed under its trusteeship as a strategic area in accordance with Articles 82 and 83 of the Charter.

Article 12

The terms of the present Trusteeship Agreement shall not be altered or amended except as provided in Articles 79, 82, 83 and 85, as the case may be, of the Charter.

Article 13

If any dispute whatever should arise between the Administering Authority and another Member of the United Nations, relating to the interpretation or the application of the provisions of the present Trusteeship Agreement, such dispute, if it cannot be settled by negotiation or other means, shall be submitted to the International Court of Justice provided for in Chapter XIV of the Charter of the United Nations.

Article 14

The Administering Authority may enter, on behalf of the Territory, any consultative regional commission, technical organ or voluntary association of States which may be constituted. It may also collaborate, on behalf of the Territory, with international public or private institutions or participate in any form of international cooperation in accordance with the spirit of the Charter.

Article 15

The present Agreement shall enter into force as soon as it has received the approval of the General Assembly of the United Nations.

8. TRUSTEESHIP AGREEMENT FOR THE TERRITORY OF NEW GUINEA, APPROVED BY THE GENERAL ASSEMBLY OF THE UNITED NATIONS ON 13 DECEMBER 1946[1]

———————

Whereas the Territory of New Guinea has been administered in accordance with Article 22 of the Covenant of the League of Nations and in pursuance of a mandate conferred upon His Britannic Majesty and exercised on his behalf by the Government of the Commonwealth of Australia; and

Whereas the Charter of the United Nations, signed at San Francisco on 26 June 1945, provides, by Article 75 for the establishment of an International Trusteeship System for the administration and supervision of such territories as may be placed thereunder by subsequent individual agreements; and

Whereas the Government of Australia now undertakes to place the Territory of New Guinea under the Trusteeship System, on the terms set forth in the present Trusteeship Agreement,

Therefore the General Assembly of the United Nations, acting in pursuance of Article 85 of the Charter, approves the following terms of trusteeship for the Territory of New Guinea, in substitution for the terms of the mandate under which the Territory has been administered:

Article 1

The Territory to which this Trusteeship Agreement applies (hereinafter called the Territory) consists of that portion of the island of New Guinea and the groups of is-

---

[1] United Nations *Treaty Series*, Vol. 8, 1947, pp. 182-187. Came into force on 13 December 1946, date of approval of the Agreement by the General Assembly of the United Nations (resolution 63 (I)).

lands administered therewith under the mandate dated 17 December 1920,[2] conferred upon His Britannic Majesty and exercised by the Government of Australia.

Article 2

The Government of Australia (hereinafter called the Administering Authority) is hereby designated as the sole authority which shall exercise the administration of the Territory.

Article 3

The Administering Authority undertakes to administer the Territory in accordance with the provisions of the Charter and in such a manner as to achieve, in the Territory, the basic objectives of the International Trusteeship System, which are set forth in Article 76 of the Charter.

Article 4

The Administering Authority shall be responsible for the peace, order, good government and defence of the Territory and for this purpose shall have the same powers of legislation, administration and jurisdiction in and over the Territory as if it were an integral part of Australia, and will be entitled to apply to the Territory, subject to such modifications as it deems desirable, such laws of the Commonwealth of Australia as it deems appropriate to the needs and conditions of the Territory.

Article 5

It is agreed that the Administering Authority, in the exercise of its powers under article 4, shall be at liberty to bring the Territory into a customs, fiscal or administrative union or federation with other dependent territories under its jurisdiction or control, and to establish common services between the Territory and any or all of these territories, if, in its opinion, it would be in the interest of the Territory and not inconsistent with the basic objectives of the Trusteeship System to do so.

Article 6

The Administering Authority further undertakes to apply, in the Territory, the provisions of such international agreements and such recommendations of the specialized agencies referred to in Article 57 of the Charter as are, in the opinion of the Administering Authority, suited to the needs and conditions of the Territory and conductive to the achievement of the basic objectives of the Trusteeship System.

Article 7

The Administering Authority may take all measures in the Territory which it considers desirable to provide for the defence of the Territory and for maintenance of international peace and security.

Article 8

The Administering Authority undertakes the discharge of its obligations under article 3 of this Agreement:

1. To co-operate with the Trusteeship Council in the discharge of all the Council's functions under Articles 87 and 88 of the Charter;

[2]*British and Foreign State Papers*, Volume 113, page 1113.

2. In accordance with its established policy:

(a) To take into consideration the customs and usages of the inhabitants of New Guinea and respect the rights and safeguard the interests, both present and future, of the indigenous inhabitants of the Territory; and in particular, to ensure that no rights over native land in favour of any person not an indigenous inhabitant of New Guinea may be created or transferred except with the consent of the competent public authority.

(b) To promote, as may be appropriate to the circumstances of the Territory, the educational and cultural advancement of the inhabitants;

(c) To assure to the inhabitants of the Territory, as may be appropriate to the particular circumstances of the Territory and its peoples, a progressively increasing share in the administrative and other services of the Territory;

(d) To guarantee to the inhabitants of the Territory, subject only to the requirements of public order, freedom of speech, of the press, of assembly and of petition, freedom of conscience and worship and freedom of religious teaching.

9. TRUSTEESHIP AGREEMENT FOR THE FORMER JAPANESE MANDATED ISLANDS, DRAWN BY THE UNITED STATES OF AMERICA AND APPROVED BY THE SECURITY COUNCIL ON APRIL 2, 1947 AND REGISTERED WITH THE SECRETARIAT ON OCTOBER 1, 1947[1]

Whereas Article 75 of the Charter of the United Nations provides for the establishment of an International Trusteeship System for the administration and supervision of such territories as may be placed thereunder by subsequent agreements; and

Whereas under Article 77 of the said Charter the Trusteeship System may be applied to territories now held under mandate; and

Whereas on 17 December 1920[2] the Council of the League of Nations confirmed a mandate for the former German islands north of the Equator to Japan, to be administered in accordance with Article 22 of the Covenant of the League of Nations; and

Whereas, Japan, as a result of the Second World War, has ceased to exercise any authority in these islands;

Now, therefore, the Security Council of the United Nations, having satisfied itself that the relevant articles of the Charter have been complied with, hereby resolves to approve the following terms of trusteeship for the Pacific Islands formerly under mandate to Japan:

Article 1

The Territory of the Pacific Islands, consisting of the islands formerly held by Japan under mandate in accordance with Article 22 of the Covenant of the League of Nations,

---

[1] United Nations *Treaty Series*, Vol. 8, 1947, pp. 190-199. Came into force on 18 July 1947, in accordance with Article 16, having been approved by the Security Council on 2 April 1947 and by the Government of the United States of America on 18 July 1947. (See United Nations documents S/P.V. 124 and S/448.)
[2] League of Nations, *Official Journal*, Volume 2 (1921), pages 87 to 88.

is hereby designated as a strategic area and placed under the Trusteeship System established in the Charter of the United Nations. The Territory of the Pacific Islands is hereinafter referred to as the Trust Territory.

Article 2

The United States of America is designated as the Administering Authority of the Trust Territory.

Article 3

The Administering Authority shall have full powers of administration, legislation, and jurisdiction over the Territory subject to the provisions of this Agreement, and may apply to the Trust Territory, subject to any modifications which the Administering Authority may consider desirable, such of the laws of the United States as it may deem appropriate to local conditions and requirements.

Article 4

The Administering Authority, in discharging the obligations of trusteeship in the Trust Territory, shall act in accordance with the Charter of the United Nations, and the provisions of this agreement, and shall, as specified in Article 83 (2) of the Charter, apply the objectives of the International Trusteeship System, as set forth in Article 76 of the Charter, to the people of the Trust Territory.

Article 5

In discharging its obligations under Article 76 a and Article 84 of the Charter, the Administering Authority shall ensure that the Trust Territory shall play its part, in accordance with the Charter of the United Nations, in the maintenance of international peace and security. To this end the Administering Authority shall be entitled:

1. To establish naval, military and air bases and to erect fortifications in the Trust Territory;

2. To station and employ armed forces in the Territory; and

3. To make use of volunteer forces, facilities and assistance from the Trust Territory in carrying out the obligations towards the Security Council undertaken in this regard by the Administering Authority, as well as for the local defense and the maintenance of law and order within the Trust Territory.

Article 6

In discharging its obligations under Article 76 b of the Charter, the Administering Authority shall:

1. Foster the development of such political institutions as are suited to the Trust Territory and shall promote the development of the inhabitants of the Trust Territory toward self-government or independence as may be appropriate to the particular circumstances of the Trust Territory and its peoples and the freely expressed wishes of the peoples concerned; and to this end shall give to the inhabitants of the Trust Territory a progressively increasing share in the administrative services in the Territory; shall develop their participation in government; shall give due recognition to the customs of the inhabitants in providing a system of law for the Territory; and shall take other appropriate measures toward these ends;

2. Promote the economic advancement and self-sufficiency of the inhabitants, and to this end shall regulate the use of natural resources; encourage the development of fisheries, agriculture, and industries; protect the inhabitants against the loss of their

lands and resources; and improve the means of transportation and communication;

3. Promote the social advancement of the inhabitants and to this end shall protect the rights and fundamental freedoms of all elements of the population without discrimination; protect the health of the inhabitants; control the traffic in arms and ammunition, opium and other dangerous drugs, and alcohol and other spirituous beverages; and institute such other regulations as may be necessary to protect the inhabitants against social abuses; and

4. Promote the educational advancement of the inhabitants, and to this end shall take steps toward the establishment of a general system of elementary education; facilitate the vocational and cultural advancement of the population; and shall encourage qualified students to pursue higher education, including training on the professional level.

Article 7

In discharging its obligations under Article 76 c of the Charter, the Administering Authority shall guarantee to the inhabitants of the Trust Territory freedom of conscience, and, subject only to the requirements of public order and security, freedom of speech, of the press, and of assembly; freedom of worship and of religious teaching; and freedom of migration and movement.

Article 8

1. In discharging its obligations under Article 76 d of the Charter, as defined by Article 83 (2) of the Charter, the Administering Authority, subject to the requirements of security, and the obligation to promote the advancement of the inhabitants, shall accord to nationals of each Member of the United Nations and to companies and associations organized in conformity with the laws of such Members, treatment in the Trust Territory no less favourable than that accorded therein to nationals, companies and associations of any other United Nation except the Administering Authority.

2. The Administering Authority shall ensure equal treatment to the Members of the United Nations and their nationals in the administration of justice.

3. Nothing in this Article shall be so construed as to accord traffic rights to aircraft flying into and out of the Trust Territory. Such rights shall be subject to agreement between the Administering Authority and the State whose nationality such aircraft possesses.

4. The Administering Authority may negotiate and conclude commercial and other treaties and agreements with Members of the United Nations and other States, designed to attain for the inhabitants of the Trust Territory treatment by the Members of the United Nations and other States no less favourable than that granted by them to the nationals of other States. The Security Council may recommend, or invite other organs of the United Nations to consider and recommend, what rights the inhabitants of the Trust Territory should acquire in consideration of the rights obtained by Members of the United Nations in the Trust Territory.

Article 9

The Administering Authority shall be entitled to constitute the Trust Territory into a customs, fiscal, or administrative union or federation with other territories under United States jurisdiction and to establish common services between such territories and the Trust Territory where such measures are not inconsistent with the basic objectives of the International Trusteeship System and with the terms of this Agreement.

Article 10

The Administering Authority, acting under the provisions of article 3 of this Agreement, may accept membership in any regional advisory commission, regional authority, or technical organization, or other voluntary association of States, may co-operate with specialized international bodies, public or private, and may engage in other forms of international co-operation.

Article 11

1. The Administering Authority shall take the necessary steps to provide the status of citizenship of the Trust Territory for the inhabitants of the Trust Territory.

2. The Administering Authority shall afford diplomatic and consular protection to inhabitants of the Trust Territory when outside the territorial limit of the Trust Territory or of the territory of the Administering Authority.

Article 12

The Administering Authority shall enact such legislation as may be necessary to place the provisions of this agreement in effect in the Trust Territory.

Article 13

The provisions of Articles 87 and 88 of the Charter shall be applicable to the Trust Territory, provided that the Administering Authority may determine the extent of their applicability to any areas which may from time to time be specified by it as closed for security reasons.

Article 14

The Administering Authority undertakes to apply in the Trust Territory the provisions of any international conventions and recommendations which may be appropriate to the particular circumstances of the Trust Territory and which would be conducive to the achievement of the basic objectives of article 6 of this Agreement.

Article 15

The terms of the present Agreement shall not be altered, amended or terminated without the consent of the Administering Authority.

Article 16

The present Agreement shall come into force when approved by the Security Council of the United Nations and by the Government of the United States after due constitutional process.

10. TRUSTEESHIP AGREEMENT FOR THE TERRITORY OF NAURU, DRAWN BY THE ADMINISTERING AUTHORITIES AND APPROVED BY THE GENERAL ASSEMBLY OF THE UNITED NATIONS ON NOVEMBER 1, 1947[1]

In pursuance of a Mandate conferred upon His Britannic Majesty the Territory of Nauru has been administered in accordance with Article 22 of the Covenant of the League of Nations by the Government of Australia on the joint behalf of the Governments of Australia, New Zealand, and the United Kingdom of Great Britain and Northern Ireland.

The Charter of the United Nations, signed at San Francisco on 26 June 1946, provides by Article 75 for the establishment of an International Trusteeship System for the administration and supervision of such territories as may be placed thereunder by subsequent individual agreements.

His Majesty desires to place the Territory of Nauru under the Trusteeship System, and the Governments of Australia, New Zealand and the United Kingdom undertake to administer it on the terms set forth in the present Trusteeship Agreement.

Therefore the General Assembly of the United Nations, acting in pursuance of Article 85 of the Charter,

Approves the following terms of Trusteeship for the Territory of Nauru, in substitution for the terms of the Mandate under which the Territory has been administered:

Article 1

The Territory to which this Trusteeship Agreement applies (hereinafter called "the Territory") consists of the island of Nauru (Pleasant Island), situated approximately 167° longitude East and approximately 0°25' latitude South, being the Territory administered under the Mandate above referred to.

Article 2

The Governments of Australia, New Zealand and the United Kingdom (hereinafter called "the Administering Authority") are hereby designated as the joint Authority which will exercise the administration of the Territory.

Article 3

The Administering Authority undertakes to administer the Territory in accordance with the provisions of the Charter and in such a manner as to achieve in the Territory the basic objectives of the International Trusteeship System, which are set forth in Article 76 of the Charter.

Article 4

The Administering Authority will be responsible for the peace, order, good government and defence of the Territory, and for this purpose, in pursuance of an Agreement made by the Governments of Australia, New Zealand and the United Kingdom, the Government of Australia will on behalf of the Administering Authority and except and

---

[1] U.N. Doc. T/Agreement/9, 21 October 1947, pp. 2-4. Original introductory note: The General Assembly of the United Nations, at the hundred and fourth plenary meeting of its second session on 1 November 1947, approved the Trusteeship Agreement, the text of which is set forth herein, by means of which, in agreement with the Government of Australia, New Zealand and the United Kingdom, the Territory of Nauru was placed under the International Trusteeship System.

until otherwise agreed by the Governments of Australia, New Zealand and the United Kingdom continue to exercise full powers of legislation, administration and jurisdiction in and over the Territory.

Article 5

The Administering Authority undertakes that in the discharge of its obligations under article 3 of this Agreement:

1. It will co-operate with the Trusteeship Council in the discharge of all the Council's functions under Articles 87 and 88 of the Charter;

2. It will, in accordance with its established policy:

(a) Take into consideration the customs usages of the inhabitants of Nauru and respect the rights and safeguard the interests, both present and future, of the indigenous inhabitants of the Territory; and in particular ensure that no rights over native land in favour of any person not an indigenous inhabitant of Nauru may be created or transferred except with the consent of the competent public authority;

(b) Promote, as may be appropriate to the circumstances of the Territory, the economic, social, educational and cultural advancement of the inhabitants;

(c) Assure to the inhabitants of the Territory, as may be appropriate to the particular circumstances of the Territory and its peoples, a progressively increasing share in the administrative and other services of the Territory and take all appropriate measures with a view to the political advancement of the inhabitants in accordance with Article 76 b of the Charter;

(d) Guarantee to the inhabitants of the Territory, subject only to the requirements of public order, freedom of speech, of the press, of assembly and of petition, freedom of conscience and worship and freedom of religious teaching.

Article 6

The Administering Authority further undertakes to apply in the Territory the provisions of such international agreements and such recommendations of the specialized agencies referred to in Article 57 of the Charter as are, in the opinion of the Administering Authority, suited to the needs and conditions of the Territory and conducive to the achievement of the basic objectives of the Trusteeship System.

Article 7

In order to discharge its duties under Article 84 of the Charter and article 4 of the present Agreement, the Administering Authority may take all measures in the Territory which it considers desirable to provide for the defence of the Territory and for the maintenance of international peace and security.

B. STATUS OF THE TRUST TERRITORIES

Trust Territory	Administering Authority	Former Status	Present Status
Cameroons	France	Mandate under French admini- stration	Became the Federal Rep. of Cameroon on Jan. 1, 1960
Cameroons	The U. K.	Mandate under British admini- stration	The Southern part merged with the Fed. Rep. of Cameroon, and the northern part, with Nigeria on Octo- ber 1, 1961
Nauru	Australia in behalf of Aus- tralia, New Zealand and the U. K.	Mandate under Australian ad- ministration in behalf of Australia, New Zealand and the U. K.	Became an independent state, on Jan. 31, 1968; not a Member of the U. N.
Ruanda-Urundi	Belgium	Mandate under Belgium admi- nistration	Became two independent states, the Rep. of Rwanda and the King- dom of Burundi on July 1, 1962
Tanganyika	The U. K.	Mandate under British admini- stration	Became an independent state, Dec. 9, 1961; merged with Zanzibar, April 26, 1964 to become Tanzania, Oct. 29, 1964
Togoland	France	Mandate under French admini- stration	Became an independent state, the Rep. of Togo, April 27, 1960
Togoland	The U. K.	Mandate under British admini- stration	Became a region of Ghana after a plebiscite in 1956; and a part of Ghana when the latter became indepen- dent on March 6, 1957
Western Samoa	New Zealand	Mandate under New Zealand's administration	Became an independent state, Western Samoa, on Jan. 1, 1962
South West Africa[1]		Mandate under the Rep. of South Africa's administration	See footnote 1

New Guinea	Australia	Mandate under Australian administration	Joined Papua to become an independent state, Papua New Guinea, on September 16, 1975, which was admitted to the United Nations on October 10, 1975
Strategic Trust Territories[2] (the Carolines, Marianas (except Guam)[3] and the Marshalls)	The U.S.A.	Mandate under Japanese administration	
Somaliland [4]	First, the U. K. and then Italy, approved by the G.A. on Nov. 21, 1949 based on the Peace Treaty with Italy	Territory detached from the enemy state	Merged with the former British protectorate of Somaliland to become an independent state, Somalia, on July 1, 1960
Ryukyu Islands[5]	The U.S.A.	Territory detached from the enemy state	Returned to Japan on May 15, 1972

---

[1] The only mandate not to be place under the trusteeship system by the mandatory power, the Republic of South Africa, but is still controlled by it in spite of the facts that the General Assembly of the United Nations terminated the mandate over the territory in 1966, established a Council of Eleven Nations to administer the territory in 1967 and changed the name of it from "South-West Africa" to "Namibia" in 1968.

[2] The strategic trust territories agreement has been approved by the Security Council which is different from the other trust territories agreements approved by the General Assembly. The relations between the strategic trust territories and the administering authority are supervised by the Security Council instead of by the General Assembly and under it the Trusteeship Council as in the case of the other trust territories.

[3] Guam is an unincorporated territory of the United States ceded from Spain after the Spanish-American War in 1898.

[4] The General Assembly established Somaliland as a trust territory under Italian administration on November 21, 1949 based on the Peace Treaty with Italy signed in February 10, 1947, which became effective on September 15, 1947.

[5] The Ryukyu Islands were placed under the trusteeship system under the Peace Treaty with Japan signed on September 8, 1951, which became effective on April 28, 1952. The Islands were returned to Japan on May 15, 1972 according to the Okinawa Reversion Treaty of June 17, 1971.

VII. IMPORTANT REGIONAL ARRANGEMENTS

A. ARRANGEMENTS AMONG AMERICAN STATES

1. ACT OF CHAPULTEPEC, DONE AT MEXICO CITY, MARCH 8, 1945[1]

(FINAL ACT OF THE INTER-AMERICAN CONFERENCE ON PROBLEMS OF WAR AND PEACE)

PURSUANT to the invitation extended on January 10, 1945, by the Government of the United Mexican States, the Delegations of the countries enumerated below met in Mexico City on February 21, 1945. The order of precedence was determined by a drawing of lots on February 21, in conformity with Article 5, paragraph (g), of the Regulations of the Conference:

RECIPROCAL ASSISTANCE AND AMERICAN SOLIDARITY

WHEREAS:

The peoples of the Americas, animated by a profound love of justice, remain sincerely devoted to the principles of international law;

It is their desire that such principles, notwithstanding the present difficult circumstances, prevail with even greater force in future international relations;

The inter-American conferences have repeatedly proclaimed certain fundamental principles, but these must be reaffirmed at a time when the juridical bases of the community of nations are being re-established;

The new situation in the world makes more imperative than ever the union and solidarity of the American peoples, for the defense of their rights and the maintenance of international peace;

The American states have been incorporating in their international law, since 1890, by means of conventions, resolutions and declarations, the following principles:

a) The proscription of territorial conquest and the non-recognition of all acquisitions made by force (First International Conference of American States, 1890);

b) The condemnation of intervention by one State in the internal or external affairs of another (Seventh International Conference of American States, 1933,[2] and Inter-American Conference for the Maintenance of Peace, 1936);[3]

c) The recognition that every war or threat of war affects directly or indirectly all civilized peoples, and endangers the great principles of liberty and justice which constitute the American ideal and the standard of American international policy. (Inter-American Conference for the Maintenance of Peace, 1936);

d) The system of mutual consultation in order to find means of peaceful cooperation in the event of war or threat of war between American countries (Inter-American Conference for the Maintenance of Peace, 1936);

e) The recognition that every act susceptible of disturbing the peace of America affects each and every one of the American nations and justifies the initiation of the procedure of consultation (Inter-American Conference for the Maintenance of Peace, 1936).

---

[1] Treaties and Other International Acts Series, No. 1543, pp. 10-14. Official English translation prepared by the Pan American Union.

[2] *Report of the Delegates of the United States of America to the Seventh International Conference of American States, Montevideo, Uruguay, December 3-26, 1933,* Department of State publication 666, Conference Series 19.

[3] *Report of the Delegation of the United States of America to the Inter-American Conference for the Maintenance of Peace, Buenos Aires, Argentina, December 1-23, 1936,* Department of State publication 1088, Conference Series 33.

f) The adoption of conciliation, unrestricted arbitration, or the application of international justice in the solution of any difference or dispute between American nations, whatever its nature or origin (Inter-American Conference for the Maintenance of Peace, 1936);

g) The recognition that respect for the personality, sovereignty and independence of each American State constitutes the essence of international order sustained by continental solidarity, which historically has been expressed and sustained by declarations and treaties in force (Eighth International Conference of American States, 1938);[1]

h) The affirmation that respect for and the faithful observance of treaties constitute the indispensable rule for the development of peaceful relations between States, and that treaties can only be revised by agreement of the contracting parties (Declaration of American Principles, Eighth International Conference of American States, 1938);

i) The proclamation that, in case the peace, security or territorial integrity of any American republic is threatened by acts of any nature that may impair them, they proclaim their common concern and their determination to make effective their solidarity, coordinating their respective sovereign wills by means of the procedure of consultation, using the measures which in each case the circumstances may make advisable (Declaration of Lima, Eighth International Conference of American States, 1938);

j) The declaration that any attempt on the part of a non-American state against the integrity or inviolability of the territory, the sovereignty or the political independence of an American State shall be considered as an act of aggression against all the American States (Declaration XV of the Second Meeting of the Ministers of Foreign Affairs, Habana, 1940);[2]

The furtherance of these principles, which the American States have constantly practised in order to assure peace and solidarity among the nations of the Continent, constitutes an effective means of contributing to the general system of world security and of facilitating its establishment;

The security and solidarity of the Continent are affected to the same extent by an act of aggression against any of the American States by a non-American State, as by an act of aggression of an American State against one or more American States;

PART I

The Governments Represented at the Inter-American Conference on Problems of War and Peace

DECLARE:

1. That all sovereign States are juridically equal among themselves.

2. That every State has the right to the respect of its individuality and independence, on the part of the other members of the international community.

3. That every attack of a State against the integrity or the inviolability of the territory, or against the sovereignty or political independence of an American State, shall, conformably to Part III hereof, be considered as an act of aggression against the other States which sign this Act. In any case invasion by armed forces of one State into the Territory of another trespassing boundaries established by treaty and demarcated in accordance therewith shall constitute an act of aggression.

---

[1]*Report of the Delegation of the United States of America to the Eighth International Conference of American States, Lima, Peru, December 9-27, 1958*, Department of State publication 1624, Conference Series 50.

[2]*Second Meeting of the Ministers of Foreign Affairs of the American Republics, Habana, July 2-30, 1940*, Department of State publication 1575, Conference Series 48, p. 71.

4. That in case acts of aggression occur or there are reasons to believe that an aggression is being prepared by any other State against the integrity or inviolability of the territory, or against the sovereignty or political independence of an American State, the States signatory to this Act will consult among themselves in order to agree upon the measures it may be advisable to take.

5. That during the war, and until the treaty recommended in Part II hereof is concluded, the signatories of this Act recognize that such threats and acts of aggression, as indicated in paragraphs 3 and 4 above, constitute an interference with the war effort of the United Nations, calling for such procedures, within the scope of their constitutional powers of a general nature and for war, as may be found necessary, including: recall of chiefs of diplomatic missions, breaking of diplomatic relations; breaking of consular relations; breaking of postal, telegraphic, telephonic, radio-telephonic relations; interruption of economic, commercial and financial relations; use of armed force to prevent or repel aggression.

6. That the principles and procedure contained in this Declaration shall become-effective immediately, inasmuch as any act of aggression or threat of aggression during the present state of war interferes with the war effort of the United Nations to obtain victory. Henceforth, and to the end that the principles and procedures herein stipulated shall conform with the constitutional processes of each Republic, the respective Governments shall take the necessary steps to perfect this instrument in order that it shall be in force at all times.

PART II

The Inter-American Conference on Problems of War and Peace

RECOMMENDS:

That for the purpose of meeting threats or acts of aggression against any American Republic following the establishment of peace, the Governments of the American Republics consider the conclusion, in accordance with their constitutional processes, of a treaty establishing procedures whereby such threats or acts may be met by the use, by all or some of the signatories of said treaty, of any one or more of the following measures: recall of chiefs of diplomatic missions; breaking of diplomatic relations; breaking of consular relations; breaking of postal, telegraphic, telephonic, radio-telephonic relations; interruption of economic, commercial and financial relations; use of armed force to prevent or repel aggression.

PART III

The above Declaration and Recommendation constitute a regional arrangement for dealing with such matters relating to the maintenance of international peace and security as are appropriate for regional action in this Hemisphere. The said arrangement, and the pertinent activities and procedures, shall be consistent with the purposes and principles of the general international organization, when established.

This agreement shall be known as the " ACT OF CHAPULTEPEC."

(Approved at the plenary session of March 6, 1945)

In testimony whereof, the Delegates of the American Republics participating in the Inter-American Conference on Problems of War and Peace, sign the present Final Act, in the Spanish language at the City of Mexico on the eighth day of March, nineteen hundred and forty-five.

The original shall be deposited by the General Secretariat in the Archives of the Ministry of Foreign Affairs of Mexico, which shall transmit certified copies to the Governments of the American Republics, to the Pan American Union, to the General Secretariat of the League of Nations, to the International Labor Office, to the Pan American Sanitary Bureau and to the Inter-American Union of the Caribbean.

The Pan American Union shall prepare the translations of this Act into the other official languages of the Conference.

[For signatories to Final Act see Spanish text.]

I hereby certify that the foregoing is a faithful English translation of the Spanish text of the Final Act of the Inter-American Conference on the Problems of War and Peace, signed at Mexico City on March 8, 1945.

WASHINGTON, D.C., *April 30, 1945*

PEDRO DE ALBA
*Secretary of the Governing Board
of the Pan American Union*

2. INTER-AMERICAN TREATY OF RECIPROCAL ASSISTANCE (RIO TREATY), DONE AT RIO DE JANEIRO, SEPTEMBER 2, 1947[1]

In the name of their Peoples, the Governments represented at the Inter-American Conference for the Maintenance of Continental Peace and Security, desirous of consolidating and strengthening their relations of friendship and good neighborliness, and
Considering:

That Resolution VIII of the Inter-American Conference on Problems of War and Peace,[2] which met in Mexico City, recommended the conclusion of a treaty to prevent and repel threats and acts of aggression against any of the countries of America;

That the High Contracting Parties reiterate their will to remain united in an inter-American system consistent with the purposes and principles of the United Nations, and reaffirm the existence of the agreement which they have concluded concerning those matters relating to the maintenance of international peace and security which are appropriate for regional action;

That the High Contracting Parties reaffirm their adherence to the principles of inter-American solidarity and cooperation, and especially to those set forth in the preamble and declaration of the Act of Chapultepec, all of which should be understood to be accepted as standards of their mutual relations and as the juridical basis of the Inter-American System;

That the American States propose, in order to improve the procedures for the pacific settlement of their controversies, to conclude the treaty concerning the "Inter-American Peace System" envisaged in Resolutions IX and XXXIX of the Inter-American Conference on Problems of War and Peace,

That the obligation of mutual assistance and common defense of the American Republics is essentially related to their democratic ideals and to their will to cooperate permanently in the fulfillment of the principles and purposes of a policy of peace;

That the American regional community affirms as a manifest truth that juridical organization is a necessary prerequisite of security and peace, and that peace is founded on justice and moral order and, consequently, on the international recognition and protection of human rights and freedoms, on the indispensable well-being of the people, and on the effectiveness of democracy for the international realization of justice and security,

---

[1] Treaties and Other International Acts Series, No. 1838, pp. 23-29.
[2] Treaties and Other International Acts Series, No. 1543; 60 Stat. 1831.

Have resolved, in conformity with the objectives stated above, to conclude the following Treaty, in order to assure peace, through adequate means, to provide for effective reciprocal assistance to meet armed attacks against any American State, and in order to deal with threats of aggression against any of them:

ARTICLE 1

The High Contracting Parties formally condemn war and undertake in their international relations not to resort to the threat or the use of force in any manner inconsistent with the provisions of the Charter of the United Nations[1] or of this Treaty.

ARTICLE 2

As a consequence of the principle set forth in the preceding Article, the High Contracting Parties undertake to submit every controversy which may arise between them to methods of peaceful settlement and to endeavor to settle any such controversy among themselves by means of the procedures in force in the Inter-American System before referring it to the General Assembly or the Security Council of the United Nations.

ARTICLE 3

1. The High Contracting Parties agree that an armed attack by any State against an American State shall be considered as an attack against all the American States and, consequently, each one of the said Contracting Parties undertakes to assist in meeting the attack in the exercise of the inherent right of individual or collective self-defense recognized by Article 51 of the Charter of the United Nations.

2. On the request of the State or States directly attacked and until the decision of the Organ of Consultation of the Inter-American System, each one of the Contracting Parties may determine the immediate measures which it may individually take in fulfillment of the obligation contained in the preceding paragraph and in accordance with the principle of continental solidarity. The Organ of Consultation shall meet without delay for the purpose of examining those measures and agreeing upon the measures of a collective character that should be taken.

3. The provisions of this Article shall be applied in case of any armed attack which takes place within the region described in Article 4 or within the territory of an American State. When the attack takes place outside of the said areas, the provisions of Article 6 shall be applied.

4. Measures of self-defense provided for under this Article may be taken until the Security Council of the United Nations has taken the measures necessary to maintain international peace and security.

ARTICLE 4

The region to which this Treaty refers is bounded as follows: beginning at the North Pole; thence due south to a point 74 degrees north latitude, 10 degrees west longitude; thence by a rhumb line to a point 47 degrees 30 minutes north latitude, 50 degrees west longitude; thence by a rhumb line to a point 35 degrees north latitude, 60 degrees west longitude; thence due south to a point in 20 degrees north latitude; thence by a rhumb line to a point 5 degrees north latitude, 24 degrees west longitude; thence due south to the South Pole; thence due north to a point 30 degrees south latitude, 90 degrees west longitude; thence by a rhumb line to a point on the Equator at

---

[1] Treaty Series 993; 59 Stat. 1031.

637

97 degrees west longitude; thence by a rhumb line to a point 15 degrees north latitude, 120 degrees west longitude; thence by a rhumb line to a point 50 degrees north latitude, 170 degrees east longitude; thence due north to a point in 54 degrees north latitude; thence by a rhumb line to a point 65 degrees 30 minutes north latitude, 168 degrees 58 minutes 5 seconds west longitude; thence due north to the North Pole.

ARTICLE 5

The High Contracting Parties shall immediately send to the Security Council of the United Nations, in conformity with Articles 51 and 54 of the Charter of the United Nations, complete information concerning the activities undertaken or in contemplation in the exercise of the right of self-defense or for the purpose of maintaining inter-American peace and security.

ARTICLE 6

If the inviolability or the integrity of the territory or the sovereignty or political independence of any American State should be affected by an aggression which is not an armed attack or by an extra-continental or intra-continental conflict, or by any other fact or situation that might endanger the peace of America, the Organ of Consultation shall meet immediately in order to agree on the measures which must be taken in case of aggression to assist the victim of the aggression or, in any case, the measures which should be taken for the common defense and for the maintenance of the peace and security of the Continent.

ARTICLE 7

In the case of a conflict between two or more American States, without prejudice to the right of self-defense in conformity with Article 51 of the Charter of the United Nations, the High Contracting Parties, meeting in consultation shall call upon the contending States to suspend hostilities and restore matters to the *statu quo ante bellum*, and shall take in addition all other necessary measures to reestablish or maintain inter-American peace and security and for the solution of the conflict by peaceful means. The rejection of the pacifying action will be considered in the determination of the aggressor and in the application of the measures which the consultative meeting may agree upon.

ARTICLE 8

For the purposes of this Treaty, the measures on which the Organ of Consultation may agree will comprise one or more of the following: recall of chiefs of diplomatic missions; breaking of diplomatic relations; breaking of consular relations; partial or complete interruption of economic relations or of rail, sea, air, postal, telegraphic, telephonic, and radiotelephonic or radiotelegraphic communications; and use of armed force.

ARTICLE 9

In addition to other acts which the Organ of Consultation may characterize as aggression, the following shall be considered as such:

a. Unprovoked armed attack by a State against the territory, the people, or the land, sea or air forces of another State;

b. Invasion, by the armed forces of a State, of the territory of an American State, through the trespassing of boundaries demarcated in accordance with a treaty, judicial decision, or arbitral award, or, in the absence of frontiers thus demarcated, invasion affecting a region which is under the effective jurisdiction of another State.

ARTICLE 10

None of the provisions of this Treaty shall be construed as impairing the rights and obligations of the High Contracting Parties under the Charter of the United Nations.

ARTICLE 11

The consultations to which this Treaty refers shall be carried out by means of the Meetings of Ministers of Foreign Affairs of the American Republics which have ratified the Treaty, or in the manner or by the organ which in the future may be agreed upon.

ARTICLE 12

The Governing Board of the Pan American Union may act provisionally as an organ of consultation until the meeting of the Organ of Consultation referred to in the preceding Article takes place.

ARTICLE 13

The consultations shall be initiated at the request addressed to the Governing Board of the Pan American Union by any of the Signatory States which has ratified the Treaty.

ARTICLE 14

In the voting referred to in this Treaty only the representatives of the Signatory States which have ratified the Treaty may take part.

ARTICLE 15

The Governing Board of the Pan American Union shall act in all matters concerning this Treaty as an organ of liaison among the Signatory States which have ratified this Treaty and between these States and the United Nations.

ARTICLE 16

The decisions of the Governing Board of the Pan American Union referred to in Articles 13 and 15 above shall be taken by an absolute majority of the Members entitled to vote.

ARTICLE 17

The Organ of Consultation shall take its decisions by a vote of two-thirds of the Signatory States which have ratified the Treaty.

ARTICLE 18

In the case of a situation or dispute between American States, the parties directly interested shall be excluded from the voting referred to in two preceding Articles.

ARTICLE 19

To constitute a quorum in all the meetings referred to in the previous Articles, it shall be necessary that the number of States represented shall be at least equal to the number of votes necessary for the taking of the decision.

ARTICLE 20

Decisions which require the application of the measures specified in Article 8 shall be binding upon all the Signatory States which have ratified this Treaty, with the sole exception that no State shall be required to use armed force without its consent.

ARTICLE 21

The measures agreed upon by the Organ of Consultation shall be executed through the procedures and agencies now existing or those which may in the future be established.

ARTICLE 22

This Treaty shall come into effect between the States which ratify it as soon as the ratifications of two-thirds of the Signatory States have been deposited.

ARTICLE 23

This Treaty is open for signature by the American States at the city of Rio de Janeiro, and shall be ratified by the Signatory States as soon as possible in accordance with their respective constitutional processes. The ratifications shall be deposited with the Pan American Union, which shall notify the Signatory States of each deposit. Such notification shall be considered as an exchange of ratifications.

ARTICLE 24

The present Treaty shall be registered with the Secretariat of the United Nations through the Pan American Union, when two-thirds of the Signatory States have deposited their ratifications.

ARTICLE 25

This Treaty shall remain in force indefinitely, but may be denounced by any High Contracting Party by a notification in writing to the Pan American Union, which shall inform all the other High Contracting Parties of each notification of denunciation received. After the expiration of two years from the date of the receipt by the Pan American Union of a notification of denunciation by any High Contracting Party, the present Treaty shall cease to be in force with respect to such State, but shall remain in full force and effect with respect to all the other High Contracting Parties.

ARTICLE 26

The principles and fundamental provisions of this Treaty shall be incorporated in the Organic Pact of the Inter-American System

In witness whereof, the undersigned Plenipotentiaries, having deposited their full powers found to be in due and proper form, sign this Treaty on behalf of their respective Governments, on the dates appearing opposite their signatures.

Done in the city of Rio de Janeiro, in four texts respectively in the English, French, Portuguese and Spanish languages, on the second of September nineteen hundred forty-seven.

RESERVATION OF HONDURAS:

The Delegation of Honduras, in signing the present Treaty and in connection with Article 9, section (b), does so with the reservation that the boundary between Honduras and Nicaragua is definitively demarcated by the Joint Boundary Commission of nineteen hundred and nineteen hundred and one, starting from a point in the Gulf of Fonseca, in the Pacific Ocean, to Portillo de Teotecacinte and, from this point to the Atlantic, by the line that His Majesty the King of Spain's arbitral award established on the twenty third of December of nineteen hundred and six.

3. CHARTER OF THE ORGANIZATION OF AMERICAN STATES, SIGNED AT BOGOTA, ON 30 APRIL 1948[1]

IN THE NAME OF THEIR PEOPLES, THE STATES REPRESENTED AT THE NINTH INTER-NATIONAL CONFERENCE OF AMERICAN STATES,

Convinced that the historic mission of America is to offer to man a land of liberty, and a favorable environment for the development of his personality and the realization of his just aspirations;

Conscious that the mission has already inspired numerous agreements, whose essential value lies in the desire of the American peoples to live together in peace, and, through their mutual understanding and respect for the sovereignty of each one, to provide for the betterment of all, in independence, in equality and under law;

Confident that the true significance of American solidarity and good neighborliness can only mean the consolidation on this continent, within the frame work of democratic institutions, of a system of individual liberty and social justice based on respect for the essential rights of man;

Persuaded that their welfare and their contribution to the progress and the civilization of the world will increasingly require intensive continental cooperation;

Resolved to persevere in the noble undertaking that humanity has conferred upon the United Nations, whose principles and purposes they solemnly reaffirm;

Convinced that juridical organization is a necessary condition for security and peace founded or moral order and on justice; and

In accordance with Resolution IX of the Inter-American Conference on Problems of War and Peace, held at Mexico City,

HAVE AGREED UPON THE FOLLOWING

CHARTER OF THE ORGANIZATION OF AMERICAN STATES

---

[1]United Nations *Treaty Series*, Vol. 119, 1952, pp. 48-92. Came into force on 13 December 1951, in accordance with article 109, the instruments of ratification of two-thirds of the signatory States having been deposited by that date with the Pan-American Union.
Following is the list of States in respect of which the Charter came into force on 13 December 1951 including the respective dates of deposit of the instruments of ratification:

State	Date	Year
Bolivia	18 October	1950
Brazil	13 March	1950
Colombia (with the following declaration)*	13 December	1951
Costa Rica	16 November	1948
Dominican Republic	22 April	1949
Ecuador	28 December	1950
Haiti	28 March	1950
Honduras	7 February	1950
Mexico	23 November	1948
Nicaragua	26 July	1950
Panama	22 March	1951
Paraguay	3 May	1950
United States of America (with the following reservation)**	19 June	1951

The Charter subsequently came into force in respect of Venezuela on 29 December 1951, the date of deposit of the instrument of ratification.

PART ONE

CHAPTER I

Nature and purposes

ARTICLE 1

The American States establish by this Charter the international organization that they have developed to achieve an order of peace and justice, to promote their solidarity, to strengthen their collaboration, and to defend their sovereignty, their territorial integrity and their independence. Within the United Nations, the Organization of American States is a regional agency.

ARTICLE 2

All American States that ratify the present Charter are Members of the Organization.

ARTICLE 3

Any new political entity that arises from the union of several Member States and that, as such, ratifies the present Charter, shall become a Member of the Organization. The entry of the new political entity into the Organization shall result in the loss of membership of each one of the States which constituted it.

ARTICLE 4

The Organization of American States, in order to put into practice the principles on which it is founded and to fulfill its regional obligations under the Charter of the United Nations, proclaims the following essential purposes;

a) To strengthen the peace and security of the continent;
b) To prevent possible causes of difficulties and to ensure the pacific settlement of disputes that may arise among the Member States;
c) To provide for common action on the part of those States in the event of aggression;
d) To seek the solution of political, juridical and economic problems that may arise among them; and
e) To promote, by cooperative action, their economic, social and cultural development.

CHAPTER II

Principles

ARTICLE 5

The American States reaffirm the following principles:

a) International law is the standard of conduct of States in their reciprocal relations;
b) International order consists essentially of respect for the personality, sovereignty and independence of States, and the faithful fulfillment of obligations derived from treaties and other sources of international law;
c) Good faith shall govern the relations between States;
d) The solidarity of the American States and the high aims which are sought through it require the political organization of those States on the basis of the effective exercise of representative democracy;

e) The American States condemn wars of aggression: victory does not give rights;

f) An act of aggression against one American States is an act of aggression against all the other American States;

g) Controversies of an international character arising between two or more American States shall be settled by peaceful procedures;

h) Social justice and social security are bases of lasting peace;

i) Economic cooperation is essential to the common welfare and prosperity of the peoples of the continent;

j) The American States proclaim the fundamental rights of the individual without distinction as to race, nationality, creed or sex;

k) The spiritual unity of the continent is based on respect for the cultural values of the American countries and requires their close cooperation for the high purposes of civilization;

l) The education of peoples should be directed toward justice, freedom and peace.

CHAPTER III

Fundamental rights and duties of States

ARTICLE 6

States are juridically equal, enjoy equal rights and equal capacity to exercise these rights, and have equal duties. The rights of each State depend not upon its power to ensure the exercise thereof, but upon the mere fact of its existence as a person under international law.

ARTICLE 7

Every American State has the duty to respect the rights enjoyed by every other State in accordance with international law.

ARTICLE 8

The fundamental rights of States may not be impaired in any manner whatsoever.

ARTICLE 9

The political existence of the State is independent of recognition by other States. Even before being recognized, the State has the right to defend its integrity and independence, to provide for its preservation and prosperity, and consequently to organize itself as it sees fit, to legislate concerning its interests, to administer its services, and to determine the jurisdiction and competence of its courts. The exercise of these rights is limited only by the exercise of the rights of other States in accordance with international law.

ARTICLE 10

Recognition implies that the State granting it accepts the personality of the new State, with all the rights and duties that international law prescribes for the two States.

ARTICLE 11

The right of each State to protect itself and to live its own life does not authorize it to commit unjust acts against another State.

ARTICLE 12

The jurisdiction of States within the limits of their national territory is exercised equally over all the inhabitants, whether nationals or aliens.

ARTICLE 13

Each State has the right to develop its cultural, political and economic life freely and naturally. In this free development, the State shall respect the rights of the individual and the principles of universal morality.

ARTICLE 14

Respect for and the faithful observance of treaties constitute standards for the development of peaceful relations among States. International treaties and agreements should be public.

ARTICLE 15

No State or group of States has the right to intervene, directly or indirectly for any reason whatever, in the internal or external affairs of any other State. The foregoing principle prohibits not only armed force but also any other form of interference or attempted threat against the personality of the State or against its political, economic and cultural elements.

ARTICLE 16

No State may use or encourage the use of coercive measures of an economic or political character in order to force the sovereign will of another State and obtain from it advantages of any kind.

ARTICLE 17

The territory of a State is inviolable; it may not be the object, even temporarily, of military occupation or of other measures of force taken by another State, directly or indirectly, on any grounds whatever. No territorial acquisitions or special advantages obtained by force or by other means of coercion shall be recognized.

ARTICLE 18

The American States bind themselves in their international relations not to have recourse to the use of force, except in the case of self-defense in accordance with existing treaties or in fulfillment thereof.

ARTICLE 19

Measures adopted for the maintenance of peace and security in accordance with existing treaties do not constitute a violation of the principles set forth in Articles 15 and 17.

CHAPTER IV
Pacific settlement of disputes

ARTICLE 20

All international disputes that may arise between American States shall be submitted to the peaceful procedures set forth in this Charter, before being referred to the Security Council of the United Nations.

ARTICLE 21

The following are peaceful procedures: direct negotiation, good office mediation, investigation and conciliation, judicial settlement, arbitration, and those which the parties to the dispute may especially agree upon at any time.

ARTICLE 22

In the event that a dispute arises between two or more American States which, in the opinion of one of them, cannot be settled through the usual diplomatic channels, the Parties shall agree on some other peaceful procedure that will enable them to reach a solution.

ARTICLE 23

A special treaty will establish adequate procedures for the pacific settlement of disputes and will determine the appropriate means for the their application so that no dispute between American States shall fail of definitive settlement within a reasonable period.

CHAPTER V

Collective security

ARTICLE 24

Every act of aggression by a State against the territorial integrity of the inviolability of the territory or against the sovereignty or political independence of an American State shall be considered an act of aggression against the other American States.

ARTICLE 25

If the inviolability or the integrity of the territory or the sovereignty or political independence of any American State should be affected by an armed attack or by an act of aggression that is not an armed attack, or by an extra-continental conflict, or by a conflict between two or more American States, or by any other fact or situation that might endanger the peace of America, the American States, in furtherance of the principles of continental solidarity or collective self-defense, shall apply the measures and procedures established in the special treaties on the subject.

CHAPTER VI

Economic standards

ARTICLE 26

The Member States agree to cooperate with one another, as far as their resources may permit and their laws may provide, in the broadest spirit of good neighborliness, in order to strengthen their economic structure, develop their agriculture and mining, promote their industry and increase their trade.

ARTICLE 27

If the economy of an American State is affected by serious conditions that cannot be satisfactorily remedied by its own unaided effort, such State may place its economic problems before the Inter-American Economic and Social Council to seek through consultation the most appropriate soultion for such problems.

CHAPTER VII

Social standards

ARTICLE 28

The Member States agree to cooperate with one another to achieve just and decent living conditions for their entire populations.

ARTICLE 29

The Member States agree upon the desirability of developing their social legislation on the following bases:

a) All human beings, without distinction as to race, nationality, sex, creed or social condition, have the right to attain material well-being and spiritual growth under circumstances of liberty, dignity, equality of opportunity, and economic security;

b) Work is a right and a social duty; it shall not be considered as an article of commerce; it demands respect for freedom of association and for the dignity of the worker; and it is to be performed under conditions that ensure life, health and a decent standard of living, both during the working years and during old age, or when any circumstances deprives the individual of the possibility of working.

CHAPTER VIII

Cultural standards

ARTICLE 30

The Member States agree to promote, in accordance with their constitutional provisions and their material resources, the exercise of the right to education on the following bases:

a) Elementary education shall be compulsory and, when provided by the State, shall be without cost;

b) Higher education shall be available to all, without distinction as to race, nationality, sex, language, creed or social condition.

ARTICLE 31

With the consideration for the national character of each State, the Member States undertake to facilitate free cultural interchange by every medium of expression.

PART TWO

CHAPTER IX

The Organs

ARTICLE 32

The Organization of American States accomplishes its purposes by means of:

a) The Inter-American Conference
b) The Meeting of Consultation of Ministers of Foreign Affairs
c) The Council
d) The Pan American Union
e) The Specialized Conferences
f) The Specialized Organizations

CHAPTER X

The Inter-American Conference

ARTICLE 33

The Inter-American Conference is the supreme organ of the Organization of American States. It decides the general action and policy of the Organization and determines the structure and functions of its Organs, and has the authority to consider any matter relating to friendly relations among the American States. These functions shall be carried out in accordance with the provisions of this Charter and of other Inter-American treaties.

ARTICLE 34

All Member States have the right to be represented at the Inter-American Conference. Each State has the right to one vote.

ARTICLE 35

The Conference shall convene every five years at the time fixed by the Council of the Organization, after consultation with the government of the country where the Conference is to be held.

ARTICLE 36

In special circumstances and with the approval of two thirds of the American Governments, a special Inter-American Conference may be held, or the date of the next regular Conference may be changed.

ARTICLE 37

Each Inter-American Conference shall designate the place of meeting of the next Conference. If for any unforeseen reason the Conference cannot be held at the place designated, the Council of the Organization shall designate a new place.

ARTICLE 38

The program and regulations of the Inter-American Conference shall be prepared by the Council of the Organization and submitted to the Member States for consideration.

CHAPTER XI

The Meeting of Consultation of Ministers of Foreign Affairs

ARTICLE 39

The Meeting of Consultation of Ministers of Foreign Affairs shall be held in order to consider problems of an urgent nature and of common interest to the American States, and to serve as the Organ of Consultation.

ARTICLE 40

Any Member State may request that a Meeting of Consultation be called. The request shall be addressed to the Council of the Organization, which shall decide by an absolute majority whether a meeting should be held.

ARTICLE 41

The program and regulations of the Meeting of Consultation shall be prepared by the Council of the Organization and submitted to the Member States for consideration.

ARTICLE 42

If, for exceptional reasons, a Minister of Foreign Affairs is unable to attend the meeting, he shall be represented by a special delegate.

ARTICLE 43

In case of an armed attack within the territory of an American State or within the region of security delimited by treaties in force, a Meeting of Consultation shall be held without delay. Such Meeting shall be called immediately by the Chairman of the Council of the Organization, who shall at the same time call a meeting of the Council itself.

ARTICLE 44

An Advisory Defense Committee shall be established to advise the Organ of Consultation on problems of military cooperation that may arise in connection with the application of existing special treaties on collective security.

ARTICLE 45

The Advisory Defense Committee shall be composed of the highest military authorities of the American States participating in the Meeting of Consultation. Under exceptional circumstances the Governments may appoint substitutes. Each State, shall be entitled to one vote.

ARTICLE 46

The Advisory Defense Committee shall be convoked under the same conditions as the Organ of Consultation, when the latter deals with matters relating to defense against aggression.

ARTICLE 47

The Committee shall also meet when the Conference or the Meeting of Consultation or the Governments, by a two-thirds majority of the Member States, assign to it technical studies or reports on specific subjects.

CHAPTER XII

The Council

ARTICLE 48

The Council of the Organization of American States is composed of one Representative of each Member State of the Organization, especially appointed by the respective Government, with the rank of Ambassador. The appointment may be given to the diplomatic representative accredited to the Government of the country in which the Council has its seat. During the absence of the titular Representative, the Government may appoint an interim Representative.

ARTICLE 49

The Council shall elect a Chairman and a Vice Chairman, who shall serve for one year and shall not be eligible for election to either of those positions for the term immediately following.

ARTICLE 50

The Council takes cognizance, within the limits of the present Charter and of Inter-American treaties and agreements, of any matter referred to it by the Inter-American Conference or the Meeting of Consultation of Ministers of Foreign Affairs.

ARTICLE 51

The Council shall be responsible for the proper discharge by the Pan-American Union of the duties assigned to it.

ARTICLE 52

The Council shall serve provisionally as the Organ of Consultation when the circumstances contemplated in Article 43 of this Charter arise.

ARTICLE 53

It is also the duty of the Council:
a) To draft and submit to the Governments and to the Inter-American Conference proposals for the creation of new Specialized Organizations or for the combination, adaptation or elimination of existing ones, including matters relating to the financing and support thereof;
b) To draft recommendations to the Governments, the Inter-American Conference, the Specialized Conferences or the Specialized Organizations, for the coordination of the activities and programs of such organizations, after consultation with them;
c) To conclude agreements with the Inter-American Specialized Organizations to determine the relations that shall exist between the respective agency and the Organization;
d) To conclude agreements on special arrangements for cooperation with other American organizations of recognized international standing;
e) To promote and facilitate collaboration between the Organization of American States and the United Nations, as well as between Inter-American Specialized Organizations and similar international agencies;
f) To adopt resolutions that will enable the Secretary General to perform the duties envisaged in Article 84;
g) To perform the other duties assigned to it by the present Charter.

ARTICLE 54

The Council shall establish the bases for fixing the quota that each Government is to contribute to the maintenance of the Pan American Union, taking into account the ability to pay of the respective countries and their determination to contribute in an equitable manner. The budget, after approval by the Council, shall be transmitted to the Governments at least six months before the first day of the fiscal year, with a statement of the annual quota of each country. Decisions on budgetary matters require the approval of two-thirds of the members of the Council.

ARTICLE 55

The Council shall formulate its own regulations.

ARTICLE 56

The Council shall function at the seat of the Pan American Union.

ARTICLE 57

The following are organs of the Council of the Organization of American States:
a) The Inter-American Economic and Social Council;
b) The Inter-American Council of Jurists; and
c) The Inter-American Cultural Council.

ARTICLE 58

The organs referred to in the preceding article shall have technical autonomy within the limits of this Charter; but their decisions shall not encroach upon the sphere of action of the Council of the Organization.

ARTICLE 59

The organs of the Council of the Organization are composed of representatives of all the Member States of the Organization.

ARTICLE 60

The organs of the Council of the Organization shall, as far as possible, render to the Governments such technical services as the latter may request; and they shall advise the Council of the Organization on matters within their jurisdiction.

ARTICLE 61

The organs of the Council of the Organization shall, in agreement with the Council, establish cooperative relations with the corresponding organs of the United Nations and with the national or international agencies that function within their respective spheres of action.

ARTICLE 62

The Council of the Organization, with the advice of the appropriate bodies and after consultation with the Governments, shall formulate the statutes of its organs in accordance with and in the execution of the provisions of this Charter. The organs shall formulate their own regulations.

The Inter-American Economic and Social Council

ARTICLE 63

The Inter-American Economic and Social Council has for its principal purpose the promotion of the economic and social welfare of the American nations through effective cooperation for the better utilization of their natural resources, the development of their agriculture and industry and the raising of the standards of living of their peoples.

ARTICLE 64

To accomplish this purposes the Council shall:

a) Propose the means by which the American nations may give each other technical assistance in making studies and formulating and executing plans to carry out the purposes referred to in Article 26 and to develop and improve their social services;

b) Act as coordinating agency for all official inter-American activities of an economic and social nature;

c) Undertake studies on its own initiative or at the request of any Member State;

d) Assemble and prepare reports on economic and social matters for the use of the Member States;

e) Suggest to the Council of the Organization the advisability of holding specialized conferences on economic and social matters;

f) Carry on such other activities as may be assigned to it by the Inter-American Conference, the Meeting of Consultation of Ministers of Foreign Affairs, or the Council of the Organization.

ARTICLE 65

The Inter-American Economic and Social Council, composed of technical delegates appointed by each Member State, shall meet on its own initiative or on that of the Council of the Organization.

ARTICLE 66

The Inter-American Economic and Social Council shall function at the seat of the Pan American Union but it may hold meetings in any American city by a majority decision of the Member States.

The Inter-American Council of Jurists
ARTICLE 67

The purpose of the Inter-American Council of Jurists is to serve as an advisory body on juridical matters; to promote the development and codification of public and private international law; and to study the possibility of attaining uniformity in the legislation of the various American countries, insofar as it may appear desirable.

ARTICLE 68

The Inter-American Juridical Committee of Rio de Janeiro shall be the permanent committee of the Inter-American Council of Jurists.

ARTICLE 69

The Juridical Committee shall be composed of jurists of the nine countries selected by the Inter-American Conference. The selection of the jurists shall be made by the Inter-American Council of Jurists from a panel submitted by each country chosen by the Conference. The Members of the Juridical Committee represent all Member States of the Organization. The Council of the Organization is empowered to fill any vacancies that occur during the intervals between Inter-American Conferences and between meetings of the Inter-American Council of Jurists.

ARTICLE 70

The Juridical Committee shall undertake such studies and preparatory work as are assigned to it by the Inter-American Council of Jurists, the Inter-American Conference, the Meeting of Consultation of Ministers of Foreign Affairs or the Council of the Organization. It may also undertake those studies and projects which, on its own initiative, it considers advisable.

ARTICLE 71

The Inter-American Council of Jurists and the Juridical Committee should seek the cooperation of national committees for the codification of international law, of institutues of international and comparative law, and of other specialized agencies.

ARTICLE 72

The Inter-American Council of Jurists shall meet when convened by the Council of the Organization, at the place determined by the Council of Jurists at its previous meeting.

The Inter-American Cultural Council

ARTICLE 73

The purpose of the Inter-American Cultural Council is to promote friendly relations and mutual understanding among the American peoples, in order to strengthen the peaceful sentiments that have characterized the evolution of America, through the promotion of educational, scientific and cultural exchange.

ARTICLE 74

To this end the principal functions of the Council shall be:

a) To sponsor inter-American cultural activities;

b) To collect and supply information on cultural activities carried on in and among the American States by private and official agencies both national and international in character;

c) To promote the adoption of basis educational programs adapted to the needy of all population groups in the American countries;

d) To promote, in addition, the adoption of special programs of training, education and culture for the indigenous groups of the American countries;

e) To cooperate in the protection, preservation and increase of the cultural heritage of the continent;

f) To promote cooperation among the American nations in the fields of education, science and culture, by means of the exchange of materials for research and study, as well as the exchange of teachers, students, specialists and, in general, such other persons and materials as are useful for the realization of these ends;

g) To encourage the education of the peoples for harmonious international relations;

h) To carry on such other activities as may be assigned to it by the Inter-American Conference, the Meeting of Consultation of Ministers of Foreign Affairs, or the Council of the Organization.

ARTICLE 75

The Inter-American Cultural Council shall determine the place of its next meeting and shall be convened by the Council of the Organization on the date chosen by the latter in agreement with the Government of the country selected as the seat of the meeting.

ARTICLE 76

There shall be a Committee for Cultural Action of which five States, chosen at each Inter-American Conference, shall be members. The individuals composing the Committee for Cultural Action shall be selected by the Inter-American Cultural Council from a panel submitted by each country chosen by the Conference, and they shall be specialists in education or cultural matters. When the Inter-American Cultural Council and the Inter-American Conference are not in session, the Council of the Organization may fill vacancies that arise and replace those countries that find it necessary to discontinue their cooperation.

ARTICLE 77

The Committee for Cultural Action shall function as the permanent committee of the Inter-American Cultural Council, for the purpose of preparing any studies that the latter may assign to it. With respect to these studies the Council shall have the final decision.

CHAPTER XIII

The Pan American Union

ARTICLE 78

The Pan American Union is the central and permanent organ of the Organization of American States and the General Secretariat of the Organization. It shall perform the duties assigned to it in this Charter and such other duties as may be assigned to it in other inter-American treaties and agreements.

ARTICLE 79

There shall be a Secretary General of the Organization, who shall be elected by the Council for a ten-year term and who may not be reelected or be succeeded by a person of the same nationality. In the event of a vacancy in the office of Secretary General, the Council shall, within the next ninety days, elect a successor to fill the office for the remainder of the term, who may be reelected if the vacancy occurs during the second half of the term.

ARTICLE 80

The Secretary General shall direct the Pan American Union and be the legal representative thereof.

ARTICLE 81

The Secretary General shall participate with voice, but without vote, in the deliberations of the Inter-American Conference, the Meeting of Consultation of Ministers of Foreign Affairs, the Specialized Conferences, and the Council and its organs.

ARTICLE 82

The Pan American Union, through its technical and information offices, shall, under the direction of the Council, promote economic, social, juridical and cultural relations among all the Member States of the Organization.

ARTICLE 83

The Pan American Union shall also perform the following functions:

a) Transmit *ex officio* to Member States the convocation to the Inter-American Conference, the Meeting of Consultation of Ministers of Foreign Affairs, and the Specialized Conferences;

b) Advise the Council and its organs in the preparation of programs and regulations of the Inter-American Conference, the Meeting of Consultation of Ministers of Foreign Affairs, and the Specialized Conferences;

c) Place, to the extent of its ability, at the disposal of the Government of the country where a conference is to be held, the technical aid and personnel which such Government may request;

d) Serve as custodian of the documents and archives of the Inter-American Conference, of the Meeting of Consultation of Ministers of Foreign Affairs, and, insofar as possible, of the Specialized Conferences;

e) Serve as depository of the instruments of ratification of inter-American agreements;

f) Perform the functions entrusted to it by the Inter-American Conference, and the Meeting of Consultation of Ministers of Foreign Affairs;

g) Submit to the Council an annual report on the activities of the Organization;

h) Submit to the Inter-American Conference a report on the work accomplished by the Organs of the Organization since the previous Conference.

ARTICLE 84

It is the duty of the Secretary General:

a) To establish, with the approval of the Council, such technical and administrative offices of the Pan American Union as are necessary to accomplish its purposes;

b) To determine the number of department heads, officers and employees of the Pan American Union; to appoint them, regulate their powers and duties, and fix their compensation, in accordance with general standards established by the Council.

ARTICLE 85

There shall be an Assistant Secretary General, elected by the Council for a term of ten years and eligible for reelection. In the event of a vacancy in the office of Assistant Secretary General, the Council shall, within the next ninety days, elect a successor to fill such office for the remainder of the term.

ARTICLE 86

The Assistant Secretary General shall be the Secretary of the Council. He shall perform the duties of the Secretary General during the temporary absence or disability of the latter, or during the ninety-day vacancy referred to in Article 79. He shall also serve as advisory officer to the Secretary General, with the power to act as his delegate in all matters that the Secretary General may entrust to him.

ARTICLE 87

The Council, by a two-thirds vote of its members, may remove the Secretary General or the Assistant Secretary General whenever the proper functioning of the Organization so demands.

ARTICLE 88

The heads of the respective departments of the Pan American Union, appointed by the Secretary General, shall be the Executive Secretaries of the Inter-American Economic and Social Council, the Council of Jurists and the Cultural Council.

ARTICLE 89

In the performance of their duties the personnel shall not seek or receive instructions from any government or from any other authority outside the Pan American Union. They shall refrain from any action that might reflect upon their position as international officials responsible only to the Union.

ARTICLE 90

Every Member of the Organization of American States pledges itself to respect the exclusively international character of the responsibilities of the Secretary General and the personnel, and not to seek to influence them in the discharge of their duties.

ARTICLE 91

In selecting its personnel the Pan American Union shall give first consideration to efficiency, competence and integrity; but at the same time importance shall be given to the necessity of recruiting personnel on as broad a geographical basis as possible.

ARTICLE 92

The seat of the Pan American Union is the city of Washington.

CHAPTER XIV

The Specialized Conferences

ARTICLE 93

The Specialized Conferences shall meet to deal with special technical matters or to develop specific aspects of inter-American cooperation, when it is so decided by the Inter-American Conference or the Meeting of Consultation of Ministers of Foreign Affairs; when inter-American agreements so provide; or when the Council of the Organization considers it necessary, either on its own initiative or at the request of one of its organs or of one of the specialized Organizations.

ARTICLE 94

The program and regulations of the Specialized Conferences shall be prepared by the organs of the Council of the Organization or by the Specialized Organizations concerned; they shall be submitted to the Member Governments for consideration and transmitted to the Council for its information.

CHAPTER XV

The Specialized Organizations

ARTICLE 95

For the purposes of the present Charter, Inter-American Specialized Organizations are the intergovernmental organizations established by multilateral agreements and having specific functions with respect to technical matters of common interest to the American States.

ARTICLE 96

The Council shall, for the purposes stated in Article 53, maintain a register of the Organizations that fulfill the conditions set forth in the foregoing Article.

ARTICLE 97

The Specialized Organizations shall enjoy the fullest technical autonomy and shall take into account the recommendations of the Council, in conformity with the provisions of the present Charter.

ARTICLE 98

The Specialized Organizations shall submit to the Council periodic reports on the progress of their work and on their annual budgets and expenses.

ARTICLE 99

Agreements between the Council and the Specialized Organizations contemplated in paragraph c) of Article 53 may provide that such Organizations transmit their budgets to the Council for approval. Arrangements may also be made for the Pan American Union to receive the quotas of the contributing countries and distribute them in accordance with the said agreements.

ARTICLE 100

The Specialized Organizations shall establish cooperative relations with world agencies of the same character in order to coordinate their activities. In concluding agreements with international agencies of a world-wide character, the Inter-American Specialized Organizations shall preserve their identity and their status as integral parts of the Organization of American States, even when they perform regional functions of international agencies.

ARTICLE 101

In determining the geographic location of the Specialized Organization the interests of all the American States shall be taken into account.

PART THREE

CHAPTER XVI

The United Nations

ARTICLE 102

None of the provisions of this Charter shall be construed as impairing the rights and obligations of the Member States under the Charter of the United Nations.

CHAPTER XVII

Miscellaneous provisions

ARTICLE 103

The Organization of American States shall enjoy in the territory of each Member such legal capacity, privileges and immunities as are necessary for the exercise of its functions and the accomplishment of its purposes.

ARTICLE 104

The Representatives of the Governments on the Council of the Organization, the representatives on the organs of the Council, the personnel of their delegations as well as the Secretary General and the Assistant Secretary General of the Organization, shall enjoy the privileges and immunities necessary for the independent performance of their duties.

ARTICLE 105

The juridical status of the Inter-American Specialized Organizations and the privileges and immunities that should be granted to them and to their personnel, as well as to the officials of the Pan American Union, shall be determined in each case through agreements between the respective organizations and the Governments concerned.

ARTICLE 106

Correspondence of the Organization of American States, including printed matter and parcels, bearing the frank thereof, shall be carried free of charge in the mails of the Member States.

ARTICLE 107

The Organization of American States does not recognize any restriction on the eligibility of men and women to participate in the activities of the various Organs and to hold positions therein.

CHAPTER XVIII

Ratification and entry into force

ARTICLE 108

The present Charter shall remain open for signature by the American States and shall be ratified in accordance with their respective constitutional procedures. The original instrument, the Spanish, English, Portuguese and French texts of which are equally authentic, shall be deposited with the Pan American Union, which shall transmit certified copies thereof to the Governments for purposes of ratification. The instruments of ratification shall be deposited with the Pan American Union, which shall notify the signatory States of such deposit.

ARTICLE 109

The present Charter shall enter into force among the ratifying States when two-thirds of the signatory States have deposited their ratifications. It shall enter into force with respect to the remaining States in the order in which they deposit their ratifications.

ARTICLE 110

The present Charter shall be registered with the Secretariat of the United Nations through the Pan American Union.

ARTICLE 111

Amendments to the present Charter may be adopted only at an Inter-American Conference convened for that purpose. Amendments shall enter into force in accordance with the terms and the procedure set forth in Article 109.

ARTICLE 112

The present Charter shall remain in force indefinitely, but may be denounced by any Member State upon written notification to the Pan American Union, which shall communicate to all the others notice of denunciation received. After two years from the date on which the Pan American Union receives a notice of denunciation, the present Charter shall cease to be in force with respect to the denouncing State, which shall cease to belong to the Organization after it has fulfilled the obligations arising from the present Charter.

IN WITNESS WHEREOF the undersigned Plenipotentiaries, whose full powers have been presented and found to be in good and due form, sign the present Charter at the city of Bogota, Colombia, on the dates that appear opposite their respective signatures.

B. ARRANGEMENTS IN THE NORTH ATLANTIC REGION

NORTH ATLANTIC TREATY, SIGNED AT WASHINGTON, D.C., APRIL 4, 1949[1]

The Parties to this Treaty reaffirm their faith in the purposes and principles of the Charter of the United Nations and their desire to live in peace with all peoples and all governments.

They are determined to safeguard the freedom, common heritage and civilization of their peoples, founded on the principles of democracy, individual liberty and the rule of law.

They seek to promote stability and well-being in the North Atlantic area.

They are resolved to unite their efforts for collective defense and for the preservation of peace and security.

They therefore agree to this North Atlantic Treaty:

Article 1

The Parties undertake, as set forth in the Charter of the United Nations, to settle any international disputes in which they may be involved by peaceful means in such a manner that international peace and security and justice are not endangered, and to refrain in their international relations from the threat or use of force in any manner inconsistent with the purposes of the United Nations.

---

[1] United Nations *Treaty Series*, Vol. 34, 1949, pp. 244-250. Came into force on 24 August 1949 in respect of all the signatory States, by the deposit with the Government of the United States of America of instruments of ratification in accordance with the provisions of article 11. Following are the dates on which an instrument of ratification was deposited on behalf of each of the signatory States:

Belgium	16 June	1949	Netherlands	12 August	1949
Canada	3 May	1949	Norway	8 July	1949
Denmark	24 August	1949	Portugal	24 August	1949
France	24 August	1949	United Kingdom of Great		
Iceland	1 August	1949	Britain and Northern		
Italy	24 August	1949	Ireland	7 June	1949
Luxembourg	27 June	1949	United States of America	25 July	1949

Article 2

The Parties will contribute toward the further development of peaceful and friendly international relations by strengthening their free institutions, by bringing about a better understanding of the principles upon which these institutions are founded, and by promoting conditions of stability and well being. They will seek to eliminate conflict in their international economic policies and will encourage economic collaboration between any or all of them.

Article 3

In order more effectively to achieve the objectives of this Treaty, the Parties, separately and jointly, by means of continuous and effective self-help and mutual aid, will maintain and develop their individual and collective capacity to resist armed attack.

Article 4

The Parties will consult together whenever, in the opinion of any of them, the territorial integrity, political independence or security of any of the Parties is threatened.

Article 5

The Parties agree that an armed attack against one or more of them in Europe or North America shall be considered an attack against them all; and consequently they agree that, if such an armed attack occurs, each of them, in exercise of the right of individual or collective self-defense recognized by Article 51 of the Charter of the United Nations, will assist the Party or Parties so attacked by taking forthwith, individually and in concert with the other Parties, such action as it deems necessary, including the use of armed force, to restore and maintain the security of the North Atlantic area.

Any such armed attack and all measures taken as a result thereof shall immediately be reported to the Security Council. Such measures shall be terminated when the Security Council has taken the measures necessary to restore and maintain international peace and security.

Article 6

For the purpose of Article 5 an armed attack on one or more of the Parties is deemed to include an armed attack on the territory of any of the Parties in Europe or North America, on the Algerian departments of France, on the occupation forces of any Party in Europe, on the islands under the jurisdiction of any Party in the North Atlantic area north of the Tropic of Cancer or on the vessels or aircraft in this area of any of the Parties.

Article 7

This Treaty does not affect, and shall not be interpreted as affecting, in any way the rights and obligations under the Charter of the Parties which are members of the United Nations, or the primary responsibility of the Security Council for the maintenance of international peace and security.

Article 8

Each Party declares that none of the international engagements now in force between it and any other of the Parties or any third State is in conflict with the provisions of this Treaty, and undertakes not to enter into any international engagement in conflict with this Treaty.

Article 9

The Parties hereby establish a council, on which each of them shall be represented, to consider matters concerning the implementation of this Treaty. The council shall be so organized as to be able to meet promptly at any time. The council shall set up such subsidiary bodies as may be necessary; in particular it shall establish immediately a defense committee which shall recommend measures for the implementation of Articles 3 and 5.

Article 10

The Parties may, by unanimous agreement, invite any other European State in a position to further the principles of this Treaty and to contribute to the security of the North Atlantic area to accede to this Treaty. Any State so invited may become a party to the Treaty by depositing its instrument of accession with the Government of the United States of America. The Government of the United States of America will inform each of the Parties of the deposit of each such instrument of accession.

Article 11

This Treaty shall be ratified and its provisions carried out by the Parties in accordance with their respective constitutional processes. The instruments of ratification shall be deposited as soon as possible with the Government of the United States of America, which will notify all the other signatories of each deposit. The Treaty shall enter into force between the States which have ratified it as soon as the ratifications of the majority of the signatories, including the ratifications of Belgium, Canada, France, Luxembourg, the Netherlands, the United Kingdom and the United States, have been deposited and shall come into effect with respect to other States on the date of the deposit of their ratifications.

Article 12

After the Treaty has been in force for ten years, or at any time thereafter, the Parties shall, if any of them so requests, consult together for the purpose of reviewing the Treaty, having regard for the factors then affecting peace and security in the North Atlantic area, including the development of universal as well as regional arrangements under the Charter of the United Nations for the maintenance of international peace and security.

Article 13

After the Treaty has been in force for twenty years, any Party may cease to be a party one year after its notice of denunciation has been given to the Government of the United States of America, which will inform the Governments of the other Parties of the deposit of each notice of denunciation.

Article 14

The Treaty, of which the English and French texts are equally authentic, shall be deposited in the archives of the Government of the United States of America. Duly certified copies thereof will be transmitted by that Government to the Governments of the other signatories.

IN WITNESS WHEREOF, the undersigned Plenipotentiaries have signed this Treaty.

DONE at Washington, the fourth day of April, 1949.

C. ARRANGEMENTS IN SOUTHEAST ASIA

1. PACIFIC CHARTER. PROCLAIMED AT MANILA, ON 8 SEPTEMBER 1954[1]

The Delegates of Australia, France, New Zealand, Pakistan, the Republic of the Philippines, the Kingdom of Thailand, the United Kingdom of Great Britain and Northern Ireland, and the United States of America,

DESIRING to establish a firm basis for common action to maintain peace and security in Southeast Asia and the Southwest Pacific,

CONVINCED that common action to this end, in order to be worthy and effective, must be inspired by the highest principles of justice and liberty,

DO HEREBY PROCLAIM:

First, in accordance with the provisions of the United Nations Charter, they uphold the principle of equal rights and self-determination of peoples and they will earnestly strive by every peaceful means to promote self-government and to secure the independence of all countries whose peoples desire it and are able to undertake its responsibilities;

Second, they are each prepared to continue taking effective practical measures to ensure conditions favorable to the orderly achievement of the foregoing purposes in accordance with their constitutional processes;

Third, they will continue to cooperate in the economic, social and cultural fields in order to promote higher living standards, economic progress and social well-being in this region;

Fourth, as declared in the Southeast Asia Collective Defense Treaty, they are determined to prevent or counter by appropriate means any attempt in the treaty area to subvert their freedom or to destroy their sovereignty or territorial integrity.

PROCLAIMED at Manila, this eighth day of September, 1954.

---

[1] United Nations *Treaty Series*, vol. 209, 1955, p. 24. The Governments of Australia, France, New Zealand and United Kingdom of Great Britain and Northern Ireland, whose respective representatives initialed the Charter, have given their acceptance or confirmation on 10 December 1954, 10 November 1954, 29 October 1954 and 8 October 1954, respectively. The Government of Pakistan has accepted the Charter on 17 February 1955.

2. SOUTHEAST ASIA COLLECTIVE DEFENSE TREATY, SIGNED AT MANILA, ON 8 SEPTEMBER 1954[1]

The Parties to this Treaty,

Recognizing the sovereign equality of all the Parties,

Reiterating their faith in the purposes and principles set forth in the Charter of the United Nations and their desire to live in peace with all peoples and all governments,

Reaffirming that, in accordance with the Charter of the United Nations, they uphold the principle of equal rights and self-determination of peoples, and declaring that they will earnestly strive by every peaceful means to promote self-government and to secure the independence of all countries whose peoples desire it and are able undertake its responsibilities,

Desiring to strengthen the fabric of peace and freedom and to uphold the principles of democracy, individual liberty and the rule of law, and to promote the economic well-being and development of all peoples in the treaty area,

Intending to declare publicly and formally their sense of unity, so that any potential aggressor will appreciate that the Parties stand together in the area, and

Desiring further to coordinate their efforts for collective defense for the preservation of peace and security,

Therefore agree as follows:

Article I

The Parties undertake, as set forth in the Charter of the United Nations, to settle any international disputes in which they may be involved by peaceful means in such a manner that international peace and security and justice are not endangered, and to refrain in their international relations from the threat or use of force in any manner inconsistent with the purposes of the United Nations.

Article II

In order more effectively to achieve the objectives of this Treaty, the Parties separately and jointly, by means of continuous and effective self-help and mutual aid will maintain and develop their individual and collective capacity to resist armed attack and to prevent and counter subversive activities directed from without against their territorial integrity and political stability.

---

[1] United Nations *Treaty Series*, vol. 209, 1955, pp. 28-34. In accordance with article IX, para. 3, the Treaty came into force on 19 February 1955 between the following States, on behalf of which the instruments of ratification were deposited with the Government of the Republic of the Philippines on the dates indicated:

Thailand	2 December 1954
Australia	19 February 1955
France	19 February 1955
New Zealand	19 February 1955
Philippines	19 February 1955
United States of America	19 February 1955
United Kingdom of Great Britain and Northern Ireland	19 February 1955

Article III

The Parties undertake to strengthen their institutions and to cooperate with one another in the further development of economic measures, including technical assistance, designed both to promote economic progress and social well-being and to further the individual and collective efforts of governments toward these ends.

Article IV

1. Each Party recognizes that aggression by means of armed attack in the treaty area against any of the Parties or against any State or territory which the Parties by unanimous agreement may hereafter designate, would endanger its own peace and safety, and agrees that it will in that event act to meet the common danger in accordance with its constitutional processes. Measures taken under this paragraph shall be immediately reported to the Security Council of the United Nations.

2. If, in the opinion of any of the Parties, the inviolability or the integrity of the territory or the sovereignty or political independence of any Party in the treaty area or of any other State or territory to which the provisions of paragraph 1 of this Article from time to time apply is threatened in any way other than by armed attack or is affected or threatened by any fact or situation which might endanger the peace of the area, the Parties shall consult immediately in order to agree on the measures which should be taken for the common defense.

3. It is understood that no action on the territory of any State designated by unanimous agreement under paragraph 1 of this Article or on any territory so designated shall be taken except at the invitation or with the consent of the Government concerned.

Article V

The Parties hereby establish a Council, on which each of them shall be represented, to consider matters concerning the implementation of this Treaty. The Council shall provide for consultation with regard to military and any other planning as the situation obtaining in the treaty area may from time to time require. The Council shall be so organized as to be able to meet at any time.

Article VI

This Treaty does not affect and shall not be interpreted as affecting in any way the rights and obligations of any of the Parties under the Charter of the United Nations or the responsibility of the United Nations for the maintenance of international peace and security. Each Party declares that none of the international engagements now in force between it and any other of the Parties or any third party is in conflict with the provisions of this Treaty, and undertakes not to enter into any international engagement in conflict with this Treaty.

Article VII

Any other State in a position to further the objectives of this Treaty and to contribute to the security of the area may, by unanimous agreement of the Parties, be invited to accede to this Treaty. Any State so invited may become a Party to the Treaty by depositing its instrument of accession with the Government of the Republic of the Philippines. The Government of the Republic of the Philippines shall inform each of the Parties of the deposit of each such instrument of accession.

Article VIII

As used in this Treaty, the "treaty area" is the general area of Southeast Asia, including also the entire territories of the Asian Parties, and the general area of the Southwest Pacific not including the Pacific area north of 21 degrees 30 minutes north latitude. The Parties may, by unanimous agreement, amend this Article to include within the treaty area the territory of any State acceding to this Treaty in accordance with Article VII or otherwise to change the treaty area.

Article IX

1. This Treaty shall be deposited in the archives of the Government of the Republic of the Philippines. Duly certified copies thereof shall be transmitted by that Government to the other signatories.
2. The Treaty shall be ratified and its provisions carried out by the Parties in accordance with their respective constitutional processes. The instruments of ratification shall be deposited as soon as possible with the Government of the Republic of the Philippines, which shall notify all of the other signatories of such deposit.
3. The Treaty shall enter into force between the States which have ratified it as soon as the instruments of ratification of a majority of the signatories shall have been deposited, and shall come into effect with respect to each other State on the date of the deposit of its instrument of ratification.

Article X

This Treaty shall remain in force indefinitely, but any Party may cease to be a Party one year after its notice of denunciation has been given to the Government of the Republic of the Philippines, which shall inform the Governments of the other Parties of the deposit of each notice of denunciation.

Article XI

The English text of this Treaty is binding on the Parties, but when the Parties have agreed to the French text thereof and have so notified the Government of the Republic of the Philippines, the French text[1] shall be equally authentic and binding on the Parties.

---

[1] The French text of the Pacific Charter, of the Southeast Asia Collective Defense Treaty and of the Protocol, as reproduced herein, was agreed upon by the signatory Governments on 14 April 1955 at Paris and later revised by agreement between those Governments. A certified copy of the above-mentioned revised French text was transmitted by the Government of the Republic of the Philippines.

a.   UNDERSTANDING OF THE UNITED STATES OF AMERICA[1]

The United States of America in executing the present Treaty does so with the understanding that its recognition of the effect of aggression and armed attack and its agreement with reference thereto in Article IV, paragraph 1, apply only to communist aggression but affirms that in the event of other aggression or armed attack it will consult under the provisions of Article IV, paragraph 2.

IN WITNESS WHEREOF, the undersigned Plenipotentiaries have signed this Treaty. DONE at Manila, this eighth day of September, 1954.

For Australia:
R.G. CASEY
For France:
G. LA CHAMBRE
For New Zealand
T. Clifton WEBB

For Pakistan:

Signed for transmission to my Government for its consideration and action in accordance with the Constitution of Pakistan

Zafrulla KHAN

For the Republic of the Philippines:
Carlos P. GARCIA
Francisco A. DELGADO
Tomas A. CABILI
Lorenzo M. TANADA
Cornelio T. VILLAREAL

For the Kingdom of Thailand:
WAN WAITHAYAKON KROMMUN NARADHIP BONGSPRABANDH

For the United Kingdom of Great Britain and Northern Ireland:
READING

For the United States of America:
John Foster DULLES
H. Alexander SMITH
Michael J. MANSFIELD

---

[1] United Nations *Treaty Series*, vol. 209, 1955, p. 34.

b. PROTOCOL TO THE SOUTHEAST ASIA COLLECTIVE DEFENSE TREATY, SIGNED AT MANILA, ON 8 SEPTEMBER 1954[1]

DESIGNATION OF STATES AND TERRITORY AS TO WHICH PROVISIONS OF ARTICLE IV AND ARTICLE III ARE TO BE APPLICABLE

The Parties to the Southeast Asia Collective Defense Treaty unanimously designate for the purposes of Article IV of the Treaty the States of Cambodia and Laos and the free territory under the jurisdiction of the State of Vietnam.

The Parties further agree that the above-mentioned states and territory shall be eligible in respect of the economic measures contemplated by Article III.

This Protocol shall enter into force simultaneously with the coming into force of the Treaty.

IN WITNESS WHEREOF, the undersigned Plenipotentiaries have signed this Protocol to the Southeast Asia Collective Denfense Treaty.

DONE at Manila, this eighth day of September, 1954.

For Australia:
R.G. CASEY
For France:
G. LA CHAMBRE
For New Zealand:
T. Clifton WEBB

For Pakistan:

Signed for transmission to my Government for its consideration and action in accordance with the Constitution of Pakistan
Zafrulla KHAN

For the Republic of the Philippines:
Carlos P. GARCIA
Francisco A. DELGADO
Tomas A. CABILI
Lorenzo M. TANADA
Cornelio T. VILLAREAL

For the Kingdom of Thailand

WAN WAITHAYAKON KROMMUN NARADHIP BONGSPRABANDH

For the United Kingdom of Great Britain and Northern Ireland:
READING

For the United States of America:
John Foster DULLES
H. Alexander SMITH
Michael J. MANSFIELD

---

[1] United Nations *Treaty Series*, vol. 209, 1955, p. 36; Came into force on 19 February 1955, in accordance with its third paragraph.

D. ARRANGEMENTS IN CENTRAL ASIA OR
THE MIDDLE EAST

1. PACT OF MUTUAL CO-OPERATION BETWEEN
IRAQ AND TURKEY, BASED ON THE PACT OF
BAGHDAD OR THE MIDDLE EAST TREATY,
SIGNED AT BAGHDAD, FEBRUARY 24, 1955[1]

Whereas the friendly and brotherly relations existing between Iraq and Turkey are in constant progress, and in order to complement the contents of the Treaty of friendship and good neighbourhood concluded between His Majesty The King of Iraq and His Excellency The President of the Turkish Republic signed in Ankara on the 29th of March, 1946,[2] which recognised the fact that peace and security between the two countries is an integral part of the peace and security of all the Nations of the world and in particular the Nations of the Middle East, and that it is the basis for their foreign policies;

Whereas Article 11 of the Treaty of Joint Defence and Economic Co-operation between the Arab League States provides that no provision of that Treaty shall in any way affect, or is designed to affect any of the rights and obligations accruing to the contracting parties from the United Nations Charter;

And having realised the great responsibilities borne by them in their capacity as members of the United Nations concerned with the maintenance of peace and security in the Middle East region which necessitate taking the required measures in accordance with Article 51 of the United Nations Charter;

They have been fully convinced of the necessity of concluding a pact fulfilling these aims and for that purpose have appointed as their Plenipotentiaries:

His Majesty King Faisal II King of Iraq:
His Excellency Al Farik Nuri As-Said
Prime Minister

His Excellency Burhanuddin Bash-Ayan
Acting Minister for Foreign Affairs

His Excellency Jalal Bayar President of the Turkish Republic:
His Excellency Adnan Menderes
Prime Minister

His Excellency Professor Fuat Koprulu
Minister for Foreign Affairs

who, having communicated their full powers, found to be in good and due form, have agreed as follows:

---

[1] United Nations *Treaty Series*, vol. 233, 1956, pp. 210-216. Came into force on 15 April 1955, by the exchange of the instruments of ratification at Ankara, in accordance with article 8. In accordance with article 5, the following States acceded to the Pact by deposit of the instruments of accession with the Ministry of Foreign Affairs of Iraq on the dates indicated:

United Kingdom of Great Britain and Northern Ireland	5 April	1955
Pakistan	23 September	1955
Iran	3 November	1955

[2] United Nations *Treaty Series*, vol. 37, p. 226.

Article 1

Consistent with Article 51 of the United Nations Charter the High Contracting Parties will co-operate for their security and defence. Such measures as they agree to take to give effect to this co-operation may form the subject of special agreements with each other.

Article 2

In order to ensure the realisation and effect application of the co-operation provided for in Article 1 above, the competent authorities of the High Contracting Parties will determine the measures to be taken as soon as the present Pact enters into force. These measures will become operative as soon as they have been approved by the Governments of the High Contracting Parties.

Article 3

The High Contracting Parties undertake to refrain from any interference whatsoever in each other's internal affairs. They will settle any dispute between themselves in a peaceful way in accordance with the United Nations Charter.

Article 4

The High Contracting Parties declare that the dispositions of the present Pact are not in contradiction with any of the international obligations contracted by either of them with any third state or states. They do not derogate from, and cannot be interpreted as derogating from, the said international obligations. The High Contracting Parties undertake not to enter into any international obligation incompatible with the present Pact.

Article 5

This Pact shall be open for accession to any member state of the Arab League or any other state actively concerned with the security and peace in this region and which is fully recognized by both of the High Contracting Parties. Accession shall come into force from the date on which the instrument of accession of the state concerned is deposited with the Ministry of Foreign Affairs of Iraq.

Any acceding State Party to the present Pact, may conclude special agreements, in accordance with Article 1, with one or more states Parties to the present Pact. The competent authority of any acceding State may determine measures in accordance with Article 2. These measures will become operative as soon as they have been approved by the Governments of the Parties concerned.

Article 6

A Permanent Council at Ministerial level will be set up to function within the framework of the purposes of this Pact when at least four Powers become parties to the Pact.

The Council will draw up its own rules of procedure.

Article 7

This Pact remains in force for a period of five years renewable for other five year periods. Any Contracting Party may withdraw from the Pact by notifying the other parties in writing of its desire to do so, six months before the expiration of any of the above-mentioned periods, in which case the Pact remains valid for the other Parties.

Article 8

This Pact shall be ratified by the Contracting Parties and ratifications shall be exchanged at Ankara as soon as possible. Thereafter it shall come into force from the date of the exchange of ratifications.

IN WITNESS WHEREOF, the said Plenipotentiaries have signed the present Pact in Arabic, Turkish and English all three texts being equally authentic except in the case of doubt when the English text shall prevail.

DONE in duplicate at Baghdad this second day of Rajab 1374 Hijri corresponding to the twenty-fourth day of February 1955.

NURI AS-SAID
BURHANUDDIN BASH-AYAN
For His Majesty the King of Iraq

Adnan MENDERES
Fuat KOPRULU
For the President of the Turkish Republic

EXCHANGE OF LETTERS

I

Baghdad 24th February, 1955

Excellency,

In connection with the Pact signed by us to-day, I have the honour to place on record our understanding that this Pact will enable our two countries to co-operate in resisting any aggression directed against either of them and that in order to ensure the maintenance of peace and security in the Middle East region, we have agreed to work in close co-operation for effecting the carrying out of the United Nations resolutions concerning Palestine.

Accept, Excellency, the assurances of my highest consideration.

NURI AS-SAID

His Excellency Adnan Menderes
Prime Minister of Turkey
Baghdad

Baghdad 24th February, 1955

Excellency,

I have the honour to acknowledge receipt of your Excellency's letter of to-day's date, which reads as follows:

[*See letter I*]

I wish to confirm my agreement to the contents of the said letter.

Accept, Excellency, the assurances of my highest consideration.

Adnan MENDERES

His Excellency Nuri As-Said
Prime Minister of Iraq
Baghdad

2. DECLARATION[1] BETWEEN THE UNITED STATES OF AMERICA, IRAN, PAKISTAN, TURKEY, AND THE UNITED KINGDOM OF GREAT BRITAIN AND NORTHERN IRELAND RESPECTING THE BAGHDAD PACT,[2] SIGNED AT LONDON ON 28 JULY 1958

1. The members of the Baghdad Pact[2] attending the Ministerial meeting in London have re-examined their position in the light of recent events and conclude that the need which called the Pact into being is greater than ever. These members declare their determination to maintain their collective security and to resist aggression, direct or indirect.

2. Under the Pact collective security arrangements have been instituted. Joint military planning has been advanced and area economic projects have been promoted. Relationships are being established with other free world nations associated for collective security.

3. The question of whether substantive alterations should be made in the Pact and its organisation or whether the Pact will be continued in its present form is under consideration by the Governments concerned. However, the nations represented at the meeting in London reaffirmed their determination to strengthen further their united defence posture in the area.

4. Article 1 of the Pact of Mutual Co-operation signed at Baghdad on February 24, 1955[2] provides that the parties will co-operate for their security and defence and that such measures as they agree to take to give effect to this co-operation may form the subject of special agreements. Similarly, the United States in the interest of world peace, and pursuant to existing Congressional authorization, agrees to co-operate with the nations making this Declaration for their security and defence, and will promptly enter into agreements designed to give effect to this co-operation.

---

[1] United Nations *Treaty Series*, vol. 335, 1959, pp. 206-208; Came into force on 28 July 1958 by signature.
[2] United Nations *Treaty Series*, vol. 233, p. 199.

E. ARRANGEMENTS AMONG THE COMMUNIST STATES IN EUROPE

TREATY OF FRIENDSHIP, CO-OPERATION AND MUTUAL ASSISTANCE BETWEEN THE PEOPLE'S REPUBLIC OF ALBANIA, THE PEOPLE'S REPUBLIC OF BULGARIA, THE HUNGARIAN PEOPLE'S REPUBLIC, THE GERMAN DEMOCRATIC REPUBLIC, THE POLISH PEOPLE'S REPUBLIC, THE ROMANIAN PEOPLE'S REPUBLIC, THE UNION OF SOVIET SOCIALIST REPUBLICS AND THE CZECHOSLOVAK REPUBLIC, SIGNED AT WARSAW ON 14 MAY 1955.[1]

The Contracting Parties,

Reaffirming their desire to create a system of collective security in Europe based on the participation of all European States, irrespective of their social and political structure, whereby the said States may be enabled to combine their efforts in the interests of ensuring peace in Europe;

Taking into consideration, at the same time, the situation that has come about in Europe as a result of the ratification of the Paris Agreements, which provide for the constitution of a new military group in the form of a "West European Union," with the participation of a remilitarized West Germany and its inclusion in the North Atlantic bloc, thereby increasing the danger of a new war and creating a threat to the national security of peace-loving States;

Being convinced that in these circumstances the peace-loving States of Europe must take the necessary steps to safeguard their security and to promote the maintenance of peace in Europe;

Being guided by the purposes and principles of the Charter of the United Nations;

In the interests of the further strengthening and development of friendship, co-operation and mutual assistance in accordance with the principles of respect for the independence and sovereignty of States and of non-intervention in their domestic affairs;

Have resolved to conclude the present Treaty of Friendship, Co-operation and Mutual Assistance and have appointed as their plenipotentiaries:

The Presidium of the National Assembly of the People's Republic of Albania: Mehmet Shehu, President of the Council of Ministers of the People's Republic of Albania;

The Presidium of the National Assembly of the People's Republic of Bulgaria: Vylko Chervenkov, President of the Council of Ministers of the People's Republic of Bulgaria;

---

[1] United Nations *Treaty Series*, vol. 49, 1955, pp. 24-32. In accordance with article 10, the Treaty came into force on 6 June 1955, the date of deposit with the Government of the Polish People's Republic of the last instrument of ratification. Following are the dates of deposit of the instruments of ratification on behalf of the signatory States:

Poland	19 May	1955
German Democratic Republic	24 May	1955
Czechoslovakia	27 May	1955
Bulgaria	31 May	1955
Union of Soviet Socialist Republics	1 June	1955
Hungary	2 June	1955
Romania	3 June	1955
Albania	6 June	1955

The Presidium of the Hungarian People's Republic: Andras Hegedus, President of the Council of Ministers of the Hungarian People's Republic;

The President of the German Democratic Republic: Otto Grotewohl, Prime Minister of the German Democratic Republic;

Council of State of the Polish People's Republic: Jozef Cyrankiewicz, President of the Council of Ministers of the Polish People's Republic;

The Presidium of the Grand National Assembly of the Romanian People's Republic: Gheorghe Gheorghiu Dej, President of the Council of Ministers of the Romanian People's Republic;

The Presidium of the Supreme Soviet of the Union of Soviet Socialist Republics: Nikolai Aleksandrovich Bulganin, President of the Council of Ministers of the Union of Soviet Socialist Republics;

The President of the Czechoslovak Republic: Viliam Siroky, Prime Minister of the Czechoslovak Republic;

who, having exhibited their full powers, found in good and due form, have agreed as follows:

Article 1

The Contracting Parties undertake, in accordance with the Charter of the United Nations, to refrain in their international relations from the threat or use of force and to settle their international disputes by peaceful means in such a manner that international peace and security are not endangered.

Article 2

The Contracting Parties declare that they are prepared to participate, in a spirit of sincere co-operation, in all international action for ensuring international peace and security and will devote their full efforts to the realization of these aims.

In this connexion, the Contracting Parties shall endeavour to secure, in agreement with other States desiring to co-operate in this matter, the adoption of effective measures for the general reduction of armaments and the prohibition of atomic, hydrogen and other weapons of mass destruction.

Article 3

The Contracting Parties shall consult together on all important international questions involving their common interests, with a view to strengthening international peace and security.

Whenever any one of the Contracting Parties considers that a threat of armed attack on one or more of the States Parties to the Treaty has arisen, they shall consult together immediately with a view to providing for their joint defence and maintaining peace and security.

Article 4

In the event of an armed attack in Europe on one or more of the States Parties to the Treaty by any State or group of States, each State Party to the Treaty shall, in the exercise of the right of individual or collective self-defence, in accordance with Article 51 of the United Nations Charter, afford the State or States so attacked immediate assistance, individually and in agreement with the other States Parties to the Treaty, by all the means it considers necessary, including the use of armed force. The States Parties to the Treaty shall consult together immediately concerning the joint measures necessary to restore and maintain international peace and security.

Measures taken under this article shall be reported to the Security Council in accordance with the provisions of the United Nations Charter. These measures shall be discontinued as soon as the Security Council takes the necessary action to restore and maintain international peace and security.

Article 5

The Contracting Parties have agreed to establish a Unified Command, to which certain elements of their armed forces shall be allocated by agreement between the Parties, and which shall act in accordance with jointly established principles. The Parties shall likewise take such other concerted action as may be necessary to reinforce their defensive strength, in order to defend the peaceful labour of their peoples, guarantee the inviolability of their frontiers and territories and afford protection against possible aggression.

Article 6

For the purpose of carrying out the consultations provided for in the present Treaty between the States Parties thereto, and for the consideration of matters arising in connexion with the application of the present Treaty, a Political Consultative Committee shall be established, in which each State Party to the Treaty shall be represented by a member of the Government or by some other specially appointed representative.

The Committee may establish such auxiliary organs as may prove to be necessary.

Article 7

The Contracting Parties undertake not to participate in any coalitions or alliances, and not to conclude any agreements, the purposes of which are incompatible with the purposes of the present Treaty.

The Contracting Parties declare that their obligations under international treaties at present in force are not incompatible with the provisions of the present Treaty.

Article 8

The Contracting Parties declare that they will act in a spirit of friendship and co-operation to promote the further development and strengthening of the economic and cultural ties among them, in accordance with the principles of respect for each other's independence and sovereignty and of non-intervention in each other's domestic affairs.

Article 9

The present Treaty shall be open for accession by other States, irrespective of their social and political structure, which express their readiness, by participating in the present Treaty, to help in combining the efforts of the peace-loving States to ensure the peace and security of the peoples. Such accessions shall come into effect with the consent of the States Parties to the Treaty after the instruments of accession have been deposited with the Government of the Polish People's Republic.

Article 10

The present Treaty shall be subject to ratification, and the instruments of ratification shall be deposited with the Government of the Polish People's Republic.

The Treaty shall come into force on the date of deposit of the last instrument of ratification. The Government of the Polish People's Republic shall inform the other States Parties to the Treaty of the deposit of each instrument of ratification.

Article 11

The present Treaty shall remain in force for twenty years. For Contracting Parties which do not, one year before the expiration of that term, give notice of termination of the Treaty to the Government of the Polish People's Republic, the Treaty shall remain in force for a further ten years.

In the event of the establishment of a system of collective security in Europe and the conclusion for that purpose of a General European Treaty concerning collective security, a goal which the Contracting Parties shall steadfastly strive to achieve, the present Treaty shall cease to have effect as from the date on which the General European Treaty comes into force.

DONE at Warsaw, this fourteenth day of May 1955, in one copy, in the Russian, Polish, Czech and German languages, all the texts being equally authentic. Certified copies of the present Treaty shall be transmitted by the Government of the Polish People's Republic to all the other Parties to the Treaty.

IN FAITH WHEREOF the Plenipotentiaries have signed the present Treaty and have thereto affixed their seals.

[L. S.] By authorization of the Presidium of the National Assembly of the People's Republic of Albania:

(Signed) M. SHEHU

[L. S.] By authorization of the Presidium of the National Assembly of the People's Republic of Bulgaria:

(Signed) V. CHERVENKOV

[L. S.] By authorization of the Presidium of the Hungarian People's Republic:

(Signed) A. HEGEDUS

[L. S.] By authorization of the President of the German Democratic Republic:

(Signed) O. GROTEWOHL

[L. S.] By authorization of the Council of State of the Polish People's Republic:

(Signed) J. CYRANKIEWICZ

[L. S.] By authorization of the Presidium of the Grand National Assembly of the Romanian People's Republic:

(Signed) G. GHEORGHIU DEJ

[L. S.] By authorization of the Presidium of the Supreme Soviet of the Union of Soviet Socialist Republics:

(Signed) N. BULGANIN

[L. S.] By authorization of the President of the Czechoslovak Republic:

(Signed) V. SIROKY

F. ARRANGEMENT AMONG THE ARAB STATES

PACT OF THE LEAGUE OF ARAB STATES,
SIGNED AT CAIRO ON 22 MARCH 1945[1]

HIS EXCELLENCY THE PRESIDENT OF THE SYRIAN REPUBLIC,
HIS ROYAL HIGHNESS THE EMIR OF TRANSJORDAN,
HIS MAJESTY THE KING OF IRAQ,
HIS MAJESTY THE KING OF SAUDI-ARABIA,
HIS EXCELLENCY THE PRESIDENT OF THE LEBANESE REPUBLIC,
HIS MAJESTY THE KING OF EGYPT,
HIS MAJESTY THE KING OF YEMEN,

With a view to strengthen the close relations and numerous ties which bind the Arab States,

And out of concern for the cementing and reinforcing of these bonds on the basis of respect for the independence and sovereignty of these States.

And in order to direct their efforts toward the goal of the welfare of all the Arab States, their common weal, the guarantee of their future and the realization of their aspirations,

And in response to Arab public opinion in all the Arab countries,

Have agreed to conclude a pact to this effect and have delegated as their plenipotentaries those whose names are given below:—

THE PRESIDENT OF THE SYRIAN REPUBLIC HAS DELEGATED FOR SYRIA:

H.E. FARIS AL KHURY, President of the Council of Ministers.
H.E. JAMIL MARDAM BEY, Minister of Foreign Affairs.

H.R.H. THE EMIR OF TRANSJORDAN HAS DELEGATED FOR TRANSJORDAN:

H.E. SAMIR AL RIFAI PASHA, President of the Council of Ministers.
H.E. SAID AL MUFTI PASHA, Minister of the Interior.
SULAIMAN AL NABULSI BEY, Secretary of the Council of Ministers.

H.M. THE KING OF IRAQ HAS DELEGATED FOR IRAQ:

H.E. ARSHAD AL UMARY, Minister of Foreign Affairs.
H.E. ALY JAWDAT AL AYYUBI, Minister Plenipotentiary of Iraq in Washington.
H.E. TAHSIN AL ASKARI, Minister Plenipotentiary of Iraq in Cairo.

---

[1] United Nations *Treaty Series*, vol. 70, 1950, pp. 248-262. Came into force on 10 May 1945, fifteen days after the deposit of the fourth instrument of ratification with the Secretary-General of the League of Arab States, in accordance with article 20. Following are the dates of deposit of the instrument of ratification and of the entry into force of the Pact in respect of each Contracting Party:

	Date of deposit of the instrument of ratification		Date of entry into force	
Transjordan	10 April	1945	10 May	1945
Egypt	12 April	1945	10 May	1945
Saudi Arabia	16 April	1945	10 May	1945
Iraq	25 April	1945	10 May	1945
Lebanon	16 May	1945	1 June	1945
Syria	19 May	1945	4 June	1945
Yemen	9 February	1946	24 February	1946

H.M. THE KING OF SAUDI-ARABIA HAS DELEGATED FOR SAUDI-ARABIA:

H.E. SHEIKH YUSUF YASIN, Assistance Minister of Foreign Affairs.
H.E. KHAIR AL DIN AL ZIRIKLY, Counsellor of the Saudi Arabian Legation in Cairo.

THE PRESIDENT OF THE LEBANESE REPUBLIC HAS DELEGATED FOR LEBANON:

H.E. ABD ALHAMID KARAMI, President of the Council of Ministers.
H.E. YUSUF SALEM, Minister Plenipotentiary of Lebanon in Cairo.

H.M. THE KING OF EGYPT HAS DELEGATED FOR EGYPT:

H.E. MAHMOUD FAHMY EL NORRACHI PASHA, President of the Council of Ministers.
H.E. ABD EL HAMID BADAWI PASHA, Minister of Foreign Affairs.
H.E. MOHAMED HUSSEIN HEIKAL PASHA, President of the Senate.
H.E. MAKRAM EBEID PASHA, Minister of Finance.
H.E. MOHAMED HAFEZ RAMADAN PASHA, Minister of Justice.
H.E. ABD AL RAZZAK AHMAD AL SANHURY BEY, Minister of Education.
H.E. ABD AL RAHMAN AZZAM REY, MINISTER Plenipotentiary in the Ministry of Foreign Affairs.

H.M. THE KING OF YEMEN HAS DELEGATED FOR YEMEN:

Who after the exchange of the credentials granting them full authority, which were found valid and in proper form, have agreed upon the following:

Article 1.—The League of Arab State shall be composed of the independent Arab States that have signed this Pact.

Every independent Arab State shall have the right to adhere to the League. Should it desire to adhere, it shall present an application to this effect which shall be filed with the permanent General Secretariat and submitted to the Council at its first meeting following the presentation of the application.

Article 2.—The purpose of the League is to draw closer the relations between member States and co-ordinate their political activities with the aim of realizing a close collaboration between them, to safeguard their independence and sovereignty, and to consider in a general way the affairs and interests of the Arab countries.

It also has among its purposes a close co-operation of the member States with due regard to the structure of each of these States and the conditions prevailing therein, in the followings matters:

(a) Economic and financial matters, including trade, customs, currency, agriculture and industry.
(b) Communications, including railways, roads, aviation, navigation, and posts and telegraphs.
(c) Cultural matters.
(d) Matters connected with nationality, passports, visas, execution of judgments and extradition.
(e) Social welfare matters.
(f) Health matters.

Article 3.—The League shall have a Council composed of the representatives of the member States. Each State shall have one vote, regardless of the number of its representatives.

The Council shall be entrusted with the function of realizing the purpose of the League and of supervising the execution of the agreements concluded between the member States on matters referred to in the preceding article or on other matters.

It shall also have the function of determining the means whereby the League will collaborate with the international organizations which may be created in the future to guarantee peace and security and organize economic and social relations.

Article 4.—A special Committee shall be formed for each of the categories enumerated in Article 2, on which the member States shall be represented. These committees shall be entrusted with establishing the basis and scope of co-operation in the form of draft agreements which shall be submitted to the Council for its consideration preparatory to their being submitted to the States referred to.

Delegates representing the other Arab countries may participate in these Committees as members. The Council shall determine the circumstances in which the participation of these representatives shall be allowed as well as the basis of the representation.

Article 5.—The recourse to force for the settlement of disputes between two or more member States shall not be allowed. Should there arise among them a dispute that does not involve the independence of a State, its sovereignty or its territorial integrity, and should the two contending parties apply to the Council for the settlement of this dispute, the decision of the Council shall then be effective and obligatory.

In this case, the States among whom the dispute has arisen shall not participate in the deliberations and decisions of the Council.

The Council shall mediate in a dispute which may lead to war between two member States or between a member State and another State in order to conciliate them.

The decisions relating to arbitration and mediation shall be taken by a majority vote.

Article 6.—In case of aggression or threat of aggression by a State against a member State, the attacked or threatened with attack may request an immediate meeting of the Council.

The Council shall determine the necessary measures to repel this aggression. Its decision shall be taken unanimously. If the aggression is committed by a member State the vote of that State will not be counted in determining unanimity.

If the aggression is committed in such a way as to render the Government of the State attacked unable to communicate with the Council, the representative of that State in the Council may request the Council to convene for the purpose set forth in the preceding paragraph. If the representative is unable to communicate with the Council, it shall be the right of any member State to request a meeting of the Council.

Article 7.—The decisions of the Council taken by a unanimous vote shall be binding on all the member States of the League; those that are reached by a majority vote shall bind only those that accept them.

In both cases the decisions of the Council shall be executed in each State in accordance with the fundamental structure of that State.

Article 8.—Every member State of the League shall respect the form of government obtaining in the other States of the League, and shall recognize the form of government obtaining as one of the rights of those States, and shall pledge itself not to take any action tending to change that form.

Article 9.—The States of the Arab League that are desirous of establishing among themselves closer collaboration and stronger bonds than those provided for in the present Pact, may conclude among themselves whatever agreements they wish for this purpose.

The treaties and agreements already concluded or that may be concluded in the future between a member State and any other State, shall not be binding on the other members.

Article 10.—The permanent seat of the League of Arab States shall be Cairo. The Council of the League may meet at any other place it designates.

Article 11.—The Council of the League shall meet in ordinary session twice a year, during the months of March and October. It shall meet in extraordinary session at the request of two member States whenever the need arises.

Article 12.—The League shall have a permanent General Secretariat composed of a

Secretary-General, Assistant Secretaries and an adequate number of officials.

The Secretary-General shall be appointed by the Council upon the vote of two-thirds of the States of the League. The Assistant Secretaries and the principal officials shall be appointed by the Secretary-General with the approval of the Council.

The Council shall establish an internal organization for the General Secretariat as well as the conditions of service of the officials.

The Secretary-General shall have the rank of Ambassador; and the Assistant Secretaries the rank of Ministers Plenipotentiary.

The first Secretary-General of the League is designated in an annex to the present Pact.

Article 13.—The Secretary-General shall prepare the draft of the budget of the League and submit it for approval to the Council before the beginning of each fiscal year.

The Council shall determine the share of each of the States of the League in the expenses. It shall be allowed to revise the share if necessary.

Article 14.—The members of the Council of the League, the members of its Committees and such of its officials as shall be designated in the internal organization, shall enjoy, in the exercise of their duties, diplomatic privileges and immunities.

The premises occupied by the institutions of the League shall be inviolable.

Article 15.—The Council shall meet the first time at the invitation of the Head of the Egyptian Government. Later meetings shall be convoked by the Secretary-General.

In each ordinary session the representatives of the States of the League shall assume the chairmanship of the Council in rotation.

Article 16.—Except for the cases provided for in the present Pact, a majority shall suffice for decisions by the Council effective in the following matters:

(a) Matters concerning the officials.

(b) The approval of the budget of the League.

(c) The internal organization of the Council, the Committees and the General Secretariat.

(d) The termination of the sessions.

Article 17.—The member States of the League shall file with the General Secretariat copies of all treaties and agreements which they have concluded or will conclude with any other State, whether a member of the League or otherwise.

Article 18.—If one of the member States intends to withdraw from the League, the Council shall be informed of its intention one year before the withdrawal takes effect.

The Council of the League may consider any State that is not fulfilling the obligations resulting from this Pact as excluded from the League, by a decision taken by a unanimous vote of all the States except the State referred to.

Article 19.—The present Pact may be amended with the approval of two-thirds of the members of the League in particular for the purpose of strengthening the ties between them, of creating an Arab Court of Justice, and of regulating the relation of the League with the International organizations that may be created in the future to guarantee security and peace.

No decision shall be taken as regards an amendment except in the session following that in which it is proposed.

Any State that does not approve an amendment may withdraw from the League when the amendment becomes effective, without being bound by the provisions of the preceding article.

Article 20.—The present Pact and its annexes shall be ratified in accordance with the fundamental form of government in each of the contracting States.

The instruments of ratification shall be filed with the General Secretariat and the present Pact shall become binding on the States that ratify in fifteen days after the Secretary-General receives instruments of ratification from four States.

The present Pact has been drawn up in the Arabic language in Cairo and dated 8 Rabi al Thani 1364 (March 22, 1945), in a single text which shall be deposited with the General Secretariat.

A certified copy shall be sent to each of the States of the League.

ANNEX ON PALESTINE

At the end of the last Great War, Palestine, together with the other Arab States, was separated from the Ottoman Empire. She became independent, not belonging to any other State.

The Treaty of Lausanne proclaimed that her fate should be decided by the parties concerned in Palestine.

Even though Palestine was not able to control her own destiny, it was on the basis of the recognition of her independence that the Covenant of the League of Nations determined a system of government for her.

Her existence and her independence among the nations can, therefore, no more be questioned *de jure* than the independence of any of the other Arab States.

Even though the outward signs of this independence have remained veiled as a result of *force majeure*, it is not fitting that this should be an obstacle to the participation of Palestine in the work of the League.

Therefore, the States signatory to the Pact of the Arab League, consider that in view of Palestine's special circumstances, the Council of the League should designate an Arab delegate from Palestine to participate in its work until this country enjoys actual independence.

ANNEX ON CO-OPERATION WITH ARAB COUNTRIES NOT MEMBERS OF THE COUNCIL OF THE LEAGUE

Whereas the member States of the League will have to deal either in the Council or in the Committees with questions affecting the interests of the entire Arab world,

And whereas the Council cannot fail to take account the aspirations of the Arab countries not members of the Council and to work toward their realization,

The States signatory to the Pact of the Arab League strongly urge that the Council of the League should co-operate with them as far as possible in having them participate in the Committees referred to in the Pact, and in other matters should not spare any effort to learn their needs and understand their aspirations and should moreover work for their common weal and the guarantee of their future by whatever political means available.

ANNEX ON THE APPOINTMENT OF SECRETARY-GENERAL OF THE LEAGUE

The States signatory to the present Pact have agreed to appoint Abd Al Rahman Azzam Bey, Secretary-General of the League of Arab States.

His appointment shall be for a term of two years. The Council of the League shall later determine the future organization of the General Secretariat.

G. ARRANGEMENT AMONG THE AFRICAN STATES

CHARTER OF THE ORGANIZATION OF AFRICAN UNITY, DONE AT ADDIS ABABA ON 25 MAY 1963[1]

We, the Heads of African States and Governments assembled in the City of Addis Ababa, Ethiopia;

CONVINCED that it is the inalienable right of all people to control their own destiny;

CONSCIOUS of the fact that freedom, equality, justice and dignity are essential objectives for the achievement of the legitimate aspirations of the African peoples;

CONSCIOUS of our responsibility to harness the natural and human resources of our continent for the total advancement of our peoples in spheres of human endeavour;

INSPIRED by a common determination to promote understanding among our peoples and co-operation among our States in response to the aspirations of our peoples for brotherhood and solidarity, in a larger unity transcending ethnic and national differences;

CONVINCED that, in order to translate this determination into a dynamic force in the cause of human progress, conditions for peace and security must be established and maintained;

DETERMINED to safeguard and consolidate the hard-won independence as well as the sovereignty and territorial integrity of our States, and to fight against neo-colonialism in all its forms;

DEDICATED to the general progress of Africa;

PERSUADED that the Charter of the United Nations and the Universal Declaration of Human Rights, to the principles of which we reaffirm our adherence, provide a solid foundation for peaceful and positive co-operation among states;

DESIROUS that all African States should henceforth unite so that the welfare and well-being of their peoples can be assured;

RESOLVED to reinforce the links between our states by establishing and strengthening common institutions;

HAVE agreed to the present Charter.

---

[1] United Nations *Treaty Series*, vol. 480, 1963, pp. 70-88. In accordance with article XXV, the Charter came into force on 13 September 1963 the instruments of ratification from two thirds of the signatory States having been deposited with the Government of Ethiopia as follows:

Ivory Coast	8 June	1963	Uganda	3 August	1963
Ethiopia	9 June	1963	Rwanda	5 August	1963
Guinea	24 June	1963	Chad	7 August	1963
Senegal	2 July	1963	Madagascar	10 August	1963
Gabon	6 July	1963	Cameroon	26 August	1963
Congo (Brazzaville)	12 July	1963	Mauritania	26 August	1963
Ghana	15 July	1963	Liberia	29 August	1963
Sudan	19 July	1963	Dahomey	7 September	1963
Mali	24 July	1963	Libya	11 September	1963
Niger	26 July	1963	Sierra Leone	11 September	1963
United Arab Republic	27 July	1963	Congo (Leopoldville)	13 September	1963

Subsequently, the Charter entered into force in respect of the following countries on the respective dates of deposit of instruments of ratification as shown below:

Tanganyika	14 September	1963	Upper Volta	29 October	1963
Tunisia	1 October	1963	Nigeria	14 November	1963

Article I

1. The High Contracting Parties do by the present Charter establish an Organization to be known as the *Organization of African Unity*.

2. The Organization shall include the Continental African States, Madagascar and other Islands surrounding Africa.

PURPOSES

Article II

1. The Organization shall have the following purposes:

a. to promote the unity and solidarity of the African States;

b. to coordinate and intensify their co-operation and efforts to achieve a better life for the peoples of Africa;

c. to defend their sovereignty, their territorial integrity and independence;

d. to eradicate all forms of colonialism from Africa; and

e. to promote international co-operation, having due regard to the Charter of the United Nations and the Universal Declaration of Human Rights.

2. To these ends, the Member States shall coordinate and harmonise their general policies, especially in the following fields:

a. political and diplomatic co-operation;

b. economic co-operation, including transport and communications;

c. educational and cultural co-operation;

d. health, sanitation, and nutritional co-operation;

e. scientific and technical co-operation; and

f. co-operation for defence and security.

PRINCIPLES

Article III

The Member States, in pursuit of the purposes stated in Article II, solemnly affirm and declare their adherence to the following principles:

1. the sovereign equality of all Member States;

2. non-interference in the internal affairs of States;

3. respect for the sovereignty and territorial integrity of each State and for its inalienable right to independent existence;

4. peaceful settlement of disputes by negotiation, mediation, conciliation or arbitration;

5. unreserved condemnation, in all its forms, of political assassination as well as of subversive activities on the part of neighbouring States or any other State;

6. absolute dedication to the total emancipation of the African territories which are still dependent;

7. affirmation of a policy of non-alignment with regard to all blocs.

MEMBERSHIP
Article IV

Each independent sovereign African State shall be entitled to become a Member of the Organization.

RIGHTS AND DUTIES OF MEMBER STATES

Article V

All Members States shall enjoy equal rights and have equal duties.

Article VI

The Member States pledge themselves to observe scrupulously the principles enumerated in Article III of the present Charter.

INSTITUTIONS

Article VII

The Organization shall accomplish its purposes through the following principal institutions:

1. the Assembly of Heads of State and Government;
2. the Council of Ministers;
3. the General Secretariat;
4. the Commission of Mediation, Conciliation and Arbitration.

THE ASSEMBLY OF HEADS OF STATE AND GOVERNMENT

Article VIII

The Assembly of Heads of State and Government shall be the supreme organ of the Organization. It shall, subject to the provisions of this Charter, discuss matters of common concern to Africa with a view to co-ordinating and harmonising the general policy of the Organization. It may in addition review the structure, functions and acts of all the organs and any specialized agencies which may be created in accordance with the present Charter.

Article IX

The Assembly shall be composed of the Heads of State and Government or their duly accredited representatives and it shall meet at least once a year. At the request of any Member State and on approval by a two-thirds majority of the Member States, the Assembly shall meet in extraordinary session.

Article X

1. Each Member State shall have one vote.
2. All resolutions shall be determined by a two-thirds majority of the Members of the Organization.
3. Questions of procedure shall require a simple majority. Whether or not a question is one of procedure shall be determined by a simple majority of all Member States of the Organization.
4. Two thirds of the total membership of the Organization shall form a quorum at any meeting of the Assembly.

Article XI

The Assembly shall have the power to determine its own rules of procedure.

THE COUNCIL OF MINISTERS

Article XII

1. The Council of Ministers shall consist of Foreign Ministers or such other Ministers as are designated by the Governments of Member States.

2. The Council of Ministers shall meet at least twice a year. When requested by any Member State and approved by two thirds of all Member States, it shall meet in extraordinary session.

Article XIII

1. The Council of Ministers shall be responsible to the Assembly of Heads of State and Government. It shall be entrusted with the responsibility of preparing conferences of the Assembly.

2. It shall take cognisance of any matter referred to it by the Assembly. It shall be entrusted with the implementation of the decision of the Assembly of Heads of State and Government. It shall coordinate inter-African co-operation in accordance with the instructions of the Assembly and in conformity with Article II (2) of the present Charter.

Article XIV

1. Each Member State shall have one vote.

2. All resolutions shall be determined by a simple majority of the members of the Council of Ministers.

3. Two thirds of the total membership of the Council of Ministers shall form a quorum for any meeting of the Council.

Article XV

The Council shall have the power to determine its own rules of procedure.

GENERAL SECRETARIAT

Article XVI

There shall be an Administrative Secretary-General of the Organization, who shall be appointed by the Assembly of Heads of State and Government. The Administrative Secretary-General shall direct the affairs of the Secretariat.

Article XVII

There shall be one or more Assistant Secretaries-General of the Organization who shall be appointed by the Assembly of Heads of State and Government.

Article XVIII

The functions and conditions of services of the Secretary-General, of the Assistant Secretaries-General and other employees of the Secretariat shall be governed by the provisions of this Charter and the regulations approved by the Assembly of Heads of State and Government.

1. In the performance of their duties the Administrative Secretary-General and the staff shall not seek or receive instructions from any government or from any other authority external to the Organization. They shall refrain from any action which might reflect on their position as international officials responsible only to the Organization.

2. Each member of the Organization undertakes to respect the exclusive character of the responsibilities of the Adminsitrative Secretary-General and the Staff and not to seek to influence them in the discharge of their responsibilities.

COMMISSION OF MEDIATION, CONCILIATION AND ARBITRATION

Article XIX

Member States pledge to settle all disputes among themselves by peaceful means and, to this end decide to establish a Commission of Mediation, Conciliation and Arbitration, the composition of which and conditions of service shall be defined by a separate Protocol to be approved by the Assembly of Heads of State and Government. Said Protocol shall be regarded as forming an integral part of the present Charter.

SPECIALIZED COMMISSIONS

Article XX

The Assembly shall establish such Specialized Commissions as it may deem necessary, including the following;
1. Economic and Social Commission;
2. Educational and Cultural Commission;
3. Health, Sanitation and Nutrition Commission;
4. Defence Commission;
5. Scientific, Technical and Research Commission.

Article XXI

Each Specialized Commission referred to in Article XX shall be composed of the Ministers concerned or other Ministers or Plenipotentiaries designated by the Governments of the Member States.

Article XXII

The functions of the Specialized Commissions shall be carried out in accordance with the provisions of the present Charter and of the regulations approved by the Council of Ministers.

THE BUDGET

Article XXIII

The budget of the Organization prepared by the Administrative Secretary-General shall be approved by the Council of Ministers. The budget shall be provided by contributions from Member States in accordance with the scale of assessment of the United Nations; provided, however, that no Member State shall be assessed an amount exceeding twenty percent of the yearly regular budget of the Organization. The Member States agree to pay their respective contributions regularly.

SIGNATURE AND RATIFICATION OF CHARTER

Article XXIV

1. This Charter shall be open for signature to all independent sovereign African States and shall be ratified by the signatory States in accordance with their respective constitutional processes.

2. The original instrument, done, if possible in African languages, in English, and French, all texts being equally authentic, shall be deposited with the Government of Ethiopia which shall transmit certified copies thereof to all independent sovereign African States.

3. Instruments of ratification shall be deposited with the Government of Ethiopia, which shall notify all signatories of each such deposit.

ENTRY INTO FORCE

Article XXV

This Charter shall enter into force immediately upon receipt by the Government of Ethiopia of the instruments of ratification from two thirds of the signatory States.

REGISTRATION OF THE CHARTER

Article XXVI

This Charter shall, after due ratification, be registered with the Secretariat of the United Nations through the Government of Ethiopia in conformity with Article 102 of the Charter of the United Nations.

INTERPRETATION OF THE CHARTER

Article XXVII

Any question which may arise concerning the interpretation of this Charter shall be decided by a vote of two thirds of the Assembly of Heads of State and Government of the Organization.

ADHESION AND ACCESSION

Article XXVIII

1. Any independent sovereign African State may at any time notify the Administrative Secretary-General of its intention to adhere or accede to this Charter.

2. The Administrative Secretary-General shall, on receipt of such notification communicate a copy of it to all the Member States. Admission shall be decided by a simple majority of the Member States. The decision of each Member State shall be transmitted to the Administrative Secretary-General, who shall upon receipt of the required number of votes, communicate the decision to the State concerned.

MISCELLANEOUS

Article XXIX

The working languages of the Organization and all its institutions shall be, possible African languages, English and French.

Article XXX

The Administrative Secretary-General may accept on behalf of the Organization gifts, bequests and other donations made to the Organization, provided that this is approved by the Council of Ministers.

Article XXXI

The Council of Minsiters shall decide on the privileges and immunities to be accorded to the personnel of the Secretariat in the respective territories of the Member States.

CESSATION OF MEMBERSHIP

Article XXXII

Any State which desires to renounce its membership shall forward a written notification to the Administrative Secretary-General. At the end of one year from the date of such notification, if not withdrawn, the Charter shall cease to apply with respect to the renouncing State, which shall thereby cease to belong to the Organization.

AMENDMENT OF THE CHARTER

Article XXXIII

This Charter may be amended or revised if any Member State makes a written request to the Administrative Secretary-General to that effect; provided, however, that the proposed amendment is not submitted to the Assembly for consideration until all the Member States have been duly notified of it and a period of one year has elapsed. Such an amendment shall not be effective unless approved by at least two thirds of all the Member States.

IN FAITH WHEREOF, We, the Heads of African State and Government, have signed this Charter.

DONE in the City of Addis Ababa, Ethiopia this 25th day of May, 1963

Algeria:
Ahmed BEN-BELLA

Burundi:
p. o. King Mwambutsa
Largio NIMOBUNA

Cameroon:
Ahmadou AHIDJO

Central African Republic:
David DACKO

Chad:
Francois TOMBALBAYE

Congo (Brazzaville):
Fulbert YOULOU

Congo (Leopoldville):
ADOULA

Dahomey:
Hubert MAGA

Ethiopia:
Haile SELASSIE I

Gabon:
Leon M'BA

Ghana:
Kwame NKRUMAH

Guinea:
Sekou TOURE

Ivory Coast:
HOUPHOUET-BOIGNY

Liberia:
William TUBMAN

Libya:
p. o. King Idris I
Hassen BIDA

Madagascar:
p. o. Philibert Tsiranana
M. SYLLA

Mali:
  Modibo KEITA

Mauritania:
  Moktar Ould DADDAH

Morocco:*
  p. o. King Hassan II
  Mehdi Mrani ZENTAR (September 19, 1963)

Niger:
  Diori HAMANI

Nigeria:
  Tafawa BALEWA

Rwanda:
  p. o. Kaibayenda HABEMENSHI

Senegal:
  p. o. Leopold Sedar Senghor
  Doudou THIAM

Sierra Leone:
  Milton MARGAI

Somalia:
  Aden Abdulla OSMAN

Sudan:
  Ibrahim ABOUD

Tanganyika:
  Julius K. NYERERE

Togo:

Tunisia:
  Habib BOURGUIBA

Uganda:
  Apollo Milton OBOTE

United Arab Republic:
  Gamal Abdel NASSER

Upper Volta:
  Maurice YAMEOGO

---

*With the following declaration:

The Government of His Majesty the King of Morocco has just signed the Charter of the Organization of African Unity, pursuant to article XXIV paragraph 1, of the Charter and in accordance with the statement made by the accrediting representative of Morocco to the Summit Conference at the closing plenary meeting to the effect that the Moroccan delegation had no power to sign the Charter at that time but reserved the right to do so as soon as possible and as an original initiator of the Charter having taken effective part in all the work of the Conference.

By this signature the Government of His Majesty records once again its dedication to the cause of African Unity written into its Constitution and to peaceful and fraternal co-operation between the peoples of Africa in every sphere, for the achievement of their objectives and aspirations and of greater African solidarity.

Nevertheless, by thus subscribing to all the objectives and to all the principles of the Charter of the Organization – principles for which it has always worked with faith and determination – the Government of His Majesty in no way renounces its legitimate rights with regard to the peaceful achievement and safeguarding of the territorial integrity of the Kingdom within its authentic frontiers.

687

VIII. IMPORTANT RESOLUTIONS ADOPTED BY THE GENERAL ASSEMBLY

A. THE UNITED NATIONS

1. OFFICIAL SEAL AND EMBLEM OF THE UNITED NATIONS[1]

The General Assembly,

1. *Recognizes* that it is desirable to approve a distinctive emblem of the United Nations and to authorize its use for the official seal of the Organization;

Resolves therefore that the design reproduced below shall be the emblem and distinctive sign of the United Nations and shall be used for the official seal of the Organization.

2. *Considers* that it is necessary to protect the name of the Organization and its distinctive emblem and official seal;

Recommends therefore:

(a) That Members of the United Nations should take such legislative or other appropriate measures as are necessary to prevent the use, without authorization by the Secretary-General of the United Nations, and in particular for commercial purposes by means of trade marks or commercial labels, of the emblem, the official seal and the name of the United Nations, and of abbreviations of that name through the use of its initial letters;

(b) That the prohibition should take effect as soon as practicable but in any event not later than the expiration of two years from the adoption of this resolution by the General Assembly;

(c) That each Member of the United Nations, pending the putting into effect within its territory of any such prohibition should use its best endeavours to prevent any use, without authorization by the Secretary-General of the United Nations, of the emblem, name, or initials of the United Nations, and in particular for commercial purposes by means of trade marks or commercial labels.

Fiftieth plenary meeting,
7 December 1946.

2. UNITED NATIONS FLAG[1]

The General Assembly

Recognizes that it is desirable to adopt a distinctive flag of the United Nations and to authorize its use and, therefore,

Resolves that the flag of the United Nations shall be the official emblem adopted by the General Assembly under the terms of its resolution 92 (I) of 7 December 1946,[2] centred on a light blue ground;

Directs the Secretary-General to draw up regulations concerning the dimensions and proportions of the flag;

---

[1] Official Records of the General Assembly, First Session, part II, pp. 185-186.
[1] Official Records of the General Assembly, Second Session, p. 91.
[2] *Resolutions adopted by the General Assembly* during the second part of its first session, pages 185-186.

Authorizes the Secretary-General to adopt a flag code, ι. ving in mind the desirability of a regulated use of the flag and the protection of its dignity

Ninety-sixth plenary meeting,
20 October 1947.

3. UNITED NATIONS DAY[1]

The General Assembly

Declares that 24 October, the anniversary of the coming into force of the Charter of the United Nations, shall henceforth be officially called "United Nations Day" and shall be devoted to making known to the peoples of the world the aims and achievements of the United Nations and to gaining their support for the work of the United Nations;

Invites Member Governments to co-operate with the United Nations in securing observance of this anniversary.

Hundred and first plenary meeting,
31 October 1947.

B. INTERNATIONAL LAW

UNITED NATIONS PROGRAMME OF ASSISTANCE IN THE TEACHING, STUDY, DISSEMINATION AND WIDER APPRECIATION OF INTERNATIONAL LAW[2]

The General Assembly,

Noting with appreciation the report of the Secretary-General on the implementation of the United Nations Programme of Assistance in the Teaching, Study, Dissemination and Wider Appreciation of International Law[3] and the recommendations made to the Secretary-General by the Advisory Committee on the United Nations Programme of Assistance in the Teaching, Study, Dissemination and Wider Appreciation of International Law, which are contained in that report,

Considering that international law should occupy an appropriate place in the teaching of legal disciplines at all universities,

Noting with appreciation the efforts made by States at the bilateral level to provide assistance in the teaching and study of international law,

---

[1] Official Records of the General Assembly, Second Session, p. 91.
[2] Official Records of the General Assembly, Thirtieth Session, Supplement No. 34 (A/10034), pp. 134-135.
[3] A/10332.

Convinced nevertheless that States, international organizations and institutions should be encouraged to give further support to the Programme and to increase their activities to promote the teaching, study, dissemination and wider appreciation of international law, in particular those activities which are of special benefit to persons from developing countries,

Recalling that, in the conduct of the Programme, it is desirable to use as far as possible the resources and facilities made available by Member States, international organizations and others,

1. *Authorizes* the Secretary-General to carry out in 1976 and 1977 the activities specified in his report, including the provision of:

(a) A minimum of 15 fellowships in 1976 and 1977 at the request of Governments of developing countries;

(b) Assistance in the form of a travel grant for one participant from each developing country invited to the regional activities to be organized in 1976 and 1977;
to be financed from budgetary provisions in the regular budget plus voluntary financial contributions which would be received as a result of the requests set out in paragraphs 7 and 8 below;

2. *Expresses its appreciation* to the Secretary-General for his constructive efforts to promote training and assistance in international law within the framework of the United Nations Programme of Assistance in the Teaching, Study, Dissemination and Wider Appreciation of International Law in 1974 and 1975;

3. *Expresses its appreciation* to the United Nations Educational, Scientific and Cultural Organization for its participation in the Programme, in particular for the efforts made to support the teaching of international law;

4. *Expresses its appreciation* to the United Nations Institute for Training and Research for its participation in the Programme, particularly in the organization of regional meetings and in the conduct of the fellowship programme in international law sponsored jointly by the United Nations and the Institute;

5. *Expresses its appreciation* to the Governments of Sierra Leone and Zaire for providing host facilities for the regional training and refresher courses held in 1975;

6. *Urges* all Governments to encourage the inclusion of courses on international law in the programmes of legal studies offered at institutions of higher learning;

7. *Requests* the Secretary-General to continue to publicize the Programme by periodically inviting Member States, universities, philanthropic foundations and other interested national and international institutions and organizations, as well as individuals, to make voluntary contributions towards the financing of the Programme or otherwise towards assisting in its implementation and possible expansion;

8. *Reiterates* its request to Member States and to interested organizations and individuals to make voluntary contributions towards the financing of the Programme and expresses its appreciation to those Member States which have made voluntary contributions for this purpose;

9. *Decides* to appoint the following thirteen Member States as members of the Advisory Committee on the United Nations Programme of Assistance in the Teaching, Study, Dissemination and Wider Appreciation of International Law, for a period of four years beginning on 1 January 1976: Barbados, Cyprus, El Salvador, France, Ghana, Hungary, Italy, Mali, Syrian Arab Republic, Union of Soviet Socialist Republics, United Kingdom of Great Britain and Northern Ireland, United Republic of Tanzania and United States of America;

10. *Requests* the Secretary-General to report to the General Assembly at its thirtieth session on the implementation of the Programme during 1974 and 1975 and, following consultations with the Advisory Committee, to submit recommendations regarding the execution of the Programme in subsequent years;

11. *Decides* to include in the provisional agenda of its thirtieth session an item entitled "United Nations Programme of Assistance in the Teaching, Study, Dissemination and Wider Appreciation of International Law."

2441st plenary meeting
15 December 1975

C. HUMAN RIGHTS

1. INTERNATIONAL BILL OF HUMAN RIGHTS[1]

A

UNIVERSAL DECLARATION OF HUMAN RIGHTS

PREAMBLE

Whereas recognition of the inherent dignity and of the equal and inalienable rights of all members of the human family is the foundation of freedom, justice and peace in the world,

Whereas disregard and contempt for human rights have resulted in barbarous acts which have outraged the conscience of mankind, and the advent of a world in which human beings shall enjoy freedom of speech and belief and freedom from fear and want has been proclaimed as the highest aspiration of the common people,

Whereas it is essential, if man is not to be compelled to have recourse, as a last resort, to rebellion against tyranny and oppression, that human rights should be protected by the rule of law,

Whereas it is essential to promote the development of friendly relations between nations,

Whereas the peoples of the United Nations have in the Charter reaffirmed their faith in fundamental human rights, in the dignity and worth of the human person and in the equal rights of men and women and have determined to promote social progress and better standards of life in larger freedom,

Whereas Member States have pledge themselves to achieve, in co-operation with the United Nations, the promotion of universal respect for and observance of human rights and fundamental freedoms,

Whereas a common understanding of these rights and freedoms is of the greatest importance for the full realization of this pledge,

Now, therefore,

The General Assembly

Proclaims this Universal Declaration of Human Rights as a common standard of achievement for all peoples and all nations, to the end that every individual and every organ of society, keeping this Declaration constantly in mind, shall strive by teaching and education to promote respect for these rights and freedoms and by progressive measures, national and international, to secure their universal and effective recognition and observance, both among the peoples of Member States themselves and among the peoples of territories under their jurisdiction.

---

[1] Official Records of the General Assembly, Third Session, Part I, pp. 71-79.

ARTICLE 1

All human beings are born free and equal in dignity and rights. They are endowed with reason and conscience and should act towards one another in a spirit of brotherhood.

ARTICLE 2

Everyone is entitled to all the rights and freedoms set forth in this Declaration, without disctinction of any kind, such as race, colour, sex, language, religion, political or other opinion, national or social origin, property, birth or other status.

Furthermore, no distinction shall be made on the basis of the political, jurisdictional or international status of the country or territory to which a person belongs, whether it be independent, trust, non-self-governing or under any other limitation of sovereignty.

ARTICLE 3

Everyone has the right to life, liberty and the security of person.

ARTICLE 4

No one shall be held in slavery or servitude; slavery and the slave trade shall be prohibited in all their forms.

ARTICLE 5

No one shall be subjected to torture or to cruel, inhuman or degrading treatment or punishment.

ARTICLE 6

Everyone has the right to recognition everywhere as a person before the law.

ARTICLE 7

All are equal before the law and are entitled without any discrimination to equal protection of the law. All are entitled to equal protection against any discrimination in violation of this declaration and against any incitement to such discrimination.

ARTICLE 8

Everyone has the right to an effective remedy by the competent national tribunals for acts violating the fundamental rights granted him by the constitution or by law.

ARTICLE 9

No one shall be subject to arbitrary arrest, detention or exile.

ARTICLE 10

Everyone is entitled in full equality to a fair and public hearing by an independent and impartial tribunal, in the determination of his rights and obligations and of any criminal charge against him.

ARTICLE 11

1. Everyone charged with a penal offence has the right to be presumed innocent until proved guilty according to law in a public trial at which he has had all the guarantees necessary for his defence.

2. No one shall be held guilty of any penal offence on account of any act or omission which did not constitute a penal offence, under national or international law, at the time when it was committed. Nor shall a heavier penalty be imposed than the one that was applicable at the time the penal offence was committed.

ARTICLE 12

No one shall be subjected to arbitrary interference with his privacy, family, home or correspondence, nor to attacks upon his honour and reputation. Everyone has the right to the protection of the law against such interference or attacks.

ARTICLE 13

1. Everyone has the right to freedom of movement and residence within the borders of each State.
2. Everyone has the right to leave any country, including his own, and to return to his country.

ARTICLE 14

1. Everyone has the right to seek and to enjoy in other countries asylum from persecution.
2. This right may not be involved in the case of prosecutions genuinely arising from non-political crimes or from acts contrary to the purposes and principles of the United Nations.

ARTICLE 15

1. Everyone has the right to a nationality.
2. No one shall be arbitrarily deprived of his nationality nor denied the right to change his nationality.

ARTICLE 16

1. Men and women of full age, without any limitation due to race, nationality or religion, have the right to marry and to found a family. They are entitled to equal rights as to marriage, during marriage and at its dissolution.
2. Marriage shall be entered into only with the free and full consent of the intending spouses.
3. The family is the natural and fundamental group unit of society and is entitled to protection by society and the State.

ARTICLE 17

1. Everyone has the right to own property alone as well as in association with others.
2. No one shall be arbitrarily deprived of his property.

ARTICLE 18

Everyone has the right to freedom of thought, conscience and religion; this right includes freedom to change his religion or belief, and freedom, either alone or in community with others and in public or private, to manifest his religion or belief in teaching, practice, worship and observance.

ARTICLE 19

Everyone has the right to freedom of opinion and expression; this right includes freedom to hold opinions without interference and to seek, receive and impart information and ideas through any media and regardless of frontiers.

ARTICLE 20

1. Everyone has the right to freedom of peaceful assembly and association.
2. No one may be compelled to belong to an association.

ARTICLE 21

1. Everyone has the right to take part in the government of his country, directly or through freely chosen representatives.
2. Everyone has the right of equal access to public service in his country.
3. The will of the people shall be the basis of the authority of government; this will shall be expressed in periodic and genuine elections which shall be by universal and equal suffrage and shall be held by secret vote or by equivalent free voting procedures.

ARTICLE 22

Everyone, as a member of society, has the right to social security and is entitled to realization, through national effort and international co-operation and in accordance with the organization and resources of each State, of the economic, social and cultural rights indispensable for his dignity and the free development of his personality.

ARTICLE 23

1. Everyone has the right to work, to free choice of employment, to just and favourable conditions of work and to protection against unemployment.
2. Everyone, without any discrimination, has a right to equal pay for equal work.
3. Everyone who works has the right to just and favourable remuneration ensuring for himself and his family an existence worthy of human dignity, and supplemented, if necessary, by other means of social protection.
4. Everyone has the right to form and to join trade unions for the protection of his interests.

ARTICLE 24

Everyone has the right to rest and leisure, including reasonable limitation of working hours and periodic holidays with pay.

ARTICLE 25

1. Everyone has the right to a standard of living adequate for the health and well-being of himself and of his family, including food, clothing, housing and medical care and necessary social services, and the right to security in the event of unemployment, sickness, disability, widowhood, old age or other lack of livelihood in circumstances beyond his control.
2. Motherhood and childhood are entitled to special care and assistance. All children, whether born in or out of wedlock, shall enjoy the same social protection.

ARTICLE 26

1. Everyone has the right to education. Education shall be free, at least in the elementary and fundamental stages. Elementary education shall be compulsory. Technical and professional education shall be made generally available and higher education shall be equally accessible to all on the basis of merit.

2. Education shall be directed to the full development of the human personality and to the strengthening of respect for human rights and fundamental freedoms. It shall promote understanding, tolerance and friendship among all nations, racial or religious groups, and shall further the activities of the United Nations for the maintenance of peace.

3. Parents have a prior right to choose the kind of education that shall be given to their children.

ARTICLE 27

1. Everyone has the right freely to participate in the cultural life of the community, to enjoy the arts and to share in scientific advancement and its benefits.

2. Everyone has the right to the protection of the moral and material interests resulting from any scientific, literary or artistic production of which he is the author.

ARTICLE 28

Everyone is entitled to a social and international order in which the rights and freedoms set forth in this Declaration can be fully realized.

ARTICLE 29

1. Everyone has duties to the community in which alone the free and full development of his personality is possible.

2. In the exercise of his rights and freedoms, everyone shall be subject only to such limitations as are determined by law solely for the purpose of security, due recognition and respect for the rights and freedoms of others and of meeting the just requirements of morality, public order and the general welfare in a democratic society.

3. These rights and freedoms may in no case be exercised contrary to the purposes and principles of the United Nations.

ARTICLE 30

Nothing in this Declaration may be interpreted as implying for any State, group or person any right to engage in any activity or to perform any act aimed at the destruction of any of the rights and freedoms set forth herein.

Hundred and eighty-third plenary meeting.
10 December 1948.

B

RIGHT OF PETITION

The General Assembly,

Considering that the right of petition is an essential human right, as is recognized in the Constitutions of a great number of countries,

Having considered the draft article on petitions in document A/C.3/306 and the amendments offered thereto by Cuba and France,

Decides not to take any action on this matter at the present session;

Requests the Economic and Social Council to ask the Commission on Human Rights to give further examination to the problem of petitions when studying the draft covenant on human rights and measures of implementation, in order to enable the General Assembly to consider what further action, if any, should be taken at its next regular session regarding the problem of petitions.

Hundred and eighty-third plenary meeting.
10 December 1948.

C

FATE OF MINORITIES

The General Assembly,

Considering that the United Nations cannot remain indifferent to the fate of minorities,

Considering that it is difficult to adopt a uniform solution of this complex and delicate problem which has special aspects in each State in which it arises,

Considering the universal character of the Declaration of Human Rights,

Decides not to deal in a specific provision with the question of minorities in the text of this Declaration;

Refers to the Economic and Social Council the texts submitted by the delegations of the Union of Soviet Socialist Republics, Yugoslavia and Denmark on this subject contained in document A/C.3/307/Rev. 2, and requests the Council to ask the Commission on Human Rights and the Sub-Commission on the Prevention of Discrimination and the Protection of Minorities to make a thorough study of the problem of minorities, in order that the United Nations may be able to take effective measures for the protection of racial, national, religious or linguistic minorities.

Hundred and eighty-third plenary meeting.
10 December 1948.

D

PUBLICITY TO BE GIVEN TO THE UNIVERSAL DECLARATION OF HUMAN RIGHTS

The General Assembly,

Considering that the adoption of the Universal Declaration of Human Rights is an historic act, destined to consolidate world peace through the contribution of the United Nations towards the liberation of individuals from the unjustified oppression and constraint to which they are too often subjected,

Considering that the text of the Declaration should be disseminated among all peoples throughout the world,

1. *Recommends* Governments of Member States to show their adherence to Article 56 of the Charter by using every means within their power solemnly to publicize the text of the Declaration and to cause it to be disseminated, displayed, read and expounded principally in schools and other educational institutions, without distinction based on the political status of countries or territories;

2. *Requests* the Secretary-General to have this Declaration widely disseminated and, to that end, to publish and distribute texts, not only in the official languages, but also, using every means at his disposal, in all languages possible;

3. *Invites* the specialized agencies and non-governmental organizations of the world to do their utmost to bring this Declaration to the attention of their members.

Hundred and eighty-third plenary meeting.
10 December 1948.

PREPARATION OF A DRAFT COVENANT ON HUMAN RIGHTS AND DRAFT MEASURES OF IMPLEMENTATION

The General Assembly,

Considering that the plan of work of the Commission on Human Rights provides for an International Bill of Human Rights, to include a Declaration, a Covenant on Human Rights and measures of implementation.

Requests the Economic and Social Council to ask the Commission on Human Rights to continue to give priority in its work to the preparation of a draft Covenant on Human Rights and draft measures of implementation.

Hundred and eighty-third plenary meeting.
10 December 1948.

2. INTERNATIONAL COVENANT ON ECONOMIC, SOCIAL AND CULTURAL RIGHTS[1]

A

The General Assembly,

Considering that one of the purposes of the United Nations, as stated in Articles 1 and 55 of the Charter, is to promote universal respect for, and observance of, human rights and fundamental freedoms for all without distinction as to race, sex, language or religion,

Considering that in Article 56 of the Charter all Members of the United Nations have pledged themselves to take joint and separate action in co-operation with the Organization for the achievement of that purpose,

Recalling the proclamation by the General Assembly on 10 December 1948 of the Universal Declaration of Human Rights as a common standard of achievement for all peoples and all nations,

Having considered since its ninth session the draft International Covenants on Human Rights prepared by the Commission on Human Rights and transmitted to it by Economic and Social Council resolution 545 B (XVIII) of 29 July 1954, and having completed the elaboration of the Covenants at its twenty-first session,

1. *Adopts* and opens for signature, ratification and accession the following international instruments:

   (a) The International Covenant on Economic, Social and Cultural Rights;

   (b) The International Covenant on Civil and Political Rights;

   (c) The Optional Protocol to the International Covenant on Civil and Political Rights;

2. *Expresses the hope* that the Covenants and the Optional Protocol will be signed and ratified or acceded to without delay and come into force at an early date;

3. *Requests* the Secretary-General to submit to the General Assembly at its future sessions reports concerning the state of ratifications of the Covenants and of the Optional Protocol which the Assembly will consider as a separate agenda item.

1496th plenary meeting,
16 December 1966.

---

[1] Official Records of the General Assembly, Twenty-first Session, Supplement No. 16, pp. 49-52.

The States Parties to the present Covenant,

Considering that, in accordance with the principles proclaimed in the Charter of the United Nations, recognition of the inherent dignity and of the equal and inalienable rights of all members of the human family is the foundation of freedom, justice and peace in the world,

Recognizing that these rights derive from the inherent dignity of the human person,

Recognizing that, in accordance with the Universal Declaration of Human Rights, the ideal of free human beings enjoying freedom from fear and want can only be achieved if conditions are created whereby everyone may enjoy his economic, social and cultural rights, as well as his civil and political rights,

Considering the obligation of States under the Charter of the United Nations to promote universal respect or, and observance of, human rights and freedoms,

Realizing that the individual, having duties to other individuals and to the community to which he belongs, is under a responsibility to strive for the promotion and observance of the rights recognized in the present Covenant,

Agree upon the following articles:

PART I

Article 1

1. All peoples have the right of self-determination. By virtue of that right they freely determine their political status and freely pursue their economic, social and cultural development.

2. All peoples may, for their own ends, freely dispose of their natural wealth and resources without prejudice to any obligations arising out of international economic co-operation, based upon the principle of mutual benefit, and international law. In no case may a people be deprived of its own means of subsistence.

3. The States Parties to the present Covenant, including those having responsibility for the administration of Non-Self-Governing and Trust Territories, shall promote the realization of the right of self-determination, and shall respect that right, in conformity with the provisions of the Charter of the United Nations.

PART II

Article 2

1. Each State Party to the present Covenant undertakes to take steps, individually and through International assistance and co-operation, especially economic and technical, to the maximum of its available resources, with a view to achieving progressively the full realization of the rights recognized in the present Covenant by all appropriate means, including particularly the adoption of legislative measures.

2. The States Parties to the present Covenant undertake to guarantee that the rights enunciated in the present Covenant will be exercised without discrimination of any kind as to race, colour, sex, language, religion, political or other opinion, national or social origin, property, birth or other status.

3. Developing countries, with due regard to human rights and their national economy, may determine to what extent they would guarantee the economic rights recognized in the present Covenant to non-nationals.

Article 3

The States Parties to the present Covenant undertake to ensure the equal right of men and women to the enjoyment of all economic, social and cultural rights set forth in the present Covenant.

Article 4

The States Parties to the present Covenant recognize that, in the enjoyment of those rights provided by the State in conformity with the present Covenant, the State may subject such rights only to such limitations as are determined by law only in so far as this may be compatible with the nature of these rights and solely for the purpose of promoting the general welfare in a democratic society.

Article 5

1. Nothing in the present Covenant may be interpreted as implying for any State, group or person any right to engage in any activity or to perform any act aimed at the destruction of any of the rights or freedoms recognized herein, or at their limitation to a greater extent than is provided for in the present Covenant.

2. No restriction upon or derogation from any of the fundamental human rights recognized or existing in any country in virtue of law, conventions, regualtions or custom shall be admitted on the pretext that the present Covenant does not recognize such rights or that it recognizes them to a lesser extent.

PART III

Article 6

1. The States Parties to the present Covenant recognize the right to work, which includes the right of everyone to the opportunity to gain his living by work which he freely chooses or accepts, and will take appropraite steps to safeguard this right.

2. The steps to be taken by a State Party to the present Covenant to achieve the full realization of this right shall include technical and vocational guidance and training programmes, policies and techniques to achieve steady economic, social and cultural development and full and productive employment under conditions safeguarding fundamental political economic freedoms to the individual.

Article 7

The States Parties to the present Covenant recognize the right of everyone to the enjoyment of just favourable conditions of work which ensure, in particular:

(a) Remuneration which provides all workers, as a minimum, with:
(i) Fair wages and equal remuneration for work of equal value without distinction of any kind, in particular women being guaranteed conditions of work not inferior to those enjoyed by men, with equal pay for equal work;
(ii) A decent living for themselves and their families in accordance with the provisions of the present Covenant;
(b) Safe and healthy working conditions;
(c) Equal opportunity for everyone to be promoted in his employment to an appropriate higher level, subject to no considerations other than those of seniority and competence;
(d) Rest, leisure and reasonable limitation of working hours and periodic holidays with pay, as well as remuneration for public holidays.

Article 8

1. The States Parties to the present Covenant undertake to ensure:

(a) The right of everyone to form trade unions and join the trade union of his choice, subject only to the rules of the organization concerned, for the promotion and protection of his economic and social interests. No restrictions may be placed on the exercise of this right other than those prescribed by law and which are necessary in a democratic society in the interests of national security or public order or for the protection of the rights and freedoms of others;

(b) The right of trade unions to establish national federations or confederations and the right of the latter to form or join international trade-union organizations;

(c) The right of trade unions to function freely subject to no limitations other than those prescribed by law and which are necessary in a democratic society in the interests of national security or public order or for the protection of the rights and freedoms of others;

(d) The right to strike, provided that it is exercised in conformity with the laws of the particular country.

2. This article shall not prevent the imposition of lawful restrictions on the exercise of these rights by members of the armed forces or of the police or of the administration of the State.

3. Nothing in this article shall authorize States Parties to the International Labour Organisation Convention of 1948 concerning Freedom of Association and Protection of the Right to Organize to take legislative measures which would prejudice, or apply the law in such a manner as would prejudice, the guarantees provided for in that Convention.

Article 9

The States Parties to the present Covenant recognize the right of everyone to social security, including social insurance.

Article 10

The States Parties to the present Covenant recognize that:

1. The widest possible protection and assistance should be accorded to the family, which is the natural and fundamental group unit of society, particularly for its establishment and while it is responsible for the care and education of dependent children. Marriage must be entered into with the free consent of the intending spouses.

2. Special protection should be accorded to mothers during a reasonable period before and after childbirth. During such period working mothers should be accorded paid leave or leave with adequate social security benefits.

3. Special measures of protection and assistance should be taken on behalf of all children and young persons without any discrimination for reasons of parentage or other conditions. Children and young persons should be protected from economic and social exploitation. Their employment in work harmful to their morals or health or dangerous to life or likely to hamper their normal development should be punishable by law. States should also set age limits below which the paid employment of child labour should be prohibited and punishable by law.

Article 11

1. The States Parties to the present Covenant recognize the right of everyone to an adequate standard of living for himself and his family, including adequate food, clothing and housing, and to the continuous improvement of living conditions. The States Parties will take appropriate steps to ensure the realization of this right, recognizing to this effect the essential importance of international co-operation based on free consent.

2. The States Parties to the present Covenant, recognizing the fundamental right of everyone to be free from hunger, shall take, individually and through international co-operation, the measures, including specific programmes, which are needed:

(a) To improve methods of production, conservation and distribution of food by making full use of technical and scientific knowledge, by disseminating knowledge of the principles of nutrition and by developing or reforming agrarian systems in such a way as to achieve the most efficient development and utilization of natural resources;

(b) Taking into account the problems of both food-importing and food-exporting countries, to ensure an equitable distribution of world food supplies in relation to need.

Article 12

1. The States Parties to the present Covenant recognize the right of everyone to the enjoyment of the highest attainable standard of physical and mental health.

2. The steps to be taken by the States Parties to the present Covenant to achieve the full realization of this right shall include those necessary for:

(a) The provision for the reduction of the stillbirth-rate and of infant mortality and for the healthy development of the child;

(b) The improvement of all aspects of environmental and industrial hygiene;

(c) The prevention, treatment and control of epidemic, endemic, occupational and other diseases;

(d) The creation of conditions which would assure to all medical service and medical attention in the event of sickness.

Article 13

1. The States Parties to the present Covenant recognize the right of everyone to education. They agree that education shall be directed to the full development of the human personality and the sense of its dignity, and shall strengthen the respect for human rights and fundamental freedoms. They further agree that education shall enable all persons to participate effectively in a free society, promote understanding, tolerance and friendship among all nations and all racial, ethnic or religious groups, and further the activities of the United Nations for the maintenance of peace.

2. The States Parties to the present Covenant recognize that, with a view to achieving the full realization of this right:

(a) Primary education shall be compulsory and available free to all;

(b) Secondary education in its different forms, including technical and vocational secondary education, shall be made generally available and accessible to all by every appropriate means, and in particular by the progressive introduction of free education;

(c) Higher education shall be made equally accessible to all, on the basis of capacity, by every appropriate means, and in particular by the progressive introduction of free education;

(d) Fundamental education shall be encouraged or intensified as far as possible for those persons who have not received or completed the whole period of their primary education;

(e) The development of a system of schools at all levels shall be actively pursued, an adequate fellowship system shall be established, and the material conditions of teaching staff shall be continously improved.

3. The States Parties to the present Covenant undertake to have respect for the liberty of parents and, when applicable, legal guardians to choose for their children schools, other than those established by the public authorities, which conform to such minimum educational standards as may be laid down or approved by the State and to ensure the religious and moral education of their children in conformity with their own convictions.

4. No part of this article shall be construed so as to interfere with the liberty of individuals and bodies to establish and direct educational institutions, subject always to the observance of the principles set forth in paragraph 1 of this article and to the requirement that the education given in such institutions shall conform to such minimum standards as may be laid down by the State.

Article 14

Each State Party to the present Covenant which, at the time of becoming a Party, has not been able to secure in its metropolitan territory or other territories under its jurisdiction compulsory primary education, free of charge, undertakes, within two years, to work out and adopt a detailed plan of action for the progressive implementation, within a reasonable number of years, to be fixed in the plan, of the principle of compulsory education free of charge for all.

Article 15

1. The States Parties to the present Covenant recognize the right of everyone:
(a) To take part in cultural life;
(b) To enjoy the benefits of scientific progress and its applications;
(c) To benefit from the protection of the moral and material interests resulting from any scientific, literary or artistic production of which he is the author.

2. The steps to be taken by the States Parties to the present Covenant to achieve the full realization of this right shall include those necessary for the conservation, the development and the diffusion of science and culture.

3. The States Parties to the present Covenant undertake to respect the freedom indispensable for scientific research and creative activity.

4. The States Parties to the present Covenant recognize the benefits to be derived from the encouragement and development of international contacts and co-operation in the scientific and cultural fields.

PART IV

Article 16

1. The States Parties to the present Covenant undertake to submit in conformity with this part of the Covenant reports on the measures which they have adopted and the progress made in achieving the observance of the rights recognized herein.

2. *(a)* All reports shall be submitted to the Secretary-General of the United Nations, who shall transmit copies to the Economic and Social Council for consideration in accordance with the provisions of the present Covenant;
(b) The Secretary-General of the United Nations shall also transmit to the specialized agencies copies of the reports, or any relevant parts therefrom, from States Parties to the present Covenant which are also members of these specialized agencies in so far as these reports, or parts therefrom, relate to any matters which fall within the responsibilities of the said agencies in accordance with their constitutional instruments.

Article 17

1. The States Parties to the present Covenant shall furnish their reports in stages, in accordance with a programme to be established by the Economic and Social Council within one year of the entry into force of the present Covenant after consultation with the States Parties and the specialized agencies concerned.

2. Reports may indicate factors and difficulties affecting the degree of fulfilment of obligations under the present Covenant.

3. Where relevant information has previously been furnished to the United Nations or to any specialized agency by any State Party to the present Covenant, it will not be necessary to reproduce that information, but a precise reference to the information so furnished will suffice.

Article 18

Pursuant to its responsibilities under the Charter of the United Nations in the field of human rights and fundamental freedoms, the Economic and Social Council may make arrangements with the specialized agencies in respect of their reporting to it on the progress made in achieving the observance of the provisions of the present Covenant falling within the scope of their activities. These reports may include particulars of decisions and recommendations on such implementation adopted by their competent organs.

Article 19

The Economic and Social Council may transmit to the Commission on Human Rights for study and general recommendation or, as appropriate, for information the reports concerning human rights submitted by States in accordance with articles 16 and 17, and those concerning human rights submitted by the specialized agencies in accordance with article 18.

Article 20

The States Parties to the present Covenant and the specialized agencies concerned may submit comments to the Economic and Social Council on any general recommendation under article 19 or reference to such general recommendation in any report of the Commission on Human Rights or any documentation referred to therein.

Article 21

The Economic and Social Council may submit from time to time to the General Assembly reports with recommendations of a general nature and a summary of the information received from the States Parties to the present Covenant and the specialized agencies on the measures taken and the progress made in achieving general observance of the rights recognized in the present Covenant.

Article 22

The Economic and Social Council may bring to the attention of other organs of the United Nations, their subsidiary organs and specialized agencies concerned with furnishing technical assistance any matters arising out of the reports referred to in this part of the present Covenant which may assist such bodies in deciding, each within its field of competence, on the advisability of international measures likely to contribute to the effective progressive implementation of the present Covenant.

Article 23

The States Parties to the present Covenant agree that international action for the achievement of the rights recognized in the present Covenant includes such methods as the conclusion of conventions, the adoption of recommendations, the furnishing of technical assistance and the holding of regional meetings and technical meetings for the purpose of consultation and study organized in conjunction with the Governments concerned.

Article 24

Nothing in the present Covenant shall be interpreted as impairing the provisions of the Charter of the United Nations and of the constitutions of the specialized agencies which define the respective responsibilities of the various organs of the United Nations and of the specialized agencies in regard to the matters dealt with in the present Covenant.

Article 25

Nothing in the present Covenant shall be interpreted as impairing the inherent right of all peoples to enjoy and utilize fully and freely their natural wealth and resources.

PART V

Article 26

1. The present Covenant is open for signature by any State Member of the United Nations or member of any of its specialized agencies, by any State Party to the Statute of the International Court of Justice, and by any other State which has been invited by the General Assembly of the United Nations to become a party to the present Covenant.

2. The present Covenant is subject to ratification. Instruments of ratification shall be deposited with the Secretary-General of the United Nations.

3. The present Covenant shall be open to accession by any State referred to in paragraph 1 of this article.

4. Accession shall be effected by the deposit of an instrument of accession with the Secretary-General of the United Nations.

5. The Secretary-General of the United Nations shall inform all States which have signed the present Covenant or acceded to it of the deposit of each instrument of ratification or accession.

Article 27

1. The present Covenant shall enter into force three months after the date of the deposit with the Secretary-General of the United Nations of the thirty-fifth instrument of ratification or instrument of accession.

2. For each State ratifying the present Covenant or acceding to it after the deposit of the thirty-fifth instrument of ratification or instrument of accession, the present Covenant shall enter into force three months after the date of the deposit of its own instrument of ratification or instrument of accession.

Article 28

The provisions of the present Covenant shall extend to all parts of federal States without any limitations or exceptions.

Article 29

1. Any State Party to the present Covenant may propose an amendment and file it with the Secretary-General of the United Nations. The Secretary-General shall thereupon communicate any proposed amendments to the States Parties to the present Covenant with a request that they notify him whether they favour a conference of States Parties for the purpose of considering and voting upon the proposals. In the event that at least one third of the States Parties favours such a conference, the Secretary-General shall convene the conference under the auspices of the United Nations. Any amendment adopted by a majority of the States Parties present and voting at the conference shall be submitted to the General Assembly of the United Nations for approval.

2. Amendments shall come into force when they have been approved by the General Assembly of the United Nations and accepted by a two-thirds majority of the States Parties to the present Covenant in accordance with their respective constitutional processes.

3. When amendments come into force they shall be binding on those States Parties which have accepted them, other States Parties still being bound by the provisions of the present Covenant and any earlier amendment which they have accepted.

Irrespective of the notifications made under article 26, paragraph 5, the Secretary-General of the United Nations shall inform all States referred to in paragraph 1 of the same article of the following particulars:

(a) Signatures, ratifications and accessions under article 26;

(b) The date of the entry into force of the present Covenant under article 27 and the date of the entry into force of any amendments under article 29.

Article 31

1. The present Covenant, of which the Chinese, English, French, Russian and Spanish texts are equally authentic, shall be deposited in the archives of the United Na-Nations.

2. The Secretary-General of the United Nations shall transmit certified copies of the present Covenant to all States referred to in article 26.

3. INTERNATIONAL COVENANT ON CIVIL AND POLITICAL RIGHTS[1]

PREAMBLE

The States Parties to the present Covenant,

Considering that, in accordance with the principles proclaimed in the Charter of the United Nations, recognition of the inherent dignity and of the equal and inalienable rights of all members of the human family is the foundation of freedom, justice and peace in the world,

Recognizing that these rights derive from the inherent dignity of the human person,

Recognizing that, in accordance with the Universal Declaration of Human Rights, the ideal of free human beings enjoying civil and political freedom and freedom from fear and want can only be achieved if conditions are created whereby everyone may enjoy his civil and political rights, as well as his economic, social and cultural rights,

Considering the obligation of States under the Charter of the United Nations to promote universal respect for, and observance of, human rights and freedoms,

Realizing that the individual, having duties to other individuals and to the community to which he belongs, is under a responsibility to strive for the promotion and observance of the rights recognized in the present Covenant,

Agree upon the following articles:

PART I

Article 1

1. All peoples have the right of self-determination. By virtue of that right they freely determine their political status and freely pursue their economic, social and cultural development.

2. All peoples may, for their own ends, freely dispose of their natural wealth and resources without prejudice to any obligations arising out of international economic co-operation, based upon the principle of mutual benefit, and international law. In no case may a people be deprived of its own means of subsistence.

---

[1] Official Records of the General Assembly, Twenty-first Session, Supplement No. 16, pp. 52-58.

3. The States Parties to the present Covenant, including those having responsibility for the administration of Non-Self-Governing and Trust Territories, shall promote the realization of the right of self-determination, and shall respect that right, in conformity with the provisions of the Charter of the United Nations.

PART II

Article 2

1. Each State Party to the present Covenant undertakes to respect and to ensure to all individuals within its territory and subject to its jurisdiction the rights recognized in the present Covenant, without distinction of any kind, such as race, colour, sex, language, religion, political or other opinion, national or social origin, property, birth or other status.

2. Where not already provided for by existing legislative or other measures, each State Party to the present Covenant undertakes to take the necessary steps, in accordance with its constitutional processes and with the provisions of the present Covenant, to adopt such legislative or other measures as may be necessary to give effect to the rights recognized in the present Covenant.

3. Each State Party to the present Covenant undertakes:

(a) To ensure that any person whose rights or freedoms as herein recognized are violated shall have an effective remedy, notwithstanding that the violation has been committed by persons acting in an official capacity;

(b) To ensure that any person claiming such a remedy shall have his right thereto determined by competent judicial, administrative or legislative authorities, or by any other competent authority provided for by the legal system of the State, and to develop the possibilities of judicial remedy;

(c) To ensure that the competent authorities shall enforce such remedies when granted.

Article 3

The States Parties to the present Covenant undertake to ensure the equal right of men and women to the enjoyment of all civil and political rights set forth in the present Covenant.

Article 4

1. In time of public emergency which threatens the life of the nation and the existence of which is officially proclaimed, the States Parties to the present Covenant may take measures derogating from their obligations under the present Covenant to the extent strictly required by the exigencies of the situation, provided that such measures are not inconsistent with their other obligations under international law and do not involve discrimination solely on the ground of race, colour, sex, language, religion or social origin.

2. No derogation from articles 6, 7, 8 (paragraph 1 and 2), 11, 15, 16 and 18 may be made under this provision.

3. Any State Party to the present Covenant availing itself of the right of derogation shall immediately inform the other States Parties to the present Covenant, through the intermediary of the Secretary-General of the United Nations, of the provisions from which it has derogated and of the reasons by which it was actuated. A further communication shall be made, through the same intermediary, on the date on which it terminates such derogation.

Article 5

1. Nothing in the present Covenant may be interpreted as implying for any State,

group or person any right to engage in any activity or perform any act aimed at the destruction of any of the rights and freedoms recognized herein or at their limitation to a greater extent than is provided for in the present Covenant.

2. There shall be no restriction upon or derogation from any of the fundamental human rights recognized or existing in any State Party to the present Covenant pursuant to law, conventions, regulations or custom on the pretext that the present Covenant does not recognize such rights or that it recognizes them to a lesser extent.

PART III
Article 6

1. Every human being has the inherent right to life. This right shall be protected by law. No one shall be arbitrarily deprived of his life.

2. In countries which have not abolished the death penalty, sentence of death may be imposed only for the most serious crimes in accordance with the law in force at the time of the commission of the crime and not contrary to the provisions of the present Covenant and to the Convention on the Prevention and Punishment of the Crime of Genocide. This penalty can only be carried out pursuant to a final judgement rendered by a competent court.

3. When deprivation of life constitutes the crime of genocide, it is understood that nothing in this article shall authorize any State Party to the present Covenant to derogate in any way from any obligation assumed under the provisions of the Convention on the Prevention and Punishment of the Crime of Genocide.

4. Anyone sentenced to death shall have the right to seek pardon or commutation of the sentence. Amnesty, pardon or commutation of the sentence of death may be granted in all cases.

5. Sentence of death shall not be imposed for crimes committed by persons below eighteen years of age and shall not be carried out on pregnant women.

6. Nothing in this article shall be invoked to delay or to prevent the abolition of capital punishment by any State Party to the present Covenant.

Article 7

No one shall be subjected to torture or to cruel, inhuman or degrading treatment or punishment. In particular, no one shall be subjected without his free consent to medical or scientific experimentation.

Article 8

1. No one shall be held in slavery; slavery and the slave trade in all their forms shall be prohibited.

2. No one shall be held in servitude.

3. (a) No one shall be required to perform forced or compulsory labour;

(b) Paragraph 3 (a) shall not be held to preclude, in countries where imprisonment with hard labour may be imposed as a punishment for a crime, the performance of hard labour in pursuance of a sentence to such punishment by a competent court;

(c) For the purpose of this paragraph the term "forced or compulsory labour" shall not include:

(i) Any work or service, not referred to in sub-paragraph (b), normally required of a person who is under detention in consequence of a lawful order of a court, or of a person during conditional release from such detention;

(ii) Any service of a military character and, in countries where conscientious objection is recognized, any national service required by law of conscientious objectors;

(iii) Any service exacted in cases of emergency or calamity threatening the life or well-being of the community;

(iv) Any work or service which forms part of normal civil obligations.

Article 9

1. Everyone has the right to liberty and security of person. No one shall be subject to arbitrary arrest or detention. No one shall be deprived of his liberty except on such grounds and in accordance with such procedure as are established by law.

2. Anyone who is arrested shall be informed, at the time of arrest, of the reasons for his arrest and shall be promptly informed of any charges against him.

3. Anyone arrested or detained on a criminal charge shall be brought promptly before a judge or other officer authorized by law to exercise judicial power and shall be entitled to trial within a reasonable time or to release. It shall not be the general rule that persons awaiting trial shall be detained in custody, but release may be subject to guarantees to appear for trial, at any other stage of the judicial proceedings, and, should occasion arise, for execution of the judgement.

4. Anyone who is deprived of his liberty by arrest or detention shall be entitled to take proceedings before a court, in order that that court may decide without delay on the lawfulness of his detention and order his release if the detention is not lawful.

5. Anyone who has been the victim of unlawful arrest or detention shall have an enforceable right to compensation.

Article 10

1. All persons deprived of their liberty shall be treated with humanity and with respect for the inherent dignity of the human person.

2. *(a)* Accused persons shall, save in exceptional circumstances, be segregated from convicted persons and shall be subject to separate treatment appropriate to their status as unconvicted persons;

(b) Accused juvenile persons shall be separated from adults and brought as speedily as possible for adjudication.

3. The penitentiary system shall comprise treatment of prisoners the essential aim of which shall be their reformation and social rehabilitation. Juvenile offenders shall be segregated from adults and be accorded treatment appropriate to their age and legal status.

Article 11

No one shall be imprisoned merely on the ground of inability to fulfil a contractual obligation.

Article 12

1. Everyone lawfully within the territory of a State shall, within that territory, have the right to liberty of movement and freedom to choose his residence.

2. Everyone shall be free to leave any country, including his own.

3. The above-mentioned rights shall not be subject to any restrictions except those which are provided by law, are necessary to protect national security, public order *(ordre public)*, public health or morals or the rights and freedoms of others, and are consistent with the other rights recognized in the present Covenant.

4. No one shall be arbitrarily deprived of the right to enter his own country.

Article 13

An alien lawfully in the territory of a State Party to the present Covenant may be expelled therefrom only in pursuance of a decision reached in accordance with law and shall, except where compelling reasons of national security otherwise require, be allowed to submit the reasons against his expulsion and to have his case reviewed by, and be represented for the purpose before, the competent authority or a person or persons especially designated by the competent authority.

Article 14

1. All persons shall be equal before the courts and tribunals. In the determination of any criminal charge against him, or of his rights and obligations in a suit at law, everyone shall be entitled to a fair and public hearing by a competent, independent and impartial tribunal established by law. The Press and the public may be excluded from all or part of a trial for reasons of morals, public order, or national security in a democratic society, or when the interest of the private lives of the parties so requires, or to the extent strictly necessary in the opinion of the court in special circumstances where publicity would prejudice the interests of justice; but any judgement rendered in a criminal case or in a suit at law shall be made public except where the interest of juvenile persons otherwise requires or the proceedings concern matrimonial disputes or the guardianship of children.

2. Everyone charged with a criminal offence shall have the right to be presumed innocent until proved guilty according to law.

3. In the determination of any criminal charge against him, everyone shall be entitled to the following minimum guarantees, in full equality:

(a) To be informed promptly and in detail in a language which he understands of the nature and cause of the charge against him;

(b) To have adequate time and facilities for the preparation of his defence and to communicate with counsel of his own choosing;

(c) To be tried without undue delay;

(d) To be tried in his presence, and to defend himself in person or through legal assistance of his own choosing; to be informed, if he does not have legal assistance, of this right; and to have legal assistance assigned to him, in any case where the interests of justice so require, and without payment by him in any such case if he does not have sufficient means to pay for it;

(e) To examine, or have examined, the witnesses against him and to obtain the attendance and examination of witnesses on his behalf under the same conditions as witnesses against him;

(f) To have the free assistance of an interpreter if he cannot understand or speak the language used in court;

(g) Not to be compelled to testify against himself or to confess guilt.

4. In the case of juvenile persons, the procedure shall be such as will take account of their age and the desirability of promoting their rehabilitation.

5. Everyone convicted of a crime shall have the right to his conviction and sentence being reviewed by a higher tribunal according to law.

6. When a person has by a final decision been convicted of a criminal offence and when subsequently his conviction has been reversed or he has been pardoned on the ground that a new or newly discovered fact shows conclusively that there has been a miscarriage of justice, the person who has suffered punishment as a result of such conviction shall be compensated according to law, unless it is proved that the non-disclosure of the unknown fact in time is wholly or partly attributable to him.

7. No one shall be liable to be tried or punished again for an offence for which he has already been finally convicted or acquitted in accordance with the law and penal procedure of each country.

Article 15

1. No one shall be held guilty of any criminal offence on account of any act or omission which did not constitute a criminal offence, under national or international law, at the time when it was committed. Nor shall a heavier penalty be imposed than

the one that was applicable at the time when the criminal offence was committed. If subsequent to the commission of the offence, provision is made by law for the imposition of a lighter penalty, the offender shall benefit thereby.

2. Nothing in this article shall prejudice the trial and punishment of any person for any act or omission which, at the time when it was committed, was criminal according to the general principles of law recognized by the community of nations.

Article 16

Everyone shall have the right to recognition everywhere as a person before the law.

Article 17

1. No one shall be subjected to arbitrary or unlawful interference with his privacy, family, home or correspondence, nor to unlawful attacks on his honour and reputation.

2. Everyone has the right to the protection of the law against such interference or attacks.

Article 18

1. Everyone shall have the right to freedom of thought, conscience and religion. This right shall include freedom to have or to adopt a religion or belief of his choice, and freedom, either individually or in community with others and in public or private, to manifest his religion or belief in worship, observance, practice and teaching.

2. No one shall be subject to coercion which would impair his freedom to have or to adopt a religion or belief of his choice.

3. Freedom to manifest one's religion or beliefs may be subject only to such limitations as are prescribed by law and are necessary to protect public safety, order, health, or morals or the fundamental rights and freedoms of others.

Article 19

1. Everyone shall have the right to hold opinions without interference.

2. Everyone shall have the right to freedom of expression; this right shall include freedom to seek, receive and impart information and ideas of all kinds, regardless of frontiers, either orally, in writing or in print, in the form of art, or through any other media of his choice.

3. The exercise of the rights provided for in paragraph 2 of this article carries with it special duties and responsibilities. It may therefore be subject to certain restriction, but these shall only be such as are provided by law and are necessary:

(a) For respect of the rights or reputations of others;

(b) For the protection of national security or of public order, or of public health or morals.

Article 20

1. Any propaganda for war shall be prohibited by law.

2. Any advocacy of national, racial or religious hatred that constitutes incitement to discrimination, hostility or violence shall be prohibited by law.

Article 21

The right of peaceful assembly shall be recognized. No restrictions may be placed on the exercise of this right other than those imposed in conformity with the law and which are necessary in a democratic society in the interests of national security or public safety, public order, the protection of public health or morals or the protection of the rights and freedoms of others.

Article 22

1. Everyone shall have the right to freedom of association with others, including the right to form and join trade unions for the protection of his interests.

2. No restrictions may be placed on the exercise of this right other than those which are prescribed by law and which are necessary in a democratic society in the interests of national security or public safety, public order, the protection of public health or morals or the protection of the rights and freedoms of others. This article shall not prevent the imposition of lawful restrictions on members of the armed forces and of the police in their exercise of this right.

3. Nothing in this article shall authorize States Parties to the International Labour Organisation Convention of 1948 concerning Freedom of Association and Protection of the Right to Organize to take legislative measures which would prejudice, or to apply the law in such a manner as to prejudice, the guarantees provided for in that Convention.

Article 23

1. The family is the natural and fundamental group unit of society and is entitled to protection by society and the State.

2. The right of men and women of marriageable age to marry and to found a family shall be recognized.

3. No marriage shall be entered into without the free and full consent of the intending spouses.

4. States Parties to the present Covenant shall take appropriate steps to ensure equality of rights and responsibilities of spouses as to marriage, during marriage and at its dissolution. In the case of dissolution, provision shall be made for the necessary protection of any children.

Article 24

1. Every child shall have, without any discrimination as to race, colour, sex, language, religion, national or social origin, property or birth, the right to such measures of protection as are required by his status as a minor, on the part of his family, society and the State.

2. Every child shall be registered immediately after birth and shall have a name.

3. Every child has the right to acquire a nationality.

Article 25

Every citizen shall have the right and the opportunity, without any of the distinctions mentioned in article 2 and without unreasonable restrictions:

(a) To take part in the conduct of public affairs, directly or through freely chosen representatives;

(b) To vote and to be elected at genuine periodic elections which shall be by universal and equal suffrage and shall be held by secret ballot, guaranteeing the free expression of the will of the electors;

(c) To have access, on general terms of equality, to public service in his country.

Article 26

All persons are equal before the law and are entitled without any discrimination to the equal protection of the law. In this respect the law shall prohibit any discrimination and guarantee to all persons equal and effective protection against discrimination on any ground such as race, colour, sex, language, religion, political or other opinion, national or social origin, property, birth or other status.

Article 27

In those States in which ethnic, religious or linguistic minorities exist, persons belonging to such minorities shall not be denied the right, in community with the other members of their group, to enjoy their own culture, to profess abd practice their own religion, or to use their own language.

PART IV

Article 28

1. There shall be established a Human Rights Committee (hereafter referred to in the present Covenant as the Committee). It shall consist of eighteen members and shall carry out the functions hereinafter provided.

2. The Committee shall be composed of nationals of the States Parties to the present Covenant who shall be persons of high moral character and recognized competence in the field of human rights, consideration being given to the usefulness of the participation of some persons having legal experience.

3. The members of the Committee shall be elected and shall serve in their personal capacity.

Article 29

1. The members of the Committee shall be elected by secret ballot from a list of persons possessing the qualifications prescribed in article 28 and nominated for the purpose by the State Parties to the present Convenant.

2. Each State Party to the present Covenant may nominate not more than two persons. These persons shall be nationals of the nominating State.

3. A person shall be eligible for renomination.

Article 30

1. The initial election shall be held not later than six months after the date of the entry into force of the present Covenant.

2. At least four months before the date of each election to the Committee, other than an election to fill a vacancy declared in accordance with article 34, the Secretary-General of the United Nations shall address a written invitation to the States Parties to the present Covenant to submit their nomination for membership of the Committee within three months.

3. The Secretary-General of the United Nations shall prepare a list in alphabetical order of all the persons thus nominated, with an indication of the States Parties which have nominated them, and shall submit it to the States Parties to the present Covenant no later than one month before the date of each election.

4. Elections of the members of the Committee shall be held at a meeting of the States Parties to the present Covenant convened by the Secretary-General of the United Nations at the Headquarters of the United Nations. At that meeting, for which two thirds of the States Parties to the present Covenant shall constitute a quorum, the persons elected to the Committee shall be those nominees who obtain the largest number of votes and an absolute majority of the votes of the representatives of States Parties present and voting.

Article 31

1. The Committee may not include more than one national of the same State.

2. In the election of the Committee, consideration shall be given to equitable geographical distribution of membership and to the representation of the different forms of civilization and of the principal legal systems.

Article 32

1. The members of the Committee shall be elected for a term of four years. They shall be eligible for re-election if renominated. However, the terms of nine of the members elected at the first election shall expire at the end of two years; immediately after the first election, the names of these nine members shall be chosen by lot by the Chairman of the meeting referred to in article 30, paragraph 4.

2. Elections at the expiry of office shall be held in accordance with the preceding articles of this part of the present Covenant.

Article 33

1. If, in the unanimous opinion of the other members, a member of the Committee has ceased to carry out his functions for any cause other than absence of a temporary character, the Chairman of the Committee shall notify the Secretary-General of the United Nations, who shall then declare the seat of that member to be vacant.

2. In the event of the death or the resignation of a member of the Committee, the Chairman shall immediately notify the Secretary-General of the United Nations, who shall declare the seat vacant from the date of death or the date on which the resignation takes effect.

Article 34

1. When a vacancy is declared in accordance with article 33 and if the term of office of the member to be replaced does not expire within six months of the declaration of the vacancy, the Secretary-General of the United Nations shall notify each of the States Parties to the present Covenant, which may within two months submit nominations in accordance with article 29 for the purpose of filling the vacancy.

2. The Secretary-General of the United Nations shall prepare a list in alphabetical order of the persons thus nominated and shall submit it to the States Parties to the present Covenant. The election to fill the vacancy shall then take place in accordance with the relevant provisions of this part of the present Covenant.

3. A member of the Committee elected to fill a vacancy declared in accordance with article 33 shall hold office for the remainder of the term of the member who vacated the seat on the Committee under the provisions of that article.

Article 35

The members of the Committee shall, with the approval of the General Assembly of the United Nations, receive emoluments from United Nations resources on such terms and conditions as the General Assembly may decide, having regard to the importance of the Committee's responsibilities.

Article 36

The Secretary-General of the United Nations shall provide the necessary staff and facilities for the effective performance of the functions of the Committee under the present Covenant.

Article 37

1. The Secretary-General of the United Nations shall convene the initial meeting of the Committee at the Headquarters of the United Nations.

2. After its initial meeting, the Committee shall meet at such times as shall be provided in its rules of procedure.

3. The Committee shall normally meet at the Headquarters of the United Nations or at the United Nations Office at Geneva.

Article 38

Every member of the Committee shall, before taking up his duties, make a solemn declaration in open committee that he will perform his functions impartially and conscientiously.

Article 39

1. The Committee shall elect its officers for a term of two years. They may be re-elected.

2. The Committee shall establish its own rules of procedure, but these rules shall provide, *inter alia,* that:

(a) Twelve members shall constitute a quorum;

(b) Decisions of the Committee shall be made by a majority vote of the members present.

Article 40

1. The States Parties to the present Covenant undertake to submit reports on the measures they have adopted which give effect to the rights recognized herein and on the progress made in the enjoyment of those rights:

(a) Within one year of the entry into force of the present Covenant for the States Parties concerned;

(b) Thereafter whenever the Committee so requests.

2. All reports shall be submitted to the Secretary-General of the United Nations, who shall transmit them to the Committee for consideration. Reports shall indicate the factors and difficulties, if any, affecting the implementation of the present Covenant.

3. The Secretary-General of the United Nations may, after consultation with the Committee, transmit to the specialized agencies concerned copies of such parts of the reports as may fall within their field of competence.

4. The Committee shall study the reports submitted by the States Parties to the present Covenant. It shall transmit its reports, and such general comments as it may consider appropriate, to the States Parties. The Committee may also transmit to the Economic and Social Council these comments along with the copies of the reports it has received from States Parties to the present Covenant.

5. The States Parties to the present Covenant may submit to the Committee observations on any comments that may be made in accordance with paragraph 4 of this article.

Article 41

1. A State Party to the present Covenant may at any time declare under this article that it recognizes the competence of the Committee to receive and consider communications to the effect that a State Party claims that another State Party is not fulfilling its obligations under the present Covenant. Communications under this article may be received and considered only if submitted by a State Party which has made a declaration recognizing in regard to itself the competence of the Committee. No communication shall be received by the Committee if it concerns a State Party which has not made such a declaration. Communications received under this article shall be dealt with in accordance with the following procedure:

(a) If a State Party to the present Covenant considers that another State Party is not giving effect to the provisions of the present Covenant, it may, by written communication, bring the matter to the attention of that State Party. Within three months after the receipt of the communication, the receiving State shall afford the State which sent the communication an explanation or any other statement in writing clarifying

the matter, which should include, to the extent possible and pertinent, reference to domestic procedures and remedies taken, pending, or available in the matter.

(b) If the matter is not adjusted to the satisfaction of both States Parties concerned within six months after the receipt by the receiving State of the initial communication, either State shall have the right to refer the matter to the Committee, by notice given to the Committee and to the other State.

(c) The Committee shall deal with a matter referred to it only after it has ascertained that all available domestic remedies have been invoked and exhausted in the matter, in conformity with the generally recognized principles of international law. This shall not be the rule where the application of the remedies is unreasonably prolonged.

(d) The Committee shall hold closed meetings when examining communications under this article.

(e) Subject to the provisions of sub-paragraph *(c)*, the Committee shall make available its good offices to the States Parties concerned with a view to a friendly solution of the matter on the basis of respect for human rights and fundamental freedoms as recognized in the present Covenant.

(f) In any matter referred to it, the Committee may call upon the States Parties concerned, referred to in sub-paragraph *(b)*, to supply any relevant information.

(g) The States Parties concerned, referred to in sub-paragraph *(b)*, shall have the right to be represented when the matter is being considered in the Committee and to make submissions orally and/or in writing.

(h) The Committee shall, within twelve months after the date of receipt of notice under sub-paragraph *(b)*, submit a report:

  (i) If a solution within the terms of sub-paragraph *(e)* is reached, the Committee shall confine its report to a brief statement of the facts and of the solution reached;

  (ii) If a solution within the terms of sub-paragraph *(e)* is not reached, the Committee shall confine its report to a brief statement of the facts; the written admissions and record of the oral submissions made by the States Parties concerned shall be attached to the report.

In every matter, the report shall be communicated to the States Parties concerned.

2. The provisions of this article shall come into force when ten States Parties to the present Covenant have made declarations under paragraph 1 of this article. Such declarations shall be deposited by the States Parties with the Secretary-General of the United Nations, who shall transmit copies thereof to the other States Parties. A declaration may be withdrawn at any time by notification to the Secretary-General. Such a withdrawal shall not prejudice the consideration of any matter which is the subject of a communication already transmitted under this article; no further communication by any State Party shall be received after the notification of withdrawal of the declaration has been received by the Secretary-General, unless the State Party concerned has made a new declaration.

Article 42

1. *(a)* If a matter referred to the Committee in accordance with article 41 is not resolved to the satisfaction of the States Parties concerned, the Committee may, with the prior consent of the States Parties concerned, appoint an *ad hoc* Conciliation Commission (hereinafter referred to as the Commission). The good offices of the Commission shall be made available to the States Parties concerned with a view to an amicable solution of the matter on the basis of respect for the present Covenant;

(b) The Commission shall consist of five persons acceptable to the State Parties concerned. If the States Parties concerned fail to reach agreement within three months on all or part of the composition of the Commission, the members of the Commission concerning whom no agreement has been reached shall be elected by secret ballot by a two-thirds majority vote of the Committee from among its members.

2. The members of the Commission shall serve in their personal capacity. They shall not be nationals of the States Parties concerned, or of a State not party to the present Covenant, or of a State Party which has not made a declaration under article 41.

3. The Commission shall elect its own Chairman and adopt its own rules of procedure.

4. The meetings of the Commission shall normally be held at the Headquarters of the United Nations or at the United Nations Office at Geneva. However, they may be held at such other convenient places as the Commission may determine in consultation with the Secretary-General of the United Nations and the States Parties concerned.

5. The secretariat provided in accordance with article 36 shall also service the commissions appointed under this article.

6. The information received and collated by the Committee shall be made available to the Commission and the Commission may call upon the States Parties concerned to supply any other relevant information.

7. When the Commission has fully considered the matter, but in any event not later than twelve months after having been seized of the matter, it shall submit to the Chairman of the Committee a report for communication to the States Parties concerned:

(a) If the Commission is unable to complete its consideration of the matter within twelve months, it shall confine its report to a brief statement of the status of its consideration of the matter;

(b) If an amicable solution to the matter on the basis of respect for human rights as recognized in the present Covenant is reached, the Commission shall confine its report to a brief statement of the facts and of the solution reached;

(c) If a solution within the terms of sub-paragraph *(b)* is not reached, the Commission's report shall embody its findings on all questions of fact relevant to the issues between the States Parties concerned, and its views on the possibilities of an amicable solution of the matter. This report shall also contain the written submissions and a record of the oral submissions made by the States Parties concerned;

(d) If the Commission's report is submitted under sub-paragraph *(c)*, the States Parties concerned shall, within three months of the receipt of the report, notify the Chairman of the Committee whether or not they accept the contents of the report of the Commission.

8. The provisions of this article are without prejudice to the responsibilities of the Committee under article 41.

9. The States Parties concerned shall share equally all the expenses of the members of the Commission in accordance with estimates to be provided by the Secretary-General of the United Nations.

10. The Secretary-General of the United Nations shall be empowered to pay the expenses of the members of the Commission, if necessary, before reimbursement by the States Parties concerned, in accordance with paragraph 9 of this article.

Article 43

The members of the Committee, and of the *ad hoc* conciliation commissions which may be appointed under article 42, shall be entitled to the facilities, privileges and immunities of experts on mission for the United Nations as laid down in the relevant sections of the Convention on the Privileges and Immunities of the United Nations.

Article 44

The provisions for the implementation of the present Covenant shall apply without prejudice to the procedures prescribed in the field of human rights by or under the constituent instruments and the conventions of the United Nations and of the specialized agencies and shall not prevent the States Parties to the present Covenant from having recourse to other procedures for settling a dispute in accordance with general or special international agreements in force between them.

Article 45

The Committee shall submit to the General Assembly of the United Nations, through the Economic and Social Council, an annual report on its activities.

PART V

Article 46

Nothing in the present Covenant shall be interpreted as impairing the provisions of the Charter of the United Nations and of the constitutions of the specialized agencies which define the respective responsibilities of the various organs of the United Nations and of the specialized agencies in regard to the matters dealt within the present Covenant.

Article 47

Nothing in the present Covenant shall be interpreted as impairing the inherent right of all peoples to enjoy and utilize fully and freely their natural wealth and resources.

PART VI

Article 48

1. The present Covenant is open for signature by any State Member of the United Nations or member of any of its specialized agencies, by any State Party to the Statute of the International Court of Justice, and by any other State which has been invited by the General Assembly of the United Nations to become a party to the present Covenant.

2. The present Covenant is subject to ratification. Instruments of ratification shall be deposited with the Secretary-General of the United Nations.

3. The present Covenant shall be open to accession by any State referred to in paragraph 1 of this article.

4. Accession shall be effected by the deposit of an instrument of accession with the Secretary-General of the United Nations.

5. The Secretary-General of the United Nations shall inform all States which have signed this Covenant or acceded to it of the deposit of each instrument of ratification or accession.

Article 49

1. The present Covenant shall enter into force three months after the date of the deposit with the Secretary-General of the United Nations of the thirty-fifth instrument of ratification or instrument of accession.

2. For each State ratifying the present Covenant or acceding to it after the deposit of the thirty-fifth instrument of ratification or instrument of accession, the present Covenant shall enter into force three months after the date of the deposit of its own instrument of ratification or instrument of accession.

Article 50

The provisions of the present Covenant shall extend to all parts of federal States without any limitations or exceptions.

Article 51

1. Any State Party to the present Covenant may propose an amendment and file it with the Secretary-General of the United Nations. The Secretary-General of the

United Nations shall thereupon communicate any proposed amendments to the States Parties to the present Covenant with a request that they notify him whether they favour a conference of States Parties for the purpose of considering and voting upon the proposals. In the event that at least one third of the States Parties favours such a conference, the Secretary-General shall convene the conference under the auspices of the United Nations. Any amendment adopted by a majority of the States Parties present and voting at the conference shall be submitted to the General Assembly of the United Nations for approval.

2. Amendments shall come into force when they have been approved by the General Assembly of the United Nations and accepted by a two-thirds majority of the States Parties to the present Covenant in accordance with their respective constitutional processes.

3. When amendments come into force, they shall be binding on those States Parties which have accepted them, other States Parties still being bound by the provisions of the present Covenant and any earlier amendment which they have accepted.

Article 52

Irrespective of the notifications made under article 48, paragraph 5, the Secretary-General of the United Nations shall inform all States referred to in paragraph 1 of the same article of the following particulars:

(a) Signatures, ratifications and accessions under article 48;

(b) The date of the entry into force of the present Covenant under article 49 and the date of the entry into force of any amendments under article 51.

Article 53

1. The present Covenant of which the Chinese, English, French, Russian and Spanish texts are equally authentic, shall be deposited in the archives of the United Nations.

2. The Secretary-General of the United Nations shall transmit certified copies of the present Covenant to all States referred to in article 48.

4. OPTIONAL PROTOCOL TO THE INTERNATIONAL COVENANT ON CIVIL AND POLITICAL RIGHTS[1]

The States Parties to the present Protocol,

Considering that in order further to achieve the purposes of the Covenant on Civil and Political Rights (hereinafter referred to as the Covenant) and the implementation of its provisions it would be appropriate to enable the Human Rights Committee set up in part IV of the Covenant (hereinafter referred to as the Committee) to receive and consider, as provided in the present Protocol, communications from individuals claiming to be victims of violations of any of the rights set forth in the Covenant,

Have agreed as follows:

Article 1

A State Party to the Covenant that becomes a party to the present Protocol recognizes the competence of the Committee to receive and consider communications from individuals subject to its jurisdiction who claim to be victims of a violation by that State Party of any of the rights set forth in the Covenant. No communication shall be received by the Committee if it concerns a State Party to the Covenant which is not a party to the present Protocol.

---

[1] Official Records of the General Assembly, Twenty-first Session, Supplement No. 16, pp. 59-60.

Article 2

Subject to the provisions of article 1, individuals who claim that any of their rights enumerated in the Covenant have been violated and who have exhausted all available domestic remedies may submit a written communication to the Committee for consideration.

Article 3

The Committee shall consider inadmissible any communication under the present Protocol which is anonymous, or which it considers to be an abuse of the right of submission of such communications or to be incompatible with the provisions of the Covenant.

Article 4

1. Subject to the provisions of article 3, the Committee shall bring any communications submitted to it under the present Protocol to the attention of the State Party to the present Protocol alleged to be violating any provision of the Covenant.

2. Within six months, the receiving State shall submit to the Committee written explanations or statements clarifying the matter and the remedy, if any, that may have been taken by that State.

Article 5

1. The Committee shall consider communications received under the present Protocol in the light of all written information made available to it by the individual and by the State Party concerned.

2. The Committee shall not consider any communication from an individual unless it has ascertained that:

(a) The same matter is not being examined under another procedure of international investigation or settlement;

(b) The individual has exhausted all available domestic remedies. This shall not be the rule where the application of the remedies is unreasonably prolonged.

3. The Committee shall hold closed meetings when examining communications under the present Protocol.

4. The Committee shall forward its views to the State Party concerned and to the individual.

Article 6

The Committee shall include in its annual report under article 45 of the Covenant a summary of its activities under the present Protocol.

Article 7

Pending the achievement of the objectives of resolution 1514 (XV) adopted by the General Assembly of the United Nations on 14 December 1960 concerning the Declaration on the Granting of Independence to Colonial Countries and Peoples, the provisions of the present Protocol shall in no way limit the right of petition granted to these peoples by the Charter of the United Nations and other international conventions and instruments under the United Nations and its specialized agencies.

Article 8

1. The present Protocol is open for signature by any State which has signed the Covenant.

2. The present Protocol is subject to ratification by any State which has ratified or acceded to the Covenant. Instruments of ratification shall be deposited with the Secretary-General of the United Nations.

3. The present Protocol shall be open to accession by any State which has ratified or acceded to the Covenant.

4. Accession shall be effected by the deposit of an instrument of accession with the Secretary-General of the United Nations.

5. The Secretary-General of the United Nations shall inform all States which have signed the present Protocol or acceded to it of the deposit of each instrument of ratification or accession.

Article 9

1. Subject to the entry into force of the Covenant, the present Protocol shall enter into force three months after the date of the deposit with the Secretary-General of the United Nations of the tenth instrument of ratification or instrument of accession.

2. For each State ratifying the present Protocol or acceding to it after the deposit of the tenth instrument of ratification or instrument of accession, the present Protocol shall enter into force three months after the date of the deposit of its own instrument of ratification or instrument of accession.

Article 10

The provisions of the present Protocol shall extend to all parts of federal States without any limitations or exceptions.

Article 11

1. Any State Party to the present Protocol may propose an amendment and file it with the Secretary-General of the United Nations. The Secretary-General shall thereupon communicate any proposed amendments to the States Parties to the present Protocol with a request that they notify him whether they favour a conference of States Parties for the purpose of considering and voting upon the proposal. In the event that at least one third of the States Parties favours such a conference, the Secretary-General shall convene the conference under the auspices of the United Nations. Any amendment adopted by a majority of the States Parties present and voting at the conference shall be submitted to the General Assembly of the United Nations for approval.

2. Amendments shall come into force when they have been approved by the General Assembly of the United Nations and accepted by a two-thirds majority of the States Parties to the present Protocol in accordance with their respective constitutional processes.

3. When amendments come into force, they shall be binding on those States Parties which have accepted them, other States Parties still being bound by the provisions of the present Protocol and any earlier amendment which they have accepted.

Article 12

1. Any State Party may denounce the present Protocol at any time by written notification addressed to the Secretary-General of the United Nations. Denunciation shall take effect three months after the date of receipt of the notification by the Secretary-General.

2. Denunciation shall be without prejudice to the continued application of the provisions of the present Protocol to any communication submitted under article 2 before the effective date of denunciation.

Article 13

Irrespective of the notifications made under article 8, paragraph 5, of the present Protocol, the Secretary-General of the United Nations shall inform all States referred to in article 48, paragraph 1, of the Covenant of the following particulars:

(a) Signatures, ratifications and accessions under article 8;

(b) The date of the entry into force of the present Protocol under article 9 and the date of the entry into force of any amendments under article 11;

(c) Denunciations under article 12.

Article 14

1. The present Protocol, of which the Chinese, English, French, Russian and Spanish texts are equally authentic, shall be deposited in the archives of the United Nations.

2. The Secretary-General of the United Nations shall transmit certified copies of the present Protocol to all States referred to in article 48 of the Covenant.

B

The General Assembly,

Considering that the text of the international Covenant on Economic, Social and Cultural Rights, the text of the International Covenant on Civil and Political Rights and the text of the Optional Protocol to the International Covenant on Civil and Political Rights should be made known throughout the world,

1. *Requests* the Governments of States and non-governmental organizations to publicize the text of these instruments as widely as possible, using every means at their disposal, including all the appropriate media of information;

2. *Requests* the Secretary-General to ensure the immediate and wide circulation of these instruments and, to that end, to publish and distribute the text thereof.

1496th plenary meeting,
16 December 1966.

C

The General Assembly,

Considering the advisability of the proposals for the establishment of national commissions on human rights or the designation of other appropriate institutions to perform certain functions pertaining to the observance of the International Covenant on Civil and Political Rights and the International Covenant on Economic, Social and Cultural Rights,

1. *Invites* the Economic and Social Council to request the Commission on Human Rights to examine the question in all its aspects and to report, through the Council, to the General Assembly;

2. *Requests* the Secretary-General to invite Member States to submit their comments on the question, in order that the Commission on Human Rights may take these comments into account when considering the proposals.

1496th plenary meeting,
16 December 1966.

5. CONVENTION ON THE PREVENTION AND PUNISHMENT OF THE CRIME OF GENOCIDE[1]

A

ADOPTION OF THE CONVENTION ON THE PREVENTION AND
PUNISHMENT OF THE CRIME OF GENOCIDE, AND
TEXT OF THE CONVENTION

The General Assembly,

Approves the annexed Convention on the Prevention and Punishment of the Crime of Genocide and propose it for signature and ratification or accession in accordance with its article XI.

Hundred and seventy-ninth plenary meeting,
9 December 1948.

ANNEX

TEXT OF THE CONVENTION

The Contracting Parties,

Having considered the declaration made by the General Assembly of the United Nations in its resolution 96 (I) dated 11 December 1946 that genocide is a crime under international law, contrary to the spirit and aims of the United Nations and condemned by the civilized world;

Recognizing that at all periods of history genocide has inflicted great losses on humanity; and

Being convinced that, in order to liberate mankind from such an odious scourge, international co-operation is required;

Hereby agree as hereinafter provided.

ARTICLE I

The Contracting Parties confirm that genocide, whether committed in time of peace or in time of war, is a crime under international law which they undertake to prevent and to punish.

ARTICLE II

In the present Convention, genocide means any of the following acts committed with intent to destroy, in whole or in part, a national, ethical, racial or religious group, as such:

(a) Killing members of the group;

(b) Causing serious bodily or mental harm to members of the group;

(c) Deliberately inflicting on the group conditions of life calculated to bring about its physical destruction in whole or in part;

(d) Imposing measures intended to prevent births within the group;

(e) Forcibly transferring children of the group to another group.

---

[1] Official Records of the General Assembly, Third Session, Part I, pp. 174-178.

ARTICLE III

The following acts shall be punishable:

(a) Genocide;
(b) Conspiracy to commit genocide;
(c) Direct and public incitement to commit genocide;
(d) Attempt to commit genocide;
(e) Complicity in genocide.

ARTICLE IV

Persons committing genocide or any of the other acts enumerated in article III shall be punished, whether they are constitutionally responsible rulers, public officials or private individuals.

ARTICLE V

The Contracting Parties undertake to enact, in accordance with their respective Constitutions, the necessary legislation to give effect to the provisions of the present Convention and, in particular, to provide effective penalties for persons guilty of genocide or any of the other acts enumerated in article III.

ARTICLE VI

Persons charged with genocide or any of the other acts enumerated in article III shall be tried by a competent tribunal of the State in the territory of which the act was committed, or by such international penal tribunal as may have jurisdiction with respect to those Contracting Parties which shall have accepted its jurisdiction.

ARTICLE VII

Genocide and the other acts enumerated in article III shall not be considered as political crimes for the purpose of extradition.

The Contracting Parties pledge themselves in such cases to grant extradition in accordance with their laws and treaties in force.

ARTICLE VIII

Any Contracting Party may call upon the competent organs of the United Nations to take such action under the Charter of the United Nations as they consider appropriate for the prevention and suppression of acts of genocide or any of the other acts enumerated in article III.

ARTICLE IX

Disputes between the Contracting Parties relating to the interpretation, application or fulfilment of the present Convention, including those relating to the responsibility of a State for genocide or any of the other acts enumerated in article III, shall be submitted to the International Court of Justice at the request of any of the parties to the dispute.

ARTICLE X

The present Convention, of which the Chinese, English, French, Russian and Spanish texts, are equally authentic, shall bear the date of 9 December 1948.

ARTICLE XI

The present Convention shall be open until 31 December 1949 for signature on behalf of any Member of the United Nations and of any non-member State to which an invitation to sign has been addressed by the General Assembly.

The present Convention shall be ratified, and the instruments of ratification shall be deposited with the Secretary-General of the United Nations.

After 1 January 1950, the present Convention may be acceded to on behalf of any Member of the United Nations and of any non-member State which has received an invitation as aforesaid.

Instruments of accession shall be deposited with the Secretary-General of the United Nations.

ARTICLE XII

Any Contracting Party may at any time, by notification addressed to the Secretary-General of the United Nations, extend the application of the present Convention to all or any of the territories for the conduct of whose foreign relations that Contracting Party is responsible.

ARTICLE XIII

On the day when the first twenty instruments of ratification or accession have been deposited, the Secretary-General shall draw up a *proces-verbal* and transmit a copy of it to each Member of the United Nations and to each of the non-member States contemplated in article XI.

The present Convention shall come into force on the ninetieth day following the date of deposit of the twentieth instrument of ratification or accession.

Any ratification or accession effected subsequent to the latter date shall become effective on the ninetieth day following the deposit of the instrument of ratification or accession.

ARTICLE XIV

The present Convention shall remain in effect for a period of ten years as from the date of its coming into force.

It shall thereafter remain in force for successive periods of five years for such Contracting Parties as have not denounced it at least six months before the expiration of the current period.

Denunciation shall be effected by a written notification addressed to the Secretary-General of the United Nations.

ARTICLE XV

If, as a result of denunciations, the number of Parties to the present Convention should become less than sixteen, the Convention shall cease to be in force as from the date on which the last of these denunciations shall become effective.

ARTICLE XVI

A request for the revision of the present Convention may be made at any time by any Contracting Party by means of a notification in writing addressed to the Secretary-General.

The General Assembly shall decide upon the steps, if any, to be taken in respect of such request.

ARTICLE XVII

The Secretary-General of the United Nations shall notify all Members of the United Nations and the non-member States contemplated in article XI of the following:

(a) Signatures, ratifications and accessions received in accordance with article XI;

(b) Notifications received in accordance with article XII;

(c) The date upon which the present Convention comes into force in accordance with article XIII;

(d) Denunciations received in accordance with article XIV.

(e) The abrogation of the Convention in accordance with article XV;

(f) Notifications received in accordance with article XVI.

ARTICLE XVIII

The original of the present Convention shall be deposited in the archives of the United Nations.

A certified copy of the Convention shall be transmitted to all Members of the United Nations and to the non-member States contemplated in article XI.

ARTICLE XIX

The present Convention shall be registered by the Secretary-General of the United Nations on the date of its coming into force.

B
STUDY BY THE INTERNATIONAL LAW COMMISSION OF THE QUESTION OF AN INTERNATIONAL CRIMINAL JURISDICTION

The General Assembly,

Considering that the discussion of the Convention on the Prevention and Punishment of the Crime of Genocide has raised the question of the desirability and possibility of having persons charged with genocide tried by a competent international tribunal.

Considering that, in the course of development of the international community, there will be an increasing need of an international judicial organ for the trial of certain crimes under international law,

Invites the International Law Commission to study the desirability and possibility of establishing an international judicial organ for the trial of persons charged with genocide or other crimes over which jurisdiction will be conferred upon that organ by international conventions;

Requests the International Law Commission, in carrying out this task, to pay attention to the possibility of establishing a Criminal Chamber of the International Court of Justice.

Hundred and seventy-ninth plenary meeting.
9 December 1948.

APPLICATION WITH RESPECT TO DEPENDENT TERRITORIES, OF THE CONVENTION ON THE PREVENTION AND PUNISHMENT OF THE CRIME OF GENOCIDE

The General Assembly recommends that Parties to the Convention on the Prevention and Punishment of the Crime of Genocide which administer dependent territories should take such measures as are necessary and feasible to enable the provisions of the Convention to be extended to those territories as soon as possible.

Hundred and seventy-ninth plenary meeting.
9 December 1948.

6. UNITED NATIONS DECLARATION ON THE ELIMINATION OF ALL FORMS OR RACIAL DISCRIMINATION[1]

The General Assembly,

Considering that the Charter of the United Nations is based on the principles of the dignity and equality of all human beings and seeks, among other basic objectives, to achieve international co-operation in promoting and encouraging respect for human rights and fundamental freedoms for all without distinction as to race, sex, language or religion,

Considering that the Universal Declaration of Human Rights proclaims that all human beings are born free and equal in dignity and rights and that everyone is entitled to all the rights and freedoms set out in the Declaration, without distinction of any kind, in particular as to race, colour or national origin,

Considering that the Universal Declaration of Human Rights proclaims further that all are equal before the law and are entitled without any discrimination to equal protection of the law and that all are entitled to equal protection against any discrimination and against any incitement to such discrimination,

Considering that the United Nations has condemned colonialism and all practices of segregation and discrimination associated therewith, and that the Declaration on the granting of independence to colonial countries and peoples proclaims in particular the necessity of bringing colonialism to a speedy and unconditional end,

Considering that any doctrine of racial differentiation or superiority is scientifically false, morally condemnable, socially unjust and dangerous, and that there is no justification for racial discrimination either in theory or in practice,

Taking into account the other resolutions adopted by the General Assembly and the international instruments adopted by the specialized agencies, in particular the International Labour Organisation and the United Nations Educational, Scientific and Cultural Organization, in the field of discrimination,

Taking into account the fact that, although international action and efforts in a number of countries have made it possible to achieve progress in that field, discrimination based on race, colour or ethnic origin in certain areas of the world continues none the less to be cause for serious concern,

Alarmed by the manifestations of racial discrimination still in evidence in some areas of the world, some of which are imposed by certain Governments by means of legislative, administrative or other measures, in the form, *inter alia,* of *apartheid,* segregation and separation, as well as by the promotion and dissemination of doctrines of racial superiority and expansionism in certain areas,

Convinced that all forms of racial discrimination and, still more so, governmental policies based on the prejudice of racial superiority or on racial hatred, besides constituting a violation of fundamental human rights, tend to jeopardize friendly relations among peoples, cooperation between nations and international peace and security,

Convinced also that racial discrimination harms not only those who are its objects but also those who practise it,

Convinced further that the building of a world society free from all forms of racial segregation and discrimination, factors which create hatred and division among men, is one of the fundamental objectives of the United Nations,

1. *Solemnly affirms* the necessity of speedily eliminating racial discrimination throughout the world, in all its forms and manifestations, and of securing understanding of and respect for the dignity of the human person;

---

[1] Official Records of the General Assembly, Eighteenth Session, Supplement No. 15, pp. 35-38.

2. *Solemnly affirms* the necessity of adopting national and international measures to that end, including teaching, education and information, in order to secure the universal and effective recognition and observance of the principles set forth below;

3. *Proclaims* this Declaration:

Article 1

Discrimination between human beings on the ground of race, colour or ethnic origin is an offence to human dignity and shall be condemned as a denial of the principles of the Charter of the United Nations, as a violation of the human rights and fundamental freedoms proclaimed in the Universal Declaration of Human Rights, as an obstacle to friendly and peaceful relations among nations and as a fact capable of disturbing peace and security among peoples.

Article 2

1. No State, institution, group or individual shall make any discrimination whatsoever in matters of human rights and fundamental freedoms in the treatment of persons, groups of persons or institutions on the ground of race, colour or ethnic origin.

2. No State shall encourage, advocate or lend its support, through police action or otherwise, to any discrimination based on race, colour or ethnic origin by any group, institution or individual.

3. Special concrete measures shall be taken in appropriate circumstances in order to secure adequate development or protection of individuals belonging to certain racial groups with the object of ensuring the full enjoyment by such individuals of human rights and fundamental freedoms. These measures shall in no circumstances have as a consequence the maintenance of unequal or separate rights for different racial groups.

Article 3

1. Particular efforts shall be made to prevent discrimination based on race, colour or ethnic origin especially in the fields of civil rights, access to citizenship, education, religion, employment, occupation and housing.

2. Everyone shall have equal access to any place or facility intended for use by the general public without distinction as to race, colour or ethnic origin.

Article 4

All States shall take effective measures to revise governmental and other public policies and to rescind laws and regulations which have the effect of creating and perpetuating racial discrimination wherever it still exist. They should pass legislation for prohibiting such discrimination and should take all appropriate measures to combat those prejudices which lead to racial discrimination.

Article 5

And end shall be put without delay to governmental and other public policies of racial segregation and especially policies of *aparthied*, as well as all forms of racial discrimination and separation resulting from such policies.

Article 6

No discrimination by reason of race, colour or ethnic origin shall be admitted in the enjoyment by any person of political and citizenship rights in his country, in particular the right to participate in elections through universal and equal suffrage and to take part in the government. Everyone has the right of equal access to public service in his country.

Article 7

1. Everyone has the right to equality before the law and to equal justice under the law. Everyone, without distinction as to race, colour, or ethnic origin, has the right to security of person and protection by the State against violence or bodily harm, whether inflicted by government officials or by any individual, group or institution.

2. Everyone shall have the right to an effective remedy and protection against any discrimination he may suffer on the ground of race, colour or ethnic origin with respect to his fundamental rights and freedoms through independent national tribunals competent to deal with such matters.

Article 8

All effective steps shall be taken immediately in the fields of teaching, education and information, with a view to eliminating racial discrimination and prejudice and promoting understanding, tolerance and friendship among nations and racial groups, as well as to propagating the purposes and principles of the Charter of the United Nations, of the Universal Declaration of Human Rights, and of the Declaration on the granting of independence to colonial countries and peoples.

Article 9

1. All propaganda and organizations based on ideas or theories of the superiority of one race or group of persons of one colour or ethnic origin with a view to justifying or promoting racial discrimination in any form shall be severely condemned.

2. All incitement to or acts of violence, whether by individuals or organizations, against any race or group of persons of another colour or ethnic origin shall be considered an offence against society and punishable under law.

3. In order to put into effect the purposes and principles of the present Declaration, all States shall take immediate and positive measures, including legislative and other measures to prosecute and/or outlaw organizations which promote or incite to racial discrimination, or incite to or use violence for purposes of discrimination based on race, colour or ethnic origin.

Article 10

The United Nations, the specialized agencies, States and non-governmental organizations shall do all in their power to promote energetic action which, by combining legal and other practical measures, will make possible the abolition of all forms of racial discrimination. They shall, in particular, study the causes of such discrimination with a view to recommending appropriate and effective measures to combat and eliminate it.

Article 11

Every State shall promote respect for and observance of human rights and fundamental freedoms in accordance with the Charter of the United Nations and shall fully and faithfully observe the provisions of the present Declaration, the Universal Declaration of Human Rights and the Declaration on the granting of independence to colonial countries and peoples.

1261st plenary meeting,
20 November 1963.

7. INTERNATIONAL CONVENTION ON THE ELIMINATION OF ALL FORMS OF RACIAL DISCRIMINATION[1]

A

The General Assembly,

Considering that it is appropriate to conclude under the auspices of the United Nations an International Convention on the Elimination of All Forms of Racial Discrimination,

Convinced that the Convention will be an important step towards the elimination of all forms of racial discrimination and that it should be signed and ratified as soon as possible by States and its provisions implemented without delay,

Considering further that the text of the Convention should be made known throughout the world,

1. *Adopts* and opens for signature and ratification the International Convention on the Elimination of All Forms of Racial Discrimination, annexed to the present resolution;

2. *Invites* States referred to in article 17 of the Convention to sign and ratify the Convention without any delay;

3. *Requests* the Governments of States and non-governmental organizations to publicize the text of the Convention as widely as possible, using every means at their disposal, including all the appropriate media of information;

4. *Requests* the Secretary-General to ensure the immediate and wide circulation of the Convention and, to that end, to publish and distribute its text;

5. *Requests* the Secretary-General to submit to the General Assembly reports concerning the state of ratifications of the Convention, which will be considered by the General Assembly at future sessions as a separate agenda item.

1406th plenary meeting,
21 December 1965.

ANNEX

International Convention on the Elimination of All Forms of Racial Discrimination

The States Parties to this Convention,

Considering that the Charter of the United Nations is based on the principles of the dignity and equality inherent in all human beings, and that all Member States have pledged themselves to take joint and separate action, in co-operation with the Organization, for the achievement of one of the purposes of the United Nations which is to promote and encourage universal respect for and observance of human rights and fundamental freedoms for all, without distinction as to race, sex, language or religion,

Considering that the Universal Declaration of Human Rights proclaims that all human beings are born free and equal in dignity and rights and that everyone is entitled to all the rights and freedoms set out therein, without distinction of any kind, in particular as to race, colour or national origin,

Considering that all human beings are equal before the law and are entitled to equal protection of the law against any discrimination and against any incitement to discrimination,

Considering that the United Nations has condemned colonialism and all practices of segregation and discrimination associated therewith, in whatever form and wherever

---

[1] Official Records of the General Assembly, Twentieth Session, Supplement No. 14, pp. 47-52.

they exist, and that the Declaration on the Granting of Independence to Colonial Countries and Peoples of 14 December 1960 (General Assembly resolution 1514 (XV)) has affirmed and solemnly proclaimed the necessity of bringing them to a speedy and unconditional end,

Considering that the United Nations Declaration on the Elimination of All Forms of Racial Discrimination of 20 November 1963 (General Assembly resolution 1904 (XVIII)) solemnly affirms the necessity of speedily eliminating racial discrimination throughout the world in all its forms and manifestations and of securing understanding of and respect for the dignity of the human person,

Convinced that any doctrine of superiority based on racial differentiation is scientifically false, morally condemnable, socially unjust and dangerous, and that there is no justification for racial discrimination, in theory or in practice, anywhere,

Reaffirming that discrimination between human beings on the grounds of race, colour or ethnic origin is an obstacle to friendly and peaceful relations among nations and is capable of disturbing peace and security among peoples and the harmony of persons living side by side even within one and the same State,

Convinced that the existence of racial barriers is repugnant to the ideals of any human society,

Alarmed by manifestations of racial discrimination still in evidence in some areas of the world and by governmental policies based on racial superiority or hatred, such as policies of *apartheid,* segregation or separation,

Resolved to adopt all necessary measures for speedily eliminating racial discrimination in all its forms and manifestations, and to prevent and combat racist doctrines and practices in order to promote understanding between races and to build an international community free from all forms of racial segregation and racial discrimination,

Bearing in mind the Convention concerning Discrimination in respect of Employment and Occupational adopted by the International Labour Organisation in 1958, and the Convention against Discrimination in Educational adopted by the United Nations Educational, Scientific and Cultural Organization in 1960,

Desiring to implement the principles embodied in the United Nations Declaration on the Elimination of All Forms of Racial Discrimination and to secure the earliest adoption of practical measures to that end,

Have agreed as follows:

PART I

Article 1

1. In this Convention, the term "racial discrimination" shall mean any distinction, exclusion, restriction or preference based or race, colour, descent, or national or ethnic origin which has the purpose or effect of nullifying or impairing the recognition, enjoyment or exercise, on an equal footing, of human rights and fundamental freedoms in the political, economic, social, cultural or any other field of public life.

2. This Convention shall not apply to distinctions, exclusions, restrictions or preferences made by a State Party to this Convention between citizens and non-citizens.

3. Nothing in this Convention may be interpreted as affecting in any way the legal provisions of States Parties concerning nationality, citizenship or naturalization, provided that such provisions do not discriminate against any particular nationality.

4. Special measures taken for the sole purpose of securing adequate advancement of certain racial or ethnic groups or individuals requiring such protection as may be necessary in order to ensure such groups or individuals equal enjoyment or exercise of human rights and fundamental freedoms shall not be deemed racial discrimination, provided, however, that such measures do not, as a consequence, lead to the maintenance of separate rights for different racial groups and that they shall not be continued after the objectives for which they were taken have been achieved.

Article 2

1. States Parties condemn racial discrimination and undertake to pursue by all appropriate means and without delay a policy of eliminating racial discrimination in all its forms and promoting understanding among all races, and, to this end:

(a) Each State Party undertakes to engage in no act or practice of racial discrimination against persons, groups of persons or institutions and to ensure that all public authorities and public institutions, national and local, shall act in conformity with this obligation;

(b) Each State Party undertakes not to sponsor, defend or support racial discrimination by any persons or organizations;

(c) Each State Party shall take effective measures to review governmental, national and local policies, and to amend, rescind or nullify any laws and regulations which have the effect of creating or perpetuating racial discrimination wherever it exists;

(d) Each State Party shall prohibit and bring to an end, by all appropriate means, including legislation as required by circumstances, racial discrimination by any persons, group or organization;

(e) Each State Party undertakes to encourage, where appropriate, integrationist multi-racial organizations and movements and other means of eliminating barriers between races, and to discourage anything which tends to strengthen racial division.

2. States Parties shall, when the circumstances so warrant, take, in the social, economic, cultural and other fields, special and concrete measures to ensure the adequate development and protection of certain racial groups or individuals belonging to them, for the purpose of guaranteeing them the full and equal enjoyment of human rights and fundamental freedoms. These measures shall in no case entail as a consequence the maintenance of unequal or separate rights for different racial groups after the objectives for which they were taken have been achieved.

Article 3

States Parties particularly condemn racial segregation and *apartheid* and undertake to prevent, prohibit and eradicate all practices of this nature in territories under their jurisdiction.

Article 4

States Parties condemn all propaganda and all organizations which are based on ideas or theories of superiority of one race or group of persons of one colour or ethnic origin, or which attempt to justify or promote racial hatred and discrimination in any form, and undertake to adopt immediate and positive measures designed to eradicate all incitement to, or acts of, such discrimination and, to this end, with due regard to the principles embodied in the Universal Declaration of Human Rights and the rights expressly set forth in article 5 of this Convention, *inter alia:*

(a) Shall declare an offence punishable by law all dissemination of ideas based on racial superiority or hatred, incitement to racial discrimination, as well as all acts of violence or incitement to such acts against any race or group of persons of another colour or ethnic origin, and also the provision of any assistance to racist activities, including the financing thereof;

(b) Shall declare illegal and prohibit organizations, and also organized and all other propaganda activities, which promote and incite racial discrimination, and shall recognize participation in such organization or activities as an offence punishable by law;

(c) Shall not permit public authorities or public institutions, national or local, to promote or incite racial discrimination.

Article 5

In compliance with the fundamental obligations laid down in article 2 of this Convention, States Parties undertake to prohibit and to eliminate racial discrimination in all its forms and to guarantee the right of everyone, without distinction as to race, colour, or national or ethnic origin, to equality before the law, notably in the enjoyment of the following rights:

(a) The right to equal treatment before the tribunals and all other organs administering justice;

(b) The right to security of person and protection by the State against violence or bodily harm, whether inflicted by government officials or by any individual, group or institution:

(c) Political rights, in particular the rights to participate in elections—to vote and to stand for election—on the basis of universal and equal suffrage, to take part in the Government as well as in the conduct of public affairs at any level and to have equal access to public service;

(d) Other civil rights, in particular:

  (i) The right to freedom of movement and residence within the border of the State;

  (ii) The right to leave any country, including one's own, and to return to one's country;

  (iii) The right to nationality;

  (iv) The right to marriage and choice of spouse;

  (v) The right to own property alone as well as in association with others;

  (vi) The right to inherit;

  (vii) The right to freedom of thought, conscience and religion;

  (viii) The right to freedom of opinion and expression;

  (ix) The right to freedom of peaceful assembly and association;

(e) Economic, social and cultural rights, in particular:

  (i) The right to work, to free choice of employment, to just and favourable conditions of work, to protection against unemployment, to equal pay for equal work, to just and favourable remuneration;

  (ii) The right to form and join trade unions;

  (iii) The right to housing;

  (iv) The right to public health, medical care, social security and social services;

  (v) The right to education and training;

  (vi) The right to equal participation in cultural activities;

(f) The right of access to any place or service intended for use by the general public, such as transport, hotels, restaurants, cafes, theatres and parks.

Article 6

States Parties shall assure to everyone within their jurisdiction effective protection and remedies, through the competent national tribunals and other State institutions, against any acts of racial discrimination which violate his human rights and fundamental freedoms contrary to this Convention, as well as the right to seek from such tribunals just and adequate reparation or satisfaction for any damage suffered as a result of such discrimination.

Article 7

States Parties undertake to adopt immediate and effective measures, particularly in the fields of teaching, education, culture and information, with a view to combating prejudices which lead to racial discrimination and to promoting understanding, tolerance and friendship among nations and racial or ethnical groups, as well as to propagating the purposes and principles of the Charter of the United Nations, the Universal

Declaration of Human Rights, the United Nations Declaration on the Elimination of All Forms of Racial Discrimination, and this Convention.

PART II

Article 8

1. There shall be established a Committee on the Elimination of Racial Discrimination (hereinafter referred to as the Committee) consisting of eighteen experts of high moral standing and acknowledged impartiality elected by States Parties from among their nationals, who shall serve in their personal capacity, consideration being given to equitable geographical distribution and to the representation of the different forms of civilization as well as of the principal legal systems.

2. The members of the Committee shall be elected by secret ballot from a list of persons nominated by the States Parties. Each State Party may nominate one person from among its own nationals.

3. The initial election shall be held six months after the date of the entry into force of this Convention. At least three months before the date of each election the Secretary-General of the United Nations shall address a letter to the States Parties inviting them to submit their nominations within two months. The Secretary-General shall prepare a list in alphabetical order of all persons thus nominated, indicating the States Parties which have nominated them, and shall submit it to the States Parties.

4. Elections of the members of the Committee shall be held at a meeting of States Parties convened by the Secretary-General at United Nations Headquarters. At that meeting, for which two thirds of the States Parties shall constitute a quorum, the persons elected to the Committee shall be those nominees who obtain the largest number of votes and an absolute majority of the votes of the representatives of States Parties present and voting.

5. *(a)* The members of the Committee shall be elected for a term of four years. However, the terms of nine of the members elected at the first election shall expire at the end of two years; immediately after the first election the names of these nine members shall be chosen by lot by the Chairman of the Committee.

(b) For the filling of casual vacancies, the State Party whose expert has ceased to function as a member of the Committee shall appoint another expert from among its nationals, subject to the approval of the Committee.

6. States Parties shall be responsible for the expenses of the members of the Committee while they are in performance of Committee duties.

Article 9

1. States Parties undertake to submit to the Secretary-General of the United Nations, for consideration by the Committee, a report on the legislative, judicial, administrative or other measures which they have adopted and which give effect to the provisions of this Convention: *(a)* within one year after the entry into force of the Convention for the State concerned; and *(b)* thereafter every two years and whenever the Committee so requests. The Committee may request further information from the States Parties.

2. The Committee shall report annually, through the Secretary-General, to the General Assembly of the United Nations on its activities and may make suggestions and general recommendations based on the examination of the reports and information received from the States Parties. Such suggestions and general recommendations shall be reported to the General Assembly together with comments, if any, from States Parties.

Article 10

1. The Committee shall adopt its own rules of procedure.
2. The Committee shall elect its officers for a term of two years.

3. The secretariat of the Committee shall be provided by the Secretary-General of the United Nations.

4. The meetings of the Committee shall normally be held at United Nations Headquarters.

Article 11

1. If a State Party considers that another State Party is not giving effect to the provisions of this Convention, it may bring the matter to the attention of the Committee. The Committee shall then transmit the communication to the State Party concerned. Within three months, the receiving State shall submit to the Committee written explanations or statements clarifying the matter and the remedy, if any, that may have been taken by that State.

2. If the matter is not adjusted to the satisfaction of both parties, either by bilateral negotiations or by any other procedure open to them, within six months after the receipt by the receiving State of the initial communication, either State shall have the right to refer the matter again to the Committee by notifying the Committee and also the other State.

3. The Committee shall deal with a matter referred to it in accordance with paragraph 2 of this article after it has ascertained that all available domestic remedies have been invoked and exhausted in the case, in conformity with the generally recognized principles of international law. This shall not be the rule where the application of the remedies is unreasonably prolonged.

4. In any matter referred to it, the Committee may call upon the States Parties concerned to supply other relevant information.

5. When any matter arising out of this article is being considered by the Committee, the States Parties concerned shall be entitled to send a representative to take part in the proceedings of the Committee, without voting rights, while the matter is under consideration.

Article 12

1. *(a)* After the Committee has obtained and collated all the information it deems necessary, the Chairman shall appoint an *ad hoc* Conciliation Commission (hereinafter referred to as the Commission) comprising five persons who may or may not be members of the Committee. The members of the Commission shall be appointed with the unanimous consent of the parties to the dispute, and its good offices shall be made available to the States concerned with a view to an amicable solution of the matter on the basis of respect for this Convention.

(b) If the States parties to the dispute fail to reach agreement within three months on all or part of the composition of the Commission, the members of the Commission not agreed upon by the States parties to the dispute shall be elected by secret ballot by a two-thirds majority vote of the Committee from among its own members.

2. The members of the Commission shall serve in their personal capacity. They shall not be nationals of the States parties to the dispute or of a State not Party to this Convention.

3. The Commission shall elect its own Chairman and adopt its own rules of procedure.

4. The meetings of the Commission shall normally be held at United Nations Headquarters or at any other convenient place as determined by the Commission.

5. The secretariat provided in accordance with article 10, paragraph 3, of this Convention shall also service the Commission whenever a dispute among States Parties brings the Commission into being.

6. The States parties to the dispute shall share equally all the expenses of the members of the Commission in accordance with estimates to be provided by the Secretary-General of the United Nations.

7. The Secretary-General shall be empowered to pay the expenses of the members of the Commission, if necessary, before reimbursement by the States parties to the dispute in accordance with paragraph 6 of this article.

8. The information obtained and collated by the Committee shall be made available to the Commission, and the Commission may call upon the States concerned to supply any other relevant information.

Article 13

1. When the Commission has fully considered the matter, it shall prepare and submit to the Chairman of the Committee a report embodying its findings on all questions of fact relevant to the issue between the parties and containing such recommendations as it may think proper for the amicable solution of the dispute.

2. The Chairman of the Committee shall communicate the report of the Commission to each of the States parties to the dispute. These States shall, within three months, inform the Chairman of the Committee whether or not they accept the recommendations contained in the report of the Commission.

3. After the period provided for in paragraph 2 of this article, the Chairman of the Committee shall communicate the report of the Commission and the declarations of the States Parties concerned to the other States Parties to this Convention.

Article 14

1. A State Party may at any time declare that it recognizes the competence of the Committee to receive and consider communications from individuals or groups of individuals within its jurisdiction claiming to be victims of a violation by that State Party of any of the rights set forth in this Convention. No communication shall be received by the Committee if it concerns a State Party which has not made such a declaration.

2. Any State Party which makes a declaration as provided for in paragraph 1 of this article may establish or indicate a body within its national legal order which shall be competent to receive and consider petitions from individuals and groups of individuals within its jurisdiction who claim to be victims of a violation of any of the rights set forth in this Convention and who have exhausted other available local remedies.

3. A declaration made in accordance with paragraph 1 of this article and the name of any body established or indicated in accordance with paragraph 2 of this article shall be deposited by the State Party concerned with the Secretary-General of the United Nations, who shall transmit copies thereof to the other States Parties. A declaration may be withdrawn at any time by notification to the Secretary-General, but such a withdrawal shall not affect communications pending before the Committee.

4. A register of petitions shall be kept by the body established or indicated in accordance with paragraph 2 of this article, and certified copies of the register shall be filed annually through appropriate channels with the Secretary-General on the understanding that the contents shall not be publicly disclosed.

5. In the event of failure to obtain satisfaction from the body established or indicated in accordance with paragraph 2 of this article, the petitioner shall have the right to communicate the matter to the Committee within six months.

6. (a) The Committee shall confidentially bring any communication referred to it to the attention of the State Party alleged to be violating any provisions of this Convention, but the identity of the individual or groups of individuals concerned shall not be revealed without his or their express consent. The Committee shall not receive anonymous communications.

(b) Within three months, the receiving State shall submit to the Committee written explanations or statements clarifying the matter and the remedy, if any, that may have been taken by that State.

7. *(a)* The Committee shall consider communications in the light of all information made available to it by the State Party concerned and by the petitioner. The Committee shall not consider any communication from a petitioner unless it has ascertained that the petitioner has exhausted all available domestic remedies. However, this shall not be the rule where the application of the remedies is unreasonably prolonged.

(b) The Committee shall forward its suggestions and recommendations, if any, to the State Party concerned and to the petitioner.

8. The Committee shall include in its annual report a summary of such communications and, where appropriate, a summary of the explanations and statements of the States Parties concerned and of its own suggestions and recommendations.

9. The Committee shall be competent to exercise the functions provided for in this article only when at least ten States Parties to this Convention are bound by declarations in accordance with paragraph 1 of this article.

Article 15

1. Pending the achievement of the objectives of the Declaration on the Granting of Independence to Colonial Countries and Peoples, contained in General Assembly resolution 1514 (XV) of 14 December 1960, the provisions of this Convention shall in no way limit the right of petition granted to these peoples by other international instruments or by the United Nations and its specialized agencies.

2. *(a)* The Committee established under article 8, paragraph 1, of this Convention shall receive copies of the petitions from, and submit expressions of opinion and recommendations on these petitions to, the bodies of the United Nations which deal with matters directly related to the principles and objectives of this Convention in their consideration of petitions from the inhabitants of Trust and Non-Self-Governing Territories and all other territories to which General Assembly resolution 1514 (XV) applies, relating to matters covered by this Convention which are before these bodies.

(b) The Committee shall receive from the competent bodies of the United Nations copies of the reports concerning the legislative, judicial, administrative or other measures directly related to the principles and objectives of this Convention applied by the administering Powers within the Territories mentioned in sub-paragraph *(a)* of this paragraph, and shall express opinions and make recommendations to these bodies.

3. The Committee shall include in its report to the General Assembly a summary of the petitions and reports it has received from United Nations bodies, and the expressions of opinion and recommendations of the Committee relating to the said petitions and reports.

4. The Committee shall request from the Secretary-General of the United Nations all information relevant to the objectives of this Convention and available to him regarding the Territories mentioned in paragraph 2 *(a)* of this article.

Article 16

The provisions of this Convention concerning the settlement of disputes or complaints shall be applied without prejudice to other procedures for settling disputes or complaints in the field of discrimination laid down in the constituent instruments of, or in conventions adopted by, the United Nations and its specialized agencies, and shall not prevent the States Parties from having recourse to other procedures for settling a dispute in accordance with general or special international agreements in force between them.

PART III

Article 17

1. This Convention is open for signature by any State Member of the United Nations or member of any of its specialized agencies, by any State Party to the Statute of the International Court of Justice, and by any other State which has been invited by the General Assembly of the United Nations to become a Party to this Convention.

2. This Convention is subject to ratification. Instruments of ratification shall be deposited with the Secretary-General of the United Nations.

Article 18

1. This Convention shall be open to accession by any State referred to in article 17, paragraph 1, of the Convention.

2. Accession shall be effected by the deposit of an instrument of accession with the Secretary-General of the Untied Nations.

Article 19

1. This Convention shall enter into force on the thirtieth day after the date of the deposit with the Secretary-General of the United Nations of the twenty-seventh instrument of ratification or instrument of accession.

2. For each State ratifying this Convention or acceding to it after the deposit of the twenty-seventh instrument of ratification or instrument of accession, the Convention shall enter into force on the thirtieth day after the date of the deposit of its own instrument of ratification or instrument of accession.

Article 20

1. The Secretary-General of the United Nations shall receive and circulate to all States which are or may become Parties to this Convention reservations made by States at the time of ratification or accession. Any State which objects to the reservation shall, within a period of ninety days from the date of the said communication, notify the Secretary-General that it does not accept it.

2. A reservation incompatible with the object and purpose of this Convention shall not be permitted, nor shall a reservation the effect of which would inhibit the operation of any of the bodies established by this Convention be allowed. A reservation shall be considered incompatible or inhibitive if at least two thirds of the States Parties to this Convention object to it.

3. Reservations may be withdrawn at any time by notification to this effect addressed to the Secretary-General. Such notification shall take effect on the date on which it is received.

Article 21

A State Party may denounce this Convention by written notification to the Secretary-General of the United Nations. Denunciation shall take effect one year after the date of receipt of the notification by the Secretary-General.

Article 22

Any dispute between two or more States Parties with respect to the interpretation or application of this Convention, which is not settled by negotiation or by the procedures expressly provided for in this Convention, shall, at the request of any of the parties to the dispute, be referred to the International Court of Justice for decision, unless the disputants agree to another mode of settlement.

Article 23

1. A request for the revision of this Convention may be made at any time by any State Party by means of a notification in writing addressed to the Secretary-General of the United Nations.

2. The General Assembly of the United Nations shall decide upon the steps, if any, to be taken in respect of such a request.

Article 24

The Secretary-General of the United Nations shall inform all States referred to in article 17, paragraph 1, of this Convention of the following particulars:

(a) Signatures, ratifications and accessions under articles 17 and 18;

(b) The date of entry into force of this Convention under article 19;

(c) Communications and declarations received under articles 14, 20 and 23;

(d) Denunciations under article 21.

Article 25

1. This Convention, of which the Chinese, English, French, Russian and Spanish texts are equally authentic, shall be deposited in the archives of the United Nations.

2. The Secretary-General of the United Nations shall transmit certified copies of this Convention to all States belonging to any of the categories mentioned in article 17, paragraph 1, of the Convention.

B

The General Assembly,

Recalling the Declaration on the Granting of Independence to Colonial Countries and Peoples contained in its resolution 1514 (XV) of 14 December 1960,

Bearing in mind its resolution 1654 (XVI) of 27 November 1961, which established the Special Committee on the Situation with regard to the Implementation of the Declaration on the Granting of Independence to Colonial Countries and Peoples to examine the application of the Declaration and to carry out its provisions by all means at its disposal,

Bearing in mind also the provisions of article 15 of the International Convention on the Elimination of All Forms of Racial Discrimination contained in the annex to resolution A above,

Recalling that the General Assembly has established other bodies to receive and examine petitions from the peoples of colonial countries,

Convinced that close co-operation between the Committee on the Elimination of Racial Discrimination, established by the International Convention on the Elimination of All Forms of Racial Discrimination, and the bodies of the United Nations charged with receiving and examining petitions from the peoples of colonial countries will facilitate the achievement of the objectives of both the Convention and the Declaration on the Granting of Independence to Colonial Countries and Peoples,

Recognizing that the elimination of racial discrimination in all its forms is vital to the achievement of fundamental human rights and to the assurance of the dignity and worth of the human person, and thus constitutes a pre-emptory obligation under the Charter of the United Nations,

1. *Calls upon* the Secretary-General to make available to the Committee on the Elimination of Racial Discrimination, periodically or at its request, all information in his possession relevant to article 15 of the International Convention on the Elimination of All Forms of Racial Discrimination;

2. *Requests* the Special Committee on the Situation with regard to the implementation of the Declaration on the Granting of Independence to Colonial Countries and

Peoples, and all other bodies of the United Nations authorized to receive and examine petitions from the peoples of the colonial countries, to transmit to the Committee on the Elimination of Racial Discrimination, periodically or at its request, copies of petitions from those peoples relevant to the Convention, for the comments and recommendations of the said Committee;

3. *Requests* the bodies referred to in paragraph 2 above to include in their annual reports to the General Assembly a summary of the action taken by them under the terms of the present resolution.

1406th plenary meeting,
21 December 1965.

8. CONVENTION ON THE POLITICAL RIGHTS OF WOMEN[1]

The General Assembly,

Considering that the peoples of the United Nations are determined to promote equality of rights for men and women, in conformity with the principles embodied in the Charter,

Believing that an international convention on the political rights of women will constitute an important step towards the universal attainment of equal rights of men and women,

Reaffirming its resolution 56 (I) of 11 December 1946,

Decides to open the attached Convention for signature and ratification at the end of the present session.

409th plenary meeting,
20 December 1952.

ANNEX

Convention on the Political Rights of Women

The Contracting Parties,

Desiring to implement the principle of equality of rights for men and women contained in the Charter of the United Nations,

Recognizing that everyone has the right to take part in the government of his country directly or through freely chosen representatives, and has the right to equal access to public service in his country, and desiring to equalize the status of men and women in the enjoyment and exercise of political rights, in accordance with the provisions of the Charter of the United Nations and of the Universal Declaration of Human Rights,

Having resolved to conclude a Convention for this purpose,

Hereby agree as hereinafter provided:

ARTICLE I

Women shall be entitled to vote in all elections on equal terms with men, without any discrimination.

ARTICLE II

Women shall be eligible for election to all publicly elected bodies, established by national law, on equal terms with men, without any discrimination.

---

[1] Official Records of the General Assembly, Seventh Session, Supplement No. 20, pp. 27-28.

ARTICLE III

Women shall be entitled to hold public office and to exercise all public functions, established by national law, on equal terms with men, without any discrimination,

ARTICLE IV

1. This Convention shall be open for signature on behalf of any Member of the United Nations and also on behalf of any other State to which an invitation has been addressed by the General Assembly.

2. This Convention shall be ratified and the instruments of ratification shall be deposited with the Secretary-General of the United Nations.

ARTICLE V

1. This Convention shall be open for accession to all States referred to in paragraph 1 of article IV.

2. Accession shall be effected by the deposit of an instrument of accession with the Secretary-General of the United Nations.

ARTICLE VI

1. This Convention shall come into force on the ninetieth day following the date of deposit of the sixth instrument of ratification of accession.

2. For each State ratifying or acceding to the Convention after the deposit of the sixth instrument of ratification or accession the Convention shall enter into force on the ninetieth day after deposit by such State of its instrument of ratification or accession.

ARTICLE VII

In the event that any State submits a reservation to any of the articles of this Convention at the time of signature, ratification or accession, the Secretary-General shall communicate the text of the reservation to all States which are or may become parties to this Convention. Any State which objects to the reservation may, within a period of ninety days from the date of the said communication (or upon the date of its becoming a party to the Convention), notify the Secretary-General that it does not accept it. In such case, the Convention shall not enter into force as between such State and the State making the reservation.

ARTICLE VIII

1. Any State may denounce this Convention by written notification to the Secretary-General of the United Nations. Denunciation shall take effect one year after the date of receipt of the notification by the Secretary-General.

2. This Convention shall cease to be in force as from the date when the denunciation which reduces the number of parties to less than six becomes effective.

ARTICLE IX

Any dispute which may arise between any two or more Contracting States concerning the interpretation or application of this Convention, which is not settled by negotiation, shall at the request of any one of the parties to the dispute be referred to the International Court of Justice for decision, unless they agree to another mode of settlement.

ARTICLE X

The Secretary-General of the United Nations shall notify all Members of the United Nations and the non-member States contemplated in paragraph 1 of article IV of this Convention of the following:

(a) Signatures and instruments of ratifications received in accordance with article IV;

(b) Instruments of accession received in accordance with article V;

(c) The date upon which this Convention enters into force in accordance with article VI;

(d) Communications and notifications received in accordance with article VII;

(e) Notifications of denunciation received in accordance with paragraph 1 of article VIII;

(f) Abrogation in accordance with paragraph 2 of article VIII.

ARTICLE XI

1. This Convention, of which the Chinese, English, French, Russian and Spanish texts shall be equally authentic, shall be deposited in the archives of the United Nations.

2. The Secretary-General of the United Nations shall transmit a certified copy to all Members of the United Nations and to the non-member States contemplated in paragraph 1 of article IV.

9. DECLARATION ON THE ELIMINATION OF DISCRIMINATION AGAINST WOMEN[1]

The General Assembly,

Considering that the peoples of the United Nations have, in the Charter, reaffirmed their faith in fundamental human rights, in the dignity and worth of the human person and in the equal rights of men and women,

Considering that the Universal Declaration on Human Rights asserts the principle of non-discrimination and proclaims that all human beings are born free and equal in dignity and rights and that everyone is entitled to all the rights and freedoms set forth therein, without distinction of any kind, including any distinction as to sex,

Taking into account the resolutions, declarations, conventions and recommendations of the United Nations and the specialized agencies designed to eliminate all forms of discrimination and to promote equal rights for men and women,

Concerned that, despite the Charter of the United Nations, the Universal Declaration of Human Rights, the International Covenant on Human Rights and other instruments of the United Nations and the specialized agencies and despite the progress made in the matter of equality of rights, there continues to exist considerable discrimination against women,

Considering that discrimination against women is incompatible with human dignity and with the welfare of the family and of society, prevents their participation, on equal terms with men, in the political, social, economic and cultural life of their countries and is an obstacle to the full development of the potentialities of women in the service of their countries and of humanity,

---

[1] Official Records of the General Assembly, Twenty-second Session, Supplement No. 16, pp. 35-37.

Bearing in mind the great contribution made by women to social, political, economic and cultural life and the part they play in the family and particularly in the rearing of children,

Convinced that the full and complete development of a country, the welfare of the world and the cause of peace require the maximum participation of women as well as men in all fields,

Considering that it is necessary to ensure the universal recognition in law and in fact of the principle of equality of men and women,

Solemnly proclaims this Declaration:

Article 1

Discrimination against women, denying or limiting as it does their equality of rights with men, is fundamentally unjust and constitutes an offence against human dignity.

Article 2

All appropriate measures shall be taken to abolish existing laws, customs, regulations and practices which are discriminatory against women, and to establish adequate legal protection for equal rights of men and women, in particular:

(a) The principle of equality of rights shall be embodied in the constitution or otherwise guaranteed by law;

(b) The international instruments of the United Nations and the specialized agencies relating to the elimination of discrimination against women, shall be ratified or acceded to and fully implemented as soon as practicable.

Article 3

All appropriate measures shall be taken to educate public opinion and to direct national aspirations towards the eradication of prejudice and the abolition of customary and all other practices which are based on the idea of the inferiority of women.

Article 4

All appropriate measures shall be taken to ensure to women on equal terms with men, without any discrimination:

(a) The right to vote in all elections and be eligible for election to all publicly elected bodies;

(b) The right to vote in all public referenda;

(c) The right to hold public office and to exercise all public functions.
Such rights shall be guaranteed by legislation.

Article 5

Women shall have the same rights as men to acquire, change or retain their nationality. Marriage to an alien shall not automatically affect the nationality of the wife either by rendering her stateless or by forcing upon her the nationality of her husband.

Article 6

1. Without prejudice to the safeguarding of the unity and the harmony of the family, which remains the basic unit of any society, all appropriate measures, particularly legislative measures, shall be taken to ensure to women, married or unmarried, equal rights with men in the field of civil law, and in particular:

(a) The right to acquire, administer, enjoy, dispose of and inherit property, including property acquired during marriage;

(b) The right to equality in legal capacity and the exercise thereof;

(c) The same rights as men with regard to the law on the movement of persons.

2. All appropriate measures shall be taken to ensure the principle of equality of status of the husband and wife, and in particular:

(a) Women shall have the same right as men to free choice of a spouse and to enter into marriage only with their free and full consent;

(b) Women shall have equal rights with men during marriage and at its dissolution. In all cases the interest of the children shall be paramount;

(c) Parents shall have equal rights and duties in matters relating to their children. In all cases the interest of the children shall be paramount.

3. Child marriage and the betrothal of young girls before puberty shall be prohibited, and effective action, including legislation, shall be taken to specify a minimum age for marriage and to make the registration of marriages in an official registry compulsory.

Article 7

All provisions of penal codes which constitute discrimination against women shall be repealed.

Article 8

All appropriate measures, including legislation, shall be taken to combat all forms of traffic in women and exploitation of prostitution of women.

Article 9

All appropriate measures shall be taken to ensure to girls and women, married or unmarried, equal rights with men in education at all levels, and in particular:

(a) Equal conditions of access to, and study in, educational institutions of all types, including universities and vocational, technical and professional schools;

(b) The same choice of curricula, the same examinations, teaching staff with qualifications of the same standard, and school premises and equipment of the same quality, whether the institutions are co-educational or not;

(c) Equal opportunities to benefit from scholarships and other study grants;

(d) Equal opportunities for access to programmes of continuing education, including adult literacy programmes;

(e) Access to educational information to help in ensuring the health and well-being of families.

Article 10

1. All appropriate measures shall be taken to ensure to women, married or unmarried, equal rights with men in the field of economic and social life and in particular:

(a) The right, without discrimination on grounds of marital status or any other grounds, to receive vocational training, to work, to free choice of profession and employment, and to professional and vocational advancement;

(b) The right to equal remuneration with men and to equality of treatment in respect of work of equal value;

(c) The right to leave with pay, retirement privileges and provision for security in respect of unemployment, sickness, old age or other incapacity to work;

(d) The right to receive family allowances on equal terms with men.

2. In order to prevent discrimination against women on account or marriage or maternity and to ensure their effective right to work, measures shall be taken to prevent their dismissal in the event of marriage or maternity and to provide paid maternity leave, with the guarantee of returning to former employment, and to provide the necessary social services, including child-care facilities.

3. Measures taken to protect women in certain types of work for reasons inherent in their physical nature, shall not be regarded as discriminatory.

Article 11

1. The principle of equality of rights of men and women demands implementation in all States in accordance with the principles of the Charter of the United Nations and of the Universal Declaration of Human Rights.

2. Governments, non-governmental organizations and individuals are urged, therefore, to do all in their power to promote the implementation of the principles contained in this Declaration.

1597th plenary meeting,
7 November 1967.

10. DECLARATION OF THE RIGHTS OF THE CHILD[1]

PREAMBLE

Whereas the peoples of the United Nations have, in the Charter, reaffirmed their faith in fundamental human rights and in the dignity and worth of the human person, and have determined to promote social progress and better standards of life in larger freedom,

Whereas The United Nations has, in the Universal Declaration of Human Rights, proclaimed that everyone is entitled to all the rights and freedoms set forth therein, without distinction of any kind, such as race, colour, sex, language, religion, political or other opinion, national or social origin, property, birth or other status,

Whereas the child, by reason of his physical and mental immaturity needs special safeguards and care, including appropriate legal protection, before as well as after birth,

Whereas the need for such special safeguards has been stated in the Geneva Declaration of the Rights of the Child of 1924, and recognized in the Universal Declaration of Human Rights and in the statutes of specialized agencies and international organizations concerned with the welfare of children,

Whereas mankind owes to the child the best it has to give,

Now therefore,

The General Assembly

Proclaims this Declaration of the Rights of the Child to the end that he may have a happy childhood and enjoy for his own good and for the good of society the rights and freedoms herein set forth, and calls upon parents, upon men and women as individuals, and upon voluntary organizations, local authorities and national Governments to recognize these rights and strive for their observance by legislative and other measures progressively taken in accordance with the following principles:

PRINCIPLE 1

The child shall enjoy all the rights set forth in this Declaration. Every child, without any exception whatsoever, shall be entitled to these rights, without distinction or discrimination on account of race, colour, sex, language, religion, political or other opinion, national or social origin, property, birth or other status, whether of himself or of his family.

---

[1] Official Records of the General Assembly, Fourteenth Session, Supplement No. 10, pp. 19-20.

744

PRINCIPLE 2

The child shall enjoy special protection, and shall be given opportunities and facilities, by law and by other means, to enable him to develop physically, mentally, morally, spiritually and socially in a healthy and normal manner and in conditons of freedom and dignity. In the enactment of laws for this purpose, the best interests of the child shall be the paramount consideration.

PRINCIPLE 3

The child shall be entitled from his birth to a name and a nationality.

PRINCIPLE 4

The child shall enjoy the benefits of social security. He shall be entitled to grow and develop in health; to this end, special care and protection shall be provided both to him and to his mother, including adequate pre-natal and post-natal care. The child shall have the right to adequate nutrition, housing, recreation and medical services.

PRINCIPLE 5

The child who is physically, mentally or socially handicapped shall be given the special treatment, education and care required by his particular condition.

PRINCIPLE 6

The child, for the full and harmonious development of his personality, needs love and understanding. He shall, wherever possible, grow up in the care and under the responsibility of his parents, and, in any case, in an atmosphere of affection and of moral and material security; a child of tender years shall not, save in exceptional circumstances, be separated from his mother. Society and the public authorities shall have the duty to extend particular care to children without a family and to those without adequate means of support. Payment of State and other assistance towards the maintenance of children of large families is desirable.

PRINCIPLE 7

The child is entitled to receive education, which shall be free and compulsory, at least in the elementary stages. He shall be given an education which will promote his general culture, and enable him, on a basis of equal opportunity, to develop his abilities, his individual judgement, and his sense of moral and social responsibility, and to become a useful member of society.

The best interests of the child shall be the guiding principle of those responsible for his education and guidance; that responsibility lies in the first place with his parents.

The child shall have full opportunity for play and recreation, which should be directed to the same purposes as education; society and the public authorities shall endeavour to promote the enjoyment of this right.

PRINCIPLE 8

The child shall in all circumstances be among the first to receive protection and relief.

PRINCIPLE 9

The child shall be protected against all forms of neglect, cruelty and exploitation. He shall not be the subject of traffic, in any form.

The child shall not be admitted to employment before an appropriate minimum age; he shall in no case be caused or permitted to engage in any occupation or employment which would prejudice his health or education, or interfere with his physical, mental or moral development.

PRINCIPLE 10

The child shall be protected from practices which may foster racial, religious and any other form of discrimination. He shall be brought up in a spirit of understanding, tolerance, friendship among peoples, peace and universal brotherhood, and in full consciousness that his energy and talents should be devoted to the service of his fellow men.

841st plenary meeting,
20 November 1959.

11. DECLARATION ON SOCIAL PROGRESS AND DEVELOPMENT[1]

The General Assembly,

Mindful of the pledge of Members of the United Nations under the Charter to take joint and separate action in co-operation with the Organization to promote higher standards of living, full employment and conditions of economic and social progress and development;

Reaffirming faith in human rights and fundamental freedoms and in the principles of peace, of the dignity and worth of the human person, and of social justice proclaimed in the Charter,

Recalling the principles of the Universal Declaration of Human Rights, the International Covenants on Human Rights, the Declaration of the Rights of the Child, the Declaration on the Granting of Independence to Colonial Countries and Peoples, the International Convention on the Elimination of All Forms of Racial Discrimination, the United Nations Declaration on the Elimination of All Forms of Racial Discrimination, the Declaration on the Promotion among Youth of the Ideals of Peace, Mutual Respect and Understanding between Peoples, the Declaration on the Elimination of Discrimination against Women and of resolutions of the United Nations,

Bearing in mind the standards already set for social progress in the constitutions, conventions, recommendations and resolutions of the International Labour Organisation, the Food and Agriculture Organization of the United Nations, the United Nations Educational, Scientific and Cultural Organization, the World Health Organization, the United Nations Children's Fund and of other organizations concerned,

Convinced that man can achieve complete fulfilment of his aspirations only within a just social order and that it is consequently of cardinal importance to accelerate social and economic progress everywhere, thus contributing to international peace and solidarity,

Convinced that international peace and security on the one hand, and social progress and economic development on the other, are closely interdependent and influence each other,

Persuaded that social development can be promoted by peaceful coexistence, friendly relations and co-operation among States with different social, economic or political systems,

---

[1] Official Records of the General Assembly, Twenty-fourth Session, Supplement No. 30, pp. 49-53.

Emphasizing the interdependence of economic and social development in the wider process of growth and change, as well as the importance of a strategy of integrated development which takes full account at all stages of its social aspects,

Regretting the inadequate progress achieved in the world social situation despite the efforts of States and the international Community,

Recognizing that the primary responsibility for the development of the developing countries rests on those countries themselves and acknowledging the pressing need to narrow and eventually close the gap in the standards of living between economically more advanced and developing countries and, to that end, that Member States shall have the responsibility to pursue internal and external policies designed to promote social development throughout the world, and in particular to assist developing countries to accelerate their economic growth,

Recognizing the urgency of devoting to works of peace and social progress resources being expended on armaments and wasted on conflict and destruction,

Conscious of the contribution that science and technology can render towards meeting the needs common to all humanity,

Believing that the primary task of all States and international organizations is to eliminate from the life of society all evils and obstacles to social progress, particularly such evils as inequality, exploitation, war, colonialism and racism,

Desirous of promoting the progress of all mankind towards these goals and of overcoming all obstacles to their realization,

Solemnly proclaims this Declaration on Social Progress and Development and calls for national and international action for its use as a common basis for social development policies:

PART I

PRINCIPLES

Article 1

All peoples and all human beings, without distinction as to race, colour, sex, language, religion, nationality, ethnic origin, family or social status, or political or other conviction, shall have the right to live in dignity and freedom and to enjoy the fruits of social progress and should, on their part, contribute to it.

Article 2

Social progress and development shall be founded on respect for the dignity and value of the human person and shall ensure the promotion of human rights and social justice, which requires:

(a) The immediate and final elimination of all forms of inequality, exploitation of peoples and individuals, colonialism and racism, including nazism and *apartheid*, and all other policies and ideologies opposed to the purposes and principles of the United Nations;

(b) The recognition and effective implementation of civil and political rights as well as of economic, social and cultural rights without any discrimination.

Article 3

The following are considered primary conditions of social progress and development:

(a) National independence based on the right of peoples to self-determination;

(b) The principle of non-interference in the internal affairs of States;

(c) Respect for the sovereignty and territorial integrity of States;

(d) Permanent sovereignty of each nation over its natural wealth and resources;

(e) The right and responsibility of each State and, as far as they are concerned,

each nation and people to determine freely its own objectives of social development, to set its own priorities and to decide in conformity with the principles of the Charter of the United Nations the means and methods of their achievement without any external interference:

(f) Peaceful coexistence, peace, friendly relations and co-operation among States irrespective of differences in their social, economic or political systems.

Article 4

The family as a basic unit of society and the natural environment for the growth and well-being of all its members, particularly children and youth, should be assisted and protected so that it may fully assume its responsibilities within the community. Parents have the exclusive right to determine freely and responsibly the number and spacing of their children.

Article 5

Social progress and development require the full utilization of human resources, including, in particular:

(a) The encouragement of creative initiative under conditions of enlightened public opinion;

(b) The dissemination of national and international information for the purpose of making individuals aware of changes occurring in society as a whole;

(c) The active participation of all elements of society, individually or through associations, in defining and in achieving the common goals of development with full respect for the fundamental freedoms embodied in the Universal Declaration of Human Rights;

(d) The assurance to disadvantaged or marginal sectors of the population of equal opportunities for social and economic advancement in order to achieve an effectively integrated society.

Article 6

Social development requires the assurance to everyone of the right to work and the free choice of employment.

Social progress and development require the participation of all members of society in productive and socially useful labour and the establishment, in conformity with human rights and fundamental freedoms and with the principles of justice and the social function of property, of forms of ownership of land and of the means of production which preclude any kind of exploitation of man, ensure equal rights to property for all and create conditions leading to genuine equality among people.

Article 7

The rapid expansion of national income and wealth and their equitable distribution among all members of society are fundamental to all social progress, and they should therefore be in the forefront of the preoccupations of every State and Government.

The improvement in the position of the developing countries in international trade resulting, among other things, from the achievement of favourable terms of trade and of equitable and remunerative prices at which developing countries market their products is necessary in order to make it possible to increase national income and in order to advance social development.

Article 8

Each Government has the primary role and ultimate responsibility of ensuring the social progress and well-being of its people, of planning social development measures as part of comprehensive development plans, of encouraging and co-ordinating or integrating all national efforts towards this end and of introducing necessary changes in the social structure. In planning social development measures, the diversity of the needs of developing and developed areas, and of urban and rural areas, within each country, shall be taken into due account.

Article 9

Social progress and development are the common concerns of the international community, which shall supplement, by concerted international action, national efforts to raise the living standards of peoples.

Social progress and economic growth require recognition of the common interest of all nations in the exploration, conservation, use and exploitation, exclusively for peaceful purposes and in the interests of all mankind, of those areas of the environment such as outer space and the sea-bed and ocean floor and the subsoil thereof, beyond the limits of national jurisdiction, in accordance with the purposes and principles of the Charter of the United Nations.

PART II

OBJECTIVES

Social progress and development shall aim at the continuous raising of the material and spiritual standards of living of all members of society, with respect for and in compliance with human rights and fundamental freedoms, through the attainment of the following main goals:

Article 10

(a) The assurance at all levels of the right to work and the right of everyone to form trade unions and workers' associations and to bargain collectively; promotion of full productive employment and elimination of unemployment and under-employment; establishment of equitable and favourable conditions of work for all, including the improvement of health and safety conditions; assurance of just remuneration for labour without any discrimination as well as a sufficiently high minimum wage to ensure a decent standard of living; the protection of the consumer;

(b) The elimination of hunger and malnutrition and the guarantee of the right to proper nutrition;

(c) The elimination of poverty; the assurance of a steady improvement in levels of living and of a just and equitable distribution of income;

(d) The achievement of the highest standards of health and the provision of health protection for the entire population, if possible free of charge;

(e) The eradication of illiteracy and the assurance of the right to universal access to culture, to free compulsory education at the elementary level and to free education at all levels; the raising of the general level of life-long education;

(f) The provision for all, particularly persons in low-income groups and large families, of adequate housing and community services.

Social progress and development shall aim equally at the progressive attainment of the following main goals.

Article 11

(a) The provision of comprehensive social security schemes and social welfare services; the establishment and improvement of social security and insurance schemes for all persons who, because of illness, disability or old age, are temporarily or per-

manently unable to earn a living, with a view to ensuring a proper standard of living for such persons and for their families and dependants;

(b) The protection of the rights of the mother and child; concern for the upbringing and health of children; the provision of measures to safeguard the health and welfare of women and particularly of working mothers during pregnancy and the infancy of their children, as well as of mothers whose earnings are the sole source of livelihood for the family; the granting to women of pregnancy and maternity leave and allowances without loss of employment or wages;

(c) The protection of the rights and the assuring of the welfare of children, the aged and the disabled; the provision of protection for the physically or mentally disadvantaged;

(d) The education of youth in, and promotion among them of, the ideals of justice and peace, mutual respect and understanding among peoples; the promotion of full participation of youth in the process of national development;

(e) The provision of social defence measures and the elimination of conditions leading to crime and delinquency, especially juvenile delinquency;

(f) The guarantee that all individuals, without discrimination of any kind, are made aware of their rights and obligations and receive the necessary aid in the exercise and safeguarding of their rights.

Social progress and development shall further aim at achieving the following main objectives:

Article 12

(a) The creation of conditions for rapid and sustained social and economic development, particularly in the developing countries; change in international economic relations; new and effective methods of international cooperation in which equality of opportunity should be as much a prerogative of nations as of individuals within a nation;

(b) The elimination of all forms of discrimination and exploitation and all other practices and ideologies contrary to the purposes and principles of the Charter of the United Nations;

(c) The elimination of all forms of foreign economic exploitation, particularly that practised by international monopolies, in order to enable the people of every country to enjoy in full the benefits of their national resources.

Social progress and development shall finally aim at the attainment of the following main goals:

Article 13

(a) Equitable sharing of scientific and technological advances by developed and developing countries, and a steady increase in the use of science and technology for the benefit of the social development of society;

(b) The establishment of a harmonious balance between scientific, technological and material progress and the intellectual, spiritual, cultural and moral advancement of humanity;

(c) The protection and improvement of the human environment.

PART III

MEANS AND METHODS

On the basis of the principles set forth in this Declaration, the achievement of the objectives of social progress and development requires the mobilization of the necessary resources by national and international action, with particular attention to such means and methods as:

Article 14

(a) Planning for social progress and development, as an integrated part of balanced over-all development planning;

(b) The establishment, where necessary, of national systems for framing and carrying out social policies and programmes, and the promotion by the countries concerned of planned regional development, taking into account differing regional conditions and needs, particularly the development of regions which are less favoured or under-developed by comparison with the rest of the country;

(c) The promotion of basic and applied social research, particularly comparative international research applied to the planning and execution of social development programmes.

Article 15

(a) The adoption of measures to ensure the effective participation, as appropriate, of all the elements of society in the preparation and execution of national plans and programmes of economic and social development;

(b) The adoption of measures for an increasing rate of popular participation in the economic, social, cultural and political life of countries through national governmental bodies, non-governmental organizations, co-operatives, rural associations, workers' and employers' organizations and women's and youth organizations, by such methods as national and regional plans for social and economic progress and community development, with a view to achieving a fully integrated national society, accelerating the process of social mobility and consolidating the democratic system;

(c) Mobilization of public opinion, at both national and international levels, in support of the principles and objectives of social progress and development;

(d) The dissemination of social information, at the national and the international level, to make people aware of changing circumstances in society as a whole, and to educate the consumer.

Article 16

(a) Maximum mobilization of all national resources and their rational and efficient utilization; promotion of increased and accelerated productive investment in social and economic fields and of employment; orientation of society towards the development process;

(b) Progressively increasing provision of the necessary budgetary and other resources required for financing the social aspects of development;

(c) Achievement of equitable distribution of national income, utilizing, *inter alia*, the fiscal system and government spending as an instrument for the equitable distribution and redistribution of income in order to promote social progress;

(d) The adoption of measures aimed at prevention of such an outflow of capital from developing countries as would be detrimental to their economic and social development.

Article 17

(a) The adoption of measures to accelerate the process of industrialization, especially in developing countries, with due regard for its social aspects, in the interests of the entire population; development of an adequate organizational and legal framework conducive to an un-interrupted and diversified growth of the industrial sector; measures to overcome the adverse social effects which may result from urban development and industrialization, including automation; maintenance of a proper balance between rural and urban development, and in particular, measures designed to ensure healthier living conditions, especially in large industrial centres;

(b) Integrated planning to meet the problems of urbanization and urban development;

(c) Comprehensive rural development schemes to raise the levels of living of the rural populations and to facilitate such urban-rural relationships and population distribution as will promote balanced national development and social progress;

(d) Measures for appropriate supervision of the utilization of land in the interests of society.

The achievement of the objectives of social progress and development equally requires the implementation of the following means and methods:

Article 18

(a) The adoption of appropriate legislative, administrative and other measures ensuring to everyone not only political and civil rights, but also the full realization of economic, social and cultural rights without any discrimination;

(b) The promotion of democratically based social and institutional reforms and motivation for change basic to the elimination of all forms of discrimination and exploitation and conducive to high rates of economic and social progress, to include land reform, in which the ownership and use of land will be made to serve best the objectives of social justice and economic development;

(c) The adoption of measures to boost and diversify agricultural production through, *inter alia,* the implementation of democratic agrarian reforms, to ensure an adequate and well-balanced supply of food, its equitable distribution among the whole population and the improvement of nutritional standards;

(d) The adoption of measures to introduce, with the participation of the Government, low-cost housing programmes in both rural and urban areas;

(e) Development and expansion of the system of transportation and communications, particularly in developing countries.

Article 19

(a) The provision of free health services to the whole population and of adequate preventive and curative facilities and welfare medical services accessible to all;

(b) The enactment and establishment of legislative measures and administrative regulations with a view to the implementation of comprehensive programmes of social security schemes and social welfare services and to the improvement and co-ordination of existing services;

(c) The adoption of measures and the provision of social welfare services to migrant workers and their families, in conformity with the provisions of Convention No. 97 of the International Labour Organisation[1] and other international instruments relating to migrant workers;

(d) The institution of appropriate measures for the rehabilitation of mentally or physically disabled persons, especially children and youth, so as to enable them to the fullest possible extent to be useful members of society—these measures shall include the provision of treatment and technical appliances, education, vocational and social guidance, training and selective placement, and other assistance required—and the creation of social conditions in which the handicapped are not discriminated against because of their disabilities.

Article 20

(a) The provision of full democratic freedoms to trade unions; freedom of association for all workers, including the right to bargain collectively and to strike, recog-

---

[1] Convention concerning Migration for Employment (Revised 1949), International Labour Office, *Conventions and Recommendations, 1919-1949* (Geneva, 1949), p. 863.

nition of the right to form other organizations of working people; the provision for the growing participation of trade unions in economic and social development; effective participation of all members of trade unions in the deciding of economic and social issues which affect their interests;

(b) The improvement of health and safety conditions for workers, by means of appropriate technological and legislative measures and the provision of the material prerequisites for the implementation of those measures, including the limitation of working hours;

(c) The adoption of appropriate measures for the development of harmonious industrial relations.

Article 21

(a) The training of national personnel and cadres, including administrative, executive, professional and technical personnel needed for social development and for overall development plans and policies;

(b) The adoption of measures to accelerate the extension and improvement of general, vocational and technical education and of training and retraining, which should be provided free at all levels;

(c) Raising the general level of education; development and expansion of national information media, and their rational and full use towards continuing education of the whole population and towards encouraging its participation in social development activities; the constructive use of leisure, particularly that of children and adolescents;

(d) The formulation of national and international policies and measures to avoid the "brain drain" and obviate its adverse effects.

Article 22

(a) The development and co-ordination of policies and measures designed to strengthen the essential functions of the family as a basic unit of society;

(b) The formulation and establishment, as needed, of programmes in the field of population, within the framework of national demographic policies and as part of the welfare medical services, including education, training of personnel and the provision to families of the knowledge and means necessary to enable them to exercise their right to determine freely and responsibly the number and spacing of their children;

(c) The establishment of appropriate child-care facilities in the interest of children and working parents.

The achievement of the objectives of social progress and development finally requires the implementation of the following means and methods:

Article 23

(a) The laying down of economic growth rate targets for the developing countries within the United Nations policy for development, high enough to lead to a substantial acceleration of their rates of growth;

(b) The provision of greater assistance on better terms; the implementation of the aid volume target of a minimum of 1 per cent of the gross national product at market prices of economically advanced countries, the general easing of the terms of lending to the developing countries through low interest rates on loans and long grace periods for the repayment of loans, and the assurance that the allocation of such loans will be based strictly on socio-economic criteria free of any political considerations;

(c) The provision of technical, financial and material assistance, both bilateral and multilateral, to the fullest possible extent and on favourable terms, and improved co-ordination of international assistance for the achievement of the social objectives of national development plans;

(d) The provision to the developing countries of technical, financial and material assistance and of favourable conditions to facilitate the direct exploitation of their national resources and natural wealth by those countries with a view to enabling the peoples of those countries to benefit fully from their national resources;

(e) The expansion of international trade based on principles of equality and non-discrimination, the rectification of the position of developing countries in international trade by equitable terms of trade, a general non-reciprocal and non-discriminatory system of preferences for the exports of developing countries to the developed countries, the establishment and implementation of general and comprehensive commodity agreements, and the financing of reasonable buffer stocks by international institutions.

Article 24

(a) Intensification of international co-operation with a view to ensuring the international exchange of information, knowledge and experience concerning social progress and development;

(b) The broadest possible international technical, scientific and cultural co-operation and reciprocal utilization of the experience of countries with different economic and social systems and different levels of development, on the basis of mutual advantage and strict observance of and respect for national sovereignty;

(c) Increased utilization of science and technology for social and economic development; arrangements for the transfer and exchange of technology, including know-how and patents, to the developing countries.

Article 25

(a) The establishment of legal and administrative measures for the protection and improvement of the human environment at both national and international levels;

(b) The use and exploitation, in accordance with the appropriate international regimes, of the resources of areas of the environment such as outer space and the sea-bed and ocean floor and the subsoil thereof, beyond the limits of national jurisdiction, in order to supplement national resources available for the achievement of economic and social progress and development in every country, irrespective of its geographical location, special consideration being given to the interests and needs of the developing countries.

Article 26

Compensation for damages, be they social or economic in nature—including restitution and reparations—caused as a result of aggression and of illegal occupation of territory by the aggressor.

Article 27

(a) The achievement of general and complete disarmament and the channelling of the progressively released resources to be used for economic and social progress for the welfare of people everywhere and, in particular, for the benefit of developing countries;

(b) The adoption of measures contributing to disarmament, including, *inter alia,* the complete prohibition of tests of nuclear weapons, the prohibition of the development, production and stockpiling of chemical and bacteriological (biological) weapons and the prevention of the pollution of oceans and inland waters by nuclear wastes.

1829th plenary meeting,
11 December 1969.

12. RESPECT FOR HUMAN RIGHTS IN ARMED CONFLICTS[1]

The General Assembly,

Conscious that a better application of existing humanitarian rules relating to armed conflicts and the development of further rules remains an urgent task in order to reduce the suffering brought about by all such conflicts,

Recalling the successive resolutions adopted in the preceding years by the United Nations relating to human rights in armed conflicts and the debates on this subject,

Noting the report of the Secretary-General on the second session of the Diplomatic Conference on the Reaffirmation and Development of International Humanitarian Law Applicable in Armed Conflicts,[2] held at Geneva from 3 February to 18 April 1975,

Noting also the note by the Secretary-General entitled "Human rights in armed conflicts: protection of journalists engaged in dangerous missions in areas of armed conflict,"[3]

Welcoming the substantial progress made at the second session of the Diplomatic Conference,

Noting that the Diplomatic Conference will continue its consideration of the use of specific conventional weapons, including any which may be deemed to be excessively injurious or to have indiscriminate effects, and its search for agreement, for humanitarian reasons, on possible rules prohibiting or restricting the use of such weapons,

1. *Calls upon* all parties to armed conflicts to acknowledge and to comply with their obligations under the humanitarian instruments and to observe the international humanitarian rules which are applicable, in particular the Hague Conventions of 1899 and 1907,[4] the Geneva Protocol of 1925[5] and the Geneva Conventions of 1949,[6]

2. *Calls* the attention of the Diplomatic Conference on the Reaffirmation and Development of International Humanitarian Law Applicable in Armed Conflicts, and of the Governments and organizations participating in it, to the need for measures to promote on a universal basis the dissemination of and instruction in the rules of international humanitarian law applicable in armed conflicts;

3. *Urges* all participants in the Diplomatic Conference to do their utmost to reach agreement on additional rules which may help to alleviate the suffering brought about by armed conflicts and to respect and protect non-combatants and civilian objects in such conflicts;

4. *Takes note with appreciation* of the decision of the Diplomatic Conference on the protection of journalists engaged in dangerous professional missions in areas of armed conflict, and of the intention of the Conference to complete its work on the subject during its next session;

---

[1] Official Records of the General Assembly, Thirtieth Session, Supplement No. 34 (A/10034), pp. 153-154.

[2] A/10195 and Corr. 1 and Add. 1.

[3] A/10147.

[4] Carnegie Endowment for International Peace, *The Hague Conventions and Declarations of 1899 and 1907* (New York, Oxford University Press, 1915).

[5] League of Nations, *Treaty Series*, vol. XCIV, No. 2138. p. 65.

[6] United Nations *Treaty Series*, vol. 75, Nos. 970-973.

5. *Expresses its appreciation* to the Swiss Federal Council for convoking the third session of the Diplomatic Conference on the Reaffirmation and Development of International Humanitarian Law Applicable in Armed Conflicts from 21 April to 11 June 1976 and to the International Committee of the Red Cross for convoking a second Conference of Government Experts on Weapons That May Cause Unnecessary Suffering or Have Indiscriminate Effects, to be held at Lugano from 28 January to 26 February 1976;

6. *Requests* the Secretary-General to report to the General Assembly at its thirty-first session on relevant developments concerning human rights in armed conflicts, in particular on the proceedings and results of the 1976 session of the Diplomatic Conference;

7. *Decides* to include in the provisional agenda of its thirty-first session the item entitled "Respect for human rights in armed conflicts."

2441st plenary meeting
15 December 1975

13. DECLARATION ON TERRITORIAL ASYLUM[1]

The General Assembly,

Recalling its resolutions 1839 (XVII) of 19 December 1962, 2100 (XX) of 20 December 1965 and 2203 (XXI) on 16 December 1966 concerning a declaration on the right of asylum,

Considering the work of codification to be undertaken by the International Law Commission in accordance with General Assembly resolution 1400 (XIV) of 21 November 1959,

Adopts the following Declaration:

DECLARATION ON TERRITORIAL ASYLUM

The General Assembly,

Noting that the purposes proclaimed in the Charter of the United Nations are to maintain international peace and security, to develop friendly relations among all nations and to achieve international co-operation in solving international problems of an economic, social, cultural or humanitarian character and in promoting and encouraging respect for human rights and for fundamental freedoms for all without distinction as to race, sex, language or religion,

Mindful of the Universal Declaration of Human Rights, which declares in article 14 that:

"1. Everyone has the right to seek and to enjoy in other countries asylum from persecution.

"2. This right may not be invoked in the case of prosecutions genuinely arising from non-political crimes or from acts contrary to the purposes and principles of the United Nations,"

Recalling also article 13, paragraph 2, of the Universal Declaration of Human Rights, which states:

---

[1] Official Records of the General Assembly, Twenty-second Session, Supplement No. 16, p. 31.

"Everyone has the right to leave any country, including his own, and to return to his country,"

Recognizing that the grant of asylum by a State to persons entitled to invoke article 14 of the Universal Declaration of Human Rights is a peaceful and humanitarian act and that, as such, it cannot be regarded as unfriendly by any other State,

Recommends that, without prejudice to existing instruments dealing with asylum and the status of refugees and stateless persons, States should base themselves in their practices relating to territorial asylum on the following principles:

Article 1

1. Asylum granted by a State, in the exercise of its sovereignty, to persons entitled to invoke article 14 of the Universal Declaration of Human Rights, including persons struggling against colonialism, shall be respected by all other States.

2. The right to seek and to enjoy asylum may not be invoked by any person with respect to whom there are serious reasons for considering that he has committed a crime against peace, a war crime or a crime against humanity, as defined in the international instruments drawn to make provision in respect of such crimes.

3. It shall rest with the State granting asylum to evaluate the grounds for the grant of asylum.

Article 2

1. The situation of persons referred to in article 1, paragraph 1, is, without prejudice to the sovereignty of States and the purposes and principles of the United Nations, of concern to the international community.

2. Where a State finds difficulty in granting or continuing to grant asylum, States individually or jointly or through the United Nations shall consider, in a spirit of international solidarity, appropriate measures to lighten the burden on that State.

Article 3

1. No person referred to in article 1, paragraph 1, shall be subjected to measures such as rejection at the frontier or, if he has already entered the territory in which he seeks asylum, expulsion or compulsory return to any State where he may be subjected to persecution.

2. Exception may be made to the foregoing principle only for overriding reasons of national security or in order to safeguard the population, as in the case of a mass influx of persons.

3. Should a State decide in any case that exception to the principle stated in paragraph 1 of this article would be justified, it shall consider the possibility of granting to the person concerned, under such conditions as it may deem appropriate, an opportunity, whether by way of provisional asylum or otherwise, of going to another State.

Article 4

States granting asylum shall not permit persons who have received asylum to engage in activities contrary to the purposes and principles of the United Nations.

1631st plenary meeting,
14 December 1967.

757

14. CONVENTION ON THE NON-APPLICABILITY OF STATUTORY LIMITATIONS TO WAR CRIMES AND CRIMES AGAINST HUMANITY[1]

The General Assembly,

Having considered the draft Convention on the Non-Applicability of Statutory Limitations to War Crimes and Crimes against Humanity,

Adopts and opens for signature, ratification and accession the Convention on the Non-Applicability of Statutory Limitations to War Crimes and Crimes against Humanity, the text of which is annexed to the present resolution.

1727th plenary meeting,
26 November 1968.

ANNEX

Convention on the Non-Applicability of Statutory Limitations to War Crimes and Crimes against Humanity

PREAMBLE

The States Parties to the present Convention,

Recalling resolutions of the General Assembly of the United Nations 3 (I) of 13 February 1946 and 170 (II) of 31 October 1947 on the extradition and punishment of war criminals, resolution 95 (I) of 11 December 1946 affirming the principles of international law recognized by the Charter of the International Military Tribunal, Nurnberg, and the judgement of the Tribunal, and resolutions 2184 (XXI) of 12 December 1966 and 2202 (XXI) of 16 December 1966 which expressly condemned as crimes against humanity the violation of the economic and political rights of the indigenous population on the one hand and the policies of *apartheid* on the other.

Recalling resolutions of the Economic and Social Council of the United Nations 1074 D (XXXIX) of 28 July 1965 and 1158 (XLI) of 5 August 1966 on the punishment of war criminals and of persons who have committed crimes against humanity,

Noting that none of the solemn declarations, instruments or conventions relating to the prosecution and punishment of war crimes and crimes against humanity made provisions for a period of limitation,

Considering that war crimes and crimes against humanity are among the gravest crimes in international law,

Convinced that the effective punishment of war crimes and crimes against humanity is an important element in the prevention of such crimes, the protection of human rights and fundamental freedoms, the encouragement of confidence, the furtherance of co-operation among peoples and the promotion of international peace and security,

Noting that the application to war crimes and crimes against humanity of the rules of municipal law relating to the period of limitation for ordinary crimes is a matter of serious concern to world public opinion, since it prevents the prosecution and punishment of persons responsible for those crimes,

Recognizing that it is necessary and timely to affirm in international law, through this Convention, the principle that there is no period of limitation for war crimes and crimes against humanity, and to secure its universal application,

Have agreed as follows:

---

[1] Official Records of the General Assembly, Twenty-third Session, Supplement No. 18, pp. 40-41.

ARTICLE I

No statutory limitation shall apply to the following crimes, irrespective of the date of their commission:

(a) War crimes as they are defined in the Charter of the International Military Tribunal, Nurnberg, of 8 August 1945 and confirmed by resolutions 3 (I) of 13 February 1946 and 95 (I) of 11 December 1946 of the General Assembly of the United Nations, particularly the "grave breaches" enumerated in the Geneva Conventions of 12 August 1949 for the protection of war victims;

(b) Crimes against humanity whether committed in time of war or in time of peace as they are defined in the Charter of the International Military Tribunal, Nurnberg, of 8 August 1945 and confirmed by resolutions 3 (I) of 13 February 1946 and 95 (I) of 11 December 1946 of the General Assembly of the United Nations, eviction by armed attack or occupation and inhuman acts resulting from the policy of *apartheid*, and the crime of genocide as defined in the 1948 Convention on the Prevention and Punishment of the Crime of Genocide, even if such acts do not constitute a violation of the domestic law of the country in which they were committed.

ARTICLE II

If any of the crimes mentioned in article I is committed, the provisions of this Convention shall apply to representatives of the State authority and private individuals who, as principals or accomplices, participate in or who directly incite others to the commission of any of those crimes, or who conspire to commit them, irrespective of the degree of completion, and to representatives of the State authority who tolerate their commission.

ARTICLE III

The States Parties to the present Convention undertake to adopt all necessary domestic measures, legislative or otherwise, with a view to making possible the extradition, in accordance with international law, of the persons referred to in article II of this Convention.

ARTICLE IV

The States Parties to the present Convention undertake to adopt, in accordance with their respective constitutional processes, any legislative or other measures necessary to ensure that statutory or other limitations shall not apply to the prosecution and punishment of the crimes referred to in articles I and II of this Convention and that, where they exist, such limitations shall be abolished.

ARTICLE V

This Convention shall, until 31 December 1969, be open for signature by any State Member of the United Nations or member of any of its specialized agencies or of the International Atomic Energy Agency, by any State Party to the Statute of the International Court of Justice, and by any other State which has been invited by the General Assembly of the United Nations to become a Party to this Convention.

ARTICLE VI

This Convention is subject to ratification. Instruments of ratification shall be deposited with the Secretary-General of the United Nations.

ARTICLE VII

This Convention shall be open to accession by any State referred to in article V.

Instruments of accession shall be deposited with the Secretary-General of the United Nations.

ARTICLE VIII

1. This Convention shall enter into force on the ninetieth day after the date of the deposit with the Secretary-General of the United Nations of the tenth instrument of ratification or accession.

2. For each State ratifying this Convention or acceding to it after the deposit of the tenth instrument of ratification or accession, the Convention shall enter into force on the ninetieth day after the date of the deposit of its own instrument of ratification or accession.

ARTICLE IX

1. After the expiry of a period of ten years from the date on which this Convention enters into force, a request for the revision of the Convention may be made at any time by any Contracting Party by means of a notification in writing addressed to the Secretary-General of the United Nations.

2. The General Assembly of the United Nations shall decide upon the steps, if any, to be taken in respect of such a request.

ARTICLE X

1. This Convention shall be deposited with the Secretary-General of the United Nations.

2. The Secretary-General of the United Nations shall transmit certified copies of this Convention to all States referred to in article V.

3. The Secretary-General of the United Nations shall inform all States referred to in article V of the following particulars:

(a) Signatures of this Convention and instruments of ratification and accession deposited under articles V, VI and VII;

(b) The date of entry into force of this Convention in accordance with article VIII;

(c) Communications received under article IX.

ARTICLE XI

This Convention, of which the Chinese, English, French Russian and Spanish texts are equally authentic, shall bear the date of 26 November 1968.

IN WITNESS WHEREOF the undersigned, being duly authorized for that purpose, have signed this Convention.

15. CONVENTION FOR THE SUPPRESSION OF THE TRAFFIC IN PERSONS AND OF THE EXPLOITATION OF THE PROSTITUTION OF OTHERS. OPENED FOR SIGNATURE AT LAKE SUCCESS, NEW YORK ON 21 MARCH 1950[1]

PREAMBLE

Whereas prostitution and the accompanying evil of the traffic in persons for the purpose of prostitution are incompatible with the dignity and worth of the human person and endanger the welfare of the individual, the family and the community,

Whereas, with respect to the suppression of the traffic in women and children, the following international instruments are in force:

1. International Agreement of 18 May 1904 for the Suppression of the White Slave Traffic, as amended by the Protocol approved by the General Assembly of the United Nations on 3 December 1948,[2]

2. International Convention of 4 May 1910 for the Suppression of the White Slave Traffic, as amended by the above-mentioned Protocol,[3]

3. International Convention of 30 September 1921 for the Suppression of the Traffic in Women and Children, as amended by the Protocol approved by the General Assembly of the United Nations on 20 October 1947,[4]

4. International Convention of 11 October 1933 for the Suppression of the Traffic in Women of Full Age, as amended by the aforesaid Protocol,[5]

Whereas the League of Nations in 1937 prepared a draft Convention[6] extending the scope of the above-mentioned instruments, and

Whereas developments since 1937 make feasible the conclusion of a convention consolidating the above-mentioned instruments and embodying the substance of the 1937 draft Convention as well as desirable alterations therein;

Now therefore
The Contracting Parties
Hereby agree as hereinafter provided:

Article 1

The Parties to the present Convention agree to punish any person who, to gratify the passions of another:

1. Procures, entices or leads away, for purposes of prostitution, another person, even with the consent of that person;

2. Exploits the prostitution of another person, even with the consent of that person.

---

[1] United Nations *Treaty Series*, Vol. 96, pp. 288; came into force on 25 July 1951, the ninetieth day following the date of deposit of the second instrument of ratification or accession, in accordance with article 24.

The following States deposited with the Secretary-General of the United Nations their instruments of ratification or accession on the dates indicated:

> *Accession.*—Israel .... 28 December 1950
> *Ratification.*—Yugoslavia .... 26 April 1951

[2] United Nations *Treaty Series*, Vol. 92, p. 19.
[3] United Nations *Treaty Series*, Vol. 98, p. 109.
[4] United Nations *Treaty Series*, Vol. 53, p. 39, Vol. 65, p. 333; Vol. 76, p. 281, and Vol. 77, p. 364.
[5] United Nations *Treaty Series*, Vol. 53, p. 49; Vol. 65, p. 334; Vol. 76, p. 281, and Vol. 77, p. 365.
[6] League of Nations, document C331.M.223.1937.IV.

Article 2

The Parties to the present Convention further agree to punish any person who:

1. Keeps or manages, or knowingly finances or takes part in the financing of a brothel;

2. Knowingly lets or rents a building or other place or any part thereof for the purpose of the prostitution of others.

Article 3

To the extent permitted by domestic law, attempts to commit any of the offences referred to in articles 1 and 2, and acts preparatory to the commission thereof, shall also be punished.

Article 4

To the extent permitted by domestic law, intentional participation in the acts referred to in articles 1 and 2 above shall also be punishable.

To the extent permitted by domestic law, acts of participation shall be treated as separate offences whenever this is necessary to prevent impunity.

Article 5

In cases where injured persons are entitled under domestic law to be parties to proceedings in respect of any of the offences referred to in the present Convention, aliens shall be so entitled upon the same terms as nationals.

Article 6

Each Party to the present Convention agrees to take all the necessary measures to repeal or abolish any existing law, regulation or administrative provision by virtue of which persons who engage in or are suspected of engaging in prostitution are subject either to special registration or to the possession of a special document or to any exceptional requirements for supervision or notification.

Article 7

Previous convictions pronounced in foreign States for offences referred to in the present Convention shall, to the extent permitted by domestic law, be taken into account for the purpose of:

1. Establishing recidivism;

2. Disqualifying the offender from the exercise of civil rights.

Article 8

The offences referred to in articles 1 and 2 of the present Convention shall be regarded as extraditable offences in any extradition treaty which has been or may hereafter be concluded between any of the Parties to this Convention.

The Parties to the present Convention which do not make extradition conditional on the existence of a treaty shall henceforward recognize the offences referred to in articles 1 and 2 of the present Convention as cases for extradition between themselves.

Extradition shall be granted in accordance with the law of the State to which the request is made.

Article 9

In States where the extradition of nationals is not permitted by law, nationals who have returned to their own State after the commission abroad of any of the offences referred to in articles 1 and 2 of the present Convention shall be prosecuted in and punished by the courts of their own State.

This provision shall not apply if, in a similar case between the Parties to the present Convention, the extradition of an alien cannot be granted.

Article 10

The provisions of article 9 shall not apply when the person charged with the offence has been tried in a foreign State and, if convicted, has served his sentence or had it remitted or reduced in conformity with the laws of that foreign State.

Article 11

Nothing in the present Convention shall be interpreted as determining the attitude of a Party towards the general question of the limits of criminal jurisdiction under international law.

Article 12

The present Convention does not affect the principle that the offences to which it refers in each State be defined, prosecuted and punished in conformity with its domestic law.

Article 13

The Parties to the present Convention shall be bound to execute letters of request relating to offences referred to in the Convention in accordance with their domestic law and practice.

The transmission of letters of request shall be effected:

1. By direct communication between the judicial authorities; or

2. By direct communication between the Ministers of Justice of the two States, or by direct communication from another competent authority of the State making the request to the Minister of Justice of the State to which the request is made; or

3. Through the diplomatic or consular representative of the State making the request in the State to which the request is made; this representative shall send the letters of request direct to the competent judicial authority or to the authority indicated by the Government of the State to which the request is made, and shall receive direct from such authority the papers constituting the execution of the letters of request.

In cases 1 and 3 a copy of the letters of request shall always be sent to the superior authority of the State to which application is made.

Unless otherwise agreed, the letters of request shall be drawn up in the language of the authority making the request, provided always that the State to which the request is made may require a translation in its own language, certified correct by the authority making the request.

Each Party to the present Convention shall notify to each of the other Parties to the Convention the method or methods of transmission mentioned above which it will recognize for the letters of request of the latter State.

Until such notification is made by a State, its existing procedure in regard to letters of request shall remain in force.

Execution of letters of request shall not give rise to a claim for reimbursement of charges or expenses of any nature whatever other than expenses of experts.

Nothing in the present article shall be construed as an undertaking on the part of the Parties to the present Convention to adopt in criminal matters any form or methods of proof contrary to their own domestic laws.

763

Article 14

Each Party to the present Convention shall establish or maintain a service charged with the co-ordination and centralization of the results of the investigation of offences referred to in the present Convention.

Such services should compile all information calculated to facilitate the prevention and punishment of the offences referred to in the present Convention and should be in close contact with the corresponding services in other States.

Article 15

To the extent permitted by domestic law and to the extent to which the authorities responsible for the services referred to in article 14 may judge desirable, they shall furnish to the authorities responsible for the corresponding services in other States the following information:

1. Particulars of any offence referred to in the present Convention or any attempt to commit such offence;

2. Particulars of any search for and any prosecution, arrest, conviction, refusal of admission or expulsion of persons guilty of any of the offences referred to in the present Convention, the movements of such persons and any other useful information with regard to them.

The information so furnished shall include descriptions of the offenders, their fingerprints, photographs, methods of operation, police records and records of conviction.

Article 16

The Parties to the present Convention agree to take or to encourage, through their public and private educational, health, social, economic and other related services, measures for the prevention of prostitution and for the rehabilitation and social adjustment of the victims of prostitution and of the offences referred to in the present Convention.

Article 17

The Parties to the present Convention undertake, in connexion with immigration and emigration, to adopt or maintain such measures as are required in terms of their obligations under the present Convention, to check the traffic in persons of either sex for the purpose of prostitution.

In particular they undertake:

1. To make such regulations as are necessary for the protection of immigrants or emigrants, and in particular, women and children, both at the place of arrival and departure and while *en route;*

2. To arrange for appropriate publicity warning the public of the dangers of the aforesaid traffic;

3. To take appropriate measures to ensure supervision of railway stations, airports, seaports and *en route*, and of other public places, in order to prevent international traffic in persons for the purpose of prostitution;

4. To take appropriate measures in order that the appropriate authorities be informed of the arrival of persons who appear, *prima facie*, to be the principals and accomplices in or victims of such traffic.

Article 18

The Parties to the present Convention undertake, in accordance with the conditions laid down by domestic law, to have declarations taken from aliens who are prostitutes, in order to establish their identity and civil status and to discover who has caused them to leave their State. The information obtained shall be communicated to the authorities of the State of origin of the said persons with a view to their eventual repatriation.

Article 19

The Parties to the present Convention undertake, in accordance with the conditions laid down by domestic law and without prejudice to prosecution or other action for violations thereunder and so far as possible:

1. Pending the completion of arrangements for the repatriation of destitute victims of international traffic in persons for the purpose of prostitution, to make suitable provisions for their temporary care and maintenance;

2. To repatriate persons referred to in article 18 who desire to be repatriated or who may be claimed by persons exercising authority over them or whose expulsion is ordered in conformity with the law. Repatriation shall take place only after agreement is reached with the State of destination as to identity and nationality as well as to the place and date of arrival at frontiers. Each Party to the present Convention shall facilitate the passage of such persons through its territory.

Where the persons referred to in the preceding paragraph cannot themselves repay the cost of repatriation and have neither spouse, relatives nor guardian to pay for them, the cost of repatriation as far as the nearest frontier or port of embarkation or airport in the direction of the State or origin shall be borne by the State where they are in residence, and the cost of the remainder of the journey shall be borne by the State of origin.

Article 20

The Parties to the present Convention shall, if they have not already done so, take the necessary measures for the supervision of employment agencies in order to prevent persons seeking employment, in particular women and children, from being exposed to the danger of prostitution.

Article 21

The Parties to the present Convention shall communicate to the Secretary-General of the United Nations such laws and regulations as have already been promulgated in their States, and thereafter annually such laws and regulations as may be promulgated, relating to the subjects of the present Convention, as well as all measures taken by them concerning the application of the Convention. The information received shall be published periodically by the Secretary-General and sent to all Members of the United Nations and to non-member States to which the present Convention is officially communicated in accordance with article 23.

Article 22

If any dispute shall arise between the Parties to the present Convention relating to its interpretation or application and if such dispute cannot be settled by other means, the dispute shall, at the request of any one of the Parties to the dispute, be referred to the International Court of Justice.

Article 23

The present Convention shall be open for signature on behalf of any Member of the United Nations and also on behalf of any other State to which an invitation has been addressed by the Economic and Social Council.

The present Convention shall be ratified and the instruments of ratification shall be deposited with the Secretary-General of the United Nations.

The States mentioned in the first paragraph which have not signed the Convention may accede to it.

Accession shall be effected by deposit of an instrument of accession with the Secretary-General of the United Nations.

For the purpose of the present Convention the word "State" shall include all the colonies and Trust Territories of a State signatory or acceding to the Convention and all territories for which such State is internationally responsible.

Article 24

The present Convention shall come into force on the ninetieth day following the date of deposit of the second instrument of ratification or accession.

For each State ratifying or acceding to the Convention after the deposit of the second instrument of ratification or accession, the Convention shall enter into force ninety days after the deposit by such State of its instrument of ratification or accession.

Article 25

After the expiration of five years from the entry into force of the present Convention, any Party to the Convention may denounce it by a written notification addressed to the Secretary-General of the United Nations.

Such denunciation shall take effect for the Party making it one year from the date upon which it is received by the Secretary-General of the United Nations.

Article 26

The Secretary-General of the United Nations shall inform all Members of the United Nations and non-member States referred to in article 23:

(a) Of signatures, ratifications and accessions received in accordance with article 23;

(b) Of the date on which the present Convention will come into force in accordance with article 24;

(c) Of denunciations received in accordance with article 25.

Article 27

Each Party to the present Convention undertakes to adopt, in accordance with its Constitution, the legislative or other measures necessary to ensure the application of the Convention.

Article 28

The provisions of the present Convention shall supersede in the relations between the Parties thereto the provisions of the international instruments referred to in sub-paragraphs 1, 2, 3 and 4 of the second paragraph of the Preamble, each of which shall be deemed to be terminated when all the Parties thereto shall have become Parties to the present Convention.

IN FAITH WHEREOF the undersigned, being duly authorized thereto by their respective Governments, have signed the present Convention, opened for signature at Lake Success, New York, on the twenty-first day of March, one thousand nine hundred and fifty, a certified true copy of which shall be transmitted by the Secretary-General to all the Members of the United Nations and to the non-member States referred to in article 23.

D. SELF-DETERMINATION AND INDEPENDENCE

1. THE RIGHT OF PEOPLES AND NATIONS TO SELF-DETERMINATION[1]

A

Whereas the right of peoples and nations to self-determination is a prerequisite to the full enjoyment of all fundamental human rights,

Whereas the Charter of the United Nations, under Articles 1 and 55, aims to develop friendly relations among nations based on respect for the equal rights and self- determination of peoples in order to strengthen universal peace,

Whereas the Charter of the United Nations recognizes that certain Members of the United Nations are responsible for the administration of Territories whose peoples have not yet attained a full measure of self-government, and affirms the principles which should guide them,

Whereas every Member of the United Nations, in conformity with the Charter, should respect the maintenance of the right of self-determination in other States,

The General Assembly recommends that;

1. The States Members of the United Nations shall uphold the principle of self-determination of all peoples and nations;

2. The States Members of the United Nations shall recognize and promote the realization of the right of self-determination of the peoples of Non-Self-Governing and Trust Territories who are under their administration and shall facilitate the exercise of this right by the peoples of such Territories according to the principles and spirit of the Charter of the United Nations in regard to each Territory and to the freely expressed wishes of the peoples concerned, the wishes of the people being ascertained through plebiscites or other recognized democratic means, preferably under the auspices of the United Nations;

3. The States Members of the United Nations responsible for the administration of Non-Self-Governing and Trust Territories shall take practical steps, pending the realization of the right of self-determination and in preparation thereof, to ensure the direct participation of the indigenous populations in the legislative and executive organs of government of those Territories, and to prepare them for complete self-government or independence.

403rd plenary meeting,
16 December 1952.

B

The General Assembly,

Considering that one of the conditions necessary to facilitate United Nations action to promote respect for the right of self-determination of peoples and nations, in particular with regard to the peoples of Non-Self-Governing Territories, is that the competent organs of the United Nations should be in possession of official information on the government of these Territories,

Recalling its resolution 144 (II) of 3 November 1947 in which it declared that the voluntary transmission of such information was entirely in conformity with the spirit of Article 73 of the Charter, and should therefore be encouraged,

---

[1] Official Records of the General Assembly, Seventh Session, Supplement No. 20, pp. 26-27.

Recalling its resolution 327 (IV) of 2 December 1949 in which it expressed the hope that such of the Members of the United Nations as had not done so might voluntarily include details on the government of Non-Self-Governing Territories in the information transmitted by them under Article 73 e of the Charter,

Considering that at the present time such information has not yet been furnished in respect of a large number of Non-Self-Governing Territories,

1. *Recommends* States Members of the United Nations responsible for the administration of Non-Self-Governing Territories, voluntarily to include in the information transmitted by them under Article 73 e of the Charter details regarding the extent to which the right of peoples and nations to self-determination is exercised by the peoples of those Territories, and in particular regarding their political progress and the measures taken to develop their capacity for self-administration, to satisfy their political aspirations and to promote the progressive development of their free political institutions;

2. *Decides* to place the present resolution on the agenda of the Committee on information from Non-Self-Governing Territories for its next session in 1953.

403rd plenary meeting,
16 December 1952.

C

The General Assembly,

Considering that it is necessary to continue the study of ways and means of ensuring international respect for the right of peoples to self-determination,

Considering that the recommendations it has adopted at its seventh session do not represent the only steps that can be taken to promote respect for such right,

1. *Requests* the Economic and Social Council to ask the Commission on Human Rights to continue preparing recommendations concerning international respect for the right of peoples to self-determination, and particularly recommendations relating to the steps which might be taken, within the limits of their resources and competence, by the various organs of the United Nations and the specialized agencies to develop international respect for the right of peoples to self-determination;

2. *Requests* the Commission on Human Rights to submit through the Economic and Social Council its recommendations to the General Assembly.

403rd plenary meeting,
16 December 1952.

2. DECLARATION ON THE GRANTING OF INDEPENDENCE TO COLONIAL COUNTRIES AND PEOPLES[1]

The General Assembly,

Mindful of the determination proclaimed by the peoples of the world in the Charter of the United Nations to reaffirm faith in fundamental human rights, in the dignity and worth of the human person, in the equal rights of men and women and of nations large and small and to promote social progress and better standards of life in larger freedom,

Conscious of the need for the creation of conditions of stability and well-being and peaceful and friendly relations based on respect for the principles of equal rights and self-determination of all peoples, and of universal respect for, and observance of, human rights and fundamental freedoms for all without distinction as to race, sex, language or religion,

---

[1] Official Records of the General Assembly, Fifteenth Session, Supplement No. 16, pp. 66-67.

Recognizing the passionate yearning for freedom in all dependent peoples and the decisive role of such peoples in the attainment of their independence,

Aware of the increasing conflicts resulting from the denial of or impediments in the way of the freedom of such peoples, which constitute a serious threat to world peace,

Considering the important role of the United Nations in assisting the movement for independence in Trust and Non-Self-Governing Territories,

Recognizing that the peoples of the world ardently desire the end of colonialism in all its manifestations.

Convinced that the continued existence of colonialism prevents the development of international economic co-operation, impedes the social, cultural and economic development of dependent peoples and militates against the United Nations ideal of universal peace,

Affirming that peoples may, for their own ends, freely dispose of their natural wealth and resources without prejudice to any obligations arising out of international economic co-operation, based upon the principle of mutual benefit, and international law,

Believing that the process of liberation is irresistible and irreversible and that, in order to avoid serious crises, an end must be put to colonialism and all practices of segregation and discrimination associated therewith,

Welcoming the emergence in recent years of a large number of dependent territories into freedom and independence, and recognizing the increasingly powerful trends towards freedom in such territories which have not yet attained independence,

Convinced that all peoples have an inalienable right to complete freedom, the exercise of their sovereignty and the integrity of their national territory,

Solemnly proclaims the necessity, of bringing to a speedy and unconditional end colonialism in all its forms and manifestations;

And to this end

Declares that:

1. The subjection of peoples to alien subjugation, domination and exploitation constitutes a denial of fundamental human rights, is contrary to the Charter of the United Nations and is as impediment to the promotion of world peace and co-operation.

2. All peoples have the right to self-determination; by virtue of that right they freely determine their political status and freely pursue their economic, social and cultural development.

3. Inadequacy of political, economic, social or educational preparedness should never serve as a pretext for delaying independence.

4. All armed action or repressive measures of all kinds directed against dependent peoples shall cease in order to enable them to exercise peacefully and freely their right to complete independence, and the integrity of their national territory shall be respected.

5. Immediate steps shall be taken, in Trust and Non-Self-Governing Territories or all other territories which have not yet attained independence, to transfer all powers to the peoples of those territories, without any conditions or reservations, in accordance with their freely expressed will and desire, without any distinction as to race, creed or colour, in order to enable them to enjoy complete independence and freedom.

6. Any attempt aimed at the partial or total disruption of the national unity and the territorial integrity of a country is incompatible with the purposes and principles of the Charter of the United Nations.

7. All States shall observe faithfully and strictly the provisions of the Charter of the United Nations, the Universal Declaration of Human Rights and the present Declaration on the basis of equality, non-interference in the internal affairs of all States, and respect for the sovereign rights of all peoples and their territorial integrity.

947th plenary meeting,
14 December 1960.

3. DECLARATION ON THE INADMISSIBILITY OF INTERVENTION IN THE DOMESTIC AFFAIRS OF STATES AND THE PROTECTION OF THEIR INDEPENDENCE AND SOVEREIGNTY[1]

The General Assembly,

Deeply concerned at the gravity of the international situation and the increasing threat to universal peace due to armed intervention and other direct or indirect forms of interference threatening the sovereign personality and the political independence of States,

Considering that the United Nations, in accordance with their aim to eliminate war, threats to the peace and acts of aggression, created an Organization, based on the sovereign equality of States, whose friendly relations would be based on respect for the principle of equal rights and self-determination of peoples and on the obligation of its Members to refrain from the threat or use of force against the territorial integrity or political independence of any State,

Recognizing that, in fulfilment of the principle of self-determination, the General Assembly, in the Declaration on the Granting of Independence to Colonial Countries and Peoples contained in resolution 1514 (XV) of 14 December 1960, stated its conviction that all peoples have an inalienable right to complete freedom, the exercise of their sovereignty and the integrity of their national territory, and that, by virtue of that right, they freely determine their political status and freely pursue their economic, social and cultural development,

Recalling that in the Universal Declaration of Human Rights the General Assembly proclaimed that recognition of the inherent dignity and of the equal and inalienable rights of all members of the human family is the foundation of freedom, justice and peace in the world, without distinction of any kind,

Reaffirming the principle of non-intervention, proclaimed in the charters of the Organization of American States, the League of Arab States and the Organization of African Unity and affirmed at the conferences held at Montevideo, Buenos Aires, Chapultepec and Bogota, as well as in the decisions of the Asian-African Conference at Bandung, the First Conference of Heads of State or Government of Non-Aligned Countries at Belgrade, in the Programme for Peace and International Co-operation adopted at the end of the Second Conference of Heads of State or Government of Non-Aligned Countries at Cairo, and in the declaration on subversion adopted at Accra by the Heads of State and Government of the African States,

Recognizing that full observance of the principle of the non-intervention of States in the internal and external affairs of other States is essential to the fulfilment of the purposes and principles of the United Nations.

Considering that armed intervention is synonymous with aggression and, as such, is contrary to the basic principles on which peaceful international co-operation between States should be built,

Considering further that direct intervention, subversion and all forms of indirect intervention are contrary to these principles and, consequently, constitute a violation of the Charter of the United Nations,

Mindful that violation of the principle of non-intervention poses a threat to the independence, freedom and normal political, economic, social and cultural development of countries, particularly those which have freed themselves from colonialism, and can pose a serious threat to the maintenance of peace,

---

[1] Official Records of the General Assembly, Twentieth Session, Supplement No. 14, pp. 11-12.

Fully aware of the imperative need to create appropriate conditions, which would enable all States, and in particular the developing countries, to choose without duress or coercion their own political, economic and social institutions,

In the light of the foregoing considerations, solemnly declares:

1. No State has the right to intervene, directly or indirectly, for any reason whatever, in the internal or external affairs of any other State. Consequently, armed intervention and all other forms of interference or attempted threats against the personality of the State and against its political, economic and cultural elements, are condemned.

2. No State may use or encourage the use of economic, political or any other type of measures to coerce another State in order to obtain from it the subordination of the exercise of its sovereign rights or to secure from it advantages of any kind. Also, no State shall organize, assist, foment, finance, incite or tolerate subversive, terrorist or armed activities directed towards the violent overthrow of the regime of another State, or interfere in civil strife in another State.

3. The use of force to deprive peoples of their national identity constitutes a violation of their inalienable rights and of the principle of non-intervention.

4. The strict observance of these obligations is an essential condition to ensure that nations live together in peace with one another, since the practice of any form of intervention not only violates the spirit and letter of the Charter of the United Nations but also leads to the creation of situations which threaten international peace and security.

5. Every State has an inalienable right to choose its political, economic, social and cultural systems, without interference in any form by another State.

6. All States shall respect the right of self-determination and independence of peoples and nations, to be fully exercised without any foreign pressure, and with absolute respect for human rights and fundamental freedoms. Consequently, all States shall contribute to the complete elimination of racial discrimination and colonialism in all its forms and manifestations.

7. For the purpose of the present Declaration, the term "State" covers both individual States and groups of States.

8. Nothing in this Declaration shall be construed as affecting in any manner the relevant provisions of the Charter of the United Nations relating to the maintenance of international peace and security, in particular those contained in Chapters VI, VII and VIII.

1408th plenary meeting,
21 December 1965.

4. STRICT OBSERVANCE OF THE PROHIBITION OF THE THREAT OR USE OF FORCE IN INTERNATIONAL RELATIONS, AND OF THE RIGHT OF PEOPLES TO SELF-DETERMINATION[1]

The General Assembly,

I

Drawing the attention of States to the fundamental obligations incumbent upon them in accordance with the Charter of the United Nations to refrain in their international relations from the threat or use of force against the territorial integrity or political independence of any State, or in any other manner inconsistent with the purposes

---

[1] Official Records of the General Assembly, Twenty-first Session, Supplement No. 16, p. 4.

of the United Nations and to develop friendly relations among nations based on respect for the principle of equal rights and self-determination of peoples,

Deeply concerned at the existence of dangerous situations in the world constituting a direct threat to universal peace and security, due to the arbitrary use of force in international relations,

Reaffirming the right of peoples under colonial rule to exercise their right to self-determination and independence and the right of every nation, large or small, to choose freely and without any external interference its political, social and economic system,

Recognizing that peoples subjected to colonial oppression are entitled to seek and receive all support in their struggle which is in accordance with the purposes and principles of the Charter,

Firmly convinced that it is within the power and in the vital interest of the nations of the world to establish genuinely sound relations between States, based on justice, equality, mutual understanding and co-operation,

Recalling the declarations contained in its resolutions 1514 (XV) of 14 December 1960 and 2131 (XX) of 21 December 1965,

1. *Reaffirms* that:

(a) States shall strictly observe, in their international relations, the prohibition of the threat or use of force against the territorial integrity or political independence of any State, or in any other manner inconsistent with the purposes of the United Nations. Accordingly, armed attack by one State against another or the use of force in any other form contrary to the Charter of the United Nations constitutes a violation of international law giving rise to international responsibility;

(b) Any forcible action, direct or indirect, which deprives peoples under foreign domination of their right to self-determination and freedom and independence and of their right to determine freely their political status and pursue their economic, social and cultural development constitutes a violation of the Charter of the United Nations. Accordingly, the use of force to deprive peoples of their national identity, as prohibited by the Declaration on the Inadmissibility of Intervention in the Domestic Affairs of States and the Protection of Their Independence and Sovereignty contained in General Assembly resolution 2131 (XX), constitutes a violation of their inalienable rights and the principle of non-intervention;

2. *Urgently appeals* to States:

(a) To renounce and to refrain from any action contrary to the above-stated fundamental principles and to assure that their activities in international relations are in full harmony with the interests of international peace and security;

(b) To exert every effort and to undertake all necessary measures with a view to facilitating the exercise of the right of self-determination of peoples under colonial rule, lessening international tension, strengthening peace and promoting friendly relations and co-operation among States;

3. *Reminds* all Members of their duty to give their fullest support to the endeavours of the United Nations to ensure respect for and the observance of the principles enshrined in the Charter and to assist the Organization in discharging its responsibilities as assigned to it by the Charter for the maintenance of international peace and security;

II

Considering that the above principles, together with the other five principles of friendly relations and cooperation among States, have been the object of a study with a view to their progressive development and codification on the basis of General Assembly resolutions 1815 (XVII) of 18 December 1962, 1966 (XVIII) of 16 December 1963 and 2103 (XX) of 20 December 1965,

Requests the Secretary-General to include the present resolution and the records of the debate on the item entitled "Strict observance of the prohibition of the threat or use of force in international relations and of the right of peoples to self-determination"

in the documentation to be considered in the further study of the principles of international law concerning friendly relations and co-operation among States in accordance with the Charter of the United Nations, with a view to the early adoption of a declaration containing an enunciation of these principles.

1482nd plenary meeting,
30 November 1966.

5. ELIMINATION OF FOREIGN MILITARY BASES IN THE COUNTRIES OF ASIA, AFRICA AND LATIN AMERICA[1]

The General Assembly,

Having received the interim report of the Conference of the Eighteen-Nation Committee on Disarmament,

Recalling its resolution 2165 (XXI) of 5 December 1966,

Noting that the Conference of the Eighteen-Nation Committee on Disarmament has not been able to give sufficient consideration to the question of the elimination of foreign military bases in the countries of Asia, Africa and Latin America,

1. *Requests* the Conference of the Eighteen-Nation Committee on Disarmament to resume consideration of the question of the elimination of foreign military bases in the countries of Asia, Africa and Latin America, in accordance with General Assembly resolution 2165 (XXI);

2. *Requests* the Conference of the Eighteen-Nation Committee on Disarmament to report to the General Assembly at its twenty-third session on the progress achieved on the question of the elimination of foreign military bases in the countries of Asia, Africa and Latin America.

1640th plenary meeting,
19 December 1967.

E. INTERNATIONAL PEACE AND SECURITY

1. ESSENTIALS OF PEACE[2]

The General Assembly

1. *Declares* that the Charter of the United Nations, the most solemn pact of peace in history, lays down basic principles necessary for an enduring peace; that disregard of these principles is primarily responsible for the continuance of international tension; and that it is urgently necessary for all Members to act in accordance with these principles in the spirit of co-operation on which the United Nations was founded;

Calls upon every nation

2. *To refrain* from threatening or using force contrary to the Charter;

3. *To refrain* from any threats or acts, direct or indirect, aimed at impairing the freedom, independence or integrity of any State, or at fomenting civil strife and subverting the will of the people in any State;

---

[1] Official Records of the General Assembly, Twenty-second Session, Supplement No. 16, p. 16.
[2] Official Records of the General Assembly, Fourth Session, p. 13.

4. *To carry out* in good faith its international agreements;

5. *To afford* all United Nations bodies full co-operation and free access in the performance of the tasks assigned to them under the Charter;

6. *To promote*, in recognition of the paramount importance of preserving the dignity and worth of the human person, full freedom for the peaceful expression of political opposition, full opportunity for the exercise of religious freedom and full respect for all the other fundamental rights expressed in the Universal Declaration of Human Rights;

7. *To promote* nationally and through international co-operation, efforts to achieve and sustain higher standards of living for all peoples;

8. *To remove* the barriers which deny to peoples the free exchange of information and ideas essential to international understanding and peace;

Calls upon every Member

9. *To participate* fully in all the work of the United Nations;

Calls upon the five permanent members of the Security Council

10. *To broaden* progressively their co-operation and to exercise restraint in the use of the veto in order to make the Security Council a more effective instrument for maintaining peace;

Calls upon every nation

11. *To settle* international disputes by peaceful means and to co-operate in supporting United Nations efforts to resolve outstanding problems;

12. *To co-operate* to attain the effective international regulation of conventional armaments; and

13. *To agree* to the exercise of national sovereignty jointly with other nations to the extent necessary to attain international control of atomic energy which would make effective the prohibition of atomic weapons and assure the use of atomic energy for peaceful purposes only.

261st plenary meeting,
1 December 1949.

2. DECLARATION ON PRINCIPLES OF INTERNATIONAL LAW CONCERNING FRIENDLY RELATIONS AND CO-OPERATION AMONG STATES IN ACCORDANCE WITH THE CHARTER OF THE UNITED NATIONS[1]

The General Assembly,

Recalling its resolutions 1815 (XVII) of 18 December 1962, 1966 (XVIII) of 16 December 1963, 2103 (XX) of 20 December 1965, 2181 (XXI) of 12 December 1966, 2327 (XXII) of 18 December 1967, 2463 (XXIII) of 20 December 1968 and 2533 (XXIV) of 8 December 1969, in which it affirmed the importance of the progressive development and codification of the principles of international law concerning friendly relations and co-operation among States,

Having considered the report of the Special Committee on Principles of International Law concerning Friendly Relations and Co-operation among States,[2] which met in Geneva from 31 March to 1 May 1970,

Emphasizing the paramount importance of the Charter of the United Nations for the maintenance of international peace and security and for the development of friendly relations and co-operation among States,

Deeply convinced that the adoption of the Declaration on Principles of International Law concerning Friendly Relations and Co-operation among States in accordance with the Charter of the United Nations on the occasion of the twenty-fifth anniversary of the United Nations would contribute to the strengthening of world peace and constitute a landmark in the development of international law and of relations among States, in promoting the rule of law among nations and particularly the universal application of the principles embodied in the Charter,

Considering the desirability of the wide dissemination of the text of the Declaration,

1. *Approves* the Declaration on Principles of International Law concerning Friendly Relations and Co-operation among States in accordance with the Charter of the United Nations, the text of which is annexed to the present resolution;

2. *Expresses its appreciation* to the Special Committee on Principles of International Law concerning Friendly Relations and Co-operation among States for its work resulting in the elaboration of the Declaration;

3. *Recommends* that all efforts be made so that the Declaration becomes generally known.

1883rd plenary meeting,
24 October 1970.

---

[1] Official Records of the General Assembly, Twenty-fifth Session, Supplement No. 2, pp. 121-124.
[2] Official Records of the General Assembly, Twenty-fifth Session, Supplement No. 18 (A/8018).

DECLARATION ON PRINCIPLES OF INTERNATIONAL LAW CONCERNING FRIENDLY RE-
LATIONS AND CO-OPERATION AMONG STATES IN ACCORDANCE WITH THE CHARTER
OF THE UNITED NATIONS

PREAMBLE

The General Assembly,

Reaffirming in the terms of the Charter of the United Nations that the maintenance
of international peace and security and the development of friendly relations and co-
operation between nations are among the fundamental purposes of the United Nations,

Recalling that the peoples of the United Nations are determined to practise tolerance
and live together in peace with one another as good neighbours,

Bearing in mind the importance of maintaining and strengthening international peace
founded upon freedom, equality, justice and respect for fundamental human rights and
of developing friendly relations among nations irrespective of their political, economic
and social systems or the levels of their development,

Bearing in mind also the paramount importance of the Charter of the United Nations
in the promotion of the rule of law among nations,

Considering that the faithful observance of the principles of international law concerning friendly relations and co-operation among States and the fulfilment in good
faith of the obligations assumed by States, in accordance with the Charter, is of the
greatest importance for the maintenance of international peace and security and for the
implementation of the other purposes of the United Nations,

Noting that the great political, economic and social changes and scientific progress
which have taken place in the world since the adoption of the Charter give increased
importance to these principles and to the need for their more effective application in
the conduct of States wherever carried on,

Recalling the established principle that outer space, including the Moon and other
celestial bodies, is not subject to national appropriation by claim of sovereignty, by
means of use or occupation, or by any other means, and mindful of the fact that consideration is being given in the United Nations to the question of establishing other
appropriate provisions similarly inspired,

Convinced that the strict observance by States of the obligation not to intervene in
the affairs of any other State is an essential condition to ensure that nations live together in peace with one another, since the practice of any form of intervention not
only violates the spirit and letter of the Charter, but also leads to the creation of situations which threaten international peace and security,

Recalling the duty of States to refrain in their international relations from military, political, economic or any other form of coercion aimed against the political independence or territorial integrity of any State,

Considering it essential that all States shall refrain in their international relations from the threat or use of force against the territorial integrity or political independence of any State, or in any other manner inconsistent with the purposes of the United Nations,

Considering it equally essential that all States shall settle their international disputes by peaceful means in accordance with the Charter,

Reaffirming, in accordance with the Charter, the basic importance of sovereign equality and stressing that the purposes of the United Nations can be implemented only if States enjoy sovereign equality and comply fully with the requirements of this principle in their international relations,

Convinced that the subjection of peoples to alien subjugation, domination and exploitation constitutes a major obstacle to the promotion of international peace and security,

Convinced that the principle of equal rights and self-determination of peoples constitutes a significant contribution to contemporary international law, and that its effective application is of paramount importance for the promotion of friendly relations among States, based on respect for the principle of sovereign equality,

Convinced in consequence that any attempt aimed at the partial or total disruption of the national unity and territorial integrity of a State or country or at its political independence is incompatible with the purposes and principles of the Charter,

Considering the provisions of the Charter as a whole and taking into account the role of relevant resolutions adopted by the competent organs of the United Nations relating to the content of the principles,

Considering that the progressive development and codification of the following principles:

(a) The principle that States shall refrain in their international relations from the threat or use of force against the territorial integrity or political independence of any State, or in any other manner inconsistent with the purposes of the United Nations,

(b) The principle that States shall settle their international disputes by peaceful means in such a manner that international peace and security and justice are not endangered,

(c) The duty not to intervene in matters within the domestic jurisdiction of any State, in accordance with the Charter,

(d) The duty of States to co-operate with one another in accordance with the Charter,

(e) The principle of equal rights and self-determination of peoples,

(f) The principle of sovereign equality of States,

(g) The principle that States shall fulfil in good faith the obligations assumed by them in accordance with the Charter, so as to secure their more effective application within the international community, would promote the realization of the purposes of the United Nations,

Having considered the principles of international law relating to friendly relations and co-operation among States,

1. *Solemnly proclaims* the following principles:

The principle that States shall refrain in their international relations from the threat or use of force against the territorial integrity or political independence of any State, or any other manner inconsistent with the purposes of the United Nations

Every State has the duty to refrain in its international relations from the threat or use of force against the territorial integrity or political independence of any State, or in any other manner inconsistent with the purposes of the United Nations. Such a threat or use of force constitutes a violation of international law and the Charter of the United Nations and shall never be employed as a means of settling international issues.

A war of aggression constitutes a crime against the peace, for which there is responsibility under international law.

In accordance with the purposes and principles of the United Nations, States have the duty to refrain from propaganda for wars of aggression.

Every State has the duty to refrain from the threat or use of force to violate the existing international boundaries of another State or as a means of solving international disputes, including territorial disputes and problems concerning frontiers of States.

Every State likewise has the duty to refrain from the threat or use of force to violate international lines of demarcation, such as armistice lines, established by or pursuant to an international agreement to which it is a party or which it is otherwise bound to respect. Nothing in the foregoing shall be construed as prejudicing the positions of the parties concerned with regard to the status and effects of such lines under their special regimes or as affecting their temporary character.

States have a duty to refrain from acts of reprisal involving the use of force.

Every State has the duty to refrain from any forcible action which deprives peoples referred to in the elaboration of the principle of equal rights and self-determination of their right to self-determination and freedom and independence.

Every State has the duty to refrain from organizing or encouraging the organization of irregular forces or armed bands, including mercenaries, for incursion into the territory of another State.

Every State has the duty to refrain from organizing, instigating, assisting or participating in acts of civil strife or terrorist acts in another State or acquiescing to organized activities within its territory directed towards the commission of such acts, when the acts referred to in the present paragraph involve a threat or use of force.

The territory of a State shall not be the object of military occupation resulting from the use of force in contravention of the provisions of the Charter. The territory of a State shall not be the object of acquisition by another State resulting from the threat or use of force. No territorial acquisition resulting from the threat or use of force shall be recognized as legal. Nothing in the foregoing shall be construed as affecting:

(a) Provisions of the Charter or any international agreement prior to the Charter regime and valid under international law; or

(b) The powers of the Security Council under the Charter.

All States shall pursue in good faith negotiations for the early conclusion of a universal treaty on general and complete disarmament under effective international control and strive to adopt appropriate measures to reduce international tensions and strengthen confidence among States.

All States shall comply in good faith with their obligations under the generally recognized principles and rules of international law with respect to the maintenance of international peace and security, and shall endeavour to make the United Nations security system based on the Charter more effective.

Nothing in the foregoing paragraphs shall be construed as enlarging or diminishing in any way the scope of the provisions of the Charter concerning cases in which the use of force is lawful.

The principle that States shall settle their international disputes by peaceful means in such a manner that international peace and security and justice are not endangered

Every State shall settle its international disputes with other States by peaceful means in such a manner that international peace and security and justice are not endangered.

States shall accordingly seek early and just settlement of their international disputes by negotiation, inquiry, mediation, conciliation, arbitration, judicial settlement, resort to regional agencies or arrangements or other peaceful means of their choice. In seeking such a settlement the parties shall agree upon such peaceful means as may be appropriate to the circumstances and nature of the dispute.

The parties to a dispute have the duty, in the event of failure to reach a solution by any one of the above peaceful means, to continue to seek a settlement of the dispute by other peaceful means agreed upon by them.

States parties to an international dispute, as well as other States, shall refrain from any action which may aggravate the situation so as to endanger the maintenance of international peace and security, and shall act in accordance with the purposes and principles of the United Nations.

International disputes shall be settled on the basis of the sovereign equality of States and in accordance with the principle of free choice of means. Recourse to, or acceptance of, a settlement procedure freely agreed to by States with regard to existing or future disputes to which they are parties shall not be regarded as incompatible with sovereign equality.

Nothing in the foregoing paragraphs prejudices or derogates from the applicable provisions of the Charter, in particular those relating to the pacific settlement of international disputes.

The principle concerning the duty not to intervene in matters within the domestic jurisdiction of any State, in accordance with the Charter

No State or group of States has the right to intervene, directly or indirectly, for any reason whatever, in the internal or external affairs of any other State. Consequently, armed intervention and all other forms of interference or attempted threats against the personality of the State or against its political, economic and cultural elements, are in violation of international law.

No State may use or encourage the use of economic, political or any other type of measures to coerce another State in order to obtain from it the subordination of the exercise of its sovereign rights and to secure from it advantages of any kind. Also, no State shall organize, assist, foment, finance, incite or tolerate subversive, terrorist or armed activities directed towards the violent overthrow of the regime of another State, or interfere in civil strife in another State.

The use of force to deprive peoples of their national identity constitutes a violation of their inalienable rights and of the principle of non-intervention.

Every State has an inalienable right to choose its political, economic, social and cultural systems, without interference in any form by another State.

Nothing in the foregoing paragraphs shall be construed as affecting the relevant provisions of the Charter relating to the maintenance of international peace and security.

The duty of States to co-operate with one another in accordance with the Charter

States have the duty to co-operate with one another, irrespective of the differences in their political, economic and social systems, in the various spheres of international relations, in order to maintain international peace and security and to promote international economic stability and progress, the general welfare of nations and international co-operation free from discrimination based on such differences.

To this end:

(a) States shall co-operate with other States in the maintenance of international peace and security;

(b) States shall co-operate in the promotion of universal respect for, and observance of, human rights and fundamental freedoms for all, and in the elimination of all forms of racial discrimination and all forms of religious intolerance;

(c) States shall conduct their international relations in the economic, social, cultural, technical and trade fields in accordance with the principles of sovereign equality and non-intervention;

(d) States Members of the United Nations have the duty to take joint and separate action in co-operation with the United Nations in accordance with the relevant provisions of the Charter.

States should co-operate in the economic, social and cultural fields as well in the field of science and technology and for the promotion of international cultural and educational progress. States should co-operate in the promotion of economic growth throughout the world, especially that of the developing countries.

The principles of equal rights and self-determination of peoples

By virtue of the principle of equal rights and self-determination of peoples enshrined in the Charter of the United Nations, all peoples have the right freely to determine, without external interference, their political status and to pursue their economic, social and cultural development, and every State has the duty to respect this right in accordance with the provisions of the Charter.

Every State has the duty to promote, through joint and separate action, realization of the principle of equal rights and self-determination of peoples, in accordance with the provisions of the Charter, and to render assistance to the United Nations in carrying out the responsibilities entrusted to it by the Charter regarding the implementation of the principle, in order:

(a) To promote friendly and co-operation among States; and

(b) To bring a speedy end to colonialism, having due regard to the freely expressed will of the peoples concerned;

and bearing in mind that subjection of peoples to alien subjugation, domination and exploitation constitutes a violation of the principle, as well as a denial of fundamental human rights, and is contrary to the Charter.

Every State has the duty to promote through joint and separate action universal respect for and observance of human rights and fundamental freedoms in accordance with the Charter.

The establishment of a sovereign and independent State, the free association or integration with an independent State or the emergence into any other political status freely determined by a people constitute modes of implementing the right of self-determination by that people.

Every State has the duty to refrain from any forcible action which deprives peoples referred to above in the elaboration of the present principle of their right to self-determination and freedom and independence. In their actions against, and resistance to, such forcible action in pursuit of the exercise of their right to self-determination, such peoples are entitled to seek and to receive support in accordance with the purposes and principles of the Charter.

The territory of a colony or other Non-Self-Governing Territory has, under the Charter, a status separate and distinct from the territory of the State administering it; and such separate and distinct status under the Charter shall exist until the people of the colony or Non-Self-Governing Territory have exercised their right of self-determination in accordance with the Charter, and particularly its purposes and principles.

Nothing in the foregoing paragraphs shall be construed as authorizing or encouraging any action which would dismember or impair, totally or in part, the territorial integrity or political unity of sovereign and independent States conducting themselves in compliance with the principle of equal rights and self-determination of peoples as described above and thus possessed of a government representing the whole people belonging to the territory without distinction as to race, creed or colour.

Every State shall refrain from any action aimed at the partial or total disruption of the national unity and territorial integrity of any other State or country.

The principle of sovereign equality of States

All States enjoy sovereign equality. They have equal rights and duties and are equal members of the international community, notwithstanding differences of an economic, social, political or other nature.

In particular, sovereign equality includes the following elements:

(a) States are juridically equal;

(b) Each State enjoys the rights inherent in full sovereignty;

(c) Each State has the duty to respect the personality of other States;

(d) The territorial integrity and political independence of the State are inviolable;

(e) Each State has the right freely to choose and develop its political, social, economic and cultural systems;

(f) Each State has the duty to comply fully and in good faith with its international obligations and to live in peace with other States.

The principle that States shall fulfil in good faith the obligations assumed by them in accordance with the Charter

Every State has the duty to fulfil in good faith the obligations assumed by it in accordance with the Charter of the United Nations.

Every State has the duty to fulfil in good faith its obligations under the generally recognized principles and rules of international law.

Every State has the duty to fulfil in good faith its obligations under international agreements valid under the generally recognized principles and rules of international law.

Where obligations arising under international agreements are in conflict with the obligations of Members of the United Nations under the Charter of the United Nations, the obligations under the Charter shall prevail.

GENERAL PART

2. *Declares* that:

In their interpretation and application the above principles are interrelated and each principle should be construed in the context of the other principles.

Nothing in this Declaration shall be construed as prejudicing in any manner the provisions of the Charter or the rights and duties of Member States under the Charter or the rights of peoples under the Charter, taking into account the elaboration of these rights in this Declaration.

3. *Declares further* that:

The principles of the Charter which are embodied in this Declaration constitute basic principles of international law, and consequently appeals to all States to be guided by these principles in their international conduct and to develop their mutual relations on the basis of the strict observance of these principles.

3. DECLARATION ON THE STRENGTHENING OF INTERNATIONAL SECURITY[3]

The General Assembly,

Recalling the determination of the peoples of the United Nations, as proclaimed by the Charter, to save succeeding generations from the scourge of war, and to this end

---

[1] Official Records of the General Assembly, Twenty-fifth Session, Supplement No. 28, pp. 22-23.

to live together in peace with one another as good neighbours and to unite their strength to maintain international peace and security,

Considering that in order to fulfil the purposes and principles of the United Nations Member States must strictly abide by all provisions of the Charter,

Recalling its resolution 2606 (XXIV) of 16 December 1969 in which the General Assembly, *inter alia*, expressed the desire that the twenty-fifth year of the Organization's existence should be marked by new initiatives to promote peace, security, disarmament and economic and social progress for all mankind and the conviction of the urgent need to make the United Nations more effective as an instrument for maintaining international peace and security,

Mindful of the observations, proposals and suggestions advanced during the debate at the twenty-fourth session of the General Assembly or presented subsequently by Governments of Member States concerning the attainment of this objective, and of the report submitted by the Secretary-General in conformity with paragraph 5 of resolution 2606 (XXIV),[2]

Having in mind the Declaration on Principles of International Law concerning Friendly Relations and Co-operation among States in accordance with the Charter of the United Nations, adopted unanimously at the current session,[3]

Conscious of its duty to examine in depth the present international situation and to study the means and recourses provided by the relevant provisions of the Charter in order to build peace, security and co-operation in the world,

1. *Solemnly reaffirms* the universal and unconditional validity of the purposes and principles of the Charter of the United Nations as the basis of relations among States irrespective of their size, geographical location, level of development or political, economic and social systems and declares that the breach of these principles cannot be justified in any circumstances whatsoever;

2. *Calls upon* all States to adhere strictly in their international relations to the purposes and principles of the Charter, including the principle that States shall refrain in their international relations from the threat or use of force against the territorial integrity or political independence of any State or in any other manner inconsistent with the purposes of the United Nations; the principle that States shall settle their international disputes by peaceful means in such a manner that international peace and security and justice are not endangered; the duty not to intervene in matters within the domestic jurisdiction of any State, in accordance with the Charter; the duty of States to cooperate with one another in accordance with the Charter; the principle of equal rights and self-determination of peoples; the principle of sovereign equality of States; and the principle that States shall fulfil in good faith the obligations assumed by them in accordance with the Charter;

3. *Solemnly reaffirms* that, in the event of a conflict between the obligations of the Members of the United Nations under the Charter and their obligations under any other international agreement, their obligations under the Charter shall prevail;

4. *Solemnly reaffirms* that States must fully respect the sovereignty of other States and the right of peoples to determine their own destinies, free of external intervention, coercion or constraint, especially involving the threat or use of force, overt or covert, and refrain from any attempt aimed at the partial or total disruption of the national unity and territorial integrity of any other State or country;

5. *Solemnly reaffirms* that every State has the duty to refrain from the threat or use of force against the territorial integrity and political independence of any other State, and that the territory of a State shall not be the object of military occupation resulting from the use of force in contravention of the provisions of the Charter, that the territory of a State shall not be the object of acquisition by another State resulting from the threat or use of force, that no territorial acquisition resulting from the threat

[2] A/7922 and Add. 1-6.
[3] Resolution 2625 (XXV).

or use of force shall be recognized as legal and that every State has the duty to refrain from organizing, instigating, assisting or participating in acts of civil strife or terrorist acts in another State;

6. *Urges* Member States to make full use and seek improved implementation of the means, and methods provided for in the Charter for the exclusively peaceful settlement of any dispute or any situation, the continuance of which is likely to endanger the maintenance of international peace and security, including negotiation, inquiry, mediation, conciliation, arbitration, judicial settlement, resort to regional agencies or arrangements, good offices including those of the Secretary-General, or other peaceful means of their own choice, it being understood that the Security Council in dealing with such disputes or situations should also take into consideration that legal disputes should as a general rule be referred by the parties to the International Court of Justice in accordance with the provisions of the Statute of the Court;

7. *Urges* all Member States to respond to the immediate need to agree on guidelines for more effective peace-keeping operations in accordance with the Charter, which could increase the effectiveness of the United Nations in dealing with situations endangering international peace and security, and consequently to support the efforts of the Special Committee on Peace-keeping Operations to reach agreement on all questions relating to such operations, as well as on provisions for their appropriate and equitable financing;

8. *Recognizes* the need for effective, dynamic and flexible measures, in accordance with the Charter, to prevent and remove threats to the peace, suppress acts of aggression or other breaches of the peace, and in particular for measures to build, maintain and restore international peace and security;

9. *Recommends* that the Security Council take steps to facilitate the conclusion of the agreements envisaged in Article 43 of the Charter in order fully to develop its capacity for enforcement action as provided for under Chapter VII of the Charter;

10. *Recommends* that the Security Council consider, in conformity with Article 29 of the Charter, whenever appropriate and necessary, the desirability of establishing subsidiary organs, on an *ad hoc* basis, and with the participation of the parties concerned, when conditions so warrant, to assist the Council in the performance of its functions as defined in the Charter;

11. *Recommends* that all States contribute to the efforts to ensure peace and security for all nations and to establish, in accordance with the Charter, an effective system of universal collective security without military alliances;

12. *Invites* Member States to do their utmost to enhance by all possible means the authority and effectiveness of the Security Council and of its decisions;

13. *Calls upon* the Security Council, including the permanent members, to intensify efforts to discharge, in conformity with the Charter, its primary responsibility for the maintenance of international peace and security;

14. *Recommends* that Member States support the efforts of the Special Committee on the Question of Defining Aggression to bring its work to a successful conclusion, thus achieving the definition of aggression as soon as possible;

15. *Reaffirms* its competence under the Charter to discuss and recommend measures for the peaceful adjustment of any situation which it deems likely to impair the general welfare or friendly relations among States, including situations resulting from a violation of the provisions of the Charter setting forth the purposes and principles of the United Nations;

16. *Urges* all Member States to implement the decisions of the Security Council in accordance with their obligations under Article 25 of the Charter and to respect, as provided for in the Charter, the resolutions of United Nations organs responsible for the maintenance of international peace and security and the peaceful settlement of disputes;

17. *Urges* Member States to reaffirm their will to respect fully their obligations under international law in accordance with the relevant provisions of the Charter and

to continue and intensify the efforts towards the progressive development and codification of international law;

18. *Call upon* all States to desist from any forcible or other action which deprives peoples, in particular those still under colonial or any other form of external domination, of their, inalienable right to self-determination, freedom and independence and to refrain from military and repressive measures aimed at preventing the attainment of independence by all dependent peoples in accordance with the Charter and in furtherance of the objectives of General Assembly resolution 1514 (XV) of 14 December 1960,[1] and render assistance to the United Nations and, in accordance with the Charter, to the oppressed peoples in their legitimate struggle in order to bring about the speedy elimination of colonialism or any other form of external domination;

19. *Affirms* its belief that there is a close connexion between the strengthening of international security, disarmament and the economic development of countries, so that any progress made towards any of these objectives will constitute progress towards all of them;

20. *Urges* all States, particularly the nuclear-weapon States, to make urgent and concerned efforts within the framework of the Disarmament Decade and through other means for the cessation and reversal of the nuclear and conventional arms race at an early date, the elimination of nuclear weapons, and other weapons of mass destruction and the conclusion of a treaty on general and complete disarmament under effective international control, as well as to ensure that the benefits of the technology of the peaceful use of nuclear energy shall be available to all States, to the maximum extent possible, without discrimination;

21. *Emphatically reiterates* the need to undertake, within the framework of the Second United Nations Development Decade, urgent and concerted international action based on a global strategy aimed at reducing and eliminating as soon as possible the economic gap between developed and developing countries, which is closely and essentially correlated to the strengthening of the security of all nations and the establishment of lasting international peace;

22. *Solemnly reaffirms* that universal respect for and full exercise of human rights and fundamental freedoms and the elimination of the violation of those rights are urgent and essential to the strengthening of international security, and hence resolutely condemns all forms of oppression, tyranny and discrimination, particularly racism and racial discrimination, wherever they occur;

23. *Resolutely condemns* the criminal policy of *apartheid* of the Government of South Africa and reaffirms the legitimacy of the struggle of the oppressed peoples to attain their human rights and fundamental freedoms and self-determination;

24. *Expresses its conviction* that the achievement of universality of the United Nations, in accordance with the Charter, would increase its effectiveness in strengthening international peace and security;

25. *Considers* that the promotion of international co-operation, including regional, subregional and bilateral co-operation among States, in keeping with the provisions of the Charter and based on the principle of equal rights and on strict respect for the sovereignty and independence of States, can contribute to the strengthening of international security;

26. *Welcomes* the decision of the Security Council to hold periodic meetings in accordance with Article 28, paragraph 2, of the Charter and expresses the hope that these meetings will make an important contribution to the strengthening of international security;

---

[1] Official Records of the Security Council, Twenty-fifth Year, 1544th meeting.

4. IMPLEMENTATION OF THE DECLARATION ON THE STRENGTHENING OF INTERNATIONAL SECURITY[1]

Date: 14 December 1976   Meeting: 98
Vote: 95-0-17 (recorded)   Report: A/31/414

The General Assembly,

Having considered the item entitled "Implementation of the Declaration on the Strengthening of International Security,"

Bearing in mind the Declaration on the Strengthening of International Security, contained in General Assembly resolution 2734 (XXV) of 16 December 1970, and the relevant resolutions of the Assembly concerning the implementation of the Declaration,

Welcoming new achievement and trends in international relations and all other efforts contributing to the strengthening of international security and the promoting of peaceful co-operation in accordance with the Charter of the United Nations,

Welcoming also, in this context, the successful results of *the Fifth Conference of Heads of State or Government of Non-Aligned Countries, held at Colombo from 16 to 19 August 1976,* which represents a further significant contribution to the strengthening of international security and development of equitable international relations,

Noting the successful outcome of the Conference on Security and Co-operation in Europe, emphasizing that the security of Europe should be considered in the broader context of world security and is closely interrelated, in particular, to the security of the Mediterranean, the Middle East and to other regions of the world, and expressing its conviction that the implementation of the Final Act of that Conference through agreed means will contribute to the strengthening of international peace and security,

Noting however with grave concern the continuing existence of focal points of crises and tensions in various regions endangering international peace and security, the continuation of the arms race as well as acts of aggression, the threat or use of force, foreign occupation and alien domination and the existence of colonialism, neo-colonialism, racial discrimination and *apartheid,* which remain the main obstacles to the strengthening of international peace and security,

Reaffirming the close link existing between the strengthening of international security, disarmament, decolonization, development and the need for a more intensive national and international effort to narrow the widening gap between the developed and the developing countries, and also stressing, in this connexion, the importance of the early implementation of the decisions adopted at its sixth and seventh special sessions,

Emphasizing the need constantly to strengthen the peace-keeping and peace-making role of the United Nations in accordance with the Charter as well as its role in promoting development through equitable co-operation,

1. *Solemnly calls upon* all States to seek strict and consistent *implementation of the purposes and the principles of the Charter of the United Nations* and of all the provisions of the Declaration on the Strengthening of International Security;

2. *Reaffirms* the legitimacy of the struggle of peoples under colonial and alien domination to achieve self-determination and independence and appeals to all States to increase their support and solidarity with them in their struggle against colonialism, racial discrimination and *apartheid;*

---

[1]Resolution adopted by the General Assembly during the first part of its Thirty-first regular session, 21 September-22 December 1976 (the Official Record is not ready at the preparing of this volume), Press Release: GA/5571, 29 December 1976, pp. 94-96.

3. *Also calls upon* all States to extend the process of relaxation of tensions, which is still limited both in scope and geographical extent, to all regions of the world, in order to help bring about just and lasting solutions to international problems with the participation of all States so that peace and security *will be based on effective respect for the sovereignty and independence of all States and the inalienable rights of all peoples to determine their own destiny freely and without outside interference, coercion or pressure;*

4. *Reaffirms* that any measure or pressure directed against any State while exercising its sovereign right freely to dispose of its natural resources constitutes a flagrant violation of the right of self-determination of peoples and the principle of non-intervention, as set forth in the Charter, which, if pursued, could constitute a threat to international peace and security;

5. *Reaffirms* its opposition to any threats or use of force, intervention, aggression, foreign occupation and measures of political and economic coercion which attempt to violate the sovereignty, territorial integrity, independence and security of States;

6. *Recommends* urgent measures to stop the arms race and promote disarmament, the dismantling of foreign military bases, the creation of zones of peace and co-operation and the achievement of general and complete disarmament and strengthening the role of the United Nations, in accordance with the Charter, in order to eliminate the causes of international tensions and ensure international peace, security and co-operation;

7. *Recommends* that the Security Council should consider appropriate steps towards carrying out effectively, as provided in the Charter and the Declaration on the Strengthening of International Security, its primary responsibility for the maintenance of international security and peace;

8. *Invites* the States parties to the Conference on Security and Co-operation in Europe to implement fully and urgently all the provisions of the Final Act, including those relating to the Mediterranean, and to consider favourably the conversion of the Mediterranean into a zone of peace and co-operation in the interests of international peace and security;

9. *Takes note* of the report of the Secretary-General,[1] requests him to submit to the General Assembly at its thirty-second session a report on the implementation of the Declaration on the Strengthening of International Security and decides to include in the provisional agenda of its thirty-second session the item entitled "Implementation of the Declaration on the Strengthening of International Security."

---

[1]A/31/185 and Add. 1.

RECORDED VOTE ON THE ABOVE RESOLUTION:

Y-YES, N-NO, A-ABSTAIN

Country	Y	N	A	Country	Y	N	A	Country	Y	N	A
Afghanistan	*			Germany, Fed. Rep.				Norway			*
Albania				Ghana				Oman	*		
Algeria	*			Greece				Pakistan	*		
Angola				Grenada				Panama	*		
Argentina				Guatemala			*	Papua New Guinea	*		
Australia			*	Guinea				Paraguay			
Austria	*			Guinea-Bissau	*			Peru	*		
Bahamas	*			Guyana	*			Philippines	*		
Bahrain	*			Haiti				Poland	*		
Bangladesh	*			Honduras	*			Portugal			*
Barbados	*			Hungary	*			Qatar	*		
Belgium			*	Iceland			*	Romania	*		
Benin	*			India	*			Rwanda	*		
Bhutan				Indonesia	*			Sao Tome and Principe			
Bolivia	*			Iran	*			Saudi Arabia	*		
Botswana	*			Iraq	*			Senegal	*		
Brazil				Ireland			*	Seychelles	*		
Bulgaria	*			Israel			*	Sierra Leone	*		
Burma	*			Italy			*	Singapore			
Burundi	*			Ivory Coast	*			Somalia			
Byelorussian SSR	*			Jamaica	*			South Africa			
Canada			*	Japan			*	Spain	*		
Cape Verde				Jordan	*			Sri Lanka	*		
Central African Rep.				Kenya				Sudan	*		
Chad				Kuwait				Surinam	*		
Chile	*			Lao Peoples Dem. Rep.	*			Swaziland	*		
China				Lebanon				Sweden			
Colombia	*			Lesotho	*			Syrian Arab Republic	*		
Comoros				Liberia	*			Thailand	*		
Congo	*			Libyan Arab Republic	*			Togo	*		
Costa Rica	*			Luxembourg			*	Trinidad and Tobago	*		
Cuba				Madagascar	*			Tunisia	*		
Cyprus	*			Malawi	*			Turkey			*
Czechoslovakia	*			Malaysia	*			Uganda	*		
Democratic Kampuchea				Maldives	*			Ukrainian SSR	*		
Democratic Yemen	*			Mali	*			USSR	*		
Denmark				Malta	*			United Arab Emirates	*		
Dominican Republic				Mauritania	*			United Kingdom			
Ecuador	*			Mauritius	*			Un. Rep. of Cameroon	*		
Egypt	*			Mexico	*			Un. Rep. of Tanzania		*	
El Salvador				Mongolia	*			United States		*	
Equatorial Guinea				Morocco	*			Upper Volta	*		
Ethiopia	*			Mozambique	*			Uruguay	*		
Fiji	*			Nepal	*			Venezuela	*		
Finland	*			Netherlands			*	Yemen	*		
France			*	New Zealand	*			Yugoslavia	*		
Gabon	*			Nicaragua	*			Zaire	*		
Gambia	*			Niger	*			Zambia			
German Dem. Rep.	*			Nigeria	*						

5. DECLARATION ON THE PROMOTION AMONG YOUTH OF THE IDEALS OF PEACE, MUTUAL RESPECT AND UNDERSTANDING BETWEEN PEOPLES[1]

The General Assembly,

Recalling that under the terms of the Charter of the United Nations the peoples have declared themselves determined to save succeeding generations from the scourge of war,

Recalling further that in the Charter the United Nations has affirmed its faith in fundamental human rights, in the dignity of the human person and in the equal rights of men and nations,

Reaffirming the principles embodied in the Universal Declaration of Human Rights,[2] the Declaration on the Granting of Independence to Colonial Countries and Peoples,[3] the United Nations Declaration on the Elimination of All Forms of Racial Discrimination,[4] General Assembly resolution 110 (II) of 3 November 1947 condemning all forms of propaganda designed or likely to provoke or encourage any threat to the peace, the Declaration of the Rights of the Child,[5] and General Assembly resolution 1572 (XV) of 18 December 1960, which have a particular bearing upon the upbringing of young people in a spirit of peace, mutual respect and understanding among peoples,

Recalling that the purpose of the United Nations Educational, Scientific and Cultural Organization is to contribute to peace and security by promoting collaboration among nations through education, science and culture, and recognizing the role and contributions of that organization towards the education of young people in the spirit of international understanding, cooperation and peace,

Taking into consideration the fact that in the conflagrations which have afflicted mankind it is the young people who have had to suffer most and who have had the greatest number of victims,

Convinced that young people wish to have an assured future and that peace, freedom and justice are among the chief guarantees that their desire for happiness will be fulfilled,

Bearing in mind the important part being played by young people in every field of human endeavour and the fact that they are destined to guide the fortunes of mankind,

Bearing in mind furthermore that, in this age of great scientific, technological and cultural achievements, the energies, enthusiasm and creative abilities of the young should be devoted to the material and spiritual advancement of all peoples,

Convinced that the young should know, respect and develop the cultural heritage of their own country and that of all mankind,

Convinced furthermore that the education of the young and exchanges of young people and of ideas in a spirit of peace, mutual respect and understanding between peoples can help to improve international relations and to strengthen peace and security,

Proclaims this Declaration on the Promotion among Youth of the Ideals of Peace, Mutual Respect and Understanding between Peoples and calls upon Governments, non-governmental organizations and youth movements to recognize the principles set forth therein and to ensure their observance by means of appropriate measures:

---

[1] Official Records of the General Assembly, Twentieth Session, Supplement No. 14, pp. 40-41.
[2] Resolution 217 A (III) of 10 December 1948.
[3] Resolution 1514 (XV) of 14 December 1960.
[4] Resolution 1904 (XVIII) of 20 November 1963.
[5] Resolution 1386 (XIV) of 20 November 1959.

Principle I

Young people shall be brought up in the spirit of peace, justice, freedom, mutual respect and understanding in order to promote equal rights for all human beings and all nations, economic and social progress, disarmament and the maintenance of international peace and security.

Principle II

All means of education, including as of major importance the guidance given by parents or family, instruction and information intended for the young should foster among them the ideals of peace, humanity, liberty and international solidarity and all other ideals which help to bring peoples closer together, and acquaint them with the role entrusted to the United Nations as a means of preserving and maintaining peace and promoting international understanding and co-operation.

Principle III

Young people shall be brought up in the knowledge of the dignity and equality of all men, without distinction as to race, colour, ethnic origins or beliefs, and in respect for fundamental human rights and for the right of peoples to self-determination.

Principle IV

Exchanges, travel, tourism, meetings, the study of foreign languages, the twinning of towns and universities without discrimination and similar activities should be encouraged and facilitated among young people of all countries in order to bring them together in educational, cultural and sporting activities in the spirit of this Declaration.

Principle V

National and international associations of young people should be encouraged to promote the purposes of the United Nations, particularly international peace and security, friendly relations among nations based on respect for the equal sovereignty of States, the final abolition of colonialism and of racial discrimination and other violations of human rights.

Youth organizations in accordance with this Declaration should take all appropriate measures within their respective fields of activity in order to make their contribution without any discrimination to the work of educating the young generation in accordance with these ideals.

Such organizations, in conformity with the principle of freedom of association, should promote the free exchange of ideas in the spirit of the principles of this Declaration and of the purposes of the United Nations set forth in the Charter.

All youth organizations should conform to the principles set forth in this Declaration.

Principle VI

A major aim in educating the young shall be to develop all their faculties and to train them to acquire higher moral qualities, to be deeply attached to the noble ideals of peace, liberty, the dignity and equality of all men, and imbued with respect and love for humanity and its creative achievements. To this end the family has an important role to play.

Young people must become conscious of their responsibilities in the world they will be called upon to manage and should be inspired with confidence in a future of happiness for mankind.

1390th plenary meeting,
7 December 1965.

6. URGENT NEED FOR CESSATION OF NUCLEAR AND THERMONUCLEAR TESTS AND CONCLUSION OF A TREATY DESIGNED TO ACHIEVE A COMPREHENSIVE TEST BAN[1]

Date: 10 December 1976   Meeting: 96
Vote: 105-2-27 (recorded)   Report: A/31/374

The General Assembly,

Reaffirming its conviction that the cessation of nuclear weapon testing would be in the supreme interest of manking, both as a major step towards controlling the development and proliferation of nuclear weapons and to relieve the deep apprehension concerning the harmful consequences of radio-active contamination for the health of present and future generations,

Gravely concerned at the continuation of both atmospheric and underground nuclear weapon testing since the thirtieth session of the General Assembly,

Recalling its previous resolutions on this subject, the most recent being resolution 3466 (XXX) of 11 December 1975,

Recalling the stated aim of the parties to the Treaty Banning Nuclear Weapon Tests in the Atmosphere, in Outer Space and under Water[2] and the Treaty on the Non-Proliferation of Nuclear Weapons[3] to seek to achieve the discontinuance of all test explosions of nuclear weapons for all time.

Noting the information concerning agreements concluded by two nuclear weapon States limiting the scope of underground nuclear weapon tests and making provision in this connexion for the control and supervision of peaceful nuclear explosions including, in certain cases, arrangements for on-site verification,[4]

Considering that conditions are favourable for these two nuclear weapon States to step up their efforts to reach agreement on the means of verifying a comprehensive test ban agreement,

Taking note of that part of the report of the Conference of the Committee on Disarmament[5] relating to the question of a comprehensive test ban treaty,

1. *Condemns* all nuclear weapon tests, in whatever environment they may be conducted;

2. *Declares* its profound concern that substantive negotiations towards a comprehensive test ban agreement have not yet begun and re-emphasizes the urgency of concluding a comprehensive and effective agreement;

---

[1] Resolutions adopted by the General Assembly during the first part of its Thirty-first regular session, 21 September–22 December 1976 (the Oficial Record is not ready at the preparing of this volume), Press Release: GA/5571, 29 December 1976, pp. 66–67.

[2] United Nations *Treaty Series,* vol. 480, No. 6964, p. 43.

[3] General Assembly resolution 2373 (XXII), annex.

[4] See A/31/125, annex.

[5] See *Official Records of the General Assembly, Thirty-first Session, Supplement No. 27* (A/31/27).

3. *Calls once again upon* all nuclear weapon States to suspend the testing of nuclear weapons by agreement, subject to review after a specified period, as an interim step towards the conclusion of a formal and comprehensive test ban agreement;

4. *Emphasizes* in this regard the particular responsibility of the nuclear weapon States which are party to international agreements in which they have declared their intention to achieve at the earliest possible date the cessation of the nuclear arms race;

5. *Calls upon* all States not yet parties to the Treaty Banning Nuclear Weapon Tests in the Atmosphere, in Outer Space and under Water to adhere to it forthwith;

6. *Urges* the Conference of the Committee on Disarmament to continue to give the highest priority to the conclusion of a comprehensive test ban agreement and to report to the General Assembly at its thirty-second session on the progress achieved;

7. *Decides* to include in the provisional agenda of its thirty-second session the item entitled "Urgent need for cessation of nuclear and thermonuclear tests and conclusion of a treaty designed to achieve a comprehensive test ban."

Y-YES, N-NO, A-ABSTAIN

Country	Y	N	A
Afghanistan	*		
Albania		*	
Algeria			*
Angola	*		
Argentina	*		
Australia	*		
Austria	*		
Bahamas	*		
Bahrain	*		
Bangladesh	*		
Barbados	*		
Belgium			*
Benin			
Bhutan	*		
Bolivia	*		
Botswana	*		
Brazil	*		
Bulgaria			*
Burma	*		
Burundi	*		
Byelorussian SSR		*	
Canada	*		
Cape Verde			
Central African Rep.	*		
Chad	*		
Chile	*		
China		*	
Colombia	*		
Comoros			*
Congo			*
Costa Rica	*		
Cuba			*
Cyprus	*		
Czechoslovakia			*
Democratic Kampuchea			
Democratic Yemen	*		
Denmark	*		
Dominican Republic	*		
Ecuador	*		
Egypt	*		
El Salvador	*		
Equatorial Guinea			*
Ethiopia	*		
Fiji	*		
Finland	*		
France			*
Gabon	*		
Gambia			*
German Dem. Rep.			*
Germany, Fed. Rep.			*
Ghana	*		
Greece			*
Grenada	*		
Guatemala			
Guinea			
Guinea-Bissau	*		
Guyana	*		
Haiti			
Honduras			
Hungary			*
Iceland	*		
India	*		
Indonesia	*		
Iran	*		
Iraq	*		
Ireland	*		
Israel	*		
Italy			*
Ivory Coast	*		
Jamaica	*		
Japan	*		
Jordan	*		
Kenya	*		
Kuwait	*		
Lao Peoples Dem. Rep.	*		
Lebanon			
Lesotho	*		
Liberia	*		
Libyan Arab Republic	*		
Luxembourg			*
Madagascar			*
Malawi	*		
Malaysia	*		
Maldives	*		
Mali	*		
Malta	*		
Mauritania			*
Mauritius	*		
Mexico	*		
Mongolia			*
Morocco	*		
Mozambique	*		
Nepal	*		
Netherlands	*		
New Zealand	*		
Nicaragua	*		
Niger	*		
Nigeria	*		
Norway	*		
Oman	*		
Pakistan	*		
Panama	*		
Papua New Guinea	*		
Paraguay	*		
Peru	*		
Philippines	*		
Poland			*
Portugal	*		
Qatar	*		
Romania	*		
Rwanda	*		
Sao Tome and Principe			
Saudi Arabia	*		
Senegal	*		
Seychelles			
Sierra Leone	*		
Singapore	*		
Somalia	*		
South Africa	*		
Spain	*		
Sri Lanka	*		
Sudan	*		
Surinam	*		
Swaziland	*		
Sweden	*		
Syrian Arab Republic	*		
Thailand	*		
Togo	*		
Trinidad and Tobago	*		
Tunisia	*		
Turkey	*		
Uganda	*		
Ukrainian SSR			*
USSR			*
United Arab Emirates	*		
United Kingdom			*
Un. Rep. of Cameroon	*		
Un. Rep. of Tanzania			*
United States			*
Upper Volta	*		
Uruguay	*		
Venezuela	*		
Yemen	*		
Yugoslavia	*		
Zaire	*		
Zambia			*

7. DECLARATION ON THE PROHIBITION OF THE USE OF NUCLEAR AND THERMONUCLEAR WEAPONS[1]

The General Assembly,

Mindful of its responsibility under the Charter of the United Nations in the maintenance of international peace and security, as well as in the consideration of principles governing disarmament,

Gravely concerned that, while negotiations on disarmament have not so far achieved satisfactory results, the armaments race, particularly in the nuclear and thermo-nuclear fields, has reached a dangerous stage requiring all possible precautionary measures to protect humanity and civilization from the hazard of nuclear and thermo-nuclear catastrophe,

Recalling that the use of weapons of mass destruction, causing unnecessary human suffering, was in the past prohibited, as being contrary to the laws of humanity and to the principles of international law, by international declarations and binding agreements, such as the Declaration of St. Petersburg of 1868, the Declaration of the Brussels Conference of 1874, the Conventions of The Hague Peace Conferences of 1899 and 1907, and the Geneva Protocol of 1925, to which the majority of nations are still parties,

Considering that the use of nuclear and thermonuclear weapons would bring about indiscriminate suffering and destruction to mankind and civilization to an even greater extent than the use of those weapons declared by the aforementioned international declarations and agreements to be contrary to the laws of humanity and a crime under international law,

Believing that the use of weapons of mass destruction, such as nuclear and thermonuclear weapons, is a direct negation of the high ideals and objectives which the United Nations has been established to achieve through the protection of succeeding generations from the scourge of war and through the preservation and promotion of their cultures,

1. *Declares* that:

(a) The use of nuclear and thermo-nuclear weapons is contrary to the spirit, letter and aims of the United Nations and, as such, a direct violation of the Charter of the United Nations;

(b) The use of nuclear and thermo-nuclear weapons would exceed even the scope of war and cause indiscriminate suffering and destruction to mankind and civilization and, as such, is contrary to the rules of international law and to the laws of humanity;

(c) The use of nuclear and thermo-nuclear weapons is a war directed not against an enemy or enemies alone but also against mankind in general, since the peoples of the world not involved in such a war will be subjected to all the evils generated by the use of such weapons;

(d) Any State using nuclear and thermo-nuclear weapons is to be considered as violating the Charter of the United Nations, as acting contrary to the laws of humanity and as committing a crime against mankind and civilization;

2. *Requests* The Secretary-General to consult the Governments of Member States to ascertain their views on the possibility of convening a special conference for signing a convention on the prohibition of the use of nuclear and thermo-nuclear weapons for war purposes and to report on the results of such consultation to the General Assembly at its seventeenth session.

1063rd plenary meeting,
24 November 1961.

---

[1] Official Records of the General Assembly, Sixteenth Session, Supplement No. 17, pp. 4-5.

8. TREATY FOR THE PROHIBITION OF NUCLEAR WEAPONS IN LATIN AMERICA (TREATY OF TLATELOLCO). DONE AT MEXICO, FEDERAL DISTRICT ON 14 FEBRUARY 1967[1]

PREAMBLE

In the name of their peoples and faithfully interpreting their desires and aspirations, the Governments of the States which sign the Treaty for the Prohibition of Nuclear Weapons in Latin America,

Desiring to contribute, so far as lies in their power, towards ending the armaments race, especially in the field of nuclear weapons, and towards strengthening a world at peace, based on the sovereign equality of States, mutual respect and good neighbourliness,

Recalling that the United Nations General Assembly, in its Resolution 808 (IX),[2] adopted unanimously as one of the three points of a coordinated programme of disarmament "the total prohibition of the use and manufacture of nuclear weapons and weapons of mass destruction of every type,"

Recalling that militarily denuclearized zones are not an end in themselves but rather a means for achieving general and complete disarmament at a later stage,

Recalling United Nations General Assembly Resolution 1911 (XVIII),[3] which established that the measures that should be agreed upon for the denuclearization of Latin America should be taken "in the light of the principles of the Charter of the United Nations and of regional agreements,"

Recalling United Nations General Assembly Resolution 2028 (XX),[4] which established the principle of an acceptable balance of mutual responsibilities and duties for the nuclear and non-nuclear powers, and

Recalling that the Charter of the Organization of American States proclaims that it is an essential purpose of the Organization to strengthen the peace and security of the hemisphere,

Convinced:

That the incalculable destructive power of nuclear weapons has made it imperative that the legal prohibition of war should be strictly observed in practice if the survival of civilization and of mankind itself is to be assured,

That nuclear weapons, whose terrible effects are suffered, indiscriminately and inexorably, by military forces and civilian population alike, constitute, through the persistence of the radioactivity they release, an attack on the integrity of the human species and ultimately may even render the whole earth uninhabitable,

That general and complete disarmament under effective international control is a vital matter which all the peoples of the world equally demand,

That the proliferation of nuclear weapons, which seems inevitable unless States, in the exercise of their sovereign rights, impose restrictions on themselves in order to

---

[1] United Nations *Treaty Series*, vol. 634, 1968, pp. 326-342. In accordance with paragraph 2 of article 28, the Treaty came into force on 22 April 1968 as between Mexico and El Salvador, on behalf of which instruments of ratification, with annexed declarations wholly waiving the requirements laid down in paragraph 1 of the same article for the entry into force of the Treaty, were deposited with the Government of Mexico on 20 September 1967 and 22 April 1968, respectively. An instrument of ratification was also deposited, on 29 January 1968, by the Government of Brazil, not availing itself of the waiver provided in article 28, paragraph 2).

[2] Official Records of the General Assembly, Ninth Session, Supplement No. 21 (A/2890), p. 3.

[3] Official Records of the General Assembly, Eighteenth Session, Supplement No. 15 (A/5515, p. 14.

[4] Official Records of the General Assembly, Twentieth Session, Supplement No. 14 (A/6014), p.7.

prevent it, would make any agreement on disarmament enormously difficult and would increase the danger of the outbreak of a nuclear conflagration,

That the establishment of militarily denuclearized zones is closely linked with the maintenance of peace and security in the respective regions,

That the military denuclearization of vast geographical zones, adopted by the sovereign decision of the States comprised therein, will exercise a beneficial influence on other regions where similar conditions exist,

That the privileged situation of the signatory States, whose territories are wholly free from nuclear weapons, imposes upon them the inescapable duty of preserving that situation both in their own interests and for the good of mankind,

That the existence of nuclear weapons in any country of Latin America would make it a target for possible nuclear attacks and would inevitably set off, throughout the region, a ruinous race in nuclear weapons which would involve the unjustifiable diversion, for warlike purposes, of the limited resources required for economic and social development,

That the foregoing reasons, together with the traditional peace-loving outlook of Latin America, give rise to an inescapable necessity that nuclear energy should be used in that region exclusively for peaceful purposes, and that the Latin American countries should use their right to the greatest and most equitable possible access to this new source of energy in order to expedite the economic and social development of their peoples,

Convinced finally:

That the military denuclearization of Latin America—being understood to mean the undertaking entered into internationally in this Treaty to keep their territories forever free from nuclear weapons—will constitute a measure which will spare their peoples from the squandering of their limited resources on nuclear armaments and will protect them against possible nuclear attacks on their territories, and will also constitute a significant contribution towards preventing the proliferation of nuclear weapons and a powerful factor for general and complete disarmament, and

That Latin America, faithful to its tradition of universality, must not only endeavour to banish from its homelands the scourge of a nuclear war, but must also strive to promote the well-being and advancement of its peoples, at the same time co-operating in the fulfilment of the ideals of mankind that is to say, in the consolidation of a permanent peace based on equal rights, economic fairness and social justice for all, in accordance with the principles and purposes set forth in the Charter of the United Nations and in the Charter of the Organization of American States,

Have agreed as follows:

OBLIGATIONS

Article 1

1. The Contracting Parties hereby undertake to use exclusively for peaceful purposes the nuclear material and facilities which are under their jurisdiction and to prohibit and prevent in their respective territories:
(a) The testing, use, manufacture, production or acquisition by any mean whatsoever of any nuclear weapons, by the Parties themselves, directly or indirectly, on behalf of anyone else or in any other way, and
(b) The receipt, storage, installation, deployment and any form of possession of any nuclear weapons, directly or indirectly, by the Parties themselves by anyone on their behalf or in any other way.
2. The Contracting Parties also undertake to refrain from engaging in encouraging or authorizing, directly or indirectly, or in any way participating in the testing, use, manufacture, production, possession or control of any nuclear weapon.

DEFINITION OF THE CONTRACTING PARTIES

Article 2

For the purposes of this Treaty, the Contracting Parties are those for whom the Treaty is in force.

DEFINITION OF TERRITORY

Article 3

For the purposes of this Treaty, the term "territory" shall include the territorial sea, air space and any other space over which the State exercises sovereignty in accordance with its own legislation.

ZONE OF APPLICATION

Article 4

1. The zone of application of this Treaty is the whole of the territories for which the Treaty is in force.
2. Upon fulfilment of the requirements of article 28, paragraph 1, the zone of application of this Treaty shall also be that which is situated in the western hemisphere within the following limits (except the continental part of the territory of the United States of America and its territorial waters): starting at a point located at 35° north latitude, 75° west longitude; from this point directly southward to a point at 30° north latitude, 75° west longitude; from there, directly eastward to a point at 30° north latitude, 50° west longitude; from there, along a loxodromic line to a point at 5° north latitude, 20° west longitude; from there, directly southward to a point at 60° south latitude, 20° west longitude; from there, directly westward to a point at 60° south latitude, 115° west longitude; from there, directly northward to a point at 0 latitude, 115° west longitude; from there, along a loxodromic line to a point at 35° north latitude, 150° west longitude; from there, directly castward to a point at 35° north latitude, 75° west longitude.

DEFINITION OF NUCLEAR WEAPONS

Article 5

For the purposes of this Treaty, a nuclear weapon is any device which is capable of releasing nuclear energy in an uncontrolled manner and which has a group of characteristics that are appropriate for use for warlike purposes. An instrument that may be used for the transport or propulsion of the device is not included in this definition if it is separable from the device and not an indivisible part thereof.

MEETING OF SIGNATORIES

Article 6

At the request of any of the signatory States or if the Agency established by article 7 should so decide, a meeting of all the signatories may be convoked to consider in common questions which may affect the very essence of this instrument, including possible amendments to it. In either case, the meeting will be convoked by the General Secretary.

Article 7

1. In order to ensure compliance with the obligations of this Treaty, the Contracting Parties hereby establish an international organization to be known as the Agency for the Prohibition of Nuclear Weapons in Latin America, hereinafter referred to as "the Agency." Only the Contracting Parties shall be affected by its decisions.

2. The Agency shall be responsible for the holding of periodic or extraordinary consultations among Member States on matters relating to the purposes, measures and procedures set forth in this Treaty and to the supervision of compliance with the obligations arising therefrom.

3. The Contracting Parties agree to extend to the Agency full and prompt co-operation in accordance with the provisions of this Treaty, of any agreements they may conclude with the Agency and of any agreements the Agency may conclude with any other international organization or body.

4. The headquarters of the Agency shall be in Mexico City.

ORGANS

Article 8

1. There are hereby established as principal organs of the Agency a General Conference, a Council and a Secretariat.

2. Such subsidiary organs as are considered necessary by the General Conference may be established within the purview of this Treaty.

THE GENERAL CONFERENCE

Article 9

1. The General Conference, the supreme organ of the Agency, shall be composed of all the Contracting Parties; it shall hold regular sessions every two years, and may also hold special sessions whenever this Treaty so provides or, in the opinion of the Council, the circumstances so require.

2. The General Conference:

(a) May consider and decide on any matters or questions covered by this Treaty, within the limits threof, including those referring to powers and functions of any organ provided for in this Treaty;

(b) Shall establish procedures for the control system to ensure observance of this Treaty in accordance with its provisions;

(c) Shall elect the Members of the Council and the General Secretary;

(d) May remove the General Secretary from office if the proper functioning of the Agency so requires;

(e) Shall receive and consider the biennial and special reports submitted by the Council and the General Secretary.

(f) Shall initiate and consider studies designed to facilitate the optimum fulfilment of the aims of this Treaty, without prejudice to the power of the General Secretary independently to carry out similar studies for submission to and consideration by the Conference.

(g) Shall be the organ competent to authorize the conclusion of agreements with Governments and other international organizations and bodies.

3. The General Conference shall adopt the Agency's budget and fix the scale of financial contributions to be paid by Member States, taking into account the systems and criteria used for the same purpose by the United Nations.

4. The General Conference shall elect its officers for each session and may establish

such subsidiary organs as it deems necessary for the performance of its functions.

5. Each Member of the Agency shall have one vote. The decisions of the General Conference shall be taken by a two-thirds majority of the Members present and voting in the case of matters relating to the control system and measures referred to in article 20, the admission of new Members, the election or removal of the General Secretary, adoption of the budget and matters related thereto. Decisions on other matters, as well as procedural questions and also determination of which questions must be decided by a two-thirds majority, shall be taken by a simple majority of the Members present and voting.

6. The General Conference shall adopt its own rules of procedure.

THE COUNCIL

Article 10

1. The Council shall be composed of five Members of the Agency elected by the General Conference from among the Contracting Parties, due account being taken of equitable geographic distribution.

2. The Members of the Council shall be elected for a term of four years. However, in the first election three will be elected for two years. Outgoing Members may not be re-elected for the following period unless the limited number of States for which the Treaty is in force so requires.

3. Each Member of the Council shall have one representative.

4. The Council shall be so organized as to be able to function continuously.

5. In addition to the functions conferred upon it by this Treaty and to those which may be assigned to it by the General Conference, the Council shall, through the General Secretary, ensure the proper operation of the control system in accordance with the provisions of this Treaty and with the decisions adopted by the General Conference.

6. The Council shall submit an annual report on its work to the General Conference as well as such special reports as it deems necessary or which the General Conference requests of it.

7. The Council shall elect its officers for each session.

8. The decisions of the Council shall be taken by a simple majority of its Members present and voting.

9. The Council shall adopt its own rules of procedure.

THE SECRETARIAT

Article 11

1. The Secretariat shall consist of a General Secretary, who shall be the chief administrative officer of the Agency, and of such staff as the Agency may require. The term of office of the General Secretary shall be four years and he may be re-elected for a single additional term. The General Secretary may not be a national of the country in which the Agency has its headquarters. In case the office of General Secretary becomes vacant, a new election shall be held to fill the office for the remainder of the term.

2. The staff of the Secretariat shall be appointed by the General Secretary, in accordance with rules laid down by the General Conference.

3. In addition to the functions conferred upon him by this Treaty and to those which may be assigned to him by the General Conference, — the General Secretary shall ensure, as provided by article 10, paragraph 5, the proper operation of the control system established by this Treaty, in accordance with the provisions of the Treaty and the decisions taken by the General Conference.

4. The General Secretary shall act in that capacity in all meetings of the General Conference and of the Council and shall make an annual report to both bodies on the work of the Agency and any special reports requested by the General Conference or the Council or which the General Secretary may deem desirable.

5. The General Secretary shall establish the procedures for distributing to all Contracting Parties information received by the Agency from governmental sources and such information from non-governmental sources as may be of interest to the Agency.

6. In the performance of their duties the General Secretary and the staff shall not seek or receive instructions from any Government or from any other authority external to the Agency and shall refrain from any action which might reflect on their position as international officials responsible only to the Agency; subject to their responsibility to the Agency, they shall not disclose any industrial secrets or other confidential information coming to their knowledge by reason of their official duties in the Agency.

7. Each of the Contracting Parties undertakes to respect the exclusively international character of the responsibilities of the General Secretary and the staff and not to seek to influence them in the discharge of their responsibilities.

CONTROL SYSTEM

Article 12

1. For the purpose of verifying compliance with the obligations entered into by the Contracting Parties in accordance with article 1, a control system shall be established which shall be put into effect in accordance with the provisions of articles 13-18 of this Treaty.

2. The control system shall be used in particular for the purpose of verifying:

(a) That devices, services and facilities intended for peaceful uses of nuclear energy are not used in the testing or manufacture of nuclear weapons;

(b) That none of the activities prohibited in article 1 of this Treaty are carried out in the territory of the Contracting Parties with nuclear materials or weapons introduced from abroad, and

(c) That explosions for peaceful purposes are compatible with article 18 of this Treaty.

IAEA SAFEGUARDS

Article 13

Each Contracting Party shall negotiate multilateral or bilateral agreements with the International Atomic Energy Agency for the application of its safeguards to its nuclear activities. Each Contracting Party shall initiate negotiations within a period of 180 days after the date of the deposit of it instrument of ratification of this Treaty. These agreements shall enter into force, for each Party, not later than eighteen months after the date of the initiation of such negotiations except in case of unforeseen circumstance or *force majeure*.

REPORTS OF THE PARTIES

Article 14

1. The Contracting Parties shall submit to the Agency and to the International Atomic Energy Agency, for their information, semi-annual reports stating that no activity prohibited under this Treaty has occurred in their respective territories.

2. The Contracting Parties shall simultaneously transmit to the Agency a copy of any report they may submit to the International Atomic Energy Agency which relates to matters that are the subject of this Treaty and to the application of safeguards.

3. The Contracting Parties shall also transmit to the Organization of American States, for its information, any reports that may be of interest to it, in accordance with the obligations established by the Inter-American System.

SPECIAL REPORTS REQUESTED BY THE GENERAL SECRETARY

Article 15

1. With the authorization of the Council, the General Secretary may request any of the Contracting Parties to provide the Agency with complementary or supplementary information regarding any event of circumstance connected with compliance with this Treaty, explaining his reasons. The Contracting Parties undertake to co-operate promptly and fully with the General Secretary.
2. The General Secretary shall inform the Council and the Contracting Parties forthwith of such requests and of the respective replies.

SPECIAL INSPECTIONS

Article 16

1. The International Atomic Energy Agency and the Council established by this Treaty have the power of carrying out special inspections in the following cases:
(a) In the case of the International Atomic Energy Agency, in accordance with the agreements referred to in article 13 of this Treaty.

9. TREATY ON THE NON-PROLIFERATION OF NUCLEAR WEAPONS[1]

The General Assembly,

Recalling its resolutions 2346 A (XXII) of 19 December 1967, 2153 A (XXI) of 17 November 1966, 2149 (XXI) of 4 November 1966, 2028 (XX) of 19 November 1965 and 1665 (XVI) of 4 December 1961,

Convinced of the urgency and great importance of preventing the spread of nuclear weapons and of intensifying international co-operation in the development of peaceful applications of atomic energy,

Having considered the report of the Conference of the Eighteen-Nation Committee on Disarmament, dated 14 March 1968,[2] and appreciative of the work of the Committee on the elaboration of the draft non-proliferation treaty, which is attached to that report,[3]

Convinced that, pursuant to the provisions of the treaty, all signatories have the right to engage in research, production and use of nuclear energy for peaceful purposes and will be able to acquire source and special fissionable materials, as well as equipment for the processing, use and production of nuclear material for peaceful purposes,

---

[1] Official Records of the General Assembly, Twenty-second Session, Supplement No. 16 A, pp. 5-7. Treaty was signed in London, Moscow and Washington on 1 July 1968.
[2] Official Records of the General Assembly, Twenty-second Session, Annexes, agenda item 28, document A/7072-DC/230.
[3] *Ibid.,* annex J

800

Convinced further that an agreement to prevent the further proliferation of nuclear weapons must be followed as soon as possible by effective measures on the cessation of the nuclear arms race and on nuclear disarmament, and that the non-proliferation treaty will contribute to this aim,

Affirming that in the interest of international peace and security both nuclear-weapon and non-nuclear-weapon States carry the responsibility of acting in accordance with the principles of the Charter of the United Nations that the sovereign equality of all States shall be respected, that the threat or use of force in international relations shall be refrained from and that international disputes shall be settled by peaceful means,

1. *Commends* the Treaty on the Non-Proliferation of Nuclear Weapons, the text of which is annexed to the present resolution;

2. *Requests* the Depositary Governments to open the Treaty for signature and ratification at the earliest possible date;

3. *Expresses the hope* for the widest possible adherence to the Treaty by both nuclear-weapon and non-nuclear-weapon States;

4. *Requests* the Conference of the Eighteen-Nation Committee on Disarmament and the nuclear-weapon States urgently to pursue negotiations on effective measures relating to the cessation of the nuclear arms race at an early date and to nuclear disarmament, and on a treaty on general and complete disarmament under strict and effective international control;

5. *Requests* the Conference of the Eighteen-Nation Committee on Disarmament to report on the progress of its work to the General Assembly at its twenty-third session.

1672nd plenary meeting,
12 June 1968.

ANNEX

Treaty on the Non-Proliferation of Nuclear Weapons

The States concluding this Treaty, hereinafter referred to as the "Parties to the Treaty,"

Considering the devastation that would be visited upon all mankind by a nuclear war and the consequent need to make every effort to avert the danger of such a war and to take measures to safeguard the security of peoples,

Believing that the proliferation of nuclear weapons would seriously enhance the danger of nuclear war,

In conformity with resolutions of the United Nations General Assembly calling for the conclusion of an agreement on the prevention of wider dissemination of nuclear weapons,

Undertaking to co-operate in facilitating the application of International Atomic Energy Agency safeguards on peaceful nuclear activities,

Expressing their support for research, development and other efforts to further the application, within the framework of the International Atomic Energy Agency safeguards system, of the principle of safeguarding effectively the flow of source and special fissionable materials by use of instruments and other techniques at certain strategic points,

Affirming the principle that the benefits of peaceful applications of nuclear technology, including any technological by-products which may be derived by nuclear-weapon States from the development of nuclear explosive devices, should be available for peaceful purposes to all Parties to the Treaty, whether nuclear-weapon or non-nuclear-weapon States,

Convinced that, in furtherance of this principle, all Parties to the Treaty are entitled to participate in the fullest possible exchange of scientific information for, and to contribute alone or in co-operation with other States to, the further development of the applications of atomic energy for peaceful purposes,

Declaring their intention to achieve at the earliest possible date the cessation of the nuclear arms race and to undertake effective measures in the direction of nuclear disarmament,

Urging the co-operation of all States in the attainment of this objective,

Recalling the determination expressed by the Parties to the 1963 Treaty banning nuclear weapon tests in the atmosphere, in outer space and under water in its Preamble to seek to achieve the discontinuance of all test explosions of nuclear weapons for all time and to continue negotiations to this end,

Desiring to further the easing of international tension and the strengthening of trust between States in order to facilitate the cessation of the manufacture of nuclear weapons, the liquidation of all their existing stockpiles, and the elimination from national arsenals of nuclear weapons and the means of their delivery pursuant to a treaty on general and complete disarmament under strict and effective international control,

Recalling that, in accordance with the Charter of the United Nations, States must refrain in their international relations from the threat or use of force against the territorial integrity or political independence of any State, or in any other manner inconsistent with the Purposes of the United Nations, and that the establishment and maintenance of international peace and security are to be promoted with the least diversion for armaments of the world's human and economic resources,

Have agreed as follows:

Article I

Each nuclear-weapon State Party to the Treaty undertakes not to transfer to any recipient whatsoever nuclear weapons or other nuclear explosive devices or control over such weapons or explosive devices directly, or indirectly; and not in any way to assist, encourage, or induce any non-nuclear-weapon State to manufacture or otherwise acquire nuclear weapons or other nuclear explosive devices, or control over such weapons or explosive devices.

Article II

Each non-nuclear-weapon State Party to the Treaty undertakes not to receive the transfer from any transferor whatsoever of nuclear weapons or other nuclear explosive devices or of control over such weapons or explosive devices directly, or indirectly; not to manufacture or otherwise acquire nuclear weapons or other nuclear explosive devices; and not to seek or receive any assistance in the manufacture of nuclear weapons or other nuclear explosive devices.

Article III

1. Each non-nuclear-weapon State Party to the Treaty undertakes to accept safeguards, as set forth in an agreement to be negotiated and concluded with the International Atomic Energy Agency in accordance with the Statute of the International Atomic Energy Agency and the Agency's safeguards system, for the exclusive purpose of verification of the fulfilment of its obligations assumed under this Treaty with a view to preventing diversion of nuclear energy from peaceful uses to nuclear weapons or other nuclear explosive devices. Procedures for the safeguards required by this article shall be followed with respect to source or special fissionable material whether it is being produced, processed or used in any principal nuclear facility or is outside any such facility or is outside any such facility. The safeguards required by this article shall be applied on all source or special fissionable material in all peaceful nuclear activities

within the territory of such State, under its jurisdiction, or carried out under its control anywhere.

2. Each State Party to the Treaty undertakes not to provide:

(a) source or special fissionable material, or *(b)* equipment or material especially designed or prepared for the processing, use or production of special fissionable material, to any non-nuclear-weapon State for peaceful purposes, unless the source or special fissionable material shall be subject to the safeguards required by this article.

3. The safeguards required by this article shall be implemented in a manner designed to comply with article IV of this Treaty, and to avoid hampering the economic or technological development of the Parties or international cooperation in the field of peaceful nuclear activities, including the international exchange of nuclear material and equipment for the processing, use or production of nuclear material for peaceful purposes in accordance with the provisions of this article and the principle of safeguarding set forth in the Preamble of the Treaty.

4. Non-nuclear-weapon States Party to the Treaty shall conclude agreements with the International Atomic Energy Agency to meet the requirements of this article either individually or together with other States in accordance with the Statute of the international Atomic Energy Agency. Negotiation of such agreements shall commence within 180 days from the original entry into force of this Treaty. For States depositing their instruments of ratification or accession after the 180-day period, negotiation of such agreements shall commence not later than the date of such deposit. Such agreements shall enter into force not later than eighteen months after the date of initiation of negotiations.

Article IV

1. Nothing in this Treaty shall be interpreted as affecting the inalienable right of all the Parties to the Treaty to develop research, production and use of nuclear energy for peaceful purposes without discrimination and in conformity with articles I and II of this Treaty.

2. All the Parties to the Treaty undertake to facilitate, and have the right to participate in, the fullest possible exchange of equipment, materials and scientific and technological information for the peaceful uses of nuclear energy. Parties to the Treaty in a position to do so shall also co-operate in contributing alone or together with other States or international organizations to the further development of the applications of nuclear energy, for peaceful purposes, especially in the territories of non-nuclear-weapon States Party to the Treaty, with due consideration for the needs of the developing areas of the world.

Article V

Each Party to the Treaty undertakes to take appropriate measures to ensure that, in accordance with this Treaty, under appropriate international observation and through appropriate international procedures, potential benefits from any peaceful applications of nuclear explosions will be made available to non-nuclear-weapon States Party to the Treaty on a non-discriminatory basis and that the charge to such Parties for the explosive devices used will be as low as possible and exclude any charge for research and development. Non-nuclear-weapon States Party to the Treaty shall be able to obtain such benefits, pursuant to a special international agreement or agreements, through an appropriate international body with adequate representation of non-nuclear-weapon States. Negotiations on this subject shall commence as soon as possible after the Treaty enters into force. Non-nuclear-weapon States Party to the Treaty so desiring may also obtain such benefits pursuant to bilateral agreements.

Article VI

Each of the Parties to the Treaty undertakes to pursue negotiations in good faith on effective measures relating to cessation of the nuclear arms race at an early date and to nuclear disarmament, and on a treaty on general and complete disarmament under strict and effective international control.

Article VII

Nothing in this Treaty affects the right of any group of States to conclude regional treaties in order to assure the total absence of nuclear weapons in their respective territories.

Article VIII

1. Any Party to the Treaty may propose amendments to this Treaty. The text of any proposed amendment shall be submitted to the Depositary Governments which shall circulate it to all Parties to the Treaty. Thereupon, if requested to do so by one third or more of the Parties to the Treaty, the Depositary Governments shall convene a conference, to which they shall invite all the Parties to the Treaty, to consider such an amendment.

2. Any amendment to this Treaty must be approved by a majority of the votes of all the Parties to the Treaty, including the votes of all nuclear-weapon States Party to the Treaty and all other Parties which, on the date the amendment is circulated, are members of the Board of Governors of the International Atomic Energy Agency. The amendment shall enter into force for each Party that deposits its instrument of ratification of the amendment upon the deposit of such instruments of ratification by a majority of all the Parties, including the instruments of ratification of all nuclear-weapon States Party to the Treaty and all other Parties which, on the date the amendment is circulated, are members of the Board of Governors of the international Atomic Energy Agency. Thereafter, it shall enter into force for any other Party upon the deposit of its instrument of ratification of the amendment.

3. Five years after the entry into force of this Treaty, a conference of Parties to the Treaty shall be held in Geneva, Switzerland, in order to review the operation of this Treaty with a view to assuring that the purposes of the Preamble and the provisions of the Treaty are being realized. At intervals of five years thereafter, a majority of the Parties to the Treaty may obtain, by submitting a proposal to this effect to the Depositary Governments, the convening of further conferences with the same objective of reviewing the operation of the Treaty.

Article IX

1. This Treaty shall be open to all States for signature. Any State which does not sign the Treaty before its entry into force in accordance with paragraph 3 of this article may accede to it at any time.

2. This Treaty shall be subject to ratification by signatory States. Instruments of ratification and instruments of accession shall be deposited with the Governments of the Union of Soviet Socialist Republics, the United Kingdom of Great Britain and Northern Ireland and the United States of America, which are hereby designated the Depositary Governments.

3. This Treaty shall enter into force after its ratification by the States, the Governments of which are designated Depositaries of the Treaty, and forty other States signatory to this Treaty and the deposit of their instruments of ratification. For the purposes of this Treaty, a nuclear-weapon State is one which has manufactured and exploded a nuclear weapon or other nuclear explosive device prior to 1 January 1967.

4. For States whose instruments of ratification or accession are deposited subsequent

to the entry into force of this Treaty, it shall enter into force on the date of the deposit of their instruments of ratification or accession.

5. The Depositary Governments shall promptly inform all signatory and acceding States of the date of each signature, the date of deposit of each instrument of ratification or of accession, the date of the entry into force of this Treaty, and the date of receipt of any requests for convening a conference or other notices.

6. This Treaty shall be registered by the Depositary Governments pursuant to article 102 of the Charter of the United Nations.

Article X

1. Each Party shall in exercising its national sovereignty have the right to withdraw from the Treaty if it decides that extraordinary events, related to the subject-matter of this Treaty, have jeopardized the supreme interests of its country. It shall give notice of such withdrawal to all other Parties to the Treaty and to the United Nations Security Council three months in advance. Such notice shall include a statement of the extraordinary events it regards as having jeopardized its supreme interests.

2. Twenty-five years after the entry, into force of the Treaty, a conference shall be convened to decide whether the Treaty shall continue in force indefinitely, or shall be extended for an additional fixed period or periods. This decision shall be taken by a majority of the Parties to the Treaty.

Article XI

This Treaty, the Chinese, English, French, Russian and Spanish texts of which are equally authentic, shall be deposited in the archives of the Depositary Governments. Duly certified copies of this Treaty shall be transmitted by the Depositary Governments to the Governments of the signatory and acceding States.

IN WITNESS WHEREOF the undersigned, duly authorized, have signed this Treaty.

10. CONVENTION ON THE PROHIBITION OF THE DEVELOPMENT, PRODUCTION AND STOCKPILING OF BACTERIOLOGICAL (BIOLOGICAL) AND TOXIN WEAPONS AND ON THEIR DESTRUCTION[1]

The General Assembly,

Recalling its resolution 2662 (XXV) of 7 December 1970,

Convinced of the importance and urgency of eliminating from the arsenals of States, through effective measures, such dangerous weapons of mass destruction as those using chemical or bacteriological (biological) agents,

Having considered the report of the Conference of the Committee on Disarmament dated 6 October 1971,[2] and being appreciative of its work on the draft Convention on the Prohibition of the Development, Production and Stockpiling of Bacteriological (Biological) and Toxin Weapons and on Their Destruction, annexed to the report,

Recognizing the important significance of the Protocol for the Prohibition of the Use in War of Asphyxiating, Poisonous or Other Gases, and of Bacteriological Methods of Warfare, signed at Geneva on 17 June 1925,[3] and conscious also of the contribution

---

[1] Official Records of the General Assembly, Twenty-sixth Session, Supplement No. 29, pp. 30-32.
[2] Official Records of the Disarmament Commission, Supplement for 1971, document DC/234.
[3] League of Nations *Treaty Series*, vol. XCIV, 1929, No. 2138.

which the said Protocol has already made, and continues to make, to mitigating the horrors of war,

Noting that the Convention on the Prohibition of the Development, Production and Stockpiling of Bacteriological (Biological) and Toxin Weapons and on Their Destruction provides for the parties to reaffirm their adherence to the principles and objectives of that Protocol and to call upon all States to comply strictly with them,

Further noting that nothing in the Convention shall be interpreted as in any way limiting or detracting from the obligations assumed by any State under the Geneva Protocol,

Determined, for the sake of all mankind, to exclude completely the possibility of bacteriological (biological) agents and toxins being used as weapons,

Recognizing that an agreement on the prohibition of bacteriological (biological) and toxin weapons represents a first possible step towards the achievement of agreement on effective measures also for the prohibition of the development, production and stockpiling of chemical weapons,

Noting that the Convention contains an affirmation of the recognized objective of effective prohibition of chemical weapons and, to this end, and undertaking to continue negotiations in good faith with a view to reaching early agreement on effective measures for the prohibition of their development, production and stockpiling and for their destruction, and on appropriate measures concerning equipment and means of delivery specially designed for the production or use of chemical agents for weapons purposes,

Convinced that the implementation of measures in the field of disarmament should release substantial additional resources, which should promote economic and social development, particularly in the developing countries,

Convinced that the Convention will contribute to the realization of the purposes and principles of the Charter of the United Nations,

1. *Commends* the Convention on the Prohibition of the Development, Production and Stockpiling of Bacteriological (Biological) and Toxin Weapons and on Their Destruction, the text of which is annexed to the present resolution;

2. *Requests* the depositary Governments to open the Convention for signature and ratification at the earliest possible date;

3. *Expresses the hope* for the widest possible adherence to the Convention.

2022nd plenary meeting,
16 December 1971.

ANNEX

Convention on the Prohibition of the Development, Production and Stockpiling of Bacteriological (Biological) and Toxin Weapons and on Their Destruction

The States Parties to this Convention,

Determined to act with a view to achieving effective progress towards general and complete disarmament, including the prohibition and elimination of all types of weapons of mass destruction, and convinced that the prohibition of the development, production and stockpiling of chemical and bacteriological (biological) weapons and their elimination through effective measures, will facilitate the achievement of general and complete disarmament under strict and effective international control,

Recognizing the important significance of the Protocol for the Prohibition of the Use in War of Asphyxiating, Poisonous or Other Gases, and of Bacteriological Methods of Warfare, signed at Geneva on 17 June 1925, and conscious also of the contribution which the said Protocol has already made, and continues to make, to mitigating the horrors of war,

Reaffirming their adherence to the principles and objectives of that Protocol and calling upon all States to comply strictly with them,

Recalling that the General Assembly of the United Nations has repeatedly condemned all actions contrary to the principles and objectives of the Geneva Protocol of 17 June 1925,

Desiring to contribute to the strengthening of confidence between peoples and the general improvement of the international atmosphere,

Desiring also to contribute to the realization of the purposes and principles of the Charter of the United Nations,

Convinced of the importance and urgency of eliminating from the arsenals of States, through effective measures, such dangerous weapons of mass destruction as those using chemical or bacteriological (biological) agents,

Recognizing that an agreement on the prohibition of bacteriological (biological) and toxin weapons represents a first possible step towards the achievement of agreement on effective measures also for the prohibition of the development, production and stockpiling of chemical weapons, and determined to continue negotiations to that end.

Determined, for the sake of all mankind, to exclude completely the possibility of bacteriological (biological) agents and toxins being used as weapons,

Convinced that such use would be repugnant to the conscience of mankind and that no effort should be spared to minimize this risk,

Have agreed as follows:

ARTICLE I

Each State Party to this Convention undertakes never in any circumstances to develop, produce, stockpile or otherwise acquire or retain:

(1) Microbial or other biological agents, or toxins whatever their origin or method or production, of types and in quantities that have no justification for prophylactic, protective or other peaceful purposes;

(2) Weapons, equipment or means of delivery designed to use such agents or toxins for hostile purposes or in armed conflict.

ARTICLE II

Each State Party to this Convention undertakes to destroy, or to divert to peaceful purposes, as soon as possible but not later than nine months after the entry, into force of the Convention, all agents, toxins, weapons, equipment and means of delivery specified in article I of the Convention, which are in its possession or under its jurisdiction or control. In implementing the provisions of this article all necessary safety precautions shall be observed to protect populations and the environment.

ARTICLE III

Each State Party to this Convention undertakes not to transfer to any recipient whatsoever, directly or indirectly, and not in any way to assist, encourage or induce any State, group of States or international organizations to manufacture or otherwise acquire any of the agents, toxins, weapons, equipment or means of delivery specified in article I of the Convention.

ARTICLE IV

Each State Party to this Convention shall, in accordance with its constitutional processes, take any necessary measures to prohibit and prevent the development, production, stockpiling, acquisition or retention of the agents, toxins, weapons, equipment and means of delivery specified in article I of the Convention, within the territory of such State, under its jurisdiction or under its control anywhere.

ARTICLE V

The States Parties to this Convention undertake to consult one another and to co-operate in solving any problems which may arise in relation to the objective of, or in the application of the provisions of, the Convention. Consultation and co-operation pursuant to this article may also be undertaken through appropriate international procedures within the framework of the United Nations and in accordance with its Charter.

ARTICLE VI

1. Any State Party to this Convention which finds that any other State Party is acting in breach of obligations deriving from the provisions of the Convention may lodge a complaint with the Security Council of the United Nations. Such a complaint should include all possible evidence confirming its validity, as well as a request for its consideration by the Security Council.

2. Each State Party to this Convention undertakes to cooperate in carrying out any investigation which the Security Council may initiate, in accordance with the provisions of the Charter of the United Nations, on the basis of the complaint received by the Council. The Security Council shall inform the States Parties to the Convention of the results of the investigation.

ARTICLE VII

Each State Party to this Convention undertakes to provide or support assistance, in accordance with the United Nations Charter, to any Party to the Convention which so requests, if the Security Council decides that such Party has been exposed to danger as a result of violation of the Convention.

ARTICLE VIII

Nothing in this Convention shall be interpreted as in any way limiting or detracting from the obligations assumed by any State under the Protocol for the Prohibition of the Use in War of Asphyxiating, Poisonous or Other Gases, and of Bacteriological Methods of Warfare, signed at Geneva on 17 June 1925.

ARTICLE IX

Each State Party to this Convention affirms the recognized objective of effective prohibition of chemical weapons and, to this end, undertakes to continue negotiations in good faith with a view to reaching early agreement on effective measures for the prohibition of their development, production and stockpiling and for their destruction, and on appropriate measures concerning equipment and means of delivery specifically designed for the production or use of chemical agents for weapons purposes.

ARTICLE X

1. The States Parties to this Convention undertake to facilitate, and have the right to participate in, the fullest possible exchange of equipment, materials and scientific and technological information for the use of bacteriological (biological) agents and toxins for peaceful purposes. Parties to the Convention in a position to do so shall also co-operate in contributing individually or together with other States or international organizations to the further development and application of scientific discoveries in the field of bacteriology (biology) for the prevention of disease, or for other peaceful purposes.

2. This Convention shall be implemented in a manner designed to avoid hampering

the economic or technological development of States Parties to the Convention or international co-operation in the field of peaceful bacteriological (biological) activities, including the international exchange of bacteriological (biological) agents and toxins and equipment for the processing, use or production of bacteriological (biological) agents and toxins for peaceful purposes in accordance with the provisions of the Convention.

ARTICLE XI

Any State Party may propose amendments to this Convention. Amendments shall enter into force for each State Party accepting the amendments upon their acceptance by a majority of the States Parties to the Convention and thereafter for each remaining State Party on the date of acceptance by it.

ARTICLE XII

Five years after the entry into force of this Convention, or earlier if it is requested by a majority of Parties to the Convention by submitting a proposal to this effect to the Depositary Governments, a conference of States Parties to the Convention shall be held at Geneva, Switzerland, to review the operation of the Convention, with a view to assuring that the purposes of the preamble and the provisions of the Convention, including the provisions concerning negotiations on chemical weapons, are being realized. Such review shall take into account any new scientific and technological developments relevant to the Convention.

ARTICLE XIII

1. This Convention shall be of unlimited duration.
2. Each State Party to this Convention shall in exercising its national sovereignty have the right to withdraw from the Convention if it decides that extraordinary events, related to the subject-matter of the Convention, have jeopardized the supreme interests of its country. It shall give notice of such withdrawal to all other States Parties to the Convention and to the United Nations Security Council three months in advance. Such notice shall include a statement of the extraordinary events it regards as having jeopardized its supreme interests.

ARTICLE XIV

1. This Convention shall be open to all States for signature. Any State which does not sign the Convention before its entry into force in accordance with paragraph 3 of this article may accede to it at any time.
2. This Convention shall be subject to ratification by signatory States. Instruments of ratification and instruments of accession shall be deposited with the Governments of the Union of Soviet Socialist Republics, the United Kingdom of Great Britan and Northern Ireland and the United States of America, which are hereby designated the Depositary Governments.
3. This Convention shall enter into force after the deposit of instruments of ratification by twenty-two Governments, including the Governments designated as Depositaries of the Convention.
4. For States whose instruments of ratification or accession are deposited subsequent to the entry into force of this Convention, it shall enter into force on the date of the deposit of their instruments of ratification or accession.
5. The Depositary Governments shall promptly inform all signatory and acceding States of the date of each signature, the date of deposit of each instrument of ratification or of accession and the date of the entry into force of this Convention, and of the receipt of other notices.

6. This Convention shall be registered by the Depositary Governments pursuant to Article 102 of the Charter of the United Nations.

ARTICLE XV

This Convention, the Chinese, English, French, Russian and Spanish texts of which are equally authentic, shall be deposited in the archives of the Depositary Governments. Duly certified copies of the Convention shall be transmitted by the Depositary Governments to the Governments of the signatory and acceding States.

IN WITNESS WHEREOF the undersigned, duly authorized, have signed this Convention.

11. TREATY ON PRINCIPLES GOVERNING THE ACTIVITIES OF STATES IN THE EXPLORATION AND USE OF OUTER SPACE, INCLUDING THE MOON AND OTHER CELESTIAL BODIES[1]

The General Assembly,

Having considered the report of the Committee on the Peaceful Uses of Outer Space covering its work during 1966,[2] and in particular the work accomplished by the Legal Sub-Committee during its fifth session, held at Geneva from 12 July to 4 August and at New York from 12 September to 16 September,

Noting further the progress achieved through subsequent consultations among States Members of the United Nations,

Reaffirming the importance of international co-operation in the field of activities in the peaceful exploration and use of outer space, including the Moon and other celestial bodies, and the importance of developing the rule of law in this new area of human endeavour,

1. *Commends* the Treaty on Principles Governing the Activities of States in the Exploration and Use of Outer Space, including the Moon and Other Celestial Bodies, the text of which is annexed to the present resolution;

2. *Requests* the Depositary Governments to open the Treaty for signature and ratification at the earliest possible date;

3. *Expresses its hope* for the widest possible adherence to this Treaty;

4. *Requests* the Committee on the Peaceful Uses of Outer Space:

(a) To continue its work on the elaboration of an agreement on liability for damages caused by the launching of objects into outer space and an agreement on assistance to and return of astronauts and space vehicles, which are on the agenda of the Committee;

(b) To begin at the same time the study of questions relative to the definition of outer space and the utilization of outer space and celestial bodies, including the various implications of space communications;

(c) To report on the progress of the work to the General Assembly at its twenty-second session.

1499th plenary meeting,
19 December 1966.

---

[1] Official Records of the General Assembly, Twenty-first Session, Supplement No. 16, pp. 13-15.
[2] Official Records of the General Assembly, Twenty-first Session, Annexes agenda items 30, 89 and 91, document A/6481.

Treaty on Principles Governing the Activities of States in the Exploration and Use of Outer Space, including the Moon and Other Celestial Bodies

The States Parties to this Treaty,

Inspired by the great prospects opening up before mankind as a result of man's entry into outer space,

Recognizing the common interest of all mankind in the progress of the exploration and use of outer space for peaceful purposes,

Believing that the exploration and use of outer space should be carried on for the benefit of all peoples irrespective of the degree of their economic or scientific development,

Desiring to contribute to broad international co-operation in the scientific as well as the legal aspects of the exploration and use of outer space for peaceful purposes,

Believing that such co-operation will contribute to the development of mutual understanding and to the strengthening of friendly relations between States and peoples,

Recalling resolution 1962 (XVIII), entitled "Declaration of Legal Principles Governing the Activities of States in the Exploration and Use of Outer Space," which was adopted unanimously by the United Nations General Assembly on 13 December 1963,

Recalling resolution 1884 (XVIII), calling upon States to refrain from placing in orbit around the Earth any objects carrying nuclear weapons or any other kinds of weapons of mass destruction or from installing such weapons on celestial bodies, which was adopted unanimously by the United Nations General Assembly on 17 October 1963,

Taking account of United Nations General Assembly resolution 110 (II) of 3 November 1947, which condemned propaganda designed or likely to provoke or encourage any threat to the peace, breach of the peace or act of aggression, and considering that the aforementioned resolution is applicable to outer space,

Convinced that a Treaty on Principles Governing the Activities of States in the Exploration and Use of Outer Space, including the Moon and Other Celestial Bodies, will further the purposes and principles of the Charter of the United Nations,

Have agreed on the following:

Article I

The exploration and use of outer space, including the Moon and other celestial bodies, shall be carried out for the benefit and in the interests of all countries, irrespective of their degree of economic or scientific development, and shall be the province of all mankind.

Outer space, including the Moon and other celestial bodies, shall be free for exploration and use by all States without discrimination of any kind, on a basis of equality and in accordance with international law, and there shall be free access to all areas of celestial bodies.

There shall be freedom of scientific investigation in outer space, including the Moon and other celestial bodies, and States shall facilitate and encourage international co-operation in such investigation.

Article II

Outer space, including the Moon and other celestial bodies, is not subject to national appropriation by claim of sovereignty, by means of use or occupation, or by any other means.

Article III

States Parties to the Treaty shall carry on activities in the exploration and use of outer space, including the Moon and other celestial bodies, in accordance with international law, including the Charter of the United Nations, in the interest of maintaining international peace and security and promoting international co-operation and understanding.

Article IV

States Parties to the Treaty undertake not to place in orbit around the Earth any objects carrying nuclear weapons or any other kinds of weapons of mass destruction, install such weapons on celestial bodies, or station weapons in outer space in any other manner.

The Moon and other celestial bodies shall be used by all States Parties to the Treaty exclusively for peaceful purposes. The establishment of military bases, installations and fortifications, the testing of any type of weapons and the conduct of military maneuvers on celestial bodies shall be forbidden. The use of military personnel for scientific research or for any other peaceful purposes shall not be prohibited. The use of any equipment or facility necessary for peaceful exploration of the Moon and other celestial bodies shall also not be prohibited.

Article V

States Parties to the Treaty shall regard astronauts as envoys of mankind in outer space and shall render to them all possible assistance in the event of accident, distress, or emergency landing on the territory of another State Party or on the high seas. When astronauts make such a landing, they shall be safely and promptly returned to the State of registry of their space vehicle.

In carrying on activities in outer space and on celestial bodies, the astronauts of one State Party shall render all possible assistance to the astronauts of other States Parties.

States Parties to the Treaty shall immediately inform the other States Parties to the Treaty or the Secretary-General of the United Nations of any phenomena they discover in outer space, including the Moon and other celestial bodies, which could constitute a danger to the life or health of astronauts.

Article VI

States Parties to the Treaty shall bear international responsibility for national activities in outer space, including the Moon and other celestial bodies, whether such activities are carried on by governmental agencies or by non-governmental entities, and for assuring that national activities are carried out in conformity with the provisions set forth in the present Treaty. The activities of non-governmental entities in outer space, including the Moon and other celestial bodies, shall require authorization and continuing supervision by the appropriate State Party to the Treaty. When activities are carried on in outer space, including the Moon and other celestial bodies, by an international organization, responsibility for compliance with this Treaty shall be borne both by the international organization and by the States Parties to the Treaty participating in such organization.

Article VII

Each State Party to the Treaty that launches or procures the launching of an object into outer space, including the Moon and other celestial bodies, and each State Party from whose territory or facility an object is launched, is internationally liable for damage to another State Party to the Treaty or to its natural or juridical persons by such object or its component parts on the Earth, in air space or in outer space, including the Moon and other celestial bodies.

Article VIII

A State Party to the Treaty on whose registry an object launched into outer space is carried shall retain jurisdiction and control over such object, and over any personnel thereof, while in outer space or on a celestial body. Ownership of objects launched into outer space, including objects landed or constructed on a celestial body, and of their component parts, is not affected by their presence in outer space or on a celestial body or by their return to the Earth. Such objects or component parts found beyond the limits of the State Party to the Treaty on whose registry they are carried shall be returned to that State Party, which shall, upon request, furnish identifying data prior to their return.

Article IX

In the exploration and use of outer space, including the Moon and other celestial bodies, States Parties to the Treaty shall be guided by the principle of co-operation and mutual assistance and shall conduct all their activities in outer space, including the Moon and other celestial bodies, with due regard to the corresponding interests of all other States Parties to the Treaty. States Parties to the Treaty shall pursue studies of outer space, including the Moon and other celestial bodies, and conduct exploration of them so as to avoid their harmful contamination and also adverse changes in the environment of the Earth resulting from the introduction of extraterrestrial matter and , where necessary, shall adopt appropriate measures for this purpose. If a State Party to the Treaty has reason to believe that an activity or experiment planned by it or its nationals in outer space, including the Moon and other celestial bodies, would cause potentially harmful interference with activities of other States Parties in the peaceful exploration and use of outer space, including the Moon and other celestial bodies, it shall undertake appropriate international consultations before proceeding with any such activity or experiment. A State Party to the Treaty which has reason to believe that an activity or experiment planned by another State Party in outer space, including the Moon and other celestial bodies, would cause potentially harmful interference with activities in the peaceful exploration and use of outer space, including the Moon and other celestial bodies, may request consultation concerning the activity or experiment.

Article X

In order to promote international co-operation in the exploration and use of outer space, including the Moon and other celestial bodies, in conformity with the purposes of this Treaty, the States Parties to the Treaty shall consider on a basis of equality any requests by other States Parties to the Treaty to be afforded an opportunity to observe the flight of space objects launched by those States.

The nature of such an opportunity for observation and the conditions under which it could be afforded shall be determined by agreement between the States concerned.

Article XI

In order to promote international co-operation in the peaceful exploration and use of outer space, States Parties to the Treaty conduction activities in outer space, including the Moon and other celestial bodies, agree to inform the Secretary-General of the United Nations as well as the public and the international scientific community, to the greatest extent feasible and practicable, of the nature, conduct, locations and results of such activities. On receiving the said information, the Secretary-General of the United Nations should be prepared to disseminate it immediately and effectively.

Article XII

All stations, installations, equipment and space vehicles on the Moon and other celestial bodies shall be open to representatives of other States Parties to the Treaty on a basis of reciprocity. Such representatives shall give reasonable advance notice of a projected visit, in order that appropriate consultations may be held and that maximum precautions may be taken to assure safety and to avoid interference with normal operations in the facility to be visited.

Article XIII

The provisions of this Treaty shall apply to the activities of States Parties to the Treaty in the exploration and use of outer space, including the Moon and other celestial bodies, whether such activities are carried on by a single State Party to the Treaty or jointly with other States, including cases where they are carried on within the framework of international intergovernmental organizations.

Any practical questions arising in connexion with activities carried on by international or intergovernmental organizations in the exploration and use of outer space, including the Moon and other celestial bodies, shall be resolved by the States Parties to the Treaty either with the appropriate international organization or with one or more States members of that international organization, which are Parties to this Treaty.

Article XIV

1. This Treaty shall be open to all States for signature. Any State which does not sign this Treaty before its entry into force in accordance with paragraph 3 of this article may accede to it at any time.

2. This Treaty shall be subject to ratification by signatory States. Instruments of ratification and instruments of accession shall be deposited with the Governments of the Union of Soviet Socialist Republics, the United Kingdom of Great Britain and Northern Ireland and the United States of America, which are hereby designated the Depositary Governments.

3. This Treaty shall enter into force upon the deposit of instruments of ratification by five Governments including the Governments designated as Depositary Governments under this Treaty.

4. For States whose instruments of ratification or accession are deposited subsequent to the entry into force of this Treaty, it shall enter into force on the date of the deposit of their instruments of ratification or accession.

5. The Depositary Governments shall promptly inform all signatory and acceding States of the date of each signature, the date of deposit of each instrument of ratification of and accession to this Treaty, the date of its entry into force and other notices.

6. This Treaty shall be registered by the Depositary Governments pursuant to Article 102 of the Charter of the United Nations.

Article XV

Any State Party to the Treaty may propose amendments to this Treaty. Amendments shall enter into force for each State Party to the Treaty accepting the amendments upon their acceptance by a majority of the States Parties to the Treaty and thereafter for each remaining State Party to the Treaty on the date of acceptance by it.

Article XVI

Any State Party to the Treaty may give notice of its withdrawal from the Treaty one year after its entry into force by written notification to the Depositary Governments. Such withdrawal shall take effect one year from the date of receipt of this notification.

Article XVII

This Treaty, of which the Chinese, English, French, Russian and Spanish texts are equally authentic, shall be deposited in the archives of the Depositary Governments. Duly certified copies of this Treaty shall be transmitted by the Depositary Governments to the Governments of the signatory and acceding States.

IN WITNESS WHEREOF the undersigned, duly authorized, have signed this Treaty.

12. INTERNATIONAL CO-OPERATION IN THE PEACEFUL USES OF OUTER SPACE[1]

Date: 8 November 1976   Meeting: 57
Adopted unanimously   Report: A/31/285

The General Assembly,

Recalling its resolution 3388 (XXX) of 18 November 1975,

Having considered the report of the Committee on the Peaceful Uses of Outer Space,[2]

Reaffirming the common interest of mankind in furthering the exploration and use of outer space peaceful purposes and in extending to States the benefits derived therefrom as well as the importance of international co-operation in this field, for which the United Nations should provide a focal point, as expressed in General Assembly resolution 1721 (XVI) of 20 December 1961,

Reaffirming the importance of international co-operation in developing the rule of law in the peaceful exploration and use of outer space,

Welcoming the entry into force on 15 September 1976 of the Convention on Registration of Objects Launched into Outer Space,[3]

1. *Endorses* the report of the Committee on the Peaceful Uses of Outer Space;

2. *Invites* States which have not yet become parties to the Treaty on Principles Governing the Activities of States in the Exploration and Use of Outer Space, including the Moon and Other Celestial Bodies,[4] the Agreement on the Rescue of Astronauts, the Return of Astronauts and the Return of Objects Launched into Outer Space,[5] the Convention on International Liability for Damage Caused by Space Objects[6] and the Convention on Registration of Objects Launched into Outer Space[3] to give early consideration to ratifying or acceding to those international agreements;

---

[1]Resolutions adopted by the General Assembly during the first part of its Thirty-first regular session, 21 September-22 December 1976 (the Official Record is not ready at the preparing of this volume), Press Release: GA/5571, 29 December 1976, pp. 59-61.
[2]Official Records of the General Assembly, Thirty-first Session, Supplement No. 20 (A/31/20).
[3]General Assembly resolution 3235 (XXIX), annex.
[4]General Assembly resolution 2222 (XXI), annex.
[5]General Assembly resolution 2345 (XXII), annex.
[6]General Assembly resolution 2777 (XXVI), annex.

3. *Notes with satisfaction* that the Legal Sub-Committee of the Committee on the Peaceful Uses of Outer Space has:

(a) Achieved considerable progress by:

(i) Formulating nine draft principles governing the use by States of artificial earth satellites for direct television broadcasting with a view to concluding an international agreement or agreements;

(ii) Formulating five draft principles and identifying three new common elements in the drafts submitted and the views expressed by Member States relating to the legal implications of remote sensing of the earth from space;

(b) Continued its work on the draft treaty relating to the moon, giving priority to the question of natural resources of the moon;

(c) Discussed questions relating to the definition and/or delimitation of outer space and outer space activities;

4. *Recommends* that the Legal Sub-Committee at its sixteenth session should:

(a) Continue, as matters of high priority:

(i) To consider the draft treaty relating to the moon;

(ii) To consider completing the elaboration of draft principles governing the use by States of artificial earth satellites for direct television broadcasting with a view to concluding an international agreement or agreements;

(iii) To give detailed consideration to the legal implications of remote sensing of the earth from space, with the particular aim of formulating draft principles on the basis of common elements identified by it;

(b) Pursue its work questions relating to the definition and/or delimitation of outer space and outer space activities in the remaining time available;

5. *Notes with satisfaction* the report of the Scientific and Technical Sub-Committee of the Committee on the Peaceful Uses of Outer Space on its thirteenth session,[1] which, *inter alia:*

(a) Examine further the question of remote sensing of the earth from space, as set out in paragraphs 26 to 81 of the report, considering in detail both the current pre-operational/experimental as well as the possible future global/operational phase of remote sensing system or systems;

(b) Continues in effect the United Nations programme on space applications;

(c) Provides for further study of a possible United Nations conference on outer space matters;

6. *Recommends* that the Scientific and Technical Sub-Committee should continue at its fourteenth session its work on the matters before it, giving priority to the three items contained in paragraph 71 of the report of the Committee on the Peaceful Uses of Outer Space;

7. *Endorses* the recommendation of the Committee on the Peaceful Uses of Outer Space that full utilization be made by the Committee and its subsidiary bodies of their existing terms of reference with regard to the establishment of an appropriate co-ordinating role for the United Nations in the field of remote sensing;

---

[1] A/AC.105/170.

8. *Further endorses* the recommendation of the Committee on the Peaceful Uses of Outer Space that the Secretary-General, for consideration by the Scientific and Technical Sub-Committee at its fourteenth session, should:

(a) Undertake the various studies and reports on remote sensing of the earth from space, as referred to in paragraph 42 of the report of the Committee;

(b) Prepare a study in depth on the question of convening a United Nations conference on space matters, as referred to in paragraphs 55 and 56 of that report;

(c) Request Member States to provide information on programmes or plans for the generation or transmission of solar energy by means of space technology, as referred to in paragraph 72 of that report;

9. *Endorses* the United Nations programme on space applications as referred to in paragraph 46 of the report of the Committee on the Peaceful Uses of Outer Space;

10. *Approves* continuing sponsorship by the United Nations of the Thumba Equatorial Rocket Launching Station in India and the CELPA Mar del Plata Station in Argentina and expresses its satisfaction at the work being carried out at those ranges in the peaceful and scientific exploration of outer space;

11. *Reiterates* its request to the World Meteorological Organization to pursue actively the implementation of its tropical cyclone project while continuing and intensifying its other related action programmes, including World Weather Watch and, especially, the efforts being undertaken towards obtaining basic meteorological data and discovering ways and means to mitigate the harmful effects of tropical storms and to remove or minimize their destructive potential, and looks forward to its report thereon in accordance with the relevant General Assembly resolutions;

12. *Requests* the specialized agencies to provide the Committee on the Peaceful Uses of Outer Space with progress reports on their work, including particular problems in the fields within their competence relating to the peaceful uses of outer space;

13. *Requests* the Secretary-General, in the light of paragraph 73 of the report of the Committee on the Peaceful Uses of Outer Space, to consider strengthening the Outer Space Affairs Division of the Secretariat;

14. *Notes* the invitation extended by the Government of Austria to hold the twentieth session of the Committee on the Peaceful Uses of Outer Space at Vienna in 1977 and accepts that invitation with appreciation;

15. *Requests* the Committee on the Peaceful Uses of Outer Space to continue its work, as set out in the present and previous resolutions of the General Assembly, and to report to the Assembly at its thirty-second session.

13. AGREEMENT ON THE RESCUE OF ASTRONAUTS, THE RETURN OF ASTRONAUTS AND THE RETURN OF OBJECTS LAUNCHED INTO OUTER SPACE[1]

The General Assembly,

Bearing in mind its resolution 2260 (XXII) of 3 November 1967, which calls upon the Committee on the Peaceful Uses of Outer Space to continue with a sense of urgency its work on the elaboration of an agreement on liability for damage caused by the launching of objects into outer space and an agreement on assistance to and return of astronauts and space vehicles,

Referring to the addendum to the report of the Committee on the Peaceful Uses of Outer Space,[1]

Desiring to give further concrete expression to the rights and obligations contained in the Treaty of Principles Governing the Activities of States in the Exploration and Use of Outer Space, including the Moon and Other Celestial Bodies,[2]

1. *Commends* the Agreement on the Rescue of Astronauts, the Return of Astronauts and the Return of Objects Launched into Outer Space, the text of which is annexed to the present resolution;

2. *Requests* the Depositary Governments to open the Agreement for signature and ratification at the earliest possible date;

3. *Expresses its hope* for the widest possible adherence to this Agreement;

4. *Calls upon* the Committee on the Peaceful Uses of Outer Space to complete urgently the preparation of the draft agreement on liability for damage caused by the launching of objects into outer space and, in any event, not later than the beginning of the twenty-third session of the General Assembly, and to submit it to the Assembly at that session.

1640th plenary meeting,
19 December 1967.

ANNEX

Agreement on the Rescue of Astronauts, the Return of Astronauts and the Return of Objects Launched into Outer Space

The Contracting Parties,

Noting the great importance of the Treaty on Principles Governing the Activities of States in the Exploration and Use of Outer Space, including the Moon and Other Celestial Bodies, which calls for the rendering of all possible assistance to astronauts in the event of accident, distress or emergency landing, the prompt and safe return of astronauts, and the return of objects launched into outer space,

Desiring to develop and give further concrete expression to these duties,

Wishing to promote international co-operation in the peaceful exploration and use of outer space,

Prompted by sentiments of humanity,

Have agreed on the following:

---

[1] Official Records of the General Assembly, Twenty-second Session, Supplement No. 16, pp. 5-7. This resolution was adopted in accordance with a decision taken by the General Assembly at its 1640th plenary meeting on 19 December 1967, the question dealt with in the addendum to the report of the Committee on the Peaceful Uses of Outer Space was examined directly in plenary meeting, and the present resolution was adopted without reference to the First Committee. See also with reference to item 32, resolutions 2260 (XXII) and 2261 (XXII).

Article 1

Each Contracting Party which receives information or discovers that the personnel of a spacecraft have suffered accident or are experiencing conditions of distress or have made an emergency or unintended landing in territory under its jurisdiction or on the high seas or in any other place not under the jurisdiction of any State shall immediately:

(a) Notify the launching authority or, if it cannot identify and immediately communicate with the launching authority, immediately make a public announcement by all appropriate means of communication at its disposal;

(b) Notify the Secretary-General of the United Nations, who should disseminate the information without delay by all appropriate means of communication at his disposal.

Article 2

If, owing to accident, distress, emergency or unintended landing, the personnel of a spacecraft land in territory under the jurisdiction of a Contracting Party, it shall immediately take all possible steps to rescue them and render them all necessary assistance. It shall inform the launching authority and also the Secretary-General of the United Nations of the steps it is taking and of their progress. If assistance by the launching authority would help to effect a prompt rescue or would contribute substantially to the effectiveness of search and rescue operations, the launching authority shall co-operate with the Contracting Party with a view to the effective conduct of search and rescue operations. Such operations shall be subject to the direction and control of the Contracting Party, which shall act in close and continuing consultation with the launching authority.

Article 3

If information is received or it is discovered that the personnel of a spacecraft have alighted on the high seas or in any other place not under the jurisdiction of any State, those Contracting Parties which are in a position to do so shall, if necessary, extend assistance in search and rescue operations for such personnel to assure their speedy rescue. They shall inform the launching authority and the Secretary-General of the United Nations of the steps they are taking and of their progress.

Article 4

If, owing to accident, distress, emergency or unintended landing, the personnel of a spacecraft land in territory under the jurisdiction of a Contracting Party or have been found on the high seas or in any other place not under the jurisdiction of any State, they shall be safely and promptly returned to representatives of the launching authority.

Article 5

1. Each Contracting Party which receives information or discovers that a space object or its component parts has returned to Earth in territory under its jurisdiction or on the high seas or in any other place not under the jurisdiction of any State, shall notify the launching authority and the Secretary-General of the United Nations.

2. Each Contracting Party having jurisdiction over the territory on which a space object or its component parts has been discovered shall upon the request of the launching authority and with assistance from that authority, of requested, take such steps as it finds practicable to recover the object or component parts.

3. Upon request of the launching authority, objects launched into outer space or

their component parts found beyond the territorial limits of the launching authority shall be returned to or held at the disposal of representatives of the launching authority, which shall, upon request. Furnish identifying data prior to their return.

4. Notwithstanding paragraphs 2 and 3 of this article a Contracting Party which has reason to believe that a space object or its component parts discovered in Territory under its jurisdiction, or recovered by it elsewhere, is of a hazardous or deleterious nature may so notify the launching authority, which shall immediately take effective steps, under the direction and control of the said Contracting Party, to eliminate possible danger of harm.

5. Expenses incurred in fulfilling obligations to recover and return a space object or its component parts under paragraphs 2 and 3 of this article shall be borne by the launching authority.

Article 6

For the purposes of this Agreement, the term "launching authority" shall refer to the State responsible for launching, or, where an international intergovernmental organization is responsible for launching, that organization, provided that that organization declares its acceptance of the rights and obligations provided for in this Agreement and a majority of the States members of that organization are Contracting Parties to this Agreement and to the Treaty on Principles Governing the Activities of States in the Exploration and Use of Outer Space, including the Moon and other Celestial Bodies.

Article 7

1. This Agreement shall be open to all States for signature. Any State which does not sign this Agreement before its entry into force in accordance with paragraph 3 of this article may accede to it at any time.

2. This Agreement shall be subject to ratification by signatory States. Instruments of ratification and instruments of accession shall be deposited with the Governments of the Union of Soviet Socialist Republics, the United Kingdom of Great Britain and Northern Ireland and the United States of America, which are hereby designated the Depositary Governments.

3. This Agreement shall enter into force upon the deposit of instruments of ratification by five Governments including the Governments designated as Depositary Governments under this Agreement.

4. For States whose instruments of ratification or accession are deposited subsequent to the entry into force of this Agreement, it shall enter into force on the date of the deposit of their instruments of ratification or accession.

5. The Depositary Governments shall promptly inform all signatory and acceding States of the date of each signature, the date of deposit of each instrument of ratification of and accession to this Agreement, the date of its entry into force and other notices.

6. This Agreement shall be registered by the Depositary Governments pursuant to Article 102 of the Charter of the United Nations.

Article 8

Any State Party to the Agreement may propose amendments to this Agreement. Amendments shall enter into force for each State Party to the Agreement accepting the amendments upon their acceptance by a majority of the States Parties to the Agreement and thereafter for each remaining State Party to the Agreement on the date of acceptance by it.

Article 9

Any State Party to the Agreement may give notice of its withdrawal from the Agreement one year after its entry into force by written notification to the Depositary Governments. Such withdrawal shall take effect one year from the date of receipt of this notification.

Article 10

This Agreement, of which the Chinese, English, French, Russian and Spanish texts are equally authentic, shall be deposited in the archives of the Depositary Governments. Duly certified copies of this Agreement shall be transmitted by the Depositary Governments to the Governments of the signatory and acceding States.

IN WITNESS WHEREOF the undersigned, duly authorized, have signed this Agreement.

OTHER DECISIONS

Notification by the Secretary-General under Article 12, paragraph 2, of the Charter of the United Nations

(Item 7)

At its 1564th plenary meeting, on 23 September 1967, the General Assembly took note of the communication dated 18 September 1967 from the Secretary-General to the President of the General Assembly.[1]

Adoption of the agenda

(Item 8)

At its 1629th plenary meeting, on 13 December 1967, the General Assembly took note of paragraph 3 of the fifth report of the General Committee,[2] concerning a correction to the French text of rule 15 of the rules of procedure of the General Assembly.

Report of the Secretary-General on the work of the Organization

(Item 10)

At its 1642nd plenary meeting, on 19 December 1967, the General Assembly took note of the report of the Secretary-General on the work of the Organization.[3]

---

[1] Official Records of the General Assembly, Twenty-second Session, Annexes, agenda item 7, document A/6819.
[2] *Ibid.*, agenda item 8, document A/6840/Add.4.
[3] *Ibid.*, Twenty-second Session, Supplement No. 1 (A/6701 and Corr. 1) and *Supplement No. 1A* (A/6701/Add.1).

The General Assembly,

Reaffirming the importance of international co-operation in the field of the exploration and peaceful uses of outer space, including the Moon and other celestial bodies, and of promoting the law in this new field of human endeavour,

Desiring that the rights and obligations pertaining to liability for damage as laid down in the Treaty on Principles Governing the Activities of States in the Exploration and Use of Outer Space, including the Moon and Other Celestial Bodies should be elaborated in a separate international instrument,

Recalling its resolutions 1963 (XVIII) of 13 December 1963, 2130 (XX) of 21 December 1965, 2222 (XXI) of 19 December 1966, 2345 (XXII) of 19 December 1967, 2453 B (XXIII) of 20 December 1968, 2601 B (XXIV) of 16 December 1969 and 2733 B (XXV) of 16 December 1970 concerning the elaboration of an agreement on the liability for damage caused by the launching of objects into outer space,

Recalling also that in resolution 2733 B (XXV) it urged the Committee on the Peaceful Uses of Outer Space to reach early agreement on a draft convention on liability, to be submitted to the General Assembly at its twenty-sixth session, embodying the principles of a full measure of compensation to victims and effective procedures which would lead to prompt and equitable settlement of claims,

Having considered the report of the Committee on the Peaceful Uses of Outer Space,[2]

Taking note with appreciation of the work accomplished by the Committee on the Peaceful Uses of Outer Space, and in particular that of its Legal Sub-Committee,

1. *Commends* the Convention on International Liability for Damage Caused by Space Objects, the text of which is annexed to the present resolution;

2. *Requests* the depositary governments to open the Convention for signature and ratification at the earliest possible date;

3. *Notes* that any State may, on becoming a party to the Convention, declare that it will recognize as binding, in relation to any other State accepting the same obligation, the decision of the Claims Commission concerning any dispute to which it may become a party;

4. *Expresses its hope* for the widest possible adherence to this Convention.

1998th plenary meeting,
29 November 1971.

ANNEX

Convention on International Liability for Damage Caused
by Space Objects

The States Parties to this Convention,

Recognizing the common interest of all mankind in furthering the exploration and use of outer space for peaceful purposes,

Recalling the Treaty on Principles Governing the Activities of States in the Exploration and Use of Outer Space, including the Moon and Other Celestial Bodies,

---

[1]Official Records of the General Assembly, Twenty-sixth Session, Supplement No. 29, pp. 25-28.
[2]Official Records of the General Assembly, Twenty-sixth Session, Supplement No. 20 (A/8420).

Taking into consideration that, notwithstanding the precautionary measures to be taken by States and international intergovernmental organizations involved in the launching of space objects, damage may on occasion be caused by such objects,

Recognizing the need to elaborate effective international rules and procedures concerning liability for damage caused by space objects and to ensure, in particular, the prompt payment under the terms of this Convention of a full and equitable measure of compensation to victims of such damage,

Believing that the establishment of such rules and procedures will contribute to the strengthening of international cooperation in the field of the exploration and use of outer space for peaceful purposes,

Have agreed on the following:

ARTICLE I

For the purposes of this Convention:

(a) The term "damage" means loss of life, personal injury or other impairment of health; or loss of or damage to property of States or of persons, natural or juridical, or property of international intergovernmental organizations;

(b) The term "launching" includes attempted launching;

(c) The term "launching State" means:

(i) A State which launches or procures the launching of a space object;

(ii) A State from whose territory or facility a space object is launched;

(d) The term "space object" includes component parts of a space object as well as its launch vehicle and parts thereof.

ARTICLE II

A launching State shall be absolutely liable to pay compensation for damage caused by its space object on the surface of the earth or to aircraft in flight.

ARTICLE III

In the event of damage being caused elsewhere than on the surface of the earth to a space object of one launching State or to persons or property on board such a space object by a space object of another launching State, the latter shall be liable only if the damage is due to its fault or the fault of persons for whom it is responsible.

ARTICLE IV

1. In the event of damage being caused elsewhere than on the surface of the earth to a space object of one launching State or to persons or property on board such a space object by a space object of another launching State, and of damage thereby being caused to a third State or to its natural or juridical persons, the first two States shall be jointly and severally liable to the third State, to the extent indicated by the following:

(a) If the damage has been caused to the third State on the surface of the earth or to aircraft in flight, their liability to the third State shall be absolute;

(b) If the damage has been caused to a space object of the third State or to persons or property on board that space object elsewhere than on the surface of the earth, their liability to the third State shall be based on the fault of either of the first two States or on the fault of persons for whom either is responsible.

2. In all cases of joint and several liability referred to in paragraph 1 of this article, the burden of compensation for the damage shall be apportioned between the first two States in accordance with the extent to which they were at fault; if the extent of the fault of each of these States cannot be established, the burden of compensation shall be apportioned equally between them. Such apportionment shall be without

prejudice to the right of the third State to seek the entire compensation due under this Convention from any or all of the launching States which are jointly and severally liable.

ARTICLE V

1. Whenever two or more States jointly launch a space object, they shall be jointly and severally liable for any damage caused.

2. A launching State which has paid compensation for damage shall have the right to present a claim for indemnification to other participants in the joint launching. The participants in a joint launching may conclude agreements regarding the apportioning among themselves of the financial obligation in respect of which they are jointly and severally liable. Such agreements shall be without prejudice to the right of a State sustaining damage to seek the entire compensation due under this Convention from any or all of the launching States which are jointly and severally liable.

3. A State from whose territory or facility a space object is launched shall be regarded as a participant in a joint launching.

ARTICLE VI

1. Subject to the provisions of paragraph 2 of this article, exoneration from absolute liability shall be granted to the extent that a launching State establishes that the damage has resulted either wholly or partially from gross negligence or from an act or omission done with intent to cause damage on the part of a claimant State or of natural or juridical persons it represents.

2. No exoneration whatever shall be granted in cases where the damage has resulted from activities conducted by a launching State which are not in conformity with international law including, in particular, the Charter of the United Nations

ARTICLE VII

The provisions of this Convention shall not apply to damage caused by a space object of a launching State to:

(a) Nationals of that launching State;

(b) Foreign nationals during such time as they are participating in the operation of that space object from the time of its launching or at any stage thereafter until its descent, or during such time as they are in the immediate vicinity of a planned launching or recovery area as the result of an invitation by that launching State.

ARTICLE VIII

1. A State which suffers damage, or whose natural or juridical persons suffer damage, may present to a launching State a claim for compensation for such damage.

2. If the State of nationality has not presented a claim, another State may, in respect of damage sustained in its territory by any natural or juridical person, present a claim to a launching State.

3. If neither the State of nationality nor the State in whose territory the damage was sustained has presented a claim or notified its intention of presenting a claim, another State may, in respect of damage sustained by its permanent residents, present a claim to a launching State.

ARTICLE IX

A claim for compensation for damage shall be presented to a launching State through diplomatic channels. If a State does not maintain diplomatic relations with the launching State concerned, it may request another State to present its claim to that launching State or otherwise represent its interests under this Convention. It may also present its claim through the Secretary-General of the United Nations, provided the claimant State and the launching State are both Members of the United Nations.

ARTICLE X

1. A claim for compensation for damage may be presented to a launching State not later than one year following the date of the occurrence of the damage or the identification of the launching State which is liable.

2. If, however, a State does not know of the occurrence of the damage or has not been able to identify the launching State which is liable, it may present a claim within one year following the date on which it learned of the aforementioned facts; however, this period shall in no event exceed one year following the date on which the State could reasonably be expected to have learned of the facts through the exercise of due diligence.

3. The time-limits specified in paragraphs 1 and 2 of this article shall apply even if the full extent of the damage may not be known. In this event, however, the claimant State shall be entitled to revise the claim and submit additional documentation after the expiration of such time-limits until one year after the full extent of the damage is known.

ARTICLE XI

1. Presentation of a claim to a launching State for compensation for damage under this Convention shall not require the prior exhaustion of any local remedies which may be available to a claimant State or to natural or juridical persons it represents.

2. Nothing in this Convention shall prevent a State, or natural or juridical persons it might represent, from pursuing a claim in the courts or administrative tribunals or agencies of a launching State. A State shall not, however, be entitled to present a claim under this Convention in respect of the same damage for which a claim is being pursued in the courts or administrative tribunals or agencies of a launching State or under another international agreement which is binding on the States concerned.

ARTICLE XII

The compensation which the launching State shall be liable to pay for damage under this Convention shall be determined in accordance with international law and the principles of justice and equity, in order to provide such reparation in respect of the damage as will restore the person, natural or juridical, State or international organization on whose behalf the claim is presented to the condition which would have existed if the damage had not occurred.

ARTICLE XIII

Unless the claimant State and the State from which compensation is due under this Convention agree on another form of compensation, the compensation shall be paid in the currency of the claimant State or, if that State so requests, in the currency of the State from which compensation is due.

ARTICLE XIV

If no settlement of a claim is arrived at through diplomatic negotiations as provided for in article IX, within one year from the date on which the claimant State notifies the launching State that it has submitted the documentation of its claim, the parties concerned shall establish a Claims Commission at the request of either party.

ARTICLE XV

1. The Claims Commission shall be composed of three members: one appointed by the claimant State, one appointed by the launching State and the third member, the Chairman, to be chosen by both parties jointly. Each party shall make its appointment within two months of the request for the establishment of the Claims Commission.

2. If no agreement is reached on the choice of the Chairman within four months of the request for the establishment of the Commission, either party may request the Secretary-General of the United Nations to appoint the Chairman within a further period of two months.

ARTICLE XVI

1. If one of the parties does not make its appointment within the stipulated period, the Chairman shall, at the request of the other party, constitute a single-member Claims Commission.

2. Any vacancy which may arise in the Commission for whatever reason shall be filled by the same procedure adopted for the original appointment.

3. The Commission shall determine its own procedure.

4. The Commission shall determine the place or places where it shall sit at and all other administrative matters.

5. Except in the case of decisions and awards by a single-member Commission, all decisions and awards of the Commission shall be by majority vote.

ARTICLE XVII

No increase in the membership of the Claims Commission shall take place by reason of two or more claimant States or launching States being joined in any one proceeding before the Commission. The claimant States so joined shall collectively appoint one member of the Commission in the same manner and subject to the same conditions as would be the case for a single claimant State. When two or more launching States are so joined, they shall collectively appoint one member of the Commission in the same way. If the claimant States or the launching States do not make the appointment within the stipulated period, the Chairman shall constitute a single-member Commission.

ARTICLE XVIII

The Claims Commission shall decide the merits of the claim for compensation and determine the amount or compensation payable, if any.

ARTICLE XIX

1. The Claims Commission shall act in accordance with the provisions of article XII.

2. The decision of the Commission shall be final and binding if the parties have so agreed; otherwise the Commission shall render a final and recommendatory award, which the parties shall consider in good faith. The Commission shall state the reasons for its decision or award.

3. The Commission shall give its decision or award as promptly as possible and no later than one year from the date of its establishment, unless an extension of this period is found necessary by the Commission.

4. The Commission shall make its decision or award public. It shall deliver a certified copy of its decision or award to each of the parties and to the Secretary-General of the United Nations.

ARTICLE XX

The expenses in regard to the Claims Commission shall be borne equally by the parties, unless otherwise decided by the Commission.

ARTICLE XXI

If the damage caused by a space object presents a large-scale danger to human life or seriously interferes with the living conditions of the population or the functioning of vital centres, the States Parties, and in particular the launching State, shall examine the possibility of rendering appropriate and rapid assistance to the State which has suffered the damage, when it so requests. However, nothing in this article shall affect the rights or obligations of the States Parties under this Convention.

ARTICLE XXII

1. In this Convention, with the exception of articles XXIV to XXVII, references to States shall be deemed to apply to any international intergovernmental organization which conducts space activities if the organization declares its acceptance of the rights and obligations provided for in this Convention and if a majority of the States members of the organization are States Parties to this Convention and to the Treaty on Principles Governing the Activities of States in the Exploration and Use of Outer Space, including the Moon and Other Celestial Bodies.

2. States members of any such organization which are States Parties to this Convention shall take all appropriate steps to ensure that the organization makes a declaration in accordance with the preceding paragraph.

3. If an international intergovernmental organization is liable for damage by virtue of the provisions of this Convention, that organization and those of its members which are States Parties to this Convention shall be jointly and severally liable; provided, however, that:

(a) Any claim for compensation in respect of such damage shall be first presented to the organization;

(b) Only where the organization has not paid, within a period of six months, any sum agreed or determined to be due as compensation for such damage, may the claimant State invoke the liability of the members which are States Parties to this Convention for the payment of that sum.

4. Any claim, pursuant to the provisions of this Convention, for compensation in respect of damage caused to an organization which has made a declaration in accordance with paragraph 1 of this article shall be presented by a State member of the organization which is a State Party to this Convention.

ARTICLE XXIII

1. The provisions of this Convention shall not affect other international agreements in force in so far as relations between the States Parties to such agreements are concerned.

2. No provision of this Convention shall prevent States from concluding international agreements reaffirming, supplementing or extending its provisions.

ARTICLE XXIV

1. This Convention shall be open to all States for signature. Any State which does not sign this Convention before its entry into force in accordance with paragraph 3 of this article may accede to it at any time.

2. This Convention shall be subject to ratification by signatory States. Instruments of ratification and instruments of accession shall be deposited with the Governments

of the Union of Soviet Socialist Republics, the United Kingdom of Great Britain and Northern Ireland and the United States of America, which are hereby designated the Depositary Governments.

3. This Convention shall enter into force on the deposit of the fifth instrument of ratification.

4. For States whose instruments of ratification or accession are deposited subsequent to the entry into force of this Convention, it shall enter into force on the date of the deposit of their instruments of ratification or accession.

5. The Depositary Governments shall promptly inform all signatory and acceding States of the date of each signature, the date of deposit of each instrument of ratification of and accession to this Convention, the date of its entry into force and other notices.

6. This Convention shall be registered by the Depositary Governments pursuant to Article 102 of the Charter of the United Nations.

ARTICLE XXV

Any State Party to the Convention may propose amendments to this Convention. Amendments shall enter into force for each State Party to the Convention accepting the amendments upon their acceptance by a majority of the States Parties to the Convention and thereafter for each remaining State Party to the Convention on the date of acceptance by it.

ARTICLE XXVI

Ten years after the entry into force of this Convention, the question of the review of this Convention shall be included in the provisional agenda of the United Nations General Assembly in order to consider, in the light of past application of the Convention, whether it requires revision. However, at any time after the Convention has been in force for five years, and at the request of one third of the States Parties to the Convention, and with the concurrence of the majority of the States Parties, a conference of the States Parties shall be convened to review this Convention.

ARTICLE XXVII

Any State Party to this Convention may give notice of its withdrawal from the Convention one year after its entry into force by written notification to the Depositary Governments. Such withdrawal shall take effect one year from the date of receipt of this notification.

ARTICLE XXVIII

This Convention, of which the Chinese, English, French, Russian and Spanish texts are equally authentic, shall be deposited in the archives of the Depositary Governments. Duly certified copies of this Convention shall be transmitted by the Depositary Governments to the Governments of the signatory and acceding States.

IN WITNESS WHEREOF the undersigned, duly authorized, have signed this Convention.

DONE in triplicate, at the cities of London, Moscow and Washington, this . . . . . . day of . . . . , one thousand nine hundred and . . . .

Looking forward to the early initiation of the substantive work of the Working Group, keeping in mind that experiments to test the feasibility of remote sensing of the earth from space platforms are scheduled to begin early in 1972,

Expressing confidence that in discharging its responsibility the Working Group would seek to promote the optimum utilization of this space application for the benefit of individual States and of the International community,

1. *Requests* Member States to submit information on their national and co-operative international activities in this field, as well as comments and working papers, through the Secretary-General to the Working Group on Remote Sensing of the Earth by Satellites;

2. *Endorses* the request of the Scientific and Technical Sub-Committee that the Working Group solicit the views of appropriate United Nations bodies and specialized agencies, and other relevant international organizations;

3. *Requests* the Secretary-General to provide the Working Group with his comments on this subject and to submit working papers on matters falling within the terms of reference of the Group;

4. *Requests* the Committee on the Peaceful Uses of Outer Space and its Scientific and Technical Sub-Committee to bring about the early initiation of the Working Group's substantive work and to keep the General Assembly informed in a comprehensive fashion on the progress of its work.

1998th plenary meeting,
29 November 1971.

15. DECLARATION OF PRINCIPLES GOVERNING THE SEA-BED AND THE OCEAN FLOOR, AND THE SUBSOIL THEREOF, BEYOND THE LIMITS OF NATIONAL JURISDICTION[1]

The General Assembly,

Recalling its resolutions 2340 (XXII) of 18 December 1967, 2467 (XXIII) of 21 December 1968 and 2574 (XXIV) of 15 December 1969, concerning the area to which the title of the item refers,

Affirming that there is an area of the sea-bed and the ocean floor, and the subsoil thereof, beyond the limits of national jurisdiction, the precise limits of which are yet to be determined,

Recognizing that the existing legal regime of the high seas does not provide substantive rules for regulating the exploration of the aforesaid area and the exploitation of its resources,

Convinced that the area shall be reserved exclusively for peaceful purposes and that the exploration of the area and the exploitation of its resources shall be carried out for the benefit of mankind as a whole,

Believing it essential that an international regime applying to the area and its resources and including appropriate international machinery should be established as soon as possible,

Bearing in mind that the development and use of the area and its resources shall be undertaken in such a manner as to foster the healthy development of the world economy and balanced growth of international trade, and to minimize any adverse economic effects caused by the fluctuation of prices of raw materials resulting from such activities,

---

[1] Official Records of the General Assembly, Twenty-fifth Session, Supplement No. 28, pp. 24-25.

Solemnly declares that:

1. The sea-bed and ocean floor, and the subsoil thereof, beyond the limits of national jurisdiction (hereinafter referred to as the area), as well as the resources of the area, are the common heritage of mankind.

2. The area shall not be subject to appropriation by any means by States or persons, natural or juridical, and no State shall claim or exercise sovereignty or sovereign rights over any part thereof.

3. No State or person, natural or juridical, shall claim, exercise or acquire rights with respect to the area or its resources incompatible with the international regime to be established and the principles of this Declaration.

4. All activities regarding the exploration and exploitation of the resources of the area and other related activities shall be governed by the international regime to be established.

5. The area shall be open to use exclusively for peaceful purposes by all States, whether coastal or land-locked, without discrimination, in accordance with the international regime to be established.

6. States shall act in the area in accordance with the applicable principles and rules of international law, including the Charter of the United Nations and the Declaration on Principles of International Law concerning Friendly Relations and Co-operation among States in accordance with the Charter of the United Nations, adopted by the General Assembly on 24 October 1970,[1] in the interests of maintaining international peace and security and promoting international co-operation and mutual understanding.

7. The exploration of the area and the exploitation of its resources shall be carried out for the benefit of mankind as a whole, irrespective of the geographical location of States, whether land-locked or coastal, and taking into particular consideration the interests and needs of the developing countries.

8. The area shall be reserved exclusively for peaceful purposes, without prejudice to any measures which have been or may be agreed upon in the contexts of international negotiations undertaken in the field of disarmament and which may be applicable to a broader area. One or more international agreements shall be concluded as soon as possible in order to implement effectively this principle and to constitute a step towards the exclusion of the sea-bed, the ocean floor and the subsoil thereof from the arms race.

9. On the basis of the principles of this Declaration, an international regime applying to the area and its resources and including appropriate international machinery to give effect to its provisions shall be established by an international treaty of a universal character, generally agreed upon. The regime shall, *inter alia*, provide for the orderly and safe development and rational management of the area and its resources and for expanding opportunities in the use thereof, and ensure the equitable sharing by States in the benefits derived therefrom, taking into particular consideration the interests and needs of the developing countries, whether land-locked or coastal.

10. States shall promote international co-operation in scientific research exclusively for peaceful purposes:

(a) By participation in international programmes and by encouraging co-operation in scientific research by personnel of different countries;

(b) Through effective publication of research programmes and dissemination of the results of research through international channels;

(c) By co-operation in measures to strengthen research capabilities of developing countries, including the participation of their nationals in research programmes.

---

[1] Resolution 2625 (XXV).

No such activity shall form the legal basis for any claims with respect to any part of the area or its resources.

11. With respect to activities in the area and acting in conformity with the international regime to be established, States shall take appropriate measures for and shall co-operate in the adoption and implementation of international rules, standards and procedures for, *inter alia:*

(a) The prevention of pollution and contamination, and other hazards to the marine environment, including the coastline, and of interference with the ecological balance of the marine environment;

(b) The protection and conservation of the natural resources of the area and the prevention of damage to the flora and fauna of the marine environment.

12. In their activities in the area, including those relating to its resources, States shall pay due regard to the rights and legitimate interests of coastal States in the region of such activities, as well as of all other States, which may be affected by such activities. Consultations shall be maintained with the coastal States concerned with respect to activities relating to the exploration of the area and the exploitation of its resources with a view to avoiding infringement of such rights and interests.

13. Nothing herein shall affect:

(a) The legal status of the waters superjacent to the area or that of the air space above those waters;

(b) The rights of coastal States with respect to measures to prevent, mitigate or eliminate grave and imminent danger to their coastline or related interests from pollution or threat thereof or from other hazardous occurrences resulting from or caused by any activities in the area, subject to the international regime to be established.

14. Every State shall have the responsibility to ensure that activities in the area, including those relating to its resources, whether undertaken by governmental agencies, or non-governmental entities or persons under its jurisdiction, or acting on its behalf, shall be carried out in conformity with the international regime to be established. The same responsibility applies to international organizations and their members for activities undertaken by such organizations or on their behalf. Damage caused by such activities shall entail liability.

15. The parties to any dispute relating to activities in the area and its resources shall resolve such dispute by the measures mentioned in Article 33 of the Charter of the United Nations and such procedures for settling disputes as may be agreed upon in the international regime to be established.

1933rd plenary meeting,
17 December 1970.

16. TREATY ON THE PROHIBITION OF THE EMPLACEMENT OF NUCLEAR WEAPONS AND OTHER WEAPONS OF MASS DESTRUCTION ON THE SEA-BED AND THE OCEAN FLOOR AND IN THE SUBSOIL THEREOF[1]

The General Assembly,

Recalling its resolution 2602 F (XXIV) of 16 December 1969,

Convinced that the prevention of a nuclear arms race on the sea-bed and the ocean

---

[1]Official Records of the General Assembly, Twenty-fifth Session, Supplement No. 28, pp. 11-13.
[2]Official Records of the Disarmament Commission, Supplement for 1970, document DC/233.

floor serves the interests of maintaining world peace, reducing international tensions and strengthening friendly relations among States,

Recognizing the common interest of mankind in the reservation of the sea-bed and the ocean floor exclusively for peaceful purposes,

Having considered the report of the Conference of the Committee on Disarmament,[2] dated 11 September 1970, and being appreciative of the work of the Conference on the draft Treaty on the Prohibition of the Emplacement of Nuclear Weapons and Other Weapons of Mass Destruction on the Sea-Bed and the Ocean Floor and in the Subsoil Thereof, annexed to the report,

Convinced that this Treaty will further the purposes and principles of the Charter of the United Nations,

1. *Commends* the Treaty on the Prohibition of the Emplacement of Nuclear Weapons and Other Weapons of Mass Destruction on the Sea-Bed and the Ocean Floor and in the Subsoil Thereof, the text of which is annexed to the present resolution;

2. *Requests* the depositary Governments to open the Treaty for signature and ratification at the earliest possible date;

3. *Expresses the hope* for the widest possible adherence to the Treaty.

1919th plenary meeting,
7 December 1970.

ANNEX

Treaty on the Prohibition of the Emplacement of Nuclear Weapons and Other Weapons of Mass Destruction on the Sea-Bed and the Ocean Floor and in the Subsoil Thereof

The States Parties to this Treaty,

Recognizing the common interest of mankind in the progress of the exploration and use of the sea-bed and the ocean floor for peaceful purposes,

Considering that the prevention of a nuclear arms race on the sea-bed and the ocean floor serves the interests of maintaining world peace, reduces international tensions and strengthens friendly relations among States,

Convinced that this Treaty constitutes a step towards the exclusion of the sea-bed, the ocean floor and the subsoil thereof from the arms race,

Convinced that this Treaty constitutes a step towards a treaty on general and complete disarmament under strict and effective international control, and determined to continue negotiations to this end,

Convinced that this Treaty will further the purposes and principles of the Charter of the United Nations, in a manner consistent with the principles of international law and without infringing the freedoms of the high seas,

Have agreed as follows:

ARTICLE I

1. The States Parties to this Treaty undertake not to emplant or emplace on the sea-bed and the ocean floor and in the subsoil thereof beyond the outer limit of a sea-bed zone, as defined in article II, any nuclear weapons or any other types of weapons of mass destruction as well as structures, launching installations or any other facilities specifically designed for storing, testing or using such weapons.

2. The undertakings of paragraph 1 of this article shall also apply to the sea-bed zone referred to in the same paragraph, except that within such sea-bed zone, they shall not apply either to the coastal State or to the sea-bed beneath its territorial waters.

3. The States Parties to this Treaty undertake not to assist, encourage of induce any State to carry out activities referred to in paragraph 1 of this article and not to participate in any other way in such actions.

ARTICLE II

For the purpose of this Treaty, the outer limit of the sea-bed zone referred to in article I shall be coterminous with the twelve-mile outer limit of the zone referred to in part II of the Convention on the Territorial Sea and the Contiguous Zone, signed at Geneva on 29 April 1958, and shall be measured in accordance with the provisions of part I, section II, of that Convention and in accordance with international law.

ARTICLE III

1. In order to promote the objectives of and ensure compliance with the provisions of this Treaty, each State Party to the Treaty shall have the right to verify through observation the activities of other States Parties to the Treaty on the sea-bed and the ocean floor and in the subsoil thereof beyond the zone referred to in article I, provided that observation does not interefere with such activities.

2. If after such observation reasonable doubts remain concerning the fulfilment of the obligations assumed under the Treaty, the State Party having such doubts and the State Party that is responsible for the activities giving rise to the doubts shall consult with a view to removing the doubts. If the doubts persist, the State Party having such doubts shall notify the other States Parties, and the Parties concerned shall co-operate on such further procedures for verification as may be agreed, including appropriate inspection of objects, structures, installations or other facilities that reasonably may be expected to be of a kind described in article I. The Parties in the region of the activities, including any coastal State, and any other Party so requesting, shall be entitled to participate in such consultation and co-operation. After completion of the further procedures for verification, an appropriate report shall be circulated to other Parties by the Party that initiated such procedures.

3. If the State responsible for the activities giving rise to the reasonable doubts is not identifiable by observation of the object, structure, installation or other facility, the State Party having such doubts shall notify and make appropriate inquiries of States Parties in the region of the activities and of any other State Party. If it is ascertained through these inquiries that a particular State Party is responsible for the activities, that State Party shall consult and co-operate with other Parties as provided in paragraph 2 of this article. If the identify of the State responsible for the activities cannot be ascertained through these inquiries, then further verification procedures, including inspection, may be undertaken by the inquiring State Party, which shall invite the participation of the Parties in the region of the activities, including any coastal State, and of any other Party desiring to co-operate.

4. If consultation and co-operation pursuant to paragraphs 2 and 3 of this article have not removed the doubts concerning the activities and there remains a serious question concerning fulfilment of the obligations assumed under this Treaty, a State Party may, in accordance with the provisions of the Charter of the United Nations, refer the matter to the Security Council, which may take action in accordance with the Charter.

5. Verification pursuant to this article may be undertaken by any State Party using its own means, or with the full or partial assistance of any other State Party, or through appropriate international procedures within the framework of the United Nations and in accordance with its Charter.

6. Verification activities pursuant to this Treaty shall not interfere with activities of other States Parties and shall be conducted with due regard for rights recognized under international law, including the freedoms of the high seas and the rights of coastal States with respect to the exploration and exploitation of their continental shelves.

ARTICLE IV

Nothing in this Treaty shall be interpreted as supporting or prejudicing the position of any State Party with respect to existing international conventions, including the 1958 Convention on the Territorial Sea and the Contiguous Zone, or with respect to rights or claims which such State Party may assert, or with respect to recognition or non-recognition of rights or claims asserted by any other State, related to waters off its coasts, including, *inter alia*, territorial seas and contiguous zones, or to the sea-bed and the ocean floor, including continental shelves.

ARTICLE V

The Parties to this Treaty undertake to continue negotiations in good faith concerning further measures in the field of disarmament for the prevention of an arms race on the sea-bed, the ocean floor and the subsoil thereof.

ARTICLE VI

Any State Party may propose amendments to this Treaty. Amendments shall enter into force for each State Party accepting the amendments upon their acceptance by a majority of the States Parties to the Treaty and, thereafter, for each remaining State Party on the date of acceptance by it.

ARTICLE VII

Five years after the entry into force of this Treaty, a conference of Parties to the Treaty shall be held at Geneva, Switzerland, in order to review the operation of this Treaty with a view to assuring that the purposes of the preamble and the provisions of the Treaty are being realized. Such review shall take into account any relevant technological developments. The review conference shall determine, in accordance with the views of a majority of those Parties attending, whether and when an additional review conference shall be convened.

ARTICLE VIII

Each State Party to this Treaty shall in exercising its national sovereignty have the right to withdraw from this Treaty if it decides that extraordinary events related to the subject-matter of this Treaty have jeopardized the supreme interests of its country. It shall give notice of such withdrawal to all other States Parties to the Treaty and to the United Nations Security Council three months in advance. Such notice shall include a statement of the extraordinary events it considers to have jeopardized its supreme interests.

ARTICLE IX

The provisions of this Treaty shall in no way affect the obligations assumed by States Parties to the Treaty under international instruments establishing zones free from nuclear weapons.

ARTICLE X

1. This Treaty shall be open for signature to all States. Any State which does not sign the Treaty before its entry into force in accordance with paragraph 3 of this article may accede to it at any time.
2. This Treaty shall be subject to ratification by signatory States. Instruments of ratification and of accession shall be deposited with the Governments of the Union of Soviet Socialist Republics, the United Kingdom of Great Britain and Northern Ireland and the United States of America, which are hereby designated the Depositary Governments.
3. This Treaty shall enter into force after the deposit of instruments of ratification

by twenty-two Governments, including the Governments designated as Depositary Governments of this Treaty.

4. For States whose instruments of ratification or accession are deposited after the entry into force of this Treaty, it shall enter into force on the date of the deposit of their instruments of ratification or accession.

5. The Depositary Governments shall promptly inform the Governments of all signatory and acceding States of the date of each signature, of the date of deposit of each instrument of ratification or of accession, of the date of the entry into force of this Treaty, and of the receipt of other notices.

6. This Treaty shall be registered by the Depositary Governments pursuant to Article 102 of the Charter of the United Nations.

ARTICLE XI

This Treaty, the Chinese, English, French, Russian and Spanish texts of which are equally authentic, shall be deposited in the archives of the Depositary Governments. Duly certified copies of this Treaty shall be transmitted by the Depositary Governments to the Governments of the States signatory and acceding thereto.

17. GENERAL AND COMPLETE DISARMAMENT[1]

Date: 21 December 1976   Meeting: 106
                          Report: A/31/386

Votes: A – 107-10-11 (recorded) C – 95-0-33 (recorded)
       B – adopted without vote D – 106-2-22 (recorded)

The General Assembly,

Recalling its resolution 2602 A (XXIV) of 16 December 1969 relating to the initiation of bilateral negotiations between the Governments of the Union of Soviet Socialist Republics and the United States of America *on the limitation of offensive and defensive strategic nuclear-weapon systems,*

Reaffirming its resolutions 2932 B (XXVII) of 29 November 1972, 3184 A and C (XXVIII) of 18 December 1973, 3261 C (XXIX) of 9 December 1974 and 3484 C (XXX) of 12 December 1975,

Bearing in mind that the above-mentioned Governments agreed on 21 June 1973 to make serious efforts to work out and sign in 1974 the agreement on more complete measures on the limitation of strategic offensive arms called for in the interim agreement of 26 May 1972, and that on the same occasion they expressed their intention to carry out the subsequent reduction of such arms,

Conscious of the fact that the interim agreement referred to above will expire next year,

---

[1] Resolutions adopted by the General Assembly during the first part of its Thirty-first regular session, 21 September-22 December 1976 (the Official Record is not ready at the preparing of this volume), Press Release: GA/5571, 29 December 1976, pp. 97-102.

Noting that, as a result of the discussions held at the highest level in November 1974 also between the Union of Soviet Socialist Republics and the United States of America, both sides reaffirmed their intention *to conclude an agreement on the limitation of strategic offensive arms to last until 31 December 1985 inclusive,*

Noting also that at the same meeting it was agreed to set ceilings both on the strategic offensive nuclear delivery vehicles as well as on such of those vehicles that may be equipped with multiple independently targetable warheads, and that both sides stated that favourable prospects existed for completing the work on the new agreement in 1975 and stressed that it would include provisions for further negotiations beginning no later than 1980-1981 on the question of further *limitations and possible reductions of strategic arms in the period after 1985.*

Noting further the information submitted by the Union of Soviet Socialist Republics and the United States of America,[2]

Reiterating its opinion that disarmament negotiations move very slowly in comparison to the obvious perils posed by the enormous arsenals of nuclear weapons,

1. *Regrets* the absence of positive results during the last three years of the bilateral negotiations between the Governments of the Union of Soviet Socialist Republics and the United States of America on the limitation of their strategic nuclear-weapons systems;

2. *Expresses its concern* for the very high ceilings of nuclear arms set for themselves by both States, *for the total absence of qualitative limitations of such arms,* for the protracted time-table contemplated for the negotiation of further limitations and possible reductions of the nuclear arsenals and for the situation thus created;

3. *Urges anew* the Union of Soviet Socialist Republics and the United States of America to broaden the scope and accelerate the pace of their strategic nuclear arms limitation talks, and stresses once again the necessity and urgency of reaching agreement on important qualitative limitations and substantial reductions of their strategic nuclear-weapon systems as a positive step towards nuclear disarmament;

4. *Reiterates its previous invitation* to both Governments to keep the General Assembly informed in good time of the progress and results of their *negotiations.*

B

The General Assembly,

Mindful that the continuation of the arms race endangers international peace and security and also diverts vast resources urgently needed for economic and social development,

Convinced that peace can be secured through the implementation of disarmament measures, particularly of nuclear disarmament, conductive to the realization of the final objective, namely, general and complete disarmament under effective international control,

Reaffirming that disarmament is one of the essential objectives of the United Nations,

Bearing in mind that the Fifth Conference of Heads of State or Government of Non-Aligned Countries, held at Colombo from 16 to 19 August 1976, called for a special ses-

---

[2]A/31/125.

sion of the General Assembly devoted to disarmament and made specific suggestions in this regard in its declaration and resolution on disarmament,[1]

1. *Decides* to convene a special session of the General Assembly devoted to disarmament, to be held in New York in May/June 1978;

2. *Further decides* to establish a Preparatory Committee for the Special Session of the General Assembly Devoted to Disarmament, composed of 54 Member States appointed by the President of the Assembly on the basis of equitable geographical distribution, with the mandate of examining all relevant questions relating to the special session, including its agenda, and to submit to the Assembly at its thrity-second session appropriate recommendations thereon;

3. *Invites* all Member States to communicate to the Secretary-General their views on the agenda and all other relevant questions relating to the special session of the General Assembly not later than 15 April 1977;

4. *Requests* the Secretary-General to transmit the replies of Member States pursuant to paragraph 3 above to the Preparatory Committee and to render it all necessary assistance, including the provision of essential background information, relevant documents and summary records;

5. *Requests* the Preparatory Committee to meet for a short organizational session not longer than one week before 31 March 1977, *inter alia*, to set the dates for its substantive sessions;

6. *Decides* to include in the provisional agenda of its thirty-second session an item entitled: "Special session of the General Assembly devoted to disarmament: report of the Preparatory Committee for the Special Session of the General Assembly Devoted to Disarmament."

C

The General Assembly,

Bearing in mind the need to allay the legitimate concern of the States of the world with regard to ensuring lasting security for their peoples,

Deeply concerned at the continuation of the arms race, in particular the nuclear arms race and the threat to mankind due to the possibility of the use of nuclear weapons,

Convinced that only nuclear disarmament resulting in the complete elimination of nuclear weapons will assure perfect security in the nuclear era,

Recognizing that the independence, territorial integrity and sovereignty of non-nuclear-weapon States need to be safeguarded against the use or threat of use of nuclear weapons,

Considering that, until nuclear disarmament is achieved on a universal basis, it is imperative for the international community to devise effective measures to ensure the security of non-nuclear-weapon States against the use, or threat of use, of nuclear weapons from any quarter,

---

[1] A/31/197, annex, p. 127.

Recalling its resolution 3261 G (XXIX) of 9 December 1974 in which it recommended to Member States to consider in all appropriate forums, without loss of time, the question of strengthening the security of non-nuclear-weapon States,

Noting that the non-nuclear-weapon States have called for assurances from nuclear-weapon Powers that they will not use or threaten to use nuclear weapons against them,

Deeply concerned over any possibility of use or threat of use of nuclear weapons in any contingency,

1. *Requests* the nuclear-weapon States, as a first step towards a complete ban on the use or threat of use of nuclear weapons, to consider undertaking, without prejudice to their obligations arising from treaties establishing nuclear-weapon-free zones, not to use or threaten to use nuclear weapons against non-nuclear-weapon States not parties to the nuclear security arrangements of some nuclear-weapon Powers;

2. *Decides* to review at its thirty-second session the progress made on the question of strengthening the security of non-nuclear-weapon States.

D

The General Assembly,

Recalling its resolution 2373 (XXII) of 12 June 1968, in which it commended the Treaty on the Non-Proliferation of Nuclear Weapons[1] and expressed the hope for the widest possible adherence to that Treaty,

Noting that 100 States now are parties to the Treaty on the Non-Proliferation of Nuclear Weapons,

Noting further that the non-nuclear-weapon States parties to the Treaty on the Non-Proliferation of Nuclear Weapons have accepted the principle of safeguards on all their peaceful nuclear activities,

Recognizing that the accelerated spread and development of peaceful applications of nuclear energy may, in the absence of an effective and comprehensive safeguards system, increase the danger of proliferation of nuclear weapons or equivalent nuclear explosive capabilities.

Noting that the objectives of the International Atomic Energy Agency, as defined in its statute, are to promote peaceful application of nuclear energy while ensuring that they are not used in such a way as to further any military purpose,

Underlining the important rule of the International Atomic Energy Agency in implementing international non-proliferation policies in connexion with the peaceful uses of nuclear energy and noting in this context the communication from Finland concerning the strengthening of the International Atomic Energy Agency safeguards on a comprehensive basis,[2]

Recognizing the necessity of continued international co-operation in the application and improvement of International Atomic Energy Agency safeguards on peaceful nuclear activities,

---

[1] General Assembly resolution 2373 (XXII), annex.
[2] A/C.1/31/6.

1. *Recognizes* that States accepting effective non-proliferation restraints have a right to enjoy fully the benefits of the peaceful uses of nuclear energy and underlines the importance of increased efforts in this field, particularly for the needs of the developing areas of the world;

2. *Requests* the International Atomic Energy Agency to give special attention to its programme of work in the non-proliferation area, including its efforts in facilitating peaceful nuclear co-operation and increasing assistance to the developing areas of the world within an effective and comprehensive safeguards system;

3. *Further requests* the International Atomic Energy Agency to continue its studies on the questions of multinational fuel cycle centres and an international regime for plutonium storage as effective means to promote the interests of the non-proliferation regime;

4. *Calls upon* the International Atomic Energy Agency to give careful consideration to all relevant suggestions aiming at strengthening the safeguards regime that have been presented to the Agency;

5. *Requests* the International Atomic Energy Agency to report on the progress of its work on this question to the General Assembly at its thirty-second session.

RECORDED VOTE ON ABOVE RESOLUTION A:

Y–YES, N–NO, A–ABSTAIN

Country	Y	N	A
Afghanistan	*		
Albania			
Algeria	*		
Angola			
Argentina	*		
Australia	*		
Austria	*		
Bahamas	*		
Bahrain	*		
Bangladesh	*		
Barbados	*		
Belgium			*
Benin			
Bhutan	*		
Bolivia	*		
Botswana	*		
Brazil	*		
Bulgaria		*	
Burma	*		
Burundi	*		
Byelorussian SSR		*	
Canada	*		
Cape Verde			
Central African Rep.	*		
Chad	*		
Chile	*		
China			
Colombia	*		
Comoros			
Congo			
Costa Rica	*		
Cuba			
Cyprus	*		
Czechoslovakia		*	
Democratic Kampuchea			
Democratic Yemen	*		
Denmark	*		
Dominican Republic	*		
Ecuador	*		
Egypt	*		
El Salvador			
Equatorial Guinea	*		
Ethiopia	*		
Fiji	*		
Finland	*		
France			*
Gabon	*		
Gambia			
German Dem. Rep.		*	
Germany, Fed. Rep.			*
Ghana	*		
Greece			*
Grenada	*		
Guatemala	*		
Guinea	*		
Guinea-Bissau	*		
Guyana	*		
Haiti			
Honduras			
Hungary		*	
Iceland	*		
India	*		
Indonesia	*		
Iran	*		
Iraq	*		
Ireland	*		
Israel			*
Italy			*
Ivory Coast	*		
Jamaica	*		
Japan	*		
Jordan	*		
Kenya	*		
Kuwait	*		
Lao Peoples Dem. Rep.			*
Lebanon	*		
Lesotho	*		
Liberia			
Libyan Arab Republic	*		
Luxembourg			*
Madagascar	*		
Malawi			*
Malaysia	*		
Maldives	*		
Mali	*		
Malta	*		
Mauritania	*		
Mauritius	*		
Mexico	*		
Mongolia		*	
Morocco			
Mozambique	*		
Nepal	*		
Netherlands	*		
New Zealand	*		
Nicaragua	*		
Niger	*		
Nigeria	*		
Norway	*		
Oman	*		
Pakistan	*		
Panama	*		
Papua New Guinea	*		
Paraguay	*		
Peru	*		
Philippines	*		
Poland		*	
Portugal	*		
Qatar	*		
Romania	*		
Rwanda	*		
Sao Tome and Principe	*		
Saudi Arabia	*		
Senegal	*		
Seychelles			
Sierra Leone	*		
Singapore	*		
Somalia			
South Africa			
Spain	*		
Sri Lanka	*		
Sudan	*		
Surinam	*		
Swaziland	*		
Sweden	*		
Syrian Arab Republic	*		
Thailand	*		
Togo	*		
Trinidad and Tobago	*		
Tunisia	*		
Turkey			*
Uganda	*		
Ukrainian SSR		*	
USSR		*	
United Arab Emirates	*		
United Kingdom			*
Un. Rep. of Cameroon	*		
Un. Rep. of Tanzania			
United States		*	
Upper Volta	*		
Uruguay	*		
Venezuela	*		
Yemen	*		
Yugoslavia	*		
Zaire	*		
Zambia	*		

Y—YES, N—NO, A—ABSTAIN

Country	Y	N	A
Afghanistan	*		
Albania			
Algeria			*
Angola			
Argentina			*
Australia			*
Austria			*
Bahamas	*		
Bahrain	*		
Bangladesh	*		
Barbados	*		
Belgium			*
Benin			
Bhutan			*
Bolivia	*		
Botswana	*		
Brazil	*		
Bulgaria			*
Burma	*		
Burundi	*		
Byelorussian SSR			*
Canada			*
Cape Verde			
Central African Rep.	*		
Chad	*		
Chile	*		
China	*		
Colombia	*		
Comoros			
Congo			
Costa Rica	*		
Cuba			
Cyprus	*		
Czechoslovakia			*
Democratic Kampuchea			
Democratic Yemen			
Denmark			*
Dominican Republic	*		
Ecuador	*		
Egypt	*		
El Salvador			
Equatorial Guinea	*		
Ethiopia	*		
Fiji	*		
Finland	*		
France			*
Gabon	*		
Gambia			
German Dem. Rep.			*

Country	Y	N	A
Germany, Fed. Rep.			*
Ghana	*		
Greece			*
Grenada	*		
Guatemala	*		
Guinea	*		
Guinea-Bissau	*		
Guyana	*		
Haiti			
Honduras			
Hungary			*
Iceland			*
India			*
Indonesia	*		
Iran	*		
Iraq			*
Ireland			*
Israel	*		
Italy			*
Ivory Coast	*		
Jamaica	*		
Japan			*
Jordan	*		
Kenya	*		
Kuwait	*		
Lao Peoples Dem. Rep.	*		
Lebanon	*		
Lesotho	*		
Liberia			
Libyan Arab Republic	*		
Luxembourg			*
Madagascar	*		
Malawi	*		
Malaysia	*		
Maldives	*		
Mali	*		
Malta	*		
Mauritania	*		
Mauritius	*		
Mexico	*		
Mongolia			*
Morocco	*		
Mozambique			
Nepal	*		
Netherlands	*		
New Zealand			*
Nicaragua	*		
Niger	*		
Nigeria	*		

Country	Y	N	A
Norway			*
Oman	*		
Pakistan	*		
Panama	*		
Papua New Guinea	*		
Paraguay	*		
Peru	*		
Philippines	*		
Poland			*
Portugal	*		
Qatar	*		
Romania	*		
Rwanda	*		
Sao Tome and Principe	*		
Saudi Arabia	*		
Senegal	*		
Seychelles			
Sierra Leone	*		
Singapore	*		
Somalia			
South Africa			
Spain	*		
Sri Lanka	*		
Sudan	*		
Surinam	*		
Swaziland	*		
Sweden			*
Syrian Arab Republic	*		
Thailand	*		
Togo	*		
Trinidad and Tobago	*		
Tunisia	*		
Turkey	*		
Uganda	*		
Ukrainian SSR			*
USSR			*
United Arab Emirates	*		
United Kingdom			*
Un. Rep. of Cameroon	*		
Un. Rep. of Tanzania			*
United States			
Upper Volta	*		
Uruguay	*		
Venezuela	*		
Yemen	*		
Yugoslavia			*
Zaire	*		
Zambia	*		

Y-YES, N-NO, A-ABSTAIN

Country	Y	N	A
Afghanistan	*		
Albania		*	
Algeria			*
Angola			
Argentina			*
Australia	*		
Austria	*		
Bahamas	*		
Bahrain	*		
Bangladesh	*		
Barbados	*		
Belgium	*		
Benin			
Bhutan			*
Bolivia			*
Botswana	*		
Brazil			*
Bulgaria	*		
Burma			*
Burundi	*		
Byelorussian SSR	*		
Canada	*		
Cape Verde			
Central African Rep.	*		
Chad	*		
Chile			*
China		*	
Colombia			*
Comoros			
Congo			
Costa Rica	*		
Cuba			
Cyprus	*		
Czechoslovakia	*		
Democratic Kampuchea			
Democratic Yemen	*		
Denmark	*		
Dominican Republic	*		
Ecuador	*		
Egypt	*		
El Salvador			
Equatorial Guinea	*		
Ethiopia	*		
Fiji	*		
Finland	*		
France			*
Gabon	*		
Gambia			
German Dem. Rep.	*		
Germany, Fed. Rep.	*		
Ghana	*		
Greece	*		
Grenada	*		
Guatemala	*		
Guinea	*		
Guinea-Bissau	*		
Guyana	*		
Haiti			
Honduras			
Hungary	*		
Iceland	*		
India			*
Indonesia	*		
Iran	*		
Iraq	*		
Ireland	*		
Israel	*		
Italy	*		
Ivory Coast	*		
Jamaica	*		
Japan	*		
Jordan	*		
Kenya	*		
Kuwait	*		
Lao Peoples Dem. Rep.	*		
Lebanon	*		
Lesotho			*
Liberia			
Libyan Arab Republic	*		
Luxembourg	*		
Madagascar	*		
Malawi	*		
Malaysia	*		
Maldives	*		
Mali	*		
Malta	*		
Mauritania	*		
Mauritius			*
Mexico			*
Mongolia	*		
Morocco	*		
Mozambique			
Nepal	*		
Netherlands	*		
New Zealand	*		
Nicaragua	*		
Niger	*		
Nigeria	*		
Norway	*		
Oman	*		
Pakistan			*
Panama			*
Papua New Guinea	*		
Paraguay			*
Peru			*
Philippines	*		
Poland	*		
Portugal	*		
Qatar	*		
Romania			*
Rwanda	*		
Sao Tome and Principe	*		
Saudi Arabia	*		
Senegal	*		
Seychelles			
Sierra Leone	*		
Singapore	*		
Somalia			
South Africa			
Spain	*		
Sri Lanka	*		
Sudan	*		
Surinam	*		
Swaziland	*		
Sweden	*		
Syrian Arab Republic	*		
Thailand	*		
Togo	*		
Trinidad and Tobago	*		
Tunisia	*		
Turkey	*		
Uganda			*
Ukrainian SSR	*		
USSR	*		
United Arab Emirates	*		
United Kingdom	*		
Un. Rep. of Cameroon	*		
Un. Rep. of Tanzania			*
United States	*		
Upper Volta	*		
Uruguay	*		
Venezuela	*		
Yemen	*		
Yugoslavia			*
Zaire	*		
Zambia			*

18. DECLARATION ON TERRITORIAL ASYLUM[1]

The General Assembly,

Recalling its resolutions 1839 (XVII) of 19 December 1962, 2100 (XX) of 20 December 1965 and 2203 (XXI) on 16 December 1966 concerning a declaration on the right of asylum,

Considering the work of codification to be undertaken by the International Law Commission in accordance with General Assembly resolution 1400 (XIV) of 21 November 1959,

Adopts the following Declaration:

DECLARATION ON TERRITORIAL ASYLUM

The General Assembly,

Noting that the purposes proclaimed in the Charter of the United Nations are to maintain international peace and security, to develop friendly relations among all nations and to achieve international co-operation in solving international problems of an economic, social, cultural or humanitarian character and in promoting and encouraging respect for human rights and for fundamental freedoms for all without distinction as to race, sex, language or religion,

Mindful of the Universal Declaration of Human Rights, which declares in article 14 that:

"1. Everyone has the right to seek and to enjoy in other countries asylum from persecution.

"2. This right may not be invoked in the case of prosecutions genuinely arising from non-political crimes or from acts contrary to the purposes and principles of the United Nations,"

Recalling also article 13, paragraph 2, of the Universal Declaration of Human Rights, which states:

"Everyone has the right to leave any country, including his own, and to return to his country,"

Recognizing that the grant of asylum by a State to persons entitled to invoke article 14 of the Universal Declaration of Human Rights is a peaceful and humanitarian act and that, as such, it cannot be regarded as unfriendly by any other State,

Recommends that, without prejudice to existing instruments dealing with asylum and the status of refugees and stateless persons, States should base themselves in their practices relating to territorial asylum on the following principles:

---

[1] Official Records of the General Assembly, Twenty-second Session, Supplement No. 16, p. 31.

Article 1

1. Asylum granted by a State, in the exercise of its sovereignty, to persons entitled to invoke article 14 of the Universal Declaration of Human Rights, including persons struggling against colonialism, shall be respected by all other States.

2. The right to seek and to enjoy asylum may not be invoked by any person with respect to whom there are serious reasons for considering that he has committed a crime against peace, a war crime or a crime against humanity, as defined in the international instruments drawn to make provision in respect of such crimes.

3. It shall rest with the State granting asylum to evaluate the grounds for the grant of asylum.

Article 2

1. The situation of persons referred to in article 1, paragraph 1, is, without prejudice to the sovereignty of States and the purposes and principles of the United Nations, of concern to the international community.

2. Where a State finds difficulty in granting or continuing to grant asylum, States individually or jointly or through the United Nations shall consider, in a spirit of international solidarity, appropriate measures to lighten the burden on that State.

Article 3

1. No person referred to in article 1, paragraph 1, shall be subjected to measures such as rejection at the frontier or, if he has already entered the territory in which he seeks asylum, expulsion or compulsory return to any State where he may be subjected to persecution.

2. Exception may be made to the foregoing principle only for overriding reasons of national security or in order to safeguard the population, as in the case of a mass influx of persons.

3. Should a State decide in any case that exception to the principle stated in paragraph 1 of this article would be justified, it shall consider the possibility of granting to the person concerned, under such conditions as it may deem appropriate, an opportunity, whether by way of provisional asylum or otherwise, of going to another State.

Article 4

States granting asylum shall not permit persons who have received asylum to engage in activities contrary to the purposes and principles of the United Nations.

1631st plenary meeting,
14 December 1967.

844

19. INTERNATIONAL CONVENTION ON THE SUPPRESSION AND PUNISHMENT OF THE CRIME OF APARTHEID[1]

Date: 30 November 1973   Meeting: 2185
Vote: 91-4-26   Report: A/9233/Add.1
    Amendment: A/L.712/Rev.1

The General Assembly,

Recalling resolution 2922 (XXVII) of 15 November 1972, in which it reaffirmed its conviction that *apartheid* constitutes a total negation of the purposes and principles of the Charter of the United Nations and is a crime against humanity,

Recognizing the urgent need to take further effective measures with a view to the suppression and punishment of *apartheid,*

Mindful of the need to conclude, under the auspices of the United Nations, an International Convention on the Suppression and Punishment of the Crime of *Apartheid,*

Convinced that the Convention would be an important step towards the eradication of the policies and practices of *apartheid,* and that it should be signed and ratified by States at the earliest possible date and its provisions implemented without delay,

Considering also that the text of the Convention should be made known throughout the world,

1. *Adopts* and opens for signature and ratification the International Convention on the Suppression and Punishment of the Crime of *Apartheid,* the text of which is annexed to the present resolution;

2. *Appeals* to all States to sign and ratify the Convention as soon as possible;

3. *Requests* all Governments and intergovernmental and non-governmental organizations to acquaint the public as videly as possible with the text of the Convention using all the information media at their disposal;

4. *Requests* the Secretary-General to ensure the urgent and wide dissemination of the Convention and, for that purpose, to publish and circulate its text;

5. *Requests* the Economic and Social Council to invite the Commission on Human Rights to undertake the functions set out under article X of the Convention.

ANNEX

International Convention on the Suppression and Punishment of the Crime of Apartheid

The States Parties to the present Convention,

Recalling the provisions of the Charter of the United Nations, in which all Members pledged themselves to take joint and separate action in co-operation with the Organization for the achievement of universal respect for, and observance of, human rights and fundamental freedoms for all without distinction as to race, sex, language or religion,

---

[1]Resolution 3068 (XXVIII) adopted by the General Assembly on November 30, 1973.

Considering the Universal Declaration of Human Rights, which states that all human beings are born free and equal in dignity and rights and that everyone is entitled to all the rights and freedoms set forth in the Declaration, without distinction of any kind, such as race, colour or national origin,

Considering the Declaration on the Granting of Independence to Colonial Countries and Peoples, [1] in which the General Assembly stated that the process of liberation is irresistible and irreversible and that, in the interests of human dignity, progress and justice, and end must be put to colonialism and all practices of segregation and discrimination associated therewith,

Observing that, in accordance with the International Convention on the Elimination of All Forms of Racial Discrimination,[2] States particularly condemn racial segregation and *apartheid* and undertake to prevent, prohibit and eradicate all practices of this nature in territories under their jurisdiction,

Observing that, in the Convention on the Prevention and Punishment of the Crime of Genocide,[3] certain acts which may also be qualified as acts of *apartheid* constitute a crime under international law,

Observing that, in the Convention on the Non-Applicability of Statutory Limitations to War Crimes and Crimes Against Humanity,[4] "inhuman acts resulting from the policy of *apartheid*" are qualified as crimes against humanity,

Observing that the General Assembly of the United Nations has adopted a number of resolutions in which the policies and practices of *apartheid* are condemned as a crime against humanity,

Observing that the Security Council has emphasized that *apartheid*, its continued intensification and expansion, seriously disturbs and threatens international peace and security,

Convinced that an International Convention on the Suppression and Punishment of the Crime of *Apartheid* would make it possible to take more effective measures at the international and national levels with a view to the suppression and punishment of the crime of *apartheid*,

Have agreed as follows:

Article I

1. The States Parties to the present Convention declare that *apartheid* is a crime against humanity and that inhuman acts resulting from the policies and practices of *apartheid* and similar policies and practices of racial segregation and discrimination, as defined in article II of the Convention, are crimes violating the principles of internatio-

---

[1] General Assembly resolution 1514 (XV).
[2] General Assembly resolution 2106 A (XX), annex.
[3] General Assembly resolution 260 A (III), annex.
[4] General Assembly resolution 2391 (XXIII), annex.

nal law, in particular the purposes and principles of the Charter of the United Nations, and constituting a serious threast to international peace and security.

2. The States Parties to the present Convention declare criminal those organizations, institutions and individuals committing the crime of *apartheid*.

Article II

For the purpose of the present Convention, the term "the crime of *apartheid*," which shall include similar policies and practices of racial segregation and discrimination as practised in southern Africa, shall apply to the following inhuman acts committed for the purpose of establishing and maintaining domination by one racial group of persons over any other racial group of persons and systematically oppressing them:

(a) Denial to a member or members of a racial group or groups of the right to life and liberty of person:

    (i) By murder of members of a racial group or groups;

    (ii) By the infliction upon the members of a racial group or groups of serious bodily or mental harm by the infringement of their freedom or dignity, or by subjecting them to torture or to cruel, inhuman or degrading treatment or punishment;

    (iii) By arbitrary arrest and illegal imprisonment of the members of a racial group or groups;

(b) Deliberate imposition on a racial group or groups of living conditions calculated to cause its or their physical destruction in whole or in part;

(c) Any legislative measures and other measures calculated to prevent a racial group or groups from participation in the political, social, economic and cultural life of the country and the deliberate creation of conditions preventing the full development of such a group or groups, in particular by denying to members of a racial group or groups basic human rights and freedoms, including the right to work, the right to form recognized trade unions, the right to education, the right to leave and to return to their country, the right to a nationality, the right to freedom pf movement and residence, the right to freedom of opinion and expression, and the right to freedom of peaceful assembly and association;

(d) Any measures, including legislative measures, designed to divide the population along racial lines by the creation of separate reserves and ghettos for the members of a racial group or groups, the prohibition of mixed marriages among members of various racial groups, the expropriation of landed property belonging to a racial group or groups or to members thereof;

(e) Exploitation of the labour of the members of a racial group or groups, in particular by submitting them to forced labour;

(f) Persecution or organizations and persons, by depriving them of fundamental rights and freedoms, because they oppose *apartheid*.

Article III

International criminal responsibility shall apply, irrespective of the motive involved, to individuals, members of organizations and institutions and representatives of the State, whether residing in the territory of the State in which the acts are perpetrated or in some other State, whenever they:

(a) Commit, participate in, directly incite or conspire in the commission of the acts mentioned in article II of the present Convention;

(b) Directly abet, encourage or co-operate in the commission of the crime of *apartheid*.

Article IV

The States Parties to the present Convention undertake:

(a) To adopt any legislative or other measures necessary to suppress as well as to prevent any encouragement of the crime of *apartheid* and similar segregationist policies or their manifestations and to punish persons guilty of that crime;

(b) To adopt legislative, judicial and administrative measures to prosecute, bring to trial and punish in accordance with their jurisdiction persons responsible for, or accused of, the acts defined in article II of the present Convention, whether or not such persons reside in the territory of the State in which the acts are committed or are nationals of that State or of some other State or are stateless persons.

Article V

Persons charged with the acts enumerated in article II of the present Convention may be tried by a competent tribunal of any State Party to the Convention which may acquire jurisdiction over the person of the accused or by an international penal tribunal having jurisdiction with respect to those States Parties which shall have accepted its jurisdiction.

Article VI

The States Parties to the present Convention undertake to accept and carry out in accordance with the Charter of the United Nations the decisions taken by the Security Council aimed at the prevention, suppression and punishment of the crime of *apartheid*, and to co-operate in the implementation of decisions adopted by other competent organs of the United Nations with a view to achieving the purposes of the Convention.

Article VII

1. The States Parties to the present Convention undertake to submit periodic reports to the group established under Article IX on the legislative, judicial, administrative or other measures that they have adopted and that give effect to the provisions of the Convention.

2. Copies of the reports shall be transmitted through the Secretary-General of the United Nations to the Special Committee on *Apartheid*.

Article VIII

Any State Party to the present Convention may call upon any competent organ of the United Nations to take such action under the Charter of the United Nations as it considers appropriate for the prevention and suppression of the crime of *apartheid*.

Article IX

1. The Chairman of the Commission on Human Rights shall appoint a group consisting of three members of the Commission on Human Rights, who are also representatives of States Parties to the present Convention, to consider reports submitted by States Parties in accordance with article VII.

2. If, among the members of the Commission on Human Rights, there are no representatives of States Parties to the present Convention of if there are fewer than three such representatives, the Secretary-General of the United Nations shall, after consulting all States Parties to the Convention, designate a representative of the State Party or representatives of the States Parties which are not members of the Commission on Human Rights to take part in the work of the group established in accordance with paragraph 1 of this article, until such time as representatives of the States Parties to the Convention are elected to the Commission on Human Rights.

3. The group may meet for a period of not more than five days, either before the

opening or after the closing of the session of the Commission on Human Rights, to consider the reports submitted in accordance with article VII.

Article X

1. The States Parties to the present Convention empower the Commission on Human Rights:

(a) To request United Nations organs, when transmitting copies of petitions under article 15 of the International Convention on the Elimination of All Forms of Racial Discrimination, to draw its attention to complaints concerning acts which are enumerated in article II of the present Convention;

(b) To prepare, on the basis of reports from competent organs of the United Nations and periodic reports from States Parties to the present Convention, a list of individuals, organizations, institutions and representatives of States which are alleged to be responsible for the crimes enumerated in article II of the Convention, as well as those against whom legal proceedings have been undertaken by States Parties to the Convention;

(c) To request information from the competent United Nations organs concerning measures taken by the authorities responsible for the administration of Trust and Non-Self-Governing Territories, and all other Territories to which General Assembly resolution 1514 (XV) of 14 December 1960 applies, with regard to such individuals alleged to be responsible for crimes under article II of the Convention who are believed to be under their territorial and administrative jurisdiction.

2. Pending the achievement of the objectives of the Declaration on the Granting of Independence to Colonial Countries and Peoples, contained in General Assembly resolution 1514 (XV), the provisions of the present Convention shall in no way limit the right of petition granted to those peoples by other international instruments or by the United Nations and its specialized agencies.

Article XI

1. Acts enumerated in article II of the present Convention shall not be considered political crimes for the purpose of extradition.

2. The States Parties to the present Convention undertake in such cases to grant extradition in accordance with their legislation and with the treaties in force.

Article XII

Disputes between States Parties arising out of the interpretation, application or implementation of the present Convention which have not been settled by negotiation shall, at the request of the States Parties to the dispute, be brought before the International Court of Justice, save where the parties to the dispute have agreed on some other form of settlement.

Article XIII

The present Convention is open for signature by all States. Any State which does not sign the Convention before its entry into force may accede to it.

Article XIV

1. The present Convention is subject to ratification. Instruments of ratification shall be deposited with the Secretary-General of the United Nations.

2. Accession shall be effected by the deposit of an instrument of accession with the Secretary-General of the United Nations.

Article XV

1. The present Convention shall enter into force on the thirtieth day after the date of the deposit with the Secretary-General of the United Nations of the twentieth instrument of ratification or accession.

2. For each State ratifying the present Convention or acceding to it after the deposit of the twentieth instrument of ratification or instrument of accession, the Convention shall enter into force on the thirtieth day after date of the deposit of its own instrument of ratification or instrument of accession.

Article XVI

A State Party may denounce the present Convention by written notification to the Secretary-General of the United Nations. Denunciation shall take effect one year after the date of receipt of the notification by the Secretary-General.

Article XVII

1. A request for the revision of this Convention may be made at any time by any State Party by means of a notification in writing addressed to the Secretary-General of the United Nations.

2. The General Assembly of the United Nations shall decide upon the steps, if any, to be taken in respect of such request.

Article XVIII

The Secretary-General of the United Nations shall inform all States of the following particulars:

(a)   Signatures, ratifications and accessions under articles XIII and XIV;

(b)   The date of entry into force of the present Convention under article XV;

(c)   Denunciations under article XVI;

(d)   Notifications under article XVII.

Article XIX

1. The present Convention, of which the Chinese, English, French, Russian and Spanish texts are equally authentic shall be deposited in the archives of the United Nations.

2. The Secretary-General of the United Nations shall transmit certified copies of the present Convention to all States.

20. PRINCIPLES OF INTERNATIONAL CO-OPERATION IN THE DETECTION, ARREST, EXTRADITION AND PUNISHMENT OF PERSONS GUILTY OF WAR CRIMES AND CRIMES AGAINST HUMANITY[1]

Date: 3 December 1973   Meeting: 2187
Report: A/9326
Amendment: A/L.711/Rev.1

The General Assembly,

Recalling its resolutions 2583 (XXIV) of 15 December 1969, 2712 (XXV) of 15 December 1970, 2840 (XXVI) of 18 December 1971 and 3020 (XXVII) of 18 December 1972,

Taking into account the special need for international action in order to ensure the prosecution and punishment of persons guilty of war crimes and crimes against humanity,

Having considered the draft principles of international co-operation in the detection, arrest, extradition and punishment of persons guilty of war crimes and crimes against humanity,[2]

Declares that the United Nations, in pursuance of the principles and purposes set forth in the Charter concerning the promotion of co-operation between peoples and the maintenance of international peace and security, proclaims the following principles of international co-operation in the detection, arrest, extradition and punishment of persons guilty of war crimes and crimes against humanity:

1. War crimes and crimes against humanity, whenever or wherever they are committed, shall be subject to investigation and the persons against whom there is evidence that they have committed such crimes shall be subject to tracing, arrest, trial and, if found guilty, to punishment.

2. Every State has the right to try its own nationals for war crimes or crimes against humanity.

3. States shall co-operate with each other on a bilateral and multilateral basis with a view to halting and preventing war crimes and crimes against humanity, and shall take the domestic and international measures necessary for that purpose.

4. States shall assist each other in detecting, arresting and bringing to trial persons suspected of having committed such crimes and, if they are found guilty, in punishing them.

5. Persons against whom there is evidence that they have committed war crimes and crimes against humanity shall be subject to trial and, if found guilty, to punishment, as a general rule in the countries in which they committed those crimes. In that connexion, States shall co-operate on questions of extraditing such persons.

6. States shall co-operate with each other in the collection of information and evidence which would help to bring to trial the persons indicated in paragraph 5 above and shall exchange such information.

7. In accordance with article 1 of the Declaration on Territorial Asylum of 14 December 1967,[3] States shall not grant asylum to any person with respect to whom there are serious reasons for considering that he has committed a crime against peace, a war crime or a crime against humanity.

---

[1] Resolution 3074 (XXVIII) adopted by the General Assembly on December 3, 1973.
[2] A/9136.
[3] General Assembly resolution 2312 (XXII).

YES - Y; NO - N; ABSTAIN - A

Country	Y	N	A
Afghanistan			*
Albania			
Algeria	*		
Argentina			*
Australia			
Austria	*		
Bahamas			
Bahrain			*
Barbados	*		
Belgium	*		
Bhutan	*		
Bolivia			*
Botswana	*		
Brazil			*
Bulgaria	*		
Burma	*		
Burundi	*		
Byelorussian SSR	*		
Cameroon			*
Canada	*		
Central African Rep.			*
Chad	*		
Chile			*
China			
Colombia			*
Congo	*		
Costa Rica	*		
Cuba	*		
Cyprus	*		
Czechoslovakia	*		
Dahomey	*		
Democratic Yemen	*		
Denmark	*		
Dominican Republic			*
Ecuador	*		
Egypt	*		
El Salvador			*
Equatorial Guinea	*		
Ethiopia	*		
Fiji	*		
Finland	*		
France	*		
Gabon	*		
Gambia	*		
German Dem. Rep.	*		
Germany, Fed. Rep.	*		
Ghana	*		
Greece	*		
Guatemala			*
Guinea	*		
Guyana	*		
Haiti	*		
Honduras	*		
Hungary	*		
Iceland	*		
India	*		
Indonesia			*
Iran	*		
Iraq	*		
Ireland	*		
Israel	*		
Italy	*		
Ivory Coast	*		
Jamaica			
Japan			*
Jordan	*		
Kenya	*		
Khmer Republic	*		
Kuwait			*
Laos	*		
Lebanon	*		
Lesotho	*		
Liberia	*		
Libyan Arab Republic	*		
Luxembourg	*		
Madagascar	*		
Malawi			*
Malaysia	*		
Maldives			
Mali	*		
Malta			
Mauritania	*		
Mauritius			
Mexico	*		
Mongolia	*		
Morocco	*		
Nepal	*		
Nertherlands	*		
New Zealand	*		
Nicaragua	*		
Niger	*		
Nigeria	*		
Norway	*		
Oman			*
Pakistan			*
Panama			
Paraguay			*
Peru	*		
Philippines	*		
Poland	*		
Portugal			*
Qatar			*
Romania	*		
Rwanda	*		
Saudi Arabia			
Senegal			
Sierra Leone	*		
Singapore	*		
Somalia	*		
South Africa			
Spain			*
Sri Lanka	*		
Sudan	*		
Swaziland			
Sweden			*
Syrian Arab Republic	*		
Thailand	*		
Togo	*		
Trinidad and Tobago			
Tunisia	*		
Turkey			
Uganda	*		
Ukrainian SSR	*		
USSR	*		
United Arab Emirates			*
United Kingdom	*		
Un. Rep. of Tanzania	*		
United States	*		
Upper Volta	*		
Uruguay			*
Venezuela			*
Yemen	*		
Yugoslavia	*		
Zaire			*
Zambia	*		

8. States shall not take any legislative or other measures which may be prejudicial to the international obligations they have assumed in regard to the detection, arrest, extradition and punishment of persons guilty of war crimes and crimes against humanity.

9. In co-operating with a view to the detection, arrest and extradition of persons against whom there is evidence that they have committed war crimes and crimes against humanity and, if found guilty, their punishment, States shall act in conformity with the provisions of the Charter of the United Nations and of the Declaration on Principles of International Law concerning Friendly Relations and Co-operation among States in accordance with the Charter of the United Nations.[4]

21. CONVENTION ON THE PREVENTION AND PUNISHMENT OF CRIMES AGAINST INTERNATIONALLY PROTECTED PERSONS, INCLUDING DIPLOMATIC AGENTS[1]

Date: 14 December 1973   Meeting: 2202
Adopted by consensus   Report: A/9407

The General Assembly,

Considering that the codification and progressive development of international law contributes to the implementation of the purposes and principles set forth in Articles 1 and 2 of the Charter of the United Nations,

Recalling that in response to the request made in General Assembly resolution 2780 (XXVI) of 3 December 1971, the International Law Commission, at its twenty-fourth session, studied the question of the protection and inviolability of diplomatic agents and other persons entitled to special protection under international law and prepared draft articles on the prevention and punishment of crimes against such persons,

Having considered the draft articles and also the comments and observations thereon submitted by States and by specialized agencies and intergovernmental organizations in response to the invitation made in General Assembly resolution 2926 (XXVII) of 28 November 1972,

Convinced of the importance of securing international agreement on appropriate and effective measures for the prevention and punishment of crimes against diplomatic agents and other internationally protected persons in view of the serious threat to the maintenance and promotion of friendly relations and co-operation among States created by the commission of such crimes,

Having elaborated for that purpose the provisions contained in the Convention annexed hereto,

1. *Adopts* the Convention on the Prevention and Punishment of Crimes against Internationally Protected Persons, including Diplomatic Agents, annexed to the present resolution;

2. *Re-emphasizes* the great importance of the rules of International law concerning the inviolability of and special protection to be afforded to internationally protected persons and the obligations of States in relation thereto;

3. *Considers* that the annexed Convention will enable States to carry out their obligations more effectively;

4. *Recognizes also* that the provisions of the annexed Convention could not in any way prejudice the exercise of the legitimate right to self-determination and independence in accordance with the purposes and principles of the Charter of the United Na-

---

[4]General Assembly resolution 2625 (XXV), annex.

[1]Resolution 3166 (XXVIII) adopted by the General Assembly on December 14, 1973.

tions and the Declaration on Principles of International Law concerning Friendly Relations and Co-operation among States in accordance with the Charter of the United Nations by peoples struggling against colonialism, alien domination, foreign occupation, racial discrimination and *apartheid;*

5. *Invites* States to become parties to the annexed Convention;

6. *Decides* that the present resolution, whose provisions are related to the annexed Convention, shall always be published together with it.

ANNEX

Convention on the Prevention and Punishment of Crimes against Internationally Protected Persons, including Diplomatic Agents

The States Parties to this Convention,

Having in mind the purposes and principles of the Charter of the United Nations concerning the maintenance of international peace and the promotion of friendly relations and co-operation among States,

Considering that crimes against diplomatic agents and other internationally protected persons jeopardizing the safety of these persons create a serious threat to the maintenance of normal international relations which are necessary for co-operation among States,

Believing that the commission of such crimes is a matter of grave concern to the international community,

Convinced that there is an urgent need to adopt appropriate and effective measures for the prevention and punishment of such crimes,

Have agreed as follows:

Article 1

For the purposes of this Convention:

1. "internationally protected person" means:

(a) a Head of State, including any member of a collegial body performing the functions of a Head of State under the constitution of the State concerned, a Head of Government or a Minister for Foreign Affairs, whenever any such person is in a foreign State, as well as members of his family who accompany him;

(b) Any representative or official of a State or any official or other agent of an international organization of an intergovernmental character who, at the time when and in the place where a crime against him, his official premises, his private accommodation or his means of transport is committed, is entitled pursuant to international law to special protection from any attack on his person, freedom or dignity, as well as members of his family forming part of his household;

2. "alleged offender" means a person as to whom there is sufficient evidence to determine *prima facie* that he has committed or participated in one or more of the crimes set forth in article 2.

Article 2

1. The intentional commission of:

(a) a murder, kidnapping or other attack upon the person or liberty of an internationally protected person;

(b) a violent attack upon the official premises, the private accommodation or the means of transport of an internationally protected person likely to endanger his person or liberty;

(c) a threat to commit any such attack;

(d) an attempt to commit any such attack; and

(e) an act constituting participation as an accomplice in any such attack shall be made by each State Party a crime under its internal law.

2. Each State Party shall make these crimes punishable by appropriate penalties which take into account their grave nature.

3. Paragraphs 1 and 2 of this article in no way derogate from the obligations of States Parties under international law to take all appropriate measures to prevent other attacks on the person, freedom or dignity of an internationally protected person.

Article 3

1. Each State Party shall take such measures as may be necessary to establish its jurisdiction over the crimes set forth in article 2 in the following cases:

(a) when the crime is committed in the territory of that State or on board a ship or aircraft registered in that State;

(b) when the alleged offender is a national of that State;

(c) when the crime is committed against an internationally protected person as defined in article 1 who enjoys his status as such by virtue of functions which he exercises on behalf of that State.

2. Each State Party shall likewise take such measures as may be necessary to establish its jurisdiction over these crimes in cases where the alleged offender is present in its territory and it does not extradite him pursuant to article 8 to any of the States mentioned in paragraph 1 of this article.

3. This Convention does not exclude any criminal jurisdiction exercised in accordance with internal law.

Article 4

States Parties shall co-operate in the prevention of the crimes set forth in article 2, particularly by:

(a) taking all practicable measures to prevent preparations in their respective territories for the commission of those crimes within or outside their territories;

(b) exchanging information and co-ordinating the taking of administrative and other measures as appropriate to prevent the commission of those crimes.

Article 5

1. The State Party in which any of the crimes set forth in article 2 has been committed shall, if it has reason to believe that an alleged offender has fled from its territory, communicate to all other States concerned, directly or through the Secretary-General of the United Nations, all the pertinent facts regarding the crime committed and all available information regarding the identity of the alleged offender.

2. Whenever any of the crimes set forth in article 2 has been committed against an internationally protected person, any State Party which has information concerning the victim and the circumstances of the crime shall endeavour to transmit it, under the conditions provided for in its internal law, fully and promptly to the State Party on whose behalf he was exercising his functions.

Article 6

1. Upon being satisfied that the circumstances so warrant, the State Party in whose territory the alleged offender is present shall take the appropriate measures under its internal law so as to ensure his presence for the purpose of prosecution or extradition.

Such measures shall be notified without delay directly or through the Secretary-General of the United Nations to:

(a) the State where the crime was committed;

(b) the State or States of which the alleged offender is a national or, if he is a stateless person, in whose territory be permanently resides;

(c) the State or States of which the internationally protected person concerned is a national or on whose behalf he was exercising his functions;

(d) all other States concerned; and

(e) the international organization of which the internationally protected person concerned is an official or an agent.

2. Any person regarding whom the measures referred to in paragraph 1 of this article are being taken shall be entitled:

(a) to communicate without delay with the nearest appropriate representative of the State of which he is a national or which is otherwise entitled to protect his rights or, if he is a stateless person, which he requests and which is willing to protect his rights; and

(b) to be visited by a representative of that State.

Article 7

The State Party in whose territory the alleged offender is present shall, if it does not extradite him, submit, without exception whatsoever and without undue delay, the case to its competent authorities for the purpose of prosecution, through proceedings in accordance with the laws of that State.

Article 8

1. To the extent that the crimes set forth in article 2 are not listed as extraditable offences in any extradition treaty existing between States Parties, they shall be deemed to be included as such therein. States Parties undertake to include those crimes as extraditable offences in every future extradition treaty to be concluded between them.

2. If a State Party which makes extradition conditional on the existence of a treaty receives a request for extradition from another State Party with which it has no extradition treaty, it may, if it decides to extradite, consider this Convention as the legal basis for extradition in respect of those crimes. Extradition shall be subject to the procedural provisions and the other conditions of the law of the requested State.

3. States Parties which do not make extradition conditional on the existence of a treaty shall recognize those crimes as extraditable offences between themselves subject to the procedural provisions and the other conditions of the law of the requested State.

4. Each of the crimes shall be treated, for the purpose of extradition between States Parties, as if it had been committed not only in the place in which it occurred but also in the territories of the States required to establish their jurisdiction in accordance with paragraph 1 of article 3.

Article 9

Any person regarding whom proceedings are being carried out in connexion with any of the crimes set forth in article 2 shall be guaranteed fair treatment at all stages of the proceedings.

Article 10

1. States Parties shall afford one another the greatest measure of assistance in connexion with criminal proceedings brought in respect of the crimes set forth in article 2, including the supply of all evidence at their disposal necessary for the proceedings.

2. The provisions of paragraph 1 of this article shall not affect obligations concerning mutual judicial assistance embodied in any other treaty.

Article 11

The State Party where an alleged offender is prosecuted shall communicate the final outcome of the proceedings to the Secretary-General of the United Nations, who shall transmit the information to the other States Parties.

Article 12

The provisions of this Convention shall not affect the application of the Treaties on Asylum, in force at the date of the adoption of this Convention, as between the States which are parties to those Treaties; but a State Party to this Convention may not invoke those Treaties with respect to another State Party to this Convention which is not a party to those Treaties.

Article 13

1. Any dispute between two or more States Parties concerning the interpretation or application of this Convention which is not settled by negotiation shall, at the request of one of them, be submitted to arbitration. If within six months from the date of the request for arbitration the parties are unable to agree on the organization of the arbitration, any one of those parties may refer the dispute to the International Court of Justice by request in conformity with the Statute of the Court.

2. Each State Party may at the time of signature or ratification of this Convention or accession thereto declare that it does not consider itself bound by paragraph 1 of this article. The other States Parties shall not be bound by paragraph 1 of this article with respect to any State Party which has made such a reservation.

3. Any State Party which has made a reservation in accordance with paragraph 2 of this article may at any time withdraw that reservation by notification to the Secretary-General of the United Nations.

Article 14

This Convention shall be open for signature by all States, until 31 December 1974 at United Nations Headquarters in New York.

Article 15

This Convention is subject to ratification. The instruments of ratification shall be deposited with the Secretary-General of the United Nations.

Article 16

This Convention shall remain open for accession by any State. The instruments of accession shall be deposited with the Secretary-General of the United Nations.

Article 17

1. This Convention shall enter into force on the thirtieth day following the date of deposit of the twenty-second instrument of ratification or accession with the Secretary-General of the United Nations.

2. For each State ratifying or acceding to the Convention after the deposit of the twenty-second instrument of ratification or accession, the Convention shall enter into force on the thirtieth day after deposit by such State of its instrument of ratification or accession.

Article 18

1. Any State Party may denounce this Convention by written notification to the Secretary-General of the United Nations.

2. Denunciation shall take effect six months following the date on which notification is received by the Secretary-General of the United Nations.

Article 19

The Secretary-General of the United Nations shall inform all States, *inter alia:*

(a) of signatures to this Convention, of the deposit of instruments of ratification or accession in accordance with articles 14, 15 and 16 and of notifications made under article 18.

(b) of the date on which this Convention will enter into force in accordance with article 17.

Article 20

The Original of this Convention, of which the Chinese, English, French, Russian and Spanish texts are equally authentic, shall be deposited with the Secretary-General of the United Nations, who shall send certified copies thereof to all States.

IN WITNESS WHEREOF the undersigned, being duly authorized thereto by their respective Governments, have signed this Convention, opened for signature at New York on 14 December 1973.

22. MEASURES TO REDUCE THE RISK OF NUCLEAR WAR OUTBREAK

Agreement signed at Washington September 30, 1971;
Entered into force September 30, 1971.[1]

AGREEMENT ON MEASURES TO REDUCE THE RISK OF OUTBREAK
OF NUCLEAR WAR BETWEEN THE UNITED STATES OF AMERICA
AND THE UNION OF SOVIET SOCIALIST REPUBLICS

The United States of America and the Union of Soviet Socialist Republics, hereinafter referred to as the Parties:

Taking into account the devastating consequences that nuclear war would have for all mankind, and recognizing the need to exert every effort to avert the risk of outbreak of such a war, including measures to guard against accidental or unauthorized use of nuclear weapons,

Believing that agreement on measures for reducing the risk of outbreak of nuclear war serves the interests of strengthening international peace and security and is in no way contrary to the interests of any other country,

Bearing in mind that continued efforts are also needed in the future to seek ways of reducing the risk of outbreak of nuclear war,

Have agreed as follows:

---

[1]Treaties and other International Agreements, No. 7186, pp. 1590-1593.

Article 1

Each Party undertakes to maintain and to improve, as it deems necessary, its existing organizational and technical arrangements to guard against the accidental or unauthorized use of nuclear weapons under its control.

Article 2

The Parties undertake to notify each other immediately in the event of an accidental, unauthorized or any other unexplained incident involving a possible detonation of a nuclear weapon which could create a risk of outbreak of nuclear war. In the event of such an incident, the Party whose nuclear weapon is involved will immediately make every effort to take necessary measures to render harmless or destroy such weapon without its causing damage.

Article 3

The Parties undertake to notify each other immediately in the event of detection by missile warning systems of unidentified objects, or in the event of signs of interference with these systems or with related communications facilities, if such occurrences could create a risk of outbreak of nuclear war between the two countries.

Article 4

Each Party undertakes to notify the other Party in advance of any planned missile launches if such launches will extend beyond its national territory in the direction of the other Party.

Article 5

Each Party, in other situations involving unexplained nuclear incidents, undertakes to act in such a manner as to reduce the possibility of its actions being misinterpreted by the other Party. In any such situation, each Party may inform the other Party or request information when, in its view, this is warranted by the interests of averting the risk of outbreak of nuclear war.

Article 6

For transmission of urgent information, notifications and requests for information in situations requiring prompt clarification, the Parties shall make primary use of the Direct Communications Link between the Governments of the United States of America and the Union of Soviet Socialist Republics.[1]

For transmission of other information, notifications and requests for information, the Parties, at their own discretion, may use any communications facilities, including diplomatic channels, depending on the degree of urgency.

Article 7

The Parties undertake to hold consultations, as mutually agreed, to consider questions relating to implementation of the provisions of this Agreement, as well as to discuss possible amendments thereto aimed at further implementation of the purposes of this Agreement.

---

[1]See TIAS 5362, 7187; 14 UST 825; *post*, p. 1598.

Article 8

This Agreement shall be of unlimited duration.

Article 9

This Agreement shall enter into force upon signature.

Done at Washington on September 30, 1971, in two copies, each in the English and Russian languages, both texts being equally authentic.

FOR THE UNITED STATES
OF AMERICA.[2]

FOR THE UNION OF SOVIET
SOCIALIST REPUBLICS.[3]

[2]William P. Rogers
[3]A. Gromyko

BIBLIOGRAPHY

Aly, B., ed. *International Organization.* Columbia, Missouri: National University Extension Association, 1952. (Its 26th Discussion and Debate Manual, 1952-1953.)

Australian Group for International Reconstruction. *The Dumbarton Oaks Proposals for World Organization: Third Statement.* Sydney: The Group, 1945.

Bentwich, Norman. *From Geneva to San Francisco: An Account of the International Organization of the New Order.* London: Gollancz, 1946.

Bhalerao, N. R. *A Plea, Urgent Entreaty for World Government.* Lashkar, Gwalior: The Author, 1950.

Bloomfield, Lincoln P. *The United States, the United Nations and the Creation of Community.* Washington: The Author, 1960.

_____ . *A World Effectively Controlled by the United Nations: A Preliminary Survey of One Form of a Stable Military Environment.* Washington: Institute for Defense Analysis, 1952. (Study Memorandum, 7)

Bowett, D.W. *The Law of International Institutions.* New York: Frederick A. Praeger, 1963.

Breitner, Thomas. *World Constitution: Study on the Legal Framework of a World Federation.* Berkeley: 1963. (Monograph on World Government, Series A-1)

Brinton, Clarence Crans. *From Many, One: The Process of Political Integration – The Problem of World Government.* Cambridge: Harvard University Press, 1948.

Carnegie Endowment for International Peace. Division of Intercourse and Education. *The General International Organization: Its Framework and Functions.* New York: The Society, 1946.

_____ . Sweetser, A., "The United States and World Organization in 1944"; Pasvolsky, L.. "Dumbarton Oaks Proposals for Economic and Social Cooperation"; Vandenberg, A.H., "Let's Win Both the War and the Peace"; Borger, G., "National Organization and International Policy"; *Report of Crimea Conference,* Yalta, February 4-11, 1945. *(International Conciliation.* No. 409, Section 2, pp. 185-222, March 1945)

Chaudhuri, Sanjib. *A Constitution for the World Government.* Calcutta: The Author, 1949.

_____ . *Steps for the Formation of the First Parliament of the World.* Calcutta: World Constitution Office, 1952.

Cheever, Daniel S. and Haviland, H. Field. *Organizing for Peace: International Organization in World Affairs.* Boston: Houghton Mifflin Company, 1954.

Claude, Inis L. *Swords into Plowshares: The Problems and Progress of International Organization.* New York: Random House, Inc., 1959.

Commission to Study the Organization of Peace. *International Safeguard of Human Rights: The Hope of the World.* New York: The Commission, 1944.

Corwin, Edward Samuel. *The Constitution and World Organization*. Princeton: Princeton University Press, 1944.

Council for World Government Organization. *Proposals Submitted to the Representatives of the United Nations Assembled at San Francisco for Establishment of a World Organization to Perpetuate Peace and to Establish Economic Cooperation and Social Progress Among All Nations*. London: The Council, 1945.

Deutsch, Karl W. *Political Community at the International Level: Problems of Definition and Measurement*. Princeton: Princeton University Press, 1953. (Princeton University Foreign Policy Analysis Project – Series 2)

_____ . *Political Community and the North Atlantic Area: International Organization in the Light of Historical Experience*. Princeton: Princeton University Press, 1957.

Doman, Nicholas. *The Coming Age of World Control: The Transition to an Organized Society*. New York: Harper & Row, Publishers, 1942.

Dulles, John Foster. *A Free Enterprise Program: A Plan for Peace – An American Federation, A European Federation and an Asiatic Federation Coordinated in One World Organization*. (A modified UNC): Dulles, J.F., "War or Peace"; Reynaud, Paul, "The Unifying Force for Europe"; Romulo, Carlos P., "The Crucial Battle for Asia." Bogota: American Federation Movement, 1951.

_____ . *War or Peace*. New York: Macmillan, Inc., 1950.

Dumbarton Oaks Conference. *Dumbarton Oaks Agreements: Statements by Secretary of State Hull and Under-Secretary Stettinius* and *Proposals for the Establishment of a General International Organization*. New York: Carnegie Endowment for International Peace, 1944. (*International Conciliation*, 1944, No. 405, pp. 729-743)

Eagleton, Clyde. *International Government*. New York: The Ronald Press Company, 1957.

_____ . *The Forces That Shape Our Future*. New York: New York University Press, 1945.

Fike, Linus R. *No Nations Alone: A Plan for Organized Peace*. New York: Philosophical Library, Inc., 1943.

Free World Research Bureau. *The Constitution and the United Nations: A Tentative and Provisional Draft of a Treaty Based on the Dumbarton Oaks Proposals*. New York: The Bureau, 1945.

Goodrich, Leland M. *The United Nations*. New York: Thomas Y. Crowell Company, Inc., 1959.

Goodspeed, Stephen S. *The Nature and Function of International Organization*. New York: Oxford University Press, 1959.

Hass, Ernest B. *Beyond the Nation-State: Functionalism and International Organization*. Stanford: Stanford University Press, 1964.

Hill, Norman L. *International Organization*. New York: Harper & Row, Publishers, 1952.

Hudson, Manley O. *Progress in International Organization*. Stanford: Stanford University Press, 1932.

862

Hughan, Jessie W. *A Study of International Government*. New York: Thomas Y. Crowell Company, Inc., 1923.

Japanese Association for International Law. *Japan and International Organizations: A Report on National Policy and Public Attitude of Japan Toward International Organizations*. Tokyo: The Association, 1955.

Jenks, Alarence W. *The Common Law of Mankind*. London: Stevens & Sons, 1958.

Johnson, Julia E. *Federal World Government*. New York: The H.W. Wilson Company, 1948.

_____. *United Nations or World Government*. New York: The H.W. Wilson Company, 1947.

Joyce, James A. *The Story of International Cooperation*. New York: Franklin Watts, Inc., 1964.

_____., ed. *World Organization: Federal or Functional? A Round Table Discussion*. London: Franklin Watts, Inc., 1945.

Kelsen, Hans. *The Law of the United Nations: A Critical Analysis of Its Fundamental Problems; with supplement, Recent Trends in the Law of the United Nations*. London: Stevens & Sons, 1951.

_____. *Peace Through Law*. Chapel Hill: The University of North Carolina Press, 1944.

King, MacKenzie. *Proposals for the Establishment of a General International Organization for the Maintenance of International Peace and Security: Statements in the House of Commons*. Ottawa: Cloutier, 1945.

Leonard, Larry. *International Organization*. New York: McGraw-Hill, Inc., 1951.

Mangone, Gerard J. *A Short History of International Organization*. New York: McGraw-Hill, Inc., 1954.

Meyer, Cord. *World Government: Necessity or Utopia?* Toronto: Canadian Institute of International Affairs, 1949.

Minor, Raleigh C. *A Republic of Nations: A Study of the Organization of a Federal League of Nations*. New York: Oxford University Press, 1918.

Monteiro, A.G. *Pantopia: A United, Permanent, Peaceful, Progressive and Just New World Order*. Bombay: Popular Book Department, 1944.

Nash, Vernon. *The World Must Be Governed*. New York: Harper & Row, Publishers, 1949.

Newfang, Oscar. *World Government*. New York: Barnes & Nobles Books, 1942.

Nussbaum, Arthur. *A Concise History of the Law of Nations*. New York: The Macmillan Company, 1954.

Pattern, Ernest M. *World Government*. Philadelphia: American Academy of Political and Social Science, 1949. (Annals, v. 264)

Plischke, Elmer. *System of Integrating the International Community*. Princeton: D. Van Nostrand Company, 1964.

Potter, Pitman B. *An Introduction to the Study of International Organization*. New York: Appleton-Century-Crofts, 1948.

Roper, Elmo. *American Attitude on World Organization*. New York: Institute of International Order, 1950.

Rudzinski, A., ed. *Selected Bibliography on International Organization*. New York: Carnegie Endowment for International Peace, 1953.

Sohn, Louis B. *Cases and Other Materials of World Law: The Interpretation and Application of the Charter of the United Nations and of the Constitutions of other Agencies of the World Community*. New York: Brooklyn Foundation Press, 1950.

Stettinius, Edward R. *What the Dumbarton Oaks Peace Plan Means*. New York: Army and Navy Department of the Young Men's Christian Association, 1945.

Tung, William L. *International Organization Under the United Nations System*. New York: Thomas Y. Crowell Company, Inc., 1969.

Union of International Associations. *International Institutions and International Organization: A Select Bibliography*. Compiled by G.P. Speechaert, Brussels, 1956. (Its Publications, 151)

United Kingdom, Central Office of Information, Reference Division. *Western Cooperation: A Reference Handbook*. London: The Office, 1955.

_____. *Guide to International Organization*. London: The Office, 1953.

United Kingdom Foreign Office. *A Commentary of the Dumbarton Oaks Proposals for the Establishment of a General International Organization*. London: The Office, 1944.

United Kingdom Parliament. House of Lords. *World Organization for Peace*. London: 1945. (Parliamentary debates. v. 135, no. 44, pp. 1107-1163).

United Nations Conference on International Organization. *Australian Delegation Report,* together with the Text of Agreement signed at San Francisco. Canberra, Commonwealth Government: Printer, 1945.

United Nations Conference on International Organization, San Francisco, California, April 25 to June 26, 1945. *Selected Documents*. Washington: U.S. Government Printing Office, 1946.

United States Congress. House Committee of Foreign Affairs. *Amendment of Certain Laws Providing for Membership and Participation by the U.S. in Certain International Organizations*. Report of J.J. Res. 334. Washington: 1949. (81st Congress, 1st Session. House Report 1257)

_____. Special Study Mission on International Organization and Movements. *Report by C.C. Merrow and others*. Washington: 1954. (83rd Congress, 2nd Session. Committee Print)

United States Department of State. *International Organization and Conference*. Series I. General. No. 1. Washington: 1948.

United States Library of Congress. Legislative Reference Service. *Legislation Relating to International Organizations* by P. Ackerman. Washington: 1951.

_____. Foreign Affairs Division. *Strengthen Free World Security: NATO and Atlantic Co-operation. The United Nations and World Government: A Collection of Excerpts and Bibliographies.* Washington: 1960. (86th Congress, 2nd Session. Committee Print)

Utrikespolitiska Institute. *Peace and Security After the Second World War; A Swedish Contribution to the Subject.* Stockholm: The Institute, 1945.

Vandenbosch, Amry. *Toward World Order.* New York: McGraw-Hill, Inc., 1963. (McGraw-Hill Series on Political Science)

Van Wagenen, Richard W. *The Need for Research on Community in the International Organization Field.* Princeton University Center for Research on World Political Institutions. Princeton: Princeton University Press, 1952.

Vinacke, Harold Monk. *International Organization.* New York: F.S. Crofts & Co., 1934.

Watkins, James T. *General International Organization: A Source Book.* Princeton: D. Van Nostrand Company, 1956.

Weik, Mary H. *The Search for World Community.* Cincinnati: American Federation of World Citizens, 1956.

Welch, John Weston. *Complete Handbook on International Organization.* Portland: The Author, 1952.

Wofford, Harris. *It Is Up to Us: Federal World Government in Our Time.* New York: Harcourt Brace Jovanovich, Inc., 1946.

World Peace Foundation. *Documents of International Organization: A Selected Bibliography.* Boston: The Foundation, 1947.

Wright, Quiney, ed. *The World Community.* Chicago: The University of Chicago Press, 1943.

Yale Law Journal. *Symposium on World Organization.* New Haven: The Journal, 1946. (Vol. 55, No. 5, pp. 865-1331, August, 1946)

Yarnell, H.E. *Proposed Modified Outline for a Charter of General International Organization.* Washington: The Author, 1944.

INDEX

867